In memory of
JC Smith and Brian Hogan

SMITH & HOGAN
CRIMINAL LAW

Eleventh Edition

David Ormerod

Professor of Criminal Law, University of Leeds,
Barrister of the Middle Temple, 18 Red Lion Court

OXFORD
UNIVERSITY PRESS

OXFORD
UNIVERSITY PRESS

Great Clarendon Street, Oxford OX2 6DP

Oxford University Press is a department of the University of Oxford.
It furthers the University's objective of excellence in research, scholarship,
and education by publishing worldwide in

Oxford New York

Auckland Cape Town Dar es Salaam Hong Kong Karachi
Kuala Lumpur Madrid Melbourne Mexico City Nairobi
New Delhi Shanghai Taipei Toronto

With offices in

Argentina Austria Brazil Chile Czech Republic France Greece
Guatemala Hungary Italy Japan Poland Portugal Singapore
South Korea Switzerland Thailand Turkey Ukraine Vietnam

Oxford is a registered trade mark of Oxford University Press
in the UK and in certain other countries

Published in the United States
by Oxford University Press Inc., New York

British Library Cataloguing in Publication Data
Data available

Library of Congress Cataloging in Publication Data
Data available

ISBN 0-40-697730-5 978-0-40-697730-4

3 5 7 9 10 8 6 4 2

Typeset by RefineCatch Limited, Bungay, Suffolk
Printed in Great Britain by
Ashford Colour Press Limited, Gosport, Hampshire

Smith & Hogan

CRIMINAL LAW

Contents

Part II Particular crimes

Preface

Smith and Hogan Criminal Law has maintained a unique position in its field for the last forty years, being held in the highest esteem by students, academics, practitioners and the judiciary. Following Brian Hogan's death in 1996, Sir John Smith (or simply JC as he was usually known) took sole responsibility for the last two editions, before he died in 2003. I was privileged to have worked with JC Smith at the University of Nottingham and subsequently to have followed in Brian Hogan's footsteps at the University of Leeds. Each left his own remarkable legacy on the law with thousands of students inspired by wonderful teaching, and a wealth of legal publications enriching the law. It is, however, principally for their collaboration in creating and developing this book that they will be remembered by generations of criminal lawyers. It was in the course of completing the tenth edition that JC paid me the great honour of inviting me to collaborate with him in writing subsequent editions. Sadly there was no opportunity to do so before he passed away, and responsibility for this eleventh edition fell to me alone. JC Smith and Brian Hogan are an impossible act to follow, but I have sought to remain true to their ideals by producing a textbook which is comprehensive, accessible and valuable to a wide legal readership, whilst providing a detailed exposition and doctrinal analysis of English criminal law. I hope that it is an edition of which they would have been proud.

Inevitably, I have made some changes, and more will no doubt follow in future editions. In particular, in this edition I have introduced more references to, and discussion of, academic scholarship. Recent years have seen a proliferation of high quality academic literature on criminal law and I have acknowledged a great deal of this without, I trust, overwhelming or distracting the reader. I have also included a full bibliography of academic references. In addition, there are numerous amendments to the text reflecting the continual pace of change in substantive criminal law, as elsewhere in criminal justice. The Sexual Offences Act 2003 necessitated a complete revision of Chapter 17, and there have been many other statutory developments to take into account including the recent Domestic Violence, Crime and Victims Act 2004. In common law there has been the landmark decision of the House of Lords in *G* (2003), overruling *Caldwell* (1981) —a result which would no doubt have delighted JC Smith and Brian Hogan—and other significant developments including those in relation to manslaughter (*Misra* (2003) and *Kennedy (No 2)* (2005)), non-fatal offences (*Dica* (2004) and *Konzani* (2005)), conspiracy (with *Harmer* (2005) and *Ali* (2005) which I have been able to include only at proofs), and duress (with *Hasan* (2005) in the House of Lords and *Safi* (2003) in the Court of Appeal). I have also drawn attention, where appropriate, to the many proposals for reform as for example with the Fraud Bill 2005, and more generally, I have made frequent reference to the valuable Reports and consultation documents produced by the Law Commission.

The manuscript was delivered to the publishers at the beginning of April 2005 but it has been possible to incorporate a few recent developments at proof stage. Further updates of significant changes in the law will be included on the Companion Web Site www.oup.com/uk/booksites/law/.

David Ormerod
June 2005

Preface

Acknowledgements

There are many friends and colleagues to thank for their assistance in the preparation of this edition. In order that the material remained accessible to a wide readership I offered drafts of chapters to academics, namely Yaman Akdeniz, Ruth Armstrong, Ben Fitzpatrick, Michael Freeman, Nick Taylor, and David Thomas, as well as barristers and solicitors of all levels of experience, including Rina Marie Hill, Simon McKay, David Perry, Peter Rook QC, Tony Shaw QC, Richard Sutton QC and Adrian Waterman. In particular, I should like to thank David Gruner who read draft chapters whilst studying criminal law on the LLB at the University of Leeds. He also provided excellent research assistance in tracking down numerous references, as did Mohammed Fakrul Islam, the librarian at 18 Red Lion Court. The valuable comments assisted me greatly, but of course any errors are mine. The Faculty of Laws at University College London generously appointed me Senior Visiting Research Fellow for the semester I spent on sabbatical leave to write this edition; the accommodation and access to facilities at the University greatly assisted.

This edition started life as a Butterworth's publication. I would like to thank Isabel Isaacson, from Butterworth's, for her support in the initial stages of writing and subsequently the team at OUP, including Kate Whetter, Jasmin Naim, Natalie Williams, Gabriella La Cava, Elissa Connor, Joy Ruskin-Tompkins and Pauline Fothergill, for seeing the project safely through to completion.

I would also like to take this opportunity to record my gratitude to the many people who have supported and encouraged me throughout my career. I have been extremely fortunate in working in law schools with a strong tradition of criminal law scholarship. At Nottingham, the roll-call at one time included JC Smith, Edward Griew, Di Birch, Mike Gunn and Paul Roberts. I am indebted to Mike Gunn who encouraged my early research and co-authored a number of articles with me, and to Di Birch who generously invited me to join the team writing commentaries in the prestigious *Criminal Law Review*. At Leeds, I am fortunate to be a member of the Criminal Justice Centre which provides a stimulating working environment with eighteen academic colleagues specialising in all aspects of criminal justice studies. In recent years I have also benefited from the experience at the Bar and have learned a great deal from colleagues in Chambers at 18 Red Lion Court, especially Peter Carter QC and my former pupil master David Huw Williams.

On a more personal note, I would like to thank Olivia for her tolerance of my endless hours in the study and my irascibility, for her invaluable assistance and unfailing encouragement.

Table of Statutes

References in **bold** type indicate where the section of an Act is set out in part or in full.

EUROPE

NEW ZEALAND

UNITED STATES

Table of Cases

Abbreviations

The following are the abbreviations used for the principal textbooks and legal journals cited in this book. References are to the latest editions, as shown below, unless it is specifically stated otherwise. The particulars of other works referred to in the text are set out in the relevant footnotes.

Andenaes, GPCL	*The General Part of the Criminal Law of Norway* (1965) by J. Andenaes.
Archbold	*Criminal Pleading, Evidence and Practice* by J. F. Archbold (2005) by P. J. Richardson and others.
Ashworth, POCL	*Principles of Criminal Law* (4th edn, 2003) by A. Ashworth.
Blackstone	*Blackstone's Criminal Practice* (2005) by P. Murphy and others.
Blackstone, *Commentaries*, i	*Commentaries on the Laws of England* by Sir William Blackstone, vol i (4 vols) (17th edn, 1830) by E. Christian.
Burchell and Hunt, SACLP	*South African Criminal Law and Procedure*, vol I, *General Principles* (1983) by F. M. Burchell, J. R. L. Milton and J. M. Burchell.
Butler	Report of the Committee on Mentally Abnormal Offenders (1975) Cmnd 6244.
CLJ	Cambridge Law Journal.
Cal Law Rev	California Law Review.
Can Bar Rev	Canadian Bar Review.
Co I Inst	*Institutes of the Laws of England* by Sir Edward Coke, vol I (4 vols) (1797).
Col LR	Columbia Law Review.
Crime, Proof and Punishment	*Crime, Proof and Punishment: Essays in Honour of Sir Rupert Cross* edited by C. F. H. Tapper (1981).
Criminal Law Essays	*Criminal Law: Essays in Honour of J. C. Smith* edited by P. F. Smith (1987).
Crim LR	Criminal Law Review.
CLP	Current Legal Problems.
CLRC/OAP/R	Criminal Law Revision Committee, Fourteenth Report, *Offences Against the Person* (1980) Cmnd 7844.
CLRC/OAP/WP	Criminal Law Revision Committee, Working Paper on Offences Against the Person (1976).
CLRC/SO/WP	Criminal Law Revision Committee, Working Paper on Sexual Offences (1980).
Draft Code	*A Criminal Code for England and Wales*, Law Com No 177 (1989).

East, I PC	*A Treatise of the Pleas of the Crown* by E. H. East, vol I (2 vols) (1803).
Edwards, *Mens Rea*	*Mens Rea in Statutory Offences* (1955) by J. Ll. J. Edwards.
Foster	*A Report on Crown Cases and Discourses on the Crown Law* by Sir Michael Foster (3rd edn, 1792) by M. Dodson.
Gordon	*Criminal Law of Scotland* (2nd edn, 1978) by G. H. Gordon.
Griew, *Theft*	*The Theft Acts 1968 and 1978* (7th edn, 1995) by E. J. Griew.
Hale, I PC	*The History of the Pleas of the Crown* by Sir Matthew Hale, vol i (2 vols) (1736).
Hall, *General Principles*	*General Principles of Criminal Law* (2nd edn, 1960) by J. Hall.
Halsbury	*The Laws of England* by the Earl of Halsbury and other lawyers (4th edn, 1973–) by Lord Hailsham of St Marylebone.
Harv LR	Harvard Law Review.
Hawkins, I PC	*A Treatise of the Pleas of the Crown* by W. Hawkins, vol I (2 vols) (8th edn, 1795) by J. Curwood.
Holdsworth, I HEL	*A History of English Law* by Sir William Holdsworth, vol i (14 vols) (1923–64).
Howard, SR	*Strict Responsibility* (1963) by Colin Howard.
J Crim L	Journal of Criminal Law (English).
J Cr L & Cr	Journal of Criminal Law and Criminology (USA).
JSPTL	Journal of the Society of Public Teachers of Law.
Kenny, *Outlines*	*Outlines of Criminal Law* by C. S. Kenny (19th edn, 1965) by J. W. C. Turner.
LQR	Law Quarterly Review.
LS	Legal Studies, the Journal of the Society of Public Teachers of Law.
MACL	*The Modern Approach to Criminal Law* edited by L. Radzinowicz and J. W. C. Turner (1948).
Med Sci & L	Medicine, Science and the Law.
MLR	Modern Law Review.
NZ Essays	*Essays on Criminal Law in New Zealand* edited by R. S. Clark (1971).
OJLS	Oxford Journal of Legal Studies.
Perkins, *Criminal Law*	*Criminal Law* (2nd edn, 1969) by R. Perkins.
Perkins and Boyce, *Criminal Law*	*Criminal Law* (3rd edn, 1982) by R. Perkins. and R. Boyce.
Pollock and Maitland, I HEL	*The History of English Law before the Time of Edward I* by Sir Frederick Pollock and F. W. Maitland, vol I (2 vols) (2nd edn).

RCCP	Report of the Royal Commission on Capital Punishment (1953) Cmd 8932.
Reshaping the Criminal Law	*Reshaping the Criminal Law: Essays in Honour of Glanville Williams* edited by P. R. Glazebrook (1978).
Russell	*Crime* by Sir W. O. Russell (12th edn, 1964) by J. W. C. Turner (2 vols).
Simester and Sullivan	*Criminal Law Theory and Doctrine* (2nd edn, 2003).
Smith, *Justification and Excuse*	*Justification and Excuse in the Criminal Law* by J. C. Smith (The Hamlyn Lectures, 1989).
Smith, *Property Offences*	*Property Offences* (1994) by A. T. H. Smith.
Smith, *Theft*	*The Law of Theft* (8th edn, 1997) by J. C. Smith.
SALJ	South African Law Journal.
Stephen, *Digest*	*A Digest of the Criminal Law* by Sir James Fitzjames Stephen (9th edn, 1950) by L. F. Sturge.
Stephen, I HCL	*A History of the Criminal Law of England* by Sir James Fitzjames Stephen, vol I (3 vols) (1883).
U Pa Law Rev	University of Pennsylvania Law Review.
Williams, CLGP	*Criminal Law: The General Part* (2nd edn, 1961) by G. L. Williams.
Williams, TBCL	*Textbook of Criminal Law* (2nd edn, 1983) by G. L. Williams.
Wilson, *Central Issues*	*Central Issues in Criminal Theory* (2002) by W. Wilson.
YLJ	Yale Law Journal.

PART I

GENERAL PRINCIPLES

1

Crime and sentence

This book is about the substantive law of crime. That is, it attempts to state and to discuss the law which determines whether any act is a crime or not. The book is not about the procedure by which the law is enforced or the evidence by which criminal offences are proved, except in so far as these matters are inseparable from the discussion of the substantive law. Procedure and evidence are subjects of equal importance which are admirably discussed in other books.

The criminal law is no more an end in itself than the law of procedure and evidence through which it is enforced. Our criminal law has grown up over many centuries and the purposes of those who have framed it, and of those who have enforced it, have undoubtedly been many and various. Consequently, it is not easy to state confidently what are the aims of the criminal law at the present day. The authors of a completely new code of criminal law are, however, in a position to state their objectives at the outset. 'The general purposes of the provisions governing the definition of offenses' in the American Law Institute's Model Penal Code[1] might be taken as a statement of the proper objectives of the substantive law of crime in a modern legal system. The purposes are:

(a) to forbid and prevent conduct that unjustifiably and inexcusably inflicts or threatens substantial harm to individual or public interests;
(b) to subject to public control persons whose conduct indicates that they are disposed to commit crimes;
(c) to safeguard conduct that is without fault from condemnation as criminal;
(d) to give fair warning of the nature of the conduct declared to be an offense;
(e) to differentiate on reasonable grounds between serious and minor offenses.[2]

The reader will judge for himself how far these purposes are fulfilled by English criminal law as he studies the general principles and particular offences discussed in the succeeding chapters. For example, whether our law is confined to forbidding conduct that is 'inexcusable', whether it adequately safeguards conduct that is without fault from condemnation as criminal, are matters which are particularly considered in the chapter on 'strict liability',[3] but which constantly arise elsewhere.

While the definition of offences can adequately *forbid* unjustifiable and inexcusable conduct, it can rarely prevent it. The Children and Young Persons (Harmful Publications)

[1] Proposed Official Draft, Art 1, 1.02 (1). Cf N. Walker, *The Aims of a Penal System.*

[2] For criticism see P. H. Robinson, 'The Modern General Part – Three Illusions', in S. Shute and A. Simester (eds), *Criminal Law Theory* (2002) 79.

[3] Below, Ch 7.

Act 1955 was said to have been 'completely successful' at a time when no prosecution had been brought under it.[4] But this is unusual. The fact that an act is known to be forbidden by the criminal law may, for many persons, be sufficient to ensure that they will not commit such an act but for others this will not be enough. Hence our need for a law of criminal procedure, of evidence – and of sentencing.[5] The mere fact of conviction, being a public condemnation of the conduct in question, has some value in the prevention of crime, but it is far from being sufficient. Some, at least, of the purposes for which the criminal law exists can be fulfilled only through the imposition of sentences. It is therefore desirable at the outset to enquire to what ends sentences are directed – or professedly directed – by those who impose them.

1. Crime and punishment

Crime has always been regarded by the courts as a moral wrong and conduct demanding retribution. The law is based on an assumption that, in the absence of evidence to the contrary, people are able to choose whether to engage in criminal conduct or not and that a person who chooses to commit a crime is responsible for the resulting wrong and deserves punishment. The courts have generally seen their task as one of fitting the penalty to the particular degree of iniquity and dangerousness of the offender's conduct on this particular occasion. The sentence should adequately reflect the revulsion felt by citizens for the particular crime. Its purpose is seen not only as punishment but also as a public denunciation of the conduct in question. It may then satisfy the demand for retaliation by the public, or some members of the public, which serious crime sometimes arouses.

The sentence must be proportionate to the offence. The business of the court is to do justice and only by achieving some measure of proportion between one sentence and another can it do justice as between one offender and another. It is difficult to say, in absolute terms, that a particular sentence of imprisonment is proportionate to a particular rape or wounding – just as in the civil law it is difficult to put a cash value on the claimant's arm when it has been lost through the defendant's negligence. We are not weighing like against like. The courts have to do the best they can. In relative terms, the notion of proportionality is more practicable. It is possible to say that one wounding is worse than another; and that, if the first deserves, say, three years' imprisonment, the other deserves two. And so, once the courts have established a point, or points, of departure, it is possible to have an approximate scale within the maximum prescribed. Sometimes a realistic statutory maximum will assist in establishing the scale. If the worst kind of case within the definition of the offence deserves the maximum, what, relatively, does this case deserve?

[4] HL, vol 299, col 451, 12 Feb 1969, quoted by G. Zellick [1970] Crim LR 192. But failure to prosecute does not mean that the harm has been eradicated. There were no prosecutions under the Prohibition of Female Circumcision Act 1985, but the practice continued and the Female Genital Mutilation Act 2003 was enacted to extend the scope of the offence.

[5] On sentencing generally, see the accounts by A. Ashworth, *Sentencing and Criminal Justice* (3rd edn, 2000), D. A. Thomas, *Principles of Sentencing* (2nd edn, 1979); and M. Wasik, *Emmins on Sentencing* (4th edn, 2001).

(a) Sentencing purposes

When a sentence is to be imposed, the first decision to be made should be as to the object to be achieved by it.[6] Is the aim simply to mete out an appropriate punishment to a wrongdoer? Or is it to deter the wrongdoer and others from committing such offences in the future? Or to protect the public by shutting the offender away? Or is it the reform of the offender? Or a combination of these objects? Numerous theories of punishment have been advanced including those of deterrence, retribution, rehabilitation, restitution, incapacitation and denunciation. Parliament has regarded various of these theories as being more influential at one time or another, and its failure to adopt a single principled approach to sentencing for any sustained period has become a matter of concern in recent years.[7] The shift in attitude is illustrated by comparison of the sentencing provisions of the Criminal Justice Act 1991 with those of the Criminal Justice Act 2003. In the 1991 Act the overriding principle was that criminals should 'get their just deserts'.[8] Retribution was central to the statutory framework for sentencing established by the Criminal Justice Act 1991.[9] The sentencing court was to have constant regard to the 'seriousness' of the offence. Custody was not to be imposed unless the seriousness of the offence required it or, in the case of a violent or sexual offence, custody was necessary to protect the public from the offender. If custody was imposed, it had to be commensurate with the seriousness of the offence unless a longer sentence was necessary to protect the public from a violent or sexual offender. If the offence was not serious enough to require custody, a non-custodial sentence involving some interference with liberty could be imposed – but only if the offence was serious enough to justify it. Under the 2003 Act, deterrence has assumed a more significant role. Section 142 of the Act provides the various aims of the sentencing court:

> (1) Any court dealing with an offender in respect of his offence must have regard to the following
>
> (a) the punishment of offenders,
>
> (b) the reduction of crime (including its reduction by deterrence),
>
> (c) the reform and rehabilitation of offenders,
>
> (d) the protection of the public, and
>
> (e) the making of reparation by offenders to persons affected by their offences.

It is difficult to see how a court can have in mind all of these purposes in any one case and apply each appropriately and consistently.

(b) Moral fault and harm done

How is the gravity of the offence to be assessed? Section 143 of the Criminal Justice Act 2003[10] is intended to provide the courts with guidance on this.

[6] See D. A. Thomas, 'Sentencing: The Basic Principles' [1967] Crim LR 455 and 503.

[7] See the amendment to the Criminal Justice Act 1991 with the Criminal Justice Act 1993, the Criminal Justice and Public Order Act 1994, the Crime (Sentencing) Act 1997, the Youth Justice and Criminal Evidence Act 1999 and the consolidation in the Powers of Criminal Courts (Sentencing) Act 2000.

[8] Crime, Justice and Protecting the Public, Cm 965, para 2.1.

[9] As consolidated in the Powers of Criminal Courts (Sentencing) Act 2000 (hereafter 'PCC(S)A 2000').

[10] D. A. Thomas, *Sentencing References 2005/2006* (2005).

(1) In considering the seriousness of any offence, the court must consider the offender's culpability in committing the offence and any harm which the offence caused, was intended to cause or might forseeably have caused.

(2) In considering the seriousness of an offence ('the current offence') committed by an offender who has one or more previous convictions, the court must treat each previous conviction as an aggravating factor if (in the case of that conviction) the court considers that it can reasonably be so treated having regard, in particular, to –

(a) the nature of the offence to which the conviction relates and its relevance to the current offence, and

(b) the time that has elapsed since the conviction.

(3) In considering the seriousness of any offence committed while the offender was on bail, the court must treat the fact that it was committed in those circumstances as an aggravating factor.

In assessing gravity the courts must therefore have regard not only to the moral fault of the offender in terms of the harm that he intended or foresaw but also the amount of harm he has done. Although the assessment involves this explicit reference to the harm intended or foreseen, or, at least, foreseeable, rather than on the chance of what actually happens, the fact is that the law attaches greater significance to the harm done,[11] and that greater significance is ever more frequently reflected in the maximum sentences prescribed for crimes. For example, it is now an offence punishable with 14 years' imprisonment to cause death by careless driving when under the influence of drink or drugs.[12] 'Joyriding', as taking a vehicle without the owner's consent is popularly and unhappily called, is punishable with six months' imprisonment but, if personal injury is caused, the maximum goes up to two years, and, if death is caused, 14 years.[13] In terms of the sentence actually handed down it has also long been accepted that the practice of the courts is to punish the attempt less severely than the complete offence. Less harm has been done.

(c) Arriving at the right sentence in a given case

(i) The statutory maximum

For many years it was the almost invariable practice of Parliament to fix a maximum but no minimum sentence and to leave it to the judge or magistrate to decide what sentence in the range from an absolute discharge to the specified maximum it is right to impose. Even where the maximum is imprisonment for life the court may grant an absolute discharge. The only significant exception to this rule was murder where the court has no discretion and is required to impose a sentence of life imprisonment in all cases. Recently, a marked unwillingness by politicians to trust the courts to impose a sufficiently severe sentence in certain types of case together with concern about persistent offenders has

11 Cf the arguments advanced in particular by Professor Ashworth, see eg 'Defining Offences Without Harm', in P. F. Smith (ed), *Essays in Honour of J. C. Smith* (1987).

12 Road Traffic Act 1988, s 3A, as amended, below, p 1017.

13 Below, p 1017.

resulted in an increase in the number of offences and circumstances in which Parliament has decreed that mandatory penalties are to be imposed. Except in these cases, the practice of Parliament is based on a recognition of the fact that the imperfections of definition are such that any definition, however carefully drafted, will embrace a wide range of culpability and that there will be some acts falling within it which are morally blameless and deserving of no punishment. Murder is no different from other crimes in this respect but it has always been treated differently for historical, emotional and, perhaps, political reasons.

(ii) The tariff

The statutory maximum gives very limited guidance to a court. It is useful only when it is not altogether out of proportion to contemporary attitudes to the crime in question. Many maxima have been revised recently but others have remained unchanged since the nineteenth century. Their origins can be traced to the terms of transportation which took the place of capital punishment in the 1820s and 1830s. Even in the case of modern revisions the practice of fixing a maximum high enough to cover the worst type of case results in maxima far above the normal range of sentences. In 1968 Parliament fixed the maximum sentence for theft at 10 years – an unrealistically long term which was never imposed. The Criminal Justice Act 1991, s 26(1) reduces it to seven years but even this reduced maximum gives no guidance whatever to a magistrates' court and very little to a Crown Court, except in a very unusual case.

This is not say that the maxima have no significance beyond the obligation not to exceed them. Where the judge imposed the maximum sentence of two years upon a man convicted of reckless driving (an offence now replaced by dangerous driving) in a case where the passengers in the other car narrowly escaped being burnt to death, the Court of Appeal reduced the sentence to 18 months, saying that it was important to bear in mind that Parliament had drawn a distinction between reckless driving and causing death by reckless driving which was punishable with five years' imprisonment.[14]

That decision also demonstrates the principle that the maximum should be reserved for the worst type of case which comes before the court and a sentence which does not allow for this is wrong in principle.[15] The inconsistency in statutory maxima can produce strange anomalies.

(iii) The sentencing exercise

In principle, in the sentencing exercise the courts need to treat like cases alike and to deal consistently and transparently with relevant differences in criminal conduct between offenders. This is not an exercise in guesswork, nor can it be an exact science. As noted above, it is an attempt to maintain proportionality in the sentences awarded. The courts rely on the guidelines issued from the Court of Appeal.[16] These guidelines are informed by reports published by the Sentencing Guidelines Council[17] after widespread

14 *Staddon* [1992] Crim LR 70.

15 Judges should not, however, use their imaginations to conjure up unlikely worst possible kinds of case: *Ambler* [1976] Crim LR 266.

16 See eg *McInerney* [2003] 1 All ER 1089 on burglary or *Billam* (1986) 82 Cr App R 347 on rape sentencing under the Sexual Offences Act 1956.

17 www.sentencing-guidelines.gov.uk/.

consultation, and the Court of Appeal has a wide opportunity to issue guidelines in appeals from the defence and, on appeals by the Attorney-General,[18] with leave of the Court of Appeal, on sentences that appear to the Attorney to be unduly lenient. In the magistrates' court the Magistrates Association Guidelines are published to assist magistrates.

The court, having considered the relevant maximum sentence and the guideline cases, having heard counsel for the defence in mitigation, and having regard to any pre-sentence reports about the offender, may impose the appropriate sentence. The courts face a difficult task in securing equal treatment in sentencing while maintaining the flexibility necessary to do justice to the factual circumstances of the case. In one sense, the task is made more complex, rather than assisted, by the range of disposal powers available to the court. Aside from discharges (conditional and absolute), there are custodial sentences which under the 2003 Act come in many forms,[19] in addition there is a range of community punishments available to the court.[20] Fines remain an enormously important disposal power for the less serious crimes. In the Crown Court fines are unlimited. The maximum fine for an either way offence tried summarily is currently £5,000.[21] There is a standard scale of maximum fines on an adult on conviction of a summary offence,[22] with the maximum currently being £5,000. The Secretary of State is empowered by s 48 of the Criminal Justice Act 1982 to vary the maximum amount of fines, including the amounts specified in the standard scale, as appears to him to be justified by the change.

References to the maximum sentence of imprisonment for an offence tried in the magistrates' court are, throughout the book, based on the law in April 2005. When the Criminal Justice Act 2003, ss 280 and 281 are brought into force, many summary offences will carry a maximum term of imprisonment of 51 weeks where the offence is summary only, and 12 months where it is an offence triable either way.

18 Criminal Justice Act 1988, s 36.

19 If brought into force these include 'intermittent custody' (weekends in prison) and 'custody plus' (short terms of imprisonment with periods on licence).

20 These are in process of change as provisions of the Criminal Justice Act 2003 come into force, but include innovative forms of disposal such as electronic tagging, curfew orders, exclusion orders, supervision orders and drug treatment and testing orders.

21 Magistrates' Courts Act 1980, s 32.

22 Criminal Justice Act 1982, s 37.

2

The definition of a crime[1]

It is now rather unfashionable to begin law books with definitions. One reason for this is the difficulty frequently encountered in defining the subject matter of a particular branch of the law; and nowhere has this been more greatly felt than in the criminal law. But a book about crimes which does not tell the reader what a crime is allows him to proceed with his own preconceived notions in the matter; and it is well recognized that there is a popular meaning of crime which is different from, less precise, and narrower than, the legal meaning. A law book must be concerned with the legal meaning of crime; and the reader is entitled to know what it is, or at least why it is so difficult to tell him. Although it is easy to trace the meaning of the word 'crime' to the Latin 'crimen' (accusation), that takes us no further forward to an understanding of the subject. Common definitions from non-legal dictionaries do not provide much help either with bland definitions such as 'an act or omission prohibited and punished by law'.

A simple definition of a crime as a wrong, prosecuted and carrying a penalty might satisfy the layman without providing any sufficient answer for the lawyer. Arguably, an exercise in further definition is futile since every lawyer knows a crime when they see it, but a ready response to this claim is that not all crimes are readily identifiable even to the lawyer. This is inevitable when there are around 8,000 crimes in England and Wales[2] covering such diverse activities as murder, rape, being in possession of an unlicensed dangerous dog[3] and obstructing a clergyman in the discharge of his duties in place of worship or on his way thither.[4] But given the importance of the criminal law in terms of what is at stake and how often it is used, surely a definition could and should be produced?

An attempt to define *a crime* at once encounters a difficulty. If the definition is a true one, it should enable us to recognize any *act* (or *omission*) as a crime, or not a crime, by seeing whether it contains all the ingredients of the definition. But reflection will show that this is impossible. When Parliament enacts that a particular act shall become a crime or that an act which is now criminal shall cease to be so, the act does not change in nature in any respect other than that of legal classification. All its observable characteristics are precisely the same before as after the statute comes into force. Any attempt at definition of a crime will thus either include the act at a time when it is not a crime, or exclude it when it is. Suicide was a crime until 3 August 1961, when, by the Suicide Act 1961,[5]

1 C. S. Kenny, *Outlines of Criminal Law* (15th edn) ch 1; G. Williams, 'The Definition of Crime' (1955) 8 CLP 107; G. Hughes, 'The Concept of Crime: An American View' [1959] Crim LR 239 and 331.

2 Not including the thousands of bye-laws created at a local level.

3 See the Dangerous Dogs Act 1991.

4 Offences Against the Person Act 1861, s 36.

5 Below, Ch 14.

it became perfectly lawful to kill oneself. The nature of the act in question, its morality or immorality and the consequence do not change overnight; but its legal nature does.

1. Sources of criminal law

The task of identifying a clear definition of crime, or even identifying common characteristics, is not assisted by the diverse range of sources from which existing offences derive, including in particular the many important and serious offences which derive from the common law rather than statute (for example, murder, manslaughter, conspiracy to defraud). It may seem surprising that the courts in the twenty-first century are still relying on definitions of offences from judicial pronouncements of centuries ago, or even from the common law writers and reporters of that antiquity – East,[6] Hale,[7] Coke,[8] Hawkins,[9] etc. The common law – with all its ambiguities and flexibility – notwithstanding, most of the English criminal law is now contained in thousands of independent statutes. These are not collected together as a catalogue of 'criminal legislation',[10] and many offences appear in an otherwise unrelated statute, as for example, with the Insolvency Act 1986. In addition, as supranational legal regimes have begun to exert more of an influence on English criminal law, the range of sources extends ever wider. The most obvious example is European Union law, which lies behind numerous offences in English law.

An important consequence of this range of sources is that it is less easy to identify any unifying thread to the criminal law: in truth there no longer is one.[11] This inhibits certainty and consistency in application of the law. As Glazebrook recently observed, 'the materials of our criminal law [are] now so voluminous, chaotic and contradictory, [that] the Law Lords are left free to decide cases as the fancy takes them.'[12]

Yet a further reason for the lack of a clear definition of crime arises from England's lack of a code of criminal law – a single scheme of offences and elements of the General Part of criminal law. This not only adds to a lack of clarity, but also to a lack of accessibility. The Law Commission's[13] declared objective in its project to create a Criminal Code for England and Wales is to enhance the law's accessibility, comprehensibility, consistency and certainty. A criminal code has obvious attractions beyond these important objectives. A code would help to ensure that national law meets its international obligations. Symbolically also, the adoption of a criminal code provides an opportunity for the State to declare its position in relation to criminal behaviour in a transparent

[6] E. H. East, *A Treatise of the Pleas of the Crown* (1803).

[7] M. Hale, *The History of the Pleas of the Crown* (1736).

[8] Co I Inst, *Institutes of the Laws of England* (1797).

[9] J. Curwood (ed), *A Treatise of the Pleas of the Crown* (8th edn, 1795).

[10] Even within the exclusively criminal statutes, it is often difficult to discern the present law since they are too readily and heavily amended without being republished in consolidated form.

[11] A. Ashworth, 'Is the Criminal Law a Lost Cause?' (2000) 116 LQR 225.

[12] P. Glazebrook, 'How Old Do You Think She Was?' [2001] CLJ 26, 30.

[13] See www.lawcommission.gov.uk.

fashion.[14] A criminal law with a single accessible authoritative source, which is internally consistent and certain would in most people's eyes be a welcome development, outweighing the risks that the code would be too inflexible and that judicial innovation would be stifled. Although historically England was a great exporter of criminal codes,[15] there is no sign of the adoption of the Draft Criminal Code produced in 1989 by a team of senior academic criminal lawyers.[16] The Law Commission has supplemented this Code with numerous draft Bills attached to its closely argued Reports on many areas of law (which are referred to at relevant points throughout the book) and there have been calls for the implementation of some of these reports by successive Lord Chief Justices,[17] and by the former Chair of the Law Commission[18] – sadly to no avail.

2. Characteristics of a crime

Despite the lack of a universally accepted definition or clear unified source of criminal law, it is possible to point to certain characteristics, which are generally found in conduct which is criminal, in particular, it usually involves a public wrong and a moral wrong.

(a) A 'public' wrong

Crimes are generally acts which have a particularly harmful effect on the public and do more than interfere with merely private rights. Sir Carleton Allen writes:

> Crime is crime because it consists in wrongdoing which directly and in serious degree threatens the security or well-being of society, and because it is not safe to leave it redressable only by compensation of the party injured.[19]

This explains why acts have been made crimes either by judicial decision or by legislation, and it does not necessarily accurately represent the present state of affairs. A crime may remain a crime long after it has ceased to be a threat to the security or well-being of society.[20] Thus Allen's proposition tells us what – as he thinks – ought to be criminal rather than what is criminal.

The 'public' nature of crimes is evidenced by the contrast between the rules of civil and criminal procedure. Any citizen can, as a general rule and in the absence of some provision to the contrary, bring a criminal prosecution, whether or not he has suffered

14 There is a considerable literature as to the advantages of a Code and what form a Code might best take: see G. de Búrca and S. Gardner, 'Codification of the Criminal Law' (1990) 10 OJLS 559; R. A. Duff, 'Rule Violations and Wrong Doings' in S. Shute and A. Simester (eds), *Criminal Law Theory* (2002); P. Alldridge, 'Making Criminal Law Known' (ibid). See also on recent developments in other jurisdictions P. R. Ferguson, 'Codifying Criminal Law: The Scots and English Draft Codes Compared' [2004] Crim LR 105; J. P. McCutcheon and K. Quinn, 'Codifying Criminal Law in Ireland' (1998) Statute Law Review 131.

15 J. F. Stephen, *A Digest of the Criminal Law* and *A History of the Criminal Law of England* (1883).

16 *A Criminal Code for England and Wales* (Law Com Report No 177, 1989).

17 See eg the statements by Lord Bingham of Cornhill, 'A Criminal Code: Must We Wait For Ever?' [1998] Crim LR 694.

18 See M. Arden, 'Criminal Law at the Crossroads: the impact on human rights from the Law Commission's perspective and the need for a Code' [1999] Crim LR 439.

19 C. K. Allen, 'The Nature of a Crime', *Journal of Society of Comparative Legislation*, Feb 1931, reprinted in *Legal Duties*, 221, at 233–234.

20 Williams, 8 CLP at 126–127.

any special harm over and above other members of the public. As a member of the public he has an interest in the enforcement of the criminal law. D steals V's watch. V may prosecute him – so may X, Y, Z or any other citizen.[21] In practice, of course, the vast majority of prosecutions are carried on by the Crown Prosecution Service or the Commissioners of Customs and Excise or other public officers who have no personal interest in the outcome. The victim of an offence cannot prevent the prosecution of the offender. The DPP's consent to a prosecution is not subject to judicial review in the absence of *mala fides.* The individual who starts a prosecution may not discontinue it at will,[22] for it is not only his concern but that of every citizen. The Crown, however, through the entry of a *nolle prosequi* by the Attorney-General, may stay the proceedings at any time[23] without the consent of the prosecutor. If the prosecution succeeds and a sentence is imposed by the court, the instigator of the prosecution has no power to pardon the offender. This power belongs exclusively to the Crown, representing the public interest in the matter. It is important not to assimilate the position of the Crown with that of the victim. The recognition of the victim in the criminal process has been marked over the last decade, but in terms of substantive law, the formal position is that the prosecution is brought by the Crown, and the Crown is not seen as a surrogate victim.[24]

All this contrasts sharply with civil wrongs – torts and breaches of contract. There, only the person injured may sue. He (and only he) may freely discontinue the proceedings at any time and, if he succeeds and an award of damages is made in his favour, he may, at his entire discretion, forgive the defendant and terminate his liability.

Crimes, then, are wrongs which the judges have held, or Parliament has from time to time laid down, to be sufficiently injurious to the public to warrant the application of criminal procedure to deal with them. Of course this does not enable us to recognize an act as a crime when we see one. Some acts are so obviously harmful to the public that *anyone* would say they should be criminal – and such acts almost certainly are – but there are many others about which opinions may differ widely. When a citizen is heard urging that, 'There ought to be a law against it . . .', he is expressing his personal conviction that some variety of act is so harmful to society that it ought to be discouraged by being made the subject of criminal proceedings. There will almost invariably be a body of opinion which disagrees. But even if *everyone* agreed with him, the act in question would not thereby become a crime. Public condemnation is ineffective without the endorsement of an Act of Parliament or a decision of a court.[25]

It is important at this point to recall one of the unique features of the criminal law. Its sanction is the most coercive method of regulating an individual's behaviour. The whole criminal justice system involves State infringements of the personal autonomy from

[21] The right of private prosecution is unaffected by the Prosecution of Offences Act 1985; but s 24 empowers the High Court, on the application of the Attorney-General, to restrain a vexatious prosecutor. The DPP may take over a private prosecution at any stage (s 6(2)) and may discontinue a prosecution during its 'preliminary stage': s 23.

[22] *Wood* (1832) 3 B & Ad 657.

[23] After the indictment has been signed: *Wylie* (1919) 83 JP 295. But the Director of Public Prosecutions may intervene and offer no evidence: *Turner v Director of Public Prosecutions* (1978) 68 Cr App R 70 (Mars Jones J), [1978] Crim LR 754; *Raymond v A-G* [1982] QB 839, [1982] 2 All ER 487, CA, [1982] Crim LR 826 and commentary.

[24] See *Weir* [2001] 1 WLR 421, HL.

[25] Witness the recent Radio 4 poll to find the listeners' law, discussed in Ch 11 below.

the possibility of investigation and surveillance, arrest, search, seizure, through the trial process, which may include pre-trial detention, to punishment including the ultimate infringement – imprisonment. The range of punishments available to the criminal courts all have one thing in common: a degree of stigma.[26] This degree of coercion is qualitatively different from that in the civil law. For the liberal at least, criminalization should be a matter of last resort because of this stigmatization and the most intrusive forms of State intervention it entails. There should be a principle of what Ashworth calls 'minimal criminalisation'.[27] The point is not so much to reduce criminal law to its absolute minimum, as to ensure that resort is only had to the criminalization in order to protect individual autonomy, or to protect those social arrangements necessary to ensure that individuals have the capacity and facilities to exercise their autonomy.[28]

(b) A 'moral' wrong

The second characteristic of crimes which is usually emphasized is that they are acts which are morally wrong.

(i) Morality

As seen above, the traditional attitude of the common law has been that crimes are essentially immoral acts deserving of punishment. In the early days of the law, when the number of crimes was relatively few and only the most outrageous acts were prohibited – murder, robbery, rape, etc – this was, no doubt, true. But experience suggests that morality and the criminal law are not co-extensive, and a review of the current range of criminal offences in England, demonstrates that this proposition is undoubtedly true. Many acts are now prohibited on the grounds of social expediency and not because of their immoral nature. This is especially so in the field of summary offences – and summary offences are crimes.[29] Moreover, many acts which are generally regarded as immoral – for example, adultery – are not crimes. The test of immorality is not a very helpful one.

There is a further difficulty which arises in classifying action as criminal on the basis of its purported immorality – whose morality should form the benchmark for criminalization? This problem is illustrated well by the problem of drawing appropriate legal limits on the level of physical harm to which a sane adult might consent being inflicted on him. Very different answers would be provided by, eg, the liberal, the paternalist, and by the legal moralist.[30]

Whether an act ought to be a crime *simply* on the ground of its immoral nature has been the subject of vigorous debate. The view of the Wolfenden Committee on

26 See N. Walker and C. Marsh, 'Do Sentences Affect Public Disapproval?' (1984) British Journal of Criminology 27; N. Walker, *Punishment, Danger and Stigma* (1980).

27 For an excellent and accessible account of the principles of criminalization see Ashworth, POCL, Ch 2 and 3.

28 N. Lacey, *Unspeakable Subjects* (1998); *State Punishment* (1988).

29 Williams (1955) 8 CLP at 110. It is true that courts have frequently declined to attribute all the normal incidents of a crime to a regulatory offence on the grounds that it is 'not truly criminal' or is 'quasi-criminal:' *Harrow London Borough Council v Shah* [1999] 3 All ER 302, [1999] Crim LR 992, DC, below, p 148. But this is a dubious argument. By any recognized test, the offence is criminal.

30 See the decision of the House of Lords in *Brown* [1994] AC 212, and Law Comm Consultation Paper No 139 (1995), Appendix C. Cf P. Roberts, 'Consent in the Criminal Law' (1997) 17 OJLS 389 and S. Shute, 'The Law Commission's Second Consultation Paper on Consent' [1996] Crim LR 684.

Homosexual Offences and Prostitution was that the enforcement of morality is not a proper object of the criminal law. The function of the criminal law, as they saw it is:

> ... to preserve public order and decency, to protect the citizen from what is offensive or injurious, and to provide sufficient safeguards against exploitation and corruption of others, particularly those who are specially vulnerable ...
>
> It is not ... the function of the law to intervene in the private lives of citizens, or to seek to enforce any particular pattern of behaviour, further than is necessary to carry out the purposes we have outlined.[31]

This view was challenged by Lord Devlin,[32] who argued that there is a public morality which is an essential part of the bond which keeps society together; and that society may use the criminal law to preserve morality in the same way that it uses it to preserve anything else that is essential to its existence. The standard of morality is that of 'the man in the jury box', based on the 'mass of continuous experience half-consciously or unconsciously accumulated and embodied in the morality of common sense'.

To this it was answered[33] that it is not proper for the State to enforce the general morality without asking whether it is based on ignorance, superstition or misunderstanding; that it is not a sufficient ground for prohibiting an act that 'the thought of it makes the man on the Clapham omnibus sick'. But if we are not to base criminal law on the general morality, does not this imply that 'our law making is or should be controlled by independent Gods of Pure Reason, installed somewhere in our political systems and endowed with power to determine such questions for society, free of the prejudices to which lesser men are subject?'[34] 'A free society is as much offended by the dictates of an intellectual oligarchy as by those of an autocrat.'[35]

In the midst of this controversy was decided the case of *Shaw v Director of Public Prosecutions*,[36] in which Lord Simonds asserted that:

> there remains in the courts of law a residual power to enforce the supreme and fundamental purpose of the law, to conserve not only the safety and order *but also the moral welfare of the state*;

and that the King's Bench was the *custos morum* of the people and had the superintendency of offences *contra bonos mores*.

> '*Shaw's* case', concludes Lord Devlin, 'settles for the purpose of the law that morality in England means what twelve men and women think it means – in other words it is to be ascertained as a question of fact.'[37]

Subsequently, however, the particular rule of law that caused the Wolfenden Committee to formulate its general principle[38] – that homosexual conduct between

31 (1957) Cmnd 247, para 13.

32 The Maccabaean Lecture, 'The Enforcement of Morals' (1959) 45 *Proc. of British Academy* 129, reprinted in *The Enforcement of Morals* (1965), 1.

33 H. L. A. Hart, *The Listener*, 30 July 1959, p 162.

34 E. V. Rostow, 'The Enforcement of Morals' [1960] CLJ 174 at 189.

35 P. Devlin, 'Law, Democracy and Morality' (1962) 110 U Pa Law Rev 635 at 642, reprinted in *The Enforcement of Morals* (1965) p 86.

36 [1962] AC 220, [1961] 2 All ER 446; below, p 390.

37 110 U Pa Law Rev at 648. See also H. L. A. Hart, *Law, Liberty and Morality*; G. Hughes, 'Morals and the Criminal Law' (1962) 71 YLJ 662. For an excellent discussion of the whole controversy, see Basil Mitchell, *Law, Morality and Religion in a Secular Society* (1967).

38 Above, n 31.

consenting male adults is an offence – was repealed by the Sexual Offences Act 1967. The House of Lords has repudiated the suggestion that it has power to extend the criminal law to enforce good morals.[39]

(ii) Harms or wrongs to others

Implicit in a requirement that a crime incorporates a moral wrong is the acceptance that a 'wrong' or harm to another or others is involved. Again, this poses a problem since it is only if there is agreement as to the moral bases for criminalizing that there is likely to be agreement as to whether the conduct involves a harm. What will be 'wrong' or 'harmful' for the paternalist will not necessarily be so for the liberal. English criminal law is based largely on the liberal principle and accordingly, wrongs are commonly assessed by reference to whether the conduct in question infringes the autonomy of another or causes serious offence to another. By far the most refined examination of this aspect of crimes has been that of Professor Feinberg, but he is not alone in recognizing the utility of the harm principle. In the late 1970s Gross dealt with the issue as had Packer a decade earlier.[40]

> The harm to others formula seems to me to have two uses that justify its inclusion in a list of limiting criteria for invocation of the criminal sanction. First, it is a way to make sure that a given form of conduct is not being subjected to the criminal sanction purely or even primarily because it is thought to be immoral. It forces an inquiry into precisely what bad effects are feared if the conduct in question is not suppressed by the criminal law. Second, it immediately brings into play a host of secular inquiries about the effects of subjecting the conduct in question to the criminal sanction. One cannot meaningfully deal with the question of harm to others without weighing benefits against detriments. In that sense, it is a kind of threshold question, important not so much in itself, as in focusing attention on the further considerations relevant to the ultimate decision. It is for these two instrumental reasons rather than for either its intrinsic rightness or ease of application that it deserves inclusion.[41]

Classification of an activity as harmful or wrong or involving a 'setback to interests' will often be a controversial question.[42] In recent years English law has, according to many commentators, too readily accepted that a form of behaviour is sufficiently harmful or wrong to warrant criminalization (rather than some alternative less coercive form of regulation).[43]

In identifying the interests to be protected by the criminal law, it is increasingly important to recognize the State's obligation to protect the rights of citizens as protected by the ECHR. Thus, where Article 3 guarantees a right to be free from inhuman and degrading treatment, it is incumbent on the State through the process of the criminal law to provide adequate protection against the infliction of such harm as corporal

39 *Knuller (Publishing, Printing and Promotions) Ltd v Director of Public Prosecutions* [1973] AC 435, [1972] 2 All ER 898, below, p 947. Such judicial offence creation would contravene Article 7 of the ECHR which protects against retrospective criminalization.

40 J. Feinberg, *Harm to Others* (1984); H. Packer, *The Limits of the Criminal Sanction* (1968), 266; H. Gross, *A Theory of Criminal Justice* (1979), 119.

41 Packer, above n 40 p 262.

42 Elaborate systems for differentiating levels of harm and relative offence seriousness have been devised, see A. von Hirsch and N. Jareborg, 'Gauging Criminal Harm: A Living Standard Analysis' (1991) 11 OJLS 1.

43 See A. Ashworth, 'Interpreting Criminal Statutes: A Crisis of Legality' (1991) 117 LQR 419.

punishment.[44] Similarly where Article 2 of the ECHR guarantees a right to life, it is incumbent on the State to provide adequate protection of that right for each citizen.[45]

3. Criminal proceedings

Because of the impossibility of defining the criminal quality of an act, most writers – and the courts – have been driven to turn to the nature of the proceedings which may follow from its commission as a means of identifying crimes.

> The criminal quality of an act cannot be discerned by intuition; nor can it be discovered by reference to any standard but one: is the act prohibited with penal consequences?[46]

The problem then becomes one of distinguishing criminal proceedings from civil proceedings. Any attempt to distinguish between crimes and torts comes up against the same kind of difficulty encountered in defining crimes generally: that most torts are crimes as well, though some torts are not crimes and some crimes are not torts. It is not in the nature of the act, but in the nature of the proceedings that the distinction consists; and both types of proceeding may follow where an act is both a crime and a tort.[47]

Kenny,[48] in perhaps the most celebrated of all attempts to define a crime, directed his attention to ascertaining the essential distinction between civil and criminal procedure. He rejected any distinction based on (i) the degree of activity manifested by the State in the two types of proceeding; for though the 'contrast is a genuine and vivid one', it was incapable of being applied with precision; (ii) the tribunals; for both civil and criminal cases may be heard in the magistrates' courts and the House of Lords; (iii) the object of the proceedings; for, while 'the object of criminal procedure is always *Punishment*', the award of exemplary damages in civil actions is also punitive; (iv) the nature of the sanctions; for, while criminal sanctions never enrich any individual, it was not true to say that all civil actions do, since some civil actions for penalties could be brought only by the Crown.

Kenny finally seized upon the degree of control exercised over the two types of proceedings by the Crown[49] as the criterion, and defined 'crimes' as:

> wrongs whose sanction is punitive and is in no way remissible by any private person, but is remissible by the Crown alone, *if remissible at all.*[50]

He thought it necessary to bring in the elements of punishment only to exclude action for the recovery of the Crown's debts or other civil rights; and the italicized words were included so as not to exclude certain crimes which cannot be pardoned.[51]

44 See below, Ch 15.

45 See the discussion below, Ch 15.

46 *Proprietary Articles Trade Association v A-G for Canada* [1931] AC 310 at 324, per Lord Atkin.

47 A civil action for assault or battery is barred by the Offences Against the Person Act 1861, ss 44 and 45 if criminal proceedings brought in the magistrates' court by or on behalf of the victim (i) have been dismissed and a certificate of dismissal has been issued; or (ii) have resulted in conviction and the defendant has paid anything he was ordered to pay or has served any imprisonment imposed. See *Stevens and Whitehouse* (1991) 155 JP 697.

48 *Outlines of Criminal Law* (15th edn), ch 1.

49 Above, p 12.

50 Above, at 1.

51 A public nuisance while still unabated and offences under Habeas Corpus Act 1679, s 11.

Kenny's definition has been much criticized. Winfield[52] thought it led to a vicious circle:

What is a crime? Something that the Crown alone can pardon. What is it that the Crown alone can pardon? A crime.[53]

Winfield thought it advisable not to accept this part of Kenny's definition; and he concentrated on the question, what is punishment? The answer he arrived at is that: 'The essence of punishment is its inevitability . . . no option is left to the offender as to whether he shall endure it or not'; whereas, in a civil case, 'he can always compromise or get rid of his liability with the assent of the injured party'.[54] Thus we seem to arrive back at the just rejected test of who can remit the sanction.

More substantial is the point made by Williams.[55] If we are going to define crime by reference to procedure, we ought to make use of the whole law of procedure, not just one item of it – the power to remit the sanction. If a court has to decide whether a particular act which has been prohibited by Parliament is a crime, it may be guided by a reference in the statute to any element which exists only in civil, or only in criminal, procedure as the case may be. A crime is:

an act that is capable of being followed by criminal proceedings, having one of the types of outcome (punishment, etc) known to follow these proceedings.[56]

This definition is by no means so unhelpful as at first sight may appear; for there are many points of distinction between civil and criminal procedure, and the specification in a statute of any one procedural feature which is peculiar either to the civil or the criminal law will therefore point to the nature of the wrong. The question in issue may well be whether a rule of criminal, or a rule of civil, procedure should be followed.[57] While it may be that no statute or decision gives guidance on this precise point, the procedure test may yet supply the answer if a statute or decision indicates, as the appropriate procedure, some other rule which is peculiar either to civil or to criminal proceedings. Of course, the definition tells us nothing about what acts *ought* to be crimes, but that is not its purpose. Writers who set out to define a crime by reference to the nature of the act, on the other hand, inevitably end by telling us, not what a crime is, but what the writer thinks it ought to be; and that is not a definition of a crime.

4. The practical test

From time to time the courts have found it necessary to determine whether a proceeding is criminal or not. Before the Criminal Evidence Act 1898, the defendant could not give evidence on oath on his own behalf in a criminal case whereas (since the Evidence Act 1851) he had been able to do so in a civil action. If he wished to give evidence the nature of the proceeding had to be ascertained.[58] The same problem could arise today if it

52 *Province of the Law of Tort*, Ch VIII. 53 Ibid, at 197.
54 Ibid, at 200. 55 8 CLP 107 at 128. 56 Ibid, at 123.
57 Cf P. J. Fitzgerald, 'A Concept of Crime' [1960] Crim LR 257 at 259–260.
58 *Cattell v Ireson* (1858) EB & E 91; *Parker v Green* (1862) 2 B & S 299.

were sought to *compel* the defendant to give evidence.[59] But much the most fruitful source of this problem has been the Judicature Act 1873, s 47, and its successor, the Judicature Act 1925, s 31(1)(a), which, until 1968,[60] provided that no appeal should lie to the Court of Appeal 'in any criminal cause or matter'. The question whether a particular proceeding is a criminal cause or matter has frequently come before the Court of Appeal and the House of Lords. In these cases the test which has regularly been applied is whether the proceedings may result in the punishment of the offender. If it may, then it is a criminal proceeding.[61] As a practical test, this seems to work well enough; but it must always be remembered that it is a rule with exceptions; for some actions for penalties are undoubtedly civil actions, and yet they have the punishment of the offender as their objective; for this reason the test of punishment is jurisprudentially unsatisfactory.[62]

The meaning of punishment itself is not easy to ascertain; for the defendant in a civil case, who is ordered to pay damages by way of compensation, may well feel that he has been punished. It has been suggested[63] that:

> What distinguishes a criminal from a civil sanction and all that distinguishes it . . . is the judgment of community condemnation which accompanies and justifies its imposition.

According to this view it is the condemnation, plus the consequences of the sentence – fine or imprisonment, etc – which together constitute the punishment; but the condemnation is the essential feature. From this, it is argued that:

> we can say readily enough what a 'crime' is:
>
> It is not simply anything which the legislature chooses to call a 'crime'. It is not simply anti-social conduct which public officers are given a responsibility to suppress. It is not simply any conduct to which a legislature chooses to attach a 'criminal' penalty. It is conduct which, if duly shown to have taken place, will incur a formal and solemn pronouncement of the moral condemnation of the community.[64]

But if 'the formal and solemn pronouncement' means the judgment of a criminal court (and what else can it mean?) we are driven back to ascertaining whether the proceeding is criminal or not. How is the judge to know whether to make 'solemn and formal pronouncement of condemnation' or to give judgment as in a civil action? Surely, only by ascertaining whether the legislature (or the courts in the case of a common law crime) have prescribed that the proceedings shall be criminal; and this must depend, primarily, upon whether it is intended to be punitive.

59 He is compellable in a civil but not in a criminal case.

60 Appeal now lies to the Court of Appeal (Criminal Division) as provided by the Criminal Appeal Act 1968.

61 Eg *Mellor v Denham* (1880) 5 QBD 467; *Seaman v Burley* [1896] 2 QB 344; *Robson v Biggar* [1908] 1 KB 672; *Re Clifford and O'Sullivan* [1921] 2 AC 570; *Amand v Home Secretary and Minister of Defence of the Royal Netherlands Government* [1943] AC 147, [1942] 2 All ER 381; *Re Osman (No 4)* [1991] Crim LR 533.

62 It is thought not to be a substantial objection that exemplary damages may be awarded in some civil cases; for this is merely ancillary to the main object and the occasions for their award are now much restricted: *Rookes v Barnard* [1964] AC 1129 at 1221, [1964] 1 All ER 367 at 407, HL; *Cassell & Co Ltd v Broome* [1972] AC 1027, [1972] 1 All ER 801, HL. *AB v South West Water Services Ltd* [1993] QB 507.

63 By H. M. Hart, 'The Aims of the Criminal Law' (1958) 23 Law and Contemporary Problems, 401, 404.

64 Ibid, 405.

5. The Human Rights Act 1998

(a) 'Criminal charge'

The meaning of a criminal offence in the context of the European Convention on Human Rights is a relatively new issue in our law. Enactment of the Human Rights Act 1998 increases the likelihood of the courts being compelled to decide whether proceedings are criminal, particularly when considering the protections of liberty in Article 5 and those of a fair trial in Article 6. However, the concept of a 'criminal charge' is an autonomous Convention concept, and the national courts can readily avoid any categorical determination for the purposes of English law.[65] The European Court has determined that if domestic law classifies the proceeding as criminal, this will be decisive, but where domestic law classifies the proceeding as non-criminal, the ECtHR will consider the true nature of the proceedings, taking into account the severity of the penalty which may be imposed looking especially at whether imprisonment is a possible penalty;[66] whether the rule applies only to a specific group or to the public generally;[67] whether there is a 'punitive or deterrent element' to the process;[68] whether the imposition of any penalty is dependent upon a finding of culpability;[69] and whether other Member States classify such conduct as criminal.[70] The impact of Article 6 in this context can be seen in domestic law: in *H*[71] the House of Lords held that proceedings to determine whether D is unfit to plead under s 4 or 4A of the Criminal Procedure (Insanity) Act 1964, do not involve the determination of a criminal charge since they do not result in a conviction or in any punishment.[72]

Ironically, this enhanced opportunity for clearer judicial definition of the concept occurs at a time when Parliament seems intent on blurring the boundaries of criminal law with the creation of quasi-criminal processes and orders such as those involving Anti-Social Behaviour Orders.[73]

(b) Convention rights and criminal law

Although the ECHR impact is most significant in the context of evidence and procedure, the ECHR also has a direct impact on the operation of the substantive criminal law in many ways.[74]

65 *Engel v Netherlands* [1976] 1 EHRR 647; *Benham v UK* [1996] 22 EHRR 293.

66 Unless the 'nature, duration or manner of execution of the imprisonment' is such that it could not be 'appreciably detrimental': ibid.

67 *Weber v Switzerland* (1990) 12 EHRR 508, para 33; *Benham v United Kingdom* (1996) 22 EHRR 293, para 56. See A. Lester and D. Pannick, *Human Rights Law and Practice* (2004), 4.6.13.

68 *Öztürk v Germany* (1984) 6 EHRR 409, para 53; *Bendenoun v France* (1994) 18 EHRR 54, para 47.

69 *Benham v United Kingdom* (1996) 22 EHRR 293, para 56.

70 *Öztürk v Germany* (1984) 6 EHRR 409, para 53.

71 [2003] 1 WLR. 411, HL.

72 See Ch 11 below.

73 Crime and Disorder Act 1998 Part 1; Anti-Social Behaviour Act 2003. Article 6 does not apply to anti-social behaviour orders: *R (McCann) v Crown Court at Manchester* [2003] 1 AC 787, HL. This trend in overcriminalization has caused Professor Ashworth to ask 'Is the Criminal Law a Lost Cause?' (2000) 116 LQR 225. See recently on 'criminal charge' *R (R) v Durham Constabulary* [2005] UKHL 21.

74 There is a substantial debate as to how significant an impact the Human Rights Act will have: for a minimalist view see Buxton LJ 'The HRA and Substantive Criminal Law' [1999] Crim LR 335; and for a more radical expectation see A. Ashworth, 'HRA 1998 and Substantive Law' [2000] Crim LR 564.

(i) Definition and interpretation

In terms of definition of crimes, the greatest impact might be through Article 7, which proscribes retrospective criminalization, including a prohibition on criminal laws which are too vague and uncertain.

Article 7 provides:

(1) No one shall be held guilty of any criminal offence on account of any act or omission which did not constitute a criminal offence under national or international law at the time when it was committed. Nor shall a heavier penalty be imposed than the one that was applicable at the time the criminal offence was committed.

(2) This Article shall not prejudice the trial and punishment of any person for any act or omission which, at the time it was committed, was criminal according to the general principles of law recognized by civilized nations.

The European Court held in *Kokkinakis v Greece*,[75] and has reiterated many times since, that:

Article 7 is not confined to prohibiting the retrospective application of the criminal law to an accused's disadvantage: it also embodies, more generally, the principle that only the law can define a crime and prescribe a penalty (*nullum crimen, nulla poena sine lege*) and the principle that the criminal law must not be extensively construed to an accused's detriment, for instance by analogy. . . . it follows that an offence must be clearly defined in the law.[76]

The Court looks to whether the individual can know from the wording of the relevant provision and, if need be, with the assistance of the courts' interpretation of it, what acts and omissions will make him criminally liable.

This is not a prohibition on the development of the common law. As the Court noted in *SW*:

However clearly drafted a legal provision may be, in any system of law, including criminal law, there is an inevitable element of judicial interpretation. There will always be a need for elucidation of doubtful points and for adaptation to changing circumstances. Indeed, in the United Kingdom, as in the other Convention States, the progressive development of the criminal law through judicial law-making is a well entrenched and necessary part of legal tradition. Article 7 of the Convention cannot be read as outlawing the gradual clarification of the rules of criminal liability through judicial interpretation from case to case, provided that the resultant development is consistent with the essence of the offence and could reasonably be foreseen.

To date the English courts have taken a very narrow view of the protection afforded by Article 7 and have failed to accept that common law crimes such as manslaughter by gross negligence[77] and public nuisance,[78] are incompatible with Article 7 on the grounds of their vagueness.

Many of the other Articles of the Convention will also affect the scope of definition of existing and future[79] crimes. As with other areas of law, the criminal court is obliged to

75 25 May 1993 (Series A no 260-A, p. 22), para 52. 76 See *SW v UK* [1995] 21 EHRR 363, para 35.

77 *Misra* [2004] EWCA Crim 2375. 78 *Goldstein* [2004] 2 All ER 589.

79 As the Minister must give an assurance to Parliament that the Bill is compatible with the ECHR: HRA 1998, s 19. Note however this is provided in the Bill in its original form when presented to Parliament. See generally A. T. H. Smith, 'The Human Rights Act and the Criminal Lawyer: The Constitutional Context' [1999] CLR 251. The Law Commission's proposals are very keenly influenced by ECHR concerns, see eg Law Comm Report No 282, *Children: Their Non-Accidental Deaths or Serious Injury* (2003).

'take account' of the ECHR jurisprudence in construing English law. This is problematic since much of the Strasbourg jurisprudence is vague and general in nature and not in the familiar form of common law case precedents. Under s 3 of the 1998 Act the courts must ensure that statutes 'so far as it is possible to do so, be read and given effect in a way which is compatible with the Convention rights'. Examples of the criminal courts' approach to that duty can be seen in numerous cases. Lord Bingham has recently summarized the position:

First, the interpretative obligation under s 3 is a very strong and far reaching one, and may require the court to depart from the legislative intention of Parliament. Secondly, a Convention-compliant interpretation under s 3 is the primary remedial measure and a declaration of incompatibility under s 4 an exceptional course. Thirdly, it is to be noted that during the passage of the Bill through Parliament the promoters of the Bill told both Houses that it was envisaged that the need for a declaration of incompatibility would rarely arise. Fourthly, there is a limit beyond which a Convention-compliant interpretation is not possible, such limit being illustrated by *R (Anderson) v Secretary of State for the Home Department* [2003] 1 AC 837 and *Bellinger v Bellinger* [2003] 2 AC 467. In explaining why a Convention-compliant interpretation may not be possible, members of the committee used differing expressions: such an interpretation would be incompatible with the underlying thrust of the legislation, or would not go with the grain of it, or would call for legislative deliberation, or would change the substance of a provision completely, or would remove its pith and substance, or would violate a cardinal principle of the legislation. . . . All of these expressions, as I respectfully think, yield valuable insights, but none of them should be allowed to supplant the simple test enacted in the Act: 'So far as it is possible to do so . . .'. While the House declined to try to formulate precise rules . . . it was thought that cases in which s 3 could not be used would in practice be fairly easy to identify.[80]

The courts have held some criminal statutes incompatible in controversial circumstances.[81]

(ii) The Convention rights

Many of the ECHR rights as specified in the Human Rights Act 1998, Sch 1 will be of importance in determining the appropriate scope and application of offences. There are numerous examples provided throughout the book, but a few simple examples show how widely the impact of the Convention could be felt in substantive criminal law: Article 2 will impact on the scope of the protection offered by the law of homicide and the qualifications on the scope of self-defence; Article 3 will regulate the parental administration of corporal punishment; Article 5 will affect the manner in which defendants found unfit to plead or not guilty by reason of insanity will be treated; Article 8 will be relevant in protecting the rights of consenting adults to engage in sexual behaviour; Article 9 could impact on the law of blasphemy or the right of a religions group to conduct a service in public; Article 10 could offer a defence to those charged with offences in which they are expressing themselves in the form of protest – criminal damage or public order; Article 11 could affect the way the public order restrictions on a meeting are enforced; and Article 14 could impact on the way that the criminal law discriminates against spouses or non-married couples.

80 *A-G's Reference (No 4 of 2002)* [2004] UKHL 43, [28].

81 See eg *A v Secretary of State for the Home Department* [2004] UKHL 56 on the Anti-Terrorism, Crime and Security Act 2001.

The relevant Articles are set out here for ease of reference.

Article 2

2. (1) Everyone's right to life shall be protected by law. No one shall be deprived of his life intentionally save in the execution of a sentence of a court following his conviction of a crime for which this penalty is provided by law.

(2) Deprivation of life shall not be regarded as inflicted in contravention of this Article when it results from the use of force which is no more than absolutely necessary:

(a) in defence of any person from unlawful violence;

(b) in order to effect a lawful arrest or to prevent the escape of a person lawfully detained;

(c) in action lawfully taken for the purpose of quelling a riot or insurrection.

Article 3

3. No one shall be subjected to torture or to inhuman or degrading treatment or punishment.

Article 5

5. (1) Everyone has the right to liberty and security of the person. No one shall be deprived of his liberty save in the following cases and in accordance with a procedure prescribed by law:

(a) the lawful detention of a person after conviction by a competent court;

(b) the lawful arrest or detention of a person for non-compliance with the lawful order of a court or in order to secure the fulfilment of any obligation prescribed by law;

(c) the lawful arrest or detention of a person effected for the purpose of bringing him before the competent legal authority on reasonable suspicion of having committed an offence or when it is reasonably considered necessary to prevent his committing an offence or fleeing after having done so;

(d) the detention of a minor by lawful order for the purpose of educational supervision or his lawful detention for the purpose of bringing him before the competent legal authority;

(e) the lawful detention of persons for the prevention of the spreading of infectious diseases, of persons of unsound mind, alcoholics or drug addicts or vagrants;

(f) the lawful arrest or detention of a person to prevent his effecting an unauthorized entry into the country or of a person against whom action is being taken with a view to deportation or extradition.

(2) Everyone who is arrested shall be informed promptly, in a language which he understands, of the reasons for his arrest and of any charge against him.

(3) Everyone arrested or detained in accordance with the provisions of paragraph (1)(c) of this Article shall be brought promptly before a judge or other officer authorized by law to exercise judicial power and shall be entitled to trial within a reasonable time or to release pending trial. Release may be conditioned by guarantees to appear for trial.

(4) Everyone who is deprived of his liberty by arrest or detention shall be entitled to take proceedings by which the lawfulness of his detention shall be decided speedily by a court and his release ordered if the detention is not lawful.

(5) Everyone who has been the victim of arrest or detention in contravention of the provisions of this Article shall have an enforceable right to compensation.

Article 6

6. (1) In the determination of his civil rights and obligations or of any criminal charge against him, everyone is entitled to a fair and public hearing within a reasonable time by an independent and impartial tribunal established by law. Judgment shall be pronounced publicly but the press and public may be excluded from all or part of the trial in the interest of morals, public order or national security in a democratic society, where the interests of juveniles or the protection of the private lives of the parties so require, or to the extent strictly necessary in the opinion of the court in special circumstances where publicity would prejudice the interests of justice.

(2) Everyone charged with a criminal offence shall be presumed innocent until proved guilty according to law.

(3) Everyone charged with a criminal offence has the following minimum rights:

(a) to be informed promptly, in a language which he understands and in detail, of the nature and cause of the accusation against him;

(b) to have adequate time and facilities for the preparation of his defence;

(c) to defend himself in person or through legal assistance of his own choosing or, if he has not sufficient means to pay for legal assistance, to be given it free when the interests of justice so require;

(d) to examine or have examined witnesses against him and to obtain the attendance and examination of witnesses on his behalf under the same conditions as witnesses against him;

(e) to have the free assistance of an interpreter if he cannot understand or speak the language used in court.

Article 8

8. (1) Everyone has the right to respect for his private and family life, his home and his correspondence.

(2) There shall be no interference by a public authority with the exercise of this right except such as is in accordance with the law and is necessary in a democratic society in the interests of national security, public safety or the economic well-being of the country, for the prevention of disorder or crime, for the protection of health or morals, or for the protection of the rights and freedoms of others.

Article 9

9. (1) Everyone has the right to freedom of thought, conscience and religion; this right includes freedom to change his religion or belief and freedom, either alone or in community with others and in public or private, to manifest his religion or belief, in worship, teaching, practice and observance.

(2) Freedom to manifest one's religion or beliefs shall be subject only to such limitations as are prescribed by law and are necessary in a democratic society in the interests of public safety, for the protection of public order, health or morals, or for the protection of the rights and freedoms of others.

Article 10

10. (1) Everyone has the right to freedom of expression. This right shall include freedom to hold opinions and to receive and impart information and ideas without interference by public authority and regardless of frontiers. This Article shall not prevent States from requiring the licensing of broadcasting, television or cinema enterprises.

(2) The exercise of these freedoms, since it carries with it duties and responsibilities, may be subject to such formalities, conditions, restrictions or penalties as are prescribed by law and are necessary in a democratic society, in the interests of national security, territorial integrity or public safety, for the prevention of disorder or crime, for the protection of health or morals, for the protection of the reputation or rights of others, for preventing the disclosure of information received in confidence, or for maintaining the authority and impartiality of the judiciary.

Article 11

11. (1) Everyone has the right to freedom of peaceful assembly and to freedom of association with others, including the right to form and to join trade unions for the protection of his interests.

(2) No restrictions shall be placed on the exercise of these rights other than such as are prescribed by law and are necessary in a democratic society in the interests of national security or public safety, for the prevention of disorder or crime, for the protection of health or morals or for the protection of the rights and freedoms of others. This Article shall not prevent the imposition of lawful restrictions on the exercise of these rights by members of the armed forces, of the police or of the administration of the State.

Article 14

14. The enjoyment of the rights and freedoms set forth in this Convention shall be secured without discrimination on any ground such as sex, race, colour, language, religion, political or other opinion, national or social origin, association with a national minority, property, birth or other status.

A detailed study of the European Court's approach to the application of these rights lies beyond the scope of this work.[82] However, key issues of interpretation are worth emphasizing. In the case of Articles 2 and 3 the rights are absolute. With Articles 8–10, the rights are qualified. Thus, although there may be a *prima facie* breach of the right, it is open to the Crown to show that the restriction on the exercise of that right is (i) prescribed by law (or in accordance with law); (ii) is necessary in a democratic society for one or more specified objectives (such as the protection of public order, health or morals, or the rights of others); and (iii) that it is a proportionate interference with the right in order to promote those specified objectives. For example, where D is prosecuted for possession of cannabis and claims his conduct was in accordance with his religion, it will be for the Crown to establish that the law relating to misuse of drugs is sufficiently clearly prescribed by law, and that the offence is necessary and proportionate to protect public order or prevent crime, etc.

(c) Burdens of proof

Woolmington v DPP[83] makes clear that the requirement for the prosecution to prove the guilt of the defendant beyond a reasonable doubt is a fundamental principle of English law. Article 6(2) of the ECHR reinforces this, providing that a person 'charged with a criminal offences shall be presumed innocent until proved guilty according to the law'. The effect of the presumption is that in any criminal trial the prosecution bear the burden of proving (beyond a reasonable doubt) that the defendant performed the relevant *actus*

[82] See B. Emmerson and A. Ashworth, *Human Rights and Criminal Justice* (2001). [83] [1935] All ER 1.

reus with the requisite *mens rea* in the crime alleged. The defendant will bear the burden of raising sufficient evidence to get any defences off the ground. For example, where it is alleged that D murdered V, the prosecution must establish all the elements of murder, and D will have an obligation to adduce sufficient evidence to raise his defence, for example, self-defence. The prosecution will then be obliged to rebut that defence to the criminal standard of proof, that is, making the jury satisfied so that they are sure that D was not acting in self-defence.

In exceptional circumstances, the defendant bears a more onerous duty: to prove a fact on the balance of probabilities, rather than merely to adduce evidence of it. The first exception is where D pleads insanity. His obligation is to prove that it is more probable than not that he was 'insane' in law.[84] A second exception is where D pleads diminished responsibility under s 2 of the Homicide Act 1957. Again, it is for D to prove that it is more probable than not that he was in a diminished state at the time of the killing. Further exceptional categories are created by Parliament, but these must be treated with caution, since all must comply with Article 6(2).[85] Finally, there are implied statutory exceptions where the offence provides any 'exception, exemption, proviso, excuse or qualification whether or not it accompanies the description of the offence in the enactment creating the offence'.[86] It is rather unsatisfactory that such an important matter as the imposition of the burden of proof turns on the matter of form in the statutory drafting.

(i) Article 6(2) of the ECHR

Where an offence imposes a *legal burden* on the accused to *prove* a matter, rather than imposing merely an *evidential burden* to *raise* evidence of a matter, the question of compatibility with Article 6(2) arises. The leading ECHR authority on the application of Article 6(2) is *Salibiaku v France*.[87] The Court recognized that:

> Presumptions of fact or of law operate in every legal system. Clearly, the Convention does not prohibit such presumptions in principle. It does, however, require the Contracting States to remain within certain limits in this respect as regards criminal law. If, as the Commission would appear to consider, paragraph 2 of article 6 merely laid down a guarantee to be respected by the courts in the conduct of legal proceedings, its requirements would in practice overlap with the duty of impartiality imposed in paragraph 1. Above all, the national legislature would be free to strip the trial court of any genuine power of assessment and deprive the presumption of innocence of its substance, if the words 'according to law' were construed exclusively with reference of domestic law. Such a situation could not be reconciled with the object and purpose of article 6, which, by protecting the right to a fair trial and in particular the right to be presumed innocent, is intended to enshrine the fundamental principle of the rule of law.
>
> Article 6(2) does not therefore regard presumptions of fact or of law provided for in the criminal law with indifference. It requires States to confine them within reasonable limits which take into account the importance of what is at stake and maintain the rights of the defence.[88]

84 See T. Jones, 'Insanity, Automatism and the Burden of Proof on the Accused' (1995) 111 LQR 475.

85 Arguably these are not so exceptional – see A. Ashworth and M. Blake, 'The Presumption of Innocence in English Criminal Law' [1996] Crim LR 306, who found around 40% of crimes imposing a burden on D.

86 See the Magistrates' Courts Act 1980, s 101 in relation to summary offences. The House of Lords has applied the same essential criteria in finding implied burdens in indictable offences: *Hunt* [1987] AC 352.

87 (1988) 13 EHRR 379.

88 Para 28.

The English courts have rapidly, though not consistently, developed a domestic jurisprudence on the imposition of a burden on the accused. No fewer than four visits to the House of Lords have failed to produce definitive guidance on the matter.[89] In the most recent pronouncement, the House held that the court's responsibility in construing statutory provisions which appear to place a burden on D is not to decide whether a reverse burden should be imposed on a defendant, but rather to evaluate whether Parliament's enactment unjustifiably infringes the presumption of innocence. In the case of a burden placed on the accused on a charge of membership of a proscribed organization under s 11 of the Terrorism Act 2000,[90] Lord Bingham, identified five reasons[91] for his conclusion that the presumption was unjustifiably infringed:

(1) the reverse burden created a real risk that innocent individuals might be convicted, since the section is capable of applying to people who have no culpability;
(2) it could be difficult for any individual to prove that he has not participated in activities, since terrorist organizations do not often keep records;
(3) if the legal burden rested on defendants, courts would in some cases convict those who could not establish their innocence;
(4) the potential punishment is up to 10 years' imprisonment;
(5) the security considerations, although important, do not absolve Member States from their duty to ensure that basic standards of fairness are observed.

This can be contrasted with their lordships' conclusion in the conjoined appeal in *Sheldrake*, dealing with s 5(2) of the Road Traffic Act 1988.[92] In relation to that offence, the House of Lords held unanimously that Parliament had not acted unjustifiably in placing the burden on the accused.[93]

> The defendant has a full opportunity to show that there was no likelihood of his driving, a matter so closely conditioned by his own knowledge and state of mind at the material time as to make it much more appropriate for him to prove on the balance of probabilities that he would not be likely to drive than for the prosecutor to prove, beyond reasonable doubt, that he would . . . If a driver tries and fails to establish a defence under section 5(2), I would not regard the resulting conviction as unfair. . . .

The guiding principles in determining the compatibility of a reverse onus provision appear to be the severity of sentence, the ease of proof for the defence and the risk of convicting the innocent.[94] These principles do not form a sufficiently solid or clear basis

[89] See *R v DPP, ex p Kebilene* [2000] 2 AC 326; *Lambert* [2002] AC 545; *Johnstone* [2003] 1 WLR 736; *A-G's Reference (No 4 of 2002)* [2004] UKHL 43.

[90] Section 11(2) provides: It is a defence for a person charged with an offence under subsection (1) to prove that the organization was not proscribed on the last (or only) occasion on which he became a member or began to profess to be a member, and that he has not taken part in the activities of the organisation at any time while it was proscribed.

[91] [51].

[92] Which provides that it is a defence for the defendant to prove that although he was in charge of the vehicle and was intoxicated beyond the legal limit 'the circumstances were such that there was no likelihood of his driving the vehicle whilst the proportion of alcohol' in his body exceeded the limit.

[93] [41].

[94] For cogent criticism see A. Ashworth, commenting in [2005] Crim LR 215.

to guide the lower courts in future decision making, and it is clear that the matter will require further appellate attention.[95]

[95] Updates on important developments on this and all other aspects of the material in the book will be published on the Companion Web Site: www.oup.com/uk/booksites/law/.

3

The classification of offences

The importance of placing the substantive criminal law in its context has already been emphasized. This is not a book about criminal process or evidence, nevertheless it is necessary to provide an outline[1] of one of the most important procedural rules governing the classification of offences.

1. Indictable and summary offences

For procedural purposes crimes are classified as indictable and summary offences. Summary offences are offences which may be tried by courts having summary jurisdiction and the trial is conducted by magistrates (whether a lay bench or a district judge) without a jury; all proceedings on indictment, which take place with a jury,[2] are now brought before the Crown Court.[3] For practical purposes it is the question of trial with or without a jury which is the important distinction between trial on indictment and summary trial. The importance of this distinction is that juries are the tribunal of fact and not law, unlike magistrates. In most other respects the course and conduct of the trial is very much the same.

The classification of offences as indictable and summary broadly reflects a distinction between serious and minor crimes. Some offences are so obviously serious that they are triable only on indictment,[4] and some offences are so obviously minor that they can be tried only summarily. But for many crimes, their gravity turns upon the particular cir-

[1] For a more detailed treatment of the criminal process see A. Ashworth and M. Redmayne, *The Criminal Process: An Evaluative Study* (3rd edn, 2005) and the practitioners' manuals *Archbold Crown Court* (2005); *Archbold Magistrates' Court* (2004–5); *Blackstone's Criminal Practice* (2005). For an accessible overview see S. Bailey, P. Ching, M. Gunn and D. Ormerod, *Smith, Bailey and Gunn, Modern English Legal System* (4th edn, 2001), ch 14.

[2] Provision to allow for non-jury trial is provided in the Criminal Justice Act 2003, Part 7 in certain circumstances including eg cases where there has been jury tampering. There is considerable pressure from the government for further extension of the exceptional categories, fuelled by collapses of lengthy trials which are claimed to be 'untriable' by a jury (see eg the 'Jubilee line fraud' which collapsed after almost two years at the Central Criminal Court, March 2005).

[3] Supreme Court Act 1981, s 46. When the Crown Court sits in the City of London it is known as the Central Criminal Court: s 8(3).

[4] And some serious offences are more serious than others; consequently provision is made in the Supreme Court Act 1981, s 75(1) as amended by the Courts' Act 2003 for the allocation of cases as between suitably experienced High Court judges, Circuit Judges, Recorders and District Judges (Magistrates' Courts). See *Practice Direction (Criminal Proceedings: Criminal Proceedings)* [2002] 1 WLR 2870, para III.21, *Classification of Crown Court business and allocation to Crown Court centres.*

cumstances of the case. Recognizing this, Parliament has from time to time provided for the summary trial of indictable offences and vice versa. Since this was done as occasion demanded without any coherent overall plan, it is not surprising that the classification which eventually emerged was found by the James Committee in 1975 to be 'confusing, complicated and anomalous'.[5] The Committee had two objectives in mind. One was to simplify the existing classification and the other was to get a better distribution of criminal business between the Crown Court and Magistrates' Courts with a view to relieving the pressure of work on the former. To these ends the Committee made a number of recommendations which were first given effect by the Criminal Law Act 1977 but are now for the most part to be found in the Magistrates' Courts Act 1980. That Act and the procedure for allocating business between the magistrates' court and the Crown Court has been the subject of repeated amendment resulting in technical and complex provisions.

The basic tripartite division as recommended by the James Committee remains: (a) offences triable only summarily; (b) offences triable only on indictment; and (c) offences triable either way.

(a) Offences triable only summarily

A summary offence is one which, if committed by an adult, is triable only summarily.[6] Such offences are entirely the creation of statute. It is of course open to Parliament to review the appropriate class for a particular offence and the opportunity was taken in the Criminal Law Act 1977, with a view to easing the workload of the Crown Court, of making certain offences (including drink-driving and assaulting constables in the execution of their duty) summary only, though they had formerly been triable either way. Subsequently the Criminal Justice Act 1988 has made summary only the offences of common assault and battery and taking vehicles without consent.

(b) Offences triable only on indictment

An 'indictable' offence means an offence which, if committed by an adult, is triable on indictment, whether it is exclusively so triable or triable either way.[7] Offences triable *only* on indictment include any offence punishable by imprisonment for life on first conviction, causing death by dangerous driving and the more serious offences under the Theft Act 1968. Generally offences are made indictable only, either because they are of such exceptional gravity or because other reasons, such as anticipated complexity of issues, make them unsuitable for summary trial. All offences at common law were triable on indictment, therefore, in the absence of any specific provision an offence will be triable on indictment. The trend has been to reserve indictable only offences for the most serious circumstances and most new offences are triable either way or summarily.

[5] *The Distribution of Criminal Business between the Crown Court and Magistrates' Courts* (1975) Cmnd 6323, para 9.

[6] Interpretation Act 1978, Sch 1. To incite the commission of a summary offence is itself a summary offence (Magistrates' Courts Act 1980, s 45(1)); to conspire to commit a summary offence is an indictable offence (Criminal Law Act 1977, s 3); it is not an offence to attempt to commit an offence which is summary only, unless the statute so provides: Criminal Attempts Act 1981, ss 1 and 3, below, Ch 12.

[7] Interpretation Act 1978, Sch 1.

(i) Procedure for indictable only offences

The Crime and Disorder Act 1998 removed the requirement for committal proceedings (where magistrates would sit as examining justices and review the evidence before committing a case to the Crown Court) for offences triable *only* on indictment.[8] Offenders charged with such offences must be 'sent' to the Crown Court for trial without committal. Section 51 of the 1998 Act and Part 6 and Sch 3 of the Criminal Justice Act 2003 result in a complex procedure whereby the court must send cases directly to the Crown Court without scrutiny of the evidence. The procedure allows for a challenge by the defence in the Crown Court for the charge to be dismissed. The judge is to dismiss charges if it appears to him that the evidence would not be sufficient for a jury to properly convict D.[9]

(c) Offences triable either way

An offence triable either way means an offence which, if committed by an adult, is triable either on indictment or summarily.[10] The class extends to (i) the offences listed in the Magistrates' Courts Act 1980, Sch I; and (ii) offences made triable either way by virtue of any other enactment.[11]

(i) Procedure for either way offences

For offences falling under this head the procedure is regulated by the Magistrates' Courts Act 1980 as amended. Save for exceptional cases, D may opt for summary trial or trial on indictment. The court may impose trial on indictment, but may (at present) not insist on summary trial if D[12] objects. The scheme obliges D to enter a plea *before* the trial allocation decision is made.[13] If D indicates that he would plead guilty at trial, the court proceeds as if this were a guilty plea received at a summary trial. If D's indication is one of not guilty, the court listens to any representations from D and from the prosecutor, including revelations about D's antecedents, and decides on the trial allocation – should it stay in the magistrates' court or be sent to the Crown Court. The court (which can now comprise one magistrate for these purposes) takes into account the adequacy of its sentencing powers and any representations of the defence and prosecution, and the allocation guidelines of the Sentencing Guidelines Council.[14] If the court considers summary trial more appropriate, that should be explained to D, as should the fact that he need not consent to summary trial but can opt for trial by jury, and that (at present) after a summary trial the magistrates have exceptional powers to send him to the Crown Court for sentence if he is found guilty of a specified offence (that is, where D is a dangerous

[8] Section 51 as substituted by the Criminal Justice Act 2003, Sch 3, para 18. There are complex provisions dealing with linked offences and offenders and linked offenders where one is a youth.

[9] Sch 3, para 2.

[10] Interpretation Act 1978, Sch 1.

[11] Magistrates' Courts Act 1980, s 17.

[12] In the case of adult joint defendants, if one consents to summary trial and the other elects for jury trial, the justices are not obliged to commit both for trial: *R v Brentwood JJ, ex p Nicholls* [1992] 1 AC 1 and see *R v Wigan JJ, ex p Layland* (1996) 160 JP 223.

[13] MCA 1980, ss 19–21 as substituted by the Criminal Justice Act 2003.

[14] Criminal Justice Act 2003, s 170.

offender).[15] D may ask for an indication as to the likely sentence he will receive if tried summarily (that is, a custodial one or not), and this may then cause him to change his indication.[16] If D consents to summary trial, the case proceeds (at a later date fixed by the court if there is to be a trial). If D elects trial on indictment, the magistrates proceed to send the case to the Crown Court.[17] If the court considers that trial on indictment is more appropriate it will proceed to send the case to the Crown Court and D effectively has no choice in the matter.[18]

(ii) Exceptional cases

The above is, in outline, the normal procedure for dealing with offences triable either way but there are exceptional cases. One such case worthy of note is where the accused is charged with a 'scheduled offence'. The James Committee had proposed,[19] again with a view to relieving pressure on the Crown Court, that minor cases of theft and criminal damage should be triable only summarily. This proposal was accepted by Parliament[20] in relation to criminal damage but not in relation to theft on the ground that a conviction for the latter involved a stigma not involved in the former. The outcome is that where on a charge of criminal damage the value of the property does not exceed the relevant sum (currently £5,000) the accused must be tried summarily but, having regard to the loss of the former right to be tried by jury, the maximum punishment which the court can impose is three months' imprisonment and/or a fine at level 4. Though triable only summarily, 'low value criminal damage' remains an indictable offence for all other purposes.[21]

2. Treasons, felonies and misdemeanours: arrestable offences

At common law a crime might be classified either as treason, felony or misdemeanour. Originally the distinction between felony and misdemeanour was a distinction between serious and minor offences (the former involving penalties of a different order from the latter)[22] but over the years this distinction, though always broadly discernible, became blurred. The practical importance of the distinction came to lie in certain consequences which turned upon whether the offence was felony or misdemeanour. For example, the general power of arrest without warrant was available only in respect of felonies; only in felonies was the distinction drawn between principals and accessories to the crime; and it

15 Under the PCC(S)A 2000, s 3A where the offence is a specified one under the Criminal Justice Act 2003, Sch 15. The Criminal Justice Act 2003, Sch 3, para 22 curtailed the power to commit for sentence to the Crown Court for sentence.

16 Clearly the provisions are designed to produce as many guilty pleas as early as possible in the system and to keep as many cases as possible from reaching the Crown Court.

17 Criminal Justice Act 2003, Sch 3, para 7.

18 Section 21.

19 Cmnd 6323, paras 74–105.

20 Magistrates' Courts Act 1980, s 22.

21 *Fennell* (2000) 164 JP 386; [2000] Crim LR 677.

22 See generally, Pollock and Maitland, II HEL, Cap VIII, s 2.

was an offence to conceal (misprision), or to agree not to prosecute (compound), a felony, though it was not an offence to conceal a misdemeanour and probably not an offence to compound one.

But now, by s 1 of the Criminal Law Act 1967, all distinctions between felony and misdemeanour are abolished and, on all matters on which a distinction has previously been drawn, the law is assimilated to that applicable to misdemeanour at the commencement of the Act. Consequently there is no distinction of substance between the former felonies, whether created at common law or by statute, and misdemeanours, and all may be conveniently called 'offences'. No doubt it would simplify things if it were possible to dispense altogether with any mention of felony and misdemeanour, but this is not possible. The terms appear regularly in pre-1968 cases and the reader must know to what they refer. Most of these cases remain unaffected by the abolition of the distinctions between felony and misdemeanour since the law is, in the main, the same for both. And even cases which raise the peculiarities of felony may remain authoritative in other respects. For example, although it is no longer necessary to draw the elaborate distinctions relating to degrees of participation in felony, the cases may remain authoritative as showing the limits of criminal participation in an offence.

It will be appreciated, however, that for some purposes, and especially for the purposes of the law of arrest without warrant, it is necessary to maintain a distinction between those (serious) offences in respect of which it is necessary that there should be a power of arrest without warrant and those (minor) offences in respect of which there is no general need for such a power. The Criminal Law Act 1967, s 2, accordingly introduced the new concept of the arrestable offence. The definition in that Act has now been replaced and modified[23] by s 24 of the Police and Criminal Evidence Act (PACE) 1984 where an arrestable offence is defined as any offence 'for which the sentence is fixed by law or for which a person (not previously convicted) may be sentenced for a term of five years (or might be so sentenced but for the restrictions imposed by s 33 of the Magistrates' Courts Act 1980), and to attempts to commit any such offence.' Included in the definition of arrestable offences are certain offences (for example, going equipped for stealing contrary to s 25 of the Theft Act 1968) which, not carrying five years' imprisonment, would not be arrestable offences in their own right but where a power of arrest without warrant was thought necessary for the proper enforcement of the law. In other respects PACE restates the law relating to arrest but does not provide a comprehensive code.[24]

Moreover, the Criminal Law Act 1967 created offences in relation to arrestable offences which cannot be committed in respect of other offences. Under s 4(1) it is an offence to assist a person guilty of an arrestable offence, and s 5(1) creates an offence of agreeing for gain to conceal information relating to an arrestable offence. These offences had their counterparts in the earlier law; the first closely resembles the former offence of being an accessory after the fact to felony, and the latter has features – though very emaciated

23 The modification is that common law misdemeanours for which no maximum sentence is prescribed are now included in the definition of arrestable offences. Statutory conspiracy to commit an arrestable offence was made an arrestable offence by s 3 of the Criminal Law Act 1977.

24 This qualification, introduced by the Criminal Law Act 1977 and continued in PACE, is to make it clear that the power of arrest remains unaffected by the fact that in certain circumstances (as to which see above, p 25) a 'scheduled' indictable offence may be triable only summarily.

features – of the former offences of misprision and compounding. The modern classification of arrestable and non-arrestable offences has thus broadly and with much modification superseded the former classification of felonies and misdemeanours.[25]

The Serious Organised Crime and Police Act 2005, s 110 replaces s 24 of PACE and abolishes the distinction between arrestable and non-arrestable offences. The provision is not yet in force and no commencement date has been set.

25 Apart from retaining the arrestable offence, PACE retains a small number of statutory powers of arrest without warrant (see Sch 2). There is no power under PACE to arrest without warrant for any other *offence* though an *offender* may be arrested without warrant if the arrest conditions specified in s 25 are met. PACE leaves unaffected the common law power to arrest for breach of the peace.

4

The elements of a crime: *actus reus*

1. Introduction

It is a fundamental principle of criminal law that a person may not be convicted of a crime unless the prosecution have proved beyond reasonable doubt both (a) that D has caused a certain event (in a result crime) or that responsibility is to be attributed to him for the existence of a certain state of affairs (in a conduct crime), which is forbidden by criminal law, and (b) that D had a defined state of mind in relation to the causing of the event or the existence of the state of affairs. The event, or state of affairs, is called the *actus reus* or the external element and the state of mind the *mens rea* or mental element of the crime. The principle that a person is not criminally liable for his conduct unless the prescribed state of mind coincides with the prohibited *actus reus* also being present is frequently stated in the form of a Latin maxim: *actus non facit reum nisi mens sit rea.*[1]

Though it is absolutely clear that D killed V – that is, he has caused an *actus reus* – he must be acquitted of murder if there is a reasonable possibility that the killing was accidental; for, if that is the case, it has not been proved beyond reasonable doubt that he had the requisite mental element. It was so laid down by the House of Lords in *Woolmington v DPP*[2] where it was held, overruling earlier authorities, that it is a misdirection to tell a jury that D must *satisfy* them that the killing was an accident. The true rule is that the jury must acquit even though they are not satisfied that D's story is true, if they think it might reasonably be true. They should convict only if satisfied beyond reasonable doubt that it is *not* true. This rule is of general application[3] and there is only one exception to it at common law – the defence of insanity.[4] To raise other defences at common law – for

[1] 'Properly translated, this means "An act does not make a man guilty of a crime, unless his mind be also guilty." It is thus not the *actus* which is "*reus*" but the man and his mind respectively' per Lord Hailsham in *Haughton v Smith* [1975] AC 476 at 491–492, [1973] 3 All ER 1109 at 1113–1114. It is, however, convenient to follow the established usage of '*actus reus*'. Cf Lord Simon in *DPP for Northern Ireland v Lynch* [1975] AC 653 at 690, [1975] 1 All ER 913 at 934 and Lord Diplock in *Miller* [1983] 2 AC 161, [1983] 1 All ER 978, 979, HL.

[2] [1935] AC 462. See Lord Cooke, 'One Golden Thread', in *Turning Points in the Common Law* (The Hamlyn Lectures 1997), p 28. See generally I. H. Dennis, *The Law of Evidence* (2nd edn, 2002) ch, C. Tapper, *Cross and Tapper on Evidence* (10th edn, 2004), ch 10.

[3] *Mancini v DPP* [1942] AC 1, [1941] 3 All ER 272; *Chan Kau v R* [1955] AC 206, [1955] 1 All ER 266; *Lobell* [1957] 1 QB 547, [1957] 1 All ER 734 (self-defence); *Bratty v A-G for Northern Ireland* [1963] AC 386, [1961] 3 All ER 523 (automatism); *Gill* [1963] 2 All ER 688, [1963] 1 WLR 841 (duress). But the onus of proving procedural bars to trial such as *autrefois convict* or *acquit*, may be on the defendant: *Coughlan* (1976) 63 Cr App R 33 at 36.

[4] Below, p 250.

example, provocation, self-defence, automatism or duress – the accused need do no more than introduce some evidence of all the constituents of the defence; whereupon it is for the Crown to satisfy the jury that at least one of those constituents did not exist. If there is evidence of a defence, though it has not been specifically raised by the accused, the judge must direct the jury to acquit unless they are satisfied that the defence has been disproved.[5] A statute may, however, expressly or impliedly[6] impose a burden of proof on the defendant and frequently does so. Since the Human Rights Act 1998 such provisions may not always be fully effective,[7] and the court will be required to examine their compatibility with Article 6(2) of the ECHR. Where an onus of proof is put upon D, he satisfies it if he proves his case on a balance of probabilities – the same standard as that on the claimant in a civil action – and he need not prove it beyond reasonable doubt.[8]

(a) Identifying elements of *actus reus* and *mens rea*

It is impossible to catalogue every type of conduct that might constitute the *actus reus* of a crime. There are many thousands of offences, and in each case it is necessary to look to the specific terms of the offence, as defined by statute or common law, to determine what the elements of *actus reus* will be. As ever, care must be taken to be precise about the form of the *actus reus* of the particular offence. For example, the *actus reus* of murder is not simply 'a killing' but rather the causing of the death of a human being under the Queen's Peace. Similarly, with conduct crimes, the *actus reus* of rape is not simply non-consensual sex, but more specifically, penile penetration of the vagina, anus or mouth of a person without consent. A key skill that the criminal lawyer must develop is the ability to identify which elements of an offence are those of *actus reus* and which relate to the *mens rea*. It is usually easier to identify the elements of a crime that comprise the *mens rea* since these are represented by common expressions – intentionally, knowingly, wilfully, recklessly, etc all of which are examined fully in the next chapter.

It should be noted that the separation of elements in this manner is principally to allow for the most convenient exposition and discussion of the crime.[9] In practical terms, there is no need for the prosecution to approach its case by breaking down the crime into constituent parts to prove each element in turn to the jury's satisfaction; it will commonly, and sensibly approach the crime as a whole. Moreover, it is not always possible to

[5] *Palmer v R* [1971] AC 814, [1971] 1 All ER 1077 at 1080; *Wheeler* (1967) 52 Cr App R 28 at 30–31; *Hamand* (1985) 82 Cr App R 65.

[6] *Hunt* [1987] 1 All ER 1 at 10, 15, HL.

[7] See above, pp 24–26.

[8] *Carr-Briant* [1943] KB 607, [1943] 2 All ER 156. The Criminal Law Revision Committee and the Law Commission have proposed that the law should be so amended that D would, in these cases, merely have to introduce sufficient evidence to raise the issue (an 'evidential burden') whereupon the onus of proof would be on the Crown: Eleventh Report, Cmnd 4991, paras 137–142; Draft Code, cl 13. Meanwhile, the House of Lords has ruled in *Lambert* [2001] 1 All ER 1014 that the Human Rights Act 1998 may require a provision expressly imposing a reverse onus to be 'read down' to an evidential burden which is satisfied by raising a reasonable doubt. See also *Johnstone* [2003] UKHL 28, [2003] 1 WLR 1736. In the most recent, but probably not the last, statement on this issue from the House of Lords, it was held that the court's task is to ascertain whether the burden of proof imposed by Parliament *unjustifiably* infringes the presumption of innocence: *A-G's Reference (No 4 of 2002)* [2004] UKHL 43, para 31, [2005] Crim LR 215.

[9] See A. T. H. Smith, 'On Actus Reus and Mens Rea' in P. Glazebrook (ed), *Reshaping the Criminal Law: Essays in Honour of Glanville Williams* (1978).

separate precisely *actus reus* from *mens rea*.[10] Sometimes a word that describes the *actus reus*, or part of it, implies a mental element. Without that mental element the *actus reus* simply cannot exist. For example, there are many offences of possession of proscribed objects (drugs, knives, etc) and it has always been recognized that 'possession', which might appear to be an element of *actus reus*, consists also in a mental element.[11] The same is true of words like 'permits',[12] 'appropriates',[13] 'cultivates',[14] 'abandons'[15] and many more that appear across the diverse range of offences. Having an offensive weapon in a public place is the *actus reus* of an offence; but whether an article is an offensive weapon depends, in some circumstances, on the intention with which it is carried. In the absence of that intention, the thing is not an offensive weapon and there is no *actus reus*.[16] The significance of this is that where the crime has an *actus reus* which incorporates a mental element, that necessarily becomes an element of the offence. It is the combination of the two which becomes an element of the offence.

(i) No conviction without *actus reus*

It is possible for the courts to dispense with *mens rea* in whole or in part, but, except in the anomalous case of an intoxicated offender,[17] they can never dispense with the *actus reus*. There are no 'thought crimes'. Thus, if an offence consists in 'possessing' or 'permitting', it cannot be proved if D cannot be shown to have 'possessed' or 'permitted'. The court may of course give effect to the word without requiring full *mens rea*, as where it has held that D was guilty of permitting the use of an uninsured vehicle where he intended to permit only the use of the vehicle (which was in fact uninsured) or cultivating a cannabis plant where he intended only to cultivate that plant (which was in fact a cannabis plant).

In some instances, the *actus reus* of a crime might be relatively minimal, and may even seem innocuous – as in conspiracy where the *actus reus* comprises 'an agreement'. This underlines the importance of keeping sight of the crime as a whole, and not allowing the fragmentation into elements of *actus reus* and *mens rea* to distort the examination of the offence.

It is important to note that all elements of the *actus reus* must be proved. For example, taking the *actus reus* of assault – causing a person to apprehend immediate unlawful personal violence[18] – that might be broken down into elements of 'causing apprehension', 'immediate', 'unlawful', 'personal violence'. If D's conduct failed to fulfil *all* of these requirements there would be no *actus reus*. Thus, if D caused V to apprehend personal violence, but not immediately, as where D telephoned V in Leeds and said 'I'm in London, but when I get back tomorrow I will hit you', there would be no assault.

(ii) Coincidence of *actus reus* and *mens rea*

Not only must the prosecution establish that all of the elements of the particular *actus reus* of the crime in question and the relevant *mens rea* were present, they must, as a

10 See A. C. E. Lynch, 'The Mental Element in the Actus Reus' (1982) 98 LQR 109.

11 See below, Ch 7. 12 Ibid.

13 See below, Ch 18. In *Gomez* [1993] 1 All ER 1, at 39, Lord Browne-Wilkinson regarded 'appropriation' as not involving any mental state; but this is hard to believe. See the discussion below, p 650.

14 *Champ* (1981) 73 Cr App R 367, [1982] Crim LR 108 and commentary.

15 *Hunt v Duckering* [1993] Crim LR 678, DC (abandoning a dog in circumstances likely to cause unnecessary suffering).

16 Below, p 583. 17 See *Lipman* [1970] 1 QB 152, [1969] 3 All ER 410. 18 See below, p 517.

general rule, establish that they occurred at the same time – that there was a coincidence of *actus reus* and *mens rea*. This principle is examined in detail in the following chapter.

The *actus reus* amounts to a crime only when it is accompanied by the appropriate *mens rea*. To cause an *actus reus* without the requisite *mens rea* is not a crime and may be an ordinary, innocent act. For example, the offence of perjury[19] consists in making a statement, whether true or not, on oath in a judicial proceeding, knowing it to be false or not believing it to be true. Thus, every statement on oath in a judicial proceeding might be seen as the *actus reus* of perjury. When we say then that a certain event is the *actus reus* of a crime what we mean is that the event would be a crime if it were caused by a person with *mens rea*. The description of the conduct as an *actus reus* does not necessarily imply any judgment whatever as to its moral or legal quality. The analysis into *actus reus* and *mens rea* is for convenience of exposition only. The only concept known to the law is the crime; and the crime exists only when *actus reus* and *mens rea* coincide.

(b) The nature of an *actus reus*

Since the *actus reus* includes all the elements in the definition of the crime except the accused's mental element,[20] it follows that the *actus reus* is not merely an act. It may indeed consist in a 'state of affairs', not including an act at all.[21] An example might be where D is charged with 'being found' drunk in a public place. Much more often, the *actus reus* requires proof of an act or an omission (which might be better described as 'conduct'). Usually, it must be proved that the conduct had a particular result. In murder, for example, it must be shown that the accused's conduct caused the death. Some crimes do not require evidence of any result. Perjury is committed as soon as D makes a statement on oath that he does not believe to be true. It is irrelevant whether his testimony is believed or not. These different types of offence have been designated[22] 'result crimes' and 'conduct crimes' respectively.

(i) Result crimes

It has been said[23] that in 'result crimes' the law is interested only in the result and not in the conduct bringing about the result. Similarly, a well-known definition of *actus reus* is 'such result of human conduct as the law seeks to prevent'.[24] But a dead man with a knife in his back is not the *actus reus* of a murder. It is putting the knife in the back thereby causing the death that is the *actus reus*. The law is no less interested in the conduct that brings about the result in a 'result crime' than in a 'conduct crime'.[25] There are many examples of result crimes, some of the most obvious being murder, manslaughter, wounding, etc. There are many others not involving offences against the person for example, obtaining property by deception.

19 Perjury Act 1911, s 1(1), Stephen, *Digest*, 95–96.

20 It should be said that this is not the only possible definition of an *actus reus*, and that a more limited view is taken of it by some writers. It is thought, however, that it is the most useful conception of the *actus reus* and is adopted throughout this book. Cf Williams, CLGP, 16 and [1958] Crim LR at 830, who suggests that the elements of *actus reus* ought also to incorporate the absence of some defences.

21 See below pp 73–75.

22 By Gordon, 61. 23 Ibid. 24 Kenny, 17.

25 See Lord Diplock in *Treacy v DPP* [1971] AC 537 at 560, [1971] 1 All ER 110 at 120.

(ii) Conduct crimes

True conduct crimes, such as perjury, are rare. The term has been interpreted more widely by Glanville Williams to include rape and abduction – in these crimes, 'you do not have to wait to see if anything happens as a result of what the defendant does.'[26] This method of classification is controversial. If the test is whether you 'have to wait to see', wounding is a conduct crime if committed with a knife but a result crime if committed with a gun, crossbow or catapult. If the distinction is to be made at all (and, while interesting, it is not clear that it has, or should have, any practical consequences) these offences are better regarded as result crimes. A result has to flow from D's physical movements, whether you have to wait for it or not.

Since the Criminal Attempts Act 1981,[27] all indictable offences are now, in a sense, potentially conduct crimes because any act, done with intent thereby[28] to commit an indictable offence may be an indictable attempt to commit it. The *actus reus* of the offence attempted need never happen and may, indeed, be impossible. Its definition serves only to define the *mens rea* of the attempt.

A case can be made that the law should always have regard only to the conduct and not to the result. Whether the conduct results in harm is generally a matter of chance and does not alter the blameworthiness and dangerousness of the actor.[29] But the law has not gone so far. If D hurls a stone, being reckless whether he injures anyone, he is guilty of an offence if the stone strikes V but of no offence – not even an attempt – if no one is injured. From a retributive point of view, it might be argued that D should be equally liable in either event. This could be achieved by the creation of general offences of reckless endangerment.[30] On utilitarian grounds, however, it is probably undesirable to turn the whole criminal law into 'conduct crimes'. The needs of deterrence are probably adequately served in most cases by 'result crimes'; and the criminal law should be extended only where a clear need is established.

It has been argued that in some offences it may be that the *actus reus* can take different forms (result or conduct) depending on the circumstances.[31] Thus, theft can be committed where D assumes only one of the rights of the owner over his property (conduct crime)[32] or where he assumes them all. This ambiguity is all the less satisfactory because the different categorization of a crime as a conduct or result crime may have implications for procedure, in terms of the form of the indictment, and for jurisdictional issues.

The fact that an offence is a 'conduct offence' does not mean that it should automatically be classified as a 'continuing' offence. The term 'conduct' is being used to distinguish

26 'The Problem of Reckless Attempts' [1983] Crim LR 365 at 366, 368.

27 As interpreted in *Shivpuri*, below, pp 422–425.

28 Ie, D intends to cause the result by that act; it is the last act D intends, and needs, to do, not a merely preparatory act. An earlier act is sufficient, if 'more than merely preparatory': below, ch 12.

29 A. Ashworth, 'Belief Intent and Criminal Liability' in J. Eekelaar and J. Bell (eds), *Oxford Essays in Jurisprudence* (1989); 'Taking the Consequences' in S. Shute, J. Gardner and J. Horder (eds), *Action and Value in Criminal Law* (1993) and 'Defining Offences Without Harm' in, P. F. Smith (ed) *Criminal Law: Essays in Honour of J. C. Smith* (1987).

30 See, *inter alia*, the discussion in K. J. M. Smith, 'Liability for Endangerment: English Ad Hoc Pragmatism and American Innovation' [1983] Crim LR 127; D. Lanham, 'Danger Down Under' [1999] Crim LR 960.

31 See M. Hirst, *Jurisdiction and the Ambit of the Criminal Law* (2003), p 128.

32 See *Morris* [1984] AC 320 below, p 649.

the type of crime from a 'result' crime. The conduct crime of perjury is completed once the testimony leaves the lips of the witness. It is not a continuing crime in any real sense. Identifying the starting and finishing points of the *actus reus* will be important in ensuring that the element of *mens rea* coincides in time, and may also be significant for procedural purposes of charging, in terms of the specific dates and actions alleged in the indictment.

(iii) *Actus reus* includes circumstances

The *actus reus* then is made up, generally but not invariably, of conduct and sometimes its consequences, and also of the circumstances in which the conduct takes place (or which constitute the state of affairs) in so far as they are relevant. Circumstances, like consequences, are relevant if they are included in the definition of the crime. The definition of theft, for example, requires that it be proved that D dishonestly appropriated property *belonging to another*. If the property belonged to no one (because it had been abandoned) D's appropriation could not constitute the *actus reus* of theft. However dishonest he might be, he could not be convicted of theft because an essential constituent of the crime is missing.[33]

(iv) Victim's conduct/state as part of the *actus reus*

Sometimes a particular state of mind on the part of the *victim* is required by the definition of the crime. If so, that state of mind is part of the *actus reus* and, if the prosecution are unable to prove its existence, they must fail. If D is prosecuted for rape, it must be proved that V did not consent to the act. The absence of consent by V is an essential constituent of the *actus reus.* But in some crimes the consent of the victim is entirely irrelevant. If D is charged with the murder of V, it is no defence for him to show that V asked to be killed.

(v) Summary

It is apparent from these examples that it is only by looking at the definition of the particular crime that we can see what circumstances are elements of the *actus reus.* We find this definition, in the case of common law crimes, in the decisions of the courts and, in the case of statutory crimes, in the words of the statute, as construed by the courts. Many factors may be relevant; for example, in bigamy, the fact that D is validly married; in treason committed abroad, that D is a British national (or under the protection of the Crown for some other reason);[34] in handling stolen goods, that the goods have, in fact, been stolen; and so on.

(c) The effect of penalty provisions in determining the elements of the *actus reus*

Sometimes it happens that Parliament provides that an offence shall be more severely punishable when a particular fact, say X, is present. When this happens, it is 'plain beyond argument that Parliament has created two offences,' according to Lord Diplock (the

[33] He might, however, be convicted of an attempt to steal. Below, p 425.
[34] *Joyce v DPP* [1946] AC 347.

whole House concurring) in *Courtie*.[35] The offence when X is present is a different and graver offence than when X is not present. X is an element in the *actus reus*, or the *mens rea*, or both, of the greater offence. This principle depends on the presumed intention of Parliament; and it is excluded if, in the particular circumstances, it would lead to such inconvenient and absurd results that, in the opinion of the courts, Parliament could not have intended it to apply: *DPP v Butterworth*.[36]

When *Courtie* applies, the effect is (i) that D can be convicted of the greater offence only if the charge alleges X, and (ii) it is for the jury to decide whether X is proved and to give their verdict accordingly, not a matter for the judge to decide after verdict. Thus, causing a person to engage in sexual activity (contrary to s 4 of the Sexual Offences Act 2003) carries a sentence of 14 years, but the sentence for that offence is increased to a maximum of life where the activity involves penetrative acts (s 4(4)) and as such, there are two forms of the offence. If D is alleged to have caused an act of sexual penetration, that should be specified in indictment.

Where Parliament provides an elaborate structure of maximum penalties, as in the case of drug offences, the substantive law is correspondingly complex.[37] But the principle is sound. Where proof of fact X entails liability to a higher penalty, the requirements of proof of X should be no less stringent than in the case of the other facts of the offence.

(d) *Actus reus* and justification or excuse

There is a longstanding debate not only as to the value of the use of terms such as *actus reus* and *mens rea*,[38] but precisely how the terminology ought to be applied. In the terminology used by Glanville Williams:[39]

> *Actus reus* includes ... the absence of any ground of justification or excuse, whether such justification or excuse be stated in any statute creating the crime or implied by the courts in accordance with general principle ...

An alternative view is that of D. J. Lanham:[40]

> As a matter of analysis we can think of a crime as being made up of three ingredients, *actus reus*, *mens rea* and (a negative element) absence of a valid defence.

35 [1984] AC 463, at 471, [1984] 1 All ER 740 at, 744, HL.

36 [1995] 1 AC 381, [1994] 3 All ER 289, HL. Section 7(6) of the Road Traffic Act 1988 on its face creates only one offence of failing to provide a specimen of breath; but there is a higher penalty where the offender was driving or attempting to drive than when he was merely in charge. Nevertheless, there is only one offence. By contrast, s 5(1)(a) of the Act (driving/attempting to/being in charge of a motor vehicle on a road after consuming so much alcohol that the proportion of it in the breath/blood/urine exceeds the prescribed limit) creates nine offences, all punishable with the same penalty: *Bolton Justices, ex p Khan* [1999] Crim LR 912.

37 *Shivpuri* [1987] AC 1, [1986] 2 All ER 334, [1986] Crim LR 536 and commentary; *Ellis, Street and Smith* (1986) 84 Cr App R 235, [1987] Crim LR 44, CA, and commentary; *Bett* [1999] Crim LR 218. *Courtie* seems to have been completely overlooked in *Leeson* [2000] 1 Cr App R 233, [2000] Crim LR 195. See commentary at p 196.

38 See P. H. Robinson, 'Should the Criminal Law Abandon the Actus Reus–Mens Rea Distinction?' in S. Shute, J. Gardner and J. Horder (eds), *Action and Value in Criminal Law* (1993), arguing for the abandonment of the oversimplistic categorization which obscures the doctrines lying beneath the overarching labels.

39 CLGP, 19. See also TBCL, ch 2.

40 [1976] Crim LR 276.

Other variations on these two basic views can be advanced including, for example, the suggestion that the *actus reus* includes the absence of any elements of justification but not those of excuse.[41]

Assuming the death penalty was still available in respect of certain crimes, if the public executioner carried out his duty to hang, say a convicted traitor, no offence would be committed – according to Williams because there is no *actus reus* (or, indeed, *mens rea*) and, according to Lanham, because, though there is both *actus reus* and *mens rea* (the intentional killing of a human being) there is a valid defence. Williams' opinion is attractive both because it seems strange to describe an act which is required or permitted by the law as an *actus reus*[42] and because there are practical difficulties in distinguishing (as Lanham's analysis requires) between the definitional elements of an offence and defence elements.[43] On the other hand, the enumeration of the elements of an offence becomes impossibly cumbersome if it has to include all conceivable defences – as the authors of the draft criminal code put it, 'the inapplicability of every exception admitted by the definition of an offence must be treated as an element of it.'[44] Moreover, defences may also require mental as well as external elements. Duress is a defence but only, of course, if D is aware of the threatening facts.[45] If the object of the Latin terminology is convenience of exposition, there is much to be said for the Lanham usage and it is generally (but not invariably) followed in this book.[46]

(e) An *actus reus* must be proved

Mens rea may exist without an *actus reus* but, if the *actus reus* of a particular crime does not exist or occur, that crime is not committed. Although D believes that he is appropriating V's property he cannot in any circumstances be guilty of theft if the property belongs to no one. D has the *mens rea* but the *actus reus*, the other fundamental element of the crime, is lacking. D may penetrate V with intent to have intercourse with her against her will but, if in fact she consents, his act cannot amount to rape. D may intend to marry during the lifetime of his wife but if, unknown to him, she is dead, he cannot commit bigamy. If D makes a statement, which he believes to be false, for the purpose of obtaining money, he cannot be convicted of obtaining by deception if the statement is, in fact, true. In each case, D may now be convicted of attempting to commit the crime in question.[47]

In *Deller*,[48] D induced V to purchase his car by representing (*inter alia*) that it was free from encumbrances that is, that D had ownership and was free to sell it. In fact, D had

[41] See M. S. Moore, *Act and Crime: The Philosophy of Action and its Implications for Criminal Law* (1993) pp 177–183.

[42] But, as noted above, *actus reus* implies no moral judgment, the only point of the analysis being convenience in exposition.

[43] Although arguably the same is true of Williams' analysis since it requires us to exclude any ground of justification or excuse.

[44] Draft Code, vol 2, 7.2, 7.3.

[45] Below, p 296.

[46] The Latin terms are frequently used by the courts but no detailed analysis has been made by them and it cannot be said that there is a standard judicial usage. The current judicial trend is to avoid Latin in the criminal trial. 'Throw Latin out of court' says Woolf: The Times, 20 July 2000.

[47] Below, p 420.

[48] (1952) 36 Cr App R 184. Cf *Brien* (1903) 3 SRNSW 410; *Dyson* [1908] 2 KB 454.

previously executed a document that purported to mortgage the car to a finance company and, no doubt, he thought he was telling a lie. He was charged with obtaining by false pretences.[49] It then appeared that the document by which the transaction had been effected was probably void in law for the technical reason that it was as an unregistered bill of sale. If the document was void the car *was* free from encumbrances '. . . quite accidentally and, strange as it may sound, dishonestly, the appellant had told the truth'.[50] D's conviction was, therefore, quashed by the Court of Criminal Appeal, for, though he had *mens rea*, no *actus reus* had been established. Under the present law, D could be convicted of an attempt to obtain by deception.[51]

(i) The problematic case of *Dadson*

A case which is sometimes said to be inconsistent with this fundamental principle, but which is worth discussing because it illustrates the difficulties that may arise in connection with its application, is *Dadson*.[52]

D was a constable, employed to watch a copse from which wood had been stolen. He carried a loaded gun. V emerged from the copse carrying wood that he had stolen, and, ignoring D's calls to stop, ran away. D, having no other means of bringing him to justice, fired and wounded him in the leg. He was convicted of shooting at V with intent to cause him grievous bodily harm. It was assumed in this case that it was lawful to wound an escaping felon[53] if this was the only way of arresting him;[54] but stealing growing wood was not, under s 39 of the Larceny Act 1827, a felony unless V had two previous convictions for the same offence. In fact V had been repeatedly convicted of stealing wood, but D did not know this. Could D rely on what would be a compelling justifying circumstance when D was unaware of its existence? Erle J told the jury that the alleged felony, *being unknown to the prisoner*, constituted no justification. On a case reserved the judges thought the conviction right: D was not justified in firing at V because the fact that V was committing a felony was not known to D at the time.

Many have argued that this case is wrong because, if we ignore D's state of mind and look at the actual facts, what he did was lawful; there was no *actus reus*.[55] It is submitted that this approach is incorrect. It is important to distinguish between two types of 'defence' that may be raised. In the first type, D merely denies the existence of an element (other than the *mens rea*) in the definition of the crime. If D makes out the defence (or more accurately successfully raises the plea) he certainly cannot be convicted, whatever his state of mind. This is what happened in *Deller*.[56] In the second type, D admits that all

49 Under the Larceny Act 1916, s 32, now replaced by the Theft Act 1968, s 15, below, p 758. The same principles are applicable.

50 (1952) 36 Cr App R 184 at 191.

51 Below, p 698.

52 (1850) 2 Den 35. Cf *Tooley* (1709) 11 Mod Rep 242 at 251, per Holt CJ; and see Williams, CLGP, 23 et seq, and Burchell and Hunt 115.

53 A term used before the Criminal Law Act 1967 to denote those committing serious offences.

54 On this point, see below, p 43.

55 See Williams, CLGP, p 22; Lady MacCauley, H. M. Trevalyen (ed), *The Works of Lord MacCauley: Volume 7* (1866) 552; P. H. Robinson, 'Competing Theories of Justification' in A. Simester and A. T. H. Smith (eds), *Harm and Culpability* (1996), 45. Cf J. Gardner, 'Justifications and Reasons' in A. Simester and A. T. H. Smith (eds), *Harm and Culpability* (1996) 103.

56 Supra.

the elements in the definition of the crime have been established and goes on to assert other facts that afford him a defence in law. As appears from the example of duress, above, the establishment of this type of defence may require D to assert the existence of a mental element as well as external facts.

In *Dadson*[57] D did not deny that he shot at V or that he intended to cause him grievous bodily harm. He admitted the necessary constituents of the crime (other than 'unlawfulness') but went on to assert other facts that, he alleged, made his act lawful. Whether his act was lawful depended on what were the constituents of the defence that he raised; and the case decided that the defence, like duress and self-defence, required the assertion not merely of external facts but also of a state of mind. A doctrine of *actus reus* which says that such a course *must* be wrong, as contravening a fundamental principle, is much too constricting. Whether the defence should consist simply in the external facts, or in the facts plus the state of mind, is a matter of policy; and it was a not unreasonable decision of policy to say that a man who deliberately shot another should be guilty of an offence unless he knew of circumstances justifying or excusing his conduct.

Dadson then, is perfectly reconcilable with *Deller.* It does not decide that a man can be convicted where there is no *actus reus.* There was an *actus reus* for D did unlawfully wound V. All that the case decided was that the defence to wounding, 'I was arresting an escaping felon', was a defence which required a mental as well as a physical element and, because the mental element was lacking, the wounding was unlawful.[58]

The Criminal Code Team and, at one time, the Law Commission assumed that *Dadson* was overruled by s 2 of the Criminal Law Act 1967 and s 24 of PACE 1984 which replaced it. Section 24 provides (prior to the Serious Organised Crime and Police Act 2005, s 110) that D may arrest V if (i) V is in the act of committing an arrestable offence, or (ii) D has reasonable grounds to suspect V to be committing such an offence. Having reasonable grounds for suspicion is a separate and distinct ground for arrest: Dadson's act would be lawful (it is said) simply because V was in the act of committing the arrestable offence. But this conclusion overlooks the common law principle, restated in s 28(3) of PACE that an arrest is lawful only if 'the person arrested is informed of the ground for the arrest at the time of, or as soon as practicable after, the arrest'. It follows that the person making an arrest must in order to be able to inform the suspect, know of, or at least suspect, the existence of valid grounds for an arrest. *Dadson* was wholly unaware of such grounds.[59] If the arrest was unlawful, the shooting to effect it was also unlawful.

This conclusion is now accepted by the Law Commission and their draft Criminal Law Bill (1993) would codify the *Dadson* principle.[60]

57 Above, p 42.

58 Below, p 553. For a defence of *Dadson*, see J. Hall, *General Principles*, 228 and R. M. Perkins, *Criminal Law*, 39. And cf the crime of perjury where D may be convicted if he makes a statement on oath which he believes to be false though it is in fact true.

59 *Edwards v DPP* (1993) 97 Cr App R 301, [1993] Crim LR 854, DC; *Chapman v DPP* [1988] Crim LR 843, DC and commentary; Smith, *Justification and Excuse*, pp 34–41. On the issue of the principle, see B. Hogan, 'The *Dadson* Principle' [1989] Crim LR 679, R. L. Christopher, 'Unknowing Justification and the Logical Necessity of the *Dadson* Principle in Self-defence' (1995) 15 OJLS 229.

60 Clause 27. See Law Comm Consultation Paper No 122 at para 20.9, especially n 295 and Law Comm No 218, para 39.11.

(ii) Explaining *Dadson* – by justification and excuse theories[61]

A distinction is sometimes made between a defence amounting to a justification and a defence amounting to an excuse. On some interpretations of this theoretical distinction, where the circumstances justify the act, it is immaterial that D is not aware of them; where they can merely excuse the act, they do so only if he is aware of them. Force used to make an arrest is said to be justified, not merely excused, so, it is argued, *Dadson* was a case of justification and is wrongly decided. Duress, which obviously requires awareness, is distinguishable because according to most commentators it merely excuses. But such an analysis based solely on justification and excuse is overly simplistic and does not provide a satisfactory explanation of *Dadson*. A boy who, knowing it is a wicked thing to do, deliberately kills his playmate has a defence if he was aged only nine at the time. Ten is the minimum age of criminal responsibility. He is excused, but no one would say he was 'justified' in killing his playmate because he was only nine. Is he to be liable for murder if he thought he was 10? Obviously not. He is excused by the fact, whether he knows of it or not. It is the policy of the law that a child under 10 shall not be convicted of crime and the child's mistake cannot be allowed to defeat that policy.

Self-defence is still governed by the common law. Suppose that D shoots at V with intent to murder him and kills him. It turns out that D did so in the nick of time because, unknown to D, V was about to shoot D dead.[62] If D had only known he would certainly have had the defence of self-defence. Is D guilty of murder? According to orthodox justification/excuse theory, it depends on whether self-defence provides a justification or an excuse for the use of force. Glanville Williams, who at one time thought self-defence merely an excuse, later concluded that it is a justification,[63] so he thought D would have a defence. But can it really be right that a person who has fired a gun at another with intent to murder should be beyond the reach of the law? One answer is that, though not guilty of murder, he is guilty of attempted murder under the Criminal Attempts Act 1981 (since, by that Act, he is to be treated for the purpose of an attempt charge as if the facts were as he believed them to be). But how can it be said that his act was both (i) justified and (ii) attempted murder? What would a jury make of a direction to that effect? The better view is that the *Dadson* principle applies and that it is generally applicable to defences unless policy (as in the case of the nine-year old, above) otherwise requires.

2. Analysis of an *actus reus*

Some writers have suggested that 'an act' is nothing more than a willed muscular movement – for example, the deliberate crooking of a finger. But if D crooked his finger around the trigger of a loaded pistol which was pointing at V, with the result that V was

61 See for further discussion Ch 11 below, and in general G. P. Fletcher, *Rethinking Criminal Law* (1978), J. C. Smith, *Justification and Excuse in the Criminal Law* (1989); M. L. Corrado (ed), *Justification and Excuse in the Criminal Law: a collection of essays* (1994); A. Eser, G. Fletcher, K. Cornils *et al.* (eds), *Justification and Excuse: comparative perspectives* (1987). For monographs and essays providing sophisticated analyses of the theories see especially R. Schopp, *Justification Defences and Just Convictions* (1988); J. Horder, *Excusing Crime* (2004).

62 This is known as the paradox of the unknowing justification – see R. L. Christopher (above).

63 Compare CLGP (1961) 25, (1982) 2 LS 233, 250.

killed, to say 'D crooked his finger' would be a most misleading way of describing D's 'act'. 'Again, suppose a person orally demands money by threats of injury. Can the action of his vocal chords be separated from the resulting sound issuing from his mouth and its intended meaning to the hearer?'[64] We naturally say, 'D shot V' or 'D demanded money from V'. This way of describing the act takes account of the circumstances surrounding the actual movement of the body (in so far as they are relevant) and its consequences (again, in so far as they are relevant), and, for ordinary purposes, it is obviously the sensible way of describing it.[65] But for the purposes of the criminal law it is sometimes necessary to break down an 'act', so comprehensively described, into the constituents of (i) the conduct which is the central feature of the crime, (ii) the surrounding material circumstances, and (iii) the consequences. One reason for so doing is that the law may require different mental elements for the various constituents. For example, when a person is charged with an attempt to commit a crime it must be proved that he intended to do the act and to cause the relevant consequence but it may be that recklessness as to circumstances will suffice.

(a) The conduct must be 'willed'[66]

If the *actus reus* of the crime includes an act, it must of course be proved that D did that act voluntarily. Although generally expressed as a requirement of 'voluntariness' there is a degree of confusion as to whether the law is truly concerned that D was 'conscious' of his actions, whether he 'willed' them, or whether they were voluntary. These terms are not synonymous, and their precise definition involves complex questions of philosophy and neurology,[67] presenting distractions which for pragmatic reasons the criminal courts are keen to avoid. The requirement of voluntariness is fundamental to the imposition of criminal liability since it reflects the underlying respect for the individual's autonomy and the principle that 'unless a man has the capacity and fair opportunity to adjust his behaviour to the law its penalties ought not to be applied to him'.[68]

The clearest cases might be thought to be those where D is unconscious. If D is unconscious or for example, asleep, he *cannot* exercise his will, so any movements of his body are involuntary. (This is subject to an important exception where the reason for the lack of consciousness is owing to voluntary intoxication.)

Even where D is conscious, there are many well-established circumstances in which the act will be found to be involuntary for the purposes of the criminal law. Suppose the act is

64 *Timbu Kolian v R* (1968) 119 CLR 47 at 69, per Windeyer J. D's act was demanding with menaces.

65 See eg the discussion of crimes involving hate speech in J. Jaconelli, 'Context-Dependent Crime' [1995] Crim LR 771.

66 See generally, R. D. Mackay, *Mental Condition Defences in the Criminal Law* (1995) Ch 1, and H. L. A. Hart, *Punishment and Responsibility* (1968) Ch 4. There is a considerable philosophical literature on the subject, including M. S. Moore, *Act and Crime: The Philosophy of Action and its Implications for Criminal Law* (1993). See also Wilson, *Central Issues*, ch 4; Norrie, *Crime, Reason and History* (2000), pp 112–120.

67 See eg D. W. Denno, 'How Psychological Research on Consciousness can Enlighten the Criminal Law' [2002] Amicus Curiae 28; R. Schopp, *Automatism, Insanity and the Psychology of Criminal Responsibility: A Philosophical Inquiry* (1991). See also B. McSherry, 'Voluntariness, Intention and the Defence of Mental Disorder: Towards a Rational Approach' (2003) 21(5) Behavioural Sciences and the Law 581; K. Saunders, 'Voluntary Acts and the Criminal Law: Justifying Culpability Based on the Existence of Volition' (1988) 49 U Pitt LR 443.

68 H. L. A. Hart, *Punishment and Responsibility*, p 181.

'wounding' and the evidence shows that, while D was holding a knife in his hand, E seized D's hand and, against D's will, plunged the knife still held by D's hand into V. Plainly D is not guilty of wounding because it was not his act. Similarly D would not be guilty of a battery if he was afflicted by St Vitus' dance and his fist shot out in an uncontrolled spasm and struck V; or if D, startled by an unexpected explosion, dropped a weight, which he was carrying carefully, on to V's foot; or if D tripped onto V. If D, while driving, is attacked by a swarm of bees and disabled from controlling the vehicle, he may be held to be no longer 'driving'.[69] In each of these cases the movement of D's limbs was involuntary in that it did not flow from an exercise by D of his will. The event happened either against or at least without his will. In these examples, note that D was conscious. Again, the involuntariness will not exclude liability if the reason for it was D's voluntary intoxication.

If D is conscious and the physical movement is voluntary, D may be liable for its consequences even though it is unintentionally misdirected, as where D put his foot on the accelerator of a bus instead of, as he intended, the brake.[70]

(i) Self-induced involutarism

As noted, there is an exception to the rule that there is no liability for an involuntary act: where the 'act' was done while in a state of self-induced intoxication.[71] The rule is a complex one to be examined in full in Ch 11 below, but in short, it will, apparently, be no defence to crimes of 'basic intent' (that is, those which do not require proof of *mens rea* of intention) that D was unconscious or otherwise 'acting' involuntarily. Thus, where D, owing to his voluntary ingestion of LSD, kills his girlfriend V, mistakenly believing that he is slaying a serpent at the centre of the earth,[72] D's prior fault by voluntarily reducing himself to that state provides a sufficient basis of fault in law to regard his subsequent involuntary conduct as blameworthy. A diabetic who fails to take sufficient food after a normal dose of insulin may rely on his consequent automatism as a defence to a charge of a crime of basic intent, unless he was actually aware of the risk of becoming aggressive, unpredictable and uncontrolled.[73] His prior conduct lacks sufficient fault to be assigned to his subsequent act. So too a person may be held liable for basic intent crimes when he is aware of the risk of becoming unpredictable or aggressive when taking valium (a soporific or sedative drug) even though not on medical prescription.[74]

It has been argued[75] that this is part of a wider rule that automatism induced by D's 'fault' is no defence in these cases. 'Fault' means doing or omitting to do something that could reasonably be foreseen to be likely to bring about such a state. There do not however, appear to be cases that do not involve the use or misuse of drink or drugs (including prescribed medicines)[76] and it is thought that this anomalous rule is properly

69 *Hill v Baxter* [1958] 1 QB 277 at 286.

70 *A-G's Reference (No 4 of 2000)* [2001] Crim LR 578 and commentary (causing death by dangerous driving).

71 *Hardie* [1984] 3 All ER 848, [1985] 1 WLR 64, CA.

72 *Lipman* [1970] 1 QB 152, [1969] 3 All ER 410; approved in *DPP v Majewski* [1977] AC 443, [1976] 2 All ER 142. See below, pp 278, 476.

73 *Bailey* [1983] 2 All ER 503, [1983] 1 WLR 760, below, p 281.

74 *Hardie*, above.

75 R. D. Mackay, 'Intoxication as a Factor in Automatism' [1982] Crim LR 146, 147. See also R. D. Mackay, *Mental Condition Defences*, above.

76 See recently *Poole* [2003] All ER (D) 448 (Mar) where D's failure to take his epilepsy medicine led to his loss of consciousness.

confined to such cases, the basis for it being the grave social danger seen to be presented by intoxicated persons.[77] One can imagine (perhaps fanciful) scenarios in which D carelessly or knowingly sets up circumstances in which he will subsequently perform an involuntary act, as where he visits a hypnotist to receive the suggestion that he should kill V and does so when in the trance, but such circumstances have not been addressed by the courts.[78]

Of course, if the 'fault' exhibited by the defendant's 'prior' conduct is in itself sufficient to found liability for the offence charged, then the defendant is properly convicted of it under ordinary principles.[79] An elementary example is where a driver, feeling sleepy, continues to drive until he falls asleep and has an accident. His failure to stop may constitute the fault necessary to convict him of careless, or even dangerous, driving.[80]

(ii) Voluntariness as *actus reus* or *mens rea*?

Writers dispute whether the voluntariness of D's conduct should be regarded as part of the *actus reus* or as part of the *mens rea*.[81] On the one hand, it is a mental element; on the other, it is said that it is an essential constituent of the act, which is part of the *actus reus*. It has been argued that the classification is important. The argument runs: some offences, known as offences of strict liability, do not require *mens rea*; so that, if voluntariness is part of the *mens rea*, a man charged with an offence of strict liability might be convicted for an involuntary act. But an *actus reus* must be proved, even for an offence of strict liability; so if voluntariness is part of the *actus reus*, no one can be convicted of any crime if his act was involuntary. As the latter result is thought to be not only desirable but to represent the law, voluntariness can only properly be regarded as an element in the *actus reus*. The fallacy in this argument lies in the proposition that offences of strict liability require 'no *mens rea*' and the assumption that this means that the whole of the mental element involved in *mens rea* may be lacking.[82] This is not so. If the mental element is part of the *actus reus* (as in, for example, possession) there is certainly no way of dispensing with it;[83] but it does not follow that it must be dispensed with where an offence is held to be one of strict liability.

For 125 years *Prince*[84] was regarded as the leading case on strict liability. Its present status, considered below,[85] is doubtful but, right or wrong, it remains a good illustration of the principle. *Prince* decided that D may be convicted of the offence under s 20 of the Sexual Offences Act 1956 (now repealed) of taking a girl under the age of 16 out of the

77 These issues are discussed in full in Ch 11 below.

78 C. Finkelstein, 'Involuntary Crimes, Voluntarily Committed' in S. Shute and A. Simester (eds). *Criminal Law Theory*, 143; P. H. Robinson, 'Causing the Condition of One's Own Defense: A Study in the Limits of the Criminal Law Doctrine' (1985) 71 Virg LR 1. See also *Finnegan v Heywood* (2000), 10 May, High Ct of Justiciary, where D's transitory state of sleep walking (and driving) was induced by his voluntary intoxication and he was aware of the likelihood of that outcome. The decision does not make it clear whether D would have had a defence of automatism if he was unaware of the likelihood.

79 The *dictum* of Martin JA in *Rabey* (1977) 79 DLR (3d) 414, 425 quoted by Mackay as a 'typical example of a dictum in support of "fault liability"' above 147, seems to be saying no more than this.

80 *Kay v Butterworth* (1945) 173 LT 191, below, p 50.

81 Turner (MACL 195 and 199 and Kenny, *Outlines*, 23) thought 'voluntariness' an element of *mens rea*. Williams, CLGP, s 8 and I. Patient, 'Some remarks about the element of voluntariness in offences of absolute liability' [1968] Crim LR 23 think it part of the *actus reus*.

82 Cf *Blackburn v Bowering*, below, p 540; Howard, SR 1; R. S. Clark, *NZ Essays* at 49; Packer, 126.

83 Above, p 36. 84 (1875) LR 2 CCR 154. 85 P 142.

possession and against the will of her father, even though D believed in good faith and on reasonable grounds that the girl he was taking was over 16. It is commonly said that no *mens rea* need be proved because the act which D *intended* – to take an 18-year-old girl (as she had told him she was) out of the possession of her parents – was not prohibited by law – it was not an *actus reus*. But even if this was an offence 'requiring no *mens rea*' it is quite clear that it involved a substantial mental element, apart from the element of voluntariness. D would have to have been proved to have intended to take a girl out of the possession of her parents. If he thought the girl was in no one's possession, he was not guilty. If he thought the girl was a boy, he was probably not guilty. No one suggests, however, that we should say that his knowledge that the girl was in the possession of her parents is part of the *actus reus*. The fact is that even in offences of strict liability, a limited degree of *mens rea* must be proved; and a jurist may, if he chooses, classify the voluntariness of the accused's act as part of the limited degree of *mens rea*. It is a matter of convenience only.

What is clear is that the voluntariness of an act is a more fundamental element of criminal liability than what we normally think of as *mens rea* – the intention to cause, or foresight of, results of the act and awareness of circumstances. If the voluntariness of the act has not been proved by the Crown there can be no conviction.

What is missing in these cases appears to most people as a vital link between mind and body; and both the ordinary man and the lawyer might well insist on this by saying that in these cases there is not 'really' a human action at all and certainly nothing for which anyone should be made criminally responsible however 'strict' legal responsibility might be.[86]

(iii) Automatism

The plea of a lack of voluntariness is described as a plea of automatism, that is, that the accused was acting as an automaton. Automatism has narrow limits as a 'defence'. It is to be confined, according to Lord Denning,[87] to acts done while unconscious and to spasms, reflex actions and convulsions.[88] It commonly arises in driving cases, particularly where diabetic defendants claim that they were suffering from hyperglycaemic or hypoglycaemic states. In *Broome v Perkins*[89] D, though in a hypoglycaemic state, was held guilty of driving without due care and attention because from time to time he apparently exercised conscious control over his car, veering away from other vehicles so as to avoid a collision, braking violently, and so on. Automatism is not a defence to a driving charge unless there is 'a total destruction of voluntary control'. A condition described by an expert witness as 'driving without awareness' was held to be no answer to a charge of

[86] H. L. A. Hart, *Jubilee Lectures*, at 137. Note that Turner, while regarding voluntariness as *mens rea*, thought it a different and more fundamental element than foresight of consequences; MACL 195–205.

[87] In *Bratty* [1963] AC 386, [1961] 3 All ER 523 at 532. It is confined to 'involuntary movement of the body or limbs of a person': *Watmore v Jenkins* [1962] 2 All ER 868 at 878, per Winn J. In a Canadian case, *Racimore* (1976) 25 CCC (2d) 143 a 'failure to remain' after an accident was held to be involuntary because D did not know there had been an accident. This seems to be an unsatisfactory device for introducing a requirement of *mens rea* into an offence of strict liability. Cf *Davey v Towle* [1973] RTR 328.

[88] See the discussion in the Scots case of *Ross v HM Advocate* (1991) SCCR 823 where the court identified four criteria: an external factor; which was not self-induced; which D was not bound to foresee; and which caused a total alienation of reason rendering him incapable of controlling or appreciating what he was doing. See on this P. Ferguson, 'The Limits of the Automatism Defence' (1991) 36 JLSS 446.

[89] [1987] Crim LR 271, DC.

causing death by reckless (or, now, dangerous) driving where it in fact amounted to merely reduced or imperfect awareness.[90] Clearly policy plays a part in the courts' adoption of such a strict approach to the degree of involuntariness constituting automatism particularly in road traffic offences. Some passages suggest that the requirement is one of a complete lack of consciousness rather than a lack of voluntariness. In relation to other crimes the courts have not consistently adopted such a strict approach. In the case of *Charlson*[91] for example, where the evidence was that D was 'acting as an automaton without any *real knowledge* of that he was doing' (emphasis added) as a result of a cerebral tumour, Barry J directed the jury to acquit if the defence might reasonably be true.

(iv) Physical involuntariness

Although the courts have confused the issue of consciousness and voluntariness in seeking to determine the scope of the defence of automatism, they have been clear and consistent in holding that the defence is of physical, not moral involuntariness. Pleas of 'irresistible impulse' have been consistently rejected as a defence even where it arises from insanity. If it is recognized as an insanity plea, *a fortiori*, it would not be recognized in the case of a sane person. The fact that, as a result of hysterical amnesia, or hysterical fugue, D was unaware of 'legal restrictions or moral concern', is no defence if he knew the facts which constitute the offence charged.[92] An irresistible craving for drink is not a defence to a charge of stealing alcohol.[93] If D has punched V it is no defence (though it may mitigate the sentence) to say that this was an immediate and irresistible reaction to provocation by V. But the borderline between this and a 'reflex action' must be a fine one. The legal nature and legal effect of a reflex action is itself uncertain. In *Ryan v R*,[94] D with one hand pointed a loaded shotgun at V whom he had robbed, while with the other hand he attempted to tie V up. V moved. D was startled and, he said, 'involuntarily' pressed the trigger because of a 'reflex action'. Barwick CJ thought that, if this story had been true, D would not have been responsible in law for the 'act' of pressing the trigger; but Windeyer J held that, while that act may have been 'involuntary' in a dictionary sense, it was one for which he was responsible in law and not properly analogous to an act done in convulsions or an epileptic seizure. With respect, however, it seems closer to these than to 'the sudden movement of a tennis player retrieving a difficult shot; not accompanied by conscious planning but certainly not involuntary'.[95]

It is of course very important to identify the precise act for which D is to be held responsible. In *Ryan v R* the pointing of the loaded gun and the placing of the finger on

[90] *A-G's Reference (No 2 of 1992)* (1993) 99 Cr App R 429. It was argued that the cause of the condition was the 'external factor' of the motorway conditions. If those conditions disclose total destruction of voluntary control, it is submitted that, assuming them to be no more than the ordinary stresses to which all drivers are subject, they would not constitute an external factor. The driver's exceptional susceptibility should result, however odd it may sound, in a special verdict of insanity. See also J. C. Smith, 'Individual Incapacities and Criminal Liability' [1999] Med L Rev 138 at 144–145 and *Rabey*, below p 261.

[91] [1955] 1 All ER 859.

[92] *Isitt* [1978] Crim LR 159, CA.

[93] *Dodd* (1974) 7 SASR 151 at 157. See generally, L. S. Tao, 'Legal Problems of Alcoholism' (1969) 37(3) Fordham LR 405; J. Tolmie, 'Alcoholism and Criminal Liability' (2001) 64 MLR 688.

[94] (1967) 40 ALJR 488, discussed by I. D. Elliott, 'Responsibility for Involuntary Acts: *Ryan v The Queen*' (1968) 41 ALJ 497.

[95] Elliott, above.

the trigger were clearly voluntary acts and, provided that it could be said that these acts caused death, the accused would be liable for homicide, whether the pressing of the trigger was an act for which he was responsible or not. Similarly in the English civil case of *Gray v Barr*[96] D approached V with a loaded gun and fired a shot to frighten V. D and V grappled together and V fell on the gun and was shot and killed. The trial judge and Salmon LJ thought that the real cause of V's death was the accident of his falling on the gun; whereas Denning MR and Phillimore LJ thought that the cause was D's deliberate act in approaching V with the gun. All the judges agreed, however, that D could properly have been convicted of manslaughter on these facts. The act for which D would be held responsible was not the firing of the fatal shot – that was not his act – but deliberately approaching V in that threatening way. Again, a man may be immune from liability for an offence involving 'driving', though he is sitting at the controls of a moving vehicle, if he is unconscious through an epileptic fit; but, depending on the degree and frequency of epilepsy and the probability that he might have an attack, he might be liable through the conscious act of starting or continuing to drive.[97]

Distinguishing sane and insane automatism

A person who was in a state of automatism (other than one induced by voluntary intoxication) at the time he is alleged to have committed the offence, cannot be guilty of it and the only question is whether he is to be found simply 'not guilty' or 'not guilty by reason of insanity'. The outcome (which is of great importance) depends on how the automatism was caused. If it was caused by 'a disease of the mind' the proper verdict is not guilty by reason of insanity. If it arose from any other cause the verdict is simply not guilty. But whether a cause is a 'disease of the mind' is a question of law and that phrase has a wide meaning. Any 'internal factor', mental or physical, is, in law, a disease of the mind. So automatism caused by a cerebral tumour or arteriosclerosis, epilepsy or diabetes arises from a disease of the mind. These are all 'internal' to the accused. External factors include concussion, the administration of an anaesthetic or other drug, or hypnosis. In a number of cases acts done while sleeping have been treated as non-insane automatism[98] but it has now been held[99] that they are the product of a disease of the mind.

It will be recalled that the one exception at common law to the rule that the burden of proof is on the prosecution is the defence of insanity. So if D claims that he was in a state of automatism because of an internal factor, he is raising the insanity defence and it will be for him to satisfy the jury on the balance of probabilities that this was so; but if he relies on an external factor and lays a proper foundation for the defence, the onus is on the prosecution to satisfy the jury beyond reasonable doubt that it was not so.[100] If he

96 [1971] 2 QB 554, [1971] 2 All ER 949; below, p 474. Cf *Jarmain* [1946] KB 74, [1945] 2 All ER 613; *Blayney v Knight* (1975) 60 Cr App R 269, DC.

97 *Hill v Baxter* [1958] 1 QB 277 at 286, [1958] 1 All ER 193 at 197, per Pearson LJ; *McBride* [1962] 2 QB 167, [1961] 3 All ER 6. Similarly where D goes to sleep: *Kay v Butterworth* (1945) 173 LT 191.

98 *Boshears* (1961) The Times, 8 Feb; *Kemp* (1986) The Times, 3 May: D strangled his wife while experiencing a condition known as 'night terror'. Note that parasomnia caused by self-induced intoxication will not provide a defence of automatism.

99 *Burgess* [1991] 2 QB 92, [1991] Crim LR 548 and see news reports for 21 March 2005 of the killing when sleepwalking which led to an acquittal.

100 See recently *Roach* [2001] EWCA Crim 2698, below p 189.

alleges that his condition was due to the administration of insulin (an external factor) inducing hypoglycaemia (too little blood sugar), he will be acquitted unless the prosecution can disprove his claim;[101] but if he alleges that it was due to diabetes (an internal factor) causing hyperglycaemia (excessive blood sugar), the onus will be on him to prove the allegation on the balance of probabilities; it must be supported by the evidence of two or more registered medical practitioners;[102] and, if he succeeds, he will be found not guilty by reason of insanity.[103]

A proper foundation for a defence of non-insane automatism may be laid by introducing evidence from which it may reasonably be inferred that the act was involuntary. Whether such a foundation has been laid is a question of law. Lord Denning has said that the accused's own word will rarely be sufficient,[104] unless it is supported by medical evidence. The difficult questions that arise where there is evidence that the automatism was caused partly by disease of the mind and partly by other factors are considered below.[105]

(v) Involuntariness not arising from automatism

A person may have full control over his body but no control over events in which it is involved. A driver's brakes fail without his fault and, consequently, he inevitably fails to accord precedence to a pedestrian on a pedestrian crossing.[106] Although it is said that this offence is absolute[107] requiring no evidence of negligence, it was held in *Burns v Bidder*[108] that such a driver has a defence. The court equated the driver's situation with that of one stunned by a swarm of bees, disabled by epilepsy,[109] or propelled by a vehicle hitting his car from behind. 'Voluntariness' is essential even in so-called crimes of 'absolute liability'.[110] On the other hand, it seems to have been held that it is no defence that the failure to accord precedence on the crossing arises inevitably from the unforeseeable behaviour of the pedestrian,[111] but the driver in such a case has no more power to avert the failure than where his brakes fail. It is submitted that D should never be held criminally liable for an 'act' or result of an act over which he has no control.[112]

101 Assuming he has not acted recklessly as to becoming automaton by failing to follow his prescription, etc.

102 Criminal Procedure (Insanity and Unfitness to Plead) Act 1991, below, p 253.

103 *Hennessy* [1989] 2 All ER 9, [1989] 1 WLR 287, CA; *Bingham* [1991] Crim LR 433. Cf *Pull* (1998) The Times, 20–21 Mar, discussed below. The distinction in terms of result highlights the unsatisfactorily incoherent nature of the law's categorization of automatism as sane or insane on the basis of its internal/external cause.

104 In *Dervish* [1968] Crim LR 37, *Cook v Atchison* [1968] Crim LR 266 and *Stripp* (1978) 69 Cr App R 318, CA it was held that D's evidence that he had a 'blackout' was insufficient to raise the defence; but D's own evidence is enough to raise the defence of provocation: *Whitfield* (1976) 63 Cr App R 39, CA.

105 Ch 11.

106 Contrary to the Zebra, Pelican and Puffin Pedestrian Crossings Regulations and General Directions 1997, SI 2400, reg 25.

107 *Hughes v Hall* [1960] 2 All ER 504, [1960] 1 WLR 733.

108 [1967] 2 QB 227, [1966] 3 All ER 29.

109 But see now *Sullivan* [1984] AC 156, [1983] 1 All ER 577.

110 An alternative explanation is the existence of a general defence of 'impossibility', below, Ch 11.

111 *Neal v Reynolds* [1966] Crim LR 393. The case is only briefly reported and may be explained on another ground.

112 See also K. J. M. Smith and W. Wilson, 'Impaired Voluntariness and Criminal Responsibility' (1993) 13 OJLS 69, considering the question of voluntariness in terms of a person's capacity to conform to the law's requirements.

3. Causation[113]

In every result crime causation is, by definition, an issue. Although the issue often arises in the context of homicide, causation is important in all result crimes.[114] In many cases it is not a contentious issue because it is not disputed. When it is disputed, the prosecution must prove that D, by his own act or unlawful omission, caused the relevant result.[115] A common approach of the courts has been[116] to assert that causation is a question of fact to be answered by the application of common sense. The view that it is so simple is belied by the existence of a book on causation in law of over 500 pages with a 24-page table of cases.[117] What D did and what happened are certainly questions of fact. Whether D's act caused what happened is more complicated. If that is a question of fact it is one which is closely circumscribed by cases deciding what is incapable in law of being a cause and what cannot reasonably be held not be a cause. Questions of fact *and law* are involved.

Whether D's act caused the result is a question that must be left to the jury, but in answering the question, they must apply legal principles, which it is the judge's duty to explain to them.[118] In one case[119] Lawton LJ said that where 'there is no conflict of evidence and all the jury has to do is to apply the law to the admitted facts, the judge is entitled to tell the jury what the result of that application will be'. Other cases[120] however show that the jury may have a substantial role in evaluating the primary facts, and that carries the attendant problems involved in their exercising moral judgment.

The judge may certainly direct the jury that they must acquit where there is no evidence that D caused the result, but it is not so clear that he may tell them that they must find that D did cause death (or any other result) even where that is the only reasonable conclusion. If it is not for the judge to decide the issue, still less is it for expert witnesses. Where the question is whether the act caused a prohibited result such as certain injuries or death, their function is to give the court their opinion on the medical issues. It is then for the jury to find the facts and apply the legal principles under the direction of the judge. Thus, cases such as *Jordan* (discussed below) have been criticized[121] because medical experts were permitted to say that certain medical treatment, and not wounds inflicted by D, were the cause of V's death.[122] Whether the wound was capable being 'a

113 See generally, H. Hart and T. Honoré, *Causation in Law* (2nd edn, 1985); A. Norrie, *Crime Reason and History* (2nd edn, 2001), ch 7; W. Wilson, *Central Issues*, ch 6.

114 Especially in cases of strict liability where, in the absence of *mens rea* elements, disputes over causation become the most critical eg in environmental offences: N. Padfield, 'Clean Water and Muddy Causation' [1995] Crim LR 683.

115 On the issue of causing an event through the use of an innocent agent see below, p 57.

116 But see now the *Empress Car* case, below, p 59.

117 H. Hart and T. Honoré, *Causation in the Law* (2nd edn, 1985).

118 *Pagett* (1983) 76 Cr App R 279, CA.

119 *Blaue* [1975] 3 All ER 446 at 450, CA, below, p 67. In *Malcherek*, below, p 66, it was held that the jury were bound to conclude that D caused V's death.

120 Eg, *Cheshire* [1991] 3 All ER 670, [1991] 1 WLR 844, below, p 65.

121 (1956) 40 Cr App R 152, below p 63. See G. Williams, 'Causation in Homicide' [1957] Crim LR 431 and F. Camps and J. Havard, 'Causation in Homicide – A Medical View' [1957] Crim LR 576.

122 Cf *Cato* [1976] 1 All ER 260 at 264, below, p 55 where the medical experts said it was not for them to state the cause of death; they spoke to facts, and deductions therefrom were for the jury.

cause', for the purpose of the decision, was a question of law, not of medicine. Certainly it was relevant and proper for the court to know if the medical treatment was effective to cause death, either in conjunction with, or independently of, the wound; and perhaps all that the witnesses intended to say was that the treatment alone was the medical cause of death.[123]

(a) The 'but for' principle

The first legal principle to apply is that D's act cannot be the cause of an event if the event would have occurred in precisely the same way had that act never been done. It must be proved that, *but for* D's act or omission, the event would not have occurred.[124] Thus, if D poisons V's drink but V dies of natural causes before it has had any effect on V, D's conduct is not a 'but for' cause of V's death.[125] When deciding whether D's act was a 'but for' cause, a simple approach is to eliminate D's behaviour from the narrative and ask whether the result would have occurred anyway. If so, D is not liable.

In the traditional Latin terminology, the act must be a *sine qua non* of the prohibited consequence (for example, death in murder). But this is only a starting point. There are many acts that are *sine qua non* of an event but are not, either in law or common sense, the cause of it. It is necessary to keep the test in perspective, otherwise blame could be attributed to D's ancestors! If D invites V to dinner and V is run over and killed on the way, V would not have died but for the invitation; but as a matter of common sense, no one would say 'D killed V', and D has not caused his death in law. In *Jordan*,[126] a wound inflicted by D was certainly a *sine qua non* of the death of V for it led directly to the (badly performed) medical treatment that, according to the medical experts, caused death. It did not necessarily follow that the treatment was, in law, the only cause of the death. That depended on the application of the further principles considered below. The 'but for' principle is a starting point in the causation inquiry, but nothing more.

(b) Contributory causes

It is clear that the act of the accused need not be the sole or the main cause of the result. It is wrong to direct a jury that D is not liable if he is, for example less than one-fifth to blame.[127] Thus, where D struck V who was suffering from meningitis and died, it was enough that the death would not have been caused by the meningitis at the time when it occurred *but for* the blows (and it was immaterial that the blows would not have caused death but for the meningitis).[128]

Contributory causes may be the acts or omissions of others including the conduct of the deceased himself. The contributory negligence of the claimant in civil actions of

123 The medical evidence may take on an additional significance in the case of an omission. See *Sinclair* (1998) below, p 82 and *Gowans* [2003] EWCA Crim 3935.

124 Even this basic rule may have exceptions, but only in very unlikely circumstances, eg, D and E, independently and simultaneously, shoot at V. D's bullet goes through V's heart and E's bullet blows his brains out. It seems safe to assume that both will be held to have caused V's death. Cf Hall, *General Principles*, 267.

125 See *White* [1910] 2 KB 124; D may be liable for the attempt.

126 Discussed in detail below, p 63.

127 *Henningan* [1971] 3 All ER 133.

128 *Dyson* [1908] 2 KB 454.

negligence was an absolute defence at common law, but no such principle applied in the criminal law. In *Swindall and Osborne*,[129] where one or other of the two accused ran over and killed an old man, Pollock CB directed the jury that it was immaterial that the victim was deaf or drunk or negligent and contributed to his own death. One or other of the two accused was a cause of death and, on the evidence, the other abetted him.

An example of a case in which third parties contributed to V's death is *Benge*.[130] D, a foreman platelayer, employed to take up a certain section of railway line, misread the timetable so that the line was up at a time when a train arrived. He placed a flagman at a distance of only 540 yards, instead of 1,000 yards as required by the company's regulations, and entirely omitted to place fog signals, although the regulations specified that these should be put at 250-yard intervals for a distance of 1,000 yards. At D's trial for manslaughter it was urged that, in spite of his mistakes, the accident could not have happened if the other servants of the company had done their duty – if the flagman had gone the proper distance or if the engine driver had been keeping a proper look-out, which he was not. Pigott B ruled that this was no defence; if D's negligence mainly or substantially caused the accident, it was irrelevant that it might have been avoided if other persons had not been negligent.

(c) Connection between fault and result

The result is not attributable to the accused if the *culpable element* in his conduct in no way contributed to the result. This is a difficult principle that is often misunderstood. A good illustration of its operation is in *Dalloway*.[131] D was driving a cart on a highway with reins not in his hands but loose on the horse's back. A three-year-old child ran into the road a few yards in front of the horse and was killed. Erle J directed the jury that, if the accused had reins and by using the reins could have saved the child, he was guilty of manslaughter; but that, if they thought he could not have saved the child by the use of the reins, then they should acquit him. If D had not been driving the cart at all the incident could not have occurred; and in that sense, he 'caused' it; but it was necessary to go further and show that the death was due to the culpable element in his conduct – his negligence in not using the reins.[132]

(d) Negligible causes

It is sometimes said[133] that D's conduct must be a 'substantial' cause but the use of the word is misleading and seems to mean only that D's contribution must be more than negligible or not be so minute that it will be ignored under the '*de minimis*' principle.[134] It may therefore be misleading to direct a jury that D is not liable unless his conduct was a

129 (1865) 4 F & F 504. *Ledger* (1862) 2 F & F 857 is contrary but was regarded by Stephen J as 'a very peculiar case': *Digest*, 161, n 4.

130 (1846) 2 Car & Kir 230. See also *Walker* (1824) 1 C & P 320 (Garrow B).

131 (1847) 2 Cox CC 273, cf *Marsh* [1997] Crim LR 205.

132 Cf the discussion of *Clarke* (1990) 91 Cr App R 69.

133 See for example, *Benge*, above, *Smith* [1959] 2 QB 35 at 42–43, [1959] 2 All ER 193 at 198 (below, p 64); Hall, *General Principles*, 283; Perkins (1946) 36 J Cr L & Cr at 393, and *Criminal Law*, 606–607.

134 *Cato* [1976] 1 All ER 260 at 265–266; '. . . it need hardly be added that [that cause] need not be substantial to render the accused guilty': *Malcherek* [1981] 2 All ER 422 at 428.

'substantial' cause.[135] For example, D and V are roped mountaineers. V has fallen over a 1,000-foot precipice and is dragging D slowly after him. D cuts the rope and V falls to his death five seconds before both V and D would have fallen. Any acceleration of death is killing but factors that produce a very trivial acceleration may be ignored. D's act is not a sufficiently substantial cause of death. Similarly, where two persons independently inflict wounds on V:

> . . . suppose one wound severed the jugular vein whereas the other barely broke the skin of the hand, and as the life blood gushed from the victim's neck, one drop oozed from the bruise on his finger . . . metaphysicians will conclude that the extra drop of lost blood hastened the end by the infinitesimal fraction of a second. But the law will apply the *substantial factor* test and for juridical purposes the death will be imputed only to the severe injury in such an extreme case as this.[136]

These are, perhaps, rather unlikely examples but the principle would apply, for example, to a person visiting a dying man and contributing to his exhaustion by talking with him; and probably to the administration of pain-killing drugs which accelerate death.[137] In the context of homicide the problems raise controversial questions of science, law and morality as to the degree of acceleration that needs to be established to constitute a cause of death.[138]

The problem of an intervening cause, which is discussed below[139] is sometimes put on the basis of substantial cause. Thus Hall writes:

> For example, a slight wound may have necessitated going to a doctor or drugstore, and *en route* the slightly injured person was struck by an automobile or shot by his mortal enemy. The slight wound, though a necessary condition of the death, did not contribute substantially to it.[140]

(e) Intervening acts or events

Although D's culpable conduct is a factual (but for) and more than *de minimis* cause of the prohibited result, he is not necessarily legally responsible for it on that basis alone. If there is an intervening event (act or omission) either as a naturally occurring phenomenon or by some human conduct, it may operate to 'break the chain of causation', precluding D's liability for the ultimate result, (although D may remain liable for an attempt in many cases).

135 *Hennigan*, above, n 127. Something more than a 'slight or trifling link' is required: *Kimsey* [1996] Crim LR.

136 R. M. Perkins and R. N. Boyce, *Criminal Law* (3rd edn), 779. But cf *Garforth* [1954] Crim LR 936.

137 Below, p 435.

138 Numerous high profile cases involved doctors who have 'eased the passing' of a terminally ill patient. Examples include: *Cox* (1992) 12 BMLR 38 (see, Editorial, 'Hard cases make bad law: Mercy killing and Dr Cox' (1992) 142 NLJ 1293) and *Adams*, H. Palmer, 'Dr Adams Trial for Murder' [1957] Crim LR 365. There has also been considerable comment following the case of David Moor: see A. Arlidge, 'The Trial of Dr David Moor' [2000] Crim LR 31; J. C. Smith, 'A Comment on Moors Case' [2000] Crim LR 41 and also J. Goss, 'A Postscript to the Trial of Dr David Moor' [2000] Crim LR 568. The trial judge, Hooper J (as he then was) was prepared to leave the question of unlawfulness to the jury – if the act was proper treatment for the illness and pain management, it would be lawful even if the effect was fatal.

139 Infra and p 57.

140 Hall, *General Principles*, at 283, 393.

An intervening act by the original actor will not break the chain of causation so as to excuse him where the intervening act is part of the same transaction;[141] but it is otherwise if the act which causes the *actus reus* is part of a completely different transaction: for example D, having wounded V, visits him in hospital and accidentally infects him with smallpox of which he dies.[142]

If, despite the intervening events, D's conduct remains a 'substantial and operative cause' of the result (for example, in murder, V's death), D will remain responsible, and if the intervention is by a person, that actor may also become liable in such circumstances. Subject to this, (and some exceptional cases), D will not be liable if:

(1) a natural event which was not *reasonably foreseeable*, supervenes; or
(2) a third party's intervening act is one of a *free deliberate and informed nature* (whether reasonably forseeable or not);[143] or, if not free, it is not reasonably forseeable; or
(3) a medical professional intervenes to treat injuries inflicted by D and the treatment is so *independent* of D's conduct and *so potent* as to preclude D's liability; or
(4) the victim's subsequent *act* in response to D's act is not within a range of responses that could be regarded as reasonable in the circumstances.

Thus, in a homicide case D, who did what would have been a fatal act but for some independent intervention, is not responsible where the intervening independent act or unforeseen event is the immediate and sufficient cause of death. D administers poison to V but, before it takes any effect on V's body, V is struck by lightning, shot dead by a burglar, or dies of a heart attack not induced by the poison. In such cases, D may be guilty of attempted murder but he cannot be convicted of murder.

The courts have struggled to produce a clear approach in this complex area. This problem is exacerbated by the diversity of factual circumstances in which such interventions arise, thereby encouraging the courts to distinguish cases too readily. Decisions have also been heavily influenced by policy considerations and this is illustrated by the willingness to conclude, for example, that interventions do not break the chain of causation where D's original conduct involves drug misuse, or where the intervention is by a health care professional. The courts have also adopted rather loose language in determining whether intervening events 'break the chain of causation', often resorting simply to the use of metaphor. The best that can be offered by way of guidance is a series of principles, some of which are openly in conflict.

(i) Naturally occurring interventions

The accepted principle in relation to naturally occurring events is illustrated by the examples given by Perkins:[144]

141 See below, p 118; Russell, 53–60, where the cases are set out; Williams, CLGP, 65; H. Hart and T. Honoré, *Causation in the Law*, 333.

142 This paragraph was cited by the court in *Le Brun* (1991) 94 Cr App R 101, below, p 117.

143 This includes acts instinctively done for self preservation and acts of an involuntary nature by the third party.

144 (1946) 36 J Cr L & Cr at 393.

> . . . if one man knocks down another and goes away leaving his victim not seriously hurt[145] but unconscious, on the floor of a building in which the assault occurred, and before the victim recovers consciousness he is killed in the fall of the building which is shaken down by a sudden earthquake, this is not homicide. The law attributes such a death to the 'Act of God' and not to the assault, even if it may be certain that the deceased would not have been in the building at the time of the earthquake, had he not been rendered unconscious. The blow was the occasion of the man's being there, but the blow was not the cause of the earthquake, nor was the deceased left in a position of obvious danger. On the other hand if the blow had been struck on the seashore, and the assailant had left his victim in imminent peril of an incoming tide which drowned him before consciousness returned, it would be homicide.[146]

In the second example, V's being drowned was a 'natural' consequence of D's action – that is, a consequence which might be expected to occur in the normal course of events. It was foreseeable as likely to occur in the normal course of events.[147] There is no break in the chain of causation by this naturally occurring intervening act and D remains liable for the result if the prosecution have established factual and legal causation as discussed in the principles above. In contrast, in the first example V's being killed by the falling building an abnormal and unforeseeable consequence. The act or event was not the natural consequence of D's act. This is sufficient to break the chain of causation. D may be liable for an attempted murder or some relevant offence against the person.

(ii) Third party interventions

Several categories of actor need to be considered.

Innocent agent

Where D employs an innocent agent[148] – for example a person who is under the age of criminal responsibility, or insane, or merely someone without *mens rea* – to commit an offence, D, in law, causes the result, though the immediate causer is the innocent agent.

Involuntariness

A truly involuntary act clearly does not break the chain: D so startles E that E involuntarily drops a weight he is carrying which causes damage to V's property. There is no true intervening 'act' and D has caused the damage.

Justified and excused responses

The principles applicable to involuntary actors have been extended beyond innocent agency, and beyond what might naturally be regarded as 'involuntariness'. It is clear that human intervention, where it consists in a foreseeable act instinctively done for the purposes of self-preservation, or in the execution of a legal duty, does not break the chain of causation. In the case of *Pagett*,[149] D, to resist lawful arrest, held a girl in front of him as a shield and shot at armed policemen. The police 'instinctively'[150] fired back and killed

145 The result would appear to be the same if he were seriously hurt.

146 Cf *Hallett* [1969] SASR 141, where the court followed this passage in relation to similar facts.

147 The courts use these terms interchangeably, but there is a difference. Not all naturally occurring events are foreseeable. In the most recent House of Lords case, *Empress Cars*, Lord Hoffmann used the term 'extraordinary' events rather than unforeseeable events in this context.

148 Below, p 167. 149 (1983) 76 Cr App R 279.

150 Is not the purpose of firearms training to avoid acts of an instinctive nature such as this?

the girl. D was held to have caused her death and to be guilty of manslaughter.[151] Though the court regarded the officers' instinctive act as 'involuntary', they also held that neither a reasonable act of self-defence nor an act done in the execution of a duty to prevent crime or arrest an offender, using such force as is reasonable in the circumstances, will break the chain of causation. It is not clear that such acts of self-defence or in the prevention of crime are necessarily in the same class as a truly 'involuntary' act. Moreover, it cannot be 'reasonable' for anyone intentionally to kill V, an innocent person, in order to save his own life[152] or to arrest X; and whether it is reasonable for him to take a risk of killing V must be doubtful. *Pagett* does not deal with the case where the officer's intervening act is unlawful. If it is, it does not necessarily follow that D's act is not a cause of death. There may be two unlawful causes.

The same principles should apply in determining whether the killing of an innocent bystander, or another policeman, by police bullets should be taken to be caused by D. It is obvious that the police marksman causes death.[153] His liability was not the issue in *Pagett*; but, if the shooting was a reasonable act of self-defence, the result, so far as he was concerned, was accidental death.[154]

Voluntary actors

If the intervening event comprises the conduct of a person acting in a 'fully voluntary' manner, the position should be straightforward. As Glanville Williams puts it:

> What a person does (if he has reached adult years, is of sound mind and is not acting under mistake, intimidation or similar pressure) is his own responsibility and is not regarded as having been caused by other people. An intervening act of this kind, therefore, breaks the causal connection that would otherwise have been perceived between previous acts and the forbidden consequence.[155]

So, in a homicide case, the 'free, deliberate and informed' intervention by a third party has been held to have the effect of relieving the accused of criminal responsibility.[156] As a matter of principle, this seems right since the voluntary actor has chosen his course of action which leads to a prohibited result, and on orthodox principles of criminal liability he is liable for his voluntary actions which are now the immediate cause.

In *Latif*,[157] British customs officers in Pakistan intercepted heroin, which D intended to import into England. The officers brought it here where D took delivery. It was held that D was not guilty of being concerned in the fraudulent evasion of the prohibition on importation because this had been effected by the 'free, deliberate and informed act' of the officers, exploiting the situation created by, but not acting in concert with, D. This broke the chain of causation. This can be contrasted with non-intentional intervening acts, for example, a failure by an employer to establish a safe system of work may remain

151 Since the jury acquitted of murder, it must be taken that they were not satisfied D had the necessary *mens rea* as was then defined in *Hyam* [1975] AC 55 – that he knew it was highly probable that the girl would suffer death or grievous bodily harm.

152 *Dudley and Stephens* (1884) 14 QBD 273, below, p 319; *Howe* [1987] AC 417, [1987] 1 All ER 771, HL. Cf commentary on *Pagett* [1983] Crim LR 394.

153 Cf *Malcherek*, below p 66.

154 The court said that its comments were confined to homicide: but the same principles must surely apply to non-fatal offences.

155 TBCL (2nd edn) 391. See, to the same effect, Hart and Honoré, 364–365.

156 *Pagett* (1983) 76 Cr App R 279, 339.

157 [1996] 2 Cr App R 92, [1996] Crim LR 414.

a legal cause of death although the fatal accident would not have occurred but for the inadvertent, probably negligent, act of an employee operating the system.[158]

This is a fundamental principle, but one that has given rise to difficulty in two categories of case that can be examined in more detail. If the cases in these two categories are regarded as correctly stating the law and are of general application, it seems that there has been a revolution within the field of criminal causation, and that it should no longer be accepted as a matter of law that the voluntary informed act of a person will break the chain of causation.

Empress Cars

In the *Empress Car* case[159] D Ltd was held by the House of Lords to have caused the pollution of a river by bringing oil on to a site and failing to take precautions against the ever-present and foreseeable possibility that someone would release the oil into the river. The escape may have been caused by the fully voluntary act of a stranger, but it was also, in the opinion of the House, caused by the company. In reaching this conclusion Lord Hoffmann appears to confuse culpability with causation.[160] A householder may be blameworthy for forgetting to lock his door and set the burglar alarm at night but he could hardly be said to have 'caused' an ensuing burglary, though it would not have occurred if he had taken the proper precautions.[161] Lord Hoffmann put the case of a factory owner who carelessly leaves a drum containing highly inflammable vapour in a place where it could easily be accidentally ignited. He thought the owner would have caused an explosion if it occurred when a workman threw in a cigarette butt, believing the drum to be empty, but he would not have done so if a man, knowing exactly what the drum contained, had thrown in a lighted match. In the former case the workman's act is not fully voluntary because he is making a fundamental mistake of fact; he is not acting with all the relevant information. In the latter case, the act is fully voluntary – and it appears to be indistinguishable from the actual facts of the *Empress Car* case. Lord Hoffmann concludes, it is submitted rightly, that, in the latter case, the carelessness of the owner had merely provided the man with an opportunity to do what he did – which appears to be equally true of the Empress Car Co Ltd. In suggesting that the chain of causation would be broken by the trespasser's act if it were an extraordinary one, but not merely by its being a free voluntary and informed act, his lordship seems to confuse the principles dealing with natural interventions and those with third party human interventions.

Lord Hoffmann further recognized in *Empress Car* that common sense is not a sufficient guide to resolving causation issues, and that legal principles are involved. This is valuable, but the guidance offered may be baffling to the courts, especially magistrates' courts, which are frequently required to decide cases like *Empress Car*. Causation, it appears, is a variable concept. According to Lord Hoffmann the answer to the question requires the court to ascertain the purpose and scope of the rule alleged to have been broken; and 'Not, only may there be different answers to questions about causation when

158 *R v DPP, ex p Jones* [2000] Crim LR 858, DC.

159 *Environmental Agency (formerly National Rivers Authority) v Empress Car Co (Abertillery) Ltd* [1998] 1 All ER 481, HL. The decision is criticized by Ashworth, POCL, 129, and by Simester and Sullivan, 99–101 as 'profoundly unsatisfactory'.

160 See his example of the irate wife at [1998] 1 All ER 487a–c.

161 As we will see below, it may be accurate to describe the householder as *a* cause where he has a duty to lock up.

attributing responsibility to different people under different rules . . . but there may be different answers when attributing responsibility to different people under the same rule'. This suggests that the principles of causation have become merely a matter of fact to be determined by the jury on a case by case basis.[162]

The principal authority relied on was that from the law of tort – Lord Hoffmann cited *Stansbie v Troman*.[163] In that case a decorator, left in charge of a house, went out to buy wallpaper, leaving the door open. He was held liable in negligence for an ensuing theft. Hart and Honoré[164] cite, along with *Stansbie v Troman*, an American case in which it was held a railway company would be liable if a girl they put down at nightfall in a dangerous area were raped. That may be true for the law of tort, but clearly, the railway or its officials could not be *criminally* liable for rape.

This construction also raises the possibility that a broader rule of causation may apply to *crimes* of negligence, such as manslaughter. Would Empress have been liable if a swimmer had swallowed the oil polluted water and died? Or if a passer-by had been killed by Lord Hoffmann's exploding oil drum? It is submitted that the case ought to be regarded as an aberrant authority[165] and ought not to be followed. It might be explained on its own facts by the House of Lords being too heavily influenced by the policy of protecting the environment. In such cases the original actor has control of the potentially hazardous product and is under a duty to protect against environmental harm.

Drug administration cases

The principle that a fully voluntary act breaks the chain of causation seems to have been overlooked, ignored and circumvented in recent cases dealing with drug administration. Again, it appears that the courts have been driven by policy – to punish those involved in drug misuse. (The cases below are considered in chronological order.)

In *Kennedy (No 1)*[166] D, at V's request, filled a syringe with heroin and water and handed it to him. V injected himself and consequently died. D's conviction for manslaughter was upheld. The court said that D was 'jointly responsible' for V's act because he had assisted and encouraged it. One who assists and encourages the commission of crime is liable to conviction of the crime but only as a secondary party. But V committed no crime! At common law suicide was a crime (now abolished) of self-murder, and anyone who aided and abetted a suicide was guilty of that; but there has never been a crime of self-manslaughter. Today V could lawfully kill himself and, *a fortiori*, take risks with his life if he so desired. It is different where V's act is not fully voluntary, as in cases where V, being terrified by D, jumped from a window or a car and suffered injury or death (see below). Then D is held to have caused the result unless V's reaction to his act was one that no reasonable man could be expected to foresee.[167] The test is objective. D's personal characteristics – age, sex, etc – are, at this stage, irrelevant.[168] If the jury are sure that they, as reasonable observers of the event, would have foreseen the possibility, causation is established. D's personal characteristics come into play when, being satisfied of the *actus reus*, the jury turn to the question of *mens rea*.

162 This might reflect Lord Hoffmann's preference for issues to be left for jury determination in the criminal trial – see also provocation below, p 455.

163 [1948] 2 KB 48.

164 P 197.

165 Ashworth uses the term, p 129.

166 [1999] 1 Cr App R 54, [1999] Crim LR 65 and commentary.

167 *Roberts* (1971) 56 Cr App R 95 at 102.

168 *Marjoram* [2000] Crim LR 372.

Subsequently, in *Dias*,[169] on similar facts to *Kennedy*, the Court of Appeal quashed the conviction for manslaughter which in that case had been based on the act of self-injection by the deceased being unlawful. Unfortunately, the court did not actually overrule *Kennedy* and left open the possibility of manslaughter based on an unlawful act of supply as the dangerous act, stating 'there may possibly be situations where the chain of causation could be established. It is however important that that issue be left to the jury to determine, as happened at the trial in *Kennedy* . . .'. It is difficult to see how 'the chain of causation could be established' in the face of the deceased's own voluntary act.[170]

Inevitably, the court's refusal to overrule *Kennedy* led to the problem resurfacing, albeit perhaps more swiftly than might have been expected. In *Rogers*,[171] D had provided the drugs for V and had held the tourniquet for V as V freely and voluntarily injected himself with what turned out to be a lethal dose of heroin. It was held that D, by holding the tourniquet, performed an unlawful administration, and that V's act did not break the chain of causation. Despite the breadth of the terms of s 23 of the Offences Against the Person Act 1861 criminalizing 'causing to be administered' and 'causing to be taken', it is difficult to see how D can be liable under this offence where V has freely and voluntarily depressed the plunger of the syringe himself.[172] The court elevated Rogers' conduct into a novel category akin to actual injection, describing D's tourniquet holding as 'active participation in the injection process'. Even if this novel interpretation of 'administration' is read restrictively as 'physical assistance' in the injection process, analogous to D holding the syringe, the final and overwhelmingly independent act of injection is still performed voluntarily by V. As such, following the decision in *Dias*, which the court purports to follow, there should, it is submitted be no offence by D.

Subsequently, the Court of Appeal appeared to be moving back to the position taken in *Kennedy*. In *Finlay*[173] the Court of Appeal took the controversial step of upholding D's conviction for unlawful act manslaughter when he merely prepared the syringe and handed it to V who self injected with heroin. Buxton LJ concluded, rightly it is submitted, that D could not be regarded as an accessory since V committed no crime by the act of self injection. This was, as his lordship put it, 'black letter law of the blackest sort'.[174] However, his lordship went on to hold that D was a joint principal in V's act. Moreover, it was held that the question of whether V's act broke the chain of causation was one of fact for the jury and, following *Empress*, involved the assessment of whether V's act was extraordinary. This creates considerable confusion in the law. It is submitted that

169 [2002] 2 Cr App R 9, [2002] Crim LR 490 and commentary by JCS.

170 See R. Heaton, 'Dealing in Death' [2003] Crim LR 497.

171 [2003] 2 Cr App R 10, [2003] Crim LR 555.

172 The cases interpreting s 23 have held that 'administration' in this context includes conduct which, although it does not involve the direct application of force to the victim, nevertheless brings the noxious thing into contact with his body: *Gillard* (1988) 87 Cr App R 189 (CS spray charged under s 24). There is no requirement that the 'administration' under s 23 involves surreptitious conduct. The 'causing to be taken' formula in s 23 might be useful for cases of surreptitious leaving of poisons for V to take, but will not work where the victim is a knowing and willing recipient of the noxious substance. Even if it could be argued that by preparing the syringe D has attempted to administer the heroin, there could be no conviction for V's death. V's voluntary act of self-administration would break the chain of causation. In any event, it is unclear whether proof of a mere attempt can be a sufficient basis for an unlawful act manslaughter conviction.

173 [2003] EWCA Crim 3868. D was found to have 'caused to be administered'.

174 Para 12.

the decision ought to be treated with caution.[175] In *Kennedy No 2*, the Court of Appeal described the decision in *Finlay* as 'departing somewhat from the approach in *Rogers*'.[176] The court seems to be suggesting that *Finlay* could be brought within the same category, on its facts, as *Rogers*, by treating D as being 'part and parcel' of V's injection process.

In the latest decision in the saga, *Kennedy No 2*,[177] the Court of Appeal returned to the conviction it had upheld in 1999, on a reference from the Criminal Cases Review Commission. The court, in a judgment which does little to clarify the law in this confusing area, upheld the conviction. The Lord Chief justice reviewed the authorities subsequent to the first appeal including *Dias, Richards*,[178] *Rogers*[179] and *Finlay*.[180] On the first appeal the court held that the supplier might be guilty as an accessory. The Court of Appeal on the second appeal accepted that basis of the decision above as being in error. However, as regards the question of V's free deliberate informed act breaking the chain, the court held that where D handed V the drugs 'for immediate injection' there was no difficulty holding D liable for manslaughter. Both parties were treated as being 'engaged in the one activity of administering the drug'. With respect, this is a conclusion which does nothing to alleviate the concerns expressed above that the courts are adopting a revolutionary approach to causation. As for *Empress*, the court was invited to consider whether the decision is of general application or confined to its own circumstances. The court merely cited Lord Hoffmann's speech in *Empress* to emphasize that 'he was very much concerned with the context in which the issue arose of decision'.

The conclusion was that 'if [D] either caused [V] to administer the drug or was acting jointly with the deceased in administering the drug [D] would be acting in concert with [V] and there would be no breach in the chain of causation'. The jury is entitled to convict if it finds that the actions of the D and V are a 'combined operation'. Is this doctrine of 'joint engagement' generally applicable or is it restricted to the drug administration cases?[181] At one point in the judgment, the Lord Chief Justice refers to the fact that D and V's acts are both 'necessary' for the completion of the injection. Does this mean that any act of D that is a 'necessary' precondition for the prescribed consequence of the offence will render him liable, irrespective of the subsequent free deliberate informed act of (the principal)? Similarly, his lordship underlines the proximity in time between the acts of the defendant and those of the intervening act, emphasizing that since D's acts are 'immediately prior' to V's injection, D remains liable as a party to the 'joint engagement'. Other problems arising from the decision – as to the undermining of principles of secondary liability,[182] and assisted suicide[183] – are addressed at relevant points elsewhere in the book.

[175] In *Kennedy No 2*, the Lord Chief Justice suggested that *Finlay* involved an unnecessarily sophisticated analysis of causation, because the court had sought to apply *Empress Cars* to the question of whether D had 'caused V to take' the noxious substance for the purposes of the offence under the OAPA 1861, s 23.

[176] Para 21. [177] [2005] EWCA Crim 685.

[178] [2002] EWCA Crim 1. [179] [2003] 1WLR 137. [180] [2003] EWCA Crim 3868.

[181] Who is the 'other' to whom the noxious substance must be administered? It would be relatively easy for the courts to create a specific category of liability here (if they are is desperate to do so on policy grounds).

[182] If D hands P a revolver and P shoots V, is D now a principal offender? Surely in such a case D becomes an accessory to P's crime of murder?

[183] Where V declares an intention to commit suicide and D being aware of that fact supplies the syringe for V's self injection, D becomes liable for murder. How can this be squared with Parliament's creation of a specific offence of assisted suicide in such cases?

It is submitted that the issue of whether a third party's free deliberate informed act is regarded in law as a break in the chain of causation deserves urgent attention by the House of Lords, which should be guided back to the course clearly set by Glanville Williams:

> the fact that [D's] own conduct, rightful or wrongful, provided the background for a subsequent voluntary act by another does not make him responsible for it. What he does may be a 'but for' cause of the injurious act, but he did not do it.[184]

(iii) Medical interventions

Largely for reasons of policy, the courts have adopted a particularly strict approach in cases where the alleged break in the chain of causation involves the conduct[185] of medical professionals. These are third parties who are intervening in a fully informed manner, (although not fully voluntarily since they are under a duty to act), but whose conduct is generally insufficient to break the chain of causation in this context.

Before the advent of a rigorous science of forensic pathology, it was less easy to establish causes of death. The nineteenth century cases[186] held that, where the immediate cause of death was the medical treatment received by V consequent upon his injury by D, D was guilty of homicide, whether the treatment was proper or improper, negligent or not. If the treatment was given *bona fide* by competent medical officers, evidence was not admissible to show that it was improper or unskilful. In the earlier cases, this rule was applied only where the wound was dangerous to life. Later, and logically, it was extended to less serious injuries. Those cases must now be regarded in the light of the modern decisions in *Jordan*,[187] *Smith*[188] and *Cheshire*.[189]

In *Jordan* D stabbed V who was admitted to hospital and died eight days later. At the trial 'it did not occur to the prosecution, the defence, the judge or the jury that there could be any doubt but that the stab caused death'.[190]

In the Court of Criminal Appeal, the fresh evidence of two doctors was allowed to the effect that in their opinion death had not been caused by the stab wound, which was mainly healed at the time of the death, but by the introduction (with a view to preventing infection) of terramycin after the deceased man had shown he was intolerant to it and by the intravenous introduction of large quantities of liquid. This treatment, according to the evidence, was 'palpably wrong'. The court held that if the jury had heard this evidence they would have felt precluded from saying that they were satisfied that the death was caused by the stab wound and they quashed the conviction. The case has been interpreted by Williams[191] as one where the medical treatment was grossly negligent, but he argues[192]

184 G. Williams, 'Finis for Novus Actus' (1989) 48 CLJ 391, 391. The article repays close reading.

185 Although usually an act, it can be an omission to act. In *R v McKechnie* (1992) Cr App R 51 where doctors discovered that V had an ulcer but decided that it would be too dangerous to operate because V was still unconscious from D's beating. V died as a result of the ulcer bursting: 'The Recorder's statement of the question of the intervening events – the doctor's decision not to operate on the duodenal ulcer because [V's] head injuries made such an operation dangerous – properly directed the jury, not to the correctness of the medical decision, but to its reasonableness.' Per Auld J at 58.

186 Discussed in the sixth edition of this work, 321.

187 (1956) 40 Cr App R 152.

188 [1959] 2 QB 35, [1959] 2 All ER 193. Followed in *Gowans* [2003] EWCA Crim 3935.

189 [1991] 3 All ER 670.

190 See (1956) 40 Cr App R 152 at 155.

191 [1957] Crim LR at 430.

192 Ibid, at 513.

that any degree of negligence which would be recognized by the civil courts should be enough. The court did not say in express terms that there was evidence of negligence, gross or otherwise, though it may reasonably be inferred that 'palpably wrong' treatment is negligent.

While anxiously disclaiming any intention of setting a precedent[193] they stated the basis of their decision in even broader terms. They were 'disposed to accept it as law that death resulting from any normal treatment employed to deal with a felonious injury may be regarded as caused by the felonious injury'; but it was 'sufficient to point out here that this was not normal treatment'. Surely treatment that is 'not normal' is not necessarily negligent, even in the civil law?[194]

The case gave rise to some concern in the medical profession and it was predicted[195] that the result of it would be that if, in future, the victim of a homicidal assault died as a result of the medical treatment instituted to save his life, it would not be considered homicide by the assailant if the treatment could be shown to be 'not normal'.

Jordan was distinguished by the Court of Criminal Appeal in *Smith*[196] and by the Court of Appeal in *Blaue*[197] as 'a very particular case depending upon its exact facts'. In *Malcherek*[198] the court thought that if a choice had to be made between *Jordan* and *Smith*, *Smith* was to be preferred; but they did not believe it was necessary to choose. In *Blaue*, *Jordan* was thought to be 'probably rightly decided on its facts'. It is submitted that this is so. *Smith* is distinguishable. In the course of a fight between soldiers of different regiments, D stabbed V twice with a bayonet. One of V's comrades, trying to carry V to the medical reception station, twice tripped and dropped him. At the reception station the medical officer, who was trying to cope with a number of other cases, did not realize that one of the wounds had pierced a lung and caused haemorrhage. He gave V treatment which, in the light of the information regarding V's condition available at the time of the trial, was 'thoroughly bad and might well have affected his chances of recovery'. D's conviction of murder was upheld and counsel's argument, that the court must be satisfied that the treatment was normal, and that this was abnormal was brushed aside.

> . . . if at the time of death the original wound is still an operating cause and a substantial cause, then the death can properly be said to be the result of the wound, albeit that some other cause of death is also operating. Only if it can be said that the original wounding is merely the setting in which another cause operates can it be said that the death does not result from the wound. Putting it in another way, only if the second cause is so overwhelming as to make the original wound merely part of the history can it be said that death does not flow from the wound.[199]

Jordan was a case where a jury might have found, in the light of the new evidence, that the wound was, or may have been, merely the setting in which medical treatment caused

[193] But no court has the right to preclude future courts from considering the effects of its decisions.

[194] See *Bolam v Friern Hospital Management Committee* [1957] 1 WLR 582 and *Bolitho v City and Hackney HA* [1998] AC 232 and the discussion in W. V. H. Rogers, *Winfield and Jolowicz on Tort* (16th edn, 2004), 195–198.

[195] By E. Camps and J. Havard, 'Causation in Homicide – A Medical View' [1957] Crim LR 576 at 582–583.

[196] [1959] 2 QB 35 at 43, [1959] 2 All ER 193 at 198.

[197] [1975] 3 All ER 446. Likewise in *Evans and Gardiner (No. 2)* [1976] VR 523 at 531.

[198] [1981] 2 All ER 422.

[199] Per Lord Parker CJ [1959] 2 QB 35 at 42–43, [1959] 2 All ER 193 at 198. The passage was applied in *Gowans* (above).

death – as if a nurse had, with gross negligence, administered a deadly poison in mistake for a sleeping pill or, as in a Kentucky case, *Bush v Commonwealth*,[200] the medical officer attending V inadvertently infected him with scarlet fever and he died of that. None of these is an act which might be expected to occur in the ordinary course of events and they free D from liability. But if the injured V is receiving proper and skilful medical attention and he dies from the treatment or the operation D will be liable.

In *Cheshire*[201] the bullet wounds which D inflicted upon V had ceased to be a threat to life and there was evidence that V's death was caused by the tracheotomy performed and negligently treated by the doctors so that it narrowed his windpipe and caused asphyxiation. The Court of Appeal held that the judge had misdirected the jury by telling them that only recklessness on the part of the doctors would break the chain of causation but upheld the conviction, asserting that 'the rare complication . . . was a direct consequence of the appellant's acts, which remained a significant cause of his death'. The test proposed by the court is not easy to apply:

> Even though negligence in the treatment of the victim was the immediate cause of his death, the jury should not regard it as excluding the responsibility of the accused unless the negligent treatment was so independent of his acts, and in itself so potent in causing death, that they regard the contribution made by his acts as insignificant.

It is difficult to know what 'so independent' and 'so potent' mean. In all these cases, D's act caused V to undergo the treatment and if that renders it 'dependent', D would be taken to have caused death, however outlandish the treatment; but it is clear that this is not intended. There is a similar problem with 'potent'. Suppose that the tracheotomy would have caused death even if the wound had been completely healed (this is not entirely clear).[202] No greater potency can then be imagined; but it is, at least, unlikely that the court intended that it should follow that D had not caused death. The wound would not have been an operating and substantial cause but the ultimate question is whether D's act was a cause and it is clear that it might be, even if the wound was not. The problem could well surface with a victim hospitalized by a wound from D who then, as the wound has healed, contracts MRSA in an unclean hospital.

It is submitted that the following propositions[203] at present represent the law:

(1) Medical evidence is admissible to show that the medical treatment of a wound was the cause of death and that the wound itself was not.[204] This is so whether or not the wound is mortal. The conflict of medical evidence may present the jury with a difficult decision as to the potency of the medical intervention.[205] Juries will need careful guidance on such issues.[206]

200 78 Ky 268 (1880) (Kentucky Court of Appeals).

201 [1991] 3 All ER 670, [1991] Crim LR 709.

202 Indeed, according to the Court of Appeal (at 678) the judge directed the jury that the prosecution must prove that 'the bullets were one operative and substantial cause of death'; but the bullets (unless they were still in V's body) could not be an *operating* cause, if that is what is meant, in the sense that a wound might be.

203 Approved in *Dear* [1996] Crim LR 595.

204 *Jordan* must be authority for this at least. Moreover at the trial in *Smith* Dr Camps gave evidence that, with proper treatment, V's chances of recovery were as high as 75 per cent.

205 See eg *Gowans* [2003] EWCA Crim 3935 where V contracted fatal septicaemia in hospital.

206 *Suratan* [2004] EWCA Crim 1246.

(2) If a wound was an operating and substantial cause of death, D is guilty of homicide, however badly the wound was treated.[207]

(3) If a wound was not an operating and substantial cause of death (for example, it was effectively healed) but V was killed by, for example, the inadvertent administration of deadly poison by a nurse, the wrongful administration of terremycin, or the ill-treatment of a tracheotomy, D may or may not be guilty of homicide. The test we must now apply is the *Cheshire* independence/potency test. A better test, it is submitted, would be whether the treatment, or the manner of administering it, was so extraordinary as to be unforeseeable – which may be much the same thing as asking whether it was grossly negligent.

Jordan and *Cheshire* were cases where the medical treatment, not the wound, may have been the cause of death. The same principle applies where the wound prevents medical treatment for an independent condition which would have saved life: *McKechnie*[208] where the injuries inflicted by D precluded medical treatment for the duodenal ulcer which killed V. Only an 'extraordinary and unusual' medical decision that the life-saving treatment was not possible would have broken the chain of causation.

It is important to keep in mind that where the question at D's trial is whether the medical professional has broken the chain of causation: the medical professional is not on trial. In *Malcherek*[209] D inflicted upon V injuries which resulted in brain damage. She was put on a life-support machine. Some days later, after carrying out five of the six tests[210] for brainstem death prescribed by the Royal Colleges, doctors disconnected the machine and half an hour later she was pronounced dead. The judge withdrew the question of causation from the jury, ruling that there was no evidence on which they could decide that D did not cause V's death. On appeal, it was argued that there was evidence on which the jury could have found that the doctors caused death by switching off the machine. The appeal was dismissed. There was no doubt that the injury inflicted by D was an operating and substantial cause of death. Whether or not the doctors were also *a* cause of death was immaterial. They were not on trial;[211] D was. It was enough that a continuing and substantial cause of V's death was the injury inflicted by D.

(iv) Victim's conduct breaking the chain of causation

General principle – D takes his victim as found

It is a well-established principle in civil law that the defendant takes the victim of his wrongdoing as he finds him – with all V's subsisting weaknesses that might exacerbate

207 But Hart and Honoré, 361, discussing *Blaue*, suppose that V had called for a blood transfusion and the doctor had refused because he wanted to play golf, whereupon V bled to death. They argue that death would have been 'caused by the doctor's callousness, not the original wound'. Surely it would have been caused by both. The wound would certainly have been an operating and substantial cause.

208 (1991) 94 Cr App R 51, [1992] Crim LR 194.

209 [1981] 2 All ER 422, [1981] 1 WLR 690. The appeal of *Steel*, heard at the same time was materially the same.

210 There were reasons for not applying the sixth test.

211 The court remarked, *obiter*, that they thought the suggestion that the doctors had caused the death 'bizarre' – they had done their skilful best to save life, but failed and so discontinued treatment. The policy dimension to causation in homicide where medical negligence is alleged is obvious.

the injury resulting from D's act, as where D pricks a haemophiliac with a pin, or slaps the head of a person with an egg-shell skull. According to *Blaue*,[212] in the criminal law, as in the civil, the defendant must 'take his victim as he finds him'.

If the principle is restricted to taking V as found in physical terms, little difficulty arises. V's subsisting conditions are all to be taken into account. V's body's 'response' to D's act might not readily be seen as an intervening 'act' between D's infliction of injury and V's death. However, controversially, the court in *Blaue* held that the principle applies so that D takes the victim as found in a holistic sense – taking the victim's *mind* as well as his body as found.

In *Blaue* D stabbed V, a young girl, and pierced her lung. She was told that she would die if she did not have a blood transfusion. Being a Jehovah's Witness, she refused on religious grounds. She died from the bleeding caused by the wound. D was convicted of manslaughter and argued that V's refusal to have a blood transfusion, being unreasonable, had broken the chain of causation. It was held that the judge had rightly instructed the jury that the wound was a cause of death. Lawton LJ said:[213]

> It has long been the policy of the law that those who use violence on other people must take their victims as they find them. This in our judgment means the whole man, not just the physical man. It does not lie in the mouth of the assailant to say that his victim's religious beliefs which inhibited him from accepting certain kinds of treatment were unreasonable. The question for decision is what caused the death. The answer is a stab wound.

In this case, the wound was 'an operating cause and a substantial cause', so the *dictum* was unnecessary to the decision. It is unclear whether the court would take the same approach if V had not previously held the religious belief, but had adopted it to spite D (an unlikely scenario). The principle stated by the court, if valid, is capable of wider application. Given that D would be liable for wounding or attempted murder, it is arguable that the principle can operate unduly harshly, but the same harshness would apply where the victim has an egg shell skull, and that rule is not commonly criticized. The true force of the criticisms of the decision is perhaps against the emphasis the law places on the result (death) rather than the blameworthiness of the conduct (unlawful wounding).[214]

Subsequent *acts* of the victim

A long line of cases has established that D will be held to have caused death or injury by so frightening V that V has jumped from a window or a car or behaved in some other manner dangerous to himself.[215] The test applied in these cases where V performs some positive act in response to D's culpable conduct is whether V's reaction was within the

212 [1975] 3 All ER 446, [1976] Crim LR 648 and commentary. *Smithers* (1976) 34 CCC (2d) 427 (Sup Ct of Canada) is to the same effect. It was immaterial that death was caused in part by malfunctioning epiglottis, where kick was a contributing cause, outside the *de minimis* range.

213 At 450.

214 See the discussion above, p 6 and A. Ashworth, 'Belief Intent and Criminal Liability' in J. Eekelaar and J. Bell (eds), *Oxford Essays in Jurisprudence* (1989); 'Taking the Consequences' in S. Shute, J. Gardner and J. Horder (eds), *Action and Value in Criminal Law* (1993) and 'Defining Offences Without Harm' in P. F. Smith (ed), *Criminal Law: Essays in Honour of J. C. Smith* (1987).

215 *Pitts* (1842) Car & M 284; *Halliday* (1889) 61 LT 701; *Curley* (1909) 2 Cr App R 96 at 109; *Lewis* [1970] Crim LR 647; *Mackie* [1973] Crim LR 54 (Cusack J); *Boswell* [1973] Crim LR 307 (Judge Gower); *Daley* (1979) 69 Cr App R 39.

range of responses which might be expected from a victim in his situation.[216] If the reaction was 'so daft as to make it [V's] own voluntary act' the chain of causation is broken. So it seems D does not have to take a 'daft' victim as he finds him – unless, presumably he knows him to be daft – that is, likely to behave in an extraordinary fashion. The range of responses to be expected will of course vary according to the age and perhaps the sex of the victim.[217]

If the victim is a contributory cause of the incident, that does not preclude D's liability if D's act is continuing and operative cause. In *People v Lewis*[218] V, having received a mortal gunshot wound from which he would have died within the hour, cut his throat and died within five minutes. D was held liable for manslaughter on the ground that the original wound was an operating cause. 'Here, when the throat was cut, [V] was not merely languishing from a mortal wound; he was actually dying; and after the throat was cut he continued to languish from both wounds. Drop by drop the life current went out from both wounds, and at the very instant of death the gunshot wound was contributing to the event.'[219] The application of this principle would have provided a different answer if V had blown his brains out and died instantly, for then the bleeding from the original wound would not have been an operating cause. The conviction could then have been upheld only by applying a different principle – that the first act provided a reason for the second[220] – and the court would indeed have decided the case on that ground if they had been satisfied that the first act *was* the cause of the second; but they thought that V's suicide might have been out of remorse or a desire to shield D.

If the victim of a rape were to be so outraged as to commit suicide by shooting herself it might be argued that it was the bullet that caused the death and not the rape. Certainly the rape is not 'an operating and substantial cause' in the same sense as the wound in *Blaue*; but according to that case the rapist must take his victim as he finds her. His act caused the act that caused her death. This may be the effect of *Dear*[221] where D's conviction for murder was upheld, even though V may have intentionally caused his own death by aggravating the wounds inflicted on him by D. If V would not have killed himself but for those injuries, D caused his death. It would have been different if V had so acted only for some reason unconnected with D's attack on him – for example, shame at his own disgraceful conduct (paedophilia) which had led D to attack him. The decision is, perhaps, not quite conclusive of the rape victim/suicide case: the wounds as well as V's acts may have been the physical cause of death, whereas in the rape case the bullet is the sole physical cause of death. In *Dear* it was apparently regarded as immaterial that V's conduct was unforeseeable. In this respect the decision is not easily reconcilable with the line of authority establishing that V's daft conduct will break the chain of causation.

216 *Williams and Davies* (1991) 95 Cr App R 1, [1992] Crim LR 198; *Corbett* [1996] Crim LR 594. Cf *Roberts* (1971) 56 Cr App R 95 at 102.

217 Presumably, following *Blaue*, religions, no matter how esoteric cannot be regarded as 'daft'. What of an irrational but entrenched fear of hospitals?

218 124 Cal 551 (1899) Sup Ct of California.

219 But was the contribution of the gunshot wound substantial or *de minimis* (slight or trifling)? Cf the example given by Perkins, above, 44 and Hart and Honoré, 243.

220 Hart and Honoré, 244.

221 [1996] Crim LR 595.

V's subsequent omissions

If V's conduct between D's act and V's death might properly be classified as an omission, will D remain liable if V's omission was a 'daft' one, or following *Blaue*, is D liable irrespective of the rationality of V's conduct?

The common law rule is that neglect or maltreatment by the injured person of himself does not exempt D from liability for his ultimate death. In *Wall's* case,[222] where the former governor of Goree was convicted[223] of the murder of a man by ordering the illegal infliction on him of a flogging of 800 lashes, there was evidence that V had aggravated his condition by drinking spirits. MacDonald LCB told the jury:[224]

> . . . there is no apology for a man if he puts another in so dangerous and hazardous a situation by his treatment of him, that some degree of unskillfullness and mistaken treatment of himself may possibly accelerate the fatal catastrophe. One man is not at liberty to put another into such perilous circumstances as these, and to make it depend upon his own prudence, knowledge, skill or experience what may hurry on or complete that catastrophe, or on the other hand may render him service.

In any event, D's act was still a continuing and operative cause of the death, and the drink might have been regarded as a merely *de minimis* cause.

A clearer case of omission by V is that of *Holland*.[225] D waylaid and assaulted V, cutting him severely across one of his fingers with an iron instrument. V refused to follow the surgeon's advice to have the finger amputated, although he was told that if he did not his life would be in great danger. The wound caused lockjaw, the finger was then amputated, but it was too late and V died of lockjaw. The surgeon's evidence was that if the finger had been amputated at first, V's life could probably have been saved. Maule J told the jury that it made no difference whether the wound was in its own nature instantly mortal, or whether it became the cause of death by reason of the deceased not having adopted the best mode of treatment. The question was whether, in the end, the wound inflicted by the prisoner was the real cause of death. *Holland* was followed in *Blaue*.[226] The argument[227] that medical science has advanced greatly since 1841 and that a refusal to undergo medical treatment, reasonable then, would be unreasonable now, did not impress the court. Whether V's conduct was reasonable or not was irrelevant.

The *Blaue* principle, if valid, would impose liability upon D for unforeseeable intervening acts causing death and is probably confined to acts or omissions by the victim in person. If the parents of the victim of the supposed rape were to kill their daughter on the ground that their religion required them to do so, it is thought that D would not be liable for the death. If, however, in *Blaue*, V had been too young to make a decision about a blood transfusion and her parents had succeeded on religious grounds in preventing a transfusion being given, it is thought that the wound would have remained an operating and substantial cause, so D would still have been liable. The parents might also have been guilty of homicide.

222 (1802) 28 State Tr 51.
223 20 years after the event.
224 Ibid, at 145.
225 (1841) 2 Mood & R 351.
226 Above, p 67. Cf *Mubila* 1956 (1) SA 31.
227 By H. Hart and T. Honoré, *Causation in the Law*, at 360.

(v) Intended consequences

It is sometimes said that intended consequences cannot be too remote, that is, that D must always be liable for them. This, however, is an oversimplification,[228] and is not always accurate because the *sine qua non* rule remains applicable. Thus, in *White*[229] the consequence intended by D – the death of his mother – occurred; but its occurrence – a fatal heart attack – had nothing to do with D's act in administering the poison and would have happened just the same if D had done nothing. Even where the *sine qua non* rule is satisfied, the consequence, though intended, may be too remote where it occurs as a result of the intervention of some new cause. So in the cases of *Bush*[230] and *Jordan*[231] it may be that D intended V's death, and V's death occurred; moreover, in neither case would death have occurred without D's act; but in the one case it was caused by scarlet fever and not by D's bullet; and in the other it was caused by medical treatment and not by D's knife.

Where the death occurs in the manner intended by D he will be guilty even if the course of events was not what he expected, for example, he shoots at V's head, but the bullet misses, ricochets and kills V by striking him in the back. The case of *Michael*[232] is perhaps a rather extreme example of this:

D's child, V, was in the care of a nurse, X. D, intending to murder the child, delivered to X a large quantity of laudanum, telling her it was a medicine to be administered to V. X did not think the child needed any medicine and left it untouched on the mantelpiece of her room. In X's absence, one of her children, Y, aged five, took the laudanum and administered a large dose to V who died. All the judges held that the jury were rightly directed that this administration by 'an unconscious agent' was murder. Hart and Honoré[233] criticize the case on the ground that the child was:

> not in any sense an agent, conscious or unconscious, of the mother, who intended [X] alone to give the poison to the child; but the decision may be justified on the ground that, in our terminology, the act of the child of five did not negative causal connexion between the prisoner's act and the death.

According to this view, the result would have been different if Y had been, not five, but 15.

It does not appear that Y knew, from the labelling of the bottle or otherwise, that this was 'medicine' for V. If she did know this, and acted on that knowledge, then there seems no difficulty in imputing the death to D, whatever Y's age. No such fact being reported, however, the case must be treated as one where Y's intervention was in no way prompted by D's instructions. Thus, if Y had taken the poison herself, her death would have been just as much caused by D's act as was V's in the actual case; but it would require an extension of the decision to hold D guilty in such a case, for Y's death was not an intended consequence.[234] If such an extension is not made, the result is quite arbitrary, for it was pure chance whether Y administered the poison to V, or to herself or another child.

228 But note the rather stronger rejection by some – 'slogans like intended consequences are never too remote simply cannot be accepted': C. Finkelstein, 'Involuntary Crimes, Voluntarily Committed', in S. Shute and A. Simester (eds), *Criminal Law Theory*, 150.

229 [1910] 2 KB 124. 230 78 Ky 268 (1880); above, p 65.

231 (1956) 40 Cr App R 152. 232 (1840) 9 C & P 356. 233 Above, at 337.

234 But the doctrine of transferred malice (below, p 113) would support such an extension.

(f) Special instances of causation

There are a few instances of causation which require special mention, by reason of the state of the authorities.

(i) Killing by mental suffering or shock

The view of earlier writers was that the law could take no cognizance of a killing caused merely by mental suffering or shock, because 'no external act of violence was offered, whereof the common law can take notice and secret things belong to God.'[235] Stephen thought that the fear of encouraging prosecutions for witchcraft was the reason for the rule and that it was 'a bad rule founded on ignorance now dispelled'.[236]

Suppose a man were intentionally killed by being kept awake till the nervous irritation of sleeplessness killed him, might not this be murder? Suppose a man kills a sick person intentionally by making a loud noise when sleep gives him a chance of life; or suppose knowing that a man has aneurysm of the heart, his heir rushes into his room and roars in his ear, 'Your wife is dead!' intending to kill and killing him, why are not these acts murder? They are no more 'secret things belonging to God' than the operation of arsenic.

This view now represents the law. Hale's proposition was first modified in *Towers*[237] where D violently assaulted a young girl who was holding a four-and-a-half-month-old child in her arms. The girl screamed loudly, so frightening the baby that it cried till it was black in the face. From that day it had convulsions and died a month later. Denman J held that there was evidence to go to the jury of manslaughter. In the case of an adult person, he said that murder could not be committed by using language so strong or violent as to cause that person to die:

mere intimidation, causing a person to die from fright by working upon his fancy, was not murder,

but that rule did not apply to a child of such tender years as this:

. . . if the man's act brought on the convulsions or brought them to a more dangerous extent, so that death would not have resulted otherwise, then it would be manslaughter.[238]

This was extended to the case of an adult person by Ridley J in *Hayward*.[239] D, who was in a condition of violent excitement and had expressed his determination to 'give his wife something', chased her from the house into the road using violent threats against her. She fell dead. She was suffering from an abnormal heart condition, such that any combination of physical exertion and fright or strong emotion might cause death. Ridley J directed the jury that no proof of actual physical violence was necessary, but that death from fright alone, caused by an illegal act, such as a threat of violence, was enough.

D was unaware of V's condition, and following the general principle above, he must take his victim as found. It is irrelevant to the issue of causation whether the fright is one that would have an effect on a reasonable person or only one of exceptional timidity. D's awareness of the likely effect of his conduct will be a relevant issue in determining his *mens rea*.

235 Hale, 1 PC 429; and see East, 1 PC 225. 236 *Digest*, 217, n 9. 237 (1874) 12 Cox CC 530.
238 Ibid, at 533. 239 (1908) 21 Cox CC 692.

(ii) Killing by perjury

With the abolition of the death penalty, discussion of D 'causing' V's death by giving false testimony leading to V's conviction for a capital crime seems now to be redundant. The principles are discussed in the 10th edition, p 57.

(b) Reform

The Criminal Law Team of the Law Commission produced a working paper on causation in 2002 as follows:

> (1) Subject to subsections (2) to (5), a defendant causes a result which is an element of an offence when –
>
> (a) he does an act which makes a substantial and operative contribution to its occurrence; or
>
> (b) he omits to do an act, which he is under a duty to do according to the law relating to the offence, and the failure to do the act makes a substantial and operative contribution to its occurrence.
>
> (2) (a) The finders of fact may conclude that a defendant's act or omission did not make a substantial and operative contribution to the occurrence of a result if compared with the voluntary intervention of another person, unless:
>
> (i) the defendant is subject to a legal duty to guard against the very harm that the intervention or event causes; and
>
> (ii) the intervention was not so extraordinary as to be unforeseeable to a reasonable person in the defendant's position; and
>
> (iii) it would have been practicable for the defendant to have taken steps to prevent the intervention.
>
> (b) The intervention of another person is not voluntary unless it is:
>
> (i) free, deliberate and informed; and
>
> (ii) performed or undertaken without any physical participation from the defendant.
>
> (3) (a) The finders of fact may conclude that a defendant's act or omission did not make a substantial and operative contribution to the occurrence of a result if compared with an unforeseeable natural event;
>
> (a) A natural event is not unforeseeable unless:
>
> (i) the defendant did not foresee it; and
>
> (ii) it could not have been foreseen by any reasonable person in the defendant's position.
>
> (4) A person who procures, assists, or encourages another to cause a result that is an element of an offence does not himself cause that result so as to be guilty of the offence as a principal except when –
>
> (a) section 26(1)(c) applies; or
>
> (b) the offence itself consists in the procuring, assisting or encouraging another to cause the result.

4. A 'state of affairs' as an *actus reus*[240]

A crime may be so defined that it can be committed although there is no 'act' in the sense considered above. There may be no necessity for any 'willed muscular movement'. Instead it may be enough if a specified 'state of affairs' is proved to exist. These offences are sometimes called 'status'[241] or 'situation'[242] offences. Under the Road Traffic Act 1988, s 4(2), for example, any person who, when in charge of a motor vehicle on a road or other public place is unfit to drive through drink or drugs, commits an offence. One cannot take charge without consciously doing so, but it is not *taking* charge of the vehicle, or *becoming* unfit which is the offence, but simply *being* in charge and *being* unfit. So long as this state of affairs continues, the *actus reus* of the crime is committed. The *actus reus* may even be in the process of being committed while D is sleeping peacefully,[243] for he may still be 'in charge'. A further example is provided by the offence under s 25 of the Theft Act 1968 whereby a person commits an offence if, when not at his place of abode, he *has with him* any article for use in the course of or in connection with burglary, etc.[244] So long as he has the article with him, he is committing the offence. Of course, in all these examples the accused will, almost invariably, have done the acts of taking charge, getting drunk, or taking up the article, but these acts are not part of the crime. Although attempts have been made to defend these offences on the basis of the accused's prior fault, these are not wholly convincing.[245]

Offences of this type are treated with great caution. They are commonly associated with tyrannical regimes in which offences of 'status' are enacted, for example, offences of being a member of a particular political organization[246] or being of a particular race or religion (criminalization of which is yet worse because the person may have made no conscious choice to become such a member).

Even in modern day England and Wales this type of offence has led to extraordinary results in offences of 'being found' in a particular situation. In *Larsonneur*[247] D was convicted under the Aliens Order 1920 in that she, 'being an alien to whom leave to land in the United Kingdom has been refused' was found in the United Kingdom. She had been brought from Ireland into the United Kingdom against her will in the custody of the police. D, having been previously ordered to depart from the UK, went to the Irish Free State, which was not a 'departure' for the purposes of the Order; but the Free State was

240 See P. Glazebrook, 'Situational Liability' in *Reshaping the Criminal Law*, 108.

241 Howard, SR, ch 3.

242 M. D. Cohen, 'The Actus Reus and Offences of Situation' (1972) 7 Israel Law Rev 186.

243 *Duck v Peacock* [1949] 1 All ER 318; but see the defence provided by Road Traffic Act 1956, s 9(1) proviso, now re-enacted in Road Traffic Act 1988, s 4(3), on which see K. Swift, *Wilkinson's Road Traffic Offences*, ch 4.

244 Theft Act 1968, s 25, below, p 829.

245 See A. Norrie, *Crime Reason and History* (2nd edn), 119.

246 See *Scales v US* 327 US 203 (1961) re communist party membership.

247 (1933) 24 Cr App R 74. Cf *Walters* [1969] 1 QB 255, [1968] 3 All ER 863 (being an incorrigible rogue). See the criticism of *Larsonneur* by Howard, *Strict Responsibility*, 47. For a spirited but unconvincing defence of the case, see D. J. Lanham, '*Larsonneur* Revisited' [1976] Crim LR 276 and R. C. Doegar, 'Strict Liability in Criminal Law and Larsonneur Revisited' [1998] Crim LR 791 with response by J. C. Smith [1999] Crim LR 100, and Lanham, Letter, [1999] Crim LR 683.

not part of the UK. She could not have been convicted of being found in the UK on 21 April if she had remained there. She was guilty of being found in UK on that day; and she was in the UK on that day because she was brought here under arrest. Notwithstanding the wide condemnation of that decision,[248] a similar result has been reached in respect of the offence under s 12 of the Licensing Act 1872 of being found drunk in a highway. In *Winzar v Chief Constable of Kent*[249] D was taken to hospital on a stretcher but was found to be drunk and told to leave. When he was seen slumped on a seat in the corridor, the police were called and they took him to a police car stationed in the highway outside the hospital. He was convicted of being found drunk in the highway. The words, 'found drunk', were held to mean 'perceived to be drunk'. But 'perceive' means 'to become aware of' and it seems that the police became aware of D's condition in the hospital and not in the highway.

Larsonneur and Winzar were convicted of offences the commission of which was in fact procured by the police;[250] and this seems peculiarly offensive. These offences of 'being found' are unusual[251] in that they require an act on the part of the finder but no act or *mens rea* of the defendant. As a matter of principle, even 'state of affairs' offences ought to require proof that D either caused the state of affairs or failed to terminate it or act in order to do so when it was within his control and possible to do so.[252] Physical impossibility of compliance with the law should be a defence, at least where it is not proved that the impossibility arose through D's own fault.[253] Thus, situational offences are rightly condemned when they do not allow the accused to adjust his behaviour to remain within the law.[254]

It has been held by the Privy Council that the offence of 'remaining' in Singapore, having been prohibited from entering that Republic, could not be committed by one who

248 'The acme of strict injustice', Hall, GPCL, 329 n14; Williams, CLGP, 11; Howard, *Strict Responsibility*, 47; Gordon, 287; Burchell and Hunt, 114. J. Horder, *Excusing Crime* (2003), explains such cases as 'far from being exceptional', rather they were 'all too characteristic of the period', p 251.

249 (1983) The Times, 28 Mar, DC. Cf *Palmer-Brown v Police* [1985] 1 NZLR 365, CA (D not 'found' behaving in a particular way when behaviour occurred some time after encounter with constable).

250 It might be argued that the police action breaks the chain of causation between any prior wrongdoing of D and the ultimate forbidden status.

251 But not unique. Being the parent of a child of compulsory school age was an offence under the Education Act 1944, s 39(1) if the child failed to attend school regularly. It was unnecessary to prove any knowledge or neglect on the part of the parent: *Crump v Gilmore* [1970] Crim LR 28. See also the Prevention of Oil Pollution Act 1971 which provided that the owner or master of a ship was liable if oil was discharged from a British ship in a prohibited sea area. P. Glazebrook, 'Situational Liability', in *Reshaping the Criminal Law*, 108, contends that *Larsonneur* type liability is by no means unusual, pointing, *inter alia*, to the similarity, from the defendant's point of view, of vicarious liability (on which see below, Ch 9).

252 I. Patient, 'Some Remarks about the Element of Voluntariness in Offences of Absolute Liability' [1968] Crim LR 23. Cf *Burns v Nowell* (1880) 5 QBD 444 at 454 '. . . before a continuous act or proceeding, not originally unlawful, can be treated as unlawful by reason of the passing of an Act of Parliament, by which it is in terms made so, a reasonable time must be allowed for its discontinuance . . .' Other jurisdictions have avoided the result in *Larsonneur: Achterdam* 1911 EDL 336 (Burchell and Hunt, 105); *O'Sullivan v Fisher* [1954] SASR 33. In the United States, similar offences have been held unconstitutional; *Robinson v California* 370 US 660, 8 L Ed 2d 758 (1962) (being addicted to the use of narcotics).

253 See A. Smart, 'Criminal Responsibility for Failing to do the Impossible' (1987) 103 LQR 532.

254 Wilson, *Central Issues*, p 83.

was ignorant of the prohibition.[255] It is implicit in the case that to 'remain' because detained would not be an offence. It is true that 'remaining' may be said to be D's act while 'being found' is the act of another; but the substance of the two offences is the same.

It was held[256] at common law that 'being in possession' was an insufficient act to constitute the *actus reus* of a crime, but there are many cases where, by statute, mere possession is enough. Thus possession of dangerous drugs,[257] explosive substances, fire-arms and forged banknotes all constitute the *actus reus* of various crimes. 'Being in possession' does not involve an act in the sense of a muscular movement at all, for a man may possess goods merely by knowingly[258] keeping them in his house. Possession which is initially lawful may become criminal because of a change of circumstances without any act by D,[259] but only after he has failed to divest himself of possession within a reasonable time.[260] 'Being in possession' is simply a state of affairs, which, in certain circumstances, involves criminal liability.

5. Omissions[261]

Considerable controversy rages over whether and to what extent the law ought to regard inactivity as a sufficient basis for criminal liability. There are powerful arguments of principle and practicality against the imposition of a general criminal liability for failing to act in circumstances which give rise to a prohibited harm. The strongest argument against imposing any such general liability is that to do so would infringe the autonomy of the citizen in a qualitatively different manner to circumstances where liability is imposed for positive action. So it is argued, it is legitimate for the law to criminalize holding someone under water so that they drown, but not to seek to compel a person to act by criminalizing, for example, his refusal to save a drowning stranger.[262] In some circumstances the law can, consistent with this principle of autonomy, impose liability for omission – as where the drowning child is not a stranger but is D's child. These categories

255 *Lim Chin Aik v R* [1963] AC 160, [1963] 1 All ER 223. See also *Finau v Department of Labour* [1984] 2 NZLR 396 (failure to leave New Zealand after revocation of permit not an offence where impossible to leave because of pregnancy). But cf *Grant v Borg* [1982] 2 All ER 257, [1982] 1 WLR 638, HL, where an immigrant was held guilty of knowingly remaining beyond the time limit although, because of a mistake of law, he may have believed the time had been extended.

256 *Heath* (1810) Russ & Ry 184; *Dugdale v R* (1853) 1 E & B 435.

257 See in particular the comprehensive analysis in R. Fortson, *Misuse of Drugs and Drug Trafficking Offences* (4th edn, 2002), ch 3.

258 A man may possess a thing in the civil law although he does not know of its existence; but knowledge will usually be required in criminal law: cf *Warner v Metropolitan Police Comr*, below, p 151; *Cugullere* [1961] 2 All ER 343, [1961] 1 WLR 858; below, p 588.

259 Cf *Buswell* [1972] 1 All ER 75, [1972] 1 WLR 64.

260 *Burns v Nowell*, above, n 250. *Levine* [1927] 1 DLR 740 is contrary but *Burns v Nowell* is followed in South Africa: Burchell and Hunt, 264.

261 There is a wealth of academic literature on the topic, see in particular: G. Fletcher, *Rethinking Criminal Law*, ch 8; G. Hughes, 'Criminal Omissions' (1958) 67 Yale LJ 590; P. Glazebrook, 'Criminal Omissions: The Duty Requirements in Offences Against the Person' (1960) 76 LQR 386; A. Ashworth, 'The Scope of Criminal Liability for Omissions' (1989) 105 LQR 424; J. C. Smith, 'Liability for Omissions in Criminal Law' (1984) 4 LS 88.

262 See G. Williams, 'Criminal Omissions – the Conventional View' (1991) 107 LQR 86.

of exceptional liability for omission are examined below. Irrespective of the existence of these exceptions, the arguments of individual autonomy have been challenged for their failure generally to respect obligations of social responsibility, particularly where the potential harm that can be averted (for example, death) is disproportionate to the infringement of the person's liberty (for example, the simple act of plucking a child from a shallow pool of water).[263]

A further argument against the imposition of general liability for omissions is that to do so would infringe principles of legality. It is questioned whether the law can impose liability with sufficient clarity, specificity and certainty to respect adequately the principles of fair warning, fair labelling, maximum certainty, coherence with civil law, etc.[264] Again, there are counter arguments to these claims. In addition, there is the suggestion that failing to act cannot be regarded as a cause of harm, so that there should be no general liability for omission in result crimes. But, these denials of causation often take an unduly simplistic approach. Further supporting arguments against the imposition of general criminal liability for omissions include the practical difficulty in defining the standard of duty which the law would impose on the person required to act, and of the potential unfairness in singling out for punishment a particular individual from the population as a whole, or a group of individuals, none of whom acted. In the discussion that follows we can examine the extent to which the law has satisfactorily overcome these objections in those exceptional categories of case in which liability for failure to act has been recognized.

(a) Offences of mere omission

Statutes frequently make it an offence to omit to do something. There are many legislative provisions requiring companies and others to submit returns of various kinds (tax, licences, etc) and making it an offence to fail to do so. This type of offence is not restricted to corporate regulation: the driver of a vehicle which is involved in an accident causing damage or injury to any person, vehicle or animal must give his name and address to any person having reasonable grounds for requiring him to do so, or report the accident to the police within 24 hours.[265] A motorist who fails to provide a police officer with a specimen of breath when properly required to do so commits an offence.[266] So does a person legally liable to maintain a child if he fails to provide him with adequate food, clothing, medical aid or lodging.[267] A person who has been temporarily released from prison under the terms of the Prison Act 1952 commits an offence if, without reasonable excuse, he remains unlawfully at large after the expiry of the period for which he was temporarily released.[268] These offences, although they provide that D is liable for a criminal offence by omission, are uncontroversial provided that they respect the general principles of criminal law. Most of them are of a regulatory nature.

263 See especially A. Ashworth, 'The Scope of Criminal Liability for Omissions' (1989) 105 LQR 424.

264 For an accessible account, see W. Wilson, *Central Issues in Criminal Theory* (2002), 82–102.

265 Road Traffic Act 1988, s 170(4).

266 Road Traffic Act 1988, s 6.

267 Children and Young Persons Act 1933, s 1(2)(a).

268 Prisoners (Return to Custody) Act 1995 as amended by the Criminal Justice Act 2003.

Offences of pure omission are also to be found, though rarely, at common law. A police officer was held to be guilty of a common law misdemeanour when, without justification or excuse, he failed to perform his duty to preserve the Queen's peace by protecting a citizen who was being kicked to death.[269] A citizen is guilty of an offence if he fails to respond to a constable's call for assistance in keeping the peace.[270] The courts appear reluctant to extend common law offences to include liability for omission.[271]

(b) Offences of omission causing a result

Where, as in the above examples, the offence is merely the failure to act itself, there are no special difficulties. Problems arise when the offence requires proof of a result as, for example, in homicide and other offences against the person. Stephen stated the rule for these offences as follows: 'It is not a crime to cause death or bodily injury, even intentionally, by any omission. . . .'[272]

He gave the following famous illustration:

A sees B drowning and is able to save him by holding out his hand. A abstains from doing so in order that B may be drowned, and B is drowned. A has committed no offence.

Stephen went on to state exceptional cases where the law imposes a duty to act. If A in the example were B's parent, A would have a duty to act and would be guilty of murder if he did not act and the child drowned. There are a number of problems which need to be considered.

- If the case is one of omission, the issue arises whether the offence in question is one under which conviction can arise for omission.
- If so, is A under a duty to act?
- If so, can we truly say that A has 'caused' the prohibited result?
- Finally, it is necessary to reflect on whether the conduct in question is properly regarded as an omission? This gives rise to particular difficulties with doctors' responsibilities to terminally ill patients.

(i) Is the offence one capable of being committed by omission?

Assuming that the conduct of the defendant can properly be described as an omission, for example, standing by and watching a person drowning, or failing to feed a person, the question to determine is whether the offence with which he is charged can be fairly interpreted to apply to omissions.

269 *Dytham* [1979] QB 722, [1979] 3 All ER 641. For a definitive modern definition of misconduct in public office see *A-G's Reference (No 3 of 2003)* [2004] EWCA Crim 868, holding that D must be subjectively aware of the duty and subjectively reckless in its fulfilment, para 30.

270 *Brown* (1841) Car & M 314, below, p 223. See D. Nicholson, 'The Citizen's Duty to Assist the Police' [1992] Crim LR 611.

271 Eg rejection of perverting the course of justice by omission: *Clark* [2003] 2 Cr App R 23; cf the extension in relation to cheating the public revenue: *Mavji* (1987) 84 Cr App R 34, which may be explained on the basis of the Court of Appeal's exceptional preparedness to extend dishonesty offences, see below, p 793.

272 J. F. Stephen, *Digest of the Criminal Law* (4th edn, 1887), art 212.

Statutes generally

In statutory offences this question becomes one of construction. Is the verb, in its context, properly construed to include an omission? Glanville Williams has written:

> In my opinion the courts should not create liability for omissions without statutory authority. Verbs used in defining offences and prima facie implying active conduct should not be stretched by interpretation to include omissions. In general the courts follow this principle. They do not say, for instance, that a person 'wounds' another by failing to save him from being wounded, or 'damages' a building by failing to stop a fire. At least, this has never been decided.[273]

But Professor Williams himself pointed out that the courts have often held offences to be capable of being committed by omission although the enactment did not expressly provide for it. As a matter of principle, it might be argued that the interpretation of a statute that is ambiguous in this regard ought to be resolved in D's favour. However, in many cases the words of the statute can be read to include omissions without straining their meaning.

There are numerous examples of the courts' construction of words to include liability for omission. In *Shama*[274] a conviction for falsifying a document required for an accounting purpose contrary to the Theft Act 1968, s 17(1)(a) was upheld where D omitted entirely to fill in a form which it was his duty to complete. In *Firth*[275] a doctor was held to have deceived a hospital contrary to the Theft Act 1978, s 2(1) by failing to inform the hospital that certain patients were private patients. 'Obstruct', 'falsify' and 'deceive' are all verbs which the courts have held to be capable of satisfaction by omission. So why not any other verb? The difficulty is to find any principle to limit such construction.

In *Ahmad*[276] it was held that the words 'does acts' in a modern statute, the Protection from Eviction Act 1977, were to be strictly construed and were not satisfied by proof of an omission. A person commits an offence if he 'does acts' likely to interfere with the peace or comfort of a residential occupier with intent to cause him to give up occupation of the premises. D, having done such acts without any such intent, omitted with the required intention, to rectify the situation he had created. He was not guilty. Yet even the word 'act' may sometimes be satisfied by an omission.[277] It has been held that a man 'commits an act of gross indecency' with a child by totally passive submission to an act done by the child.[278] As noted, the courts often sidestep the issue by treating the whole of the circumstances as forming the basis for liability as in *B*[279] where the issue was whether D 'acted with or towards a child' by remaining motionless as the boy pressed his erect penis against D.

Homicide

The courts have long accepted without debate that murder and manslaughter are capable of commission by omission. Most cases of homicide by omission have resulted in convic-

273 Letter to the Editor, [1982] Crim LR 773.

274 [1990] 2 All ER 602, [1990] Crim LR 411.

275 (1990) 91 Cr App R 217, [1990] Crim LR 326.

276 (1986) 84 Cr App R 64, [1986] Crim LR 739. It will be noted that the court did not regard the act plus omission as an act. Cf 'Creating a danger', below, p 83.

277 This has particular significance because the entire law of attempts is based on the requirement of an 'act': Criminal Attempts Act 1981.

278 *Speck* [1977] 2 All ER 859.

279 [1999] Crim LR 594.

tions for manslaughter but there is at least one reported case of murder. In *Gibbons and Proctor*[280] a man and the woman with whom he was living were convicted of murder of the man's child by withholding food. By living with the man and receiving money from him for food the woman had assumed a duty towards the child (see below). The judge was held to have rightly directed that they were guilty of murder if they withheld food with intent to cause the child grievous bodily harm, as a result of which she died. If the child had sustained grievous bodily harm but not died, it is difficult to suppose that the court would not have held the defendants guilty of an offence under s 18 of the Offences Against the Person Act 1861.[281] The commission of this offence seems to have been an essential constituent of the defendant's liability, as the case was left to the jury. It would be strange indeed if causing death should be capable of commission by omission and causing grievous bodily harm not. It would mean that D was not in breach of a duty to act until death occurred when the duty was retrospectively imposed. That is surely unacceptable.

Non-fatal offences against the person

Although the courts have accepted that homicide can be perpetrated by omission, they have assumed that assault or battery, other offences at common law, require an act.[282] The words 'kill' and 'slay' in an indictment have been held to be satisfied by proof of an omission, so why not 'assault' or 'battery'? It is said that if D digs a pit for V to fall into, he commits an assault.[283] Why should it be different if he digs the pit without any such intention and then leaves it unfilled, intending V to fall in? Glanville Williams argues in respect of a similar case that 'in such circumstances of act-omission the total conduct should be regarded as an act . . .'.[284] But 'should be regarded as' suggests a fiction and criminal liability should not turn on fictions. And it would not meet the case where the hole has been dug by D's gardener and D, hearing that V is coming, decides to leave it unfilled.

Why should not the court legitimately interpret this as D causing V immediate unlawful violence? This view may derive some support from the decision in *Ireland*[285] that D's silent telephone call can constitute an assault. Again however, it is likely that the courts would regard the assault as deriving from D's whole course of conduct by making the call coupled with his remaining silent. It is submitted that it would be realistic for the courts to recognize that one can 'assault', no less than 'kill', by omission.[286]

As for committing battery by omission, whereas assault only requires proof that D caused V to apprehend unlawful violence, battery requires the application of unlawful violence. Can it be said that D can apply force by omission? Such an interpretation of

280 (1918) 13 Cr App R 134, CCA.

281 Below, p 559.

282 Leaving aside for now the case where D creates a dangerous situation and fails to take steps within his power to avert that: *Santana Bermudez* [2004] Crim LR 471.

283 The 'indirect violence' cases are doubted by M. Hirst, 'Assault, Battery and Indirect Violence' [1999] Crim LR 577. Cf J. C. Smith (1984) 4 LS 88.

284 G. Williams, 'What should the Code do about Omissions?' (1987) 7 LS 92.

285 [1998] AC 147.

286 Cf Wilson, *Central Issues*, 101.

'apply' might be a more difficult extension than with assault where the word 'cause' is the operative one.[287]

The discussion in the previous two paragraphs has dealt with the issue of whether there can be liability for assault and battery by omission, assuming that the elements of duty and causation can be established. As a separate matter, there can be liability for supervening fault in assault or battery – where D's course of conduct creates a dangerous situation towards any person and he omits to avert the risk. In *Fagan v Metropolitan Police Commissioner*,[288] where D accidentally drove his car onto a policeman's foot and then intentionally left it there, the majority of the court held that there was an assault (technically a battery) on the ground that, because D remained sitting in the car, there was a continuing act, not a mere omission. This again suggests, if not a fiction, a straining of words. Why should it be different if D had got out immediately, leaving the car on the officer's foot? The case would nowadays be decided under the exceptional category of duty recognized in *Miller*,[289] namely that D had created a dangerous situation by his act of driving onto V's foot and he then came under a duty to take reasonable steps to alleviate that danger. In *Santana Bermudez*,[290] this reasoning was applied to uphold D's conviction for assault occasioning actual bodily harm where D told a police officer who was about to search him that there were no needles on his person. The officer was pricked by a needle in D's pocket.

On the basis of *Gibbons* (above), it would seem that causing grievous bodily harm contrary to s 18 of the 1861 Act may be committed by omission. Although under s 20 of the 1861 Act the offence of grievous bodily harm would require proof of an 'infliction' of a 'wound', it is not clear that the words would be construed more narrowly than 'cause' in this context.[291] Since the offence under s 47 of the 1861 Act requires proof of an assault or battery and the 'occasioning', that is, 'causing' of actual bodily harm subject to what was said above regarding assault, there is no reason to assume that the offence cannot be committed by omission.

The CLRC recommended that liability for omissions in offences against the person should be confined to murder, manslaughter, and their proposed offences of causing serious injury with intent, unlawful detention, kidnapping, abduction and aggravated abduction.[292] The Home Office in its most recent reform proposals[293] redrafts the offences against the person in terms of causing injury and serious injury. This approach would present few problems in relation to liability for commission by omission.

Offences against property

The Code Team, being obliged to accept the CLRC recommendations, concluded that, if injury to the person was to be incapable of commission by omission, so, *a fortiori*, should be damage to property. This leads to the following illustration:[294]

D is employed as a night watchman at a factory. His duties are to take all reasonable steps to ensure the safety of the building. D sees that a small fire has broken out. There is an adjacent

287 See Lord Hope in *Ireland* [1998] AC 147, 165.
288 [1969] 1 QB 439, [1968] 3 All ER 442, DC.
289 [1983] 2 AC 161.
290 [2004] Crim LR 471.
291 *Mandair* [1995] AC 208.
292 Fourteenth Report, paras 252–255.
293 *Violence: Reforming the Law of Offences Against the Person* (1998).
294 Law Com No 143, 212, 20(v).

bucket of sand with which, as he knows, he could easily put out the fire. Having a grievance against his employer, he walks away and lets the fire burn. The factory is destroyed. He is not guilty of arson.

Such a conclusion may be unacceptable to the courts. If so, the remedy is in their hands. 'Destroy' and 'damage' in the Criminal Damage Act 1971[295] are capable of being construed to include omissions. It is submitted that in light of the shift in the proposals for reform of offences against the person this approach also needs to be reconsidered.

(ii) Who owes a duty?

Assuming that the offence itself is one capable of being committed by omission, the next question is, whether the individual defendant is one who may be under a duty to act?[296] Since most cases of omission have concerned homicide, the duties so far recognized[297] have been examined in the context of the duty to preserve life. This is important because there is an enhanced danger that the courts will find a duty in previously unrecognized circumstances where the inquiry involves an entirely *ex post facto* rationalization of the relationships involved when a fatality occurred.

Parents and other relations

Parents owe such a duty to their children. Presumably children above the age of responsibility owe a corresponding duty to their parents.[298] Other close relationships, whether of a family,[299] domestic, business, or other nature, possibly impose similar duties. The criminal law is increasingly willing to protect wide categories of individuals on the basis of their existence within an extended family,[300] but it is unclear whether it would be as willing to extend liability so broadly. The courts have managed to avoid identifying with precision those relationships which can be sufficient to ground liability. Indeed, they have failed to identify what is significant about those relationships in which a duty has been imposed. As a matter of principle, it can be argued that the important issue is not one of blood or formal legal relationship, but of interdependence.[301]

A further unresolved issue is what the relationship duty obliges D to do if it does arise. This would seem to be resolved on a case by case basis. One important issue will be whether the offence can be committed where D performed an act which he believed to be sufficient to fulfil the duty, or if he had a reasonable belief that what he was doing was sufficient. These issues will become intertwined with the *mens rea* of the offence.

It is equally unclear, when, if ever, the relationship duty ends. In the case of a parent and child for example, a parent of a normal child may well be absolved on the attainment of the child's majority, but this could hardly be so in the case of a disabled dependent child.

295 Below, p 890.

296 See generally, L. Alexander, 'Criminal Liability for Omissions: An Inventory of Issues', in S. Shute and A. Simester (eds), *Criminal Law Theory: Doctrines of the General Part* (2000).

297 Other than in cases of 'Supervening Fault', below, p 83.

298 See eg, a muscular 14-year-old leaves his fainting mother to drown in the notorious shallow pool.

299 Eg marriage – in *Hood* [2004] 1 Cr App R (S) 431: D was convicted of gross negligence manslaughter for failing to call medical assistance for his wife for three weeks after she fell and broke bones.

300 See eg the extensive definition of family in the Sexual Offences Act 2003, s 27.

301 Fletcher, above, 613.

Voluntary undertakings

The need to define precisely the categories of relationship which trigger a duty has often been avoided by the courts because the particular case calling for adjudication has involved a number of overlapping bases of liability including, significantly, the fact that the accused has voluntarily undertaken a position of responsibility towards V. For example, a person who has undertaken to care for a helpless and infirm relative[302] who has become dependent on him may be held to owe a duty, particularly where he is to receive some reward for caring for the other.[303] The holder of a public office requiring him to care for others may also incur criminal liability by failing to do so.

This category of duty would surely extend to unrelated persons who voluntarily undertake responsibility. It is arguable therefore that D who sees a stranger V drowning, but who voluntarily begins to go to V's assistance could be liable should D then abandon the rescue. Underlying bases for this category of duty includes the argument that in such cases D may be the best placed to act and that V may have relied to his detriment on D's actions – in the case of the drowning swimmer, V may be worse off by relying on D since he may have stopped calling for assistance from other potential rescuers.[304]

The extent to which the voluntary assumption of responsibility is a free-standing basis for the imposition of a duty, and the scope of circumstances in which it might apply remain unresolved. One of the most controversial cases may well turn on the existence of this duty. In *Stone and Dobinson*, although the defendants' liability for manslaughter arose in part from their family relationship, and their cohabitation with the victim, their voluntary undertaking of responsibility for the victim seems to have been significant in the courts conclusion that a duty was owed, although it seems that the voluntary undertaking was implied.

As in other categories of duty, the courts have failed to define the content of the duty. The conviction of the defendants in *Stone and Dobinson*, both of whom had limited mental capacity, suggests that the courts might adopt a strict line when faced with claims that the accused had done what he believed to be sufficient to fulfil his duty. In terms of the termination of such a duty, one who has undertaken the duty can probably divest himself of it only by passing it on to some responsible authority or other person.

It is submitted that people who jointly engage in a hazardous activity whether lawful – like mountaineering – or unlawful – like drug abuse[305] – may also owe duties to one another. The courts have exhibited reluctance to impose obligations on this basis alone. In *Sinclair Johnson and Smith*[306] manslaughter convictions were upheld against those who failed to seek medical care for a comatose fellow drug-taker, but the duty was based on the previous friendship and bond between the individuals rather than the joint act of

302 *Marriott* (1838) 8 C & P 425; *Nicholls* (1874) 13 Cox CC 75 (D was V's grandmother).

303 *Instan* [1893] 1 QB 450 (D was V's niece, living in V's house, consuming food provided at V's expense but not supplying any to V); *Stone and Dobinson* [1977] QB 354, [1977] 2 All ER 341.

304 See for analysis of the problems G. Mead, 'Contracting into Crime: A Theory of Criminal Omissions' (1991) OJLS 147.

305 The point was not decided in *Dalby* [1982] 1 All ER 916. Cf *People v Beardsley* (1967) 113 NW 1128.

306 See eg *Sinclair Johnson and Smith* (1998) 21 Aug, CA.

drug administration. In *Ruffell*,[307] a manslaughter conviction was upheld where D had been jointly involved in drug taking with the deceased. D, who had placed V outside in temperatures of six degrees, had also been a friend and host to V, and it is unclear on precisely which basis his duty arose.

Contractual duties

A contract may found a duty under criminal law to persons, including those not party to the contract but likely to be injured by failure to perform it. The most obvious examples in this category are those who are employed as carers or healthcare professionals. In *Pittwood*[308] a railway crossing gate-keeper opened the gate to let a cart pass and went off to his lunch, forgetting to shut it again. Ten minutes later a haycart was struck by a train while crossing the line. D was convicted of manslaughter. It was argued on his behalf that he owed a duty of care only to his employers, the railway company, with whom he contracted. Wright J held, however, that:

> there was gross and criminal negligence, as the man was paid to keep the gate shut and protect the public . . . A man might incur criminal liability from a duty arising out of contract.[309]

Again, the courts have not addressed the issue of whether the duty owed under a contract exists strictly within the bounds of the terms of that contract. If D is a lifeguard whose terms of employment stipulate that he finishes at 5 pm daily, is he under a duty to save V who is drowning at 5.05 pm? It seems clear at least that the duty will terminate when the relationship ends, as when an employee leaves the service of his employer.

Creating a dangerous situation/supervening fault

Where D *does an act* which puts in peril V's person, his property, his liberty or any other interest protected by the criminal law and D is aware that he has created the peril, he has a duty to take reasonable steps to prevent the harm in question resulting. The act may be done without any kind of fault but, if D fails to intervene, it is undoubtedly his act which is the cause of the harm. For this reason the principle may apply to a wider range of offences than can be committed by simple omission. This category of liability might therefore be treated as entirely separate from the four bases for imposing liability previously discussed.

The principle derives from *Miller*,[310] where D, a squatter in V's house, went to sleep holding a lighted cigarette. He awoke to find the mattress smouldering. He did nothing to put it out but moved into an adjoining room and went to sleep there. The house caught fire. D was convicted of arson contrary to s 1(1) and (3) of the Criminal Damage Act

307 [2003] EWCA Crim 122. 308 (1902) 19 TLR 37.

309 Wright J said that this was not a mere case of nonfeasance, but of misfeasance. However D's breach of duty was not in opening the gate, but in omitting to close it again. Cf, however, *Smith* (1869) 11 Cox CC 210, where Lush J ruled that there was no duty because D's employer had no duty to provide a watchman. (If D makes a practice of seeing old ladies across the road, he is not responsible if one day he fails to be present and an old lady is killed.) H. Beynon [1982] Crim LR at 22 suggests that opening and not shutting might be regarded as one 'act'; but would it really have been different if the gate had been opened by D's colleague who had just gone off duty? One hopes not.

310 [1983] 2 AC 161, [1983] 1 All ER 978. See [1982] Crim LR 527 and 773–774. The principle is replicated in the Home Office Draft Bill, cl 16 in *Violence: Reforming the Law of Offences Against the Person* (1998).

1971. The House of Lords held that the recorder had rightly directed the jury that, when D woke up, he was under a duty to take some action to put the fire out. Lord Diplock said:[311]

> I see no rational ground for excluding from conduct capable of giving rise to criminal liability conduct which consists of failing to take measures that lie within one's power to counteract a danger that one has oneself created, if at the time of such conduct one's state of mind is such as constitutes a necessary ingredient of the offence.

The Court of Appeal had upheld the conviction on a different basis:

> We would only say that an unintentional act followed by an intentional omission to rectify it or its consequences, or a reckless omission to do so when recklessness is a sufficient *mens rea* for the particular case, should only be regarded in toto as an intentional or reckless act when reality and common sense so require; this may well be a matter to be left to the jury. Further, in the relevant analysis we think that whether or not there is on the facts an element of adoption on the part of the alleged offender of what he has done earlier by what he deliberately or recklessly fails to do later is an important consideration.

The application of this 'continuous act' theory would apparently have produced a different result in *Ahmad*.[312] If the appellant could be deemed to have acted intentionally (that is, with intent to cause the residential occupier to give up occupation) when he rendered the flat uninhabitable, the difficulty of convicting him would have disappeared. This theory, however, involves an undesirable legal fiction. Fictions should have no place in the criminal law. Lord Diplock preferred the 'duty' to the 'continuous act' theory but only on the ground that the former is easier to explain to a jury. It is submitted, however, that they are different in substance as the example based on *Ahmad* shows.[313] It is vital to note that for this principle to apply, D must have the *mens rea* required for the crime with which he is charged at the time of the omission to avert the danger he has created.

Again, one issue to be resolved is the extent of any such duty. Although expressed in terms of 'reasonable' steps, it is unclear how objective this test is to be in application, and in particular whether it is sufficient that D believes on the facts as he sees them that the remedial measures he took are sufficient. Moreover, it is unclear how the law would deal with an individual who claimed impossibility of performance of such a duty.[314]

It is necessary to invoke the *Miller* principle only in the case of a result crime requiring fault where the act causing the result is done without that fault. Where the offence requires no fault, there is no need to rely on it. In *Wings Ltd v Ellis*[315] D Ltd, a tour operator, published a brochure which, unknown to D, contained misrepresentations. On discovering the truth, D did all they could to correct the errors but, subsequently, V read an uncorrected brochure and booked a holiday in reliance on it. D was convicted under the Trade Descriptions Act 1968, s 14(1)(a), of making a statement which they knew to be false and, s 14(1)(b), recklessly making a false statement. The statement was 'made' when

311 At [1983] 2 AC 176, [1983] 1 All ER 981. See recently on Scots law application of the principle, J. Chalmers, 'Fireraising by Omission' (2004) SLT 59.

312 Above, p 78.

313 See commentary [1982] Crim LR 527 and 773–774 and (1984) 4 LS 88 at 91.

314 See A. Smart, 'Criminal Responsibility for Failing to do the Impossible' (1987) 103 LQR 532.

315 [1984] 1 All ER 1046, [1984] 1 WLR 731; revsd [1985] AC 272, [1984] 3 All ER 577, HL.

it was read by V and, by then, D knew it was false. The Divisional Court, applying *Miller*, quashed both convictions. D had done all that could reasonably be expected to correct the false trade descriptions. The prosecutor appealed in respect of the offence under s 14(1)(a) only. The appeal was allowed. Subject to a statutory defence which was not pleaded, the House held that s 14(1)(a) created an 'absolute' offence.[316] D knew the statement was false and no other fault was required. There was no room for the application of *Miller*. Though any reader of s 14 would suppose that s 14(1)(a) is the more serious offence, 14(1)(b) requires some element of fault, however 'reckless' is interpreted, and Lord Hailsham thought that *Miller* might have been properly held applicable to that.[317]

Where the offence is one requiring fault, whether *mens rea* strictly so-called or negligence, it is submitted that the *Miller* principle is of general application.[318] If D, sitting alone in the passenger seat of a car, were accidentally to knock off the handbrake, so that the car rolled away, it is submitted that he could be convicted of murder if he wilfully omitted to put the brake on again, intending the car to run over and kill or cause grievous bodily harm to V. D locks the door of a room, not knowing that V is inside. Having learned that V is within, he omits to unlock the door. Should he not be liable for false imprisonment?[319] Since the principle requires the appropriate element of fault at the time of the subsequent omission, it is submitted that liability should arise in such a case.[320]

In the case of *Lewin v CPS*,[321] a decision not to prosecute was upheld where D left his heavily intoxicated friend, V, asleep in a car in the summer heat in Spain where he died. The court observed that D's responsibility for the welfare of his passenger 'persisted for so long as the vehicle was in motion, but . . . would normally have come to an end as soon as the vehicle was properly parked in a safe place at the end of its journey . . . [it] could only persist in a way which would be relevant to the offence of manslaughter if a reasonable person would have foreseen [the risk of death]'. The court went on 'the young man who was left in the unlocked car was an adult, not a small child or dog'.[322] Had not D created a dangerous situation by leaving V, heavily intoxicated, in the car without summoning help when D realised the temperature had risen so high?

316 See below, p 139.

317 Lord Scarman thought the analogy with *Miller* 'ingenious, if far-fetched' and (it is submitted unfairly) an 'unhelpful and over-elaborate approach to the interpretation of an Act intended to protect the public . . .' [1984] 3 All ER 590–591.

318 *Green v Cross* (1910) 103 LT 279 – D innocently caught a dog in a trap. Instead of releasing it he left it until it was freed two hours later by the police. Held, Channell J dissenting, that there was evidence on which he could be convicted of 'cruelly ill-treating' the dog.

319 Andenaes, GPCL of Norway, 135; and see *Fagan v Metropolitan Police Comr* [1969] 1 QB 439, [1968] 3 All ER 442; above, p 80. See also the unusual case of *Bowell* [2003] EWCA Crim 3896 in which D falsely imprisoned V in his car, V jumped from the car and escaped, but D put V back in the car and falsely imprisoned her again before taking her to hospital several hours later: she was rendered paraplegic by these actions. The court suggested that D 'could have left her in the road without committing an offence' when she had jumped out.

320 What of the case in which D hosts a party and X imbibes alcohol to excess. If D allows X to drive home and X kills V, should D be liable? See the discussion of prosecutions under French law (2004) The Times, 26 Oct.

321 [2002] EWHC Crim 1049.

322 para 24.

(iii) Causation and omissions[323]

Once it has been determined that there is an offence that can be committed by omission and a defendant who can be held liable owing to the existence of a relevant duty, there remains the question of whether his failure to act has caused the prohibited harm.

Considering again the example of the child, B, left to drown by his parent A, it is obvious that Stephen saw no difficulty in saying that the death (or bodily injury) was caused by A's omission. Others have taken a different view.[324] Thus, it has been argued that B's death would have occurred in precisely the same way if his parent, A, had not come on the scene for any reason so how can A be said to have caused it? He simply allowed it to happen. The cause of B's death could be said to be simply his falling into the water. Nothing else had to happen. He just drowned. If A and strangers, C, D and E had walked by the pool together it is impossible to say that, as a matter of fact, A has caused the death but C, D and E have not.

There is a danger of oversimplifying things and seeking to resolve the entire issue of liability on the basis of causation without regard to the prior question of duty.[325] In the case of A, C, D and E, it is possible to describe their failure as *a* factual cause of B's death, and if A is under a duty towards B, it is therefore possible to say that A's failure to act may be *a* legal cause of B's death.[326] Thus, in law, as the Draft Code puts it:

> a person causes a result which is an element of an offence when . . . (b) he omits to do an act which might prevent its occurrence and which he is under a duty to do according to the law relating to the offence. (Cl 17 (b))

It may be that this provision goes beyond the present law (and beyond what is desirable) in one respect: it extends liability to results which the act D omitted to do *might have* prevented. Arguably it should be limited to results which that act *would have* prevented.[327] Thus, in the drowning child example, if A is B's parent and fails to act, under the present law it is submitted that the prosecution would have to establish that the failure on A's part *would* have, not might have, prevented B's death.

(iv) Act or omission?

It is not always easy to distinguish between an act and an omission. If a doctor is keeping a patient alive by cranking the handle of a machine and he stops, this looks like a clear case of omission. So too, if the machine is electrically operated but switches itself off every 24 hours and the doctor deliberately does not restart it. Switching off a functioning machine looks like an act; but is it any different in substance from the first two cases?[328] On the other hand, is it any different from cutting the high-wire on which a tight-rope

323 See Wilson, *Central Issues*, pp 186–192; H. Beynon, 'Causation, Omissions and Complicity' [1987] Crim LR 539.

324 See B. Hogan, 'Omissions and the Duty Myth', in P. F. Smith (ed), *Criminal Law: Essays in Honour of J. C. Smith* (1987).

325 See A. Leavens, 'A Causation Approach to Criminal Omissions' (1988) 76 Cal LR 547.

326 As considered above, it is sufficient that D's conduct is a substantial and operative cause of V's death for homicide; there is no need to prove that D's conduct is the sole cause of death.

327 Glanville Williams, 'What Should the Code do about Omissions?' 7 (1987) LS 92 at 106–107, citing *Morby* (1882) 15 Cox CC 35.

328 Examples put by Williams [1977] Crim LR 443–452.

walker is balancing?[329] – which is an act, if ever there was one. Is the ending of a programme of dialysis an omission, while switching off a ventilator is an act? Is the discontinuance of a drip feed, which is keeping a patient alive, by withdrawing the tube from his body an act[330] and failure to replace an emptied bag an omission? It seems offensive if liability for homicide is so heavily dependent on distinctions of this kind; but it appears to be so.

A doctor is, no doubt, under a duty to make reasonable efforts, in the light of customary medical practice and all other relevant factors, to keep a patient alive.[331] Unfortunately, this does not solve the problem because the content of any duty there may be to 'keep alive' is different from that of the duty 'not to kill'. The issue has become further complicated with recognition that public authorities must respect not only the right to life under Article 2 of the ECHR but also the right to be free, in the course of treatment, from inhuman and degrading treatment under Article 3. The doctor must also respect the Article 8 privacy rights of the patient which might involve a declared wish to die or for treatment to be withheld in specific circumstances.

There is no doubt that parents owe a duty to their children; yet, where parents refuse their consent to an operation on a newborn baby, suffering from Down's Syndrome, knowing that without the operation it will die, they are not necessarily guilty of a criminal homicide if death ensues. If it were an offence, it would (in the absence of diminished responsibility) be murder because the parents intend the death of the child. In *Re B (A Minor)*,[332] when the parents refused their consent, the child was made a ward of court, and the court gave consent as being in the interests of the child. Dunn LJ said that the decision of the parents to allow the child to die was one which everyone accepted as 'entirely responsible'. It was a decision, it seems, that the parents could lawfully take, so that the death of the child, if it had followed, would not have been an *actus reus*. Templeman LJ thought there might possibly be cases 'where the future is so certain and where the life of the child is bound to be full of pain and suffering that the court might be driven to a different conclusion' – that is, to allow the child to die.[333] Yet there is no doubt that if the parents – or anyone – did any positive act to kill the child, they would be guilty of murder, subject to a relevant defence of necessity.[334] The undoubted duty of parents to preserve the life of their child is different from, and more restricted than, their duty not to kill it.

In *Arthur*,[335] a doctor, having noted that the parents of a Down's Syndrome child did not wish the child to survive, ordered 'nursing care only' and the administration of a drug, allegedly to stop the child seeking sustenance. At the trial of the doctor for attempted murder of the child, Farquharson J directed the jury that it was for them to decide whether 'there was an act properly so-called on the part of Dr Arthur, as distinct from simply allowing the child to die'. Simply allowing the child to die would apparently

329 I. Kennedy, 'Switching Off Life Support Machines: The Legal Implications' [1977] Crim LR 443 at 452. See the discussion by H. Beynon, 'Doctors as Murderers' [1982] Crim LR 17.

330 Beynon, ibid.

331 Williams, TBCL (1st edn, 1978) 236. See the discussion in *R (Burke) v GMC* [2004] EWHC 1879 (Admin).

332 [1981] 1 WLR 1421.

333 Cf the views in *R (Burke) v GMC* [2004] EWHC 1879 (Admin).

334 See the discussion of *Re A* [2001] Fam 147, below.

335 (1981) 12 BMLR 1, discussed by M. Gunn and J. C. Smith, 'Arthur's Case and the Right to Life of a Down's Syndrome Child' [1985] Crim LR 705 and I. Kennedy, *Treat Me Right*, ch 8.

have been lawful,[336] and withholding food was, according to the medical evidence put by the judge to the jury, 'a negative act' – a mere omission. It is submitted that a better view is that an omission to provide such a child with food and the ordinary necessities of life ought to be equated with an act causing death rather than with an omission to perform an operation or to take some other extraordinary action. The position seems to be the same with a helpless, elderly person, incapable of taking decisions. It may be lawful for his family and the doctor to decide that an operation which would prolong a useless and painful life should not be performed; but it surely cannot be lawful to starve him to death, whether with the assistance of drugs or not?

Terminating life

The distinction between act and omission was the basis of the important decision in *Airedale National Health Service Trust v Bland*.[337] B, a victim of the Hillsborough stadium disaster, had been in a persistent vegetative state for three and a half years and medical opinion was that there was no hope of improvement or recovery. The Trust, with the support of B's parents, applied for a declaration that they might lawfully discontinue ventilation, nutrition and hydration by artificial means and end medical treatment except to allow B to die peacefully. The application was resisted by the Official Solicitor, who argued that the withdrawal of artificial feeding would constitute murder. The judge made the declaration and the House of Lords, affirming the Court of Appeal, upheld it. There was no doubt about the intention to kill. The object of the exercise was to terminate B's life. It was accepted that to kill by administering a lethal injection or any similar act would be murder; but what was proposed was held to be not an act but an omission. Lord Goff said:

> The question is not whether the doctor should take a course which will kill his patient, or even take a course which has the effect of accelerating his death. The question is whether the doctor should or should not continue to provide his patient with medical care which, if continued, will prolong his patient's life.

Lord Goff added that it might be difficult to say that it was in the patient's best interests that the treatment should be ended but that it could sensibly be said that it was not in his best interests that it should be continued. 'Ending' and 'not continuing' look uncommonly like the same thing; but the former expresses the conduct as an act, which could not be justified, and the latter as an omission, which could. In *Re A (Conjoined Twins: Surgical Separation)* the Court of Appeal held, rightly, it is submitted that surgery to separate twins was an act. [338]

[336] It is submitted that nothing turned on the fact that the charge had been reduced from murder to attempted murder – see [1986] Crim LR 760–762 and D. Poole, 'Arthur's Case: A Comment' [1986] Crim LR 383; D. Brahams, 'Putting Arthur's Case in Perspective' [1986] Crim LR 387.

[337] [1993] 1 All ER 821, [1993] Crim LR 877, HL. See J. Keown, 'Restoring Moral and Intellectual Shape to the Law After *Bland*' (1997) 113 LQR 481. The Scottish courts have reached the same result by a different route: *Law Hospital NHS Trust v Lord Advocate* [1996] 2 FLR 407. *Bland's* case was distinguished in *Re A (Children; Conjoined Twins: Surgical Separation)*, below, p 321. Note that the termination by non-feeding of a patient in a persistently vegetative state should normally only occur with the sanction of the High Court: *Practice Direction* [1994] 2 All ER 413. The approach has been held to be compatible with the obligations of the State to secure the right to life under Article 2 of the ECHR: *NHS Trusts, A v M* [2001] 1 All ER 801.

[338] For criticism of the approach of the House of Lords in *Bland* and the consequences for the conjoined twin case see also J. McEwan, 'Murder by Design: The Feel-Good Factor and the Criminal Law' [2001] Med LR 246.

ECHR concerns

In *R (Burke) v GMC*[339] the court recognized that a withdrawal of artificial feeding and hydration which a competent patient wishes to continue or which an incompetent person has previously, when competent, directed to continue would infringe Article 8 of the ECHR.[340] The court declined to decide whether there would be such a breach of Article 8 once the patient was in a coma, but suggested that withdrawal once the patient was in a coma and being treated with dignity might be legitimate if it was in the final stages of life and serving no purpose.

In *NHS Trust A v M, NHS Trust B v H*[341] it was held that the withdrawal of nutrition and hydration by artificial means from a patient in a persistent vegetative state would not infringe Article 2.

In *Burke* it was held that withdrawal of treatment would breach Article 3 if it exposed the patient to acute mental and physical suffering irrespective of the awareness of the patient to that suffering. The court in *Burke* also suggested that it would be difficult to envisage circumstances in which the withdrawal of artificial feeding from a sentient patient would be compatible with the Convention. Further refinement of the BMA/GMC guidance in the light of advances in medical care seems inevitable.

It will be appreciated from the discussion of these difficult medical cases that the courts struggle to distinguish between acts and omissions. The difficulty all too often leads to distinctions without any apparent difference, or in some cases a sidestepping of the issue by a convenient treatment of the *actus reus* as the defendant's conduct viewed *in toto*.

(v) 'Easy rescue' statutes

As noted, there are hotly contested philosophical arguments about the desirability of creating liability for omissions in general, and much of the academic discussion has centred on the liability for failing to rescue.[342] Many jurisdictions have dealt with the 'shallow pool' case by creating a specific offence for anyone to fail to take steps which he could take without any personal risk, to save another from death or injury.[343] It is important to note that these statutes do not equate omissions with acts. The offender is liable for the specific statutory offence of failing to rescue (with its own penalty) and not the harmful result which D may have prevented and has allowed to happen. Thus, he is not necessarily guilty of homicide if the victim dies.[344] Criticisms have been levelled at the generality of the offences but a strong case has been put for English law to consider such.[345]

339 [2004] EWHC 1879 (Admin).

340 On the GMC Guidelines see J. Keown, 'Beyond *Bland*: A critique of the BMA Guidance on Withholding and Withdrawing Medical Treatment' (2000) 20 LS 66; cf. D. Price, 'Fairly Bland: An Alternative View of a Supposed New "Death Ethic" and the BMA Guidelines' (2001) 21 LS 618.

341 [2001] Fam 348.

342 See especially J. Feinberg, *Harm to Others* (1984), ch 4. See also M. Menlove, 'The Philosophical Foundations of a Duty to Rescue' and A. McCall Smith, 'The Duty to Rescue and the Common Law', in M. Menlove and A. McCall Smith (eds), *The Duty to Rescue: The Jurisprudence of Aid* (1993).

343 See for detailed examination of the French system A. Ashworth and E. Steiner, 'Criminal Omissions and Public Duties: The French Experience' (1990) 10 LS 153.

344 Andanaes, GPCL, 132.

345 See especially Ashworth, above, and POCL, ch 4.4.

5

The elements of a crime: *mens rea*[1]

1. Introduction

In the preceding chapter the *actus reus* or external element of the offence were examined. This chapter deals with the *mens rea* or mental fault of the accused. An *actus reus* is, in the eyes of the law, a 'bad' thing. It is not necessarily a bad thing in everyone's eyes or even in the eyes of the majority of people. But the law requires us to accept its legal 'badness'. Many people think that, in certain circumstances, mercy killing is morally right. In law it is the *actus reus* of murder, legally very bad indeed. It follows from the fact that an *actus reus* is treated in law as a bad thing that an intention to cause it is, in law, a bad intention, a guilty mind. Similarly, consciously taking a risk of causing an *actus reus* – that is being reckless whether the *actus reus* be caused – is also a bad state of mind, though less so than intentionally causing the *actus reus*. Inadvertently causing an *actus reus* by failing to take reasonable care – negligence – may also be regarded as legally blameworthy, though still less so. Intention, recklessness and negligence imply different degrees of 'fault' in the criminal law. This is set out concisely and clearly in the draft Criminal Code Bill, cl 6, which provides:

fault element; means an element of an offence consisting –

(a) of a state of mind with which a person acts; or

(b) of a failure to comply with a standard of conduct; or

(c) partly of such a state of mind and partly of such a failure. . . .

All serious crimes and most minor offences require proof that D had the relevant blameworthy state of mind that is, fault element but some – which we call 'offences of strict liability' – do not require proof of fault with respect to all the elements of the *actus reus*. For example, in the offence of assault, D must be shown to have caused V to apprehend immediate unlawful personal violence (the *actus reus*) and to have intended or been reckless as to whether his conduct would cause V to apprehend immediate unlawful violence. If D intended V to apprehend violence, but not that the apprehension was of

[1] For classic writings on the topic see: J. W. G. Turner, 'The Mental Element in Crimes at Common Law', MACL 195; G. Williams, *The Mental Element in Crime* and CLGP, in ch 2; H. L. A. Hart, 'Negligence, *Mens Rea* and Criminal Responsibility', in *Oxford Essays in Jurisprudence*, 29; J. C. Smith, 'The Guilty Mind in the Criminal Law' (1960) 76 LQR 78; A. Ashworth, 'Reason, Logic and Criminal Liability' (1975) 91 LQR 102. R. A. Duff, 'Certifying Criminal Fault', in *Criminal Law and Justice*, 93; G. Williams, 'Oblique Intention' [1987] CLJ 417.

immediate violence, he would be acquitted. The fault element for that part of the *actus reus* would not have been established. Contrast this with a case where D is charged with rape of a child under 13. The prosecution must establish that D penetrated V's vagina, anus or mouth with his penis, and that at the time V was under 13. However, the prosecution is only required to prove that D intended to penetrate V with his penis. There is no requirement to prove that D knew or was reckless as to V being under 13 – liability as to that element of the *actus reus* relating to age is strict.

The traditional term for the state of mind which must be proved, '*mens rea*', is unfortunately sometimes used by courts to include all degrees of fault, including failure to comply with a standard of conduct – negligence. Frequently the terminology is of no consequence but it can lead to confusion.[2] In this book we use '*mens rea*' to mean the state of mind, intention or recklessness, required by the particular crime and 'negligence' to describe failures to comply with a standard of conduct.

(a) Subjective and objective fault

There is an ongoing debate between: (i) 'subjectivists' who assert that, for serious crimes at least, the mental element should require proof that the defendant has personal awareness of his actions and has himself perceived the relevant circumstances and consequences comprising the *actus reus* of the offence; and (ii) 'objectivists', for whom it is sufficient to prove that the reasonable person would have perceived the relevant circumstances/consequences comprising the *actus reus*, irrespective of whether the defendant himself was aware of them. This is of course a grossly over-simplistic summary of the competing positions. A more realistic view is that there are shades of subjectivism and objectivism along a spectrum. There are competing claims as to the merits of the approaches, both in terms of their principled foundations and their practical application.[3] The subjectivists argue that the requirement of personal awareness on the part of the defendant respects the autonomy of the individual: D is punished where he has chosen to act in a way contrary to law. Objectivists point out that D might also be regarded as sufficiently culpable to deserve criminal punishment where his inadvertence related to a substantial and obvious risk of the proscribed harm, which D had the capacity to perceive.

Despite weighty academic opinion that 'the torch of orthodox subjectivism carried by Glanville Williams and Smith and Hogan and then by the Law Commission should be doused',[4] the subjective approach is that favoured by the judiciary, at least in serious crimes, and this has been emphasized recently in the clearest terms. In the landmark case of *G*[5] Lord Bingham stated that:

it is a salutary principle that conviction of serious crime should depend on proof not simply that the defendant caused (by act or omission) an injurious result to another but that his state of mind

[2] Commentary on *Seaboard Offshore Ltd v Secretary of State for Transport* [1993] Crim LR 611; affd [1994] 2 All ER 99; *Peterssen v RSPCA* [1993] Crim LR 852.

[3] The major proponents of the subjectivist view have been Glanville Williams and Sir John Smith. The subjectivist view has been challenged by prominent academic writers including A. Ashworth, POCL, Anthony Duff, *Intention Agency and Criminal Liability* (1990), A. Norrie, *Crime Reason and History* (2000) and J. Horder, see the articles cited below in this chapter. For an excellent account of the positions in the context of manslaughter see the Law Commission's Report No 237 on *Involuntary Manslaughter* (1996) Part IV.

[4] Ashworth, POCL, p 253.

[5] [2003] UKHL 50, [2004] 1 AC 1034.

when so acting was culpable. This, after all, is the meaning of the familiar rule *actus non facit reum nisi mens sit rea.* The most obviously culpable state of mind is no doubt an intention to cause the injurious result, but knowing disregard of an appreciated and unacceptable risk of causing an injurious result or a deliberate closing of the mind to such risk would be readily accepted as culpable also. It is clearly blameworthy to take an obvious and significant risk of causing injury to another. But it is not clearly blameworthy to do something involving a risk of injury to another if (for reasons other than self-induced intoxication: *R v Majewski* [1977] AC 443) one genuinely does not perceive the risk. Such a person may fairly be accused of stupidity or lack of imagination, but neither of those failings should expose him to conviction of serious crime or the risk of punishment.[6]

However, despite this strong endorsement of the subjectivist position from the House of Lords, Parliament has demonstrated a willingness to create serious offences in which the fault element is explicitly objective. Recent examples include many sexual offences in the Sexual Offences Act 2003 and some of the money laundering offences in the Proceeds of Crime Act 2002.

(b) *Mens rea* concerns legal not moral guilt

The literal meaning of '*mens rea*' – 'a guilty mind' – is misleading unless it is kept in mind that we are concerned with legal, not moral guilt. A person may – though only in exceptional circumstances – have *mens rea* though neither he nor any reasonable person would regard his state of mind as blameworthy.[7] *Mens rea* is the mental element required by the definition of the particular crime – typically, intention to cause the *actus reus* of that crime, or recklessness whether it be caused. The word '*rea*' refers to the criminality of the act, not its moral quality.

In *Yip Chiu-cheung*[8] D was charged with conspiring with E to export drugs from Hong Kong to Australia. E was an undercover drug enforcement officer who was called as a prosecution witness and testified that he made the agreement with D and intended, with the authority of his superiors, to carry it out. He was going to take the drugs to Australia to entrap other drug dealers. It takes two conspirators to make a conspiracy and D's unsuccessful defence was that E was not a conspirator because he lacked *mens rea.* It was held that E *did* have the *mens rea* of conspiracy – that is, an intention to commit the agreed crime. Neither E's good motives nor the superior orders under which he was acting would have been a defence if he had been charged. *Yip* was followed in *Kingston.*[9]

In *Kingston*[10] D, a paedophile, was charged with indecent assault on a 15-year-old boy, V. D and V had both been drugged surreptitiously by P. P knew of D's tendencies, and he drugged D and V in the hope that D would indecently assault V and that he, P, would be able to video-record the events so as to blackmail D. D did indeed indecently assault V and P video-recorded the events. The House of Lords reinstated D's conviction; simply because blame or moral fault was absent did not mean that the necessary *mens rea* was also absent. Lord Mustill stated that:

6 Per Lord Bingham [32].

7 *Dodman* [1998] 2 Cr App R 338, C-MAC, holding that 'Mens rea does not . . . involve blameworthiness', citing this work and disapproving the *Manual of Air Force Law*, s 69, n 2.

8 [1995] 1 AC 111. 9 [1994] 3 WLR 519. 10 Ibid.

Each offence consists of a prohibited act or omission coupled with whatever state of mind is called for by the statute or rule of the common law which creates the offence. In those offences which are not absolute the state of mind which the prosecution must prove to have underlain the act or omission – the 'mental element' – will in the majority of cases be such as to attract disapproval. The mental element will then be the mark of what may properly be called a 'guilty mind'. The professional burglar is guilty in a moral as well as a legal sense; he intends to break into the house to steal, and most would confidently assert that this is wrong. But this will not always be so. In respect of some offences the mind of the defendant, and still less his moral judgment, may not be engaged at all. In others, although a mental activity must be the motive power for the prohibited act or omission the activity may be of such a kind or degree that society at large would not criticize the defendant's conduct severely or even criticize it at all. Such cases are not uncommon. Yet to assume that contemporary moral judgments affect the criminality of the act, as distinct from the punishment appropriate to the crime once proved, is to be misled by the expression 'mens rea', the ambiguity of which has been the subject of complaint for more than a century.[11]

The circumstances of these two cases are exceptional. An *actus reus* generally is, or includes, some very undesirable result – killing, wounding, theft or damage to property, etc – and an intention to cause it is nearly always a state of mind which ordinary people would regard as blameworthy; but moral blameworthiness is not the legal test. 'Fault terms' require further scrutiny.

2. Forms of *mens rea*

(a) Intention[12]

Numerous offences are defined so as to require proof of 'intention' to cause specified results. It might be expected that the meaning of such a fundamental term would have been settled long ago but this is not so. The cases are inconsistent, judicial opinion has recently changed and there is still some measure of uncertainty.[13] We may begin, however, with one well-settled proposition. Everyone agrees that a person intends to cause a result if he acts with the purpose of doing so. If D has resolved to kill V and he fires a loaded gun at him with the object of doing so, he intends to kill. It is immaterial that he is aware that he is a poor shot, that V is nearly out of range, and that his chances of success are small. It is sufficient that killing is his object or purpose, that he wants to kill, that he acts in order to kill.[14]

One view is that 'intention' should be limited to the narrow definition of purposive or

[11] At 526.

[12] The literature on this topic is voluminous. See, *inter alia*, J. C. Smith, 'Intention in Criminal Law' (1974) 27 CLP 93; Lord Goff, 'The Mental Element in the Crime of Murder' (1988) 104 LQR 30; G. Williams, 'The mens rea for murder – Leave it alone' (1989) 105 LQR 387; J. Buzzard, 'Intent' [1978] Crim LR 5 and J. C. Smith, 'A Reply' [1978] Crim LR 14; A. R. White, *Misleading Cases*, 47, J. Finnis (1993) 109 LQR 329; N. Lacey, 'A Clear Concept of Intention' (1993) 56 MLR 621; J. Horder, 'Intention in the Criminal Law – A Rejoinder' (1995) MLR 678; N. Lacey, 'In(de)terminable Intentions' (1995) 58 MLR 692; M. C. Kaveny, 'Inferring Intention from Foresight' (2004) 120 LQR 81.

[13] The fact that the main cases defining intention are all murder cases, with the difficult policy issues that offence entails, exacerbates inconsistency and uncertainty.

[14] Duff suggests that this can be ascertained by asking: would D treat his action as a failure if he did not achieve the result? If so, D intended the result. R. A. Duff, *Intention, Agency and Criminal* (1990) 61.

direct intention – that a result should never be regarded as intended unless it was the actor's purpose, that is, unless he acted in order to bring about the result. This is often considered to be the ordinary meaning given to the word by people generally.[15] However, the courts have frequently given the word a wider meaning, sometimes described as 'oblique' as distinct from 'direct' intention.[16] Under this alternative approach, it is sufficient that the accused has foreseen the prohibited result as one which is highly probably, or virtually certain to occur, even if achieving that result is not his purpose.[17]

(i) Current legal position

Until recently, the predominant judicial view was that an actor intended a result if he knew that it was a highly probable (or perhaps merely probable) result of his act, although it was not his purpose or object to cause that result. In 1979 Lord Diplock said that the matter had been finally settled in this sense by the decision of the House of Lords in *Hyam v DPP*.[18] A majority of the House in *Hyam* was certainly of the opinion that this was the law but the actual decision was that foresight of high probability of serious bodily harm was a sufficient *mens rea* for murder, not that such a state of mind necessarily amounted to an intention to cause serious bodily harm. In *Moloney*,[19] however, the House held that the *mens rea* of murder is intention to cause death or serious bodily harm so it was essential to determine the meaning of 'intention'. *Moloney* must be read in the light of the explanation of it by the House in *Hancock and Shankland*,[20] the Court of Appeal in *Nedrick*[21] and by the House in *Woollin*.[22] When it is so read it appears that the current state of the law is:

(1) A result is intended when it is the actor's purpose to cause it.

(2) A court or jury *may also find* that a result is intended, though it is not the actor's purpose to cause it, when –

(a) the result is a virtually certain consequence of that act, and
(b) the actor knows that it is a virtually certain consequence.

It seems clear that (1) and (2) are distinct forms of intention. In *MD*[23] the Court of Appeal described the second form of intention – oblique intention – as:

> designed to help the prosecution fill a gap in the rare circumstances in which a defendant does an act which caused death without the purpose of killing or causing serious injury, but in circumstances where death or serious bodily harm had been a virtual certainty (barring some unforeseen intervention) as a result of the defendant's action and the defendant had appreciated that such was the case. *Woollin* is not designed to make the prosecution's task more difficult, many murderers whose purpose was to kill or cause serious injury would escape conviction if the jury was only [directed under (2)]. The man who kills another with a gun would be able to

15 On the problems of using the ordinary language approach in this context see Lacey above, n 12.

16 Cf J. Bentham, *Principles of Morals and Legislation* (Harrison edn, 207).

17 G. Williams, 'Oblique Intention' [1987] CLJ 417. See also A. W. Norrie, 'Oblique Intention and Legal Politics' [1989] Crim LR 793; A. W. Norrie, 'Intention – More Loose Talk' [1990] Crim LR 642; R. A. Duff, 'The Politics of Intention: A Response to Norrie' [1990] Crim LR 637.

18 [1975] AC 55, [1974] 2 All ER 41, below, p 99. See [1979] AC at 638.

19 [1985] AC 905, [1985] 1 All ER 1025.

20 [1986] AC 455, [1986] 1 All ER 641.

21 [1986] 3 All ER 1, [1986] 1 WLR 1025.

22 [1999] AC 82, [1998] Crim LR 890.

23 [2004] EWCA Crim 1391.

escape liability for murder if he could show[24] that he was such a bad shot that death or serious bodily harm was not a virtual certainty or that the defendant had thought that death or serious bodily harm was not a virtual certainty.[25]

(ii) Criticisms of the present law

The blurring of evidence and substantive law

The fact that the result was a virtually certain consequence of D's act is very good evidence that he knew that it was a virtually certain consequence; but it is difficult to see why it should be regarded as a necessary condition as a matter of substantive criminal law.[26] If D thinks he knows that the result is virtually inevitable because he is making a mistake, why should he be held not to have intended it because it was not, in fact, inevitable? His state of mind is the same in either case. If D fires a gun pointed at V's heart, his intention can hardly be affected by the fact, unknown to D, that V is wearing a bullet-proof vest. The state of mind of a person who thinks he knows is the same as that of a person who actually knows. The difference is in the external circumstances. This point may not be of great practical importance because the best evidence that D knew that the consequence was virtually certain will be the fact that it *was* virtually certain; but this is not invariably so.

'Finding' intention

The second major criticism with the present description of the law offered in *Woollin* concerns the House's use of the phrase, italicized above, 'may also find'. *Woollin* amended the much-criticized proposition in *Nedrick* that foresight of virtual certainty is merely evidence *from which intention may be inferred.* At one point Lord Steyn said that, 'The effect of the critical direction is that a result foreseen as virtually certain is an intended result.'

That seemed to be unequivocal and was welcomed by many commentators who concluded that there was no room for any 'finding' of intention by the jury because on a literal reading it ought to follow that a court or jury, when satisfied of such foresight, *must* (not 'may') find that the result is intended. In terms of optimizing the certainty and consistency in application of this important *mens rea* element, equating foresight of virtual certainty with intention is clearly an advantageous approach.

An alternative view was that *Woollin* did leave a degree of flexibility for the jury; the definition was that the jury 'may' find intention. This suggests there is something further for the jury to decide – that there is some ineffable, apparently undefinable notion of intent locked in the breast of jurors, if not magistrates. It has been suggested by, amongst others, Professor Norrie, that a test in which foresight of virtual certainty was intention, rather than something from which intention may be found, would be over-inclusive and would not reflect the degree of 'moral malevolence' in D's act. The argument is that the jury, having decided that D did foresee some prohibited consequence as certain, should

[24] Surely this is a slip and the burden is on the Crown to rebut such a defence?

[25] The extended *Woollin* direction is only rarely needed. It is needed where D denies his purpose, not where eg D denies any part in the crime: *Phillips* [2004] EWC Crim 112. The trial judge is best placed to make the decision on the appropriate direction. See also *Allen* [2005] EWCA Crim 17/5/05.

[26] This criticism as stated in the 10th edition was acknowledged by the Court of Appeal in *MD* [2004] EWCA Crim 1391.

go on to consider whether, in all the circumstances, he was so wicked that an intention to cause the evil should be attributed to him.[27] Although this might enhance the prospects of achieving justice in the individual case, it does little to secure certainty and consistency in general application.

It seems that the Court of Appeal at least are unwilling to interpret *Woollin* as laying down a clear rule that foresight of virtually certain consequences is intention. In *Matthews and Alleyne*[28] M and A were convicted of robbery, kidnapping and murder. V was attacked on leaving a club in the early hours of the morning, and ultimately thrown off a bridge 25 feet high into a river 64 feet wide. V could not swim and drowned. A co-accused gave evidence that V had said he could not swim. One ground of appeal against their conviction for murder was that the judge had directed the jury that foresight of virtual certainty of consequences *was* intention. The Court of Appeal held that *Woollin* did not reach or lay down such a rule of substantive law; *Woollin* was concerned with the law of evidence. The judge had gone further than permitted.

> [T]he law has not yet reached a *definition* of intent in murder in terms of appreciation of a virtual certainty . . . On the contrary, it is clear from the discussion in *Woollin* as a whole that *Nedrick* was derived from the existing law, at that time ending in *Moloney* and *Hancock*, and that the critical direction in *Nedrick* was approved, subject to the change of one word.

The proper direction should have been in the terms from *Woollin* quoted above. However, the court acknowledged that once it was accepted that what was required was appreciation of virtual certainty, and not a lesser foresight of probable consequences, there was very little to choose between evidence and substantive law.

It seems then that the jury retain their 'moral elbow room'.[29] A person who admits to having seen the result as virtually certain will not necessarily be found to have intended the result; the jury will have the discretion to find that he did. This is, it is submitted an unsatisfactory position, leaving undefined a key term of fault applicable in the most serious crimes. The potential for inconsistent decisions on identical facts is stark. This approach does not merely pose problems of a practical nature. If this 'moral threshold' test is to be applied to oblique intention so as to save hard cases from conviction, why should it not also apply to direct intention – that is, purpose? The typical mercy-killer acts with the purpose of killing – and his may be the hardest case of all.

Lord Lane CJ recognized the force of the criticism of his judgment in *Nedrick* in the debate on the Report of the House of Lords Select Committee on Murder[30] when he stated:

> in *Nedrick* the court was obliged to phrase matters as it did because of earlier decisions in your Lordships' House by which it was bound. We had to tread very gingerly indeed in order not to tread on your Lordships' toes. As a result, *Nedrick* was not as clear as it should have been. However, I agree with the conclusions of the committee that 'intention' should be defined in the terms set out in paragraph 195 of the report on page 50. That seems to express clearly what in *Nedrick* we failed properly to explain.[31]

27 A. Norrie, 'After *Woollin*' [1999] Crim LR 532; see also *Crime Reason and History* (2nd edn, 2000) 47–50.

28 [2003] 2 Cr App R 30 [2003] Crim LR 553.

29 J. Horder, 'Intention in the Criminal Law: A Rejoinder' [1995] MLR 678, 688.

30 HL Paper 78-I, 1989.

31 HL, vol 512, col 480 (6 Nov 1989).

The definition referred to is that stated in cl 18 (b) of the Draft Code:

A person acts 'intentionally' with respect to . . . a result when he acts either in order to bring it about or being aware that it will occur in the ordinary course of events.

In *Woollin* Lord Steyn, stressing '*will* occur', noted the similarity to the virtual certainty test. In *Moloney* Lord Bridge gave a notable example of a man who boards a plane which he knows to be bound for Manchester – the last place he wants to be – in order to escape pursuit: by boarding the Manchester plane, the man '*conclusively* demonstrates his intention to go there, because it is a moral certainty that that is where he will arrive'.[32] There is nothing here about this being merely evidence upon which the jury may find intention – intention is *conclusively* demonstrated.[33] Nevertheless, the Court of Appeal in *Matthews and Alleyne* having been referred to the above passage in the 10th edition of this work remained unconvinced that the law had yet reached that position.

(iii) Intention and results known to be condition of achievement of purpose

It may be said that no one can ever know that a result is certain to follow from an act. This is why courts and writers are driven to speak of 'virtually' or 'morally' or 'almost' certain results. But a person may know that he cannot achieve his purpose, A, without bringing about some other result, B. If he is to bring about A, he knows he must also, at the same time or earlier, bring about B. It may be that, in any other circumstances, he would much rather B did not happen, indeed its occurrence may be abhorrent to him. But, the choice being between (i) going without A and (ii) having A and B, he decides to have A and B. It seems fair to say that he intends to cause B as well as A. Suppose that V has made a will, leaving the whole of his large estate to D. D loves V but he has an overwhelming desire to enjoy his inheritance immediately. If he gives V what he knows to be a fatal dose of poison, he intends to kill V, though he says truthfully that it causes him anguish. D wishes to injure his enemy, X, who is standing inside the window of the house of D's friend, Y. If, knowing the window to be closed, he throws the stone through it at X, can it be doubted that he intends to break his friend's window?

Since result 'A' is the actor's purpose, it is immaterial that he is not certain that it will happen. He is not a good shot and he knows the stone may miss – but he intends to strike X. And, since he knows that, if he strikes X, it will be because he has broken Y's window, he intends to break the window. It seems from these examples that we might safely say that a result known or believed to be a condition of the achievement of the actor's purpose is intended.

Yet even this modest conclusion is not beyond doubt. In *Moloney*[34] Lord Bridge referred with approval to *Steane*[35] where D, who, during the Second World War, gave broadcasts which would assist the enemy in order to save himself and his family from the horrors of the concentration camp, was held not to have had an 'intent to assist the enemy'. Steane may have been a loyal citizen who, in other circumstances, would have wished to do nothing to assist the enemy; but, being faced with the choice, 'Assist us – or back to the concentration camp', he chose to assist the enemy. Of course, his purpose was

32 [1985] AC at 296 (authors' italics).

33 This was the view taken by Ward and Brooke LJJ in *Re A (Conjoined Twins)* [2000] 4 All ER 961.

34 [1985] AC 905 at 929.

35 [1947] KB 997, [1947] 1 All ER 813.

to stay out of the camp; but it seems plain that he knew that his purpose could only be achieved by assisting the enemy. Reading the script was assisting the enemy.[36] There are numerous similar cases. In *Ahlers*,[37] a German consul who assisted German nationals to return home after the declaration of war in 1914 was held to have intended only to do his duty as consul. In *Sinnasamy Selvanayagam*[38] the Privy Council said, *obiter*, that if D remained in occupation of his home in defiance of a lawful order to quit, knowing that the owner of the property would be annoyed, his 'dominant intention' was simply to retain his home and he was not guilty under the Ceylon Penal Code [as it then was] of remaining in occupation with intent to annoy the owner. In *Gillick*'s case[39] some of the judges seem to have been of the opinion that a doctor, who knew that his provision of contraceptive advice to a girl under 16 would encourage a man to have sexual intercourse with her, would not be guilty of abetting the offence, because his intention was to protect the girl, not to encourage sexual intercourse with her.

In some of these cases, it seems that the concept of intention is strained to do a job for which it is not fitted. The courts appear to examine the motives of the defendant. Steane's acquittal would more properly have been based on duress and the case envisaged in *Gillick* seems to have been, in substance, one of necessity – a minor encouragement of sexual intercourse was a lesser evil than an unwanted pregnancy in the young girl.[40] In each of these cases, D had an 'honourable' purpose. Where D's purpose is disreputable, the court is most unlikely to interpret intention so narrowly. If Steane, being a chain smoker deprived of cigarettes, had read the script in order to get a packet, it is probable that Lord Goddard CJ would have had no hesitation in holding that, of course, he intended to assist the enemy. Yet, from the point of view of intention, there seems to be no difference between the cases.[41] If this is so, it produces an undesirable distortion of the concept of intention and it would be better if the true reason for the decision were articulated. *Moloney*, however, encourages such decisions – the jury appears to be left a measure of discretion to say whether they think the state of mind should be categorized as intention or not.

It is arguable that intention, in law, should extend to results known or believed by the actor to be conditions of the achievement of his purpose but should go no further. This would give effect to the constantly reiterated opinion of the courts that intention is different from desire. Result 'B' is not desired, at least it is not desired for its own sake; but it is intended. And any overlap with recklessness is avoided. D is not merely taking a risk of causing B; he *knows* or thinks he knows that, if he achieves his aim of causing 'A', 'B' will happen or will have already happened.

36 It might be argued that, even in these circumstances, B is not necessarily a condition of A. Someone might open the window while the stone is in flight towards it. The microphone into which Steane spoke might have been disconnected or the transmitter broken down. Lord Bridge's man who boards the plane for Manchester (the last place he wishes to go) to escape arrest intends (as Lord Bridge says [1985] AC at 986) to go to Manchester although it is possible that the plane will be diverted to Luton. Even in the case of D who gives V the fatal dose of poison to accelerate his inheritance, it is possible that V will die of natural causes before the poison takes effect: cf *White* [1910] 2 KB 124, CCA.

37 [1915] 1 KB 616.

38 [1951] AC 83.

39 *Gillick v West Norfolk and Wisbech Area Health Authority* [1986] AC 112, [1985] 3 All ER 402, [1986] Crim LR 113, HL and commentary. See also *Salford Health Authority, ex p Janaway* [1989] AC 537.

40 See now the Sexual Offences Act 2003, s 73 (below).

41 Glanville Williams, *The Mental Element in Crime*, 21.

(iv) Results known to be virtually certain to accompany achievement of purpose

Result B may also be intended, according to *Moloney*, where B is not a condition of A. It is possible for A (D's purpose) to occur without B also happening, but as D knows, causing A is virtually certain to cause B as well. D, wishing to collect the insurance on a cargo (result A), puts a time bomb in a plane to blow up in mid-Atlantic. He has no wish to kill the crew. It is *possible* for the plane and cargo to be destroyed and the crew to escape – people do occasionally fall from aircraft at great heights and survive – but the possibility is so remote as to be negligible; and D knows that.[42] There is certainly a strong argument for saying that he intends to kill. This is so even if, as D knows, this type of bomb has a 50 per cent failure rate. There is an even chance that nothing will happen. But he wants the explosion (result A) to happen and, if it does, killing (result B) is, as he knows, a virtual certainty. So a jury may (not must) find that there is an intention to kill.[43]

The difficulty is that once we depart from absolute certainty, there is a question of degree and an uncertain boundary between intention and recklessness. In *Hyam*[44] D, in order to frighten Mrs Booth, her rival for the affections of X, put blazing newspaper through the letter box of Booth's house and caused the death of two of her children. Ackner J directed the jury that D was guilty if she knew that it was highly probable that her act would cause at least serious bodily harm; and by their verdict of guilty the jury must be taken to have found that she did know that. In the light of *Moloney*, that direction was wrong but Lord Bridge[45] thought that, on a proper direction, no reasonable jury could have failed to convict Hyam. Is that really so? Might not a jury have been satisfied that D knew this was a highly probable result without being satisfied that she knew it was virtually certain?

In *Moloney*,[46] Lord Hailsham and Lord Bridge put the case of a terrorist who plants a time bomb in a public building and gives a warning to enable the public to be evacuated. He knows that it is virtually certain that a bomb disposal squad will attempt to defuse the bomb. The squad does so, the bomb explodes and a member of the squad is killed. It is assumed that this is murder.[47] The bomber intends to endanger the squad's lives (because he knows that it is virtually certain they will attempt to defuse the bomb) but he does not, surely, know that it is virtually certain that one of them will be killed or even seriously injured. It is doubtful if this would be murder even under the 'highly probable' formula of *Hyam*. It looks like recklessness which is not enough for murder. The example might be justified if it could be proved that the terrorist wants the bomb to go off *at a time* when he knows it is virtually certain that the squad will be attempting to defuse it. That would be indistinguishable from the 'bomb-in-the-plane' case, above, where the bomber wants the bomb to go off in mid-Atlantic.

42 These examples have prompted a voluminous literature of their own, see A. Pedain, 'Intention and the Terrorist Example' [2003] Crim LR 579 and the references therein.

43 Cf the view of I. Kugler, 'Conditional Oblique Intention' [2004] Crim LR 284, seemingly suggesting that the question will depend on whether D has a guilty motive or Parliament's motive in creating an offence of that form or the degree of harm actually caused. It is difficult to see how these issues affect D's intention in substantive law.

44 [1975] AC 55, [1974] 2 All ER 41.

45 [1985] AC at 926, [1985] 1 All ER at 1037.

46 [1985] AC at 913, 927.

47 Cf A. Pedain, above, suggesting that this is a form of 'purposive' intent because of D's 'motive'.

In *Moloney*, D shot his stepfather, whom he loved, when, in the course of a drunken game to establish who was quicker 'on the draw' with loaded shotguns, he pulled the trigger in response to a challenge, 'if you have [the guts] pull the trigger'. He may not have realized that the gun was aimed, at point-blank range, at V's head. His conviction was quashed because the judge misdirected the jury that D intended serious bodily harm if he foresaw that it would 'probably' happen. Lord Bridge insisted on the need for 'a moral certainty', a probability which is 'little short of overwhelming' and an act that 'will lead to a certain event unless something unexpected supervenes to prevent it'.[48] Unfortunately, in summing up his opinion in the form of guidelines for trial judges, he used the term, 'natural consequence', to mean a consequence that is virtually certain to ensue.

In *Hancock and Shankland*[49] two striking miners pushed from the parapet of a bridge heavy concrete blocks which struck a taxi taking a working miner to work and killed the taxi-driver. They said they intended to push the blocks on to the middle lane, not the inside lane in which the taxi was travelling, and that they intended to frighten the working miner and prevent him going to work, but not to hurt anyone. At their trial for murder, the judge closely followed the *Moloney* 'guidelines'. The Court of Appeal held that the conviction must be quashed. The guidelines were defective. The jury might well have understood 'natural consequence' to mean 'direct consequence' and not to convey the notion of moral certainty or overwhelming probability of which Lord Bridge spoke. The House of Lords agreed. Both courts stressed that even awareness that the consequence is virtually certain is not intention, but only evidence from which a jury may infer intention, if they are satisfied beyond reasonable doubt that this is the right inference. The difficulty of applying this rule is considered above.

Although the House in *Moloney* said that they were laying down the law not only for murder but for offences requiring 'specific intent' generally (which, here, seems to mean merely offences requiring intent), their approval of *Steane* and the difficulty of reconciling the illustration of the bomber suggests that the word may well be held to bear different shades of meaning in different contexts.

An act may be intentional with respect to circumstances as well as consequences. Intention here means either hope that the circumstance exists – which corresponds to purpose in relation to consequences – or knowledge that the circumstance exists – which corresponds to foresight of certainty in relation to consequences.

He who steals a letter containing a cheque, intentionally steals the cheque also if he hopes that the letter may contain one, even though he well knows that the odds against the existence of such a circumstance are very great.[50]

If D receives a car which he knows to be stolen, that is an intentional handling of stolen goods even though D would, perhaps, much prefer that the car was not stolen. If, however, D believed merely that it was probable, or highly probable, that the car was stolen, this would not be an intentional handling.

[48] [1985] AC at 925, 926, 929.

[49] [1986] AC 455, [1986] 1 All ER 641.

[50] J. Salmond, *Jurisprudence* (11th edn, 1957), 411.

(v) Intention in crimes other than murder

Nearly all the leading cases relate to murder and Lord Steyn prefaced his decision in *Woollin* by remarking that 'intent' does not necessarily have precisely the same meaning in every context of the criminal law. Sometimes the context may indicate a narrower meaning – that nothing less than purpose will do. This may be the explanation of *Steane*, though that decision has been regularly cited in murder cases. A strong case can be made that the very nature of an attempt involves purpose, and that 'intent' in the Criminal Attempts Act[51] should be construed accordingly. The Code recognizes that the context may require some modification of its proposed definition. But, while the context may require a narrower meaning, it is submitted that a court should be slow to give the term a narrower one. *Woollin* draws a clear line between intention and recklessness and it is desirable to preserve that clarity throughout the criminal law.

(vi) Reform

The definition in cl 18 (b) of the Draft Code provides:

> A person acts 'intentionally' with respect to . . . a result when he acts either in order to bring it about or being aware that it will occur in the ordinary course of events.

There were two possible defects in the definition proposed in the Draft Code: (i) It did not provide for the case where D knows that the relevant result will occur if, but only if, he succeeds in achieving some other purpose[52] and he is not certain that he will achieve that other purpose. This is exemplified by the case of the bomb with the 50 per cent failure rate.[53] (ii) In certain, admittedly rather unlikely, circumstances, the definition might mean that a person intended a result which it was his purpose to avoid – which does not seem to be very good sense. To avoid these difficulties, the Law Commission[54] proposed a definition for the purposes of non-fatal offences against the person, which slightly modified, is included in the draft Bill, cl 14 (1) in the Home Office Consultation Paper of February 1998:[55]

> . . . a person acts intentionally with respect to a result if –
> (a) it is his purpose to cause it; or
> (b) although it is not his purpose to cause it, he knows that it would occur in the ordinary course of events if he were to succeed in his purpose of causing some other result.

Woollin, however, shows that this may be too narrow. D lost his temper and threw down his three-month-old son on to a hard surface, killing him. The Crown did not contend that his purpose was to kill or cause serious injury. He was convicted of murder on a direction that it was enough that he knew there was a 'substantial risk' that he would cause serious injury. His conviction was upheld by the Court of Appeal but quashed by the House of Lords. Even if Woollin knew that serious bodily injury was certain, he would not have an intention to cause it within cl 14 – it was not his purpose and he had no other purpose, except to vent his anger, which is not a purpose to cause a result. To meet this

51 Below, p 400. 52 Above, p 97. 53 Above, p 99.

54 Law Com No 218 7.1–7.14 and Cl 1 of draft Bill, following Law Com No 122 (1992) 5.4–5.11 and J. C. Smith, 'A Note on Intention' [1990] Crim LR 85.

55 J. C. Smith, 'Offences Against the Person: The Home Office Consultation Paper' [1998] Crim LR 317.

point it is submitted that the clause should be amended to read '. . . he knows that it *will occur in the ordinary course of events, or* that it would do so if he were to succeed in his purpose of causing some other result'.

Parliament has accepted in one context at least that a person has intention in relation to a consequence where he means to cause the consequences or is aware that it will occur in the ordinary course of events.[56]

(b) Recklessness

For many crimes, either intention to cause the proscribed result or recklessness as to whether that result is caused is sufficient to impose liability. A person who does not intend to cause a harmful result may take an unjustifiable risk of causing it. If he does so, he may be held to be reckless. Not all risk-taking constitutes recklessness. Sometimes it is justifiable to take a risk of causing harm to another's property or his person or even of causing his death. The operator of an aircraft, the surgeon performing an operation and the promoter of a tightrope act in a circus must all know that their acts might cause death but none of them would properly be described as reckless unless the risk he took was an unreasonable one. The law allows the use of reasonable force in the lawful arrest of an offender or in private defence. If D forces V's car off the road, that cannot be reckless driving if it was reasonable to use that degree of force lawfully to arrest V.[57] If D, doing an act of reasonable self-defence, damages V's window, he is not guilty of reckless criminal damage.[58] Whether it is justifiable to take a risk depends on the social value of the activity involved relative to the probability and the gravity of the harm which might be caused. The question is whether the risk was one which a reasonable and prudent person might have taken. It might be reasonable for D to shoot V's ferocious dog which is attacking his sheep, but it does not follow that it would be reasonable to take a risk of causing injury or death to V – still less a bystander, X. The test is objective – that is to say, the court or jury lays down the required standard of care. It is impossible to say in general terms that recklessness requires any particular degree of probability of the occurrence of the harm in question.[59] If the act is one with no social utility – for example, a game of 'Russian roulette' or an armed robbery – the slightest possibility of any harm should be enough. If the act has a high degree of social utility – for example, the performance of a surgical operation – then only such a very high degree of probability of grave harm as outweighs that utility will suffice to condemn it as a reckless act.[60]

(i) Subjective recklessness

To establish recklessness it is necessary in all cases to show that D took an unjustifiable risk; but the prosecution must go further. The standard test of recklessness – traditionally called '*Cunningham*' recklessness after the case of that name – requires not only proof of a

56 See the International Criminal Courts Act 2001, s 66(3)(a).

57 *Renouf* [1986] 2 All ER 449, [1986] 1 WLR 522, 82 Cr App R 344.

58 *Sears v Broome* [1986] Crim LR 461, DC.

59 See *Vehicle Inspectorate v Nuttall* [1999] 1 WLR 629.

60 See A. Norrie, 'Subjectivism, Objectivism and the Limits of Criminal Recklessness' (1992) 12 OJLS 45; P. H. Robinson, 'The Modern General Part: Three Illusions' in S. Shute and A. Simester (eds), *Criminal Law Theory* (2002), 88–91.

taking of an unjustified risk, but proof that D was aware of the existence of the unreasonable risk. It is a subjective form of *mens rea*, focused on the defendant's own perceptions of the risk. In *Cunningham*[61] D tore a gas meter from the wall of the cellar of an unoccupied house to steal the money in it. He left the gas gushing out. It seeped into a neighbouring house and was inhaled by V whose life was endangered. D was convicted under s 23 of the Offences Against the Person Act 1861[62] of maliciously administering a noxious thing so as to endanger life. Because the judge directed the jury that 'malicious' meant simply 'wicked', D's conviction was quashed. The Court of Criminal Appeal quoted with approval the principle first propounded by Kenny in 1902.[63]

> . . . in any statutory definition of a crime 'malice' must be taken not in the old vague sense of 'wickedness' in general, but as requiring either (i) an actual intention to do the particular *kind* of harm that in fact was done, or (ii) recklessness as to whether such harm should occur or not (ie the accused has foreseen that the particular kind of harm might be done, and yet has gone on to take the risk of it). It is neither limited to, nor does it indeed require, any ill-will towards the person injured.

The court reiterated: 'In our opinion, the word "maliciously" in a statutory crime postulates foresight of consequence.' Cunningham was not guilty unless *he knew*, when he broke off the gas meter, or left the broken pipe with the gas gushing out,[64] that it might be inhaled by someone. In cases requiring 'malice' it is not sufficient that, if D had stopped to think, it would have been obvious to him that there was a risk. He must actually know of the existence of the risk and deliberately take it.

In a series of cases, of which the most important is *Parmenter*,[65] convictions of malicious wounding have been quashed because the judge, in directing the jury, took the words of Diplock LJ, 'should have foreseen', out of their context in *Mowatt*,[66] thus leading the jury to think that it is enough that D ought to have foreseen. It is not. To be 'malicious', D must actually foresee some harm and the fact that he ought to have foreseen is, at best, some evidence that he did foresee.

In *Cunningham* the court was considering the requirement of 'malice', a form of recklessness, but the definition adopted in *Cunningham* applies generally.[67]

It is well established that where D closes his mind to the risk he can be found reckless within the subjective definition, as where he claims that his extreme anger blocked out of his mind the risk involved in his action. As Lord Lane put it, 'Knowledge or appreciation of a risk of the [proscribed harm] must have entered the defendant's mind even though he may have suppressed it or driven it out.'[68]

In the recent case of *G* Lord Bingham based his definition of recklessness for the Criminal Damage Act 1971 on the Draft Criminal Code, cl 18(c):

[61] [1957] 2 QB 396, [1957] 2 All ER 412. [62] Below, p 563.

[63] *Outlines of Criminal Law* (16th edn, 1952), 186.

[64] See omissions, above, p 84. [65] [1991] 4 All ER 698 at 706, HL.

[66] [1968] 1 QB 421 at 426.

[67] In one sense the definition in *Cunningham* is defective since it fails to make explicit that not only must D foresee the risk of the proscribed harm, but he must take it *unjustifiably* as discussed above, p 102.

[68] *Stephenson* [1979] QB 695, 704. See also the comments of Lord Bingham in *G* [2004] 1 AC 1034 [39] and Lord Steyn [58].

A person acts recklessly within the meaning of section 1 of the Criminal Damage Act 1971 with respect to –

(i) a circumstance when he is aware of a risk that it exists or will exist;

(ii) a result when he is aware of a risk that it will occur;

and it is, in the circumstances known to him, unreasonable to take the risk.

It is submitted that this subjective definition of recklessness ought to be applied in all statutory offences of recklessness unless Parliament has explicitly provided otherwise.[69]

(ii) The rise and fall of objective recklessness

The *Cunningham*, subjective approach to recklessness or 'advertent recklessness' as it is also called, was the accepted definition until a controversial, and, it is now accepted, erroneous turn by the House of Lords in the 1980s. Although the House of Lords has recently restored orthodoxy by affirming that the definition of recklessness is as stated in *Cunningham*, it is valuable to examine briefly,[70] the temporary shift of English law towards objective recklessness in some offences.

Caldwell v MPC[71]

It was accepted that the *Cunningham* definition of recklessness applied, *inter alia*, to the offence of damage to property under the Malicious Damage Act 1861. The Law Commission in their Report on Criminal Damage[72] made many proposals for the reform of the law but they considered that the mental element, as interpreted in *Cunningham*, was satisfactory. They proposed only that it be 'expressed with greater simplicity and clarity' and that this should be achieved by using 'intentionally or recklessly' in place of the archaic and misleading 'maliciously'. Parliament adopted their proposals in the Criminal Damage Act 1971. Unfortunately, the Commission proposed no definition of recklessness and the Act contains none. Before 1981, the Court of Appeal held, though after some hesitation, that 'reckless' in the 1971 Act bore the *Cunningham* meaning but in that year, the House of Lords decided in *Caldwell*[73] (Lords Wilberforce and Edmund-Davies dissenting) and in *Lawrence*[74] that, where the statute uses the word 'reckless', a different test applies. In *Caldwell* Lord Diplock said that a person is reckless whether any property would be destroyed or damaged:

> . . . if (1) he does an act which in fact creates an obvious risk that property would be destroyed or damaged and (2) when he does the act he (i) either has not given any thought to the possibility

69 Cf the offences relating to the Enrichment Technology (Prohibition on Disclosure) Regulations 2004, SI 1818, made under the Anti-Terrorism Crime and Security Act 2001, s 80(2) where *Caldwell* recklessness is expressly adopted.

70 For a full examination and compelling critique of the *Caldwell* definition and its implications see the 10th edition of this work, and the references cited therein.

71 [1982] AC 341. See especially, E. Griew, 'Reckless Damage and Reckless Driving – Living with *Caldwell* and *Lawrence*' [1981] Crim LR 743; J. McEwan and J. Robilliard, 'Recklessness: the House of Lords and the Criminal Law' (1981) LS 267; G. Syrota, 'A Radical Change in the Law of Recklessness?' [1982] Crim LR 97; G. Williams, 'Recklessness Redefined' [1981] CLJ 252; G. Williams, 'The Unresolved Problem of Recklessness' (1988) 8 LS 74.

72 Law Com No 29 (1970), confirming proposals in Working Paper No 23 (1969).

73 [1982] AC 341, [1981] 1 All ER 961.

74 [1982] AC 510, [1981] 1 All ER 974. For discussion of these decisions see also the commentaries at [1981] Crim LR 393 and 410.

of there being any such risk or (ii) has recognized that there was some risk involved and has nonetheless gone on to do it.[75]

Under both limbs (i) and (ii) of the direction, as formulated, it must be proved that the risk taken was an 'obvious [and serious][76] risk'. The further element of culpability is either –

(a) D's failure to give thought to whether there was 'such a risk' (which might be designated 'inadvertent recklessness'); or

(b) D's knowledge that there was 'some risk' ('advertent recklessness').

This represented a very different test to that in *Cunningham*.[77] It was sufficient to convict D for an offence to which the *Caldwell* reckless test applied where the reasonable person would have seen the risk even if D did not, nor even where D could not see the risk because of some limitation in his capacity.[78]

The 'model direction' contained inconsistencies and lacked precision,[79] in particular it left the knotty question whether there was a loophole or lacuna so that D would not be reckless if he had considered the matter and decided that there was no risk.[80] There were more principled objections to the test. First, it resulted in an indefensible distinction in law between the tests of recklessness applicable to various offences. To take an example based on *W (A Minor) v Dolbey*,[81] if D took an air rifle and, not even considering the possibility that it might be loaded (as was the fact), aimed and fired it at V, breaking V's spectacles and destroying his eye, D would, under *Caldwell*, have been be liable for causing criminal damage to the spectacles but would not have been criminally liable at all for the destruction of the eye. The law appeared to give greater protection to spectacles than to eyes.

Secondly, it failed to respect the principle that for serious crimes at least, the defendant should be proved to have a culpable state of mind. *Caldwell* allowed for conviction on the basis of D having no state of mind as to the risk of the proscribed harm. This most significant principled failing of the *Caldwell* approach was its potential to create injustice, and this led, ultimately to its downfall. The test worked harshly in cases of young people and those whose capacity to see risk was diminished for reasons which involved no fault on their part. For example, in *Stephenson*[82] a tramp sheltered in a hollow in a haystack. Feeling cold, he lit a fire in the hollow. The haystack was destroyed. Any reasonable person would have been aware of the risk but Stephenson was suffering from schizophrenia and may not have been aware of it. Because this was not clearly left to the

75 [1981] 1 All ER at 967. '(i)' and '(ii)' have been inserted by the authors.

76 According to the definition in *Lawrence* decided in the House on the same day.

77 The difference can be seen by considering post *G* cases applying *Cunningham* to overturn convictions where the direction had, erroneously, been based on *Caldwell*: eg *Castle* [2004] All ER (D) 289 (Oct); *Cooper* [2004] EWCA Crim 1382.

78 See S. Field and M. Lynn, 'The Capacity for Recklessness' (1992) 12 LS 74; S. Field and M. Lynn, 'Capacity Recklessness and the House of Lords' [1993] Crim LR 127.

79 To whom must the risk be obvious? Was it always necessary for the risk to be obvious to a reasonable person? What if D was an expert who would have foreseen the risk but the reasonable person would not have done. (See further the commentary on the decision of the Court of Appeal in *Reid* (1989) 91 Cr App R 263 at [1991] Crim LR 269, 271.) Was the degree of risk that ought to have been foreseen restricted to serious risks?

80 D. J. Birch, 'The Foresight Saga: The Biggest Mistake of All' [1988] Crim LR 4.

81 (1983) 88 Cr App R 1, [1983] Crim LR 681.

82 [1979] QB 695, [1979] 2 All ER 1198.

jury, the court – pre-*Caldwell* – quashed his conviction. Even if he had stopped to think it is possible that, because of his condition, he might not have realized that there was a risk of damage. *Stephenson* would have been decided differently under *Caldwell*. The objective test therefore had the potential to criminalize the blind person who damaged property being unaware of a risk which would have been obvious to a sighted person. And those with temporary handicaps – the person who strikes a match, being unaware because of his heavy cold, that the premises reek with petrol fumes could be convicted. *Caldwell* created a slippery slope to intolerable injustice with no obvious exit. Sir John Smith wrote of *Caldwell*: 'The decision sets back the law concerning the mental element in criminal damage in theory to before 1861.'[83]

R v G[84]

In *G*, Ds, aged 11 and 12 went camping without their parents' permission. During the night they set fire to newspapers in the yard at the back of a shop and threw the lit newspapers under a bin. They left without putting out the fire. The fire spread to the wheelie bin and to the shop causing £1m worth of damage. Ds' case was that they expected the newspapers to burn themselves out on the concrete floor. Neither appreciated the risk of the fire spreading as it did. They were charged with arson contrary to s 1(1) and (3) of the 1971 Act. The judge directed the jury in accordance with *Caldwell*, expressing reservations about that being a harsh test. The Court of Appeal upheld the convictions stating that *Caldwell* had been rightly applied and certified the issue of recklessness as one of general public importance. The House of Lords reviewed the history of the term 'recklessness' and unanimously overruled *Caldwell*. It was recognized that having regard to the Law Commission Report No 29 on which the Criminal Damage Act 1971 was based and the Parliamentary intent, the majority in *Caldwell* erred in concluding that 'reckless' in s 1 of the Act meant something different from 'maliciously' under the previous law. That subjective test of recklessness required proof that the accused had foreseen the risk and yet had gone on to take it.[85] That was a much broader conclusion than was necessary to dispose of the certified question. The decision in *Caldwell* was acknowledged to be based on 'fragile foundations' because the House of Lords were not referred to the Law Commission Report. Moreover, Lord Bingham in *G*, noted the fact that the majority decision in *Caldwell* had been in the face of a powerful dissent from Lord Edmund Davies, and had been subjected to sustained and cogent academic[86] and judicial criticism.[87]

Acknowledging the force of the principled criticisms outlined above, the House of Lords in *G* concluded that it should depart from *Caldwell* because it was 'just' to do so. *Caldwell* was castigated as being 'unfair', Lord Bingham referred to it as 'neither just nor

83 [1981] Crim LR 393.

84 For criticism see A. Halpin, *Definition in the Criminal Law* (2004), ch 3, especially pp 102–121. See also M. Davies, 'Lawmakers, Law Lords and Legal Fault' (2004) J Crim L 130, noting the 'delicious irony' that *G* was decided at a time when Parliament was introducing objective fault elements for serious sex offences in the Sexual Offences Act 2003.

85 *Cunningham* [1957] 2 QB 396.

86 See n 71 above.

87 Notably, Ackner LJ in *Stephen Malcolm R* (1984) 79 Cr App R 334, and Goff LJ in *Elliott v C (A Minor)* (1983) Cr App R 103.

moral', and Lord Steyn as a 'cynical strategy'. Lord Steyn also cited treaty obligations and the general shift in recent years towards greater subjectivity in *mens rea* as supporting the outright overruling of *Caldwell*. In short, as Lord Bingham observed, whilst it is clearly blameworthy to take a risk obvious to the individual, it is not 'clearly blameworthy' to do something involving a risk of harm when D has not perceived that risk.[88]

Their lordships rejected the narrower solution of a capacity-based exception to the *Caldwell* test. This approach had been suggested as a compromise between the subjectivism of *Cunningham* and the objectivism of *Caldwell*. It would have restricted *Caldwell* recklessness to cases in which D himself, having regard to his capacity to see risk, ought to have foreseen the risk of the proscribed harm. The House of Lords held that such an exception would be likely to create further difficulties in defining the relevant exceptional category, and would still impose liability generally on those who caused damage inadvertently. Lord Bingham noted that:

> . . . this refinement also has attractions, although it does not meet the objection of principle and does not represent a correct interpretation of the section. It is, in my opinion, open to the further objection of over-complicating the task of the jury (or bench of justices). It is one thing to decide whether a defendant can be believed when he says that the thought of a given risk never crossed his mind. It is another, and much more speculative, task to decide whether the risk would have been obvious to him if the thought had crossed his mind. The simpler the jury's task, the more likely is its verdict to be reliable.[89]

In practical terms, the House of Lords expressed concern at the complexity of *Caldwell* directions. Their lordships were confident that juries could be trusted to apply the *Cunningham* test without blindly accepting a defendant's assertion that he never thought of a certain risk when all the circumstances and probabilities and evidence of what he did and said at the time showed that he did or must have done. It was noted that there is nothing to suggest that this was seen as a problem before *Caldwell*.[90]

The decision is also welcome for its explicit adoption of the key provision from the Draft Criminal Code defining recklessness. Lord Bingham based his conclusion on the Draft Criminal Code, cl 18(c) as quoted above.

Does *Caldwell* still have a role to play?

At one stage in the mid-1980s it looked as if the *Caldwell* test was destined to be the principal form of recklessness in English law. Lord Roskill, when holding the *Caldwell/Lawrence* test to be applicable to manslaughter, said that 'reckless' should be given the *Caldwell* meaning in all offences, 'unless Parliament has otherwise ordained'.[91] Even before *G* it was clear that its application was much more limited. Lord Bingham explicitly limited his judgment in that case to overruling *Caldwell* in its application to criminal damage,[92] so the question remains, post-*G*, are there any offences to which the *Caldwell* formula applies? Other offences to which *Caldwell* had been applied included the Data

[88] Cf. Lord Rodger of Earlsferry, [69], 'there is much to be said for treating as reckless D who does not trouble his mind to a risk that would have been obvious to him', and see J. Horder, 'Two Histories and Four Hidden Principles of *Mens Rea*' (1997) 113 LQR 95.

[89] [38]. [90] [39].

[91] *Seymour* [1983] 2 All ER 1058 at 1064, HL. [92] [28].

Protection Act 1984, s 5[93] but that has now been repealed by the Data Protection Act 1998. *Halsbury's Laws* suggests *Caldwell* applies to the offence of recklessly providing false answers on being summoned for jury service,[94] and *Blackstone's Criminal Practice* (2003), immediately prior to *G* suggested *Caldwell* applied to recklessly making a declaration, etc which is false in a material particular;[95] recklessly giving false information in purported compliance with any obligation under the Misuse of Drugs Act,[96] and recklessly making a misleading or deceptive statement or forecast.[97] Although some authority supported these propositions, and it is submitted that there is now no basis for applying anything other than the test set out in the Draft Criminal Code, cl 18 as applied in *G*, to each of these offences.

In *Attorney-General's Reference (No 3 of 2003)*,[98] the Court of Appeal emphasized that although the House of Lords in *G* had stated that their decision was one specifically on recklessness under the Criminal Damage Act, 'general principles were laid down'. It was established that a defendant could not be culpable under the criminal law of doing something involving a risk of injury to another or damage to property if he genuinely did not perceive the risk.[99] The court refused to restrict the application of *G* to cases of positive action rather than those where liability arose by D's omission, and applied the subjective test to D's foresight of circumstances as well as consequences.

(iii) Subjective vs objective recklessness

The decision in *G* is important in reasserting the primacy of subjectivism, echoing other recent decisions in the House of Lords.[100] Lord Rodger acknowledged that there are academic arguments of substantial pedigree in favour of an objective approach to recklessness.[101] The choice is not simply between strict subjective and objective approaches. Many commentators have put forward a compromise position in which the unacceptable harshness of a purely objective test is avoided. These approaches seek to reflect D's culpability in failing to advert to a risk that would have been obvious *to him*, that is, one that to was within his capacity to recognize.[102] Alternative suggestions have included tests of 'practical indifference'.[103]

93 *Data Protection Registrar v Amnesty International* [1995] Crim LR 633.

94 Juries Act 1974, s 2.

95 Customs and Excise Management Act 1979, s 167(1).

96 Misuse of Drugs Act 1971, s 18(3).

97 Financial Services and Markets Act 2000, s 397(1)(c).

98 [2004] 2 Cr App R 367.

99 [12].

100 *DPP v B* [2000] AC 428; *R v K* [2002] 1 AC 462 (strict liability); *(Morgan) Smith* [2001] 1 AC 146 (provocation).

101 See Horder, above, n 71.

102 See H. L. A. Hart, 'Negligence, *Mens Rea* and Criminal Responsibility' in *Punishment and Responsibility* (1968).

103 R. A. Duff, *Intention, Agency and Criminal Liability* (1990), arguing that a test of practical indifference could be applied where D's conduct, 'including any conscious risk taking, any failure to notice an obvious risk created by her action and any unreasonable beliefs on which she acted, display a seriously culpable practical indifference to the interests which the agent's actions in fact threatened', p 172.

(iv) Indifference

'Indifference' is not required in the Law Commission's definitions. A person who knowingly takes an unreasonable risk of causing a forbidden result may hope, sincerely and fervently, that it will never happen; but he is, surely, reckless. In *Reid* Lord Goff suggested that a person may be indifferent to a risk without being aware of its existence.[104] Surely, however, the most we can say is that D would have been indifferent to the risk if he had been aware of it. Such a conclusion could usually be drawn only from evidence as to his general character and habits which the law of evidence does not allow.[105] It is submitted that indifference to a particular risk, where it is proved to exist, is an aggravating factor, but not an element in the definition of the required fault.[106]

(v) Reform

The Law Commission's draft Criminal Law Bill (cl 1) reproducing, with a slight modification, the definition in the Draft Code (cl 18(b)) provides that –

> a person acts –
>
> (b) 'recklessly' with respect to –
>
> (i) a circumstance, when he is aware of a risk that it exists or will exist, and
>
> (ii) a result when he is aware of a risk that it will occur,
>
> and it is unreasonable, having regard to the circumstances known to him, to take that risk . . .

The draft Criminal Law Bill would apply this definition to non-fatal offences against the person, and the draft Code Bill would apply it to criminal offences generally. That would result in a great simplification of the law. It is submitted that it would also be a great improvement.

(c) Negligence[107]

After *G* and the eradication of *Caldwell* and *Lawrence* it is possible once again confidently to draw a clear distinction between recklessness and negligence. Recklessness is the conscious taking of an unjustifiable risk, negligence the inadvertent taking of an unjustifiable risk. If D is aware of the risk and decides to take it, he is reckless; if he is unaware of the risk, but ought to have been aware of it, he is negligent. Where D did consider whether or not there was a risk and concluded, wrongly and unreasonably, that there was no risk, or so small a risk that it would have been justifiable to take it, he is negligent.

(d) Intention, recklessness and negligence as to circumstances

Intention, recklessness and negligence may all exist with respect to circumstances as well as consequences. Sometimes the law may require intention as to one or more elements of a crime yet be satisfied with recklessness or negligence as to another or others. In

104 (1992) 95 Cr App R 391, HL. L. Leigh, 'Recklessness after *Reid*' (1993) 56 MLR 208.

105 Cf the proposals by V. Tadros, 'Recklessness and the Duty to Take Care' in S. Shute and A. Simester (eds), *Criminal Law Theory* (2002) arguing that D should be liable if he did not fulfil his duty of investigating the risks which his 'background beliefs' led him to realize were present.

106 Cf *Gardiner* [1994] Crim LR 455 and commentary.

107 See Ch 6 below, and J. Brady, 'Recklessness, Negligence, Indifference and Awareness' (1980) 43 MLR 381.

obtaining by deception[108] D must intend to obtain, but he may be merely reckless whether the statement he makes is true or false. It would seem that, in determining whether D's fault amounted to intention, recklessness or negligence, the same criteria should be applied to circumstances as to consequences. So an act is intentional as to a circumstance[109] when D wants the circumstance to exist (where he hopes, perhaps faintly, that the letter he steals contains money, he intends to steal money)[110] or knows that it exists; or, if the broader view of intention[111] is accepted, he is virtually certain that it exists. He is reckless whether a circumstance exists or will exist when it is obvious that it may do so and he knows that. He is negligent with respect to a circumstance when, as a reasonable person, he ought to know that it exists or will exist and fails to do so, whether he has given thought to the question or not.

(e) Blameless inadvertence

Finally, a person may reasonably fail to foresee a consequence that follows from his act – as when a slight slap causes the death of an apparently healthy person; or reasonably fail to consider the possibility of the existence of a circumstance – as when goods, which are in fact stolen, are bought in the normal course of business from a trader of high repute.

3. Further principles of *mens rea*

Mens rea is a term which has no single meaning. Every crime has its own *mens rea* which can be ascertained only by reference to its statutory definition or the case law. The most we can do is to state a general principle, or presumption, which governs its definition. Since *G* we can say with confidence that, in crimes requiring *mens rea*, as distinct from negligence, the defendant should be liable only for that which he had *chosen* to bring about, or to take the risk of bringing about, that is, that he intended, or was reckless (in the subjective sense) as to whether all the elements of the offence, both results and circumstances, should occur or exist. Because he had so chosen, he could fairly be held responsible for the occurrence of the *actus reus*. His intention or recklessness as to all the elements of the offence was *mens rea* or the basic constituent of it.

The general principle is expressed in the draft Code as follows:

24—(1) Unless a contrary intention appears, a person does not commit a Code offence unless he acts intentionally, knowingly or recklessly in respect of each of its elements . . .

(a) The correspondence principle and constructive crime

The justification for requiring awareness of at least the possibility of *every* element is that it must be presumed that every element contributes to the criminality of it. If it does

[108] Below, p 742.

[109] This is not the same as saying that the circumstance is intended, because that implies a belief by D that he may be able to influence the existence of the circumstance; below, p 854.

[110] Salmond, *Jurisprudence* (11th edn), 411.

[111] Above, p 94.

not, it should not be there.[112] The requirement is therefore described as one of correspondence between the elements of *actus reus* and *mens rea*. This is an important aspect of the subjective approach to *mens rea*. The present law falls far short of precise correspondence in many offences. In many offences there are elements of the *actus reus* to which no corresponding *mens rea* attaches.

A concept similar to that embodied in cl 24(1) has been designated 'basic intent' by Lord Simon in *DPP v Morgan*:[113] 'By "crimes of basic intent" I mean those crimes whose definition expresses (or, more often implies) a *mens rea* which does not go beyond the *actus reus*.' Lord Simon's 'basic intent' does not go beyond but (it seems) does not necessarily go as far as the *actus reus* – it may not extend to every element of it. For this reason, and because it involves recklessness as well as intention, the term 'basic *mens rea*' is preferred.

Basic *mens rea*, as so defined, is not required for all crimes, for (i) even at common law there were many exceptions to it and (ii) statutory crimes are frequently interpreted so as to exclude the necessity for either intention or recklessness with respect to some one or more elements in the *actus reus*.

Sometimes the common law is satisfied by proof of the basic *mens rea* of a lesser offence than that charged – sometimes called 'constructive' crime. An intention to cause serious bodily harm is the *mens rea* of murder. There is no need to prove that D intended to cause, or was reckless whether he caused, death – although death is the crucial element in the definition. Lords Mustill and Steyn have criticized this rule as a 'conspicuous anomaly' and an example of 'constructive crime'.[114] Constructive crime (that is, where the *mens rea* of a lesser offence suffices for a greater) is, however, the general rule in offences against the person. Manslaughter may be committed by doing an unlawful and dangerous act which happens to cause death.

Statutes are sometimes similarly interpreted. D may be convicted of inflicting grievous bodily, if he foresaw some harm, not necessarily 'grievous', or of an assault occasioning actual bodily harm even though he foresaw no harm – the *mens rea* of common assault is enough.[115]

Some offences are so defined that intention with respect to only one or more elements in the definition of the *actus* is sufficient. Sometimes it is enough to prove only negligence; sometimes even this is not necessary and D may be convicted although he was blamelessly inadvertent as to a circumstance of the *actus reus*. In the latter case we shall say that the crime imposes 'strict liability' as to that circumstance.[116] The courts have long paid lip-service to, and sometimes applied, the presumption in favour of *mens rea*, but in the last few years *B* and *K* have given that presumption a new force. It is to apply unless it is excluded expressly or by *necessary* implication. It is not enough that the court thinks

112 A view criticized by J. Horder in writing eg on the requirement of *mens rea* as to age in sex crimes, [2001] Crim LR 15. See also the more general debate about the application of the correspondence principle and its merits: J. Horder, 'A Critique of the Correspondence Principle' [1995] Crim LR 759; B. Mitchell, 'In Defence of a Principle of Correspondence' [1999] Crim LR 195.

113 [1975] 2 All ER 347 at 363; contrasting the term with 'ulterior intent' as used in the third edition of this work and considered below.

114 In *A-G's Reference (No 3 of 1994)* [1998] 1 Cr App R 91, below, p 432 and *Powell and Daniels* [1999] AC 1, [1998] 1 Cr App R 261, below, p 191.

115 Cf the proposals of the Law Commission in its Report No 218, on offences against the person where the correspondence principle is respected in full. See Ch 16 below.

116 See Ch 7.

it would reasonable for Parliament to have excluded it. Though we have moved substantially closer to cl 24(1) this is far from being the end of strict liability, for example, the Sexual Offences Act 2003 introduces many offences where liability is strict in relation to a key element such as the age of the victim. Clause 24 remains an aspiration.

Recklessness and indifference to circumstances

There is a particular difficulty in requiring proof of subjective recklessness as to an *actus reus* element which is of a morally indifferent nature. The definition of a crime sometimes draws an arbitrary line, as to a person's age, or as to time, weight, size and other matters of degree. Ignorance of the law is no defence but there is no reason why a person who is unaware of the law should direct his mind to the question whether the arbitrary line has been crossed in the particular case.[117] The possessor of a shotgun has no reason to consider whether the barrel is less than 24 inches in length unless he knows that, if it is, possession without a firearms certificate is an offence.[118] The case is different in a material respect from that of the person who has a positive but mistaken belief that the shotgun is under that length. Williams[119] sought to resolve the difficulty by distinguishing between cases of 'mistaken belief' (where there is a positive belief) which will negative recklessness and 'simple ignorance' (where there is no advertence to the question) which will not. This distinction gained some support from *Caldwell.*[120] D can truly be said to be indifferent as to the circumstance – he does not care whether the barrel of the gun is more or less than 24 inches, because he is unaware that it matters. This principle, however, could only be properly applicable in respect of age, time, weight, size and other circumstances which everyone knows to exist in some degree. D knows that the barrel has length and, *ex hypothesi*, he does not care what it is. Where the circumstance is not simply a matter of degree but of kind, it is no longer possible to say that D was indifferent.[121] D may buy and deliver to V a book with an attractive cover without looking at the contents and without considering whether it might contain blasphemous and obscene material, but to infer that he was indifferent would be quite unwarranted. It might be that, when he learned the facts, he might be quite horrified.[122] An objective form of *mens rea* may be appropriate in such a case.[123]

(b) Ulterior intent

The principle stated in cl 24(1), by itself, would amount to a definition of the *mens rea* of many crimes, but it does not meet all cases. A crime is frequently so defined that the *mens rea* includes an intention to produce some further consequence beyond the *actus reus* of the crime in question. Burglary is an example. It is not enough that D intended to

[117] Cf Horder, above [2001] Crim LR 15.

[118] Firearms Act 1968, s 1.

[119] Williams, CLGP (1st edn) 122, (2nd edn) 151. Cf *A-G's Reference (No 1 of 1995)* [1996] 2 Cr App R 320, [1996] Crim LR 575.

[120] Above, p 104; cf *Pigg* (1982) 74 Cr App R at 358–359.

[121] There is an argument that in relation to sex offences V's being 16 renders D's acts towards her qualitatively different. See Horder, above.

[122] The possessor of the shotgun might be equally horrified when they learned the *law*, but that is not the same thing. We are considering recklessness as to facts, not law. Cf *Mousir* [1987] Crim LR 561 and commentary.

[123] Above, p 109.

enter a building as a trespasser, that is, to achieve the *actus reus* of burglary. It is necessary to go further and to show that D had the intention of committing one of a number of specified offences in the building. The actual commission of one of those offences is no part of the *actus reus* of burglary which is complete as soon as D enters. Causing grievous bodily harm with intent to resist the lawful apprehension of any person,[124] placing gunpowder near a building with intent to do bodily injury to any person,[125] are instances of similar crimes. Where such an ulterior intent must be proved, it is sometimes referred to as a 'specific intent'.[126] This term, however, is one which should be regarded with caution.[127] It is variously used to mean (i) whatever intention has to be proved to establish guilt of the particular crime before the court;[128] (ii) a 'direct' as distinct from an 'oblique' intention;[129] or (iii) an intention ulterior to the *actus reus*; or (iv) a crime where D may successfully plead lack of the prescribed *mens rea* notwithstanding the fact that he relies on evidence that he was intoxicated at the time.[130] The phrase 'ulterior intent' is therefore preferred to describe the third concept. The nature of the ulterior intent required varies widely from crime to crime – an intention to commit one of a number of specified offences in burglary, an intention to cause V to act to his prejudice in forgery, an intent permanently to deprive the owner in theft and so on.[131]

Where an ulterior intent is required, it is obvious that recklessness is not enough. On a charge of wounding with intent to cause grievous bodily harm, proof that D was reckless whether he caused grievous bodily harm will not suffice.[132]

It should again be emphasized that most crimes require only basic *mens rea* and no ulterior intent. In rape, for example, it is enough that the accused intentionally or recklessly perpetrated the *actus reus* – penile penetration of a person without her consent – and no ulterior intention need be proved. The result is that the best we can do by way of a general definition of *mens rea* is as follows: 'Intention, knowledge or recklessness with respect to all the elements of the offence *together with any ulterior intent which the definition of the crime requires.*'

(c) Transferred malice[133]

If D, with the *mens rea* of a particular crime, does an act which causes the *actus reus* of the same crime,[134] he is guilty, even though the result, in some respects, is an unintended one. D intends to murder X and, in the dusk, shoots at a man whom he believes to be X. He hits and kills the man at whom he aims, who is in fact V. In one sense this is obviously an

124 Offences Against the Person Act 1861, s 18. 125 Ibid, s 30.

126 See R. Perkins, 'A Rationale of *Mens Rea*' (1939) 52 Harv L Rev 905, 924.

127 See R. Cross, 'Specific Intent' [1961] Crim LR 510.

128 *DPP v Beard* [1920] AC 479 at 501–502; below, p 276.

129 Above, p 94. *Steane* [1947] KB 997 at 1004, [1947] 1 All ER 813 at 816.

130 Below, pp 276–281.

131 See J. Horder, 'Crimes of Ulterior Intent' in A. Simester and A. T. H. Smith (eds), *Harm and Culpability* (1996) 153, arguing for more crimes of this nature to reflect more accurately the moral differences in wrongdoing.

132 *Belfon* [1976] 3 All ER 46, where this passage was cited at p 49, [1976] 1 WLR 741, 744.

133 See A. Ashworth in *Reshaping the Criminal Law*, 77–94 and in *Crime, Proof and Punishment*, 45–70; G. Williams, 'Convictions and Fair Labelling' [1983] CLJ 85.

134 See *Hussain* [1969] 2 QB 567, [1969] 2 All ER 1117, [1969] Crim LR 433 and commentary; *Ellis, Street and Smith* [1987] Crim LR 44 and commentary; cf *Kundeus* (1976) 24 CCC (2d) 276 at 282–283.

unintended result; but D did intend to cause the *actus reus* which he has caused and he is guilty of murder. Again, D intends to enter a house, No 6 King Street, and steal therein. In the dark he mistakenly enters No 7. He is guilty of burglary.[135]

The law, however, carries this principle still farther. Suppose, now, that D, intending to murder X, shoots at a man who is in fact X, but *misses* and kills V[136] who, unknown to D, was standing close by. This is an unintended result in a different – and more fundamental – respect than the example considered above. Yet, once again, D, with the *mens rea* of a particular crime, has caused the *actus reus* of the same crime; and, once again, he is guilty of murder. So, where D struck X, who fell against V, who also fell and sustained a fatal injury, D was guilty of manslaughter: 'The criminality of the doer of the act is precisely the same whether it is [X] or [V] who dies.'[137] The application of the principle to cases of this second type is known as the doctrine of 'transferred malice'.

In *Latimer*,[138] D had a quarrel in a public house with X. He took off his belt and aimed a blow at X which struck him lightly, but the belt bounded off and struck V who was standing close by and wounded her severely. The jury found that the blow was unlawfully aimed at X, but that the striking of V 'was purely accidental and not such a consequence of the blow as the prisoner ought to have expected' – that is, he was not even negligent with respect to this result. It was held, on a case reserved, that D was properly convicted of unlawfully and maliciously wounding V.

It is important to notice the limitations of this doctrine. It operates only when the *actus reus* and the *mens rea* of the *same* crime coincide. If D, with the *mens rea* of one crime, does an act which causes the *actus reus* of a different crime, he cannot, as a general rule, be convicted of either offence. D shoots at V's dog with intent to kill it but misses and kills V who, unknown to D, was standing close by. Obviously he cannot be criminally liable for killing the dog, for he has not done so; nor can he be convicted of murder,[139] for he has not the *mens rea* for that crime. A similar result follows where D shoots at V with intent to kill him and, quite accidentally, kills V's dog: D is guilty of neither crime. In such a case D would be liable for attempting to murder V and the availability of the attempt charge in most cases prompts Ashworth to question whether the transferred malice doctrine is needed.[140]

In *Pembliton*[141] D was involved in a fight outside a public house, and, as a result, was charged with maliciously breaking a window. The jury found:

> that the prisoner threw the stone which broke the window, but that he threw it at the people he had been fighting with, intending to strike one or more of them with it, but not intending to break the window.[142]

His conviction was quashed by the Court for Crown Cases Reserved, for there was no finding that he had the *mens rea* of the crime, the *actus reus* of which he had caused. Lord Coleridge pointed out that it would have been different if there had been a finding that he

135 See *Wrigley* [1957] Crim LR 57.

136 What of the situation where D shoots at V intending to kill and does so, but the bullet continues and causes grievous bodily harm to X? Can D be convicted of grievous bodily harm to X? Or attempted murder of X?

137 *Mitchell* [1983] QB 741, [1983] 2 All ER 427, CA. Cf *Haystead v Chief Constable of Derbyshire* [2000] Crim LR 758, DC.

138 (1886) 17 QBD 359.

139 As to whether it could be manslaughter, see below, pp 472–482.

140 See n 133 above.

141 (1874) LR 2 CCR 119.

142 Ibid, at p 120.

was reckless as to the consequence which had occurred – but there was no such finding.[143] The intent which is transferred must be a *mens rea*, whether intention or recklessness. If D shoots X with intent to kill, because X is making a murderous attack on him and this is the only way in which he can preserve his own life, he does not intend an *actus reus* (in the broader sense, p 41, above), for to kill in these circumstances is justified. If, however, D misses X and inadvertently kills V, an innocent bystander, he does cause an *actus reus* but he is not guilty of murder for there is no *mens rea* (in the broader sense) to transfer; the result which he intended was a perfectly lawful one.[144]

In *A-G's Reference (No 3 of 1994)*[145] the Court of Appeal gave full effect to the doctrine as described above, declining to impose two limitations advocated by Glanville Williams:[146] (i) that 'an unexpected difference of mode will be regarded as severing the chain of causation if it is sufficiently removed from the intended mode'; and (ii) that the doctrine 'should be limited to cases where the consequence was brought about by negligence in relation to the actual victim'. In that case, D stabbed a pregnant woman whose child was born prematurely as a result of the stabbing and died in consequence of the premature birth. The fact that death resulted from premature birth, not directly from the stab wound, 'an unexpected difference of mode', was immaterial; as was the question whether D was negligent in relation to the child. In fact, D knew that the woman was pregnant but it seems that it would have made no difference if he had not known, and had had no reason to know that. His 'malice' against the mother was transferred to the child whose death he had in fact caused.

The House of Lords, unenthusiastically, confirmed the existence of this ancient principle of transferred malice but declined to extend it to what they regarded as a double transfer of intent – from the mother to the foetus, and from the foetus to the child. D was not guilty of murder. Remarkably, however, they held he might be convicted of manslaughter by an unlawful and dangerous act – the assault on the mother. This looks like the application of the just rejected doctrine of transferred malice. But D did not intend a merely unlawful and dangerous act. He intended to cause grievous bodily harm; and the act, done with that intention, admittedly caused death – which looks like murder.

(d) Coincidence of *actus reus* and *mens rea*[147]

The *mens rea* must coincide in point of time with the act which causes the *actus reus*.[148] 'If I happen to kill my neighbour accidentally, I do not become a murderer by thereafter expressing joy over his death. My happiness over the result is not the same as a willingness to commit the illegal act.'[149] *Mens rea* implies an intention to do a present act, not a future

143 Under *Caldwell*, recklessness was easy to establish in such a case and there was less need to rely on the doctrine of transferred malice.

144 Below, p 329; and cf *Gross* (1913) 23 Cox CC 455.

145 [1996] 1 Cr App R 351, [1996] Crim LR 268, below, p 432.

146 CLGP, 48. He would abolish the doctrine for criminal damage. It results in 'unfair labelling' where the property damaged is more valuable than the property D intended to damage. He would retain it for offences against the person: [1983] CLJ 85. Injury to one person is (presumably) as bad as the same injury to any other person.

147 G. Marston, 'Contemporaneity of Act and Intention' (1970) 86 LQR 208; A. R. White, 'The Identity and Time of the *Actus Reus*' [1977] Crim LR 148.

148 *Jakeman* (1982) 76 Cr App R 223, [1983] Crim LR 104 and commentary thereon.

149 Andanaes, CLGP of Norway, 194.

act.[150] Suppose that D is driving to V's house, bent on killing V. A person steps under the wheels of D's car, giving D no chance to avoid him, and is killed. It is V. Clearly, D is not guilty of murder. One who walks out of prison while in a state of automatism does not commit the offence of escape[151] by deliberately remaining at large.[152] Suppose that D, having resolved to kill his wife, V, prepares and conceals a poisoned apple with the intention of giving it to her tomorrow. She finds the apple today, eats it and dies. D is not guilty of murder. He might be guilty of manslaughter on the ground that the act of leaving the apple where it might be found was reckless or grossly negligent.[153] However, if D does an act with intent thereby to cause the *actus reus*, and does so, it is immaterial that he has repented before the *actus reus* occurs. Where D dispatched suitcases which she knew to contain cannabis from Ghana to London, her repentance before the importation took place was no defence.[154]

Where however D has, with *mens rea*, gone beyond mere preparation and is in the course of committing an offence, it should be no answer that the final step was involuntary or accidental – as where D is on the point of pulling the trigger with intent to murder and, being startled by an explosion, does so involuntarily.[155]

Where the *actus reus* of the crime charged is a continuing act, it is sufficient that D has *mens rea* during its continuance.[156] Where the *actus reus* is part of a larger transaction, it may be sufficient that D has *mens rea* during the transaction, though not at the moment the *actus reus* is accomplished. D inflicts a wound upon V with intent to kill him. Then, believing that he has killed V, he disposes, as he thinks, of the 'corpse'. In fact V was not killed by the wound but dies as a result of the act of disposal. D has undoubtedly caused the *actus reus* of murder by the act of disposal but he did not, at that time have *mens rea*. In an Indian and a Rhodesian[157] case it has been held, accordingly, that D must be acquitted of murder and convicted only of attempted murder. But in *Thabo Meli*[158] the Privy Council held that it was:

> impossible to divide up what was really one series of acts in this way. There is no doubt that the accused set out to do all these acts in order to achieve their plan, and as parts of their plan: and it is much too refined a ground of judgment to say that, because they were at a misapprehension at one stage and thought that their guilty purpose was achieved before it was achieved, therefore they are to escape the penalties of the law.

This suggests that the answer might be different where there was no antecedent plan to dispose of the body. *Thabo Meli* was distinguished on this ground in New Zealand[159] and, at first, in South Africa.[160] But in England, in *Church*[161] the Court of Criminal Appeal

150 'There is no law against a man's intending to commit a murder the day after tomorrow. The law only deals with conduct': R. M. Holmes, *The Criminal Law* (John Harvard edn) 54.

151 Sixth edition of this work, p 756.

152 *Scott* [1967] VR 276; discussed by C. Howard 'Escaping from Gaol' in [1967] Crim LR at 406.

153 Cf *Burke* [1987] Crim LR 480 and commentary at 484.

154 *Jakeman*, above. Cf *Wings Ltd v Ellis*, above, p 84.

155 See commentary on *Burke* [1987] Crim LR 480. Note the possibility of applying the *Miller* principle (above, Ch 4) where D has created the dangerous situation and comes under a duty to avert risk.

156 *Fagan v Metropolitan Police Comr* [1969] 1 QB 439, [1968] 3 All ER 442; above, p 84. Cf *Miller* [1983] 2 AC 161, [1983] 1 All ER 978, HL; *Singh (Gurdev) v R* [1974] 1 All ER 26, [1973] 1 WLR 1444, CA.

157 *Khandu* (1890) ILR 15 Bom 194; *Shorty* [1950] SR 280.

158 [1954] 1 All ER 373. Followed in *Moore and Dorn* [1975] Crim LR 229.

159 *Ramsay* [1967] NZLR 1005.

160 *Chiswibo* 1960 (2) SA 714.

161 [1966] 1 QB 59, [1965] 2 All ER 72.

applied *Thabo Meli* where D, in a sudden fight, knocked V unconscious and, wrongly believing her to be dead, threw her into the river where she drowned. He was charged with murder and his conviction for manslaughter was upheld. Here there was no antecedent plan. The point was not considered by the court, but it was apparently thought to be enough that the accused's conduct constituted 'a series of acts which culminated in [V's] death'. This is an extremely flexible approach to the principle of concurrence or contemporaneity as it is sometimes called, and it facilitates convictions in awkward fact scenarios.

In *Le Brun*[162] the court followed *Church*, holding that it was immaterial that there was no preconceived plan and that the same principles apply to manslaughter as to murder.[163] D, in a quarrel, knocked his wife unconscious and while attempting to drag her body away dropped and killed her. The jury were rightly told that they could convict of murder or manslaughter, depending on the intention with which the blow was struck, if D accidentally dropped V while (i) attempting to move her to her home against her wishes and/or (ii) attempting to dispose of her body or otherwise cover up the assault. The court appears to uphold the conviction on both of two alternative principles.

The transaction principle

This appears to be that D is guilty of homicide if he kills during the continuance of the transaction, the sequence of events initiated by the unlawful blow, and that the transaction continues at least during the conduct described under (i) and (ii) above. This suggests that it certainly continues while D is engaged in some kind of wrongdoing arising out of, and immediately following, the unlawful blow. Though the case does not decide this, the result might have been different if D had dropped V in the same manner and at the same time and place while attempting to get her to hospital, or to her home if he had thought that was where she would wish to be taken; or, if he believed her to be dead, while he was attempting to deliver the corpse to the police. Under this principle it is immaterial that the second act is the sole cause of death.

The causation principle

This holds that the initial blow is a cause of death. As that blow was struck with *mens rea*, there is no further problem – D is guilty of murder or manslaughter as the case may be. The second event was also a cause of death but it is clear that there may be more than one cause. This may suggest that Le Brun would have been guilty if V had been similarly dropped by a passer-by who was trying to get her to hospital. But it may be that an intervening act by a third party is regarded as breaking the chain of causation, particularly where it is unforeseeable, whereas the same thing done by the original actor is not.[164] The causation principle was the *ratio decidendi* of the South African case of *S v Masilela.*[165] D, intending to kill V, knocked him unconscious and, believing him to be dead, set fire to the house. V died from the fumes. If he had not been unconscious he would have been able to walk out, so knocking him unconscious was a cause of death. But

162 [1992] QB 61, [1991] 4 All ER 673.

163 In *A-G's Reference (No 4 of 1980)* [1981] 2 All ER 617 at 620, the court left open the question whether the principle applies to manslaughter and whether it was part of the *ratio decidendi* of *Church* that it does so.

164 See the passage, above, cited by the court in *Le Brun.*

165 1968 (2) SA 558 (AD).

it is probable that the chain of causation would be regarded as broken if the house had been set on fire by a tramp who happened to come along after D's departure.

In all these cases the second act was a cause of the death. Where it is impossible to say which act caused death, it has been held that D may be convicted only if it can be proved that he acted with *mens rea* (or other appropriate degree of fault) on both occasions. Where D knocked V downstairs and then, believing that he had killed her, cut her throat in order to dispose of the body, and it was impossible to say which act caused death, it was held that the jury should have been directed that they should convict of manslaughter if they were satisfied *both* (i) that knocking V downstairs was an intentional act which was unlawful and dangerous;[166] *and* (ii) that the act of cutting the throat was one of gross criminal negligence.[167] If manslaughter was committed, it was immaterial that it was impossible to prove on which of these two closely related occasions it occurred.[168] If the jury were not satisfied on both points, there was a 50 per cent chance that this was a case of accidental death, in which case acquittal must follow. But if *Thabo Meli* applies to manslaughter,[169] the direction is too favourable. Assuming it was all one 'transaction', it should have been enough to prove that D had the required *mens rea* on the first occasion.

(e) The relevance of motive

If D causes an *actus reus* with *mens rea*, he is guilty of the crime and on the orthodox view it is entirely irrelevant to his guilt that he had a good motive. The mother who kills her disabled and suffering child out of motives of compassion is just as guilty of murder as is the man who kills for gain or hatred. On the other hand, if either the *actus reus* or the *mens rea* of any crime is lacking, no motive, however evil, will make a man guilty of a crime. The orthodox view that motive should not be confused with *mens rea* has come under challenge.[170] An American writer has argued:[171]

> Suppose a grave felony is about to be committed under such circumstances that the killing of the offender to prevent the crime would be justified by law, and at that very moment he is shot and killed. If the slayer was prompted by the impulse to promote the social security by preventing the felony he is guilty of no offence; if he had no such impulse but merely acted upon the urge to satisfy an old grudge by killing a personal enemy, he is guilty of murder. The intent is the same in either case – to kill the person; the difference between innocence and guilt lies in the motive which prompted this intent.

It is submitted, however, that (assuming that D knew of the facts which justified the killing) this view is contrary to principle. If it were correct, it would seem to follow that D, the public executioner, would be guilty of murder in hanging X, who had been condemned to death by a competent court, if it were shown that D had postponed his retirement to carry out this particular execution because he had a grudge against X and

166 This is manslaughter. Below, p 474.

167 This may be considered to be manslaughter and indeed, was held to be so in this case. Below, p 474.

168 *A-G's Reference (No 4 of 1980)* [1981] 2 All ER 617, [1981] 1 WLR 705, CA, [1981] Crim LR 493 and commentary.

169 This question was left open. *Church* suggests that it does; and that seems right in principle.

170 See W. Wilson, *Central Issues* (2002), ch 5; A. Norrie, *Crime Reason and History* (2nd edn, 2000) 35–43; J. Horder, 'On the Irrelevance of Motive in Criminal Law' in J. Horder (ed), *Oxford Essays in Jurisprudence* (2000).

171 R. M. Perkins and R. N. Boyce, *Criminal Law* (3rd edn), 930.

derived particular pleasure from hanging him. This can hardly be the law. If a surgical operation, though dangerous to life, is clearly justifiable on medical grounds, a surgeon who performs it with all proper skill cannot be said to be guilty of attempted murder, or, if the patient dies, murder, because he hopes the patient will die so that he can marry his wife, or inherit his property, or so that the patient will avoid the thoroughly miserable life he will face if he survives.[172]

One of the difficulties in determining the relevance of motive in criminal law lies in the ambiguity of language. Sometimes, when we speak of motive, we mean an emotion such as jealousy or greed, and sometimes we mean a species of intention. For example, D intends (i) to put poison in his uncle's tea, (ii) to cause his uncle's death, and (iii) to inherit his money. We would normally say that (iii) is his motive. Applying our test of 'desired consequence' (iii) is certainly also intended. The reason why it is considered merely a motive is that it is a consequence ulterior to the *mens rea* and the *actus reus*; it is no part of the crime. If this criterion as to the nature of motive be adopted then it follows that motive, by definition, is irrelevant to criminal responsibility – that is, a person may be lawfully convicted of a crime whatever his motive may be, or even if he has no motive. The courts are not always consistent in their terminology. If D dismisses E, an employee, who has given evidence against him, in accordance with the terms of E's contract, D will be guilty of contempt of court, it is said, if his 'motive' was to punish E for his evidence but not if it was for any other reason – for example, incompetence or redundancy.[173] Consistency in terminology would suggest that in such a case we should speak of intent or purpose rather than motive. For example, if this variety of contempt were to be defined, the definition might say, 'with intent to punish the witness'.

In some exceptional cases motive does form an element of an offence. A new and conspicuous example is the 'racially aggravated offence' created by the Crime and Disorder Act 1998. Any of the existing offences specified in the Act[174] becomes a new racially aggravated offence with an enhanced penalty if, *inter alia*, 'the offence is motivated (wholly or partly) by hostility towards members of a racial group, based on their membership of that group.' In blackmail, contrary to the Theft Act 1968, s 21,[175] the accused's motive may be relevant in ascertaining whether his demand was unwarranted.[176] There are other circumstances in which motive may feature in the offence (for example, dishonesty) and defence (for example, the denial of provocation to the revenge killer).[177]

As *evidence*, motive is always relevant.[178] This means simply that, if the prosecution can prove that D had a motive for committing the crime, they may do so since the existence of a motive makes it more likely that D in fact did commit it. People do not usually act without a motive.

Motive is important again when the question of punishment is in issue. When the law allows the judge a discretion in sentencing, he will obviously be more leniently disposed towards the convicted person who acted with a good motive.

172 See A. T. H. Smith in *Reshaping the Criminal Law*, 95.

173 *A-G v Butterworth* [1963] 1 QB 696, [1962] 3 All ER 326, CA. Cf *Rooney v Snaresbrook Crown Court* (1978) 68 Cr App R 78, [1979] Crim LR 109.

174 See below, pp 557–559.

175 See below, Ch 20.

176 Cf *Adams*, below, p 803; *Chandler v DPP* [1964] AC 763.

177 This restriction is made explicit in the Law Commission's latest proposals, Ch 15 below.

178 *Williams* (1986) 84 Cr App R 299, CA, not following *Berry* (1986) 83 Cr App R 7.

(f) Ignorance of the law is no defence[179]

In our discussion of the general principles of *mens rea* nothing has been said about whether the accused knows his act is against the law, for, in the great majority of cases, it is irrelevant whether he knows it or not: '. . . the principle that ignorance of the law is no defence in crime' said Lord Bridge, 'is so fundamental that to construe the word "knowingly" in a criminal statute as requiring not merely knowledge of facts material to the offender's guilt, but also knowledge of the relevant law, would be revolutionary and, to my mind, wholly unacceptable.'[180] It must usually be proved that D intended to cause, or was reckless whether he caused, the event or state of affairs which, as a matter of fact, is forbidden by law; but it is quite immaterial to his conviction (though it may affect his punishment) whether he *knew* that the event or state of affairs was forbidden by law. This is so even though it also appears that D's ignorance of the law was quite reasonable and even, apparently, if it was quite impossible[181] for him to know of the prohibition in question. It was no defence for a native of Baghdad, charged with a sexual offence on board a ship lying in an English port, to show that the act was lawful in his own country and that he did not know English law.[182] It was held that a Frenchman might be guilty of murder in the course of duelling in England, even if he did not know that duelling was against English law.[183] In *Bailey*,[184] D was convicted of an offence created by a statute which was passed while he was on the high seas although he committed the act before the end of the voyage when he could not possibly have known of the statute.[185] In each of these cases it might be argued that D at least intended something immoral; but that makes no difference. A motorist's mistaken belief that a constable has no right in the particular circumstances to require a specimen of breath is not a reasonable excuse for not providing the specimen.[186] A mistaken belief that a firearms certificate was current was held to be incapable of being a reasonable excuse under the Firearms Act 1968, on the ground that it was a mistake of law.[187] Ignorance that certain banking transactions require the consent of the Bank of England is no defence to a charge of unauthorized deposit-taking.[188]

[179] See Ch 10, and A. Ashworth, 'Excusable Mistake of Law' [1974] Crim LR 652; M. Matthews, 'Ignorance of the Law is no Excuse' (1983) 3 LS 174.

[180] *Grant v Borg* [1982] 2 All ER 257 at 263, HL but cf *Curr* [1968] 2 QB 944, [1967] 1 All ER 478, below, p 355 where the court thought that a woman improperly receiving a family allowance payment was guilty only if she knew that what she was doing 'amounted to an offence'. But the section required only that she should know that the allowance was not 'properly payable'. Acts done by D to V in the reasonable belief that V was committing a bye-law offence may be justified even if it turns out that the byelaw was void for uncertainty: *Percy v Hall* [1997] QB 924, [1996] 4 All ER 523, CA (Civ Div).

[181] *Bailey*, below.

[182] *Esop* (1836) 7 C & P 456.

[183] *Barronet and Allain* (1852) Dears CC 51.

[184] (1800) Russ & Ry 1.

[185] But the judges recommended a pardon. Where a continuing act was made unlawful it was held that a reasonable time must be allowed for its discontinuance and that ignorance of the law was relevant to determine this question: *Burns v Nowell* (1880) 5 QBD 444. Cf above, p 74, n 252.

[186] *Reid* [1973] 3 All ER 1020, [1973] 1 WLR 1283, CA: '. . . if you choose at the street side to act out the part of Hampden, you have got to be right': per Scarman LJ.

[187] *Jones* [1995] 1 Cr App R 262. But was not this really a mistake of fact – though probably an unreasonable one?

[188] *A-G's Reference (No 1 of 1995) (B and F)* [1996] 2 Cr App R 320. The more difficult question was whether the ignorant directors 'consented' to the commission of the offence. Held, they did.

Few distinctions have given more difficulty than that between mistake of fact and mistake of law but the point has been little discussed in the present context. The decision in *Brutus v Cozens*[189] that the meaning of an ordinary word in a statute is not a question of law opens up exciting possibilities. If D studies the Public Order Act and concludes that the conduct in which he proposes to indulge is not 'insulting', but the court takes a different view, why cannot D rely on his mistake 'of fact'? It is thought that such a defence would be unsympathetically received by the courts and, indeed, regarded as subversive of the criminal law;[190] but, if it is accepted that *Brutus v Cozens* applies, it is difficult to see that it is bad in principle.

In the case of the most serious crimes the problem does not arise; everyone knows it is against the law to murder, rob or rape. In the case of many less serious crimes, however, a person may very easily, and without negligence, be ignorant that a particular act is a crime. In such cases there will usually be nothing immoral about the act; and the conviction of a morally innocent person requires justification. Various justifications for the rule have been advanced. Blackstone[191] thought that 'every person of discretion' may know the law – a proposition which is manifestly untrue today. Austin[192] based the rule upon the difficulty of disproving ignorance of the law, while Holmes,[193] who considered this no more difficult a question than many which are investigated in the courts, thought that to admit the plea would be to encourage ignorance of the law. A modern writer, Jerome Hall,[194] argues that to allow the defence would be to contradict one of the fundamental postulates of a legal order: that rules of law enforce objective meanings, to be ascertained by the courts:

> If that plea [*sc.* ignorance of the law] were valid, the consequence would be: whenever a defendant in a criminal case thought that the law was thus and so, he is to be treated as though the law were thus and so, that is, *the law actually is thus and so.*[195]

As Hall points out, the criminal law represents an objective code of ethics which must prevail over individual convictions and he therefore argues:[196]

> Thus, while a person who acts in accordance with his honest convictions is certainly not as culpable as one who commits a harm knowing it is wrong, it is also true that conscience sometimes leads one astray. *Mens rea* underlines the essential difference. Penal liability based on it implies the objective wrongness of the harm proscribed – regardless of motive or conviction. This may fall short of perfect justice but the ethics of a legal order must be objective.

Much modern legislation is devoid of moral content, apart from the moral obligation to obey the law. One who, being ignorant of the law, sells goods at a price in excess of the maximum fixed by statute could hardly be said to have been led astray by his conscience while the 'harm proscribed' lacks 'objective wrongness'.

189 [1973] AC 854, [1972] 2 All ER 1297, HL.

190 Cf *Sancoff v Halford* [1973] Qd R 25. (Belief that books were not obscene is a mistake of law.)

191 Commentaries, iv, 27.

192 *Lectures on Jurisprudence*, 497.

193 *The Common Law*, 48.

194 'Ignorance and Mistake in Criminal Law' (1957) 33 Ind LJ 1. Cf *General Principles*, 382–383.

195 33 Ind LJ at 19. In *Cooper v Simmons* (1862) 7 H & N 707 at 717 Martin B thought that to allow the defence would be 'to substitute the opinion of a person charged with a breach of the law for the law itself'.

196 Above at 22.

The common law rule is not universally followed and the arguments by which it is supported have been found 'not very convincing to those used to another system'.[197] In Scandinavian criminal law, ignorance of the law is, in varying degrees, a defence. Thus, in Norway, a man will not be excused for ignorance of 'the general rules of society which apply to everybody' or 'the special rules governing the business or activity in which the individual is engaged'. But 'a fisherman need not study the legislation on industry'; a servant may be excused for *bona fide* and reasonable obedience to illegal orders of his master; or a stranger for breaking a rule which he could not be expected to know about; or liability may be negatived because the legislation is very new, or its interpretation doubtful. Such rules seem to have much to commend them, compared with the rigid and uncompromising attitude of English law. They seek to relate guilt to moral responsibility in a way in which our rule does not.[198]

(g) Mistake of law may negative *mens rea*[199]

If D, with *mens rea*, causes the *actus reus*, he is guilty and it will not avail him to say that he did not know the *actus reus* was forbidden by the criminal law. But the *actus reus* may be so defined that a mistake of law may result in D's not being intentional or reckless with respect to some element in it and so in his not having *mens rea*. In such a case, his mistake, whether reasonable or not, is a defence. '... an honest belief in a certain state of things does afford a defence, including an honest though mistaken belief about legal rights.'[200] Unless the prosecution can prove that the mistake was not made, they have not established the requisite *mens rea*. If D is charged with intentionally or recklessly damaging property belonging to another, his honest belief, arising from a mistake of law, that the property is his own, is a defence. The court so held, in *Smith*,[201] not because of any special provision in the Criminal Damage Act but by 'applying the ordinary principles of *mens rea*'. In *Roberts v Inverness Local Authority*[202] D was acquitted of moving a cow from one district to another without a licence because he believed the two districts had been amalgamated into one. Likewise in *National Coal Board v Gamble*[203] it was accepted that a mistake by the weighbridge operator about his right to withhold the ticket (a question of civil law) might be 'a genuine belief in the existence of circumstances

197 Andenaes., '*Ignorantia Juris* in Scandinavian Law', in *Essays in Criminal Science* (ed Mueller), 217 at 222. For South African Law see *S v De Blom* 1977 (3) SA 513 (AD) discussed by C. Turpin [1978] CLJ 8.

198 An exception to the general rule is created by the Statutory Instruments Act 1946, s 3. See D. Lanham, 'Delegated Legislation and Publication' (1974) 37 MLR 510. On a charge brought under a statutory instrument it is a defence for D to prove that the instrument had not been issued at the time of the alleged offence; unless the Crown then proves that reasonable steps had been taken to bring it to the notice of the public, or persons likely to be affected by it, or D. See *Defiant Cycle Co Ltd v Newell* [1953] 2 All ER 38. The Privy Council has held that, in a jurisdiction where there is no similar provision, a person who is unaware that a ministerial order applying a prohibition to him has been made may set up his ignorance as a lack of *mens rea: Lim Chin Aik v R* [1963] AC 160, [1963] 1 All ER 223; above, p 75.

199 See Ch 10, p 290 below.

200 *Barrett and Barrett* (1980) 72 Cr App R 212 at 216, CA, below, p 127.

201 [1974] QB 354, [1974] 1 All ER 632, CA; below, p 283.

202 (1889) 27 SLR 198, discussed by Widgery LCJ in *Cambridgeshire and Isle of Ely County Council v Rust* [1972] 3 WLR 226 at 231. The LCJ treats the mistake as one of fact; but surely the boundaries of districts are determined by civil law.

203 [1959] 1 QB 11 at 25, per Devlin J. The facts are set out below, p 181.

which, if true, would negative an intention to aid.' A person does not 'act as auditor of a company at a time when he knows that he is disqualified for appointment to that office' if, through ignorance of the statutory provisions, he does not know he is disqualified.[204]

The crucial question will be, what is the *mens rea* required by the crime? A mistake negativing *mens rea* as to some element in the *actus reus* is no defence if the law does not require *mens rea* as to that element. Bigamy provides a good illustration. The *actus reus* is committed by one who 'being married, marries'. If D, knowing that he was already married to X, were to marry V, it would certainly be no defence for him to say that he thought the law allowed him more than one wife. That would be a mistake of criminal law. He intends, being married, to marry – the *actus reus* – and would simply be saying that he did not know that the *actus reus* was forbidden by the criminal law. If, misunderstanding the law of divorce, he wrongly supposed that his first marriage had been dissolved, he would not intend the *actus reus.* His mistake as to the law of divorce would negative basic *mens rea*; and, if bigamy required basic *mens rea*, it would be a defence. That would be a mistake of civil law. The leading case of *Tolson*,[205] however, decided that bigamy does not require *mens rea* as to the element, 'being married': the Crown need prove only that D intended to go through the alleged second ceremony; whereupon D had a defence if he believed, or may have believed, on reasonable grounds, that he was not married. It is probable that, after the cases of *B (A Minor) v DPP*[206] and *K*[207] an unreasonable mistake would excuse, if it may have been honestly made but no case has yet so decided. In an Australian case[208] D, a landlord, was charged with wilfully demanding as rent a sum which was irrecoverable under the relevant statute. D wrongly believed that he was entitled to charge any rent he pleased. Three judges thought the belief no defence: it was sufficient that D wilfully demanded that sum of money. But two judges thought that D's belief precluded the *mens rea* required; that a person cannot wilfully demand an *irrecoverable* rent unless he knows it is irrecoverable. 'The defendant who is not shown in such a case to know that the act is unlawful needs no excuse. The offence has not been proved against him.'[209]

This principle will operate only when the definition of the *actus reus* contains some legal concept like 'property belonging to another'. It has no application where the law fixes a standard which is different from that in which D believes. If he kills a trespasser it is no defence for him to assert that he believed the law allows deadly force to be used to expel trespassers.[210] It does not apply where D refuses, however honestly, to accept the judgment of a court,[211] just as it would be hopeless for him to argue that he did not accept the validity of an Act of Parliament. The principle is probably also confined to the case where the legal concept belongs to the civil law – as the notion of property ownership does – and not to the criminal law.[212] Suppose that X obtains goods from V by deception

204 *Secretary of State for Trade and Industry v Hart* [1982] 1 All ER 817, [1982] 1 WLR 481. Cf Juries Act 1974, s 20(5)(d).

205 (1889) 23 QBD 168, CCR.

206 [2000] 1 All ER 833, HL, at 836–838.

207 [2001] 3 All ER 897, HL, at 907.

208 *Iannella v French* (1968) 119 CLR 84.

209 At p 97, per Barwick CJ.

210 Cf *Barrett and Barrett* (1980) 72 Cr App R 212; below, p 127.

211 Ibid.

212 It seems that a distinction between mistakes of civil and mistakes of criminal law was found to be untenable in German law: *Honig* (1963) 54 J Cr L & Cr at 285. But the distinction taken in the text seems to be a necessary consequence of the concept of *mens rea.*

and gives them to D, who knows all the facts. We have already seen that it will not avail D to say he does not know handling stolen goods is a crime. Equally, it is thought it will not avail him to say that he did not know that it is against the criminal law to obtain goods by deception and that goods so obtained are 'stolen' for this purpose. 'Stolen' is a concept of the criminal, not the civil law, and ignorance of it is no defence.

On the other hand, the 'leave' granted to a visitor to remain in the United Kingdom looks like a civil law concept, but the House of Lords has held that a mistake of law is no answer to a charge of knowingly remaining without leave.[213]

(h) Absence of a 'claim of right' as an element in *mens rea*

Sometimes the *mens rea* of an offence is so defined as to require the absence of a claim of right. In other words, if D believed he had a right to do the act in question, he had no *mens rea* and therefore was not guilty of the crime. This defence will prevail even if D's belief is mistaken and is based upon an entirely wrong view of the law. It is available in a number of important crimes, including theft,[214] criminal damage to property,[215] and a number of other offences requiring wilfulness or fraud. This is in accordance with the ordinary principle that a mistake of law may, indirectly, operate as a defence by preventing the accused from having *mens rea* in acting as he did. It is important to notice the limits within which this defence operates. The mistake must be one which leads the accused to believe he has a right to act as he does; it is not enough that he simply believes his act is not a crime. Here too, the distinction between mistake as to the criminal and as to the civil law seems to be important. Thus if D, having read in an out-of-date book on criminal law that it is not stealing to take another's title deeds to land,[216] were to take V's deeds, thinking that this was a way in which he could injure V without any risk of being punished, he could, no doubt, be convicted of theft under s 1 of the Theft Act 1968. He had no claim of right. It would be otherwise if D, owing to a misunderstanding of the law of property, thought that the title deeds were his, and that V was wrongfully withholding them from him. Here, clearly, he had a claim of right. Thus, while a mistake as to the criminal law only will not give rise to a claim of right, an error as to the civil law may do so.

It certainly cannot be asserted with confidence that the absence of a claim of right is a *general* requirement of *mens rea*, as it is in the case of theft and the other crimes referred to above. The question will therefore be considered in relation to specific crimes discussed below.

(i) Proof of intention and foresight

There was formerly high authority[217] for the view that there is an irrebuttable presumption of law that a person foresees and intends the natural consequences of his acts. Proof that he did an act the natural consequence of which was death, was conclusive proof that

213 *Grant v Borg* [1982] 2 All ER 257, [1982] 1 WLR 638.

214 Below, p 645.

215 Below, p 890.

216 This was the rule at common law.

217 *DPP v Smith* [1961] AC 290, [1960] 3 All ER 161; below, p 437. The decision cannot be technically overruled by the Privy Council but five judges, all members of the House of Lords, declared that it was wrongly decided in *Frankland* [1987] AC 576, PC.

he intended to kill, in the absence of evidence of insanity or incapacity to form an intent. To what extent, if at all, this actually represented the law was disputed: but it is now clear beyond all doubt that it is not the law. The question in every case is as to the actual intention of the person charged at the time when he did the act. Section 8 of the Criminal Justice Act 1967 provides:

A court or jury in determining whether a person has committed an offence,

(a) shall not be bound to infer that he intended or foresaw a result of his actions by reason only of its being a natural and probable consequence of those actions; but

(b) shall decide whether he did intend or foresee that result by reference to all the evidence drawing such inferences from the evidence as appear proper in the circumstances.

To what extent intention or foresight need be proved in any particular case depends on the law relating to the crime which is in issue. Section 8 is concerned with *how* intention or foresight must be proved, not *when* it must be proved.[218] On a charge of unlawful act manslaughter, for example, it remains unnecessary to prove that D intended or foresaw that death was likely to result from his act.[219] The section was once construed so as to affect the substantive law of murder[220] but this was exceptional and it is now clear that it applies only to proof and never affects the substantive law.

Section 8 is confined to the *result* of D's actions. But no satisfactory distinction can be made between the results of an action and the relevant surrounding circumstances. In this connection at least, no attempt need be made to draw such a distinction because the decision of the House of Lords in *DPP v Morgan*[221] establishes that, as a matter of common law, the same principle applies to circumstances. It used to be said that a mistake of fact could be a defence only if it was reasonable but that is refuted by *Morgan*. It may now be taken to be settled that, once it is established that the definition of a crime requires a state of mind – intention, knowledge or *Cunningham* recklessness – with respect to particular elements of an offence, a mistake of fact or of law which is inconsistent with that state of mind is also incompatible with guilt and must lead to an acquittal. The significance of *Morgan*, as the courts have now belatedly recognized,[222] affects matters far beyond the law of rape (and indeed no longer affects the law of rape).

The first question in every case is, what *mens rea* does the definition of the crime in question require? Neither s 8 nor *Morgan* affect the answer to this question. What s 8 and *Morgan* do establish is that a failure to foresee consequences, whether reasonable or not (s 8), or a failure to know of circumstances, whether reasonable or not (*Morgan*) which negatives the *mens rea* of the offence requires acquittal. Where, on the other hand, the law does not require *mens rea*, s 8 and *Morgan* have no application. *Prince* and *Tolson*[223] were distinguished[224] and appeared to be unaffected, but, after *B* and *K*[225] it now appears that both concerned crimes requiring *mens rea*.

218 *DPP v Majewski* [1976] 2 All ER 142 at 151, 170.

219 *DPP v Newbury* [1977] AC 500, [1976] 2 All ER 365, HL.

220 *Hyam v DPP* [1975] AC 55, [1974] 2 All ER 41; above, p 99.

221 [1976] AC 182, [1975] 2 All ER 347; below, p 126.

222 *Beckford v R* [1988] AC 130, [1987] 3 All ER 425, PC. See J. C. Smith, 'The Triumph of Inexorable Logic' in Eoin O'Dell (ed), *Leading Cases of the Twentieth Century* (2000), p 294.

223 Above, p 123. 224 Lord Hailsham at 361–362. 225 Above, p 108.

The fundamental principle of *Morgan* is in no way inconsistent with the existence of crimes of negligence, where unreasonable mistakes will be no defence. That is a matter of policy and one which, ideally, should be decided in Parliament when the statutory definitions of crimes are approved.

It was said, with some justification, in 1982 that there had been a 'Retreat from *Morgan*'.[226] There was a tendency for the courts to say that *Morgan* was concerned only with the law of rape and laid down no general principle. In one case,[227] the Court of Appeal said, *obiter*, that D might have been convicted of doing an act with intent to evict a residential occupier although he believed that the person he intended to evict was not a residential occupier but a squatter, because there was no reasonable basis for his belief. So to hold would be to defy the 'inexorable logic' which Lord Hailsham found compelling in *Morgan*. Happily, the 'retreat' has now been stemmed and in *Beckford v R* the Privy Council has said:

> Looking back, *Morgan* can now be seen as a landmark decision in the development of the common law, returning the law to the path upon which it might have developed but for the inability of an accused to give evidence on his own behalf.[228]

It may now perhaps be safely assumed that the courts will give full effect to the principle of the case as described above.

(j) *Morgan* and defences

Beckford v R is of great importance in that it takes the principle of *Morgan* even further than the majority of the House were at that time prepared to go. In *Morgan* the defence was a simple denial of the prosecution's case. By charging rape, the prosecution alleged that D had intercourse with a person who did not consent and that he either knew that she did not consent or was reckless (at that time subjective recklessness was the prescribed *mens rea* for rape) whether she did so. D denied that he knew or was reckless, as alleged. There is another type of plea, more accurately described as a defence, where D admits the allegations made by the prosecution but asserts further facts which, in law, justify or excuse his action. Self-defence is an example. D admits that he intentionally killed or wounded V but asserts that he did so because V was making a deadly attack on him and this was the only way he could save his own life. It may transpire that D was mistaken. V was not in fact making a deadly attack. The law has long recognized that D's defence is still good if his mistaken belief of fact was based on reasonable grounds. Directions to juries and *dicta* in higher courts were consistent in asserting that the defence failed if there were no reasonable grounds for his belief. The majority of the House of Lords in *Morgan* did not intend to interfere with this rule. They were concerned with a mistake as to an element of the offence, this question related to a mistake as to an element of a defence. In *Beckford* the Privy Council rejected this distinction. They approved the ruling of Lane LCJ in *Gladstone Williams*.[229] Discussing the offence of assault, he said:

226 D. Cowley [1982] Crim LR 198.
227 *Phekoo* [1981] 3 All ER 84, [1981] 1 WLR 1117.
228 [1987] 3 All ER 425 at 431.
229 [1987] 3 All ER 411, 78 Cr App R 276, CA.

The mental element necessary to constitute guilt is the intent to apply unlawful force to the victim. We do not believe that the mental element can be substantiated by simply showing an intent to apply force and no more.[230]

If D believed, reasonably or not, in the existence of facts which would justify the force used in self-defence, he did not intend to use *unlawful* force. *Beckford* clearly applies to all instances of private defence.[231] However, in duress, for example, the courts continue to state that D's belief in the alleged compelling facts must be based on reasonable grounds.[232] If, however, D is to be judged on the facts as he believed them to be when he sets up self-defence it is difficult to see why it is different in principle when he sets up duress. In both cases D is saying that, on the facts as he believed them to be, his act was not an offence. It is submitted that the principle of *Beckford* should be applicable to defences generally.

Of earlier cases, that of the Divisional Court in *Albert v Lavin*[233] must, since *Beckford*, be taken to be wrong in making a distinction in relation to assault between the definitional elements of an offence and the definitional elements of a defence. The same subjective test applies to both, *Barrett and Barrett*[234] is more complex.

D was convicted of assault occasioning actual bodily harm to bailiffs who were executing a warrant to take possession of his house. D intended to assault the bailiffs but claimed that he was justified because he believed the court order had been obtained by fraud, though his application to have it set aside had been unsuccessful. Not surprisingly, this refusal to accept the judgment of the courts was held to be no defence. If D was making a mistake, it was one of law, admittedly the civil law,[235] but of a rather special kind. It does not necessarily follow that the result would have been the same if D had believed the men were not bailiffs at all but imposters, or that the court had made no order. He was entitled to use force to repel a trespasser. An honest belief arising from a mistake of fact, reasonable or not, that the men were trespassers should certainly have been an answer;[236] *Morgan* was discussed, in relation not to this, but to a second point. It was argued that D was justified because he honestly believed that the force the bailiffs were using was excessive. But a mistake as to the amount of force which the law permits is certainly a mistake of law which is incapable of founding a defence. If it were otherwise, every person would, in effect, fix his own standards, whereas standards are fixed by law. *Morgan*, properly understood, had nothing to do with either of these points and the court's remark that it was inapplicable because it related to rape was inapt. Indeed, the court spoke with approval of the *Tolson*[237] principle but, as they phrased it, it was the *Morgan*[238] principle – 'an honest belief in a certain state of things does afford a defence, including an honest though mistaken belief about legal rights' – not, be it noted, an honest *and reasonable* belief. The subjectivist could not ask for more; but the principle

230 This important ruling may be threatened by the Human Rights Act, Art 2 (right to life), setting a more demanding standard than 'honest belief', see below, Ch 11.B5.

231 Below, Ch 11.B5.

232 *Hasan* [2005] Crim LR (Oct); [2005] UKHL, below, Ch 11.B5.

233 [1982] AC 546, [1981] 1 All ER 628, DC.

234 (1980) 72 Cr App R 212.

235 See above, p 122.

236 *Blackburn v Bowering*, below, p 540.

237 See above, p 123, below, p 131.

238 Above, p 111.

was inapplicable here because (i) refusal to accept the validity of a court order, if it is properly called a mistake at all, is not the sort of mistake that a court can, as a matter of policy, admit as a defence; and (ii) standards are conclusively settled by the law.

Although s 8 requires the court to have regard to *all* the evidence, that is, all the evidence relevant to the question whether D did intend or foresee, the courts have consistently held that evidence that D did not intend or foresee because he had taken drink or drugs is no defence, except in the case of crimes requiring 'specific intent'. This practice has been reconciled with the words of s 8 by holding that there is a rule of substantive law that the prosecution need prove no *mens rea* where D relies on evidence that he had taken drink or drugs for the purpose of showing that he lacked any *mens rea*, not being a 'specific intent', which the definition of the crime requires in all other circumstances.[239]

It might be thought, at first sight, that proof of intention, foresight and knowledge presents almost insuperable difficulties. Direct evidence of a person's state of mind, except through his own confession, is not available. But the difficulties, in practice, are not so great. If D points a loaded gun at V's head, pulls the trigger and shoots him dead, it is reasonable to infer that D intended and foresaw V's death. A jury might well be convinced by such evidence that D intended to kill. If D offered an explanation of any kind – he thought the gun was unloaded, or he intended to fire above V's head – and the jury thought that it might reasonably be true, then they should acquit him of an intention to kill. If he offered no explanation, as s 8 makes clear, the jury would not be bound to convict him of having such an intention; they would have to ask themselves whether, in the light of all the evidence, they were satisfied beyond reasonable doubt. Sometimes D's acts may afford apparently overwhelming evidence of his intention to produce a particular result but evidence to the contrary is always admissible and the question must be left to the jury.[240] Similarly, the fact that any reasonable person would, in the circumstances, have known of a fact is cogent evidence that D knew of it.

The difficulty of distinguishing between 'he foresaw' and 'he ought to have foreseen', 'he knew' and 'he ought to have known', is not a good reason for not drawing the line at this point. It is an inescapable difficulty when we have a law which requires us to look into individual's minds; and such a requirement is essential to a civilized system of criminal law.

> ... a lack of confidence in the ability of a tribunal correctly to estimate evidence of states of mind and the like can never be sufficient ground for excluding from enquiry the most fundamental element in a rational and humane criminal code.[241]

239 *DPP v Majewski* [1977] AC 443, [1976] 2 All ER 142, HL.

240 *Riley* [1967] Crim LR 656, is a striking instance of the rebuttal of apparently conclusive evidence of an intent. Expert evidence was admitted that D was suffering from psychoneurosis; but in the case of a normal person expert evidence as to the operation of the mind is not admissible. It is a question for the jury: *Chard* (1971) 56 Cr App R 268, CA. Cf *Turner* [1975] QB 834, [1975] 1 All ER 70.

241 *Thomas v R* (1937) 59 CLR 279 at 309, per Dixon J.

6

Crimes of negligence[1]

1. Negligence as failure to comply with an objective standard

Intention, recklessness and negligence all involve a failure to comply with an objective standard of conduct; that is, they are all forms of fault. Where intention or *Cunningham/G* recklessness[2] is required, a state of mind must also be proved. The now discredited form of *Caldwell* recklessness was also said by the House of Lords to involve proof of a state of mind; but this is misleading. *Caldwell* recklessness was only a state of mind in the sense that *not* giving thought is a state of mind.[3] An important distinction between *Caldwell* recklessness and negligence was the subject of much of the debate over that much-maligned case. Whereas under *Caldwell* recklessness, D would not have been liable if he had given thought to the matter of risk, and wrongly concluded that there was no risk,[4] in a crime of negligence D would be liable. The evidence of D's personal state of mind is no answer. Negligence may be conclusively proved by simply showing that D's conduct failed to measure up to an objective standard. It is no answer for him to say, 'I considered whether there was a risk and decided there was none'. Where the risk is one that he ought to have foreseen, that is an admission of negligence.[5]

It is not necessary to prove that D did not foresee the risk. It could never be a defence to a charge of negligence to show that the dangerous/careless act was done recklessly or intentionally. If D were charged with manslaughter and the prosecution's case was that he killed V by gross negligence it is inconceivable that it could be a defence for him to say convincingly, 'I wasn't negligent; I *intended* to kill him' – or 'I took a quite deliberate risk of killing him'. The more blameworthy state of mind must include the less; so, if D failed to comply with the objective standard, he is liable whatever his state of mind.

(a) Purely objective standards?

Negligence is *conduct* that departs from the standard to be expected of a reasonable person. This is not to say that a person's state of mind is always completely irrelevant

[1] See generally, H. L. A. Hart, in *Punishment and Responsibility* (1968), ch VI, 'Negligence, *Mens Rea* and Criminal Responsibility'; liability for negligence in manslaughter and road traffic offences is considered in detail below, Ch 28.

[2] Above, p 102.

[3] Above, p 104. See G. Williams [1981] CLJ 252 at 256–258.

[4] Above, p 103.

[5] See generally J. Brady, 'Recklessness, Negligence, Indifference and Awareness' (1980) 43 MLR 381. Note also the conclusion in *A-G's Reference (No 2 of 1999)* [2000] QB 796, that it is not necessary to produce evidence of the 'state of mind' of the accused in a charge of gross negligence manslaughter.

when negligence is in issue. He may, for example, have special knowledge that an ordinary person would not possess. The question then is, whether a reasonable person, *with that knowledge*, would have acted as he did. For example, behaviour with a revolver that is possibly not negligent in the case of an ordinary person with no special knowledge might be grossly negligent if committed by a firearms expert.[6] However, this situation has to be treated with care. If D has *less* knowledge or capacity for foresight than the reasonable person this, it seems, will not generally help him; but if he has *more* knowledge or capacity for foresight, a higher standard will be expected of him. This principle receives statutory recognition in the Road Traffic Act 1988, s 2A(3), defining dangerous driving.[7] In deciding whether a driver drove dangerously, the standard is 'what would be expected of a competent and careful driver'; and, in determining that standard:

> . . . regard shall be had not only to the circumstances of which he could be expected to be aware, but also to any circumstances shown to be within the knowledge of the accused.

In the offence of harassment under the Protection from Harassment Act 1997, s 1(1)(b) read with s 1(2) imposes a requirement that the course of conduct (which is alleged to amount to harassment) must be one which D knew *or ought to have known* amounts to harassment and that the test of whether he knew or ought to have known is whether a reasonable person *in possession of the same information* would think the course of conduct did amount to harassment. In *C*,[8] the defendant, who was a paranoid schizophrenic, had performed the conduct for the offence by sending offensive letters to his MP, on at least two occasions. D was convicted and appealed on the basis that the judge should have directed the jury to consider his mental disorder as a relevant condition of the hypothetical reasonable man in s 1(2). The Court of Appeal held that s 1(2) involved a purely objective test relating to the reasonable person and reasonable conduct. D's illness was not relevant to that question. Section 1(2) seeks to endow the reasonable person with knowledge of circumstances that would render otherwise seemingly innocuous conduct harassing (for example, when D knows that previous advances towards V have been rejected and continues to send gifts). In such cases Ds inculpatory state of mind is taken into account. Why then should the reasonable person not also be possessed with knowledge about Ds *exculpatory* states of mind in order to assess whether the conduct is harassment? This is not the same as asking whether a reasonable person with the characteristics of the accused would regard it as harassment, particularly where the characteristic inhibits cognition of the wrongdoing.[9]

(b) Negligence as *mens rea*

Writers differ as to whether negligence can properly be described as *mens rea*. If the term is used simply as a compendious expression for the varieties of fault that may give rise to criminal liability, then it does of course include negligence. If it is taken in its more literal sense of 'guilty mind', the usage is inappropriate. It is sometimes argued that the absence

6 *Cf Lamb* [1967] 2 QB 981, [1967] 2 All ER 1282; below, p 473.

7 Below, p 1012.

8 [2001] Crim LR 845.

9 Arguably the strong policy grounds of protection on which the Act is founded justify the court's rejection of any attempt to diminish the objective stance under this offence.

of foresight or knowledge is just as much a state of mind as its presence;[10] but, since negligence may be proved without establishing anything as to what was going on in D's mind, it seems more appropriate and convenient to restrict the term to intention and recklessness and that is the sense in which it is used in this book. Crimes requiring *mens rea* are contrasted with crimes of negligence.

2. Negligence as the basis of liability

There are few serious crimes in English law in which negligence is the gist of the offence. Manslaughter and public nuisance are the most conspicuous examples, although arguably manslaughter is a separate form of offence because it requires 'gross negligence'. Generally, in serious crimes, intention or recklessness is required as to the central features of the offence, but negligence with respect to some subsidiary element in the *actus reus* is sometimes enough. So under s 9 of the Sexual Offences Act 2003, it is an offence intentionally to touch a person, B, under 16 where that touching is sexual and either B is under 16 and D *does not reasonably believe* that B is 16 or over, or B is under 13. The 'touching' at the core of the offence has to be shown to be intentional, but as to the circumstance of B's age (where between 13 and 16), it is expressly provided that D is guilty if he does not reasonably believe B to be over 16. An honest but unreasonable belief that B is over 16 is no excuse. Negligence with respect to that circumstantial element of the *actus reus* will suffice. Such a provision, as well as catching the negligent person, disposes of another difficult case. It deals satisfactorily with the case of D who does not advert to B's age at all (simple ignorance), for he cannot say that he reasonably believed B to be over 16.

It should be noted that the Sexual Offences Act, although moving from a purely subjective approach to recklessness as to consent has not produced an offence of rape (nor other offences in which the fault element is exclusively one of negligence). The question for the jury in rape is whether the prosecution has made them sure that the particular defendant did not have a reasonable belief in consent in all the circumstances including whether any steps *he* took to ascertain consent were reasonable, and whether he intentionally penetrated the victim.

(a) Negligent mistakes

The rule, once supposed to exist, that a mistake was never a defence unless it was reasonable, was capable of turning almost any crime into a crime of negligence; but *Morgan*,[11] *B (A Minor)*[12] and *K*[13] have established that there is no such general rule. For example, it was held that if D goes through a ceremony of marriage, believing wrongly but without reasonable grounds that she is not married because her husband is dead, or her marriage has been dissolved or annulled, she is guilty of bigamy.[14] This, in effect, was to turn bigamy into a crime of negligence so far as this element of the offence is concerned. D was to be held liable because he did not take sufficient care to ascertain that his first marriage

[10] Salmond on *Jurisprudence* (11th edn), 329. See also P. Brett, *An Inquiry into Criminal Guilt* (1963), 99.
[11] Above, p 125. [12] Above, p 87. [13] Above, p 123.
[14] *Tolson* (1889) 23 QBD 168, CCR; *Gould* [1968] 2 QB 65, [1968] 1 All ER 849.

was at an end, before going through the second ceremony. It appears that these cases would be decided differently today. D would be guilty only if she knew that her husband was or might be alive, or that her first marriage was or might be subsisting, as the case may be.

Occasionally, negligence *is* the central feature of the crime. Under the Road Traffic Act 1988, s 3, for example, it is an offence to drive a mechanically propelled vehicle on a road without due care and attention or without reasonable consideration for other persons using the road. On a charge of driving without due care, it is clear that negligence is the gist of the offence. This section, it has been held, establishes:

an objective standard, impersonal and universal, fixed in relation to the safety of other users of the highway. It is in no way related to the degree of proficiency or degree of experience to be attained by the individual driver.[15]

So a learner driver, who was 'exercising all the skill and attention to be expected from a person with his short experience' but who failed to attain the required standard, was held guilty. The offence may be committed by making an error of judgment of a kind that a reasonably prudent and skilful driver would not make. It will be noted that it is not necessary to prove that any harmful consequence ensued; it is enough to show that D drove in a manner in which a reasonable person would not have driven because he would have realized it involved an unjustifiable risk. The same considerations apply to the more serious offence of dangerous driving.

3. Degrees of negligence

It has been said that there can be no 'degrees of inadvertence when that word is used to denote a state of mind, since it means that in the man's mind there has been a complete absence of a particular thought, a nullity; and of nullity there can be no degrees'.[16]

It is true that there can be no degrees of inadvertence but there can be degrees of fault in failing to advert. The more obvious the risk and the greater D's capacity to advert to it, the greater the fault in failing to be aware of it. If negligence is regarded as non-attainment of a required standard of conduct then it is clear that there are degrees of it. One person may fall just short of the required standard, another may fall far short. The existence of degrees of negligence is recognized by s 2A of the Road Traffic Act 1988 (as substituted by the Road Traffic Act 1991)[17] when it provides that a person drives dangerously if:

(a) the way he drives falls far below what would be expected of a competent and careful driver, and

(b) it would be obvious to a competent and careful driver that driving in that way would be dangerous.

15 *McCrone v Riding* [1938] 1 All ER 157.

16 Kenny, *Outlines*, 39, criticized by Hart, above, who writes: 'Negligence is gross if the precautions to be taken against harm are very simple, such as persons who are but poorly endowed with physical and mental capacities can easily take'.

17 Below, Ch 28.

A driver whose driving falls below, but not *far* below what would be expected of a competent and careful driver is negligent and probably guilty of careless driving contrary to s 3 of the 1988 Act; but he is not sufficiently negligent to be guilty of the more serious offence of dangerous driving.

The fault required for the present offence of causing death by dangerous driving probably falls short of that required by the law of manslaughter as restated in *Adomako*:[18] that is, '. . . whether, having regard to the risk of death involved, the conduct of the defendant was so bad as in all the circumstances as to amount in [the jury's] judgment to a criminal act or omission'. There are two possible distinctions. First, driving may fall far below what would be expected of a competent and careful driver without involving any apparent risk *to life*. The only apparent risk may be to property but, if the driving unforeseeably causes death, that will amount to the Road Traffic Act offence. Second, the Road Traffic Act offence is not subject to the jury's assessment of its 'badness'. True, the jury find, or, more accurately, have to accept the judge's direction, that even careless driving is a 'criminal act'; but the principle in *Adomako* has to be read against the background that the crime charged is manslaughter; and clearly the jury will be looking to see whether the conduct is bad enough to amount to that very serious crime, not careless driving. Conceivably, a jury of motorists might think that the particular driving, though falling far below the standard expected of a competent and careful driver, ought *not* to amount to a crime. It would be their duty to convict of causing death by dangerous driving, but not of manslaughter.[19]

4. Should negligence be a ground of liability?

Distinguished academic writers have strongly contended that negligence should have no place in criminal liability.[20] Their arguments for the most part assume a clear-cut distinction between conscious and inadvertent risk-taking that clearly distinguishes *Cunningham/G* recklessness from negligence. *Caldwell* brought much inadvertent risk-taking within the criminal law, but it no longer has any application (although there are numerous serious offences with an objective element including for example: manslaughter, dangerous driving, many sexual offences under the Sexual Offences Act 2003, and money laundering offences under the Proceeds of Crime Act 2002). Turner acknowledges that negligence connotes that D was 'in some measure blameworthy, and that we should expect an ordinary reasonable man to foresee the possibility of the consequences and to regulate his conduct so as to avoid them';[21] however, he also contends that the moral test, on which criminal liability should be (and, indeed, is) based, is the proof of subjective fault of foresight of the consequences of one's conduct. Hall goes further and finds it difficult to accept that negligently caused harm reflects a moral fault.[22] He rejects the view that punishment stimulates care, arguing that the deterrent theory postulates a

[18] [1995] 1 AC 171, [1994] 3 All ER 79, [1994] Crim LR 757, HL, below, p 482.

[19] There has to be a risk of death for gross negligence manslaughter: *Misra* [2004] EWCA Crim 2375, [2005] Crim LR 234. Below Ch 14.

[20] See eg J. Hall, 'Negligent Behaviour Should be Excluded from Criminal Liability' (1963) 63 Col LR 632.

[21] MACL 207.

[22] *General Principles* 136.

person who weighs the possibility of punishment in the balance before acting; but the inadvertent harm-doer, by definition, does not do this. Hall appears to suggest that the courts themselves do not really believe that punishment deters negligence, pointing out that sentences, even for negligent homicides, are relatively light. He rejects the thesis that negligent persons may be ethically blameworthy in so far as they are insensitive to the rights of others. In the case of negligently caused car accidents, for example, he argues that it seems much more probable that a dull mind, slow reactions, awkwardness and other ethically irrelevant factors were the underlying cause.

Glanville Williams acknowledges that 'it is possible for punishment to bring about greater foresight, by causing the subject to stop and think before committing himself to a course of conduct'; but thinks that this justification does not go very far and that the law is wise in penalising negligence only exceptionally.

Lord Nicholls, rejecting the former rule that only a reasonable mistake will excuse, invoked a presumption against liability for mere negligence.

When [a person is held liable because his mistake, though negativing *mens rea*, was made without reasonable grounds] the defendant's 'fault' lies exclusively in falling short of an objective standard. His crime lies in his negligence. A statute may so provide expressly or by necessary implication. But this can have no place in a common law principle, of general application, which is concerned with the need for a mental element as an essential ingredient of a criminal offence.[23]

Hart, however, challenges the commonly accepted criterion of foresight. The reason why it is thought proper to punish (in most cases) the person who foresees the forbidden harm is that he can choose to cause it or not; but in some cases of negligence, at least, it may be said:

'he could have thought about what he was doing' with just as much rational confidence as one can say of an intentional wrong-doing, 'he could have done otherwise'.[24]

Hart's approach to negligence, however, differs from that so far generally adopted by the courts. He would not enforce an objective, external and impersonal standard which took no account of the individual's lack of capacity. He would recognize that punishment might be proper only if two questions are answered in the affirmative:[25]

(i) Did the accused fail to take those precautions which any reasonable man with normal capacities would in the circumstances have taken?

(ii) Could the accused, given his mental and physical capacities, have taken those precautions?

The only English case following this approach seems to be *Hudson*.[26] In deciding whether a man who had sexual intercourse with a defective woman, contrary to s 7 of the Sexual Offences Act 1956 (repealed) had 'no reason to suspect her to be a defective', the court was bound:

23 [2000] 1 All ER 833 at 837.

24 *Oxford Essays in Jurisprudence*, 29.

25 Ibid at 46. Hart was not advocating the punishment of negligence, only seeking to dispel the belief that negligence is a form of strict liability.

26 [1966] 1 QB 448, [1965 1 All ER 721. But see now the many offences under the Sexual Offences Act 2003 where the issue turns on the reasonableness of D's belief.

to take into account the accused himself. There may be cases of which this is not one, where there is evidence before the jury that the accused himself is a person of limited intelligence, or possibly suffering from some handicap which would prevent him from appreciating the state of affairs which an ordinary man might realize.

The decisions in *Caldwell* and *Lawrence* in 1981 were open to the interpretation that an 'obvious' risk meant obvious to the particular defendant but the courts soon put paid to that notion. 'Obvious' under that test meant obvious to the reasonable person, even if the defendant was a 14-year-old schoolgirl with a learning disability.[27] Some academics rely on the cases decided under *Caldwell* to support the argument that the courts are (and ought to be) amenable to an interpretation of the concept of the reasonable person that is not entirely objective. Thus, Simester and Sullivan argue that the reasonable man ought to be endowed with the personal physical characteristics of the particular accused.[28] Some further support for this might derive from the House of Lords decision in *G*. However, a response to this claim might be that these cases[29] are merely examples of the courts' desperate attempts to mitigate the harshness of the *Caldwell* formulation of recklessness which applied to serious offences, and that the cases do not provide support for any broader judicial willingness to subjectivise the test of negligence. In other contexts the court has rejected an opportunity to endow the reasonable man with the personal characteristics of the accused.[30] Attempts in other contexts to dilute the concept of the reasonable man have resulted in an unsatisfactory state of affairs.[31]

Hall[32] argues that negligence should be controlled in other ways – by re-examining whether negligent persons should be able to escape completely from the consequences of civil liability by insurance; by more vigorous control of licences to operate dangerous instrumentalities; and by more education and instruction.

The negligent handling of certain instruments – notably motor vehicles – can have such drastic consequences that society is almost bound to adopt any measures that seem to have a reasonable prospect of inducing greater care; and it seems reasonable to suppose that the threat of punishment does have an effect on the care used in the handling of such instruments.

(a) A halfway house?

In some Commonwealth jurisdictions there is a trend towards replacing strict liability by liability for negligence – the so-called 'halfway house' but the English courts have not followed that trend.[33] Courts in the Commonwealth have moved ahead of those in England. The lead came from Australia.[34] In Canada, the Supreme Court, in a notable

[27] *Elliott v C (A Minor)* [1983] 2 All ER 1005, DC, (1984) 79 Cr App R 334. *Stephen Malcolm R* (1984) 79 Cr App R 334.

[28] *Criminal Law Theory and Doctrine*, p 152.

[29] And those relating to driving such as *Reid* (1992) 95 Cr App R 391, HL.

[30] See eg *C* [2001] Crim LR 845 above. See more generally on negligence as an element of harassment, under the Protection from Harassment Act 1997, E. Finch, 'Stalking the Perfect Stalking Law: An Evaluation of the Efficacy of the Protection from Harassment Act 1997' [2002] Crim LR 703, 714.

[31] See the discussion in relation to provocation, below, p 451.

[32] 'Negligent behaviour should be excluded from Penal Liability' (1963) 63 Col LR 632.

[33] Below, p 161.

[34] *Maher v Musson* (1934) 52 CLR 100; *Proudman v Dayman* (1941) 67 CLR 536.

judgment delivered by Dickson J, held that public welfare offences *prima facie* fall into an intermediate class between offences requiring *mens rea* and offences 'of absolute liability'. The prosecution need prove only that D caused the *actus reus* but he may escape liability by proving that he took all reasonable care to avoid the commission of the offence.[35] Without going so far as to establish any general principle, in England Parliament has shown some inclination to move in this direction. The Trade Descriptions Act 1968 creates a number of offences, some of which replace earlier offences of strict liability, and s 24 provides that it is a defence to prove (i) that the commission of the offence was due (*inter alia*) to a mistake or accident and (ii) that D 'took all reasonable precautions and exercised all due diligence to avoid the commission of such an offence by himself or any person under his control'.[36] Thus, though the prosecution do not have to prove negligence, it is a defence for D to show that he was not negligent. Similar steps have been taken in the Misuse of Drugs Act 1971.[37]

Where there is no such express due diligence provision in a statute, it is unlikely that the courts will hold it to be implied. It is true that the House of Lords in *Sweet v Parsley*[38] looked favourably on the doctrine developed in Australia:[39]

> When a statutory prohibition is cast in terms which at first sight appear to impose strict responsibility, they should be understood merely as imposing responsibility for negligence but emphasising that the burden of rebutting negligence by affirmative proof of reasonable mistake rests upon the defendant.[40]

However, the courts have shown no inclination to put such a principle into practice. In *Gammon (Hong Kong) Ltd v Attorney-General of Hong Kong*,[41] the Privy Council, while stressing the need for very high standards of care, regarded the choice as a straight one between *mens rea* and strict liability. The decisions of the House of Lords in *B (A Minor) v DPP* and *K*[42] have probably ruled out any such 'halfway house' in English law. This is discussed in more detail in the next chapter.

35 *City of Sault Ste Marie* (1978) 40 CCC (2d) 353.

36 See generally D. L. Parry, 'Judicial Approaches to Due Diligence' [1995] Crim LR 695.

37 Below, p 152.

38 [1969] 1 All ER 347 at 351, per Lord Reid, at 357, per Lord Pearce and at 362, per Lord Diplock.

39 N 34, above.

40 G. Orchard, 'The Defence of Absence of Fault in Australasia and Canada', *Criminal Law Essays*, 114.

41 [1985] AC 1, [1984] 2 All ER 503 at 509.

42 Above, p 123.

7

Crimes of strict liability

1. The nature of strict liability

Crimes which do not require intention, recklessness or even negligence as to one or more elements in the *actus reus* are known as offences of strict liability or, sometimes, 'of absolute prohibition'.[1] An example is the Medicines Act 1968, s 58(2) which provides that no person shall sell by retail specified medicinal products except in accordance with a prescription given by an appropriate medical practitioner. In *Pharmaceutical Society of Great Britain v Storkwain Ltd*[2] D supplied specified drugs on prescriptions purporting to be signed by a Dr Irani. The prescriptions were forged. There was, therefore, no prescription given by an appropriate medical practitioner. There was no finding that D acted dishonestly, improperly or even negligently in acting on that prescription. So far as appeared, the forgery was sufficient to deceive the pharmacists without any shortcoming on their part. Yet the House of Lords held that the Divisional Court was right to direct the magistrate to convict.

The case which has been said[3] to be the first to impose strict liability is *Woodrow*.[4] D was found guilty of having in his possession adulterated tobacco, although he did not know it was adulterated. The prosecution emphasized the purpose of the statute – it was for the protection of the revenue – and the absence of 'knowingly' or any similar word in the form of the offence. The court relied on a section of the Act which empowered the Commissioners of Excise to forbear to prosecute where there was no 'intention of fraud or of offending against this Act' – the implication being that the crime was still committed even when there was no fraud or intention of offending against the Act. Parke B thought that the prosecution would very rarely be able to prove knowledge; and that the public inconvenience which would follow if they were required to do so would be greater

[1] For discussions of these offences, see J. Ll. Edwards, *Mens Rea*; F. Sayre, 'Public Welfare Offences' (1933) 33 Col LR 55; Howard, SR; Smith and Pearson, 'The Value of Strict Liability' [1969] Crim LR 516; Carson, 'Some Sociological Aspects of Strict Liability and the Enforcement of Factory Legislation' (1970) 33 MLR 396; B. Hogan, 'Criminal Liability without Fault' (1969, Leeds Univ Press); J. C. Smith, 'Responsibility in Criminal Law', in *Barbara Wootton, Essays in Her Honour* (ed Bean and Whynes, 1986) – hereinafter '*Wootton*' – 141; P. Brett, 'Strict Responsibility: Possible Solutions' (1974) 37 MLR 417; L. Leigh, *Strict and Vicarious Liability* (1982); J. Horder, 'Strict Liability, Statutory Construction and the Spirit of Liberty' (2002) 118 LQR 458.

[2] [1986] 2 All ER 635, HL discussed by B. S. Jackson in 'Storkwein: A Case Study in Strict Liability and Self Regulation' [1991] Crim LR 892, who shows that the Society's policy was to prosecute only where the pharmacist had not acted with due diligence; but the Society does not have a monopoly of the right to prosecute; and if, in practice, fault is required, should not the decision whether it exists be made in court? See also R. Cooke, 'Turning Points' (Hamlyn Lectures, 1997) 40.

[3] By F. Sayre, 'Public Welfare Offences' (1933) 33 Col LR 55.

[4] (1846) 15 M & W 404.

than the injustice to the individual if they were not. Even the exercise of reasonable care would not have saved D; according to Parke B, he was liable even if the adulteration was discoverable only by a 'nice chemical analysis'.[5] Notwithstanding the subsequent mass of case law, the considerations taken into account in this early case are very much the same as those which influence the decisions of the courts today: the purpose of the legislation, the precise statutory form of words in creating the offence and whether the offence would otherwise be impossible or almost impossible to prove.

In *Hobbs v Winchester Corpn*,[6] the plaintiff, a butcher, was suing for compensation for certain unsound meat which had been destroyed under the Public Health Act 1875. That Act provided that, where any person sustained damage in relation to any matter as to which he was not himself in default, full compensation should be paid. The question was: was the plaintiff in default? He was unaware, and he could not have discovered by any examination which he could reasonably be expected to make, that the meat was unsound. It was held by the Court of Appeal, reversing Channell J that the plaintiff was in default because he was guilty of the crime of selling unsound meat. Kennedy LJ said:[7]

> the clear object, the important object [of the statute] . . . is as far as possible to protect the buyer of that which, in the opinion at all events of most people, is a necessity of human life, from buying and consuming meat that is unwholesome and unfit for the food of man; and I should say that the natural inference from the statute and its object is that the peril to the butcher from innocently selling unsound meat is deemed by the legislature to be much less than the peril to the public which would follow from the necessity of proving in each case a *mens rea*.
>
> I think that the policy of the Act is this: that if a man chooses for profit to engage in a business which involves the offering for sale of that which may be deadly or injurious to health he must take that risk, and that it is not a sufficient defence for anyone who chooses to embark on such a business to say 'I could not have discovered the disease unless I had an analyst on the premises'.

In *Cundy v Le Cocq*[8] D was convicted of selling intoxicating liquor to a drunken person contrary to s 13 of the Licensing Act 1872. It was proved that D did not know the person was drunk and nothing had occurred to show that he was drunk. While some sections of the Act contained the word 'knowingly', s 13 did not do so. The Divisional Court held that it was not necessary to consider whether D knew, or had means of knowing, or could with ordinary care have detected, that the person served was drunk. If he served a drink to a person who was in fact drunk, he was guilty.

It was established in each of these cases that D was not even negligent. He intended to sell medicine or meat or liquor or to possess tobacco; but he was blamelessly unaware of the crucial fact in the *actus reus*.

Where an offence is one of strict liability, the prosecution not only *need* not tender evidence of *mens rea* as to that matter of strict liability, they *must* not. The evidence is

[5] The judges suggested that D might have taken a warranty from the person from whom he bought the tobacco, indemnifying him against the consequences of a prosecution (fine and forfeiture). But there are difficulties about this. In *Askey v Golden Wine Co Ltd* [1948] 2 All ER 35 at 38, Denning J said: 'It is . . . a principle of our law that the punishment inflicted by a criminal court is personal to the offender and that the civil courts will not entertain an action by the offender to recover an indemnity against consequences of that punishment'.

[6] [1910] 2 KB 471, CA.

[7] Ibid, at 483. Note the modern statutory defence, below, p 161.

[8] (1884) 13 QBD 207.

irrelevant and, as it shows the defendant to be at fault, it is prejudicial. In *Sandhu*,[9] D was charged with the strict liability offence of causing a listed building to be altered without authority. The prosecution were allowed to prove, over his objection, that he knew the work went beyond what was permitted. His conviction was quashed.

(a) Distinction from absolute liability

The term 'absolute prohibition' is misleading in so far as it suggests that an accused whose conduct has caused[10] an *actus reus* will necessarily be held liable. It is commonly said that 'no *mens rea*' need be proved in the case of these offences: 'D can be convicted on proof by P of *actus reus* only'.[11] It is only in an extreme case[12] that this is true. Lord Edmund-Davies said that '. . . an offence is regarded – and properly regarded – as one of strict liability if no *mens rea* need be proved as to a single element in the *actus reus*'.[13] By this test, even murder is an offence of strict liability because no *mens rea* is required as to the crucial element of death.[14] Murder, however, does require an intention to cause grievous bodily harm, the *mens rea* of a lesser offence and a substantial *mens rea*. *Prince*,[15] which was for so long regarded as the leading case on strict liability, always required a substantial mental element; liability was strict only as to the age of the girl. Liability as to one element (for example, the age of V) is also strict in many of the offences in the Sexual Offences Act 2003 (see below).

The single element as to which no *mens rea* is required will usually be one of great significance; but it by no means follows that *mens rea* should not be required as to the remaining constituents of the offence. In one of the leading cases, *Gammon (Hong Kong) Ltd v Attorney-General of Hong Kong*, construing the Hong Kong Building Ordinance, Lord Scarman said: 'Each provision clearly requires a degree of *mens rea*, but each is silent whether it is required in respect of all the facts which together constitute the offence created'. The Privy Council held that D was liable for deviating in a material way from the approved plan, even though there was no evidence that he knew that his act constituted a material deviation from the plan – liability as to that element was strict.[16] Liability is thus not 'absolute' and the term 'strict liability' will be preferred throughout this book.

9 [1997] Crim LR 288 and commentary. See *Hill* [1997] Crim LR 459 for commentary on the sentencing implications.

10 In *Kilbride v Lake* [1962] NZLR 590, discussed by M. Budd and A. Lynch, 'Voluntariness, Causation and Strict Liability' [1978] Crim LR 74. D was acquitted of permitting a vehicle not displaying a current warrant of fitness to be on the highway, when the warrant was detached during his absence. The court took the view that there was an *actus reus* (*sed quaere?*) but that D had not caused it and he was not liable even if the offence was one of strict liability. Cf *Parker v Alder* [1899] 1 QB 20; below, p 163; *Strowger v John* [1974] RTR 124.

11 Howard, SR 1.

12 *Larsonneur*, above, p 73.

13 *Whitehouse v Gay News Ltd* [1979] AC 617 at 656, [1979] 1 All ER 898 at 920, quoting the 4th edition of this book at 79.

14 It is for this reason that some eminent judges regard murder as an anomaly and an instance of 'constructive crime'. Above, p 112.

15 Above, p 125. The misleading proposition that an offence of strict liability requires no *mens rea* seems to have been the cause of the trial judge's difficulties in *Blackburn v Bowering* [1994] 3 All ER 380, below, p 540.

16 *Gammon (Hong Kong) Ltd v A-G of Hong Kong* [1985] AC 1, [1984] 2 All ER 503, PC.

(b) Common law and statute

Crimes of strict liability are almost invariably found in statutes. There are many thousands of these offences both triable on indictment[17] and in the magistrates' court.[18] Some commentators identify an increased use of such offences by Parliament in the regulatory sector.[19] It used to be said that there were only two exceptions at common law to the rule requiring *mens rea.* These were public nuisance and criminal libel. In the former any employer might be held liable for the act of his employee even though he himself did not know it had taken place; while in the latter a newspaper proprietor was liable for libels published by his employees without his authority or consent. Public nuisance, however, is an anomalous crime and is treated in several respects rather as if it were a civil action than an indictable offence; while in criminal libel the rule has been modified by the Libel Act 1843 which makes it a defence for the defendant to prove that the publication was without his authority, consent or knowledge and did not arise from want of due care or caution on his part. It will be noted, moreover, that both cases are instances of vicarious liability. To these two instances, we must add a third – contempt of court.[20] It is an offence to publish inaccurate reports of the evidence at a trial in such a manner that the jurors might be influenced in their decision, even though the publisher believes in good faith and on reasonable grounds that the reports are accurate.[21] Parliament has expressly recognized the existence of strict liability in this offence by the Contempt of Court Act 1981. 'The Strict Liability Rule', as the Act calls it, continues to be a rule of the common law, though it is to some extent qualified by the Act.

According to one view, blasphemy is another example of strict liability at common law. A minority of the House of Lords in *Lemon and Gay News Ltd*[22] thought that was the effect of the decision of the majority. The majority denied that this was so. A writing is blasphemous when it has a tendency to shock and outrage Christians. *Lemon* decides that it is unnecessary to prove that D was aware of this tendency. It is sufficient that he intentionally used words which, in fact, are likely to shock and outrage. It is submitted that the minority were right to regard this as the imposition of strict liability. D may be convicted although he is quite unaware that his act has the quality which makes it criminal. No one would deny that strict liability is imposed when a butcher is convicted of selling meat which is unfit for human consumption although he is unaware of the dangerous character of the meat. The case of the blasphemous libel seems to be the same in principle.[23] A similar decision has been made in respect of the related common law offence of outraging public decency.[24]

Apart from these instances, the common law generally required *mens rea,* though sometimes, the *mens rea* of a lesser offence as in the case of murder where intention to cause grievous bodily harm is sufficient. It is very different with statutory offences. In a

[17] A. Ashworth and M. Blake, 'The Presumption of Innocence in English Criminal Law' [1996] Crim LR 306 found almost half of the offences in *Archbold* were strict on one sense.

[18] See Justice, *Breaking the Rules* (1980).

[19] See R. Baldwin, 'The New Punitive Regulation' (2004) 67 MLR 351.

[20] *Evening Standard Co Ltd* [1954] 1 QB 578, [1954] 1 All ER 1026. D. Eady and A. T. H. Smith (eds), *Arlidge Eady and Smith on Contempt* (2nd edn, 1999), para 4–10.

[21] This too is sometimes said to be an instance of vicarious liability.

[22] [1979] AC 617, [1979] 1 All ER 898, [1979] Crim LR 311 and commentary.

[23] See [1979] Crim LR at 312.

[24] *Gibson* [1991] 1 All ER 439, below.

great many cases, the courts have held that Parliament intended to impose strict liability and have convicted defendants who lacked *mens rea*, not merely as to some subsidiary matter, but as to the central feature of the *actus reus* and who did not have the *mens rea* of any other offence. The validity of the imposition of strict liability was recognized by the House of Lords in *Warner v Metropolitan Police Comr*,[25] the first case on the point to reach the highest tribunal.

2. The presumption of *mens rea*

Since strict liability offences are almost always found in statutes, the courts, in enforcing them, profess merely to be implementing the intention of Parliament, express or implied, as they find it in the statute. This has frequently been mere lip-service. In 1958 Devlin J wrote:

> The fact is that Parliament has no intention whatever of troubling itself about *mens rea*. If it had, the thing would have been settled long ago. All that Parliament would have to do would be to use express words that left no room for implication. One is driven to the conclusion that the reason why Parliament has never done that is that it prefers to leave the point to the judges and does not want to legislate about it.[26]

The courts then have a fairly free hand in this matter. It is only rarely that the statute ruled out *mens rea* expressly or by necessary implication. When strict liability has been imposed, it has usually been because the judges considered it necessary or desirable in the public interest – exercising a legislative function. Whether the courts are prepared to continue to do Parliament's work for it seems, after recent developments, to be in doubt. In the past they have usually begun with a ritual incantation of the presumption in favour of *mens rea*, commonly the well-known statement by Wright J in *Sherras v De Rutzen*:[27]

> There is a presumption that *mens rea*, or evil intention, or knowledge of the wrongfulness of the act, is an essential ingredient in every offence; but that presumption is liable to be displaced either by the words of the statute creating the offence or by the subject-matter with which it deals, and both must be considered.

The courts have been very ready to find the presumption rebutted. The doctrine of *mens rea* is said[28] to have reached its nadir when even bigamy was held to be a crime of strict liability in *Wheat* (1921),[29] now happily overruled. The trend in the years before *Warner*[30] seems to have been in favour of strict liability; but Lord Reid in that case (where he dissented) and in *Sweet v Parsley*[31] powerfully reaffirmed the presumption: '. . . whenever a section is silent as to *mens rea* there is a presumption that, in order to give effect to

25 [1969] 2 AC 256, [1968] 2 All ER 256, Lord Reid (whose speech deserves careful study) dissenting on this issue. The case is more fully considered below, p 151.

26 *Samples of Lawmaking*, at 71. Cf G. C. Thornton, *Legislative Drafting*, at 264. Lord Reid in *Sweet v Parsley* [1969] 1 All ER 347 at 351.

27 [1895] 1 QB 918 at 921, below, p 147.

28 Williams, CLGP, 178.

29 [1921] 2 KB 119, overruled by *Gould* [1968] 2 QB 65, [1968] 1 All ER 849.

30 *Warner v Metropolitan Police Comr*, below, p 151.

31 [1970] AC 132, [1969] 1 All ER 347, HL, below, p 153 but the House again imposed strict liability in *Alphacell Ltd v Woodward* [1972] AC 824, [1972] 2 All ER 475; below, p 154.

the will of Parliament, we must read in words appropriate to require *mens rea*'; and '. . . it is a universal principle that if a penal provision is reasonably capable of two interpretations, that interpretation which is most favourable to the accused must be adopted'.[32] In 1980, in *Sheppard*,[33] Lord Diplock noted that, 'The climate of both parliamentary and judicial opinion has been growing less favourable to the recognition of absolute offences over the last few decades . . . '.[34]

Again, the effect on the practice of the courts does not seem to have been great. But we may well have reached a turning point with the decisions of the House in *B (A Minor) v DPP*[35] and *K*.[36] The case of *Prince* which had exercised so much influence for 125 years was declared to be discredited and a spent force.

(a) A twenty-first century revitalized presumption of *mens rea*[37]

In *B* Lord Hutton said: '. . . the test is not whether it is a reasonable implication that the statute rules out *mens rea* as a constituent part of the crime – the test is whether it is a *necessary* implication'.[38]

And in *K*, the House was as good as its word. Section 14 of the Sexual Offences Act 1956 (now repealed – indecent assault on a woman)[39] provided that neither a girl under 16 (s 14(2)) nor a defective (s 14(4)) could give a consent which would prevent an act being an assault for the purposes of the section. It was, however, a defence for the person who had acted indecently towards a consenting defective to prove that he did not know, and had no reason to suspect, her to be a defective. It necessarily followed that a person who failed to prove this was guilty although he honestly believed the woman was not a defective; that is, subject to the statutory defence, the section imposed strict liability on that person. Section 14(3) provided that where D had gone through a ceremony of marriage with V which was invalid because she was under 16, it was a defence for him to prove that he believed, and had reasonable cause to believe, her to be his wife. Again, it necessarily followed that a person who was unable to prove that is guilty, although he honestly believed the girl to be his wife; subject to the statutory defence, the section imposed strict liability. But in contrast, there was no statutory defence for the person who 'assaulted' the consenting girl under 16. Previous decisions over many years had held that, in this scenario, the section imposed unmitigated strict liability.

In *K* the House overruled those cases and decided that it was for the prosecution to prove that D did not have the honest belief he asserted that V was 16 or over. Full *mens rea* with respect to age was not excluded expressly or by necessary implication so it was required. Lord Bingham thought this result was not absurd but Lord Millett thought that, 'To afford a defendant who has not married the girl a more generous defence than one who believes he has is grotesque'.[40] Nevertheless, he concurred without reluctance in the

32 Per Lord Reid at 349–350.
33 [1980] 3 All ER 899 at 906.
34 [1969] 2 AC 256, [1968] 2 All ER 356.
35 [2000] 2 AC 428.
36 [2001] 3 All ER 897.
37 For strong criticism see J. Horder, 'How Culpability Can, and Cannot, Be Denied in Under-Age Sex Crimes' [2001] Crim LR 15, commenting that the decision in *B v DPP* 'flies in the face of legislation and case law across much of the rest of the common law world'; P. R. Glazebrook, 'How Old Do You Think She Was?' [2001] CLJ 26.
38 [2000] 1 All ER at 855 d–e.
39 Below, Ch 17.
40 [2001] 3 All ER 897 [43].

decision to do justice in the case before him. He, at least, seemed ready to abandon all pretence that he was implementing the intention of Parliament. Parliament had signally failed to discharge its responsibility.

Although the Sexual Offences Act 2003 reverses the effect of the decision by creating offences in which liability as to age is strict, the decisions afford a pre-eminence to the presumption which, if applied generally, could result in a substantial diminution of strict liability in English law. The principle of these decisions is not confined to offences of this type. The judges thought that: 'In principle, an age-related ingredient of a statutory offence stands on no different footing from any other ingredient'.[41]

The strength of the presumption of *mens rea* and of a requirement of *mens rea* in the subjective sense was endorsed in the strongest terms in *G*.[42] Lord Bingham observed:

> . . . it is a salutary principle that conviction of serious crime should depend on proof not simply that the defendant caused (by act or omission) an injurious result to another but familiar rule *actus non facit reum nisi mens sit rea*. The most obviously culpable state of mind is no doubt an intention to cause the injurious result, but knowing disregard of an appreciated and unacceptable risk of causing an injurious result or a deliberate closing of the mind to such risk would be readily accepted as culpable also. It is clearly blameworthy to take an obvious and significant risk of causing injury to another. But it is not clearly blameworthy to do something involving a risk of injury to another if (for reasons other than self-induced intoxication: *R v Majewski* one genuinely does not perceive the risk. Such a person may fairly be accused of stupidity or lack of imagination, but neither of those failings should expose him to conviction of serious crime or the risk of punishment.[43]

All offences of strict liability are vulnerable to challenge by the revitalized presumption.[44] A note of caution is, however, required because of the refusal, *obiter*, of some of their lordships in *K*[45] to apply the presumption to what was the offence of sexual intercourse with a girl under 13, an offence punishable with a maximum of life imprisonment, although there was nothing in the words of that section itself which could possibly exclude it. But, in *Kumar*[46] the Court of Appeal applied *B* and *K* to hold that the offence of buggery (under the 1956 Act, now repealed by the Sexual Offences Act 2003) did not impose strict liability as to the age of the participants. It would, however, be misleading to think that since *B* and *K*, the courts have consistently rejected strict liability. Far from it. There are numerous instances of provisions being interpreted as imposing strict liability as for example, in *Muhammed*[47] (materially contributing to insolvency by gambling carrying two years' imprisonment); *Matudi*,[48] (importing prohibited animal products); and *Hart v Anglian Water Services Ltd*[49] (causing sewage effluent to be discharged).

41 Lord Nicholls in *B* [2000] 2 AC 463, [2000] 1 All ER at 839. Lord Hobhouse in *K* [2001] 3 All ER at 911.

42 [2003] UKHL 50; [2004] 1 AC 1034.

43 [32]. Lord Steyn observed that the 'general tendency in modern times is towards adopting a subjective approach' [55].

44 A key contender must be the strictness as to age in offences of possession of indecent images of children, following *Land* [1999] QB 65, cf the commentary on *Smith and Jayson* [2002] Crim LR 659.

45 [2000] 1 All ER at 843g–h per Lord Steyn and 854h–j per Lord Hutton; [2001] 3 All ER [33] per Lord Bingham.

46 [2005] Crim LR 470.

47 [2003] EWCA Crim 1852, 2 WLR 1050.

48 [2004] EWCA Crim 697.

49 [2003] EWCA Crim 224.

(b) What *mens rea* is presumed

In stating the presumption the courts do not usually tell us what they mean by *mens rea*. A much cited statement is that of Cave J in *Tolson*:[50]

> At common law an honest . . .[51] belief in the existence of circumstances, which, if true, would make the act for which a prisoner is indicted an innocent act has always been held to be a good defence.

This is ambiguous. Does 'an innocent act' mean:

(a) not the crime charged or

(b) neither the crime charged nor some lesser offence or

(c) not a civil wrong or

(d) not a moral wrong?

Even the dissenting judge in *Prince*, Brett J, thought the *mens rea* of a lesser offence, if it had existed, (option (b)) would have been enough; and some judges thought (d) sufficed. In their view, Prince had *mens rea* because taking even an 18-year-old girl out of her father's possession would have been an immoral act.

The draft Criminal Code, cl 20, 'General requirement of fault', would provide a clear rule based on (a):

> (1) Every offence requires a fault element of recklessness with respect to each of its elements other than fault elements, unless otherwise provided.

If that were enacted, we would know exactly where we stood with respect to offences to which the Code applied. In the meantime there remains a degree of uncertainty.

3. Recognizing offences of strict liability

In divining the will of Parliament relating to the elements of *mens rea*, the courts have not adopted a clear and consistent approach. Indeed, Glazebrook has suggested that there is an 'all too familiar litany of vague overlapping criteria which from time out of mind has signally failed to compel from judges predictable consensus'.[52]

(a) The offence in its statutory context

One of the principal methods of determining if the presumption of *mens rea* is displaced is by reference to statutory formula. The decisions in *B* and *K* illustrate the supreme importance attached to the words of the statute. The presumption, we are told, 'can only be displaced by specific language, that is an express provision or a necessary implication'.[53] If that is taken literally many, if not most, cases of strict liability were wrongly decided; but it would be premature to jump to that conclusion.

50 (1889) 23 QBD 168, CCCR, at 181.

51 The words 'and reasonable' are omitted as being no longer applicable in the light of *B v DPP*.

52 'How Old Did You Think She Was?' [2001] CLJ 25.

53 Per Lord Steyn in *K*, para [32].

(i) Verbs importing a mental element

We have already noticed that a particular verb may imply a mental element.[54] The use of such a verb in the definition of an offence may import a requirement of fault when the use of a different verb with no such implication would result in an offence of strict liability.

A good illustration is provided by the offence for a person to 'use or cause or permit to be used' a motor vehicle in contravention of certain regulations. 'Using', 'causing' and 'permitting' are three separate offences. In *James & Son Ltd v Smee*[55] the court held that *using* a vehicle in contravention of a regulation (in that it had a defective braking system) was an offence of strict liability; but D was charged with *permitting* the use which, said the court, 'in our opinion, at once imports a state of mind'. A person might use a vehicle with defective brakes although he had no idea that the brakes were defective; but he would not properly be said to permit use with defective brakes unless he knew that the brakes were defective or, at least, was turning a blind eye to that fact. Unfortunately, the courts act inconsistently in their interpretation of this and similar words.

Another example is the offence of permitting a vehicle to be used without insurance, which is committed by a person who lends his car to another on condition that it is only driven by an insured driver, if it is in fact driven by a person who is uninsured. The court ignores the ordinary meaning of the word 'permit'. D who says: 'Here is my car, but you must not drive it until you have insurance' is taken to permit what he actually forbids driving without insurance.[56] In what appears to be the first case to reach the House of Lords, *Vehicle Inspectorate v Nuttall*[57] (employer (D) permitting driver to contravene rules regarding rest periods) it is said that the meaning depends on the context but it remains difficult to discern how and why the context operates. In *Nuttall* two judges held that D had a duty to take reasonable steps to detect and prevent breaches and that, if he failed to do so, he 'permitted'. Two judges thought that a mental element of recklessness, in the sense of not caring whether a breach took place, was required. What is reasonable is an objective question and D's opinion is irrelevant.[58]

Similar inconsistency is to be found in the interpretation of the verbs, 'suffer', 'allow' and 'cause'. It seems that the courts will generally give verbs their natural meaning, including any mental element they imply, unless they consider that social policy requires them to decide otherwise. Probably the danger to the public of uninsured driving is the reason for the courts' refusal to give effect to what they recognize in another social context to be the natural meaning of the words used by Parliament. But is uninsured driving a greater social evil than driving with defective brakes?

Knowledge is not necessarily the only mental element required. Does a person who knows that his premises are being used for producing or supplying drugs 'permit' if he does nothing about it? Is mere acquiescence enough?[59] Perhaps this is a case where the alternative verb, 'suffer', more appropriately describes the conduct.

54 Above, ch 5.
55 [1955] 1 QB 78, [1954] 3 All ER 273, DC. Cf *Lomas v Peek* [1947] 2 All ER 574.
56 *DPP v Fisher* [1991] Crim LR 787, distinguishing *Newbury v Davis* [1974] RTR 367.
57 [1999] 1 WLR 629, HL. Cf *Yorkshire Traction Co v Vehicle Inspectorate* [2001] RTR 518, DC.
58 *Brock and Wyner* [2001] Crim LR 320 (permitting premises to be used for supplying drugs).
59 *Bradbury* [1996] Crim LR 808.

(ii) The use of adverbs

'Knowingly'

The use of an adverb is a more explicit way of making clear that *mens rea* is required. The clearest word is 'knowingly'. Devlin J has said that 'knowingly' only says expressly what is normally implied[60] – it does expressly what the presumption in favour of *mens rea* would do by implication. The use of the word suggests that Parliament wanted to make sure that the courts would not find some reason for holding the presumption to be excluded – similarly where Parliament provides that it is an offence to 'knowingly permit' something to be done. Perhaps the word 'permit' would have been sufficient to import *mens rea* – but the draftsman was taking no chances.

When 'knowingly' is used, it should be difficult for any court to hold that *mens rea* is not required as to all the elements of the offence, though it might not extend to an exception clause in the definition of the crime.[61]

The requirement of 'knowingly' is satisfied by proof of what is sometimes called 'wilful blindness': 'it is always open to the tribunal of fact, when knowledge on the part of a defendant is required to be proved, to base a finding of knowledge on evidence that the defendant had deliberately shut his eyes to the obvious or refrained from enquiry because he suspected the truth but did not want to have his suspicion confirmed'.[62] Sometimes, however, the courts take a stricter view, as in handling stolen goods, below, Ch 22. In *Kwan Ping Bang*[63] it was accepted that proof of knowledge by inference is possible provided the inference was compelling – 'one (and the only one) that no reasonable man could fail to draw from the direct facts proved'.

'Wilfully'

The word 'wilfully' looks like a '*mens rea* word' and it is sometimes treated as such. D does not 'wilfully' obstruct a police officer simply because he does a deliberate act which in fact obstructs the officer; an intention to obstruct must be proved.[64] There are, however, cases in which the courts have imposed strict liability notwithstanding the use of this word. 'Wilful' in these cases is held to apply only to the act but not to some circumstance or consequence which is an element of the crime. D was held guilty of wilfully fishing in private water, although he believed there was public right to fish there;[65] of wilfully killing a house pigeon when he shot a bird, believing it was a wild pigeon;[66] and of wilfully destroying an oak tree in contravention of a tree preservation order when he was unaware of the order and believed that permission had been given for the tree to be felled.[67] In these cases, the fishing, the killing of a bird, the cutting down of a tree were all 'wilful' acts; but in none of them was the commission of the crime 'wilful'.

60 *Roper v Taylor's Central Garage (Exeter) Ltd* [1951] 2 TLR 284 at 288. See also S. Shute, 'Knowledge and Belief in the Criminal Law', in S. Shute and A. Simester (eds), *Criminal Law Theory* (2002).

61 Cf *Brooks v Mason* [1902] 2 KB 743, DC and *Wings Ltd v Ellis*, above p 84.

62 *Westminster City Council v Croyalgrange Ltd* [1986] 2 All ER 353 at 359, HL; *Manifest Shipping Co Ltd v Uni-Polaris Shipping Co Ltd* [2001] 1 All ER 743, HL.

63 [1979] AC 609, 615.

64 *Willmott v Atack* [1977] QB 498, [1976] 3 All ER 794, DC.

65 *Hudson v MacRae* (1863) 4 B & S 585, DC.

66 *Cotterill v Penn* [1936] 1 KB 53.

67 *Maidstone Borough Council v Mortimer* [1980] 3 All ER 552, DC.

In the most important recent authority, *Sheppard*,[68] Lord Diplock said that if the word is given such a narrow meaning it is otiose because, in the absence of the word and even in offences of strict liability, the law requires a voluntary – that is, a wilful – act. Its use should therefore imply that something more is required. In *Sheppard* it was held that 'wilfully' in s 1 of the Children and Young Persons Act 1933 was not to be limited to requiring an intention to do one of the physical acts described in the section (assault, ill-treat, etc) but must extend to the consequences ('in a manner likely to cause him unnecessary suffering or injury to health'). D was guilty of 'wilful neglect' by refraining from getting medical aid only if he knew there was a risk that the child's health might suffer or, where he was unaware of the risk, if he did not care whether the child might be in need of medical treatment or not. Following *Sheppard*, it is arguable that 'wilfully' should be construed to mean wilfully committing the crime; but in practice it is unlikely that the courts will consistently so hold. In *Attorney-General's Reference (No 3 of 2003)*[69] the court considered the House of Lords' interpretation of 'wilful neglect' in *Sheppard* in light of the decision in *G*.[70] The Court of Appeal emphasized that in its view *Sheppard* imposed a subjective test in which the characteristics of the individual defendant were to be taken into consideration in determining whether he 'did not care'.

(iii) Effect of usage of *mens rea* words in some sections but not others

Where a *mens rea* word is used in one section of a statute but not in another that may suggest that the second creates an offence of strict liability; but Lord Reid has said:

> It is also firmly established that the fact that other sections of the Act expressly require *mens rea*, for example because they contain the word 'knowingly', is not itself sufficient to justify a decision that a section which is silent as to *mens rea* creates an absolute offence.[71]

In *Sherras v De Rutzen*,[72] D was charged with supplying liquor to a constable on duty, contrary to s 16(2) of the Licensing Act 1872. The policeman was not wearing his armlet which, it was admitted, was an indication that he was off duty. D, who was in the habit – quite lawfully – of serving constables in uniform but without their armlets, made no enquiry and took it for granted that the policeman was off duty. Section 16(1) of the Act made it an offence for a licensee *knowingly* to harbour or suffer to remain on his premises any constable on duty. Section 16(2) did not include the word 'knowingly'. Yet D's conviction was quashed. Day J said that the only inference to be drawn was that under s 16(1) the prosecution had to prove knowledge, while under s 16(2) the defendant had to prove he had no knowledge.[73] Wright J made no attempt to reconcile the two subsections, contenting himself with pointing out that:[74]

68 [1981] AC 394, HL.

69 [2004] EWCA Crim 868, [2004] 2 Cr App R 23.

70 [2004] AC 1034.

71 *Sweet v Parsley* [1970] AC 132 at 149, [1969] 1 All ER 347.

72 [1895] 1 QB 918. Cf *Harding v Price* [1948] 1 KB 695, [1948] 1 All ER 283, DC (a defence to failure to report an accident to show that D did not know accident had occurred, even though word 'knowingly' in the Motor Car Act 1903 was omitted when the section was repealed and replaced by the Road Traffic Act 1930). Reliance was unsuccessfully placed on the effect of additional new sections on the meaning of the original provisions of an Act in *Blake* [1997] Crim LR 207.

73 This view was doubted by Devlin J in *Roper v Taylor's Central Garage* (above). If Day J intended to refer to the *evidential* burden only, the *dictum* is unobjectionable. See J. L. Edwards, *Mens Rea*, 90–97.

74 [1895] 1 QB 918 at 923.

if guilty knowledge is not necessary, no care on the part of the publican could save him from conviction . . . since it would be as easy for the constable to deny that he was on duty when asked, or to produce a forged permission from his superior officer as to remove his armlet before entering the public house.[75]

(b) The offence in its social context

In addition to the statutory form of the offence, the court must have regard to the context of the legislation and the purpose it was designed to serve, and this will be highly influential. Cases where strict liability was imposed primarily on social grounds may be even more vulnerable to attack after *B and K*. If *mens rea* is not ruled out expressly or by necessary implication from the text, it cannot, according to *dicta* in *K*, be excluded. As noted, this has not prevented the Court of Appeal imposing strict liability in *Muhammed* and *Matudi*.

(i) 'Real' or 'quasi' crime?[76]

Here an important matter is whether the court considers the offence to be a 'true' or 'real' crime or a 'quasi-crime'. Parliament makes no such distinction. An act either is, or it is not, declared by Parliament to be a crime.[77] Mitchell J said that he did not regard the offence of selling a lottery ticket to a child under 16 as 'truly criminal in character' although it was punishable on indictment with two years' imprisonment.[78] This is a peculiar notion of 'truth'. The truth is that it is a crime. It is the courts which take it upon themselves to decide whether it is 'real' or 'quasi' crime. They do so on the basis that an offence which, in the public eye, carries little or no stigma and does not involve 'the disgrace of criminality',[79] is only a quasi-crime. Then, strict liability may be imposed because 'it does not offend the ordinary man's sense of justice that moral guilt is not of the essence of the offence'.[80] In *Hart v Anglian Water*, the Court of Appeal suggested that breaches of the Water Resources Act 1991, were not of a 'non criminal' character.[80a] In *Sherras v De Rutzen* Wright J distinguished 'a class of acts . . . which are not criminal in any real sense, but are acts which in the public interest are prohibited under a penalty'.[81] Since we are assuming a defendant who is morally blameless, no stigma ought to attach to him anyway. In determining whether the offence involves a 'stigma', it is necessary to consider the case where the offence is committed intentionally. If Parliament prohibits the causing of results because it deems them in some measure harmful, the intentional causing of the harm in question probably deserves some measure of moral condemnation. Stigma attaches to, or should attach to, the person who deliberately sells lottery tickets to children or even the motorist who deliberately leaves his car in a parking space for longer than is permitted by law – it is an anti-social act, likely to cause inconvenience

75 A recent example of this criterion as a determinant of strict liability is the case of *Matudi* [2003] EWCA Crim 697, (2004) J Crim L 186 dealing with the importation of endangered species.

76 See J. Horder, 'Strict Liability, Statutory Construction and the Spirit of Liberty' (2002) 118 LQR 458, noting that regulatory offences are also stigmatizing for the accused.

77 See Ch 2, above.

78 *London Borough of Harrow v Shah* [2000] Crim LR 692, DC.

79 Per Lord Reid in *Warner v Metropolitan Police Comr* [1969] 2 AC 256 at 272.

80 Ibid cf *Wings Ltd v Ellis*, above, p 84. See also *Matudi* [2003] EWCA Crim 697.

80a [2003] EWCA Crim 224.

81 [1895] 1 QB 918 at 922.

to others. But few people, even 'right-thinking' people, would consider such an act so iniquitous, even when done intentionally, that the actor ought to be locked up or even shunned and avoided. Since offences of strict liability do not distinguish between degrees of fault and no fault at all, the conviction fixes the offender with whatever stigma might attach to an intentional offender.[82]

(ii) A crime of general or special prohibition?

A second factor which may be of great significance is whether the provision is of general application or relates only to those following a particular trade, profession or special activity (especially where D has voluntarily engaged in that activity). In the latter type of case, the court may be much more ready to hold such a 'regulatory offence' to impose strict liability. Lord Diplock put it as follows:[83]

> Where penal provisions are of general application to the conduct of ordinary citizens in the course of their everyday life, the presumption is that the standard of care required of them in informing themselves of facts which would make their conduct unlawful is that of the familiar common law duty of care. But where the subject-matter of a statute is the regulation of a particular activity involving potential danger to public health, safety or morals, in which citizens have a choice whether they participate or not, the court may feel driven to infer an intention of Parliament to impose, by penal sanctions, a higher duty of care on those who choose to participate and to place on them an obligation to take whatever measures may be necessary to prevent the prohibited act, without regard to those considerations of cost or business practicability which play a part in the determination of what would be required of them in order to fulfil the ordinary common law duty of care.

So we find most instances of strict liability in statutes regulating the sale of food, and drugs, the management of industrial activities, the conduct of licensed premises and the like. But the 'particular activity' may be one in which citizens generally engage, like driving a car. However, this is something which we choose to do and, as it involves potential danger to others, it is not inconsistent with this statement of principle that some offences regulating the conduct of motorists should be strict.

(iii) Possibility of compliance

According to Devlin J, it is:

> a safe general principle to follow . . . that where the punishment of an individual will not promote the observance of the law either by that individual or by others whose conduct he may reasonably be expected to influence, then, in the absence of clear and express words, such punishment is not intended.[84]

This principle has been restated many times, for example by the Privy Council in both *Lim Chin Aik*[85] and *Gammon (Hong Kong) Ltd v Attorney-General of Hong Kong*[86] and by the Divisional Court in *Pharmaceutical Society of Great Britain v Storkwain Ltd.*[87] But, if

[82] See J. C. Smith, in *Wootton*, 141 and in commentary on *B* at [2000] Crim LR 408. And see *Harrow v Shah*, above n 78.

[83] In *Sweet v Parsley* [1970] AC 132 at 163.

[84] *Reynolds v G. H. Austin & Sons Ltd* [1951] 2 KB 135, [1951] 1 All ER 606, DC.

[85] [1963] AC 160 at 174, [1963] 1 All ER 223 at 228.

[86] [1985] AC 1 at 14–15, [1984] 2 All ER 503 at 508–509.

[87] [1985] 3 All ER 4, approved by the House of Lords [1986] 2 All ER 635 at 640.

implemented, it would seem to require negligence, though not perhaps of a high degree, rather than impose strict liability. D, it appears, must be shown to have fallen short in some respect of the standard to be expected of him. But was the principle applied in *Storkwain*? Are pharmacists expected to keep a handwriting expert on the premises to scrutinize the prescriptions? Or to telephone the doctor each time they receive a prescription for confirmation that he wrote it?[88] In *Harrow v Shah* it was acknowledged that D had done all they could to ensure compliance with the law. What else could they do, except stop selling lottery tickets? Obviously the courts do not expect such wholly unreasonable steps to be taken – but how then can the principle be satisfied in such cases? The evidence from empirical studies is that strict liability is not necessarily successful in securing compliance with regulations.[89]

(iv) Social danger

Fourthly, and by no means least, the courts are influenced by the degree of social danger which, in their opinion, will follow from breach of the particular prohibition. They take judicial notice of the problems with which the country is confronted. The greater the degree of social danger, the more likely is the offence to be interpreted as one of strict liability. Inflation, drugs, road accidents and pollution are constantly brought to our attention as pressing evils; and in each case the judges have at times invoked strict liability as a protection for society.

Economic dangers and inflation

The economic dangers through which the country was passing were the basis of the decision in *St Margaret's Trust Ltd.*[90] In this case D Ltd, a finance company, was charged with disposing of a car on hire purchase without a deposit of at least 50 per cent of the purchase price having been paid as required by the Hire Purchase Order[91] then in force. A car dealer and his customers had fraudulently misled D Ltd into advancing more than 50 per cent by stating a falsely inflated price for the cars which were the subjects of the transactions. It was admitted that D Ltd had acted innocently throughout and supposed that a deposit of at least 50 per cent had been paid. The company was, nevertheless, convicted.

The reasons given by the court had very little to do with the words of the statute. It is true Donovan J said: 'The words of the order themselves are an express and unqualified prohibition of the acts done in this case by St Margaret's Trust Ltd.' But this means no more than that no such word as 'knowingly' was used. He went on:

> The object of the order was to help to defend the currency against the peril of inflation which, if unchecked, would bring disaster on the country. There is no need to elaborate this. The present generation has witnessed the collapse of the currency in other countries and the consequent chaos, misery and widespread ruin. It would not be at all surprising if Parliament, determined to

[88] It appears that in *Storkwain* the pharmacist, not knowing Dr Irani, *did* telephone the number on the prescription but it was false and he was deceived by the forger or his accomplice who answered: B. S. Jackson [1991] Crim LR at 895.

[89] G. Richardson, 'Effective Means of Regulating Industry Strict Liability for Regulating Crime: the empirical evidence' [1987] Crim LR 295.

[90] [1958] 2 All ER 289, [1958] 1 WLR 522.

[91] SI 1956/180. Revoked – no corresponding order in force.

prevent similar calamities here, enacted measures which it intended to be absolute prohibitions of acts which might increase the risk in however small a degree. Indeed that would be the natural expectation. There would be little point in enacting that no one should breach the defences against a flood, and at the same time excusing anyone who did it innocently.[92]

Dangerous drugs[93]

Legislation concerning dangerous drugs has had a chequered recent history. Lord Parker declared in 1966[94] that he took judicial notice of the fact that drugs are a great danger and the Divisional Court imposed strict liability of a most draconian character in a number of cases about that time. D was held to be guilty of being 'concerned in the management of premises used for the purpose of smoking cannabis' though he did not know and had no means of knowing that such smoking was taking place.[95] In other cases, it was held that D was guilty of being in unauthorized possession of a drug contrary to s 1(1) of the Drugs (Prevention of Misuse) Act 1964 if he knew he had control of a thing which was in fact a dangerous drug, even though he did not know, and had no reason to know, that it was either dangerous or a drug.[96] He might have reasonably believed that he had a bottle of sweets, but that would have been no defence.

Problems of possession

The first case on strict liability ever considered by the House of Lords, *Warner v Metropolitan Police Comr*[97] concerned possession of prohibited drugs. D, who sold scent as a sideline, collected two boxes which had been left for him at a cafe. One box contained scent, the other controlled drugs. D said he assumed both boxes contained scent. The jury were told that such a belief went only to mitigation. The Court of Appeal agreed. If D was in possession of the box and he knew the box contained something, he was in possession of the contents, whatever they were; and, as it was an 'absolute' offence, that was all the prosecution had to prove.

The House of Lords, Lord Reid dissenting, agreed with the courts below that s 1(1) of the 1964 Act created an 'absolute' offence, not requiring any *mens rea* as such. But it was, of course, necessary to prove the *actus reus*, that is, possession, and that involved proving a mental element. Lord Guest agreed with the Court of Appeal – D's knowledge that he had a box containing *something* under his control was enough – but the other judges held that more was required. Though D's possession of the box gave rise to a strong inference that he was in possession of the contents, that inference might be rebutted. Their Lordships' opinions are obscure and various but it seems that the inference certainly would be rebutted if (i) D believed the box contained scent, (ii) scent was something of 'a wholly different nature' from the drugs, (iii) D had no opportunity to ascertain its true nature, and (iv) he did not suspect there was 'anything wrong' with the contents. These issues (or at least some of them, for the majority of the House were far from being in complete

92 [1958] 2 All ER 289 at 293. Would the floodgates really have opened in this way, if the case had been decided differently?

93 See generally R. Fortson, *The Misuse of Drugs and Drug Trafficking Offences* (4th edn, 2002).

94 In *Yeandel v Fisher* [1966] 1 QB 440 at 446, [1965] 3 All ER 158 at 161.

95 *Yeandel v Fisher*, above.

96 Eg *Lockyer v Gibb* [1967] 2 QB 243, [1966] 2 All ER 653.

97 [1969] 2 AC 256, [1968] 2 All ER 356.

accord) ought to have been left to the jury and, as they had not, three judges held that there had been a misdirection but upheld the conviction under the proviso.

Possession is a neutral concept, not implying any kind of blame or fault but experience, especially in the old law of larceny, has shown that, when it becomes the determinant of guilt, it tends to acquire a refined and artificial meaning of great complexity. It seems the most obvious common sense to say that a person firmly grasping a parcel is in possession of it and a distinction between the parcel and its contents is too absurd to contemplate; but, if it is a grave offence merely to possess the contents, courts will strive to find means to say that an innocent person is not in possession, by refining the meaning of that concept. Of course, this problem would not arise if it were held that the offence required some element of fault – possession, as observed, is neutral and in itself incapable of being 'fault' – but, sadly, of all the judges involved, only Lord Reid was willing to take this sensible course. The result was another calamitous decision by the House.

The five speeches delivered in *Warner* differ so greatly and it is so difficult to make sense of parts of them that courts in later cases have found it impossible to extract a *ratio decidendi.* The law has been modified by the Misuse of Drugs Act 1971 but the onus remains on the Crown to prove possession and the Act has nothing to say about that concept. It has, however, influenced the approach of the courts. In *McNamara*[98] the Court of Appeal, while paying lip-service to the House of Lords, has gone back to the view of the Court of Appeal and the (on this issue) dissenting opinion of Lord Guest. D was in possession of a cardboard box containing cannabis resin. He said he thought it contained pornographic material. Because he knew he was in control of the box and that the box contained something he was in possession of cannabis. The court was able to reach this conclusion without qualm because it no longer followed that D was guilty of the offence. Under the Misuse of Drugs Act 1971, s 28, it was a defence to prove[99] that he neither believed nor suspected nor had reason to suspect that the thing of which he was in possession was a controlled drug.

McNamara provides a welcome simplification of the law where D knows he has the thing or a container with something in it but claims he thought it was something else. It does not solve the problem when he claims he was unaware of its existence. In *Warner*[100] there was unanimous agreement about a hypothetical case posed earlier by Lord Parker CJ[101] – if something is slipped into a woman's shopping basket and she has no idea that it is there, she is not in possession of it. It is easy to find authority in the vast case law on possession to contradict that proposition but Parker LCJ, the Court of Appeal and the House were entirely confident about it: the woman is in possession of the basket and the known contents but not the thing secretly inserted. The judges shrank from saying that the hypothetical woman was in possession of the thing because they were thinking of a packet of controlled drugs and, if she was in possession, she would have been guilty of a grave offence. If the thing were a box of chocolates dropped in by a friend as a birthday present it is unlikely that they would have hesitated to hold that she was in possession of it. Suppose that, before she discovered it, the box had been removed by a pickpocket,

98 (1988) 87 Cr App R 246, [1988] Crim LR 440 and commentary.

99 Interpreted, *obiter*, by the House of Lords in *Lambert* [2001] 3 All ER 577, [2002] AC 545 to mean not 'prove' but 'introduce evidence of' so as to comply with the Human Rights Act 1998.

100 [1969] 2 AC at 282, 286, 300, 303 and 311.

101 *Lockyer v Gibb* [1967] 2 QB 243 at 248.

would they have hesitated to hold that it was stolen from her (it was not stolen from anyone else) and that the pickpocket was a thief? Of course not. So far as possession is concerned, there is no rational distinction between the drugs and the chocolates.

In *Lewis*[102] it was held that the judge had not misdirected the jury by telling them that the tenant of a house might be found to be in possession of drugs found on the premises although he did not know they were there, provided he had had an opportunity to find out that they were. But there is no material difference between planting drugs in a person's house and planting them in her basket.[103] The decision seems to contradict the one thing on which their Lordships in *Warner* were unanimous. In introducing the idea of opportunity, the court relied on a statement of Lord Morris. But Lord Morris was dealing with a quite different question: possession, he said, was 'being *knowingly in control of a thing* in circumstances which have involved an opportunity (whether availed of or not) to learn or discover, at least in a general way, *what the thing is*'.[104] In *Lewis*, D was not knowingly in control of the thing.

Warner does not affect the law where the drug was not in a container. D must know he has the thing, but it is not necessary that he should know or comprehend its nature.[105] In *Marriott*[106] D was convicted of being in possession of 0.03 grains of cannabis adhering to a penknife. It was held that the jury had been wrongly directed that he was guilty if he knew he was in possession of the penknife. It was necessary to prove at least that he knew that there was some foreign matter adhering to the knife. The court thought that no further *mens rea* was necessary – so that the accused would be guilty if he thought the matter was tobacco or toffee – but now, under the Misuse of Drugs Act, it would be a defence for him to prove[107] that he neither believed, nor suspected, nor had reason to suspect, that the matter was a controlled drug.

Being concerned in the management of premises

The second case concerning strict liability to reach the House of Lords was *Sweet v Parsley*.[108] On this occasion, the House overruled the cases which decided that being 'concerned in the management of premises used for the purpose of smoking cannabis' is an offence of strict liability. D, a schoolmistress, was the subtenant of a farmhouse in the country. She let the rooms, retaining one room for her own use and visiting the farm occasionally to collect rent and see that all was well. Cannabis was smoked in the farmhouse but it was found as a fact that she had no knowledge whatever of this. The Divisional Court nevertheless dismissed her appeal. She was 'concerned in the management' and that was enough. The House quashed her conviction. The 'purpose' referred to in the section must be that of the person concerned in the management; and D had no such purpose. Only Lord Wilberforce was content to stop with this 'prosaic interpretation

102 (1987) 87 Cr App R 270, [1988] Crim LR 517 and commentary.

103 'First of all man does not have possession of something which has been put into his pocket or into his house without his knowledge': *McNamara* (1988) 87 Cr App R 246 at 248.

104 [1969] 2 AC at 289 (authors' italics).

105 *Boyesen* [1982] AC 768, [1982] 2 All ER 161. (It is immaterial how minute the quantity is provided only that it amounts to something and D knows he has it.)

106 [1971] 1 All ER 595, [1971] 1 WLR 187.

107 Interpreted, *obiter*, by the House of Lords in *Lambert* [2001] 3 All ER 577 to mean not 'prove' but 'introduce evidence of' so as to comply with the Human Rights Act 1998.

108 [1970] AC 132, [1969] 1 All ER 347.

of the paragraph'. The remainder relied, in varying degrees, on a presumption in favour of *mens rea*. The actual decision in *Warner* was not affected,[109] but the attitude of the House, with the exception of Lord Reid, who saw no reason to alter what he had said in the earlier case, is very different. The judges are no less sensitive to the public's view of injustice than to their need for protection; and, for once, a case of strict liability had excited public interest. The public outcry and sense of injustice may not have been without influence.[110]

The corresponding provisions of the Misuse of Drugs Act require *mens rea* and leave the onus of proof, where it belongs, with the Crown. It is an offence if an occupier[111] or person concerned in the management of premises 'knowingly permits or suffers' the smoking of cannabis and other specified activities in connection with drugs. The word 'knowingly' was introduced for the first time in the Act; but it does not alter the rule under the Dangerous Drugs Act 1965 that knowledge or wilful blindness is enough, but reasonable grounds for suspicion are not.[112]

Pollution[113]

In view of the current concern about pollution it is scarcely surprising that a modern example of strict liability should come from that area. In *Alphacell Ltd v Woodward*[114] the House of Lords held that D Ltd was guilty of causing polluted matter to enter a river, contrary to s 2(1)(a) of the Rivers (Prevention of Pollution) Act 1951.[115] They had built and operated settling tanks with an overflow channel into the river and provided pumps designed to prevent any overflow taking place. Because the pumps became obstructed with vegetation, an overflow of polluted water occurred. There was no evidence that D knew that pollution was taking place or that they had been in any way negligent. Lord Salmon stressed the public importance of preventing pollution and the risk of pollution from the vast and increasing number of riparian industries and said:[116]

> If . . . it were held to be the law that no conviction could be obtained under the 1951 Act unless the prosecution could discharge the often impossible onus of proving that the pollution was caused intentionally or negligently, a great deal of pollution would go unpunished and undeterred to the relief of many riparian factory owners. As a result, many rivers which are now filthy would become filthier still and many rivers which are now clean would lose their cleanliness.

109 *Fernandez* [1970] Crim LR 277 where it was held to be enough that D knew a package might contain some prohibited article and was prepared to take it, whatever the contents were.

110 '. . . fortunately the press in this country are vigilant to expose injustice . . .' per Lord Reid, *Sweet v Parsley*, above at 150.

111 The occupier is a person whose degree of control is sufficient to enable him to exclude anyone likely to commit an offence under the Act. It is not limited to persons in legal possession and includes a student with rooms in college: *Tao* [1977] QB 141, [1976] 3 All ER 65.

112 *Thomas* (1976) 63 Cr App R 65, [1976] Crim LR 517.

113 See recently C. Abbott, 'The Appropriateness of Strict Liability in Environmental Law' (2004) Environmental Law and Management 67.

114 [1972] AC 824, [1972] 2 All ER 475. Cf *Empress Car Co (Abertillery) Ltd v National Rivers Authority* [1998] 1 All ER 481, HL, above, p 59; *Maidstone Borough Council v Mortimer* [1980] 3 All ER 552, *Kirkland v Robinson* [1987] Crim LR 643, DC (possession of live wild birds an offence of strict liability under the Wildlife and Countryside Act 1981, s 1(1)(a), taking into account the outstanding social importance of an Act designed to protect the environment).

115 See now Water Resources Act 1991, s 85(1).

116 [1972] AC at 848.

In *Atkinson v Sir Alfred McAlpine & Son Ltd*[117] it was held that the company was guilty of failing to give written notice, as required by the Asbestos Regulations 1969, that they were going to undertake work involving crocidolite though they neither knew nor had reason to know that the work involved crocidolite. The court distinguished *Harding v Price*[118] where Lord Goddard CJ, holding that D was not guilty of failing to report an accident, the happening of which he was unaware, said:

If a statute contains an absolute prohibition against the doing of some act, as a general rule *mens rea* is not a constituent of the offence, but there is all the difference between prohibiting an act and imposing a duty to do something on the happening of a certain event. Unless a man knows that the event has happened, how can he carry out the duty imposed? . . . Any other view would lead to calling on a man to do the impossible.

In *McAlpine*, the court said that, unlike the accident, it was 'probably possible' to ascertain whether crocidolite was involved; but since they held that the mischief would not be met if 'knows or ought to know' were read into the regulation, it is clear that impossibility would not be regarded as a defence.

(c) The severity of the punishment

It is often argued that the provision for a severe maximum punishment shows that strict liability could not have been intended by Parliament. To some extent, this is in conflict with the principle previously discussed, since the provision for only a slight punishment would suggest that Parliament thought the social danger involved to be slight. In the recent case of *Muhammed*[119] accepting that materially contributing to the extent of insolvency by gambling was an offence of strict liability, the seriousness of the offence was described as the 'starting point' for the court in its determination. The court explained that the more serious the offence the greater the weight to be attached to the *mens rea* presumption and vice versa.

However, the courts do not seem to have been deterred in recent years from imposing strict liability in the case of offences carrying heavy maximum sentences – the offence under the Dangerous Drugs Act 1965 of which Sweet was convicted was punishable on indictment with 10 years' imprisonment and causing death by dangerous driving was punishable with five. The fact that an offence under s 58(2) of the Firearms Act 1968 was punishable with three years' imprisonment did not deter the court from holding that an honest and reasonable belief that the firearm was an antique was no defence.[120] In *Gammon (Hong Kong) Ltd v Attorney-General of Hong Kong*[121] the Privy Council admitted that the fact the offence was punishable with a fine of HK$250,000 and imprisonment for three years was 'a formidable point'; but found 'there is nothing inconsistent with the purpose of the ordinance in imposing severe penalties for offences of strict liability'. The House of Lords in *B and K* contemplated with equanimity strict

117 (1974) 16 KIR 220, [1974] Crim LR 668, DC.

118 [1948] 1 KB 695, [1948] 1 All ER 283, DC.

119 [2003] 2 WLR 105.

120 *Howells* [1977] QB 614, [1977] 3 All ER 417. Section 19 of the Act (carrying a firearm in a public place) also imposes strict liability, although the penalty is seven years: *Vann and Davis* [1996] Crim LR 52.

121 [1985] AC 1 at 17, [1984] 2 All ER 503 at 511.

liability for having sexual intercourse with a girl under 13 although the offence was punishable with life imprisonment.[122]

(d) Other factors

It is impossible to catalogue all factors but in addition to those above, factors influencing the court's decision as to whether the presumption is necessarily rebutted, include the presence of due diligence defences, the stigma of the offence,[123] and the ease of proof for the prosecution unless strict liability is imposed. This factor must be treated with caution since logically, it would allow for strict liability in for example murder because the prosecution face a difficult task in proving D's *mens rea* of intention.

(i) Liability is strict, not 'absolute'

It was observed at the beginning of this chapter that the need for a mental element is not ruled out completely by the fact that an offence is one of strict liability. It may be necessary to prove that D was aware of all the circumstances of the offence save that in respect of which strict liability was imposed. When the court holds that it is an offence of strict liability to sell meat which is unfit for human consumption, it decides that a reasonable mistake as to that particular fact is not a defence. It does not decide that any other defence is unavailable to D; and indeed, we have seen that a mistake as to other circumstances of the *actus reus* may afford a defence.[124] There is no reason why all other defences should not be available as they are in the case of offences requiring full *mens rea.* Even when the former offence of dangerous driving was thought to impose strict liability,[125] it was held to be a defence if D was in a state of automatism when he 'drove' the vehicle.[126] It is perfectly clear that a child under the age of 10 could in no circumstances be convicted of an offence of strict liability[127] and it is submitted that a child between 10 and 14 could before 1998 be convicted only if it were proved that he knew his act was 'wrong'.[128] It is submitted, therefore, that other general defences – insanity,[129] necessity,[130] duress[131] and coercion – should be available equally on a charge of an offence of strict liability as in the case of any other offence.[132]

122 *B and K*, above, p 142.

123 See *Barnfather* (below, n 137). In terms of the potential use of strict liability offences as evidence of D's bad character see *Goss* [2005] Crim LR 61.

124 Above, p 122.

125 Cf *Gosney* [1971] 3 All ER 220.

126 *Hill v Baxter* [1958] 1 QB 277, [1958] 1 All ER 193; *Budd* [1962] Crim LR 49; *Watmore v Jenkins* [1962] 2 QB 572, [1962] 2 All ER 868.

127 Below, p 295.

128 Below, p 296. Cf Cave J in *Tolson* (1889) 23 QBD 168 at 182 and Lord Diplock in *Sweet v Parsley* [1969] 1 All ER 347 at 361.

129 See *H v DPP* [1997] 1 WLR 1406 below in which insanity was wrongly regarded as a defence displacing *mens rea.*

130 But see *Cichon v DPP* [1994] Crim LR 918 (defence of necessity not open under Dangerous Dogs Act 1991, s 1(2)(d), because an 'absolute' offence).

131 See *Eden DC v Baird* [1998] CODS 209.

132 For discussion of this question see F. Sayre, 'Public Welfare Offences' (1933) 33 Col LR 55 at 75–78; S. Howard, *SR*, ch 9.

Larsonneur[133] and *Winzar v Chief Constable of Kent*[134] establish that *lawful* compulsion is not a defence to offences of 'being found'. It does not follow that unlawful duress would not be a defence. If D, being drunk, were forced at gunpoint into the highway he should not be guilty of being found drunk there. Nor does it follow that even lawful compulsion may not found a defence to other, less extreme, cases of strict liability than those of 'being found'.

(ii) ECHR

It has been noted in Chapter 2 that the European Convention's impact on the substantive criminal law has been relatively muted, even since the enactment of the Human Rights Act 1998. One guarantee afforded by the ECHR is the presumption of innocence under Article 6(2). It has been argued that strict liability offences offend against Article 6(2) because once the prohibited act is proved, D is presumed to be liable. Although there is some faint support in the ECHR case law for the application of Article 6(2) to strict liability offences,[135] the European Court has held that strict liability offences are compatible with the Article: 'in principle the contracting States may, under certain conditions, penalize a simple or objective fact as such irrespective of whether it results from criminal intent or from negligence'.[136]

The English courts have taken account of that conclusion in holding that Article 6(2) is restricted to providing procedural protection and does not render the imposition of strict liability incompatible with Article 6(2).[137]

4. Arguments for and against strict liability

The proliferation of offences of strict liability, while generally deplored by legal writers, was welcomed by the distinguished social scientist, Lady Wootton, on the ground that 'nothing has dealt so devastating a blow at the punitive concept of the criminal process . . .'.[138]

> If, however, the primary function of the courts is conceived as the prevention of forbidden acts, there is little cause to be disturbed by the multiplication of offences of strict liability. If the law says that certain things are not to be done, it is illogical to confine this prohibition to occasions on which they are done from malice aforethought; for at least the material consequences of an action, and the reasons for prohibiting it are the same whether it is the result of sinister malicious plotting, of negligence or of sheer accident.[139]

Accepting that the primary function of the courts is the prevention of forbidden acts, there remains the question, what acts should be regarded as forbidden? Surely only such

133 (1933) 24 Cr App R 74; above, p 73.

134 (1983) The Times, 28 Mar, above, p 74. Cf *O'Sullivan v Fisher* [1954] SASR 33, discussed by Howard, above at 193; *Achterdam* 1911 EDL 336 (Burchell and Hunt, 114).

135 See *Hansen v Denmark* 28971/95.

136 *Salibaku v France* (1998) 13 EHRR 379, Emmerson and Ashworth, para 9–64.

137 *Barnfather v Islington LBC* [2003] EWHC 418 (Admin) and see the valuable comment by B. Fitzpatrick, (2004) J Crim L 16; *Muhammed* [2003] EWCA Crim 1852. On the issue more broadly see P. Roberts, 'The Presumption of Innocence Brought Home? Kebilene Deconstructed' (2002) 118 LQR 41.

138 *Crime and the Criminal Law* (2nd edn), 44. See also at 63, criticized by B. Hogan, 'Criminal Liability without Fault' (Leeds Univ Press, 1967); H. L. A. Hart, *The Morality of the Criminal Law*, 13 et seq.

139 Ibid, at 51.

acts as we can assert ought not to have been done. Suppose that a butcher, who has taken all reasonable precautions, has the misfortune to sell some meat which is unfit for human consumption. That it was so unfit is undiscoverable by any precaution which a butcher can be expected to take. Ought the butcher to have acted as he did? Unless we want butchers to stop selling meat, or to take precautions so extreme as to be unreasonable (like employing an analyst)[140] it would seem that the answer should be in the affirmative; we want butchers, who have taken all reasonable precautions, to sell meat – the act of this butcher was not one which the law should seek to prevent. The imposition of strict liability rather than negligence seems wholly inappropriate.

Some of the judges who upheld the conviction of *Prince* did so, on the ground that men should be deterred from taking girls out of the possession of their parents, whatever the girl's age. This reasoning can hardly be applied to many modern offences of strict liability. We do not wish to deter people from driving cars, being concerned in the management of premises, financing hire purchase transactions or canning peas.[141] These acts, if done with all proper care, are not such acts as the law should seek to prevent. The fallacy in the argument lies in looking at the harm done in isolation from the circumstances in which it was brought about. Many acts, which have in fact caused harm, *ought* to have been done. The surgeon performing a justified operation with all proper skill may cause death.

Another argument that is frequently advanced in favour of strict liability is that, without it, many guilty people would escape – 'that there is neither time nor personnel available to litigate the culpability of each particular infraction'.[142] This argument assumes that it is possible to deal with these cases without deciding whether D had *mens rea* or not, whether he was negligent or not. Certainly D may be convicted without deciding these questions, but how can he be sentenced? Clearly the court ought to deal differently with (i) the butcher who knew that the meat was tainted; (ii) the butcher who did not know, but ought to have known; and (iii) the butcher who did not know and had no means of finding out. Sentence cannot properly be imposed without deciding into which category the convicted person falls. Treating the offence as one of strict liability, in the case of jury trial, merely removes the decision of these vital questions of fact from the jury and puts them in the hands of the judge; in the case of summary trial, it removes the questions from the sphere of strict proof according to law and leaves them to be decided in the much more informal way in which questions of fact relating purely to sentence are decided.[143] If the offence is one of strict liability, evidence is not admissible at the trial

140 See Kennedy LJ cited above, p 138 and see below, p 161.

141 See *Smedleys Ltd v Breed* [1974] AC 839. 'Obviously any consequence is avoidable by the simple expedient of not engaging in the process at all. But that clearly is not what is meant unless the process itself is open to serious criticism as unnecessary or inefficient', per Lord Hailsham [1974] 2 All ER 21 at 28.

142 H. Wechsler, 'The Model Penal Code', in *Modern Advances in Criminology* (ed J. Ll. Edwards, 1965), 73. The argument was met by the authors of the code by 'the creation of a grade of offence which may be prosecuted in a criminal court but which is not denominated criminal and which entails upon conviction no severer sentence than a fine or civil penalty or forfeiture'.

143 Disputed facts affecting sentence may be decided by the judge in a 'Newton hearing' after conviction – see *Newton* (1982) 77 Cr App R 13, [1983] Crim LR 198. In some cases judges have preferred the use of additional counts to obtain the jury's decision on important issues of culpability which would not appear from a verdict of guilty on a single count. See *Hoof* (intentional or reckless arson?), below, ch 24. This course is not open where the offence is one of strict liability. In *Warner* (above, p 151) the recorder asked the jury after verdict whether D knew the box contained drugs but they said, reasonably, that they had not decided that question.

either to show that D was blameworthy – *Sandhu*[144] – or that he was not: *Gosney*.[145] On the assumption (held, on appeal, to be wrong) that the former offence of dangerous driving was one of strict liability, the judge, no doubt rightly, excluded evidence alleged to show that D was blameless. If the rules relating to proof at the trial have any value at all, it is extraordinary that they should not be applied to the most important facts in the case. That the sentence should be imposed by the judge on a basis of fact different from that on which the jury convicted is deplorable; but it is always possible in the case of strict liability unless the judge questions the jury as to the grounds of their decision – and there are difficulties about this.[146]

The argument which is probably most frequently advanced by the courts for imposing strict liability is that it is necessary to do so in the interests of the public. Now it may be conceded that in many of the instances where strict liability has been imposed, the public does need protection against negligence and, assuming that the threat of punishment can make the potential harm-doer more careful, there may be a valid ground for imposing liability for negligence as well as where there is *mens rea*. This is a plausible argument in favour of strict liability if there were no middle way between *mens rea* and strict liability – that is liability for negligence – and the judges have generally proceeded on the basis that there is no such middle way. Liability for negligence has rarely been spelled out of a statute except where, as in driving without due care, it is explicitly required. Lord Devlin has explained this:[147]

> It is not easy to find a way of construing a statute apparently expressed in terms of absolute liability so as to produce the requirement of negligence. Take, for example, an offence like driving car while it has defective brakes. It is easy enough to read into a statute a word like 'wilfully' but you cannot just read in 'carelessly'. You cannot show that no one should carelessly drive a car with defective brakes; you are not trying to get at careless driving. What you want to say is that no one may drive a car without taking care to see that the brakes are not defective. That is not so easy to frame as a matter of construction and it has never been done.

The case against strict liability then is, first, that it is unnecessary. It results in the conviction of persons who have behaved impeccably and who should not be required to alter their conduct in any way. Secondly, that it is unjust. Even if an absolute discharge can be given (as in *Ball*)[148] D may feel rightly aggrieved at having been formally convicted of an offence for which he bore no responsibility. It is significant that Ball thought it worthwhile to appeal. Moreover, a conviction may have far-reaching consequences outside the courts,[149] so that it is no answer to say that only a nominal penalty is imposed.[150]

The imposition of liability for negligence would in fact meet the arguments of

144 [1997] Crim LR 288.

145 [1971] 2 QB 674, [1971] 3 All ER 220.

146 Cf comment on *Lockyer v Gibb* [1966] Crim LR 504 and on *Sheppard* [1981] Crim LR 171 at 172; *Dalas* [1966] Crim LR 692; *Warner* [1967] 3 All ER 93, [1967] Crim LR 528; *Lester* [1976] Crim LR 389; *Foo* [1976] Crim LR 456 and commentaries on these cases.

147 *Samples of Lawmaking*, 76.

148 (1966) 50 Cr App R 266. (Blameless driver guilty of causing death by dangerous driving.)

149 As in the case of *Sweet v Parsley* [1970] AC 132, [1969] 1 All ER 347.

150 This was accepted by the Privy Council in *Lim Chin Aik* [1963] AC 160 at 175 and by Lord Reid in *Warner* [1968] 2 All ER 356 at 366.

most of those who favour strict liability. Thus Roscoe Pound, in a passage which has been frequently and uncritically accepted as a justification for such offences, wrote:[151]

> The good sense of the courts has introduced a doctrine of acting at one's peril with respect to statutory crimes which expresses the needs of society. Such statutes are not meant to punish the vicious but to put pressure upon the thoughtless and inefficient to do their whole duty in the interest of public health or safety or morals.

The 'thoughtless and inefficient' are, of course, the negligent. The objection to offences of strict liability is not that these persons are penalized, but that others who are completely innocent are also liable to conviction. Though Lord Devlin was sceptical about the possibility of introducing the criterion of negligence in the lecture from which the above quotation is taken, in *Reynolds v Austin*[152] he stated from the bench the principle that strict liability should only apply when there is something that the defendant can do to promote the observance of the law – which comes close to requiring negligence.

If there were something which D could do to prevent the commission of the crime and which he had failed to do, he might generally be said to have failed to comply with a duty – perhaps a high duty – of care; and so have been negligent. One would have thought that what D ought to do would necessarily be limited by what was reasonable. A law requiring one to act unreasonably would seem odd indeed; but Lord Salmon was prepared to take this step in *Alphacell*. The section, he thought, 'encourages riparian factory owners not only to take reasonable steps to prevent pollution but to do everything possible to ensure that they do not cause it'.[153]

This suggests that, however vast the expenditure involved, and however unreasonable it may be in relation to the risk, D is under a duty to take all *possible* steps. The factory owner might prefer to take the chance of paying the maximum fine of (then) £200; but a 'repetition or continuation of an earlier offence' may lead to liability to imprisonment for six months.[154] By now, the offence might be thought to have lost its character of being 'not criminal in any real sense' but it could not cease to be an offence of strict liability; and it would still be no defence that reasonable steps (or, indeed, all possible steps) had been taken. Clearly Lord Salmon was right in saying that there was a great deal more in the case than the fine and costs of the trial, amounting to £44. Yet it may be doubted whether factory owners will in fact do more than is reasonable; and it is questionable whether they ought to be required to do so, at the risk – even though it be unlikely – of imprisonment. The contrary argument is that: '. . . the existence of strict liability does induce organisations to aim at higher and higher standards'.[155]

151 *The Spirit of the Common Law*, 52.

152 [1951] 2 KB 135 at 150, [1951] 1 All ER 606 at 612; above, p 149.

153 [1972] 2 All ER at 491. Cf *Smedleys Ltd v Breed* [1974] AC 839.

154 Criminal Law Act 1967, s 2(7). See G. Richardson, 'Effective Means of Regulating Industry, Strict Liability for Regulating Crime: The Empirical Evidence [1987] Crim LR 295.

155 M. Smith and A. Pearson, 'The Value of Strict Liability' [1969] Crim LR 5 at 16.

(a) Why strict? Defence burdens and due diligence

(i) The 'halfway house'?

In some common law jurisdictions there has developed a 'halfway house' between strict liability and full *mens rea*. Once the *actus reus* has been proved an onus is imposed on D, sometimes to introduce evidence and sometimes to prove, that he had reasonable grounds for his failure to be aware of, or to foresee, relevant facts, as the case may be. This approach, as practised in New Zealand, has the approval of Lord Cooke of Thorndon:

It does seem odd that in the home of Woolmington absolute (or strict) liability is so extensively accepted by the courts, and with some equanimity. It is as if the great case has created a judicial mindset which recoils at a shifting of the onus, yet tolerates a harsher solution.[156]

There is great force in this criticism. We have cited Lord Devlin's opinion as to the difficulties he saw in the way of implying a requirement of negligence instead of one of *mens rea* but, just as the judges invented the presumption in favour of *mens rea*, they could have invented a presumption of a negligence requirement in particular types of case. They chose not to do so. There is nothing wrong, it is submitted, with the 'judicial mindset' which recoils at a shifting of the onus – that reflects a healthy commitment to the presumption of innocence – but when combined with a refusal to imply a requirement of either *mens rea* or negligence, it does indeed lead to an unduly harsh solution. The opportunity to adopt the halfway house was presented to the House of Lords in *B (A Minor) v DPP*[157] but was declined in favour of a requirement of full *mens rea*. It seems the halfway house has no future in England and Wales, except where it is embodied in a statute.

(ii) Due diligence defences

It is common for the drastic effect of a statute imposing strict liability to be mitigated by the provision of a statutory defence. It is instructive to consider one example.[158] Various offences relating to the treatment and sale of food are enacted by the first 20 sections of the Food Safety Act 1990. Many, if not all, of these are strict liability offences. Section 21(1), however, provides that it shall be a defence for the person charged with any of the offences to prove that he took all reasonable precautions and exercised all due diligence to avoid the commission of the offence by himself or by a person under his control; but, (s 21(5)), where this defence involves an allegation that the offence was due to the act or default of another person, the defendant may not, without the leave of the court, rely on it unless within a prescribed period he has served on the prosecutor a notice in writing giving such information identifying or assisting in the identification of the other person as was then in his possession.

The section goes on to provide for ways in which the defence may be established by a person who neither prepared the food in question nor imported it into Great Britain. In

156 'One Golden Thread' in *Turning Points of the Common Law* (Hamlyn Lectures, 1997) 28 at 47. See also *City of Sault Ste Marie* (1978) 85 DLR 3d 161 (Can). On defences of due diligence see G. Orchard, 'The defence of absence of fault in Australia and Canada' in P. Smith (ed), *Essays in Honour of J. C. Smith*, (1987).

157 [2000] 2 AC 428.

158 For a comprehensive treatment of a similar defence in the context of consumer protection see D. Parry, 'Judicial Approaches to Due Diligence' [1995] Crim LR 675.

respect of offences under s 14 (selling food not of the nature or substance or quality demanded) and s 15 (falsely describing or presenting food) such a person is taken to have established the defence under subsection (1) if he satisfies the requirements of subsection (3) or (4):

(3) A person satisfies the requirements of this subsection if he proves –

(a) that the commission of the offence was due to an act or default of another person who was not under his control, or to reliance on information supplied by such a person;

(b) that he carried out all such checks of the food in question as were reasonable in all the circumstances, or that it was reasonable in all the circumstances for him to rely on checks carried out by the person who supplied the food to him; and

(c) that he did not know and had no reason to suspect at the time of the commission of the alleged offence that his act or omission would amount to an offence under the relevant provision.

(4) A person satisfies the requirements of this subsection if he proves –

(a) that the commission of the offence was due to an act or default of another person who was not under his control, or to reliance on information supplied by such a person;

(b) that the sale or intended sale of which the alleged offence consisted was not a sale or intended sale under his name or mark; and

(c) that he did not know, and could not reasonably have been expected to know, at the time of the commission of the alleged offence that his act or omission would amount to an offence under the relevant provision.

So if a shopkeeper sells a toffee with a nail in it and is charged with selling food not of the nature or substance or quality demanded,[159] contrary to s 14, he must satisfy the court that he took whatever precautions a shopkeeper can reasonably be expected to take to avoid such an event and, as this defence apparently alleges that the offence was due to the act or default of the manufacturer, he must have served the required notice on the prosecutor. He may then rely on subsection (3) and, if he can prove the three matters stated in the subsection on the balance of probabilities, the defence is made out. Though the requirements look formidable, this might not be too difficult in this particular example. (a) *Someone* not under the defendant's control was responsible for letting the nail get into the toffee and the defendant is not apparently required to identify the defaulter; (b) a shopkeeper cannot reasonably be expected to unwrap and dissect the toffees he sells; and (c) if the manufacturer is reputable and does not have a record of selling sweets containing foreign bodies, he had no reason to suspect it on this occasion. There may be other circumstances in which it is not so easy to get over the three hurdles but, as subsections (2) to (4) are without prejudice to the generality of the defence under subsection (1), it is open to the defendant to satisfy the court in any other way that, as a matter of fact, he took all reasonable precautions and exercised all due diligence. If he prepared or imported the food, he must do this anyway.

This defence substantially mitigates the requirements of earlier legislation under which the shopkeeper would have had to bring the manufacturer before the court and prove,

159 Cf *Lindley v G. W. Horner & Co Ltd* [1950] 1 All ER 234.

presumably beyond reasonable doubt, that the offence was due to his act or default. The manufacturer was then strictly liable, however diligent he might have been.[160] He would still be liable to conviction because, by s 20 of the 1990 Act, 'Where the commission by any person of an offence under any of the preceding provisions of this Part is due to act or default of some other person, that other person shall be guilty of the offence . . .'.

However, he might now rely on the defence of due diligence provided by s 21.

The new section might also provide a defence in another notorious case. In *Parker v Alder*[161] a milk salesman, in pursuance of a contract of sale, delivered some milk in a pure and unadulterated condition to a railway station for carriage to London. Under this contract the ownership in the milk passed when it was delivered in London. When delivered it was found to be adulterated. Some unknown person had added nine per cent of water. The unlucky defendant, without any fault on his part, had sold adulterated milk and was convicted of an offence which is now replaced by s 14 of the 1990 Act. Statutory defences provided in subsequent food legislation would not have helped him because they required him to identify the person to whose act or default the contravention was due, and that he plainly could not do. Now the only requirements are that he is to supply such information as is in his possession and prove that he took all reasonable precautions, etc.

Statutory defences do not always take such a complicated form. But they usually impose on the defendant a burden of proving both that he had no *mens rea* and that he took all reasonable precautions and exercised all due diligence to avoid the commission of an offence. Thus one who sells feeding stuffs containing deleterious ingredients is liable even if he proves that the commission of the offence was due to a mistake or an accident or some other cause beyond his control unless he also proves that he took all reasonable precautions, etc.[162] The effect of such provisions is that the prosecution need do no more than prove that the accused did the prohibited act and it is then for him to establish, if he can, that he did it innocently. Such provisions are a distinct advance on unmitigated strict liability; but they are still a deviation from the fundamental principle that the prosecution must prove the whole of their case; and an extensive use of offences of strict liability, even when so qualified, is to be deplored.

160 *Lindley v G. W. Horner & Co Ltd*, above.

161 [1899] 1 QB 20.

162 Agriculture Act 1970, ss 73 and 82. See too Weights and Measures Act 1985, s 34; Trade Descriptions Act 1968, s 24. See *Richards* [2004] EWCA Crim 192, failing to exercise due diligence to check cars on sale are not 'clocked'. The provision of a statutory defence may be an indication to the court that an offence of strict liability is intended. Cf Obscene Publications Act 1959, s 2(5), below, p 954.

8

Parties to crime[1]

The person who directly and immediately causes the *actus reus* of a crime, (the principal offender, in this chapter, P) is not necessarily the only one who is criminally liable for it. A person, in this chapter, D, might also be liable as an accessory or secondary party. The law of secondary parties is applicable to all offences, unless expressly or impliedly excluded. It is possible that it is impliedly excluded where statute creates offences of 'using or causing or permitting to be used'.[2] Occasionally, helping to commit, or encouraging someone to commit a crime is made a principal offence – as with the offence of assisting suicide.[3]

1. Basis of liability

By the Accessories and Abettors Act 1861, s 8 as amended by the Criminal Law Act 1977:

> Whosoever shall aid, abet, counsel or procure the commission of any indictable offence whether the same be an offence at common law or by virtue of any act passed or to be passed, shall be liable to be tried, indicted and punished as a principal offender.[4]

The section does not create an offence. It specifies the procedure and punishment for the aiders, abettors, counsellors and procurers, conveniently designated 'secondary parties'.

It has always been sufficient to prove that the defendant was either the principal or a secondary party.[5] A person who is simply charged with an offence, say theft, may be convicted on that indictment or information whether the evidence proves that he committed the theft, or aided, abetted, counselled or procured it. But the charge should, wherever possible, specify the actual mode of participation alleged.[6] This rule can operate extremely harshly since the prosecution can obtain a conviction without specifying precisely which part they allege the accused played. Thus, in *Gianetto*, it was sufficient for the prosecution to allege that the defendant killed his wife or that he was an accessory to her

1 See generally K. J. M. Smith, *A Modern Treatise on Complicity* (1991), and the discussion in the Law Commission's Consultation Paper No 131, *Assisting and Encouraging Crime* (1993).

2 *Carmichael & Sons (Worcester) Ltd v Cottle* [1971] RTR 11. Cf *Farr* [1982] Crim LR 745, CA, and commentary.

3 See Suicide Act 1961, below, p 493 and see also eg Female Genital Mutilation Act 2003.

4 Similar provisions relating to summary trial are to be found in the Magistrates' Courts Act 1980, s 44.

5 *Mackalley's Case* (1611) 9 Co Rep 61b, *Fitzgerald* [1992] Crim LR 660.

6 *DPP for Northern Ireland v Maxwell* [1978] 3 All ER 1140, HL; *Taylor* [1998] Crim LR 582.

death (by contracting a killer to do so).[7] The lack of precision in such indictments does not render them incompatible with Article 6 of the ECHR on the basis of the requirement for a defendant to know 'in detail' the nature of the case against him.[8]

Although the law treats the accessory in identical terms for the purposes of procedure and punishment as the principal, it is important for several reasons to identify who the principal offender and the secondary party are.

(1) The primary importance of identifying the principal offender lies in the fact that the secondary party is liable once the principal has committed the crime. Secondary liability is derivative; that is, it derives from the liability of the principal.[9]

> [W]hen the law relating to principals and accessories as such is under consideration there is only one crime, although there may be more than one person criminally liable in respect of it . . . There is one crime and that it has been committed must be established before there can be any question of criminal guilt of participation in it. . . .[10]

With a murder for example, D may supply the weapon to P, who kills V, but it is not until that killing takes place that D becomes liable as a secondary party. D's liability derives from the principal offence. This can be compared with a regime of punishing those who assist or encourage crime on the basis of inchoate liability. On such a regime, D who supplies the weapon would be liable as soon as he had performed that blameworthy conduct, irrespective of whether P went on to kill V. In English law, such conduct can be punished as a possible incitement or conspiracy if there is an agreement, but it is not a basis for imposing liability as an 'accessory'.[11]

It is also necessary to distinguish what used to be called the 'principal in the first degree'[12] (hereafter, merely 'principal') from secondary participants because:

(2) in the case of all offences of strict liability secondary parties must be proved to have *mens rea*;[13]

[7] [1997] 1 Cr App R 1, CA. See J. C. Smith's commentary [1996] Crim LR 722 for criticism.

[8] *Mercer* [2001] All ER (D) 187. See Ashworth, POCL, 415.

[9] See Fletcher, *Rethinking Criminal Law* (1978) ch 8; K. J. M. Smith, above, ch 4; D. Lanham, 'Primary and Derivative Criminal Liability: An Australian Perspective' [2000] Crim LR 707. The law in application fails to remain true to this theory: W. Wilson describes English law as 'fudging' the theoretical basis: *Central Issues in Criminal Theory* (2002), ch 7. An alternative analysis sees the secondary as causally responsible for the principal's crime (see K. J. M. Smith, above, ch 3).

[10] Russell 128, approved in *Surujpaul v R* [1958] 3 All ER 300 at 301, PC. This is now subject to the rule in *Millward* [1994] Crim LR 527, below, p 206.

[11] For a radical proposal to criminalize conduct on an inchoate basis focused on what D did rather than what P did, see Law Com Consultation Paper No 131, above, n 1. See also R. Buxton, 'Complicity in the Criminal Code' (1969) 85 LQR 252. The Law Commission Report on *Assisting and Encouraging Crime* is due to be published in 2005.

[12] The common law of felonies designated the actual perpetrator 'the principal in the first degree' and distinguished secondary parties into principals in the second degree – those who participated at the time when the felony was actually perpetrated – and accessories before the fact – those who participated at an earlier time. It was traditional to state that the distinction was that the principal in the second degree was *present* at the commission of the offence; but in fact he might be a considerable distance away – in an American case (*State v Hamilton and Lawrie* 13 Nev 386 (1878) – signals from mountain top), 30–40 miles, so long as he was assisting or available to assist, at the time. Hawkins II PC c 29, ss 7 and 8; Foster 350.

[13] Below, p 179. In road traffic offences, where disqualification of the principal is obligatory, disqualification of secondary parties is discretionary: Road Traffic Offenders Act 1988, s 34(5).

(3) in some cases the offence is so defined that it can be committed as a principal only by a member of a specified class (for example, the holder of a justices' licence);[14]

(4) in some offences vicarious liability may be imposed for the act of another who is a principal or does the act of a principal; but there is no vicarious liability for the act of a secondary party.[15]

2. The principal

Where there are several participants in a crime the principal is the one whose act is the most immediate cause of the *actus reus*. In murder, for example, he is the person who, with *mens rea*, fires the gun or administers the poison which causes death; in theft, the person, who, with *mens rea*, appropriates the thing which is stolen; in bigamy, the person who, knowing himself to be already married, goes through a second ceremony of marriage; and so on. In the case of statutory offences, the scope of principal liability will turn on the precise form of words used in the offence.[16]

It is a fundamental principle that criminal liability arises from wrongdoing for which a person is himself responsible and not for the wrongdoing of others. If, by performing acts of assistance a secondary party were taken to have caused the commission of the offence for all purposes he would become a principal. If D, having procured P to murder V, were taken to have caused V's death, that is, killed V, he would satisfy the definition of murder as a principal. Anyone whose assistance or encouragement in fact caused another to commit a crime would be a principal. The separate body of law of accessory liability is based on the assumption that the accessory does not cause the *actus reus*.[17]

The Draft Code, cl 17(3), accordingly provides:

> A person who procures, assists or encourages another to cause a result that is an element of an offence does not himself cause that result so as to be guilty of the offence as a principal except when –
>
> (a) section 26(1)(c) [innocent agency] applies; or
>
> (b) The offence itself consists in the procuring, assisting or encouraging another to cause the result.[18]

It is therefore assumed for the purposes of this chapter that the decision in *Finlay*[19] is confined to its own circumstances. If it were of general application, there would be no need for a separate law relating to secondary parties: the sole question would be whether D is a cause of the prohibited result. The principal's free deliberate informed act directly causing the prohibited harm would not, according to *Finlay*, render D a mere accessory unless P's act were 'extraordinary'.

14 Below, p 225. 15 Below, p 233.

16 See eg *Corporation of London v Eurostar* [2004] EWHC 187 (Admin), where Eurostar were guilty as principals for 'landing' an Alsatian dog as prohibited under anti-rabies legislation.

17 H. Hart and T. Honoré, *Causation in the Law* (2nd edn, 1985), 380; S. H. Kadish, *Essays*, 143–144.

18 See on the shortcomings of cl 17 in general, G. Williams, '*Finis for Novus Actus*' [1989] CLJ 391.

19 [2003] EWCA Crim 3868. D liable for manslaughter by supply of drugs to V who, as sane adult freely self injects and dies as a result.

In *Kennedy No 2*,[20] the Court of Appeal held that where D hands V a syringe and V self injects, the jury are entitled to find that they are jointly engaged in the offence of administering heroin.[21] It is submitted that the decision ought to be read in its specific and very narrow context. D had handed the syringe to the deceased 'for immediate injection' and D was found by the jury to have been 'engaged' in the administration. It would be premature to apply the case beyond this narrow bound by suggesting for example that by supplying the gun to P (a sane adult acting of his own volition) for him to execute V, D becomes a murderer rather than an accessory to murder.

How the jury are to be assisted in determining whether D and P are 'jointly engaged'[22] is not examined by the court, nor is it clear to what extent D's actions must be 'necessary' in order for him to be regarded as jointly engaged. One such situation might be that in *Rogers*[23] where D had the tourniquet for V to self inject. These cases are discussed in Chapter 4.

(a) Innocent agency[24]

The *actus reus* may be directly brought about by the act of someone who is not a participant in the crime at all (that is, who has no *mens rea*, or who has some defence, such as infancy or insanity). Such a person is usually described as an 'innocent agent' and, in such a case, the principal is the participant in the crime whose act is the most immediate cause of the innocent agent's act. If D sends through the post a letter-bomb to V who is injured by the explosion, the postman who delivers the letter is an innocent agent. So if D, intending to kill V, gives to V's daughter a poison which, he says, will cure V's cold, and she innocently administers the poison, causing V's death, then D is guilty as the principal offender.[25] If the daughter had had *mens rea* then she would, of course, have been the principal.

Where D, a collector of money, makes a false statement to his employer's book-keeper, knowing that the statement will be entered in the books, and it is so entered by the innocent book-keeper, D is guilty, as a principal, of falsifying his employer's accounts.[26] Where D dishonestly sets in motion a chain of actions by innocent fellow employees which he intends to result, and which does result, in his employer's account being debited he may be guilty of theft of the thing in action represented by the bank balance.[27] Where D induced a child, aged 11, to take money from a till and give it to D, D was a principal only if the child was exempt from criminal liability which, at that time, depended on whether he knew the act was wrong.[28] If the child is liable to conviction, then he is the principal and D is a secondary party.[29]

20 [2005] EWCA Crim 685.

21 See discussion above in Ch 4.

22 [29].

23 [2003] Crim LR 555, [2003] 1 WLR 1374.

24 See P. Alldridge, 'The Doctrine of Innocent Agency' (1990) 2 Criminal Law Forum 45; G. Williams, 'Innocent Agency and Causation' (1992) Criminal Law Forum 289.

25 *Anon* (1634) Kel 53; *Michael* (1840) 9 C & P 356.

26 *Butt* (1884) 15 Cox CC 564.

27 *Stringer and Banks* [1991] Crim LR 639.

28 See below, p 296. And see *Tyler* (1838) 8 C & P 616 (liability for act of lunatic).

29 *Manley* (1844) 1 Cox CC 104. The child was actually nine. A child under 10 is now incapable of crime, so D would be the principal whether the nine-year-old knew the act was wrong or not. In *DPP v K & B* [1997] 1 Cr App R 36, DC, it was said, *obiter*, that if D procured a child under 10 to have sexual intercourse without consent, D could not be guilty of rape because there would be no *actus reus*. That seems wrong: see [1997] Crim LR 121, 122. See also *Mazeau* (1840) 9 C & P 676.

There are some crimes to which the doctrine of innocent agency is inapplicable because it is impossible to say that D has personally committed the *actus reus.*[30] Bigamy – except in the case of a marriage by proxy – is a good example. Compare it with murder. If D causes an innocent person, say the postman E, to kill V by delivering a letter which he does not know contains a bomb, it is right for the law to take the view that *D has killed V* – the *actus reus* of murder; but if D induces E, an innocent person who has no knowledge of D or F's marital status, to go through a marriage with F, which D knows to be bigamous, it is impossible to say that *D has married during the lifetime of his wife* – the *actus reus* of bigamy. He has not done so. In the same category, it is submitted, are rape and other crimes involving sexual intercourse and the *dicta* in *Cogan and Leak*[31] that rape may be committed through an innocent agent are contrary to principle.

(b) Joint principals

There may be more than one cause of an *actus reus* and more than one causer. So there may be two or more principals in the same crime. If D1 and D2 make an attack on V intending to murder him and the combined effect of their blows is to kill him, both are guilty of murder[32] as joint principals. For this purpose, causing another person, X, (not an *innocent* agent), by persuasion or otherwise, to commit the crime is not causing the *actus reus.* X's voluntary intervening act 'breaks the chain of causation'. However, following *Kennedy No 2*,[33] D may be 'jointly engaged' with P if the jury concludes that they were 'engaged in the one activity' in the sense of 'carrying out a combined operation' for which they were jointly responsible. It is unclear to what extent this doctrine will be applied beyond the narrow circumstances of drug administration. A different type of joint responsibility is that where each of two or more parties does an act which is an element of, or part of, the *actus reus.*[34]

What is the position when the principal himself is not present at the moment of the completion of the crime? If two or more persons conspire to employ an innocent agent both are liable as principals for the agent's acts and it is immaterial that the agent was instructed by the one in the absence of the other. The innocent agent's acts are considered the acts of both conspirators.[35] Where there is no innocent agent, the same considerations cannot apply. P, in pursuance of an agreement with D, leaves poison to be taken by V, or sets a trap into which V falls. D is liable as a secondary party.

(i) Joint enterprise

The distinction between a joint principal and an aider or abettor is sometimes a fine one. There is a view that all participants in a 'joint enterprise' – that is, persons acting with a common purpose – are principals. This appears to be so in Australia.[36] Parties who are

30 Cf *Woby v AJB and LCO* [1986] Crim LR 183, DC (boys under 18 not guilty of buying intoxicating liquor in licensed premises when they sent in an adult to buy it).

31 [1976] QB 217, [1975] 2 All ER 1059, [1975] Crim LR 584 and commentary thereon; below, p 205.

32 *Macklin and Murphy's Case* (1838) 2 Lew CC 225.

33 [2005] EWCA Crim 685.

34 *Bingley* (1821) Russ & Ry 446 (A and B each forged part of a banknote).

35 *Bull and Schmidt* (1845) 1 Cox CC 281.

36 *Osland v R* (1998) 73 ALJR 173, HC of A. See further J. C. Smith, 'Joint Enterprise and Secondary Liability' (1999) 50 NILQ 153.

present at the commission of the offence are all 'principals in the first degree.' A similar opinion has appeared here in the judgments of Hobhouse LJ, considered below.[37] But this is contrary to all English authority. Stephen in his *Digest*, article 37, stated that 'whoever aids or abets the actual commission of a crime, either at the place where it is committed or elsewhere, is a principal in the second degree in that crime'; and, in article 38:

When several persons take part in the execution of a common criminal purpose, each is a principal in the second degree, in respect of every crime committed by any one of them in the execution of that purpose.

Generally it is immaterial in which capacity D1 is alleged to have participated in the crime. Either way, he is equally responsible and liable to conviction. When it is necessary to distinguish, the test would seem to be: did D1 by his own act (as distinct from anything done by D1 with D2's advice or assistance) contribute to the causation of the *actus reus*? If he did, he is a principal. The distinction may be important where, as in *Osland*, the jury acquit D1 and convict D2. If D2 caused the *actus reus* by his own act, he is a principal and there is no problem. But, if he did not, there is a difficulty. If D1 is innocent, there is no crime for him to aid and abet. The difficulty can be overcome (i) if D1 can be regarded as an innocent agent, or (ii) under a somewhat uncertain principle[38] that it is an offence to procure the commission of an *actus reus*;[39] but it is surely wrong to overcome it by a fiction, a pretence that D2 'did it', if he did not.

Where the *actus* is a 'state of affairs',[40] the test for determining a principal is: ignoring D, does the statutory description of the state of affairs fit P?

3. Secondary participation

To be liable, a person who is not the principal must be proved to have aided, abetted, counselled or procured, though it is quite sufficient to show that he did one of these things.[41] All four expressions imply the commission of the offence.[42]

Secondary parties are liable when and where the offence aided, abetted, counselled or procured is committed. So an employer who sends a lorry, which he knows to be in a dangerous condition, from Scotland to England may be held liable in England for a death caused here because of the lorry's condition.[43]

As noted above, the crucial difference between inchoate and secondary liability is that with inchoate offences D's liability arises as soon as he has completed the acts of incitement, etc, irrespective of whether it leads to the commission of the substantive offence. With secondary liability D's act of encouragement only gives rise to liability once the person encouraged, P, performs the offence.

37 P 191. 38 Below, p 205. 39 *Millward*, below, p 206. 40 Above, p 206.

41 *Ferguson v Weaving* [1951] KB 814.

42 'Counselling' must not be taken literally. Mere incitement to commit an offence, not followed by its actual commission, is not 'counselling' – *Assistant Recorder of Kingston-upon-Hull, ex p Morgan* [1969] 2 QB 58, [1969] 1 All ER 416, DC.

43 *Robert Millar (Contractors) Ltd* [1970] 2 QB 54, [1970] 1 All ER 577.

A principal in a conspiracy to commit an offence, who, *ex hypothesi*, intends the offence to be committed, is guilty of the offence when it is committed by a co-conspirator, unless he has effectively withdrawn from the conspiracy in the meantime: *Rook*.[44] There is one possible exception: there may be a 'wheel' or 'chain' conspiracy in which conspirator A has no contact with, and is even unaware of the existence of conspirator B. If A commits the planned offence, it is *arguable* that B has not aided, abetted, counselled or procured – he has not in fact caused, assisted or encouraged – A to commit the offence. In that case B might be convicted of, for example, conspiracy to murder, but not of the intended murder when it was committed by A. Another qualification is necessary if, as is probable, there is such a thing as secondary participation in conspiracy – for example, B intentionally assists the making of an agreement to murder by providing a room, telephone numbers, etc, but is entirely indifferent whether murder be committed. It is arguable that even this should entail liability for the murder when it is committed; but perhaps the better view is that an act which does not assist or encourage the offender in the course of the commission of the offence is not enough.

(a) *Actus reus* of the secondary party

Where D aids P in the commission of say a murder, P's *actus reus* and *mens rea* as the principal will be prescribed by the law of murder (killing a human being with malice aforethought, etc). D's liability as a secondary party comprises the *actus reus* of aiding, abetting, counselling or procuring, with the relevant *mens rea* of a secondary party (intention to assist, knowledge of the relevant circumstances rendering P's act criminal). The contrast between the conduct sufficient to satisfy these elements and the requirements of the principal offence will often be stark. In a case of murder, D may have aided and abetted by driving the get-away car, being aware that an armed robbery was to take place. P will only be liable if he has killed with intent to kill or commit grievous bodily harm. Both will be convicted as murderers, labelled as such and punished as such.

It is important to remember that one whose participation in the relevant events does not involve advice or encouragement to commit the crime, and who does not assist the commission in any way, is not liable as a secondary party. Accepting a lift on a motorcycle known to have been taken without consent does not amount to aiding and abetting the use of the vehicle without insurance.[45] It would be different if the taking had been a joint enterprise (discussed below).[46]

(i) Aid, abet, counsel, procure

In *Attorney-General's Reference (No 1 of 1975)* Lord Widgery CJ said:

We approach s 8 of the 1861 Act on the basis that the words should be given their ordinary meaning, if possible. We approach the section on the basis also that if four words are employed here 'aid, abet, counsel or procure', the probability is that there is a difference between each of

44 [1993] 2 All ER 955, [1993] Crim LR 698 and commentary. Cf Stephen, *Digest of the Criminal Law* (9th edn), art 28; Williams, CLGP, 363; *Pinkerton v United States* 328 US 640 (1946). See, however, D. Lanham, 'Complicity, Concert and Conspiracy' [1980] 4 Crim LJ 276.

45 *D (Infant) v Parsons* [1960] 2 All ER 493, [1960] 1 WLR 797.

46 *Ross v Rivenall* [1959] 2 All ER 376n, [1959] 1 WLR 713. Cf the Theft Act 1968, s 12(1) and *Boldizsar v Knight* [1980] Crim LR 653, below, p 721.

those four words and the other three, because, if there were no such difference, then Parliament would be wasting time in using four words where two or three would do.[47]

The four words had previously been regarded as technical terms and it is clear that they cannot be given their ordinary meaning in all respects. Under the law of felonies, 'aiding and abetting' was used to describe the activity of the principal 'in the second degree' (not being present) and 'counselling and procuring' that of the accessory before the fact.[48] 'Aid and abet' has however sometimes been used in relation to acts committed before the actual perpetration of the crime. If we are to have regard to the natural meaning of the words instead of regarding them as technical terms, this is understandable because some such acts are not very happily described either as counselling or as procuring, though they merit criminal liability. Where it is necessary to distinguish between them, 'abet' and 'counsel' will be used henceforth to describe these two types of secondary participation.

In the modern law, secondary participation almost invariably consists simply in assisting or encouraging the commission of the crime. This can be by practically any means – supply of weapons, tools, information, support and encouragement, keeping watch, etc. It is generally irrelevant whether the secondary participant is present or absent or whether his assistance or encouragement was given before or at the time of the commission of the offence. The only possible exception may be the procurer who succeeds in causing the principal to commit the crime (as in the *Attorney-General's Reference*) without doing anything which could be fairly described as encouragement or assistance.

All four words may be used together to charge a person who is alleged to have participated in an offence otherwise than as a principal.[49] So long as the evidence establishes that D's conduct satisfied one of the words, that is enough. Where the indictment uses only one term – for example, 'procures' – it is necessary to prove that D's conduct fits that term.

Each element of *actus reus* deserves further brief examination to consider three particular issues: (i) what forms of conduct constitute aiding, abetting, counselling and procuring; (ii) whether there need be a causal link between the aiding etc and the principal offence; and, (iii) whether there need be a meeting of minds or consensus between the aider, etc and the principal.

Aiding

It has sometimes been said[50] that 'aid and abet' is a single concept, 'aid' denoting the *actus reus* and 'abet' the *mens rea*. The natural meaning of s 8 is however that stated in *Attorney-General's Reference*. Moreover the words do connote a different kind of activity. The natural meaning of to 'aid' is to 'give help, support or assistance to.'[51] The courts have taken a broad view of what suffices for 'aid'. Although historically it was limited to one who was present assisting or encouraging the principal at the time of the offence,[52] there

47 [1975] 2 All ER 684 at 686.

48 *Ferguson v Weaving*, above, at 818–819; Stephen, *Digest* (4th edn), arts. 37–39; *Bowker v Premier Drug Co Ltd* [1928] 1 KB 217 ('aid and abet' implies presence).

49 *Re Smith* (1858) 3 H & N 227; *Ferguson v Weaving* [1951] KB 814, [1951] 1 All ER 412.

50 *Lynch v DPP for Northern Ireland* [1975] 1 All ER 913 at 941, per Lord Simon quoting the 3rd edition of this work and Devlin J in *National Coal Board v Gamble* [1959] 1 QB 11 at 20.

51 *Oxford English Dictionary.*

52 Per Lowry CJ in *DPP v Maxwell* [1978] 3 All ER 1140, 1158.

is now no such restriction and it could be satisfied by any act of assistance before or at the time of the offence.[53] Supplying a weapon or transporting P to the scene of the crime are obvious examples.

Aiding, does not imply any causal connection. D may come to the assistance of P and enable him to commit the offence more easily, earlier, or with greater safety and, if so, he is surely guilty even if the same offence would have been committed if he had not intervened.[54] In *Bryce*[55], however, the Court of Appeal held that where D had transported the killer P to the scene of the crime, but the killing had not occurred until 13 hours later, there was no 'break in the chain of causation' which would absolve D.

Aiding does not imply any consensus between D and P. If D sees P committing a crime and comes to his assistance by, for example, restraining the policeman who would have prevented P from committing the crime, D is surely guilty even though his assistance is unforeseen and unwanted by P and unknown to him. The same might apply to aid given beforehand. D, knowing that P is going to meet a blackmailer, V, slips a gun into P's pocket in the hope that he will kill V – which he does.

Abetting

The natural meaning of 'abet' is 'to incite, instigate or encourage'.[56] Abetting is usually defined in term of encouragement. There is little to distinguish this method of secondary participation from counselling. Perhaps there is no difference except that at common law 'abet' connoted incitement at the time of the offence and 'counsel' incitement at an earlier time. It is entirely clear that either type of activity is sufficient to found liability as a secondary party.

The requirement of causation for abetting is best considered alongside that of counselling.[57] The natural meaning of 'abet' does not imply any causal element because, the word, (as with counselling) does not even imply that the offence has been committed. Instigation, incitement, encouragement, counselling, may all be unsuccessful and they have occurred no less because the offence is not committed. Of course, the law is that the offence must have been committed before anyone can be convicted as an abettor or counsellor of it; but, when the offence has been committed, it is certainly still true to say that D 'counselled' it, in the ordinary meaning of the word, even if his counsel was ignored by P; and the same seems to be true of abetting. There is nevertheless the high authority of Stephen for the view that one who counsels or commands (as well as procures) is liable and, by implication liable only, for an offence 'which is committed *in consequence* of such counselling, procuring, or commandment'.[58]

It is clearly the law that an attempt to counsel does not amount to counselling. Proffered advice or encouragement which has no effect on the mind of the principal offender is not counselling.[59] This is not to say that the counselling must be a cause of the commission of the offence. So to require would be to insist that, but for the counselling,

53 *Coney* (1882) 8 QBD 534.

54 See W. R. Le Fave and A. W. Scott, *Criminal Law*, 504.

55 [2004] EWCA Crim 1231.

56 *Oxford English Dictionary*.

57 See eg *Wilcox v Jeffery* [1951] 1 All ER 464; below, p 176; *Du Cros v Lambourne* [1907] KB 40.

58 Stephen, *Digest* (4th edn), art 39.

59 *Clarkson* [1971] 3 All ER 344, [1971] 1 WLR 1402, C-MAC.

the offence would not have been committed.[60] This would confine counselling (and abetting) much too narrowly. D may be liable although, when he encouraged P, he knew that P had already made up his mind to commit the offence.[61] If it were incumbent on the prosecution to prove that the offence would not have been committed 'but for' D's advice or encouragement of P it seems safe to say that the point would figure much more prominently in the law reports. On the contrary, the facts of many cases where D has been held liable suggest that the offence would have been committed by P whether D had participated or not and no one seems to have suggested that this should be a defence.

In *Bryce*[62] D was convicted of murder as a secondary when in the course of a drug dealers' dispute he assisted P, who was acting on the orders of the drugs baron B, by transporting P and a gun to a caravan near V's home. More than 12 hours later, P, acting alone, shot V. D's ground of appeal was that the delay meant that what D did (transporting P) was too remote in time and place to the killing particularly since at that stage P had not formed the intention to commit the offence. The Court of Appeal, after a comprehensive survey of the case law, upheld the conviction concluding that no intervening event occurred hindering the plan, this despite the fact that in the 12-hour plus delay P's gun barrel was shortened and B visited P to encourage him. The court concluded that there was no 'overwhelming supervening event' sufficient to break the chain of causation, nor had D effected a withdrawal in that time. This implies a casual requirement.

As for consensus, there must be some connection between the abetting or counselling and the commission of the offence. It is probably not necessary to prove that D was influenced in any way by P, but he must at least be aware that he has the authority, or the encouragement, or the approval, of P to do the relevant acts.

> For example, if the principal offender happened to be involved in a football riot in the course of which he laid about him with a weapon of some sort and killed someone who, unknown to him, was the person whom he had been counselled to kill, he would not, in our view, have been acting within the scope of his authority; he would have been acting outside it, albeit what he had done was what he had been counselled to do.[63]

It was suggested in *Attorney-General's Reference (No 1 of 1975)* that in the case of abetting and counselling the concepts might require a meeting of minds of secondary party and principal. If counselling and abetting must be, in some degree, operative, as suggested above, this is clearly right.

Counselling

To 'counsel' means to advise or solicit or encourage. The relevance of causation and consensus have been examined in the discussion of abetting above.

60 '... it does not make any difference that the person [*sc*, the person counselled] would have tried to commit suicide anyway': *A-G v Able* [1984] 1 All ER 277 at 288, per Woolf J.

61 *Giannetto* [1997] 1 Cr App R 1, [1996] Crim LR 722. Trial judge's example: 'I am going to kill your wife'; husband: 'Oh goody'.

62 [2004] EWCA Crim 1231, [2004] Crim LR 936.

63 *Calhaem* [1985] QB 808, [1985] 2 All ER 266, CA, per Parker LJ. *Schriek* [1997] 2 NZLR 139, 149. Cf the view taken in W. Wilson, *Criminal Law Doctrine* (2003) 587.

Procuring

'To procure means to produce by endeavour'.[64] 'You cannot procure an offence unless there is a causal link between what you do and the commission of the offence'.[65] In *Attorney-General's Reference*, D who had added alcohol to P's drink without P's knowledge or consent was held to have procured P's offence of driving with a blood/alcohol concentration above the prescribed limit[66] if it was proved that D knew that P was going to drive and that the ordinary and natural result of the added alcohol would be to bring P's blood/alcohol concentration above the prescribed limit. D had caused the commission of the offence. This is in accordance with the natural meaning of 'procure'.[67]

Glanville Williams writes of the *Attorney-General's Reference* that 'in so far as [it] purports to decide that merely causing an offence can be said to be a procuring of it, it should be regarded as too incautious a generalisation'. He quotes the famous case of *Beatty v Gillbanks*[68] where it was held that the Salvation Army was acting lawfully in holding its meeting in Weston-super-Mare although its officers knew from experience that this would cause a hostile organization, the Skeleton Army, to attack them. It would be absurd to hold that the Salvationists were liable as secondary parties for the attack on themselves, but they might have known that the attack would result in damage to others, for example, broken shop windows. There are two possible answers to this criticism: (i) Lord Widgery did not say that 'procure' means merely 'cause'. He said 'To procure means to produce by endeavour'. The Salvationists may have caused the Skeletons to make the attack (and to break the supposed windows) but these were certainly not results that they were 'endeavouring' to produce. Against this, it might be said that in *Attorney-General's Reference* D's awareness that he was causing the commission of the offence also fell short of proof of an endeavour to cause it; and in *Blakely*[69] the court thought that D 'procured' a result if he contemplated it as a possible result of his act – which is far removed from endeavouring to produce it. (ii) The Skeletons knew exactly what they were doing and in *Attorney-General's Reference* Lord Widgery made it clear the decision would not necessarily be the same where a driver knew that his drink was laced. The unaware driver 'in most instances . . . would have no means of preventing the offence from being committed', the aware driver would. Lord Widgery thus contemplated that the act of the aware driver might break the chain of causation even for the purposes of secondary liability.

A procurer of an innocent agent to commit a crime is taken to have caused the *actus reus* for all purposes. An alleged procurer of a guilty agent must be proved to have in fact caused the act of the guilty agent; but, in law, he is not regarded as having caused the *actus reus*.

In *Attorney-General's Reference (No 1 of 1975)* D's act of procuring was done without the knowledge or consent, and perhaps against the will, of P. The case decides that consensus is immaterial where 'procuring' is relied on.

64 *A-G's Reference (No 1 of 1975)* [1975] 2 All ER 684 at 686; *Reed* [1982] Crim LR 819. See K. J. M. Smith, 'Complicity and Causation' [1986] Crim LR 663; H. Beynon, 'Causation, Omissions and Complicity' [1987] Crim LR 539.

65 Ibid, at 687.

66 Road Traffic Act 1972, s 6(1), now replaced by Road Traffic Act 1988, s 5.

67 Cf P. Glazebrook, 'Attempting to Procure' [1959] Crim LR 774.

68 (1882) 9 QBD 308; *TBCL* 339.

69 Below, p 184.

How many modes of participation?

These terminological difficulties with four possible methods of participating in crime complicate the statement of the law. The Draft Code uses the terms 'procures, assists or encourages' to describe the whole of the activities which amount to secondary participation. It has been suggested[70] that in substance there are only two kinds of action involved – 'intentionally influencing the decision of the primary party to commit the crime and intentionally helping the primary actor to commit the crime'. But this does not seem to cover a case like *Attorney-General's Reference*,[71] where the principal is strictly liable. D 'procured' P to drive with excess alcohol by secretly lacing P's drink. There was no 'decision of the primary party to commit the crime'; and 'helping the primary actor to commit the crime' also seems to imply that the purpose of the primary actor is to commit the crime, which was not so. If that kind of case is to be covered, the notion of procuring must also be included.

(ii) The timing of the *actus reus*

Assistance given before the offence is committed will ground liability so it is only as regards the conclusion of the offence that time becomes important. Assistance given when the principal is no longer in the course of the commission of the offence – to enable him to escape or to reap the benefits of the commission of the offence – does not amount to abetting. Where P broke into a warehouse, stole butter and deposited it in the street 30 yards from the warehouse door, D who came to assist in carrying it off was held not guilty of abetting in larceny.[72] Assistance given to a murderer, after his victim is dead, to a rapist after the act of penetration has concluded,[73] or to a bigamist after the second ceremony of marriage, cannot ground liability for the crime in question. One who, without any pre-arranged plan, joins in an attack on V after V has received a fatal injury, is not guilty of homicide (though he may be guilty of an attempt) if his action in no way contributes to V's subsequent death.[74]

(iii) Presence at the crime as a sufficient *actus reus* for secondary liability?

A person is not guilty merely because he is present at the scene of a crime and does nothing to prevent it.[75] D who stands outside a building while his friends commit a burglary inside cannot, without proof of some assistance such as being a look out, be convicted of burglary.[76] To continue to sit beside the driver of a car until the end of a journey after learning that he is uninsured does not amount to abetting his uninsured

[70] Kadish, *Essays*, 151, supported by G. Williams, 'Complicity, Purpose and the Draft Code – 1' [1990] Crim LR 4, 'Letters to the Editor – Criminal Complicity' [1991] Crim LR 930.

[71] Above, p 171.

[72] *King* (1817) Russ & Ry 332; see also *Kelly* (1820) Russ & Ry 421.

[73] The act is a continuing one: Sexual Offences Act 2003, s 79.

[74] *S v Thomo* 1969 (1) SA 385 (AD); Burchell and Hunt, 352. Some fine distinctions have begun to be drawn. In *Grundy* (1989) 89 Cr App R 333, it was held that if D struck a blow to V after P had caused grievous bodily harm, D might still be liable for assisting grievous bodily harm. In *Percival* [2003] EWCA Crim 1561, D who punched V after P had wounded V could not be liable as an aider and abettor to wounding.

[75] *Atkinson* (1869) 11 Cox CC 330; but it is an offence to refuse to assist a constable to suppress a breach of the peace when called upon to do so: *Brown* (1841) Car & M 314.

[76] *S v DPP* [2003] EWHC 2717 (Admin). See also *Rose* [2004] EWCA Crim 764 [2004] All ER (D) 222 (Mar) where D's only actions at the scene were to discourage P from his attack on V.

driving.[77] Continuing to share a room with a person known to be in unlawful possession of drugs is not evidence of abetting, unless encouragement or control is proved.[78] If prohibited drugs, found in a van belonging to a party of tourists, are the property of and under the exclusive control of one of them, the others are not guilty of abetting simply because they are present and know of the existence of the drugs.[79] The abettor must either (i) be present in pursuance of an agreement that the crime be committed, or (ii) give assistance or encouragement in its commission.[80]

Both assistance or encouragement in fact *and* an intention to assist or encourage must be proved.[81] When this is proved, it is immaterial that D joined in the offence without any prior agreement.[82] In *Allan*[83] it was held that one who remains present at an affray, nursing a secret intention to help if the need arises but doing nothing to evince that intention, does not thereby become an abettor. Where two drivers, without any previous arrangement between them, enter into competitive driving on the highway so as knowingly to encourage each other to drive at a dangerous speed or in a dangerous manner, the one is liable as a secondary party for a death or other criminal result caused by the other.[84] In the leading case of *Coney*[85] it was held that proof of mere voluntary presence at a prize-fight, without more, is, at the most, only *prima facie* and not conclusive evidence of abetting the battery of which the contestants are guilty. Presence at such an event is certainly capable of amounting to an actual encouragement. If there were no spectators there would be no fight and, therefore, each spectator, by his presence, contributes to the incentive to the contestants. As Mathew J (dissenting) said:[86]

> The chief incentive to the wretched combatants to fight on until (as happens too often) dreadful injuries have been inflicted and life endangered or sacrificed, is the presence of spectators watching with keen interest every incident of the fight.

Voluntary presence at such an event, then, is some evidence on which a jury might find that the accused was there with the intention of encouraging the fight. Coney's conviction was quashed because the majority of the court thought that the chairman's direction was capable of being understood to mean that voluntary presence was *conclusive* evidence of an intention to encourage. If the direction had made it clear that presence was *prima facie* evidence only, no doubt the conviction would have been sustained. So in *Wilcox v Jeffrey*[87] it was held that D's presence at a public performance by P, a celebrated American performer on the saxophone, who had been given permission to enter the UK only on

77 *Smith v Baker* [1971] RTR 350.

78 *Bland* [1988] Crim LR 41.

79 *Searle* [1971] Crim LR 592 and commentary thereon.

80 It is insufficient to prove that D arrived even only 30 seconds after P has finished attacking V if there is no evidence of D encouraging P: *Rose* [2004] EWCA Crim 764.

81 *Clarkson* [1971] 3 All ER 344, [1971] 1 WLR 1402; *Jones and Mirrless* (1977) 65 Cr App R 250, CA.

82 *Rannath Mohan v R* [1967] 2 AC 187, [1967] 2 All ER 58.

83 [1965] 1 QB 130, [1963] 2 All ER 897; see also *Tansley v Painter* (1968) 112 Sol Jo 1005; *Danquah* [2004] EWCA Crim 1248 (presence alone insufficient to show that Ds formed part of the gang that robbed V when no evidence of contribution to the intimidation or threats).

84 *Turner* [1991] Crim LR 57 and commentary. (Williams, *TBCL* 360, thinks otherwise, citing *Mastin* (1834) 6 C & P 396.) If one of two racing drivers is killed, the other may be convicted of causing death by dangerous driving; and it is immaterial whether his act or that of the deceased was the immediate cause of death: *Kimsey* [1996] Crim LR 35.

85 (1882) 8 QBD 534.

86 Ibid, at 544.

87 [1951] 1 All ER 464.

condition that he would take no employment, was a sufficient aiding and abetting of P in his contravention of the relevant immigration provisions – the Aliens Order 1920. D's behaviour before and after the performance supplied further evidence of his intention to encourage; for he had met P at the airport and he afterwards reported the performance in laudatory terms in the jazz periodical of which he was the proprietor.

Public order offences often raise particular problems in this context since the principal offence will often be dependent on proof of acts by a specific number of individuals, and in cases of spontaneous violence between groups, it is difficult to identify who is a principal involved in the fight, who is present encouraging, and who is merely present.[88]

Where the evidence establishes mere presence without any positive act, a prior agreement that the crime be committed must be proved. But if some positive act of assistance or encouragement is voluntarily done, with knowledge of the circumstances constituting the offence, it is irrelevant that it is not done with the motive or purpose of encouraging the crime.[89] So if D handed a gun to P knowing that P intended to shoot V, it would not avail D to say that he hoped that P would not use the gun.[90] Nevertheless, the onus on the Crown to prove D's intent can be a heavy one where liability is based on D's presence at the scene.[91]

(iv) Omission as a sufficient *actus reus* of secondary liability?

The law does not generally impose criminal liability for a failure to act, as discussed in Chapter 4. In the context of secondary liability, the question arises whether D's omission to prevent P committing the crime is sufficient to trigger liability. Two categories need to be distinguished.

First, there are the established categories in which the law imposes a duty on an individual to act. Thus, a husband who stands by and watches his wife drown their children is guilty of abetting the homicide.[92]

Secondly, there are circumstances in which D has a *right to control* the actions of another and he deliberately refrains from exercising it, his inactivity *may* be a positive encouragement to the other to perform an illegal act, and, therefore, an aiding and abetting. If a licensee of a public house stands by and watches his customers drinking after hours, he is guilty of aiding and abetting them in doing so.[93]

In *Du Cros v Lambourne*,[94] it was proved that D's car had been driven at a dangerous speed but it was not proved whether D or E was driving. It was held that, nevertheless, D could be convicted. If E was driving she was doing so in D's presence, with his consent and approval; for he was in control and could and ought to have prevented her from driving in a dangerous manner. D was equally liable whether he was a principal or an

[88] See *Blackwood and others* [2002] EWCA Crim 3102.

[89] *National Coal Board v Gamble* [1959] 1 QB 11, [1958] 3 All ER 203; below, p 181.

[90] Cf, however, *Fretwell* (1864) Le & Ca 443; below, p 180.

[91] Eg *Miah* [2004] EWCA Crim 63.

[92] *Russell* [1933] VLR 59.

[93] *Tuck v Robson* [1970] 1 All ER 1171, [1970] 1 WLR 741, DC. The principal offence is committed by the drinkers, not the licensee.

[94] [1907] 1 KB 40; cf also *Rubie v Faulkner* [1940] 1 KB 571, [1940] 1 All ER 285; *Harris* [1964] Crim LR 54. See D. Lanham, 'Drivers Control and Accomplices' [1982] Crim LR 419; M. Wasik, 'A Learner's Careless Driving' [1982] Crim LR 411.

abettor.[95] The result would presumably have been different if it had been E's own car, for D would then have had no right of control, and could only have been convicted if active instigation to drive at such speed had been proved. In such cases it must be proved that D2 knew of those features of P's driving which rendered it dangerous and failed to take action within a reasonable time.[96] In *Baldessare*,[97] P and D unlawfully took X's car and P drove it recklessly and caused V's death. It was held that D was guilty of manslaughter as an abettor. In this case (as prosecuting counsel put it):

> The common purpose to drive recklessly was . . . shown by the fact that both men were driving in a car which did not belong to them and the jury were entitled to infer that the driver was the agent of the passenger. It matters not whose hand was actually controlling the car at the time.

It is not necessary that the inactive participator be present at the commission of the offence. A company and its directors may be convicted of abetting the false making of tachograph records by the company's drivers if they knew that their inactivity was encouraging the practice.[98]

(v) A problem of proof in the *actus reus*

If all that can be proved is that the offence was committed either by D1 or by D2, both must be acquitted.[99] Only if it can be proved that the one who did not commit the crime must have aided and abetted it can both be convicted.[100] This is as true where parents are charged with injury to their child as it is in the case of any other defendants. The only difference is that one parent may have a duty to intervene to prevent the ill-treatment of their child by the other when a stranger would have no such duty. It is for the prosecution to prove that the parent who did not inflict the injuries must have aided and abetted the infliction by failure to fulfil that duty or otherwise. Following detailed consideration by the Law Commission, proposals for new offences and procedural changes were made, and provisions based on, though differing significantly from those recommendations were implemented in the Domestic Violence, Crime and Victims Act.[101] Section 6 of the Act introduces controversial procedural changes whereby inferences can be drawn from a defendant's silence even where no case to answer would otherwise be established. Section 5 introduces the new offence of causing the death of a child or vulnerable adult in household, considered below, p 501.

95 Cf *Swindall and Osborne* (1846) 2 Car & Kir 230: *Salmon* (1880) 6 QBD 79; *Iremonger v Wynne* [1957] Crim LR 624; Williams, *CLGP*, 137, n 23. There is, however, a difference regarding disqualification; above, p 165, n 13 *Smith v Mellors* [1987] Crim LR 421.

96 *Dennis v Pight* (1968) 11 FLR 458 at 463.

97 (1930) 22 Cr App R 70.

98 *J. F. Alford Transport Ltd* [1997] 2 Cr App R 326, [1997] Crim LR 745, citing the 8th edition of this book at 334. See also *Gaunt* [2003] EWCA Crim 3925, where D, the manager, failed to control P (employees) in racial harassment of V (employee).

99 *Richardson* (1785) 1 Leach 387; *Abbott* [1955] 2 QB 497, 39 Cr App R 141.

100 *Russell and Russell* [1987] Crim LR 494; *Lane and Lane* (1985) 82 Cr App R 5. For a valuable direction where one of two interrogating police officers has caused injury, see *Forman* [1988] Crim LR 677 (Judge Woods). See generally, G. Williams, 'Which of you did it?' (1989) 52 MLR 179; E. Griew, 'It Must Have Been One of Them' [1989] Crim LR 129. *Gibson and Gibson* (1984) 80 Cr App R 24 is misleading and should be used with care. See commentary [1984] Crim LR 615.

101 The Law Commission proposed a new offence of aggravated child cruelty under s 1 of the Children and Young Persons Act 1933, and an offence which dealt with both serious injury and death in relation to children only. For comment see P. Glazebrook, 'Insufficient Child Protection' [2003] Crim LR 541.

(b) *Mens rea* of the secondary party

The *mens rea* requirements of the secondary party are complex, but can be summarized thus:

(1) the secondary party must intend to assist or encourage the principal's act, or in the case of procuring, to bring the offence about;

and

(2) the secondary party must have knowledge as to the facts forming the essential elements of the principal's offence, (including any facts as to which the principal bears strict liability). This includes an awareness that the principal will act with *mens rea.*

(i) Intention to aid, etc

It must be proved that D intended to do the acts which he knew to be capable of assisting or encouraging the commission of the crime. There are therefore two elements – an intention to perform the act and an intention that the act will be of assistance. Where D supplies a weapon to P, which P uses in a murder, proof of his intention will turn on whether D meant to hand it over (as opposed to accidentally leaving it and P discovering it) and whether D intended that this assist P. There is no further third element of intention – that the crime be committed. As Devlin J said:[102]

If one man deliberately sells to another a gun to be used for murdering a third, he may be indifferent whether the third man lives or dies and interested only in the cash profit to be made out of the sale, but he can still be an aider and abettor.

So it is the intention to do the acts of assistance or encouragement which must be proved.

Intention to perform the act of assistance

This element of the *mens rea* is unlikely to give to difficulty. D must intend to perform the act that does in fact provide assistance. Only in circumstances of potential involuntariness is there likely to be a problem.

Intention to assist

Whilst it is unnecessary for the prosecution to prove that D intended the commission of the principal offence, proof that D intended by his voluntary act to assist is necessary. The courts have failed to define with any precision what this second element of intention means: should it require proof only that D knew his acts would assist P or should it be proved that D acted in order to assist P?[103] It seems to be generally accepted that D's knowledge that his act will assist is sufficient.[104] The weight of authority certainly supports the view that it is not necessary to prove that D had as his purpose or desire to assist

[102] [1959] 1 QB 11 at 23, [1958] 3 All ER 203, applied in *J. F. Alford Transport Ltd* [1997] 2 Cr App R 326, 334–335.

[103] See R. A. Duff, 'Can I help You? Accessorial Liability and the Intention to Assist' (1990) LS 165. See generally, K. J. M. Smith, above, ch 5.

[104] Cf I. H. Dennis, 'The Mental Element for Accessories', in *Essays in Honour of J. C. Smith* (1987); cf G. Sullivan, 'Intent, Purpose and Complicity' [1988] Crim LR 641; and I. H. Dennis, 'Intention and Complicity: A Reply' [1988] Crim LR 649; G. Williams, 'Complicity, Purpose and the Draft Code – 1' [1990] Crim LR 4, 12.

and if D had the intention, it is no excuse that D's motives in performing the act of assistance were unimpeachable.[105]

Intention to assist not restricted to D's purpose

In *Lynch v DPP for Northern Ireland*, where D drove P to the place where he knew that P intended to murder a policeman, D's intentional driving of the car was aiding and abetting, 'even though he regretted the plan or indeed was horrified by it'.[106] There is some difficulty in reconciling the implications of the decision in *Gillick's Case*[107] (a civil action for a declaration) with this principle. The House of Lords held that, in certain circumstances, a doctor may lawfully give contraceptive advice or treatment to a girl under the age of 16 without her parents' consent. The conditions of lawful treatment could include cases where the doctor, D, knew that the provision of the advice or treatment would encourage or facilitate sexual intercourse by the girl with a man, P. The man would commit an offence.[108] The doctor's motives would no doubt be unimpeachable, but that is generally no answer.

Why is not the doctor (and the parents if they concurred in the advice, for they have no more right than the doctor to aid and abet crime) guilty of aiding and abetting the man's offence?[109] His act may well be facilitated (through the girl's being more ready to have intercourse) and (if he knows of the contraception) encouraged by the doctor's acts.[110] The decision that the doctor's advice is lawful clearly implies that he does not aid and abet a crime but the reason is nowhere clearly stated. It seems most likely that Woolf J and the majority of the House thought he lacked the necessary intention. As noted above,[111] this seems to put an undue strain on the concept of intention if to be liable as a secondary party D must not only intend to provide the assistance, but intend that the principal offence be committed. If a mother, knowing that her son is about to embark on an armed robbery and cannot be dissuaded, gives him a bullet-proof vest, with the sole and admirable motive of saving him from death or serious injury, is not her intention to enable him to perpetrate the robbery more safely an intention to aid and abet it? This should be a sufficient basis for her liability without proof that she intended that the robbery took place. It is submitted that *Gillick's Case* is better regarded as being based impliedly, if not expressly,[112] on necessity.

In *Fretwell*,[113] D reluctantly supplied an abortifacient to a woman when she threatened to kill herself if he did not do so. He hoped she would not use it but she did so and died. This was self-murder at common law but D was held not liable as an accessory because he was 'unwilling that the woman should take the poison'. A distinction between indifference and unwillingness of this nature is, however, too uncertain to form the basis of a

[105] Woolf J in *Gillick v West Norfolk and Wisbech Area Health Authority* [1984] QB 581 at 589, [1984] 1 All ER 365 at 373. Woolf J's discussion of the criminal aspects of this case was adopted by Lords Scarman and Bridge in the House of Lords [1986] AC 112.

[106] [1975] AC 653 at 678, [1975] 1 All ER 913, per Lord Morris, approving the judgment of Lowry LCJ on this point. *Fretwell* (1862) Le & Ca 161, below, appears to be a merciful decision and unsound in principle.

[107] Above, n 105.

[108] Sexual Offences Act 2003, below, p 628.

[109] Although see now the exceptions in the Sexual Offences Act 2003, s 73.

[110] For a full discussion of this question, see [1985] Crim LR 114.

[111] P 98.

[112] See J. R. Spencer in *Criminal Law Essays* 148, 164.

[113] Above, n 105; cf Williams, CLGP, s 124.

legal rule. Applying the principles outlined above, D intentionally/voluntarily supplied the product and he intended to assist. *Fretwell* is perhaps best regarded as a case in which the court strained the principles governing the liability of accessories in order to mitigate the severity of the rule which treated suicide as murder.[114] Woolf J regards it 'as confined to its own facts'.[115]

Oblique intention to assist

In its most recent pronouncement, *Bryce*[116] the Court of Appeal has confirmed that D can be found to be intending to assist even if it is not D's purpose or desire that his acts will assist. The court refers to an extract from *Blackstone's Criminal Practice* suggesting that the definition of intention in this context should reflect that in the law of murder. On this approach, the jury can 'find' an intention to assist from the evidence of D's intended performance of the act of assistance, even though his purpose or desire is not to assist. In *Bryce*, D had transported P to the scene of the crime, he clearly had intended to perform that act of assistance, but D claimed that he lacked any intention to assist since he did not know whether P would carry out the killing, indeed, D claimed that P himself did not finally decided to do so until 12 hours after D had left. The Court of Appeal held that the jury were entitled to find, from the evidence of his performing that intentional act of transportation and the knowledge D had of P's potential crime, that D had a sufficient intention to assist.

Recklessness insufficient

Mere recklessness, still less negligence, whether assistance be given, is probably not enough. D's realization that he may have left his gun-cupboard unlocked and that his son has a disposition to commit armed robbery, is probably not sufficient to fix D with liability for the armed robbery and homicide which the son commits using one of D's guns. There was no intention to do any act of advice or assistance.

'Intention' in cases of supply

In *National Coal Board v Gamble*,[117] P, a lorry driver, had his employer's lorry filled with coal at a colliery belonging to the defendant Board. When the lorry was driven on to the weighbridge operated by the defendants' employee, D2, it appeared, and D2 so informed P, that its load exceeded by nearly four tons that permitted by the relevant Motor Vehicles (Construction and Use) Regulations 1955. P said he would take the risk, D2 gave him a weighbridge ticket and P committed the offence as principal by driving the overloaded lorry on the highway. The property in the coal did not pass until the ticket was handed over and, therefore, P could not properly have left the colliery without it. It was held that the Board, D1, through D2,[118] was guilty of the misdemeanour. The decision was based on the assumption that D2 knew he had the right to prevent the lorry leaving the colliery with the coal. Had D2 not known this, he should have been acquitted. Presumably D2 was indifferent whether P drove his overloaded lorry on the road or not – he probably thought that it was none of his business – but D2's motive was irrelevant and it was

114 As to which, see below, p 493.

115 *A-G v Able* [1984] 1 All ER 277 at 287, citing the 4th edition of the work (1978) at 120–121. But cf *Gillick*, above p 180 and *Janaway v Salford Health Authority*, below, p 513.

116 [2004] EWCA Crim 1231.

117 [1959] 1 QB 11, [1958] 3 All ER 203 DC, Slade J dissenting.

118 See, however, below, p 182, n 123.

enough that a positive act of assistance had been voluntarily done (that is intentional performance of the act of assistance) with knowledge that by doing so he would be assisting P and knowledge of the circumstances constituting the offence.

This result is in accord with two previous decisions. In *Cook v Stockwell*,[119] D, a brewer, intentionally supplied large quantities of beer to some cottages, knowing very well that they were reselling it, without being licensed to do so, to soldiers quartered nearby. In *Cafferata v Wilson*,[120] D, a wholesaler, voluntarily sold a firearm to P, who kept a general shop, but was not registered as a firearms dealer. Presumably D knew that P was going to resell the firearm, which in fact he did. In both cases D was held liable as an accessory to the illegal sale. In these cases the suppliers were indifferent whether the crime was committed or not. Both had voluntarily performed acts of assistance and had sufficient knowledge from which a jury could find that they intended by the act to assist.

'Intention' when D obliged to supply

National Coal Board v Gamble suggests a distinction between the cases:

(1) where the seller (D) is aware of the illegal purpose of the buyer (P) before ownership has passed to the buyer; and
(2) where the seller (D) learns of that purpose for the first time after ownership has passed but before delivery.

In (1) delivery amounts to abetting; in (2) it does not. The seller is merely complying with his legal duty to give the buyer his own property.

> In a sense a man who gives up to a criminal a weapon which the latter has a right to demand from him aids in the commission of the crime as much as if he sold or lent the article, but this has never been held to be aiding in law.[121]

This seems a scarcely satisfactory distinction. If D delivers weedkiller to P, knowing that P intends to use it to murder his wife, it would be remarkable if D's guilt turned on whether the ownership passed before or after D learned of P's intention. The important thing is that D knows of P's intention when he makes delivery. It should not be an answer that P has a right to possession of the thing in the civil law because the civil law should not afford a right in such a case.[122] In *Garrett v Arthur Churchill (Glass) Ltd*[123] D, who had bought a goblet as agent of P, was held guilty of being knowingly concerned in the exportation of goods without a licence, when, on P's instructions, he delivered P's own goblet to P's agent who was to take it to America.

> . . . albeit there was a legal duty in ordinary circumstances to hand over the goblet to the owners once the agency was determined, I do not think that an action would lie for breach of that duty if the handing over would constitute the offence of being knowingly concerned in its exportation.[124]

119 (1915) 84 LJKB 2187. 120 [1936] 3 All ER 149.

121 [1959] 1 QB 11 at 20, per Devlin J.

122 See Williams, CLGP, s 124 and J. C. Smith, 'Civil Law Concepts in the Criminal Law' [1972]B CLJ 197 at 208.

123 [1970] 1 QB 92, [1969] 2 All ER 1141. How far does this go? If X lends a picture to a museum, does the museum really commit an offence if, on demand, it returns the picture to X, knowing that he intends to export it without the licence required by law?

124 [1969] 2 All ER at 1145, per Parker LCJ.

Probably then the seller is liable whether or not the ownership has passed before delivery. Williams's view, however, is that the seller ought to be liable in neither case. He argues:[125]

The seller of an ordinary marketable commodity is not his buyer's keeper in criminal law unless he is specifically made so by statute. Any other rule would be too wide an extension of criminal responsibility.

A rule based on the nature of the thing as 'an ordinary marketable commodity' is not workable. Weedkiller is an ordinary marketable commodity but it may be acquired and used to commit murder. A more feasible distinction is one based on the seriousness of the offence contemplated. This is the American approach:

The gravity of the social harm resulting from the unlawful conduct is used to determine whether mere knowledge of the intended use will be sufficient to carry the taint of illegality.[126]

The disadvantage of this rule is its uncertainty and no such distinction has been taken in English law. The cases suggest a general rule of liability of sellers. This is *a fortiori* the case with lenders or letters of articles or premises intended for unlawful purposes for here the owner has a continuing interest in and right to control the property.[127]

(ii) Knowledge of circumstances[128]

The second, more complex element of the secondary party's *mens rea* is that he must have knowledge, or at least turn a blind eye to, any circumstance which is an element of the principal offence.

Before a person can be convicted of aiding and abetting the commission of an offence he must at least know the essential matters which constitute that offence. He need not actually know that an offence has been committed, because he may not know that the facts constitute an offence and ignorance of the law is not a defence.[129]

This raises two questions:

(1) What does 'knowledge' mean in this context?
(2) As to what must D have knowledge – what are the 'essential matters that constitute the principal offence'?

Knowledge/foresight/wilful blindness

Determining whether D's state of mind was one of knowledge is especially difficult in the context of secondary liability since the question is really whether D has foreseen the likelihood of certain events and conduct on the part of P. At best they may be happening at that time, but commonly D's acts of assistance will have occurred before the

125 CLGP, s 124 at 373. *TBCL* (1st edn), 293–294.

126 R. M. Perkins and R. N. Boyce (3rd edn) 746. See also G. Williams, 'Obedience to Law as a Crime' (1990) 53 MLR 445.

127 For example, the hotelier who lets a room to a man accompanied by a 14-year-old girl, knowing that he intends to seduce her.

128 See generally K. J. M. Smith, above, ch 6.

129 *Johnson v Youden* [1950] 1 KB 544 at 546, [1950] 1 All ER 300 at 302, per Lord Goddard CJ. See also *Ackroyds Air Travel Ltd v DPP* [1950] 1 All ER 933 at 936; *Thomas v Lindop* [1950] 1 All ER 966 at 968; *Ferguson v Weaving* [1951] 1 KB 814, [1951] 1 All ER 412; *Bateman v Evans* [1964] Crim LR 601; *Smith v Jenner* [1968] Crim LR 99; *Dial Contracts Ltd v Vickers* [1971] RTR 386; *D. Stanton & Sons Ltd v Webber* [1973] RTR 87, [1972] Crim LR 544 and commentary thereon.

commission of the crime by P and D cannot really have 'knowledge' of something that has yet to occur.[130] The courts have therefore interpreted 'knowledge' as equivalent to D foreseeing (or in some cases turning a blind eye to) the likelihood of the essential matters. Thus, in *Bryce*, the court held that it was sufficient that D knowingly did the act of assistance transporting P to the scene, and at the time of doing that act 'contemplated' the commission of an offence of the type that P committed.

In *Carter v Richardson*[131] where D, the supervisor of a learner driver, P, was convicted of abetting P's driving with excess alcohol, the court said that it was sufficient that D knew that it was 'probable' that P was 'over the limit' – that he was, in effect, 'reckless' in the *Cunningham* sense[132] – to the essential element of P's being over the limit. It may be that this was *obiter* because the magistrates were satisfied that D, though obviously unaware of the precise amount of alcohol in P's blood, knew that it was so great as to be above the limit.

In *Carter v Richardson*, the principal's offence comprised two main elements: driving with excess alcohol. D intentionally encouraged the act of driving and was reckless as to the circumstance of the excess alcohol, that was sufficient render him liable. In *Blakely and Sutton v DPP*,[133] D's intention was to create the circumstance (P's excessive alcohol level), being at worst reckless whether the act of driving, which it was her object to prevent, occurred. In that case D, wanting P to stay the night with her, laced his drink without his knowledge. D knew that P would not drive home when she told him, as she intended, of the alcohol he had consumed, but he drove off before she could tell him. D's conviction for procuring P's driving with excess alcohol was quashed because the justices may have convicted, wrongly applying *Caldwell/Lawrence* recklessness, on the assumption that it was enough that D had not given thought to the possibility of an obvious and serious risk that he would do so. Though the court deplored the use of the word, 'reckless', it seems that the conviction would have been upheld if it had been proved that D was aware of a risk that P would drive with excess alcohol. If so, this would go further than the decision or *dicta* (as the case may be) in *Carter v Richardson.* It seems that subjective recklessness as to a circumstance in the principal's crime is enough, although because of the common misuses of the word 'reckless', it is better to speak in terms of awareness of probability.

As noted, the courts have been prepared to accept that knowledge can be satisfied by proof of wilful blindness but not negligence. 'Knowledge includes what ought to be known, so that wilful blindness cannot excuse. There is a vast distinction between deliberately refraining from making inquiries, the result of which the person does not care to have, and mere negligence. Negligence cannot amount to sufficient *mens rea*'.[134]

130 For discussion of the philosophical nature of knowledge and its relevance to the criminal law see S. Shute, 'Knowledge and Belief in the Criminal Law' at 171 and G. R. Sullivan, 'Knowledge, Belief and Culpability' at 207 both in S. Shute and A. Simester (eds), *Criminal Law Theory: Doctrines of the General Part* (2002). See also the essay by R. Bagshaw, 'Legal Proof of Knowledge', in P. Mirfield and R. Smith (eds), *Essays in Honour of Colin Tapper* (2003) on evidential influences of substantive law definitions of knowledge.

131 [1974] RTR 314, discussed by G. Williams [1975] CLJ 182 and *TBCL*, 309. But in *Giogianni* (1984) 156 CLR 473 the High Court of Australia held that recklessness is not sufficient on a charge of aiding and abetting.

132 It is quite clear that inadvertent *Caldwell/Lawrence* recklessness was never enough: *Blakely and Sutton v DPP* [1991] Crim LR 763, DC.

133 [1991] RTR 405, [1991] Crim LR 763, DC.

134 Per Collins J *R v Roberts and George* [1997] RTR 462; [1997] Crim LR 55.

Knowledge in abetting an offence of strict liability

This same *mens rea* – knowledge of the essential elements of P's wrongdoing – is required for secondary participation in an offence of strict liability as for any other offence. The principal offender may, but a secondary party may not, be convicted without *mens rea.* The reason is that secondary participation is a common law notion. It was never necessary for a statute creating an offence to specify that it should also be an offence to aid, etc, its commission. The common law, now codified in the Accessories and Abettors Act 1861,[135] was that so to act created liability to conviction of the offence aided. It is natural that the normal principles of liability at common law should apply. The result, however, is to emphasize the anomalous nature of offences of strict liability, for the alleged aider who has no *mens rea* must be acquitted even if he was negligent[136] whereas the principal who has caused the *actus reus* must be convicted even if he took all proper care.

In *Callow v Tillstone,*[137] D, a veterinary surgeon, was charged with abetting the exposure for sale of unsound meat. At the request of a butcher, P, he examined the carcase of a heifer which had eaten yew leaves and been killed by the farmer just before it would have died of yew poisoning. He gave P a certificate that the meat was sound. The examination had been negligently conducted and the meat was tainted. P, relying on the certificate, exposed the meat for sale and was convicted. The justices, holding that D's negligence had caused the exposure, convicted him of abetting. It was held that his conviction must be quashed.[138] Thus, if *Prince*[139] had been assisted in his taking of V out of the possession of her parents by a friend, D, who had driven him away with the girl in a hansom cab, it would have been a defence for D (even though it was not for Prince) to show that he believed the girl to be over 16 or even (at least if he was unaware of the relevance of the age of 16) that he did not know what age she was. The same principle must apply, *a fortiori*, to offences where negligence as to circumstances will found liability. If D encourages P to marry, both believing honestly but mistakenly and on unreasonable grounds that P's husband is dead, P may be convicted of bigamy but D cannot be convicted of abetting. This principle applies only to D's negligence as to circumstances forming part of P's crime. Whether a secondary party may be liable for unforeseen consequences of P's crime is considered below.[140]

'Essential matters' of P's offence of which D must 'know'

'The essential matters which constitute the offence' are the circumstances existing at the time when the act of secondary participation is done. D need not know that the essential elements of P's conduct constitute a crime since ignorance of the criminal law is no defence; rather D must know of the existence of the essential matters. The essential matters clearly comprise the *actus reus* of P's offence. The circumstances of the *actus reus* must be known, but the *actus reus* may also include certain consequences, but these cannot be 'known' by D before they happen. It is more accurate to speak of the

[135] Above, p 164. Cf *McCarthy* [1964] Crim LR 225.

[136] *Carter v Mace* [1949] 2 All ER 714, DC, is to the contrary, but in *Davies, Turner & Co Ltd v Brodie* [1954] 3 All ER 283, [1954] 1 WLR 1364, DC, that case was said to lay down no principle of law and to be decided on its own particular facts. See J. Montgomerie in 'Aiding and Abetting Statutory Offences' (1950) 66 LQR 222.

[137] (1900) 83 LT 411, DC.

[138] See also *Bowker v Premier Drug Co Ltd* [1928] 1 KB 217 at 227.

[139] Above, p 139.

[140] Below, p 194.

requirement that D foresees the possibility (not necessarily a probability)[141] of the consequences occurring.[142] This aspect of the *mens rea* of D is considered in full below, p 195. The essential matters should, logically, also include P's *mens rea.* Thus, if D foresees/knows that P might beat V up, but does not foresee/know that P will perform that action with the intention of killing or causing V grievous bodily harm, D will not have knowledge of the 'essential matters' comprising the principal offence of murder. (There is however, some authority for the view that the *mens rea* of the principal offender need not be known or foreseen by D. This is discussed below, p 194.) It is important to note that D need not have the same *mens rea* as P, that is, that required for the principal offence; D must have knowledge/foresight of P's *mens rea.* Difficulties involved in proving one person's contemplation of another's state of mind are obvious. The difficulty is even more apparent when it is realized that D may be found to have the relevant *mens rea* relating to P's *mens rea* even though at the time D performs the *actus reus* of assistance P has not yet formed that *mens rea.*[143]

Knowledge of type of crime

The courts have struggled to identify accurately the degree or specificity of knowledge that D must have as to P's crime. Three principles have evolved.

(1) If D aids, abets, counsels or procures P to commit a crime of a certain type, neither party specifying any particular victim, time or place, D may be convicted as a secondary party to any crime of that type which P commits.

(2) If D aids, abets, counsels or procures P to commit a crime against a particular person, or in respect of a particular thing, D is not liable if P *intentionally* commits an offence of the same type against some other person, or in respect of some other thing, unless D foresaw that P might do as he did.[144]

(3) D is, however, equally liable with P for any acts done by P in the course of endeavouring to carry out their common purpose. If the common purpose is to cause grievous bodily harm to V, and D, endeavouring to do so, kills V, both D and P are guilty of murder. If the common purpose is to injure V and P, endeavouring to do so, kills him, both P and D are guilty of manslaughter. If the common purpose is to wound V (so the case is within principle (2) above) and P, endeavouring to wound V, wounds X, P is liable under the doctrine of transferred malice;[145] and so, therefore, is D.

Principle (1) A leading case is *Bainbridge.*[146] D purchased some oxygen-cutting equipment which was used six weeks later for breaking into a bank at Stoke Newington. D's story was that he had bought the equipment for one Shakeshaft, that he suspected Shakeshaft wanted it for something illegal – perhaps melting down stolen goods – but that he did not know that it was going to be used for any such purpose as it was in fact used. It was held that it was essential to prove that D knew the *type of crime* that was going to be committed: it was not enough that he knew that some kind of illegality was contemplated; but that, if D knew breaking and entering and stealing was intended, it was not

[141] *Powell* [1999] AC 1.
[142] See generally *Day* [2001] Crim LR 984, discussed below.
[143] *Bryce* [2004] Crim LR 963.
[144] *Powell* [1999] AC 1, [1997] 4 All ER 545, HL.
[145] Above, p 113.
[146] [1960] 1 QB 129, [1959] 3 All ER 200, CCA.

necessary to prove that D knew that the Midland Bank, Stoke Newington, was going to be broken into. That would be too great a degree of specificity for the prosecution to establish and would narrow the scope of accessorial liability unduly. It is the same where information on how to commit a crime of a particular type is given, though neither adviser nor advised has any particular crime in view when the advice is given.[147] Where D opened a bank account for P, giving P a false name, D was convicted of aiding and abetting P in the fraudulent use of the particular forged cheque which P subsequently drew upon the account. D had evinced an intention that the account be used as a vehicle for presenting forged cheques like the one in fact presented.[148] D knew the type of crime. This principle might be regarded as unduly broad. Can it really be said that where D does not even know the precise crime P will commit he knows the 'essential elements'?

The House of Lords carried the principle to its logical conclusion in *DPP for Northern Ireland v Maxwell*.[149] If D gives assistance to P, knowing that P intends to commit a crime, but being uncertain whether P has crime X, or crime Y, or crime Z, in mind, D will be liable as a secondary party to whichever of those crimes P in fact commits. D drove P to an inn, realizing that P intended either to plant a bomb or to shoot persons at the inn. In fact, P intended to plant, and did plant a bomb. D was liable for that offence (as a secondary party). He would have been liable for murder if P had shot and killed. It would be otherwise if P had committed another type of crime which was not in D's contemplation when he did the relevant act. Nor is a 'general criminal intention' enough. So an intention to abet another in the possession of a bag, whatever its contents may be, is insufficient to found an indictment for abetting the possession of cannabis.[150] If D had guessed that the bag contained either cannabis or some other article, proscribed or not, that should have been enough.

Where are the limits to such liability? If D has supplied P with the means of committing or information on how to commit a crime of a particular type, is he to be held liable for all the crimes of that type which P may thereafter commit? What if the Midland at Stoke Newington was the second, third or fourth bank which P had feloniously broken and entered with Bainbridge's apparatus? Glanville Williams questioned whether D should be subject to such unforeseeable and perhaps far-reaching liability.[151] Yet, once it is conceded that D need not know the details of any specific crime, it is difficult to see why he should be liable for any one crime of *the type* contemplated and not for others.[152]

Bainbridge and *Maxwell* leave some unsolved problems. Whether a crime is of the 'same type' as another may not always be easy to discover. If D lends a jemmy to P, contemplating that P intends to enter a house in order to steal, is D guilty of any offence if P enters a house intending to commit grievous bodily harm? Clearly, D cannot be convicted of grievous bodily harm, because that is an offence of a different type; but he is probably guilty of burglary, because burglary was the crime he had in view – though this

147 *Baker* (1909) 28 NZLR 536. G. Williams thinks the case is wrongly decided: CLGP s 125. But is it distinguishable in principle from *Bainbridge*? Cf *McLeod and Georgia Straight Publishing Co Ltd* (1970) 75 WWR 161 (newspaper liable for incitement through article on how to cultivate marijuana).

148 *Thambiah v R* [1966] AC 37, [1965] 3 All ER 661, PC.

149 [1978] 3 All ER 1140, [1978] 1 WLR 1350, HL.

150 *Patel* [1970] Crim LR 274 and commentary thereon. Cf *Fernandez* [1970] Crim LR 277.

151 CLGP, s 124.

152 On the question of the withdrawal of an accessory before the fact, see below, p 208.

particular variety of burglary may be abhorrent to him. If D contemplates theft and P commits robbery, D is not guilty of robbery but might be convicted of the theft which is included in it. Is theft an offence of the same type as removing an article from a place open to the public[153] or taking a motor vehicle without authority?[154] Is robbery an offence of the same type as blackmail? What of D who provides a stolen credit card to P assuming it will be used in deception, but P uses it to slip the latch on V's door and commit theft. Is it sufficient that these are both dishonesty offences?

This is an aspect of the law desperately in need of clarification. That is now only likely on any substantial scale from Parliament.

Principle (2) This principle is most clearly expressed by Hawkins:[155]

> But if a man command another to commit a felony on a particular person or thing and he do it on another; as to kill A and he kill B or to burn the house of A and he burn the house of B or to steal an ox and he steal an horse; or to steal such an horse and he steal another; or to commit a felony of one kind and he commit another of a quite different nature; as to rob J S of his plate as he is going to market, and he break open his house in the night and there steal the plate; it is said that the commander is not an accessory because the act done varies in substance from that which was commanded.

The principle applies where there is a substantial variation from the proposed course of conduct. Hawkins also stated:[156]

> [I]f the felony committed be the same in substance with that which was intended, and variant only in some circumstance, as in respect of the time or place, at which, or the means whereby it was effected, the abettor of the intent is altogether as much an accessory as if there had been no variance at all between it and the execution of it; as where a man advises another to kill such a one in the night, and he kills him in the day, or to kill him in the fields, and he kills him in the town, or to poison him, and he stabs or shoots him.

The distinction depends on whether the variation is one 'of substance' and any such distinction must produce difficult borderline cases. In *Dunning and Graham*, an unreported case at Preston Crown Court,[157] D had a grievance against V. P offered to set fire to V's house. D accepted the offer and gave P V's address. P went to V's house, changed his mind, and set fire to V's Mercedes instead. D did not know that V owned such a car. Nevertheless, Macpherson J held that it was open to the jury to convict D on the ground that she must have authorized or envisaged the possibility of property such as a car in the driveway being damaged by fire. If the car had been so damaged as a consequence of P's setting fire to the house, D would have been liable for arson of the car under principle (3), below. The actual case, however, seems to involve a deliberate variation from the plan. The result might be justified on this basis that D had authorized P to take revenge on V by damaging his property and that it did not really matter to her what the property was. Whether the variation is, or is not, one of substance, depends on the purpose of D as expressed to P.

The South African case of *S v Robinson*[158] provides a further controversial illustration of the difficulties of applying these principles. D1, D2 and P agreed with V that P should

[153] Theft Act 1968, s 11. Below, p 716. [154] Theft Act 1968, s 12. Below, p 719.

[155] 2 PC c 29, s 21. See also Foster, 369. Stephen, *Digest* (4th edn), art 43. [156] Ibid, s 20.

[157] December 1985, unreported. [158] 1968 (1) SA 666.

kill V to procure the money for which V's life was insured and to avoid V's prosecution for fraud. At the last moment, V withdrew his consent to die but P nevertheless killed him. It was not proved that D1 and D2 foresaw the possibility that P might kill V even if he withdrew his consent or that they had been reckless whether he did so kill him. It was held that the common purpose was murder with the consent of the victim and that P had acted outside that common purpose. D1 and D2, accordingly, were not guilty of murder – though they were guilty of attempted murder, since P had reached the stage of an attempt before V withdrew his consent. Holmes JA, dissenting, thought '. . . looking squarely at the whole train of events, the conspiracy was fulfilled in death, and there is no room for exquisite niceties of logic about the exact limits of the mandate in the conspiratorial common purpose'. The division of judicial opinion in this case highlights the problem. What constitutes a change of 'substance' could be interpreted narrowly, being limited to changes which would alter the nature of the criminal charge that could be prosecuted. In *Robinson*, the offence planned was murder, that committed was murder, but we know from other high authority that a fundamental change might involve something that would not alter the nature of the charge – as where the manner of infliction is different.[159] A broader view of change of 'substance' seems more desirable, but the problem then arises of how to delimit 'changes of substance'. If P knows that a condition precedent of the agreement has not been performed (whether or not forming part of the definition of the crime), he might naturally be said to be no longer engaged on the joint enterprise. If D agrees with P that P shall murder V if he finds out that V is committing adultery with D's wife and P, having discovered that V is *not* committing adultery, nevertheless kills him, D should not be liable for murder, though, if this conditional intention is enough, he may be liable for conspiracy to murder.

Principle (3) The doctrine of transferred malice applies to secondary parties as it does to principals.[160] Where P, intending to follow D's advice to kill V, mistakes X for V and kills X, D is guilty as a secondary party, and P as a principal, of murder. If D advises P to burn V's house and P does so but the flames spread and burn Y's house, D as well as P is guilty of arson of Y's house. The difference between these cases and those falling under principle (2) is that here P has not *deliberately* departed from the course that D advised or assisted him to follow; P was attempting to put the agreed plan into execution and D is as responsible for the unintended results of the acts he has authorized or encouraged as P.

In *Reardon*[161] P shot two men, X and Y, in the bar of a pub and carried them, both dying, into the garden. He returned to the bar, said to D that one of them was still alive, and asked D for the loan of his knife. Medical evidence established that both men died from wounds inflicted by P with D's knife. D was charged with both murders. It was accepted[162] that if D intentionally gives assistance to P to kill an identified person, X, D is not liable if P *deliberately* kills a different person, Y. But in *Reardon* the intended victim was not identified. There being no way of distinguishing between the victims, it was a case

159 *English* [1999] AC 1.

160 Hawkins, PC, ch 29, s 22; Foster, *Crown Law*, 370; Stephen, *Digest* (4th edn), art 41, illustration (1). See also D. Lanham, 'Accomplices and Transferred Malice' (1980) 96 LQR 110.

161 [1999] Crim LR 392, CA. In *Gilmour* D was roused from his bed and told to drive the car 'which he did not do willingly'. It seems his purpose was not to throw petrol bombs but to save his own skin; but he was treated as a party to a joint enterprise.

162 Referring to the 8th edition of this book, at p 142.

of liability for both murders or neither. The convictions were upheld on the ground that the jury must have found that D foresaw 'at least the strong possibility that if [P] found the other deceased alive, he might use the knife in the same way . . .'. D intended to assist one murder and he knew there was a real risk that there might be two.

The old and famous case of *Saunders and Archer*,[163] in its result at least, is reconcilable with this principle. P, intended to murder his wife. Following the advice of D, P gave her a poisoned apple to eat. She ate a little of it and gave the rest to their child. P loved the child, yet he stood by and watched it eat the poison, of which it soon died. It was held that P was guilty of murder of the child, but the judges agreed that D, who, of course, was not present when the child ate the apple, was not an accessory to this murder.

If P had been absent when the child ate the apple it is thought that this would have been a case of transferred malice and D would have been liable; but P's presence and failure to act made the killing of the child, in effect, a deliberate, and not an accidental, departure from the agreed plan. It was – as it is well put in Kenny, 'as if Saunders had changed his mind and on a later occasion had used such poison as Archer had named in order to murder some quite different person of whom Archer had never heard'.[164]

At one time the authorities stated that a person was liable for the commission of an offence which was a probable consequence of the offence counselled or abetted – an objective test. In the leading case of *Chan Wing-Siu*, however, it was accepted that the test is now subjective and the only issue in that case was whether the prosecution had to prove that D foresaw that the commission of the offence was more probable than not, or whether, as the Privy Council decided, it was enough that he foresaw it as something which 'might well' happen. The matter is considered further under 'Joint enterprise' below.

(c) Joint enterprise and secondary liability[165]

Difficulties arise in fixing the secondary party's liability in a case of joint enterprise, as for example where D and P set out to commit a crime, say burglary, and in the course of the commission of that crime P commits a further offence. In what circumstances will D be liable for the further offences committed by P? It is in these situations that the question of D's foresight of 'essential matters' becomes most complex. In summary, the law has now settled that D will be liable for P's further offences, provided that those further offences are of the type that D contemplated P might commit with *mens rea*, and, that D contemplated that P might commit them in a manner not fundamentally different from the way that P did in fact commit them.

(i) Joint enterprise – an aspect of aiding and abetting

Cases where two or more parties have embarked on the commission of a criminal offence – a joint criminal enterprise – have concerned the courts greatly in recent years. It is submitted that these cases are governed by the ordinary principles of secondary parti-

163 (1573) 2 Plowd 473.

164 *Outlines* at 112. See the perceptive jury questions and clear directions in *Gordon-Butt* [2004] EWCA Crim 961 on changes of victim.

165 J. C. Smith, 'Criminal Liability of Accessories: Law and Law Reform' (1997) 113 LQR 453, J. Burchell, 'Joint Enterprise and Common Purpose' (1997) SACJ 125.

cipation. It is important to notice at the outset that in *Rook*[166] it was held that the same ordinary principles of secondary liability apply to a party who is absent as to one who is present – and rightly so, because the absent party may well be the 'mastermind' and the most culpable party. In the House of Lords in *Powell Daniels and English* their lordships consistently treated parties to the joint enterprise as accessories.

However, a new theory appeared in the Law Commission's Consultation Paper No 131, 'Assisting and Encouraging Crime',[167] and in *Stewart and Schofield*[168] – that a party to a joint enterprise is different from a 'mere aider or abettor, etc' or secondary party. Distinguishing secondary participation, Hobhouse LJ said: 'In contrast, where the allegation is joint enterprise, the allegation is that one defendant participated in the criminal act of another'.[169]

But this theory presents problems, if D and P set out together to rape (or to murder),[170] how does D 'participate' in P's act of penile penetration of V (or P's shooting V) except by assisting him or encouraging him – that is, aiding, abetting, counselling or procuring him – to do the act? It is submitted there is no other way. The only peculiarity of joint enterprise cases is that, once a common purpose to commit the offence in question is proved, there is no need to look further for evidence of assisting and encouraging. The act of combining to commit the offence satisfies these requirements of aiding and abetting. Frequently it will be acts of encouragement which provide the evidence of the common purpose. It is simply necessary to apply the ordinary principles of secondary liability to the joint enterprise, as follows.

(ii) Joint enterprise and joint principals

It will be recalled that D1 and D2 are joint principals where each does an act which is a cause of the *actus reus*; for example, each stabs V who dies from the combined effect of the wounds; or D1 and D2 together plant a bomb which goes off and kills V; but then each is liable for his own act, not because he has 'participated' in the act of another; and each is liable to the extent of his own *mens rea.* Suppose that, in the bomb case, D2 intends (and believes that D1 intends) that ample warning will be given to allow the area to be cleared, whereas D1 intends that no warning shall be given. The bomb goes off

166 [1993] 2 All ER 955. *Wan and Chan* [1995] Crim LR 296.

167 Criticized by J. C. Smith, 'Secondary participation in crime – can we do without it?' (1994) 144 New LJ 679. The Law Commission propose the abolition of the law of aiding, abetting, counselling and procuring and its replacement by two substantive offences of (i) assisting and (ii) encouraging the commission of crime. The proposals have many attractive features but involve serious practical difficulties. A puzzling aspect of the paper is that it contemplates the possibility of retaining joint enterprise liability while abolishing aiding, abetting, etc. It is submitted that this is impossible. A Report on Assisting and Encouraging is to be produced by the Law Commission in 2005 available from www.lawcom.gov.uk/163.htm#57/40.

168 [1995] 1 Cr App R 441, [1995] Crim LR 420 and commentary.

169 Hobhouse LJ returned to this theme in a civil proceeding, *Crédit Lyonnais Bank Nederland NV v Export Credits Guarantee Department* [1998] 1 Lloyd's Rep 19 at 42–44. The effect seems to be the same as the opinion in *Osland,* above, n 36, that all the parties to a joint enterprise are principals in the first degree. The Australian approach is considered by the High Court in *McAuliffe v The Queen* (1995) 183 CLR 108 and *Gillard v The Queen* [2003] HCA 64, paras 108–113.

170 There is no justification for limiting the joint enterprise principles to murder, cf the statement in *Bryce* that it arises when 'two persons have already embarked upon and actually engaged in a course of criminal conduct in the course of which someone is killed', para 29, is too narrow.

prematurely and kills V. D1 is *prima facie* guilty of murder, D2 of manslaughter.[171] Similarly where they jointly release a gas canister which D2 believes to contain tear gas and D1 knows to contain a deadly gas. There are two principals and two offences.

(iii) Principal and accessory with a common purpose

Where the parties have a common purpose to commit an offence but the act of P alone is the immediate cause of its commission, then –

(1) D is liable for the commission by P of that crime (X) which D intended and assisted or encouraged him to commit. For purposes of exposition, it is convenient to call this 'basic accessory liability'.[172]

(2) D is also liable for crime (Y) which he did *not* intend or assist or encourage P to commit, if D knew that in the course of[173] committing crime (X) which D was encouraging or assisting, P *might* do – that is, there was a real risk that P would do – an act of the kind which P did and which resulted in crime (Y). It is convenient to call this 'parasitic accessory liability'. The principle was stated by the Privy Council in *Chan Wing-Siu v R*,[174] as interpreted in *Hyde* and *Hui Chi-ming* and approved by the House of Lords in *Powell and Daniels*.[175]

> [The principle] turns on contemplation . . . It meets the case of a crime foreseen as a possible incident of the common unlawful enterprise. The criminal culpability lies in participating in the venture with that foresight.[176]

For example, D assists or encourages P to commit burglary or robbery, contemplating that in the course of committing that offence P 'might well' do an act with intent to cause grievous bodily harm. If P does an act of the kind foreseen/contemplated and causes grievous bodily harm, D, as well as P, is guilty of the offence of causing grievous bodily harm with intent, contrary to s 18 of the Offences Against the Person Act. If V dies of the injury, D, as well as P, is guilty of murder. If D assists or encourages P, contemplating that P may act with intent

[171] Earlier editions of this book (see 6th edn at 152–3) treated *Murtagh and Kennedy* [1955] Crim LR 315 as if it were a case of joint principals, a case where both parties were the cause of the *actus reus*. P, the driver, and D, the passenger in a car, were charged with murder by running down V. Glyn Jones J directed the jury that to drive a car at a person with intent to kill or cause grievous bodily harm was murder; but wilfully to drive on the pavement, not intending to hit anyone but intending to terrorize, would be manslaughter. The jury convicted P of murder and D of manslaughter. Both convictions were quashed on grounds which are immaterial for present purposes. The verdicts imply that P intended to run V down but D intended that he should not be run down but merely frightened. Are not driving at V to kill him, and driving close to V to frighten him, fundamentally different acts? And if D did not intend that, nor foresee a risk that, P would, drive at V, was not the act outside the scope of the joint enterprise and one for which D was not responsible? Only P did an act causing death and D could only be made liable if he foresaw that *that act* might be done: *Mahmood*, below, p 193.

[172] Described by Lord Hoffmann as 'plain vanilla' joint enterprise: *Brown and Everitt v The Queen* [2003] UKPC 10 [13].

[173] Irrespective of whether it is completed.

[174] (1985) 80 Cr App R 117. See the 7th edition of this book, at 143–145, for an account of the cases ending in the final acceptance of the principle of *Chan Wing-Siu* in *Hyde* (1991) 92 Cr App R 131 and the decision in *Hui Chi-ming* (1992) 94 Cr App R 236, PC, that that result need not be authorized but merely foreseen.

[175] [1999] AC 1, [1997] 4 All ER 545, HL. See also the comment by G. Virgo [1998] CLJ 3.

[176] See for a recent reaffirmation in terms of contemplation *Bryce* [2004] EWCA Crim 1321, [2004] Crim LR 963.

to kill and P does so, both are guilty of attempted murder.[177] The question is one of contemplation. In *Gordon*,[178] it was held that a lack of surprise expressed by D as to the principal crime by P is not necessarily to be equated with foresight by D that the crime was one that P might commit.

(3) D is not liable for a crime (Z) committed by P in the course of committing crime (X) if the relevant act done by P was of a *fundamentally different kind* from any act that D foresaw or contemplated that P might commit. In *English*[179] both D and P armed themselves with wooden stakes to attack a police officer. D knew that P might cause grievous bodily harm with a stake, and if he had done and V had died D would have been guilty of murder. But P killed V with a knife which D did not know he had. The House of Lords quashed D's conviction because it was not left to the jury to decide whether the killing with a knife was an act of a fundamentally different kind from any foreseen by D. An earlier illustration is *Mahmood*.[180] A and B took a car without the consent of the owner. There followed the usual police chase. A, the driver, abandoned the car in gear with the engine running so that the car went on and killed a baby. The jury convicted B as well as A of manslaughter. Although the jury, being properly directed, must have found as a fact that B *did* foresee that A might do such an act, the Court of Appeal quashed B's conviction, holding there was no evidence on which they could find that B foresaw such an exceptional act of gross negligence. It would probably have been different if A had killed by excessive speed, going through a red light, etc, acts which commonly occur in cases of this kind and which a jury might properly have found that B did foresee.

(iv) 'Parasitic' liability where an accessory does not share the common purpose?

Probably most accessories have a common purpose with the principal, but not all. The question is whether parasitic liability extends to a person who, though he is an accessory, does not share the principal's purpose. Examples we have already encountered are the cases where:

(1) D knowingly gives assistance to P (for example, by selling an intending murderer a gun) but is completely indifferent to whether P goes on to commit the offence contemplated. According to *Reardon*[181] (discussed above), in which P shot the two men, X and Y, in the bar, carried them dying, into the garden, borrowed D's knife and killed both X and Y. D was charged with both murders. D's convictions for both murders were upheld on the ground that D intended to assist one murder and he knew there was a real risk that there might be two – that is, by applying the principle of parasitic liability.

(2) D merely encourages P who has already made up his mind to commit the offence.

(3) D procures P, without P's knowledge or consent, to commit the crime.[182]

[177] *O'Brien* [1995] 2 Cr App R 649, [1995] Crim LR 734.

[178] [2004] EWCA Crim 961.

[179] An appeal heard together with *Powell and Daniels*, above n 175.

[180] [1995] RTR 48, [1994] Crim LR 368.

[181] [1999] Crim LR 392, CA. In *Gilmour* D was roused from his bed and told to drive the car 'which he did not do willingly'. It seems his purpose was not to throw petrol bombs but to save his own skin; but he was treated as a party to a joint enterprise.

[182] *A-G's Reference (No 1 of 1975)*, above, p 170.

(4) D participates unwillingly because he fears the consequences to himself if he does not.[183]

There seems to be no difference in principle between cases (1) and (2), above, and the question does not arise in case (3) since P has no purpose to commit an offence. In case (4) it was assumed without argument that parasitic liability applied. Present authority thus supports the opinion that parasitic liability is applicable to accessory liability generally.

(v) Liability for unforeseen consequences

It is apparent from the foregoing discussion that, where D is liable for an act done by P, he is liable for the unforeseen *consequences* of that act to the same extent as P. D foresees that P may do an act with intent to cause grievous bodily harm. P does so and kills: both are guilty of murder even if neither foresaw the possibility of death.

If two persons participate in an event, but it is not proved that each intends to assist or encourage the other, neither is liable for acts done by the other which he did not assist or encourage the other to commit: *Petters and Parfitt.*[184] If one or other of them caused injury or death but it is not possible to prove which, neither can be convicted. If, however, D intentionally assists P, even though without P's knowledge, D will be liable for the crime which he intended to assist P to commit and, it is submitted, any crime committed by P which D foresaw P might commit.

(vi) Where D is not responsible for the offence committed by P, may he be convicted of a lesser offence arising out of the same act?

If D is acquitted of the offence committed by P on the ground that he did not foresee that P might do an act *of that kind*, may he be convicted of a lesser offence, resulting from that act? In principle, the answer would appear to be no: D is not in law responsible for *that act* or its consequences.[185] It seems that the courts have now recognized that principle, although its application is far from straightforward. In *English* the court could have substituted a conviction for manslaughter if they had thought that D was guilty of that offence. They did not do so. Subsequently in *Uddin*[186] the court said: 'If the jury conclude that the death of the victim was caused by the actions of one participant which can be said to be of a completely different type to those contemplated by the others, they are not to be regarded as parties to the death whether it amounts to murder of manslaughter'.

Authorities rejecting D's liability for lesser offence

In *Dunbar*[187] the prosecution's case was that D had hired P to kill V. The jury, who convicted P of murder and D of manslaughter, must be presumed to have found that D authorized P to cause harm less than serious harm. D's conviction for manslaughter was quashed. D was not responsible for P's unauthorized and unforeseen act. It is submitted that that was right. A series of other cases supports this view.[188] More recent authorities

[183] *Gilmour*, below, p 195.

[184] [1995] Crim LR 501. Cf *Mohan* [1967] 2 AC 187, PC.

[185] For a different opinion, see C. Clarkson, 'Complicity, Powell and Manslaughter' [1998] Crim LR 556.

[186] [1998] 2 All ER 744 at 752. See also *Crooks* [1999] NI 226, 234, per Carswell LCJ.

[187] [1988] Crim LR 693.

[188] *Anderson and Morris* (1966) 50 Cr App R 216, *Lovesey and Peterson* (1969) 53 Cr App R 461, as well as *Uddin, Dunbar* and probably *English.*

subsequent to *English* such as *Mitchell and King*,[189] also take the view that D may not be convicted of manslaughter.

Authorities supporting D's liability for lesser offence

In *Stewart and Schofield*, the court distinguished *Dunbar*, where D was not present, as not properly a case of joint enterprise. But *Rook* (which establishes that it is irrelevant whether a party is present or absent) was not cited. *Stewart and Schofield* is supported by *Betty*[190] and *Reid*,[191] but these cases are inconsistent with those cited in the previous paragraph.

D's contemplation of the nature of P's conduct

Are these strands of conflicting authority reconcilable? Returning to the principle stated above, the question is whether D has contemplated that P's act would be *of the type* or *kind* that is in fact committed. Since this is such a vague and fact-dependent test, it may be possible to reconcile the conflicting decisions on their facts.[192] The problems echo those discussed in relation to basic accessorial liability above as to what constitutes the essential matters of P's conduct of which D must have knowledge. In the circumstances of a joint enterprise the question becomes with what degree of precision must D have contemplated the 'type of conduct' that P commits.

The difficulty in applying this vague and ill-articulated principle is illustrated by reference to three recent cases. In the Northern Irish case of *Gilmour*,[193] D drove P to a place where he knew P intended to petrol-bomb a house. Petrol bombs, surprisingly, rarely cause injury to the person but this was an exceptionally large bomb which caused a great conflagration and three deaths. The lethal nature of the bomb satisfied the judge (in a 'Diplock' court – that is, one without a jury) that P intended, not merely to cause serious injury but to kill, that is, P must have known that it was virtually certain to do so. There was, however, no evidence that D was aware that this was not an 'ordinary' bomb. P was obviously guilty of murder and the judge convicted D as well on the ground that, knowing that the family was to be petrol-bombed, he remained near the scene in his car to enable P to escape. D's conviction for murder was quashed but a conviction for manslaughter substituted on the ground that a 'person acting as an accessory to a principal who carries out the very deed contemplated by both [is] guilty of the degree of offence appropriate to the intent with which he so acted.'[194] On the facts, it is submitted that it is difficult to see that the use of the big bomb was the 'very deed' contemplated by D. In an English (as opposed to a 'Diplock') court, it would have to be left to the jury to say whether they were satisfied that P's act was not fundamentally different from that contemplated by D. It seems unlikely that they would find that an act that was virtually certain to kill was not fundamentally different from one that was unlikely to cause injury, or that such a finding could be upheld.[195]

[189] [1999] Crim LR 496. See also *Crooks* [1999] NI 266, CA.

[190] (1963) 48 Cr App R 6.

[191] (1975) 62 Cr App R 109.

[192] See Professor Taylor in *Blackstone's Criminal Practice* 2001, para A.5.5.

[193] [2000] NI 367, [2000] Crim LR 763, NI CA.

[194] Per Carswell LCJ, applying the principle stated (by Professor Richard Taylor) in *Blackstone* 2001, para A5.5.

[195] The criticism of the case in the 10th edition was cited with approval in the case of *Van Hoogstraaten* (2 Dec 2003), CCC (Sir Stephen Mitchell). See also *Jairan* [2005] UKPC 19.

The principle adopted in *Gilmour* was applied, though without reference to any authority, in *Roberts, Day and Day*:[196] P, D and C made a concerted attack on V, punching and kicking. The jury convicted P and D of murder and C of manslaughter. It was unsuccessfully argued on appeal that the jury must have misunderstood the direction and that C's conviction was unsafe: 'The subject-matter of a joint enterprise is not a state of mind or intention but an objective act which it is contemplated will or might be done'. The jury may have found that P, the killer, intended the act to cause serious injury, D foresaw that it might, whereas C foresaw no more than slight harm. Again, the principle may be sound, but it is hard to see how the verdict could be justified on the evidence. The cases highlight how difficult it is when such issues are left to be determined as matters of fact.[197]

The difficulty in identifying the relevant circumstances and components of P's crime of which D must have contemplation is illustrated by the case of *Van Hoogstraaten.*[198] In that case the act of the principal causing death was a deliberate shot aimed at V with a firearm. D had knowledge of P's possession of the firearm. In addition, D knew, indeed he intended that P would use the firearm. However, D contemplated only that P would use the firearm in V's presence to frighten V. In a comprehensive review of the authorities, the learned judge identified the crucial question as being: 'how is the act which caused death to be correctly defined?'[199] The prosecution submitted that the relevant act by P was the discharge of the firearm, and D contemplated that act. The defence submitted that the relevant act by P was a *deliberate shot intended to kill.* The trial judge ruled that the act was of a fundamentally different character to any that D had contemplated.

In the case of some crimes, particularly murder committed by P, where the question arises as to D's liability for manslaughter, a test based on the contemplation of a 'type of act' seems particularly imprecise since the distinction between murder and manslaughter turns exclusively on *mens rea.* Can the 'act' of P, which D must be proved to have contemplated, become a fundamentally different 'act' because of the change of mental state of 'P' when performing it?

How significant is the state of mind of the principal? In *O'Brien*[200] D's conviction for attempted murder was upheld only because he knew P might shoot *with intent* to kill. Consider the following case, P administers to V a particular drug, call it XYZ, which P knows is certain to kill, and is assisted and encouraged by D who knows the drug is XYZ but believes XYZ's only effect will be to give V a headache. V is killed. P is guilty of murder. Whether D is guilty of manslaughter depends on whether the act done by P was 'fundamentally different' from any act contemplated by A. The administration of a deadly drug is fundamentally different from the administration of a drug which will cause mere discomfort. If the drug administered by P were a different drug – PQR – the answer, it is submitted, would be clear – D is not liable for the consequences of that unforeseen and fundamentally different act. Should it be different where D's mistake or

196 CA, No 2000/174/Y4, 22 June 2001.

197 See the correspondence between J. C. Smith and R. D. Taylor [2001] Crim LR 333.

198 (2 Dec 2003), CCC (Sir Stephen Mitchell).

199 p 25E of the ruling. In that case the prosecution were stymied from alleging that D had contemplated that P might deliberately kill V or cause V serious injury with intent, because D had been acquitted of murder. The prosecution could, arguably, have led those facts as evidence of manslaughter.

200 [1995] 2 Cr App R 649.

ignorance relates not to the identity of the thing but to its attributes? If P and D had both believed that the only effect of XYZ was to cause a headache, then both would certainly be guilty of manslaughter. P has agreed to and assisted the mischievous act which caused death. He has not agreed to or foreseen a murderous act which causes death.[201]

(vii) The relevance of the weapon used by P

Great importance has always been attached to whether D knew that P was carrying the weapon with which the deed was done. If he knew,[202] that is cogent evidence that he contemplated an act of the kind done. But it is only evidence.[203] Some of the cases, however, give the fact a wider, substantive significance. In *Powell and Daniels* Lord Hutton approved the decision of Carswell J in the Northern Irish case of *Gamble*.[204] D, who agreed to participate in 'kneecapping' V with a gun, was not guilty of murder when P cut V's throat with a knife – an act D had not foreseen. But Lord Hutton added: 'whether a secondary party who foresees the use of a gun to kneecap, and death is then caused by the deliberate firing of the gun into the head or body of the victim, is guilty of murder is more debatable . . . '.[205] If D foresaw that P might use the gun in this way, then he would certainly be liable; but otherwise, surely not. 'Kneecapping', abominable though it is, is unlikely to cause death, whereas blowing a man's brains out is certain to do so. D should not be liable (for murder or manslaughter) simply because he foresaw the use of a gun and a gun was used.[206]

Where, however, it can be proved that D and P have agreed to kill V, the nature of the weapon used should surely not matter. If they have agreed that P should shoot V, and P cuts his throat or strangles him, D should be guilty of murder.[207] Their joint purpose has been accomplished. An exception might be a case where the means used by P involved exceptional cruelty to which D would never have agreed. The dangerousness of the weapon is significant where, in a murder case, the prosecution can prove no more than a joint intent to do grievous bodily harm or in a manslaughter case, an intention to commit a battery. If, however, the weapon used by P was different from, but as dangerous as, the weapon contemplated by D, the difference is immaterial. So in *Greatrex*[208] it should have

[201] Professor Taylor raises objections, discussed by J. C. Smith in 'Commentary on *Day*' [2001] Crim LR 984: D's liability for manslaughter might depend on the prosecution proving that P did not have the *mens rea* for murder; and that, if the jury were not sure that P had the *mens rea* of murder and convicted him only of manslaughter, they could not be sure that D was guilty of manslaughter and would have to acquit him altogether.

[202] The prosecution is obliged to prove knowledge, which can not be inferred from, eg, the closeness of D and P and their having been together for the hours prior to the attack in which P used a knife: *Parchment* [2003] EWCA Crim 2428.

[203] *Roberts* [1993] 1 All ER 583 at 590.

[204] [1989] NI 268, NI Crown Court.

[205] [1997] 4 All ER 565h–j.

[206] In an unreported pre-English case, *Wei*, 96/5461/W3, 25 July 1997, five members of a Triad gang set out, four intending to murder V, the fifth, S, believing that the common intention was only to frighten him, but by the firing of a loaded shotgun. When V was shot dead, the four were convicted of murder and S of manslaughter. The jury were not satisfied that S was aware of a real risk that the gun would be fired with intent to kill, S's conviction was upheld: he had 'authorized' the use of a loaded gun. But, surely, firing a gun at a person is fundamentally different from firing over his head in order to frighten him; and, if that is so, S was not responsible for that unforeseen act: *Bamborough* [1996] Crim LR 744 is similar. See also *Van Hoogstraaten* above, where it is doubted that *Wei* survives *Powell and Daniels* above.

[207] Cf Lord Hutton in *Powell* [1997] 4 All ER 566e–f.

[208] [1999] 1 Cr App R 126, CA.

been left to the jury to decide whether kicking with 'a shod foot', which was contemplated by D, was fundamentally different from striking with a bar or spanner, which was not contemplated.

In *O'Flaherty and others*[209] the Court of Appeal emphasized that the question whether use of a weapon is fundamentally different from any act which D realized P might perform is a question of fact for the jury. 'The principles set out in *Uddin* are not stated to be principles of law as opposed to matters of evidence, and it would be unfortunate if they crystallised as such'. D's foresight of P's possession and use of a weapon may give rise to significant difficulties of proof. It may have to be left as a matter of inference from the surrounding circumstances. Particular problems arise if in the course of the enterprise P arms himself (for example, with a kitchen knife at the scene of the burglary). D may not have foreseen or be aware of P's possession of such a weapon.[210]

(viii) Spontaneous behaviour

'Joint enterprise' suggests a planned offence. The principles expounded above are readily applicable to such offences, less easily to the spontaneous conduct of two or more without pre-planning – usually an attack on person or property. The law, it is submitted, is the same. Beldam LJ has said:[211]

> From the behaviour of individuals joining together as a group in a concerted attack on a single victim, it is often the only reasonable inference that they individually and collectively unite with each other in an assault on the victim with intent to do him really serious harm. In pursuance of that intent one or usually all, attack the victim and do acts with the necessary intent to make them individually guilty of inflicting grievous bodily harm with intent. But it is also the case that by combining together in their attacks each encourages and assists the others in the commission of similar offences . . . Thus where the participants in a united attack individually inflict serious harm, by taking part with others at the same time they encourage and assist them to commit a similar crime on the victim. From the evidence of the onset of the combined assault and from the actions of the participants, a jury is asked to infer not only that there was concerted action by the participators but the intent with which the acts done by them was carried out and whether the conduct of those who do not actually infict serious harm is such as to have encouraged the conduct of those who do.

Some may be both principals and accessories to the acts of others, some only accessories. So long as the jury are satisfied that a particular defendant was one or the other, they should convict him.

(ix) The effect of provocation in the course of a joint enterprise

In *McKechnie*[212] where the killer acted under a provocation received in the course of carrying out the joint enterprise, it was held that this ruled out any liability of the other parties to it. Presumably the reason is that a person who has lost his self-control can no longer be said to be acting in pursuance of a common purpose. If so, there is some

209 [2004] EWCA Crim 526, [2004] Crim LR 751.

210 See *C* [2002] EWCA Crim 3154.

211 *Greatrex*, above, at 138. Beldam LJ made a similar analysis in *Uddin* [1998] 2 All ER 744 at 751. See also *MCarthy* [2003] EWCA Crim 484, and *Reid* [2005] EWCA Crim 595.

212 [1992] Crim LR 194.

difficulty in reconciling the decision with *Calhaem*.[213] *McKechnie* was distinguished in *Pearson*.[214] There the alleged provocation occurred before the joint enterprise began. A and B, acting in concert, attacked their father, V. B first struck V with a sledgehammer and A then delivered further blows which killed him. Both pleaded provocation. The jury convicted B of murder and A (the younger brother who had suffered more from his father) of manslaughter. B's conviction was reduced to manslaughter because of misdirection on the evidence of provocation; but the court said the verdicts were not inconsistent: the notion of provocation affecting one but not the other was consistent with joint enterprise. Probably the distinction from *McKechnie* is that A was a principal and his liability was not dependent on that of B. He made his own causal contribution to the death.[215] If so, joint enterprise was not an element of A's offence; he was liable because he killed V.

(x) Is the law too strict?

There is a strongly held view that the present law is too strict.[216] D may be liable for an offence requiring proof of an intention on the part of the principal, P, although D is only reckless. Recklessness whether death be caused is a sufficient *mens rea* for manslaughter but not for murder; yet D may be convicted of murder because he was reckless as to whether P committed murder. This is certainly a controversial point; but recklessness *whether murder be committed* is a different and more culpable state of mind than recklessness *whether death be caused* – a point which was regarded as persuasive by Lord Steyn in *Powell and Daniels*.[217]

Some argue that D should not be held liable because he foresaw that P *might* do the act with intent in question, but only if he foresaw that P *would* do that act with that intent. This was the effect of some cases[218] decided after *Hancock* and *Nedrick*[219] but they seem to have been based on a misunderstanding of the effect of decisions on the *mens rea* of the principal in murder, which do not affect the principles of secondary liability. A further misunderstanding by some of the critics was that *Chan Wing-Siu* made the law stricter. On the contrary, it seems that the earlier common law rule was that an accessory to felony was liable, not only for that felony which he incited and encouraged, but also for any other felony committed by the principal that was a *probable* consequence of what he ordered or advised – an objective test.[220] In *Chan Wing-Siu* the Crown acknowledged that the test was subjective. The issue was a narrow one: whether it was sufficient that D foresaw that P 'might well' do the fatal act, or that they must prove that he foresaw that it

213 [1985] QB 808, [1985] 2 All ER 266 (D liable as a counsellor of P's act where P killed after 'going berserk'), above, p 173.

214 [1992] Crim LR 193, below, p 446.

215 Cf *Osland*, above, n 36, where Gaudron and Gunmow JJ suggested that either B 'participated' in A's acts or (surely better) that his own acts substantially contributed to the death.

216 An argument that it violated Article 6 of the ECHR was firmly rejected in *Concannon* [2002] Crim LR 211.

217 [1997] 4 All ER at 550–551.

218 *Barr* (1986) 88 Cr App R 362; *Smith* [1988] Crim LR 616 and see David Poole QC, 'Letter to the Editor – Joint Enterprise and Intent: A Comment' [1989] Crim LR 236.

219 Above, p 94.

220 Foster, *Crown Law* 370; Stephen, *Digest* (4th edn), art 20, KJM Smith, above, 210–214.

was more probable than not, as the appellant argued. The Privy Council decided in favour of the Crown – it is sufficient that D foresaw that P 'might well' do the fatal act.

(xi) The theory of liability in joint enterprise

No less an authority than Lord Hobhouse has criticized[221] the above opinion that the law of joint enterprise is an application of the principles of accessory liability. He argues that the true basis is the civil law concept of agency which is also part of the criminal law: the party who does the deed (the principal in criminal law) is the agent of the others. Sometimes this is true, as where B and C hire P, a 'contract killer', to do the deed. But if P decides to commit murder and recruits B, C and D for reward to assist him by providing a weapon, driving him to and from the scene and keeping watch, it seems quite inaccurate to describe P as the agent of B, C and D. They are his agents. P is here the principal in the civil as well as in the criminal law. B, C and D are rightly held responsible for P's act; but their responsibility is surely not explicable on the ground that P is their agent. They are responsible because they aided and abetted him.

(d) Secondary participation and inchoate offences

It is an offence to incite, or to conspire, or to attempt, to commit an offence.[222] It is not an offence to attempt[223] or, it is submitted, to incite or to conspire[224] to do an act which would involve no more than secondary liability for the offence if it were committed. Secondary liability is triggered by the commission of the substantive principal offence. Knowing that P intends to drive his car, D2 urges D1 to 'lace' P's drink with so much alcohol that P will inevitably commit an offence under s 5(1) of the Road Traffic Act 1988[225] if P drives after consuming the drink. D1 agrees to do so and attempts to, or does, lace the drink. If P consumes the drink, drives his car and thus commits the offence under the Road Traffic Act 1988, D2 and D1 will be guilty as secondary parties;[226] but if P declines the drink, or does not drive the car, D2 is guilty neither of incitement nor of conspiracy and D1 is guilty neither of conspiracy nor of attempt to commit the offence. The act incited, agreed upon, attempted and indeed done, lacing the drink, is not the offence.[227]

In this example, P could be guilty as the principal offender, notwithstanding his lack of *mens rea*, on the ground that the offence is assumed to be one of strict liability. Where the offence is one requiring *mens rea*, which the actual perpetrator of the *actus reus* lacks, then those who procured him to act will be liable because they, or one of them, will be principals. D2 urges D1 to stage his death and disappears so that D1's wife,

221 'Agency and the Criminal Law', in *Lex Mercatoria (Essays in Honour of Francis Reynolds)* (2000).

222 Ch 12, below.

223 Criminal Attempts Act 1981, s 1(4)(b); *Dunnington* [1984] QB 472, [1984] 1 All ER 676, [1984] Crim LR 98, CA. Cf *Chief Constable of Hampshire v Mace* (1986) 84 Cr App R 40, [1986] Crim LR 752.

224 *Hollinshead* [1985] 1 All ER 850 at 857–858, CA. The House of Lords left the question open: [1985] AC 975, [1985] 2 All ER 769. See J. C. Smith, 'Secondary Participation and Inchoate Offences' in *Crime, Proof and Punishment*, 21. *Po Koon Tai*, Criminal Appeal No 836 of 1979, Supreme Court of Hong Kong, is to the contrary so far as conspiracy is concerned.

225 Driving or being in charge of a motor vehicle with an alcohol concentration above a prescribed limit.

226 *A-G's Reference (No 1 of 1975)*, above, p 107.

227 The adulteration of the drink might possibly amount to the administration of a noxious thing, contrary to the Offences Against the Person Act 1861, s 24, below, Ch 16.

P, may claim the insurance money on D1's life. If P was not a party to the fraud and was intended to obtain the money innocently, D2 would be guilty of inciting D1 to obtain for another by deception as the principal offender; D2 and D1 would be guilty of conspiring to commit the offence; and D1 would be guilty of an attempt to commit it at the latest when the news of his death reached the insurers.[228] If P were a party to the fraud, D1's acts would not be an offence[229] but the three would be guilty of conspiracy to defraud.

Where P is guilty of incitement to commit a crime, D1 may be liable for abetting or counselling the incitement. Where P is guilty of an attempt to commit a crime, D1 may be liable for abetting or counselling the attempt.[230] In the case of conspiracy, however, one who abets or counsels the commission of the crime appears to be a principal in the conspiracy.

(e) Conviction of secondary party and acquittal of principal offender/no principal

Even if the alleged principal has been acquitted, a conviction of another as a secondary party may be logical. This is so even if it is assumed[231] that a secondary party may be convicted only when the principal himself is guilty. The acquittal of the alleged principal, so far from being conclusive that no crime was committed, is not even admissible in evidence at a subsequent trial of the secondary parties.[232] A second jury may be satisfied beyond reasonable doubt that the crime was committed upon evidence which the first jury found unconvincing; evidence may be admissible against the secondary party which was not admissible against the principal, or fresh evidence may have come to light or the principal may have been acquitted because the prosecution offered no evidence against him.

The position would seem to be the same where the secondary party is tried first and convicted and the principal is subsequently acquitted[233] and when the parties are jointly indicted. In *Hughes*,[234] after the prosecution had offered no evidence against P, he was acquitted and called as a witness for the Crown, with the result that D was convicted by the same jury as an accessory to P's alleged crime. Where principal and secondary party are tried separately, this result is supported by the analogous rule laid down in *DPP v Shannon*[235] that the acquittal of one party to a conspiracy does not invalidate the conviction of the only other party on an earlier or later occasion. *Shannon* left open the question whether the one party may be convicted of conspiracy when the other is acquitted at the

228 *DPP v Stonehouse* [1978] AC 55, [1977] 2 All ER 909, HL, below, p 418.

229 This assumes that *Robinson* [1915] 2 KB 342, CCA, is rightly decided and that these would be preparatory acts and not an attempt to obtain. Below, p 412.

230 *Hapgood and Wyatt* (1870) LR 1 CCR 221, CCR; *S v Robinson* 1968 (1) SA 666. Cf Sexual Offences (Amendment) Act 1976, s 7(2) (aiding, etc attempted rape).

231 Contrary to the view expressed below, p 205.

232 *Hui Chi-ming v R* [1991] 3 All ER 897, PC. Under the Police and Criminal Evidence Act 1984, s 74, a conviction is now admissible to prove the commission of the offence by the principal: *Turner* [1991] Crim LR 57.

233 In *Rowley* [1948] 1 All ER 570, D's conviction was quashed when, after he had pleaded guilty as an accessory after the fact, the alleged principals were acquitted by the jury. But the decision is criticized in *Shannon* [1974] 2 All ER 1009 at 1020 and 1049; below n 235.

234 (1860) Bell CC 242.

235 [1975] AC 717, [1974] 2 All ER 1009, HL; below, Ch 12.

same trial;[236] and in *Anthony*[237] it was said, *obiter*, that a jury cannot acquit P and at the same time find D guilty of counselling him to commit the crime.

If P and D are tried together and the evidence tending to show that P committed the crime is the same against both, then it would be inconsistent to acquit P and convict D.[238] Where, however, there is evidence admissible against D but not against P that P committed the crime (as, for example, a confession by D that he counselled P to commit the crime and saw him commit it) it would be perfectly logical to acquit P and convict D of counselling him (and of conspiring with him). In *Humphreys and Turner*,[239] which was just such a case, Chapman J held that D might be convicted as a secondary party, distinguishing the *dicta* in *Anthony* as applicable only to felonies. It is submitted that, since the Criminal Law Act 1967 came into force, the rule stated in *Humpheys and Turner* is applicable to all offences.

It is one thing for a court which is trying D alone to reject or ignore the holding of another court that P was not a principal and to hold that he was; and that, therefore, D might be convicted as a secondary party to P's crime. It is quite another thing for a court to hold at one and the same time, (i) that P was, in law, not guilty[240] and (ii) that D was guilty, as a secondary party, of P's crime. These propositions seem, at first sight, to be inconsistent with the derivative nature of secondary liability.[241]

(i) Secondary party guilty of a greater offence than the principal

Since secondary liability is said to derive from that of the principal, it is hard to see how the secondary party can legally be held to be greater than that of the principal. Hawkins[242] thought that the offence of the *accessory* can never 'rise higher' than that of the principal, 'it seeming incongruous and absurd that he who is punished only as a partaker of the guilt of another, should be adjudged guilty of a higher crime than the other'. But Hawkins was speaking of an accessory in the strict sense and he saw no incongruity or absurdity in a principal in the second degree being guilty of a greater offence than the principal in the first degree. Such a distinction, depending on whether the secondary party is present at, or absent from, the commission of the crime does not seem acceptable. If it ever had any validity it depended on the distinction in the law of felonies between a principal in the second degree and an accessory which has been abolished.

There are some cases where it seems obvious that a person who, at least, appears to be a secondary party ought to be convicted of a greater offence than the immediate perpetrator of the *actus reus*. We have already noticed that offences may be committed through innocent agents and that if D, with intent to kill, sends a letter-bomb through the post to V who is killed by the explosion, D is guilty of murder as a principal and E, the postman,

[236] The point is now settled by the Criminal Law Act 1977, and *Longman and Cribben* (1980) 72 Cr App R 121, below, p 397; but *Shannon* is relevant to the common law governing secondary participation.

[237] [1965] 2 QB 189, [1965] 1 All ER 440. Cf *Surujpaul v R* [1958] 3 All ER 300 at 302–303.

[238] *Surujpaul v R* [1958] 3 All ER 300, [1958] 1 WLR 1050.

[239] [1965] 3 All ER 689 (Liverpool Crown Court). Following in *Sweetman v Industries and Commerce Department* [1970] NZLR 139. Cf *Davis* [1977] Crim LR 542, CA and commentary and *Fuller* [1998] Crim LR 61.

[240] Not merely that there was not enough evidence to convict him, but that there was evidence which established his innocence.

[241] Above, p 165.

[242] 2 PC s 29, s 15.

is an innocent agent. Suppose, however, that E notices some wires sticking out of the parcel and that he is aware that a number of letter-bombs have been sent by terrorists lately with fatal results. He thinks, 'This could be a letter bomb – but it's not likely and I'm in a hurry, I'll risk it', and pushes the letter through V's letter box where it explodes and kills V. If these facts are proved, E behaved recklessly and is guilty of manslaughter. He is no longer an innocent agent. But it would be absurd if D who sent the letter with intent to kill should escape liability for murder.

Glanville Williams suggests that a person like our postman should be regarded as a semi-innocent agent – 'he is an innocent agent in respect of part of the responsibility of the secondary party'.[243] Kadish does not like this – 'the ideas of a "semi-innocent agent" and of responsibility as a composite of parts seems only to add to the conceptual mystery'[244] – but the expression 'semi-innocent agent' is useful for describing this situation. It does not, however, explain how the greater can derive from the less.

Kadish discusses the example of D who, intending that P shall kill V, fabricates provocation which causes P to lose his self-control and kill V. P, because of the provocation, is guilty only of manslaughter. Kadish's solution is that here D can properly be said to have caused V's death. Because P's actions are not 'fully voluntary' they do not break the chain of causation. Once it is established that D caused V's death, 'it follows that the nature of his crime is determined by the culpability with which he acted'. According to Kadish's explanation (though he does not spell this out), this is not a case of the liability of an accessory rising above that of the principal. There is no accessory. There is only one homicide but it is well settled that there may be two causes – and two causers – of a result.[245] D and P have both caused the death and it is both manslaughter, in respect of which P is the principal, and murder, in respect of which D is the principal. This theory would also explain other hypothetical cases that have been discussed.

> [D] hands a gun to [P] informing him that it is loaded with blank ammunition only and telling him to go and scare [V] by discharging it. The ammunition is in fact live (as [D] knows) and [V] is killed. [P] is convicted only of manslaughter. . . . It would seem absurd that [D] should thereby escape conviction for murder.[246]

P's act would be regarded as not 'fully voluntary' because, through his ignorance of material facts, he was not fully aware of what he was doing or its consequences; so D has caused the death, intending to kill and is a principal murderer.[247]

The absurd result postulated above was thought to follow from *Richards*,[248] which the Court of Appeal and Lord Mackay considered to be wrongly decided. D, a woman, hired P1 and P2 to beat up her husband 'bad enough to put him in hospital for a month'.

243 *TBCL*, 373. 244 *Blame and Punishment*, 183.

245 Eg P shoots at V, intending to kill but only wounds. D treats the wound recklessly and V dies of the maltreated wound. P and D have both caused V's death. P is guilty of murder and D of manslaughter. Both are principals.

246 *Burke* [1986] QB 626 at 641–642, [1986] 1 All ER 833 at 839–840, CA. Lord Mackay agreed with the Court of Appeal who found this example convincing: [1987] AC 417, [1987] 1 All ER 771, HL. See the similar examples in the 5th edition of this work, at p 140.

247 It is not so clear that the causation theory is a satisfactory explanation of the case where D intends the result and E is reckless whether he causes it – eg the postman case, above. It seems to be straining a bit to say that the postman's act is not 'fully voluntary'.

248 [1974] QB 776, [1973] 3 All ER 1088, CA.

She signalled to P1 and P2 when V left the house. They inflicted a wound upon V, not amounting to a serious injury. D was convicted of wounding with intent to cause grievous bodily harm but P1 and P2 were acquitted of that offence and convicted of the lesser offence of unlawful wounding. Following the opinion of Hawkins, D's conviction was quashed and a conviction for unlawful wounding substituted. It was assumed that, under the old law of felonies, D would have been an accessory and not a principal in the second degree.[249]

Richards was heavily criticized and, in view of the disapproval expressed in *Burke*, though only *obiter*, may not be followed in future. *Richards* found a belated defender in Professor Kadish who argues (i) that D did not cause the actions of P1 and P2 because they were not her unwitting instruments but chose to act freely as they did and (ii) she could not be held liable 'for an aggravated assault [ie an assault with intent to cause grievous bodily harm] that did not take place'.[250] Of course D did in one sense cause the actions of P1 and P2 – they would never have harmed V if she had not set them on to him; but it is a fair point that she would not be regarded as having caused the result under the ordinary principles of secondary participation (above, p 171). The postman example is distinguishable because the postman there did exactly what the murderer intended him to do. P1 and P2 did not.

The anomaly of holding D liable for the greater offence is emphasized if it is supposed that V, by some unforeseeable mischance, had died of the slight injury inflicted by P1 and P2. This would have been manslaughter by P1 and P2. If D was guilty of the s 18 offence, it would follow logically that she was guilty of murder. It may be argued that this would be wrong (though she had the necessary *mens rea*), because no act was ever done with *intent thereby* to kill or cause serious bodily harm – there was no 'murderous act'. If, however, P1 and P2 had acted with intent to do serious bodily harm but succeeded in inflicting only a slight injury it would have been murder by all three if V had died of that. But then the act would have been done in pursuance of a joint enterprise to cause serious bodily harm. In fact it was not so done. For that reason, though not for the reasons given, it may be that the decision in *Richards* was right after all.

The position is more straightforward where D and P both have the *mens rea* for the greater offence but P's liability is reduced for some reason to that of a lesser offence. If P causes the *actus reus* in carrying out the agreed plan but his liability is reduced 'for some reason special to himself',[251] such as provocation or diminished responsibility,[252] it seems clearly right that D should not be able to shelter behind P's personal exemption from liability for the greater offence. In the case considered in *Burke*, however, the reduction in P's liability did not depend on a personal consideration of this kind. P's defence was that he had agreed to shoot V out of fear of D, but that, when it came to the event, the gun went off accidentally. The killing was therefore unintentional and amounted to no more than manslaughter. The judge, following *Richards*, directed that, if the jury found P guilty only of manslaughter, then D could at most be guilty of manslaughter. The implication of the decision of the House is that this was wrong. It is submitted that it is

249 Above, p 171.

250 'Complicity and Causation' (1985) 73 Cal Law Rev 323 at 329.

251 The phrase used by Lord Mackay in *Burke*, above, n 246.

252 This case is covered by s 2(4) of the Homicide Act 1957. D's liability for murder is not affected by E's diminished responsibility.

correct; that the true position is that if P has gone beyond a merely preparatory act and is attempting to commit the crime when he 'accidentally' kills, both D and P are guilty of murder; but, if P is doing only a preparatory act when he happens to kill – he is driving to V's house with intent to blow it up when the bomb in his car goes off and kills V who has unexpectedly gone out for a walk – P is liable only for manslaughter and so is D. The killing which occurs is not the killing he intended, though the victim happens to be the same.[253]

(ii) Where the 'principal' is not guilty

Here we are concerned with cases where the immediate perpetrator of the *actus reus* is not guilty of the offence alleged and the offence is one which is incapable of being committed by a person acting through an innocent agent such as rape and other offences involving sexual intercourse, driving offences and bigamy (except where the bigamous marriage is by proxy). There are three possible situations:

(1) P has committed the *actus reus* of the offence with *mens rea* but has a defence;

(2) P has committed the *actus reus* but has no *mens rea*;

(3) P has not committed the *actus reus*.

(1) *Bourne*[254]

D, by duress compelled his wife (P) to have sexual connection with a dog. His conviction of abetting her to commit buggery was upheld although it was assumed that the wife, if she had been charged, would have been acquitted on the ground of coercion.[255] Sir Rupert Cross[256] argued that this was in accordance with principle because 'The wife committed the "*actus reus*" with the "*mens rea*" required by the definition of the crime in question and the husband participated in that "*mens rea*".' The wife had *mens rea* in the sense that she knew exactly what she was doing, though she was to be excused for doing it. Where the defence relied upon by the principal is excusatory, that does not preclude the secondary party from being convicted, according to some theorists.

(2) *Cogan and Leak*[257]

D terrorized his wife, V, into submitting to sexual intercourse with P. P was convicted of rape and D of abetting him, but, on appeal, P's conviction had to be quashed because the jury had not been directed correctly, and it may have been that P lacked the *mens rea* as to V's consent. D's conviction was upheld but primarily on the ground that D was the principal offender acting through an innocent agent. The agency theory is misconceived. If it were right, a woman could be convicted of rape as the principal and it is plain that she cannot commit that offence; she does not have a penis. To suggest that D raped his wife V using P's penis is nonsense. The court's second reason was that D was rightly convicted as a procurer because V had been raped ('no one outside a court of law would say she had not been') and 'therefore the particulars of offence accurately stated what [D]

[253] See commentary [1987] Crim LR 481 at 484.

[254] (1952) 36 Cr App R 125. See J. Ll. Edwards, 'Duress and Aiding and Abetting' (1953) 69 LQR 297; R. Cross, 'Duress and Aiding and Abetting (A Reply)' (1953) 69 LQR 354.

[255] Below, p 326.

[256] (1953) 68 LQR 354.

[257] [1976] QB 217, [1975] 2 All ER 1059, [1975] Crim LR 584 and commentary.

had done, namely that he procured [P] to commit the offence'. But if P believed V was consenting, V had not, as a matter of law, been raped. If X's bike is taken from the place he left it by Y who owns an exactly similar model and thinks this is his, X, who has lost his bike for ever, reasonably believes it has been stolen, but he is wrong. The court's distinguishing of *Walters v Lunt*[258] (trike not stolen goods because taken by seven-year-old) was erroneous. If the hypothetical bike and trike were not stolen, and plainly they were not, V was not raped by P in *Cogan*. The court's opinion that D had procured not merely the *actus reus* but the offence of rape is wrong.

If a conviction is to be upheld in such a case – and policy and justice seem to require it – this could be on the ground that it is an offence to procure the commission of an *actus reus*; and this step was taken in *Millward*.[259] D instructed his employee, P, to drive on a road a vehicle which D knew, but P did not know, was in a dangerous condition. It was assumed that the *actus reus* of reckless driving was committed simply by the driving of the vehicle on the road. The condition of the vehicle resulted in a collision causing death. P was charged with causing death by reckless driving and D of abetting him. P was acquitted, D was convicted and his conviction upheld on the ground that he had procured the *actus reus*. This solution was advocated in the first seven editions of this book and it seems the best available to the courts; but there is force in the opinion of Kadish[260] that it 'at least technically . . . amounts to creating a new crime'. As there is no principal, there is no question of participation in the guilt of another or of 'secondary liability' and it becomes, in effect, a substantive offence to procure the commission of the *actus reus* of any crime.

Bourne, Cogan and Leak and *Millward* were all cases of alleged procuring and it is not certain whether the principle of *Millward* extends to other modes of secondary participation. Procuring is narrower than the other modes in that (i) it must be the cause of the *actus reus* and, perhaps, (ii), it must be the procurer's purpose to cause the result – 'To procure means to produce by endeavour'[261] – but that may be too restrictive. Bourne and Leak were endeavouring to bring about the whole *actus reus*; but Millward, while he was 'endeavouring' to have the dangerous vehicle driven on the road, which was assumed to amount to reckless driving, was certainly not endeavouring to have anyone killed. If the driver had been guilty of reckless driving, then both he and Millward would certainly have been guilty of causing death by reckless driving; but it does not necessarily follow that Millward should be guilty of that offence when the driver is not guilty. If 'procure' does imply purpose and if the principle is limited to procuring, then he ought to have been convicted only of reckless driving and not of causing death.

258 [1951] 2 All ER 645, below, p 295.

259 [1994] Crim LR 527. *Millward* was soon followed in *Wheelhouse* [1994] Crim LR 756. D dishonestly procured E to take V's car from V's garage. E believed the car belonged to D. D was guilty of burglary although E was not. But it has been established at least from the time of Hale that burglary may be committed by an innocent agent: Hale 1 PC 555 (1736). It was not necessary to rely on the new principle in *Millward*. In *DPP v K and B* [1997] 1 Cr App R 36, [1997] Crim LR 121, DC, the female procurers of 'rape' by an unidentified boy who may have been under 14, and may have been *doli incapax* (ie at that time incapable of committing the crime), were held guilty of rape. It was said that it would have been different if the unidentified boy had been, or may have been, under 10 because then there would have been no *actus reus* of rape. It is submitted that that is wrong. The *actus reus* was the voluntary penetration of the vagina by the penis, whatever the age of the boy.

260 *Essays in Criminal Law*, 180.

261 Above, p 174.

The cases may also be approached in terms of justification and excuse, although it is doubtful that this sheds any greater light on the issue – the principal offender in each case was acquitted on the basis of an excusing factor (duress or lack of *mens rea*), and according to the theory this does not preclude secondary liability.[262]

(3) *Morris v Tolman*[263]

D was charged with abetting the owner of a vehicle in using that vehicle for a purpose for which the vehicle had not been licensed. The statute (the Roads Act 1920) was so phrased that the offence could be committed only by the licence-holder. It was held that, there being no evidence that the licence-holder, P, had used the vehicle for a purpose other than that for which it was licensed, D must be acquitted. Though he, in fact, had so used the vehicle, that was not an *actus reus*. Again, in *Thornton v Mitchell*,[264] D, a bus conductor, negligently signalled to the driver of his bus, P, to reverse, so that two pedestrians, whom it was not possible for the driver to see, were knocked down and one of them killed. The driver having been acquitted of careless driving, it was held that the conductor must be acquitted of abetting. Again, there was no *actus reus*. The driver's acquittal shows that he committed no *actus reus*, for careless driving is a crime which requires no *mens rea* beyond an intention to drive and D could not be said to have driven the bus. There would have been no such obstacle in the way of convicting D for manslaughter. That would, at that time, simply have raised the question whether D's negligence was sufficiently great.[265]

Thornton and Mitchell was distinguished in *Millward* on the ground that there was no *actus reus* of careless driving in the former case. And in *Loukes*[266] where the facts were similar to those in *Millward*, D's conviction for procuring the offence of causing death by *dangerous* driving was quashed. The *actus reus* of the new offence[267] is more precisely defined and a condition of the liability of the driver, P, in this situation is that 'it would be obvious to a competent and careful driver that driving the vehicle in its current state would be dangerous'. The judge directed an acquittal of the driver on the ground that there was no evidence that the dangerous condition of the vehicle would have been obvious to a competent and careful driver. The conviction of Loukes, who was responsible for the maintenance of the vehicle, for procuring the commission of the offence, was quashed. There being no *actus reus*, he could not be held to have procured one.[268]

Again, these decisions can be approached by reference to the theory of justifications and excuses.[269]

262 See J. C. Smith, *Justifications and Excuses in Criminal Law* (1989); G. Williams, 'Theory of Excuses' [1982] Crim LR 722, especially 735–738; R. Taylor, 'Complicity and Excuses' [1983] Crim LR 656.

263 [1923] 1 KB 166.

264 [1940] 1 All ER 339. See R. D. Taylor, 'Complicity and Excuses' [1983] Crim LR 656, for another way of looking at the problems raised by this case.

265 See above, ch 5, and below, p 482.

266 [1996] Crim LR 341. See commentary doubting whether there was an *actus reus* in *Millward*. And cf *Roberts and George* [1997] Crim LR 209.

267 Below, p 1012. It seems that there is no room for procuring the *actus reus* as distinct from the offence because there is no *actus reus* unless the fault element is present – ie the full offence is committed: *Roberts and George* [1997] Crim LR 209 and commentary.

268 In *Pickford* [1995] 1 Cr App R 420, 429–430 it was held that it was not an offence to aid and abet a boy under the age of 14 (at that time presumed to be incapable of sexual intercourse) to commit incest with his mother. The act would not be an *actus reus*.

269 See n 262 above.

(f) Withdrawal by a secondary party[270]

Where D has counselled P to commit a crime, or is present, aiding P in the commission of it, it may yet be possible for him to escape liability by withdrawal before P goes on to commit the crime. An effective withdrawal will not, however, affect any liability he may have already incurred for incitement, or conspiracy, or, if the withdrawal took place after P had done a more than merely preparatory act,[271] attempt, to commit the crime.[272]

Although the principle that 'a person who unequivocally withdraws before the moment of the actual commission of the crime by the principal should not be liable for that crime,[273] is clear, it is less easy to identify on what basis the defence operates. It is unclear whether it is designed primarily to serve as an incentive to D to withdraw or to reflect his diminished degree of blameworthiness.[274] There are at least three bases for constructing such a defence:

(i) That the defence operates only where D brings to an end the *actus reus* of assisting or encouraging P. On this interpretation the defence would be relatively narrowly constructed.

(ii) The defence may operate because D's withdrawal negates his *mens rea* of intention to assist or encourage. Such an approach would create an extremely broad defence, potentially D's unannounced unilateral decision to take no part would suffice. That would be unworkable.

(iii) Thirdly, it is possible to construe the defence as a 'true' defence operating despite the presence of D's continuing *actus reus* and *mens rea* as a secondary party.

English law has yet to address these issues directly.

(i) An effective withdrawal?

For any withdrawal to be effective, it must be voluntary. If D is arrested, he can hardly be said to have 'withdrawn'. His arrest does not necessarily demonstrate any repentance on his part, nor undo any aid, advice or encouragement he may have already given.[275] Of course, it usually precludes any future secondary participation by him;[276] but in this section we are concerned with absolution from the potential liability arising from D's past acts.

In addition to a general voluntary awareness, a clear precondition for the defence to operate is an unequivocal communication of withdrawal. This can be communication to the principal, and if more than one to all principals, or by communication with the law enforcement agency.

270 See D. Lanham, 'Accomplices and Withdrawal' (1981) 97 LQR 575, Williams, TBCL, 310–311, K. J. M. Smith, 'Withdrawal and Complicity' [2001] Crim LR 769.

271 Below, p 410.

272 Withdrawal does not affect liability for an attempt; below, p 419.

273 *O'Flaherty* [2004] EWCA Crim 526, [2004] Crim LR 751.

274 For a comprehensive discussion of these approaches see K. J. M. Smith, 'Withdrawal in Complicity: A Restatement of Principles' [2001] Crim LR 769.

275 *Johnson and Jones* (1841) Car & M 218. *Jackson* (1673) 1 Hale PC 464 at 465 appears contra but is an obscure and unsatisfactory case. See Lanham, above at 577.

276 For a case where it did not, see *Craig and Bentley* (1952) The Times, 10–13 Dec.

Mere repentance, without any action, is not a sufficient or necessary condition for the defence.[277] D's 'innocent' state of mind at the time of the commission of the crime is no answer if he had *mens rea* when he did the act of counselling or aiding. English courts are generally reluctant to inquire into questions of motive. D may have seen the light, or he may be acting out of malice against his accomplices or because of fear of detection or because he has decided that the risks outweigh the possible rewards. It is submitted that it should make no difference. It has been recognized, for example, that if D neutralizes the effect of any assistance or encouragement he has given, he is not liable, even if he did not intend to neutralize its effect.[278]

Preventing or attempting to prevent the crime?

To be effective must D's withdrawal involve his taking all reasonable steps to prevent the crime? It is submitted that this is not a necessary, although clearly it should be a *sufficient* basis for the defence. Where D gives timely warning to the police, the effect ought in most cases to be that the crime will be prevented; but this may not always be so and, even where it is, there remains D's potential liability for abetting P's attempt, if P has gone beyond mere preparation. Surely, however, efforts to prevent the commission of the crime by informing the police ought to be an effective withdrawal, whether D has or has not attempted to persuade E to desist. Apart from being the best evidence of repentance, it is conduct which the law should and does encourage.[279]

Withdrawal by cancelling assistance provided

The question of withdrawal is usually approached by ascertaining whether D has 'neutralized' any input his assistance or encouragement might have had irrespective of whether that will in fact prevent the crime being committed. However, this is a difficult test to apply. For example, where D has supplied information it may be impossible in any meaningful sense to cancel the effect of that assistance by merely communicating withdrawal to P and suggesting that D will have no further part to play. In such cases D's communicated countermand must go further if it is to be effective in neutralizing *the effect* of the assistance. It may be that D in such cases would be obliged to inform the police or do some act to prevent the crime, but the courts have not insisted on this.

Although no clear test has evolved, what seems to be involved in these cases is an unarticulated proportionality test, assessing the exculpatory conduct (what was done or said, to whom, at what stage of the criminal conduct), and the mode of D's participation in the contemplated offence (supply of weapons or advice, mere encouragement, presence at the crime). In the recent case of *O'Flaherty*, the court suggested that in evaluating the effectiveness of the withdrawal, account will be taken of 'the nature of the assistance and encouragement already given and how imminent the [principal offence], as well as the nature of the action said to constitute the withdrawal'.[280] The court

277 Hale, 1 PC 618; Stephen, *Digest* (4th edn), art 42; Williams, CLGP, s 127; *Croft* [1944] 1 KB 295, [1944] 2 All ER 483; *Becerra*, below, n 283.

278 *Rook* [1993] 2 All ER at 963.

279 Cf the large 'discounts' on sentence which may be earned for information given after D has become liable for and been convicted of the offence.

280 Para 60.

emphasized that it is not necessary for D have taken reasonable steps to prevent the crime in order to have successfully withdrawn.

If D's assistance consisted only in advising or encouraging P to commit the crime, it may be enough for him to tell P to desist.[281] If P then commits the crime he does so against D's advice and without his encouragement. It may be that P would never have committed the crime if D had not put it into his head in the first place; but then D may be properly and adequately dealt with by conviction of incitement. If D has counselled more than one person, then it seems that he must communicate his countermand to all of those who perpetrate the offence, for otherwise his counselling remains operative.[282] To be effective, the communication must be such as 'will serve unequivocal notice upon the other party to the common unlawful cause that if he proceeds upon it he does so without the further aid and assistance of those who withdraw.'[283] The position might be different where D has supplied P with the means of committing the crime. Aid may be no less easily neutralized than advice.

In *Grundy*[284] D had supplied P, a burglar, with information which was presumably valuable to P in committing the crime; but, for two weeks before P did so, D had been trying to stop him breaking in. It was held that there was evidence of an effective withdrawal which should have been left to the jury. In *Whitefield*[285] there was evidence that D had served unequivocal notice on E that, if he proceeded with the burglary they had planned together, he would do so without D's aid or assistance. The jury should have been told that, if they accepted the evidence, that was a defence.

If a rejected countermand may be an effective withdrawal, as in *Grundy*, it is arguable that an attempt to countermand should be the same. D has done all in his power to communicate his countermand to P but failed. In all these cases, the countermand has, *ex hypothesi*, failed; and, if the question is whether D has done his best to neutralize his input, the answer does not depend on the reasons for the failure.[286] It could be argued that, where D has failed to communicate, he can escape only by going to the police; but this was not insisted on in *Grundy* when persuasion failed. This suggests that the basis for the defence lies not in neutralizing the *actus reus* performed by D, but on some broader principle operating to exculpate D despite his continuing *actus reus*.

An effective withdrawal may often be made more easily at the preparatory stage than where the crime is in the course of commission. Thus, in *Beccara* where D handed P a knife so that he could use it on anyone interfering in a burglary, D did not make a sufficient communication of withdrawal when, on the appearance of V, he said 'Come on, let's go', and got out through a window. Something 'vastly different and vastly more effective' was required and, possibly, nothing less than physical intervention to stop P committing the crime would be required.[287] In that case, the 'withdrawal' occurred at a very late stage. When the knife is about to descend, the only effective withdrawal may be physical intervention to prevent it reaching its target.

281 *Saunders and Archer* (1573) 2 Plowd 473.

282 *State v Kinchen* (1910) 52 So 185, quoted by Lanham, above, at 591.

283 *Whitehouse* [1941] 1 WWR 112, per Sloan JA (Court of Appeal of British Columbia) approved in *Becerra* (1975) 62 Cr App R 212, CA. Cf *Fletcher* [1962] Crim LR 551; *Grundy* [1977] Crim LR 543, CA.

284 [1977] Crim LR 543.

285 (1984) 79 Cr App R 36.

286 Lanham, above at 590.

287 *Becerra*, above, n 283. Cf *Baker* [1994] Crim LR 444.

Spontaneous violence

In all the cases discussed above the offence was pre-planned. It has been held in *Mitchell and King* that cases of spontaneous violence are different.[288] If A and B spontaneously attack V, they are aiding and abetting one another, so long as each is aware that he is being assisted and encouraged by the other; but, if B simply withdraws, his participation in the offence apparently ceases without the need for any express communication to A, so that he will not be liable for acts done by A thereafter.

The appropriateness of this test depends on which basis the defence rests. If it is regarded as a defence which operates by D neutralizing his *actus reus*, it can be doubted: if A was encouraged by B's participation and was unaware that B had withdrawn, A continues to be encouraged. There is still an effective *actus reus*. As noted above, there are cases in which the defence has been successful where D has failed to neutralize the effect of his acts of assistance.

Fortunately, in the case of *Robinson*,[289] the Court of Appeal explained *Mitchell and King* as an exceptional case. Referring to the criticisms above, the court stated that:

> it can only be in exceptional circumstances that a person can withdraw from a crime he has initiated. Similarly in those rare circumstances communication of withdrawal must be given in order to give the principal offenders the opportunity to desist rather than complete the crime. This must be so even in situations of spontaneous violence unless it is not practicable or reasonable so to communicate as in the exceptional circumstances pertaining in *Mitchell* where the accused threw down his weapon and moved away before the final and fatal blows were inflicted.

More recently however, in *O'Flaherty*, the court followed the distinction between 'planned' and 'spontaneous' violence drawn in *Mitchell and King*. The Court of Appeal concluded that 'in a case of spontaneous violence such as this where there has been no prior agreement, the jury will usually have to make inferences as to the scope of the joint enterprise from the knowledge and actions of individual participants'.[290]

The issue surely deserves clarification from the House of Lords.

(g) Victims as parties to crime[291]

It has been noted[292] that when a statute creates a crime it does not generally provide that it shall be an offence to aid, abet, counsel or procure it. Such a provision is unnecessary, for it follows by implication of law. There is, however, one exception to this rule. Where the statute is designed for the protection of a certain class of persons it may be construed as excluding by implication the liability of any member of that class who is the victim of the offence, even though that member does in fact aid, abet, counsel or procure the offence. The principle is clearly stated in the Draft Code (cl 27(7)) in general terms:

[288] *Mitchell and King* (1998) 163 JP 75, [1999] Crim LR 496, DC.

[289] [2000] 5 Archbold News 2, CA. [290] Para 65.

[291] B. Hogan, 'Victims as Parties to Crime' [1962] Crim LR 683; G. Williams, 'Victims as Parties to Crimes – A Further Comment' [1964] Crim LR 686; G. Williams, 'Victims and Other Exempt Parties in Crime' (1990) 10 LS 245; Criminal Law Revision Committee, Fifteenth Report (Cmnd 9213), Appendix B.

[292] Above, p 167.

Where the purpose of an enactment creating an offence is the protection of a class of persons no member of that class who is a victim of such an offence can be guilty of that offence as an accessory.

But this has been applied, so far, only in respect of certain sexual offences.

In *Tyrrell*[293] D, a girl between the ages of 13 and 16, abetted P to have unlawful sexual intercourse with her. This was an offence by P under the Criminal Law Amendment Act 1885, s 5.[294] It was held, however, that D could not be convicted of abetting because the Act 'was passed for the purpose of protecting women and girls against themselves'.[295]

In *Pickford*[296] the court held (though it was probably not necessary to the decision) that *Tyrrell* was applicable to the case of a woman committing incest with her 13-year-old son, but it is not obvious that s 11 of the Sexual Offences Act 1956 (which made it an offence for the woman to permit 'her grandfather, father, brother or son' to have intercourse with her) was intended for the protection of anyone. Under the Sexual Offences Act 2003, there is nothing to prevent the boy being treated as a principal offender.

It has been held that a woman who is not pregnant can be convicted of abetting the use upon herself by another of an instrument with intent to procure her miscarriage, although the clear implication of the statute[297] is that such women cannot be convicted of *using* an instrument on herself with that intent.[298] However, a pregnant woman can be convicted under the same section of using an instrument on herself so it cannot be argued that this section was passed for the protection of *women* and it would be curious that Parliament should have intended to protect non-pregnant women from themselves, but not pregnant women.

How far the rule in *Tyrrell* extends has not been settled. The court referred to 'women' as well as girls and it may well be that it extends to the offences of procuration of women to be prostitutes and of brothel keeping which were in the 1885 Act and then in the Sexual Offences Act 1956.[299] It was held that it applied to the prostitute who abets a man who is living off her earnings.[300]

In all these cases, it seems clear that the protection of the law extended only to a person of the class who is a *victim*. Thus, a child under 16 could be convicted of abetting P in having intercourse with another child under 16; a boy under 14 could be convicted, even before the Sexual Offences Act 1993, of abetting P in intercourse with another boy under 14; a prostitute could abet P in keeping a brothel in which she was not a participant, or of living on the earnings of another prostitute.

There are many instances outside sexual offences where laws are passed for the protection of a particular class of persons. For example, there is much legislation protecting tenants from rapacious landlords. In the civil law a tenant who has paid a premium

[293] [1894] 1 QB 710.

[294] See now Sexual Offences Act 2003, s 9; below, Ch 17.

[295] Per Lord Coleridge CJ at 712. Both the Chief Justice and Mathew J pointed out that there was nothing in the Act to say that the girl should be guilty of aiding and abetting; but, it is submitted, no importance could be attached to that, for statutes hardly ever do.

[296] [1995] 1 Cr App R 420, 428.

[297] Offences Against the Person Act 1861, s 58; below, Ch 16.

[298] *Sockett* (1908) 72 JP 428; below, p 507.

[299] Sections 22–24, 28 and 29. Repealed see now Sexual Offences Act 2003, ss 52–55.

[300] *Congdon* [1990] NLJR 1221 (Judge Addison); Hogan [1962] Crim LR at 692–693; G. Williams, 'Victims and other exempt parties in crime' (1990) 10 LS 245 at 248–249. The offence is repealed by the Sexual Offences Act 2003, under which children are a protected class, but liable to conviction for participating in the sexual activity. *Tyrell* seems to be largely ignored in the 2003 Act.

illegally demanded by her landlord is not so tainted with his criminality as to be disabled from asserting her rights under the tenancy;[301] and it is possible that a principle similar to that in *Tyrrell* might be applied if a tenant were charged with abetting the landlord's offence.

(h) Instigation for the purpose of entrapment[302]

Police or other law enforcement officers or their agents sometimes do acts for the purpose of entrapping, or getting evidence against offenders, which would certainly amount to counselling or abetting an offence if they were not done for that purpose. The difficult question is how far an officer may go without himself incurring liability for the offence. Law enforcement officers have no general licence to aid and abet crime.

Two separate questions are involved: (i) in what circumstances will the law enforcement agency official have committed a crime by his encouragement?; (ii) in what circumstances will the person encouraged by the officer be entitled to rely on such entrapment to excuse his conduct? We are concerned here only with the first of those questions, the second being a matter of defence (and in English law only by way of procedural defence in terms of stay of proceedings).[303]

(i) Secondary liability for the agent provocateur

As long ago as 1929, the Royal Commission on Police Powers expressed:[304]

> As a general rule, the police should observe only, without participating in an offence, except in cases where an offence is habitually committed in circumstances in which observation by a third party is *ex hypothesi* impossible. Where participation is essential it should only be resorted to on the express and written authority of the Chief Constable.

In *Sang*[305] Lord Salmon said:

> I would now refer to what is, I believe and hope, the unusual case, in which a dishonest policeman, anxious to improve his detection record, tries very hard with the help of an agent provocateur to induce a young man with no criminal record to commit a serious crime; and ultimately the young man reluctantly succumbs to the inducement . . . The policeman and the informer who had acted together in inciting him to commit the crime should . . . both be prosecuted and suitably punished.

It is not clear that the word 'dishonest' adds anything to the postulated facts and it should make no difference that the policeman's motive is hatred of crime. It can hardly be necessary that the man induced to act should be 'young'; and it might be even more serious to induce a man with a bad record who was 'going straight', for the consequences for him would be worse. These matters go to sentence, not liability.

301 *Grace Rymer Investments Ltd v Waite* [1958] Ch 831, [1958] 2 All ER 777.

302 Williams, CLGP, s 256.

303 See below, p 345. See generally the decision of the House of Lords in *Looseley* [2001] UKHL 53, [2002] 1 Cr App R 360; A. Ashworth, 'Redrawing the Boundaries of Entrapment' [2002] Crim LR 161; D. Ormerod and A. Roberts, 'The Trouble with *Teixera*: Developing a principled approach to entrapment (2002) Int J E & P 38; A. Ashworth, 'Testing Fidelity to Legal Values: Official Involvement in Criminal Justice' (2000) 63 MLR 633, 642–652.

304 Cmd 3297 (1928), 116.

305 (1979) 69 Cr App R 282 at 296.

The essence of the *dictum* seems to be that a person who would not otherwise have committed a particular crime is induced to do so,[306] and the House of Lords in *Looseley* confirmed that this is the essential basis of the concept of entrapment in English law –

> Whether the police conduct preceding the commission of the offence was no more than might be expected from others in the circumstances?[307]

An officer who agrees, and intends, to participate in such an offence is guilty of conspiracy.[308] Merely to provide the opportunity for, and temptation to commit an offence will be lawful,[309] as is participation in an offence which has already been 'laid on' and is going to be committed in any event, in order to trap the offenders.[310] In such a case it makes no difference that the police intervention may have affected the time or other circumstances of the commission of the offence.[311]

By these standards, judges in the past may have shown undue tolerance to incitement of offences by the police. In *Mullins*[312] when D, apparently acting with the authority of the police, attended a treasonable conspiracy, endeavoured to persuade strangers to join in and advocated the use of violence, Maule J rejected an argument that D's evidence required corroboration as that of an accomplice. He said that a person employed by the government as a spy does not deserve to be blamed 'if he instigates offences no further than by pretending to concur with the perpetrators'. That *dictum* is of course acceptable; but D's conduct seems to have gone well beyond this, particularly in trying to persuade strangers to join in. Where there is a continuing general conspiracy – for example, to supply drugs to anyone asking for them – it seems that a law enforcement officer commits no offence by inducing the general conspirators to enter into a particular conspiracy within the ambit of the general conspiracy, for example, to supply him with specified drugs.

It cannot be the law that the police may properly participate in a crime to the point at which irreparable damage is done. A policeman who assists P to commit murder in order to entrap him must be guilty of murder. It is submitted that the same must be true of any injury to the person, unless it is trivial and V consents to it; and probably to any damage to property, unless the owner consents.

(i) Reform

The Law Commission is due to produce a Report on assisting and encouraging offenders in 2005. Comment will be placed on the updates website.

306 Cf *Birtles* [1969] 2 All ER 1131n, [1969] 1 WLR 1047.

307 Lord Nicholls, para 23.

308 *Yip Chiu-cheung v R*, above, p 00.

309 *Williams v DPP* (1993) 98 Cr App R 209, DC where the 'bait' was cartons of cigarettes left in a vulnerable position. The court said that the police had not aided, abetted, etc: but had they not procured the commission of the offence? They would have regarded the operation as a failure if no one had stolen the cartons.

310 *McCann* (1971) 56 Cr App R 359.

311 *McEvilly* (1973) 60 Cr App R 150.

312 (1848) 3 Cox CC 526.

9

Assistance after the offence

1. Impeding the apprehension or prosecution of arrestable offenders[1]

At common law anyone who gave to any party to a felony any assistance whatever, tending to and having the object of, enabling him to evade arrest, trial or punishment, was guilty of the felony as accessory after the fact. The whole of the law relating to accessories after the fact was repealed by the Criminal law Act 1967 and replaced by s 4 of that Act:

(1) Where a person has committed an arrestable offence,[2] any other person who, knowing or believing him to be guilty of the offence or of some other arrestable offence, does without lawful authority or reasonable excuse any act with intent to impede his apprehension or prosecution shall be guilty of an offence.

[(1A) In this section and section 5 below 'arrestable offence' has the meaning assigned to it by section 24 of the Police and Criminal Evidence Act 1984.]

(2) If on the trial of an indictment for an arrestable offence the jury are satisfied that the offence charged (or some other offence of which the accused might on that charge be found guilty) was committed, but find the accused not guilty of it, they may find him guilty of any offence under subsection (1) above of which they are satisfied that he is guilty in relation to the offence charged (or that other offence).

(3) A person committing an offence under subsection (1) above with intent to impede another person's apprehension or prosecution shall on conviction on indictment be liable to imprisonment according to the gravity of the other person's offence, as follows: –

(a) if that offence is one for which the sentence is fixed by law, he shall be liable to imprisonment for not more than ten years;

(b) if it is one for which a person (not previously convicted) may be sentenced to imprisonment for a term of fourteen years, he shall be liable to imprisonment for not more than seven years;

(c) if it is not one included above but is one for which a person (not previously convicted) may be sentenced to imprisonment for a term of ten years, he shall be liable to imprisonment for not more than five years;

(d) in any other case, he shall be liable to imprisonment for not more than three years.

(4) No proceedings shall be instituted for an offence under subsection (1) above except by or with the consent of the Director of Public Prosecutions.

1 G. Williams, 'Evading Justice' [1975] Crim LR 430; K. J. M. Smith, *A Modern Treatise on Complicity* (1991), ch 1.

2 When the Serious Organised Crime and Police Act 2005 is in force, by Sch 7, Part 3, 'arrestable offence' will be replaced by 'relevant offence' to reflect the abolition of the concept of 'arrestable offence'.

The effect of *Courtie*[3] is that the section creates four offences, punishable with 10, seven, five and three years' imprisonment, respectively. In many instances the decision is made to charge those who have assisted offenders with perverting the course of justice.[4]

(a) *Actus reus*

There are two elements in the *actus reus*: (i) an arrestable offence must have been committed by the person (O) whose apprehension or prosecution D is charged with impeding; and (ii) D must have done 'any act' with the appropriate intent. No one may be convicted of an attempt to commit this offence.[5]

(i) Proof of an arrestable offence

The arrestable offence alleged to have been committed by O must be specified in the indictment.[6] If, however, it turns out that O was not guilty of the specified offence, D may still be convicted if O was guilty of another arrestable offence of which he might have been convicted on the indictment for the specified offence, under s 6(3) of the Criminal Law Act 1967.[7] If, for example, it is alleged that O committed murder and it transpires at D's trial that O was not guilty of murder but was guilty of manslaughter or attempted murder, D may be convicted. It is not necessary to direct the jury to find what offence D thought O had committed, though this may be a material factor in the imposition of sentence.[8] It is immaterial that O has been acquitted at an earlier trial if it can be proved at D's trial that O was guilty. Even where O and D are tried together, O's acquittal should not, in principle, be conclusive if it can be proved, as against D, that O committed the offence.[9] But O's conviction is presumptive evidence that he committed the offence: PACE 1984, s 74.

(ii) An act of assistance

Once the arrestable offence has been proved, the remaining element in the *actus reus* – any act – is almost unlimited. There must be an *act* – an omission will not suffice – but it need not be an act having a natural tendency to impede the apprehension or prosecution of an offender. Where the act does not have such a tendency, however, it will be difficult to prove the intent, in the absence of a confession. The common instances of the offence will undoubtedly correspond to the typical ways of becoming an accessory after the fact under the old law – by concealing the offender, providing him with a car, food or money to enable him to escape, or destroying evidence against him. According to the Criminal Law Revision Committee,[10] 'The requirement that there should be an attempt to "impede" a

3 Above, p 40.

4 On which see recently S. M. Edwards, 'Perjury and Perverting the Course of Justice Considered' [2003] Crim LR 525.

5 Criminal Attempts Act 1981, s 1(4)(c).

6 Presumably this can include O's liability for secondary or inchoate offences.

7 *Morgan* [1972] 1 QB 436, [1972] 1 All ER 348. *Quaere* whether the same principle is applicable to other provisions allowing conviction of offences other than that charged? NB: n 2 above.

8 Ibid.

9 Cf *Shannon* [1975] AC 717, [1974] 2 All ER 1009, HL; *Donald* (1986) 83 Cr App R 49, [1986] Crim LR 535. *Williams* [1975] Crim LR at 432. On the use of an offender's incriminating statements at a joint trial see *Hayter* [2005] UKHL 6, [2005] Crim LR (Sept).

10 Cmnd 2659, para. 28.

prosecution will exclude mere persuasion not to prosecute'. Yet words are no doubt a sufficient act; so that the offence would be committed by intentionally misdirecting police who were pursuing an offender, or making a false statement to a detective.[11] An act done through an agent would be sufficient. Indeed, the mere authorization of the agent would be a sufficient act, when done with intent to impede, to constitute the offence, though the agent never acted on it.

(iii) Relationship to escape

Under the old law, D was guilty as an accessory after the fact if he assisted a felon to evade his punishment by enabling him to escape or to remain at large. It is clearly not an offence under s 4 to enable a convicted arrestable offender (as opposed to one awaiting trial) to escape from gaol; but this is not important as such acts will amount to other offences.[12] Whether it is an offence to assist such an arrestable offender who has escaped to remain at large depends on the interpretation of 'apprehension'. Does it extend beyond its obvious meaning of apprehension with a view to prosecution and include the rearrest of the escaped convicted prisoner? There seems to be no reason why it should not be so interpreted.

(b) *Mens rea*

There are two elements in the *mens rea*: (i) D must know or believe the offender to be guilty of the arrestable offence which he had actually committed, or some other arrestable offence; and (ii) D must intend to impede the apprehension or prosecution of the offender.

(i) Know or believe

D must *know or believe.* Where the allegation is that D know or believed of the '. . . the offence' – the arrestable offence which has actually been committed – the *mens rea* is probably governed both by 'knowing' and 'believing', but, if 'believing' is construed as in handling, it adds little to 'knowing'.[13] If the word 'believing' had not been included, 'knowing' might well have been construed to include wilful blindness.[14] If D has a mere suspicion that O is an arrestable offender and, shutting his eyes to an obvious means of knowledge, assists him, he can hardly be said to 'believe' in O's guilt. Thus recklessness may not be enough and, arguably, the subsection is unduly narrow in this respect.[15] Where the allegation is that the knowledge or belief relates to some 'other arrestable offence' the issue must be governed only by 'believing' since, *ex hypothesi*, the offence has not been committed and, therefore, D cannot 'know' it has.

(ii) Knowledge or belief as to what?

In order to know or believe that an arrestable offence has been committed, D need not know the law. It will be enough that he believes in the existence of facts which, whether he

[11] This would amount to other offences as well; see below, p 853.

[12] Prison breaking, escape and rescue are offences at common law. See 6th edition of this work at ch 19.3, p 756.

[13] *Ismail* [1977] Crim LR 557, CA; *Grainge* [1974] 1 All ER 928, CA; *Griffiths* (1974) 60 Cr App R 14; CA; below, p 854.

[14] *Williams* [1975] Crim LR at 435.

[15] Above, p 108.

knows it or not, amount in law to an arrestable offence.[16] His ignorance of the law cannot afford a defence. The position is, perhaps, not quite so obvious where D has a positive mistaken belief. D knows that there is a duty not to conceal arrestable offenders, but, knowing what O has done, is wrongly informed that it does not constitute an arrestable offence. Arguably, he now has no *mens rea* on the ground that he has made a mistake of civil law,[17] whether there is a right to arrest being a civil and not a criminal matter.

It is immaterial that D is unaware of O's identity.[18] What if he makes a mistake of identity? If D thinks he sees R committing an arrestable offence and acts, intending to impede his apprehension or prosecution, is he guilty under s 4 if it was in fact O whom he observed? Perhaps the question should be answered by making a distinction. If D does an act which he intends to assist the person whom he in fact observed, his mistake of identity should be immaterial. For example, he sends a constable, who is pursuing the offender, in the wrong direction. Here D knows that the *person he is assisting* has committed an arrestable offence, and that person has in fact done so. Suppose, on the other hand, that D fabricates evidence the following day so as to provide an alibi for R and this evidence could not, and was of course not intended to assist O, of whom D has never heard. Here he does not intend to assist the person whom he in fact observed. An indictment charging D with doing an act, knowing O to be guilty of an arrestable offence and with intent to impede his prosecution is plainly bad. If R has never committed an arrestable offence, it would seem that D is not guilty under the section;[19] if R once did commit an arrestable offence, then D is guilty unless the limitation tentatively suggested in the previous paragraph be imposed.

(iii) Some other arrestable offence

'Some other arrestable offence' must refer to an offence which O has not committed, for otherwise the words are redundant (NB: n 2 above). If D thinks he has seen O commit a robbery and acts with intent to conceal this, he will be guilty, though O had in fact committed a murder and not a robbery. This is obviously as it should be, where, as in this example, D's belief relates to the transaction which constituted the actual offence. Suppose, however, that unknown to D, O committed murder last week. D believes, wrongly, that O committed bigamy two years ago. If D does an act with intent to impede O's prosecution of bigamy – such as burning O's letters – it would seem very odd indeed that he should be liable only because O committed murder last week – the murder has nothing to do with the case. This suggests that the supposed offence must arise from the same transaction as the actual offence (and, undoubtedly, this will normally be the case) but so to hold would require the imposition of some limitation on the express words of the section.[20]

(iv) With intent

The act must be done with intent to impede the arrestable offender's apprehension or prosecution. It seems that it must be proved that D's *purpose* was to impede, and that it is

16 Cf *Sykes v DPP* [1962] AC 528 at 563, [1961] 3 All ER 33 at 42. But cf n 2 above now.

17 Above, p 122. But see Draft Code, cl 25(3)(b), Law Com No 143.

18 *Brindley* [1971] 2 QB 300, [1971] 2 All ER 698.

19 Nor could D be convicted of an attempt to commit the offence. See Criminal Attempts Act 1981, s 1(4)(c), below, p 416.

20 Cf the discussion of s 5, below, p 220.

not enough that he knew his act would certainly impede if that was not his object or one of his objects; or, as it has been put above, that a 'direct' and not merely an 'oblique' intention is required.[21] At all events, this seems to be the Criminal Law Revision Committee's view of the clause which became s 4. Discussing the case of harbouring, they wrote:

> If the harbouring is done with the object of impeding apprehension or prosecution . . . it will be within the offence; if it is done merely by way of providing or continuing to provide the criminal with accommodation in the ordinary way, it will not; and juries will be able to tell the difference.[22]

If this be the correct interpretation of the section, then, as under the old law of accessories after the fact, a handler of stolen goods will not be guilty of an offence under s 4, even where he knows that his conduct has the effect of impeding the apprehension or prosecution of the thief, if that is not his object.[23] Nor is D guilty if, by acts done with the object of avoiding his own arrest or prosecution, he knowingly impedes the arrest or prosecution of another.[24] Where there is *prima facie* evidence of the necessary intent, it is for D to lay a foundation for a defence by introducing evidence that his sole purpose was of a different character. In the absence of such evidence, there is no duty to direct a jury to consider whether D might have had a different intent.[25] If D has the dual object of saving himself and the other from arrest or prosecution then, no doubt, he is guilty.

(v) Lawful authority

Even though the act is done with intent to impede, it is not an offence if there is 'lawful authority or reasonable excuse' for it. According to the Criminal Law Revision Committee:[26]

> The exception for 'lawful authority' will cover an executive decision against a prosecution, and that for 'reasonable excuse' will avoid extending the offence to acts such as destroying the evidence of an offence (for example a worthless cheque) in pursuance of a legitimate agreement to refrain from prosecuting in consideration of the making good of loss caused by that offence.

It is possible that the exception may have some application outside this situation.[27] As with the Prevention of Crime Act,[28] it enables the courts to afford a defence in circumstances in which they think it reasonable to do so.

(c) The sentence

Section 4(3)[29] provides for a sliding scale of sentences which is related to the arrestable offence which has actually been committed. Where D believes that some other arrestable offence has been committed, the punishment to which he is liable is fixed according to the *actus reus*, not according to the *mens rea*. If D acts with intent to impede the apprehension

[21] Above, pp 93–94. [22] Cmnd 2659, para 30. [23] *Andrews and Craig* [1962] 3 All ER 961n.
[24] *Jones* [1949] 1 KB 194, [1948] 2 All ER 964. [25] *Brindley* [1971] 2 QB 300 at 304.
[26] Cmnd 2659, para 28.
[27] Would a wife have a reasonable excuse for assisting her husband? See P. Pace, ' "Impeding Arrest". A Wife's Right as a Spouse?' [1978] Crim LR 82. According to *Lee Shek Ching v R* Hong Kong, CA, 1985, No 53, being O's wife is not, as such, a reasonable excuse.
[28] Below, p 582. [29] Above, p 216.

of O whom he believes to have committed malicious wounding[30] (maximum, five years), he is liable to three years' imprisonment if his belief is correct; but if O has in fact committed murder, he is liable to 10 years.

It is clear that the arrestable offence which fixes the maximum under s 4 must have been committed when the act of impeding takes place. D, rightly believing O to be guilty of malicious wounding, acts to impede his arrest. Subsequently, O's victim, V, dies, and O becomes guilty of murder. D is liable to only three and not 10 years' imprisonment.

2. Compounding an arrestable offence[31]

The abolition of felonies by the Criminal Law Act 1967 eliminated two common law misdemeanours known respectively as 'compounding a felony' and 'misprision of felony'.[32] The former consisted in an agreement for consideration not to prosecute, or to impede a prosecution for, a felony. The latter consisted simply in an omission to report a felony to the police. In place of these offences s 5(1) of the Criminal Law Act enacts an offence, triable either way, as follows:

> Where a person has committed an arrestable offence,[33] any other person who, knowing or believing that the offence or some other arrestable offence has been committed, and that he has information which might be of material assistance in securing the prosecution or conviction of an offender for it, accepts or agrees to accept for not disclosing that information any consideration other than the making good of loss or injury caused by the offence, or the making of reasonable compensation for that loss or injury, shall be liable on conviction on indictment to imprisonment for not more than two years.

This provision is much less far-reaching than the previous law. It is narrower than misprision in that the offence is committed only if D accepts or agrees to accept a consideration for not disclosing the information relating to the arrestable offence. It is narrower than compounding in that it is not now criminal to accept or agree to accept consideration for not disclosing information relating to the arrestable offence, if the consideration is no more than the making good of loss or injury caused by the offence or the making of reasonable compensation for that loss or injury. No one may be convicted of attempting to commit an offence under s 5(1).[34]

(a) *Actus reus*

There are two elements in the *actus reus*: (i) an arrestable offence must actually have been committed; and (ii) D must accept or agree to accept consideration for not disclosing information which he knows or believes to be material.

The new offence is wider than misprision and compounding in that it extends to all arrestable offences which, of course, includes crimes which were not felonies; but it is provided by s 5(5): 'The compounding of an offence other than treason shall not be an

30 Below, p 553. 31 G. Williams, 'Evading Justice' [1975] Crim LR at 609.
32 See the 1st edition of this book, at 539–544.
33 When the Serious Organised Crime and Police Act 2005 is in force, by Sch 7, Part 3 'arrestable offence' is replaced by 'relevant offence'.
34 Criminal Attempts Act 1981, s 1(4)(c), below, p 416.

offence otherwise than under this section'. It is thus clear that it is not an offence to agree to accept any consideration for not prosecuting a non-arrestable offence, though whether the resulting contract is enforceable is another matter.

The offence is committed only where D 'accepts or agrees to accept' the consideration. The situation envisaged is that where an offer is made to D. If the offer comes from D, then he would seem to be guilty also of the much more serious offence of blackmail.[35] Consideration presumably bears much the same meaning as in the law of contract and extends to money, goods, services, or any act or forbearance.

The Act makes no provision for any privileged relationships (such as may have existed under the law of misprision) but proceedings may not be instituted without the consent of the Director of Public Prosecutions.[36]

(b) *Mens rea*

There are two elements in the *mens rea*. It must be proved that (i) D knew or believed that an arrestable offence (once SOCPA 2005 is in force 'relevant') had been committed and (ii) D intended to accept or to agree to accept consideration other than the making good of loss or the making of reasonable compensation.

(i) Knowledge as to what?

Where D's knowledge or belief relates to the arrestable offence A which has actually been committed, the application of the section seems quite straightforward. But D's belief may relate to some other arrestable offence B which, *ex hypothesi*, has not been committed. Here D's acceptance, or agreement to accept consideration, must relate to the offence B which he believes to have been committed and thus not to the offence which has actually been committed since they are different. Under this section D's belief need not – as, under s 4, it probably must[37] – be that an arrestable offence has been committed by the same person who has in fact committed such an offence. If D wrongly supposes that he has seen an arrestable offence committed by R and accepts consideration for not disclosing what he saw, he will be guilty if in fact he saw O committing an arrestable offence.

The argument advanced in connection with s 4, that D's belief must relate to the transaction which resulted in the actual offence, is much stronger in relation to s 5. If D wrongly supposes that R has committed an arrestable offence and accepts consideration for not disclosing that fact, his guilt can hardly be established by proving that some time, somewhere, someone committed an arrestable offence – for example, that Dr Crippen committed murder. The offence which D supposes to have been committed must have something to do with the offence which has actually been committed. The most obvious point of connection is that the real and the supposed offence must both arise out of the same transaction. An alternative view might be that it is sufficient if either (i) the two offences arise out of the same transaction or (ii) they both relate to the same person. Unknown to D, O committed murder last week. D believes, wrongly, that O committed bigamy two years ago. O offers money to D 'to keep his mouth shut'. D, believing that O is talking about the bigamy, accepts. According to the first view put above, D is not guilty; according to the alternative view, he is. It is submitted that the first view is better; according to the second, D's liability depends entirely on chance.

[35] Below, Ch 20. [36] Section 5(3). [37] See above, p 218.

If D's acceptance of consideration relates to the transaction in question, then it seems that it will be immaterial that he is mistaken as to both (i) the nature of the arrestable offence and (ii) the identity of the perpetrator. He supposes he saw R perpetrating a robbery. Actually, he saw O committing murder. If he accepts consideration for not disclosing what he saw he should be guilty.

The Criminal Law Revision Committee stated:[38]

> . . . the offence will not apply to a person who refrains from giving information because he does not think it right that the offender should be prosecuted or because of a promise of reparation by the offender. It would be difficult to justify making the offence apply to those cases.

It is difficult to see, however, how it can be a defence for D simply to say that he did not 'think it right that the offender should be prosecuted', if he has accepted consideration for not disclosing information. Even if he convinces the court of his views as to the impropriety of the contemplated prosecution he still falls within the express words of the section. He could be acquitted only if the section were interpreted so as to require that D's object or motive be the acquisition of the consideration. As we have seen,[39] on a charge under s 4, it is probable that a *purpose* of impeding must be proved, but this may be justified by giving a narrow meaning to the ulterior intent specified in that section. No ulterior intent is specified in s 5 and, consequently, it is difficult to see how the section can be limited in the same way.

(ii) Relationship with advertising for return of stolen goods

In the light of the rules about compounding, it is perhaps a little surprising that the offence of advertising rewards for the return of goods stolen or lost has been retained.[40] Section 23 of the Theft Act provides:

> Where any public advertisement of a reward for the return of any goods which have been stolen or lost uses any words to the effect that no questions will be asked, or that the person producing the goods will be safe from apprehension or inquiry, or that any money paid for the purchase of the goods or advanced by way of loan on them will be repaid, the person advertising the reward and any person who prints or publishes the advertisement shall on summary conviction be liable to a fine not exceeding one hundred pounds.

In so far as an advertisement states that 'no questions will be asked' this is only proposing what is perfectly lawful under s 5(1) of the Criminal Law Act.[41] It is not clear why this should be an offence because it is done through a public advertisement. Nor is it clear why it should be an offence to offer a reward for the return of stolen goods, even their return by the thief. The promise to pay the reward might be unenforceable for lack of consideration but, if it were actually paid, there would be nothing unlawful about that. Possibly the theory is that, if such advertisements were common, theft might be encouraged in that thieves would have an easy and safe way of disposing of the stolen

38 Cmnd 2659, para 41. 39 Above, p 219.

40 The section replaces the Larceny Act 1861, s 102 which provided for a penalty of £50 recoverable by a common informer. This was changed to a fine of £100 by the Common Informers Act 1951. The CLRC hesitantly recommended the retention of the provision 'as advertisements of this kind may encourage dishonesty': Cmnd 2977, para 144.

41 Above, p 220.

goods for reward. This cannot apply to an advertisement addressed to the bona fide purchaser offering to recompense him if he will return the stolen goods; this seems quite a reasonable thing to do, especially since the bona fide purchaser commits no offence by retaining the goods for himself.[42]

The section creates what the courts are pleased to call a quasi-criminal offence, not requiring *mens rea*, so the advertising manager of a company was liable for the publication of an advertisement which he had not read.[43] 'Stolen' bears the wide meaning given to that word by s 24(4) of the Theft Act so the bona fide purchaser may indeed have become the absolute owner of the goods where, for example, they have been obtained by deception and the property passed.

3. Refusal to aid a constable[44]

It is a common law misdemeanour to refuse to go to the aid of a constable who, on seeing a breach of the peace, calls on D to assist him in restoring the peace. A ticket collector was held to be guilty of the offence when he failed to come to the assistance of a policewoman struggling with a thief. His defence that he had obeyed instructions not to leave his post was not accepted.[45] There must be a reasonable necessity for the constable to request assistance. It is no defence that D's aid would have been ineffective. So where a constable requested D to assist him in suppressing a breach of the peace among four or five hundred people at a prize fight, Alderson B directed that D's refusal was an offence.[46] It seems that it was no answer that he had his horses to take care of. Alderson B[47] recognized that physical impossibility or a lawful excuse would be an answer; but it is not clear what would constitute 'lawful excuse'. Is the citizen required to act where there would be a grave risk of death or serious injury? Surely the State cannot criminalize D for a failure to put his life on the line?

42 Below, p 665.

43 *Denham v Scott* (1983) 77 Cr App R 210, [1983] Crim LR 558, DC.

44 On which see the valuable article by D. Nicholson, 'The Citizen's Legal Duty to Assist the Police' [1992] Crim LR 611.

45 *Waugh* (1976) The Times, 1 Oct (Knightsbridge Crown Court).

46 *Brown* (1841) Car & M 314. Cf *Sherlock* (1866) LR 1 CCR 20.

47 In *Brown*, above.

10

Vicarious liability and liability of associations

1. Vicarious liability[1]

(a) Nature and scope of doctrine

The doctrine of 'vicarious liability' is a mechanism by which the law attributes blame for the acts of another. Common examples include retail companies being responsible for the sale of items by managers and shop assistants in their stores, and of licensees being responsible for the acts of their employees.

It is important to distinguish vicarious liability from liability for breach of a personal duty. Many statutes, particularly dealing with regulatory offences create specific offences that can be committed by the specified person (for example, the employer) in person. If the specified person is in breach of that duty, he commits the *actus reus* of the offence and, if it imposes strict liability, he is personally, not vicariously, guilty of the offence, though he may say with truth that he would not have been in breach but for the fault of his employees or agents. A good example is the Health and Safety at Work etc Act 1974. By s 3(1) the Act imposes on every employer a duty 'to conduct his undertaking in such a way as to ensure, so far as is reasonably practicable' that persons not in his employment are not exposed to risk. In *British Steel plc*[2] D's sub-contractor, negligently conducting D's undertaking, caused V's death. D had not ensured so far as was, in the opinion of the court, reasonably practicable, that persons were not exposed to risk and D was therefore guilty. D was liable, not vicariously for the acts of the sub-contractor which caused death, but for his own failure to ensure that there was no risk of such a thing happening. This was a case of personal liability being imposed by the statute.[3]

1 G. Williams, CLGP, ch 7, and '*Mens Rea* and Vicarious Responsibility' (1956) 9 CLP 57; P. Glazebrook, 'Situational Liability', in *Reshaping the Criminal Law*, 108; P. J. Pace, 'Delegation – a Doctrine in Search of a Definition' [1982] Crim LR 627; L. H. Leigh, *Strict and Vicarious Liability* (1982); F. B. Sayer, 'Criminal Responsibility for the Acts of Another' (1930) 43 Harv LR 689; T. Baty, *Vicarious Liability* (1916), especially ch X. For proposals for the reform of the law, see Law Commission Working Paper No 43.

2 [1995] 1 WLR 1356, [1995] Crim LR 654. If work is part of D's undertaking – a question of fact – D is in breach of his duty if independent contractors whom he engages to perform it unreasonably expose others to risk: *Associated Octel Ltd* [1996] 4 All ER 846, HL. *Alphacell Ltd* (above p 154) was, it is submitted, a case of personal liability and wrongly treated as a precedent for vicarious liability in *National Rivers Authority v Alfred McAlpine Homes (East) Ltd* [1994] 4 All ER 286, DC, [1994] Crim LR 960 and commentary.

3 See also *Nottingham City Council v Wolverhampton and Dudley Breweries* [2004] 2 WLR 820, holding the owner of the premises liable under s 14 Food and Safety Act 1990.

(i) Relationship with tortious doctrine

True vicarious liability is the general rule in the law of tort. An employer is held liable for all acts of his employee performed in the course of his employee's employment. In the criminal law, an employer is generally not so liable. In the leading civil case of *Lloyd v Grace, Smith & Co*,[4] a solicitor's managing clerk, without the knowledge of his employer, induced a widow to give him instructions to sell certain property, to hand over the title deeds and to sign two documents which were neither read over nor explained to her, but which she believed were necessary for the sale. The documents were, in fact, a conveyance to the clerk of the property, of which he dishonestly disposed for his own benefit. It was held that, since the clerk was acting within the scope of his authority, his employer was liable. Now it is very likely that the clerk was guilty of certain criminal offences – perhaps in those days larceny of the title deeds and fraudulent conversion of the money; but it is perfectly clear that his employer could never have been made criminally liable for those acts for which the employer bore civil liability.

An employer is similarly liable in tort where the employee acting in the course of his employment commits a fraud involving a forgery,[5] and for acts which amount to obtaining by deception, assault and battery, manslaughter and so on; but in none of these cases would the employer be *criminally* liable simply on the ground that his employee was acting in the course of his employment. The doctrine of vicarious liability in tort developed in the early part of the eighteenth century, but it was made clear by the leading case of *Huggins*[6] that there was to be no parallel development in the criminal law. Huggins, the warden of the Fleet, was charged with the murder of a prisoner whose death had been caused by the servant of Huggins' deputy. It was held that, though the servant was guilty, Huggins was not, since the acts were done without his knowledge. Raymond CJ said:[7]

> It is a point not to be disputed, but that in criminal cases the principal is not answerable for the act of the deputy as he is in civil cases: they must each answer for their own acts, and stand or fall by their own behaviour. All the authors that treat of criminal proceedings proceed on the foundation of this distinction; that to affect the superior by the act of his deputy, there must be the command of the superior which is not found in this case.

An employer can be held liable for his employee's crimes, as a general rule, only where he is a participant in them within the rules stated in the preceding chapter. Three exceptions to the general rule have already been noted:[8] in public nuisance, criminal libel and contempt of court an employer has been held liable for his employee's acts although he is, personally, perfectly innocent. These were the only exceptions at common law; but now, by statute, there are many such offences. Parliament is of course always at liberty

[4] [1912] AC 716, HL. As approved by the House of Lords in *Lister v Hesley Hall* [2001] UKHL 22. Note also the recent approach of the House of Lords in *Dubai Aluminium v Salaam* [2003] AC 366, where their lordships held that it is not a condition of vicarious liability that all the wrongful acts for which an employee was responsible had to have been committed in the course of employment, rather vicarious liability would not be imposed unless all the acts or omissions which were necessary to make him personally liable had taken place in the course of employment. See generally on tortious liability, P. S. Atiyah, *Vicarious Liability in the English Law of Torts* (1967); W. V. H. Rogers, *Winfield and Jolowicz on Tort* (16th edn, 2002), ch 20.

[5] *Uxbridge Permanent Building Society v Pickard* [1939] 2 KB 248, [1939] 2 All ER 344.

[6] (1730) 2 Stra 883.

[7] Ibid, at 885.

[8] Above, p 140.

to impose vicariously criminal liability. Atkin J in *Mousel Brothers Ltd v London and North-Western Railway Co*[9] provided guidance on the identification of statutory vicarious liability:

> . . . while prima facie a principal is not to be made criminally responsible for the acts of his servants, yet the legislature may prohibit an act or enforce a duty in such words as to make the prohibition or the duty absolute; in which case the principal is liable if the act is in fact done by his servants. To ascertain whether a particular Act of Parliament has that effect or not regard must be had to the object of the statute, the words used, the nature of the duty laid down, the person upon whom it is imposed, the person by whom it would in ordinary circumstances be performed, and the person upon whom the penalty is imposed.

The decision of the House of Lords in *Environment Agency v Empress Cars*[10] also has an impact in this area. As noted above, their lordships took an unorthodox, and it is submitted erroneous approach to the issue of causation in the strict liability offences of 'causing' pollution under the Water Resources Act 1991. The House held that the conduct of a third party unknown to the defendants that released the pollutant from the defendant's storage tanks did not break the chain of causation, leaving the defendants liable. Applying this interpretation, an employer can be personally liable for the acts of his employee who is the cause of the pollution, even where that act is the direct cause of the wrongdoing and unauthorized.[11]

(ii) Strict liability and vicarious liability distinguished

Vicarious liability is by no means the same thing as strict liability.[12] The point requires emphasis for there is an unhappy judicial tendency to confuse the two concepts. A statute may require *mens rea* and yet also impose vicarious responsibility. It has already been noted that supplying liquor to a constable on duty is an offence requiring *mens rea*,[13] yet a licensee may be vicariously liable for his agent's act in so doing[14] and the same considerations apply to the offence of suffering gaming to be carried on in licensed premises.[15] Conversely, it is clearly possible for a statute to create strict liability without imposing vicarious responsibility. Once a statute has been held to impose a duty with strict liability on a particular person, it is likely to be held that that person is liable for the acts of anyone through whom he performs that duty.[16] Where, however, the duty with strict liability is not imposed on particular persons but on the public generally, vicarious liability is inappropriate. For example, the former offence of causing death by dangerous driving was, at one time, held to be an offence of strict liability, but it is surely inconceivable that vicarious liability would have been imposed.

9 [1917] 2 KB 836 at 845. 10 [1999] 2 AC 22.

11 See *Milford Haven Port Authority* [2000] 2 Cr App R (S) 423.

12 *Seaboard Offshore Ltd v Secretary of State for Transport* [1993] Crim LR 611; affd [1994] 2 All ER 99, HL.

13 *Sherras v De Rutzen*, above, p 141.

14 *Mullins v Collins* (1874) LR 9 QB 292.

15 *Bosley v Davies* (1875) 1 QBD 84 (*mens rea* required); *Bond v Evans* (1888) 21 QBD 249 (licensee liable for servants' act); Licensing Act 1872, s 16.

16 *Dicta* to the effect that an offence of strict liability necessarily imposes vicarious responsibility are not difficult to find: see eg *Barker v Levinson* [1951] 1 KB 342 at 345, [1950] 2 All ER 825 at 827; *James & Son Ltd v Smee* [1955] 1 QB 78 at 95, [1954] 3 All ER 273 at 280, per Slade J; *Bradshaw v Ewart-James* [1983] 1 All ER 12 at 14.

(b) Basis of liability

As in the case of strict liability, so with vicarious liability it appears that the development is the work of the courts rather than of Parliament. Statutes do occasionally say, in terms, that one person is to be liable for another's crimes.[17] It is more common, however, for the courts to 'detect' such an intention in statutes. This judicial willingness to impose vicarious liability arises particularly in summary offences. The reason most commonly advanced by the judges for holding a person (usually an employer, but independent contractors may also be caught)[18] liable is that the statute would be 'rendered nugatory'[19] – and the will of Parliament thereby defeated – if he were not. It may seem rather odd for the courts to be willing to impose liability for the acts of another on grounds of expediency when the foundation of the criminal law is that a person should be liable only for his personal wrongdoing. This would be particularly unsatisfactory in the absence of clear evidence that the prosecution of an employer will render the legislation more effective by deterring that and other employers from similar breaches.

Two quite distinct principles, differing somewhat in their effect, underlie the various decisions on vicarious liability. In the first place, a person may be held liable for the acts of another where he has delegated to that other the performance of certain duties cast on him by Act of Parliament. In the second place, an employer may be held liable because acts which are done physically by his employee may, in law, be the employer's acts. These two types of case require separate consideration.

(i) The delegation principle[20]

A good illustration of the application of this principle may be found in the case of *Allen v Whitehead*.[21] The Metropolitan Police Act 1839, s 44, provides an offence for a keeper of a refreshment house to 'knowingly permit or suffer prostitutes or persons of notoriously bad character to meet together and remain in a place where refreshments are sold and consumed'.

D, the occupier of a café, while receiving the profits of the business, did not himself manage it, but employed a manager. Having had a warning from the police, D instructed his manager that no prostitutes were to be allowed to congregate on the premises and had a notice to that effect displayed on the walls. He visited the premises once or twice a week and there was no evidence that any misconduct took place in his presence. Then, on eight consecutive days, a number of women, known to the manager to be prostitutes, met together and remained there between the hours of 8 pm and 4 am. It was held by the Divisional Court, reversing the Metropolitan Magistrate, that D's ignorance of those facts was no defence. The acts of the manager and his *mens rea* (knowing that the women

[17] A striking example is the Road Traffic Offenders Act 1988, s 64(5), which provides that the owner of a vehicle (even if a corporation) shall be conclusively presumed to have been the driver at the time of the commission of certain offences and, 'accordingly, that acts or omissions of the driver of the vehicle at the time were his acts or omissions'.

[18] See eg *Quality Dairies (York) Ltd v Pedley* [1952] 1 KB 275.

[19] *Mullins v Collins* (1874) LR 9 QB 292 at 295, per Blackburn and Quain JJ; *Coppen v Moore (No 2)* [1898] 2 QB 306 at 314, per Lord Russell CJ; *Allen v Whitehead*, below.

[20] See P. J. Pace, 'Delegation – A Doctrine in Search of a Definition' [1982] Crim LR 627.

[21] [1930] 1 KB 211.

present were prostitutes) were both to be imputed to his employer, not simply because he was an employee, but because the management of the house had been delegated to him.

So in *Linnett v Metropolitan Police Comr*[22] it was held, following *Allen v Whitehead*,[23] that one of two co-licensees was liable for the acts of the other in knowingly permitting disorderly conduct in the licensed premises, contrary to s 44 of the same Act, although the other was neither his servant nor his partner,[24] but simply his delegate in 'keeping' the premises.

The argument that vicarious responsibility is necessary if the statute is to be effective applies with especial force to cases of this type. Where the statute is phrased in such a way that the offence can be committed only by the delegator, there would indeed be a real difficulty in making the statute effective without vicarious liability. For example, under the Metropolitan Police Act 1839, s 44 (above), the offence may be committed only by a person 'who shall *have or keep* any house . . .'. Presumably the mere manager in *Allen v Whitehead* was not such a person and if, therefore, the absentee 'keeper' were not liable for his manager's acts, the statute could be ignored with impunity. The position is the same in many of the offences under the Licensing Acts;[25] only the licensee can commit the offences. The difficulty has been well put by Lord Russell CJ:[26]

> We may take as an illustration the case of a sporting publican who attends race-meetings all over the country, and leaves a manager in charge of his public-house; is it to be said that there is no remedy under this section[27] if drink is sold by the manager in charge to any number of drunken persons? It is clear that there is no machinery by which the person actually selling can be convicted; a penalty can only be inflicted on the licensee.

Sub delegation

It has been recognized that vicarious liability might be extended to cover the case where A delegates his responsibilities to B who sub-delegates them to C. Thus, if the licensee's delegate sub-delegates his responsibilities, the licensee is liable for the sub-delegate's acts,[28] but he is not liable for the acts of an inferior servant to whom control of the premises has not been delegated.[29]

What constitutes effective delegation?

There is some doubt as to the degree of delegation which is necessary to bring the principle into operation. In a leading case, *Vane v Yiannopoullos*,[30] Parker LCJ said that: 'It must be shown that the licensee is not managing the business himself but has delegated the management to someone else . . . .'[31]

22 [1946] KB 290, [1946] 1 All ER 380.

23 Above, n 21.

24 Both were, in fact, the employees of a limited company. The company was not charged, no doubt for the good reason that it was not the licensee.

25 See generally, S. Mehigan, J. Phillips and J. Saunders (eds), *Paterson's Licensing Acts 2005* (113th edn, 2005), and by the same authors, *The Licensing Act 2003* (2004), paras 8.11–8.12.

26 In *Police Comr v Cartman* [1896] 1 QB 655 at 658. Yet when Parliament adds 'or his servant' the court holds that the delegation still applies to the licensee: *Howker v Robinson*, below.

27 Licensing Act 1872, s 13. Cf *Cundy v Le Cocq*, above, p 138, which establishes that the offence is also one of strict liability.

28 *Crabtree v Hole* (1879) 43 JP 799; *Sopp v Long* [1970] 1 QB 518, [1969] 1 All ER 855.

29 *Allchorn v Hopkins* (1905) 69 JP 355.

30 [1965] AC 486, [1964] 3 All ER 820, HL.

31 [1964] 2 QB 739 at 745, [1964] 2 All ER 820 at 823.

Lord Evershed[32] agreed with that and Lord Hodson said that the principle '. . . has never so far been extended so as to cover the case where the whole of the authority of the licensee has not been transferred to another'.[33]

Lord Reid appears to have confined the principle to cases where the licensee is absent from the premises leaving another in charge.[34] It was held that the principle was inapplicable in that case where the licensee was on the premises at the time of the offence, but not on the floor where a waitress, whom he had instructed as to her rights to sell intoxicating liquor, made an illegal sale. But in *Howker v Robinson*[35] a licensee who was serving in one room of the pub (the public bar) was held liable for an illegal sale made by his barman in another room (the lounge). This does not seem to be a case where the whole authority of the licensee had been transferred or where he was not managing the business himself. The court regarded the question whether there had been delegation as one of fact, which had been properly decided by the magistrates. *Winson*,[36] which the court followed, was entirely different, for there the licensee visited the premises only occasionally and had a manager who was in control.

In *Howker v Robinson* the degree of delegation was no greater than is essential in any public house with more than one bar and it is submitted that not only does it go too far but it leaves the law in an uncertain state; for it is apparently open to the magistrates to find as 'a fact' that there has or has not been delegation where the licensee is on the premises. The principle ought to be confined to the case where the licensee is not 'doing his job', but has handed it over to another. Where a licensee who is employed by a brewery is suspended, his employer has the right, under an implied term in the contract of employment, to delegate the rights and duties of licensee to another employee. Thus sales of liquor on the licensed premises continue to be lawful and, presumably, the suspended licensee is liable for offences committed by the delegate.[37]

No delegation principle in strict liability offences?

According to Lord Parker, the delegation principle comes into play *only* in the case of offences requiring *mens rea*.[38] Where liability is strict, 'the person on whom liability is thrown is responsible whether he has delegated or whether he has acted through a servant'. According to this view, if D, the licensee, not having delegated his duties, is serving in the bar and E, the barmaid, without his knowledge, sells liquor (i) to a constable on duty and (ii) to a drunken person, D is liable for the latter but not the former offence, since (i) requires *mens rea* but (ii) does not. If this is right, the cases of offences of strict liability are dealt with under the 'attributed act' principle (below).

Legitimacy of the delegation principle

Some doubt was cast on the validity of the delegation principle by the House of Lords in *Vane v Yiannopoullos*.[39] Since there was no delegation in that case their Lordships' remarks were *obiter*. Lords Morris and Donovan could find no statutory authority for the doctrine and, though they did not find it necessary to pronounce on its validity, Lord Donovan thought that 'If a decision that "knowingly" means "knowingly" will make the

32 [1965] AC at 505.
33 Ibid, at 510.
34 At 497; cf Pace, above, 629, 636.
35 [1973] QB 178, [1972] 2 All ER 786, DC. Contrast *McKenna v Harding* (1905) 69 JP 354.
36 [1969] 1 QB 371, [1968] 1 All ER 197.
37 *DPP v Rogers* [1992] Crim LR 51, DC.
38 *Winson* [1969] 1 QB 371 at 382, [1968] 1 All ER 197.
39 [1965] AC 486, [1964] 3 All ER 820, HL.

provision difficult to enforce, the remedy lies with the legislature'. Lord Reid found the delegation principle hard to justify; but while it may have been unwarranted in the first instance, it was now too late to upset such a long standing practice. Lord Evershed thought that a licensee may 'fairly and sensibly' be held liable where he has delegated his powers and Lord Hodson expressed no opinion. Subsequent cases[40] show that the doctrine continues unimpaired. Such a long standing principle is perhaps unlikely now to be overruled by the House of Lords. It should not, however, be extended.[41] In *Bradshaw v Ewart-James*[42] the court declined to apply it to the case where the master of a ship delegated the performance of his statutory duty to his chief officer. That, however, was not a case of the full delegation which the doctrine seems to require, for the master remained on board and in command. As the master cannot personally direct the ship for 24 hours a day, some delegation is inevitable.

(ii) The 'attributed act' principle

This second principle occurs usually in cases of strict liability where the *actus reus* of the employee, etc is attributed to D. It occurs in the many cases where 'selling' is the central feature of the *actus reus*, under statutes like the Trade Descriptions Act, the Food and Drugs Acts, etc. A 'sale' consists in the transfer of property in goods from A to B[43] and the seller, in law, is necessarily the person in whom the property is vested at the commencement of the transaction. It is not a great step and no surprise, therefore, for the court to say that the employer has committed the *actus reus* of 'selling' even though he was nowhere near when the incident took place. In *Coppen v Moore (No 2)*,[44] D owned six shops, in which he sold 'American hams'. He gave strict instructions that these hams were to be described as 'breakfast hams' and were not to be sold under any specific name of place of origin. In the absence of D, and without the knowledge of the manager of the branch, one of the assistants sold a ham as a 'Scotch ham'. D was convicted, under the Merchandise Marks Act 1887, s 2(2), of selling goods 'to which any . . . false trade description is applied'. Lord Russell CJ said:[45]

> It cannot be doubted that the appellant [the owner] sold the ham in question, although the transaction was carried out by his servants. In other words he was the seller, although not the actual salesman. It is clear also, as already stated, that the ham was sold with a 'false trade description' which was material. If so, there is evidence establishing a prima facie case of an offence against the Act having been *committed by the appellant.*

The court was clearly influenced by the fact that D (like many other employers) carried on his business in a number of branches and could not possibly be in direct control of each one so that, if actual knowledge of the particular transaction had to be proved, he could hardly ever be made liable. The court did not, however, apply the principle of

40 *Ross v Moss* [1965] 2 QB 396, [1965] 3 All ER 145; *Winson* [1969] 1 QB 371, [1968] 1 All ER 197.

41 Cf *Howker v Robinson*, above, p 229. Yet Bristow J, while considering himself bound by the authorities to apply the delegation principle, hoped that it might be overturned by the House of Lords: [1972] 2 All ER at 791.

42 [1983] QB 671, [1983] 1 All ER 12, DC.

43 This is so in the criminal as well as the civil law: *Watson v Coupland* [1945] 1 All ER 217.

44 [1898] 2 QB 306. One partner may similarly be liable for the acts of another: *Davies v Harvey* (1874) LR 9 QB 433. Cf *Parsons v Barnes* [1973] Crim LR 537.

45 [1898] 2 QB 306 at 313.

delegation which is to be found in the licensing cases. By construing the Act in accordance with the principles of the civil law and so holding that D had himself committed an *actus reus*, the court introduced a more far-reaching principle. Comparison with *Allchorn v Hopkins*[46] will show that, under the delegation principle, D would not have been liable for the act of the assistant to whom control of the premises had not been delegated.[47]

A modern instance of the application of the attributed act principle is *Harrow London Borough Council v Shah and Shah.*[48] The Shahs, newsagents, were convicted of selling a national lottery ticket to a boy under 16, contrary to the National Lottery Act 1993, s 13(1)(c) although they had taken all reasonable steps to ensure that the regulations were complied with and, though one of them was on the premises, neither was present in the shop when the ticket was sold by their employee, H, who reasonably believed the boy was at least 16 years old.

The limits of the attribution principle

There are many cases not involving a sale where a similar principle has been invoked. Just as it is the employer who, in law, 'sells' goods with which his employee is actually dealing, so too is he 'in possession' of goods which are actually in his employee's hands[49] and so can be made liable for offences of 'being in possession' (of which there are many)[50] through his employees. A producer of plays 'presents' a play even though he may be miles away when it is performed and was liable, under s 15 of the Theatres Act 1843 (now repealed),[51] if words were introduced into the performance, even without his knowledge, which had not been allowed by the Lord Chamberlain.[52]

More controversially, it has been held that the owners of a van which they have supplied to a bailiff of their farm, nevertheless commit the offence of 'keeping' a van which is not 'used solely for the conveyance of goods or burden in the course of trade' without a licence[53] if the bailiff uses it, without their knowledge or authority, to take his wife for a day out at Clacton.[54] A master 'uses' his vehicle in contravention of the Motor Vehicles (Construction and Use) Regulations if his servant so uses it.[55] It is quite understandable that a court should hold that an employer 'presents' a play or 'keeps' a vehicle, for these verbs are apt to describe his function and inapt to describe that of his employees. It is less clear that this is so in the case of 'uses'. This could very well refer to the employee's use.

[46] Above, p 228, n 29.

[47] It was within the scope of the servant's authority in *Coppen v Moore*, above, to sell hams. A master is not liable where a servant boy, who has no authority to sell anything, supplies his master's whisky to a customer out of hours: *Adams v Camfoni* [1929] 1 KB 95. In this case there was no sale by the master.

[48] [1999] 3 All ER 302, [2000] Crim LR 992, DC. It is submitted that the court attributed excessive authority to *Moussell Bros Ltd v London and North-Western Rly Co Ltd* [1917] 2 KB 836, DC in holding that the offence imposed vicarious liability. The ruling of strict liability is also questionable, in the light both of the terms of the section and the subsequent decisions in *B (A Minor) v DPP* and *K* above, p 142. See [2000] Crim LR 694–696.

[49] Below, p 232.

[50] For examples, see above, p 151.

[51] See Theatres Act 1968; below, p 964.

[52] *Grade v DPP* [1942] 2 All ER 118. The defendant had in fact been called up for service in the RAF. The result would have been different if D had been charged with 'causing' the play to be presented: *Lovelace v DPP* [1954] 3 All ER 481, [1954] 1 WLR 1468.

[53] Contrary to the Revenue Act 1869, s 27 (repealed).

[54] *Strutt v Clift* [1911] 1 KB 1.

[55] *Green v Burnett* [1955] 1 QB 78, [1954] 3 All ER 273; but not where a partner, or person authorized ad hoc, uses the vehicle, if there is also an offence of permitting: *Crawford v Haughton* [1973] QB 1, [1972] 1 All ER 535, DC; *Garrett v Hooper* [1973] Crim LR 61; *Cobb v Williams* [1973] Crim LR 243.

A recent case serves to illustrate the proper limits of the doctrine and the need for the statute to be considered in its context. In *Attorney-General's Reference (No 2 of 2003)*,[56] D was held not to be vicariously liable for 'keeping' an embryo contrary to s 3(1)(b) and s 41(2)(a) of the Human Fertilisation and Embryology Act 1990 ('keeping or using' an embryo, except in pursuance of a licence) where he was the consultant responsible for the supervision of two clinics licensed under the 1990 Act. The embryologist working within one of the clinics was convicted of offences, but D was unaware of those activities and had not participated in them. In approving the trial judge's decision to acquit D, Judge LJ commented that the offence is committed by the person who contravenes s 3(1), and regarded it as difficult to see how the language could extend to create criminal liability for 'keeping' to D, who 'notwithstanding his statutory responsibilities, does not in fact keep the embryo at all'.[57]

Sales by a licensee

A new principle seemed to have emerged in *Goodfellow v Johnson*:[58] a licensee is liable for the act of another which can lawfully be performed only by virtue of the licence, even though the other is not his servant or employee. D, a licensee, employed by a brewery, was held liable for the sale of watered gin made, contrary to the Food and Drugs Act 1955, by a barmaid employed, not by D, but by the brewery. *Coppen v Moore* did not apply since D (licensee) was not the owner of the gin; and the delegation principle did not apply because there was no delegation. It was thought that this case precludes the prosecution of the owner whose beer the licensee is selling.[59] It is submitted that that is wrong. The brewery was certainly the seller in law, but it was not charged. The offence in question was not a licensing offence. If the barmaid had sold adulterated lemonade (a sale for which no licence is required) it would be absurd to say that the brewery (and the barmaid) was guilty of selling adulterated lemonade but not adulterated gin. In *Nottingham City Council v Wolverhampton and Dudley Breweries*[60] it was acknowledged that the owner (brewery) could be convicted of an offence of selling intoxicating liqueur below the tolerance allowed in the Food Labelling Regulations, of the Food Safety Act 1990. Kennedy LJ, accepted that in *Goodfellow*, Lord Parker had misunderstood the provisions of the Food and Drugs Act 1955 by treating them as absolute offences, and had misunderstood *Hotchin v Hindmarsh*. Kennedy LJ observed that the owner (brewery) through the barmaid could make an effective sale regardless of the licensee and that such a sale could involve the owner and not just the licensee in criminal liability.[61] The responsibility of the licensee under licensing legislation does not relieve the owner of responsibility in relation to all other products.

(c) Mode of participation of employer and employee

In those cases where the statute creates an offence specifically for licensees, keepers of refreshment houses, or other designated people to do the act in question, it is apparent that the licensee, etc, who is held vicariously liable for the acts of his employee is a

56 [2004] EWCA Crim 785.
57 [20].
58 [1966] 1 QB 83, [1965] Crim LR 304 and commentary.
59 *Allied Domecq Leisure Ltd v Paul Graham Cooper* [1999] Crim LR 230 and commentary.
60 [2004] 2 WLR 820.
61 [18].

principal for he alone possesses the personal characteristic which is an essential part of the *actus reus* and no one else is qualified to fill that role. The employee who actually performs the act is plainly incapable of being a principal, but it seems that he may be convicted as an abettor[62] – strange though this appears when he is the only participant in the crime who is present.

Where the *actus reus* does not include a personal characteristic of the employer and the employee is capable of being a principal, then it seems that he may be held to be a joint principal with his employer. In crimes of 'selling' and being 'in possession' the court allows the prosecution the best of both worlds by having regard to the legal act when dealing with the employer and the physical act when dealing with the employee. So it is held that the employee, as well as the employer, 'sells'[63] or is 'in possession';[64] and the employee whose 'use' of a vehicle was held to be use by his employer was convicted in *Green v Burnett* (above) as a principal. It is submitted that when the employee is capable of being a principal it is logical to hold him liable as such (for he is the real offender) and not as an abettor.

Determining whether the delegate is a principal or abettor, etc is of more than academic interest for two reasons. First, if the crime is one of strict liability, *mens rea* must nevertheless be proved if he is to be convicted as an abettor but not if he is a principal.[65] Secondly, where there is a statutory defence enabling someone held vicariously liable to escape if he can bring the 'actual offender' before the court, it is difficult to suppose that the production of an abettor (even though he is the real offender) will suffice. However, a joint principal certainly will in this scenario.[66]

(d) No vicarious liability for abetting, or attempting crimes

Abetting is a common law notion and therefore, as we have seen,[67] requires *mens rea* even where the offence abetted is one of strict liability. For the same reasons there can be no vicarious responsibility for abetting an offence, even though the offence itself may be one imposing vicarious liability. In *Ferguson v Weaving*[68] D, a licensee, was charged with abetting several of her customers in consuming liquor on the licensed premises outside the permitted hours, contrary to the Licensing Act 1921, s 4. It appeared that she had taken all proper means to ensure that drinking ceased when 'Time' was called. But the waiters in the concert room, contrary to their instructions, made no attempt to collect the customers' drinks and, while D was visiting the several other rooms in the premises, the offence was committed. It was assumed that control of the concert room had been delegated. While accepting that the waiters might have been guilty of abetting the customers who were the principal offenders, the court was emphatic that D could not be. Lord Goddard CJ said:[69]

62 *Griffiths v Studebakers Ltd* [1924] 1 KB 102; *Ross v Moss* [1965] 2 QB 396, [1965] 3 All ER 145.

63 *Hotchin v Hindmarsh* [1891] 2 QB 181. Cf *Goodfellow v Johnson* [1966] 1 QB 83, [1965] 1 All ER 941 but note the *Nottingham* case above.

64 *Melias Ltd v Preston* [1957] 2 QB 380, [1957] 2 All ER 449.

65 Above, p 185.

66 *Melias Ltd v Preston* [1957] 2QB 830.

67 Above, p 185.

68 [1951] 1 KB 814, [1951] 1 All ER 412. See also *Thomas v Lindop* [1950] 1 All ER 966; *John Henshall (Quarries) Ltd v Harvey* [1965] 2 QB 233, [1965] 1 All ER 725. *Provincial Motor Club Co Ltd v Dunning* [1909] 2 KB 599 overlooks this principle and is a doubtful decision.

69 [1951] 1 KB 814 at 821, [1951] 1 All ER 412 at 415.

She can aid and abet the customers if she knows that the customers are committing an offence, but we are not prepared to hold that their knowledge can be imputed to her so as to make her, not a principal offender, but an aider and abettor. So to hold would be to establish a new principle in criminal law and one for which there is no authority.

Had there been a substantive offence of *permitting* drinking on licensed premises after hours, it is fairly clear that the court could have held D guilty; for in that case the acts, and the *mens rea*, of the servant would have been attributed to her. Likewise it has been said that there can be no vicarious liability for attempting to commit a crime, even though the crime attempted imposes vicarious liability.[70]

(e) Reform

Clause 29 of the Law Commission Draft Criminal Code would restrict the application of vicarious liability to those circumstances in which Parliament expressly imposed such.

2. Liability of corporations[71]

(a) Introduction

As the number of corporations has grown and the involvement they have in diverse aspects of daily life has expanded, the pressure for the imposition of criminal liability for their wrongdoing has increased. The debate has been brought into an acute focus by various disasters each with large loss of life: in particular the *Herald of Free Enterprise* ferry disaster and various rail crashes (Southall, Ladbrooke Grove, Paddington, Hatfield). It is a widely held view that the law's present approach to criminal punishment of corporations is unsatisfactory at a fundamental level since the law has not sought to create a specific model of criminalization to reflect accurately the reality of the modern day corporation. Rather, it has relied on strained fictions in an attempt to fit the corporate wrongdoing within the model which has evolved for criminalising and prosecuting the individual human actor.

Historically, it was thought that a corporation could not be indicted for a crime at all.[72] Personal appearance was necessary at court in the assizes and quarter-sessions and the corporation, having no physical person, could not appear. In the Court of King's Bench, however, appearance by attorney was allowed and the difficulty was circumvented by removing the indictment into that court by writ of *certiorari*;[73] but now all this is unnecessary and, by statute,[74] a corporation may appear and plead through a representative. Further objections which have been raised to imposing criminal liability are that, since a corporation is a creature of the law, it can only do such acts as it is legally

70 *Gardner v Akeroyd* [1952] 2 QB 743, [1952] 2 All ER 306.

71 See C. Wells, *Corporations and Criminal Responsibility* (2nd edn, 2001); D. Bergman, *The Case for Corporate Responsibility* (2000); J. Gobert and M. Punch, *Rethinking Corporate Crime* (2003); J. Gobert, 'Corporate Criminality: New Crimes for the Times' [1994] Crim LR 722; G. R. Sullivan, 'Expressing Corporate Guilt (1995) 15 OJLS 281.' For proposals for reform, see below, p 245.

72 *Anon* (1701) 12 Mod Rep 560, per Holt CJ.

73 *Birmingham and Gloucester Rly Co* (1842) 3 QB 223.

74 Criminal Justice Act 1925, s 33.

empowered to do, so that any crime is necessarily *ultra vires*; and that the corporation, having neither body nor mind, cannot perform the acts or form the intents which are a prerequisite of criminal liability. The *ultra vires* doctrine, however, seems to have been ignored in both the law of tort and crime and to apply only in the law of contract and property.[75]

(i) Bases of criminal liability

A corporation is a legal person but it has no physical existence. As a legal entity, a corporation may be placed under a duty to conduct itself in a particular way on pain of criminal sanction for non-compliance. The type of case where it is most obviously proper that a corporation should be held liable arises where a statute imposes a duty upon a corporation to act and no action is taken. It was in such cases that the earliest developments took place. In 1842, in *Birmingham and Gloucester Rly Co*,[76] a corporation was convicted for failing to fulfil a statutory duty. Four years later, in *Great North of England Rly Co*,[77] counsel sought to confine the effect of that decision to cases of non-feasance where there was no agent who could be indicted, arguing that, in the case of misfeasance, only the agents who had done the wrongful acts were liable. The court held that the distinction was unfounded. Even if it were discoverable, it was incongruous that the corporation should be liable for the one type of wrong and not the other.

Aside from these cases in which the duty is specifically imposed on the corporation as a legal person, prosecuting the corporation within the orthodox model of criminal law – an *actus reus* and *mens rea* with an absence of defences – creates difficulties since the corporate legal entity cannot either act or form an intention of any kind except through its directors or employees. The criminal law's solution to the lack of a corporate body to perform the *actus reus* and mind capable of forming *mens rea* has been to treat the minds and bodies of the officers and servants of the corporation as supplying its mental and physical faculties. This has been done in two distinct ways:

(1) By holding a corporation vicariously liable for the acts of its employees and agents where a natural person would similarly be liable for such acts; for example, in public nuisance at common law,[78] or when a statute imposes vicarious responsibility.[79] Vicarious liability has been considered above. It was not a great step forward from holding that a corporation could be liable for breach of statutory duty, to the courts imposing liability vicariously in these circumstances.[80]

(2) By holding that in every corporation there are certain persons (designated 'controlling officers' in the draft Criminal Code)[81] who are the 'directing mind

[75] Cf W. V. H. Rogers, *Winfield and Jolowicz on Tort* (16th edn, 2002), 292–293, 834–837.

[76] (1842) 3 QB 223. Cf *British Steel plc* [1995] Crim LR 654.

[77] (1846) 9 QB 315.

[78] *Great North of England Rly Co* (1846) 9 QB 315.

[79] *Griffiths v Studebakers Ltd* [1924] 1 KB 102; *Mousell Bros Ltd v London and North-Western Rly Co* [1917] 2 KB 836.

[80] *Mousell Bros Ltd v London and North-Western Rly Co* [1917] 2 KB 836; *Griffiths v Studebakers Ltd* [1924] 1 KB 102.

[81] Law Com No 143, para 11–6, and cl 34.

and will'[82] of the corporation and who, when acting in the company's business, are considered to be the 'embodiment of the company'.[83] Their acts and states of mind are the company's acts and states of mind and it is held liable, not for the acts of others, but for what are deemed to be its own acts.

(b) Non-vicarious liability of corporations

(i) The identification doctrine

The courts' willingness to attribute to the company the blameworthy acts and *mens rea* of the controlling officers developed rapidly in criminal law in the mid-1940s. In *DPP v Kent and Sussex Contractors Ltd*[84] the offence required an intention to deceive and it was held that the transport manager's intent was the intent of the company. *Kent* was approved in *ICR Haulage Ltd*[85] where the company was convicted of a common law conspiracy to defraud, the act and intent of the managing director being the act and intent of the company. The doctrine was memorably described by Denning LJ:[86]

> A company may in many ways be likened to a human body. It has a brain and a nerve centre which controls what it does. It also has hands which hold the tools and act in accordance with directions from the centre. Some of the people in the company are mere servants and agents who are nothing more than hands to do the work and cannot be said to represent the mind or will. Others are directors and managers who represent the directing mind and will of the company and control what it does. The state of mind of these managers is the state of mind of the company and is treated by the law as such.[87]

A person is not a 'controlling officer' simply because his work is 'brain' work (as opposed to physical work) and he exercises some managerial discretion, since not all such persons 'represent the directing mind and will of the company and control what it does'.[88] The manager of a supermarket belonging to a company owning hundreds of supermarkets is not the company's 'brains' and does not act as the company.[89] This illustrates one of the major shortcomings of the identification doctrine – that is, that it fails to reflect the reality of the modern day large multi-national corporation. It produces what many regard as an unsatisfactorily narrow scope for criminal liability. Companies have been

82 *Lennard's Carrying Co Ltd v Asiatic Petroleum Co Ltd* [1915] AC 705, 713 per Viscount Haldane LC. Applied in *J. F. Alford Transport Ltd* [1997] 2 Cr App R 326 at 331.

83 *Essendon Engineering Co Ltd v Maile* [1982] RTR 260, [1982] Crim LR 510.

84 [1944] KB 146, [1944] 1 All ER 119.

85 [1944] KB 551, [1944] 1 All ER 691. Cf *McDonnell* [1966] 1 QB 233, [1966] 1 All ER 193, below p 242.

86 *H. L. Bolton (Engineering) Co Ltd v T. J. Graham & Sons Ltd* [1957] 1 QB 159 at 172. Though this *dictum* has been frequently followed, the Privy Council has said in the *Meridian* case, below, p 238 that the anthropomorphism distracts attention from what the Board regarded as the true principle determining whether acts should be attributed to the corporation – ie, the interpretation of the particular statute.

87 Thus, it is thought that a company could be guilty of abetting an offence through its managing director – though there is no *vicarious* liability in abetting (above, p 232. See *Robert Millar (Contractors) Ltd* [1970] 2 QB 54.

88 *Tesco Supermarkets Ltd v Nattrass* [1972] AC 153 at 171, HL, per Lord Reid, at 187 per Lord Dilhorne, at 200 per Lord Diplock. See Gobert, above, 59–70.

89 Ibid.

held to be not criminally liable for the acts of a depot engineer[90] or a weighbridge operator,[91] of the European Sales Manager of the company.[92]

In the leading case of *Tesco Supermarkets Ltd v Nattrass*[93] it was said that the company may be criminally liable for the acts only of:

'. . . the board of directors, the managing director and perhaps other superior officers of a company [who] carry out the functions of management and speak and act as the company', per Lord Reid,[94]

or of a person:

'. . . who is in actual control of the operations of a company or of part of them and who is not responsible to another person in the company for the manner in which he discharges his duties in the sense of being under his orders', per Viscount Dilhorne.[95]

Lord Diplock[96] thought that the question is to be answered by:

'. . . identifying those natural persons who by the memorandum and articles of association or as a result of action taken by the directors or by the company in general meeting pursuant to the articles are entrusted with the exercise of the powers of the company'.

Lord Pearson too thought that the constitution of the company concerned must be taken into account; and Lords Dilhorne, Pearson and Diplock thought that the reference in the 'common form' provision, discussed below,[97] to 'any director, manager, secretary or other similar officer of the body corporate' affords a useful indication. If those persons who are responsible for the general management of the company delegate their duties to another, then the acts of that other will be the acts of the company.[98]

Once the facts have been ascertained, it is a question of law whether a person in doing particular things is to be regarded as the company or merely as the company's employee or agent.[99] Accordingly the judge should direct the jury that if they find certain facts proved then they must find that the act and intention of the agent is the act and the intention of the company. It is not sufficient to direct that the company is liable for its 'responsible agents' or 'high executives', for such persons are not necessarily the company.[100] The test is the same whether the offence be serious or trivial.

In the *Tesco* case, the company, being charged with an offence under the Trade Descriptions Act 1968, relied on the statutory defence that they had taken all reasonable precautions and exercised all due diligence and that the commission of the offence was due to the act or default of 'another person', namely the branch manager, who had failed to supervise the assistant who actually committed the offence. Since the manager was the 'hands' and not the 'brains' of the company, it was held that the defence was available. It would have been otherwise if it had been not the manager but a director who had failed in his duty.

90 *Magna Plant Ltd v Mitchell* [1966] Crim LR 394.

91 *John Henshall (Quarries) Ltd v Harvey* [1965] 2 QB 233, [1965] 1 All ER 725.

92 *Redfern and Dunlop Ltd (Aircraft Division)* [1993] Crim LR 43.

93 Above, n 88. 94 At 171. 95 At 187.

96 At 200, followed in *Seaboard Offshore Ltd v Secretary of State for Transport* [1994] 2 All ER 99, 104, HL.

97 See below, p 242. 98 [1972] AC 153 at 193.

99 [1972] AC 153 at 170, 173, per Lord Reid. 100 *Sporle* [1971] Crim LR 706.

Meridian – all a matter of construction?

In the recent *Meridian* case[101] the Privy Council, in a valuable review of the nature of corporate liability, has said that whether an act is to be attributed to a corporation is a question of the construction of the particular statute under which proceedings are brought, so that the statute may impose corporate liability in respect of an employee who could not be said to be the 'directing mind and will' of the corporation under the primary rules of attribution. This is a controversial extension of the potential scope of corporate liability. For many it represents a welcome relaxation of the identification doctrine, with the potential to impose corporate liability in a broader range of circumstances, but in doing so it reduces the degree of certainty in the law. Indeed, Buxton LJ in a powerful dissent in the Court of Appeal (Civil Division) has commented that *Meridian* represented an 'imperfect guide to the approach to the rule for attribution of a crime'.[102]

The Board in *Meridian* contrasted the *Tesco* case with *Re Supply of Ready Mixed Concrete.*[103] In the latter case the House of Lords held a company liable for contempt of court for the act of an employee in making an arrangement in breach of an undertaking given by the company to the Restrictive Practices Court. The board of directors knew nothing of the arrangement and had given instructions that no such arrangements were to be made. But the arrangement made by X was an agreement binding on the company.[104] The offending arrangement was made by the company no less than the sale was made by the employer in *Coppen v Moore* (the Scotch Ham case).[105] The company had given an undertaking that no such arrangement would be made and it had made such an arrangement. Should it not have been exactly the same if the undertaking had been given by an individual employer and the arrangement made by an employee with ostensible authority?[106] *Ready Mixed Concrete* was a case of civil contempt of court and the result would not necessarily have been the same if it had been a criminal offence requiring *mens rea*. In *Meridian* itself, it was held that the acts of the company's investment manager were properly attributed to the company for the purposes of the New Zealand Securities Act 1988. Perhaps all that these cases demonstrate is that a statute imposes liability if that appears to be the intention of the legislature. The Court of Appeal has subsequently emphasized that the *Meridian* approach is only applicable to offences of statutory origin.[107]

It is unclear how far the *Meridian* approach does go. The case of *Moore v I Bresler Ltd*,[108] which has been criticized for going too far down the scale in identifying a controlling officer,[109] was approved in *Meridian* by the Privy Council as an example of its 'construction' principle. The company was convicted of making false returns with intent to deceive, contrary to the Finance (No 2) Act 1940, when the returns were made by the

101 *Meridian Global Funds Management Asia Ltd v Securities Commission* [1995] 2 AC 500.

102 *Re Odyssey (London) Ltd v OIC Run Off Ltd* (2000) The Times, 3 Mar, Court of Appeal (Civ Div).

103 [1995] 1 AC 456. See C. Wells, 'A Quite Revolution in Corporate Liability for Crime' (1995) 145 NLJ 1326.

104 Lord Nolan [1995] 1 All ER at 150–151.

105 Above, p 230.

106 'In my opinion . . . the act [in breach of an injunction] need not be done by the person himself': Warrington J in *Stancomb v Trowbridge UDC* [1910] 2 Ch 190 at 193–4, a decision which Lord Nolan said should have been followed in *Ready-Mixed Concrete.*

107 *A-G's Reference (No 2 of 1999)* [2000] QB 796.

108 [1944] 2 All ER 515, DC.

109 By R. Welsh, 'The Criminal Liability of Corporations' (1946) 62 LQR 345 at 358, Williams, TBCL (2nd edn), 973.

company secretary and a branch sales manager.[110] The decision is also subject to criticism because the object was to conceal the fraudulent sale by these two officers of the company's property.[111] The Draft Code, cl 30(6), would reverse it by providing that a corporation is not liable for the act of a controlling officer when it is done with the intention of doing harm, or concealing harm done, to the corporation.

A corporation's 'state of mind'

Having identified the relevant controlling individual with whom the corporation may be identified, it is necessary to prove that he had performed the relevant *actus reus* with the accompanying *mens rea*. Where the offence is one of strict liability, the corporation may be held liable for the acts of any of its employees or agents where those acts are, in law, the company's acts, under the attribution principle discussed above (p 235).[112] Wherever the offence requires *mens rea*, it must be proved that a controlling officer had the *mens rea*.[113] Similarly, where a defence requires evidence of a belief or other state of mind, this must usually be the belief or state of mind of a controlling officer;[114] but the belief of one will not suffice if another, especially if he is superior to the first, knows that that belief is ill founded.[115] Probably, as the Draft Code states, all controlling officers who are concerned in the offence must have the required state of mind. If, however, no controlling officer is involved and all the employees or agents who are involved do have the required state of mind, the defence ought clearly to be available. If a branch manager, not being a controlling officer, finds a controlled drug in supplies delivered to his branch and takes control of it, intending to hand it to the police, the company may surely rely on this intention to establish the defence provided by s 5(4) of the Misuse of Drugs Act 1971, if it is charged with unlawful possession of the drug.[116]

No aggregation of controlling individuals' conduct[117]

A question that was raised by many critics of the identification doctrine was whether it must be proved that an individual controlling officer (whether identifiable or not) was guilty of the crime charged or whether it is permissible to 'aggregate' the conduct of a number of officers, none of whom would individually be guilty, so as to constitute in sum, the elements of the offence. It is submitted that it is not possible artificially to create a *mens rea* in this way.[118] Two innocent states of mind cannot be added together to produce a guilty state of mind. Any such doctrine could certainly have no application in offences requiring knowledge, intention or recklessness. It is in relation to offences of

110 But the company secretary might perhaps be regarded, when acting within the scope of his authority, as the company's 'directing mind and will' for this purpose. *Kent and Sussex Contractors* [1944] KB 146, [1944] 1 All ER 119, seems more doubtful in this respect, as only the transport manager was involved.

111 Williams, TBCL (2nd edn), 973, refers to *Belmont Finance Corpn Ltd v Williams Furniture Ltd* [1979] Ch 250 as 'a much more sensible decision of a civil court'.

112 Agent's act the principal's act in law.

113 *Tesco Supermarkets Ltd v Nattrass* [1972] AC 153, [1971] 2 All ER 127. Draft Criminal Code, cl 34(2).

114 *GJ Coles & Co Ltd v Goldsworthy* [1985] WAR 183. See G. Orchard in *Criminal Law Essays*, 114, 117, 118–119.

115 *Brambles Holdings Ltd v Carey* (1976) 15 SASR 270 at 280.

116 See Law Com No 177, Draft Criminal Code, Appendix B, Example 30 (vi).

117 See especially C. Wells, 'Culture, Risk and Criminal Liability' [1993] Crim LR 551, 563.

118 Cf *Armstrong v Strain* [1952] 1 KB 232, [1952] 1 All ER 139, Devlin J: 'You cannot add an innocent state of mind to an innocent state of mind and get as a result a dishonest state of mind'.

negligence (particularly gross negligence) that the aggregation principle has been most forcefully advocated. The argument proceeds as follows: a company owes a duty of care and if its operation falls far below the standard required it is guilty of gross negligence. A series of minor failures by officers of the company might add up to a gross breach by the company of its duty of care. There is authority for such a doctrine in the law of tort[119] and the concept of negligence is the same in the criminal law, the difference being one of degree – criminal negligence must be 'gross'. It is immaterial that the doctrine of vicarious liability in tort does not apply in criminal law, because this is a case not of vicarious, but of personal, liability and that is a proper concern of the criminal law. Thus a corporation ought to be open to prosecution for manslaughter on the aggregation principle, now that it is established that that offence may be committed by gross negligence.[120] This argument has been rejected by the Court of Appeal in the *Attorney-General's Reference (No 2 of 1999)*.[121] The prosecution arose from the Southall train crash in which seven passengers died. The trial judge ruled that the gross negligence manslaughter offence required negligence to be proved under the identification doctrine. The Court of Appeal approved that ruling, holding that unless an identified individual's conduct, characterized as gross criminal negligence could be attributed to the company, the company was not, in the present state of the common law liable for manslaughter.[122]

(c) Limits of corporate liability

When any statute makes it an offence for 'a person' to do or omit to do something, that offence is capable of commission by a corporation, unless the contrary appears: the Interpretation Act 1889 defined 'person' to include 'a body of persons corporate or unincorporate' unless the contrary appears and provided that the definition, so far as it includes bodies corporate, applies to any provision of an Act whenever passed, relating to an offence punishable on indictment or summary conviction.[123] The nature of the offence may be such that a corporation is physically incapable of committing it even through its controlling officers. The fact that the offence requires *mens rea* does not preclude corporate liability since, as discussed above, the state of mind of the corporation's controlling officers, as well as their acts, may be attributed to the corporation.

There are numerous limitations on the liability of a corporation.

Penalty and punishment

It can only be convicted of offences which do not carry a physical punishment such as imprisonment. These include most offences; but exclude murder. The lack of imagination

119 *W. B. Anderson & Sons Ltd v Rhodes (Liverpool) Ltd* [1967] 2 All ER 850, Cairns J, discussed by M. Dean, 'Hedley Byrne and the Eager Business Man' (1968) 31 MLR 322; *Salmond on Torts* (21st edn, 1996), 406–409; *Fleming on Torts* (8th edn, 1992), 376–385.

120 See below, p 482. In the *P & O* case Turner J seems to have proceeded on the basis that recklessness must be proved.

121 [2000] QB 796; considering *Great Western Trains Co* (1999) 3 June, CCC. It was also rejected in Scotland in *Transco v HM Advocate* [2004] SLT 41.

122 The court's conclusion that there can *in general* be no corporate liability in the absence of an identified human offender ignores the principle discussed above of corporate liability where a duty is specifically imposed on the corporation as a legal person: *Birmingham & Gloucester Railway* (1840) 3 QB 223.

123 See the Interpretation Act 1978 s 5 and Sch 1.

in the law's response to sentencing corporations when they are found liable has been cogently criticized.[124]

Categories of offence

There are other offences which it is extremely unlikely that an official of a corporation could commit within the scope of his employment; for example, bigamy,[125] rape, incest and, possibly, perjury.[126]

Manslaughter[127]

It was at one time thought[128] that a corporation could not be convicted of an offence involving personal violence but in *P & O European Ferries Ltd*[129] Turner J held that an indictment for manslaughter would lie against the company in respect of the Zeebrugge disaster. The persuasive authority of this ruling is not impaired by the judge's subsequent decision that, on the evidence before him, the company had no case to answer. The rejected argument was based on the fact that, from the time of Coke (1601), authoritative books had described manslaughter as 'the killing of a human being by a human being'.[130]

This definition found its way into the law of some states of the USA and, via Stephen's draft Code Bill of 1880, into the New Zealand Crimes Acts of 1908 and 1961. The effect was that the New Zealand Court of Appeal decided in *Murray Wright Ltd*[131] that a corporation could not be guilty of manslaughter as a principal. Turner J did not follow that decision. Coke's purpose in using the phrase 'by a human being' was not to exclude corporations from liability – corporations were not indictable for any crime at that time – but to distinguish killings by an inanimate thing or an animal without the fault of any person. Such killings then had legal consequences but were not murder or manslaughter. Moreover, the requirement of an act or omission by a human being is not peculiar to manslaughter. All crimes are acts or omissions, or the results of acts or omissions, by

124 See generally on the sentencing of corporations Gobert above, n 1, ch 7; and for a review of the punishments that might be available see M. Jefferson, 'Corporate Criminal Liability: The Problems of Sanctions' (2001) 65 J Crim L 235.

125 Even in some of these cases it is not inconceivable that a corporation might be held liable as a secondary party. Eg the managing director of an incorporated marriage advisory bureau negotiates a marriage which he knows to be bigamous. Or a pornographic film company liable as an accessory to rape.

126 In *Re Odyssey (London) Ltd v OIC Run Off Ltd* (2000) The Times, 3 Mar, Court of Appeal (Civ Div), the majority considered, *obiter*, that a company could be liable for perjury through acts of director and managing director, if he had the 'status' of the company when testifying.

127 See generally Wells, above n 1, ch 5; G. Forlin (ed), *Butterworths Corporate Killing Service* (2002); M. Childs, 'Medical Manslaughter and Corporate Liability' (1999) LS 316 raising the possible application to trust hospitals.

128 *Cory Bros Ltd* [1927] 1 KB 810 (Finlay J, holding that a corporation could not be indicted for manslaughter or an offence under the Offences Against the Person Act 1861, s 31), a ruling of which Stable J said in *ICR Haulage Ltd* [1944] KB 551, 'if the matter came before the court today, the result might well be different'.

129 (1990) 93 Cr App R 72, [1991] Crim LR 695 and commentary. Streatfield J ruled that an indictment for manslaughter would lie in *Northern Strip Mining Construction Co Ltd* (Glamorgan Assizes, 1 Feb 1965, unreported) but the corporation was acquitted on the merits. Maurice J's decision in a civil action, *S and Y Investments (No 2) Pty Ltd v Commercial Co of Australia Ltd* (1986) 21 App R 204 at 217, required a ruling that a company was guilty of manslaughter. A company, *OLL Ltd*, was convicted of manslaughter at Winchester Crown Court, 8 Dec 1994, following a canoeing tragedy in Lyme Bay.

130 See, eg, Stephen, *Digest of the Criminal Law* (1st edn, 1877, Art. 218 and subsequent editions), *Halsbury's Laws of England* (4th edn, 1990 reissue), 613.

131 [1970] NZLR 476.

human beings. It is not manslaughter if a person is killed by an earthquake or a thunderbolt or a wild animal in the jungle. Conspiracy is committed contrary to s 1 of the Criminal Law Act 1977 'if a person agrees with any other person' but an agreement between two human beings is required to make a conspiracy.[132] A corporation can be convicted of conspiracy but only if at least one of the human beings is a controlling officer of the corporation acting within the scope of his authority.

There have been a number of successful prosecutions of companies for manslaughter. To date these have all involved small companies in which the identification doctrine has been relatively easy to apply.[133]

(d) Statutory liability of corporate officers

It is now common form to include the following provision in statutes creating offences likely to be committed by corporations:[134]

> Where an offence . . . committed by a body corporate is proved to have been committed with the consent or connivance of, or to be attributable to any neglect on the part of, any director, manager, secretary or other similar officer of the body corporate or any person who was purporting to act in any such capacity, he as well as the body corporate shall be guilty of that offence and shall be liable to be proceeded against and punished accordingly.

Whether a director or other officer is under a duty is a question which can be answered only by looking at the facts of each case; and the onus of proving that there was a duty which has been neglected is on the prosecution.[135]

So far as 'consent' and 'connivance' are concerned the provision probably effects only a slight extension of the law; for the officer who expressly consents or connives at the commission of the offence will be liable as a secondary party under the principles considered above. There may be a consent which does not amount to counselling or abetting, however; and the words 'attributable to any neglect on the part of'[136] clearly impose a wider liability in making the officer liable for his negligence in failing to prevent the offence.

The common form provision does not create an offence. It creates an extended form of secondary liability for an offence committed by a body corporate under some other provision of the relevant Act. It is submitted that, like the general law of secondary liability, it applies automatically and does not have to be, and indeed is incapable of being, charged as an offence.[137]

[132] *McDonnell* [1966] 1 QB 233, [1966] 1 All ER 193.

[133] See eg *Kite and OLL Ltd*, Winchester Crown Court, 8 Dec 1994, reported in *The Independent*, 9 Dec 1994; *R v Jackson Transport (Ossett) Ltd* reported in Health and Safety at Work, Nov 1996, p 4; *R v Great Western Trains Company (GWT)*, Central Criminal Court, 30 June 1999; *Roy Bowles Transport Ltd* (1999) The Times, 11 Dec.

[134] Eg Outer Space Act 1986, s 11(3).

[135] *Huckerby v Elliott* [1970] 1 All ER 189. 'Manager' means someone managing the affairs of the company and not, eg, the manager of a store: *Tesco Supermarkets Ltd v Nattrass* [1972] AC 153 at 178.

[136] These words are omitted from the Theft Act 1968, s 18.

[137] Contra, *Wilson* [1997] Crim LR 53. See commentary.

(e) Unincorporated bodies

An unincorporated association is not a legal person at common law and therefore could not incur criminal liability though its members could. This is still the position for common law offences. Statutory offences are different. The effect of the Interpretation Act 1889 was that in all enactments relating to offences, whenever passed, the word 'person' includes bodies corporate (s 2) and, in enactments passed after 1889, both bodies corporate *and unincorporate* (s 19). The Interpretation Act 1978 preserves this position.[138] Since 1889 unincorporated bodies have been able to commit any offence under an enactment passed after 1889 which makes it an offence for a 'person' to do or omit to do anything which an unincorporated body is capable of doing. The potential liability of unincorporated bodies seems to have been little noticed. In *Attorney-General v Able* Woolf J, dealing with an alleged offence under the Suicide Act 1961 said, 'It must be remembered that the [Voluntary Euthanasia Society] is an unincorporate body and there can be no question of the society committing an offence';[139] but since the offence may be committed by 'a person' it seems that it may be committed by an unincorporated body. An unincorporated body, being the registered keeper of a vehicle, was held capable of liability as a 'person' to fixed penalties for illegal parking under the Transport Act 1982.[140]

Sometimes statutes have made express provision for the liability of unincorporated bodies but it seems that this is unnecessary when the word 'person' is used in the definition of the offence.

When an unincorporated association is prosecuted, presumably the court must proceed by analogy to the law relating to corporations. Such associations have officials corresponding to the controlling officers of corporations and it is inconceivable that the association is liable for the act of any one of its members who has no part in the general management of its affairs.

(f) Rationale and reform of corporate criminal liability

The English courts have created the identification principle through which corporate liability might be imposed without addressing the broader social purposes of imposing such liability,[141] nor of the effectiveness of the punishments administered. The fines imposed are ultimately borne by the shareholders who, in most cases, are not responsible, in any sense, for the offence. If they really had control over the directors and so over the management of the company, this might afford some justification; but it is generally recognized that they have little control over large, public companies.[142] Moreover fines may be inflicted on the Boards of nationalized industries, where there are no shareholders and the consumers of the product, who ultimately pay the fine, have no rights whatever to appoint or dismiss the officials concerned.

138 Schedule 2, para 4(5) maintains the existing application of 'person' to corporate bodies (and, implicitly, its non-application to unincorporated bodies) in pre-1889 statutes creating offences. The definition of 'person' in Sch 1 applies to all statutes passed after the commencement of the 1889 Act, so that they continue to be capable of commission by unincorporated bodies.

139 [1984] QB 795, [1984] 1 All ER 277.

140 *Clerk to Croydon Justices, ex p Chief Constable of Kent* [1989] Crim LR 910, DC.

141 Cf other jurisdictions, and eg J. Gobert and E. Mugnai, 'Coping with Corporate Criminality – Some Lessons from Italy' [2002] Crim LR 617.

142 Pennington, *Company Law* (8th edn, 2001), Part III.

Since the persons actually responsible for the offence may, in the great majority of cases be convicted it has been questioned whether there is any need to impose this additional penalty. Arguments in favour of corporate liability include that there may be difficulty in fixing individuals with liability where someone among the 'brains' of the corporation has undoubtedly authorized the offence. Corporate liability of course ensures that the offence will not go unpunished and that a fine proportionate to the gravity of the offence may be imposed, when it might be out of proportion to the means of the individuals concerned. Further, the imposition of liability on the organization gives all of those directing it an interest in the prevention of illegalities – and they are in a position to prevent them, though the shareholders are not. Since, moreover, the names of the officers will mean nothing to the public only the conviction of the corporation itself will serve to warn the public of the wrongful acts – operating buses with faulty brakes, trains on defective tracks, or selling mouldy pies – which are committed in its name.

(i) Alternative models of corporate responsibility

As noted in the introduction to this chapter, the courts have taken a relatively simplistic approach to imposing criminal liability on corporations by shoehorning them into the orthodox model of criminal liability via the identification doctrine.[143] This has pre-empted discussion of the more fundamental question namely whether an entirely separate model of criminal responsibility ought to be created to reflect corporate structures and activities. For some the company is no more than the collection of individuals which make it up, for others the company has a distinct personality which should be reflected in the law's treatment. A model of criminality based on the acts of the individuals which make up the company may in fact prove to be the most effective approach, but the issue has not been considered otherwise than in the academic literature. The issues raised extend well beyond the scope of this work, but four options for criminal liability should be noted.[144]

Aggregation

This approach has been noted above and involves aggregating the *mens rea* of various individuals within the corporation to combine as a sufficient blameworthy 'state of mind' of the company. This approach has been considered and rejected by the Court of Appeal.[145] This approach would not require radical deviation from the orthodox model of criminal responsibility.

Extended vicarious liability

An alternative model would be to extend the approach to vicarious liability, as in some other jurisdictions such as some States in the USA, and introduce due diligence defences

143 See A. Norrie, *Crime Reason and History* (2nd edn, 2000), ch 5.

144 J. Gobert, 'Corporate Criminality: four models of fault' (1994) 14 LS 393; J. Gobert, 'Corporate Criminality: New Crimes for the Times' [1994] Crim LR 722; R. Grantham, 'Corporate Knowledge: Identification or Attribution?' (1996) 59 MLR 732.

145 *A-G's Reference (No 2 of 1999)* [2000] QB 796. See also Bingham LJ in *R* v *HM Coroner for East Kent, ex p Spooner* (1989) 88 Cr App R 10.

available to corporations.[146] Again, this may not involve a drastic change from the present position.

Corporate *mens rea*

Professor Wells rejects the identification doctrine as too narrow and advocates an extension of the availability of direct corporate liability. Having regard to the organizational structures of corporations and the corporate policies and practices, she argues that the law should recognize that 'responsibility can both flow from the individual to the corporation *and* be found in the corporation's structures themselves'.[147] Under this proposal a corporation can be responsible for the corporation's acts. Wells concludes that there should be a form of corporate *mens rea* approach. The difficulty with such a proposal lies in determining how errant the policy and/or practice of the company must be to be treated in law as being equally deserving of blame as is the *mens rea* of the individual offender.

Reactive corporate fault

A more radical approach derives from the work of Australian academics, Fisse and Braithwaite.[148] In short, they propose a model under which the company can become liable to court orders to investigate and remedy its conduct where there is an alleged criminal wrongdoing. Criminal liability would follow where the company subsequently failed to take adequate remedial measures.

(ii) Reform

The Law Commission,[149] responding in part to the growing public disquiet about numerous fatal incidents, recommended the creation of a new offence of 'corporate killing'. A corporation would commit this offence if a 'management failure' by it were a cause of a person's death, and that failure fell far below what could reasonably be expected of the corporation in the circumstances. This represents a fundamental change, as Wells notes, the corporate manslaughter proposals provide 'the scholarly foundation for a shift in the legal form of corporate liability' away from individual liability and identification.[150]

A 'management failure' would occur if the way in which the corporation's activities are managed or organized failed to ensure the health and safety of persons employed in or affected by those activities. The offence would be punishable with a fine and no individual would be liable to be convicted as a secondary party to this offence, but without prejudice to his being guilty of any other offence in respect of the death in question. A corporation might also be guilty of either of the two new general offences proposed by the Commission to replace involuntary manslaughter.[151]

146 See G. R. Sullivan, 'The Attribution of Culpability to a Limited Company' [1996] CLJ 515.

147 C. Wells, *Corporations and Criminal Responsibility* (2nd edn 2001) p 157.

148 *Corporations, Crime and Accountability* (1993).

149 *Legislating the Criminal Code: Involuntary Manslaughter*, Law Com No 237 (1996). H. Keating, 'The Law Commission Report on Involuntary Manslaughter: (1) The Restoration of a Serious Crime' [1998] Crim LR 535; A. McColgan, 'Heralding Corporate Liability' [1994] Crim LR 547. See also S. Field and N. Jorg, 'Corporate Liability and Manslaughter: should we be going Dutch?' [1991] Crim LR 156.

150 'The Corporate Manslaughter Proposals: Pragmatism, Paradox or Peninsularity' [1996] Crim LR 545, 553.

151 Below, p 488.

In 2000, the government accepted the need for reform:[152]

The government considers that while there may prove to be difficulties in proving a 'management failure' there is a need to restore public confidence that companies responsible for loss of life can properly be held accountable in law. The government believes the creation of a new offence of corporate killing would give useful emphasis to the seriousness of health and safety offences and would give force to the need to consider health and safety as a management issue.[153]

It preferred to extend the offence to all 'undertakings' including unincorporated associations and other trades or businesses. The government sought views on the application of the offence to groups of companies, Crown immunity to the offence of corporate killing, who might investigate it and the availability of legal aid.

In May 2003 the government announced its intention to introduce a Corporate Homicide Bill to honour its manifesto commitment and finally, in March 2005, a draft Bill was produced 'to introduce a new offence for holding organisations to account for gross failings by their senior management that have had fatal consequences. This would complement, not replace, other forms of accountability such as prosecutions under health and safety legislation. And it would be . . . linked to the standards required under those laws.'[154]

152 *Reforming the Law on Involuntary Manslaughter: The Government's Proposals* (2000): www.homeoffice.gov.uk/docs/invmans.html#A%20preferred%20alternative%20-%20. See J. Gobert, 'Corporate Killing at Home and Abroad: Reflections on the Government Proposals' (2002) 118 LQR 72; G. R. Sullivan, 'Corporate Killing – Some Government Proposals' [2001] Crim LR 31. For a different proposal based on causing death in the course of a specified 'scheduled' offence (such as one contrary to the Health and Safety at Work Act) see P. R. Glazebrook, 'A Better Way of Convicting Businesses of Avoidable Deaths and Injuries' (2002) CLJ 405.

153 Para 3.1.9.

154 See www.homeoffice.gov.uk/docs4/con_corp_mans.html for the draft Bill and relevant consultation documents.

11

Defences

1. Introduction

There is no accepted hierarchy of defences in English law and none is adopted here.[1] Equally, it should be noted, there is considerable debate about the precise theoretical lines between elements which ought properly to be regarded as part of the offence and those comprising defences.[2] For ease of exposition and convenience, the chapter is divided into two parts.

Part A deals with 'defences' or pleas based on a denial of capacity or status deserving of criminal sanction. It would be misleading to treat all of these as 'defences' in the true sense of the word since some involve a plea which simply puts the Crown to proof of the relevant issue. At the core of the topics considered in Part A – insanity, intoxication, mistake and infancy – is the basic principle of English criminal law that the defendant should be held liable only where he is of sufficient capacity. As Professor Hart famously explained, a person is only to be blamed if he has the 'capacity and fair opportunity to change or adjust his behaviour to the law.[3]

Part B, deals with defences in the true sense – where D has caused an *actus reus* with the appropriate *mens rea*, but despite both these elements of the offence being proved by the Crown, D is entitled to an acquittal owing to some justifying or excusing circumstance or condition. There are special defences which apply to particular crimes (for example, provocation and diminished responsibility in murder), there are also defences applicable to crimes generally. They are dealt with separately although where appropriate their interrelationship is considered.

(a) Theories of justification and excuse

The common law of homicide distinguished between justification and excuse. Some homicides, like that done by the public hangman in carrying out the sentence of the court, were justifiable. Others, like killing by misadventure and without culpable negligence, were merely excusable. In both cases the accused who successfully raised the

[1] See however the theoretical approach in P. Robinson, 'Criminal Law Defences: A Systematic Analysis' (1982) 82 Col LR 199; and for a ladder of defences see J. Horder, *Excusing Crime* (2003), 103.

[2] See generally G. Williams, 'Offences and Defences' (1982) 2 LS 233; K. Cambell, 'Offence and Defence' in I. Dennis (ed), *Criminal Law and Criminal Justice* (1987).

[3] *Punishment and Responsibility* (1968), p 181.

defence was acquitted of felony but, if the homicide was merely excusable, his goods were forfeited. In 1828 forfeiture was abolished and, ever since, there has been no difference, so far as the defendant is concerned, between the various general defences. If successfully raised, they result in a verdict of not guilty.

There has been a revival of interest in a distinction between justification and excuse.[4] On one simple form of the theory, an act is justified when society positively approves of it. It is merely excused when society disapproves of it but thinks it is not right to punish D. Whereas the justification speaks to the rightness of the act, the excuse relates to the circumstances of the individual actor. Clearly such a distinction exists in fact. There are examples which obviously fall into one category or the other. The nine-year-old child who deliberately kills his playmate is excused but no one would say he is justified. In contrast, nearly everyone would approve of the conduct of a man who wounds an aggressor when that is the only way he can save the lives of his family.

However, these systems of classification into justifications and excuses suffer from a number of drawbacks. First, there is no agreement on the precise model that the classifications should take. A number of sophisticated models of justification and excuse have been developed by academic lawyers.[5] Secondly, there is no consensus as to which classification applies to which defence – for example, many see duress as excusatory but some as justificatory. Thirdly, there seems to be little agreement as to what difference, if any, would result in practical terms from classification of a particular defence into one category or another. Few suggest that there is any difference so far as the acquittal of the person relying on the defence is concerned[6] but it has been argued more widely that the distinction affects third parties in that (i) it is lawful to resist an aggressor whose aggression is merely excused but not one whose aggression is justified; and (ii) there may be a conviction for aiding and abetting one who is merely excused[7] but not one who is justified. Some would also argue that particular judicial decisions on excuses are not to be regarded as being of any wider significance in precedent terms.[8] As Fletcher (whose work inspired the current interest) acknowledges,[9] Anglo-American criminal law has never expressly recognized these (as he thinks) fundamental distinctions. The proposed distinctions bear little resemblance to the justifiable and excusable homicides of the old common law.

Applying the theory as expounded by Fletcher, a person arresting 'anyone who is in the act of committing an arrestable offence' would be justified but a person arresting 'anyone

[4] G. Fletcher, *Rethinking Criminal Law* (1978), ch 10; S. Yeo, *Compulsion in the Criminal Law* (1990); J. C. Smith, *Justification and Excuse* (1989); G. Williams, 'The Theory of Excuses' [1982] Crim LR 732; P. Robinson, 'Criminal Law Defences: A Systematic Analysis' (1982) 82 Col LR 199; J. Gardner, 'The Gist of Excuses' (1998) Buffalo Crim LR 575; J. Horder, above.

[5] Debate continues as to whether D who relies on a justification should be seen as having done no wrong, or as having done wrong but being justified in doing it (see G. Fletcher, 'The Nature of Justifications' in S. Shute, S. Gardner and J. Horder (eds), *Action and Value in Criminal Law* (1993), 175). As for excuses, there is debate over whether D is excused because he has acted 'out of character' or because he lacked capacity (ie he has not lived up to the standards we can reasonably expect of someone in his circumstances). See generally, J. Gardner, 'The Gist of Excuses' (1998) (above); V. Tadros, 'The Characters of Excuses' (2001) 21 OJLS 495; and J. Horder, above, ch 3.

[6] Cf Robinson above considering special verdicts for those who are excused.

[7] As in *Bourne* (1952) 36 Cr App R 125 and *Cogan and Leak* [1976] QB 217, [1975] 2 All ER 1059, above, p 205.

[8] Robinson, above.

[9] N 5, above.

whom he has reasonable grounds for suspecting to be [but who is not in fact] committing such an offence' is merely excused. But both acts are equally 'justified' by the law – the Police and Criminal Evidence Act 1984, s 24(4)(a) and (b), declares that both are acts that a person *may* do. In doing so, he incurs no civil or criminal liability. It is true, however, that the first 'arrestee' would not be entitled to use force in self-defence (if the arrestor was using only reasonable force) whereas the second might be.[10]

The law does recognize that a person's act may be excused in the criminal law, while incurring civil liability. A person who makes an unreasonable mistake of fact which, if it were true, would amount to reasonable grounds for suspecting another to be in the act of committing an arrestable offence, has a defence to a criminal prosecution for false imprisonment or assault (because he lacks *mens rea*) but remains liable for the corresponding torts: the act done is not the act which the 1984 Act says he *may* do. Here the terminology of justification and excuse seems appropriate. The act is 'unlawful', but the actor is excused from criminal liability.

Any attempt to rely on the theories of justifications or excuses as the guiding principle by which to structure an analysis of defences would, in the present state of the law, be premature, and no such attempt is made in this chapter in either Part A or B.

SECTION A **CAPACITY AND MENTAL CONDITIONS**

1. Introduction

In this part, the pleas of insanity, intoxication, mistake and infancy are considered. Examination of the first three involves a degree of overlap since they are all concerned with D's denial that he was a responsible actor at the time of the commission of the offence. Their interrelationship may be usefully summarized at the outset. In short, there are three situations:

(1) Those tending to an acquittal on the ground of insanity – diseases of the mind. These are internal factors treated in law as a disease of the mind but extending to such everyday conditions as sleepwalking, epilepsy and diabetes.

(2) Those tending to an absolute acquittal, such as concussion, the taking (in accordance with instructions) of a *medically prescribed* drug or anaesthetic, and other 'external' factors. These may give rise to a defence of automatism, but that defence is hedged with qualification and approached by the courts with considerable scepticism. A defence of automatism is available only where D suffers a complete loss of control. In addition, where the automatism is self-induced by taking alcohol or drugs, it will be a defence only to crimes of specific intent (as explained below) or in relation to basic intent offences where D's conduct in inducing the state of automatism is not reckless.

[10] Below, p 333.

(3) Those not amounting to a defence at all – in the case of crimes not requiring specific intent, intoxication arising from the voluntary taking of drink or drugs (discussed below p 275).

2. Insanity[11]

There are two ways in which an accused person's sanity may be relevant in a criminal trial. First, is where the accused is claiming that he was insane at the time of the commission of the acts alleged to constitute the criminal offence. Secondly, the accused may be claiming that he is insane at the time of trial and therefore not fit to be tried. It is convenient to deal with this second category here because of their very close relationship with the defence of insanity, although technically it is a matter not of substantive law but of procedure.

(a) Insanity and unfitness to be tried

There are two stages to consider in this category.

(i) Mental condition rendering trial impracticable

Where D has been committed in custody for trial, and the Home Secretary is satisfied by reports from at least two medical practitioners that he is suffering from mental illness, or severe mental impairment,[12] he may order that D be detained in a hospital, if he is of opinion having regard to the public interest that it is expedient to do so.[13] The Home Secretary exercises this power only:

> where the prisoner's condition is such that immediate removal to a mental hospital is necessary, that it would not be practicable to bring him before a court, or that the trial is likely to have an injurious effect on his mental state.[14]

The defendant is normally brought to trial when he is well enough.[15] The basis for this practice is:

> that the issue of insanity should be determined by the jury whenever possible and the power should be exercised only when there is likely to be a scandal if the prisoner is brought up for trial. . . .[16]

Clearly to maintain compatibility with Article 5(1) and Article 6 of the ECHR it is essential that the power to detain is exercised in accordance with law and sparingly.[17]

[11] See the excellent discussion in R. D. Mackay, *Mental Condition Defences in Criminal Law* (1998). Proposals for the reform of the law are made in the Report of the Committee on Mentally Abnormal Offenders (The Butler Report – hereinafter Butler), Cmnd 6244, 1975.

[12] For definitions, see Mental Health Act 1983, s 1(1).

[13] Mental Health Act 1983, ss 47, 48. See Archbold (2005) ss 3–81.

[14] RCCP, Cmd 8932, at 76 referring to the corresponding power under the Criminal Lunatics Act 1884. See Butler, para 3.38.

[15] Butler, para 3.38.

[16] RCCP, Cmd 8932, above.

[17] Cf the statistics revealed by R. D. Mackay and D. Machin, *Transfers from Prison to Hospital – the operation of s 48 of the Mental Health Act 1983* (Home Office Research Directorate) No 84.

(ii) Unfitness to be tried[18]

The second stage is when the accused is brought up for trial. It might then be alleged by the defence or the prosecution that D is unfit to plead. If this issue is raised on arraignment the Crown Court must follow the procedure to determine his fitness under ss 4 and 4A of the Criminal Procedure (Insanity) Act 1964.[19] The issue may also arise where D has been found unfit, his condition has improved and he is brought back to court to determine whether he remains unfit.[20] In the magistrates' court and the Youth Court[21] the procedure is contained in s 37 of the Mental Health Act 1983.

The question at this stage is whether D is able to understand the charge and the difference between pleas of guilty and not guilty, to challenge jurors, to instruct counsel and to follow the evidence. In the recent case of *M*[22] the trial judge directed that the defendant had to have sufficient ability in relation to six things: (i) to understand the charges, (ii) to understand the plea, (iii) to challenge jurors, (iv) to instruct counsel and his solicitor, (v) to understand the course of the trial, and (vi) to give evidence if he chooses. If he is able to do these things, he has *a right* to be tried if he so wishes, even though he is not capable of acting in his best interests.[23] The same principle must, theoretically, be applicable where the prosecution contend that D is fit to plead and he denies it; but it might be more leniently applied in such a case.

What constitutes unfitness?

It was held in *Podola*[24] that a person is fit to plead where an hysterical amnesia prevents him from remembering events during the whole of the period material to the question whether he committed the crime alleged, but whose mind is otherwise completely normal. The court was prepared to concede that a deaf mute is 'insane' – the word used in the Criminal Lunatics Act 1800 – but declined,

> to extend the meaning of the word to include persons who are mentally normal at the time of the hearing of the proceedings against them and are perfectly capable of instructing their solicitors as to what submission their counsel is to put forward with regard to the commission of the crime.[25]

18 See Mackay, above, ch 5; for trends in the use of the plea see R. D. Mackay and G. Kearns, 'An Upturn in Unfitness to Plead?' [2000] Crim LR 532.

19 As substituted by the Criminal Procedure (Insanity and Unfitness to Plead) Act 1991 and amended by the Domestic Violence, Crime and Victims Act 2004, discussed by S. White, 'The Criminal Procedure (Insanity and Unfitness to Plead) Act 1991' [1992] Crim LR 4; P. Fennell, 'The Criminal Procedure (Insanity and Unfitness to Plead) Act 1991' (1992) 55 MLR 547. The 1964 Act replaced the Criminal Lunatics Act 1800.

20 Section 4A is mandatory and must be complied with in full in such cases: *Ferris* [2004] EWHC 1221 (Admin).

21 *P v Barking Youth Court* [2002] EWHC 734, [2002] Crim LR 637.

22 [2003] EWCA Crim 3452.

23 *Robertson* [1968] 3 All ER 557, [1968] 1 WLR 1767, CA. See also *R (Kenneally) v Snaresbrook Crown Court* [2002] QB 1169.

24 [1960] 1 QB 325, [1959] 3 All ER 418. The jury had found that Podola was not suffering from hysterical amnesia and the question before the Court of Criminal Appeal concerned the onus of proof of that issue; but the court held that this question could only arise if the alleged amnesia could in law bring Podola within the scope of s 2 of the Criminal Lunatics Act 1800. The court's decision on this point thus appears to be part of the *ratio decidendi* of the case.

25 [1960] 1 QB at 356, [1959] 3 All ER at 433. The word 'insane' is not used in s 4 of the 1964 Act; but the law is unchanged. Cf Cmd 2149, at 7.

But is a person suffering from hysterical amnesia so capable? If the actual facts justify a defence of accident or alibi but D is unable to remember them, the defence, in the absence of volunteer witnesses, cannot be raised. On the other hand it would be unsatisfactory if, for example, there could be no trial of a motorist who had suffered concussion in an accident, alleged to have been caused by his reckless driving, and who could not remember what he did. It would be still less satisfactory in the case of one whose failure to recall the relevant events arose from drunkenness.[26]

The test has been cogently criticized for its focus on D's communicative ability and its failure to address the true problem – whether D is capable of providing a rational account of the incident to instruct his lawyer.[27] A test of decisional competence has been recommended.[28]

The procedure

The issue may be raised by the judge on his own initiative or at the request of the prosecution or the defence. Where neither party raises the issue, the judge should do so if he has doubts about the accused's fitness.[29] He may resolve his doubts by reading the medical reports, but it is undesirable for him to hear medical evidence.

If the question is raised by either party, or if the judge has doubts, the issue used to be tried by a jury.[30] Following the Domestic Violence Crime and Victims Act 2004, s 22, the issue is now to be determined by a court without a jury. Before the 2004 Act it was held that such proceedings did not constitute 'criminal proceedings' since they cannot result in a conviction; the procedure is to ensure the protection of the defendant and the public. Accordingly, Article 6 of the ECHR does not apply.[31] Although the reasoning by which their Lordships reached that conclusion is unconvincing, the conclusion seems right and the same conclusion must apply after the 2004 Act.

The general rule is that the question of fitness is to be determined as soon as it arises. If the accused is found by the judge to be fit and the trial proceeds it will be tried by a jury in the normal way. Where, exceptionally, the question falls to be determined at a later time the issue is to be determined by the same jury by which the accused is being tried.[32] The defendant may not be found unfit to plead unless there is written or oral evidence to that

26 *Broadhurst v R* [1964] AC 441 at 451, [1964] 1 All ER 111 at 116, PC. Butler (by majority) recommends the retention of the *Podola* rule.

27 See also the psychiatrist's view – D. Grubin, 'What Constitutes Unfitness to Plead' [1993] Crim LR 748, cf R. A. Duff, 'Fitness to Plead and Fair Trials' [1994] Crim LR 419.

28 See R. D. Mackay, 'On Being Insane in Jersey Part Three – the Case of the *Attorney General v O'Driscoll*' [2004] Crim LR 219.

29 *MacCarthy* [1967] 1 QB 68, [1966] 1 All ER 447, discussed by A. R. Poole, 'Standing Mute and Fitness to Plead' [1966] Crim LR 6.

30 Criminal Procedure (Insanity) Act 1964, s 4(5). Particular problems arose in cases with co-defendants: V. Baird and C. Wade, 'The Criminal Procedure (Insanity and Unfitness to Plead) Act 1991 and the Juries Act 1974: Irreconcilable problems' [1999] Crim LR 656.

31 *H* [2003] UKHL 1, [2003] Crim LR 817, affirming *M Kerr and H* [2002] Crim LR 57. On ECHR concerns with the operation of the procedure see E. Baker, 'Human Rights and McNaughten and the 1991 Act' [1994] Crim LR 84; R. D. Mackay, 'On Being Insane in Jersey Part Three – the Case of the *Attorney General v O'Driscoll*' [2004] Crim LR 219; 'On Being Insane in Jersey Part Two' [2002] Crim LR 728.

32 Section 22 of the 2004 Act, amending the Criminal Procedure (Insanity) Act 1964, s 4(5) as substituted by the Criminal Procedure (Insanity and Unfitness to Plead) Act 1991, s 2.

effect by two or more registered medical practitioners at least one of whom is approved by the Home Secretary as having special experience in the field of mental disorder.[33]

The general view expressed by witnesses before the Royal Commission on Capital Punishment was that:

> someone who is certifiably insane may often nevertheless be fit to plead to the indictment and follow the proceedings at the trial and that, if he is, he should ordinarily be allowed to do so, because it is in principle desirable that a person charged with a criminal offence should, whenever possible, be tried, so that the question whether he committed the crime may be determined by a jury.[34]

Time of trial of fitness to plead

The case against a person who is undoubtedly unfit to plead may be weak and capable of demolition by cross-examination of the prosecution witnesses by his lawyers. It would be wrong if he were to be found unfit and subjected to the restraints (including detention) which may follow from that finding without having an opportunity to test the prosecution's case. The matter is now regulated by the Criminal Procedure (Insanity) Act 1964, as amended by the Criminal Procedure (Insanity and Unfitness to Plead) Act 1991 and the Domestic Violence, Crime and Victims Act 2004. As we have seen, the general rule is that the question of fitness is to be determined by the judge as soon as it arises; but if the judge, having regard to the nature of the supposed disability, thinks that it is expedient and in the interests of the accused to do so, he may postpone consideration of the question of fitness to be tried until any time up to the opening of the case for the defence.

This gives the defence the opportunity to test the prosecution's case. If it is insufficient to justify a conviction, the jury will be directed to acquit and the question of fitness to plead will not arise. If there is a case to answer, that question will then be determined by the jury by whom D is being tried.

The trial of the facts

Where D is found to be unfit, either on arraignment or at the end of the prosecution case, the trial shall not proceed, or proceed further.[35] If the matter rested there, D might again be subject to restraint though he has done nothing wrong. Even if the prosecution's evidence has been heard and amounts to a case to answer, there may be an answer to it in the shape of evidence – for example, of alibi – available to the defence. Section 4A (introduced by the 1991 Act, and amended by the 2004 Act) therefore provides that the court shall decide on the evidence (if any) already given and such evidence as is adduced

[33] The 1964 Act as amended, s 4(6). See *Borkan* [2004] EWCA Crim 1642.

[34] Report, Cmd 8932, at 78. The judge must generally exercise this discretion to postpone where there is a reasonable chance that the prosecution case will be successfully challenged: *Webb* [1969] 2 QB 278, [1969] 2 All ER 626. On the other hand, 'the case for the prosecution may appear so strong and the suggested condition of the prisoner so disabling that postponement of the trial of the issue would be wholly inexpedient': *Burles* [1970] 2 QB 191, [1970] 1 All ER 642, per Parker LCJ.

[35] The judge in *O'Donnell* [1996] 1 Cr App R 286 went wrong at this point by allowing the trial to proceed, by failing to appoint someone to put the case for the defence and by not directing the trial jury that, now, the only question for them was whether D did the act. Conviction annulled and *venire de novo* ordered.

by the prosecution or the defence whether D 'did the act or made the omission charged against him as the offence'.[36]

It was held in *Antoine*[37] that the words 'act' and 'omission' mean the *actus reus* of the offence and that, accordingly, D could not rely on the defence of diminished responsibility. That defence applies only when the *actus reus* (and, indeed, the *mens rea*) of murder has been established. The decision creates problems by its presumption that all offences divide neatly into elements (only) of *actus reus* and *mens rea* that can be readily identified. The confusion is exemplified in the judgment, for example, Lord Hutton, with whom all their Lordships agreed, said that the jury should take into account any objective evidence of mistake, accident or self-defence and should not find that D did the act unless it is sure that the prosecution has negatived the defence. But the 'defences' of mistake and accident are simply denials of *mens rea*, not of the *actus reus*, and self-defence has a vital mental element. If this *dictum* is right, it is hard to see why any other evidence, other than of a defect of reason from disease of the mind, suggesting the absence of *mens rea*[38] should not be admissible, thus undermining the whole decision. Subsequently it has been held that D cannot invoke the defence of provocation.[39] That defence applies only where all the elements of murder are proved so 'the act' of murder and of manslaughter by reason of provocation seems to be identical. It appears that his Lordship was anticipating that the s 4A inquiry is directed not merely to the *actus reus*, not to the full offence of *actus reus* and *mens rea*, but to an 'unlawful act'. It is possible to envisage some relatively straightforward cases where 'objective defences' ought to be pleaded. Difficult examples to test the precise limits of Lord Hutton's 'objective defences' might include a case in which the defence of sane automatism would have been advanced at trial. For example, where D has been hit on the head and in a state of concussion hit and killed V. D has by trial become so traumatized by the event that he is unfit. Is the plea a denial of *mens rea* and forbidden? Or is it a denial of a 'voluntary act' and expressly recognized by Lord Hutton? Or is it in some third category of 'not unlawful act'? The Court of Appeal acknowledged the problem in *M*[40] where it was accepted that the *actus reus/mens rea* distinction was not one that could be rigidly adhered to in every case given the diverse nature of crimes. It also poses special problems in cases of secondary liability.

The broader problem lies in defining with sufficient precision the level of inquiry that is appropriate at a trial of the facts under s 4A so as to (a) avoid assessment of the accused's mental state at the time of the offence, because although he is the person best

36 Problems arise where D has been found unfit to plead and his condition improves so that by the time of the trial of the facts he is potentially fit to stand trial. There is no power to reverse the decision on unfitness: *Omara* [2004] EWCA Crim 431.

37 [2001] 1 AC 340, HL, [2000] Crim LR 621, overruling *Egan* [1998] 1 Cr App R 121 which had 'held' that the words meant all the ingredients of the offence – a surprising construction, but that intended by the Butler Committee (Cmnd 6244, 1975, para 10.24) on whose recommendations these provisions are based. R. D. Mackay and G. Kearns, 'The Trial of the Facts and Unfitness to Plead' [1997] Crim LR 644, however, demonstrated that this was not the meaning intended by ministers who introduced the Bill in Parliament. The same words used in the Trial of Lunatics Act 1883, s 2, refer only to the *actus reus: Felstead* [1914] AC 534, HL. An application to Strasbourg was rejected as manifestly ill-founded: *Antoine v UK* 62960/00. See also R. D. Mackay, 'On Being Insane in Jersey Part Two' [2002] Crim LR 728.

38 Clearly, the finding of an act or omission may include some elements of *mens rea* where they are a composite element of the *actus reus. R (Young) v Central Criminal Court* [2002] 2 Cr App R 12, [2002] Crim LR 588 and commentary by J. C. Smith.

39 *Grant (Heather)* [2002] QB 1030.

40 [2003] 2 Cr App R 21.

able to know that, by definition, he is now unfit to provide such evidence, or rebut allegations, and (b) prevent the detention of those who would have secured a complete acquittal at a normal trial for reasons other than those of mental illness. The irony is that by seeking to protect defendants from a full trial and inquiry into a mental state that they are unable to defend, the system might place them in a worse position, particularly with offences carrying a fixed sentence.

Where D has been found to be unfit and to have committed the *actus reus*, but his condition then improves and the question arises whether he is fit to be tried, the determination of his fitness and of whether he performed the *actus reus* must both be re-litigated. The prior determination of the *actus reus* being satisfied cannot be relied upon.[41]

Onus of proof

Podola's case decides, overruling earlier authorities, that, where D raises the issue of fitness to plead, the onus of proving that he is unfit is on him. By analogy to the rule prevailing when a defence of insanity is raised at the trial,[42] D is required to prove his case, not beyond reasonable doubt, but on a balance of probabilities. If the issue is raised by the prosecution and disputed by the defence then the burden is on the prosecution and the matter must be proved beyond reasonable doubt.[43] If the issue is raised by the judge and disputed by D, presumably the onus is again on the prosecution.[44]

The effect of *Podola*'s case is that a man may be convicted although a court was not satisfied that he was capable of making out a proper defence at his trial. Moreover the reasoning of the court has been criticized[45] on the ground, *inter alia*, that the prosecution, in bringing the charge at all, is implicitly alleging that D is fit to stand his trial; and that he, in denying that he is so fit, is merely denying that the prosecution have established all the elements in their case.

Disposal powers in relation to a person unfit to plead who 'did the act'

Until the reforms made by the 1991 Act took effect the court had to order that any person found unfit to plead had to be admitted to the hospital specified by the Home Secretary where he might be detained without limitation of time, the power to discharge him being exercisable only with the Home Secretary's consent. Since the 1991 Act a person who is found unfit to plead but not to have done the act or made the omission charged simply goes free. Where he is found to be unfit *and* to have done the act or made the omission a wider range of disposals is now generally available. Where, however, the sentence for the offence to which the finding relates is fixed by law – in effect, murder[46] – the court was, until the Domestic Violence, Crime and Victims Act 2004 obliged to make a hospital order restricting discharge without limitation of time. It was recognized by the Court of Appeal that the imposition of such an order may well breach Article 5(1) of the ECHR unless D is on the facts mentally disordered to such an extent that detention would be

[41] *Ferris* [2004] EWHC 1221 (Admin).

[42] Per Edmund Davies J at first instance, [1960] 1 QB 325 at 329, [1959] 3 All ER 418 at 442; *Robertson* [1968] 3 All ER 557, [1968] 1 WLR 1767, CA.

[43] *Antoine* [2001] AC 340. According to Podola's counsel, Mr Lawton, it had been the normal practice in recent years for the prosecution to call the evidence.

[44] By M. Dean, 'Fitness to Plead' [1960] Crim LR 79 at 82.

[45] Section 5 of the 1964 Act as amended.

[46] But presumably also other 'automatic' sentences triggered by the particular offence with which D is now charged.

proportionate. Since 'unfitness' may be based on D's inability to communicate and other matters falling far short of such mental disorder, there would be many cases in which the order was incompatible with Article 5.[47] Under s 24 of the 2004 Act inserting a new s 5 into the 1964 Act, in any case other than one of a fixed sentence, the court may make:

(i) a hospital order (with or without a restriction order);[48]

(ii) a supervision order; or

(iii) an order for absolute discharge.

(b) A plea of insanity raised at trial[49]

If the accused is found fit to plead or, if that issue is not raised, he may raise the defence of insanity at his trial. The plea will be that D was insane at the time of the commission of the offence alleged. Insanity is a defence at common law and, though rarely raised in a magistrates' court, applies in a summary trial as well as a trial on indictment. The statutory procedure considered below applies only in trials on indictment and the unamended common law operates in magistrates' courts.[50] A successful defence results in a simple acquittal. A successful defence at a trial on indictment formerly resulted in a mandatory order that the defendant be admitted to a special hospital where he might be detained indefinitely, but now, by the 1991 Act as amended by the Domestic Violence Crime and Victims Act 2004, the same powers of disposal are available as for a person found unfit to plead, stated above.

(i) Operation of the defence

It is important to notice that, whereas at the two preliminary stages above, the concern was with the accused's sanity *at the time of the inquiry*, at the trial the question concerns the accused's sanity *at the time when he did the criminal act*. The fact that he was insane in the medical sense is not in itself sufficient to afford a defence. It seems surprising that in the twenty-first century the law is based not on any medical understanding of mental illness but on a distinct legal criterion of responsibility defined by the common law and set out in authoritative form in the 'M'Naghten Rules', formulated by the judges as long ago as 1843.[51] Daniel M'Naghten, intending to murder Sir Robert Peel, killed Peel's secretary by mistake. His acquittal of murder[52] on the ground of insanity provoked controversy and was debated in the House of Lords, which sought the advice of the judges and submitted to them a number of questions. The answers to those questions became the famous Rules. Answers to hypothetical questions, even by all the judges, are not, strictly speaking, a source of law; but in *Sullivan*[53] it was accepted by the House of Lords that the Rules have provided a comprehensive definition since 1843.

47 *Grant* [2002] Crim LR 403.

48 *See Narey v Customs and Excise* [2005] All ER (D) 199 (Apr).

49 See generally Mackay, above, ch 2.

50 *Horseferry Road Magistrates' Court, ex p K* [1996] 2 Cr App R 574, [1997] Crim LR 129. See T. Ward, 'Magistrates, Insanity and the Common Law' [1997] Crim LR 796.

51 (1843) 4 St Tr NS 847.

52 (1843) 10 Cl & Fin 200.

53 *Sullivan* [1983] 2 All ER 673 at 676.

In one sense the importance of the Rules has diminished greatly since the abolition of the death penalty and the introduction of the defence of diminished responsibility. On charges other than for murder, where diminished responsibility is not available, defendants are generally unwilling to rely on the defence, preferring to risk conviction and sentence rather than incur the stigma of an insanity verdict and the indefinite detention which used to follow. However, although reliance on the defence was rare for a number of years, it has recently become a more common plea.[54]

Some who, on the evidence before the court, were not guilty of the offence, have preferred to plead guilty when it was ruled that the evidence amounted to a plea of insanity and not, as they had claimed, non-insane automatism. The propriety of accepting a plea of guilty by a person who, on the evidence, is not guilty seems doubtful but it has not been questioned in the Court of Appeal and the House of Lords has left the matter open. It is regrettable that the state of the substantive law is such that innocent people suffering from a mental condition feel compelled to plead guilty. One element of deterrent to invoking the Rules has been removed because the court now has wider powers of disposal. Whereas committal to a special hospital may be regarded as worse than the consequences of conviction, other disposal options such as an absolute discharge or a supervision and treatment order may not be. A defendant who is advised that one of these orders is likely to be made in the event of a successful defence may now be willing to raise it, whereas formerly he would not have done so – but the stigma of 'insanity' remains. Even the label is strikingly inappropriate in the present day when so much progress has been made to inform public attitudes to mental illness.

(ii) The test of insanity

Whatever the effect of the recent changes, the M'Naghten Rules remain of great importance both because they provide the legal test of responsibility of the mentally abnormal and because they set a limit to the defences of automatism and, in theory, of diminished responsibility. These are legal questions and not questions of medicine or psychiatry. The basic propositions of the law are to be found in the answers to Questions 2 and 3:[55]

> . . . the jurors ought to be told in all cases that every man is presumed to be sane, and to possess a sufficient degree of reason to be responsible for his crimes, until the contrary be proved to their satisfaction; and that to establish a defence on the ground of insanity, it must be clearly proved that, at the time of the committing of the act, the party accused was labouring under such a defect of reason, from disease of the mind, as not to know the nature and quality of the act he was doing, or, if he did know it, that he did not know he was doing what was wrong.

It will be seen that there are two lines of defence open to an accused person:

(i) he must be acquitted if, because of a disease of the mind, he did not know the nature and quality of his act;

(ii) even if he did know the nature and quality of his act, he must be acquitted if, because of a disease of the mind, he did not know it was 'wrong'.

54 See R. D. Mackay, 'Fact and Fiction About the Insanity Defence' [1990] Crim LR 247; R. D. Mackay and G. Kearns, 'The Continued Underuse of Unfitness to Plead and the Insanity Defence' [1994] Crim LR 546; R. D. Mackay and G. Kearns, 'More Facts(s) about the Insanity Defence' [1999] Crim LR 714.

55 10 Cl & Fin at 210.

The two limbs of the rule require separate consideration but the first question, under either limb, is whether D was suffering from 'a defect of reason from disease of the mind'. If D was unaware of the nature and quality of his act for some other reason, he will usually be entitled to a simple acquittal on the ground that he lacked the necessary *mens rea*. Moreover the onus of proof will remain on the Crown, whereas it will shift to D once he tenders evidence of a defect of reason arising from disease of the mind. If D was unaware that his act was 'wrong' for some other reason, this will generally not amount to a defence at all, for neither ignorance of the law, nor will good motive normally afford a defence.[56]

When a defendant puts his state of mind in issue, the question whether he has raised the defence of insanity is one of law for the judge.[57] Whether D, or indeed his medical witnesses, would call the condition on which he relies, 'insanity' is immaterial. The expert witnesses may testify as to the factual nature of the condition but it is for the judge to say whether that is evidence of 'a defect of reason, from disease of the mind', because, as will appear, these are legal, not medical, concepts. In the leading case of *Sullivan*,[58] the defence to a charge of assault occasioning actual bodily harm was that D attacked V while recovering from a minor epileptic seizure and did not know what he was doing. The House of Lords held that the judge had rightly ruled that this raised the defence of insanity. D had then pleaded guilty to the charge of which he was manifestly innocent, and his conviction was upheld.

Disease of the mind

Whether a particular condition amounts to a disease of the mind within the Rules is not a medical but a legal question to be decided in accordance with the ordinary rules of interpretation. It seems that any disease which produces a malfunctioning of the mind is a disease of the mind.[59] It need not be a disease of the brain. Arteriosclerosis, a tumour on the brain, epilepsy, diabetes, sleepwalking, pre-menstrual syndrome and all physical diseases, may amount in law to a disease of the mind if they produce the relevant malfunction. The focus on the definition in legal terms with no direct correlation with medical definitions renders this aspect of the test potentially incompatible with Article 5(1)(e) of the ECHR (see below) where it results in D's loss of liberty.

Sane automatism and insanity distinguished

It is critical to distinguish between pleas of insanity and pleas of non-insane automatism. A malfunctioning of the mind is not a disease of the mind when it is caused by some external factor – a blow on the head causing concussion, the consumption of alcohol or drugs, or the administration of an anaesthetic. In such a case the plea is one of non-insane automatism. That 'defence' imposes no burden of proof on the accused and if successful results in a complete acquittal. Insanity on the other hand must be proved by D (on the balance of probabilities) and results in a special verdict of not guilty by reason of insanity.

56 The application of the burden of proof in these cases is critically explored by T. Jones, 'Insanity, Automatism and the Burden of Proof on the Accused' (1995) 111 LQR 475.

57 See *Roach* [2001] EWCA Crim 2698.

58 [1984] AC 156, [1983] 2 All ER 673, HL.

59 *Kemp* [1957] 1 QB 399 at 406, [1956] 3 All ER 249 at 254, per Devlin J, approved by Lord Denning in *Bratty*, below, p 260.

In determining whether D suffers a disease of the mind it is clear that the law considers not only the state of mind in which D was, but how it came about.[60] Devlin J thought that the object of the inclusion of the words 'disease of the mind' was to exclude 'defects of reason caused simply by brutish stupidity without rational power'; but it seems the words exclude more than that. In *Quick*[61] D who had inflicted actual bodily harm called medical evidence to show that he was a diabetic and that he was suffering from hypoglycaemia and was unaware of what he was doing. Bridge J ruled that he had raised a defence of insanity, whereupon D pleaded guilty. On appeal it was held that the alleged mental condition was caused not by D's diabetes but by his use of insulin prescribed by the doctor. This was an external factor and the defence of automatism should have been left to the jury. If the condition had been caused by the diabetes then it would seem that the defence would have been insanity. The case illustrates the fine line between the two defences although the consequence of pleading them successfully is markedly different.[62] The unsatisfactory nature of this distinction is discussed in the next section.

In *Kemp* D made an entirely motiveless and irrational attack on his wife with a hammer. He was charged with causing grievous bodily harm to her with intent to murder her. It appeared that he suffered from arteriosclerosis which caused a congestion of blood in his brain. As a result he suffered a temporary lapse of consciousness during which he made the attack. It was conceded that D did not know the nature and quality of his act and that he suffered from a defect of reason but it was argued on his behalf that this arose, not from any mental disease, but from a purely physical one. It was argued that, if a physical disease caused the brain cells to degenerate (as in time, it might), then it would be a disease of the mind; but until it did so, it was said, this temporary interference with the working of the brain was like a concussion or something of that sort and not a disease of the mind. Devlin J rejected this argument and held that D was suffering from a disease of the mind. He said:

> The law is not concerned with the brain but with the mind, in the sense that 'mind' is ordinarily used, the mental faculties of reason, memory and understanding. If one reads for 'disease of the mind' 'disease of the brain,' it would follow that in many cases pleas of insanity would not be established because it could not be proved that the brain had been affected in any way, either by degeneration of the cells or in any other way. In my judgment the condition of the brain is irrelevant and so is the question of whether the condition of the mind is curable or incurable, transitory or permanent.[63]

In the earlier case of *Charlson*[64] where the evidence was that D was 'acting as an automaton without any real knowledge of that he was doing' as a result of a cerebral tumour, Barry J directed the jury to acquit if the defence might reasonably be true. Devlin J distinguished *Charlson* on the ground that there the doctors were agreed that D was not

60 Contrary to the *dictum* of Devlin J in *Kemp* [1957] 1 QB 399 at 407.

61 [1973] QB 910, [1973] 3 All ER 347, [1973] Crim LR 434 and commentary; cf *Hennessy* and *Bingham*, below, p 260.

62 See *Bingham* [1991] Crim LR 433.

63 [1957] 1 QB at 407, [1956] 3 All ER at 253.

64 [1955] 1 All ER 859, [1955] 1 WLR 317.

suffering from a mental disease.[65] As this is a question of law the distinction seems unsound and in *Bratty*[66] Lord Denning approved *Kemp* and disagreed with *Charlson.* Lord Denning put forward his own view of a disease of the mind:

it seems to me that any mental disorder which has manifested itself in violence and is prone to recur is a disease of the mind. At any rate it is the sort of disease for which a person should be detained in hospital rather than be given an unqualified acquittal.

Quick casts some doubt on this *dictum*, and it is surely right to do so. The definition might fit a diabetic, but 'no mental hospital would admit a diabetic merely because he had a low blood sugar reaction', and it might be felt to be 'an affront to common sense' to regard such a person as insane; yet the court saw the weakness of the argument, agreeing with Devlin J that the disease might be 'curable or incurable . . . transitory or permanent'; and the fact that the Home Secretary might have a difficult problem of disposal did not affect the matter. Lord Denning's *dictum* has also been criticized on the ground that it is tautologous and that a disease of the mind may manifest itself in wrongful acts other than violence, such as theft.[67]

'External' and 'internal' factors

The distinction between external causes, which may give rise to a defence of non-insane automatism, and internal factors which can only give rise to a defence of insanity has been subjected to sustained and cogent criticism.[68] The supposed justification is that the internal factor will usually be a continuing condition which may cause a recurrence of the prohibited conduct whereas the external factor – the blow on the head, the injection, the inhalation of toxic fumes,[69] etc will usually have a transitory effect. Such a precise correlation between the source and likelihood of recurrence is inaccurate. The blow on the head may inflict permanent damage, in which case that damage will be an internal factor, giving rise to a defence of insanity. In cases of diabetes, it can hardly be suggested that there is a greater risk of recurrence from the diabetes itself causing a hyperglyacaemic state (insanity) than from D forgetting to eat after taking insulin and going into a hypoglycaemic state (non-insane automatism). Distinguishing between external and internal causes is an unsatisfactory and deficient way of addressing the true mischief – the likelihood of danger posed by uncontrolled recurrence of the mental condition. The deficiency is exposed in Lord Lane's judgment in *Burgess*:

if there is a danger of recurrence that may be an added reason for categorising the condition as a disease of the mind. On the other hand, the absence of the danger of recurrence is not a reason for saying that it cannot be a disease of the mind.[70]

The passage serves to emphasize that the underlying basis for the courts' approach is policy.

[65] A similar argument was rejected in *Sullivan* [1983] 2 All ER 673 at 677. The nomenclature adopted by the medical profession may change but the meaning of 'disease of the mind' in the Rules remains unchanged.

[66] *Bratty v A-G for Northern Ireland* [1963] AC 386 at 410–412, [1961] 3 All ER 523 at 533–534, HL.

[67] N. Walker, *Crime and Insanity in England* (1963), 117.

[68] See the dissent by Dickson J in *Rabey* (1981) 114 DLR (3d) 193; R. D. Mackay, 'Non-Organic Automatism' [1980] Crim LR 350; Williams, TBCL, 671.

[69] *Oakley* (1986) 24 CCC (3d) 351 at 362, per Martin JA.

[70] [1991] WLR 1206 at 1212.

Range of conditions treated in law as 'a disease of the mind'

The reach of the M'Naghten Rules in extending to epileptics,[71] diabetics,[72] pre-menstrual syndrome sufferers,[73] sleepwalkers,[74] is astonishingly wide. However, it should be noted that all the reported cases involve apparently purposive conduct and it may be that the Rules should be limited to cases of that type. A convulsive movement of a person in an epileptic fit may result in injury to person or property but it would seem absurd either to convict the epileptic or hold him to be insane.

In *Bratty v Attorney-General for Northern Ireland*,[75] D took off a girl's stocking and strangled her with it. There was medical evidence that he was suffering from psychomotor epilepsy which might have prevented him from knowing the nature and quality of his act. It was held to be evidence of insanity. This seems very far removed from a convulsive movement of the body of an epilepsy sufferer. It is a complex operation which has every appearance of being controlled by the brain. Whether or not D could have prevented himself from acting in this way, he appears to be a very dangerous person and, in the absence of some other form of protection for the public, a simple verdict of acquittal seems inappropriate. Sullivan's conduct, like that of Kemp, Charlson, Quick and Rabey (below) also seems to have been apparently purposive and, though he was less obviously a danger to the public than Bratty, his case may be indistinguishable in principle.

It is unrealistic to suggest that the law has only ever been applied in circumstances of purposive conduct, and miraculously only in cases in which there is agreement that the verdict was appropriate. It remains deeply unsatisfactory for the law to remain so ill-defined as to leave exposed to the risk of such a verdict a person with a mental condition of what may be a trivial nature and who poses no real future risk to society. The challenge to the overbroad definition of disease of the mind may arise under the ECHR. Article 5(1)(e), in guaranteeing protection against arbitrary detention, allows for the detention of those suffering from mental illness where it is necessary for the protection of the public. The European Court has accepted that the State's power to detain in these circumstances is limited to cases where the mental illness is one recognized by objective medical expertise, and where the medical and legal definitions of mental illness have a close correlation.[76] In cases where a defendant is detained as a result of a special verdict of insanity when the 'disease' he was suffering from was one which lawyers but not medical professionals would classify as insanity there would seem to be an incompatibility.

Psychological blow – disease of mind (insanity) or external factor (non-insane automatism)?

Cases in other jurisdictions have raised the question whether a 'dissociative state' resulting from a 'psychological blow' amounts to insane or non-insane automatism. In *Rabey*[77]

[71] *Sullivan* [1984] AC 156. [72] *Hennessey* [1989] 2 All ER 9.

[73] *Smith* [1982] Crim LR 531 and see V. St John, 'Premenstrual Syndrome in the Criminal Law' [1997] Auckland Uni LR 331; S. M. Edwards, 'Mad Bad or Pre-Menstrual' (1988) 138 NLJ 456.

[74] *Burgess* [1991] 2 All ER 769. Irene Mackay, 'The Sleepwalker is not Insane' (1992) 55 MLR 714. Cf the Canadian Supreme Court in *Parks* (1990) 95 DLR (4th) 27.

[75] [1963] AC 386, [1961] 3 All ER 523.

[76] *Winterwerp v Netherlands* [1979] 2 EHRR 387. See P. Sutherland and C. Gearty, 'Insanity and the ECHR' [1992] Crim LR 418; E. Baker, above; B. Emmerson and A. Ashworth, *Human Rights and Criminal Justice* (2001). On the success of challenges in Jersey see R. D. Mackay, 'On Being Insane in Jersey Part Two' [2002] Crim LR 728.

[77] (1977) 37 CCC (2d) 461; affd [1980] SCR 513, 54 CCC (2d) 1. See also *Parnerkar* [1974] SCR 449, 10 CCC (2d) 253 and cases discussed by R. D. Mackay, 'Non-Organic Automatism' [1980] Crim LR 350.

D, a student who had become infatuated by a girl, V, discovered that V did not regard him particularly highly and reacted by hitting her on the head with a rock that he had taken from a geology laboratory. He was acquitted of causing bodily harm with intent on the ground of automatism. The trial judge accepted that D was in a dissociative state consequent upon the psychological blow of his rejection, which, he held, was an external factor, analogous to a blow to the skull, where the skull is thin, causing concussion. The Ontario Court of Appeal allowed the prosecution's appeal and ordered a new trial. A further appeal to the Supreme Court of Canada was dismissed. That court approved the judgment of Martin J, who took the view that 'the ordinary stresses and disappointments of life which are the common lot of mankind do not constitute an external cause . . .'.[78] The exceptional effect which this ordinary event had on D 'must be considered as having its source primarily in the [D's] psychological or emotional make-up'. Notwithstanding the powerful dissent by Dickson J, it is submitted that this is right and that in such a case if the evidence as to the dissociative state is accepted at all,[79] it should be treated as evidence of insanity. Once the judge has so categorized the defence, the onus of proving on a balance of probabilities that he was in a dissociative state is on D. If he and his medical witnesses are to be believed, he was not guilty, but he is a highly dangerous person.[80] Who is to say that the next ordinary stress of life will not lead him unconsciously to wield a deadly weapon? Policy clearly has a significant part to play here.

Martin J left open the question of the effect of an extraordinary event of such severity that it might reasonably be expected to cause a dissociative state in the average person. This, it is submitted, is a case of non-insane automatism because D has done nothing to show that he is any more dangerous to others than anyone else; and he should be simply acquitted. It is difficult to identify what should constitute such a degree of extraordinariness. In *T*[81] where the defendant had committed a robbery when suffering from Post Traumatic Stress Disorder as a result of being raped, the trial judge ruled that the rape was to be treated as an external factor. It would be uncontroversial to regard the rape as an extraordinary event, but it is unclear which if any other traumatic events will suffice. Further judicial clarification of the scope of this exceptional category of non-insane automatism would be welcome.

Defect of reason

The disease of the mind must have given rise to a defect of reason. It seems that the powers of reasoning must be impaired and that a mere failure to use powers of reasoning which one has is not within the M'Naghten Rules. When D claimed that she had taken articles from a supermarket without paying for them because of absentmindedness resulting from depression, it was held that, even if she was suffering from a disease of the mind (which is arguable), she had not raised the defence of insanity but was simply denying that she had *mens rea*.[82]

78 (1980) 54 CCC (2d) at 7.

79 Cf the scepticism of Williams about the acceptance of the evidence of 'over enthusiastic psychiatrists' in relation to the similar case of *Parnerkar* [1974] SCR 449, 10 CCC (2d) 253; Williams, TBCL (1st edn), at 612–613.

80 In fact, D's expert witness said D had no predisposition to dissociate; but the court, while bound to take account of medical evidence, may also take account of the facts of the case and apply its common sense to all the evidence.

81 [1990] Crim LR 256. And see *Huckerby* [2004] EWCA Crim 3251.

82 *Clarke* [1972] 1 All ER 219.

The nature and quality of his act

The phrase 'nature and quality of his act' refers to the physical nature and quality of the act and not to its moral or legal quality.[83] In modern terms, it means simply that D 'did not know what he was doing'.[84] It is of narrow application; illustrations given by leading writers are:

A kills B under an insane delusion that he is breaking a jar[85]

and

the madman who cut a woman's throat under the idea that he was cutting a loaf of bread.[86]

Of course, a person who was under such a delusion as these, apart altogether from insanity, could never be convicted of murder, simply because he had no *mens rea*. The important practical difference, however, is that, if the delusion arose from a disease of the mind, he will be liable to be (though no longer necessarily) indefinitely detained in a special hospital whereas, if it arose from some other cause, he will go entirely free. A person whose acts are involuntary because he is unconscious does not 'know the nature and quality of his act'.[87]

Knowledge that the act is wrong

This question is not whether the accused is able to distinguish between right and wrong in general, but whether he was able to appreciate the wrongness of the particular act he was doing at the particular time. It has always been clear that if D knew his act was contrary to law, he knew it was 'wrong' for this purpose. Thus in their first answer the judges in *M'Naghten*'s case said:[88]

. . . notwithstanding the party accused did the act complained of with a view, under the influence of insane delusion, of redressing or revenging some supposed grievance or injury, or of producing some public benefit, he is nevertheless punishable, according to the nature of the crime committed, if he knew at the time of committing such crime that he was acting contrary to law; by which expression we understand your lordships to mean the law of the land.

Even if D did not know his act was contrary to law, he was still liable if he knew that it was wrong 'according to the ordinary standard adopted by reasonable men'.[89] The fact that the accused thought his act was right was irrelevant if he knew that people generally considered it wrong. This again seems to be supported by the Rules:[90]

If the question were to be put as to the knowledge of the accused solely and exclusively with reference to the law of the land, it might tend to confound the jury, by inducing them to believe that an actual knowledge of the law of the land was essential to lead to a conviction: whereas the law is administered upon the principle that everyone must be taken conclusively to know it, without proof that he does know it. If the accused was conscious that the act was one which he ought not to do, and if that act was at the same time contrary to the law of the land, he is punishable.

83 *Codère* (1916) 12 Cr App R 21.
84 *Sullivan* [1983] 2 All ER 673 at 678.
85 Stephen, *Digest* (8th edn), at 6.
86 Kenny, *Outlines*, 76.
87 *Sullivan* [1983] 2 All ER 673 at 678, HL.
88 (1843) 10 Cl & Fin at 209.
89 *Codère* (1916) 12 Cr App R 21 at 27.
90 (1843) 10 Cl & Fin at 210.

A modern case, however suggests that the courts are concerned only with the accused's knowledge of legal wrongness. In *Windle*,[91] D was unhappily married to a woman, V, who was always speaking of committing suicide and who, according to medical evidence at the trial, was certifiably insane. D killed V by the administration of 100 aspirins. He then gave himself up to the police, saying, 'I suppose they will hang me for this'. A medical witness for the defence said that D was suffering from a form of communicated insanity known as *folie à deux*. Rebutting medical evidence was called, but the doctors on both sides agreed that he knew he was doing an act which the law forbade. Devlin J thereupon withdrew the issue from the jury. So far the decision accords perfectly with the law as stated above but, in the Court of Criminal Appeal, Lord Goddard CJ, in upholding the conviction, said:[92]

> Courts of law can only distinguish between that which is in accordance with the law and that which is contrary to law. . . . The law cannot embark on the question and it would be an unfortunate thing if it were left to juries to consider whether some particular act was morally right or wrong. The test must be whether it is contrary to law. . . .
>
> In the opinion of the court there is no doubt that in the M'Naghten Rules 'wrong' means contrary to law and not 'wrong' according to the opinion of one man or of a number of people on the question whether a particular act might or might not be justified.

It is thought that *Windle* is in accordance with authority in rejecting the arguments of the defence that D should be acquitted if, knowing his act to be against the law, he also believed it to be morally right. In practice it seems that juries commonly accept the defence in such cases.[93] The effect of the *obiter dictum* – it was no more than that – in *Windle* is that 'wrong' means only 'legally wrong', would seem to be to widen the defence by making it available to a person, who knows that his act is morally wrong but, owing to disease of the mind, fails to appreciate that it is also legally wrong. Such a case was not before the court.

The High Court of Australia has refused to follow *Windle*. In *Stapleton v R*[94] they made a detailed examination of the English law, before and after *M'Naghten* and came to the conclusion that *Windle* was wrongly decided. Their view was that if D believed his act to be right according to the ordinary standard of reasonable men he was entitled to be acquitted even if he knew it to be legally wrong. This would extend the scope of the defence, not only beyond what was laid down in *Windle*, but beyond what the law was believed to be before that case. While such an extension of the law may be desirable, it is difficult to reconcile with the M'Naghten Rules and to justify on the authorities.[95] It is unlikely to be followed by the courts in England. Should the defence be available where D kills a prostitute, knowing that to do so is murder, but believing that God has told him to rid the streets of such women?[96]

Whereas the defence of insanity is excessively broad in defining diseases of the mind, it is unsatisfactorily narrow in respect of what constitutes a sufficient awareness of wrongdoing.

[91] [1952] 2 QB 826, [1952] 2 All ER 1.

[92] [1952] 2 QB 826 at 833, 834, [1952] 2 All ER 1 at 1, 2.

[93] See R. D. Mackay and G. Kearns, 'More Fact(s) About the Insanity Defence' [1999] Crim LR 714 at 722.

[94] (1952) 86 CLR 358; see also *Weise* [1969] VR 953, especially at 960 et seq, per Barry J.

[95] *Stapleton v R* is discussed in a note by N. Morris, ' "Wrong" in the M'Naghten Rules' (1953) 16 MLR 435, which is criticized by J. Montrose, 'The M'Naghten Rules' (1954) 17 MLR 383.

[96] Cf Peter Sutcliffe (1981) 30 Apr, CCC. See A. Norrie, *Crime, Reason and History* (2nd edn, 2000), at 192–3.

Insane delusions and insanity

The judges were asked in *M'Naghten*'s case:

If a person under an insane delusion as to existing facts commits an offence in consequence thereof, is he thereby excused?

They replied:[97]

. . . the answer must, of course, depend on the nature of the delusion: but making the same assumption as we did before, namely, that he labours under such partial delusion only, and is not in other respects insane, we think he must be considered in the same situation as to responsibility as if the facts with respect to which the delusion exists were real. For example, if under the influence of his delusion he supposes another man to be in the act of attempting to take away his life, and he kills that man, as he supposes, in self-defence, he would be exempt from punishment. If his delusion was that the deceased had inflicted a serious injury to his character and fortune, and he killed him in revenge for such supposed injury, he would be liable to punishment.

This seems to add nothing to the earlier answers. The insane delusions that the judges had in mind seem to have been factual errors of the kind which prevent a man from knowing the nature and quality of his act or knowing it is wrong. The example given seems to fall within those rules.

The proposition that the insane person 'must be considered in the same situation as to responsibility as if the facts with respect to which the delusion exists were real' must be treated with caution. It must always be remembered that there must be an actual *actus reus*, accompanied by the appropriate *mens rea*, for a conviction. Suppose that D strangles his wife's poodle under the insane delusion that it is her illegitimate child. If the supposed facts were real he would be guilty of murder – but that is plainly impossible as there is no *actus reus.*[98] Nor is there any crime in respect of the dog, for there is no *mens rea*. The rule seems merely to emphasize that delusions which do not prevent D from having *mens rea* will afford no defence. As Lord Hewart CJ rather crudely put it, 'the mere fact that a man thinks he is John the Baptist does not entitle him to shoot his mother'. A case often discussed is that of a man who is under the insane delusion that he is obeying a divine command. Some American courts have held that such a belief affords a defence. Yet if the accused knows that his act is forbidden by law, it seems clear he is liable. Stephen certainly thought that this was so:

My own opinion is that if a special divine order were given to a man to commit murder, I should certainly hang him for it, unless I got a special divine order not to hang him.[99]

Irresistible impulse

It is recognized by psychiatrists that a man may know the nature and quality of an act, may even know that it is wrong, and yet perform it under an impulse that is almost or quite uncontrollable. Such a man has no defence under the M'Naghten Rules. The matter was considered in *Kopsch*:[100] D, according to his own admission, killed his uncle's wife. He said that he strangled her with his necktie at her own request. (If this was an insane

97 (1843) 10 Cl & Fin at 211.

98 Nor, notwithstanding *Shivpuri*, below, p 424, should an insane delusion entail liability for an attempt.

99 2 HCL 160, n 1.

100 (1925) 19 Cr App R 50, CCA. See also *True* (1922) 16 Cr App R 164; *Sodeman* [1936] 2 All ER 1138, PC.

delusion, it would not, of course, afford a defence under the rules stated above.) There was evidence that he had acted under the direction of his subconscious mind. Counsel argued that the judge should have directed the jury that a person under an impulse which he cannot control is not criminally responsible. This was described by Lord Hewart CJ as a 'fantastic theory . . . which if it were to become part of our criminal law, would be merely subversive'.[101]

The judges have steadily opposed the admissibility of such a defence on the ground of the difficulty – or impossibility – of distinguishing between an impulse which proves irresistible because of insanity and one which is irresistible because of ordinary motives of greed, jealousy or revenge. The view has also been expressed that the harder an impulse is to resist, the greater is the need for a deterrent.[102]

The law does not recognize irresistible impulse even as a symptom from which a jury might deduce insanity within the meaning of the Rules.[103] If, however, medical evidence were tendered in a particular case that the uncontrollable impulse, to which the accused in that case had allegedly been subject, was a symptom that he did not know his act was wrong, it would be open to the jury to act on that evidence.[104] But it is not permissible for a judge to make use in one case of medical knowledge which he may have acquired from the evidence in another, in his direction to the jury.[105]

Although the M'Naghten Rules remain unaltered a partial defence of irresistible impulse has now been admitted into the law through the new defence of diminished responsibility (see below).[106]

Burden of proof

The M'Naghten Rules laid down that:

> every man is presumed to be sane, and to possess a sufficient degree of reason to be responsible for his crimes, until the contrary be proved to [the jury's] satisfaction; and that to establish a defence on the ground of insanity, it must be clearly proved, etc.[107]

It seems from these words that the judges were intending to put the burden of proof squarely on the accused, and so it has always been subsequently assumed.[108] Insanity is stated to be the one exception at common law to the rule that it is the duty of the prosecution to prove the accused's guilt in all particulars.[109] He does not have to satisfy that heavy onus of proof beyond reasonable doubt which rests on the prosecution but is entitled to a verdict in his favour if he proves his case on a balance of probabilities, the standard which rests on the claimant in a civil action. If the jury think it is more likely than not that he is insane within the meaning of the Rules, then he is entitled to their verdict.

When, however, consideration is given to what has to be proved to establish insanity

101 (1925) 19 Cr App R 50 at 51.

102 As Canadian judge, Riddell J, put it: 'If you cannot resist an impulse in any other way, we will hang a rope in front of your eyes, and perhaps that will help': *Creighton* (1909) 14 CCC 349.

103 *A-G for State of South Australia v Brown* [1960] AC 432, [1960] 1 All ER 734, PC.

104 Ibid. See also *Sodeman* (1936) 55 CLR 192 at 203.

105 [1960] AC 432 at 449. 106 See p 464. 107 (1843) 10 Cl & Fin at 210.

108 *Stokes* (1848) 3 Car & Kir 185; *Layton* (1849) 4 Cox CC 149; *Smith* (1910) 6 Cr App R 19; *Coelho* (1914) 30 TLR 535; *Bratty v A-G for Northern Ireland* [1963] AC 386, [1961] 3 All ER 523.

109 *Woolmington v DPP* [1935] AC 462.

under the first limb of the Rules, there is an apparent conflict with the general rule requiring the prosecution to prove *mens rea.* This requires proof that the accused was either intentional or reckless with respect to all those consequences and circumstances of his act which constitute the *actus reus* of the crime with which he is charged. But this, in effect, is to prove that the accused *did* know the nature and quality of his act. The general rule, therefore, says that the prosecution must prove these facts; the special rule relating to insanity says that the defence must disprove them![110] Williams argued[111] that the only burden on the accused is the 'evidential' one of introducing sufficient evidence to raise a reasonable doubt in the jury's minds; and that the burden of *proof* is on the prosecution. This solution appears to be the best way of resolving the inconsistency.[112]

This problem does not arise when the accused's defence takes the form that he did not know that his act was wrong. Here he is setting up the existence of facts which are quite outside the prosecution's case and there is no inconsistency in putting the onus on the accused. It is very strange that the onus of proof should be on the Crown if the defence is based on the first limb of the Rules and on the accused if it should be on the second. Yet the authorities[113] seem clearly to establish that the onus in the case of the second limb is on the accused. It is not possible to argue that the courts really meant the evidential burden for they have said very clearly that the burden is one of proof 'on balance of probabilities', the same standard that the claimant in a civil action must satisfy. Whatever may be the position regarding the first limb of the defence then, it seems clear that, under the second, the onus is on the accused.

The anomaly is emphasized by the decision of the House of Lords in *Bratty v Attorney-General for Northern Ireland*[114] that, where the defence is automatism arising otherwise than through a disease of the mind, the burden of proof is on the prosecution. It is difficult to see why a man whose alleged disability arises from a disease of the mind should be convicted whereas one whose alleged disability arises from some other cause, would, in exactly the same circumstances, be acquitted.[115]

The scope of the defence

Hale[116] thought insanity was a defence only to capital charges but that opinion is no longer tenable. In *Horseferry Road Magistrates' Court, ex p K*[117] the court accepted the proposition in *Archbold*,[118] relied on by the applicant, that the defence of insanity 'is based on the absence of *mens rea*'. This may be true where D asserts that he did not know the nature and quality of his act, but it is not true where he asserts that he did not know the act was wrong.[119] Awareness of 'wrongness' is not an element in *mens rea.* It seems that *Ex p K* misled the court in *DPP v H*[120] into holding that the defence does not

110 See further, T. Jones, above, n 56.

111 CLGP, at 165.

112 Cf however, *Cottle* [1958] NZLR 999 at 1019, per North J.

113 *Sodeman v R* [1936] 2 All ER 1138: *Carr-Briant* [1943] KB 607, [1943] 2 All ER 156.

114 [1963] AC 386, [1961] 3 All ER 523.

115 The Butler proposals on onus of proof appear below, p 271.

116 I PC, c 4, and N. Walker, *Crime and Insanity in England*, I, 80; S. White (1984) 148 JPN 412 at 419.

117 Above, p 256, n 50.

118 1996 edn, at 17–109.

119 See also *Moore v The State* [2001] UKPC 4.

120 [1997] 1 WLR 1406. This is perhaps another manifestation of the fallacy that an offence of strict liablity requires 'no *mens rea*'. The error of the trial judge in *Blackburn v Bowering*, below, p 540.

apply to an offence of strict liability – in that case driving with excess alcohol. It is submitted that the defence is of general application. Hawkins,[121] cited by the court in *Ex p K*, states: 'those who are under a natural disability of distinguishing between good and evil, as . . . ideots and lunaticks . . . are not punishable *by any criminal prosecution whatsoever*' [the court's italics].

The special verdict of insanity and the right of appeal

The Trial of Lunatics Act 1883 now provides that if it appears to jury that the defendant 'did the act or made the omission charged but was insane as aforesaid at the time the jury shall return a special verdict that the accused is not guilty by reason of insanity.' In *Attorney-General's Reference (No 3 of 1998)*[122] it was held that the words 'act' and 'omission' mean the *actus reus* of the offence as defined in the 8th edition of this book, p 28.[123] The prosecution do not have to prove *mens rea*. To require them to do so would be inconsistent with the rule that the onus is on D to prove that he did not know the nature and quality of his act.

Although it may seem, at first sight, highly illogical to give the accused a right of appeal from an acquittal, this was a highly desirable reform which was affected by the 1964 Act. If it were the case that a special verdict of insanity could be found only where D himself had so pleaded, it would be reasonable that there should be no appeal; but this was not the case. Thus it will be recalled that in *Kemp*[124] D's contention was that he should be entirely acquitted, but it was held that the medical evidence established insanity within the M'Naghten Rules. The issue was decided against D, yet he had no right of appeal. A similar position arose where, after the Homicide Act 1957, D raised the defence of diminished responsibility and the prosecution were thereupon allowed to introduce evidence of insanity within the M'Naghten Rules.[125] For these reasons, a right of appeal to the Court of Appeal and the House of Lords is provided by s 12 of the Criminal Appeal Act 1968, subject to the same conditions as apply in criminal appeals generally. The right of appeal is not limited to the case where the issue is decided against D's contention in the court below. It is now possible for D to appeal against the finding (no longer express but now implicit in the verdict) that he did the act or against the finding that he was insane when he did so.

Function of the jury

It has been laid down for defences of both insanity and diminished responsibility that:[126]

> . . . it is for the jury and not for medical men [*sic*] of whatever eminence to determine the issue. Unless and until Parliament ordains that this question is to be determined by a panel of medical men, it is to a jury, after a proper direction by a judge, that by the law of this country the decision is to be entrusted.

121 Hawkins 1 PC 1–2.

122 [1999] 3 All ER 40, [1993] Crim LR 986.

123 See above, p 9.

124 Above, p 259.

125 *Rivett* (1950) 34 Cr App R 87 at 94; *Latham* [1965] Crim LR 434; *Walton v R* [1978] AC 788, [1978] 1 All ER 542; [1977] Crim LR 747, PC.

126 *Matheson* [1958] 2 All ER 87, 42 Cr App R 145; *Bailey* (1961) 66 Cr App R 31n, [1961] Crim LR 828, *Sanders* [1991] Crim LR 781 – all cases concerning diminished responsibility – but the same principle surely applies to insanity.

The law regarding insanity, however, is now modified by s 1 of the 1991 Act which provides that a jury shall not return a special verdict of not guilty by reason of insanity except on the written or oral evidence of two or more registered medical practitioners of whom at least one is approved by the Home Secretary as having special experience in the field of mental disorder. The jury may still have to decide between conflicting medical evidence; but if the medical evidence is wholly in favour of a special verdict (or of diminished responsibility) and there is nothing in the facts or surrounding circumstances which could lead to a contrary conclusion, then a verdict of guilty (or guilty of murder as the case may be) will be upset. If there are facts which, in the opinion of the court, justify the jury in coming to a conclusion different from that of the experts, their verdict will be upheld.

(iii) Proposals for reform of insanity defence[127]

Almost from the moment of their formulation the Rules have been subjected to vigorous criticism, primarily by doctors, but also by lawyers. The Rules, being based on outdated psychological views, are too narrow, it is said, and exclude many persons who ought not to be held responsible. They are concerned only with defects of reason and take no account of emotional or volitional factors whereas modern medical science is unwilling to divide the mind into separate compartments and to consider the intellect apart from the emotions and the will.

In 1923 a committee under the chairmanship of Lord Atkin recommended that a prisoner should not be held responsible 'when the act is committed under an impulse which the prisoner was by mental disease in substance deprived of any power to resist'.[128]

The recommendation was not implemented. In 1953 the Royal Commission on Capital Punishment[129] made much more far-reaching proposals. They thought that the question of responsibility is not primarily a matter of law or of medicine, but of morals and, therefore, most appropriately decided by a jury of ordinary people. They thought that the best course would be to abrogate the rules altogether and 'leave the jury to determine whether at the time of the act the accused was suffering from disease of the mind (or mental deficiency) to such a degree that he ought not to be held responsible'.[130]

This meant abandoning the assumption that it is necessary to have a rule of law defining the relation of insanity to criminal responsibility; but the Commission thought this assumption had broken down in practice anyway.[131] As an alternative, which they thought less satisfactory but better than leaving the Rules unchanged, the Commission recommended that a third limb be added to the Rules: that the accused 'was incapable of preventing himself from committing it . . .'.[132]

The Butler Committee proposed a new approach which has been substantially incorporated in the Draft Code. There would be a new verdict of 'not guilty on evidence

127 S. Dell, 'Wanted; An Insanity Defence that Can be Used' [1983] Crim LR 431.

128 Cmd 2005. 129 Cmd 8932.

130 Ibid, para 333. Cf Walker's criticism, above, at 110–111: 'By what criterion could one tell whether this or that case "ought" to have been included? Could the criterion be expressed in words, or was it ineffable?'

131 The Commission was impressed by Lord Cooper's view that 'However much you charge a jury as to the M'Naghten Rules or any other test, the question they would put to themselves when they retire is – "Is this man mad or is he not?" '; Report, para 3.22.

132 Cmd 2005.

of mental disorder' – 'a mental disorder verdict'. As under the M'Naghten Rules, such a verdict would be returned in two types of case: (i) where the mental disorder precludes the required fault (corresponding to the 'nature and quality' limb), and (ii) where all the elements of the offence are proved but the mental disorder nevertheless should result in an acquittal (corresponding to the 'wrong' limb). The Code reverses the order.[133] Clause 35 provides:

(1) A mental disorder verdict shall be returned if the defendant is proved to have committed an offence but it is proved on the balance of probabilities (whether by the prosecution or by the defendant) that he was at the time suffering from severe mental illness or severe mental handicap.

'Severe mental illness' is defined in the terms proposed by Butler as follows:

'Severe mental illness' means a mental illness which has one or more of the following characteristics –

(a) lasting impairment of intellectual functions shown by failure of memory, orientation, comprehension and learning capacity;
(b) lasting alteration of mood of such degree as to give rise to delusional appraisal of the defendant's situation, his past or his future, or that of others, or lack of any appraisal;
(c) delusional beliefs, persecutory, jealous or grandiose;
(d) abnormal perceptions associated with delusional misinterpretation of events;
(e) thinking so disordered as to prevent reasonable appraisal of the defendant's situation of reasonable communication with others.

'Severe mental handicap' means: 'a state of arrested or incomplete development of mind which includes severe impairment or intelligence and social functioning', a definition adapted from that in the Mental Health Act 1959.

If the Code had stopped here, as Butler intended, this would have involved a major change of principle in that there need be no causal connection between the mental disorder and the commission of the act. Butler thought that the disorders specified are of such severity that a causal connection could safely be presumed. D's belief that he was John the Baptist, presumably 'a grandiose delusional belief', would be a defence to a charge of murdering his mother.[134] More realistically, D would have a defence to a charge of robbing a bank or of dangerous driving because he had a jealous delusional belief that his wife was committing adultery. The Law Commission thought such a result unacceptable and so cl 35(2) provides:

Subsection (1) does not apply if the court or jury is satisfied beyond reasonable doubt that the offence was not attributable to the severe mental illness or severe mental handicap.

The effect is that there is a presumption that the commission of the offence was attributable to the disorder but it is rebuttable by proof beyond reasonable doubt.

Clause 36 provides the other limb of the defence:

A mental disorder verdict shall be returned if –

133 For an alternative approach to reform see the recent Scottish proposals – *Insanity and Diminished Responsibility*, Report No 195 (2004) in which the M'Naghten approach is rejected in favour of a model found in the USA where the defence is based on a lack of criminal responsibility due to mental disorder.

134 Above, p 265, n 98.

(a) the defendant is acquitted of an offence only because, by reason of evidence of mental disorder or a combination of mental disorder and intoxication, it is found that he acted or may have acted in a state of automatism, or without the fault required for the offence, or believing that an exempting circumstance existed; and

(b) it is proved on the balance of probabilities (whether by the prosecution or by the defendant) that he was suffering from mental disorder at the time of the act.

The clause applies only where the mental disorder (or mental disorder combined with intoxication) is the *sole* cause of D's condition, lack of fault, or mistake. Like the Rules, it applies to a person who, because of mental disorder, is under a delusion that he is the victim of a deadly attack and kills, as he supposes, in self-defence ('an exempting circumstance').

Onus of proof under the Code

The onus of proving *mens rea* or, when the issue has been raised, of disproving automatism or belief in an exempting circumstance, is on the prosecution. If they fail in this respect, D must be acquitted and the only question (where there is some evidence of mental disorder) is whether there should be an absolute acquittal or an acquittal on evidence of mental disorder. It seems right in principle that D should be entitled to an absolute acquittal, unless the jury are satisfied (either by the prosecution or the defence) that he was suffering from mental disorder; and cl 36(b), following Butler, so provides. Under cl 35 the choice for the jury is between conviction ('the defendant is proved to have committed an offence') and a mental disorder verdict so it might be thought the onus should be on the prosecution to prove one or the other. Butler, however, proposed that, to avoid confusing the jury, the onus of proving mental disorder should again be on the party alleging it, whether prosecution or defence; and cl 35 follows that proposal.

The Code would produce substantial improvements on the present position. It has been suggested however that it would still be incompatible with Article 5 of the ECHR.[135]

As for the present rules, it should be noted that there are some defenders, and the case for them has been most cogently put by Lord Devlin:

> As it is a matter of theory, I think there is something logical – it may be astringently logical, but it is logical – in selecting as the test of responsibility to the law, reason and reason alone. It is reason which makes a man responsible to the law. It is reason which gives him sovereignty over animate and inanimate things. It is what distinguishes him from the animals, which emotional disorder does not; it is what makes him man; it is what makes him subject to the law. So it is fitting that nothing other than a defect of reason should give complete absolution.[136]

3. Non-insane automatism

A claim by the defendant that his consciousness was so impaired that he was acting in a state of physical involuntariness is a claim of automatism. This concept – a denial of a

[135] See Ashworth, POCL, at 212.

[136] 'Mental Abnormality and the Criminal Law' in *Changing Legal Objectives* (ed, R. St J. MacDonald, Toronto, 1963) 71 at 85. Cf A. F. Goldstein, *The Insanity Defence* (1967).

voluntary act – has been discussed in Chapter 4 above in the context of the *actus reus*.[137] This summary is presented here in juxtaposition to the analysis of insanity and intoxication to assist in understanding all three. It should be noted that where the defendant makes this claim the defence will only succeed if his loss of control was complete; an impaired consciousness is not automatism.[138] This is arguably an unduly strict approach. The plea of automatism can be made in relation to all offences (subject to what is said below regarding self-induced automatism).

The defence of non-insane automatism can arise only where D's loss of consciousness is caused by the operation of some *external* factor on D. Automatism may arise where D suffers: a reflex spasm in response to being attacked by a swarm of bees,[139] a blow to the head causing concussion, an injection of insulin,[140] a rape or other serious violent attack causing post traumatic stress disorder, etc.[141] This requirement is critical in distinguishing non-insane automatism from insanity and is discussed in the preceding section.

(a) Self-induced automatism

Where D's state of automatism arises from his voluntary conduct (usually, ingesting substances), the operation of the defence falls into four categories.

(1) Where the automatism arises from D's taking a substance in *bona fide* compliance with his[142] medical prescription the defence is a complete one to all crimes, provided D's loss of control is complete and he is automaton. D who has an adverse reaction to an anaesthetic or prescribed drug and hits V will be acquitted on charges (whether they be murder or assault) if he was automaton at the time.

(2) Where the crime with which D is charged is one of specific intent (discussed below p 278) and the automatism arises from D's taking a substance otherwise than in accordance with a medical prescription, the defence will result in acquittal if D's loss of consciousness was complete to the extent that he was automaton.

(3) Where the crime with which D is charged is one of basic intent (below, p 278), and the automatism arises from D's voluntarily taking a substance otherwise than in accordance with his medical prescription the defence will fail if the substance ingested was one commonly known to create states of unpredictability or aggression (alcohol, heroin, cannabis, cocaine, etc). Thus, D charged with reckless criminal damage will have no success with a defence based on his claim that he was 'completely out of it' and unconscious when he swung his leg out and damaged the property.

137 See the discussion in Scots law as to whether the defence is one of a denial of *mens rea* or *actus reus* (P. R. Ferguson, 'The Limits of the Automatism Defence' (1991) 36 J Law Soc Scotland 446; I. MacDougall 'Automatism – Negation of *Mens Rea*' (1992) 37 J Law Soc Scotland 57). It is surely the latter.

138 *A-G's Reference (No 2 of 1992)* [1992] QB 91. This is not always easy to establish see *Nelson* [2004] EWCA Crim 333 (reliance on hearsay). The Draft Code would permit the defence in circumstances of impaired consciousness (cl 33.)

139 *Hill v Baxter* [1958] 1 QB 277.

140 *Quick* [1973] QB 910.

141 *R v T* [1990] Crim LR 256.

142 See the odd acceptance of the defence where D took his friend's 'pills' and mixed them with alcohol: *Buck* (2002), discussed by K. Roberts (2002) 99 Law Soc Gaz 40.

(4) Where the crime with which D is charged is one of basic intent, and the automatism arises from D's taking a substance otherwise than in accordance with his medical prescription but where the substance is not commonly known to create a state of unpredictability or aggression the defence will result in an acquittal only if in taking the substance D was not subjectively reckless as to the effect it would have. Thus, D who is charged with reckless criminal damage after taking a soporific drug will not succeed in his plea of automatism if he was aware when taking the drug that it posed the risk for him of a state of unpredictability of aggression.

Although the defence of automatism operates to deny the *actus reus* of the offence, in cases of self-induced automatism, the approach is founded on the same policy concerns that underpin the rules relating to the plea of intoxication which, if accepted at all, operates as a denial of *mens rea*.

4. Intoxication[143]

It will come as no surprise to hear that the law in this area is heavily policy based. There is often little by way of principle underpinning the operation of the law. The relationship between intoxication and crime, particularly violent crime and public disorder needs no elucidation here. The following discussion analyses the three key distinctions drawn by the courts in their application of the plea of intoxication:

(1) Is the intoxication voluntary or involuntary?

(2) If voluntary, is the crime charged one of specific 'intent' or 'basic' intent?

(3) If basic intent, is the drug involved one of a dangerous nature (is it one known to create states of unpredictability or aggression)?

Before analysing these three issues, it is important to emphasize the general limits on the plea of intoxication. Intoxication is not, and never has been, a 'defence' in itself. It is never a defence for D to say, however convincingly, that but for the drink he would not have behaved as he did.[144] Because alcohol and other drugs weaken the restraints and inhibitions which normally govern our conduct, a person may do things when drunk that he would never dream of doing when sober.

(a) Intoxication as a denial of *mens rea*

Intoxication impairs a person's perception and judgment so he may fail to be aware of facts, or to foresee results of his conduct, of which he would certainly have been aware, or have foreseen, if he had been sober. So, intoxication may be the reason why the defendant lacked the *mens rea* of the crime charged. When D relies on evidence of intoxication he does so for the purpose of showing he lacked *mens rea*. This is its only relevance so far as liability to conviction (as opposed to sentence) is concerned.

143 The focus here is exclusively on D's intoxication. V's intoxication may affect the substantive law, for example, in relation to sexual offences discussed below, p 606.

144 *DPP v Beard* [1920] AC 479 at 502–504.

It must always be borne in mind when considering intoxication that if D had the *mens rea* for the crime charged he is guilty. A drunken or drugged intent suffice for a crime of intention, a drunken or drugged awareness of a risk of the prohibited harm will suffice for a crime of recklessness. This is so even though drink impaired or negatived D's ability to judge between right and wrong or to resist temptation or provocation and even though, in his drunken state, he found the impulse to act as he did irresistible.

In many of the cases where drunkenness is relevant, the defence, in substance, is one of mistake and the evidence of drunkenness is circumstantial evidence that the mistake was made. Two examples quoted by Lord Denning[145] are: (i) where a nurse got so drunk at a christening that she put the baby on the fire in mistake for a log of wood;[146] and (ii) where a drunken man thought his friend, lying in bed, was a theatrical dummy and stabbed him to death.[147] Lord Denning said there would be a defence to murder in each of these cases. These mistakes were highly unreasonable and, in the case of a sober person, it would be extremely difficult to persuade a jury that they were made. The relevance of the evidence of drunkenness is simply that it makes these mistakes much more credible. Similarly where D denies that he foresaw some obvious consequence of his action. A denial which would be quite incredible in the case of a sober person may be readily accepted when there is evidence that D was drunk.

In *Beard* it was said that intoxication was a defence only if it rendered D *incapable* of forming the *mens rea*.[148] This goes too far. Proof of a lack of capacity to form *mens rea* is of course conclusive that *mens rea* was not present; but it is now established that it is not necessary to go so far. It is sufficient that D lacked *mens rea* on that occasion even though he was capable of forming the necessary intent. Equally, a drunken person may be capable, notwithstanding his drunkenness, of forming the intent to kill and yet not do so. The nurse at the christening was capable of forming the intent to tend the fire, so she was probably capable of forming an intention to kill. The important thing is that she did not do so – and the drunkenness was highly relevant to rebut the inference which might otherwise have arisen from her conduct. The question is, taking D's intoxicated state into account did he in fact form the necessary *mens rea*?[149] The onus of proof – again contrary to certain *dicta* in *Beard*[150] – is clearly on the Crown to establish that, notwithstanding the alleged intoxication, D formed the intent.[151]

In a spate of recent cases the courts have taken the unwelcome and it is submitted unduly restrictive approach to the question of when an intoxication plea gets off the ground. In *Soolkal and another v The State*,[152] *McKnight*[153] and *P*[154] the courts have

[145] In *A-G for Northern Ireland v Gallagher* [1963] AC 349 at 381m, [1961] 3 All ER 299 at 313.

[146] (1748) 18 *Gentleman's Magazine*, 570; quoted in Kenny, *Outlines*, 29.

[147] (1951) The Times, 13 Jan.

[148] [1920] AC 479 at 501–502, HL.

[149] *Pordage* [1975] Crim LR 575, CA, following *dicta* in *Sheehan* [1975] 2 All ER 960, [1975] Crim LR 339 and commentary, CA, *Cole* [1993] Crim LR 300. To the same effect are *Menniss* [1973] 2 NSWLR 113 and *Kamipeli* [1975] 2 NZLR 610. But cf *Groark* [1999] Crim LR 669.

[150] [1920] AC 479 at 502.

[151] *Sheehan*, above. *Bowden* [1993] Crim LR 379. When evidence emerges, whatever its source, of such intoxication as might have prevented D's forming a specific intent the judge must direct the jury on it: *Bennett* [1995] Crim LR 877. Cf *McKinley* [1994] Crim LR 944, where the point was left open. The absence of a *Sheehan* direction seems to be a fertile ground of appeal: see *Golding* [2004] EWCA Crim 858.

[152] [1999] 1 WLR 2011, PC.

[153] (2000) The Times, 5 May.

[154] [2004] EWCA Crim 1043.

suggested that D is required to provide specific evidence to show that he was intoxicated and that he lacked *mens rea*. This burden is not satisfied by evidence that he had consumed so much alcohol that he was intoxicated or by a loss of memory owing to intoxication. The courts are surely imposing to onerous a duty on D who is not raising a defence in the true sense but rather denying the element of *mens rea* which it is always incumbent on the Crown to prove.

(i) Intoxicated *mens rea*

If D had the *mens rea* for the crime charged it makes no difference whether his intoxication was voluntarily or involuntary, nor whether the crime was one of specific or basic intent, nor whether the drug was of a dangerous or non-dangerous variety. In *Kingston*[155] D may have given way to his paedophiliac inclinations only because E had surreptitiously laced his drink with intent that he should do so. D, however, knew what he was doing; he intended to commit a sexual assault on a 15-year-old boy. That was the *mens rea* of the offence. The judge had rightly directed the jury that a drugged intention is still an intention. The fact that, but for the secretly administered drug, he would not have formed the intent was a matter going only to mitigation of the penalty.[156]

(b) Involuntary intoxication

Where, as a result of involuntary intoxication, D lacks the *mens rea* of the offence, it is submitted that he must be acquitted. This is so whether the crime charged is one of specific or basic intent. The offence has not been committed and there is absolutely no reason why the law should pretend that it has. On a charge of strict liability, the involuntary intoxication will not avail D since there is no *mens rea* for it to displace. In cases of alleged negligence, in principle, D ought only to be liable if the reasonable person would have acted in the same way had he suffered the effects of the involuntary intoxication.

In *Kingston* Lord Mustill referred to a number of Scottish decisions to the effect that a defence is made out if it is 'based . . . on an inability to form *mens rea* due to some external factor which was outwith the accused's control and which he was not bound to foresee'. The *dicta* quoted all required an inability to form the intent. Inability is certainly a conclusive answer; but, it is submitted that, whatever the position in Scotland, in England the ultimate question is whether D did form the *mens rea* and, if he did not – perhaps because he made a drunken mistake of fact – he must be acquitted, even though he was capable of forming the intent. This is the law in those cases where voluntary intoxication may be the basis of defence to an offence of specific intent, and it ought to apply, *a fortiori*, to involuntary intoxication.

Involuntary intoxication is narrowly defined. If D knew he was drinking alcohol, he could not claim that the resulting intoxication was involuntary merely because he

155 [1994] 3 All ER 353, HL, above, p 92. See J. Horder, 'Pleading Involuntary Lack of Capacity' (1993) 52 CLJ 298; R. Smith and L. Clements, 'Involuntary Intoxication, The threshold of inhibition and the instigation of crime' (1995) 46 NILQ 210.

156 The case prompted interesting calls for a new defence applicable where D acted out of character. See G. R. Sullivan, 'Involuntary Intoxication and Beyond' [1994] Crim LR 272; 'Making Excuses', in S. Shute and A. Simester (eds), *Harm and Culpability* (1996) 131; V. Tadros, 'The Character of Excuse' (2001) 21 OJLS 495;

under-estimated the amount he was consuming[157] or the effect it would have on him. Intoxication is probably 'involuntary' only if D was unaware that he was taking an intoxicant. It covers the case where D's lemonade is laced with vodka and he is unaware that he has consumed any alcohol, he can rely on evidence of his drunken condition.[158] Similarly, perhaps, where he has taken drink under duress.[159] It also covers the special case where a person becomes intoxicated through taking drugs (presumably including alcohol) voluntarily in *bona fide* pursuance of medical treatment or prescription. This is likely to be rarely applicable to drink but it might apply where, for example, brandy is administered to D after an accident.

As intoxication is nearly always voluntary, it is probably for D to raise the issue if he wishes to contend that it is involuntary. The onus of proof will then generally be on the Crown:[160] but the Public Order Act 1986, s 6(5), for the purposes of offences under that Act, requires D to 'show' that his intoxication was not self-induced or caused by medical treatment. This was presumably intended to put the onus of proof on D; but 'show', in contrast with 'prove' which is used in other sections of the Act, might be taken to impose no more than an evidential burden – more especially under the Human Rights Act 1998 giving force to Article 6(2) of the ECHR.[161]

(c) Voluntary intoxication

(i) Basic and specific intent crimes

D is entitled to an acquittal where his voluntary intoxication is such that he did not form the *mens rea* for the offence of specific intent. It must be emphasized that this applies where there is a lack of *mens rea*, not merely a reduction of inhibition; a drunken intent is nevertheless an intent.

In the case of a crime not requiring 'specific intent' D may be convicted if he was voluntarily intoxicated by a dangerous drug at the time of committing the offence, though he did not have the *mens rea* required in all other circumstances for that offence and even though he was in a state of automatism at the time of doing the act.

(ii) The rule in *Majewski*

In *DPP v Majewski*[162] the House of Lords has confirmed the rule, obscurely stated in *Beard*,[163] that evidence of self-induced intoxication negativing *mens rea* is a defence to a charge of a crime requiring a specific intent but not to a charge of any other crime.

157 *Allen* [1988] Crim LR 698.

158 Above, p 275. In *Majewski*, below, the Lord Chancellor pointed out that the drugs taken were not medically prescribed.

159 Cf *Kingston*, above. But what of the much more common case where D has voluntarily taken some drink and his companions surreptitiously add more? Probably, the jury should be told to convict only if satisfied that the drink voluntarily taken *contributed* to his lack of awareness.

160 *Stripp* (1978) 69 Cr App R 318 at 323; *Bailey* [1983] 2 All ER 503 at 507.

161 Cf *Lambert* [2001] 3 All ER 577; *A-G's Reference (No 4 of 2002)* [2004] UKHL 40; [2005] Crim LR 200 above, p 26.

162 [1977] AC 443, [1976] 2 All ER 142, [1976] Crim LR 374, and commentary. G. Williams, 'Intoxication of Specific Intent' (1976) 126ii NLJ 658; A. D. Gold, 'An Untrimmed Beard' (1976) 19 Crim LQ 34; A. Dashwood, 'Logic and the Lords in *Majewski*' [1977] Crim LR 532 and 591.

163 [1920] AC 479.

On one interpretation, the case imposes a rule of substantive law that, where D relies on voluntary intoxication as a defence to a charge of a crime not requiring 'specific intent', the prosecution need not prove any intention or foresight, whatever the definition of the crime may say, nor indeed any voluntary act. It follows that s 8 of the Criminal Justice Act 1967[164] has no application. There is, it appears, an implied qualification to every statute creating an offence and specifying a *mens rea* other than a specific intent. The *mens rea* must be proved – except, we must infer, where the accused was intoxicated through the voluntary taking of drink or drugs.

On this view it is fatal for a person charged with a crime not requiring specific intent who claims that he did not have *mens rea* to support his defence with evidence that he had taken drink and drugs. By so doing he dispenses the Crown from the duty, which until that moment lay upon them, of proving beyond reasonable doubt that he had *mens rea. Mens rea* ceases to be relevant. Can the Crown escape from this duty by leading evidence, or extracting an admission in cross-examination, that D had taken drink so as to diminish his capacity to foresee the consequences of his acts? According to Lord Salmon[165] in *Majewski* the question the House was deciding was whether the accused could rely *by way of defence* on the fact that he had voluntarily taken drink. But there are other *dicta* which suggest that D is held liable without the usual *mens rea* because he has taken the drink – the taking of the drink is the foundation of his liability[166] – a variety of *mens rea* – though not in the sense in which that term is used in this book. It is a form of 'prior fault'. If that be right, there is no reason why the Crown should not set out to prove it instead of seeking to prove *mens rea* in the sense of intention or recklessness.

The difficulty in principled terms with this approach is that it deems the defendant's negligence or recklessness in becoming voluntarily intoxicated his 'prior fault' to be sufficient *mens rea* for the crime. This is despite the fact that there is no contemporaneity between the fault in becoming intoxicated and the commission of the *actus reus* of the crime. And more importantly, despite the fact that the degree of fault in becoming intoxicated (foresight or awareness of becoming intoxicated) bears no correlation to the *mens rea* that would normally be required – foresight or awareness of a risk of a prohibited harm specified in the offence.

It seems that this rule applies whatever the degree of intoxication, if D claimed that it prevented him from foreseeing or knowing what he would have foreseen or known had he been sober. It is true that Lord Elwyn-Jones at one point[167] posed the question before the House much more narrowly – as that of a person who 'consciously and deliberately takes alcohol and drugs not on medical prescription, but in order to escape from reality, to go "on a trip", to become hallucinated . . .'. Such a person is readily distinguishable from the ordinary 'social drinker' who becomes intoxicated in the course of a convivial evening. The former, intending to reduce himself to a state in which he

164 Above, p 125.
165 [1977] AC 443
166 'His course of conduct in reducing himself by drugs and drink to that condition in my view supplies the evidence of *mens rea*, of guilty mind, certainly sufficient for crimes of basic intent': per Lord Elwyn-Jones LC [1976] 2 All ER 142 at 150. 'There is no juristic reason why mental incapacity (short of M'Naghten insanity) brought about by self-induced intoxication to realize what one is doing or its probable consequences should not be such a state of mind stigmatized as wrongful by the criminal law; and there is every practical reason why it should be': per Lord Simon at 153.
167 [1977] AC 443 at 471.

will have no control over his actions, might well be said to be in some sense reckless as to what he will do while in that state. The same cannot be said of the latter. But the general tenor of the speeches, as well as earlier and subsequent cases, is against any such distinction.[168]

An alternative view is that *Majewski* does not create a rule of substantive law, but one of evidence. On this view, once D has been shown to be voluntarily intoxicated in a basic intent crime the evidence of intoxication is irrelevant to the question whether D held the *mens rea*, but the prosecution is still obliged to prove that D had the relevant *mens rea*. There is some authority that a jury must be directed to decide whether D was reckless, disregarding the evidence that he was intoxicated. In *Woods*[169] D, charged with rape under the pre-2003 law, claimed that he was so drunk that he did not realize V was not consenting. He relied on s 1(2) of the Sexual Offences (Amendment) Act 1976[170] which required the jury to have regard to the presence or absence of reasonable grounds for a belief that the woman was consenting, 'in conjunction with any other relevant matters'. He said his intoxication was a relevant matter. The court said that self-induced intoxication is not 'a legally relevant matter' but 'the subsection directs the jury to look carefully at all the other relevant evidence before making up their minds on this issue'. The evidence of intoxication is undoubtedly logically relevant and may be the most cogent evidence. To ignore it, in coming to a conclusion, is to answer a hypothetical question. It is no longer, 'did he believe she was consenting?' and must become, 'would he have known she was consenting if he had not been drunk?' This is most obviously so in the case where D's intoxication has rendered him unconscious. In *Richardson and Irwin*,[171] where DD dropped a fellow student from a balcony when drunk causing him grievous bodily harm, they were charged under s 20 of the 1861 Act. Their convictions were quashed by the Court of Appeal holding that the trial judge should have directed that the jury had to be sure that DD would have foreseen the risk of injury had they been sober.

This interpretation of *Majewski* as a rule of evidence also poses problems. Take *Lipman* where D strangled V after taking LSD and believing that he was fighting off a serpent at the centre of the earth.[172] How can a judge seriously tell a jury to decide whether D *did* intend to do an unlawful and dangerous act to V – ignoring the undisputed evidence that he was unconscious at the time? Without this 'legally irrelevant' evidence, the *only* question the jury can sensibly answer is, 'would he have known that such an act was dangerous if he had not been intoxicated'? On facts like those in *Lipman*, there is only one possible answer. It is most regrettable that juries should be faced with questions which are, with all respect, nonsensical, even if their common sense will lead them to consider the only matter really in issue.

(iii) Distinguishing specific and basic intent crimes[173]

In view of the rule in *Majewski*, the nature of 'specific intent' is a matter of great importance but a careful scrutiny of the authorities, particularly *Majewski* itself, fails to

168 A. C. E. Lynch, 'The Scope of Intoxication' [1982] Crim LR 139 makes a quite different distinction between 'complete intoxication' (to which *Majewski* would apply) and 'partial intoxication' (to which it would not); but there are many degrees of intoxication and the suggested distinction seems unworkable.

169 (1981) 74 Cr App R 312.

170 Now repealed.

171 [1999] 1 Cr App R 192.

172 [1970] 1 QB 152.

173 A. Ward, 'Making Some Sense of Self Induced Intoxication' [1986] CLJ 247.

reveal any consistent principle by which specific and basic are to be distinguished.[174] In *Majewski*, 'specific' was contrasted with 'basic intent';[175] but some crimes requiring no ulterior intent – conspicuously murder – are also treated as crimes of 'specific intent'. Lord Simon suggested that the distinguishing factor is that 'the *mens rea* in a crime of specific intent requires proof of a purposive element': yet there need be no purposive element in the *mens rea* of murder; and rape, which is said not to be a crime of specific intent, obviously requires a purposive element. Lord Elwyn-Jones LC suggested that the test is that crimes not requiring specific intent are crimes that may be committed recklessly. Lord Edmund-Davies, a party to *Majewski*, was dismayed to think that, as a result of *Caldwell*, this opinion prevailed.[176] It certainly seems likely that any offence which may be committed recklessly will be held an offence of 'basic' and not 'specific' intent.

The only safe conclusion seems to be that 'crime requiring specific intent' means a crime where evidence of voluntary intoxication negativing *mens rea* is a defence; and the designation of crimes as requiring, or not requiring, specific intent is based on no principle but on policy. In order to know how a crime should be classified for this purpose we can look only to the decisions of the courts. These tell us that the following are crimes requiring specific intent.

Specific intent crimes

Murder,[177] wounding or causing grievous bodily harm with intent,[178] theft,[179] robbery,[180] burglary with intent to steal,[181] handling stolen goods,[182] endeavouring to obtain money on a forged cheque,[183] causing criminal damage contrary to s 1(1) or (2) of the Criminal Damage Act 1971 where only intention to cause damage or, in the case of s 1(2), only intention to endanger life, is alleged,[184] an attempt to commit any offence requiring specific intent, and possibly some forms of secondary participation in any offence.[185]

174 Cf S. Gardner, above, and J. Horder, 'Intention in the Criminal Law – A Rejoinder' (1995) 58 MLR 678, who views the specific intent crimes as those in which the intent is integrally bound up with the nature and definition of the wrong involved.

175 Above, p 276.

176 [1982] AC 341 at 361, [1981] 1 All ER 961 at 972.

177 *Beard*, above; *Gallagher* [1963] AC 349, [1961] 3 All ER 299; *Sheehan* [1975] 2 All ER 960, [1975] 1 WLR 739, CA.

178 *Bratty v A-G for Northern Ireland* [1963] AC 386, [1961] 3 All ER 523, per Lord Denning; *Pordage* [1975] Crim LR 575; *Davies* [1991] Crim LR 469.

179 *Ruse v Read* [1949] 1 KB 377, [1949] 1 All ER 398 and *Majewski* per Lord Simon at 152.

180 As a corollary of theft.

181 *Durante* [1972] 3 All ER 962, [1972] 1 WLR 1612.

182 *Durante*, above.

183 *Majewski*, per Lord Salmon at 158.

184 *Caldwell* [1981] 1 All ER 961 at 964.

185 *Clarkson* [1971] 3 All ER 344 at 347. But in *Lynch v DPP for Northern Ireland* [1975] 1 All ER 913 at 942, Lord Simon said, approving the decision of the Northern Irish Court of Criminal Appeal, that they held that the *mens rea* of aiding and abetting did not involve a 'specific intent'. But (i) he may have used the term in a different sense; and (ii) there may be a difference depending on the nature of the alleged secondary liability – an intent to procure is different from an intent to aid; above, p 170.

Basic intent crimes

The following are crimes not requiring a specific intent: manslaughter (apparently in all its forms);[186] rape,[187] maliciously wounding or inflicting grievous bodily harm;[188] kidnapping and false imprisonment;[189] assault occasioning actual bodily harm;[190] assault on a constable in the execution of his duty;[191] common assault;[192] taking a conveyance without the consent of the owner;[193] criminal damage where intention or recklessness, or only recklessness, is alleged[194] and possibly an attempt to commit an offence where recklessness is a sufficient element in the *mens rea*,[195] as in attempted rape.[196]

It will be noted that for most specific intent offences there exists a basic intent offence that can be charged in the alternative (murder and manslaughter, ss 18 and 20 of the OAPA, etc). The prosecution are usually therefore able to avoid an acquittal in cases of self-induced intoxication. Two problems arise in this regard however. First, the jury will face confusing directions on charges such as ss 18 and 20 as to what use they may make of the evidence of intoxication. Secondly, there are some specific intent offences for which there is no basic intent equivalent. Theft is the obvious example.

(iv) Specific and basic – a legitimate basis of distinction?

A classification of all crimes as offences of either specific or basic intent is over simplified. Consider the offence under s 18 of the Offences Against the Person Act 1861 of unlawfully and maliciously wounding with intent to resist lawful apprehension. There is abundant authority to the effect that the words 'unlawfully and maliciously' when used in s 20 import only a basic intent, that is, *Cunningham* recklessness. Presumably they have the same effect in s 18. So as far as wounding goes, s 18 is an offence of basic intent. But the intent to resist lawful apprehension seems a clear case of specific intent. So it seems that a drunken person who intends to resist lawful arrest but, because of his drunkenness, does not foresee the risk of wounding, might be convicted, notwithstanding his lack of *Cunningham* recklessness. If, on the other hand, because of drunkenness, he does not realize that he is resisting lawful arrest, he must be acquitted.[197] Possibly rape is another example. A reasonable belief whether the person is consenting is a basic intent; but presumably there must be an actual intention to perform the penile penetration. But it is difficult to envisage a man, however drunk, having sexual intercourse without intending to do so. In *Fotheringham*, D had intercourse with the 14-year-old babysitter who was in his matrimonial bed. She did not resist, but did not in fact consent. D, who was drunk,

[186] *Beard, Gallagher* and *Bratty v A-G Northern Ireland* [1961] 3 All ER at 533, per Lord Denning; *Lipman* [1970] 1 QB 152, [1969] 3 All ER 410.

[187] *Majewski*, above, per Lords Simon and Russell and *Leary v R* (1977) 74 DLR (3d) 103, SCC, discussed, 55 Can Bar Rev 691. But if this is right, *Cogan and Leak* above, p 205 is wrongly decided; and *Morgan* above, pp 111, 125 might have been decided simply on this ground. Cf *Fotheringham* (1988) 88 Cr App R 206, [1988] Crim LR 846 and commentary. See now Ch 17 below.

[188] *Bratty* at 533, per Lord Denning; *Majewski*, above, per Lords Simon and Salmon.

[189] *Hutchins* [1988] Crim LR 379.

[190] *Bolton v Crawley* [1972] Crim LR 222; *Majewski*, above.

[191] *Majewski*, above.

[192] *A fortiori.*

[193] *MacPherson* [1973] RTR 157, *Gannon* (1987) 87 Cr App R 254. *Diggin* (1980) 72 Cr App R 204 is not, as at first appeared: [1980] Crim LR 656, an authority on intoxicated taking: [1981] Crim LR 563; but see S. White, 'Taking the Joy out of Joyriding' [1980] Crim LR 609.

[194] Below, Ch 27.

[195] Commentary on *Pullen* [1991] Crim LR 457 at 458.

[196] Below, p 403.

[197] *Davies* [1991] Crim LR 469.

said that he believed she was his wife. It was then not rape for a man to have intercourse with his wife without consent. His appeal was dismissed. His drunken belief that V was his wife was no more a defence than his belief that she was consenting.[198]

It is regrettable that the distinction is so obscure that the Law Commission felt unable confidently to state what the law was.[199]

(v) Intoxication and *Caldwell* recklessness

Where the offence is one of *Caldwell* recklessness, assuming that any such offences still exist, the impact of *Majewski* is reduced. Where, because he was intoxicated, D gave no thought to the existence of the risk, he was reckless and is liable to conviction without the invocation of the rule in *Majewski*.[200] This was the position in *Caldwell* itself. But *Majewski* may still have a significant sphere of operation.[201] D might say that he did consider whether there was a risk and decided there was none. He was then not *Caldwell*-reckless. But, if he would have appreciated the existence of the risk had he been sober, he will still be liable because of *Majewski*.

(d) Dangerous or non-dangerous drugs in basic intent crime

In the case where D has become voluntarily intoxicated and the offence with which he is charged is one of basic intent, there remains one important issue to consider – whether the substance ingested is dangerous, that is, commonly known to create states of unpredictability or aggression.

The law in this area has developed principally in cases where D was intoxicated by alcohol. In *Lipman*[202] it was held that the same principles apply to intoxication by other drugs but two later cases, *Bailey*[203] and *Hardie*,[204] suggest that drugs must be divided into two categories. Where it is common knowledge that a drug is liable to cause the taker to become aggressive or do dangerous or unpredictable things, that drug is to be classed with alcohol. Where there is no such common knowledge, as in the case of a merely soporific or sedative drug, different rules apply. There are obvious difficulties about classifying drugs in this way and, if the distinction survives at all, it would not be surprising if it leads to further case law.

In *Bailey*[205] a diabetic failed to take sufficient food after insulin. He caused grievous bodily harm and his defence to charges under ss 18 and 20 of the Offences Against the Person Act was that, because of this failure, he was in a state of automatism. The recorder's direction to the jury that this was no defence was obviously wrong so far as s 18 was concerned for that is an offence of specific intent. The Court of Appeal held that it was also wrong for s 20 because 'self-induced automatism, other than that due to intoxication from alcohol or drugs, may provide a defence to crimes of basic intent'.[206]

198 (1988) 88 Cr App R 206, [1988] Crim LR 846. But, according to *Richardson and Irwin* [1999] 1 Cr App R 392, [1999] Crim LR 494, D may rely on a drunken mistaken belief in consent, where consent would be a defence to a charge under OAPA 1861, s 20. Since this is a basic intent offence, the decision seems doubtful.

199 See Law Com Report No 229, para 3.27.

200 This point was overlooked in *Cullen* [1993] Crim LR 936.

201 This is overlooked by Lord Diplock at [1981]1 All ER 968a.

202 [1970] 1 QB 152, [1969] 3 All ER 410; below, p 476.

203 [1983] 2 All ER 503, [1983] 1 WLR 760.

204 [1984] 3 All ER 848, [1985] 1 WLR 64.

205 [1983] 2 All ER 503, [1983] 1 WLR 760, CA.

206 P 271.

The court went on:

The question in each case will be whether the prosecution has proved the necessary element of recklessness. In cases of assault, if the accused knows that his actions or inaction are likely to make him aggressive, unpredictable or uncontrolled with the result that he may cause some injury to others and he persists in the action or takes no remedial action when he knows it is required, it will be open to the jury to find that he was reckless.

The automatism seems to have been treated as arising from the failure to take food, rather than from the taking of the insulin, but the court hinted at a distinction between two types of drug:

It is common knowledge that those who take alcohol to excess or certain sorts of drugs may become aggressive or do dangerous or unpredictable things. . . . But the same cannot be said, without more, of a man who fails to take food after an insulin injection.

In *Hardie*[207] D's defence to a charge of damaging property with intent to endanger the life of another or being reckless whether another's life be endangered, was that he had taken valium, a sedative drug, to calm his nerves and that this had resulted in intoxication precluding the *mens rea* for the offence. The judge, following *Majewski* and *Caldwell*, directed that this could be no defence. The Court of Appeal quashed the conviction. *Majewski* was not applicable because valium:

is wholly different in kind from drugs which are liable to cause unpredictability or aggressiveness. . . . if the effect of a drug is merely soporific or sedative the taking of it, even in some excessive quantity, cannot in the ordinary way raise a conclusive presumption against the admission of proof of intoxication for the purpose of disproving *mens rea* in ordinary crimes, such as would be the case with alcoholic intoxication or incapacity or automatism resulting from the self-administration of dangerous drugs.[208]

These cases then appear to apply where intoxication is self-induced otherwise than by alcohol or dangerous drugs. In these cases the test of liability is stated to be one of recklessness: 'If he does appreciate the risk that [failure to take food/taking the non-dangerous drug] may lead to aggressive, unpredictable and uncontrollable conduct and he nevertheless deliberately runs the risk or otherwise disregards it, this will amount to recklessness'.[209]

It is clear that the recklessness which must be proved is:

(i) subjective, an actual awareness of the risk of becoming aggressive, but

(ii) 'general' – not requiring foresight of the *actus reus* of any particular crime, such as is required in the case of a sober person charged with an offence of *Cunningham* recklessness. D will be liable for any crime of recklessness the *actus reus* of which he happens to commit under the influence of the self-induced intoxication. This flows from the rule in *Majewski*.

207 [1984] 3 All ER 848, [1985] 1 WLR 64.

208 This overlooks the fact that the *Majewski* principle is stated to be a rule of substantive law and that the Criminal Justice Act 1967, s 8, precludes conclusive presumptions of intention or foresight. Above, p 277. The distinction is also unsatisfactory in pharamacological terms: M. Weller and W. Somers, 'Differences in the Medical and Legal viewpoint illustrated by *Hardie*' [1991] 31 Med Sci Law 152.

209 *Bailey* [1983] 2 All ER 503 at 507.

Further:

(iii) being aware that one may lose consciousness may be sufficient where a failure to exercise control may result in the *actus reus* of a crime, as in the case of careless or reckless driving.

(e) Intoxication and defences

(i) Statutory defences prescribing a belief in circumstances

The *Majewski* rule has been held inapplicable where statute expressly provides that a particular belief shall be a defence to the charge. If D held that belief, he is not guilty, even though it arose from a drunken mistake that he would not have made when sober. In *Jaggard v Dickinson*[210] D had a friend, H, who had invited her to treat his house as if it were her own. When drunk, D went to a house which she thought was H's but which in fact belonged to R, who barred her way. D gained entry by breaking windows and damaging the curtains. Charged with criminal damage, contrary to s 1(1) of the Criminal Damage Act 1971, she relied on s 5(2) of that Act[211] which provides that a person has a lawful excuse if he believed that the person entitled to consent to the damage would have done so had he known of the circumstances. D said that she believed that H would, in the circumstances, have consented to her damaging his property. Since s 1(1) creates an offence not requiring specific intent, D could not have relied on her drunkenness to negative her recklessness whether she damaged the property of another, but, it was held, she could rely on it to explain what would otherwise have been inexplicable and give colour to her evidence about the state of her belief. The court thought this was not the same thing as using drunkenness to rebut an inference of intention or recklessness. It seems, however, to be exactly the same thing.[212] Moreover, thought the court, s 5(2) provides that it is immaterial whether a belief is justified or not if it is honestly held, and it was not open to the court to add the words 'and the honesty of the belief is not attributable only to self-induced intoxication'. Yet the courts have not hesitated to add similar words to qualify Parliament's express requirement of 'malice', that is, *Cunningham* recklessness. The result is anomalous. Where the defendant did not intend any damage to property he may be held liable because he was drunk; but where he did intend damage to property but thought the owner would consent he is not liable, however drunk he may have been. Suppose that D, because he is drunk, believes that certain property belonging to V is his own and damages it. His belief is not a matter of defence under s 5(2)[213] but negatives recklessness whether property *belonging to another* be damaged.[214] If D, being drunk, destroys X's property believing that it is the property of Y who would consent to his doing so, this is a defence; but if he destroys X's property believing that it is his own, it is not.

210 [1981] QB 527, [1980] 3 All ER 716. Cf the unsatisfactory case of *Gannon* (1987) 87 Cr App R 254, criticized by G. Williams, 'Two Nocturnal Blunders' (1990) 140 NLJ 1564.

211 Below, p 901.

212 See above, pp 276–277.

213 *Smith (DR)* [1974] QB 354, [1974] 1 All ER 632.

214 Ibid.

(ii) Common law defences

In relation to common law defences, the law has gone quite the other way. Although it is now settled that when D sets up self-defence, he is to be judged on the facts as he believed them to be, whether reasonably or not,[215] a mistake arising from voluntary intoxication cannot be relied on, according to *O'Grady*[216] even on charge of murder or other crime requiring specific intent. This was plainly *obiter* because the appellant had been acquitted of murder and was appealing only against his conviction for manslaughter; but in *O'Connor*[217] the court, inexplicably, treated it as binding, while quashing the conviction of murder on another ground. The *dictum* assumes that if self-defence is a defence to murder it must also be a defence to manslaughter, but this is not necessarily so because an act done in self-defence arising from a grossly negligent mistake (which a drunken mistake almost certainly is) should be manslaughter by gross negligence.[218] The decision is difficult to defend. The court's attention does not appear to have been drawn to the recommendations of the Criminal Law Revision Committee, complementing those which the court followed in *Gladstone Williams.*[219] The better view, it is submitted, is that a mistake arising from voluntary intoxication by alcohol or dangerous drugs may found a defence to crime requiring specific intent but not to one of basic intent if the prosecution prove that but for the intoxication the defendant would not have made the mistake.

(f) Intoxication induced with the intention of committing crime

Has D a defence if, intending to commit a crime, he takes drink or drugs in order to give himself 'Dutch courage' and then commits the crime, having, at the time of the act, induced insanity within the M'Naghten Rules or such a state of drunkenness as to negative a 'specific intent'? The problem was raised by *Attorney-General for Northern Ireland v Gallagher.*[220] D, having decided to kill his wife, bought a knife and a bottle of whisky. He drank much of the whisky and then killed his wife with the knife. The defence was that he was either insane or so drunk as to be incapable of forming the necessary intent at the time he did the act. The Court of Criminal Appeal in Northern Ireland reversed his conviction for murder on the ground that the judge had misdirected the jury in telling them to apply the M'Naghten Rules to D's state of mind at the time before he took the alcohol and not at the time of committing the act. The majority of the House of Lords apparently did not dissent from the view of the Court of Criminal Appeal that such a direction would be 'at variance with the specific terms of the M'Naghten Rules which definitely fix the crucial time as the time of committing the act'.[221]

They differed, however, in their interpretation of the summing up and held that it did direct the jury's attention to the time of committing the act. In that case, of course, it was not necessary to decide the problem because the jury, by their verdict, had found that D had *mens rea* and was not insane.

215 *Gladstone Williams* [1987] 3 All ER 411, 78 Cr App R 276, below, p 329.

216 [1987] QB 995, [1987] 3 All ER 420, criticized by the Law Commission, Law Com No 177, para 8.42, by H. Milgate [1987] CLJ 381 and J. C. Smith [1987] Crim LR 706.

217 [1991] Crim LR 135.

218 Below, p 482.

219 See above, n 215.

220 [1963] AC 349, [1961] 3 All ER 299.

221 See [1963] AC 349 at 376, [1961] 3 All ER 299 at 310.

Lord Denning, however, seems to have taken the view that the Court of Criminal Appeal's interpretation of the summing up was correct and that the direction, so interpreted, was right in law. He said:[222]

> My Lords, I think the law on this point should take a clear stand. If a man, whilst sane and sober, forms an intention to kill and makes preparation for it knowing it is a wrong thing to do, and then gets himself drunk so as to give himself Dutch courage to do the killing, and whilst drunk carries out his intention, he cannot rely on this self-induced drunkenness as a defence to a charge of murder, nor even as reducing it to manslaughter. He cannot say he got himself into such a stupid state that he was incapable of an intent to kill. So also, when he is a psychopath, he cannot by drinking rely on his self-induced defect of reason as a defence of insanity. The wickedness of his mind before he got drunk is enough to condemn him, coupled with the act which he intended to do and did do.

The difficulty about this is that an intention to do an act some time in the future is not *mens rea*.[223] The *mens rea* must generally coincide with the conduct which causes the *actus reus*. If D, having resolved to murder his wife at midnight, drops off to sleep and, while still asleep, strangles her at midnight, it is thought that he is not guilty of murder (though he may be liable for manslaughter on the ground of his negligence). The case of deliberately induced drunkenness, however, is probably different. The true analogy, it is thought, is the case where a man uses an innocent agent as an instrument with which to commit crime. It has been seen[224] that if D induces an irresponsible person to kill, D is guilty of murder. Is not the position substantially the same where D induces in himself a state of irresponsibility with the intention that he shall kill while in that state?[225] Should not the responsible D be liable for the foreseen and intended acts of the irresponsible D? So regarded, a conviction would not be incompatible with the wording of the M'Naghten Rules. The result, certainly, seems to be one required by policy and it is thought the courts will achieve it if the problem should be squarely raised before them.

(g) *Majewski* in the commonwealth

Majewski was followed by the Supreme Court of Canada by a majority of four to three in *Leary*[226] but that court, by a majority of six to three, then held, in *Daviault*,[227] that *Leary*, that is, the *Majewski* rule, violates the Canadian Charter of Rights and Freedoms in that it eliminates the fundamental requirements of voluntariness and of *mens rea* in offences of basic intent. The High Court of Australia rejected *Majewski* in *O'Connor*,[228] holding that evidence of voluntary intoxication is admissible in all cases to show that an act was involuntary or that any required mental element was lacking, and approving the New Zealand Court of Appeal decision in *Kamipeli*[229] to similar effect. In South Africa the Appellate Division reached the same conclusion in *Chrétien*.[230] In Scotland the position is less clear.[231]

222 [1963] AC 349 at 382, [1961] 3 All ER 299 at 314. 223 Above, p 36.
224 Above, p 166. 225 See the discussion in Ch 4, p 47.
226 (1994) 118 DLR (4th) 469. 227 [1978] 1 SCR 29, 33 CCC (2d) 473.
228 (1980) 146 CLR 64. 229 [1975] 2 NZLR 610. 230 1981 (1) SA 1097 (A).
231 See S. Gough, 'Surviving without *Majewski*' [2000] Crim LR 719; J. Chalmers, 'Letter to the Editor' [2001] Crim LR 258.

(h) Reform of intoxication

England is becoming isolated in the Commonwealth in clinging to the *Majewski* principle. Its abolition elsewhere does not seem to have led, as some anticipated, to increased crime or a collapse in respect for the law.[232] The Law Commission reached a provisional conclusion that *Majewski* should be abolished in a Consultation Paper.[233] The radical proposal was to introduce a new offence of criminal intoxication which would better reflect, in terms of label, the responsibility of the individual who commits a crime in a state of voluntary intoxication.[234] The consultation however persuaded the Commission to change its mind and they now recommend[235] the codification of the rule with minor amendment and attempted clarification, but in a draft Bill so complex and clumsy that it is impossible to commend it.[236]

The Home Office has now proposed a simplified model based on the Law Commission's Report which it intends to enact in relation to offences against the person.

19.–(1) For the purposes of this Act a person who was voluntarily intoxicated at any material time must be treated –

(a) as having been aware of any risk of which he would have been aware had he not been intoxicated, and

(b) as having known or believed in any circumstances which he would have known or believed in had he not been intoxicated.

(2) Whether a person is voluntarily intoxicated for this purpose must be determined in accordance with the following provisions.

(3) A person is voluntarily intoxicated if –

(a) he takes an intoxicant otherwise than properly for a medicinal purpose,

(b) he is aware that it is or may be an intoxicant, and

(c) he takes it in such a quantity as impairs his awareness or understanding.

(4) An intoxicant, although taken for a medicinal purpose, is not properly so taken if –

(a) the intoxicant is not taken on medical advice, and the taker is aware that the taking may result in his doing an act or making an omission capable of constituting an offence of the kind in question, or

(b) the intoxicant is taken on medical advice, but the taker fails then or afterwards to comply with any condition forming part of the advice and he is aware that the failure may result in his doing an act or making an omission capable of constituting an offence of the kind in question.

(5) Intoxication must be presumed to have been voluntary unless there is adduced such evidence as might lead the court or jury to conclude that there is a reasonable possibility that the intoxication was involuntary.

(6) An intoxicant is any alcohol, drug or other thing which, when taken into the body, may impair the awareness or understanding of the person taking it.

232 G. Orchard, 'Surviving without *Majewski*' [1993] Crim LR 426.

233 Law Com Consultation Paper No 127 (1993).

234 For a defence see G. Virgo, 'Reconciling Principle and Policy' [1993] Crim LR 415; for criticism see S. Gardiner, 'The Importance of *Majewski*' (1994) 14 OJLS 279.

235 Law Com No 229 (1995). See J. Horder, 'Sobering Up' (1995) 58 MLR 534; E. Paton, 'Reformulating the Intoxication Rule' [1995] Crim LR 382.

236 See S. Gough, 'Intoxication and Criminal Liability' (1996) 112 LQR 335.

(7) A person must be treated as taking an intoxicant if he permits it to be administered to him.

The proposal in cl 19(a) clarifies the position by asserting that the intoxication is treated as *mens rea* in the case of a basic intent offence. Clause 19(b) is however problematic since it restricts the defence by allowing D to be convicted by attributing to him beliefs which he did not in fact possess.[237]

It is submitted that if we are to have legislation substantially re-enacting the present law, it would be better to base it upon the much simpler clauses in the draft Criminal Code,[238] perhaps slightly modified or, better still, those in the Code Team's report[239] to the Commission.

Other proposals for a *via media* have been made[240] but have not attracted support and are not pursued here. The choice seems to be between complete abolition of the *Majewski* principle and its retention. So far as English law is concerned, it seems to be here to stay for the indefinite future.

5. Combined, consecutive and concurrent causes of loss of capacity

The internal and external factors which cause an individual defendant to lack capacity may operate consecutively or concurrently. There is little authority on the complex questions which may arise and such as there is does not seem well thought out. It is sufficient to demonstrate, however, that this is a practical and not merely an academic problem. Some answers to the questions which may arise are suggested here.

(a) Consecutive operation

(i) Intoxication causes automatism

D, because he is drunk, sustains concussion and does the allegedly criminal act in a state of automatism resulting from the concussion. In *Stripp*[241] the Court of Appeal thought, *obiter*, that D should be acquitted on the ground of automatism. That seems right – the intoxication is too remote from the act. The Law Commission concluded that the case suggests '*obiter*, the possibility that where there is a course of automatism clearly separable in time or effect from the intoxication and supported by a foundation of evidence, then a defence of automatism may be available, but when the causal factors are less easily separable it would seem that the presence of the intoxication will on policy grounds adopted in *Majewski* exclude reliance on automatism'.[242] Distinguishing the degree of separateness of the factors will not always be easy.

237 See J. C. Smith, 'Offences Against the Person: The Home Office Consultation Paper' [1998] Crim LR 317.

238 Clauses 22 and 33.

239 Law Com No 143 (1985), cl 26.

240 See the 7th edition of this book, at 230.

241 (1979) 69 Cr App R 318,323, CA. No foundation for automatism was laid.

242 Law Com Consultation Paper No 127 (above), para 2.33, Report (above) para 6.44.

(ii) Automatism causes intoxication

D having sustained concussion, drinks a bottle of vodka under the impression that it is water and does the allegedly criminal act, not knowing what he doing because he is intoxicated. Since the intoxication is involuntary, both causes lead to an acquittal and D must be acquitted.

(iii) Intoxication causes insanity

Beard settles that insanity caused by drink operates in the same manner as insanity arising from any other cause. If excessive drinking causes actual insanity, such as delirium tremens, then the M'Naghten Rules will be applied in exactly the same way as where insanity rises from any other causes: 'drunkenness is one thing and the diseases to which drunkenness leads are different things; and if a man by drunkenness brings on a state of disease which causes such a degree of madness, even for a time, which would have relieved him from responsibility if it had been caused in any other way, then he would not be criminally responsible'.[243]

It has already been seen[244] that there are serious difficulties in defining a 'disease of the mind' and the distinction between temporary insanity induced by drink and simple drunkenness is far from clear-cut. The distinction becomes important in the case of a person who does not know that his act is wrong because of excessive drinking. If he is suffering from temporary insanity he is entitled to a verdict of not guilty on the ground of insanity; but if he is merely drunk he should be convicted.[245]

(iv) Insanity causes intoxication or automatism

'Insanity' in the *M'Naghten* sense can strictly have no application here because it applies only in relation to a particular criminal act, whereas getting drunk or causing oneself concussion is probably not a criminal act at all and certainly not the criminal act with which we are concerned. However, D may not know the nature and quality of the act which causes the condition. The intoxication is involuntary, so D should be acquitted. In so far as automatism is caused by insanity, it is the result of an internal cause which looks as if the net result should be, not guilty on the ground of insanity; but it would seem odd that, if D's insanity leads him to drink excessively, he should be acquitted absolutely whereas if it takes the form of banging his head against a wall until he does not know what he is doing he should be subject to restraint. Policy may be best served by a verdict of not guilty on the ground of insanity in both cases.

(v) Automatism causes insanity

Such cases will surely be rare, but, if one should arise, probably the answer should be as in the case where automatism and insanity are concurrent causes and for the same reason.[246]

243 *Davis* (1881) 14 Cox CC 563 at 564, per Stephen J approved by the House of Lords in *DPP v Beard* [1920] AC 479 at 501.

244 Above, pp 258–260.

245 In a case of simple drunkenness the judge should not introduce the question whether the prisoner knew he was doing wrong – for 'it is a dangerous and confusing question' – per Lord Birkenhead in *DPP v Beard* [1920] AC 479 at 506. Note that in the Scots case of *Finegan v Heywood* (2000) The Times, 10 May, a defence of sleepwalking triggered by intoxication was treated as not being one of 'automatism'.

246 Below, p 289.

(b) Concurrent operation

(i) Intoxication and automatism

The circumstances of non-insane automatism being pleaded where D's level of intoxication renders him automaton are discussed above (pp 271–273).

(ii) Intoxication and insanity

D does not know what he is doing, partly because of a disease of the mind and partly because he is drunk. The choice is (or should be) between a verdict of not guilty on the ground of insanity and, in a crime not requiring specific intent, one of guilty. This view is supported by the Law Commission.[247] Two difficult cases cast doubt on this and illustrate the difficulty in dealing with combined causes in practice.

In *Burns*[248] D was charged with indecent assault, a crime not requiring specific intent. He may not have been aware of what he was doing, partly because of brain damage and partly because of drink and drugs. It is unclear whether the drugs were prescribed to B.[249] The court accepted that, if D did not know what he was doing, he was entitled to an absolute acquittal. If the only causes are alcohol and insanity it is difficult to see how this can be right, since neither of the concurrent causes entitled D to be absolutely acquitted. If the causes are alcohol, prescribed drugs and insanity the position is more complex. Since the crime is one of basic intent, it is arguable that the non-dangerous drugs that D was taking require the prosecution to establish that D was not reckless in becoming aggressive and unpredictable.[250] Williams took the view that in such a case insanity was the correct verdict,[251] and analogy with *Beard* might suggest that this is the right verdict, but the House of Lords in *Attorney-General for Northern Ireland v Gallagher*[252] thought otherwise, unless the alcohol caused some quite different type of disease, such as delirium tremens.[253]

(iii) Automatism and insanity

In *Roach*,[254] the Court of Appeal adopted a more pragmatic approach, focusing on which of the multiple concurrent causes of the lack of control was dominant. D was convicted of wounding with intent to cause grievous bodily harm having attacked V with a knife after a minor dispute. D claimed to have no knowledge or memory of the incident. D claimed that his voluntary intoxication by alcohol, coupled with his prescribed drugs might have had some causative effect on his latent mental illness being triggered leading to his lack of awareness. The expert evidence described a 'disease of the mind' and not surprisingly that was treated by the prosecution as the basis of a plea of insanity. Defence counsel argued that the 'disease of the mind' should lead to a defence of automatism, but the judge did not leave that defence to the jury.[255] The

247 Law Com Consultation Paper No 127, para 2.31.

248 (1973) 58 Cr App R 364, [1975] Crim LR 155 and commentary.

249 In earlier editions, it was suggested that the combination of the causes was intoxication and insanity alone. Prof Mackay, *Mental Condition Defences*, p 158 criticizes that narrow view of the facts.

250 See Mackay, p 159.

251 TBCL, 681.

252 [1963] AC 349, [1961] 3 All ER 299, above, p 284 (effect of drink on a psychopath).

253 Combination of mental abnormality and drink resulting in a substantial impairment of mental responsibility does not amount to a defence of diminished responsibility: *Fenton* below, p 473.

254 [2001] EWCA Crim 2698.

255 [17].

Court of Appeal upheld the appeal, accepting that automatism was sufficiently widely defined that if external factors were operative on an 'underlying condition which would not otherwise produce a state of automatism', then a defence of non-insane automatism ought to be left to the jury.[256] The court considered this to be a borderline case identified in *Quick* where the 'transitory effect caused by the application to the body of some external factor such as violence, drugs, including anesthetics, alcohol and hypnotic inferences cannot fairly be said to be due to disease'. With respect, this seems to be a confusing application of that principle. In *Quick* the lack of control was due to hypoglycaemia, caused by taking insulin. It was not hyperglycaemia caused by diabetes. The court seems to accord precedence to the prescribed drugs rather than the internal cause and the voluntary intoxication. The lack of control seems to have been a combination of (i) the 'psychogenic' personality (which would alone result in a special verdict); (ii) prescribed drugs (which alone if taken as per the prescription would have resulted in acquittal); and (iii) the voluntary intoxication (which on a specific intent charge such as this could have resulted in acquittal). It is submitted that the decision in *Roach* should be approached with considerable caution. It may be regarded as correctly decided on its facts since the judge gave confusing directions as to the relevant burdens of proof.

6. Mistake[257]

The rules relating to mistake are simply an application of the general principle that the prosecution must prove its case, including the *mens rea* or negligence which the definition of the crime requires and rebuttal of excuses raised. The so-called 'defence' is simply a denial that the prosecution has proved its case. Accordingly, only mistakes which deny *mens rea* or raise an excuse will have any bearing on D's liability.

(a) Mistakes as denials of *mens rea*

The 'landmark decision'[258] in *DPP v Morgan* endorsed by the House of Lords in *DPP v B*,[259] holds that D's mistake of fact will result in acquittal in all crimes of *mens rea* where it prevents D from possessing the relevant *mens rea* which the law requires for the crime with which he is charged. Historically, mistake had been treated as a special defence and there were many *dicta* by eminent judges that *only* reasonable mistakes would excuse. Lord Lane CJ[260] and the House of Lords,[261] in the light of *Morgan*, doubted these

256 [28].

257 E. Keedy, 'Ignorance and Mistake in the Criminal Law' (1908) 22 Harv LR 75; G. Williams, CLGP, ch 5; J. Hall, *General Principles*, ch XI; G. Williams, 'Homicide and the Supernatural' (1949) 65 LQR 491; Howard, 'The Reasonableness of Mistake in the Criminal Law' (1961), 4 Univ QLJ 45.

258 [1976] AC 182, [1975] 2 All ER 347; above, p 125.

259 And subsequently by its ringing endorsement in *R v K* [2002] 1 AC 462 and *G* [2003] UKHL 50.

260 *Taaffe* [1983] 2 All ER 625, 628.

261 *Westminster City Council v Croyalgrange Ltd* [1986] 2 All ER 353 at 399.

pronouncements and the House in *B v DPP*[262] has now made it very clear that they are wrong. Lord Hailsham had explained in *Morgan*:

Once one has accepted . . . that the prohibited act in rape is non-consensual sexual intercourse, and that the guilty state of mind is an intention to commit it, it seems to me to follow as a matter of inexorable logic that there is no room either for a defence of honest belief or mistake, or of a defence of honest and reasonable belief or mistake. Either the prosecution proves that the accused had the requisite intention, or it does not. In the former case it succeeds, and in the latter it fails.[263]

Where the law requires intention or recklessness with respect to some element in the *actus reus*, a mistake, whether reasonable or not, which precludes both states of mind will excuse. Thus, where D genuinely though unreasonably believes that the thing he is shooting at is a scarecrow and not a human, he will lack the *mens rea* for murder – an intention to kill or do grievous bodily harm *to a person in being*.

Where the natural inference from D's conduct in the particular circumstances is that he intended or foresaw a particular result, the jury are very likely to convict him if he introduces no testimony that he did not in fact foresee; but the onus of proof remains throughout on the Crown and, technically, D does not bear even an evidential burden,[264] as he does when he raises a defence of automatism.

Although D's belief need not be reasonable to excuse him, as a matter of practice, the more unreasonable it is, the jury are less likely to accept that it was genuinely held.

(i) Mistakes and crimes of negligence

Where the law requires only negligence in respect of an element of the *actus reus*, then only a *reasonable* mistake can afford a defence; for an unreasonable mistake, by definition, is one which a reasonable person would not make and is, therefore, negligent.[265] In cases of gross negligence manslaughter, D's unreasonable mistake may excuse provided it is not regarded by the jury as a grossly unreasonable mistake. Parliament may, of course, specify in relation to any crime that only reasonable beliefs will excuse. A recent example of this is the Sexual Offences Act 2003 (see below).

(ii) Mistakes in crimes of strict liability

Where crime is interpreted as imposing strict liability, then even a reasonable mistake as to that element of the *actus reus* for which liability is strict will not excuse. It is an oversimplification to say that mistakes are irrelevant in strict liability crimes since there are few such crimes in which every element of *actus reus* is regarded as strict. Thus, in a

262 See particularly Lord Nicholls at [2000] 1 All ER 836–839.

263 Per Lord Hailsham at 214. For criticism see J. Horder, 'Cognition, Emotion and Criminal Culpability' (1990) 106 LQR 469.

264 G. Williams, 'The Evidential Burden' (1977) 127 NLJ 156 at 158. But there is an evidential burden on D to get a particular mistake before the jury. 'Mistake is a defence in the sense that it is raised as an issue by the accused. The Crown is rarely possessed of knowledge of the subjective factors which may have caused an accused to entertain a belief in a fallacious set of facts': *Pappajohn v R* (1980) 52 CCC (2d) 481 at 494, per Dickson J. The judge does not have to direct the jury in every case of murder: 'You must be satisfied that D did not believe V was a turkey'; but he must give such a direction if D has testified that, when he fired, he thought V was a turkey.

265 Above, Ch 6.

sexual offence such as sexual assault of a child under 13 where liability as to the age of the victim is strict, D will still have to be proved to have intentionally assaulted V. Where he claims that because of a mistake he had not meant intentionally to touch a person, he will be denying *mens rea*, and an honest mistake will excuse.

(iii) Identifying the *mens rea* to which mistakes relate

On the explanation so far, the application of the principles of mistake would seem to be straightforward. However, there are skeletons lurking in the common law cupboard which suggest that in some cases D's mistake as to an element of *actus reus* must always be reasonable to excuse.

One particular problem relates to the cases on bigamy. In *Morgan*, the House showed no inclination to interfere with the line of authority[266] which asserted that D's mistaken belief in the death of his first spouse, or the dissolution or nullity of his first marriage, was a defence only if it was reasonable. If that is so, to be consistent with the *Morgan* principle, these cases must be taken to establish that neither intention nor recklessness but only negligence with respect to the existence of the first marriage need be proved. But in *B v DPP* Lord Nicholls expressly disapproved of the requirement of reasonableness in the leading case of *Tolson*.[267] The discussion of the bigamy cases in *Morgan* must be seen in the context of an unsatisfactorily strict approach in that case to the problem of the implication of *mens rea* into statutory offences. The House was concerned with the common law offence of rape; but Lord Cross said that if the Sexual Offences Act 1956 had enacted explicitly that a man who has sexual intercourse with a woman without her consent (the *actus reus* of rape) is guilty of an offence, he might well have held that only a reasonable mistake would be a defence. Presumably the only intention which Lord Cross would have required in his hypothetical case would have been an intention to have intercourse with a woman.

The *dicta* in *Morgan* on bigamy suggest that, where a statute uses no words expressly importing *mens rea*, the mental element which the court will require the prosecution to prove will be minimal – to go through a ceremony of marriage, to have sexual intercourse, etc, and that it will then be for the accused to introduce evidence sufficient to raise a doubt whether he did not, on reasonable grounds, have a belief inconsistent with some material element in the *actus reus*. It is submitted that a genuine though unreasonable belief ought now to be a sufficient excuse on a charge of bigamy. In general terms the *Tolson* approach may be tolerable where we are concerned with so-called 'quasi-criminal', 'regulatory' or 'welfare' offences; but it should have no place in serious crimes – and, after *B v DPP*, *K* and *G* it seems less likely to do so.

What the discussion on bigamy exposes is the broader problem in many crimes of identifying which elements of *actus reus* require a corresponding *mens rea* requirement. In most serious offences there will usually be a strong if not complete correspondence. For example, in *Westminster City Council v Croyalgrange Ltd*[268] Robert Goff LJ referred

[266] *Tolson* (1889) 23 QBD 168, CCR. *King* [1964] 1 QB 285; *Gould* [1968] 2 QB 65. As the opinions in *Morgan* relating to defences have been reconsidered (above p 125) so too may the opinions regarding bigamy, if the matter ever arises. The House also accepted the requirement of reasonable grounds for believing the use of force to be necessary in self-defence, but see *Beckford* and *Williams*, below, p 331.

[267] (1889) 23 QB 168 CCR.

[268] [1986] 83 Cr App R 155, [1986] Crim LR 693.

to 'the ordinary principle that, where it is required that an offence should have been knowingly committed, the requisite knowledge must embrace all the elements of the offence'. On orthodox subjective principles intention or recklessness is required as to all the elements of the *actus reus* unless that is excluded expressly or by implication; and the more serious the crime, the more reluctant should the court be to find an implied exclusion.[269]

The shift in the common law, as evidenced by the House of Lords decisions in *B*, *K* and *G*, is to endorse this subjective approach to *mens rea*. As Lord Nicholls observed in *B v DPP*, 'considered as a matter of principle, the honest belief approach must be preferable. By definition the mental element in crime is concerned with a subjective state of mind such as intent or belief.'[270]

(b) Mistakes and defences

Morgan also left untouched the traditional requirement that mistakes as to the elements of defences were to be reasonable if they were to operate to excuse the accused. However, subsequently the courts have adopted the subjective principle in some categories (for example, self-defence),[271] but not others (for example, duress).[272] Some commentators seek to distinguish the categories on the basis of whether the defence is one of a justificatory or excusatory kind, or whether the defence relates to a 'definitional element' of the offence. Since the law does not adopt such classifications, and they cannot be universally applied, it seems that these may confuse rather than illuminate matters.[273] Whether the law recognizes the mistake made by D as to facts which if they existed would provide a valid defence, and whether to be recognized the mistake must be one of a reasonable or merely genuine nature, must be considered in the context of each defence (see the next part of this chapter). Intoxicated mistake has been discussed above (p 284).

(c) Irrelevant mistakes

A mistake which does not preclude *mens rea* (or negligence where that is in issue) is irrelevant and no defence. Suppose D believes he is smuggling a crate of Irish whiskey. In fact the crate contains Scotch whisky. Duty is, of course, chargeable on both. D believes he is importing a dutiable item and he is importing a dutiable item. The *actus reus* is the same whether the crate contains Irish or Scotch. He *knows*, because his belief and the facts coincide in this respect, that he is evading the duty chargeable on the goods in the crate. If D had believed the crate to contain only some non-dutiable item, for example, foreign currency (even if he had mistakenly believed it was dutiable) he would have lacked the *mens rea* for the offence.[274]

269 There are, admittedly, many exceptions to this principle.

270 P 70. For criticism see J. Horder, 'How Culpability can and cannot be denied in under-age sex crimes' [2001] Crim LR 15, arguing that D's mistake should be relevant if it relates to his 'guiding moral reason'.

271 *Williams* [1987] 3 All ER 441.

272 *Graham* [1982] 1 All ER 801; *Hasan* [2005] UKHL 22.

273 See TBCL, 138; R. Tur, 'Subjectivism and Objectivism : Towards Synthesis' in S. Shute, J. Gardner and J. Horder (eds), *Action and Value in Criminal Law* (1993), 213.

274 See commentary on *Taaffe* [1983] Crim LR 536 at 537, CA; affd [1984] AC 539. See *Forbes* [2001] UKHL 40 where D believed he was importing prohibited goods (adult pornography) and he was importing prohibited goods (child pornography). D evaded the prohibition on imports and intended to do so. See also *Matrix* [1997] 8 Archbold News.

(d) Mistakes of law

Mistake of criminal law is generally no defence,[275] for usually knowledge that the act is forbidden by law is no part of *mens rea.* This applies where, for example D, a visitor to England believes that his actions are lawful because they do not constitute a crime in his homeland.[276] The harshness of this rule is tempered by the fact that most serious criminal offences are also well recognized as moral 'wrongs'. It is however a harsh rule in application to the many thousands of regulatory offences, ameliorated only slightly by s 3(2) of the Statutory Instruments Act 1946 providing a defence for an accused charged with an offence created by Statutory Instrument to prove that, at the time of the offence, the instrument had not been published nor reasonable steps taken to bring its contents to the notice of the public or the accused.[277] Where D has relied on erroneous advice provided by the relevant State authority he may be successful in an application to stay proceedings as an abuse of process.[278]

Identifying whether the mistake is one of criminal law or fact is not always easy. For example, if D mistakenly believes that the person grabbing hold of him is a thug about to rob him and he resists, he has made a mistake of fact and cannot be guilty of assaulting a police officer with intent to resist arrest. Where however, D is aware that the person who is grabbing him is a police officer, but mistakenly believes that the officer has no power of arrest on the facts as they exist, D has made a mistake of criminal law. But what of D who makes a mistake as to antecedent facts which, if as he believed them to be, would indeed preclude the officer's power of arrest?[279]

Where the *mens rea* involves some legal concept[280] or the absence of a claim of right then mistake may negative mens rea and be a defence.

An honest though unreasonable mistake as to the civil law may lead to acquittal where it prevents D from holding the *mens rea* of the criminal offence. For example, in *Smith (David)*[281] D damaged property in his rented flat believing it was his own property – he made a mistake as to the ownership of the property. His conviction for criminal damage was quashed since D had no intent to damage property *belonging to another.* His mistake as to ownership prevented him having the relevant *mens rea.* As James LJ explained:

> Applying the ordinary principles of *mens rea,* the intention and recklessness and the absence of lawful excuse required to constitute the offence have reference to property belonging to another. It follows that in our judgment no offence is committed under this section if a person destroys or causes damage to property belonging to another if he does so in the honest though mistaken belief that the property is his own, and provided that the belief is honestly held it is irrelevant to consider whether or not it is a justifiable belief.[282]

275 Above, p 120. 276 See *Esop* (1836) 7 C & P 456.

277 Cf A. Ashworth, 'Excusable Mistake of Law' [1974] Crim LR 652 and p 122, n 128 above.

278 See A. Ashworth, 'Testing Fidelity to Legal Values' (2000) 63 MLR 633, 635–642 identifying the importance of Article 7 of the ECHR. One of the strongest examples is *Postermobile v LBC* (1997) 8 Dec and the Editorial at [1998] Crim LR 435 (D receiving erroneous information from planning agency). See also G. Williams, 'The Draft Code and Relevance of Official Statements' (1989) 9 LS 177.

279 See *Lee* [2001] Cr App R 193, below p 541. 280 Above, p 122. 281 [1974] QB 354.

282 At p 360.

7. Infancy[283]

Infants or, in more modern terminology, minors, are persons under 18 years of age. As such, they are (with some exceptions) incapable of making contracts or wills but the law imposes no such limitations on their ability to commit crimes, for, as Kenny put it, 'a child knows right from wrong long before he knows how to make a prudent speculation or a wise will'.[284]

The common law, for the purposes of the criminal liability, divided infants into three categories, now possibly reduced to two.

(a) Children under 10 years

A child was entirely exempt from criminal responsibility at common law until the day before his seventh birthday.[285] By statute, responsibility now begins on the child's tenth birthday.[286] The common law rule was stated as a conclusive presumption that the child is *doli incapax*, and the statute uses the same language: 'It shall be conclusively presumed that no child under the age of 10 years can be guilty of any offence.' Even though there may be the clearest evidence that the child caused an *actus reus* with *mens rea*, he cannot be convicted once it appears that he had not, at the time he did the act, attained the age of 10. Nor is this a mere procedural bar; no crime is committed by the child with the result that one who instigated him to do the act is a principal and not a secondary party.[287] And where a husband and wife were charged with receiving from their son (aged seven years) a child's tricycle, knowing it to have been stolen, it was held that they must be acquitted on the ground that, since the child could not steal, the tricycle was not stolen.[288] Ten is a comparatively low age for the beginning of criminal responsibility, it is certainly much lower than many other European states; but, as the Ingleby Committee pointed out:[289]

> In many countries the 'age of criminal responsibility' is used to signify the age at which a person becomes liable to the 'ordinary' or 'full' penalties of the law. In this sense, the age of criminal responsibility in England is difficult to state: it is certainly much higher than [ten].[290]

283 See more generally on youth crime, C. Ball, 'Youth Justice: Half A Century of Responses to Youth Offending' [2004] Crim LR 167; and for an historical account see G. Williams, The Criminal Responsibility of Children' [1954] Crim LR 493.

284 Kenny, *Outlines*, 80.

285 A person now attains a particular age at the commencement of the relevant anniversary of the date of his birth: Family Law Reform Act 1969, s 9(1).

286 Children and Young Persons Act 1933, s 50, as amended by the Children and Young Persons Act 1963, s 16, which raised the age from eight. The Ingleby Committee had recommended that the age be raised to 12. Cmnd 1911 (1960).

287 Above, p 166.

288 *Walters v Lunt* [1951] 2 All ER 645; and cf *Marsh v Loader* (1863) 14 CBNS 535.

289 Cmnd 1191, at 30. For the special rules governing the sentencing of children see *Archbold Magistrates* (2004–5) ch 34. For comparative materials on child prosecution see A. Nicol in *Child Offenders: UK and International Practice* (1995) Howard League for Penal Reform.

290 The age then was eight. Above, n 286.

(b) Children aged 10 and above

At common law there was a *rebuttable* presumption that a child aged not less than 10 but under 14 years ('a young person') was *doli incapax*, incapable of committing crime. The presumption was rebutted only if the prosecution proved beyond reasonable doubt, not only that the child caused an *actus reus* with *mens rea*, but also that he knew that the particular act was not merely naughty or mischievous, but 'seriously wrong'. If there was no evidence of such knowledge, other than that implicit in the act itself, the child had no case to answer. In *C v DPP*[291] the Divisional Court held that this ancient rule of the common law was outdated and no longer law; but the House of Lords reversed this, ruling that it was not open to the courts so to hold. That decision was followed by a series of acquittals which caused disquiet.

In the Crime and Disorder Act 1998, Parliament responded by abolishing the rebuttable presumption.[292] This was intended to put children aged 10 and above on an equal footing with adults, so far as liability (but not sentencing or mode of trial and procedure) is concerned. The Act is not well drafted and it has been cogently argued by Professor Walker that the section does not affect the substantive law,[293] leaving it open to a child under 14 to introduce evidence that he did not know that what he did was seriously wrong, whereupon it will be for the prosecution to prove, not only the usual *mens rea*, but also that the child did know that.[294] Even this less far-reaching construction would probably remove most of the difficulties which previously arose. A 13-year-old might be expected to find great difficulty in inducing a jury to doubt that he did not know it was seriously wrong to rape someone – a fact formerly presumed in his favour.

The presumption still poses problems in prosecutions for historic sexual abuse alleged against defendants who were between the ages of 10–14 at the time of their commission.[295]

SECTION B GENERAL DEFENCES

1. Duress

(a) Duress by threats and circumstances[296]

For centuries the law has recognized a defence of duress by threats. The typical case is where D is told, 'Do this [an act which would be a crime if there were no defence of

291 [1996] AC 1, [1995] 2 All ER 43, HL. See the 8th edition of this book for detail, at 195.

292 Crime and Disorder Act 1998, s 34. See L. Gelsthorpe, 'Much Ado About Nothing' (1999) CFLQ 209; J. Fonda, 'New Labour, Old Hat: Youth Justice and the Crime and Disorder Act 1998' [1999] Crim LR 36.

293 See Nigel Walker, 'The end of an old song' (1999) 149 NLJ 64.

294 This is supported by the Solicitor General's statements in Parliament, as cited by Walker.

295 *R v Andrew N* [2004] EWCA Crim 1236, CA.

296 See generally the discussion of the defences in the Law Com Consultation Paper No 122, *Legislating the Criminal Code: Offences Against the Person and General Principles* (1992) and Law Com No 218, *Legislating the Criminal Code: Offences Against the Person and General Principles* (1993).

duress] – or you will be killed', and, fearing for his life, he does the required act. Quite recently, the law has recognized another form of duress – duress of circumstances. Again, D does the act alleged to constitute the crime out of fear, but this time no human being is demanding that he do it.[297] D does it because his life is threatened and his only way of escape is to do the act, which, but for the duress, would be a crime. The compulsion on D to do the act is exactly the same whether the threat comes from someone demanding that he do it, or from an aggressor, or other circumstances. His moral culpability, or lack of it, seems exactly the same.[298] The relationship of duress, duress of circumstances and necessity is postponed until each has been examined in detail (p 324 below).

The law relating to duress by threats is now well-developed. Duress of circumstances is still relatively new, but it has developed by analogy to duress by threats so that there is a ready-made set of principles to govern it. By a strange coincidence, all the early cases on duress of circumstances concerned road traffic offences but there was no reason why it should be limited to such offences. *Pommell*[299] (possession of a prohibited weapon without a certificate) now decides that it has the same range and is governed by the same principles as duress by threats. The result is that either form of duress is a general defence, except that neither applies to some forms of treason, or to murder or attempted murder, whether as a principal or a secondary party.

(i) Duress and voluntariness[300]

It has often been said that the duress must be such that D's act is not 'voluntary'. We are not, however, concerned here with the case where a person is compelled by physical force to go through the motions of an *actus reus* without any choice on his part. In such cases he will almost invariably[301] be guilty of no offence on the fundamental ground that he did no act.

> If there be an actual forcing of a man, as if A by force takes the arm of B and the weapon in his hand and therewith stabs C whereof he dies, this is murder in A but B is not guilty.[302]

Nor are we concerned with the kind of involuntariness which arises from automatism where D is unable to control the movement of his body. When D pleads duress (or necessity) he admits that he was able to control his actions and chose to do the act with which he is charged, but denies responsibility for doing so. He may say, 'I had no choice' but that is not strictly true.[303] The alternative to committing the crime may have been so exceedingly unattractive that no reasonable person would have chosen it; but there was a choice. The courts recognize this. Where D is required to kill an innocent person, they insist that he must choose to defy the threat or threatening circumstance – and 'threaten' him with conviction for murder and life imprisonment if he does not. In Canada, the Supreme Court (holding that necessity may be an excuse, but not a justification)

[297] *Cole* [1994] Crim LR 582; *Ali* [1995] Crim LR 303.

[298] See the judicial affirmation that the defences are this closely linked: *Safi* [2003] Crim LR 721; *Shayler* [2001] 1 WLR 2206, citing the 6th edition of this work, but note p 324 below.

[299] [1995] 2 Cr App R 607.

[300] See M. Wasik, 'Duress and Criminal Responsibility' [1977] Crim LR 453; A. Norrie, *Crime Reason and History* (2nd edn, 2000), 165–170; A. T. H. Smith, 'On *Actus Reus* and *Mens Rea*' in P. Glazebrook (ed), *Reshaping the Criminal Law* (1978), at 104–106.

[301] Cf *Larsonneur*, above, p 73.

[302] Hale, 1I PC 534.

[303] *Hasan* [2005] UKHL 22, per Baroness Hale [73].

described the act as 'morally involuntary', the 'involuntariness' being 'measured on the basis of society's expectation of appropriate and normal resistance to pressure'.[304] This seems to mean only that even a person of goodwill and reasonable fortitude might have chosen to do the 'criminal' act. Since a person, yielding to duress which would have been a defence to any other crime, may (see below) be convicted of murder or attempted murder, it is clear that, in law, duress is not inconsistent with a voluntary act or with an intention to do that act and to cause the results which the actor knows will follow. The conviction implies both that the act was voluntary and the result intended.[305] D intends to do the act which, but for the duress, would be a crime. It has been recognized by the Court of Appeal that the defence is not a denial of *mens rea*, but a true defence operating despite the existence of the *actus reus* and *mens rea* of the offence.[306]

In short, duress is a defence because '. . . threats of immediate death or serious personal violence so great as to overbear the ordinary powers of human resistance should be accepted as a justification for acts which would otherwise be criminal'.[307]

Lord Bingham in *Hasan*, summarized the elements of the defence:[308] (i) there must be a threat of death or serious injury; (ii) made to D or his immediate family or someone close to him or, someone for whom D would reasonably regard himself as responsible; (iii) D's perception of the threat and his conduct in response are to be assessed objectively; (iv) the conduct it is sought to excuse must have been directly caused by the threats D relies on; (v) there must have been no evasive action D could reasonably take; (vi) D cannot rely on threats to which he has voluntarily laid himself open; (vii) the defence is unavailable to murder, attempted murder or treason.

(ii) The onus of proof

The onus of disproving duress of either kind is on the Crown.[309] If no facts from which duress might reasonably be inferred appear in the prosecution's case, then D has the 'evidential burden' of laying a foundation for the defence by introducing evidence of such facts.[310] There is considerable judicial scepticism regarding defences of duress and the defendant's burden to get the defence on its feet will not always be straightforward.[311] There is a particular judicial anxiety when the defence is raised late in the trial process.

304 *Perka* (1984) 13 DLR (4th) 1.

305 *Howe* [1987] 1 All ER 771 at 777, HL, per Lord Hailsham, LC, citing Lords Kilbrandon and Edmund-Davies in *DPP for Northern Ireland v Lynch* [1975] AC 653 at 703 and 709–710.

306 *Fisher* [2004] EWCA Crim 1190, [2004] Crim LR 938; *Hasan* [2005] UKHL 22 per Lord Bingham [18].

307 *A-G v Whelan* [1934] IR 518, per Murnaghan J (Irish CCA). The judge probably did not have in mind any distinction between justification and excuse. If there is a material distinction, duress seems to be an excuse. Cf R. A. Duff, 'Rule Violations and Wrongdoing', in S. Shute and A. Simester (eds), *Criminal Law Theory* (2002) 63.

308 [21].

309 *Gill* [1963] 2 All ER 688, [1963] 1 WLR 841, CCA; *Giaquento* [2001] EWCA Crim 2696; *Bianco* [2002] 1 Archbold News 2.

310 Radically, the Law Commission proposal would reverse the burden of proof on this defence. 'We repeat that in our view the reasons we have given for recommending that the defendant should bear the persuasive burden of proving duress are unique to the case of that defence. We also believe that they are sufficient to justify that step, and that it would not result in injustice to the defendant who genuinely acted under duress. The closing words of cl 25(2) and cl 25(4) of the Criminal Law Bill provide accordingly'. Report, para 33.16. It is doubtful whether this would be compatible with the ECHR (Article 6(2)). See the doubts expressed by Lord Bingham in *Hasan* [20].

311 See *Hasan* [20].

(iii) The nature of the threat

The type of qualifying threat or danger

As a matter of policy the law places strict limits on the type of threat sufficient to trigger the defence. It is not simply a question of balancing in each case the gravity of the threat against the gravity of the offence D causes. There is a minimum threshold below which the threats will never be sufficient to allow the defence of duress to operate. That threshold is set at a high level. The only threat or danger which will found a defence in either type of duress is one of death or serious[312] personal injury.[313] It has been held that serious psychiatric injury can be grievous bodily harm for the purposes of the Offences Against the Person Act and it is probable that a threat to cause such injury could amount to duress.[314] A threat to make a person a nervous wreck could be just as terrifying as a threat to cause serious physical injury. This criterion of serious injury is narrowly construed by the courts. In *Brown*[315] the court refused leave to appeal a conviction for possession of drugs when D, suffering from MS was cultivating cannabis for personal use to alleviate pain. The court regarded the threat of 'injury' he faced as being only that additional pain he would suffer by having to rely on prescribed medication rather than the lower level of pain suffered with his condition if he used cannabis. The difference between the two levels of pain was not sufficient to constitute serious injury.[316]

The Draft Criminal Code (cl 42 and cl 43) and most modern codes require a threat of death or serious injury.[317] Lord Goddard in *Steane*[318] spoke of violence or imprisonment but in that case duress was held not to be in issue. Widgery LJ in *Hudson*,[319] Lord Lane CJ in *Graham*,[320] and Woolf LJ in *Conway*,[321] all required a threat of death or serious personal injury. Hale required threats of death and so did the judges in *M'Growther*[322] and *Purdy*[323] but those were cases of treason. While the present law appears to be that a threat of serious personal injury is the minimum which is acceptable to found a defence to *any* crime, a higher minimum may be required for crimes of great gravity.

The following *dictum* of Lords Wilberforce and Edmund-Davies no longer applies to killing but is good for other acts:

> . . . the realistic view is that, the more dreadful the circumstances of the killing, the heavier the evidential burden of an accused advancing such a plea, and the stronger and more irresistible the duress needed before it could be regarded as affording any defence.[324]

Threats of blackmail, no matter how effective, are not sufficient.[325] There is no modern[326]

[312] In *Aikens* [2003] EWCA Crim 1573 it was doubted that a threat to punch V in the face would suffice.
[313] *Radford* [2004] EWCA Crim 2878. Cf the Criminal Damage Act 1971, s 5(2)(b).
[314] *Baker v Wilkins* [1997] Crim LR 497. [315] [2003] EWCA Crim 2637 CA (Crim Div).
[316] A duress of circumstances case. See also, *Quayle* [2005] EWCA Crim 1415.
[317] Law Commission Report, para 29.1: 'the overwhelming tendency of the authorities as of modern codes, is to limit the defence to cases where death or serious injury is threatened. . . . Consultation strongly supported that limitation on the defence of duress, which is imposed by clause 25(2)(a) of the Criminal Law Bill'.
[318] [1947] KB 997 at 1005. [319] [1971] 2 QB 202, [1971] 2 All ER 244.
[320] [1982] 1 All ER 801, [1982] 1 WLR 294. [321] [1989] QB 290, [1988] 3 All ER 1025.
[322] (1746) Fost 13. [323] (1946) 10 JCL 182.
[324] *Abbott v R* [1976] 3 All ER at 152. [325] *Singh* [1973] 1 WLR 1600.
[326] Cf *Crutchley* (1831) 5 C & P 133.

case in which a threat of injury to property has been admitted.[327] In *M'Growther*[328] D, who was a tenant of the Duke of Perth, called witnesses who proved that the Duke had threatened to burn the houses and drive off the cattle of any of his tenants who refused to follow him. Lee CJ directed that this could be no defence. But that was a case of treason and it does not necessarily follow that such a threat would not be enough on some lesser charge. If the evil D caused by submitting to the threat was clearly less than that which would have been inflicted had he defied it, there are cogent reasons for allowing a defence; even if the threat was not of death or even grievous bodily harm. Williams has argued strongly in favour of such a principle, which is, of course, closely analogous to that adopted in the American Model Penal Code in relation to necessity.[329] But this would deny a defence to D even though the injury threatened was one which no ordinary person could be expected to endure; and there would be grave difficulty in balancing the two evils against one another when they are of a completely different character.[330] 'Proportionality' may be requisite for necessity[331] but it seems inappropriate for duress.

Threats against whom?

Most of the cases naturally involve a threat or danger to the life or safety of the defendant himself, but the defences are not limited to that situation. In *Hurley and Murray*[332] the Supreme Court of Victoria held that threats to kill or seriously injure D's *de facto* wife amounted to duress. In *Conway*[333] the threat was to the passenger in D's car; and in *Martin*[334] D's wife's threat to commit suicide if he did not drive while disqualified was held capable of founding a defence of duress of circumstances – though in fact it seems to have been one of duress by threats – 'Drive or else . . .'. So threats against the life or safety of D's family and others to whom he owes a duty almost certainly will, and threats to a stranger probably will, be sufficient evidence of duress. If a bank robber threatens to shoot a customer in the bank unless D, the clerk, hands him the keys, D surely has a defence to a charge of abetting the robbery. The Draft Code allows the defence where the threat is made to the life or safety of D 'or another'.

In *Shayler*,[335] the Lord Chief Justice, approving a statement of Rose LJ in *Hussain*, stated that:

> the evil must be directed towards the defendant or a person or persons for whom he has responsibility or, we would add, persons for whom the situation makes him responsible; . . . [this extends], by way of example, [to] the situation where the threat is made to set off a bomb unless the defendant performs the unlawful act. The defendant may have not have had any previous connection with those who would be injured by the bomb but the threat itself creates the defendant's responsibility for those who will be at risk if he does not give way to the threat.

327 '. . . the threat may be to burn down [D's] house unless the householder merely keeps watch against interruption while a crime is committed. Or a fugitive from justice may say, "I have it in my power to make your son bankrupt. You can avoid that merely by driving me to the airport." Would not many ordinary people yield to such threats, and act contrary to their wish not to perform an action prohibited by law? Faced with such anomaly, is not the only answer, "Well, the law must draw a line somewhere; and, as a result of experience and human valuation, the law draws it between threats to property and threats to the person" ', per Lord Simon [1975] 1 All ER at 932.

328 Above, p 299. 329 Below, p 323. 330 Law Com Working Paper No 55, paras 14–17.

331 *S (DM)* [2001] Crim LR 986 below, p 334. 332 [1967] VR 526.

333 [1989] QB 290, [1988] 3 All ER 1025, CA.

334 [1989] 1 All ER 652. See also *Wright* [2000] Crim LR 510.

335 [2001] 1 WLR 2206, para 49. This was accepted in *Hasan* [2005] UKHL 22, per Lord Bingham.

An extraneous threat

The threat must have some source extraneous to the defendant himself. In *Rodger and Rose*[336] D who was serving a life sentence was informed that his tariff had been substantially increased. He broke out of prison and raised duress as a defence to prison-breaking. It was conceded for the purpose of the appeal that he broke out because he had become suicidal and would have committed suicide had he not done so. So there was a threat to his life, but since the threat did not come from an extraneous source, it was no defence. To allow it, said the court, 'could amount to a licence to commit crime dependent on the personal characteristics and vulnerability of the offender'. The Court of Appeal in *Brown* relied upon this limitation to the defence to preclude the defence of duress of circumstances where D cultivated cannabis for personal use to alleviate pain for his MS.[337]

An imminent threat

The Court of Appeal has recently reiterated the 'requirement that the accused must know or believe that the threat is one which will be carried out immediately or before the accused or the other person threatened, can obtain official protection'.[338] But in *Abdul-Hussain*,[339] where Iraqis hijacked an aircraft because they feared they would be killed if they were returned to Iraq, the court reinterpreted the requirement of immediacy, holding that the question was whether D's response to the 'imminent' threat was proportionate and reasonable.[340] In *Hasan* Lord Bingham was at pains to reassert the primacy of the immediacy requirement. His lordship opined that the defence would not be available with a delay of a day between D being threatened with being shot and his commission of the crime.

Threats as a concurrent cause of the crime

It is said that D's will, must have been 'overborne' by the threat.[341] Presumably this means only that he would not have committed the offence 'but for' the threat and that the threat was one which might cause a person of reasonable fortitude to do as he did. If the prosecution can prove that he would have done the same act even if the threat had not been made, it seems that the defence will fail.[342] But the threat need not be the only motive for D's action. In *Valderrama-Vega*[343] D was under financial pressure and had

336 [1998] 1 Cr App R 143.

337 P 299, n 316. See M. Watson, 'Cannabis and the defence of necessity' (1998) 148 NLJ 1260. See for a philosophical consideration of such matters S. J. Morse, 'Diminished Capacity' in S. Shute, S. Gardner and J. Horder (eds), *Action and Value in Criminal Law* (1993), at 250–263.

338 *Hurst* [1995] 1 Cr App R 82, 93; *Flatt* [1996] Crim LR 576.

339 [1999] Crim LR 570.

340 See *Abdul-Hussain* [1999] Crim LR 570, where the court added '. . . if Anne Frank had stolen a car to escape from Amsterdam and been charged with theft, the tenets of English law would not, in our judgment, have denied her a defence of duress of circumstances, on the ground that she should have waited for the Gestapo's knock on the door'. But the requirement of proportionality is questionable.

341 Cf the discussion of *Steane* [1947] KB 997, [1947] 1 All ER 813. See also G. R. Rubin, 'New Light on Steane's Case' (2003) Legal History 143.

342 In *DPP v Bell (Derek)* [1992] Crim LR 176, DC, D, in terror of an aggressor, began to drive with excess alcohol. Although he admitted that, before the threat, he intended to drive, it was found as a fact (a finding with which the divisional court could not interfere) that he drove because of terror and so had a defence of duress of circumstances. But for the threat he might have changed his mind or been persuaded by his passengers not to drive.

343 [1985] Crim LR 220 and commentary.

been threatened with disclosure of his homosexual inclinations – neither matter being capable of amounting to duress – but it was wrong to direct the jury that the threats of death or serious injury also alleged to have been made must have been the sole reason for his committing the offence. If he would not have committed the offence but for the latter threats the defence was available even if he acted because of the cumulative effect of all the pressure on him. It is probably going too far to say that it is enough that the threats of death were 'the last straw' because the law will look for something more substantial than 'a straw' for an excuse; but threats of death or serious bodily harm can never be trivial, so it is probably sufficient to tell the jury that D has the defence if he would not have acted but for the threats. A direction that the defence was available only if D acted *solely* because of the relevant threats was upheld where it was suggested that he might also have been influenced by greed but the court thought it inadvisable to use that word in a summing up.[344]

No threat need exist in fact

There is no requirement for there to be a threat in fact. It is sufficient that D believes that there is a threat of the relevant gravity. If the defence was only available where there was a threat in fact, D could not plead duress where threatened with an unloaded gun, nor where D escaped from prison erroneously believing it to be on fire. This would be unduly restrictive.

In *Safi and others*[345] Afghan hijackers who had landed at Stansted airport claimed that their fear of persecution at the hands of the Taliban constituted a defence of duress of circumstances. The trial judge directed that the defence failed unless there was evidence that there was in fact, or might in fact have been, an imminent peril to the defendants or their families. S appealed on the basis that the defence should be available if he *reasonably* believed that if he had not acted in the way he had, he (and /or the family) would have been killed or seriously injured. The Court of Appeal allowed the appeal. Duress of circumstances does not depend on there being an actual risk of death or serious injury to the accused; the defence can be made out if the accused was impelled to act as he did because, as a result of what he reasonably believed to be the situation, he had good cause to fear that otherwise death or serious injury would result.

The situation of the defendant who is not personally aware of the threat but which would cause a reasonable person to commit crime has not been addressed.[346]

(Risk of) Threat not one knowingly courted

A further important limitation on the defence is that the threat must not be one that arises from D's voluntary involvement in a violent criminal enterprise. This has become an increasingly problematic area and the courts have sought to prevent the defence being too readily available to those involved in drug related and terrorist crime in particular where their involvement demonstrates a degree of prior culpability. The restriction is hedged in with qualifications. In the recent House of Lords decision in *Hasan*[347] the

[344] *Ortiz* (1986) 83 Cr App R 173.

[345] [2003] EWCA Crim 1809, [2003] Crim LR 721.

[346] Cf *O'Too* [2004] EWCA Crim 945 CA where D2 in cross examination suggested that D1 was threatened with death if he did not comply with demands to deal drugs. D1's defence was a denial of involvement and therefore the defence was not raised and not left to the jury.

[347] [2005] UKHL 22.

House expressed concern at the way in which the defence was being relied on more readily by defendants in more cases and that there was a danger that the restrictive elements of the offence were not being applied rigorously enough.[348]

Voluntary membership

D will be denied the defence if he voluntarily joined the criminal gang, as in *Sharp* where D was a party to a conspiracy to commit robberies who said that he wanted to pull out when he saw his confederates equipped with guns, whereupon E threatened to blow his head off if he did not carry on with the plan. In the course of the robbery, E killed V. D's conviction for manslaughter was upheld after a jury, had rejected his defence of duress. This had been the approach adopted in the Court of Criminal Appeal in Northern Ireland in *Fitzpatrick* (duress no defence to a charge of robbery committed as a result of threats by the IRA because D had voluntarily joined that organization)[349] and the *dicta* of Lords Morris, Wilberforce and Simon in *Lynch*.[350] It would be different of course if D was compelled to join the violent organization by threats of death or serious bodily harm then, in principle, he should not be deprived of the defence. Whether any lesser threat should suffice at this stage has not been decided. As Baroness Hale put the matter in *Hasan* the question ought to be whether D by his joining exposed himself to the risk as considered below 'without reasonable excuse'.[351]

The types of organization

It is impossible to specify precisely for which types of organization D's membership will preclude his pleading duress. In *Sharp* the gang were armed robbers; in *Fitzpatrick*, a paramilitary organization. In *Lewis*[352] the court construed this limitation on the defence strictly to be limited to association to be 'a para-military or gangster-tyrant style of organization' In *Shepherd*,[353] where D voluntarily joined a gang of burglars but wanted to give up after his first outing and raised the defence of duress by the gang to a charge of a later burglary, it should have been left to the jury to decide whether he was taking a risk of being subjected to such a threat of violence when he joined the gang. If a strict approach to this element is taken a drug user's association with a drug dealer might preclude his subsequent reliance on the defence.[354]

Active membership

D's attempt to withdraw from the organization, when the particular enterprise which resulted in the charge is in contemplation, is too late. But a person who joined a para-military organization in his youth can hardly be held to have forfeited his right to plead duress by that organization for life. If he has done all he can to sever his connection with it before the particular incident was in contemplation, should he not be able to rely on the defence?

The risk to which D was exposing himself?

In *Lewis*, D, who was serving a sentence for armed robbery, was savagely attacked in the prison yard by E, who was serving a sentence for the same robbery. D refused to testify

[348] See especially Lord Bingham's speech at [22]. [349] [1977] NI 20.
[350] [1975] AC 653. [351] [78].
[352] (1992) 96 Cr App R 412; *Kleijn* [2001] All ER (D) 143 (May).
[353] (1987) 86 Cr App R 47. [354] Are there any non-violent drug dealers?

against E because he was terrified of reprisals and was charged with contempt. It was held that duress ought to have been left to the jury. There was no evidence that D knew that he was exposing himself to the risk of this *sort of threat* when he participated in the armed robbery.

In subsequent cases a point of controversy arose as to whether D would be denied the defence only where voluntarily put himself in a position where he was aware of the risk of being subjected to pressure by way of violence *to commit offences of the type alleged*, or whether he would be denied the offence if he exposed himself to unlawful threats more generally. In *Baker and Ward*,[355] the Court of Appeal favoured the first view, which was more generous to the accused. However, in *Heath*,[356] the Court of Appeal took a more restrictive view, holding that the defence of duress would be denied if when D voluntarily associated with the group he knew that by doing so he was likely to be pressured by threats of violence to compel him to commit *any crime*. This was followed in *Harmer*.[357] Despite the cogent academic criticism of this approach,[358] the House of Lords in *Hasan* has now confirmed that *Baker* was wrongly decided. Lord Bingham explained that:

> The defendant is, *ex hypothesi*, a person who has voluntarily surrendered his will to the domination of another. Nothing should turn on foresight of the manner in which, in the event, the dominant party chooses to exploit the defendant's subservience. There need not be foresight of coercion to commit crimes, although it is not easy to envisage circumstances in which a party might be coerced to act lawfully.[359]

D's awareness of the risk to which he is exposing himself

Hasan confirms that the defence is unavailable where the risk to which D exposes himself is pressure to commit any crime. A further question arises whether the defence can only be denied D where he is proved to have been aware of that risk (subjectively), or whether it is sufficient that he ought to have been aware of that risk (objectively). As a matter of policy the House of Lords in *Hasan* suggests that the test is whether D ought to have known. Again this restricts the availability of the defence.[360]

> The policy of the law must be to discourage association with known criminals, and it should be slow to excuse the criminal conduct of those who do so. If a person voluntarily becomes or remains associated with others engaged in criminal activity in a situation where he knows or ought reasonably to know that he may be the subject of compulsion by them or their associates, he cannot rely on the defence to excuse any act which he is thereafter compelled to do by them. It is not necessary in this case to decide whether or to what extent that principle applies if an undercover agent penetrates a criminal gang for bona fide law enforcement purposes and is compelled by the gang to commit criminal acts.[361]

355 [1999] 2 Cr App R 355.

356 *Heath* [2000] Crim LR 109 (indebted drug user, aware that he might be subjected to threats, required to transport £300k of cannabis), distinguishing *Baker and Ward* (above) (inadequate direction).

357 [2002] Crim LR 401.

358 As J. C. Smith noted in commenting on *Heath*, 'it is one thing to be aware that you are likely to be beaten up if you do not pay your debts, it is another that you may be aware that you may be required under threat of violence to commit other, though unspecified crimes, if you do not'.

359 Cf Baroness Hale's example of the battered woman compelled to perform lawful tasks of ironing.

360 Cf Baroness Hale commenting on the attractions of the subjectivist approach advanced by the Law Commission.

361 Lord Bingham [38].

A nominated crime

In the paradigmatic case of duress, the defendant will have been told 'perform this crime or else'. The question has arisen how specific the nomination of the crime must be for D to be able to rely on the threats. In *Cole*[362] D was convicted of robbing two building societies and pleaded duress on the basis that he had been threatened by money lenders to whom he was in debt. The Court of Appeal held that a plea of duress was not available as the money lenders had not stipulated that he commit robbery to meet their demands. There was not the degree of immediacy and directness required between the peril threatened and the offence charged. Subsequently in *Ali*[363] D, a heroin addict, was convicted of robbing a building society and D claimed that his supplier, X, who had a reputation for violence, had demanded repayment of the monies D owed him. Further, that X had provided D with a gun and told D to get the money by the following day from a bank or a building society. The Court of Appeal upheld his conviction but appeared to accept that a threat is capable of amounting to duress when the duressee is charged with robbing a particular building society not specified by the duressor.

(iv) Evaluating D's response to the threat

Several difficult issues arise in determining whether by committing the crime in response to the threats D's conduct should be excused. In particular, the courts have struggled with questions of whether it is sufficient that the particular defendant regarded it as a reasonable response to the threat he believed that he faced, or whether the defence is only available if the reasonable person would have responded in the same way if faced with the threat D genuinely believed he faced.

In *Howe* the House of Lords answered in the affirmative the question–

> Does the defence of duress fail if the prosecution prove that a person of reasonable firmness sharing the characteristics of the defendant would not have given way to the threats as did the defendant?

The House held that the correct direction was that stated by Lane LCJ in *Graham.*[364]

> (1) Was [D], or may he have been, impelled to act as he did because, as a result of what he reasonably believed [E] had said or done, he had good cause to fear that if he did not so act [E] would kill him or . . . cause him serious physical injury? (2) If so, have the prosecution made the jury sure that a sober person of reasonable firmness, sharing the characteristics of [D], would not have responded to whatever he reasonably believed [E] said or did by taking part in the killing?

The direction contains three objective elements.

(1) D must have *reasonably* believed in the circumstances of the threat;[365]

(2) D's belief must have amounted to *good cause* for his fear;

(3) D's response must be one which might have been expected of a *sober person of reasonable firmness.*

362 [1994] Crim LR 582. In *Hasan*, Lord Bingham regarded the threat as lacking immediacy in this case.

363 [1995] Crim LR 303.

364 [1982] 1 All ER 801 at 806, 74 Cr App R 235 at 241. Cf *Lawrence* [1980] 1 NSWLR 122.

365 This is part subjective. But the test of reasonableness was firmly endorsed in *Hasan*, [23] per Bingham.

A fourth element is usually considered although not deriving from the *Graham* judgment:

(4) D must have had no *reasonable* opportunity to escape the threat.

In imposing this objective regime on the defence Lord Lane in *Graham* equated duress with self-defence which, it was then generally accepted, imposed an objective test. But less than two years later in *Gladstone Williams*[366] Lord Lane, influenced by the judgment of Lawton LJ in *Kimber*,[367] held that an unreasonable belief, if honestly held, might found self-defence. Lawton LJ appreciated and applied the general effect of *DPP v Morgan*[368] which was not cited in *Graham*. Logically, if *Morgan* applies to self-defence, it ought equally to apply to duress.[369] It is arguable that the defences are distinguishable in this respect since duress is generally regarded as excusatory and self-defence as justificatory in nature.[370] The decision in *Graham* may thus have been an unfortunate accident – but, since it has been approved by the House of Lords and the House of Lords in *Hasan* certainly did not seem to be inclined to depart from it.[371]

It is submitted that, in the first two respects, the direction in *Graham* lays down too strict a rule. D should surely be judged on the basis of what he honestly believed and what he genuinely feared.[372] If his genuine fear was such that no person of reasonable firmness could have been expected to resist it, he should be excused. He may have been unduly credulous or stupid, but he is no more blameworthy than a person whose fear is based on reasonable grounds.[373] *Martin (DP)*[374] holds that D's characteristics – in that case a schizoid affective disorder, making him more likely to regard things said as threatening and to believe that threats would be carried out – must be taken into account. This seems to be a substantial mitigation of the objective test.

As with mistake generally, lack of faith in the jury to detect the 'bogus defence' and the additional hardship for the prosecution probably lies at the root of the objective requirements. But this attitude has been strongly repudiated recently in relation to offences. In *B v DPP*[375] and *K* and the requirement of reasonable grounds for D's claimed belief may

366 Below, p 329.

367 [1983] 3 All ER 316 (an honest belief that V was consenting was a defence to indecent (now sexual) assault).

368 Above, p 125. See J. C. Smith, 'The Triumph of Inexorable Logic' in *Leading Cases of the Twentieth Century* (2000).

369 In *Martin (DP)* [2000] 2 Cr App R 42, CA, (discussed in Archbold News [2000] Issue 7, p 6) Mantell LJ said at 49 – apparently in error – that the subjective test in self-defence had been applied to duress in *Cairns* [1999] 2 Cr App R 137 where Mantell LJ also gave the judgment. See generally on the merits of the subjective and objective approaches P. Alldridge, 'Developing the Defence of Duress' [1986] Crim LR 433.

370 See S. Yeo, *Compulsion in the Criminal Law* (1990).

371 Lord Bingham rejected comparison with other defences.

372 See recently W. Wilson, 'The Structure of Defences' [2005] Crim LR 108, 115–116.

373 In *DPP v Rogers* [1998] Crim LR 202, DC, Brooke LJ seems wrongly to have assumed that this is now the law, apparently anticipating a reform proposed by the Law Commission. Cf *Abdul-Hussain*, [1999] Crim LR 570. If D reasonably believes there is a threat, it is immaterial that there is no threat in fact: *Cairns* [1999] 2 Cr App R 137, CA. For a criticism of the Commission's 'slavish adherence to subjectivism' see J. Horder, 'Occupying the Moral High Ground' [1994] Crim LR 334 at 341 and comments by J. C. Smith, 'Individual incapacities and criminal liability' [1998] Med L Rev 138 at 155–157.

374 [2002] 2 Cr App R 42, CA.

375 [2000] 2 Cr App R 65. See especially Lord Nicholls [2000] 1 All ER 833 at 839–840.

now be vulnerable. As with mistake generally, the more tenuous the grounds for his claim, the less likely is D to be believed.

The confusion in this area is illustrated by the case of *Safi* (above). At the first trial the judge directed the jury that D's genuine belief in the threat of death was sufficient, on a retrial the second judge adopted an objective formulation. The Court of Appeal failed to clarify the position but seemed implicitly to be adopting an objective test.[376] In *M*, the Court of Appeal adopted an apparently subjective approach to the first question. In *M*[377] it was held that the jury should be instructed that the defence fails if the prosecution satisfied them of any of the following:

(a) that the defendant did not genuinely believe that unless she committed the offence there was a real possibility of at least serious harm to herself or her family,
(b) that an ordinary person of reasonable firmness, sharing the accused's characteristics, would not in reaction to threats, real or perceived, have acted as she did, or that there was a rejected opportunity to escape or avoid the threat without injury to herself or her family which a reasonable person, in a like situation, would have taken.

In two subsequent cases the Court of Appeal has again endorsed the objective approach in the first limb.[378] Further clarification from the House of Lords was not forthcoming in *Hasan*, but the tenor of the speech of Lord Bingham leaves little doubt that the objective formulation would be preferred.

The person of reasonable firmness[379]

Since duress is (*pace* Lord Hailsham) a concession to human frailty[380] and some are frailer than others, it is arguable that the standard of fortitude required should also vary.[381] *Graham* is however consistent with a common approach of the law in deciding that this is fixed. It is for the law to lay down standards of conduct. When attacked, D may use only a reasonable degree of force in self-defence. Under provocation, D must display a reasonable degree of self-restraint. Similarly, *Graham* decides, a person under duress is required to display 'the steadfastness reasonably to be expected of the ordinary citizen in his situation'.[382] The court relied particularly on the analogy with the law of provocation as laid down in *Camplin*.[383] That test, as now relaxed in favour of the accused by the decision in *Smith (Morgan)*,[384] suggests that the threat must be one which would overcome the will of a person having the ability to resist threats reasonably to be expected of an ordinary person of the sex and age of the defendant and in other respects sharing such of the

376 Para 25. 377 [2003] EWCA Crim 1170. See also *Sewell* [2004] EWCA Crim 2322.
378 *Blake* [2004] EWCA Crim 1238, para 18; *Bronson* [2004] EWCA Crim 903 para 23.
379 See K. J. M. Smith, 'Duress and Steadfastness: In Pursuit of the Unintelligible' [1999] Crim LR 363.
380 *Howe* [1987] 1 All ER 771 at 779–780.
381 'It is arguable that the standard should be purely subjective and that it is contrary to principle to require the fear to be a reasonable one': per Lord Simon [1975] 1 All ER at 931. Cf Law Commission Working Paper No 55, paras 11–13 and Law Com Report No 83 at paras 2.27–2.28. Cf *Hudson* [1965] 1 All ER 721 at 724.
382 (1982) 74 Cr App R at 241. 383 [1978] AC 705, [1978] 2 All ER 168, below, p 451.
384 [1999] 1 Cr App R 256, below, p 454.

defendant's characteristics[385] as would affect, not only the gravity of the threat to him, but also of his ability to resist it. The courts may, however, adopt a more restrictive approach to the full defence of duress than to the partial defence of provocation.

In *Bowen*[386] it was held that a low IQ, short of mental impairment or mental defectiveness, is not relevant: a person of low IQ may be expected to be as courageous and able to withstand threats as anyone else. That does not necessarily answer the argument – belatedly advanced on appeal – that D's ability to seek the protection of the police might have been impaired. Age[387] and sex may be relevant, depending on the circumstances, as may pregnancy and serious physical disability. In *Bowen*[388] the court added to the list 'recognized mental illness or psychiatric condition, such as post traumatic stress disorder leading to learned helplessness'.[389] The last condition refers to *Emery*,[390] a case of cruelty to a child, where it was said, *obiter*, that it would be right to admit 'an expert account of the causes of the condition of dependent helplessness, the circumstances in which it might arise and what level of abuse would be required to produce it'. 'A woman of reasonable firmness suffering from a condition of dependent helplessness' is a contradiction in terms; but the point appears to be that the alleged history of violence by D's partner, said to have produced that condition, was part of the duress. That explanation does not however seem to have appealed to the court in *Bowen*. This is a question for the jury and expert evidence has been held inadmissible to show that D was 'emotionally unstable' or in 'a grossly elevated neurotic state',[391] or that he is unusually pliable or vulnerable to pressure;[392] nor is evidence of sexual abuse as a child, resulting in lack of firmness, not amounting to psychiatric disorder: *Hurst*,[393] where Beldam LJ said, 'we find it hard to see how the person of reasonable firmness can be invested with the characteristics of a personality which lacks reasonable firmness . . .'.

It is no less hard when the condition is a 'recognized mental illness'. The acceptance of such an illness as a relevant characteristic suggests that the objective test has broken down and that we are moving closer to the test proposed by the Law Commission: 'the threat is one which in all the circumstances (including any of [the defendant's] characteristics that affect its gravity) he cannot reasonably be expected to resist'.[394]

The court will be faced with drawing some fine distinctions between unusual vulnerability and recognized psychiatric conditions affecting the ability to withstand pressure.[395] The increasing shift towards subjectivity in this limb of the defence stands in contrast to the increased objectivity in the first limb. It highlights the incoherence of the defence as it has evolved at common law, underlining the need for a legislative response.

385 Such as the schizoid affective disorder afflicting *Martin (DP)* above.

386 [1996] 2 Cr App R 157, [1996] Crim LR 577. In *Flatt* [1996] Crim LR 576 it was held that drug addiction was a self-induced condition, not a characteristic. For criticism of the approach in general for its failure to reflect psychiatric understanding see A. Buchanan and G. Virgo, 'Duress and Mental Abnormality' [1999] Crim LR 517.

387 Cf *Ali* [1989] Crim LR 736, above p 305.

388 [1996] 2 Cr App R 157.

389 This was held to be insufficient in *Moseley* [1999] 7 Archbold News 2.

390 (1992) 14 Cr App R (S) 394.

391 *Hegarty* [1994] Crim LR 353.

392 *Horne* [1994] Crim LR 584.

393 [1995] 1 Cr App R 82, 90.

394 Draft Criminal Law Bill, cl 25, Law Com No 218.

395 See *Antar* [2004] EWCA Crim 2708.

An effective threat at the time D acts

The only force that doth excuse, is a force upon the person, and present fear of death; and his force and fear must continue all the time the party remains with the rebels. It is incumbent on every man, who makes force his defence to show an actual force, and that he quitted the service as soon as he could.[396]

If the person under the compulsion is able reasonably to resort to the protection of the law, he must do so or the defence will be lost. In *Hasan* Lord Bingham regarded the 'immediacy of the threat' and D's inability to avoid it as the 'cardinal feature' of the defence.[397] His lordship observed that it should be made clear to juries that unless D reasonably expects the threats to be carried out 'immediately or almost immediately' the defence may be lost because there may be little room for doubt that the could take evasive action. The question whether D had a reasonable opportunity to take evasive action ought not in his lordship's opinion to be subsumed within the question whether D had a reasonable belief in the existence of the threat and whether a reasonable person in D's circumstances would have responded as D did.[398] When the threat is withdrawn or becomes ineffective, D must desist from committing the crime as soon as he reasonably can. If, having consumed excess alcohol, he drives off in fear of his life, he commits an offence only if the prosecution can prove that he continued to drive after the terror ceased.[399]

Where the threats operate, or D reasonably perceives them as operating on someone other than himself, the question whether the threat is still operative may be more difficult to determine. For example, in *Hurley* D had ample opportunity to place himself under the protection of the police but the court held that the defence of duress might still be available because his *de facto* wife was held as a hostage by his oppressors. Though he himself was physically out of range, the threats against her were presently operative on his mind. *Hudson*[400] goes further. Two young women, called as witnesses for the prosecution, gave false evidence because they had been threatened by a gang with serious physical injury if they told the truth, and they saw one of the gang in the public gallery of the court. Duress was accepted as a defence to a charge of perjury. DD could have put themselves under the protection of the law by informing the court; and there were no threats to third parties. The court thought it immaterial that the threatened injury could not follow at once since (in its opinion) there was no opportunity for delaying tactics and they had to make up their minds whether to commit the offence while the threat was operating. The threat was no less compelling because it could not be carried out there if it could be effected in the streets of Salford the same night. The case thus turns on the point that police protection could not be effective. It was recognized to extend the possible ambit of the defence widely for there would be few cases where the police can offer effective and permanent protection against such threats.[401]

396 *M'Growther* (1746) Fost 13 at 14, per Lee CJ.

397 [25–26].

398 [24].

399 *DPP v Bell (Derek)*, above, p 301.

400 [1971] 2 All ER 244; followed by *Lewis* (1992) 96 Cr App R 412, 415.

401 See comment in [1971] Crim LR 359 and (by Goodhart) in 87 LQR 299 and 121 NLJ 909 and (by Zellick) in 121 NLJ 845. In *K* (1983) 78 Cr App R 82, CA, it was held that duress might be available as a defence to contempt of court committed in the witness box by a prisoner who had been threatened with reprisals against himself and his family, by the accused, a fellow prisoner. The Law Commission propose: 'The threat must be, or the defendant must believe that it is, one that will be carried out immediately, or before he

However, in *Hasan*, Lord Bingham regarded *Hudson and Taylor* as having had 'the unfortunate effect of weakening the requirement that execution of a threat must be *reasonably* believed to be imminent and immediate'[402] Such a strict standard may be supported by the need to prevent the defence being misused and pleaded in spurious cases, but is it right that a defendant who reasonably fears he will be shot tomorrow after perjuring himself today ought not to be allowed a defence of duress?

As with the question whether the reasonable person would have withstood the pressure, similar principles apply to the doctrine requiring D to escape from duress if possible. His defence will fail if an ordinary person of his sex, age and other relevant characteristics would have taken an opportunity to escape. Obviously, physical disabilities, for example that he was lame, would be taken into account.[403] Following *Graham*, however, he must presumably be taken to have been aware of opportunities of which he ought reasonably to have been aware at the time the opportunity arose.[404] A better view, it is submitted, is that if he was not in fact aware of the opportunity to escape, he should not be penalized for his stupidity or slow-wittedness. In the current judicial climate this would be seen as too generous to the accused.

(v) Offences to which duress/duress of circumstances not available

Duress by threats has been accepted as a defence to manslaughter,[405] criminal damage,[406] arson,[407] theft,[408] handling,[409] perjury and contempt of court,[410] offences under the Official Secrets Acts[411] and drug offences;[412] and courts have assumed that it would apply to buggery[413] (presumably therefore to sex offences under the 2003 Act) and conspiracy[414] to defraud. It is available to strict liability crimes.[415]

Duress of circumstances has been held to be a defence to various road traffic offences to hi-jacking, contrary to s 1(1) of the Aviation Security Act 1982[416] and to unlawful possession of a firearm. It now seems safe to say that either kind of duress may be a defence to any crime, except some forms of treason, murder and, attempted murder.[417]

(or the person under threat) can obtain official protection: Criminal Law Bill, clause 25(2)(b). This provision, by allowing the defence if the defendant believes that official protection will be ineffective, differs from previous treatments of the point' – Report, para 29.2.

402 [27]. Lord Bingham at one point suggests that the defence in *Hudson* should fail because there was no question that DD had 'no opportunity to avoid' the threat. That is surely too strict a view. The question is whether they had a reasonable chance to avoid the threats.

403 But the fact that he was voluntarily drunk or drugged might be considered irrelevant.

404 *Aikens* above.

405 *Evans and Gardiner* [1976] VR 517 and (*No 2*) 523.

406 *Crutchley* (1831) 5 C & P 133.

407 *Shiartos* (Lawton J, 19 Sept 1961, unreported but referred to in *Gill*, below).

408 *Gill* [1963] 2 All ER 688, [1963] 1 WLR 841, CCA.

409 *A-G v Whelan* [1934] IR 518.

410 *K* (1983) 78 Cr App R 82, CA; *Lewis* (1992) 96 Cr App R 412.

411 *Shayler* [2001] Crim LR 986.

412 *Valderrama-Vega* [1985] Crim LR 220; *Ortiz* (1986) 83 Cr App R 173.

413 *Bourne* (1952) 36 Cr App R 125.

414 *Verrier* [1965] Crim LR 732. In *Abdul-Hussain*, [1999] Crim LR 570, the court doubted whether duress can be a defence to conspiracy; but if it is a defence to doing the act, it must surely be a defence to agreeing to do it.

415 *Eden DC v Braid* [1998] COD 259.

416 *Abdul-Hussain* [1999] Crim LR 570.

417 It is not available to civil tax penalties: *Mu v Customs and Excise* [2001] STI VADT.

Duress and treason

Although it is not uncommon for treason to be mentioned as a crime where duress is not a defence, it is quite clear that it may be a defence to at least some forms of treason.[418]

As long ago as 1419 in *Oldcastle*'s case[419] the accused, who were charged with treason in supplying victuals to Sir John Oldcastle and his fellow rebels, were acquitted on the ground that they acted through fear of death and desisted as soon as they could. The existence of the defence was admitted, *obiter*, by Lee CJ in *M'Growther*,[420] a trial for treason committed in the 1745 rebellion and by Lord Mansfield in *Stratton*:[421]

> ... if a man is forced to commit acts of high treason, if it appears really force, and such as human nature could not be expected to resist and the jury are of that opinion, the man is not guilty of high treason.

Much more recently, in *Purdy*[422] Oliver J directed a jury that fear of death would be a defence to a British prisoner of war who was charged with treason in having assisted with German propaganda in the second world war. Against this, Lord Goddard CJ said in *Steane*[423] that the defence did not apply to treason, but this remark appears to have been made *per incuriam*. Treason is an offence which may take many forms varying widely in seriousness and it would be wrong to suppose that threats, even of death, will necessarily be a defence to every act of treason. In *Oldcastle*'s case[424] Hale emphasizes that the accuseds' act was *only* furnishing of victuals and he appears to question whether, if they had taken a more active part in the rebellion, they would have been excused. Stephen thought the defence only applied where the offender took a subordinate part.

Duress and murder

It was stated in the books from Hale onwards that duress could not be a defence to a charge of murder. As Blackstone put it, a man under duress 'ought rather to die himself than escape by the murder of an innocent'.[425] There was, however, no clear judicial authority in point and in 1969 in *Kray*[426] an inroad was made into the supposed rule when Widgery LJ said that a person charged as an accessory before the fact to murder might rely on duress. In 1975, in *Lynch v DPP for Northern Ireland*[427] the House of Lords, by a majority of three to two, held that a person charged with aiding and abetting murder – one who would have been a principal in the second degree under the law of felonies – could have a defence of duress. The position of the actual killer was left open and in *Abbott*[428] in 1976, again by three to two, the Privy Council distinguished *Lynch* and held that the defence was not available to the principal offender, the actual killer. This was an illogical and unsatisfactory position because it is by no means always the case that the actual killer is the most dominant or culpable member of a number of accomplices, but he alone was now excluded from the defence. The distinctions involved were technical

[418] [1975] 1 All ER at 920, per Lord Morris; 940, per Lord Simon; 944, per Lord Kilbrandon. In *Gotts* [1992] 2 WLR 284 at 300, Lord Lowry excepts 'most forms of treason'. This passage was cited by Lord Bingham in *Hasan*.

[419] (1419) Hale I PC 50, East I PC 70.

[420] (1746) Fost 13, 18 State Tr 391.

[421] (1779) 21 State Tr 1045.

[422] (1946) 10 JCL 182.

[423] [1947] KB 997 at 1005, [1947] 1 All ER 813 at 817.

[424] (1419) Hale I PC 50.

[425] Blackstone, *Commentaries*, iv, 30.

[426] [1970] 1 QB 125, [1969] 3 All ER 941.

[427] [1975] AC 653.

[428] [1977] AC 755, [1976] 3 All ER 140.

and absurd.[429] Accordingly, when the matter came before the House in *Howe*[430] there was a strong case for either going forward and allowing the defence to all alleged parties to murder, or backward, and allowing it to none. The House chose the latter course, overruling its own decision in *Lynch.* The speeches emphasize different aspects, but the following reasons for the decision appear among them.

(1) The ordinary person of reasonable fortitude, if asked to take an innocent life, might be expected to sacrifice his own.[431] Lord Hailsham would not 'regard a law as either "just"; or "humane" which withdraws the protection of the criminal law from the innocent victim and casts the cloak of its protection on the coward and the poltroon in the name[432] of a "concession to human frailty".'

(2) One who takes the life of an innocent person cannot claim that he is choosing the lesser of two evils.[433]

(3) The Law Commission had recommended[434] 10 years previously that duress should be a defence to the alleged principal offender, but Parliament had not acted on that recommendation.[435]

(4) Hard cases could be dealt with by not prosecuting – in some cases the person under duress might be expected to be the principal witness for the prosecution[436] – or by the action of the Parole board in ordering the early release of a person who would have had a defence if duress had been an available defence.[437]

It is submitted that none of these reasons is at all convincing.[438]

(i) If the defence were available, it would apply only when a jury thought a person of reasonable fortitude *would* have yielded to the threat. The criminal law should not require heroism. Moreover, there are circumstances in which the good citizen of reasonable fortitude not only would, but probably should, yield to the threat because –

(ii) to do so might clearly be to choose the lesser of two evils, as where the threat is to kill D and all his family if he does not do, or assist in, an act which he knows will

[429] *Graham* [1982] 1 All ER 801 at 804 per Lane LCJ. See also I. H. Dennis, 'Duress Murder and Criminal Responsibility' [1980] 106 LQR 208.

[430] [1987] AC 417, [1987] 1 All ER 771, [1987] Crim LR 480 (sub nom *Burke*) and commentary. See also H. Milgate, 'Duress and the Criminal Law; Another About Turn by the House of Lords' [1988] CLJ 61; L. Walters, 'Murder under Duress and Judicial Decision Making in the House of Lords' (1988) 18 LS 61; see also J. Horder, *Excusing Crime* (above), at 133–137.

[431] *Howe* [1987] 1 All ER 771 at 779–780.

[432] Referring to the 5th edition of this work at 215.

[433] Lord Hailsham, *Howe* (above) at 780.

[434] Lord Bridge, ibid, at 784 and Lord Griffiths at 788.

[435] Law Commission, *Defences of General Application* (Law Com No 83).

[436] Lord Griffiths, *Howe* (above) at 790.

[437] Lord Griffiths, ibid, at 791 and Lord Hailsham at 780–781. In non-murder cases the suggestion that the defence should be kept within strict limits and that no injustice will result because of the availability of sentencing discretion met with approval from Lord Bingham in *Hasan,* [22] but cf Baroness Hale for convincing arguments against.

[438] This opinion was endorsed by Judge Stephen who, with Judge Cassese, was, however, dissenting in *Prosecutor v Drazen Erdemovic* (Case No IT–96–22-A) in the Appeals Chamber of the International Tribunal for the Prosecution of Persons for Serious Violations of International Humanitarian Law in the Former Yugoslavia.

cause grievous harm but not death (though, *ex hypothesi*, it has resulted in death and so constitutes murder).

(iii) Parliament's failure to act on the Law Commission recommendation proves nothing. The government has not given Parliament the opportunity to consider the matter. By parity of reason, Parliament might be taken to have approved of *Lynch*'s case, because there has been no move to overrule it.

(iv) Even if he were not prosecuted, the 'duressee' would be, in law, a murderer and, if he were called as a prosecution witness, the judge would, at that time, have been required to tell the jury that he was an accomplice in murder on whose evidence it would be dangerous to act in the absence of corroboration. A morally innocent person should not be left at the mercy of administrative discretion on a murder charge.

There is clearly a strong argument for reversing *Howe*.[439] Lord Bingham recently suggested that the logic of the argument is 'irresistible'.[440] The Law Commission in its Report recommended allowing the defence to the charge of murder, but radically, recommended reversing the burden of proof.

Attempted murder and other related offences

In *Howe* only Lord Griffiths[441] expressed a clear view that duress is not a defence to attempted murder but it has since been so held by a majority of three to two in *Gotts*.[442] This is logical. If it were otherwise the effect would be that an act, excusable when done, would become inexcusable if death resulted. But logic would also require the exclusion of the defence on a charge under s 18 of the Offences Against the Person Act 1861 of causing grievous bodily harm with intent because here also, the offence becomes murder if death results from it. A distinction might be taken between murder committed with intent to kill, where duress would not be a defence, and murder committed with intent to cause serious bodily harm, where it would. This would be reconcilable with the traditional statement of the law – a man 'ought rather to die himself than escape by the murder of an innocent' – which seems to postulate a decision to kill; but *Howe* seems too emphatic and uncompromising a decision to allow of any such refinement. *Gotts* indicates that the line is to be drawn below attempted murder, leaving the defence applicable to incitement and conspiracy to murder.

There is no point in raising the defence of duress to a murder charge; but suppose, as is frequently the case, that the evidence is such that the jury might properly acquit of murder and convict of manslaughter. If there is evidence that D may have been acting under duress[443] it is submitted that the judge should direct the jury that they must not convict of manslaughter either, unless they are sure that D was not acting under duress.

439 On the need for reform see A. Reed, 'The Need for a New Anglo American approach to Duress' [1996] J Crim L 209.

440 *Hasan* [21].

441 *Howe* (above) at 780 and 790.

442 [1992] 2 AC 412, [1992] 1 All ER 832, HL. Lord Lowry, dissenting, thought it is 'the stark fact of death' which distinguishes murder from all other offences. See S. Gardiner, 'Duress in Attempted Murder' (1991) 107 LQR 389.

443 Cf *Gilmour*, [2000] 2 Cr App R 407 where D was roused from his bed and, unwillingly, drove the terrorist murderers to and from the scene of the crime.

(b) Duress of circumstances

(i) The emergence of the defence[444]

The recognition of this defence occurred, more or less by accident, in *Willer.*[445] D was charged with reckless driving after he had driven very slowly on a pavement in order to escape from a gang of youths who were obviously intent on doing violence to him and his passengers. The trial judge declined to leave the defence of necessity to the jury. The Court of Appeal quashed D's conviction. They said that there was no need to decide on any defence of necessity that might have existed because 'the defence of duress[446] arose but was not pursued', as it ought to have been. It should have been left to the jury to say whether D drove 'under that form of compulsion, ie, under duress'. But this was not an instance of the previously recognized defence of duress by threats – the youths were not saying, 'Drive on the pavement – or else . . .'. There is a closer analogy with private defence.[447] But in substance the court was simply allowing the defence of necessity which it purported to dismiss as unnecessary to the decision. It should surely make no difference whether D drove on the pavement to escape from the youths, or a herd of charging bulls, a runaway lorry, or a flood, if he did so in order to escape death or serious bodily harm.

Subsequent cases have not dismissed *Willer* as a case decided *per incuriam.* They have treated it as rightly decided but have recognized that it is not the long-established defence of duress but an extension of it, 'duress of circumstances,' the relationship of which to necessity has not been settled (see below). In *Conway,*[448] another case of reckless driving, D's passenger, Tonna, had been the target of an attack on another vehicle a few weeks earlier when another man was shot and Tonna had a narrow escape. According to D, when two young men in civilian clothes came running towards D's parked car, Tonna shouted hysterically, 'Drive off'. D drove off because he feared a deadly attack on Tonna. Being pursued by the two men in an unmarked vehicle, he drove in a manner which the jury adjudged to be reckless. The two men were police officers who wished to interview Tonna. D's conviction was quashed because the defence of duress of circumstances had not been left to the jury.

Willer and *Conway* were followed in *Martin (Colin).*[449] D, while disqualified, drove his stepson, who had overslept, to work. He said that he did so because his wife feared that the boy would lose his job if he were late and threatened to commit suicide if D did not drive him. The wife had suicidal tendencies and a doctor stated that it was likely that she would have carried out her threat. The defence ought to have been left to the jury. According to the Court of Appeal the defence:

> can arise from other objective dangers threatening the accused or others . . . . the defence is available only if, from an objective standpoint, the accused can be said to be acting reasonably and proportionately in order to avoid a threat of death or serious injury. . . . [The] jury should be directed to determine these two questions: First, was the accused, or may he have been impelled to act as he did as a result of what he reasonably believed to be the situation he had good cause to

444 See S. Gardner, 'Necessity's Newest Invention' (1991) 11 OJLS 125.

445 (1986) 83 Cr App R 225.

446 The 'very different' defence of duress according to the court in *Denton* (1987) 85 Cr App R 246 at 248.

447 Below, p 335.

448 [1989] QB 290, [1988] 3 All ER 1025.

449 [1989] 1 All ER 652.

fear that otherwise death or serious physical injury would result; Second, if so, would a sober person of reasonable firmness, sharing the characteristics of the accused, have responded to that situation by acting as the accused acted?[450]

On the facts, the case seems to be strictly a case of duress by threats, where D is told, 'Commit the crime or else . . .'. The defence, as with duress by threats, is available only so long as the 'circumstances' continue to threaten. It may have been available (though the court did not decide the point) to a driver who drove off with excess alcohol in his blood to escape assailants; but it was not necessary for him to drive the two and a half miles to his home.[451] But where it was found that D, having consumed excess alcohol, drove off in fear of his life, he was guilty of an offence only if the prosecution could prove that he continued to drive after the terror ceased.[452]

In a recent controversial case of *Jones*,[453] involving intentional criminal damage to an air-force base in an attempt to prevent the USAF and UK services continuing their bombardment of Iraq, the defendants sought to rely, *inter alia*, on defences of duress of circumstances to the charges. In particular, the defendants argued that the war on Iraq was illegal in international law and that their actions were therefore necessary to avert that crime being committed on civilians in Iraq. On an interlocutory appeal the Court of Appeal held that the defence was not available, declaring that it is limited to a case of D being faced with a crime in national law. With respect, that cannot be right. The defence was available to *Martin* when his wife was threatening suicide (not a crime), moreover one can envisage many circumstances in which D or those for whom he is responsible face a threat of death or serious injury by non-criminal means (for example, a rapidly engulfing forest fire leads D to steal a car to escape to safety).

2. Necessity

As with duress, we are again concerned with situations in which a person is faced with a choice between two unpleasant alternatives, one involving his committing a breach of the criminal law and the other some evil to himself or others. If the latter evil outweighs any evil involved in the breach of the letter of the law, it is arguable that the actor should have a defence of necessity. The courts have never recognized a defence in these broad terms and to what extent a defence of necessity prevails in English law is uncertain. As early as 1552 Sergeant Pollard in an argument which apparently found favour with the judges of the Exchequer Chamber said that breaking the letter of laws might be justified 'where the words of them are broken to avoid greater inconveniences, or through necessity, or by compulsion . . .'.[454] More than 300 years later Stephen thought the law so vague that it was open to the judges to lay down any rule they thought expedient; and that the expediency of breaking the law in some cases might be so great that a defence should be allowed – but these cases could not be defined in advance.[455]

In spite of these doubts, Williams in 1953 submitted 'with some assurance' that the

450 Per Simon Brown J at 653.

451 *DPP v Jones* [1990] RTR 34, DC. Nor to drive 72 miles when intoxicated to escape a threat *DPP v Tomkinson*, above.

452 *DPP v Bell (Derek)*, above, p 301.

453 [2005] Crim LR 122.

454 *Reniger v Forgossa* (1552) 1 Plowd 1 at 18.

455 2 HCL 108.

defence of necessity is recognized by English law[456] and, particularly, by the criminal law,[457] arguing that the 'peculiarity of necessity as a doctrine of law is the difficulty or impossibility of formulating it with any approach to prevision'.

Williams' confidence was entirely justified. Lord Goff has, on several occasions recognized the existence of the defence and it was applied by the House of Lords in the *Bournewood Trust* case[458] to justify the detention of a person suffering from mental disorder where there was no statutory authority in point. Such persons might be detained where they were a danger or potential danger to themselves or others. From an early period other particular instances of necessity were recognized. It was justifiable (in the conditions of those days) to pull down a house to prevent a fire from spreading,[459] for a prisoner to leave a burning gaol contrary to the express words of a statute and for the crew of a ship or a passenger[460] to jettison the cargo in order to save the lives of the passengers. It was once held that prison officials may – indeed, must – forcibly feed prisoners if that is necessary to preserve their health and, *a fortiori*, their lives.[461] It was a defence to the statutory felony of procuring an abortion to show that the act was done in good faith for the purpose only of preserving the life of the mother,[462] although at that time there was no provision for such a defence in any statute.[463] More recently it has been recognized that a constable may direct other persons to disobey traffic regulations if that is reasonably necessary for the protection of life and property.[464]

An important case law development is the emergence of duress of circumstances above, which in many cases is treated simply as an instance of necessity. The relationship of the defences is discussed below. Despite the explicit recognition of the defence the courts adopt a persistently restrictive approach to the defence. There is an underlying anxiety that the defence must be kept within strict limits to prevent defendants claiming generally that they thought their actions in breaking the law were reasonable and represented the lesser of two evils. This would be a Trojan horse[465] for anarchy. The speech of Lord Bingham in *Hasan* underlined these judicial anxieties with defences of circumstantial pressure.

(a) Nature of threat

The traditional examples of necessity – escaping from the burning gaol, etc – do, like duress and duress of circumstances involve danger to life. In relation to lesser threats, writers from Hale[466] onwards have denied that necessity can be defence to a charge of

456 6 CLP, 216. 457 CLGP, 724, et seq. 458 [1998] 3 All ER 289, HL, at 297–298, 301–302.

459 See now the Criminal Damage Act 1971, below, Ch 28. 460 *Mouse's Case* (1608) 12 Co Rep 63.

461 *Leigh v Gladstone* (1909) 26 TLR 139 (Alverstone LCJ), not followed by Thorpe J in *Secretary of State for the Home Department v Robb* [1995] 1 All ER 677. The decision is heavily criticized – see G. Zellick, 'The Forcible Feeding of Prisoners: An Examination of the Legality of England Therapy' [1976] PL 153 at 159 – and no longer applied in practice.

462 *Bourne* [1939] 1 KB 687, [1938] 3 All ER 615. Cf *Morgentaler* (1975) 20 CCC (2d) 449 (SCC), discussed by L. Leigh, 'Necessity and the Case of Dr. Morgentaler' [1978] Crim LR 151.

463 See now Abortion Act 1967, below, Ch 15 and *T v T* [1988] 1 All ER 613, Fam Div.

464 *Johnson v Phillips* [1975] 3 All ER 682, [1976] 1 WLR 65, DC. Cf *Wood v Richards* [1977] RTR 201, [1977] Crim LR 295, DC.

465 Cf A. Norrie, *Crime Reason and History* (2nd edn, 2000), at 160.

466 I PC, 54, and see Blackstone, *Commentaries*, iv, 31.

theft of food or clothing. In modern times Lord Denning has justified the rule on the ground that '. . . if hunger were once allowed to be an excuse for stealing, it would open a door through which all kinds of lawlessness and disorder would pass'.[467]

In that case, a civil action, it was held that homelessness did not justify even an orderly entry into empty houses owned by the local authority: 'If homelessness were once admitted as a defence to trespass, no one's house could be safe. Necessity would open a door which no man could shut'.[468]

Probably it is now the law that if the taking or the entry was necessary to prevent death or serious injury through starvation or cold there would be a defence of duress of circumstances; but if it were merely to prevent hunger, or the discomforts of cold or homelessness, there would be no defence.

There are some cases where what was in substance a defence of necessity was allowed without identifying a threat to life or serious injury. In *Gillick*'s case one of the conditions stated of the lawfulness of the contraceptive advice or treatment given to a girl under 16 was that, unless she receives it, 'her physical or mental health or both are likely to suffer'.[469] In *F v West Berkshire Health Authority*[470] it was held that it was lawful to carry out a sterilization operation on a woman who lacked the mental capacity to consent because otherwise there would be a grave risk of her becoming pregnant which would be disastrous from a psychiatric point of view. Lord Goff founded his judgment on necessity. These cases would, however, involve at most a slight extension of duress of circumstances – comparable to MacNaghten J's interpretation of 'preserving the life of the mother' to include preserving her from becoming 'a physical or mental wreck' in *Bourne*,[471] a case which must now be regarded as one of duress of circumstances. Lord Goff has also said, 'That there exists a defence of necessity at common law, which may in some circumstances be invoked to justify what would otherwise be a trespass to land, is not in doubt. But the scope of the defence is by no means clear'. He found it unnecessary to decide the important question raised in that case, whether the defence could justify forcible entry (which would otherwise be a crime) into the private premises of another in the *bona fide*, but mistaken, belief that there exists an emergency on the premises by reason of the presence there of a person who has suffered injury and who may require urgent attention.[472]

(i) Statutory implication or exclusion of necessity defence

In England it has been argued that there is a principle of statutory interpretation:

> . . . that it requires clear and unambiguous language before the courts will hold that a statutory provision was intended to apply to cases in which more harm will, in all probability, be caused by complying with it than by contravening it.[473]

467 *Southwark London Borough v Williams* [1971] 2 All ER 175 at 179.

468 Ibid.

469 Per Lord Fraser [1986] AC 112, at 174.

470 [1989] 2 All ER 545, HL.

471 [1939] 1 KB 687, [1938] 3 All ER 615, below, p 504.

472 *Richards and Leeming* (on appeal from 81 Cr App R 125) (10 July 1986, unreported), HL. The House agreed with Lord Goff's speech. (We are indebted to Anthony Hooper for drawing our attention to this case.) By s 17(5) of the Police and Criminal Evidence Act 'all the rules of common law under which a constable has power to enter premises without a warrant are hereby abolished'. But does this abolish a justification which (if it exists at all) is available, not only to constables, but to persons generally?

473 P. Glazebrook, 'The Necessity Plea in English Criminal Law' [1972A] CLJ 87 at 93.

This principle, if it exists, seems to be little noticed in modern times. In *Buckoke v Greater London Council*[474] Lord Denning MR said, *obiter*:

> A driver of a fire engine with ladders approaches the traffic lights. He sees 200 yards down the road a blazing house with a man at an upstairs window in extreme peril. The road is clear in all directions. At that moment the lights turn red. Is the driver to wait for 60 seconds or more, for the lights to turn green? If the driver waits for that time, the man's life will be lost.

Lord Denning accepted the opinion of both counsel that the driver would at that time commit an offence against the Road Traffic Regulations if he crossed the red light. But the threat to the fictional man at the upstairs window seems to be no less than the threat to Willer, to the passenger in Conway's car or to Martin. Lord Denning was stating the effect of the law as he then believed it to be; but he added that the hypothetical driver 'should not be prosecuted. He should be congratulated' – so he might welcome this development. As Professor Packer says:

> . . . it seems foolish to make rules (or to fail to make exceptions to rules) that discourage people from behaving as we would like them to behave. To the extent that the threat of punishment has deterrent efficacy, rules such as these would condition people confronted with dilemmas to make the wrong choice, either through action or inaction. And the actual imposition of punishment would serve no useful purpose since we assume these people are not in need of either restraint or reform.[475]

The terms of a statute may, in effect, 'build in' a defence of necessity or, on the other hand, positively exclude one; and in either of these situations there is no room for the application of a general, common law defence.

(ii) Necessity and responses to non-criminal threats

As noted in the case of *Jones* above, the Court of Appeal sought to limit the defence to cases where D faced a criminal threat (in fact it was stipulated that the crime must be one under national law not international law). It is submitted that no such restriction applies. D may rely on the defence where he is faced with naturally occurring disasters, accidents caused by human actors or criminal threats.

(iii) Necessity and negligence?

In *DPP v Harris*[476] McCowan LJ was inclined to think that necessity can never be a defence to what would otherwise be the offence of driving without due care because 'due' admits of consideration of all the circumstances that would be taken into account if the general defence applied. In *Backshall*[477] the court preferred the opinion of Curtis J who thought it contrary to common sense to allow the defence in relation to the graver offence of reckless (now dangerous) driving and not to the lesser offence of careless driving; but

474 [1971] 1 Ch 655, [1971] 2 All ER 254 at 258. Statutory regulations now exempt the driver of the fire engine; but a contractor with a ladder on his lorry might find himself in the same position.

475 H. Packer, *The Limits of the Criminal Sanction* (1969), 114.

476 [1995] 1 Cr App R 170, [1995] Crim LR 73, DC. Curtis J thought that if necessity (in effect, duress of circumstances) applied to reckless driving, it must apply to the lesser offence of careless driving. Cf *Symonds* [1998] Crim LR 280.

477 [1999] 1 Cr App R 35 at 41.

the court recognized that it may make no difference. A person driving as a necessity, as required, is not failing to exercise 'due' care.

The reasoning of McCowan LJ might be applicable to any crime where the prosecution must prove that an act was done unreasonably: if it was necessary so to act, it could hardly be unreasonable to do so. In *Harris* the court was concerned with a statutory regulation which prescribes the circumstances in which a fire, police or ambulance vehicle may cross a red light; and such a specific provision may well be taken to exclude a defence of necessity when such a vehicle crosses in other circumstances. In *Harris* all was *obiter* because the court found that there was no necessity for D to drive as he did.

(iv) Necessity in strict and absolute liability offences

In *Cichon v DPP*[478] the court held that prohibition against allowing a pit bull terrier to be unmuzzled in a public place was 'absolute' and said that it followed that Parliament had excluded any defence of necessity; but if a general defence such as self-defence, duress – or necessity – is available even in offences requiring *mens rea*, it should *a fortiori* be available to an offence of strict liability. If the owner had removed the dog's muzzle on the orders of an animal rights fanatic armed with a sawn-off shotgun, he would surely have had a defence of duress. So too is that with necessity – though the fact that the dog in *Cichon* was afflicted with kennel cough might well be held insufficient to ground any such defence.

(v) Necessity and murder

One of the reasons given by the House of Lords in *Howe*[479] for refusing to allow a defence of duress to murder was that it had been decided in the famous case of *Dudley and Stephens*[480] that necessity was not a defence to murder. Whether that was the *ratio decidendi* of the case has been debated. One interpretation of the judgment is that the court found that no necessity existed. But the House of Lords has now held that the case does decide the point and it is fruitless to discuss that question further. Three men and a boy of the crew of a yacht were shipwrecked. After 18 days in an open boat, having been without food and water for several days, the two accused suggested to the third man that they should kill and eat the boy. He declined but, two days later Dudley killed the boy who was now very weak. The three men then fed on the boy's body and, four days later, they were rescued. The accused were indicted for murder. The jury, by a special verdict, found that the men would probably have died within the four days had they not fed on the boy's body, that the boy would probably have died before them and that, at the time of the killing, there was no appreciable chance of saving life, except by killing one for the others to eat.

The accused were convicted of murder, but the sentence was commuted to six months' imprisonment.

In *Dudley and Stephens*[481] Lord Coleridge CJ examined the pronouncements of writers of authority and found nothing in them to justify the extension of a defence to such a

478 [1994] Crim LR 918, DC.

479 [1987] AC 417 at 429, 453, above, p 312.

480 (1884) 14 QBD 273. On the instructions of Huddleston B the jury found the facts in a special verdict and the judge then adjourned the assizes to the Royal Courts of Justice where the case was argued before a court of five judges (Lord Coleridge CJ, Grove and Denman JJ, Pollock and Huddleston BB).

481 On the case generally, see A. W. B. Simpson, *Cannibalism and the Common Law* (1984).

case as this. Killing by the use of force necessary to preserve one's own life in self-defence was a well-recognized, but entirely different, case from the killing of an innocent person. Moreover, '[i]f . . . Lord Hale is clear – as he is – that extreme necessity of hunger does not justify larceny, what would he have said to the doctrine that it justified murder?'[482]

Apart from authority, the court clearly thought that the law ought not to afford a defence in such a case. They thought, first, that it would be too great a departure from morality; and, secondly, that the principle would be dangerous because of the difficulty of measuring necessity and of selecting the victim. The second reason is more convincing:

> Who is to be the judge of this sort of necessity? By what measure is the comparative value of lives to be measured? Is it to be strength or intellect, or what? It is plain that the principle leaves to him who is to profit by it to determine the necessity which will justify him in deliberately taking another's life to save his own.[483]

Williams finds as the 'one satisfying reason' in the judgment that it was no more necessary to kill the boy than one of the grown men and adds: 'To hinge guilt on this would indicate that lots should have been cast . . .'.[484] If the boy had agreed to be bound by the casting of lots, he would have been consenting to die; and arguably, consent in such a situation may be a defence. Captain Oates took his life when he left Scott and his companions; yet he was regarded, not as a felon, but as a hero.[485] If the boy had not consented, the drawing of lots would be hardly more rational than trial by ordeal – yet more civilized than a free-for-all. In fact, the court disapproved, *obiter*, of a ruling in an American case, *United States v Holmes*,[486] that the drawing of lots in similar circumstances would legalize a killing. Holmes, a member of the crew of a wrecked ship, was cast adrift in an overcrowded boat. In order to prevent the boat sinking, the mate gave orders to throw the male passengers overboard and Holmes assisted in throwing over 16 men. No doubt, if his act was criminal at all, it was murder; but a grand jury refused to indict him for murder and so he was charged with manslaughter. The judge directed that the law was that passengers must be preferred to seamen; only enough seamen to navigate the boat ought to have been saved; and the passengers whom necessity requires to be cast over must be chosen by lot. As this had not been done (none of the officers or crew went down with the ship) the jury found him guilty.

Stephen thought the method of selection 'over refined'[487] and Lord Coleridge thought this 'somewhat strange ground . . . can hardly . . . be an authority satisfactory to a court in this country'.[488]

The English judges offered no alternative solution and, presumably, their view was that, in the absence of a self-sacrificing volunteer, it was the duty of all to die. This was also the view of the distinguished American judge, Cardozo J:

> Where two or more are overtaken by a common disaster, there is no right on the part of one to save the lives of some, by the killing of another. There is no rule of human jettison.[489]

The principle in *Dudley and Stephens* is distinguishable if there is no problem of selection. D, a mountaineer who cuts the rope seconds before he would be dragged over a

[482] 14 QBD at 283. [483] 14 QBD at 287. [484] CLGP, 744.
[485] Should it matter that Oates killed himself? [486] 26 Fed Cas 360 (1841).
[487] 2 HCL 108. [488] 14 QBD at 285. [489] *Selected Writings*, 390.

precipice by E, his falling companion, surely commits no offence. There is no question of choosing between D and E. E is going to die in a matter of seconds anyway. The question is whether he alone should die a few seconds earlier, or whether they should both die seconds later.

At the inquest following the Zeebrugge disaster a witness, an army corporal, gave evidence that he and numerous other passengers were trapped in the stricken ferry and in grave danger of drowning. A possible way of escape up a rope ladder was barred by a man, petrified by cold or fear, who could move neither up nor down. After fruitless attempts to persuade him to move, the corporal ordered those nearer to push him off the ladder. They did so, he fell into the water and was not seen again. The trapped passengers were then able to climb up the ladder to safety. The coroner expressed the opinion that a reasonable act of self-preservation, or the preservation of others, is 'not necessarily murder'. So far as is known, no legal proceedings against the corporal were ever contemplated. Unlike the cabin boy, but like the falling mountaineer, the man on the ladder was chosen by fate as the potential victim by his immobility there. He was preventing the passengers from going where they had a right and a most urgent need to go. He was, unwittingly, imperilling their lives.[490]

Similarly the commander of an Australian naval ship 'took the decision to save the rest of his crew by sealing four sailors in the blazing engine room, consigning them to certain death, after rescuers were beaten back by the flames'.[491] It seems likely that the decision taken by the officer is that which any prudent officer of sound judgement would have taken. If so, it is inconceivable that he would ever be charged with, or convicted of, murder. Surely the law should recognize this. In these examples the evil avoided outweighs that caused – one dies instead of two, or instead of many – not only is there extreme duress – the conduct is justified. Indeed the Australian officer would probably have been in breach of his duty if he had allowed his ship and most of her crew to be lost. So, notwithstanding the approval of *Dudley and Stephens* by *Howe*, it would be premature to conclude that necessity can never be a defence to murder. See eg recently the recommendation of the Victoria Law Reform Commission[492] that duress and necessity should be available to murder when D faces 'a sudden and extraordinary emergency'.

Re A – the conjoined twins

In the case of the conjoined twins[493] the court held that, in the special circumstances of that case, it was lawful to kill the weaker twin, B, in order to save the life of the stronger, A. But this was not a simple choice between A and B, which the court would have been unwilling to make. The situation presented to the court was that if the operation was performed B would be killed but A would probably live – as indeed occurred – but, if the operation was not performed, both would die. Brooke LJ based his decision on necessity. The three requirements for the defence were stated to be: (i) the act is needed to avoid

490 See further, Smith *Justification and Excuse*, ch 3. And cf, self-defence against a nine-year-old or insane person.

491 (1998) The Times, 5 May.

492 Final report, *Defences to Homicide* (2004).

493 *Re A (Children)* [2000] 4 All ER 961, [2001] 400 and commentary, below p 338. Cf the approach of the Canadian Supreme Court in *Latimer* [2001] 1 SCR 3, denying D a defence where he killed his severely disabled daughter. The court pronounced a defence based on three criteria: (i) imminent peril; (ii) no reasonable legal alternative being available; (iii) D's reaction being proportionate.

inevitable and irreparable evil; (ii) no more should be done than is reasonably necessary for the purpose to be achieved; and (iii) the evil inflicted must not be disproportionate to the evil avoided.[494]

His lordship distinguished *Dudley and Stephens.* There was no problem of selection in this case. Like the man on the rope in the Zeebrugge case and the falling mountaineer dragging his companion to his death, A was selected by the circumstances. Brooke LJ preferred necessity to private defence (discussed below) because here there was no 'unjust' aggression by B. But B was imperilling A's life and the private defence solution avoids the argument, valid or not, that necessity can never justify killing. Whatever its basis, the principle appears to be that it is lawful for D to kill B where, as D knows, B is doomed to imminent death but even the short continuation of his life will kill A as well.

Following the destruction of the World Trade Center in New York by hijacked aircraft it now appears to be recognized that it would be lawful to shoot down a plane, killing all the innocent passengers and crew if this were the only way to prevent a much greater impending disaster. Even if duress cannot be a defence to murder, it seems quite clear that necessity can.

(vi) A doctor's defence of necessity

Without expressly acknowledging it, the courts appear to have recognized a special defence to murder by doctors. Although a doctor knows that treatment will accelerate the death of his patient significantly – that is, kill him – he is not guilty of murder if his purpose is to give what, in the circumstances as he understands them, is proper treatment to relieve pain.[495] Even if this is right, there remains the possibility, where the doctor has made a grossly negligent assessment of the circumstances, of a conviction for manslaughter.

(vii) Necessity and a duty to act

Where D owes a duty of care to E it seems that necessity may impose on him a duty to act to the detriment of – even to kill – others. In the *Bournewod Trust* case it seems there was a duty to detain the dangerous patient. The Australian naval officer referred to above probably had a duty to kill the four sailors. While the doctors in the conjoined twins remained in control, they apparently had a duty to kill the weaker twin. When the 'conflict of duties'[496] is resolved, D must fufil the prevailing duty. If A, B and C are members of a mountaineering party and A sees that B is dragging C to the deaths of both, is he not bound to cut the rope, accelerating B's death but saving the life of C, if he can do so without risk? But what about a passer-by, D, who found himself in the same position as A? Presumably he would be justified in cutting the rope but probably not bound to do so.[497]

494 P 1051.

495 Dr Moor's case, discussed by A. Arlidge QC, 'The Trial of Dr. David Moor' [2000] Crim LR 31 and a comment by J. C. Smith, 'A Comment on Dr. Moor's Case' [2000] Crim LR 41. See also A. Ashworth, 'Criminal Liability in a Medical Context: the Treatment of Good Intentions' in A. Simester and A. P. H. Smith (eds), *Harm and Culpability* (1996).

496 See the discussion of the judgment of Wilson J in *Perka v R* (1984) 13 DLR (4th) 1 at 36 by Ward LJ at [2000] 4 All ER 1015–1016, by Brooke LJ at 1048–1050 and by Walker LJ at 1065–1066.

497 On the 'duty' to assist in such cases see Ch 4 above.

(viii) Necessity in other jurisdictions

In other parts of the common law world a general defence of necessity is now recognized. The courts of Victoria have recognized the existence of a general, if limited, defence in *Loughnan*[498] where D's defence to a charge of escaping from prison was that he feared he would otherwise be killed by other prisoners – but the defence was not made out on the facts. In *Perka*[499] the Supreme Court of Canada held that necessity may be an 'excuse' but not a 'justification' (there seems to be no practical difference except that it perhaps made the court feel better) for an act which is 'inevitable, unavoidable and afford(s) no reasonable opportunity for an alternative course of action that does not involve a breach of the law'.

The American Model Penal Code, which has been adopted in many states of the USA, propounds a general defence of necessity:

> Conduct which the actor believes to be necessary to avoid a harm or evil to him or to another is justifiable, provided that:
>
> (a) the harm or evil sought to be avoided by such conduct is greater than that sought to be prevented by the law defining the offence charged. . . .[500]

No such general principle exists or is likely to be developed by English courts. Edmund Davies LJ has clearly formulated the judicial attitude:

> . . . the law regards with the deepest suspicion any remedies of self-help, and permits these remedies to be resorted to only in very special circumstances. The reason for such circumspection is clear – necessity can very easily become simply a mask for anarchy.[501]

Until recently, it seemed that, except in cases where necessity had already been recognized as a defence, the courts were likely to be satisfied by their power to grant an absolute discharge in hard cases.[502] Recent developments suggest they may now be more adventurous.

(ix) Reform

The Law Commission, departing from the views of its Working Party, at one time recommended that there should be no general defence of necessity; and that, for the avoidance of doubt, it should be enacted that any such defence as does exist is abolished.[503] They thought that provision should be made by statute for a defence to particular offences where appropriate. The Commission is now persuaded that the defence of duress of circumstances should be provided and it is to be found in cl 43 of their Draft Code. More recently the Law Commission[504] has also accepted that as part of

498 [1981] VR 443. 499 (1984) 13 DLR (4th) 1.

500 Article 3, s 3.02. It is subject to qualifications not necessary to be noted here.

501 *Southwark London Borough v Williams* [1971] Ch 734, [1971] 2 All ER 175 at 181.

502 P. Glazebrook, above, 118–119.

503 Law Com No 83, *Defences of General Application* (1977); criticized by G. Williams, 'Necessity' [1978] Crim LR 128 under the Crim LR heading Defences of General Application: The Law Commission's Report No 83; R. Huxley, 'Proposals and Counter-Proposals on the Defence of Necessity' [1978] Crim LR 141.

504 Law Com No 218, *Legislating the Criminal Code: Offences Against the Person and General Principles* (1992).

the policy of retaining common law defences, a 'specific defence of necessity should be kept open as something potentially separate from duress. That is provided for by clause 36(2) of the Criminal Law Bill, which expressly saves "any distinct defence of necessity" when abrogating the common law defences of duress by threats and of circumstances.'

The Code would leave it open to the courts to develop such a defence at common law and Lord Mustill in *Kingston*[505] recognized the ability of the courts to establish new defences, though he found no justification for doing so in that case. The conjoined twins case illustrates a more open judicial approach.

(b) The relationship between duress, duress of circumstances and necessity[506]

It seems now to be generally accepted that duress and duress of circumstances will be treated as identical by the courts as regards all elements other than the obvious one of the source of the threat. This seems unobjectionable. However, in *S (DM)*[507] it was stated that *Abdul-Hussain* 'reflects other decisions which have treated the defences of duress and necessity as being part of the same defence and the extended form of the defence [that is, duress of circumstances] as being different labels for essentially the same thing'.[508] But there are strong objections to this view.

(1) It is established that duress cannot be a defence to murder or attempted murder but, following *Re A* (the case of the conjoined twins) it is now clear that necessity may.

(2) Imminent threats of death or grievous bodily harm are the only occasions for a defence of duress but not for necessity. It is surely a defence to a charge of battery that D was pushing a child to save him from some quite minor injury or even damage to his clothing. Suppose that in *Martin (Colin)* D's wife's threat had been, not to kill herself but to leave D; and suppose further that the consequences of her doing so would have been disastrous for D and his family. Duress of circumstances is not open. Should it be a defence for D to demonstrate that the break-up of his marriage would be a social disaster beside which any effect of his driving a short distance while disqualified would pale into insignificance?

(3) Necessity is a defence only if the evil D seeks to avoid would be greater than that which he knows he is causing whereas if D yields to torture which no ordinary person could be expected to resist, he should be excused however grave the consequences.

(4) Recent cases allowing evidence of the vulnerability to duress of the particular defendant have nothing to do with the proportionality of evils which is said to be

505 Above, p 275.

506 See also W. Wilson, *Central Issues* (2002), ch 10, pp 303 et seq.

507 [2001] Crim LR 986.

508 C. Clarkson, 'Necessary Action: A New Defence' [2004] Crim LR 81 (50th Anniversary article), has recently made a more radical suggestion that the defences of duress, necessity, duress of circumstances and self-defence should be collapsed into one defence of 'necessary action'. This would succeed in achieving its aim of avoiding the inconsistencies of the present law, but only by adopting a lowest common denominator for the defences which seems to be simply that the jury scrutinizes D's conduct to ascertain whether he faced a crisis and responded proportionately. It would be most unlikely to be adopted by the courts since they would be concerned that it opens the floodgates for spurious claims and perverse verdicts.

required for necessity but highly relevant to whether he should be excused for giving way to threats.

(5) Necessity may create a duty to act but mere duress can hardly do so.

(6) Duress is (generally accepted to be) an excuse, but necessity is a justification. It is quite inappropriate to talk of a surgeon's will being 'overborne' when he decides that it is necessary to carry out a sterilization or other operation, as in the *West Berkshire case*,[509] on a person who is unable to consent. The surgeon is making a reasoned and reasonable decision. Lord Brandon thought that not only would it be lawful, but that it would be the doctor's duty to operate. There is no question of excusing 'human frailty'. All this is true, *a fortiori*, of the decision of the court when it authorizes such an operation as in *Re A* (the conjoined twins).

It is disappointing that the appellate courts, including recently the Lord Chief Justice, are prepared to state that 'the distinction between duress of circumstances and necessity has, correctly, been by and large ignored or blurred by the courts'.[510]

3. Marital coercion

Though the terminology used by judges and writers is by no means uniform, the term 'coercion' is generally reserved for a special defence that was available at common law only *to a wife* who committed certain crimes in the presence of her husband. It was then presumed that she acted under such coercion as to entitle her to be excused, unless the prosecution were able to prove that she took the initiative in committing the offence. The exact extent of the defence at common law is uncertain. It did not apply to treason or murder; Hale[511] excluded manslaughter as well and Hawkins ruled out robbery.[512]

Earlier authorities allowed the defence only in the case of felonies but later it seems to have been extended to misdemeanours – but excluding brothel-keeping; 'for this is an offence touching the domestic economy or government of the home in which the wife has a principal share'.[513]

Various theoretical justifications were advanced for the rule – the identity of husband and wife, the wife's subjection to her husband and her duty to obey him – but the practical reason for its application to felonies was that it saved a woman from the death penalty when her husband was able, but she was not, to plead benefit of clergy.[514] This reason disappeared in 1692 when benefit of clergy was extended to women, yet the rule continued and its scope increased.

In 1925, however, the presumption was abolished by the Criminal Justice Act 1925, s 47:

> Any presumption of law that an offence committed by a wife in the presence of her husband is committed under the coercion of the husband is hereby abolished, but on a charge against a wife

509 Above, p 317.

510 *Shayler* (above), para 55; in *Hasan* [2005] UKHL 22, Lord Bingham seems to use the term necessity interchangeably with duress eg [22].

511 I PC 45.

512 I PC 4; but the editor of the 8th edition (J. Curwood) doubted this.

513 Blackstone, *Commentaries*, iv, 29.

514 Hale, I PC 45; 2 Lew CC 232n.

for any offence other than treason or murder, it shall be a good defence to prove that the offence was committed in the presence of, and under the coercion of, the husband.

At first sight, it would seem that all Parliament has done is to shift the burden of proof. But there are difficulties about this, for the question at once arises, proof of what? And it is not very easy to answer. 'Coercion' at common law was really a fiction applied when the wife committed a crime in the presence of the husband and there was no evidence of initiative by the wife. The common law gives little guidance as to what is required now coercion is a matter of affirmative proof. In *Shortland*,[515] a case of procuring a passport by deception, the court said that the wife must prove on the balance of probabilities that her will was overborne by the wishes of her husband so that she was forced unwillingly to participate in the offence. Neither physical force nor the threat of it is required.

(a) Coercion

Coercion is a wider defence than duress and is available to wives in addition to that general defence.[516] 'The Act can be regarded as merely an incomplete statement of the common law, and the common law still exists to supplement its deficiency'.[517] In the debate on the Bill the Solicitor-General told the House that the section gives the married woman:

a rather wider and more extended line of defence than pure compulsion, because coercion imports coercion in the moral, possibly even in the spiritual realm, whereas compulsion imports something only in the physical realm.[518]

The recommendation of the Avory Committee[519] that wives should be put in the same position as persons generally was not adopted. Far from there being the 'endless litigation' which one member feared there are only four reported cases[520] in which the defence has been relied on.[521] It is by no means clear what a wife has to prove to succeed – moral and spiritual, as distinct from physical, coercion are somewhat intangible.

(b) Restriction of marriage

The defence is available only to a woman who is validly married to her coercer. The woman must prove on the balance of probabilities that she is married to him. It is not enough that she believes on reasonable grounds that she is validly married: *Ditta*[522] where Lord Lane seems to have questioned whether the defence applies in the case of an Islamic polygamous marriage. There are obvious difficulties with such a discriminatory definition of the defence. It is questionable whether it would be regarded as compatible with Article 14 of the ECHR if D was convicted and imprisoned (therefore suffering

515 [1996] 1 Cr App R 116, [1995] Crim LR 893.

516 CLGP, 765. See *Richman* [1982] Crim LR 507 (Bristol Crown Court).

517 CLGP, 765, approved by Lord Edmund-Davies [1975] 1 All ER 954. See also Lord Wilberforce at 930.

518 HC, vol 188, col 875 (1925).

519 Cmd 1677.

520 *Pierce* (1941) 5 JCL 124, *Richman, Ditta* and *Shortland*, supra. Cf *Bourne* (above, p 205) where duress rather than coercion seems to have been relied on.

521 Perhaps the view of Mr Greaves-Lord, MP, has proved correct: '. . . how many women are there who have been coerced like that, who dare go into the witness box in order to convict the very persons under whose coercion the woman had committed the crime?' HC, vol 188, col 870 (1925).

522 [1988] Crim LR 43.

deprivation of liberty) or suffering some other penalty infringing her right to respect for private life (Article 8) when facing coercion which would have entitled her to rely on the defence had she been married to the threatening party. The defence seems to be restricted to the 'wife' but ought to be available to a party in a civil partnership under the Civil Partnerships Act 2004.

(c) Reform

If the defence has any rational basis in the modern law, it must (however unfounded in fact) be that wives are, or may be, under such domination by their husbands that they ought to be excused from criminal liability by threats of much less gravity than will avail persons generally. If so, it ought to be available to a woman who has an honest and reasonable (or even unreasonable) belief that she is married to her coercer. There is no reason to suppose that a wife by an Islamic polygamous marriage is any less under this supposed domination by her husband than a wife by a monogamous marriage; or a woman who lives as the 'partner' of a man under his domination. The defence is a relic of the past which ought to have been abolished long ago.

The Law Commission has recommended its abolition.[523]

4. Superior orders

It is not a defence for D merely to show that the act was done by him in obedience to the orders of a superior, whether military or civil. Where a security officer caused an obstruction of the highway by checking all the vehicles entering his employer's premises, it was no defence that he was obeying his employer's instructions.[524] Both the House of Lords and the Privy Council have asserted, probably *obiter*, that there is no defence of superior orders in English law.[525] Both approved the statement of the High Court of Australia[526] that 'It is fundamental to our legal system that the executive has no power to authorize a breach of the law and that it is no excuse for an offender to say that he acted under the authority of a superior officer'.

The fact that D was acting under orders may, nevertheless, be very relevant. It may negative *mens rea* by, for example, showing that D was acting under a mistake of fact or that he had a claim of right[527] to do as he did, where that is a defence; or, where the charge is one of negligence,[528] it may show that he was acting reasonably.

(a) Military law

Since 1944 the Manual of Military Law[529] has asserted that the fact that a war crime was committed in pursuance of superior orders does not deprive the act in question of its

523 Law Com No 83 (1977), paras 3.1–3.9. 524 *Lewis v Dickson* [1976] RTR 431, DC.

525 *Clegg* [1995] 1 All ER 334 at 344, HL, below, p 342; *Yip Chiu-cheung* [1994] 2 All ER 924 at 928, PC, below, p 342. The implications of *Clegg* for firearms officers and servicemen are considered in S. Skinner, 'Citizens in Uniform: Public Defence, Reasonableness and Human Rights' [2000] PL 266.

526 *A v Hayden (No 2)* (1984) 156 CLR 532 at 540.

527 *James* (1837) 8 C & P 131. 528 *Trainer* (1864) 4 F & F 105.

529 *Manual of Military* Law Part 1 (1972), ch VI, para 24; Part III, para 627. See Ministry of Defence, *The Manual of the Law of Armed Conflict* (2004). See generally, A. P. Rogers, *Law on the Battlefield* (1996), at 143–147.

character as a crime. The rule is capable of operating particularly harshly in the case of military orders. A soldier may be 'liable to be shot by a court-martial if he disobeys an order and to be hanged by a judge and jury if he obeys it'.[530] Servicemen are trained to obey orders instantly so that their response to commands is almost a reflex action. Although it would not be realistic to suggest that the action was involuntary, there is a cogent argument that the serviceman should have a defence if he did not know that the order was illegal and it was not so manifestly illegal that he ought to have known it.[531] Stephen J, remarking that the point had never been fully considered and determined – and it is still so – thought that 'Probably . . . it would be found that the order of a military superior would justify his inferiors in executing any orders for giving which they might fairly suppose their superior officer to have good reasons'.[532]

Thus it might be right to treat servicemen somewhat differently from civilians, though perhaps only when engaged in military or quasi-military operations and not, for example, when speeding in driving the colonel to the officers' mess.

In a South African case[533] which has been much cited, Solomon J said:

> I think it is a safe rule to lay down that if a soldier honestly believes he is doing his duty in obeying the commands of his superior, and if the orders are not so manifestly illegal that he must or ought to have known they are unlawful, the private soldier would be protected by the orders of his superior officer. . . .

The only English authority[534] directly on the point holds that it is not a defence to a charge of murder for D to show that he fired under the mistaken impression that it was his duty to do so. D was, no doubt, making a mistake of law, but there is no finding as to its reasonableness.

(b) Other provisions dealing with the defence

In an international context, the Statute of the International Criminal Court provides in Article 30 that 'the commission of a crime pursuant to an order of a government or of a superior does not relieve a person of criminal responsibility unless: (a) that person is under a legal obligation to obey orders of the government or the superior in question; (b) the person did not know that the order was unlawful; (c) the order was not manifestly unlawful'.[535]

530 A. V. Dicey, *Introduction to the Study of the Law of the Constitution* (10th edn, 1959), 303. Cf Stephen I HCL, 204–206, Williams, CLGP, 105, TBCL, 455–456, and Commander J Blackett (1944) RUSI Journal, Feb, p 12. See also D. B. Nichols, 'Untying the Soldier by Refurbishing the Common Law' [1976] Crim LR 181.

531 See I. Brownlee, 'Superior Orders – Time for a New Realism' [1989] Crim LR 396.

532 I HCL 205.

533 *Smith* (1900) 17 SCR 561, 17 CGH 561. But the case has not always been followed in South Africa. See Burchell and Hunt, 298–9.

534 *Thomas* (1816) Ms of Bayley J, Turner and Armitage, *Cases on Criminal Law* (1964), 67. For an instance of a concealed defence of superior orders, see *Salford Area Health Authority, ex p Janaway* [1989] AC 537, [1988] 2 WLR 442, CA; affd sub nom *Janaway v Salford Area Health Authority* on other grounds [1989] AC 537, [1988] 3 All ER 1079, HL, discussed, Smith *Justification and Excuse*, 70–72.

535 By Article 33(2) all orders to commit genocide or crimes against humanity are manifestly unlawful.

5. Public and private defence

Force causing personal injury, damage to property, or even death may be justified or excused because the force was reasonably used in the defence of certain public or private interests. Public and private defence is therefore a general defence to any crime of which the use of force is an element or which is alleged to have been committed by the use of force.[536] The use of the word 'unlawfully' in a statutory definition is a reminder of the existence of the general defences but they apply whether or not the statute uses that word[537] unless expressly or impliedly excluded. It is clear that the burden of disproving claims of public or private defence rests on the prosecution.[538] The law is to be found in a variety of sources. Defence of the person, whether one's own or that of another, is still regulated by the common law, defence of property by the Criminal Damage Act 1971, and arrest and the prevention of crime by s 3 of the Criminal Law Act 1967. Because of its haphazard growth, the law contains some inconsistencies and anomalies.

(a) General principle

The general principle is that the law allows such force to be used as is reasonable in the circumstances as the accused believed them to be, whether reasonably or not. For example, if D believed that he was being attacked with a deadly weapon and he used only such force as was reasonable to repel such an attack, he has a defence to any charge of an offence arising out of his use of that force. It is immaterial that he was mistaken and unreasonably mistaken.

The question, 'Was the force used reasonable in the circumstances as D supposed them to be?' is, with one exception,[539] a question, to be answered by the jury or magistrates. If D's use of force was reasonable to cause any harm which could reasonably have been foreseen, it is justified or excused, even if it results in some greater harm. For example, D wrestles with V who is trying to steal D's wallet. V dies of a heart attack. If it was reasonable to wrestle with him but would not have been reasonable to kill him, D commits no offence.

The defences can be conveniently described in terms of trigger and response – the trigger being D's belief that the circumstances render it reasonable for him to use force, and the response being the amount of force he uses.[540]

(i) D's belief in need for force subjectively assessed

The authority for the proposition that D is to be judged on the facts as he believed them to be is *Gladstone Williams*,[541] repeatedly applied in the Court of Appeal[542] and by the

536 *Renouf* [1986] 2 All ER 449 (reckless driving). Force was not an element of the offence of reckless driving (now abolished) but the use of force was alleged to constitute the recklessness in that case.

537 *Renouf*, supra; *Rothwell* [1993] Crim LR 626.

538 The judge must give clear direction on the issue: *O'Brien* [2004] EWCA Crim 2900.

539 See s 5 of the Criminal Damage Act 1971, below, pp 900–901.

540 See recently W. Wilson, 'The Structure of Defences' [2005] Crim LR 108.

541 (1984) 78 Cr App R 276, CA. But, where D is drunk, see *O'Grady* [1987] QB 995.

542 *Jackson* [1985] RTR 257; *Asbury* [1986] Crim LR 258, CA; *Fisher* [1987] Crim LR 334, CA; *Beckford v R* [1988] AC 130, [1987] 3 All ER 425, PC.

Privy Council in *Beckford v R*. Williams was charged with an assault occasioning actual bodily harm to V. D's defence was that he was preventing V from committing an assault on X. But V may have been lawfully arresting X. The jury was directed that if V was acting lawfully, D had a defence only if he believed *on reasonable grounds* that V was acting unlawfully. It was held that this was a misdirection. D had a defence if he honestly held that belief, reasonably or not. The court referred to the recommendation of the Criminal Law Revision Committee: 'The common law of self-defence should be replaced by a statutory defence providing that a person may use such force as is reasonable in the circumstances as he believes them to be in the defence of himself or any other person'.[543] The court declared that this proposition represented the common law, as stated in *Morgan*[544] and *Kimber*.[545]

(ii) Reasonableness of the force used to be assessed objectively

The reasonableness of D's response and the amount of force used are to be assessed objectively on the facts as D believes them to be. D's belief that he is doing only what is reasonable may be evidence, but no more, that it was reasonable.[546] Lord Morris has said:[547]

> If there has been an attack so that defence is reasonably necessary it will be recognized that a person defending himself cannot weigh to a nicety the exact measure of his necessary defensive action. If a jury thought that in a moment of unexpected anguish a person attacked had only done what he honestly and instinctively thought was necessary that would be most potent evidence that only reasonable defensive action had been taken. A jury will be told that the defence of self-defence, where the evidence makes its raising possible, will only fail if the prosecution show beyond doubt that what the accused did was not by way of self-defence.

These cases relate to self-defence but similar considerations apply to force used to prevent crime or to effect an arrest, etc.

(iii) Evidence of D's beliefs

There may be an issue as to what circumstances D genuinely believed to exist, especially where the claimed belief is, viewed objectively, an unreasonable one. In such a case evidence of D's personal characteristics must, in principle, be admissible in so far as they bear upon his ability to be aware of, or to perceive, the circumstances. But *Martin (Anthony)*,[548] decides, on policy grounds, that psychiatric evidence that D would have

543 *Fourteenth Report* (Cmnd 7844), para 72(a). The phrase 'may use' is inappropriate. The CLRC was concerned only with establishing a defence in criminal proceedings. The act should not be regarded as justified in the civil law; and, if the mistake was grossly negligent and caused death, it might be manslaughter.

544 [1976] AC 182.

545 [1983] 3 All ER 316, CA (D guilty of indecent assault only if he did not believe V was consenting and 'couldn't care less').

546 *Scarlett* [1993] 4 All ER 629 appeared to have significantly modified this rule but *Owino* [1996] 2 Cr App R 128, [1995] Crim LR 743, CA and *DPP v Armstrong-Braun* [1999] Crim LR 416, DC, decide that *Scarlett* in no way qualifies the law as stated in *Gladstone Williams* (1984) 78 Cr App R 276.

547 *Palmer v R* [1971] 1 All ER 1077 at 1078, PC, applied in *Shannon* (1980) 71 Cr App R 192, [1980] Crim LR 438 and *Whyte* [1987] 3 All ER 416.

548 [2002] Crim LR 136; and see *Shaw (Norman) v R* [2002] Crim LR 140, [2002] 1 Cr App R 10, PC, in which the Board appears to accept a much wider proposition that D is to be judged on the circumstances *and danger* as he believed them to be. This is, it is submitted a preferable approach.

perceived the supposed circumstances as being a greater threat than would a normal person is not admissible. The court rejected an analogy with provocation[549] because provocation applies only to murder and is not a complete defence. But the court did not consider duress which applies to virtually all crimes except murder and is a complete defence. In *Martin (DP)*[550] psychiatric evidence was admitted that D was suffering from a schizoid affective disorder which made him more likely than a normal person to regard things said as threatening, and to believe that threats would be carried out. Are the policy considerations for private defence and duress different? Or is one of these cases wrong? The court in *Martin (Anthony)* conceded that evidence of D's physical characteristics may be admissible. Circumstances which would not be seen as threatening by a robust young man may appear so to a frail elderly woman.

The balancing of the characteristics of the individuals can give rise to difficult issues. What of the relatively slight woman who uses lethal force against a physically stronger male whom she believes is about to attack her? The Law Commission in its recent 2004 consideration of the Partial Defence to Murder recognized the difficulty that this posed in many trials and recommended a new Judicial Studies Board Direction:

> It is insufficient to weigh the weapons used on each side; sometimes there is an imbalance in size and strength. You must also consider the relationship between the defendant and [the other party]. A defendant who has experienced previous violence in a relationship may have an elevated view of the danger that they are in. They may honestly sense they are in greater danger than might appear to someone who has not lived through their experiences. All these matters should be taken into account when considering the reasonableness of the force used.[551]

(iv) The effect of the Human Rights Act 1998

There are arguments of some force[552] that the effect of Article 2 of the ECHR – the right to life – may be to invalidate the principle of *Gladstone Willams* and *Beckford* that a defendant is to be judged on the facts as he genuinely, though unreasonably believed them to be. Article 2 provides:

> (1) Everyone's right to life shall be protected by law. No one shall be deprived of his life intentionally save in the execution of a sentence of a court following his conviction of a crime for which this penalty is provided by law.
>
> (2) Deprivation of life shall not be regarded as inflicted in contravention of this article when it results from the use of force which is no more than absolutely necessary:
>
> a in defence of any person from unlawful violence;
>
> b in order to effect a lawful arrest or to prevent the escape of a person lawfully detained;
>
> c in action lawfully taken for the purpose of quelling a riot or insurrection.

549 See *Smith (Morgan)* [2001] 1 AC 146, HL, below, p 454.

550 [2000] 2 Cr App R 42, above, p 307.

551 Law Com No 290, *Partial Defences to Murder* (2004), para 4.14 (adapted from suggested formulation by Justice For Women).

552 By A. Ashworth, commenting on *Andronicou and Constantinou v Cyprus*, ECHR, 9/10/97, [1998] Crim LR 823. But see Buxton LJ [2000] Crim LR 331 at 336–337. See F. Leverick [2002] Crim LR 347; J. C. Smith, 'The Use of Force in Public or Private Defence and Article 2' [2002] Crim LR 958; and F. Leverick, 'The Use of Force in Public or Private Defence and Article 2: A Reply to Professor Sir John Smith' [2002] Crim LR 963.

It is argued that the present English law is incompatible with this provision since a person's right to life is not sufficiently protected if he may be killed by force used without reasonable grounds. From a subjectivist standpoint, this would be a grave setback to the prevailing approach to criminal liability in England.

The arguments of incompatibility highlight a number of issues. First, the Article allows for life to be taken only where 'absolutely necessary'. A defendant in England could be acquitted even though his attack turns out to have been completely unnecessary. Furthermore, the European Court has underlined the restrictive nature of the exceptional circumstances in which killing is permitted by observing that the accused must have had 'good grounds' to use force.[553] Finally, it is noted that Article 2 restricts the circumstances in which a life may be taken to purposes of quelling riots, etc or in defence of unlawful *violence*. In English law, it is possible for a defendant to be acquitted where he uses lethal force in response to an attack on property.

It is not clear that Article 2 or the ECtHR's jurisprudence (which is customarily vague) *demands* a change in the law to an objective test. The test of 'absolute necessity' seems in practice not to be an inflexible one. Moreover, the ECtHR has not condemned English law which it has had opportunity to do. Notwithstanding some unguarded language by the CLRC and the courts, English law does not say that D may take the life of another where there are no reasonable grounds for doing so. It says only that he is not guilty of a criminal offence, if he believes honestly though unreasonably that such ground exists. Where D's belief is unreasonable that will of course be a powerful reason for disbelieving his account and convicting him. The killing is unlawful, but not criminal. D remains liable in tort. But that is not all. The criminal law itself provides protection. If D's mistake is so unreasonable as to amount to gross negligence, D will be guilty of manslaughter.[554] That is, D will be guilty of criminal homicide if the jury think his conduct bad enough to amount to a crime – or, as is submitted below, bad enough to deserve condemnation as manslaughter. The right to life of the road user can hardly be said to be insufficiently protected against the reckless or dangerous motorist because he is guilty only of manslaughter and not murder. Moreover, most force used in public or private defence is not intended to, and does not have, fatal results. Is the *Beckford* principle to be outlawed only where it has fatal results? There would not seem to be any reason in that. The alternative is that it is invalidated entirely. It is submitted that this would be an undesirable and unnecessary conclusion and the English courts should not arrive at it unless compelled to do so. The present law, at least as regards protection against violence to the person, balances the need to protect life – and limb – against the ordinary rights of persons accused of crime.

(b) Force used in the course of preventing crime or arresting offenders

The common law on this subject was both complex and uncertain;[555] but now, by the Criminal Law Act 1967, s 3:

553 See *Andronociou*, para 171; *Gul v Turkey* (2002) 34 EHRR 28, para 77; *McCann v UK* (1996) 21 EHRR 95.

554 Cf Leverick [2002] Crim LR 347 at 361.

555 See the 1st edition of this book at 230–238.

(1) A person may use such force as is reasonable in the circumstances in the prevention of crime, or in effecting or assisting in the lawful arrest of offenders or suspected offenders or of persons unlawfully at large.

(2) Subsection (1) above shall replace the rules of the common law on the question when force used for a purpose mentioned in the subsection is justified by that purpose.

Section 3 states a rule both of civil and criminal law. When the force is 'reasonable in the circumstances' it is justified in every sense. No civil action or criminal proceeding will lie against the person using it. The section says nothing specifically about any criminal liability of the user of the force. When that is in issue the ordinary principles of *mens rea* should apply. The use of force may be unjustified in the civil law because it is not in fact 'reasonable in the circumstances'; but D, while liable in tort, may nevertheless be excused from criminal liability if it was 'reasonable in the circumstances *as he believed them to be*'. It has been held in a civil action in Northern Ireland[556] that, for the purpose of an identical provision, the objectives of the use of force are to be determined, not by the evidence of the user of the force, but by the court, applying an objective test. D, a soldier, said that his purpose in shooting was to arrest the occupants of a vehicle whom he believed on reasonable grounds to be determined terrorists who would probably continue to commit terrorist offences if they got away; but the court held that the use of force was not reasonable to make an arrest but was justified because it was reasonable to prevent crime.[557] If this is right (and it is a persuasive opinion) in a civil action, it is also right in criminal law. The only difference is that in the criminal case, D need not have reasonable grounds for his honest belief in the circumstances.

(i) What is a crime?

Section 3 operates only where D responds to prevent a 'crime'. In *Jones*,[558] the Court of Appeal concluded that the concept of 'crime' in this context can only have been intended to mean a 'domestic' crime (that is, not a crime only in international law). The Criminal Law Revision Committee[559] explained the proposed s 3 in very broad terms:

> the court, in considering what was reasonable force, would take into account all the circumstances, including in particular the nature and degree of force used, the seriousness of the evil to be prevented and the possibility of preventing it by other means; but there is no need to specify in the clause the criteria for deciding the question. Since the clause is framed in general terms, it is not limited to arrestable or any other class of offences, though in the case of very trivial offences it would very likely be held that it would not be reasonable to use even the slightest force to prevent them.

Despite the breadth of this statement the Court of Appeal's limitation in *Jones* seems warranted if the defence is to retain the degree of certainty desirable.

The definition of 'crime' may also cause problems at a more mundane level where the question arises whether the offence has been completed before D uses any force. In

556 *Kelly v Ministry of Defence* [1989] NI 341. But cf *Thain*, below, p 339.

557 The European Court of Human Rights (App No 17579/90) observed that the 'prevention of crime' does not appear in the justifications for taking life in Article 2 of the ECHR, but held that the shooting was justified to effect a lawful arrest. This decision is cogently criticized by J. C. Smith, 'The right to life and the right to kill in law enforcement' (1994) 144 NLJ 354.

558 [2005] Crim LR 122.

559 Cmnd 2659, para 23.

Bowden, for example, the issue was whether V had completed the appropriation of the keys before D used violence to prevent what he understood to be a theft.[560]

(ii) When is the use of force reasonable?

The Criminal Law Revision Committee,[561] the authors of the section, described it as set out in the last paragraph: 'reasonable force, would take into account all the circumstances, including in particular the nature and degree of force used, the seriousness of the evil to be prevented and the possibility of preventing it by other means.'

It cannot be reasonable to cause harm unless (i) it was *necessary* to do so in order to prevent the crime or effect the arrest and (ii) the evil which would follow from failure to prevent the crime or effect the arrest is so great that a reasonable person might think himself justified in causing that harm to avert that evil. It is likely, therefore, that even killing will be justifiable to prevent unlawful killing or grievous bodily harm, or to arrest a person where there is an imminent risk of his causing death or grievous bodily harm if left at liberty. The whole question is somewhat speculative. Is it reasonable to kill or cause serious bodily harm in order to prevent rape? Or robbery, when the property involved is very valuable, and when it is of small value?[562] How much force may be used to prevent the destruction of a great work of art? It seems that the question, 'what amount of force is reasonable in the circumstances?' is always for the jury and never a point of law for the judge.[563] If the prosecution case does not provide material to raise the issue, there is an evidential burden on the accused. If that burden is satisfied, that question for the jury is:

> . . . Are we satisfied that no reasonable person (a) with knowledge of such facts as were known to the accused or [reasonably][564] believed by him to exist (b) in the circumstances and time available to him for reflection (c) could be of the opinion that the prevention of the risk of harm to which others might be exposed if the suspect were allowed to escape, justified exposing the suspect to the risk of harm to him that might result from the kind of force that the accused contemplated using.[565]

The standard of reasonableness should, as noted above, take account of the nature of the crisis in which the necessity to use force arises for, in circumstances of great stress, even the reasonable person cannot be expected to judge the minimum degree of force required to a nicety. In holding quite considerable force to be justified to prevent an obstruction of the highway by a violent and abusive driver, Geoffrey Lane J said:

'In the circumstances one did not use jewellers' scales to measure reasonable force . . .'.[566]

560 [2002] EWCA Crim 1279.

561 Cmnd 2659, para 23.

562 Where a butcher used a butcher's knife to frustrate the robber of his takings, his action met with the approval of the coroner, though the robber died: (1967) The Times, 16 Sept. See the more recent cases discussed by E. Tennant (2003) 167 JP 804.

563 *Reference under s 48A of the Criminal Appeal (Northern Ireland) Act 1968 (No 1 of 1975)* [1976] 2 All ER 937 at 947, HL, per Lord Diplock.

564 Lord Diplock used the word 'reasonably' and, in the light of his often stated opinion, it is likely that he would wish to continue to use it, were he still alive; but his remarks, in the light of *Gladstone Williams* and the cases following it, should be read as if 'reasonably' were omitted.

565 Ibid.

566 *Reed v Wastie* [1972] Crim LR 221.

(iii) Defence only if force used

Section 3 excuses only the use of *force*. In *Blake v DPP*[567] D, demonstrating against the Iraq war, wrote with a felt pen on a concrete pillar near the Houses of Parliament. He was charged with criminal damage and argued that his act was justified by, *inter alia*, s 3. The court held that his act was 'insufficient to amount to the use of force within the section'. This suggests that the defence might not have been ruled out in this ground (though it almost certainly would on other grounds) if D had used a hammer and chisel. It is odd that force should be excused when less serious acts might not be; but that is the effect of the section.[568]

(c) Force used in private defence

The Criminal Law Act 1967 made no reference to the right of private defence – the right to use force in defence of oneself or another against an unjustifiable attack.[569] The right of private defence still exists at common law; but if, and in so far as, it differed in effect from s 3 of the 1967 Act, it has probably been modified by that section. Private defence and the prevention of crime are sometimes indistinguishable. If D goes to the defence of E whom V is trying to murder, he is exercising the right of private defence but he is also seeking to prevent the commission of a crime. It would be absurd to ask D whether he was acting in defence of E or to prevent murder being committed and preposterous that the law should differ according to his answer. He was doing both.[570] The law cannot have two sets of criteria governing the same situation and it is submitted that s 3 of the Criminal Law Act is applicable. The Act may be taken to have clarified the common law. Before the Criminal Law Act, the Court of Criminal Appeal equated the defence of others with the prevention of crime. In *Duffy*[571] it was held that a woman would be justified in using reasonable force when it was necessary to do so in defence of her sister, not because they were sisters, but because 'there is a general liberty as between strangers to prevent a felony'. That general liberty now extends to all offences. The principles applicable are the same whether the defence be put on grounds of self-defence or on grounds of prevention of crime. The degree of force permissible should not differ, for example, in the case of an employer defending his employee from the case of a brother defending his sister – or, indeed, that of a complete stranger coming to the defence of another under unlawful attack. The position is the same where D acts in defence of property, whether his own or that of another, which V seeks to steal, destroy or damage.

Where D is acting in defence of his own person it may be less obvious that he is also acting in the prevention of crime but this will usually be in fact the case. D's purpose is not the enforcement of the law but his own self-preservation; yet the degree of force which is permissible is the same.[572] An enquiry into D's motives is not practicable.[573]

567 [1993] Crim LR 586, DC.

568 The illogicality of this restriction as noted by Brooke LJ in *Bayer v DPP* [2003] EWHC 2567 (Admin); [2004] Crim LR 663, calling for reform of the defences.

569 Thus where D knows that the actual or imminent danger he faces is not from an unlawful or criminal act he cannot rely on the defence: *Bayer v DPP* [2003] EWHC 2567 (Admin).

570 See *Clegg* [1995] 1 All ER 334 at 343.

571 [1967] 1 QB 63, [1966] 1 All ER 62, CCA.

572 *Devlin v Armstrong* [1971] NI 13 at 33; *McInnes* [1971] 3 All ER 295 at 302.

573 Above, p 118.

As with s 3, the private law defence is limited to cases in which D responds to an unjustified attack by using force. However, there is no requirement that D is responding to a 'crime'. Thus where D believes that V's actions are unjustified because they are, for example, unlawful in international law, his use of force to prevent V's action may be justified.

(d) Further elements of the defences

(i) A duty to retreat?

There were formerly technical rules about the duty to retreat before using force, or at least fatal force. This is now simply a factor to be taken into account in deciding whether it was necessary to use force, and whether the force was reasonable.[574] If the only reasonable course is to retreat, then it would appear that to stand and fight must be to use unreasonable force. There is, however, no rule of law that a person attacked is bound to run away if he can.

A demonstration by D at the time that he did not want to fight is, no doubt, the best evidence that he was acting reasonably and in good faith in self-defence; but it is no more than that. A person may in some circumstances so act without temporizing, disengaging or withdrawing; and he should have a good defence.[575]

(ii) A pre-emptive strike

It has been accepted that a defendant need not wait for the attacker to strike the first blow before he defends himself. In *Devlin v Armstrong*[576] following serious disturbances in Londonderry, D exhorted crowds of people who were stoning the police to build a barricade and keep the police out and fight them with petrol bombs. D claimed that she had acted in this manner because she honestly believed that the police were about to behave unlawfully in assaulting people and damaging property in the area. The Court of Appeal acknowledged that a 'plea of self-defence may afford a defence [where D used force] not merely to counter an actual attack, but to ward off or prevent an attack which he honestly anticipated. In that case, however, the anticipated attack must be imminent'.[577] In *Beckford*[578] the Privy Council also acknowledged that circumstances may justify a pre-emptive strike in self-defence. The availability of the defence in circumstances of pre-emptive strike has been narrowly construed by the courts. Where there is no evidence to support a suggestion that D has acted in pre-emptive defence, no direction on the issue is needed.[579]

The requirement of imminence, strictly construed, prevents the widespread reliance on the defence where battered spouses kill their abusive partners. Commonly the physical disparity between the parties means that the woman will seize her opportunity to kill the abuser when he is not poised about to strike her, but in a position of vulnerability. This

574 *McInnes*, above. But cf *Whyte* [1987] 3 All ER 416 at 419, CA.

575 This passage was approved by the Court of Appeal in *Bird* [1985] 2 All ER 513 at 516.

576 [1971] NI 13.

577 Per Lord MacDermott LCJ at 33.

578 [1987] 3 All ER 425 PC.

579 *Williams* [2005] EWCA Crim 669, cf *Carter* [2005] All ER (D) 372 (Apr).

has caused such individuals to rely on the partial defences of provocation and diminished responsibility.[580]

The Law Commission has responded to this problem in its latest 2004 proposals from the Partial Defences to Murder project by including within its broad provocation defence, a defence where D kills through fear of serious violence to himself or another.[581]

(1) Unlawful homicide that would otherwise be murder should instead be manslaughter if the defendant acted in response to:

(a) gross provocation (meaning words or conduct or a combination of words and conduct which caused the defendant to have a justifiable sense of being seriouslywronged); or

(b) fear of serious violence towards the defendant or another;

or

(c) a combination of (a) and (b); and

a person of the defendant's age and of ordinary temperament, that is, ordinary tolerance and self-restraint, in the circumstances of the defendant might have reacted in the same or a similar way.

(iii) Defence against a provoked attack

In *Browne*[582] Lowry LCJ said, with regard to self-defence, 'The need to act must not have been created by conduct of the accused in the immediate context of the incident which was likely or intended to give rise to that need'.

Self-defence is clearly not available where D deliberately provoked the attack with the intention of killing purportedly in self-defence.[583] Where D's act was merely 'likely' to give rise to the need, the proposition, with respect, is more questionable. If D did not foresee that his actions would lead to an attack on him, it is submitted that he should not be deprived of his usual right of self-defence. Even if he did foresee the attack, he may still be entitled to act in self-defence if he did not intend it. D intervenes to stop V from ill-treating V's wife. He knows that V may react violently. V makes a deadly attack on D. Surely D's right of self-defence is unimpaired. This suggestion was cited *obiter* with approval in *Balogun*.[584] It seems clear that there is no rule preventing D who initiates an attack from relying on self-defence. D will not be entitled to rely on self-defence in such circumstances where the person attacked is using only reasonable force to fend off D's initial attack.

(iv) Defence against lawful force

Lowry LCJ also stated in *Browne*:[585]

[580] See generally the discussion below, p 464 and C. Wells, 'Battered Woman Syndrome and Defences to Homicide: where now?' (1994) 14 LS 266; A. McColgan, 'In Defence of Battered Women Who Kill' (1993) OJLS 508; J. Dressler, 'Battered Women Who Kill Their Sleeping Tormentors' in S. Shute and A. Simester (eds), *Criminal Law Theory* (2002) arguing for a duress type defence and J. Horder, ' 'Killing the Passive Abuser: A Theoretical Defence' in S. Shute and A. Simester (eds), *Criminal Law Theory* (2002), 285.

[581] Recommendation 3.168.

[582] [1973] NI 96 at 107, CCA, discussed 24 NILQ 527. On 'prior fault' generally, see S. Yeo, *Compulsion* (1990), ch 5.

[583] Cf *Mason* (1756) Fost 132; and the corresponding problem in provocation, at 377.

[584] [1999] 98/6762/X2.

[585] [1973] NI 96 at 107.

Where a police officer is acting lawfully and using only such force as is reasonable in the circumstances in the prevention of crime or in effecting the lawful arrest of offenders or suspected offenders, self-defence against him is not an available defence.

Again it may respectfully be questioned whether this proposition is not too wide. If D, an innocent person, is mistaken, even reasonably, by the police for a notorious gunman and they so attack him that he can preserve his life only by killing or wounding – an attack which would be reasonable if he were the gunman – does the law really deny him the right to resist?[586] Again, if D reasonably supposes that the police are terrorists, he surely commits no crime by resisting, even if the police are in fact acting lawfully and reasonably.

A person is not to be deprived of his right of self-defence because he has gone to a place where he might lawfully go, but where he knew he was likely to be attacked. There is no question of any duty to retreat at least until the parties are in sight of one another and the threat is imminent.[587]

In a very few cases the attacker may not be committing a crime because, for example, he is a child under 10, insane, in a state of automatism or under a material mistake of fact. If D is unaware of the circumstances which exempt the attacker, then s 3 of the Criminal Law Act will still, indirectly, afford him a defence to any criminal charge which may be brought, provided he is acting reasonably in the light of the circumstances as they appear, reasonably or not, to him; for he intends to use force in the prevention of crime, as that section allows, and therefore has no *mens rea.*

Where D does know of the circumstances in question, then s 3 is inapplicable, but it is submitted that the question should be decided on similar principles. A person should be allowed to use reasonable force in defending himself or another against an unjustifiable attack, even if the attacker is not criminally responsible.[588] Authority can now be found in the case of the conjoined twins, *Re A (Children).*[589] The court granted a declaration that it would be lawful to carry out an operation to separate the twins to enable A to live even though the operation would inevitably kill B. B's heart and lungs were too deficient to keep her alive. She lived only because A was able to circulate sufficient oxygenated blood for both. The evidence was that, if the operation was not done, both would die. The *ratio decidendi* of the three judges differed but it is submitted that Ward LJ rightly held that this was a case of self-defence. B was, of course, completely innocent but she was killing A. He equated the case with that of a six-year-old boy shooting all and sundry in a playground. It would be lawful to kill him if that was the only way to prevent the deaths of others. There is a great difference between the boy's active conduct and the pathetic inactivity of B; but neither is committing a crime. Whatever the position regarding

586 The judgment of Winn LJ in *Kenlin v Gardiner* [1967] 2 QB 510, [1966] 3 All ER 931 is ambivalent. *Albert v Lavin* [1982] AC 546, [1981] 1 All ER 628, DC (reversed by the House of Lords on another point) supports the view in the text. And see the draft Criminal Code, cl 47 (3)(b) and (6) (Law Com No 143) and *Ansell v Swift* [1987] Crim LR 194 (Lewes Crown Court). The question is elaborately discussed in *Lawson and Forsythe* [1986] VR 515. Young CJ thought it may be reasonable to assume that, in some circumstances, D may defend himself against a lawful attack; McGarvie J said that he may do so, approving the 5th edition of this work, at 327–328, but Ormiston J thought self-defence was only lawful against an unlawful attack. Cf *Fennell* [1971] 1 QB 428, [1970] 3 All ER 215, [1970] Crim LR 581 and commentary; below, p 547.

587 *Field* [1972] Crim LR 435; cf *Beatty v Gillbanks* (1882) 9 QBD 308.

588 *Bayer v DPP*, above.

589 [2000] 4 All ER 961, [2001] Crim LR 400, CA (Civ Div) and commentary.

necessity and duress, it has always been held that private defence may be an answer to a charge of murder.

(v) D's reliance on unknown justifying circumstances[590]

What of D who seeks to rely on facts that existed and would justify his use of force, but of which he was unaware at the time of acting? The test proposed in the CLRC's Fourteenth Report and adopted as the law in *Gladstone Williams* is stated exclusively in terms of the defendant's belief. Its terms do not apply where D is unaware of existing circumstances which, if he knew of them, would justify his use of force. This line of reasoning accords with *Dadson*.[591] This is no accident. The Committee gave careful consideration to the matter and concluded that the *Dadson* principle was correct.[592] Although s 2 of the Criminal Law Act and s 24 of PACE[593] which replaced it appear to justify arrest and therefore the use of force necessary to effect it both (i) where the circumstances of justification in fact exist, and (ii) where the arrester suspects on reasonable grounds that they exist, it is clear that no arrest can be lawful unless the arrester suspects, whether on reasonable grounds or not, that the arrestee is committing, or has committed, or is about to commit, an arrestable offence. Under s 28(3) of PACE, restating the common law, the arrest is unlawful unless the arrestee is informed of the grounds for it at the time of, or as soon as is practicable after, the arrest. The arrester cannot state such grounds unless he at least suspects their existence. So a person like Dadson who has no suspicion of any valid ground for making an arrest is acting unlawfully, even though such grounds, unsuspected by him, exist in fact. An arrester who suspects without reasonable grounds will not be justified under (ii) above, but he will be justified under (i) if his unreasonable suspicion is well founded. To that extent an arrest on 'hunch' is justified.

Although the spheres of private defence and arrest overlap there are clearly occasions when one applies to the exclusion of the other. An officer pursuing an escaping criminal is unlikely to be able to claim that he was acting in private defence. Where a soldier who had killed the man he was pursuing disclaimed any intention to make an arrest and relied on a claim that he was acting in self-defence which proved to be unfounded, it was no answer to a charge of murder that he would have been justified in shooting in order to make an arrest.[594] A person cannot rely on powers of arrest unless he was acting with the purpose of arresting.

(vi) Defence of property[595]

Where D is charged with criminal damage and his defence is that he was acting in defence of his own property – as where he kills V's dog which, he claims, was attacking his sheep, the matter is regulated by the Criminal Damage Act 1971, which is considered below,

[590] See T. M. Funk, 'Justifying Justifications' (1999) OJLS 630, arguing that *Dadson* represents a 'very principled, precedented, coherent and logically compelling decicion'. See also P. H. Robinson, 'Competeing Theories of Justification: Deeds v Reasons' in S. Shute and A. Simester (eds), *Criminal Law Theory* at 45; R. Christopher, 'Unknowing Justification and the logical necessity of the *Dadson* principle in self-defence' (1995) 15 OJLS 229.

[591] Above, p 42.

[592] The discussion is not included in the Report, Cmnd 7844, paras 281–287.

[593] The Serious Organised Crime and Police Act 2005, s 110, see pp 32–33 above.

[594] *Thain* [1985] NI 457 (NI CA), discussed in Smith, *Justification and Excuse*, 34. Cf *Kelly v Ministry of Defence*, above, p 333.

[595] See D. Lanham, 'Defence of Property in the Criminal Law' [1966] Crim LR 368.

p 902. Where D is charged with an offence against the person, or any other offence, and his defence is that he was defending his property, he will generally be acting in the prevention of crime and, as in defence of the person, s 3 is likely to be held to provide the criterion. It can rarely, if ever, be reasonable to use deadly force merely for the protection of property. Would it have been reasonable to kill even one of the Great Train Robbers to prevent them from getting away with their millions of pounds of loot, or to kill a man about to destroy a priceless painting? – even assuming that no means short of killing could prevent the commission of the crime. It will be recalled that Article 2 of the ECHR does not permit the use of lethal force otherwise than in preventing riot, etc – or unlawful 'violence'.

In the case of *Hussey*[596] it was stated that it would be lawful for a person to kill one who would unlawfully dispossess him of his home. Even if this were the law at the time, it would seem difficult now to contend that such conduct would be reasonable; for legal redress would be available if the householder were wrongly evicted. In so far as the householder was preventing crime, his conduct would be regulated by s 3 of the Criminal Law Act 1967 which replaces the rules of common law. It is thought that, in any event, the rule in *Hussey* would not extend to a trespasser who did not intend to dispossess the householder, even if the trespasser were guilty of an offence under Part II of the Criminal Law Act 1977.[597]

Following the conviction for murder of the Norfolk farmer Anthony Martin when he killed a burglar entering his deserted farmhouse,[598] there was considerable public concern, fuelled by misinformed newspaper reports, and a resulting clamour for a new law to protect the rights of householders.[599] Not surprisingly the issue became a political one, and a number of excessively wide defences were drafted as Private Members' Bills.[600] There has been no change to the substantive law.[601]

(vii) To what offences is public or private defence an answer?

These defences are most naturally relied on as answers to charges of homicide, assault, false imprisonment and other offences against the person. It is not clear to what extent public or private defence may be invoked as defences to other crimes. Clause 44 of the Draft Code ('Use of force in public or private defence') would not justify or excuse any criminal conduct not involving the use of force (except acts immediately preparatory to the use of such force); but the Code would leave it open to the courts to develop a wider defence at common law. It is not clear to what extent the present law allows these defences to crimes other than those involving the use of force. In *Attorney-General's Reference (No 2 of 1983)*[602] D made and retained in his shop petrol bombs at a time when extensive rioting was taking place in the area. He was acquitted of an offence under s 4(1) of the Explosive

596 (1924) 18 Cr App R 160, CCA.

597 Cf *Taylor v Mucklow* [1973] Crim LR 750 and commentary. See also the civil law case of *Revill v Newbury* [1996] All ER 291.

598 See S. Yeo, 'Killing in Defence of Property' (2000) 150 NLJ 730.

599 The poll on the Radio 4 programme, 'Today' in 2004 revealed that this was the listeners' most desired legislative change.

600 See the Criminal Justice (Justifiable Conduct) Bill 2004, and the Criminal Law (Amendment) (Householder Protection) Bill 2004.

601 See Law Com No 290, *Partial Defences to Murder* (2004) Parts 3 and 4.

602 [1984] QB 456, [1984] 1 All ER 988, [1984] Crim LR 289 and commentary, CA.

Substances Act 1883 of possessing an explosive substance in such circumstances as to give rise to a reasonable suspicion that he did not have it for a lawful object. It was a defence under the terms of the section for D to prove that he had it for a lawful object. The Court of Appeal held that there was evidence on which a jury might have decided that the use of the petrol bombs would have been reasonable force in self-defence against an apprehended attack. If so, D had the bombs for 'a lawful object' and was not guilty of the offence charged. Yet it was assumed[603] that he was committing offences of manufacturing and storing explosives contrary to the Explosives Act 1875. The court agreed with the Court of Appeal in Northern Ireland in *Fegan*[604] that possession of a firearm for the purpose of protecting the possessor may be possession for a lawful object, even though the possession was unlawful being without a licence. The judgment is strangely ambivalent.

> [D] is not confined for his remedy to calling in the police or boarding up his premises. He may still arm himself for his own protection, if the exigency arises, although in so doing he may commit other offences. That he may be guilty of other offences will avoid the risk of anarchy contemplated by the reference.

To say 'He may do it – but he will commit an offence if he does' seems inconsistent. There is, however, a clear statement that acts immediately preparatory to justifiable acts of self-defence are also justified. This must surely be right. If D becomes caught up in a shoot-out between police and dangerous criminals, picks up a revolver dropped by a wounded policeman and fires in order to defend his own and police lives, it would be astonishing if he had a defence to a charge of homicide but not to possessing a firearm without a licence.[605] Possibly, then, the passage above refers to preparatory, but not immediately preparatory acts. This does not resolve the ambivalence. The law must say whether a person may, or may not, do such acts; and if it says they are crimes, he may not.

The matter must now be considered in the light of the defence of duress of circumstances. A person may save himself from injury by an attacker by using force or by running away and *Willer* and *Conway*[606] are cases where this form of self-defence was an answer to a charge of reckless driving. In *Symonds*[607] where a driver, charged under s 20 of the OAPA and with dangerous driving, raised self-defence it was held that the same considerations applied to the driving charge as to the s 20 offence. Calling the defence to driving charge 'duress of circumstances' may make no difference – but sometimes it may, because duress requires an objective test where the test for self-defence (*Gladstone Williams*) is certainly subjective. As a matter of policy there is a great deal to be said for encouraging a threatened person to escape, even where that involves committing a minor offence, rather than using force against the aggressor. It now seems that those defendants would have had a defence if they had driven through a red light, or while disqualified, or with excess alcohol, providing that it was necessary to do so in order to escape death or serious bodily harm. The hypothetical user of the revolver was also acting under duress of circumstances. A successful defendant will not care whether his defence is called 'duress of circumstances' or 'private defence'; but whether the defence succeeds may well depend on how it is categorized, for the former is limited to threats to the person whereas the

603 *A-G's Reference (No 2 of 1983)* [1984] 1 All ER 988 at 992–993.

604 [1972] NI 80. Cf *Emmanuel* [1998] Crim LR 347.

605 Cf *Georgiades* [1989] Crim LR 574.

606 Above, p 300. See D. W. Elliott, 'Necessity, Duress and Self-defence' [1989] Crim LR 611.

607 [1998] Crim LR 280.

latter extends to defence of property; and the former is governed by an objective test whereas a subjective test is applied to the latter. A disqualified driver who drove his Rolls Royce to avoid its destruction by an aggressor could not plead duress; nor would possession of the revolver without a licence be excused by duress if the possessor's honest belief that life was in danger was not based on reasonable grounds – though his defence to a charge of homicide would not be impaired. For the avoidance of such anomalies, acts immediately preparatory to public or private defence are better regarded as justified or excused by those defences.

The fears of the courts regarding a general defence of necessity[608] probably militate against a recognition that public and private defence may constitute a defence to crime generally; but, where contravention of *any* law is (i) necessary to enable the right of public or private defence to be exercised, and (ii) reasonable in the circumstances, it ought to be excused. It is open to the courts to move in this direction.

(viii) Use of force, excessive in the known circumstances

Where D, being under no mistake of fact, uses force in public or private defence, he either has a complete defence or if he uses excessive force, no defence. If the charge is murder, he is guilty of murder or not guilty of anything. He may have believed the force was reasonable but if, even by the relaxed standard applied in this context,[609] it was not, he was making a mistake of law, which is not a defence, and he is guilty of murder. That is the law of England, affirmed by the House of Lords in *Clegg*.[610] D, a soldier on duty in Northern Ireland, fired four shots at a car (in fact stolen) which did not stop at a checkpoint. The judge, sitting in a 'Diplock court' without a jury, accepted that the first three shots had been fired in self-defence or defence of a colleague but that the fourth, which killed, was not, as the car had passed the soldiers and was already 50 feet down the road. D's conviction of murder was affirmed by the House of Lords, holding that it is established law that killing by excessive force in self-defence is murder and that if a change is to be made, it is for Parliament, not the courts, to make it. There is no partial defence resulting in a manslaughter conviction, as with provocation and diminished responsibility. The possibility was considered and rejected immediately after the *Clegg* decision.[611]

For 30 years a line of cases in Australia held that killing by excessive force, even where there is no mistake of fact, should be manslaughter and not murder, if some force was justified:

> . . . if the occasion warrants action in self-defence or for the prevention of felony or the apprehension of the felon but the person taking action acts beyond the necessity of the occasion and kills the offender the crime is manslaughter – not murder.[612]

The defence, as stated by the High Court in *Howe*[613] in relation to self-defence, applied where (i) D honestly and reasonably thought he was defending himself; and (ii) homicide

608 Above, p 323. 609 Above, p 333.

610 [1995] 1 All ER 334, [1995] Crim LR 418 and commentary. See also M. Kaye, 'Excessive Force in Self Defence After *Clegg*' (1996) J Crim L 448.

611 See the *Inter-Departmental Review of the law on lethal force in self-defence or the prevention of crime* (1996) paras 83–84.

612 *McKay* [1957] ALR 648 at 649, per Lowe J.

613 (1958) 100 CLR 448; *Bufalo* [1958] VR 363; *Haley* (1959) 76 WNNSW 550; *Tikos* [1963] VR 285; *Tikos (No 2)* [1963] VR 306.

would have been justified if excessive force had not been used; but (iii) D used more force than was reasonably necessary. This principle was mainly applied in self-defence cases,[614] but it originated in *McKay*,[615] which concerned the use of excessive force in the arrest of a felon and the defence of property and it is logical that, if it applies at all, it should apply to any of the defences now being considered.[616]

In *Palmer*[617] the Privy Council explained why they saw no need for this refinement of the law:

> If there has been an attack so that defence is reasonably necessary it will be recognized that a person defending himself cannot weigh to a nicety the exact measure of his necessary defensive action. If a jury thought that in a moment of unexpected anguish a person attacked had only done what he honestly and instinctively thought was necessary that would be most potent evidence that only reasonable defensive action had been taken. A jury will be told that a defence of self-defence, where the evidence makes it raising possible, will only fail if the prosecution show beyond doubt that what the accused did was not by way of self-defence.[618]

In *Zecevic*[619] the Australian High Court overruled its previous decisions and followed *Palmer*, bringing Australian law into line with that of England. It did so, not because it thought the principle applied in those cases was a bad one, but because of the complexity which had arisen from the court's attempt to state the law in a form which took account of the onus of proof. The law was to be changed because it was too difficult for juries to understand and apply. The principle of *Gladstone Williams*[620] – which has not yet been followed in Australia – removes some of the complexity from the law and it ought to be capable of being stated in a form readily comprehensible by juries.

The CLRC was persuaded that *Howe* was right in principle and recommended its adoption in relation to private defence of person and property and the prevention of crime.[621] It is submitted that the soundness of this recommendation is not impaired by *Zekevic* or by *Clegg*. The Law Commission in cl 59 of the Draft Code would implement the recommendation.

(e) Reform

The Law Commission's latest proposals in respect of the defences is contained in Report No 218 which provides:

> Cl 27(1) The use of force by a person for any of the following purposes, if only such as is reasonable in the circumstances as he believes them to be, does not constitute an offence –

614 Ibid. 615 [1957] VR 560.

616 It has been argued the principle is of general application and should govern duress, coercion and necessity. Thus, even if duress, coercion and necessity do not afford a complete defence to murder, they might reduce the offence to manslaughter: Morris and Howard, above, 142. The idea is undeniably attractive but it is as yet unsupported by authority.

617 [1971] AC 814, [1971] 1 All ER 1077.

618 On the importance of this direction and the potential for it to be underestimated see the Law Com No 290, Part 4, paras 4.11–4.14.

619 *Zecevic v DPP for Victoria* (1987) 61 ALJR 375. See Editorial [1988] Crim LR 1; D. Lanham, 'Death of a Doubtful Defence' (1988) 104 LQR 239.

620 Above, p 284.

621 CLRC/OAP/R, para 228. Cf P. F. Smith, 'Excessive Defence—A Rejection of Australian Initiative' [1972] Crim LR 524.

(a) to protect himself or another from injury, assault or detention caused by a criminal act;

(b) to protect himself or (with the authority of that other) another from trespass to the person;

(c) to protect his property from appropriation, destruction or damage caused by a criminal act or from trespass or infringement;

(d) to protect property belonging to another from appropriation, destruction or damage caused by a criminal act or (with the authority of the other) from trespass or infringement; or

(e) to prevent crime or a breach of the peace.

(6) Where an act is lawful by reason only of a belief or suspicion which is mistaken, the defence provided by this section applies as in the case of an unlawful act, unless –

(a) D knows or believes that the force is used against a constable or a person assisting a constable, and

(b) the constable is acting in the execution of his duty.

(i) Partial defences to murder – the latest proposals

Despite the furore over the Tony Martin conviction and the calls for greater protection of householders who kill the government now seems to have ruled out any statutory reform of the law. In an unprecedented move, the CPS has however recently drafted 'new' guidance as to when a prosecution may be appropriate.[622] This advises prosecutors that, *inter alia*, 'if the degree of force used is not very far beyond the threshold of what is reasonable, a prosecution may not be needed in the public interest.' On the other hand, prosecutors are also required to take account of the 'final consequences of the action taken', so that: 'Where the degree of force used . . . is assessed as being excessive, and results in death or serious injury, it will be only in very rare circumstances indeed that a prosecution will not be needed in the public interest. Minor or superficial injuries may be a factor weighing against prosecution'.

The Law Commission recently concluded that no new partial defence to murder should be created for the defendant who kills by using excessive force. A defendant will, in appropriate circumstances, be able to advance a 'pure' self-defence plea and the new broader provocation based plea. Under the proposed scheme, if the jury rejects the self-defence plea, they might still return a manslaughter verdict on the application of the new defence.

(1) Unlawful homicide that would otherwise be murder should instead be manslaughter if the defendant acted in response to (a) gross provocation (meaning words or conduct or acombination of words and conduct which caused the defendant to have a justifiable sense of being seriously wronged); or (b) fear of serious violence towards the defendant or another; or (c) a combination of (a) and (b); and a person of the defendant's age and of ordinary temperament, that is, ordinary tolerance and self-restraint, in the circumstances of the defendant might have reacted in the same or a similar way.

(2) In deciding whether a person of ordinary temperament in the circumstances of the defendant might have acted in the same or a similar way, the court should take

622 See www.cps.gov.uk.

into account the defendant's age and all the circumstances of the defendant other than matters whose only relevance to the defendant's conduct is that they bear simply on his or her general capacity for self-control.

(3) The partial defence should not apply where (a) the provocation was incited by the defendant for the purpose of providing an excuse to use violence, or (b) the defendant acted in considered desire for revenge.

(4) A person should not be treated as having acted in considered desire for revenge if he or she acted in fear of serious violence, merely because he or she was also angry towards the deceased for the conduct which engendered that fear.

(5) The partial defence should not apply to a defendant who kills or takes part in the killing of another person under duress of threats by a third person (pending a wider review of the law of murder).

(6) A judge should not be required to leave the defence to the jury unless there is evidence on which a reasonable jury, properly directed, could conclude that it might apply.

6. Entrapment[623]

Unlike some jurisdictions such as the USA[624] there is no defence of entrapment in English law in the sense of a substantive law plea advanced at trial.[625] Originally it was thought to be a necessary corollary that a judge has no discretion to exclude evidence of the commission of an offence which was induced by the trap for such exclusion would indirectly provide the defence which the law did not allow. While the substantive law is unchanged, it is now clear that that the judges' duty to ensure that the accused receives the fair trial as emphasized by the Human Rights Act entitles or requires the judge in some circumstances to stay proceedings as an abuse of process[626] or exclude the evidence in the discretion under s 78 of PACE.

(a) Basis of stay for abuse of process

As the remedy is one properly regarded as a matter of criminal procedure and is dealt with here in only brief outline.[627] In short, the question is whether the State officials[628]

623 J. D. McClean, 'Informers and Agents Provocateurs' [1969] Crim LR 527; J. Heydon, 'The Problems of Entrapment' [1973] CLJ 268; Law Com Working Paper No 55 and Law Com No 83, *Report on Defences of General Application* (1977) where it is recommended that there should be no defence of entrapment but that consideration should be given to the creation of a new *offence* of entrapment. See A. Ashworth, 'Entrapment' [1978] Crim LR 137.

624 *Jacobsen v US* 112 S Ct 1535 (1992).

625 *Sang* [1980] AC 402; *Latif* [1996] 1 WLR 104; *Looseley* [2001] UKHL 53. For consideration of the merits of a defence see A. Choo, *Abuse of Process and Judicial Stays of Criminal Proceedings* (1993).

626 See generally D. Corker and D. Young, *Abuse of Process* (2001).

627 Since the remedy is by way of a stay (a terminating ruling) it will, under the Criminal Justice Act 2003, be appealable by the prosecution.

628 Where the entrapment is from a private citizen – usually the 'fake Sheikh' of the *News of the World* newspaper – the abuse of process argument has not often proved successful (see *Shannon* [2001] 1 WLR 51; *Hardwicke and Thwaites* [2001] Crim LR 220). Arguably it should since the court and prosecuting authorities as agencies of the State are endorsing the impropriety of the private individual and that in itself could be seen as an abuse of process. The possibility that a prosecution based on private entrapment could infringe Article 6 has been confirmed in *Shannon v UK* [2005] Crim LR 133.

have done more than afford the accused an opportunity to break the law, of which he freely took advantage, or whether they have persuaded him by shameful or unworthy conduct to commit an offence which he would not otherwise have committed.[629] If the latter the court should stay proceedings in order to avoid bringing the administration of justice into disrepute and respect the fact that it is not fair to try the defendant for a State-created crime. Determining whether the State has overstepped the mark or merely offered D an 'unexceptional' opportunity to commit crime will give rise to difficult decisions particularly since there will not always be an objective benchmark on what is an unexceptional opportunity. This may be easier to discover in the case of a drug deal (have the police offered a better deal than the average local price for that drug) than in cases of police offering to act as contract killers (price dependent on victim and means of killing). Numerous factors will be influential in determining whether the case should be stayed including: the type of crime involved, the degree of pressure or inducement offered, the circumstances in which it is offered, the particular vulnerability of the accused, the circumstances of the police operation – was it based on reasonable suspicion of a particular target and was it an authorized operation in accordance with the Regulation of Investigatory Powers Act, Part II.[630] The House of Lords in *Looseley* rejected the emphasis placed on the accused's 'predisposition' to commit the crime in the European Court in *Teixeira de Castro v Portugal*.[631] It is submitted the House was right to do so and that that decision, although followed more recently by the ECtHR,[632] ought to be regarded with caution.[633]

(i) Sentencing

Entrapment is also matter which may be taken into account in fixing the sentence so, where there was a possibility that a theft might not have been committed but for a police trap, D was sentenced as if he had been convicted of a conspiracy to steal rather than the actual theft.[634] But if the police have given D an unexceptional opportunity to deal drugs which he has taken there is no obligation to discount the sentence.[635]

7. Impossibility[636]

Where the law imposes a duty to act, it has sometimes been held that it is a defence that, through no fault of his own, it was impossible for D to fulfil that duty. A driver is not liable for failure to report an accident if he does not know the accident has happened.[637] The secretary of a limited company is not liable for failure to annex to an annual return,

629 *A-G's Reference (No 3 of 2000)* [2002] Crim LR 301 and commentary; *Nottingham City Council v Amin* [2000] 2 All ER 946, DC; A. Ashworth, 'Redrawing the Boundaries of Entrapment' [2002] Crim LR 161; S. Mackay, 'Entrapment, Competing Views on the Effect of the HRA on the English Criminal Law' [2002] EHRLR 764.

630 See eg the decision to allow the appeal in *Moon* [2004] All ER (D) 167 (Nov) where D had dealt drugs to an undercover officer in an unsupervised operation when there was no prior suspicion against D; cf *Procter* [2004] EWCA Crim 1984.

631 (1998) 28 EHRR 101.

632 *Eurofin* [2005] Crim LR 134.

633 See D. Ormerod and A. Roberts, 'The Trouble with *Teixera*: Developing a principled approach to entrapment' [2002] Int Jnl E & P 38.

634 *McCann*, above, p 332.

635 See *Thornton and Hobbs* [2003] EWCA Crim 919.

636 CLGP, at 746–748. See A. Smart, 'Responsibility for failing to do the impossible' (1987) 103 LQR 532.

637 *Harding v Price* [1948] 1 KB 695, [1948] 1 All ER 283, DC.

as required by the Companies Act 1985, a copy of a balance sheet laid before the company in general meeting where there is no such balance sheet in existence: 'nobody ought to be prosecuted for that which it is impossible to do'.[638] A person is not liable for failure to leave a particular place if he is unaware of the order requiring him to do so.[639] In New Zealand it has been held that a failure to leave the country after a revocation of a permit was not an offence if no airline would carry D because of the advanced state of her pregnancy.[640] Impossibility is a defence to a charge of failure to assist a constable to preserve the peace when called upon to do so.[641]

On the other hand, the failure of a driver to produce a test certificate is not excused by the fact that it is impossible for him to do so, the owner of the vehicle being unable or unwilling to produce it.[642] Failure by the owner of a vehicle to display the excise licence is not excused by the fact that, without any negligence or default on his part, it has become detached in his absence.[643]

We find here the inconsistency which is so common in relation to strict liability. It cannot be asserted, therefore, that any *general* defence of impossibility is recognized at the present time. It has to be regarded as a question of the interpretation of the particular provision, with all the uncertainty that this entails.

When impossibility might be available as a defence, it will presumably fail if the impossibility has been brought about by D's own default.[644] The defence would also seem to be confined to cases where the law imposes a duty to act and not to cases of commission where the corresponding defence, if any, is necessity.[645]

8. Non-compliance with EU law[646]

A form of defence, which at one time it was anticipated would become commonplace but which remains a relative rarity, is that the criminal provision under which the defendant is charged is invalid because it conflicts with the law of the European Union.[647] This is not to say that the defence is never used. The Court of Appeal has recently confirmed that the trial judge is obliged to consider a defence put forward under EU legislation. In *Searby Ltd*[648] the defendant company was charged with offences under the Control of Pesticides Regulations 1986 pursuant to the Food and Environment Protection Act 1985 alleging that it had stored and sold pesticides in the UK without Ministerial order. The company's claim that, by reference to the classification of the pesticides under EU law it was not obliged to obtain such an order was not considered by the trial judge. The Court of

638 *Stockdale v Coulson* [1974] 3 All ER 154 at 157, DC, per Melford Stevenson J.

639 *Lim Chin Aik v R* [1963] AC 160, [1963] 1 All ER 223, PC.

640 *Finau v Department of Labour* [1984] 2 NZLR 396.

641 *Brown* (1841) Car & M 314, per Alderson B.

642 *Davey v Towle* [1973] RTR 328, DC.

643 *Strowger v John* [1974] RTR 124, DC; cf *Pilgram v Dean* [1974] 2 All ER 751, DC.

644 But cf *Stockdale v Coulson*, above, and comment at [1974] Crim LR 375.

645 See *Canestra* 1951 (2) SA 317 (AD) and Burchell and Hunt, 293–296.

646 E. Baker, 'Taking European Criminal Law Seriously' [1998] Crim LR 361; H. Jung, 'Criminal Justice – a European Perspective' [1993] Crim LR 237; J. Dine, 'European Community Criminal Law' [1993] Crim LR 246; N. Bridge, 'The European Communities and the Criminal Law' [1976] Crim LR 88.

647 See T. C. Hartley, 'The Impact of European Community Law on the Criminal Process' [1981] Crim LR 75.

648 [2003] EWCA Crim 1910.

Appeal quashed the conviction, since the trial judge had failed to give effect to 'directly applicable' EU law.[649]

With regards to specific EC Treaty articles, pleaded in defence, *Dearlove*[650] provides an example. V charged a substantially higher price for goods which the buyer intended to sell on the home market than for goods intended for export. It was accepted that this policy contravened Article 85(1) of the EEC Treaty.[651] D conspired to obtain goods from V at the lower price by dishonestly representing that he intended to export them outside the EU to Bulgaria. His conviction was upheld because the Theft Act 1968 could not be regarded as a statutory support of the offending pricing policy and the prosecution was brought by the Crown to protect the public. The result would have been the same if V had brought a private prosecution – the nature of the criminal proceedings would have been the same. But the court accepted that, if the prosecution had undermined the effectiveness of Article 85(1) or favoured or reinforced the contravention, the appeal would have been allowed. And it might also have been different if the prosecution had been brought under a regulation made to enforce the offending policy. Other examples of the EU defence in operation include unsuccessful attempts to rely on provisions of the Treaty which secure rights of free movement of goods as a defence to the importation of obscene articles.[652]

The relative paucity of domestic jurisprudence on EU defences is not to say that EU law does not have an important influence on certain areas of criminal law, as for example in some aspects of cartels in competition law that are now criminalized by the Enterprise Act 2002,[653] and in areas of VAT evasion and carousel frauds. Furthermore, in relation to regulatory offences the EU has a far more significant impact. In short, criminal law in England will continually require further examination in the light of EU developments.[654]

There is a growing influence of EU law on the criminal process in the UK in more general terms following the gradual expansion of the EU's laws on Common Foreign and Security Policy as well as its laws on Police and Judicial Co-operation in Criminal Matters (formerly, Justice and Home Affairs). In particular, the impact will be felt, in combating terrorism, corruption and fraud, immigration, trafficking of persons and drugs, and through the implementation of a uniform and EU-wide arrest warrant, through immigration and border control, and corruption and fraud.[655]

649 See European Communities Act 1972, s 2(1).

650 *Dearlove, Druker* (1988) 88 Cr App R 279, CA.

651 Ie, restrictive agreements and concerted practices, now Article 81(1) following Amsterdam's EC Treaty 1999.

652 Case 34/79, R v Henn and Darby [1979] ECR 3795; see also Case 121/85, *Conegate Ltd v Commissioners of Customs and Excise* [1986] ECR 1007. There is a vast amount of case law regarding free movement under the EC Treaty, with regard to 'market access', to which refer to Craig and de Búrca, below, n 655.

653 C. Graham, 'The Enterprise Act 2002 and Competition Law' (2004) 67 MLR 273. C. Harding and J. Joshua, 'Breaking up the Hand Core: the Prospects for the Proposed Cartel Offence' [2002] Crim LR 933. See generally, Arts 81–89 EC Treaty, but specifically that of Art 81, EC Treaty (above), Art 82, EC Treaty (abuse of a dominant position) and Art 87, EC Treaty (state aid) which are in force so as to not distort anti-competitiveness and allow punishment of those that do in and around the EU.

654 See G. Corstens, 'Criminal law in the first Pillar?' (2003) 11 Euro Jnl of Crime, Criminal Law and Criminal Justice 131.

655 See S. Peers, *EU Justice and Home Affairs Law* (2000), esp ch 9; D. Dinan, *Ever Closer Union* (2nd edn, 1999); T. Tridimas, *The General Principles of EC Law* (1999); T. C. Hartley, *The Foundations of European Community Law* (5th edn, 2003), at 261–267; P. Craig and G. De Búrca, *EU Law: Text, Cases and Materials* (3rd edn, 2003), esp ch 1 and 301–312.

12

Incitement, conspiracy and attempt

1. Introduction

Incitements, conspiracies and attempts are known collectively as 'inchoate offences'. 'Inchoate' means 'just begun, incipient; in an initial or early stage . . .'. Criminalizing inchoate offences raises particular difficulties because the conduct involved will often be far removed from the type of harm that would be needed to give rise to a charge under the relevant substantive offence. For example where A and B agree to burgle V's house, a conspiracy to burgle is complete even though they have never been near the house and have taken no further steps to perpetrate that crime. It does not follow that inchoate offences will never involve a tangible harm – attempted murder can be charged as appropriately where D shoots V who survives as where D is arrested before he has taken aim to shoot.

The *actus reus* of inchoate offences can extend to cover a wide range of behaviour, sometimes seemingly innocuous, as for example with 'an agreement' in conspiracy, or mere words of encouragement in incitement. However, there are sound reasons of policy and principle for punishing these types of wrongdoing, a central one being that the defendant has demonstrated by his actions his willingness that a substantive offence be committed. Since the *actus reus* is so broad, it is important that inchoates are kept within reasonable limits by requirements of strict *mens rea*. But, this emphasis on *mens rea* does not mean that inchoates can be regarded as thought-crime; there remains a requirement that the defendant's blameworthy state of mind manifests itself by some words or conduct.

Inchoate offences always relate to a substantive offence. Thus, there is no crime of attempt *per se*, only crimes of, for example, attempted theft, attempted murder, etc. It should also be noted that liability for inchoate offences exists quite independently of accessorial liability. In the latter, the secondary party's liability derives from the commission of the full offence by the principal offender. Inchoate offences are completed and can be prosecuted before the commission of any full offence. Significant consequences flow from this difference. For example, there are defences of withdrawal for secondary parties who demonstrate a change of heart before the commission of the principal offence; inchoate liability is complete with the act of incitement, conspiracy or attempt and any subsequent withdrawal goes only to mitigation in sentencing.[1] Arguably, inchoate offences better respect the principle of fair labelling since the description of D's conduct

[1] There have been suggestions that by analogy with counselling, such a defence should be available to an inciter. For discussion see Ashworth, POCL, 467, and Wilson, *Central Issues* (2002), 243–249.

accurately reflects his personal behaviour whereas in secondary liability the accessory's conduct may be fundamentally mis-described being derivative on the conduct of another – the principal (as where the getaway driver in a fatal armed robbery is convicted as a 'murderer').[2]

It is likely that inchoate offences will be of increasing importance in the future, especially in prosecuting certain types of crime, the obvious example being the supply and importation of prohibited drugs. A number of other factors suggest that inchoates will become more commonplace, including in particular, the recent shift from coercive to 'intelligence-led' policing where new powers and technological advances allow the police to gather evidence and intervene before substantive crimes are committed. Aside from their prevalence, the study of inchoate offences is also of increased importance because of Parliament's willingness to enact new forms of substantive offence that take the form of inchoate offences. Recent examples include the offence of 'grooming' (seducing children to a meeting),[3] offences of 'inciting' another to engage in sexual activity,[4] expansive terrorist offences[5] and the wide ranging offences under the Proceeds of Crime Act 2002.[6]

2. Incitement

It is a common law misdemeanour to incite another to commit an offence triable in England and Wales.[7] The definition of incitement in the draft Criminal Code,[8] cl 47, as recently approved by the Divisional Court and the Court of Appeal,[9] is:

(1) A person is guilty of incitement to commit an offence or offences if –

(a) he incites another to do or cause to be done an act or acts which, if done, will involve the commission of the offence or offences by the other; and

(b) he intends or believes that the other, if he acts as incited,

(c) shall, or will do so with the fault required for the offence or offences.

[2] See above, Ch 8, and the discussion of the Law Commission proposals in respect of secondary liability, Law Com Consultation Paper No 131 (1993), on which see J. C. Smith, 'Secondary Participation in Crime – Can we do without it?' (1994) 144 NLJ 679. See further the report of the Law Com [insert when published May 2005]

[3] See s 15 of the Sexual Offences Act 2003, and Ch 17 below, 593. On the prevalence of this, see A. Gillespie, [2002] CFLQ 411; 'Children, Chatrooms and the Law' [2001] Crim LR 435, and Gallagher *et al.*, 'International and internet child sexual abuse and exploitation – issues emerging from research' [2003] CFLQ 353–370.

[4] Sexual Offences Act 2003, s 8, see above, p 629.

[5] See eg Terrorism Act 2000, s 59; Anti-Terrorism, Crime and Security Act 2001, s 50, discussed by C. Walker, *The Anti-Terrorism Legislation* (2002).

[6] See the discussion at p 862, below and references therein.

[7] The Sexual Offences (Conspiracy and Incitement) Act 1996, extended jurisdiction to include incitement and conspiracy in England to commit sexual offences outside the United Kingdom against a person under 16, (Ch 17, below), provided that the act is an offence under the law of the place where it is to be done. See generally P. Alldridge, 'The Sexual Offences (Conspiracy and Incitement) Act 1996' [1997] Crim LR 30, 35–36; R. Ticehurst, 'Jurisdiction in sex tourism cases' (1996) 146 NLJ 1826. See also the specific statutory extensions in relation to inciting terrorist activity outside the UK: Anti-Terrorism, Crime and Security Act 2001.

[8] Law Com No 177, I, 63.

[9] *DPP v Armstrong* [2000] Crim LR 379, DC, and *Goldman* [2001] Crim LR 894, CA. *Armstrong* is welcomed by J. Holroyd, 'Incitement, A Tale of Three Agents' (2001) J Crim Law 515.

(a) *Actus reus*

The Code does not further define 'incite'. At common law it is recognized that the *actus reus* can be committed by non-hostile encouragement. Thus, an inciter includes:

> . . . one who reaches and seeks to influence the mind of another to the commission of a crime. The machinations of criminal ingenuity being legion, the approach to the other's mind may take various forms, such as suggestion, proposal, request, exhortation, gesture, argument, persuasion, inducement, goading or the arousal of cupidity.[10]

In *Marlow*[11] the court observed that this 'gamut of words' omits 'encourage' which, it thought, 'represents as well as any modern word can the concept involved;' but then added the proviso that it must be clear that the encouragement involved a positive step 'aimed at inciting another to commit a crime'. So it is not every encouragement which necessarily amounts to incitement. Perhaps the best single word is 'incite' itself. In directing a jury it is important that they are left with no doubt as to the meaning of this essential element of the offence, but care must be taken not to use inappropriate synonyms.[12] The Court of Appeal in *Smith* were inclined to think that fewer rather than more synonyms should be used in directing the jury.[13] Incitement can be committed by hostile threats or pressure as well as by friendly persuasion.[14]

Incitement may be implied as well as express. To advertise an article for sale, representing its potential to be used to do an act which is an offence, is an incitement to commit that offence[15] – even when accompanied by a warning that the act is an offence. But the mere intention to manufacture and sell, wholesale, a device which has no function other than one involving the commission of an offence is not an intention to incite the commission of that offence.[16] The distinction seems appropriate since the defendant's mere intention to manufacture seems too remote from the possible commission of the full offence by the anticipated purchaser to warrant criminal sanction.

In a recent expansion of the offence, the Court of Appeal held that there can be an incitement where E, the incitee, invites D, the incitor, to ask him, E, to commit an offence.

10 Holmes, JA in *Nkosiyana* 1966 (4) SA 655 at 658, AD, approved in *Goldman*, above, n 9.

11 [1997] Crim LR 897; [1998] 1 Cr App R (S) 273. (A statutory offence of incitement, contrary to the Misuse of Drugs Act 1971, s 19.)

12 See *Smith* [2004] EWCA Crim 2187, referring to the 10th edition of this work and suggesting that use of the word 'stimulation' did not render the conviction for inciting rape unsafe where D and E had met to examine a pair of girl's knickers and to urge each other on to commit paedophile offences.

13 Ibid, [15].

14 *Race Relations Board v Applin* [1973] QB 815 at 827, CA, Civil Div, per Lord Denning MR, followed in *Invicta Plastics Ltd v Clare* [1976] RTR 251, [1976] Crim LR 131.

15 *Invicta Plastics*, above. (Indication that 'Radatex' may be used to detect police radar traps was incitement to an offence under s 1(1) of the Wireless Telegraphy Act 1949. Note that the licensing requirement was removed by SI 1989 No 123, and that no offence of 'obtaining information' is committed by the user of the apparatus: *R v Knightsbridge Crown Court, ex p Foot* [1999] RTR 21.) Cf the reports in, The Times, 6 Aug 1998 that a student was convicted of 'inciting speeding offences' by the sale of a 'speed trap jammer'. In *Parr-Moore* [2003] 1 Cr App R (S) 425, the court described the appellants' publication of disclaimer as serving only to illustrate their realization that the trade was illegal [3].

16 *James and Ashford* (1985) 82 Cr App R 226 at 232, distinguishing *Invicta Plastics*, above. See also *Maxwell-King* (2001) The Times, 2 Jan: incitement to commit offence contrary to Computer Misuse Act 1990, s 3 by supply of device to allow unauthorized access to satellite TV channels.

Thus, in *Goldman*[17] it was held that it was immaterial that E published an advertisement inviting readers to buy indecent photographs of children. D replied to the advertisement offering to buy the photographs of children under 16. D was guilty of attempting[18] to incite E to distribute indecent photographs of children under 16,[19] contrary to s 1 of the Protection of Children Act 1978. If E in this scenario is a State official, care must be taken to avoid a plea of 'entrapment', which if successful will lead to the proceedings being stayed as an abuse of process. Entrapment itself is not, however, a substantive law defence in England.[20]

More recently, in *O'Shea*,[21] it was accepted by the court that there was a *prima facie* case that by subscribing to a website with indecent images of children D had incited or encouraged E, the business offering for supply on the site, to continue even though his communication had been with a wholly automated computer system. This is not an authority for any startling proposition that incitement can be committed in respect of a machine. The court's acceptance of the broad proposition that there can be an incitement because there is a business behind the computer has however the potential to undermine the clear acknowledgement that there must be 'another' who is the incitee. It is respectfully submitted that this broad-brush approach to incitement would create an undesirable extension to the law. Similarly, it is submitted that arguments that the person incited was for these purposes the programmer who had set up the wholly automated system whereby the computer would provide D with the indecent images on receipt of relevant information are also flawed. The person involved in programming has performed the task before D's communication. A more palatable argument is that D's communication with E can be proved from evidence that the business responded for example, by producing bi-weekly updates to the website to reflect requests. Obviously, the *mens rea* requirement remains that D intends to encourage a person to engage in conduct that constitutes a crime. In some cases therefore D might deny *mens rea*, claiming that he was sufficiently well informed of the workings of the system of a website to believe that he was not communicating with any person. The essence of an incitement is reaching and seeking to influence another's mind.[22]

In principle, it is necessary that the incitement should have been communicated,[23] but the matter is of small practical importance[24] since, in the case of a failure of communica-

17 [2001] Crim LR 894, CA.

18 There is no explanation as to why the acts were not charged as incitement *per se*. They should have been.

19 See now the Sexual Offences Act 2003, s 45.

20 A full discussion of the plea of entrapment, lies beyond the scope of this work. See Ch 11 above for brief consideration. In short, if E, as a police officer has induced D to commit an offence that he would not have committed but for the exceptional nature of E's inducement, D has been entrapped. See *Loosely* [2001] UKHL 53, [2002] Crim LR 301.

21 [2004] Crim LR 948.

22 The court in *O* did not discuss whether a corporation might be incited.

23 *Banks* (1873) 12 Cox CC 393 (letter, suggesting the murder of a child not yet born, intercepted. Held an attempt to incite under Offences Against the Person Act 1861, s 4; (repealed)). Statutory offences of 'soliciting' may be different; cf *Horton v Mead* [1913] 1 KB 154.

24 *Ransford* (1874) 13 Cox CC 9. Section 19 of the Misuse of Drugs Act 1971 expressly makes it an offence to attempt to incite another to commit an offence under that Act.

tion,[25] there would at least be an attempt to incite.[26] An offence of attempting to incite may seem fanciful, but can be the most appropriate charge, as where for example at a football match D shouts encouragement to E to wound a police officer. E does not hear this because of the noise from the crowd. D is guilty of attempting to incite.[27]

Technological advances such as the internet produce the potential for simultaneous communication with thousands of individuals, across many jurisdictions.[28] In law, there is no limitation on the number of individuals who may be incited. Thus, a newspaper advertisement or other media broadcasts would constitute the offence.[29] Examples of this nature also underline the fact that not all incitements constitute an attempt to conspire (see below).

(i) No need for incitee to be persuaded

If there is communication with an intended incitee, the offence can be committed irrespective of whether D's incitement succeeds in persuading E to commit, or to attempt to commit the offence. It was so held in *Higgins*[30] where Lord Kenyon said:[31]

> But it is argued, that a mere intent to commit evil is not indictable, without an act done; but is there not an act done, when it is charged that the defendant solicited another to commit a felony? The solicitation is an act: and the answer given at the Bar is decisive, that it would be sufficient to constitute an overt act of high treason.

More recently in *Marlow*, the offence involved the publication of a book about the cultivation and production of cannabis. Witnesses were called to testify that they had been influenced by reading the book. The offence of incitement, however, was committed as soon as the book was published and read[32] by anyone, whether influenced by it or not. Evidence of being influenced was relevant only to establish the book's persuasive quality, and perhaps, circumstantially and remotely, that of the author's intention. It follows that the offence can be committed where the incitee is a police officer involved in the suppression of the type of crime incited.[33]

(b) *Mens rea*

The *mens rea* of incitement is crucial to the offence and has given rise to confusion in the courts resulting in an unfortunate lack of clarity in the law. It comprises two elements. First, as with attempts, D must intend the consequences specified in the *actus reus*. It is not enough that D intends that his communication reach E and that its message is understood. The essence of incitement seems to be an intention to bring about the criminal

25 It is of *some* importance, because a magistrates' court has no power to convict of an attempt on a charge of the full offence. A separate information of attempt would have to be laid.

26 An offence at common law: *Chelmsford Justices, ex p Amos* [1973] Crim LR 437, DC; *Cope* (1921) 16 Cr App R 17.

27 But note that there is no offence of incitement to conspire: Criminal Law Act 1977, s 5(7).

28 This can give rise to all sort of problems, see eg *Association Union des Etudiants Juifs de France v Yahoo! Inc* (2000) International Internet Law Review 2, where a French court ordered that to respect French laws on inciting racism, Yahoo (a US company) must prohibit French users from accessing Nazi websites.

29 See *El Faisal* [2004] EWCA Crim 343 (convictions for soliciting murder upheld where D encouraged audience to kill Jews and 'unbelievers').

30 (1801) 2 East 5.

31 Ibid, at 170.

32 See p 358, below. See also the broad definition in *Most* (1881) 7 QBD 244, 258 per Huddleston B.

33 *DPP v Armstrong*, above, n 9; *Krause* (1902) 66 JP 121.

result by the act of another. There is therefore an important difference from accessorial liability. If D incites E to inflict grievous bodily harm upon V, D is guilty of inciting grievous bodily harm. D is not guilty of incitement to murder, though if death results from the infliction of the intended harm both D and E will be guilty of murder under the law governing participation.[34] The second element of *mens rea* is that, as in the case of counselling and abetting, the prosecution must prove that D knew of (or deliberately closed his eyes to) all the circumstances of the act incited which are elements of the crime in question.

(i) Intention

In this context, the concept of intention has not been judicially defined. At one extreme, it has been argued that the prosecution must establish that it is D's purpose (direct intent) that the crime incited will occur. In *Marlow* the court used the word 'aim,' thereby supporting this narrow approach. There is some academic support for this view,[35] suggesting that D's foresight of virtual certainty is an insufficient basis to convict where, for example, D knows that by telling E that E's wife is having an affair E is virtually certain to kill her.[36] Arguably, in such a case there is in any event no *actus reus* because there is no element of persuasion or pressure.[37] This is an important element of incitement but is not necessary in the case of counselling or abetting. If D sells a gun to E, knowing that E intends to murder V, it is probable that D is guilty of murder if E does kill V;[38] but, if E does not kill V, it would seem impossible, on those facts alone, to convict D of incitement.[39]

The more generally accepted view is that intention in this context includes oblique intention: it is sufficient that D knew, not necessarily that his advice would be followed, but that if it was the commission of the crime would be the virtually certain result.[40] Thus, Marlow may have been quite indifferent whether anyone followed the advice given he may have had only one purpose in mind – making money – as might the manufacturers of Radatec in *Invicta Plastics.*[41]

A more extreme view which has no judicial support is that the *mens rea* of incitement should be satisfied on proof of recklessness as to the incited offence being committed.[42]

34 Cf *Whybrow* (1951) 35 Cr App R 141.

35 See also the American Model Penal Code, para 5.02(1) which refers to D acting 'the purpose of promoting or facilitating . . .'.

36 V. Tadros (2002) LS 448, 454 argues that since D takes no responsibility for the action or potential action of E if he has not 'identified' with it, D ought not to be convicted of the incitement. It is not clear what this additional requirement that D 'associate himself' with the incitee by treating the substantive crime 'as a reason for his action' would add to the offence.

37 Above, 351; *Hendrickson and Tichner* [1977] Crim LR 356; *Christian.* Cf Buxton (1969) 85 LQR 252 at 256.

38 Above, p 182.

39 Cf *James and Ashford* (1985) 82 Cr App R 226 at 232, above, 291.

40 The Law Commission Consultation Paper No 131, *Assisting and Encouraging Crime* (1993) seems to accept this interpretation, see, at 129 and the recommendation at 133. See also the Law Reform Commission of Canada Working Paper No 29, *Secondary Liability: Participation in Crime and Inchoate Offences* (1982) referring to 'intent (direct or indirect)' as the relevant *mens rea*, 30–31.

41 Above, p 351, n 15.

42 This argument is founded on the claim that the inciter is more dangerous than the conspirator and attempter since he creates a risk that the incitee will act in a way over which the inciter has no control: see L. Alexander and D. Kessler, '*Mens Rea* and Inchoate Crimes' (1997) 87 J Crim L and Criminology 1138, 1156. The Draft Scots Criminal Code treats recklessness as to E's commission of the crime as sufficient for incitement: cl 19(1)(b).

If D did not intend that the substantive offence would be committed, as where D is an undercover police officer, there will be no liability.

(ii) Knowledge of circumstances

The second element of *mens rea* requires that among the circumstances of which D must be proved to know (or to have deliberately closed his eyes) is the *mens rea* of the person incited. If D believes that E will do the act without the *mens rea* for the crime in question, then D intends to commit that crime through an innocent agent, if it is capable of being so committed, and may become guilty as the principal or an abettor if the *actus reus* is completed by E,[43] but D is not guilty of incitement.

In the odd case of *Curr*,[44] D was acquitted of inciting women to commit offences under the Family Allowances Act 1945 because it was not proved that the women had the guilty knowledge necessary to constitute that substantive offence. The real question, it is submitted, should have been, not whether the women incited actually had the knowledge, but whether D knew that they had. In that event he should have been guilty. But if he knew that they did not have the guilty knowledge, he was not guilty of incitement, whether they had the guilty knowledge or not.[45] Thus, if D urges E to accept the gift of a necklace, which is in fact stolen, D is not guilty of inciting E to handle stolen goods unless D believes E to be aware that the necklace is stolen; even though in fact E is so aware.

Although D must intend E to act with *mens rea* of the crime incited, it is not necessary that D should have the *mens rea* of that substantive crime. If D incites E to steal V's property, it is no defence that D intended to ensure that V would get his property back again – that is, that D did not have the intent permanently to deprive V which is an element of the *mens rea* of theft. It is enough that D intends E to have that intention permanently to deprive. This principle was overlooked in *Shaw*[46] where D incited E to obtain property by deception from their employer, V. D was held not guilty of incitement to obtain if his purpose was, as he said, to demonstrate the insecurity of V's system and he did not intend V to suffer any permanent loss. D intended E to commit the offence and it should have been no answer that he intended to tell him afterwards that it was all in a good cause.

D need not know that the actions he intends that E will perform with *mens rea* constitute a crime. Ignorance of the criminal law is no defence.

(c) Other issues

(i) Incitement must relate to an offence

The act incited must be one which, when done, would involve the commission of the full offence by the person incited or his innocent agent. This can cause difficulties, as for example in *Whitehouse* where it was not an offence at common law for a man to incite a girl of 15 to permit him to have incestuous sexual intercourse.[47] Thus he could not be convicted of the incitement. In response to this case, the Criminal Law Act 1977, s 54,

[43] Above, p 166. [44] [1968] 2 QB 944, [1967] 1 All ER 478, CA.

[45] Cf *Bourne* (1952) 36 Cr App R 125; above, p 205.

[46] [1994] Crim LR 365, not followed in *DPP v Armstrong*, above, n 9. Cf the Draft Criminal Code (Law Com No 177) cl 47, above, p 350.

[47] (1977) 65 Cr App R 33, followed in *Pickford* [1995] 1 Cr App R 420, below, p 358.

made it an offence for a man to incite a girl under 16 to have incestuous sexual intercourse with him[48] but the general principle is unaffected.

By analogy with *Millward*[49] it is arguable that incitement to commit merely the *actus reus* of the full offence should be sufficient to constitute the offence of incitement.[50] D encourages E to rape V, telling E, falsely, that V will be consenting to such activity even though she might pretend otherwise. If E penetrates V (but reasonably believing in V's consent, E acts without *mens rea*) D has aided and abetted rape. If E's act is not committed,[51] why should D's encouragement not constitute incitement to rape? The present law is that D must know or believe that the person incited has,[52] or intend that he shall have, the *mens rea* of the full offence. As such, if D believed that E believed in V's consent D would lack *mens rea* for incitement (because E would lack *mens rea*). Similarly, where D threatens F with grievous harm if she does not commit a sex act with a dog, if she performed the act and had the *mens rea* of that offence, she would be able to rely on the defence of duress. Imposing liability on D for his incitement in such a case seems in principle no less objectionable than in the case of the rape. F's bestiality is committed under duress and can be viewed as 'excused' conduct which falls to be treated in the same way as E's excuse in the form of his denial of the *mens rea* for rape.

In these examples D has generated the excusing condition by respectively lying to E, and threatening F. Distinguishable from both cases is, arguably, that of D who incites G to perform acts that will be justified, as for example where D incites G an abused spouse, to use violence against V in self-defence. In *El Faisal*[53] a similar argument failed on its facts because D's exhortations to his audience to kill Jews, Hindus, Americans and 'unbelievers' were not limited to encouraging attacks in self-defence as D claimed.[54] To date, the courts have not adopted any distinction based on justification and excuses in this context.

This argument which proceeds by analogy with *Millward* would not affect the principle derived from cases like *Whitehouse* because there is no *actus reus* on the part of the person incited. In general terms, the argument to extend the law when merely the *actus reus* has occurred may be less compelling with incitement – when the full offence is merely in prospect – than with aiding and abetting. Nevertheless, many may regard it as a justifiable extension.

Inciting other inchoate offences

An indictment would lie at common law for inciting to conspire but the offences of incitement and attempt to conspire were abolished by s 5(7) of the Criminal Law Act 1977. A charge of incitement to attempt to commit an offence would generally be inept because to incite to attempt is to incite to commit the full offence. Where, however, in the circumstances known to D, but not to E, the completed act will amount only to an

48 See now the Sexual Offences Act 2003, ss 10, 24, 25, below, ch 17.

49 Discussed in the context of 'Participation', above, p 206.

50 See R. Leng, 'Incitement – An Objective Approach to the Definition of Crime' (1978) 41 MLR 725.

51 See *Bourne* (1952) 36 Cr App R 125 and *Cogan and Leak* [1976] QB 217.

52 *Curr* [1968] 2 QB 944, [1967] 1 All ER 478, CA, below, p 359.

53 [2004] EWCA Crim 343.

54 See also *Devlin v Armstrong* [1977] NI 13 where MacDermott LCJ rejected the defence to a charge of inciting riots. The rejection was based on the absence of any belief that the incitees had a belief in the need for self-defence. Arguably, if D believes that there will be a need for self-defence that is sufficient.

attempt, the contrary is arguable. For example, D gives E a substance which he knows to be harmless, telling E that it is poison and urging him to administer it to V. If E does as requested he will be guilty of an attempt to murder.[55] D could scarcely be said to have incited murder but it is arguable that he should be liable for inciting an attempt to murder.

An incitement to incite is an offence except, possibly, when it amounts to an incitement to conspire which, following s 5(7) of the Criminal Law Act 1977 is no offence. To allow an indictment for incitement to incite in the latter case would, it has been said, amount to an illegitimate evasion of that section.[56] But the distinction is absurd and a better view would be that incitement to incite is untouched by the 1977 Act.[57]

Incitement of a person to commit an offence is not the offence of attempting to commit that offence; but the incitement of an innocent agent might be.[58]

Inciting, counselling and abetting

There is probably no offence of incitement to counsel or abet an offence.[59] It is true that, in *Whitehouse*, the court did not quash the conviction on that short ground as they might have done; but the Criminal Law Act 1977, s 30(4), seems to be drafted on the assumption that there is no such offence and there is one decision to that effect by a circuit judge.[60] D paid E £50 to find someone to assault V. It was held that there was no case to answer on an indictment alleging that D incited E to assault V and that it is not an offence to incite another to become 'an accessory before the fact'. The point is certainly open to challenge since D's wrongdoing in encouraging E appears no less blameworthy, and the potential harm is not obviously less serious, than in an incitement for E to commit the substantive offence himself. The argument against extending incitement in this manner is that D's actions are very remote from the commission of the substantive offence.[61] There may, as noted, be an incitement to incite, so D could have been charged with that unless (possibly) E was incited to conspire with X, a person yet unknown. A charge of conspiracy to incite is permissible in law.[62]

(ii) ECHR concerns

Since an incitement can be committed by mere words or publication, there is the potential for a 'defence' to be raised under Article 10 of the ECHR.[63] However, since Article 10

55 Below, p 400.

56 *Evans* [1986] Crim LR 470, CA; *Sirat* (1986) 83 Cr App R 41, [1986] Crim LR 245, CA.

57 The Draft Criminal Code would resurrect the offence of incitement to conspire: cl 47. Conspiracy to incite is indictable: *Booth* [1999] Crim LR 144.

58 See *Cromack* [1978] Crim LR 217 and commentary, and J. C. Smith, *Crime, Proof and Punishment*, 21. The cases posed in the text are different, being, arguably, attempts by D to do the act himself.

59 See J. C. Smith, *Crime, Proof and Punishment*, 21 at 29.

60 *Bodin and Bodin* [1979] Crim LR 176 and commentary (Judge Geoffrey Jones).

61 K. J. M. Smith argues that a further problem is that D's wrongdoing is contingent on the actions of his incitees, but this would undermine liability for incitement generally (see *A Modern Treatise on the Law of Complicity* (1991), 54, n 147).

62 Incitement to conspire was abolished on the recommendation of the Law Commission's Working Party by s 5(7) of the Criminal Law Act 1977; but the Commission saw no reason why conspiracy to incite should not continue in the law (Law Com No 76, para 1.44) and it is unaffected by the 1977 Act. The Commission now recommends 'that neither incitement nor conspiracy should be excluded from the scope of incitement': Law Com No 177, para 13.15.

63 Freedom of expression – see above p 23. Similar guarantees are contained in the International Covenant on Civil and Political Rights (ICCPR) Article 19.

provides only a qualified right to freedom of expression, provided the law of incitement is carefully prescribed and published, and its application is necessary and proportionate to the protection of the rights of others or the prevention of crime, such a challenge will fail. The Divisional Court has recognized the potential significance of such a defence.[64] A number of such claims have been considered in Strasbourg, often dealing with incitement offences of a much broader application than those found in English law.[65] A challenge against the decision in *Marlow* was held by the European Court to be inadmissible.[66] Notwithstanding the interference with the freedom of expression, this was in pursuit of a legitimate aim and the risk of committing the crime was foreseeable. Moreover, in terms of the necessity and proportionality of criminalizing such conduct, this was within the United Kingdom's margin of appreciation.[67]

(iii) Withdrawal

The offence is complete on communication with the incitee. Withdrawal goes only to mitigation in sentence. The courts' strict approach to withdrawal can be seen in the related context of 'offering' to supply drugs contrary to s 4 of the Misuse of Drugs Act 1971. In *Prior*[68] D's phone calls offering to sell drugs (to an undercover officer) was sufficient even though D later withdrew the offer in the course of that same phone call.

(iv) Jursidiction

Since the crime is complete upon D's acts of incitement, irrespective of whether they have any impact on the mind of the incitee, the offence would appear to be committed when and where that communication occurs. An incitement abroad to commit an offence in England is indictable in England.

(v) Incitor cannot be the 'victim'

Under the rule in *Tyrrell*[69] a victim is incapable of being an abettor; he is equally incapable of incitement.[70] The concept of 'victim' has never been adequately defined in this context, and it remains unclear whether, for example, the masochist who incites the sadist to inflict actual bodily harm on him commits the offence of inciting actual bodily harm.[71] Any procedural requirements relating to the ulterior offence – such as the consent of the Director of Public Prosecutions[72] – do not necessarily apply to a charge of incitement.

64 See *Rusbridger et al. v Attorney-General* [2002] Crim LR 800. R (the editor of *The Guardian*) published articles calling for republicanism without violence and sought a declaration that his conduct would not be prosecuted under s 3 of the Treason Felony Act 1848.

65 See the consideration of offences of incitement to racial hatred including *Incal v Turkey* (1998) 4 BHRC 476; *Garaudy v France* [2003] EHRLR 672. For consideration of an incitement to religious hatred offence see M. Idriss, 'Religion and the Anti-terrorism, Crime and Security Act 2001' [2002] Crim LR 890 and below Ch 27.

66 [2001] EHRLR 444.

67 The court was influenced by the fact that the trial had involved assessment of the impact of the book on purchasers, although as noted this is strictly irrelevant to the offence.

68 [2004] 6 Archbold News 1.

69 Above, p 212. Tyrrell was acquitted of incitement as well as abetting.

70 Serious inroads into this principle have been made in the Sexual Offences Act 2003 see below, Ch 17.

71 Cf *Brown* [1994] 1 AC 212.

72 *Assistant Recorder of Kingston-upon-Hull, ex p Morgan* [1969] 2 QB 58, [1969] 1 All ER 416.

If the offence incited is actually committed, then, as seen above, D becomes a participant (accessory) in the offence and may be dealt with accordingly.

(vi) Procedure and mode of trial

Incitement to commit any criminal offence, even an offence triable only summarily, amounted to a misdemeanour at common law. It followed that the incitement was triable on indictment and punishable with a fine and imprisonment at the discretion of the court.[73] It was highly anomalous that the mere incitement should be regarded as more serious than the actual commission of the (summary) offence, even though the use of the greater powers of sentencing might be defensible where the incitement was to commit a large number of offences.[74] Now, by the Magistrates' Courts Act 1980, s 45, any offence consisting in the incitement to commit a summary offence is triable *only* summarily. Incitement to commit an offence triable either way is itself triable either way.[75] Incitement to commit an offence triable only on indictment continues to be triable only on indictment. Where incitement is tried summarily the offender is not liable to any greater penalty than he would be liable to on summary conviction of the completed offence, whether it is a summary offence[76] or an offence triable either way.[77] Where incitement is tried on indictment, it continues to be punishable with fine and imprisonment at the discretion of the court, whatever the penalty for the crime incited. In principle, it would be desirable for Parliament to provide a structure of maximum sentences for incitement. This is a further argument for the need to replace common law crimes in a modern code.

3. Conspiracy

Conspiracy was a misdemeanour at common law. It was classically, if loosely, defined[78] as an agreement to do an unlawful act or a lawful act by unlawful means. The word 'unlawful' was used in a broad sense. It included not only all crimes triable in England, even crimes triable only summarily, but also at least (i) fraud, (ii) the corruption of public morals, (iii) the outraging of public decency, and (iv) some torts. In this respect it went far beyond the other inchoate offences of incitement and attempt, where the result incited or attempted must be a crime. For many years the crime of conspiracy was believed to be even more extensive and to include any agreement to effect a public mischief; but in 1974 in *DPP v Withers*[79] the House of Lords held that an agreement which did not come within one of the heads referred to above was not indictable as a public mischief.

[73] By the Magistrates' Courts Act 1952, s 19(8) and Sch 1, para 20, incitement to commit a summary offence could be dealt with summarily with the consent of the accused.

[74] As in *Curr* [1968] 2 QB 944, [1967] 1 All ER 478, CA.

[75] Magistrates' Courts Act 1980, s 17.

[76] Criminal Law Act 1977, s 30(4).

[77] Ibid, s 28(1).

[78] By Lord Denman in *Jones* (1832) 4 B & Ad 345 at 349. But a few years later in *Peck* (1839) 9 Ad & El 686 at 690 he declared, 'I do not think the antithesis very correct'.

[79] [1975] AC 842, [1974] 3 All ER 984. Conspiracy to commit the common law offence of public nuisance continues to be a potential source of expansion of the criminal law. See commentary on *Soul* (1980) 70 Cr App R 295, [1980] Crim LR 233, CA. The Court of Appeal has recently confirmed the ECHR compatibility of the offence of public nuisance: *Goldstein* [2003] EWCA Crim 3450, [2004] Crim LR 303.

It is the ultimate aim of the Law Commission that conspiracy shall be confined to agreements to commit crimes.

The crime of conspiracy should be limited to agreements to commit criminal offences: an agreement should not be criminal where that which it was agreed to be done would not amount to a criminal offence if committed by one person.[80]

This aim has received general approval. Its immediate implementation, however, was not thought to be appropriate because the abolition of conspiracy to defraud would leave an unacceptably wide gap in the law. It was therefore recommended that conspiracy to defraud should be preserved until the Law Commission could make recommendations for more comprehensive offences of fraud and these could be implemented. Ironically, although the Home Office, following a subsequent Law Commission Report, *Fraud*,[81] has finally recommended general offences of fraud (discussed in Ch 19 below), it has also recommended the retention of conspiracy to defraud as a separate offence – for no other reason than to ensure that no gaps are left in the law. Perhaps the offence will be with us forever.

It was further decided by the Law Commission that, pending the outcome of a review of the law relating to obscenity and indecency, it was undesirable to interfere with the law of conspiracy to corrupt public morals or to outrage public decency and that these too, should for the present, be preserved. The reform effected by the Criminal Law Act 1977 is therefore a limited and provisional reform. Notwithstanding some amendment by the Criminal Attempts Act 1981 and the Criminal Justice Act 1987, it remains an ill-drafted piece of legislation presenting numerous problems of interpretation. The arguments for urgent reform to clarify the position seem compelling.

(a) Summary of present law

(i) Statutory conspiracy

It is an offence of conspiracy triable only on indictment to agree to commit any criminal offence triable within the jurisdiction, even an offence triable only summarily. This is a 'statutory' conspiracy under the Criminal Law Act 1977. It is not limited to agreements to commit a statutory crime – agreements to commit the common law offence of murder are charged under this offence – rather the term 'statutory conspiracy' is used to distinguish it from common law conspiracies.

(ii) Common law conspiracies

It is an offence triable only on indictment to agree:

(ii) to defraud, whether or not the fraud amounts to a crime or even a tort;

(ii) to do an act which tends to corrupt public morals or outrage public decency, whether or not the act amounts to a crime.

The 1977 Act has no part to play in the prosecution of such offences. Whether a particular agreement is a conspiracy at common law or a statutory conspiracy under the Criminal Law Act, or both, is considered below. In all cases, however, the *actus reus* is the agreement

80 Law Com No 76, para 1.113; see also Law Com Working Paper No 50.

81 Law Com No 276.

which, of course, is not a mere mental operation, but must involve spoken or written words or other overt acts. If D repents and withdraws immediately after the agreement has been concluded, he is guilty[82] and his repentance is a matter of mitigation only. This is the crucial distinction between inchoate offending and liability for encouraging and assisting.

Relationship between common law and statutory conspiracies

Section 1(1) of the 1977 Act creates the offence of statutory conspiracy. It provides in effect that it is a conspiracy to agree to commit *any* offence. On a literal reading this would mean that it dealt with common law conspiracies to defraud etc, but s 1(1) is subject to the following provisions of Part I of the Act. These include s 5(1) and (2) which[83] provide:

(1) Subject to the following provisions of this section, the offence of conspiracy at common law is hereby abolished.

(2) Subsection (1) above shall not affect the offence of conspiracy at common law so far as relates to conspiracy to defraud.

The Act, as originally enacted, caused great difficulty and controversy over the relationship between statutory conspiracy and conspiracy to defraud at common law. Eventually the House of Lords decided in *Ayres*[84] that if the alleged agreement would involve the commission of an offence it must be indicted as a statutory conspiracy to commit that offence under the 1977 Act and not as a conspiracy to defraud. Statutory conspiracy and conspiracy to defraud were mutually exclusive. This presented difficulties for prosecutors. Indictments and convictions for conspiracy to defraud had to be quashed because it was discovered that the carrying out of the agreement necessarily involved the commission of some offence, however trivial. The House substantially modified the effect of *Ayres*, as generally understood, in the decision in *Cooke*.[85] That decision brought new difficulties,[86] but, happily, these need not be pursued here because the Criminal Justice Act 1987, s 12, restores the full scope of conspiracy to defraud at common law:

(1) If–

(a) a person agrees with any other person or persons that a course of conduct shall be pursued; and

(b) that course of conduct will necessarily amount to or involve the commission of any offence or offences by one or more of the parties to the agreement if the agreement is carried out in accordance with their intentions.

the fact that it will do so shall not preclude a charge of conspiracy to defraud being brought against any of them in respect of the agreement.

[82] As in the *Bridgewater Case*, unreported, referred to by Lord Coleridge CJ in the *Mogul Steamship Case* (1888) 21 QBD 544 at 549.

[83] As amended by the Criminal Justice Act 1987.

[84] [1984] AC 447, [1984] 1 All ER 619.

[85] [1986] AC 909, [1986] 2 All ER 985.

[86] See [1987] Crim LR 114 and *Levitz* (1989) 90 Cr App R 33, [1989] Crim LR 714, where Bingham LJ pointed out that the problems apply to conspiracies entered into between the coming into force of the 1977 Act and 20 July 1987 when s 12 of the Criminal Justice Act 1987 took effect – probably by now (2005) very few in number.

Statutory conspiracy and conspiracy to defraud are no longer mutually exclusive. An agreement to commit a crime involving fraud or dishonesty is both a statutory conspiracy and a conspiracy to defraud. The prosecutor will frequently have a choice[87] which should be exercised in accordance with the guidance in the Code for Crown Prosecutors issued by the Director of Public Prosecutions under s 10(1) of the Prosecution of Offences Act 1985.[88] The broad and flexible nature of the conspiracy to defraud offence ensures its continued popularity with prosecutors.

Statutory conspiracies and common law conspiracies to corrupt public morals or to outrage public decency remain mutually exclusive, as the Act makes plain. Where the conduct in which the parties have agreed to engage would amount to the commission of one of these offences if carried out by a single person, the agreement is a statutory conspiracy. Where it would not amount to such an offence if carried out by a single person, it is conspiracy at common law. Cases since the 1977 Act confirming that it is an offence for a single person to do acts tending to corrupt public morals create a doubt whether there is any scope for the operation of common law conspiracy to do these things.[89]

(b) Statutory conspiracy[90]

The offence of statutory conspiracy is defined by s 1(1) and s 1(2) of the Act. Section 1(1) (as amended by s 5 of the Criminal Attempts Act 1981) provides:

> Subject to the following provisions of this part of the Act, if a person agrees with any other person or persons that a course of conduct shall be pursued which, if the agreement is carried out in accordance with their intentions, either –
>
> (a) will necessarily amount to or involve the commission of any offence or offences by one or more of the parties to the agreement, or
>
> (b) would do so but for the existence of facts which render the commission of the offence or any of the offences impossible,
>
> he is guilty of conspiracy to commit the offence or offences in question.

(i) *Actus reus*

The agreement

Surprisingly, the courts have failed to define with precision what conduct suffices to constitute the completed agreement which lies at the core of the offence. It may be that an

87 In the recent case of *Mohammed* [2004] EWCA Crim 678, the Court of Appeal was prepared to uphold a conviction on an erroneous charge of conspiracy to defraud contrary to s 1 of the 1977 Act.

88 See Archbold (2005) at paras 1–262 and 1–263. See further www.cps.gov.uk.

89 *May* (1989) 91 Cr App R 157, CA; *Gibson* [1990] 2 QB 619, CA; *Rowley* [1991] 4 All ER 649, [1991] Crim LR 785, CA, below, p 390.

90 For the background to Part I of the Criminal Law Act, see Law Com Working Papers Nos 50 (*Inchoate Offences*, 1973), 56 (*Conspiracy to Defraud*, 1974), 57 (*Conspiracies Relating to Morals and Decency*, 1974) and 63 (*Conspiracies to Effect a Public Mischief and to Commit a Civil Wrong*, 1975); and Report, *Conspiracy and Criminal Law Reform* (Law Com No 76, 1976). For the interpretation of the Act, see E. J. Griew, 'Annotations on the Act', in *Current Law Statutes*; J. C. Smith, 'Conspiracy under the Criminal Law Act 1977' [1977] Crim LR 598 and 638; D. W. Elliott, '*Mens rea* in statutory conspiracy' [1978] Crim LR 202; and G. Williams, 'The New Statutory Offence of Conspiracy' (1977) 127 NLJ 1164 and 1188.

agreement in the strict sense required by the law of contract is not necessary[91] but the parties must at least have reached a decision[92] to perpetrate their unlawful object. A failure to direct the jury carefully on this requirement will render the conviction unsafe.[93] In *Walker*[94] a conviction was quashed although it was 'perfectly clear' that D had discussed with others the proposition of stealing a payroll, because it was not proved that they had got beyond the stage of negotiation when D withdrew. Once the parties have agreed, the conspiracy is complete, even if they take no further action, because, for example they are arrested.

If A agrees to sell B certain goods, known to both to be stolen, at 'a price to be agreed between us', they have not (apart from the question of illegality) reached the stage of a concluded contract.[95] Is there an indictable conspiracy? It is thought that there probably is; though it is arguable that the situation is no different from that where the parties are bargaining as to the price of stolen goods and are clearly, therefore, still at the stage of negotiation. What of the position where A and B agree that they will, say, import drugs, but only if they can find a suitable courier? Is there a completed agreement? (See also the discussion below, p 372.)

A single agreement between A and B may involve them in two or more conspiracies. There is nothing to prevent their being charged as such. Where the defendants agreed to buy cannabis in Thailand and import it into the UK, a conviction in Thailand for conspiracy to possess cannabis for sale did not bar a prosecution in England for conspiracy to import the cannabis into England. There were two distinct conspiracies and it was immaterial that the evidence proving both might be the same.[96] A further example of this principle arises in cases involving conspiracy to defraud. An agreement by British Rail stewards to sell their own food on trains instead of British Rail's and keep the profits is a conspiracy to defraud British Rail and, it seems, a second conspiracy to cheat the passengers.[97] But where there is a general conspiracy to commit offences of a certain type perhaps extending over a lengthy period, agreements to commit particular offences of that type may be treated simply as evidence of the general conspiracy.[98]

Conspiracy is a continuing offence.[99] The opportunity conspiracy offers to roll together a course of criminal conduct under one charge and on one indictment is a significant attraction for prosecutors. It has been held that a single agreement can embrace conduct involving several offences, without infringing the rules against duplicity.[100] Thus D can be indicted for example, for conspiracy to rob *and* murder as part of one agreement. Moreover, *Hussain*[101] and subsequent cases confirm that there is

91 See G. Orchard, 'Agreement in Criminal Conspiracy' [1974] Crim LR 297 at 335.

92 Cf Williams, CLGP, 212.

93 *Webster* [2003] EWCA Crim 1946 (conspiracy to cheat the Revenue).

94 [1962] Crim LR 458; *Mulcahy v R* (1868) LR 3 HL 306 at 317.

95 *May and Butcher Ltd v R* [1934] 2 KB 17n, HL.

96 *Lavercombe* [1988] Crim LR 435.

97 *Cooke* [1986] AC 909, [1986] 2 All ER 985, HL.

98 *Hammersley* (1958) 42 Cr App R 207, 'the Brighton Conspiracy Case', discussed in [1958] Crim LR 422–429 where the acts alleged ranged over a period of eight years and involved numerous illegal agreements with other persons, yet the court contrived to hold that only one conspiracy to obstruct the course of justice, evidenced by a large number of overt acts, was disclosed by the indictment. *Barratt and Sheehan* [1996] Crim LR 495 is a similar case. Cf *Edwards* [1991] Crim LR 45.

99 *DPP v Doot* [1973] AC 807, [1973] 1 All ER 940, HL.

100 *Roberts* [1998] 1 Cr App R 441; *Greenfield* [1973] 1 WLR 1151; *Taylor* [2002] Crim LR 205.

101 [2002] Crim LR 407; *El-Kurd* [2001] Crim LR 234; and *Singh* [2003] EWCA Crim 3712.

nothing in the Act to prevent charges being laid for conspiracy to commit offences 'X *or* Y' as one agreement. Thus, an indictment is not necessarily invalid for conspiracy to commit an offence of money laundering, even though it is unclear which of the distinct substantive offences of money laundering was involved (below, p 372). These cases on the procedure for indicting conspiracy effect significant extensions of an already broad offence.

It is probably not essential that the agreement should have been made prior to the concerted action. If, when D1 is taking steps towards the commission of a crime, D2 comes to his assistance and the two work in concert, they might thereby be held to have conspired;[102] but if D1 is unaware of, or rejects D2's assistance, there is no conspiracy,[103] though D2 might be held to be an abettor of any offence or attempt consummated by D1.[104] Although some of these principles are derived from case law on the common law conspiracies, it is submitted that they apply equally to statutory conspiracy.

Although the commission of the *actus reus* in terms of agreement may be committed by words, there does not appear to be any reported defence challenge on the basis of an alleged infringement of Article 10,[105] but this is unsurprising given the breadth of the qualifications in Article 10(2) to the protection afforded in Article 10(1), including the prevention of crime.

Proof of the agreement

The question of what conduct amounts to a sufficient agreement to found a charge of conspiracy is one of several questions in the criminal law that are aggravated by a confusion between the substantive law and the law of evidence. The actual agreement in most cases will probably take place in private and direct evidence of it, even perhaps in an age of intelligence-led policing with undercover surveillance and telephone tapping, will rarely be available. A very frequent way of proving the agreement is by showing that the parties concerted in the pursuit of a common object in such a manner as to show that their actions must have been co-ordinated by arrangement beforehand.[106] The danger is that the importance attached to the acts done may obscure the fact that these acts do not in themselves constitute a conspiracy, but are only evidence of it. If the jury are left in reasonable doubt, when all the evidence is in, whether the two accused persons were acting in pursuance of an agreement, they should acquit, even though the evidence shows that they were simultaneously pursuing the same object.[107] A further problem with

102 *Leigh* (1775) 1 Car & Kir 28n; *Tibbits and Windust* [1902] 1 KB 77, CCR.

103 *State v Tally* (1894) 102 Ala 25; *Michael and Wechsler's Cases* 699; *Hawkesley* [1959] Crim LR 211 (QS).

104 *Rannath Mohan v R* [1967] 2 AC 187, [1967] 2 All ER 58, PC.

105 Or perhaps, Article 11 in terms of the right to associate with others.

106 *Cooper and Compton* [1947] 2 All ER 701; *Hammersley* (1958) 42 Cr App R 207. Lord Diplock thought that it is 'a legal fiction' (*DPP v Bhagwan* [1970] 3 All ER 97 at 104) and 'the height of sophistry' (*Knuller (Publishing, Printing and Promotions) Ltd v DPP* [1972] 2 All ER 898 at 921) that the offence lies not in the concerted action but in the inferred anterior agreement; but the law is clear that it is the agreement that is the offence. The concerted action is evidence of the crime, but not the crime itself. Cf J. C. Smith, 'Proving Conspiracy' [1996] Crim LR 386, J. C. Smith, 'More on Proving Conspiracy' [1997] Crim LR 333.

107 Where there are counts for both conspiracy and the ulterior crime and the only evidence of conspiracy is the collaboration of the parties in the completion of the ulterior crime, the only logical verdicts are guilty of both conspiracy and the ulterior crime or not guilty of both. Thus in *Cooper and Compton* [1947] 2 All ER 701, the court quashed a verdict of guilty of conspiracy as inconsistent with a verdict of not guilty of larceny. Conversely, in *Beach and Owens* [1957] Crim LR 687, a verdict of guilty of attempt to pervert the course of justice was quashed as inconsistent with a failure to agree on a conspiracy count. See below on the use of substantive and conspiracy counts.

proving agreement by reliance on the defendants' course of conduct in performing the agreement is that it undermines one of the principal reasons for the offence of conspiracy – to allow the investigating agency to intervene in the criminal conduct when it is inchoate, before it poses a greater danger of tangible harm.

Wheel and chain conspiracies

It may not be necessary to show that the persons accused of conspiring together were in direct communication with one another. Thus, it may be that the conspiracy revolves around some third party, X, who is in touch with each of D1, D2, D3, though they are not in touch with one another (a 'wheel conspiracy'). Provided that the result is that they have a common design – for example, to rob a particular bank – D1, D2 and D3 may properly be indicted for conspiring together though they have never been in touch with one another until they meet in the dock. The same is true of a chain conspiracy where D1 communicates with D2, D2 with D3 etc. In either case it must be proved, of course, that each accused has agreed with another guilty person in relation to that single conspiracy.[108]

> What has to be ascertained is always the same matter: is it true to say . . . that the acts of the accused were done in pursuance of a criminal purpose held in common between them?[109]

These propositions, for which there is ample authority,[110] are stated in the case of *Meyrick*,[111] though that case itself seems a questionable application of them. D1 and D2, nightclub proprietors, each offered bribes to a police sergeant, E, to induce him to connive at breaches of the licensing laws. They were convicted of conspiring, *inter alia*, to contravene the licensing laws. The jury were directed that there must be a 'common design' and, by their verdict of guilty, they so found, but it is difficult to see how the evidence justified this finding. The design of each nightclub proprietor was simply to evade the licensing laws in respect of his own premises.

Meyrick was distinguished in *Griffiths*[112] on the rather unconvincing ground that:

> . . . the conspiracy alleged [in *Meyrick*] was . . . in relation to a comparatively small geographical area, namely Soho. In view of the size and nature of the locality, there were clearly facts upon which a jury could come to the conclusion that the night club proprietors in that district well knew what was happening generally in relation to the police.[113]

Even if D1 and D2 each knew that the other had made a similar agreement with E, it would seem that there were two separate and specific conspiracies not one general one. Paull J has put the following example:

> I employ an accountant to make out my tax return. He and his clerk are both present when I am about to sign the return. I notice an item in my expenses of £100 and say: 'I don't remember incurring this expense.' The clerk says: 'Well, actually I put it in. You didn't incur it, but I didn't think you would object to a few pounds being saved.' The accountant indicates his agreement to this attitude. After some hesitation I agree to let it stand. On those bare facts I cannot be charged with fifty others in a conspiracy to defraud the Exchequer of £100,000 on the basis that this accountant and his clerk have persuaded 500 other clients to make false returns, some being false

108 *Ardalan* [1972] 2 All ER 257 at 261.

109 *Meyrick* (1929) 21 Cr App R 94 at 102 and *Griffiths* [1966] 1 QB 589, [1965] 2 All ER 448 applied in *Chrastny* [1992] 1 All ER 189, [1991] 1 WLR 1381, CA; *Mintern* [2004] EWCA Crim 07.

110 See eg *Cooper and Compton*, above; *Sweetland* (1957) 42 Cr App R 62.

111 See above, n 109.

112 (1965) 49 Cr App R 279.

113 Ibid, at 291.

in one way, some in another, or even all in the same way. I have not knowingly attached myself to a general agreement to defraud.[114]

It is submitted that the position would be no different if the accountant had said: 'We do this for all our clients'; there would still have been a series of conspiracies, not one general conspiracy. The convictions in *Griffiths* were indeed quashed on the ground that the evidence, while perhaps sufficient to establish a series of separate conspiracies, did not establish the single 'wheel conspiracy' alleged.

A count charging a general conspiracy is not bad because the evidence offered to prove it includes subsequent subsidiary conspiracies.[115] If A and B set up an organization to plant bombs, that is a conspiracy and indictable as such, though the overt acts offered to prove it consist in further agreements to plant particular bombs. Those further agreements are indictable as separate conspiracies, notwithstanding the existence of the general conspiracy;[116] and acquittal or conviction of one such alleged conspiracy is no bar to trial for another.

The meaning of 'course of conduct' which has been agreed

The words, 'the agreement', mean the agreement that a 'course of conduct' shall be pursued. We thus have to envisage the contemplated course of conduct as having been pursued and to ask, would it, when completed, necessarily amount to or involve the commission of any offence?[117] But the phrase, 'course of conduct', is ambiguous. It might mean only the actual physical acts which the parties propose shall be done; or it might include the consequences which they intend to follow from their conduct and the relevant circumstances which they know, or believe, or intend, to exist. In *DPP v Nock*,[118] a case of common law conspiracy committed before, but decided after, the Act came into force, the House of Lords used the same phrase, 'course of conduct', and gave it the former meaning. The defendants resolved to extract cocaine from a particular substance in their possession by subjecting it to a certain process. The substance contained no cocaine. They were held not guilty of conspiracy to produce a controlled drug. The 'course of conduct' was the application of that process to that substance; and this would necessarily *not* amount to or involve the commission of the offence of producing a controlled drug.

Section 1(1)(b), above, which was added by the Criminal Attempts Act 1981, is designed to ensure that this result does not follow in a case of statutory conspiracy. *Nock* is a case where the 'existence of facts' – that is, that there was no cocaine in the substance – rendered the commission of the offence of producing a controlled drug impossible; and, but for that fact, the course of conduct would necessarily have resulted in the production of a controlled drug. The agreement in *Nock* would therefore now amount to a statutory conspiracy to produce a controlled drug. The phraseology is unhappy – the *absence* of cocaine must be regarded as the existence of a fact – but the effect seems to be that we look at the facts at the time of the agreement as the defendants believed them to be.

114 Ibid. Cf the argument of Maddocks in *Meyrick* (1929) 45 TLR 421 at 422.
115 *Greenfield* [1973] 3 All ER 1050, [1973] 1 WLR 1151.
116 *Coughlan (Martin)* (1976) 63 Cr App R 33, [1976] Crim LR 631, CA.
117 Cf *Barnard* (1979) 70 Cr App R 28, [1980] Crim LR 235, CA and commentary.
118 [1978] AC 979, [1978] 2 All ER 654, [1978] Crim LR 483 and commentary.

Section 1(1)(b) removes any problem concerning the existence of facts at the time of the agreement and, as a corollary, consequences which depend on the existence of those facts – for example, the production of cocaine. The subsection has nothing to say, however, about (i) other consequences, not dependent on the existence of facts believed by the defendants to exist or (ii) the existence of facts precluding the commission of the crime at the time it is to be carried out.

Consequences as part of the course of conduct?

Suppose the defendants D and E agree to kill V by putting poison in his tea. This, surely, must be conspiracy to murder; but the act of putting poison in the tea will not necessarily result in murder. V may decide not to drink it. So, if the course of conduct is putting poison in the tea, it is not conspiracy to murder – which is absurd.[119] Subsection (1)(b) has nothing to say in the matter because there is no question of impossibility. To avoid the absurdity, 'course of conduct' must be read to include the intended consequences – in this case, the death of V.[120] So persons deceiving a building society into giving authority for a mortgage are guilty of conspiracy to procure the execution of a valuable security if they believe that this will be the result of their 'course of conduct' even though it will not happen because the society now uses an electronic device not amounting to a 'valuable security'.[121] 'Course of conduct' it is submitted must include the contemplated result.

Circumstances as part of the course of conduct

In determining whether conspiracy is committed, we have to look forward from the time of the agreement – will the pursuance of the agreed course of conduct necessarily amount to or involve the commission of an offence? Circumstances change. The commission of the offence may be perfectly possible at the time of the agreement and become impossible by the time it is to be performed. Where this may happen, how can we say that the pursuance of the course of conduct will *necessarily* amount to or involve the commission of an offence? Defendants agree to receive certain goods, which they know to be stolen, next Monday; but, before next Monday, the goods may cease to be stolen goods by being restored to lawful custody. D1 and D2 may agree to marry next Tuesday, knowing that D1's wife is alive; but, before next Tuesday, she may die. These events may be unlikely, but they are possible, and therefore it cannot be said that the receipt of the goods or the going through the marriage ceremony will necessarily amount to, or involve the offences of handling stolen goods and bigamy respectively. If the contemplated receipt of the goods, or the marriage ceremony, is the 'course of conduct', the agreements do not amount to conspiracy to handle or commit bigamy.[122] Clearly they ought to do so.

The obvious way out of this difficulty is to construe 'course of conduct' to include material circumstances *which the parties believe will (not may) exist.*

[119] It would be conspiracy to attempt to commit murder, since putting poison in the tea necessarily amounts to an attempt. The Criminal Attempts Act 1981 does not rule out the possibility of such an offence, but it is an absurd concept. An agreement to attempt to do something is in practical terms an agreement to do it.

[120] This argument is more fully developed in [1977] Crim LR at 601–602. See also G. Williams (1977) 127 NLJ 1164 at 1165.

[121] *Bolton* (1991) 94 Cr App R 74, [1992] Crim LR 57.

[122] They might be conspiracies to attempt. See, n 119, above.

There are two difficulties about this approach. One is s 1(2) of the Act.[123] This provides that a person is not guilty of conspiracy to commit an offence unless he 'intends or knows' that circumstances necessary for the commission of the offence shall or will exist at the time when the conduct constituting the offence is to take place. In the examples just given, D cannot 'know' that the circumstances will exist because, as we have seen, they may not do so; and it seems strange to say that he 'intends' that they shall exist when he has, and knows he has, no control over their existence.[124] He 'believes' they will exist; but s 1(2) does not use that word.[125] The circumstance may be held to be intended because it is part of an intended result; or 'know' may be construed broadly.

The second difficulty, which applies to both consequences and circumstances, is a new one, arising from the amendment made by the Criminal Attempts Act 1981, which added s 1(1)(b). If 'course of conduct' includes the circumstances believed by the parties to exist, this provision is entirely unnecessary. It is necessary only if the narrow *Nock*[126] interpretation of 'course of conduct' is right. Arguably, by enacting s 1(1)(b) Parliament has accepted that interpretation, but to have taken the sting out of it so far as impossibility at the time of the agreement is concerned. The trouble with this approach is that it leaves other stings elsewhere. However, the argument that course of conduct must include intended consequences and foreseen circumstances is so compelling that s 1(1)(b) might reasonably be regarded as an 'avoidance of doubt' provision, strictly unnecessary, but there for the guidance of the unwary. *Nock* is a discredited, though not overruled,[127] decision on the common law and should not be applied in interpreting the 1977 Act.

The object of the conspiracy

An agreement to commit any offence, even an offence triable only summarily, is a conspiracy contrary to s 1 of the Act, triable on indictment.[128] Proceedings for conspiracy to commit any summary offence or offences may not be instituted except by or with the consent of the Director of Public Prosecutions[129] or, where prosecution for the summary offence itself so requires, by or with the consent of the Attorney-General.[130] Probably discretion will be exercised in the light of the reasons given by the Law Commission[131] for retaining the apparently anomalous rule that an agreement to commit a summary offence should be indictable. 'We think that the only justification for prosecuting as conspiracy an agreement to commit summary offences is the social danger involved in the deliberate planning of offences on a widespread scale.'

123 Below.

124 For a further discussion of 'intend or know', see the 4th edition of this book, 220–222 and [1977] Crim LR 602–605.

125 Cf *Ali* [2005] EWCA Crim 87, below p 372.

126 Above, p 366.

127 See below, p 421.

128 There is one exception. An agreement to commit a summary offence, not punishable with imprisonment, is not a conspiracy if the offence is to be committed in contemplation or furtherance of a trade dispute within the Trade Union and Labour Relations (Consolidation) Act 1992, s 242: s 1(3). Section 3 of the Conspiracy and Protection of Property Act 1875 is repealed: s 5(11). J. C. Smith, 'Conspiracy under the Criminal Law Act 1977' [1977] Crim LR 638.

129 Section 4(1).

130 Section 4(2).

131 Law Com No 76, para 1.85. The Commission refer to *Blamires Transport Services Ltd* [1964] 1 QB 278, [1963] 3 All ER 170 as a typical example of the sort of case they had in mind. The conspiracy to contravene certain provisions of the Road Traffic Acts extended over two years and included a large number of offences, all triable only summarily.

Such indictments at common law were particularly objectionable because they enabled the conspiracy to be punished so much more heavily than the actual commission of the summary offence and because they enabled the indictment to be brought after the time limit for the institution of summary proceedings had expired. As appears below, the 1977 Act goes some way towards meeting these objections.[132]

There was an exception at common law where the summary offence was itself defined so as to comprise an agreement and that agreement would not be a conspiracy at common law or to commit an offence under some other statute. In such a case a conspiracy charge would allege 'the very offence which is created by the [relevant] Act . . . and which the Act makes triable only as a summary offence'; and, therefore, no indictment would lie.[133] Such an agreement appears not to be a conspiracy under s 1(1)[134] of the 1977 Act because it is the agreement itself, and not any course of conduct to be pursued, which amounts to the commission of an offence.[135]

Although technically possible, conspiracies to commit other inchoate offences – for example, conspiring to incite – would be rare and objectionable in principle since the remoteness from the substantive offence is substantial.

An agreement to break a law that might be made in the future was not indictable at common law.[136] Suppose, however, that the parties agree to pursue a course of conduct that will offend against a statute passed but not in force at the time of the agreement. If, at the time of the agreement, a date has been fixed on which the statute will come into force (which is increasingly unlikely with modern criminal legislation) and, if that date is before the agreed date of the course of conduct, it appears that there is a conspiracy. If the commencement date is fixed after the agreement and is before the agreed date of performance, the continuing agreement will become a conspiracy as soon as the date of commencement is fixed.

Agreement to do acts of secondary participation

Persons may agree to do an act that would render them liable to conviction as secondary parties if that offence were committed. Is an agreement to aid and abet an offence a conspiracy? The Criminal Attempts Act 1981[137] makes it clear that there can be no attempt to aid and abet an offence but it leaves open the question whether there can be a conspiracy to do so.[138]

D1 and D2, knowing that E intends to commit a burglary, agree to leave a ladder in a place where it will assist him to do so. E is not a party to that agreement. If E uses the

[132] In *Blamires* the prosecution was brought several years after the offences had been committed. That would not be possible under the Act; but if the proceedings were instituted within the six-month limitation period, a heavy fine would still be possible. It may be that the agreement, or part of it, amounted to a conspiracy to defraud (it was an agreement to make false records, presumably to deceive inspectors, cause them to act contrary to their duty and thereby, according to *Welham v DPP* [1961] AC 103, [1960] 1 All ER 805, to defraud them) in which case it might be indicted as such, and the limitation period would be inapplicable.

[133] *Barnett* [1951] 2 KB 425, [1951] 1 All ER 917, CCA, holding that there could be no indictment for a conspiracy amounting to a bidding agreement under the Auctions (Bidding Agreements) Act 1927. The agreement was not unlawful apart from the Act. (Offences under the Act are now triable on indictment: Auctions (Bidding Agreements) Act 1969 s 1(1).)

[134] It would, in any case, probably be a conspiracy to defraud, if it were a conspiracy at all.

[135] Cf s 5(6) which declares that *conspiracies* under the enactments shall be governed by the rules laid down by ss 1 and 2 but shall not also be offences under s 1.

[136] *West* [1948] 1 KB 709, [1948] 1 All ER 718.

[137] Section 1(4)(b).

[138] The question is discussed by J. C. Smith in *Crime, Proof and Punishment*, 21, 35–36 and 40–41.

ladder and commits burglary, D1 and D2 will be guilty of aiding and abetting him to do so. Are they guilty of conspiracy to commit burglary? Conspiracy requires an agreement that will involve 'a course of conduct' amounting to or involving 'the commission of an offence'. If the course of conduct is placing the ladder, it seems clear that they are not guilty. Placing the ladder is not an offence, not even an attempt to aid and abet burglary, since the Criminal Attempts Act 1981[139] makes it clear that this is not an offence known to the law. However, it is argued above[140] that 'course of conduct' should be interpreted to include the consequences intended to follow from the conduct agreed upon, including the action of a person not a party to the agreement – for example, V, who takes up poisoned tea left by D and E and drinks it. So it might be argued, consistently with that, that the course of conduct ought to include E's use of the ladder in committing burglary. If that should be accepted, the next question would be whether the burglary is 'the commission of any offence by one or more of the parties to the agreement'. E is not a party to the agreement, so the question becomes, do the words 'commission of any offence' include participation in the offence as a secondary party? Since all the parties to a conspiracy to commit an offence will be guilty of that offence if it is committed, but s 1(1) contemplates that it may be *committed* by only one of them, it is clear that 'commission' means commission by a principal in the first degree. It is submitted therefore that an agreement to aid and abet an offence is not a conspiracy under the Act.

The previous paragraphs were approved by the Court of Appeal in *Hollinshead*.[141] DD agreed to sell to X 'black boxes', devices for altering electricity meters to show that less electricity had been used than was the fact. They expected X to re-sell the devices to consumers of electricity for use in defrauding the electricity supplier. The House of Lords[142] did not find it necessary to decide the matter and Lord Roskill said that it should be treated as open for consideration *de novo* if the question arises again. But there was clearly an agreement to aid and abet the consumers to commit offences under s 2 of the Theft Act 1978 against the electricity supplier and, if that agreement were a statutory conspiracy, it could not under the then prevailing (though now repealed) rule in *Ayres*,[143] be a conspiracy to defraud. By upholding the conviction for conspiracy to defraud, the House implicitly decided that there was no statutory conspiracy and therefore that an agreement to aid and abet the consumers to commit an offence against the suppliers was not a statutory conspiracy.[144] This, it is submitted, is the position under the Act.

The Supreme Court of Hong Kong has held that there may be a *common law* conspiracy to aid and abet an offence. In *Po Koon-tai*,[145] the defendants, the owners of a ship in Hong Kong and the captain and crew on the high seas, agreed to land in Hong Kong certain refugees whom they had picked up at sea in desperate circumstances. The refugees were not alleged to be parties to the conspiracy but they committed the principal offence by landing in Hong Kong without permission. It was held that landing the refugees was 'an unlawful act'. The concept of the unlawful act in common law conspiracy was one of notorious elasticity but an English court might be reluctant to extend it to acts of aiding and abetting if the Criminal Law Act has been correctly interpreted above. The question arises only in the fields of fraud, corruption of morals and outraging public decency.

139 Below, p 400.
140 P 367.
141 [1985] 1 All ER 850 at 858.
142 [1985] AC 975.
143 Above, p 361.
144 See commentary on *Hollinshead* [1985] Crim LR 653 at 656.
145 [1980] HKLR 492.

Conditional intention

The question of conditional intention requires separate consideration, particularly in the light of s 1(1) of the Act. The parties may agree on alternative courses of action depending on the existence of some fact to be ascertained or some event which may or may not happen. If one of these courses of action involves the commission of a crime and the other does not, is this a conspiracy to commit the crime? Can it be said that, if the agreement is carried out in accordance with their intentions, the course of conduct pursued will *necessarily* amount to or involve the commission of an offence? Is not the agreement carried out in accordance with their intentions if, in the event, they take the non-criminal course?

Agreement to commit crime – subject to opportunity

One straightforward case that can be dealt with immediately is that where the parties' objective is to commit a crime – but not if it proves too difficult or too dangerous – as where A and B agree that they will abandon their intention to commit burglary in No 10, King Street if they find the house surrounded by police. This will amount to a conspiracy. If they go through with the agreement they must, of necessity, commit burglary. The fact that an agreement to commit a crime is subject to express or implied reservations does not necessarily preclude conspiracy.[146] What if D1 and D2 agree to have V killed if they can find a suitable contract killer for a reasonable price? To what extent does the contingent condition have to lie within the control of the conspirators?

Agreements where objective is criminal vs agreements where criminality is incidental

The most difficult to analyse are the cases where the agreement is to perform acts which may be criminal in the event of certain conditions arising, but where it is possible for the object of the agreement to be performed without necessarily perpetrating a crime. There are three decisions on the point. In *Reed*[147] A and B were held guilty of conspiring to aid and abet suicide[148] where they agreed that A would visit individuals contemplating suicide and either discourage them or actively help them, depending on his assessment of the appropriate course of action. In *Jackson*[149] A and B agreed with C that C should be shot in the leg so that, if he was convicted of the burglary for which he was being tried, the court would deal with him more leniently. They were guilty of conspiring to pervert the course of justice. In *O'Hadhmaill*,[150] it was held that an agreement by members of the IRA during the period of the IRA ceasefire to make bombs with a view to causing explosions, if, but only if, the ceasefire came to an end was a conspiracy to cause an explosion.

In the first two cases, the court held that the following hypothetical case is distinguishable: A and B agree to drive from London to Edinburgh in a time which can be achieved without exceeding the speed limits, but only if the traffic which they encounter is exceptionally light. In this example, as in the two decisions, the parties have apparently

146 *Mills* (1963) 47 Cr App R 49, [1963] Crim LR 181, CCA, and commentary. Cf *Hussein* [1978] Crim LR 219, CA, and commentary, below, p 372.

147 [1982] Crim LR 819, CA.

148 Aiding and abetting suicide is a substantive offence, so the rule that there is no offence of conspiracy to aid and abet an offence does not apply. Above, p 369.

149 [1985] Crim LR 442, CA.

150 [1996] Crim LR 509.

agreed that, in a certain event, they will commit a crime. The difference appears to be that exceeding the speed limit is only incidental to the main object of the agreement – getting from London to Edinburgh in a certain time. In the decided cases, procuring the suicide, perverting justice or causing an explosion is, in a certain event, to be 'the object of the exercise'.

Agreement to commit crime A, and if necessary, crime B also

Are burglars guilty of conspiracy to murder if they set out to commit burglary, having agreed that, if it is necessary to do so in order to complete the burglary or to escape, they will shoot to kill? On the analysis in the previous paragraph, arguably not – shooting to kill would be incidental to the achievement of an objective which might be achieved without it. On a natural interpretation of the expression the agreement will not 'necessarily' involve murder.

However, the courts appear to have concluded differently. It has been suggested that, for example, if conspirators agree that they will steal a particular item and that they will, if necessary, either commit burglary or robbery to obtain that item, that will amount to an agreement to commit the offences of theft, burglary *and* robbery.[151] At the time they make the agreement, their course of conduct will not *necessarily* involve burglary *or* robbery. It may constitute two agreements to burgle and rob. It is submitted that the issue deserves clarification from the House of Lords.

Agreements to commit crime A or crime B

A different type of conditional intention is encountered when the parties agree on a course of conduct which might amount to crime A or crime B. This is commonly encountered in the old law (pre-Proceeds of Crime Act 2002) on money laundering. D1 and D2 might agree to commit crime A (laundering the proceeds of drug trafficking) or crime B (laundering the proceeds of crime other than drug trafficking). The prosecution are often unsure whether the illicit source is drugs or other criminality, and the actors are therefore charged with conspiring to launder *drug* money (an offence under s 49(2) of the Drug Trafficking Act 1994) and/or illicit money from other criminal activity (an offence under s 93C(2) of the Criminal Justice Act 1988). Clearly they ought to be guilty of something but it is hard to see how the carrying out of the course of conduct can be said *necessarily* to amount to either crime. Logically it will not do so,[152] but the courts have upheld convictions based on indictments alleging that D has conspired to launder either drug money 'or' other criminal proceeds.[153] In some cases D1 and D2 will have made two agreements, eg, D1 and D2 can be indicted for conspiracy to rob and murder where they agree that if the next person who walks around the corner is a man they will rob him and if it is a woman they will rape her.

151 *A-G's Ref (No 4 2003)* [2004] EWCA Crim 1944, para 14; *Hussain* [2002] 2 Cr App R 26, para 27.

152 In *El-Kurd* [2001] Crim LR 234, CA, the court contrived to avoid the problem. Similarly where the parties agree to import 'prohibited drugs' which might be Class A or B or C – three separate offences. See *Taylor (RJ)* [2002] Crim LR 203.

153 See *Hussain, A-G's Ref (No 4 2003)*, above. Cf *Ali* [2005] EWCA Crim 87.

Jurisdiction

The situation where there is an agreement in England to commit an offence abroad is now regulated by s 1A[154] of the Criminal Law Act 1977. The section applies where the pursuit of the agreed course of conduct would involve an act by one or more the parties, or the happening of some event, in a place outside the UK which (a) would be an offence by the law of that place and (b) would be an offence triable here but for the fact that it was committed abroad. Then, if, in England or Wales, (i) a person became a party to the agreement, or (ii) a party to the agreement did anything in relation to it before its formation, or did or omitted anything in pursuance of it, the agreement is a indictable as a conspiracy, contrary to s 1(1) of the 1977 Act. There is, in effect, a presumption that the act or event is an offence by the foreign law unless the defence gives notice that, in their opinion, for which they must show grounds, it is not, and requiring the prosecution to prove it.[155] In the Crown Court the question is to be treated as one of law to be decided by the judge. This is a significant extension of the scope of the already broad reaching offence of conspiracy. It is indicative of Parliament's approach to extending the scope of the criminal law beyond the physical limits of the jurisdiction in general.[156]

The Act makes no express provision for agreements abroad to commit an offence in England. It has been clear since 1973[157] that, at common law, an agreement abroad to commit a crime in England is indictable here if an overt act is done in England in pursuance of the agreement. The Privy Council held in *Somchai Liangsiriprasert v United States Government*[158] that it is unnecessary to prove that any overt act was done in England. The only purpose of requiring an overt act could be to establish the link between the conspiracy and England or to show that the conspiracy was continuing and any other evidence that establishes this is just as good.

Agreements abroad to commit offences abroad deserve a brief mention. D1 and D2, British citizens in France, agree to kill V in France or to go through a ceremony of marriage there, both knowing that D1 is married. The offences contemplated are triable in England so, literally, these are indictable conspiracies under the Act. It may be, however, that the presumption against the extra-territorial application of the criminal law will exclude agreements not made within the jurisdiction and not intended to have any effect therein but this seems less likely after *Liangsiriprasert.*[159]

[154] Inserted by the Criminal Justice (Terrorism and Conspiracy) Act 1998, s 5(1)(4). See on this C. Campbell, 'Two Steps Backwards: The Criminal Justice (Terrorism and Conspiracy) Act 1998' [1999] Crim LR 941; J. Holroyd, 'The Reform of Jurisdiction over International Conspiracy' (2000) 64 J Crim L 323. For the previous law, see the 9th edition of this work at 286.

[155] Section 1A(8).

[156] See generally M. Hirst, *Jurisdiction and the Ambit of the Criminal Law* (2003), 142–148 for critical analysis of the provisions.

[157] *DPP v Doot* [1973] AC 807, [1973] 1 All ER 940.

[158] (1990) 92 Cr App R 77, PC (a case of extradition from Hong Kong to USA, but applying the common law of England), followed in *Sansom* [1991] Crim LR 126 where, however, one of the conspirators had acted in England in pursuance of the conspiracy. *Somchai* was applied in *Re Goatley* [2002] EWHC 1209 (Admin) to a case of cannabis importation.

[159] Cf the corresponding problem in attempts, below, p 417.

(c) *Mens rea*

Conspiracy is a crime where it is more difficult than usual to distinguish between *actus reus* and *mens rea*, some of the elements discussed below in the context of *mens rea* might have been dealt with as easily as *actus reus*. The *actus reus* may be said to be an agreement: but agreement is essentially a mental operation, though it must be manifested by acts of some kind. 'In the case of conspiracy as opposed to the substantive offence, it is what was agreed to be done and not what was in fact done which is all important.'[160] In short, the requirements of *mens rea* are: (i) an intention to agree, (ii) an intention to carry out the agreement, (iii) intention or knowledge as to any circumstances forming part of the substantive offence.

(i) Intention to agree

Clearly, if D1 is unaware that his conduct is being construed by D2 as an assent or agreement to a criminal proposal he will have no liability for conspiracy since he will not be intending to form the necessary agreement. There might be argued to be two elements to this part of the *mens rea*. First, it must be shown that D intended to perform the acts/speak the words that were capable of constituting an offer or acceptance of the agreement. This provides a very limited scope for denial of *mens rea*, but this might succeed where D is so intoxicated that he uses language or actions without being aware of their likely interpretation. Secondly, the requirement of *actus reus* that there is an agreement suggests a corresponding *mens rea* requirement that D intentionally used conduct that he was aware might be understood to constitute an offer/acceptance in the non-contractual sense.[161]

(ii) Intention to carry out the agreement

The section assumes the existence of an intention of the parties not merely to agree, but also to carry out their agreement. This is not surprising because the essence of conspiracy, like incitement and attempt, is the intent to cause the forbidden result. The Law Commission understood this well enough and their Report[162] was quite unequivocal. The draft Bill, and the Bill which was introduced into Parliament, provided that, where a person was charged with conspiracy to commit an offence, 'both he and the other person or persons with whom he agrees must intend to bring about any consequence which is an element of that offence, even where the offence in question may be committed without that consequence actually being intended by the person committing it'. Unwisely, this provision was deleted from the Bill because it was thought too complex; but, in agreeing to the amendment, the Lord Chancellor stated: 'What has been sought to be done, and what I think has been conceded in the speeches made today, is that the law should require full intention and knowledge before conspiracy can be established'.[163]

160 *Bolton* (1991) 94 Cr App R 74 at 80, per Woolf LJ.

161 Cf *Prior* [2004] Crim LR 849 and commentary discussing the *mens rea* for an 'offer' to supply drugs.

162 *Report on Conspiracy and Criminal Law Reform* (Law Com No 76), paras 1.25–1.41. For the common law, see *Mulcahy* (1868) LR 3 HL 306 at 317, per Willes J. *Yip Chiu-cheung*, above, p 92, assumes that a person is guilty of conspiracy at common law only if he intends to carry out the agreement. See per Lord Griffiths [1994] 2 All ER at p 928c.

163 HL, vol 379, col 55.

However, in *Anderson*,[164] Lord Bridge, in a speech with which all of the House agreed, said that it was sufficient that an alleged conspirator had agreed that the criminal course of conduct be pursued and that he would play his role, but that it was not necessary to prove in addition that he intended the crime to be committed. He was, he said –

> clearly driven by consideration of the diversity of roles which parties may agree to play in criminal conspiracies to reject any construction of the statutory language which would require the prosecution to prove an intention on the part of each conspirator that the criminal offence or offences which will necessarily be committed by one or more of the conspirators if the agreed course of conduct is fully carried out should in fact be committed.

Lord Bridge was concerned with cases like that of the owner of a car, D, who agrees with a gang to hire it to them for use in a robbery. D may be quite indifferent whether the robbery is committed or not. The answer to that situation is that the gang are certainly guilty of conspiracy for they do intend to carry out the robbery; and D is guilty of abetting the conspiracy by giving encouragement to its continuance. There is no need to dilute the requirement that the conspirators must intend the commission of crime.

In *Anderson*, D was convicted of conspiring with a number of other persons to effect the escape of one of them from prison. D had agreed to supply diamond wire to cut bars. He had certainly intended to be a party to that agreement. But D said that he never intended the plan to be put into effect and believed that it could not possibly succeed. It was held that this was no defence. It was clear in that case that two or more of the alleged conspirators did intend to carry out the agreement, so D's conviction could have been upheld on the ground that he aided and abetted that conspiracy – which he undoubtedly did, encouraging the making or continuance of it by his offer to help.[165]

The decision that no intention need be proved on the part of one alleged principal offender in conspiracy would significantly alter the scope of the offence. If no intention needs to be proved on the part of conspirator A, then none needs to be proved on the part of another, B. But if A and B are the only parties, and neither has the intention that it should be carried out, how can there be a crime of conspiracy: a conspiracy which no one intends to carry out is an absurdity, if not an impossibility. Moreover, s 1(2)[166] of the Act requires the conspirators to have intention or knowledge as to facts or *circumstances* constituting an offence, and it would be very remarkable indeed if intention or knowledge were required for the circumstances of the principal offence and not for its *consequences.*

It is submitted that *Anderson* should not be followed in this respect. It has been overlooked or ignored more than once by the Court of Appeal.[167] In *Edwards* where D had agreed to supply amphetamine but there was a possibility that he intended to supply ephedrine, it was held that the judge had rightly directed the jury that they could convict of conspiracy to supply amphetamine only if D intended to supply amphetamine – that is, it was not sufficient that D agreed to supply amphetamine unless he intended to carry

[164] [1986] AC 27, [1985] 2 All ER 961, [1985] Crim LR 651, HL and commentary. See also P. W. Ferguson, 'Intention Agreement and Statutory Conspiracy' (1986) 102 LQR 26.

[165] See commentary on the decision of the Court of Appeal, [1984] Crim LR 551, and, on conspiracy to aid and abet, above, p 200.

[166] Below, p 377.

[167] *Edwards* [1991] Crim LR 45; *Ashton* [1992] Crim LR 667; *Harvey* [1999] Crim LR 70.

out the agreement. In *McPhillips*[168] the Court of Appeal of Northern Ireland, while citing *Anderson*, accepted the proposition in this book[169] that s 1(1) of the 1977 Act[170] assumes the existence of an intention of the parties to carry out the agreement. Lord Lowry CJ held that D, who had joined in a conspiracy to plant a bomb, timed to explode on the roof of a hall at 1 am when a disco would be at its height, was not a party to the conspiracy to murder of which his accomplices were guilty because, unknown to his accomplices, he intended to give a warning enabling the hall to be cleared. He did not intend that anyone should be killed. *Anderson* was distinguished relying on Lord Bridge's *dictum* that a 'perfectly respectable citizen' who joins in an agreement 'without the least intention of playing any part in the ostensibly agreed criminal objective but rather with the purpose of frustrating and exposing the objective of the other parties' is not guilty of conspiracy. The *dictum* may be correct[171] but hardly seems to fit McPhillips, whose convictions, arising out of the same facts, for conspiracy to cause explosions and offences under the Explosive Substances Act 1883, were upheld. He was rightly acquitted of conspiracy to murder as a principal offender simply because he lacked the required intention. More debatable is the decision that he was not guilty as an abettor of the conspiracy to murder. He intentionally gave assistance or encouragement to what he knew to be a conspiracy to murder and that is normally sufficient for liability. This suggests that an intention to frustrate the object of the conspiracy is a special defence. There are clear public policy grounds for allowing such a defence, although any such withdrawal-type defence will need to be carefully prescribed in the context of inchoate liability. Arguably it should be limited to conduct of the conspirator which serves unequivocal notice of withdrawal on his co-conspirators and seeks to nullify the effects of any overt acts D has performed as part of the conspiracy.[172] It has been held that where D1 intends that the offence should be carried out he is guilty of conspiracy although he had an ulterior motive to gather evidence of the criminal wrongdoing and expose it.[173]

Intention to play some part in carrying out the agreement

According to Lord Bridge in *Anderson*[174] the *mens rea* of conspiracy is established:

> . . . if, and only if, it is shown that the accused, when he entered into the agreement, intended to play some part in the agreed course of conduct in furtherance of the criminal purpose which the agreed course of conduct was intended to achieve.

No authority was cited for this novel *dictum* and the Court of Appeal has subsequently held that Lord Bridge is not to be taken as saying what he plainly did say (above); the court in *Siracusa* said that participation in conspiracy can be active or passive and D's

---

168 (1990) 6 BNIL. 169 See the 6th edition of this work at 259.

170 Article 9(1) of the Criminal Attempts and Conspiracy (Northern Ireland) Order 1983 is identical with s 1(1).

171 *Edwards* [1991] Crim LR 45, above, p 375. But cf *Yip Chiu-cheung v R*, above, p 92, and *Somchai Liangsiriprasert v United States Government* (1990) 92 Cr App R 77 at 82 where the Privy Council left open the question whether law enforcement officers who entered into an agreement to import drugs into the USA with the object of trapping the dealers should be regarded as conspirators. For valuable discussion on the liability of state officials A. Ashworth, 'Testing Fidelity to Legal Values: Official Involvement and Criminal Justice' in S. Shute and A. Simester (eds), *Criminal Law Theory: Doctrines of the General Part* (2002), 299, 324–5.

172 Cf the discussion above in relation to secondary withdrawal, p 208.

173 *R v Jones and Warburton* [2002] EWCA Crim 735.

174 [1986] AC 27 at 39, [1985] 2 All ER 961 at 965.

intention to participate 'is established by his failure to stop the unlawful activity'.[175] D's liability is, however, complete when he joins the agreement, intending that it be carried out, and his failure to stop it is, at most, evidence of his agreement and intention. In truth, O'Connor LJ in *Siracusa* appears to have been using this as a mechanism to circumvent *Anderson.*

It is submitted that the correct statement of the law is that there is nothing in the section, nor in the common law, to require participation in the carrying out of the agreement by each conspirator. All that need be contemplated is the commission of the offence 'by one or more of the parties to the agreement'. So an agreement between A and B that A will supply a proscribed drug to B is a conspiracy between them to supply the drug.[176]

Unforeseen but inevitable consequences

As noticed above, Parliament deleted the provision in the Bill requiring an intention to cause any consequence which is an ingredient in the crime the parties are alleged to have conspired to commit. It is, however, submitted above that, notwithstanding *Anderson*, the parties must intend that at least one of them will pursue the course of conduct agreed upon. If so, they must be proved to have intended the foreseen consequences. Exceptionally, the agreed course of conduct may be such that it will necessarily cause a consequence not foreseen by the parties. For example, they agree to inflict a particular type of bodily harm, not appreciating that it will necessarily cause death. On a literal interpretation of the Act they are guilty of conspiracy to murder. In principle, that would be a wrong result, because killing is not intended and possibly not even foreseen as a possibility. It is thought that, as in interpreting other aspects of the offence, the answer lies in the construction of 'course of conduct'.[177] This should be read not only to include the consequences which are intended by the parties, but also to be limited to such consequences, whether they will in fact necessarily result or not. This is justifiable because it is the *agreed* course of conduct that we are concerned with; and the agreement does not include causing death.

If D1 and D2 agree to cause grievous bodily harm to V they are guilty of conspiring to commit an offence under s 18 of the Offences Against the Person Act 1861 but they are not guilty of conspiracy to murder although, if they carry out their intention and consequently V dies, they will be guilty of murder.[178] Similarly, an agreement to behave with gross negligence towards V is not a conspiracy to commit manslaughter, even though the parties will be guilty of manslaughter if they carry out the agreement and kill V.[179]

(iii) Knowledge as to circumstances

Section 1(2) of the Act provides:

Where liability for any offence may be incurred without knowledge on the part of the person committing it of any particular fact or circumstance necessary for the commission of the offence,

[175] *Siracusa* (1989) 90 Cr App R 340, [1989] Crim LR 712.

[176] *Drew* [2000] 1 Cr App R 91, [1999] Crim LR 581. But an indictment alleging a conspiracy to supply 'another' will be taken to mean a conspiracy to supply someone other than the conspirators: cases cited in commentary at [1999] Crim LR 582.

[177] Above, p 366.

[178] For an argument to the contrary, see 4th edition of this work, 222–223 and [1977] Crim LR 638–639. Cf Williams, 127 NLJ at 1169 and Williams, TBCL (1st edn, 1978), 357–359.

[179] A conspiracy to commit manslaughter seems a theoretical possibility in the case of a suicide pact or where the party to do the killing is suffering from diminished responsibility. Below, p 442.

a person shall nevertheless not be guilty of conspiracy to commit that offence by virtue of subsection (1) above unless he and at least one other party to the agreement intend or know that the fact or circumstance shall or will exist at the time when the conduct constituting the offence is to take place.

The provision is intended to reflect the general principle that elements of *mens rea* in inchoate offences ought not to be diluted since that *mens rea* often forms the core of the wrongdoing in the absence of any tangible harm resulting from the *actus reus.* The aim therefore of this section is to ensure that even if strict liability and recklessness as to circumstances are sufficient *mens rea* for the substantive crime, these are to have no place in conspiracy. Intention or knowledge as to *all* the circumstances of the *actus reus* is required *even* where the agreement is to commit a crime which in its substantive form may be committed recklessly, or is a crime of strict liability or one committed on the basis of D's suspicion or negligence. Although its aim is clear enough, a number of problems arise in its interpretation.

Scope of application

First, there is no express provision in s 1(1) requiring intention or knowledge as to circumstances. Section 1(2) is expressed to apply *only* to those conspiracies which involve an offence which in its substantive form has an element of strict liability as to a circumstance or requires only recklessness as to a circumstance. A strict interpretation could thus lead to the conclusion that the section does not apply where the conspiracy alleged is one involving a substantive crime in which there is a requirement of intention or knowledge (and not mere recklessness) as to a circumstance. On that interpretation, the conspirators need *not* be shown to have an intention or knowledge because the principal offence would not be within s 1(2) because it *does* require knowledge.

An example to demonstrate the absurdity of this position has been much debated and although outdated because the offence has been repealed,[180] the principle is unaffected. If D1 and D2 agree to take V out of the possession of her parents without their consent and D1 knows that she is only 15, there is no conspiracy if D2 believes she is 16 (or has no idea what age she is). This is so even if D2 will liable to conviction of the substantive offence if he actually takes the girl. The following case has been put.

But suppose in the same situation, D2's belief is that the girl is not in the possession of a parent or guardian (although D1 is under no misapprehension). It seems that D2 is guilty of conspiracy to commit the offence in section 20, Sexual Offences Act 1956 [repealed], although if they did take the girl, D2 would not be guilty of that offence. Indeed it is precisely because he would not be so guilty, that he is guilty of conspiracy to commit the offence in section 20. Section 1(2) fails to protect him because it only applies where liability for any offence may be incurred without knowledge . . . of any fact or circumstance, and *Hibbert*[181] holds that there is no liability for the offence in section 20 without knowledge of the existence of a parent or guardian.[182]

It is difficult to suppose, however, that Parliament intended that the requirement of *mens rea* should be greater on a charge of conspiring to commit an offence of strict liability or recklessness than on a charge of conspiring to commit an offence requiring knowledge.[183]

180 Sexual Offences Act 1956, s 20 as interpreted in *Prince* (1875) LR 2 CCR 154, probably overruled by *B (A Minor)*, above, p 143 repealed by the Sexual Offences Act 2003.

181 (1869) LR 1 CCR 184.

182 D. W. Elliott [1978] Crim LR 204.

183 J. C. Smith [1977] Crim LR 606; G. Williams 127 NLJ 1166.

To avoid the 'scandalous paradox',[184] reliance should be placed on the word 'nevertheless' in s 1(2). Parliament might therefore be taken to be saying '*even* where liability for any offence may be incurred without knowledge, knowledge or intent is required on a charge of conspiracy'; and thus implying that, *a fortiori*, such knowledge or intent is required on a charge of conspiracy to commit an offence requiring knowledge.

That begs two questions – (i) what comprises knowledge, and (ii) knowledge of what?

What is knowledge?[185]

The knowledge required relates to the fact or circumstance which must be proved as part of the *actus reus*. It was noted above that the 'course of conduct' agreed upon may have to be construed as including material circumstances *which the parties believe will exist* (otherwise there could be problems with conspiracy to commit bigamy two days hence, etc). The full reading of s 1(2) might be, though it is unclear, that the parties are not liable for conspiracy to commit any crime where the *actus reus* includes proof of a circumstance which they do not know does exist, or intend, or know, or believe will exist.

What are the 'facts or circumstances' which must be known?

Suppose that D1 agrees to help D2 move out of his flat. D2 is unsure whether the cabling he has installed for his hi-fi belongs to him or to his landlord. D1 and D2 confer together and are uncertain, but agree, nevertheless, to remove it knowing their actions will result in damage in the process. They therefore have an intention to cause damage, and are reckless as to whether the property belongs to another. The substantive offence of criminal damage requires that D intends or is reckless as to the causing of damage (the result), *and* that D knows or is reckless as to whether the property belongs to another (circumstance).[186] If D1 and D2 went ahead, they would have sufficient *mens rea* to be convicted of the substantive offence. As for the conspiracy, in the *actual* circumstances that exist, the carrying out of the agreement 'will necessarily amount' to criminal damage; but on an orthodox reading of s 1(2), it is not a conspiracy to commit criminal damage. It would not be criminal damage in the circumstances which the parties *intend, or know, shall or will exist*. Ds' are reckless as to the circumstance. Recklessness as to the circumstance of the *actus reus* (property belonging to another) is not a sufficient *mens rea* on a charge of conspiracy to commit a crime (criminal damage) even where it is a sufficient *mens rea* for the crime itself.

As a general point, it seems that the courts have struggled in identifying the relevant fact or circumstance in the substantive offence. For the section to bite there must be a fact or circumstance in the *actus reus* on which liability is strict or for which D's recklessness in the substantive offence suffices. The problems of the operation of this section can be illustrated by reference to two different categories of case: those involving the conspiracies to commit criminal damage being reckless as to whether life is endangered; and those involving money laundering under the pre-Proceeds of Crime Act 2002 law.

Taking the criminal damage example, in a series of cases,[187] the court offered confusing

184 D. W. Elliott, above.

185 See generally S. Shute, 'Knowledge and Belief in the Criminal Law' (at 187) and G. R. Sullivan, 'Knowledge, Belief and Culpability' (at 215) in S. Shute and A. Simester (eds), *Criminal Law: Doctrines of the General Part* (2002), chs 8, 9 respectively.

186 *Smith (David Raymond)* [1974] QB 354. See below, p 897.

187 *Mir* (1994) 22 Apr; *Browning* (1998) unreported, *Ryan* (1999) The Times, 13 Oct.

guidance as to the relevant circumstances in the substantive offence about which D must be proved to have knowledge when charged with a conspiracy. The Court of Appeal has held that on a charge of conspiracy to commit criminal damage being reckless as to whether life is endangered thereby (s 1(2) of the Criminal Damage Act 1971) it is sufficient to establish recklessness (rather than knowledge) on the part of the conspirators. These cases are based on the false assumption that the substantive offence requires proof of a fact that life is endangered. It does not: *Parker*.[188] Since life endangerment is not 'a circumstance' that needs to exist for the full offence, it is unnecessary in a conspiracy to prove that Ds 'knew of' or intended it.[189]

Section 1(2) has also given rise to an acute problem with prosecutions under the former money laundering legislation. In *Sakavickas*[190] conspiracies to commit a s 93A Criminal Justice Act 1988 offence (facilitating money laundering knowing or suspecting the source of money is criminal) were upheld. The facts or circumstance in the substantive offence include that the retention of X's proceeds was facilitated, and that the proceeds were from a criminal source. In the substantive offence neither of these circumstances requires proof of intention or knowledge (they are strict or satisfied by proof of mere suspicion). In a conspiracy, by logical application of s 1(2) the prosecution ought to prove that D and at least one other conspirator had knowledge of these two circumstances. In a strange interpretation of the section, the Court of Appeal held that for a conspiracy, D needs to have knowledge (and nothing less) of his own state of mind of reasonable suspicion as to the provenance of the money, but need not have knowledge of the circumstance that the money is of an illegal provenance. This is clearly not how s 1(2) was intended to be interpreted. If the substantive offence were being charged, no one would suggest for one minute that D must be shown to have both a suspicion as to the provenance of the money and knowledge of his own state of mind of suspicion![191] It is submitted that the conclusion that D's knowledge or awareness of his own state of mind is itself a fact or circumstance that needs to be proved for the conspiracy offence is incorrect.[192]

Even more problematical were conspiracies involving the more draconian substantive offences of laundering someone else's *drug* money under s 49(2) of the Drug Trafficking Act 1994 and laundering someone else's money from other criminal activity under s 93C(2) of the Criminal Justice Act 1988. As substantive charges these can only lead to conviction on the prosecution proving that D knew or had reasonable grounds to suspect

188 [1993] Crim LR 856.

189 See now *Ali* [2005] EWCA Crim 87, para 129. There are two arguments that these cases are not wrongly decided. First, they were all heard at a time when *Caldwell* recklessness was a sufficient *mens rea* for criminal damage. As such, although the offence did not require proof of a circumstance of a life being endangered, it did require proof of the reasonable person's awareness of a risk of life endangerment. That it is said could be a 'circumstance' in the substantive offence for which D must be held to have knowledge for the charge of conspiracy. Secondly, since *G* [2004] 1 AC 1034, the *mens rea* as to the endangerment of life is subjective. Arguably, however, there is still an 'objective circumstance' that must exist because even in a case of subjective recklessness, there must be proof that D 'unreasonably' took the risk he foresaw. Thanks are due to Rudi Fortson for discussions on this point.

190 [2004] EWCA Crim 2686, [2005] Crim LR 293. See now *Ali* [2005] EWCA Crim 87, para 129–131.

191 No one in a murder trial would suggest that the accused has to intend to kill or do grievous bodily harm and be aware that he has a state of mind of intention.

192 See further the commentary at [2005] Crim LR 293.

that the money in whole or in part directly or indirectly represented another person's proceeds of drug trafficking/other criminal activity respectively. The relevant circumstances are (i) that the money is of an illicit provenance,[193] (ii) of the type specified (drug or other), (iii) that it is someone else's money, (iv) that D had possession of the facts that would cause a reasonable person to suspect the illicit provenance and (v) that the reasonable person would have formed a suspicion on the facts available to D. In the substantive offence the prosecution need not prove that D had intention or knowledge as to these circumstances. Therefore, on a conspiracy, an orthodox application of s 1(2) of the 1977 Act would require that D, and at least one other conspirator had knowledge as to each of these elements. Sadly the courts have not adopted such a straightforward approach. The Court of Appeal in *Harmer*[194] has now accepted that the consequence of *M* in the House of Lords is that the prosecution is obliged to prove that the property was illicit and that D had knowledge as to that illicit provenance. Thankfully, the Proceeds of Crime Act 2002, ss 327 and 340 reduces the problem in the particular context of drugs because the prosecution is now obliged to prove only that the property is 'criminal property'. Clarification of the scope and application of s 1(2) is, nevertheless, urgently needed from the House of Lords.[195]

Conspiring to import prohibited drugs

The offences of evading the prohibition on the importation of drugs come within s 1(2).[196] They are offences for which liability may be incurred without knowledge on the part of the defendant that the drug was of a particular class. For the substantive offence, it is sufficient that D knew the goods were subject to a prohibition on importation. If he is charged with importing pethidine (a Class A drug – penalty, life imprisonment) it is no defence that he believed the drug to be pemoline (a Class C drug – penalty, five years). But that the drug *was* pethidine is, of course, a fact necessary for the commission of the offence. On a charge of conspiracy, it must be proved that the defendant and at least one other party intended or knew that that fact should or would exist.[197] An indictment for conspiracy to import 'prohibited drugs' is different. It embraces agreements to import Class A, B and C drugs and, as these are different offences carrying different penalties, it appears at first sight to allege three distinct conspiracies. But s 1, defining statutory conspiracy, speaks of 'any offence or offences' and s 3 provides that, where the penalties for the substantive offences differ, the maximum for the conspiracy is the longer or longest of these.[198]

193 See the House of Lords decision in *M* [2004] UKHL 50, [2005] Crim LR 479.

194 [2005] Crim LR 482.

195 A point was certified in *Ali* [2005] EWCA Crim 87.

196 Above, p 379.

197 *Siracusa* [1989] Crim LR 712 and commentary. In *Patel* (89/4351/S1, CA, 7 Aug 1991), Archbold, para 34–16, it was said that an agreement to deal with a drug believing it to be of a higher class than was in fact the case would be a conspiracy to deal in the drug of the lower class. That seems irreconcilable with s 1(2). But the parties appear to be guilty of a conspiracy to deal with the drugs of the higher class! The commission of the offence is impossible, but that is immaterial. See further *Taylor (RJ)* [2002] Crim LR 203 and commentary, and 301; *Hussain* [2002] 2 Cr App R 363, [2002] Crim LR 407 and commentary.

198 Conspiracy thus appears to be a statutory exception to the rule in *Courtie* [1984] AC 463, that, when Parliament provides that an offence shall be more severely punishable when a particular fact is present, it necessarily creates two offences. See also the interesting decision of the Privy Council in *Karpavicius* [2002] UKPC 59 construing the New Zealand drugs legislation, although the ruling turns largely on the particular statutory words in s 6(2A)(c) of the Misuse of Drugs Act 1975 (NZ) which are not present in the English legislation. See also J. Evans, 'Dilemma of Proof and the Extension of Criminal Statutes' [2003] Crim LR 181.

(iv) Where only one party has *mens rea*

Section 1(2) makes it clear that, so far as the relevant circumstances are concerned, both parties to the agreement (or, where there are more than two parties, at least two of them) must have *mens rea*. If D1 and D2 agree to touch V sexually and D1 knows that she is only 15, there is no conspiracy if D2 reasonably believes that she is 16.

The Law Commission's rejected subsection would have made similar provision for foresight of consequences, but there is no such provision in the Act. If, however, 'course of conduct' is construed, as suggested above, to include intended consequences, and only intended consequences, the result is the same. As Lord Griffiths said in *Yip Chiu-cheung*,[199] 'The crime of conspiracy requires an agreement between two or more persons to commit an unlawful act with the intention of carrying it out. It is the intention to carry out the crime that constitutes the *mens rea* of the offence'. If D1 intends death and D2 intends grievous bodily harm, this is a conspiracy to cause grievous bodily harm but not a conspiracy to murder.

Ignorance of criminal law no defence

There is no requirement that Ds have knowledge of the relevant criminal law which renders their proposed conduct illegal.[200]

(d) Common law conspiracies

All common law conspiracies require proof of an agreement as considered in relation to statutory conspiracies above.

(i) Conspiracy to defraud[201]

This offence is one of the most controversial in English criminal law, and there has been sustained pressure for its abolition.[202] It is excessively broad, vague, and criminalizes conduct by two or more that would not be criminal or even tortious when performed by an individual. It offends against the principles of legality, certainty and fair warning, and results in an offence which is commonly defined by reference only to the concept of dishonesty – a concept that is ill-suited to shoulder that responsibility.[203] The Law Commission commented recently that the offence is 'so wide that it offers little guidance

199 [1994] 2 All ER 924, PC at 928.

200 *Churchill v Walton* [1967] 2 AC 224; *Broad* [1997] Crim LR 666.

201 See Smith, *Property Offences* (1994), ch 19; A. Arlidge, J. Parry, and I. Gatt, *On Fraud* (2nd edn, 1996), ch 2; R. Sutton and L. Dobbs, *Fraud Law, Practice and Procedure* (2004), ch 3. For an historical account see T. Hadden, 'Conspiracy to Defraud' [1996] CLJ 248. See also J. C. Smith, 'Fraud and the Criminal Law', in P. Birks (ed), *Pressing Problems in the Law* (1995), vol 1, 49.

202 See for discussion the Law Commission Working Papers No 56 (1974); No 104 (1988) and A. T. H. Smith, 'Conspiracy to Defraud [1988] Crim LR 508; Law Com Report No 228, *Conspiracy to Defraud* (1994) and J. C. Smith, 'Conspiracy to Defraud: Some Comments on the Law Commission's Report' [1995] Crim LR 209. The Law Commission offered a defence of its approach: S. Silber, 'The Law Commission, Conspiracy to Defraud and the Dishonesty Project' [1995] Crim LR 461, and see J. C. Smith, Letter [1995] Crim LR 519.

203 See the discussion below in Ch 18. As noted by the Law Commission in its Consultation Paper No 155, *Legislating the Criminal Code: Fraud and Deception* (1999) in rejecting the idea of an offence based on an element of dishonesty because of anxiety that it would not be compatible with Article 7. See also D. Ormerod, 'A Bit of a Con' [1999] Crim LR 789.

on the difference between fraudulent and lawful conduct'.[204] Even the Home Office has acknowledged that the offence was 'arguably unfairly uncertain and wide enough potentially to encompass sharp business practice'.[205] The Commission's conclusion was that the offence should be abolished, to be replaced by three specific fraud offences, but the Home Office has recently recommended that although the new fraud offences will be implemented, conspiracy to defraud will be retained – as a safeguard against lacunae being revealed in the new scheme.

Scope of the offence

It was stated by the House of Lords in *Scott v Metropolitan Police Comr*[206] that:

> . . . it is clearly the law that an agreement by two or more by dishonesty to deprive a person of something which is his or to which he is or would be or might be entitled[207] and an agreement by two or more by dishonesty to injure some proprietary right of his, suffices to constitute the offence of conspiracy to defraud.[208]

In *Scott*, D agreed with the employees of cinema owners that in return for payment, they would abstract films without the consent of their employers, or of the owners of the copyright, in order that D might make copies infringing the copyright, and distribute them for profit. It was held that D was guilty of a conspiracy to defraud. It was held to be immaterial that no one was deceived. The offence is one of defrauding. Although the well-known definition of 'defraud' by Buckley J in *Re London and Globe Finance Corpn Ltd*,[209] includes a reference to deceit ('to defraud is by deceit to induce a course of action'), there can be fraud without deceit. For example, larceny was an offence which had to be committed 'fraudulently', but deceit has never been a necessary ingredient of theft.

There are two versions of the offence of conspiracy to defraud. The most commonly encountered is that involving economic prejudice.

Defrauding by imperilling economic interests

The majority of the authorities relied on in *Scott* were in fact conspiracies to steal or to do acts which included theft, though the defrauding was not necessarily confined to theft. In *Button*[210] DD were convicted of conspiracy to use their employer's vats and dyes to dye articles which they were not permitted to dye in order to make profits for themselves and so to defraud their employer of the profit. The dyes were no doubt stolen; but the employer did not have a proprietary interest in the profit so that the appropriation of it

204 Law Com Report No 276, *Fraud* (2002), para 1.6.

205 See Home Office, *Fraud Law Reform: Consultation on Proposals for Legislation* (2004) para 6. www.homeoffice.gov.uk/docs3/fraudlawreform.html. For comment, see P. Binning, 'When Dishonesty is not Enough' (2004) 154 NLJ 1042 and the references cited in Ch 19 below on fraud reform.

206 [1975] AC 819, [1974] 3 All ER 1032.

207 In *Tarling v Government of the Republic of Singapore* (1978) 70 Cr App R 77, [1978] Crim LR 490 the House of Lords by a majority held that the intention of company directors to make and retain a secret profit for which they would have been accountable to the shareholders was not evidence of an intention to defraud. See, however, J. C. Smith, 'Theft, Conspiracy and Jurisdiction: Tarling's case' [1979] Crim LR 220 at 225–226. In *Adams v R* [1995] 1 WLR 52, PC, the court seems to have been of the view that, even if the agreement to make and retain the secret profit is not an offence, the agreement to take positive steps to conceal it is. See commentary [1995] Crim LR 561, 562.

208 Per Viscount Dilhorne at 1039.

209 [1903] 1 Ch 728 at 732, 733.

210 (1848) 11 QB 929.

did not constitute a substantive offence.[211] The great majority of agreements to defraud in this category will be agreements to commit offences under the Theft Acts but clearly there are cases amounting to fraud within the definition in *Scott* that are not substantive offences. An example is the appropriation of the profit in *Button*. The Criminal Law Revision Committee considered whether such conduct should be brought within the definition of theft and concluded:

> . . . although the conduct, when it occurs, is reprehensible enough to deserve punishment, it does not seem to us that it occurs often enough to involve a substantial problem or to require the creation of a new criminal offence.[212]

Parliament presumably accepted this view, as it certainly accepted, after full debate, that temporarily to deprive another of his property should not be theft; yet an agreement so to do is clearly capable of amounting to conspiracy under the *dictum*[213] in *Scott*. Likewise was the case where D1 and D2 agree to shift D1's boundary fence so as to appropriate V's land – an act which is not, by specific decision of Parliament, theft, but evidently a conspiracy to defraud.

It is clear that V is defrauded if he is induced to take an economic risk which he would not have taken but for a deception.[214] It is no answer that D believed that the speculation was a good one and that V had a good chance of making a profit. If V is induced to part with something of economic value, he is probably defrauded even if he does receive the promised return.[215] The breadth of the offence proves useful in prosecuting high yield investment frauds and other investment scams. Its breadth and flexibility are its vice and its virtue. The Law Commission in its Report No 276 catalogued those forms of conduct that are capable of being prosecuted only as conspiracy to defraud.[216]

Agreement to deceive V to act contrary to public duty

The proposition in *Scott* is not an exclusive definition of conspiracy to defraud. It is confined to economic prejudice; but a person is also defrauded if he is deceived

211 J. C. Smith, 'Embezzlement and the Disobedient Servant' (1956) 19 MLR 39. But see *A-G for Hong Kong v Reid*, below, p 662.

212 Cmnd 2977, para 29.

213 The defendants intended to deprive the owners temporarily of the films but permanently of the profits the owners would otherwise have made; and the defrauding was the loss of the profits: [1974] 3 All ER 1032 at 1038.

214 *Allsop* (1976) 64 Cr App R 29, [1976] Crim LR 738, CA and commentary; cf *Hamilton* (1845) 1 Cox CC 244; *Carpenter* (1911) 22 Cox CC 618.

215 *Potger* (1970) 55 Cr App R 42; Smith, *Theft*, para 4–35.

216 These include: deception which obtains a benefit which does not count as property, services or any of the other benefits defined in the Theft Acts; deception which causes a loss and obtains a directly corresponding gain, where the two are not the same property (other than a transfer of funds between bank accounts); deception which causes a loss and obtains a gain where the two are neither the same property nor directly correspondent; deception which does not obtain a gain, or cause a loss, but which prejudices another's financial interests; deception for a non-financial purpose; deception to gain a temporary benefit; deceptions which do not cause the obtaining of a benefit; conduct involving a view to gain or an intent to cause loss, but not deception; making a secret gain or causing a loss by abusing a position of trust or fiduciary duty; obtaining a service by giving false information to a machine; 'fixing' an event on which bets have been placed; dishonestly failing to fulfill a contractual obligation; and, dishonestly infringing another's legal right.

into acting contrary to his public duty.[217] So it would be a conspiracy to defraud if DD agree by deception to induce a public official to grant an export licence,[218] or to supply information[219] or to induce a professional body to accept an unqualified person as a member,[220] assuming, in each case, that it was the duty of the person so deceived not to do as asked in the actual circumstances of the case. If the public official is persuaded by means other than deception – for example, bribes or threats – to act contrary to his duty, he is obviously not defrauded and the agreement is not a conspiracy to defraud unless it can be said that those affected by the breach of duty have been defrauded – for example, those persons about whom the confidential information is disclosed or, more likely, perhaps, the official's superiors whose duty to keep the information secret has been vicariously violated. Most conspiracies to pervert the course of justice consist in agreements to deceive a public official so that he acts contrary to his duty and are conspiracies to defraud.

Some of their lordships in *Withers*[221] thought that this principle was strictly confined to public officials, and did not extend to the case, for example of a bank manager deceived into breaking his contractual duty.[222] However in *Wai Yu-tsang v R*[223] the Privy Council said that the cases concerned with public duties are not to be regarded as a special category but as examples of the general principle that conspiracy to defraud does not require an intention to cause economic loss. The Board, disapproving Lord Diplock's more restrictive statement in *Scott*,[224] preferred the broad propositions of Lord Denning – 'If anyone may be prejudiced in any way by the fraud, that is enough' – and Lord Radcliffe, who agreed with Lord Denning and used similar language, in *Welham*.[225] This seems to open a very broad vista of potential criminal liability.

'Intention' to defraud

If a person is defrauded when he is 'prejudiced', conspirators clearly have a sufficient *mens rea* if it is their purpose to cause that prejudice by carrying out their agreement. There are *dicta* to the effect that such direct intention in the form of a purpose is required, but in *Wai Yu-tsang* the Privy Council thought this too restrictive and that it is enough that the parties have *agreed to cause* the prejudice. If they have agreed to cause it, that is, to defraud, they intend to defraud, and it is immaterial that defrauding is not their purpose.

The purpose of fraudsters is almost always to make a profit for themselves and not to cause loss to another. They act out of greed, not spite. Since they know that they can make

217 *Welham v DPP* [1961] AC 103, [1960] 1 All ER 805. *Welham* was followed in *Terry* [1984] AC 374, [1984] 1 All ER 65, HL. (D, who uses an excise licence belonging to another vehicle intending to cause police officers to act on the assumption that it belongs to his vehicle, has an intention to defraud, even though he intends to pay the licence fee.)

218 *Board of Trade v Owen* [1957] AC 602, [1957] 1 All ER 411.

219 *DPP v Withers* [1975] AC 842, [1974] 3 All ER 984.

220 *Bassey* (1931) 22 Cr App R 160, CCA.

221 [1975] AC 842, [1974] 3 All ER 984.

222 On the broad interpretation of public duty in the offence of misconduct in public office, see *A-G's Reference (No 3 of 2003)* [2004] EWCA Crim 868.

223 [1991] 4 All ER 664 at 670, PC.

224 [1975] AC 819 at 840–841. But the court in *Wai* made no reference to *Withers* [1975] AC 842, decided by the same judicial committee at the same time as *Scott*, where Lords Simon and Kilbrandon agreed with Lord Diplock.

225 [1961] AC 103 at 133 and 124 respectively.

a gain only by causing loss or prejudice, they intend to cause the loss or prejudice, even though they have no 'wish' to cause it and perhaps regret the 'necessity' of doing so in order to achieve their object.

In the light of these principles *Attorney-General's Reference (No 1 of 1982)* (the 'whisky-label case')[226] is a doubtful decision. The defendants were charged with conspiracy to defraud X Co by causing loss by unlawful labelling, sale and supply of whisky, falsely purporting to be 'X label' products. The agreement was made in England but the whisky was to be sold in Lebanon. The *ratio decidendi* was that the trial judge had rightly held that he had no jurisdiction to try the indictment because the contemplated crime in Lebanon (obtaining by deception from the purchasers of the whisky) would not have been indictable in England (see now below on jurisdiction). One reason for holding that there was no conspiracy to defraud X Co was that this was not the 'true object' of the agreement. Damage to X Co would have been 'a side effect or incidental consequence of the conspiracy and not its object'.[227] This must now be considered in the light of the decision of the House of Lords in *Cooke.*[228] British Rail stewards boarded a train, equipped with their own food which they dishonestly sold to passengers, instead of that provided by their employers, intending to keep the proceeds of sale for themselves. They were probably guilty in law of going equipped to cheat the passengers and, when they sold food to them, of obtaining the price by deception.[229] Whether this was so or not, the House had no difficulty in holding that they were guilty of conspiracy to defraud British Rail. It is true that the House was preoccupied with the problem of distinguishing *Ayres*, the 'whisky-label case' was not cited and it does not appear that it was argued that the loss to British Rail was 'a side effect or incidental consequence'. Nevertheless, it is clear that this was a case where the object of the conspirators was to make a profit out of the customers, not to defraud British Rail.

Of course, one must agree with Lord Lane CJ in the 'whisky-label case'[230] that, 'it would be contrary to principle, as well as being impracticable for the courts, to attribute to defendants constructive intentions to defraud third parties based on what the defendants should have foreseen as probable or possible consequences.' Constructive intentions are to be abhorred; but presumably the House in *Cooke* thought that a jury could properly find that the defendants must have known that their conduct would, inevitably, cause loss to British Rail. If so, it was right to hold that they *intended*[231] to defraud British Rail and it should be immaterial that this was not their purpose.

The intention must always be proved. Thus, the use abroad of a stolen cheque book and cheque card is capable of being fraud on a bank in England because the effect is to cause the bank in England to meet its legal or commercial obligation to honour the cheque; but, if D is charged with conspiracy to defraud the bank, the jury must be directed that he appreciated that his conduct would have this effect.[232] Subject to the jurisdictional problem, considered below, it is submitted that, on a proper direction,

226 [1983] QB 751, [1983] 2 All ER 721, [1983] Crim LR 534 and commentary.

227 [1983] 2 All ER 724. But in *Governor of Pentonville Prison, ex p Osman* (1990) 90 Cr App R 281 at 298 it was held, distinguishing the whisky-label case, that a conspiracy to deprive V of dollars in the United States was only the means to effecting the 'true object' of the conspiracy which was the defrauding of V in Hong Kong. The distinction is not blindingly obvious.

228 [1986] AC 909, [1986] 2 All ER 985, [1987] Crim LR 114.

229 Below, p 769.

230 [1983] 2 All ER at 724.

231 Above, p 94, Ch 5.

232 *McPherson and Watts* [1985] Crim LR 508.

the whisky-label conspirators might properly have been convicted of conspiracy to defraud the X Co. They might have been more sophisticated in this respect than the stewards in *Cooke* and better able to appreciate the effect of their actions on third parties. This applies equally to the 'Chanel case',[233] where the facts were similar.

Prejudice includes putting at risk

If the conspirators know that the effect of carrying out the agreement will be to put V's property at risk, then they intend prejudice to V and, if they are dishonest, they are guilty of conspiracy to defraud him. This is so notwithstanding that it turns out that V's property is unimpaired, or even that he makes a profit out of the transaction. A clear example would be where the conspirators agree to take V's money without his consent and then bet with it on a horse with odds at 20 to 1. They have agreed to defraud him and the conspiracy is not undone even if the horse wins and, as they intended throughout, they pay half the winnings into his bank account. This, it is submitted is the best explanation of *Allsop*.[234] The judgment is difficult because of its reliance on two *dicta* of Lord Diplock which were mutually inconsistent and have both since been disapproved; but the decision on the facts is readily explicable. D was a 'sub-broker' for a hire-purchase finance company, V. His function was to introduce prospective hire-purchasers who wished to acquire cars. In collusion with others, he filled in application forms with false statements about the value of the cars and the payment of deposits so as to cause V to accept applications for hire-purchase finance which, otherwise, they might have rejected. He expected and believed that the transactions he introduced would be duly completed, so that V would achieve their contemplated profit to the advantage of all concerned, including D who got his commission. His defence was that he did not intend V to suffer any pecuniary loss or be prejudiced in any way. The court found that V was defrauded when he was induced to do the very acts which D intended him to do. V paid an excessive price for cars and advanced money to persons who were not as creditworthy as they were alleged to be. This not merely put him at risk of being defrauded, but actually defrauded him: 'Interests which are imperilled are less valuable in terms of money than those same interests when they are secure and protected'.[235] The result intended by D was, in law, the defrauding of V; and V was in law defrauded. It is wholly immaterial whether D would have regarded that result as 'fraud'. If he did not, he was making a mistake of law.

According to this explanation D intended to prejudice V. The facts admitted of no other interpretation. But the judge had directed the jury that they could convict if they were satisfied that D realized that his conduct was *likely to lead* to the detriment or prejudice of V. If this is taken literally, it is sufficient that D is reckless (in the *Cunningham/G* sense) whether prejudice – that is, defrauding – occurs. It is submitted that this would be going too far and take common law conspiracy out of line with statutory conspiracy. In *Wai Yu-tsang* the Privy Council expressed a reluctance 'to allow this part of the law to become enmeshed in a distinction, sometimes artificially drawn between intention and recklessness'; but they then said, of *Allsop* and the instant case, that it is enough that:

[233] Section 2(3) of the Act. [234] (1976) 64 Cr App R 29. [235] (1976) 64 Cr App R at 32.

the conspirators have dishonestly agreed to bring about a state of affairs which they realize will *or may* [authors' italics] deceive the victim into so acting, or failing to act, that he will suffer economic loss or his economic interests will be put at risk.

The use of the words, 'or may', admit recklessness as a sufficient *mens rea* – it is enough that the parties have taken a conscious risk of causing prejudice. This was probably not necessary to the decision since the trial judge had directed the jury that D was guilty if he knew what he had done 'would cause detriment or prejudice to another'.

Dishonesty in putting property at risk

The intention to defraud is readily discernible in *Allsop* where there could be no question of V believing he had any right to do what he did. More difficult is the case where company directors take a risk with the company's property, perhaps hoping to make a large profit and so benefit the shareholders. If the risk taken was such that 'no director could have honestly believed . . . it was in the interest of that company that the risk should be taken',[236] then the company is defrauded. Whether a risk is unjustifiable is a question of judgement and a matter of degree. There is no clear dividing line between right and wrong, such as was crossed in *Allsop* when false statements were made or in *Wai Yu-tseng* where the dishonouring of cheques was concealed in a bank account. Whether the risk is so grave that no director could believe it justified is equally a matter of judgement and degree. Conspiracy to defraud thus lacks the precision that we should normally look for in any offence, and certainly in one of this seriousness. In *Landy*[237] the Court of Appeal proposed a model of how an indictment should be drawn for the facts of that case. The words italicized illustrate these points:

Causing and permitting the Bank to make *excessive* advances to *insubstantial* and *speculative* trading companies incorporated in Liechtenstein and Switzerland, such advances being *inadequately* guaranteed and without *proper* provision for payment of interest.[238]

The courts have reiterated the need for greater care in the framing of indictments for conspiracy to defraud in particular making clear a distinction between the agreement alleged and the reasonable information given in respect of it.[239] Where the prosecution provides further particulars to clarify the allegations, these do not form part of the ingredients of the offence in the indictment unless they relate to the *agreement* not the method of implementation and as such there need not be jury unanimity on them.[240]

Dishonesty is an essential constituent of the *mens rea* but there has been controversy about what 'dishonesty' means in this context. In *Landy*[241] the court appeared to think that the ultimate test was whether the *defendant* thought his conduct dishonest. In *McIvor*[242] the court reiterated this view, holding that the test in theft is different; but, shortly afterwards in *Ghosh*[243] it was held that the same test should be applied in con-

236 *Sinclair* [1968] 3 All ER 241, (1968) 52 Cr App R 618.

237 [1981] 1 All ER 1172, (1981) 72 Cr App R 237.

238 [1981] 1 All ER at 1179.

239 *K* [2004] EWCA Crim 2685, [2005] Crim LR 298. It was noted however that it is only necessary to specify in detail in the indictment the agreement, and not how the participants intended individually to go about (or had gone about) defrauding V.

240 Ibid; cf *Fussell* [1997] Crim LR 812.

241 [1981] 1 All ER 1172 at 1181.

242 [1982] 1 All ER 491, [1982] 1 WLR 409.

243 [1982] QB 1053, [1982] 2 All ER 689. See *Cox and Hodges* [1983] Crim LR 167 and commentary (fraudulent trading).

spiracy to defraud as in theft. The standard of honesty is that of ordinary decent people and D is dishonest if he realizes he is acting contrary to that standard. In theft, D is not dishonest if he believes he has a right to do the act in question and this must also apply in conspiracy. If, however, he knows for example, that no 'ordinary decent company director' would take the risk in question, then he knows that the risk is an unjustifiable one and it is dishonest for him to take it.[244] The test proposed in *Sinclair*[245] accords with this. If *no* director could have believed the risk was justified, it follows that the defendant did not; but it would seem right that the jury should be directed that they must find this is so.

Fraud – by whom?

In statutory conspiracy it is expressly provided that the contemplated offence is to be committed 'by one or more of the parties to the agreement'.[246] In *Hollinshead*,[247] the Court of Appeal held that this was a restatement of the common law, so the same principle applied to conspiracy to defraud: the contemplated fraud must be one which is to be perpetrated by one of the parties to the agreement in the course of carrying it out. But complete execution of the agreement to sell the black boxes in that case would not defraud anyone. The parties contemplated that the fraud would be carried out by other persons, not yet ascertained who would buy the boxes and use them to defraud the electricity suppliers. The court therefore quashed the convictions for conspiracy to defraud – but they were restored by the House of Lords. The House held that the 'purpose' of the defendants was to cause economic loss to the electricity suppliers. This is difficult to understand. Their purpose was to make a profit by selling the devices to the (as they thought) middleman. Presumably they did not care what happened to the boxes after that. If they had been accidentally destroyed in a fire, they would not consider that their enterprise had failed. On the contrary they might have been pleased at the prospect of selling some more. The House seems to have been much influenced by the fact that the boxes were 'dishonest devices' with only one 'purpose', which was to cause loss. But 'purpose' is here used in the sense of 'function'. An inanimate thing cannot have a 'purpose' (any more than it can be 'dishonest') in the sense in which that word is used in the law of conspiracy. However that may be, *Hollinshead* seems to broaden the law of conspiracy to defraud to include the case where the defendants contemplate that the execution of their agreement will enable some third party to perpetrate a fraud.

Jurisdiction over conspiracy to defraud[248]

An agreement in England or Wales to carry out a fraud abroad is not indictable at common law in England or Wales as a conspiracy to defraud. This is now regulated by s 5(3) of the Criminal Justice Act 1993 which provides that, where the conspiracy would be triable in England but for the fraud which the parties had in view not being

244 For a remarkable difference of opinion in the House of Lords as to whether there was evidence of dishonesty, see *Tarling v Government of the Republic of Singapore* (1978) 70 Cr App R 77. See, on this case, J. C. Smith, 'Theft Conspiracy and Jurisdiction: Tarling's case' [1979] Crim LR 220.

245 Above, n 387.

246 Criminal Law Act 1977, s 1(1)(a), above, p 362.

247 [1985] 1 All ER 850 at 857, above, p 370.

248 See generally M. Hirst, *Jurisdiction and the Ambit of the Criminal Law* (2003), 175–178.

intended to take place in England and Wales, a person may be guilty of conspiracy to defraud if:[249]

(a) a party to the agreement constituting the conspiracy, or a party's agent, did anything in England and Wales in relation to the agreement before its formation, or
(b) a party to it became a party in England and Wales (by joining it either in person or through an agent), or
(c) a party to it or a party's agent, did or omitted anything in England and Wales in pursuance of it.

Conspiracy to defraud and cartels

One particular form of conduct, that was previously only charged, if at all, as a conspiracy to defraud involved the dishonest agreement between suppliers, to fix prices or limit production. Such anti-competitive cartels are now proscribed by a series of specific offences introduced by the Enterprise Act 2002. Sections 188–202 create offences involving agreements to fix prices, limit production or supply, rig bids, etc where the agreement is a horizontal one between providers.[250] The offences ensure compliance with the Article 81 obligations under the EU Treaty.

(ii) Conspiracy to corrupt public morals

In *Shaw v DPP*,[251] the House of Lords (Lord Reid dissenting) held that a conspiracy to corrupt public morals is an offence. D published the Ladies' Directory which advertised the names and addresses of prostitutes with, in some cases, photographs and, in others, particulars of sexual activities which they were willing to practice. He was convicted of (1) conspiring to corrupt public morals; (2) living on the earnings of prostitution[252] and (3) publishing an obscene article, contrary to the Obscene Publications Act 1959, s 2(1).[253] His conviction on all counts was upheld by the Court of Criminal Appeal and the House dismissed his further appeal in respect of counts (1) and (2). Lord Tucker, with whose speech the majority agreed, was of the opinion that there was an offence of conspiring to commit a public mischief and that the corruption of public morals was a public mischief; but he did not reject the view of the Court of Criminal Appeal that to corrupt public morals is a substantive offence. Lord Simon in *DPP v Withers*[254] concluded that there were three possible *rationes decidendi.*

(i) There is a substantive offence of corrupting public morals, so an agreement to do so is a conspiracy.
(ii) The corruption of public morals is a separate head of conspiracy.

249 Hirst argues that s 5(3) should be charged separately from and in addition to conspiracy to defraud, above, 178.

250 For detailed analysis see C. Harding and J. Joshua, 'Breaking up the Hardcore' [2002] Crim LR 933; M. Furse and S. Nash, 'Partners in Crime – the General Cartel Offence in UK law' (2004) Int Company and Commerical Law Review 138; K. MacDonald and R. Thompson, 'Dishonest Agreements' (2003) Competition Law Journal 94.

251 [1962] AC 220, [1961] 2 All ER 446.

252 Contrary to s 30 of the Sexual Offences Act 1956 (since repealed).

253 Considered below, p 944. Leave to appeal on that count was refused by the Court of Criminal Appeal. See the puzzling remarks by Lord Reid [1962] AC 220 at 280, [1961] 2 All ER 446 at 460; and see [1961] Crim LR 473, n 2a.

254 [1974] 3 All ER 984 at 1003. Above, p 359.

(iii) There is an offence of conspiracy to affect a public mischief and the corruption of public morals is a public mischief.

Lord Simon held that it was open to the House to reject *ratio* (iii) and, indeed, the decision does so. Since Lord Tucker did not decide that there is a substantive offence of corrupting public morals, it seems clear that the *ratio* must be taken to be (ii).

It is therefore uncertain whether an agreement to corrupt public morals is a statutory conspiracy which should be charged under the 1977 Act; but judges of first instance may consider themselves bound by the decision of the Court of Criminal Appeal to hold that it is. *Shaw* was followed in *Knuller*[255] where, Lord Diplock dissenting, the House held that an agreement to publish advertisements to facilitate the commission of homosexual acts between adult males in private was a conspiracy to corrupt public morals, although such conduct was no longer a crime.[256] Lord Reid maintained his view that *Shaw* was wrongly decided but held that it should nevertheless be followed in the interests of certainty in the law. Given the existence of the offence, he thought there was sufficient evidence of its commission here:

> . . . there is a material difference between merely exempting certain conduct from criminal penalties and making it lawful in the full sense . . . I read [the Sexual Offences Act 1967[257]] as saying that, even though it may be corrupting, if people choose to corrupt themselves in this way that is their affair and the law will not interfere. But no licence is given to others to encourage the practice.[258]

In *Shaw*, Lord Simonds used language which suggested that the House was asserting the right to expand the scope of the criminal law:[259]

> In the sphere of criminal law I entertain no doubt that there remains in the courts of law a residual power to enforce the supreme and fundamental purpose of the law, to conserve not only the safety and order but also the moral welfare of the State, and that it is their duty to guard it against attacks which may be the more insidious because they are novel and unprepared for.

In *Knuller*, however, the House was emphatic that there is no residual power to create new offences. That is a task for Parliament. 'What the courts can and should do (as was truly laid down in *Shaw*'s case) is to recognize the applicability of established offences to new circumstances to which they are relevant'.[260] Moreover, a finding that conduct is liable to corrupt public morals is one not lightly to be reached. It is not enough that it is liable to 'lead morally astray'. Lord Simon of Glaisdale went so far as to say that, 'The words "corrupt public morals" suggest conduct which a jury might find to be destructive of the very fabric of society'.[261]

There are very strong objections of principle to an offence based on such vague notions of morality. It is doubtful whether such an offence would withstand challenge under Article 7 of the ECHR for its uncertainty. If the allegations involve the publication of material it may also be that a defence under Article 10 arises.[262] In view of the range of

[255] [1973] AC 435, [1972] 2 All ER 898.

[256] Below, Ch 17. [257] See now Ch 17. [258] [1972] 2 All ER at 904.

[259] [1962] AC 220 at 267, [1961] 2 All ER 446 at 452. For a judicial view to the contrary, see Stephen, III HCL 359. See S. Davies, *Annual Survey of English Law* (1932) 276–277. For criticism of *Shaw*, see D. Seaborne Davies (1962) 6 JSPTL (NS) 104; A. Goodhart (1961) 77 LQR 560; H. Williams (1961) 24 MLR 626; and [1961] Crim LR 470.

[260] [1972] 2 All ER at 932, per Lord Simon of Glaisdale. [261] Cf Lord Devlin's views, above, p 14.

[262] This is discussed below in Ch 26 on 'Obscenity'.

specific statutory offences dealing with obscenity and indecent images, it is doubtful whether there is any need to retain the offence of conspiracy to corrupt public morals.[263] Unfortunately, the offence did not form part of the comprehensive review of sexual offences recently conducted.[264]

(iii) Conspiracy to outrage public decency

A majority of the House in *Knuller* (Lords Reid and Diplock dissenting) held that there is a common law offence of outraging public decency[265] and, consequently, it is an offence to conspire to outrage public decency. The particular offences previously recognized – keeping a disorderly house, mounting an indecent exhibition and indecent exposure – were particular applications of a general rule. It is not an answer to show that outrageously indecent matter is only on the inside pages of a book or magazine which is sold in public. But:

> . . . 'outrage', like 'corrupt' is a very strong word. 'Outraging public decency' goes considerably beyond offending the susceptibilities of, or even shocking, reasonable people . . . [T]he offence is concerned with recognized minimum standards of decency, which are likely to vary from time to time . . . [N]otwithstanding that 'public' in the offence is used in a locative sense, public decency must be viewed as a whole; and . . . the jury should be invited, where appropriate, to remember that they live in a plural society, with a tradition of tolerance towards minorities, and that this atmosphere of tolerance is itself part of public decency.[266]

Lords Simon and Kilbrandon (Lord Morris dissenting) thought that the jury had not been adequately directed in accordance with these principles and, accordingly, that the conviction must be quashed. In the recent case of *Choi*[267] the defendant had secretly filmed women using a public lavatory in a supermarket. The court considered the meaning of the expression 'outraging public decency' and concluded that it involved activity which 'fills the onlooker with loathing or extreme distaste or causes them extreme annoyance'.

Following the recent decisions of the Court of Appeal recognising the existence of a substantive offence of outraging public decency, it may well be prudent to charge the offence under s 1 of the 1977 Act. Statutory conspiracies and common law conspiracies to corrupt public morals or to outrage public decency remain mutually exclusive, under s 5(3) of the 1977 Act. The prosecutor cannot therefore hedge his bets.

(e) Procedural issues relating to conspiracies

(i) Conspiracy where the contemplated offence is committed

The courts discourage the charging of conspiracy where there is evidence of the complete crime:

> . . . when the proof intended to be submitted to a jury is proof of the actual commission of crime, it is not the proper course to charge the parties with conspiracy to commit it, for the course operates, it is manifest, unfairly and unjustly against the parties accused; the prosecutors are thus

263 A. Hamilton, 'Live streamed sex videos' (2003) 14(2) Computers and the Law 29, considers the possibility of prosecution for live video broadcasts on the internet.

264 See especially *Setting the Boundaries* (2001) and the discussion in Ch 17, below.

265 See below pp 965–967; following *Mayling* [1963] 2 QB 717, [1963] 1 All ER 687, CCA.

266 [1972] 2 All ER at 936, per Lord Simon.

267 [1999] 8 Archbold News 3.

enabled to combine in one indictment a variety of offences, which, if treated individually, as they ought to be, would exclude the possibility of giving evidence against one defendant to the prejudice of others, and which deprive defendants of the advantage of calling their co-defendants as witnesses.[268]

Though these sentiments have been approved by the Court of Criminal Appeal,[269] it is not at all clear that evidence is admissible on a conspiracy charge which would not be admissible on a joint trial for the complete crime. In both cases D1 may be prejudiced by evidence admissible only against D2. The real objection to conspiracy, as it has been commonly used in recent years, has been pointed out by Williams.[270] It is:

> . . . to the use of a conspiracy count to give a semblance of unity to a prosecution which, by combining a number of charges and several defendants, results in a complicated and protracted trial. The jury system is unworkable unless the prosecution is confined to a relatively simple issue which can be disposed of in a relatively short time.

The length and complexity of trials for conspiracy in cases like *Griffiths*[271] raises doubts whether justice can be done. Even that case is outclassed by more recent trials. In *Wright*[272] an indictment of 29 counts charging fraudulent trading and asset stripping resulted in the then longest criminal jury trial in English history, occupying 252 working days extending over a period of 17 months. More than 300 witnesses gave evidence and the documents covered more than 10,000 pages. The summing-up lasted 11 days and the jury were sent out to consider their verdicts more than seven weeks after they had heard counsels' speeches and three months after the evidence was completed.[273] The Court of Appeal was nevertheless satisfied that the convictions were not unsafe or unsatisfactory. But can any ordinary person absorb, remember and evaluate such a mass of evidence and argument? Is it fair to a defendant to be on a trial for so long?

(ii) Requirement of two or more parties

Corporations

A company may be convicted of an offence of conspiracy.[274] It must be proved that D conspired with another but the other need not be identified.[275] If the managing director of a company resolves to perpetrate an illegality in the company's name, but communicates this to no one, there is no conspiracy between him and the company. To allow an indictment would be to 'offend against the basic concept of a conspiracy, namely an agreement of two or more to do an unlawful act . . . it would be artificial to take the

268 Cockburn CJ, in *Boulton* (1871) 12 Cox CC 87 at 93.

269 *West* [1948] 1 KB 709 at 720, [1948] 1 All ER 718 at 723 and see *Gray* [1995] 2 Cr App R 100, sub nom *Liggins* [1995] Crim LR 45, and Archbold (2005), para 34–47.

270 CLGP, 684; and see *The Proof of Guilt* (3rd edn), ch 9 and 'The Added Conspiracy Count' (1978) 128 NLJ 24.

271 Above, p 365. The headnote is wrong in stating that a 'wheel conspiracy' is not known to the law: *Ardalan* [1972] 2 All ER 257 at 262.

272 [1995] Crim LR 251.

273 See also the recent Jubilee Line fraud case at the Central Criminal Court, 2003–2005: News Report 20 Mar 2005.

274 *R v ICR Haulage Co Ltd* [1944] KB 551, CCA.

275 *Phillips* (1987) 86 Cr App R 18, discussed, [1988] Crim LR at 338.

view that the company, although it is clearly a separate legal entity can be regarded here as a separate entity or a separate mind . . . .'[276]

Statutory exceptions

In statutory conspiracies there are three cases in which the requirement of two parties is not satisfied. By s 2(2) of the Act, a person is not guilty of a statutory conspiracy –

> . . . if the only other person or persons with whom he agrees are (both initially and at all times during the currency of the agreement) persons of any one or more of the following descriptions, that is to say –
>
> (a) his spouse [or civil partner];
>
> (b) a person under the age of criminal responsibility; and
>
> (c) an intended victim of that offence or of each of those offences.

Spouses

Paragraph (a) almost certainly states the rule of the common law, although no English case has ever so decided.[277] The common law rule was based upon the fiction that husband and wife were one person with one will. The application of the rule to statutory conspiracies is based upon a social policy of preserving the stability of marriage.[278] The common law rule applies only where the parties are married at the time of the agreement. Marriage after the conspiracy or during its continuance is no defence.[279] Clearly the same rule applies under the Act. A wife is guilty, though she agrees only with her husband, if she knows that there are other parties to the conspiracy.[280] There is no protection against prosecution should the married couple be charged with the substantive offence having perpetrated the offence as they agreed. The protection extends only to conspiracies exclusive to the married couple; if they agree with a third party the conspiracy can be prosecuted.[281]

Infants

For the purposes of paragraph (b) a person is under the age of criminal responsibility 'so long as it is conclusively presumed by section 50 of the Children and Young Persons Act 1933,[282] that he cannot be guilty of any offence'[283] – that is, he is under the age of 10. The Act makes no provision for the case of a child between 10 and 14.[284] Following the abolition of the *doli incapax* presumption (see below), children of 10 and above are *prima facie* in the same position as adults.

276 *McDonnell* [1966] 1 QB 233, [1966] 1 All ER 193 (Nield J). Cf *ICR Haulage Co* [1944] KB 551. A conviction might ensue if D agrees with his company in his capacity as a person responsible for the acts of another corporation rather than as the person responsible for his company: see the Canadian cases cited in *McDonnell*.

277 See, eg, Hawkins I PC, c 27, s 8 and *Mawji v R* [1957] AC 126, [1957] 1 All ER 385, PC. There may be a conspiracy between husband and wife in the civil law: *Midland Bank Trust Co Ltd v Green (No 3)* [1979] Ch 496, [1979] 2 All ER 193 (Oliver J).

278 Law Com Consultation Paper No 76, paras 1.46–1.49.

279 *Robinson's Case* (1746) 1 Leach 37.

280 *Chrastny* [1992] 1 All ER 189, [1991] 1 WLR 1381, CA; *Lovick* [1993] Crim LR 890.

281 *Chrastny* [1992] 1 All ER 189.

282 Above, p 295.

283 Section 2(3) of the Act.

284 Above, p 296.

Victims

The Act does not define 'victim'. It is suggested that a person is a victim of an offence when the offence is held to exist for his protection with the effect that he is not a party to that offence when it is committed by another with his full knowledge and co-operation.[285] Thus there would be no conspiracy where D agreed with a person to kidnap him with his consent. There will be an offence of conspiracy where D and V agree on a course of conduct that would involve their both being guilty of an offence if the act takes place. It is unclear whether D and V who agree to engage in sadomasochistic activity would commit a conspiracy to commit gbh or abh at the time of the agreement.[286]

Again there seems to be no common law authority in point and the question seems unlikely to arise on a charge of conspiracy at common law since an agreement to defraud with the victim of the fraud is difficult to imagine.

Solo conspirators?

The 1977 Act does not deal with other cases where one of two parties to the agreement would not be liable to prosecution for the ulterior offence. It is clear that there may be a conspiracy although only one party is capable of committing the ulterior offence as a principal. If, for example, the offence can be committed only by the holder of a justices' licence and A, a licensee, agrees with B, a customer who is incapable of committing the offence as a principal, that he, A, will do so, there is a conspiracy to contravene the licensing legislation. The course of conduct will necessarily amount to the commission of the offence by one of the parties. B will be liable as a secondary party if the offence is committed. The controversial case of *Whitchurch*[287] is thus readily explicable. D, believing herself to be pregnant, agreed with two others that they would procure her miscarriage. It was not proved that D was in fact pregnant. A person who unlawfully uses instruments on a woman to procure an abortion commits an offence whether the woman is pregnant or not; but a woman who does the same acts to herself is guilty only if she is in fact pregnant. It was held that all three were guilty of conspiracy and it is submitted that the result would be the same if D had agreed with only one other person. D is guilty as a secondary party if the ulterior offence is committed by using the instruments on her,[288] so she is not a 'victim' under the principle of *Tyrrell*.[289]

In *Duguid*[290] D agreed with E to remove a child of whom E was the mother from the possession of her lawful guardian. This would have been a crime by D under the Offences Against the Person Act 1861, s 56, but it was provided that a mother should not be liable to prosecution on account of taking her own child. It was held that E's 'immunity from prosecution for an act done by herself' was no bar to the conviction of D for conspiracy. The court did not find it necessary to decide whether E could have been convicted of the

285 Above, p 212. 286 See *Brown* [1994] AC 212, below, p 517.

287 (1890) 24 QBD 420, criticized by Williams as 'gravely wrong for it sets at naught the limitation upon responsibility imposed by Parliament': CLGP, 673. But see B. Hogan, 'Victims as Parties to Crime' [1962] Crim LR 683.

288 *Sockett* (1908) 72 JP 428. 289 Above, p 212.

290 (1906) 21 Cox CC 200. Cf *Sherry and El Yamani* [1993] Crim LR 537.

conspiracy.[291] This suggests that there may be a conspiracy with only one guilty party but the case is far from clear because the court may have accepted the argument of the prosecution that any bar to the prosecution of E was of a procedural nature. The better view is that there must be two conspirators.[292]

The Act does not deal with an agreement with a mentally disordered person so the common law, whatever it may be, applies to all conspiracies. The Law Commission thought express provision unnecessary because 'a purported agreement with a person who is so mentally disordered as to be incapable of forming the intent necessary for the substantive offence will not be an agreement within clause 1(1) of the draft Bill [now, in substance, section 1(1) of the Act].'[293] This seems to be right in the case of a mentally disordered person who does not know the nature and quality of the proposed act; but a person who, through mental disorder, does not know the proposed act is 'wrong' may be perfectly capable of forming the intent to commit it with full knowledge of the facts and circumstances.[294] In such a case it is arguable that a mentally normal party to the agreement is guilty of a statutory conspiracy though the mentally abnormal person is not because it is sufficient that the carrying out of the agreement will amount to an offence by *one of the parties*.[295] What is the position where there is an agreement by D1 and D2 to kill where D2 would have a defence of diminished responsibility on a charge of murder? If the killing is to be done by D1 it will be murder and so the agreement is a conspiracy to murder. If it is to be done by D2, D1 will still be guilty of murder by virtue of s 2(4) of the Homicide Act 1957.[296] However if, as submitted above,[297] 'commission of any offence' means commission as principal in the first degree, this appears to be a conspiracy to commit manslaughter.

Another case with which the 1977 Act does not deal specifically is that where E purports to conspire with D but has no intention of going through with the plan. The question was formerly of no practical importance because D could be convicted of an attempt to conspire, but the Act rules that out. The point has not arisen in England but in some jurisdictions it has been decided that there is no conspiracy.[298] It might be argued that, looking at the facts objectively, there is such an agreement as (apart from the illegality) would be enforceable in the law of contract and that therefore there is an *actus reus*. D, who, with *mens rea*, has caused the *actus reus* should be guilty. An answer to this argument is that there is no *actus reus* unless E agrees in fact, that is, that an actual subjective agreement is required. If *Anderson*[299] is followed and E held to be guilty of conspiracy notwithstanding his lack of intention, the problem disappears.

291 The language used suggests that she might well have been guilty of conspiracy and of secondary participation in the ulterior offence if D had committed it, whether or not she could have been prosecuted. Section 56 has been repealed by the Child Abduction Act 1984, below, p 580, but the similar problems which could arise under that Act should be resolved in the same way.

292 Cf *Yip Chiu-cheung*, above, p 382.

293 Law Com No 76, 22, n 67.

294 Cf *Matusevich v R* (1977) 51 ALJR 657 at 670, per Aickin J.

295 Section 1(1), above, p 375.

296 Below, Ch 14.

297 Above, p 367.

298 *Harris* [1927] NPD 347 (South Africa); *O'Brien* [1954] SCR 666 (Canada); *Delaney v State* 164 Tenn 432 (1932) (Tennessee); *State v Otu* [1964] NNLR 113 (Nigeria). Cf *Thomson* (1965) 50 Cr App R 1. See G. H. L. Fridman in (1956) 19 MLR 276.

299 Above, p 375.

Acquittal of the other alleged conspirators

Where D is alleged to have conspired with one other person, E, the acquittal of E, either before or after the trial of D, was no bar to, or ground for quashing, as the case may be, the conviction of D.[300] This was where the parties were tried separately. Where they were tried together there was some doubt whether it was ever right to convict D and acquit E – or vice versa.[301] These doubts are resolved by s 5(8) and (9) of the Act, which governs both common law and statutory conspiracies:

5—(8) The fact that the person or persons who, so far as appears from the indictment on which any person has been convicted of conspiracy, were the only other parties to the agreement on which his conviction was based have been acquitted of conspiracy by reference to that agreement (whether after being tried with the person convicted or separately) shall not be a ground for quashing his conviction unless under all the circumstances of the case his conviction is inconsistent with the acquittal of the other person or persons in question.

(9) Any rule of law or practice inconsistent with the provisions of subsection (8) above is hereby abolished.

There may be evidence – usually a confession, but not necessarily so[302] – which is admissible against D but not against E, which shows that D conspired with E. In these circumstances it is perfectly logical for the jury to be satisfied, as against D, that he conspired with E, but not satisfied, as against E, that he conspired with D. It is only when the evidence against D and E is of equal weight, or nearly so, that the judge should direct the jury that they must either acquit both or convict both – being careful to add that, if they are unsure about the guilt of one, both must be acquitted.[303] The difficult question for the judge remains in deciding whether there is a sufficient inequality between the weight of the cases against each conspirator. The required degree of difference has been explained as 'marked'[304] or 'substantial'.[305] Ultimately the question would seem to be whether the difference is sufficient to displace a juror's reasonable doubt that they might otherwise have had. There is nothing to prevent the conviction of one conspirator at a retrial where his co-conspirator was acquitted at the original trial.[306]

(iii) Onus of proof

The onus of proof of conspiracy, whether common law or statutory, is on the Crown even where, on a charge of committing the ulterior offence, it would be on the defendant. So on a charge of conspiring to produce a controlled drug (an offence under s 4(2) of the Misuse of Drugs Act 1971) the prosecution must prove that D knew that the thing he was producing was the controlled drug alleged although on a charge of committing

300 *DPP v Shannon* [1975] AC 717, [1974] 2 All ER 1009, HL. See also C. W. Coulter, 'The Unnecessary Rule of Consistency in Conspiracy Trials' (1986) 135 U Pa LR 223.

301 Ibid.

302 See *Testouri* [2004] Crim LR 372.

303 *Longman and Cribben* (1980) 72 Cr App R 121, [1981] Crim LR 38 and commentary. Cf the similar problem which arises with secondary parties, above, p 201. *Roberts* (1983) 78 Cr App R 41, [1985] Crim LR 218.

304 *Longman*, 125.

305 *Roberts*, 47.

306 *James* [2002] EWCA Crim 1119.

the offence under the Misuse of Drugs Act the onus of proving lack of knowledge or suspicion would, by s 28 of that Act, have been on D.[307]

(iv) Sentence

A person convicted of a common law conspiracy was liable to imprisonment and a fine at the discretion of the court; but under the Criminal Justice Act 1987, s 12, conspiracy to defraud is now punishable with a maximum of 10 years' imprisonment.

A person convicted of a statutory conspiracy is liable to a sentence of imprisonment for a term not exceeding the maximum provided for the offence which he has conspired to commit.[308] Where the conspiracy is to commit more than one offence, the maximum is the longer or longest of the sentences provided for. Where the offence is triable either way the maximum for conspiracy is the maximum provided for conviction on indictment. Power to impose life imprisonment is provided in the case of conspiracy to commit (i) murder or any other offence the sentence for which is fixed by law; (ii) any offence for which a sentence of imprisonment for life is provided; and (iii) an indictable offence punishable with imprisonment for which no maximum term is provided.[309]

The power to impose a fine without limit is unaffected by the Act. Section 3(1) provides the general power of the Crown Court, under what is now the Powers of Criminal Courts (Sentencing) Act, to impose a fine in lieu of or in addition to dealing with the offender in any other way. A conspiracy to commit an offence punishable with a maximum fine of £100 is thus punishable with a fine without limit except, of course, that it must not be unreasonable in all the circumstances.

(v) Powers of arrest

When the Police and Criminal Evidence Act 1984, s 24(1), came into force all offences carrying a maximum of five years' imprisonment or more became arrestable offences,[310] whether the maximum derives from an enactment or from the common law. As conspiracy to defraud is now punishable with a maximum of 10 years' imprisonment under the Criminal Justice Act 1987, s 12(3), it is an arrestable offence. So are common law conspiracies to corrupt public morals or outrage public decency because they are punishable at common law with imprisonment at the discretion of the court. Under the Serious Organised Crime and Police Act 2005 all such offences are arrestable (s 110).

Statutory conspiracies are arrestable offences under the Serious Organised Crime and Police Act 2005.

(vi) Periods of limitation

Section 4(4) of the Act provides that where –

(a) an offence has been committed in pursuance of any agreement; and

(b) proceedings may not be instituted for that offence because any time limit applicable to the institution of such proceedings has expired, proceedings under section 1 above for con-

307 *McGowan* [1990] Crim LR 399; *R v A-G, ex p Rockall* [1999] All ER (D) 726 (statutory presumption of corruption under the Prevention of Corruption Act 1916, s 2 not applicable on conspiracy charge) adopting the view in the 8th edition of this book at 285.

308 Section 3(3). 309 Section 3(2). 310 See above, p 31.

spiracy to commit that offence shall not be instituted against any person on the basis of that agreement.

One of the objections to conspiracy charges at common law, especially charges of conspiracy to commit a summary offence, is that they enable a limitation period to be evaded. This provision meets that criticism, at least to some extent. Section 4(4) only applies where the offence has been committed. Thus an agreement to commit an offence which is subject to a period of limitation remains indictable indefinitely if the offence is never committed and never will be committed because the parties have abandoned the plan. There is no point from which the period of limitation can begin to run.

(f) Rationale of conspiracy

Why should the mere agreement to commit an offence be a crime?[311] A commonly accepted reason is that it enables the criminal law to intervene at an early stage to prevent the harm involved in the commission of the ulterior offence.[312] This argument is not completely convincing, however, for it does not explain why agreements differ from other acts manifesting an intention to commit a crime, which are not offences unless sufficiently proximate to amount to attempts. A declaration by one person of his unshakeable resolution to commit a crime and the taking of preparatory steps (not in themselves offences) do not amount to a crime. The law thus attaches importance to the act of agreement, 'over and above its value as an indicator of criminal intent'.[313] It is a step towards the commission of a crime to which the law has long attached a peculiar significance. The combination of minds, bent on the commission of the unlawful act, is taken to dispense with the need for proximity where only one person is involved.

It is argued that the effect of the combination of two individuals is to increase the risk that the crime will be committed and the danger to the proposed victim, or to the public. Yet the risk and the danger are not necessarily greater than those arising from the resolve and the preparatory acts of a determined sole individual. Perhaps the basis, never clearly articulated by our courts, is that there is something inherently wicked in a 'plot' to commit crime.[314]

None of this explains why an agreement to do an act, which is not a crime, may be a conspiracy. The traditional explanation is as follows.

> The general principle on which the crime of conspiracy is founded is this, that the confederacy of several persons to effect any injurious object creates such a new and additional power to cause injury as requires criminal restraint; although none would be necessary were the same thing proposed, or even attempted to be done, by any person singly.[315]

This, however, does not explain why the confederacy, however powerful, should be criminal when even the actual achievement of the same injurious object by an individual

[311] See I. H. Dennis, 'The Rationale of Criminal Conspiracy' (1977) 93 LQR 39; Williams, CLGP, para 226; F. Sayre (1922) Harv LR 393; P. E. Johnson, 'The unnecessary crime of conspiracy' (1973) Calif LR 1137, Ashworth, POCL, 458–460. Cf D. Fitzpatrick, 'Variations on Conspiracy'(1993) 143 NLJ 1180, suggesting wider use of aiding and abetting conspiracy.

[312] Law Com Working Paper, para 12: 'the most important rationale'. The Law Commission agreed: Law Com No 76, para 1.5.

[313] Dennis, above, n 309.

[314] See Dennis, above, 51–52.

[315] Criminal Law Commission, *Seventh Report* (1843), 90.

– or, indeed, by the confederates – is not in itself an offence. The rationale of this aspect of conspiracy is now generally rejected and we are moving to a stage where it will be of historical interest only: '. . . the offence of conspiracy to do an unlawful, though not criminal, act ought to have no place in a modern system of law'.[316] The only significant exception to this principle is now the law of conspiracy to defraud.

In practical prosecution terms, the opportunity to charge counts of conspiracy, presenting the jury with a clear picture of the combined course of conduct of multiple defendants in one indictment is undeniable. There are in addition evidential advantages of cross admissibility of material against each of the conspirators.

(g) Reform

It has been suggested that the scope of the offence may need to be extended yet further, and in a radically different form, in order to meet the activities of 'multi-faceted criminal enterprises'. In particular, there have been expressions of anxiety that the limitations of the present offence hinder prosecution because each defendant has to be shown to be a party to the same agreement, which does not reflect the common organization of modern criminal enterprises.[317] One possibility for reform would be a new style of conspiracy offence, modelled on the US Racketeer Influenced and Corrupt Organisations (RICO) legislation. This could be achieved by creating an offence in the form of the Customs and Excise Management Act 1979 offences of 'being knowingly concerned in . . .' followed by a schedule of proscribed activities.[318]

4. Attempt[319]

An attempt to commit any indictable offence was a misdemeanour at common law. The common law[320] was repealed by the Criminal Attempts Act 1981 (in this section of the book referred to as 'the Act').[321] Section 1(1) of the Act creates a new statutory offence:

> If, with intent to commit an offence to which this section applies, a person does an act which is more than merely preparatory to the commission of the offence, he is guilty of attempting to commit the offence.

(a) *Mens rea* in attempts[322]

Exceptionally, *mens rea* is here discussed before *actus reus* because, as has often been remarked,[323] the mental element assumes paramount importance in attempts. The *actus reus* may be a perfectly innocent and harmless act, as where D puts sugar in V's tea. If D

316 Law Com No 76, para 1.9.

317 See M. Levi and A. Smith, *Comparative analysis of organized crime conspiracy legislation and practice and their relevance to England and Wales* (2002), Home Office Research Study No 17/02, 16.

318 See further the discussion in M. Levi and A. Smith, above.

319 For a theoretical examination of the offence see R. A. Duff, *Criminal Attempts* (1996).

320 See the fourth edition of this book at 246–264.

321 See generally, I. H. Dennis, 'The Criminal Attempts Act 1981' [1982] Crim LR 5. See also P. Glazebrook, 'Should we have a law of attempted crime' (1969) 85 LQR 28. Wilson, *Central Issues*, ch 8.

322 See Duff, above ch 1.

323 See eg, *Whybrow* (1951) 35 Cr App R 141.

intends to murder V and believes that the substance is a deadly poison when it is in fact sugar, he has committed attempted murder. The *actus reus* may be *any* act, provided it is done with intent to commit the offence and goes beyond mere preparation (see below). Although the terms of s 1 suggest that the *mens rea* requirement is straightforward – 'with intent' – the position is more complex, and requires discussion of a number of elements of fault.

(i) 'Intentional' conduct

Clearly, D must intend to perform the relevant *act* that goes beyond mere preparation towards the commission of the full offence within s 1. This can only sensibly be understood to mean purposive intent.

(ii) Intention as to consequences

Where the substantive offence requires proof of a result or consequence, the offence of attempt will require proof of an intention as to that consequence. This is straightforward enough where the *mens rea* of the substantive offence requires an intention as to the consequence. Whilst, many substantive offences require proof of some mental element short of intention (for example, recklessness) as to consequences, the requirements of the law on a charge of attempt are stricter. Recklessness whether the relevant harm is caused is a sufficient *mens rea* for most non-fatal offences against the person, for criminal damage and many other offences but it is not a sufficient *mens rea* on a charge of attempting to commit any of them.[324] Equally, although an intention to cause grievous bodily harm is a sufficient *mens rea* for murder, that is plainly not an intent to commit murder and so is insufficient on a charge of attempted murder. Nothing less than an intention to kill will do on that charge.[325]

Purposive or oblique intention as to consequences?

As has been seen,[326] intention has a variable meaning in the criminal law so the question arises, what does 'intent to commit an offence' mean in s 1(1) of the Act? It was held in *Pearman*[327] that the word 'intent' in s 1 has the same meaning as in the common law of attempts. The court applied *Mohan*[328] where the Court of Appeal held that there must be proved:

> . . . a decision to bring about, in so far as it lies within the accused's power, the commission of the offence which it is alleged the accused attempted to commit, no matter whether the accused desired that consequence of his act or not.

324 *Millard and Vernon* [1987] Crim LR 393. Cf D. Stuart, '*Mens Rea*, Negligence and Attempts' [1968] Crim LR 647.

325 Cf *Whybrow, O'Toole* [1987] Crim LR 759, CA. As the Court of Appeal accepted in *Morrison* [2003] All ER (D) 281 (May), an indictment containing a count of attempted murder includes, implicitly, an intention to cause grevious bodily harm with intent which can therefore be left as an alternative count. For academic comment on the need for proof in attempts of an intention as to the completed offence see J. Horder, 'Varieties of Intention, Criminal Attempts and Endangerment' (1994) 14 LS 335.

326 Above, Ch 5.

327 (1984) 80 Cr App R 259, CA. For the common law position see R. Buxton, 'Inchoate Offences: Incitement and Attempt' [1973] Crim LR 656.

328 [1976] QB 1, [1975] 2 All ER 193, CA.

The concluding words are difficult to reconcile with the main proposition, which certainly seems to embody the notion of 'trying' to cause, or striving for, a result.[329]

In *Pearman* the court thought that these words:

are probably designed to deal with a case where the accused has, as a primary purpose, some other object, for example, a man who plants a bomb in an aeroplane, which he knows is going to take off, it being his primary intention that he should claim the insurance on the aeroplane when the freight goes down into the sea. The jury would not be put off from saying that he intended to murder the crew simply by saying that he did not want or desire to kill the crew, but that was something that he inevitably intended to do. Similarly, for example, a man who is cornered by the police when he is in a car may have the primary purpose of simply escaping from that situation. If he drives straight at the police officers at high speed, a jury is likely to conclude that he intended to injure a police officer and maybe cause him serious grievous bodily harm.[330]

This is the meaning given to intention in criminal law generally after the series of cases culminating in *Woollin*[331] and applied by the Court of Appeal in *Walker*,[332] a case of attempted murder. The court condoned the use by the judge of the phrase, 'very high degree of probability', but it is now clear that foresight of 'virtual certainty' is required. It seems therefore that the requirement of intention as to consequences is satisfied by proof of oblique intention.

On the facts of *Walker* these refinements may not have been in point, since the jury had convicted on a direction that they must be satisfied that D was *trying* to kill. If he was trying to kill it was immaterial, as a matter of law, whether death was, or was known by D to be, virtually certain, highly probable, or merely possible: a person may intend to kill even though the possibility of doing so is, and he knows it is, remote. Probability is no more than relevant evidence of the sufficient state of mind – it is easier to infer that D was trying to kill if he threw V from the window of the 20th floor than if he threw him from the window of ground floor. It was only if he was *not* trying to kill that the degree of probability assumed the character of a rule of law, and then *Woollin* requires foresight of virtual certainty and nothing less will do.[333]

Further guidance on the appropriate definition of intention as to consequences is provided by the Home Office in its Consultation Paper on reform of offences of violence, which included a definition of intent in its attached Bill:

A person acts with intent with respect to a result if it is his purpose to cause it, or if he knows it would occur in the ordinary course of events if he were to succeed in his purpose of causing some other result.[334]

(iii) Intention as to circumstances forming part of *actus reus*?

Where the substantive offence requires proof of intention or knowledge as to a circumstance, and recklessness will not suffice for the complete offence, it is clear that it will not

329 See the discussion in Duff, above.

330 (1984) 80 Cr App R 259 at 263.

331 [1998] 4 All ER 103, above, p 94.

332 (1989) 90 Cr App R 226, [1990] Crim LR 44.

333 For discussion of the philosophical dimensions of a distinction between trying to do something and trying to succeed see J. Hornby, 'On What's Intentionally Done', in S. Shute, J. Gardner and J. Horder, *Action and Value in Criminal Law* (1993), 60; J. Horder, 'Varieties of Intention, Criminal Attempts and Endangerment' (1994) 14 LS 335, suggesting those who try without an intention to succeed are equivalent to those who recklessly endanger.

334 Clause 20.

suffice for the attempt. So if D attempts to receive goods, being reckless whether they are stolen, he is not guilty of an attempt to handle stolen goods because the full offence of handling requires knowledge or belief as to the circumstance that the goods are stolen goods.

(iv) Recklessness or less as to circumstances forming part of the *actus reus*

Where the fault element relating to circumstances forming part of the *actus reus* of the offence is specified to be less than intention or knowledge, is it necessary always to prove an intention as to that circumstance on a charge of attempt? The short answer is no, but the precise nature of the relevant *mens rea* is far from easy to specify.

It is clear that although an attempt requires an intended result, it does not necessarily require intention with respect to material circumstances. So for example in *Pigg*,[335] before the Act, it was assumed without argument that a man might be guilty of attempted rape if he tried to have sexual intercourse with a woman (with intention as to penetration), being reckless whether or not she consented to his doing so (that is, the circumstance of her consent). Though the point was not spelt out in any case, it is submitted that this was right in principle. The *mens rea* of the complete crime should be modified only in so far as it is necessary in order to accommodate the concept of attempt. If advertent subjective recklessness as to circumstances is a sufficient *mens rea* for the complete crime, it should be so for an attempt.

If D, seeking to remove hi-fi wiring from his rented accommodation sets out to damage the cable (intention as to a result), and at the time is reckless as to the ownership of the cable (a circumstance) because he is aware of the risk that it is the landlord's but is prepared to run that risk unjustifiably, he ought to be open to conviction for attempted criminal damage once he has gone beyond an act of mere preparation. The counter argument to this is that as with all inchoate crimes, liability might arise where the defendant has caused little if any tangible harm, and to avoid overbreadth, the offence ought therefore to require proof of a high level of culpability – in *mens rea* terms intention, (perhaps even purposive intention) or knowledge.[336]

The Law Commission at one time assumed that any distinction between the requirements of *mens rea* as to consequences and circumstances would be unworkable and proposed that intention should be required as to *all* the elements of the offence. The first version of the Draft Criminal Code[337] followed that opinion and stated the rule expressly, using rape as an example. This was criticized as undesirably narrow.[338] The Commission found the criticism persuasive and the Draft Code, cl 49 (2), now provides:

For the purposes of subsection (1) [attempt to commit an offence], an intention to commit an offence is an intention with respect to all the elements of the offence other than fault elements,

335 [1982] 2 All ER 591, 74 Cr App R 352, [1982] Crim LR 446 and commentary. See also S. White, 'Three Points on *Pigg*' [1989] Crim LR 539, 541.

336 See G. R. Sullivan, 'Intent, Subjective Recklessness and Culpability' (1992) 12 OJLS 381, 385 (relying on a concept of 'knowledge in the second degree'). Cf R. A. Duff, 'The Circumstances of an Attempt' (1991) 50 CLJ 100, 100–101.

337 Law Com No 143.

338 R. Buxton, 'The Working Party on Inchoate Offences: Incitement and Attempt' [1973] Crim LR 656, 662.

except that recklessness with respect to circumstances suffices where it suffices for the offence itself.[339]

In *Khan*[340] the court, after considering the conflicting opinions, held that, for the purposes of the Criminal Attempts Act, a man has an intention to commit rape if he intends to have sexual intercourse with a person, being reckless whether V consents.[341] As Duff argues, D would be liable for the full offence if he succeeded in doing what he was trying to do with that level of *mens rea* as to circumstance, and it is logical therefore that he should be guilty of the attempt.[342] In practical terms it would be virtually impossible to prove that D intended that the person with whom he had intercourse did not consent. The valuable protection offered by the offence of attempt would be severely curtailed.

Unfortunately, the courts have subsequently complicated the picture. *Khan* was followed (and arguably extended) in *Attorney-General's Reference (No 3 of 1992)*[343] where the offence charged was attempted arson being reckless whether life be endangered, contrary to s 1(2) of the Criminal Damage Act 1971. DD had thrown petrol bombs at an occupied car and missed. The Court of Appeal stated a general principle:

> . . . a defendant, in order to be guilty of an attempt, must be in one of the states of mind required for the commission of the full offence, and did [*sic*] his best, so far as he could, to supply what was missing from the completion of the offence. It is the policy of the law that such people should be punished notwithstanding that in fact the intentions of such a defendant have not been fulfilled.[344]

Several comments must be made about this approach.[345] First, the decision goes beyond *Khan* and the Draft Code (above) by allowing a conviction for attempt where D's *mens rea* comprises only recklessness as to the existing consequences if there is an intention as to the missing circumstances. The full offence under s 1(2) of the Criminal Damage Act 1971 requires proof of a consequence: that property is damaged. There has never been a requirement in s 1(2) of an actual endangerment of any life. The required circumstance is that the property belonged to someone (not necessarily another). In addition, there was a requirement that an ordinary prudent observer would have realized that life might be

339 For criticism on this see G. Williams, 'Intents in the Alternative' [1991] 50 CLJ 120.

340 [1990] 2 All ER 783, (1990) 91 Cr App R 29. See further G. Williams, 'The Problem of Reckless Attempts' [1983] Crim LR 365; R. Buxton, 'Circumstances, Consequences and Attempted Rape' [1984] Crim LR 25; R. A. Duff, 'The Circumstances of Attempt' (1991) CLJ 100 and the response by Williams, 'Intents in the Alternative' (1991) CLJ 120.

341 Note that there is a serious deficiency in drafting in the Sexual Offences Act 2003, s 77. The definitions and application of rebuttable and conclusive presumptions as to consent in ss 75 and 76 are, by s 77, applicable only in respect of the substantive offences, not inchoate versions. What then of D charged with attempted rape and rape, where the prosecution are unsure with what V was penetrated if anything, and D pleads consent, whereas the complaint alleges that the penetration occurred while she was sleeping? See below Ch 17.

342 Above pp 112–113.

343 (1993) 98 Cr App R 383, [1994] Crim LR 348. For cogent criticism see D. W. Elliott, 'Endangering Life by Destroying or Damaging Property' [1997] Crim LR 382, 393.

344 See further on this approach J. Stannard, 'Making up for the missing element: A sideways look at attempts' (1987) 7 LS 194.

345 See R. A. Duff, 'Recklessness in Attempts (Again)' (1995) 15 OJLS 309 for an approach which seeks to explain the decision without distinctions between consequences and circumstances, focusing instead on the question whether D would have necessarily committed the full offence if he had carried out the actions.

endangered by the damage.[346] Since the court in the *Attorney-General's Reference* concluded that it was sufficient if D was [*Caldwell*] reckless as to that element of life endangerment, it would seem that recklessness as to present consequences (where that is sufficient *mens rea* for the full offence) may also suffice for the *mens rea* of an attempt. This is, it is submitted, contrary to the clear wording of the Act.

Secondly, the statement is overbroad. Read literally this approach would lead to the conviction for attempt of D who is merely reckless as to a consequence element of the offence provided he had an intention as to the relevant missing circumstance element(s). This is clearly not what the Act was intended to mean. Consider D who is reckless as to whether his slapdash DIY will damage the hi-fi cabling he is just about to try to remove (reckless as to consequence), but who intends/knows that it is property belonging to his landlord (intention as to circumstance).

Thirdly, even if the case does not extend the law as regards the *mens rea* for consequences in attempt, it produces problems for the *mens rea* as to circumstances. On a broad interpretation, the case would introduce strict liability into the law of attempts. If D tries to touch sexually a girl, V, whom he believes on reasonable grounds to be aged 16 but who is in fact only 12, he would be guilty of an attempt to commit the offence under s 7 of the Sexual Offences Act 2003. He has the state of mind required for the commission of the full offence (an intention to touch a person, who is in fact, whether he knows it or not, under the age of 13); and he has done his best 'to supply [in the quaint language of the court] what was missing from the commission of the full offence' – sexual touching. There is a logical argument in favour of such an extension of inchoate liability;[347] but it goes beyond anything actually decided and beyond any recommendation of the Law Commission. It seems unlikely that the court appreciated the point and the *dictum* should be regarded with reserve.

Finally, at the time, it was settled that *Caldwell* recklessness was sufficient for the full offence under the Criminal Damage Act and the court held that this was also the right test on the attempt charge. Advertent recklessness (*Cunningham/G* recklessness) has long been thought to be an acceptable *mens rea* as to circumstances in attempt because it is a true state of mind. However, a person may be *Caldwell* reckless even if the possibility of the relevant risk (danger to life), never enters his head. Arguably, this is an unacceptable extension of liability for an inchoate offence.[348] The point does not appear to have been considered explicitly by the court. Given the overruling of *Caldwell* in *G*[349] the issue assumes less significance in relation to criminal damage, but if it is interpreted more broadly so that recklessness, negligence or even strict liability as to a circumstance suffice, it remains of fundamental importance.

346 The latter requirement flowed from the application of the objective test in *Caldwell* as in *Sangha* (1988) 87 Cr App R 88. It is worth noting that since *Caldwell* has been overruled by *G*, it is arguable that the requirement relating to the endangerment of life is not purely one of D's *mens rea* – that D intends or is subjectively reckless as to that danger – because recklessness requires also that the risk taking is unjustified, which implicitly requires that the risk is objectively present.

347 See J. C. Smith, 'Two Problems in Criminal Attempts' (1957) 70 Harv LR 422 at 433 and 'Two Problems in Criminal Attempts Re-examined' [1962] Crim LR 135. See for further discussion R. A. Duff, 'Recklessness in Attempts (Again)' (1995) 15 OJLS 309, defending the more radical view.

348 What of the person who does not give a thought to the relevant circumstance? Perhaps he should be held sufficiently reckless if he was indifferent? Cf commentary on *Mousir* [1987] Crim LR 561 at 562.

349 [2004] 1 AC 1034.

In addition to exposing the lack of clarity and certainty on the *mens rea* of attempts, the *Attorney-General's* case highlights the absence of any general offence of reckless endangerment in English criminal law. If such an offence existed, it might serve as an alternative charge where D failed to bring about the proscribed harm of the substantive offence, but had exhibited a sufficient degree of culpability to deserve criminal sanction. A conviction could be achieved without straining the natural scope and meaning of the law of attempts. The argument for such an offence might be at its most compelling when the conduct creates a risk of injury, rather than mere risk to property.[350]

(v) Conditional intention

Great practical difficulty and much academic debate was caused by the decision of the Court of Appeal in *Husseyn.*[351] The defendants opened the door of a van in which there was a holdall containing valuable sub-aqua equipment. They were charged with attempted theft of the equipment. The judge directed the jury that they could convict if the defendants were about to look into the holdall and, if in the defendants' opinion its contents were valuable, to steal them. The Court of Appeal held that this was a misdirection: 'it cannot be said that one who has it in mind to steal only if what he finds is worth stealing has a present intention to steal'. This caused particular difficulties in the law of burglary because most persons charged with that crime intend to steal, not some specific thing, but anything they find which they think is worth stealing.[352] The Court of Appeal[353] got over this difficulty by holding that *Husseyn* applied only where, as in that case, the indictment named the specific thing which the defendant was alleged to have attempted to steal (the sub-aqua equipment). It would have been different, apparently, if the indictment had charged an attempt to steal 'some or all of the contents' of the holdall – or car, handbag or house, as the case may be. This purely procedural device was rightly criticized. In *Husseyn*, for example, the only thing in the holdall was the sub-aqua equipment. If the defendant was guilty of attempting to steal 'some or all of the contents' he was obviously guilty of attempting to steal the sub-aqua equipment – there were no other contents; but if the indictment charged him with that he had to be acquitted!

Conditional intent under the 1981 Act

The Act does not expressly do anything about this absurd and unworthy distinction, and it remains part of the law.[354] The Act does, however, remove the major obstacle to a

350 See the Scots model in the Draft Code, cl 43, 'a person who intentionally or recklessly causes a risk of injury to another person is guilty of an offence of causing an unlawful risk of injury.' As the commentary makes clear this deals with the person who, for example, drops a heavy object from a tall building onto a busy road, missing all road users. See generally K. J. M. Smith, 'Liability for Endangerment: English Ad Hoc Pragmatism and American Innovation' [1983] Crim LR 127.

351 (1977) 67 Cr App R 131n, [1978] Crim LR 219 and commentary; A. White, *Misleading Cases*, 63. See also G. Williams, 'The Three Rogues Charter' [1980] Crim LR 263.

352 Similarly a person may be guilty of attempted burglary with intent to commit gbh if he attempts to enter, hoping to find someone inside whom he would wish to beat up. It is immaterial that there is no one in the house: *Toothill* [1998] Crim LR 876.

353 *A-G's References (Nos 1 and 2 of 1979)* [1980] QB 180, [1979] 3 All ER 143, [1979] Crim LR 585; see also *Walkington* [1979] 2 All ER 716, [1979] Crim LR 526 and commentary.

354 *Smith and Smith* [1986] Crim LR 166, CA.

rational solution to the problem, namely the decision in *Haughton v Smith*.[355] So long as this case remained law, the defendant could only be convicted of attempting to steal something that was in the holdall, car, room or other place, because there could be no attempt to steal something that was not there.[356] In *Husseyn* the jury must have found that D intended to steal anything in the holdall that he found to be of value. If he would have taken the sub-aqua equipment had he found it, he had certainly done an act that was more than merely preparatory to stealing it and he ought to be found guilty of attempting to do so. It might not, however, be possible for the jury to be satisfied that he would have taken that item. If he would not have taken it, it follows that he was looking for other things – we know not what and perhaps he did not know either – which were not there. He was attempting to steal all right, but his attempt was doomed to failure. This no longer matters since the Act reversed *Haughton v Smith*. He was no different in this respect from the person who attempts to steal from an empty pocket.

The only difficulty is the form of the indictment. The formula approved by the Court of Appeal, 'some or all of the contents', is unsatisfactory because the jury may not be satisfied that he intended to steal *any* of the actual contents and may indeed be satisfied that he did not intend to steal any of them. The indictment would be accurate, however, if it simply stated, 'attempted to steal from a holdall'. This represents the truth, whether there is anything there that he would have stolen or not. The failure to specify any subject matter is not an objection because there is in fact no subject matter to be specified. The defendant must be dealt with on the basis that he intended to take anything he thought worth taking, whatever it might be. The problem is exactly the same in the empty pocket case.

In *Husseyn*, the court followed *Easom*,[357] where D picked up a woman's handbag in a theatre, rummaged through the contents and put it back having taken nothing. The handbag was attached by a thread to a policewoman's wrist. D's conviction for stealing the handbag and the specified contents – tissues, cosmetics, etc, was quashed because there was no intention permanently to deprive the owner of these. Consequently, the court held, he was not guilty of attempting to steal the handbag or contents. Whether he was rightly acquitted of theft is debated[358] but, assuming he was, he was also innocent of attempting to steal the specific contents, but he was clearly guilty of an attempt to steal what was not there. Plainly, he was looking for money and therefore the handbag was, in effect, empty. *Easom*, too, seems a suitable case for a charge of attempting to steal from a handbag. The court posed a much-discussed example. 'If a dishonest postal sorter picks up a pile of letters intending to steal any which are registered, but, on finding that none of them are, replaces them, he has stolen nothing.' This is true; but he was then (before *Haughton v Smith*) and is now, guilty of attempting to steal registered letters.

355 [1975] AC 476, [1973] 3 All ER 1109, below, p 704.

356 Though there was an understandable inclination on the part of the Court of Appeal to carry on as if that case did not exist. See *Bayley and Easterbrook* [1980] Crim LR 503 and commentary.

357 [1971] 2 QB 315, [1971] 2 All ER 945.

358 See Williams, TBCL, 651–653 and [1979] Crim LR 530; below, p 704.

(b) *Actus reus* in attempt[359]

Although the *mens rea* of the offence is of primary importance, the *actus reus* of attempts remains significant. It ensures that the offence does not extend to criminalizing thought, but rather applies only when D has exhibited some willingness to bring his criminal intentions to fruition. This of course begs the question how much of a physical manifestation of that intention it is necessary for D to perform in order for his conduct to be regarded as an attempt to commit the crime. This is an extremely controversial issue on many levels. On a theoretical level there is a division between the 'subjectivist' and 'objectivist' schools of thought. In short, it has been said that 'subjectivists require the relevant acts to manifest an *intention* to commit the substantive offence whereas objectivists require the relevant acts to manifest the *actual* attempt.'[360] The more broadly the law extends the scope of attempt liability to include even the slightest conduct towards the commission of an offence the greater the protection that can be afforded and the earlier the police can intervene. The cost of that approach is in potentially overbroad criminalization and oppressive policing.[361]

There exists a substantial literature on the question whether the criminal law is right to place as much emphasis as it does on the *consequences* of the criminal actor's conduct. In the context of attempt, this raises specific questions whether and why D ought to be treated differently in terms of liability and punishment when he embarks on carrying out his criminal intentions, but the proscribed harm does not occur.[362]

(i) Common law

Before the 1981 Act there was a sufficient *actus reus* for an attempt if the defendant had taken such steps towards the commission of the offence as were properly described as 'an attempt' to commit it, in the ordinary meaning of that term. This did not maximize certainty and clarity in the law. Many steps may be taken towards the commission of a crime that could not properly be described in this fashion. D, intending to commit murder, buys a gun and ammunition, does target practice, studies the habits of his intended victim, reconnoitres a suitable place to lie in ambush, puts on a disguise and sets out to take up his position. These are all acts of preparation but could scarcely be described as attempted murder. D takes up his position, loads the gun, sees his victim approaching, raises the gun, takes aim, puts his finger on the trigger and squeezes it. He has now certainly committed attempted murder; but he might have desisted or been interrupted at any one of the stages described. At what point had he gone far enough to be guilty of an attempt? The answer given by the common law was that it was a matter of

359 See R. A. Duff, *Criminal Attempts* (1996), ch 2. D. Stuart, 'The Actus Reus in Attempts' [1970] Crim LR 505.

360 Wilson, *Central Issues*, 237.

361 For a discussion of an even broader approach in which attempt liability is founded not on D's physical manifestation to commit crime but his disposition to do so, see P. H. Robinson, 'The Modern General Part: Three Illusions' in S. Shute and A. Simester, *Criminal Law Theory: Doctrines of the General Part* (2003), 92–93.

362 See generally, Duff, above ch 12; J. C. Smith, 'The Element of Chance in the Criminal Law' and in particular the writings of Professor Ashworth: 'Belief Intent and Criminal Liability' in J. Eekelaar and J. Bell (eds) *Oxford Essays in Jurisprudence* (1987), 'Criminal Attempts and the Role of Resulting Harm under the Code and under the Common Law' (1988) 19 Rutgers LR 725.

fact: was the act sufficiently proximate to murder to be properly described as an attempt to commit it?

More detailed formulations of the principle proved unsuccessful, being capricious in their operation or simply unhelpful.[363] This is not surprising when it is recalled that the principle has to apply to all crimes and that crimes are very diverse in their nature. The only well-settled rule was that if D had done the 'last act' that, as he knew, was necessary to achieve the consequence alleged to be attempted, he was guilty.[364] The converse, however, did not apply. An act might be sufficiently proximate although it was not necessarily the last act to be done. In *White*[365] D was held guilty of attempted murder by the attempted administration of a dose of poison though he may well have contemplated further doses, and further doses may have been necessary, to kill.

(ii) Common law and 1981 Act compared

The test stated in s 1(1) of the Act is in substance that proposed by the Law Commission.[366] The Commissioners found that there is no 'magic formula' to define precisely what constitutes an attempt and that there is bound to be some degree of uncertainty in the law. The proximity test was the only one broadly acceptable. Even its imprecision was not without advantages: 'its flexibility does enable difficult cases to be reconsidered and their authority questioned'; and 'where cases are so dependent on what are sometimes fine differences of degree, we think it is eminently appropriate for the question whether the conduct in a particular case amounts to an attempt to be left to the jury'. The purpose of the proximity test was to prevent too great an extension of criminal liability, by excluding mere acts of preparation. The Commission thought it 'undesirable to recommend anything more complex than a rationalisation of the present law'.

The Law Commission rejected a definition in terms of proximity because of the danger of a formula which suggested that only the 'last act' could be an attempt.[367] They therefore decided that the formula should direct attention, not to when the commission of the offence begins, but to when mere preparation ends. The resulting preparatory act test is more apt in one respect. 'Proximity' suggested that the attempter had to come 'pretty near'[368] to success; yet, where the attempt is to do the impossible (as where D attempts to murder using sugar that he believes to be poison), success is an infinity away. In contrast, there is no such conceptual difficulty about preparatory acts to do the impossible – by one who does not know it is impossible, of course!

It seems that no substantial change in the law was intended by the introduction of the test of going beyond mere preparation. If any change has been made, it is to extend the scope of attempts because, if there is any 'middle ground' between mere preparation and

363 The most interesting effort was called the 'equivocality theory'. This is discussed in the fourth edition of this book at 253–255, but it is probably now of only historical interest, so far as English law is concerned.

364 Even this, not very ambitious, rule was doubted by Lord Edmund-Davies in *Stonehouse* [1978] AC 55 at 86, [1977] 2 All ER 909 at 933, but his Lordship's doubts seem to relate to the last act of a secondary party which, admittedly, does not necessarily constitute an attempt. See [1977] Crim LR 547–549.

365 [1910] 2 KB 124; see also *Linneker* [1906] 2 KB 99.

366 See Law Com No 102, 2.45–2.52. Criticized by G. Williams, 'Wrong Turnings on the Law of Attempt' [1991] Crim LR 416.

367 In particular a test based on whether D had taken 'substantial steps' cf the American Model Penal Code 5.01(1)(c).

368 O. W. Holmes J, *Commonwealth v Kennedy* 170 Mass 18 (1897).

a proximate act, an act in the middle ground now constitutes an attempt whereas formerly it did not do so. It might be suggested for example that the assassin in the example above was not proximate when he merely left home to the site of the assassination, but that conduct might now be regarded as being beyond mere preparation. However, it seems more likely that preparation and commission overlap than that there is any gap between them.

(iii) Interpreting 'beyond mere preparation'

Every step towards the commission of an offence, except the last one, could properly be described as 'preparatory' to the commission of the offence. The assassin crooks his finger around the trigger preparatory to pulling it. If the section were so interpreted, only the last act would amount to an attempt – a result which the Law Commission's formula was intended to, and does, avoid: a man may be guilty of attempted rape though he has not physically attempted to penetrate the woman's vagina or the person's mouth or anus.[369]

The key word is 'merely'.[370] Not all preparatory acts are excluded. When does an act cease to be *merely* preparatory? The answer, it seems, must be when the actor is engaged in the commission of the offence which he is attempting – as Rowlatt J put it many years ago, when he is 'on the job'.[371] Whether he is still, seems to be, as it was before the Act, the ultimate question.

The first step for the court should be to determine precisely the nature of the crime alleged to be attempted. In *Nash*,[372] D, who had left notes for paper boys inviting them to meet him and perform indecent acts with him, was held to be guilty of attempting to procure acts of gross indecency.[373] What the court overlooked was that an act is not 'procured' until it is committed; so the charge was, in substance, one of attempting to *commit* an act of gross indecency.[374] D's conduct fell far short of that. The nature of the crime is also important since it has been recognized that where the substantive offence turns on the commission of a single act (for example, killing or wounding) early acts are less likely to be regarded as beyond mere preparation than where the crime in question is one continuing over time (for example, fraud), where the 'moment of embarkation' may arise far earlier. This depends of course on the method by which the killing or the fraud is

369 *A-G's Reference (No 1 of 1992)* (1992) 96 Cr App R 298, [1993] Crim LR 274. Cf *Paitnaik* [2000] 3 Archbold News 2, CA, D straddled V and attempted to subdue her but had yet to remove his or her clothes or perform unequivocal sexual acts – sufficient evidence of attempt to be left to jury. See also *MH* [2004] WL 137 2419 where D struck the complainant, dragged her to a quiet lane, removed her trousers and boots and struggled with her asking her to make love: sufficient evidence of attempt to rape.

370 E. Griew, *Current Law Statutes*, says that, 'If "merely" adds anything at all, it is only emphasis'; but elsewhere in his note he recognizes that all acts but the last are in one sense preparatory and that the phrase, 'merely preparatory', indicates that 'there may, in any criminal transaction, be a point before which it is appropriate to describe the actor as not yet engaged in the commission of the offence but as *only* preparing to commit it' (our italics). 'Only' equals 'merely'. Thus, Griew seems to agree that not all preparatory acts are excluded, but only those that are 'only' or 'merely' preparatory. In *Tosti* [1997] Crim LR 746 the court held that D's acts were 'preparatory, but not merely so'.

371 *Osborn* (1919) 84 JP 63.

372 [1999] Crim LR 308 and commentary. Cf *Toothill*, below, p 406 where the act which had to be attempted was the entry, not the intended rape. See now the offence of committing an offence with intent to commit a sex offence under the Sexual Offences Act 2003, s 62.

373 An offence under the Sexual Offences Act 1956, s 13 now repealed (see the offences of inciting a child under 13 to engage in sexual activity, below, p 632.

374 See P. R. Glazebrook [1959] Crim LR 774, commenting on *Miskell* (1954) 37 Cr App R 214.

to be achieved.[375] Particular care is needed if the charge is one of an attempt to commit an offence which has in its substantive form an inchoate nature.[376]

Having identified the nature of the crime and the nature of the conduct alleged to constitute acts beyond mere preparation, the court must determine whether the acts are indeed 'more than merely preparatory to the commission of the offence'. This is a question of fact. In a jury trial, it is of course for the judge to decide whether there is evidence sufficient in law to support such a finding and it is then for the jury to decide (i) what acts the defendant did and (ii) whether they were more than merely preparatory.[377] If the judge decides there is not sufficient evidence, he directs a verdict of not guilty. Where he decides there is sufficient evidence, he must leave both questions of fact to the jury, even where the only possible answer in law is that the defendant is guilty.[378] Where, for example, the evidence is that the defendant has done the 'last act', he may not tell the jury that, if they find that D did that act, that *is* an attempt even though, in law, this is so. The judge may express a strong opinion, but he must not appear to take the question of fact out of the hands of the jury.[379]

It has been argued[380] that the judge and jury, in performing their respective functions, are not entitled to have regard to the word 'attempt'. The question to be determined is, in the words of s 4(3), simply whether the defendant 'did an act falling within subsection (1) of [section 1]'; and that subsection does not use the word 'attempt'. While there is great force in this argument, it is submitted that it should not prevail. As observed above, all acts but the last are preparatory. How then are we to determine whether an act is more than *merely* preparatory? To be more than merely preparatory, it must also be something else. What? Some other concept not mentioned in the section must be invoked to give it a sensible meaning. The answer seems to be that the act must be part of the commission of the intended offence, an act that is done by a defendant 'on the job', that it is, in a word, an 'attempt'.

The Act is, in this respect, a codifying Act so, applying *Bank of England v Vagliano Bros*,[381] 'the correct approach is to look first at the natural meaning of the statutory words, not to turn back to earlier case law and seek to fit some previous test to the words of the section'.[382] The citation of pre-Act cases has been discouraged; but the rule in *Vagliano* recognizes that where a provision is 'of doubtful import' resort to the previous law is perfectly legitimate – and there is a good deal of doubt about the import of this

375 *Qadir* [1997] 9 Archbold News, 1, CA.

376 See *Shergill* [2003] CLY 871 where the court rejected an indictment alleging an attempt to be knowingly concerned in the making of arrangements for facilitating entry of illegal entrants in to the UK (contrary to the Immigration Act 1971, s 25).

377 See s 4(3) of the Act, which, in substance, codifies the common law as to the functions of judge and jury: *Stonehouse* [1978] AC 55, [1977] 2 All ER 909. On the difficulty in application for jurors see J. A. Andrews, 'Uses and Misuses of the Jury', in *Reshaping the Criminal Law*, pp 55–56.

378 *Wang* [2005] UKHL 9.

379 *Griffin* [1993] Crim LR 515, CA. If the judge does and the jury convict, the Court of Appeal used to have an easy route to upholding the conviction under the proviso to the Criminal Appeal Act 1968, s 2. Since the Criminal Appeal Act 1995, there is no proviso, and the court would have to quash the conviction if it was regarded as unsafe.

380 E. Griew, *Current Law Statutes* (1997).

381 [1891] AC 107 at 144.

382 *Jones* (1990) 91 Cr App R 351 at 353, discussed by K. J. M. Smith, 'Proximity in Attempt: Lord Lane's Midway Course' [1991] Crim LR 576.

provision. Since the Act provides for the first time a statutory definition of attempt, the cases on attempt at common law are no longer binding. They may, however, be regarded as persuasive because the Act is (in this respect) intended to be no more than a rationalization of the common law.

Judicial interpretation of the test

The test of proximity at common law was expressed in various ways. One way, which gave attempts very narrow scope,[383] was that of Lord Diplock in *Stonehouse* where, having cited the opinion in *Eagleton*[384] that only acts 'immediately connected' with the offence can be attempts, he continued:[385] 'In other words the offender must have crossed the Rubicon and burnt his boats.'

The 'Rubicon test' was at first accepted as representing the law under the 1981 Act[386] but was rejected in *Gullefer.*[387] In *Jones,*[388] applying *Gullefer,* the court upheld D's conviction of attempted murder where he got into V's car and pointed a loaded sawn-off shot gun at him, despite an argument by D that he had at least three acts to do: remove the safety catch, put his finger on the trigger and pull it. When he pointed the gun, there was evidence to leave to the jury. In the same vein is *Litholetovs*[389] where D had done sufficient to be guilty of attempted arson by pouring petrol on V's door. It was unnecessary to prove that he had gone further by producing and operating the cigarette lighter he was carrying.

In *Gullefer* Lord Lane also referred to an alternative 'test' formulated by Stephen:[390] 'An attempt to commit a crime is an act done with intent to commit that crime and forming part of a series of acts which would constitute its actual commission, if it were not interrupted.'

Lord Lane recognized the unhelpful nature of this test. It does not define where the 'series of acts' begins. Moreover, many acts that are obviously merely preparatory could be said to be part of such a series. Lord Lane said the Act requires a 'midway course' and that the attempt begins 'when the defendant embarks on the crime proper'. This seems the same as Rowlatt J's 'on the job' test.

It was thought that some pre-Act cases which were considered by judicial and academic critics to take too restrictive a view of attempts might be decided differently under the Act. This now seems unlikely. Notable among the cases is *Robinson.*[391] D, a jeweller, having insured his stock against theft, concealed some of it on his premises, tied himself up with string and called for help. He told a policeman who broke in that he had been knocked down and his safe robbed. The jewellery was insured for £1,200. The policeman was not satisfied with the story and discovered the property concealed on the premises. D confessed that he had hoped to get money from the insurers. His conviction for attempting to obtain by false pretences was quashed. If this case still represents the law, a judge, on these facts, should direct a jury to acquit of the attempt. Notwithstanding the criticisms of the result, it is by no means clear that this conduct ought to be regarded as more than merely

383 On which see Duff, p 390. 384 (1855) Dears CC 376, 515. 385 [1978] AC 55 at 68.

386 *Widdowson* (1985) 82 Cr App R 314 at 318–319.

387 [1990] 3 All ER 882, 91 Cr App R 356n. Cf *Boyle* (1986) 84 Cr App R 270. Cf *Stevens v R* [1985] L.R.C. (Crim) discussed by L. Blake (1986) J Crim Law 247.

388 Above, n 380. 389 [2002] EWCA Crim 1154.

390 *Digest of Criminal Law* (5th edn, 1894), Art 50.

391 [1915] 2 KB 342, (1915) 11 Cr App R 124, CCA. Cf *Button* [1900] 2 QB 597, CCR.

preparatory. The stage had been set; but the business of obtaining money from the insurance company was yet to begin. D was undoubtedly preparing to commit a crime but it is not obvious that he had yet begun to commit it. *Widdowson*, decided under the Act, was a rather similar case and the conviction was quashed.

In *Gullefer* D, seeing that the dog he had backed in a greyhound race was losing, jumped onto the track to stop the race. He hoped that the stewards would declare 'no race' whereupon punters would be entitled to have their money back and he would recover his £18 stake. His conviction for attempting to steal the £18 was quashed. His act was merely preparatory. It remained for him to go to the bookmaker and demand his money. Like Robinson, he had prepared the ground for his demand but, until he began to make it, he had not, apparently, 'embarked on the crime proper', he was not 'on the job'.

The strict interpretation of the Act appears most vividly in *Campbell*[392] where D was arrested by police when, armed with an imitation gun, he approached within a yard of the door of a post office with intent to commit a robbery therein. His conviction for attempted robbery was quashed: there was no evidence on which a jury could 'properly and safely' find that his acts were more than merely preparatory. From the viewpoint of public safety it is an unhappy decision. Though the police may lawfully arrest a person doing such preparatory acts because he is, or they have reasonable grounds for suspecting that he is, about to commit an arrestable offence,[393] they may feel obliged to wait until he has entered the post office and approached the counter before arresting him. The extra danger to post office staff, the public and the officers themselves is obvious.[394]

Geddes[395] is similar. D was found in the boys' toilet of a school, equipped in such a way as to suggest strongly that his purpose was kidnapping. His conviction for attempted false imprisonment was quashed. Even clear evidence of what D had in mind 'did not throw light on whether he had begun to carry out the commission of the offence'. Lord Bingham, distinguished between evidence that D was 'trying to commit the offence . . . [and that] he had only got himself ready to put himself in a position or equipped himself to do so.'

In *Comer v Bloomfield*[396] the defendant went a step further than Robinson. Having crashed his van, he pushed it into a nearby wood, reported to the police that it had been stolen and wrote to his insurers stating that the van had been stolen and enquiring whether he could claim for it. He was acquitted by magistrates of attempt to obtain money by deception and the Divisional Court held that the magistrates were entitled to conclude that the making of a preliminary enquiry was insufficiently proximate to the

392 [1991] Crim LR 268. But cf *Kelly* [1992] Crim LR 181. 393 PACE, s 24(7) below, p 572.

394 Campbell was convicted of the offence of carrying an imitation firearm and in similar cases it may be possible to convict of 'going equipped'; but the police may not know whether the suspect is armed or equipped and, whether they know or not, they will naturally wish to obtain a conviction for the more serious offence which they believe he intends to commit.

395 [1996] Crim LR 894, per Bingham LCJ. The offence would now be one of trespass with intent to commit a sex offence contrary to the Sexual Offences Act 2003, s 63. This case is not easy to reconcile with *Tosti* [1997] Crim LR 746, where DD were examining a door to decide how best to break in, it was held to fall on the other side of the line and to be sufficient evidence of attempted burglary.

396 (1970) 55 Cr App R 305.

actual obtaining. If the magistrates had convicted the defendant, it may be that the conviction would have been upheld on the ground that there was evidence on which they might find that the act was sufficiently proximate (under the old law). Some such inconsistency in result must be anticipated when the question is treated as one of fact. Even if *Robinson* does represent the law under the 1981 Act, Bloomfield's enquiry might well be held to be evidence of a more than merely preparatory act; D had set about the business of getting money from the insurers. He was on the job.

This might be compared with the recent case of *Bowles and Bowles*[397] in which DDs had befriended a vulnerable old lady and completed her last will and testament naming themselves as beneficiaries, but had not sought to execute the document and had it languishing for months in a drawer. The Court of Appeal held that there was insufficient evidence of an act more than merely preparatory to making a false instrument.

Perhaps the most striking case of all the common law cases is *Komaroni and Rogerson*[398] where the defendants followed a lorry for 130 miles, waiting in vain for the driver to leave it unattended so that they could steal it. Streatfeild J held that this was mere preparation. It seems likely that this would, rightly, be held to be evidence of an attempt under the Act.

(c) Attempt by omission

Section 1 of the 1981 Act is drafted in terms of an 'act' being more than merely preparatory. A crime of omission where the *actus reus* does not include any consequence resulting from the omission is by its nature incapable of being attempted.[399] This is not true of an offence including a consequence that may be committed by one having a duty to act. If the parents of a child deliberately withhold food from the child with the intent to kill it, they have set out to commit murder.[400] In fact, they are attempting to commit murder but, in the rare case where it cannot be proved that they did any act contributing to the death, it seems probable that, under the Criminal Attempts Act, they are no longer guilty of that offence.[401] They have done no 'act', as required by s 1(1). Though the government seems to have supposed that an attempt could be charged in such a case,[402] it would require bold judicial interpretation to read 'act' to include 'omission', although reference to the Parliamentary debates would support liability for omissions in such a case.[403] Cases will be rare where an intention to commit an offence by omission can be proved. Where it can be so proved, there seems to be an unfortunate gap in the law.

397 [2004] EWCA Crim 1608.
398 (1953) 103 L Jo 97.

399 Below, p 415. For discussion of inchoate crimes as result or conduct crimes see M. Hirst, *Jurisdiction and the Ambit of the Criminal Law* (2003), 134 et seq.

400 *Gibbins and Proctor* (1918) 13 Cr App R 134, above, p 79. Cf M. Gunn and J. C. Smith [1985] Crim LR 705 at 706.

401 They are of course guilty of the offence of wilful neglect of a young person under the Children and Young Persons Act 1933. See also the new offence under the Domestic Violence, Crime and Victims Act 2004, s 5 discussed in Ch 15.

402 See I. Dennis [1982] Crim LR 5, 7.

403 See also the discussion of the nurse who intending to kill a terminally ill patient, omits to replace a life sustaining drip: P. Palmer, 'Attempt by Act or Omission: Causation and the Problem of the Hypothetical Nurse' (1999) 63 J Crim L 158.

(d) Successful attempts

It has sometimes been argued that failure is essential to the very nature of an attempt so that success precludes a conviction for attempting to commit a crime.[404] For a rather technical reason, this was true of attempts to commit felonies at common law.

There was a rule that a misdemeanour committed in the course of committing a felony 'merged' in the felony. Since an attempt to commit a felony was a misdemeanour, it ceased to exist when the felony was committed. This doctrine was almost certainly abolished, so far as trial on indictment is concerned, as long ago as 1851,[405] though the matter was disputed. With the abolition of felonies by the Criminal Law Act 1967 this doctrine of merger disappeared and s 6(4) of the Act provided:

> . . . where a person is charged on indictment with attempting to commit an offence or with an assault or other act preliminary to an offence, but not with the completed offence, then (subject to the discretion of the court to discharge the jury with a view to the preferment of an indictment for the completed offence) he may be convicted of the offence charged notwithstanding that he is shown to be guilty of the completed offence.

This provision does not extend to summary trial and there was some doubt about the position in magistrates' courts until the Divisional Court held in *Webley v Buxton*[406] that an attempt to commit a misdemeanour does not merge in the completed offence at common law. D, sitting astride a motor-cycle, used his feet to push it eight feet across a pavement. He was charged with attempting to take a conveyance for his own use without the consent of the owner. The slightest movement of the conveyance is enough to constitute the full offence.[407] It was held that, though the justices were satisfied that he was guilty of the full offence, they had properly convicted him of the attempt.

The 1981 Act makes no provision for this problem, following the recommendation of the Law Commission,[408] so the matter is governed by the common law as stated in *Webley v Buxton.* As a matter of principle, this seems right. At a certain point in the transaction, D is guilty of an attempt. The attempt may fail for many reasons, or it may succeed. There is no reason why, if it succeeds, it should cease to be the offence of attempt which, until that moment, it was. The greater includes the less. If D is convicted of attempted murder while his victim, V, is still alive and V then dies of injuries inflicted by D, D is now liable to be convicted of murder; but the conviction for attempt is not invalidated. It would, of course, be improper to convict D of both the attempt and the full offence at the same time. To that extent, the attempt merges in the completed offence.

(e) Categories of offence which may be subject to an attempt

There are a number of limitations on the scope of the liability for attempt.

404 Hall, GPCL, 577: '. . . attempt implies failure . . .'. Fletcher *Rethinking,* 131. In *Commonwealth v Crow* 303 Pa 91 (1931) at 98, the court said 'A failure to consummate a crime is as much an essential element of an attempt as the intent and performance of an overt act towards its commission.'

405 By the Criminal Procedure Act 1851, s 12, now repealed by the Criminal Law Act 1977.

406 [1977] QB 481, [1977] 2 All ER 595, [1977] Crim LR 160, overlooked in *Velasquez* [1995] 7 Archbold News 3, which is therefore wrong.

407 Below, p 720.

408 Law Com Consultation Paper No 102, 2.113.

(i) No liability for attempts at summary only offences

At common law it was doubtful whether an attempt to commit an offence triable only summarily was a crime. Under the Act, it is clear that it is not, unless the provision creating the offence expressly provides that it shall be. The indictable offence of criminal damage is now triable only summarily if the damage is not more than £5,000,[409] but it has been held that such 'low-value' criminal damage remains an indictable offence.[410] It is, therefore still an offence to attempt to commit it, however low the value of the damage attempted.

Since 1981 the policy aimed at disposing of more cases in magistrates' courts has resulted in an increase in the number of offences that are triable only summarily, including common assault and battery. The effect was to abolish the former offence of attempted assault, which leaves an undesirable gap in the law. There seems to be no good reason why it should not be an offence to attempt to commit a summary only offence and the policy should be reconsidered.

(ii) Limits on liability for attempts of conspiracy and other secondary liability

By section 1(4),[411] there can be no liability for attempting to commit crimes of conspiracy, whether common law or statutory,[412] and offences of assisting an arrestable offender or compounding an arrestable offence contrary to ss 4(1) and 5(1) respectively of the Criminal Law Act 1967.[413] Liability for attempting these offences would be a considerable extension of the law, with the conduct involved being doubly remote from the substantive offence. Nevertheless, somewhat illogically, it remains an offence under the Act, as it was at common law, to attempt to commit the common law offence of incitement.[414] This covers the case where a communication, which would be an incitement if it arrived, is intercepted. The Act makes clear that it is not an offence to attempt to aid, abet, counsel, procure or suborn the commission of an offence:[415] s 1(4)(b). Where, however, aiding, etc, is the principal offence as in s 2(1) of the Suicide Act 1961,[416] an attempt to aid, etc is an offence. Section 1(4)(b) does not apply because these are not instances of aiding, etc, *an offence*. An 'attempt under a special statutory provision' (s 3(1) of the Act) is now governed by the same principles as attempts under the Act.

(iii) Other exceptional cases where no liability for attempt

Apart from the statutory exceptions there may be other crimes where an attempt charge cannot be pursued. Stephen thought there was a large number of such offences[417] but his examples are not wholly convincing. In addition to those cases discussed above

[409] Magistrates' Courts Act 1980, s 22 and Sch 2. Only damage to the property itself is relevant, not any consequential damage: *R (On the Application of Abbott) v Colchester Magistrates' Court* [2001] Crim LR 564, DC.

[410] *Bristol Magistrates' Court, ex p E* [1999] Crim LR 161, DC; *Fennell* [2000] Crim LR 677.

[411] This result is achieved, rather curiously by s 8 of the Computer Misuse Act 1990.

[412] Above, Ch 9. Cf the statements in *Harmer* [2005] Crim LR 482 and comment.

[413] Above, Ch 9. Reasons for excluding the offences under the Criminal Law Act 1967 are given in Law Com Consultation Paper No 102 at 2.124–2.126.

[414] Above, 350.

[415] *Dunnington* [1984] QB 472, [1984] 1 All ER 676, (1984) 78 Cr App R 171. For the common law, see J. C. Smith, 'Secondary Participation and Inchoate Offences', in *Crime, Proof and Punishment*, 21.

[416] Below, Ch 15. *McShane* (1977) 66 Cr App R 97, [1977] Crim LR 737. See also *S* [2005] All ER (D) 339 (Mar). J. C. Smith in *Crime, Proof and Punishment* at 32.

[417] II HCL 227.

(summary only offences, conspiracy and aiding and abetting), offences where no attempt charge is possible include:

(1) Where any act done with the appropriate intent amounts to the complete crime.[418] Such crimes are rare but one may be the form of treason known as compassing the Queen's death. The offence requires proof of an overt act but it seems that any act done with intent to kill the Queen would be enough.

(2) A crime defined as an omission[419] where the *actus reus* does not include any consequence of the omission, as in the case of misprision of treason or some statutory offences of omission.

(3) It is difficult to conceive of an attempt where the *actus reus* is a state of affairs, such as 'being found' in particular circumstances.[420]

(4) It has been argued that there ought to be no liability for an offence that may be committed recklessly or negligently but not intentionally. The example most often used which comes readily to mind is involuntary manslaughter. The essence of this crime is that the killing is unintentional. An intentional killing (in the absence of diminished responsibility, the conditions for infanticide, provocation[421] or a suicide pact) is necessarily murder. Section 1(1) of the Act requires an intent to commit the offence which D is charged with attempting and on this view an intent to commit involuntary manslaughter is not a concept known to law. What however of D who intends to commit a strict liability offence but is foiled in the process – why should he not be liable of attempting to commit that offence? If liability can arise for strict liability, why not for offences of manslaughter?[422]

(f) Jurisdictional issues[423]

(i) Attempt in England to commit an offence abroad[424]

The Act now[425] allows for the prosecution for attempt of an offence intended by the defendant to be committed outside England and Wales, provided that the more than merely preparatory act is done in England and Wales and the result attempted would be both an indictable offence as defined by our law and an offence by the law of that place.

If D, a British citizen, in England posts a letter bomb to V in France, intending to kill V, he is liable to conviction for attempted murder as soon as the letter is posted;[426] but, if he intends only to injure V, he is not guilty of an attempt to cause him grievous or actual bodily harm. This is because murder abroad by a British citizen is triable in England but

[418] In *Rogers v Arnott* [1960] 2 QB 244, [1960] 2 All ER 417 it was said that, for this reason, there could be no attempt to commit fraudulent conversion under s 20 of the Larceny Act 1916; but it is clear that there may be an attempt to appropriate property belonging to another, ie, to steal, contrary to s 1 of the Theft Act 1968, which has repealed fraudulent conversion.

[419] Attempt by omission generally is considered, above, p 414. [420] Above, p 73.

[421] For attempted infanticide, see K. A. Smith [1983] Crim LR 739, below, p 499; and for attempt under provocation, *Bruzas* [1972] Crim LR 367, below, p 443 and *Campbell* [1997] Crim LR 495 (Sedley J) and commentary.

[422] Cf A. Simester and G. Sullivan, *Criminal Law* at 302.

[423] See generally M. Hirst, *Jurisdiction and the ambit of the criminal law* (2003), ch 4.

[424] Cf conspiracy, above, p 359.

[425] Subsection (1A), inserted by Criminal Justice Act 1993, s 5(2), 1 June 1999.

[426] Below, p 429.

lesser offences against the person are not. If D were an alien, then he could not be tried in England for attempted murder. This seems anomalous, particularly since two aliens acting in concert could since 1977 be convicted of conspiracy in England to commit murder abroad.[427]

The jurisdiction of the court has been extended to certain cases where an act is done in England and Wales that would be an indictable attempt under the Act, but for the fact that the offence, if completed, would not be triable in England and Wales.[428] If D posted a letter in England, attempting to obtain property by deception from V in France, he would always have been guilty of an attempt, triable here, if he intended that the ownership or possession of the property should be transferred to him in England for then the completed offence would be committed here;[429] but if both property and possession were to be transferred in France (for example to a third party there) the completed offence would not be triable in England, in which case the attempt would not have been triable here either. Now it would.

(ii) Attempt abroad to commit an offence in England

It was settled before the Act by the decision of the House of Lords in *DPP v Stonehouse*[430] that an act done abroad with intent thereby to cause the commission of an offence in England was indictable here, at least if it had an effect in England. If D, being abroad, incites E, whom D knows or believes to be an innocent agent, to do a criminal act here, he is guilty of an attempt, provided that the offence is one capable of commission by an agent.[431] D, in Miami, falsely staged his death by drowning with the intent that his innocent wife in England should claim life assurance monies. He was guilty of attempting to enable his wife to obtain by deception. The 'effect', to which the majority of the House attached importance, was the communication through the media to her and the insurance companies of the false statement that he had died. Lord Keith insisted that an effect within the jurisdiction was essential but Lord Diplock thought otherwise. Why should the result have been different if D had been rescued from the sea and confessed before any report of his death appeared in England? In *Somchai Liangsiriprasert v United States Government*[432] the Privy Council, holding that a conspiracy abroad to commit an offence in England is indictable even though no overt act has been done within the jurisdiction, said, *obiter*, that the same rule applies to the other inchoate offences of incitement and attempt. The Act has nothing to say on the question so it remains a matter of common law. This may be taken to have been settled by *Liangsiriprasert.*

(iii) Attempt abroad to commit an offence abroad

D, a British citizen, being in France, attempts to kill V in France or, knowing himself to be married, attempts to go through a ceremony of marriage there with X. If he succeeds

427 Above, p 373.

428 This applies to an offence under s 3 of the Computer Misuse Act 1990: s 1(1A) and (1B) of the Act; and to a 'Group A offence' as defined in Part 1 of the Criminal Justice Act 1993: s 1A of the Act. This includes all the major offences under the Theft Acts 1968 and 1978, the Forgery and Counterfeiting Act 1981 and the common law offence of cheating the public revenue.

429 *Smith* [1996] 2 Cr App R 1.

430 [1978] AC 55, [1977] Crim LR 544.

431 Cf *Latif* [1996] 2 Cr App R 92, HL, 414, [1996] Crim LR 414 and commentary. But if D knows or believes E to have *mens rea,* he is guilty, not of an attempt, but of incitement.

432 (1991) 92 Cr App R 77 at 87–90.

he will be liable to conviction in England of murder and bigamy. Exceptionally, English law assumes jurisdiction over these crimes when committed abroad by a British citizen. Literally, then, the attempt is an offence under the Act. It has been argued that the presumption against the extra-territorial operation of the criminal law[433] requires the words 'does an act' to be construed as applicable only to acts done within the jurisdiction, or having, or being intended to have, some effect therein; but this argument has less weight after *Liangsiriprasert*. If the court has jurisdiction over the full offence when wholly committed abroad, why not over the attempt?

(g) Withdrawal[434]

It is logical that, once the steps taken towards the commission of an offence are sufficiently far advanced to amount to an attempt, it can make no difference whether the failure to complete the crime is due to a voluntary withdrawal by the prisoner, the intervention of the police, or any other reason. In *Taylor*[435] it was held that an attempt was committed where D approached a stack of corn with the intention of setting fire to it and lighted a match for that purpose but abandoned his plan on finding that he was being watched. In some jurisdictions, logic has given way to policy and a defence of free and voluntary desistance is allowed.[436] Following the recommendation of the Law Commission,[437] the 1981 Act made no change to the common law in this respect. The principal argument in favour of a withdrawal defence is that it might induce the attempter to desist – but this seems unlikely. The existence of the defence would add to the problems of law enforcement authorities.

5. Inchoate crime and impossibility[438]

The problem of impossibility is peculiar to the 'inchoate' offences that are the subject of this chapter. If it is impossible to commit a crime, obviously no one can be convicted of committing it. It does not follow that no one can be convicted of inciting another, or conspiring or attempting to commit the crime. It is a fact that people sometimes do incite, conspire and attempt to do what is impossible. This happens only when the defendant does not realize that what he has in view is impossible, that is, he is making a mistake of some kind, as when he tries to kill someone who unknown to him is already dead.

The law has long recognized that, in some circumstances, a conviction for incitement, conspiracy or attempt to commit an offence might be proper, although the commission of that offence was impossible. There has been great controversy about the

433 See E. Griew, *Current Law Statutes*, General Note.

434 See M. Wasik, 'Abandoning Criminal Intent' [1980] Crim LR 785. Duff, above 65–75.

435 (1859) 1 F & F 511; see also *Lankford* [1959] Crim LR 209. It is doubtful whether Taylor's desistance was 'free and voluntary' in the sense that he was motivated by a desire to avoid detection.

436 See D. Stuart, 'The *Actus Reus* in Attempts' [1970] Crim LR at 519–521. See the Draft Scots Code which provides a defence where D 'voluntarily abandons his attempt as a result of repentance before all acts necessary for the commission of the offence were done.' Cl 18(2). Ashworth favours such a defence: POCL, 467–468.

437 Law Com No 102, 2.131–2.133.

438 See generally Duff, above, ch 3.

circumstances in which impossibility will afford a defence and those in which it will not.

Several different categories of impossibility need to be considered in detail.

(a) Impossibility and non-existent crimes

One category of case can be disposed of easily. That is where the crime is 'impossible' in the sense that the intended result is not a crime at all but D, because of his ignorance or mistake of criminal law, believes that it is. Here, the law is the same for all three inchoate offences and it is clear that none of them is committed. Suppose that D comes from a country where adultery is a crime and he thinks that it is a crime in England. He may incite the commission of adultery, agree to commit adultery and attempt to commit adultery. The 'offence' he has in mind is non-existent in England, its 'commission' is impossible and he has committed no inchoate offence.

In *Taaffe*,[439] D imported into the United Kingdom certain packages which he believed to contain foreign currency. He thought it was a crime to import foreign currency. It was not. He could not, on those facts, be convicted of any offence or of an attempt to commit any offence. The intention to import foreign currency, believing it to be a crime, though morally reprehensible, was not the *mens rea* of any crime. The conduct he had in mind was not the *actus reus* of any offence. In fact, Taaffe had committed the *actus reus* of a crime because the contents of the package were cannabis and it is an offence to import cannabis; but he had no *mens rea* to complement that *actus reus*.

(b) Impossibility in fact

In all the other cases to be considered below, there is a crime that exists and is capable of being committed and D has the *mens rea* of the ulterior offence – he intends that it shall be committed; but because of some *fact* as to which he is ignorant or mistaken, either –

(i) the result he intends cannot be achieved, or
(ii) the result he intends, if achieved, will not be the crime that he believed would be committed.

Into category (i) fall cases where the means used are inadequate to achieve the intended result and where the subject matter or victim of the intended offence does not exist. Category (ii) comprises cases where some circumstance, which is an element of the intended crime, does not exist. D believes that he is committing a crime, because he is making a mistake, not of criminal law, but of fact. For example, he intends that he (or the person incited or with whom he conspires) shall have sexual intercourse with V, whom he believes to be 15. V is 16 and consequently the 'result' (intercourse with V) will not be the crime that D intended. At one time,[440] it was thought that the distinction between categories (i) and (ii) was material but, as the law now stands, it has no part to play.

439 [1983] 2 All ER 625, CA; affd [1984] AC 539, [1984] 1 All ER 747, HL. See commentary on the decision of the Court of Appeal [1983] Crim LR 536.

440 See the first three editions of this work. See also, R. A. Duff, 'Attempts and the Problem of the Missing Circumstance' (1991) 42 NILQR 87 and A. White, *Misleading Cases*.

It might be expected that the same general principles of the common law would apply to all cases of incitement, conspiracy and attempt and this probably was the case.[441] The law now, however, is that:

(a) incitement and common law conspiracy are governed by the common law;
(b) statutory conspiracy and attempt are governed by the Criminal Law Act 1977, s 1(1), as amended,[442] and the Criminal Attempts Act 1981, s 1(2) and (3), respectively.

(i) Impossibility in incitement and common law conspiracies

The common law was laid down, for attempts, in *Haughton v Smith*,[443] and for conspiracy, in *DPP v Nock*.[444] The result of these decisions is that impossibility *is* a general defence at common law. It seems that the only exception is that D may be convicted where the impossibility results merely from the inadequacy of the means used, or to be used, to commit the offence.

So, for example, D will *not* be guilty of incitement where –

(i) The subject matter of the offence does not exist. D incites E to steal from V's safe. V's safe is empty.
(ii) The victim of the offence does not exist. D incites E to murder V. V is already dead.[445]
(iii) The subject matter of the offence lacks some quality which is an element of the offence. D and E believe a certain diamond to have been stolen. D incites E to receive it. It had not been stolen.[446]
(iv) The victim of the offence lacks some quality which is an element of the offence. D and E reasonably believe V to be aged 15. In fact she is 16. D incites E to have consensual sexual intercourse with her.

On the other hand, D *may be* guilty of incitement where –

(i) He gives E a jemmy and urges him to use it to break into V's safe and steal a diamond. The diamond is in the safe, but it is impossible to break in with the jemmy.
(ii) He gives E some poison and tells him to administer it to V so as to kill him. The dose is inadequate to kill anyone.

But where D incited E to supply him with indecent photographs of young children, being unaware that E was a police officer engaged in detecting pornographic offences, D's plea

441 In *Fitzmaurice* [1983] QB 1083, [1983] 1 All ER 189. CA, followed in *Sirat* (1985) 83 Cr App R 41, [1986] Crim LR 245, it was held that the principles stated in *Haughton v Smith* and *Nock* apply to incitement. See I. Cohen, 'Inciting the Impossible' [1979] Crim LR 239.

442 Above, p 373.

443 [1975] AC 476, [1973] 2 All ER 896. H. L. A. Hart, 'The House of Lords on Attempting the Impossible' in C. Tapper (ed), *Crime Proof and Punishment: Essays in Honour of Sir Rupert Cross* (1981), 1; J. Temkin, 'Impossible Attempts: Another View' (1976) 39 MLR 55.

444 [1978] AC 979, [1978] 2 All ER 654, above, p 366.

445 *Sirat* (1985) 83 Cr App R 41 at 43.

446 *Haughton v Smith*, above.

of impossibility failed.[447] The court observed that the commission of the offence was not impossible because E had access to child pornography, though he would never have dreamed of distributing it to D.[448]

(ii) Statutory conspiracies and attempts

For statutory conspiracies the law is to be found in the Criminal Law Act 1977, s 1(1)[449] as amended by the Criminal Attempts Act 1981 and, for attempts, it is in the Criminal Attempts Act 1981, s 1(2) and (3) which provides:

> (2) A person may be guilty of attempting to commit an offence to which this section applies even though the facts are such that the commission of the offence is impossible.
>
> (3) In any case where –
>
> (a) apart from this subsection a person's intention would not be regarded as having amounted to an intent to commit an offence; but
>
> (b) if the facts of the case had been as he believed them to be, his intention would be so regarded, then for the purposes of subsection (1) above he shall be regarded as having an intent to commit that offence.

Subsection (3) is strictly unnecessary but it was wise to include it as a matter of caution. It is unnecessary because under it no one will 'be regarded as having an intent to commit that offence' who does not in fact have that intent. It would be wholly wrong to impute a non-existent intent to a defendant and the Act does not do so. In other words the subsection does nothing – except forestall the following fallacious argument:

(i) D (believing them to be stolen) intends to handle certain goods.
(ii) Those goods are not stolen.
(iii) Therefore D does not intend to handle stolen goods.

Subsection (3) says he shall be regarded as having an intention to handle stolen goods. Of course, he has such an intention anyway. The fact that the goods are not stolen, being unknown to him, is wholly irrelevant in determining his intention.

The gist of the two provisions is that for both conspiracy and attempt there must be an intention to commit the offence[450] contemplated, whereupon it is immaterial that it is *in fact* impossible to commit that offence if, in the case of conspiracy, there has been an agreement to commit it and in the case of an attempt, a more than merely preparatory step towards its commission. The provisions have no application to the cases considered above where there is no crime to commit despite D's intention to do so, for example, adultery in England and the *Taaffe* case.

The proper construction of the Criminal Attempts Act has been a matter of acute controversy but it is now settled by the decision of the House of Lords in *Shivpuri*.[451] It

447 The same is true for common law conspiracy to defraud. Cf *Gleeson* [2003] EWCA Crim 3557, [2004] 1 Cr App R 29.

448 *DPP v Armstrong* [2000] Crim LR 379, DC, where the above list was considered relevant – but it is not necessarily exhaustive.

449 Above, p 373.

450 For conspiracy, pace Lord Bridge in *Anderson*, above, p 375.

451 [1987] AC 1, [1986] 2 All ER 334, [1986] Crim LR 536.

seems reasonable to assume that the same interpretation will be put on the amended s 1(1) of the Criminal Law Act 1977 (statutory conspiracy) for that section was amended by the Criminal Attempts Act 1981, s 5, to keep the law of attempt and conspiracy in line in this respect.

In the case of attempts, it must be proved that D had an intention to commit the crime in question. Once that is established, the only question is whether, with that intent, he has done an act which is 'more than merely preparatory' to the commission of the offence. Since, *ex hypothesi*, the offence is impossible, it is the offence envisaged by D to which the act in question must be more than merely preparatory. The effect is that the court must ask, 'would the act have been more than merely preparatory to the commission of the offence if the facts had been as D believed them to be?'

In the case of conspiracy, it must be proved that D agreed with another or others that a course of conduct is to be pursued which, in the circumstances believed by the parties to exist, will, in the event of their intention being achieved, amount to or involve the commission of the offence. It has been argued above[452] that this is the only sensible interpretation of the phrase, 'course of conduct', and that the amendment by the 1981 Act was strictly unnecessary. The 1981 amendment may, however, be taken to reinforce this opinion. It is then immaterial that the circumstances are in fact such that the offence is impossible, or that the results can never be achieved.

In the following examples, D *will be guilty* both of statutory conspiracy and attempt:

(i) D and E agree that they will use D's jemmy to break into V's safe and steal a diamond. D tries to do so. It is quite impossible to break into the safe with that jemmy. D and E are guilty of conspiracy and D of an attempt to steal the diamond. (It is immaterial whether the diamond is in the safe or not.)

(ii) D and E agree that they will administer a poison, which D has acquired, to V in order to kill him. D administers the poison. The poison would not kill anyone. D and E are guilty of conspiracy, and D of an attempt, to murder V.

(iii) D and E agree that they will steal from V's safe. D attempts to break open the safe. It is empty. D and E are guilty of conspiracy, and D of attempt, to steal from the safe.

(iv) D and E agree that they will murder V. D shoots at V's heart but V is already dead. D and E are guilty of conspiracy to murder and D of attempted murder.[453]

(v) D and E agree that they will receive from F certain goods which they believe to be stolen goods. D takes possession of the goods. The goods are not stolen goods. D and E are guilty of conspiracy, and D of an attempt, to handle stolen goods.

(vi) D and E agree that D will have consensual sexual intercourse with V, a girl whom they believe to be aged 15. D has sexual intercourse with her. In fact she is 16. D and E are guilty of conspiracy, and D of an attempt, to engage in sexual activity with a child under the age of 16.

452 P 366.

453 See also the example of *Brown* [2004] Crim LR 665 where D was rightly convicted of attempting to pervert the course of justice having put in train the machinery of public justice (by alleging he had been abused by V) which, if the matter were carried through in a way he wished or foresaw, would cause a risk to an innocent person (who was unknown to D already dead).

Examples (iii) and (iv) would not have been offences at common law under the principles established in *Haughton v Smith* and *Nock* but those decisions are now generally recognized to have been unduly restrictive. It is the cases exemplified by illustrations (v) and (vi) which have been the subject of much controversy.[454] The reason is that, in these cases, if D succeeds in doing the precise thing that he set out to do, he will not commit a crime. D takes possession of the very goods he intended to take possession of – no other – and that is no offence, for the goods are not stolen goods. D has sexual intercourse with the girl he intends to have intercourse with. She is 16 and consents so there is nothing unlawful. How then can his taking steps towards the accomplishment of something that is no crime be a conspiracy or an attempt to commit it? Bramwell B ridiculed the idea in *Collins*[455] in 1864. He put the case of D who takes an umbrella from his club, intending to steal it, but it turns out to be his own umbrella. Bramwell B thought it absurd that D should be convicted of attempting to steal it. Arguments of this kind prevailed in the House of Lords in *Anderton v Ryan*[456] but were then rejected in *Shivpuri*[457] barely a year later.

In *Anderton v Ryan*, D bought a video recorder for £110. Later she said to police, 'I may as well be honest, it was a stolen one I bought . . .'. She was charged with handling and attempted handling. The prosecution, presumably believing that they were unable to prove that the video had in fact been stolen, offered no evidence on the first charge. The magistrates were not satisfied that the video had been stolen, though D believed it had. They dismissed the charge. The Divisional Court allowed the prosecution's appeal[458] but the House of Lords, Lord Edmund-Davies dissenting, restored the decision of the magistrates. The Criminal Attempts Act 1981, s 1(3), said Lord Roskill, 'does not compel the conclusion that an erroneous belief in the existence of facts which, if true, would have made his completed act a crime makes him guilty of an attempt to commit that crime'. Because the House thought the conclusion absurd, they were not going to reach it unless compelled to.

In *Shivpuri*, D was arrested by customs officials while in possession of a suitcase. He admitted that he knew it contained prohibited drugs. Analysis showed that the material in the suitcase was not a prohibited drug but a vegetable material akin to snuff. He was convicted of attempting to be knowingly concerned in dealing with a prohibited drug, contrary to s 1(1) of the Criminal Attempts Act 1981 and s 170(1)(b) of the Customs and Excise Management Act 1979. His appeal was dismissed by the Court of Appeal[459] and, overruling *Anderton v Ryan*, by the House of Lords. No distinction is to be drawn between 'objectively innocent' acts (taking one's own umbrella, receiving non-stolen goods, handling snuff) and 'guilty' acts, for the purposes of the law of attempts. The law is as stated above.[460]

Since it must be proved that D intended to commit the crime in question, he is morally at least as bad as the person who actually commits the offence and, where the offence may

[454] The powerful article which influenced the decision in *Shivpuri* is Glanville Williams, 'The Lords and Impossible Attempts' [1986] CLJ 33. For earlier writing, see B. Hogan, 'The Criminal Attempts Act and Attempting the Impossible' [1984] Crim LR 584, 'Attempting the Impossible and the Principle of Legality' (1985) 135 NLJ 454; G. Williams, 'Attempting the Impossible – the Last Round?' (1985) 135 NLJ 337 and commentaries at [1985] Crim LR 44, 504, [1986] Crim LR 51.

[455] (1864) 9 Cox CC 497 at 498.

[456] [1985] AC 560, [1985] 2 All ER 355.

[457] [1987] AC 1, [1986] 2 All ER 334.

[458] [1985] 1 All ER 138, [1984] Crim LR 483.

[459] [1985] QB 1029, [1985] 1 All ER 143.

[460] P 422.

be committed with some lesser degree of *mens rea*, perhaps worse; and he is as dangerous to whatever interest the particular law is designed to protect as the person who actually commits the offence. It is sometimes objected that he is punished solely for his thoughts but this is not true because it must be proved (in the case of an attempt) that he has taken such steps to put his intention into execution as would (if the facts were as he believed) be more than merely preparatory to the commission of the offence. In the case of conspiracy (not expressly considered in *Shivpuri* but presumably governed by the same principles) he must have agreed with another that the offence be committed – the usual *actus reus* of conspiracy. It is also argued that the conclusion offends against the principle of legality (no one shall be convicted of doing something which has not been declared by the law to be an offence).[461] But the issue in these cases was the proper construction of the statute. If Parliament has said (and the House ultimately decided that it has) that it is to be an offence (attempt) to do any act which is more than a merely preparatory with intent to commit an offence, the law may be criticized for being too wide-ranging; but the conviction of one who does any such act with that intent can no longer be criticized for breaching the principle of legality.

The breadth of the law is such that there may be cases where prosecution would be ill-advised. Bramwell B's man who took his own umbrella would no doubt be surprised to find himself charged with attempting to steal his own umbrella. D who has *succeeded* in having sexual intercourse with V, a 16-year-old, might be astonished to find himself charged in consequence with *attempting* to commit an offence against a person under 16. As such acts are objectively innocent, the offence is unlikely to come to light unless D advertises the fact that he acted with *mens rea*. There will be other cases, however, where a prosecution is in the public interest. The would-be drug smuggler, exemplified by *Shivpuri*, is an instance. It may well be that their Lordships' change of mind was not uninfluenced by the fact that *Anderton v Ryan* would have required them to turn such dangerous persons loose on the public. Perhaps the most important case in practice is that of the person who receives goods wrongly believing them to be stolen. Mrs Ryan's was an unusual and trivial case. Typical of the case where a prosecution is likely to be brought is *Haughton v Smith* itself. A van, heavily laden with stolen corned beef, was intercepted by the police. Having discovered that the intended recipient was D, the police allowed it to proceed on its way, but under the control of disguised policemen. D received the goods, believing them to be stolen. But the beef ceased to be stolen goods when the police took control of it.[462] The House held that he was not guilty of attempted handling but now he could plainly be convicted. The public interest called for his conviction no less than if the police had never intercepted the goods.

Two doubtful cases

Mistakes of civil law

It has been noted that an intention to commit a non-existent crime arising from a mistake as to the criminal law involves no liability.[463] More arguable is the case where D has an intention to commit an existing offence because he is making a mistake of civil law. Believing that the law requires him to use money for a particular purpose, D dishonestly

[461] B. Hogan, 'The Principle of Legality' (1986) NLJ 267.
[462] Below, p 839. [463] Above, p 420.

uses the money for another purpose. If his belief was true, he would be guilty of theft. Actually the law allows him to do what he likes with the money and he commits no substantive offence.[464] He intends to steal and has done his best to do so. In principle, the case is difficult to distinguish from those where the intent to commit an offence is attributable to a mistake of fact; but the use of 'facts' in s 1(3)(b) is likely to exclude liability.

Reckless impossible attempts

The recognition in *Khan*[465] of the reckless-as-to-circumstances attempt raises the spectre of the reckless/impossible attempt.[466] D has intercourse with V who consents, but D is not sure whether she consented or not. Is he guilty of attempted rape? Glanville Williams thought he must be, but that he should not be prosecuted. A possible answer is that s 1(3) of the Act requires us to treat D as if the facts were 'as he *believed* them to be' removes the impossibility defence, this affords some ground for holding that the reckless/impossible attempt is still no offence.

(c) Reform

It would be rash to predict that *Shivpuri* solves all the problems relating to impossibility except the doubtful cases noted above. The fact that Lord Hailsham, with whom Lord Elwyn-Jones and Lord MacKay concurred, offered reasons why *Anderton v Ryan* was distinguishable (even though they concurred in overruling it) may encourage subsequent attempts to distinguish *Shivpuri* on similar lines. To do so would, however, be to resurrect in a slightly different form arguments which were in substance rejected in *Shivpuri*.[467] It is, of course, anomalous that for incitement, impossibility should continue to be governed by the common law, particularly as that was left in such an unsatisfactory state by *Haughton v Smith* and *Nock*. It is submitted that the matter would be put on a sound basis by the enactment of the proposal of the Draft Criminal Code, cl 50(1):[468]

> A person may be guilty of incitement, conspiracy or attempt to commit an offence although the commission of the offence is impossible, if it would be possible in the circumstances which he believes or hopes exist or will exist at the relevant time.

[464] Commentary on *Huskinson* [1988] Crim LR 620 at 622.
[465] Above, p 404.
[466] Glanville Williams [1983] Crim LR 365 at 375.
[467] See the analysis of Lord Hailsham's speech at [1986] Crim LR 539–541. See attempts to reconcile the two decisions see R. A. Duff, 'Regarding Intention: The Criminal Attempts Act 1981 s 1(3)' [1990] XII(2) Liverpool Law Review 161, and Duff, *Criminal Attempts*, 378–384.
[468] See Law Com Consultation Paper No 177, paras 13.50–13.53.

PART II

PARTICULAR CRIMES

13

Murder

1. Definition

Although it is generally regarded as the most serious crime (apart perhaps from treason), the offence has not been defined by statute. Indeed, the classic definition dates from the seventeenth century. That definition provided by Coke is:

> Murder is when a man of sound memory, and of the age of discretion, unlawfully killeth within any county of the realm any reasonable creature *in rerum natura* under the king's peace, with malice aforethought, either expressed by the party or implied by law, [so as the party wounded, or hurt, etc die of the wound or hurt, etc within a year and a day after the same][1].

(a) Who can commit murder

'A man of sound memory and of the age of discretion' means simply a person who is responsible according to the general principles which have been discussed above. Such a person is over the age of nine. If the act was done before 30 September 1998 and he was then under 14, he must be proved to have had a 'mischievous discretion'.[2] The other limitations are that the offender is not insane within the M'Naghten Rules, and since 1957,[3] he does not suffer from diminished responsibility. A corporation cannot be tried for murder because it cannot suffer the only penalty allowed by law, life imprisonment.

(b) Where murder can be committed[4]

If the killing is by a British citizen, it need no longer take place within 'any county of the realm'. Murder and manslaughter are among the exceptional cases where the English courts have jurisdiction over offences committed abroad. By s 9 of the Offences Against the Person Act 1861 and s 3 of the British Nationality Act 1948 a murder or manslaughter committed by a British citizen on land anywhere out of the United Kingdom may be tried in England or Northern Ireland as if it had been committed there.[5] Homicides on a

1 3 Inst 47. As to the words in parentheses, see below, p 434.

2 The Crime and Disorder Act 1998, s 35 abolished the *doli incapax* rules from that date.

3 See s 2 of the Homicide Act 1957, below Ch 14.

4 See generally on jurisdiction M. Hirst, *Jurisdiction and the Ambit of the Criminal Law* (2003), 226–232.

5 See CLRC, Offences Against the Person Working Paper 67; Offences Against the Person Report 125. There is no provision enabling a murder committed in Scotland to be tried in England. See for discussion M. Hirst, 'Murder in England or Murder in Scotland' [1995] CLJ 488. Homicides committed abroad by non-British citizens may be tried here if the offences are under the War Crimes Act 1991, see *Sawoniuk* [2000] Cr App R 220.

British ship[6] or aircraft[7] are also triable here, whether committed by a British subject or not; those on a foreign ship, (outside territorial waters[8]) may be triable if committed by a British citizen who 'does not belong' to that ship.[9] There are other statutory extensions under which murder may be tried in England and Wales irrespective of the killer's nationality.[10]

(c) Who can be the victim[11]

Though this matter is traditionally discussed only in relation to murder and does not seem to have arisen in other contexts, it is clear that, in principle, the same rules must apply to assaults and offences against the person generally,[12] Coke's 'reasonable creature in *Rerum natura*' is simply the 'person' who is the victim of an offence in the modern law of offences against the person – that is, any human being.[13] The problems are at what stage in the process of birth a foetus becomes a person; and at what stage in the process of death a person becomes a corpse. Article 2 of the ECHR provides a right to life, and this imposes on the State certain obligations to protect life, and investigate the taking of life, but the European Court has not directly addressed the issue of when life begins and ends.[14]

(i) Child or foetus?

It is not murder to kill a child in the womb or in the process of leaving the womb. At common law it was a 'great misprision' (misdemeanour)[15] and it is now an offence under s 58 of the Offences Against the Person Act 1861,[16] or, where the child is capable of being born alive, under the Infant Life (Preservation) Act 1929.[17] The question is whether the child has 'an existence independent of its mother'. To kill a child before it has such an existence is, under the 1929 Act, child destruction and not murder. To have such an existence the child must have been wholly expelled from its mother's body and be alive.[18]

6 As defined in the Merchant Shipping Act 1995, s 1. The jurisdiction applies not only when sailing on the high seas, but also when in the rivers of a foreign territory at a place below bridges, where the tide ebbs and flows and where great ships go: *Anderson* (1868) LR 1 CCR 161. See further the Merchant Shipping Act 1995, ss 281–282.

7 Civil Aviation Act 1982, s 92. The Civil Aviation (Amendment) Act 1996, s 1(2) extends the jurisdiction to offences on foreign aircraft in specified circumstances. See also the Aviation Security Act 1982, s 6.

8 Jurisdiction over offences within territorial waters is given by the Territorial Waters Jurisdiction Act 1878, s 2.

9 Merchant Shipping Act 1995, ss 281–282. 10 See especially the Suppression of Terrorism Act 1978, s 4.

11 D. Seaborne Davies, 'Child-killing in English Law' (1937) 1 MLR 203; G. Williams, *Sanctity of Life and the Criminal Law* (1957), 19–23; S. B. Atkinson, 'Life, Birth and Live Birth' (1904) 20 LQR 134.

12 In *Tait* (1990) Cr App R 44, the court held that the offence of threatening to kill under s 16 of the OAPA 1861 was not made out by threats to kill a foetus.

13 Draft Code, cl 53.

14 See generally B. Emmerson and A. Ashworth, *Human Rights and Criminal Justice*, paras 18.30–18.34.

15 3 Co Inst 50. According to Hale, I PC 433, 'a great crime'. Willes J said in 1866 (BPP 21 at 274) that the crime was obsolete. (See MACL at 310.)

16 Below, p 502. Prescription, supply, administration or use of the contraceptive pill, mini-pill and morning-after pill does not contravene s 58 of the OAPA. *R (On the Application of Smeaton) v Secretary of State for Health* [2002] All ER (D) 115 (Apr); [2002] Crim LR 664. Abortion in compliance with the 1967 Act does not contravene Article 2 of the ECHR: *Paton v UK* [1980] 3 EHRR 408.

17 Below, p 502. See generally D. M. Katkin and R. Ogle, 'A Rationale for Infanticide Laws' [1993] Crim LR 903.

18 See *Poulton* (1832) 5 C & P 329; *Enoch* (1850) 5 C& P 539.

The cord and after-birth need not have been expelled from the mother nor severed from the child.[19] The tests of independent existence which the courts have accepted are that the child should have an independent circulation, and that it should have breathed after birth. But there are difficulties about both these tests.

In *Brain* Park J said:[20]

> . . . it is not essential that it should have breathed at the time it was killed; as many children are born alive and yet do not breathe for some time after their birth.

It appears that there is no known means of determining at what instant the foetal and parental circulations are so dissociated as to allow the child to live without the help of the parental circulation; and this dissociation may precede birth. There is thus some uncertainty about the precise moment at which the child comes under the protection of the law of murder, though the question does not seem to have troubled the courts in recent years. The last reported case that the CLRC could trace was in 1874.[21] The committee recommends that the test should be that the victim should have been born and have an existence independent of its mother. With the rapid developments in medical science and the increasing ability to keep alive children born prematurely, the law should be careful to avoid any more rigid form of definition. As Brooke LJ observed in holding that a conjoined twin with useless heart and lungs, dependent on her twin was protected by the law of murder, '[a]dvances in medical treatment of deformed neonates suggest that the criminal law's protection should be as wide as possible, and a conclusion that a creature in being was not reasonable would be confined only to the most extreme cases of which this is not an example.[22]

The European Court of Human Rights has declined to decide directly whether the foetus is protected by the right to life in Article 2. In *Vo v France*[23] a doctor negligently caused fatal injury to a viable foetus after mistaking the mother's identity for that of another patient. The French Criminal Court acquitted him on the basis that the foetus was not a human being for the purposes of the offence. On application to the ECtHR, the Court ruled that the issue of life's commencement was within the margin of appreciation. The Court acknowledged that in:

> the circumstances examined to date by the Convention institutions – that is, in the various laws on abortion – the unborn child is not regarded as a 'person' directly protected by Article 2 of the Convention and that if the unborn do have a 'right' to 'life', it is implicitly limited by the mother's rights and interests. The Convention institutions have not, however, ruled out the possibility that in certain circumstances safeguards may be extended to the unborn child . . . It is also clear from an examination of these cases that the issue has always been determined by weighing up various, and sometimes conflicting, rights or freedoms claimed by a woman, a mother or a father in relation to one another or *vis-à-vis* an unborn child.[24]

The interpretation of Article 2 has involved the Court in balancing the legal, medical, philosophical, ethical and religious dimensions, and since there is no consensus on the

19 *Reeves* (1839) 9 C & P 25.

20 (1834) 6 C & P 349 at 350. But see *C v S* and *Rance v Mid-Downs Health Authority*, below, p 503.

21 *Handley* (1874) 13 Cox CC 79, followed by Wright J in *Pritchard* (1901) 17 TLR 310. Cmnd 7844, para 35.

22 Per Brooke LJ in *Re A* [2001] Fam 147, [2001] 2 WLR 480.

23 [2004] 2 FCR 577.

24 Para 80.

matter at national level, it is unsurprising that the Court has left the State with considerable discretion in the matter – the issue of when the right to life begins comes within the margin of appreciation.[25]

(ii) Prenatal injury

Where D intentionally causes injury to, or attempts to kill, the foetus, but the child is born alive and dies of the injury sustained, D has caused the death of a person in being – the *actus reus* of murder. Coke[26] stated that he was guilty of murder. In *West* (1848), Maule J directed the jury that a woman was guilty of murder if, in attempting to procure an abortion, she caused the premature birth of her child who, consequently, died five hours later. The basis of that decision, however appears to be that D caused the death by a felonious act, a type of 'constructive murder', which was abolished by the Homicide Act 1957. In *Attorney-General's Reference (No 3 of 1994)*,[27] the House of Lords accepted, *obiter*, as an established rule, that 'Violence towards a foetus which results in harm suffered after the baby has been born alive can give rise to criminal responsibility even if the harm would not have been criminal (apart from statute) if it had been suffered in utero'. But, since an intention to cause death or injury to the foetus is not the *mens rea* of murder,[28] it seems that it could not be that offence. The Draft Criminal Code would make that clear. If D intended the child to be born alive and then die, that would be murder. And it might be manslaughter by gross negligence, if there was an obvious and unjustifiable risk of, for example, premature birth and consequent early death.

In the *Attorney-General's Reference*, the Court of Appeal held that the foetus before birth is an integral part of the mother, no less than her arm or leg. If that were so, an intention to kill or cause serious harm to the foetus would be an intention to cause such harm to the mother – the *mens rea* of murder. This would have settled the issue discussed in the last paragraph; but the House held that it was wrong. 'The mother and foetus were two distinct organisms living symbiotically, not a single organism with two aspects'.

In the *Attorney-General's Reference* D stabbed his girlfriend, V, who was 26 weeks' pregnant with his child, X. V recovered but, because of the wound, X was born prematurely and, as a result of the premature birth, died after 120 days. The Court of Appeal held that there was evidence to go to a jury that D murdered X, his intention to cause serious harm to V being 'transferred' to X. But the House declined to extend the doctrine of transferred malice to what it regarded as a double transfer of intent – from the mother to the foetus and from the foetus to the child. It was not murder. Oddly, they went on to hold that it was manslaughter of the child by the unlawful and dangerous act of stabbing the mother – which looks exactly like transferred malice. Moreover the act was not merely unlawful and dangerous – it was done with the *mens rea* of murder and, as it is acknowledged that it caused the death of the child, it is hard to see why it is not murder.

[25] In *X v Norway*, App No 867/60; *X v Austria* (1976) 7 DR 87; *X v UK* (1980) 1 DR 244 the Convention institutions declined to determine the issue of the time at which life begins.

[26] 3 Co Inst 50; Hawkins, I PC, c 31, s 16; East, I PC 228; contra Hale, I PC 433; *West* (1848) 2 Cox CC 500. See also *Kwok Chak Ming* (Hong Kong, 1963) discussed in [1963] Crim LR 748 and Temkin, below n 28.

[27] [1997] 3 All ER 936 at 942, HL, reversing [1996] 1 Cr App R 351, [1996] Crim LR 268, CA.

[28] Cf J. Temkin, 'Pre-natal Injury, Homicide and the Draft Criminal Code' [1986] CLJ 414, and the Draft Code, cl 53.

It was held in *Senior*[29] that where the pre-natal injury was caused by gross negli[gence] or with a *mens rea* sufficient only for manslaughter, and death after birth resulted from it, a conviction for manslaughter was appropriate. It would be logical to go on to hold that gross pre-natal neglect of the child by the mother, resulting in death after birth, should also be manslaughter; but the courts have stopped short of this conclusion.[30] Neglect of the child by the mother after birth may give rise to liability, neglect before the birth does not. A woman is entitled to refuse medical treatment, even though she knows that the result may be the death of the foetus, or the child if it is born alive.[31]

(iii) Death

Similar problems could arise in determining the moment at which life ends, though these do not seem, in practice, to have troubled the courts. Is V dead, and therefore incapable of being murdered, if his heart has stopped beating but a surgeon confidently expects to start it again, by an injection or mechanical means?[32] Is V dead if he is in a 'hopeless' condition and 'kept alive' only by an apparatus of some kind?[33] There is, at present, no certain answer to these questions. The current medical view is that the test is one of brainstem death and that this can be diagnosed with certainty.[34] The law has not yet evolved a definition of its own and the CLRC declined to propose one[35] both because of the fluid state of medical science and the repercussions that such a definition might have on other branches of the law.[36]

(iv) Under the Queen's peace

All persons appear to be 'under the Queen's peace' for this purpose, even an alien enemy, 'unless it be in the heat of war, and in the actual exercise thereof'.[37] In *Page*[38] an argument that an Egyptian national who had been murdered in an Egyptian village by a British soldier was not within the Queen's peace, was rejected.[39] Enemy soldiers

29 (1832) 1 Mood CC 346.

30 *Knights* (1860) 2 F & F 46; *Izod* (1904) 20 Cox CC 690 (Channell J); and see the discussion by Davies, MACL at 308–309.

31 *St George's Healthcare NHS Trust v S* [1998] 3 All ER 673, 685–692 (Civ Div).

32 G. Williams, *Sanctity of Life and the Criminal Law* (1957), 18.

33 I. M. Kennedy and A. Grubb, *Medical Law Text with Materials* (2000), chs 16, 17, 18 and references therein; I. M. Kennedy, 'Alive or Dead?' (1969) 22 CLP 102; 'Switching Off Life Support Machines' [1977] Crim LR 443; B. Hogan 'A Note on Death' [1972] Crim LR 80; P. Skegg, 'Irreversibly Comatose Individuals: Alive or Dead?' [1964] CLJ 130; Report of the Broderick Committee (1969), Cmnd 4810, paras. 808–812 and Law Com No 230 (1995).

34 *Re A* [1992] 3 Med LR 303; *British Medical Journal* and *The Lancet*, 21 Feb 1979. Cf *Malcherek* [1981] 2 All ER 422, [1981] 1 WLR 690, above, p 66. For detailed medical discussion on the test see C. Pallis and D. Harley, *ABC of Brain Stem Death* (2nd edn, 1996) and recently, M. D. Bell, E. Moss and P. G. Murphy, 'Brainstem death testing in the UK-time for reappraisal?' (2004) 92 Br J Anaesthesia 633–40. See further I. Kennedy and A. Grubb, *Medical Law* (3rd edn, 2000), 2141.

35 CLRC/OAP/R, para 37.

36 See also the discussion above relating to omissions and the termination of patients' life sustaining treatment, pp 87–88 in omissions.

37 Hale, I PC 433.

38 [1954] 1 QB 170, [1953] 2 All ER 1355 (C–MAC). See further P. Rowe, 'Murder and the Law of War' (1991) NILQ 216.

39 The real issue in that case was whether the court-martial assembled in the Canal Zone had jurisdiction to try the case. It was admitted that, if D had been brought to this country and tried here, no question could have arisen as to the nationality of the victim. The court-martial was held to have jurisdiction under the Army Act.

who have been taken prisoner or have surrendered are protected by the law of murder.[40]

(d) Death within a year and a day[41]

The rule stated by Coke that the death must occur within a year and a day has been abolished by the Law Reform (Year and a Day Rule) Act 1996. If an act can be shown to be the cause of death, it may now be murder, any other homicide offence, or suicide, however much time has elapsed between the act and the death. The Act, however, requires the consent of the Attorney-General to the prosecution of any person for murder, manslaughter, infanticide, or any other offence of which one of the elements is causing a person's death, or aiding and abetting suicide, (i) where the injury alleged to have caused the death was sustained more than three years before the death occurred or (ii) where the accused has previously been convicted of an offence committed in circumstances alleged to be connected with the death. So consent is required if D has been convicted of wounding V, who has subsequently died of the wound within three years of D's causing it and it is proposed to prosecute D for murder or manslaughter. Similarly, it would seem, if D has been convicted of a robbery, burglary or driving offence in the course of which V sustained an injury of which he subsequently died.

The year-and-a-day[42] rule continues to apply where any act or omission causing death was committed before 17 June 1996.

(e) Unlawful

The requirement that the killing is unlawful is an important element of the offence. The most obvious example of its application is where the killing is in self-defence. The element applies to protect others, for example, it was accepted by the Court of Appeal in the *Attorney-General's Reference (No 3 of 1994)*[43] that the doctor who performed a lawful abortion would not be liable for murder should the foetus be born alive and die from injuries sustained in the termination procedure. The doctor in such a case would have performed a lawful act under the Abortion Act. Consent, which in many offences will render conduct lawful, has no part to play in the context of murder. So also it is murder at common law if a man condemned to death be executed by someone other than the officer lawfully appointed, or if the officer lawfully appointed carries out the execution by an unauthorized method, as where he beheads a man condemned to be hanged.[44]

[40] Note also that a civilian of an enemy state in the custody of British forces is protected by Article 2 of the ECHR: *R (Mazin Jumaa Gatteh Al SKeina) v Secretary of State for Defence* [2004] EWHC 2911 (Admin).

[41] For historical material on the rule see D. Yale, 'A Year and A Day in Homicide' [1989] CLJ 202, and on the reform see Law Comm Consultation Paper No 136, *The Year and a Day Rule in Homicide* (1994).

[42] For further details see 7th edition of this work, at 330.

[43] [1996] 2 All ER 10.

[44] Ibid. The death penalty was abolished for all crimes in England and Wales: Crime and Disorder Act 1998 s 36.

(f) Causing death[45]

It must be proved that D, by his own act or unlawful omission, caused death. For this purpose, D, who, for example, procures E to murder D's wife, does not cause her death. D does not kill; E does. D is guilty of murder but as a secondary party. The principles of causation apply to 'result crimes' generally and are considered in detail in Chapter 4, above. In fact, most of the leading cases concern causing death in homicide offences.

(i) Accelerating death

It is noted, here, however, that what must be caused is some acceleration of death. Since everyone must die sooner or later, it follows that every killing is merely an acceleration of death; and it makes no difference for this purpose that the victim is already suffering from a fatal disease or injury or is under sentence of death. Thus, in *Dyson*[46] Lord Alverstone CJ said:[47]

> The proper question to have been submitted to the jury was whether the prisoner accelerated the child's death by the injuries which he inflicted in December, 1907. For if he did the fact that the child was already suffering from meningitis from which it would in any event have died before long, would afford no answer to the charge of causing its death.

The administration of pain-saving drugs presents difficult problems. In the case of *Adams*[48] Devlin J directed the jury that there is no special defence justifying a doctor in giving drugs which would shorten life in the case of severe pain: 'If life were cut short by weeks or months it was just as much murder as if it were cut short by years.' He went on:

> But that does not mean that a doctor aiding the sick or dying has to calculate in minutes or hours, or perhaps in days or weeks, the effect on a patient's life of the medicines which he administers. If the first purpose of medicine – the restoration of health – can no longer be achieved, there is still much for the doctor to do, and he is entitled to do all that is proper and necessary to relieve pain and suffering even if measures he takes may incidentally shorten life.

These passages are not easy to reconcile. If the doctor gives drugs with the sole object of relieving suffering of a dying man knowing that the drugs will certainly shorten his life, then he intends to shorten life, that is, to kill. If, as Devlin J held, the doctor has a defence it cannot be because his act has not caused death nor because he did not intend so to do. It seems that the courts now do recognize a special defence for a doctor in these circumstances.[49] In *Airedale NHS Trust v Bland*[50] Lord Goff referred, *obiter*, to:

45 H. Hart and T. Honoré, *Causation in the Law* (2nd edn, 1985), especially chs XII–XIV; G. Williams, 'Causation in Homicide' [1957] Crim LR 429 and 510; F. Camps and J. Harvard, 'Causation in Homicide – A Medical View' [1957] Crim LR at 576. See also the discussion above, Ch 4 and references therein.

46 [1908] 2 KB 454 at 457.

47 [1908] 2 KB 454. And see Hale, I PC 428; *Fletcher* (1841) Russell 417; *Martin* (1832) 5 C & P 128 at 130.

48 [1957] Crim LR 365; S. Bedford, *The Best We Can Do* (1958), 192; P. Devlin, *Easing the Passing* (1985); H. Hart and T. Honoré, above, at 344.

49 Cf *Moor* (Hooper J) discussed by A. Arlidge, 'The Trial of Dr. David Moor' [2000] Crim LR 31 and J. C. Smith, 'A Comment on Moor's Case' [2000] Crim LR 41, above, p 323. See also J. Goss, 'Postscript on the trial of David Moor' [2000] Crim LR 568. The broader issues raised by assisted suicide and euthanasia lie beyond the scope of this work. See in particular, R. Dworkin, *Life's Dominion* (1993); Kennedy, above, ch 17; H. Briggs, *Euthanasia, Death with Dignity and the Law* (2002); J. Glover, *Causing Death and Saving Lives* (1977).

50 [1993] 1 All ER 821 at 868h–j.

> . . . the established rule that a doctor may, when caring for a patient who is, for example, dying of cancer, lawfully administer painkilling drugs, despite the fact that he knows that an incidental effect of that application will be to abbreviate the patient's life.

Lord Goff added:

> Moreover, where the doctor's treatment of his patient is lawful, the patient's death will be regarded in law as exclusively caused by the injury or disease to which his condition is attributable.

But this is surely a fiction and therefore undesirable. It is not the doctor's *purpose* to kill but the brutal truth is that the doctor (according to the general principles of law) *intends* to kill, and does kill, his patient. If an unqualified and unauthorized person did the same act with the same knowledge he would presumably be guilty of murder. For the doctor, it is an intentional, but justifiable, killing.

It is not however permissible, even for a doctor acting in good faith, purposely to kill in order to terminate pain. When pain-killing drugs were no longer effective, Dr Cox,[51] in order to end the great suffering of his patient, administered a drug to stop her heart and end her suffering, not by the palliative effect of drugs but by death. He was held guilty of attempted murder (it was no longer possible to prove the actual cause of death). If he had administered a large dose of sedative causing her to lapse into a coma, he would probably have been on the right side of the law – even though that would have shortened life.

(g) The *mens rea* of murder[52]

(i) Malice aforethought

The *mens rea* of murder is traditionally called 'malice aforethought'. This is a technical term and it has a technical meaning quite different from the ordinary popular meaning of the two words. The phrase, it has been truly said, 'is a mere arbitrary symbol . . ., for the "malice" may have in it nothing really malicious; and need never be really "aforethought".'[53]

Thus a parent who kills a suffering child out of motives of compassion is 'malicious' for this purpose; and there is sufficient aforethought if an intention to kill is formed only a second before the fatal blow is struck. Neither ill-will nor premeditation[54] is necessary.

The meaning of the term is of the utmost importance, for it is the presence or absence of malice aforethought which determines whether an unlawful killing is murder or manslaughter.

> Murder is unlawful homicide with malice aforethought. Manslaughter is an unlawful homicide without malice aforethought.[55]

51 (1992) 12 BLMR 38.

52 See Lord Goff, 'The Mental Element in the Crime of Murder' (1988) 104 LQR 30 and G. Williams, 'The *Mens Rea* for Murder: Leave it Alone' (1989) 105 LQR 387. For discussion of the comparative approaches to the fault element in murder see S. Yeo, *Fault in Homicide* (1997), and the helpful but brief summary in the Law Commission's Report No 290, *Partial Defences to Murder* (2004), ch 2.

53 Kenny, *Outlines* (15th edn), 153.

54 For a suggestion for reform on this basis see B. Mitchell 'Thinking About Murder' (1992) J Crim L 78. See also the support for such a view derived from the research by Prof Mitchell appended to Law Com Report No 290, *Partial Defences to Murder* (2004).

55 Per Stephen J in *Doherty* (1887) 16 Cox CC 306 at 307.

Malice aforethought is a concept of the common law. It has a long history but, since *Moloney*,[56] it is no longer necessary to explore this in order to expound the modern law. We can now state that it consists in –

(i) an intention to kill any person or,

(ii) an intention to cause grievous bodily harm to any person.

'Intention' has the meaning attributed to it in *Woollin*[57] as applied in *Matthews and Alleyne*.[58]

'Grievous bodily harm', at one time broadly interpreted to mean any harm sufficiently serious to interfere with health and comfort, must now be applied in its ordinary natural meaning. 'Grievous' means 'really serious'[59] and the word 'really' probably adds nothing but emphasis to the fact that the harm intended must be (actually or really) serious.[60] Although the expression is ambiguous and forms a core element of the definition of such a serious offence carrying a unique sentence and stigma, it has been held, in Northern Ireland at least, to be compatible with the requirement in Article 7 of the ECHR of certainty.[61] There seems little doubt that this view would be followed by the courts in England.

In 1960 in the notorious case of *DPP v Smith*, the House of Lords laid down a largely objective test of liability in murder – the test was 'not what the defendant contemplated, but what the ordinary reasonable man or woman would in all the circumstances of the case have contemplated as the natural and probable result'. In *Hyam*[62] the House declined to overrule *Smith*, holding that its effect had been modified by s 8 of the Criminal Justice Act 1967; but in *Frankland and Moore v R*[63] the Privy Council (comprising five judicial members of the House of Lords), acting on the *dicta* of Lord Diplock in *Hyam*,[64] Lord Bridge in *Moloney*[65] and Lord Scarman in *Hancock*,[66] held that in so far as it laid down an objective test, *Smith* did not represent the common law of England. Though the Privy Council cannot formally overrule a decision of the House of Lords, it can probably be taken, for all practical purposes, that *Smith* is overruled. Section 8 did not, after all, modify the law of murder; and the function of that section in relation to murder, as to all other crimes, is not to define what *mens rea* must be proved, but only *how* the *mens rea* required by the common law or other statutes, is to be proved.

(ii) Constructive malice

Although the common law of malice aforethought is now fully stated in the rule requiring an intention to cause death or grievous bodily harm, it is necessary to refer to s 1 of the Homicide Act 1957 which modified the common law.

(1) Where a person kills in the course or furtherance of some other offence, the killing shall not amount to murder unless done with the same malice aforethought

56 [1985] AC 905, [1985] 1 All ER 1025, above, p 94.

57 [1999] 1 Cr App R 8.

58 [2003] 2 Cr App R 30, [2003] EWCA Crim 192.

59 *DPP v Smith* [1961] AC 290 at 334, [1960] 3 All ER 161 at 171.

60 *Saunders* [1985] Crim LR 230. It is for the judge to decide in each case whether it is necessary to direct the jury that the harm intended must be 'really serious'. Where the act was stabbing with a five and half inch knife blade, it was not necessary: *Janjua* [1999] 1 Cr App Rep 91.

61 *Anderson* [2003] NI 12, CA.

62 [1975] AC 55 at 70–71.

63 [1987] AC 576.

64 [1975] AC 55 at 94.

65 [1985] AC 905 at 921 and 928.

66 [1986] AC 455 at 473.

(express or implied) as is required for a killing to amount to murder when not done in the course or furtherance of another offence.

(2) For the purposes of the foregoing subsection, a killing done in the course or for the purpose of resisting an officer of justice, or of resisting or avoiding or preventing a lawful arrest, or of effecting or assisting an escape or rescue from legal custody, shall be treated as a killing in the course of furtherance of another offence.

The purpose of this section was, as the side-note indicates, to limit malice aforethought by the 'Abolition of "constructive malice" '. This took two forms. (i) It was murder to kill in the course or furtherance of a violent felony (or possibly any felony) so that an intention to commit the felony (for example, rape or robbery) was a sufficient *mens rea* where death resulted.[67] (ii) It was murder to kill while attempting to prevent lawful arrest or bring about escape from lawful arrest or custody, so that an intention to do these things was also malice aforethought where the act caused death. Subsection (1) abolishes the first, and subs (2) the second form of constructive malice. While eliminating constructive malice, the section leaves in existence 'express' and 'implied' malice. Although these terms have been used for centuries, their meaning is obscure and is certainly not any ordinary natural meaning that they might bear.[68] In the light of the common law, as we know it to be, 'express malice' must be taken to mean the intention to kill and 'implied malice' the intention to cause grievous bodily harm. Though the terms remain on the 'statute book', there is in practice no need to use them and the sooner they are buried the better.

It was at one time argued that s 1 also abolished intention to cause grievous bodily harm as a head of malice aforethought – an argument which required some other meaning to be given to 'implied malice' since that is expressly preserved. The argument was that the only reason why intention to cause grievous bodily harm was malice aforethought before 1957 was that in 1803 Lord Ellenborough's Act created a felony of causing grievous bodily harm with intent to do so. If death resulted, that was murder because, and only because, the killing was in the course or furtherance of that felony. The argument was rejected in *Vickers*[69] but accepted by Lords Diplock and Kilbrandon in *Hyam* where the matter was left open because Lord Cross was not prepared to decide between the conflicting views. In *Cunningham*[70] the House confirmed that intention to cause grievous bodily harm survived the Homicide Act as a head of *mens rea*, having ante-dated Lord Ellenborough's Act as a form of malice aforethought, distinct from constructive malice.

Recently Lords Mustill and Steyn have criticized the rule that an intention to cause serious bodily harm is a sufficient *mens rea* for murder as a 'conspicuous anomaly' and an example of 'constructive crime'.[71] Lord Steyn spoke of the result of the present definition being defendants 'classified as murderers who are not in truth murderers'.[72] The grievous bodily harm rule has been defended by some academic commentators, either as reflecting a general principle that the law imposes an obligation on an attacker to take the

[67] This form of murder exists in some US States and in former British Colonies, see eg *Griffith* [2004] UKPC 58 (Barbados).

[68] See Lord Hailsham in *Cunningham* [1981] 2 All ER 863 at 867.

[69] [1957] 2 QB 664, [1957] 2 All ER 741, CCA (a court of five judges).

[70] [1982] AC 566, [1981] 2 All ER 863, HL.

[71] *A-G's Reference (No 3 of 1994)* [1998] 1 Cr App R 91, 93, HL; *Powell and Daniels* and *English* [1998] 1 Cr App R 261, 267–268, and *Woollin* [1999] 1 Cr App R 8, 13.

[72] Ibid.

unforeseen consequences of his actions,[73] or as an appropriate response in cases of death caused by an 'attack'.[74]

The House of Lords missed its opportunity in *Cunningham* to rid the law of the anomaly by requiring at least awareness of the risk of causing death. It seems unlikely that the House will go to the lengths of overruling its own previous decisions in this area and Parliament is unlikely to do anything to narrow the law of murder.

2. The sentence for murder

Until the Homicide Act 1957[75] all persons convicted of murder were automatically sentenced to death. By s 5 of that Act certain types of murder were singled out and designated 'capital murder'. These continued to be punishable by death, while the remaining types of murder were punishable by imprisonment for life. In effect there were two degrees of murder.

The distinction between the two degrees of murder proved to be most unsatisfactory, and the death penalty for murder was suspended by the Murder (Abolition of Death Penalty) Act 1965.[76] All persons convicted of murder must now be sentenced to imprisonment for life. The mandatory sentence for murder was then unique in English law and the CLRC considered whether or not the judge should have discretion as in all other crimes. They were deeply and almost evenly divided on the issue. Their Report[77] set out the arguments on both sides in some detail but made no recommendation.

Subsequently the matter was considered by a Select Committee of the House of Lords (the Nathan Committee) which recommended, with one dissentient, that the mandatory sentence be abolished. Murder should be punishable with a maximum sentence of life but the judge should have the same discretion to impose lesser sentences as he has for other crimes.[78] The arguments in favour of this course are overwhelming. Murders vary as greatly in their gravity and murderers in their dangerousness, as for any other crime. The recommendation has not, however, found favour with the government and there seems to be no prospect of its implementation at the present time.

On sentencing a murderer, formerly the judge would make a recommendation to the Home Secretary of the minimum period which should elapse before the prisoner is released on licence.[79] That power was successfully challenged as incompatible with Articles 5 and 6 of the ECHR since the Minister was not an independent and impartial arbiter of the term of imprisonment.[80] The mandatory sentence itself has been held not

73 J. Horder, 'Two Histories and Four Hidden Principles of *Mens Rea*' [(1997)] 113 LQR 9.

74 W. Wilson, 'Murder and the Structure of Homicide', in A. Ashworth and B. Mitchell (eds), *Rethinking English Homicide Law* (2000).

75 See M. Wasik, 'Sentencing in Homicide' in A. Ashworth and B. Mitchell (eds), *Rethinking English Homicide Law* (2000), 167.

76 This, by virtue of affirmative resolutions of both Houses of Parliament on 16 and 18 Dec 1969, was to be permanently in force. See L. Blom-Cooper, 'Life Until Death' [1999] Crim LR 899.

77 *Fourteenth Report* CLRC/OAP/R, 19–27.

78 HL Paper 78–I, (1989). See A. Ashworth, 'Reform of the Law of Murder' [1990] Crim LR 75.

79 See the review of the process over the last 50 years – S. Shute, 'Punishing Murderers: release procedures and the "tarriff" ' [2004] Crim LR 873.

80 *R v Home Secretary, ex p Anderson* [2002] UKHL 46; *Stafford v UK* [2002] 35 EHRR 121.

to be incompatible with Articles 3 and 5 of the ECHR.[81] The Criminal Justice Act 2003 imposes a new regime for the sentencing and procedure for release of those sentenced to life imprisonment.[82]

3. Proposals for reform

Given the seriousness involved in the offence,[83] the unique stigma and the mandatory sentence it is surprising that the offence remains so ill-defined in so many respects. The Law Commission in its recent Report on *Partial Defences to Murder*[84] concluded that 'the law of murder in England and Wales is a mess'[85] and recommended 'a thorough consideration of the constituent elements of murder and its sentencing regime'.[86] The Home Office has recently accepted that recommendation, but as yet no detailed explanation of the scope terms of reference, reviewing body, or time frame have been announced.

Three main areas have been the subject of sustained criticism and focus for reform proposals. First, there is the ambiguity over the definition of the concept of intention (as examined above). This increases the opportunity for inconsistency in application and generates uncertainty in the law. Secondly, there is the grievous bodily harm rule which, in creating a constructive crime, carries with it all of the criticisms normally levelled at such offences for a failure to respect principles of fair labelling and correspondence between *actus reus* and *mens rea*.[87] Thirdly, there is the sustained and cogent criticism of the mandatory sentence.[88] It is often assumed that the mandatory sentence is retained to reflect the will of the populus, but research does not bear out such a conclusion.[89] Care must be taken when relying on (small scale) research findings, but when it is also noted that the Law Commission found a 'profound ignorance of the breadth of unlawful and lethal conduct which falls within the meaning of murder'[90] it seems that the mandatory sentence might be something favoured largely by politicians.

A number of options for reform might be postulated. One unlikely way forward would be to replace murder and manslaughter with a single offence of unlawful killing in which the sentence is at the discretion of the trial judge (within guidelines). This view had some judicial support (from Lord Kilbrandon in *Hyam*) but was rejected by the CLRC.[91] Since

[81] *Pyrah* [2003] 1 AC 903, [2003] 1 Cr App R 33.

[82] See *Practice Direction (Crime: Mandatory Life Sentence)* [2004] 1 WLR 1874; *Practice Direction (Crime: Mandatory Life Sentence) No 2* [2004] WLR 2551; and Criminal Justice Act 2003, s 269 et seq. For academic comment see N. Padfield, 'Tariffs in Murder' [2002] Crim LR 192.

[83] See Fletcher, *Rethinking Criminal Law*, 352.

[84] Law Com No 290 (2004).

[85] Para 2.74.

[86] Para 2.8.

[87] As regards labelling, Lord Steyn cited above, n 72 that people are labelled murderers who are in truth not such. As for correspondence, the *mens rea* of intent to do gbh does not correspond with the *actus reus* – death. See in particular B. Mitchell, 'In defence of the Correspondence Principle' [1999] Crim LR 195; J. Horder, 'A Critique of the Correspondence Principle in Criminal Law' [1995] Crim LR 759. See also N. Lacey, 'Partial Defences to Homicide', in A. Ashworth and B. Mitchell, above, ch 5.

[88] See generally B. Mitchell, *Murder and Penal Policy* (1990).

[89] See the reports of Professor Mitchell's research as appended to the Law Commission Report No 290, revealing that 62.9% of the population surveyed thought that there ought *not* to be a mandatory sentence.

[90] Para 2.20.

[91] In its Fourteenth Report on *Offences Against the Person* (1980). See R. Buxton, 'The New Murder' [1980] Crim LR 521.

this would remove the specific label and uniqueness that attaches to it, the option is unlikely ever to find much general support.[92] A second alternative would be to reintroduce the felony murder rule with specified categories of offence during the commission of which the causing of an unintended death would be murder.[93] This has few supporters. A third alternative is to extend the meaning of intention so as to include foresight of a probability of death or gbh. Since this is a retreat from the narrower approach introduced in *Woollin*, it is unlikely to receive much judicial support. A fourth alternative is to define murder so as to include cases in which death is intended (as presently defined), and those cases in which the defendant intentionally causes serious injury and in doing so demonstrates an indifference to life.[94] A fifth, similar, alternative is for murder to encompass intended killings and those where death follows an intended grievous bodily harm coupled with foresight of the life threatening nature of the injury. This is the latest proposal offered by the CLRC and incorporated in the Law Commission's Draft Code as follows:

A person is guilty of murder if he causes the death of another –

(a) intending to cause death; or

(b) intending to cause serious personal harm and being aware that he may cause death. . . .

This recommendation was endorsed by the Nathan Committee which made its own independent study of, and received much evidence on, the law of murder. The recommendation would make a relatively small change in the law of murder, excluding a person who, notwithstanding his intention to cause serious harm, did not foresee any risk of death. Of greater practical significance was Nathan's endorsement of the Code definition of intention.[95] The decision in *Woollin*,[96] goes some way towards effecting that reform. The 1998 Home Office Consultation Paper, which would have applied that definition to non-fatal offences, did not extend to murder.

[92] For fascinating studies into the public perceptions of the scope of the offence see B. Mitchell, 'Public Perceptions of Homicide and Criminal Justice' (1998) 38 Cr J Crim, 453; 'Further Evidence of the Relationship Between Legal and Public Opinion on the Homicide Law' [2000] Crim LR 814.

[93] For discussion see W. Wilson, 'Murder and the Structure of Homicide' in A. Ashworth and B. Mitchell (eds), *Rethinking English Homicide Law* (2000).

[94] See for discussion Goff, above, B. Mitchell, 'Culpably Indifferent Murder' (1996) 25 Anglo Am LR 64.

[95] Above, p 96.

[96] Above, p 94.

14

Manslaughter

At common law, all unlawful homicides which are not murder are manslaughter. There are now numerous statutory forms of unlawful killing including, for example, causing death by dangerous driving.

Manslaughter includes many types of homicide. This is an inevitable consequence of it being limited in scope only by murder at one extreme and accidental killings at the other. Despite the enormous range of conduct treated in law as manslaughter, it is customary and useful to divide manslaughter into only two main groups: 'voluntary' and 'involuntary' manslaughter. The distinction is that in voluntary manslaughter D may have the malice aforethought of murder, but the presence of some defined mitigating circumstance reduces his crime to the less serious grade of criminal homicide. Where these circumstances are present D may actually intend to kill and do so in pursuance of that intention and yet not be guilty of murder.[1] At common law, voluntary manslaughter occurred in one category of case only, where the killing was done under provocation. Under the Homicide Act 1957 the provocation defence was put on a statutory footing and two further categories of voluntary manslaughter were added: killing is now manslaughter and not murder, notwithstanding the fact that D can be proved to have had the necessary malice aforethought at the time of the conduct, where (i) D is suffering from diminished responsibility;[2] and (ii) where D kills in pursuance of a suicide pact.[3] The problem of the suicide pact is looked at in connection with the statutory crime of abetting suicide.[4]

1. Voluntary manslaughter

(a) Provocation[5]

The common law rule was stated by Devlin J in what the Court of Criminal Appeal described as a 'classic direction', as follows:

1 *A-G of Ceylon v Perera* [1953] AC 200, PC; *Lee Chun-Chuen v R* [1963] AC 220, [1963] 1 All ER 73; *Parker v R* [1964] AC 1369, [1964] 2 All ER 641; *Smith (Clean) v R* [2002] 1 Cr App R 92; contra, per Lord Simon in *Holmes v DPP* [1946] AC 588 at 598, HL.

2 Section 2.

3 Section 4, below.

4 Below, p 493.

5 There is a wealth of literature on the topic. The Law Commission's Report No 290, *Partial Defences to Murder* (2004) is an excellent starting point. For a comprehensive academic review of the theoretical issues and the historical context of the defence, see J. Horder, *Provocation and Responsibility* (1992). Valuable articles and essays include A. Ashworth, 'The Doctrine of Provocation' [1976] CLJ 292; J. M. Kaye, 'Early History of Murder and Manslaughter' (1967) 83 LQR 365; J. Horder, 'Reshaping the Subjective Element in the Provocation Defence' (2005) OJLS 123.

Provocation is some act, or series of acts, done by the dead man to the accused, which would cause in any reasonable man, and actually causes in the accused, a sudden and temporary loss of self-control, rendering the accused so subject to passion as to make him or her for the moment not master of his mind'.[6]

The common law rule has been modified by the Homicide Act 1957, s 3, which provides:

> Where on a charge of murder there is evidence on which the jury can find that the person charged was provoked (whether by things done or by things said or by both together) to lose his self-control, the question whether the provocation was enough to make a reasonable man do as he did shall be left to be determined by the jury; and in determining that question the jury shall take into account everything both done and said according to the effect which, in their opinion, it would have on a reasonable man.

Section 3 does not create or codify, but assumes the existence of, and amends, the common law defence. It does not state the effect of a successful defence – it is by virtue of the common law that the offence is reduced to manslaughter. The section assumes the existence of the dual test:

(1) was the defendant provoked to lose his self-control? (a subjective question); and
(2) was the provocation enough to make a reasonable man do as he did? (an objective question).

The defence is available only to a charge of murder whether as a principal or accessory.[7] Provocation is not a defence to a charge of wounding or any charge other than murder according to *Cunningham*.[8] In *Bruzas*[9] Eveleigh J held that it was not a defence to a charge of attempted murder at common law[10] and it is clear that it is not a defence under the Criminal Attempts Act 1981.[11] The defence has no relevance to the determination of whether D committed the acts causing death when he has been found unfit to plead under s 4A of the Criminal Procedure (Insanity) Act 1964.[12]

On a murder charge, in deciding whether D intended death or grievous bodily harm, the jury must consider evidence of provocation with all other relevant evidence.[13] If they are not satisfied that he had the necessary *mens rea*, they must acquit. But even if they decide he did have *mens rea*, provocation may still be a defence to a charge of murder at common law, entitling D to be convicted of manslaughter.

Whether the defendant was provoked to lose his self-control is a question of fact. In accordance with the general rule, it is for the judge to say whether there is any evidence of that fact. In one tragic case, where the defendant yielded to the entreaties of his incurably ill and suffering wife to put an end to her life, it was held that there was no evidence of provocation: D had not lost his self-control, indeed the evidence was that he was so in

6 *Duffy* [1949] 1 All ER 932n.

7 *Marks* [1998] Crim LR 676.

8 [1959] 1 QB 288, [1958] 3 All ER 711.

9 *Bruzas* [1972] Crim LR 367, on which see P. English, 'Provocation and Attempted Murder' [1973] Crim LR 727.

10 See commentary and CLRC/OAP/R, para 98.

11 *Campbell* [1997] Crim LR 495 (Sedley J) above, p 417.

12 *Grant* [2001] EWCA Crim 261; [2002] QB 1030.

13 Section 8 of the Criminal Justice Act 1967, above, p 125, *Williams* [1968] Crim LR 678; *Ives* [1970] 1 QB 208, [1969] 3 All ER 470.

control as to stop immediately when he thought, wrongly, that she had changed her mind.[14] The case highlights the arbitrariness of a defence partially absolving those who kill in a state of anger or outrage, but not in exercising mercy.

Sufficient evidence of provocation may appear in the case presented by the Crown. If not, there is an evidential burden on the defendant.[15] If no evidence that the defendant was provoked to lose his self-control is adduced by the Crown or the defendant, then the judge will withdraw the defence from the jury. Since the burden of proof is on the Crown, evidence which might leave a reasonable jury in reasonable doubt whether or not the defendant was provoked is sufficient. There must be evidence of provocation, mere speculation will not suffice.[16]

Once the judge has decided there is sufficient evidence that the defendant was provoked, whether or not the defence has been raised expressly by D or his counsel,[17] he must leave it to the jury to answer the questions, (i) *was* the defendant provoked to lose his self-control? and (ii) was the provocation enough to make a reasonable man do as he did? Since the 1957 Act, the judge may not withdraw the defence from the jury on the ground that in his well-founded opinion there is no evidence on which they could answer the second question in the affirmative.[18] Although the court in *Dhillon*[19] was unwilling to admit it, the effect of the 1957 Act plainly is that D must not be deprived of his chance that the jury will return a perverse verdict; but the right is an imperfect one since the court said, *obiter*, that the conviction of murder is 'safe' and will be upheld if the court is sure that 'at least 10 members of the jury would be drawn to that conclusion'.

(i) Provocation by 'things done or said'

Since provocation continues to be a defence at common law it might have been held that the words 'provoked' and 'provocation' in s 3 bear the limited meaning they had at common law, subject only to the limited changes expressly made by the section. This has not been the approach of the courts. These words have been given their ordinary natural meaning, free of the technical limitations of the common law. One of the starkest examples of this is *Doughty*[20] in which it was held that the judge was bound by the plain words of the section to leave provocation to the jury where there was evidence that the persistent crying of his baby had caused D to lose his self-control and kill it. Whatever the position may have been at common law, the provocation does not have to be an illegal or wrongful act. There must be 'things done or things said' and the crying of the baby was presumably regarded as a 'thing done'. The court rejected an argument that the decision would open the floodgates: the decision did not mean that baby-killers would easily be able to avoid conviction for murder on the basis of provocation: '. . . because reliance can

14 *Cocker* [1989] Crim LR 740, discussed by P. R. Taylor, 'Provocation and Mercy Killing' [1991] Crim LR 111.

15 Mixed statements of the accused may be relied on: *Jama* [2004] EWCA Crim 960. Care needs to be taken with reliance on D's lies: *Davies* [2004] EWCA Crim 1914.

16 *Miao* [2003] 3 All ER (D) 218 (Nov).

17 *Mancini v DPP* [1942] AC 1, [1941] 3 All ER 272.

18 This seems to be a unique exception to the rule that the judge must not allow a matter of fact (or opinion) to be decided when there is no evidence of it. The CLRC recommends repeal of this rule: CLRC/OAP/R, para 88. Cf the position before the Act as discussed in *Franco v The Queen* [2001] UKPC 38 and *Fox v The Queen* [2001] UKPC 41.

19 [1997] 2 Cr App R 104 at 114–115, [1997] Crim LR 295 and commentary.

20 (1986) 83 Cr App R 319. See J. Horder, 'The Problem of Provocative Children' [1987] Crim LR 655.

be placed upon the common sense of juries upon who the task of deciding the issue is imposed by s 3 and that common sense will ensure that only in cases where the facts fully justified it would their verdict be likely to be that thy would hold a defendant's act in killing a crying child would be the response of a reasonable man within the section'.[21] This broad interpretation of the trigger for the defence means that there is no requirement that the provoking acts or words were performed consciously, let alone with the deliberate intent to provoke. This dilution of the concept of 'provocation' to mean merely words or conduct that *cause* the loss of control in the defendant has been heavily criticized by academics.[22]

In *Acott*[23] it was held by the House of Lords that it is not enough that D's loss of temper may possibly have been the result of some unidentified words or actions by another. In such a case, there would be no material on which the jury could make the objective judgement demanded by the Act. There must be 'some evidence of *what* was done or *what* was said to provoke the homicidal reaction' (the court's italics). The trial judge is best placed to make this assessment.

Mere circumstances, however provocative, do not constitute a defence to murder. Loss of control by a farmer on his crops being destroyed by a flood, or his flocks by foot-and-mouth, a financier ruined by a crash on the stock market or an author on his manuscript being destroyed by lightning, could not, it seems, excuse a resulting killing. 'Act of God' could hardly be regarded as 'something done' within s 3. Since, where there is a provocative act, it no longer need be done by the victim, this distinction begins to look a little thin. If D may rely on the defence where the crops or the manuscript were destroyed by an unknown arsonist or the stock exchange crash was engineered by other anonymous financiers, why should it be different where no human agency was involved? The 'provocation' is no more and no less.

By whom the provocation may be given[24]

Section 3 removes certain limitations on the defence as formulated in *Duffy*. That formulation limited the nature of operative provocation to acts done (i) by the dead person (ii) to the accused. Evidence would thus not be admissible of acts done (i) by third parties or (ii) to third parties. Under s 3, however, there is no such limitation and the only question seems to be whether the evidence is relevant to the issue – namely whether D was provoked to lose his self-control. The test of relevance should be – would a reasonable man (or ordinary person as the House of Lords would prefer despite the statutory formula)[25] regard the act in question as having a provocative effect on the person charged? So it was held in *Davies*, where D killed his wife, V, following upon her adultery with X, that the judge was wrong to direct that V's conduct and, by implication, not X's, was to be taken into account.[26]

21 Per Stocker LJ at 326.

22 See in particular, T. Macklem and J. Gardner, 'Provocation and Pluralism' (2001) 64 MLR 815. See Law Com No 173, paras 4.8–4.11.

23 [1996] Crim LR 664; affd [1997] 1 All ER 706, HL. See also *Bharj* [2005] All ER (D) 330 (Feb), emphasizing that the jury would be looking at *all* the evidence.

24 See R. S. O'Regan, 'Indirect Provocation and Misdirected Retaliation' [1968] Crim LR 319.

25 See the discussion of *Morgan Smith* below p 454.

26 [1975] QB 691, [1975] 1 All ER 890. Cf the earlier decision to the same effect by Lawton J in *Twine* [1967] Crim LR 710, where D's girlfriend's conduct caused D to lose his self-control and strike and kill the man she was with.

The defence was available, even at common law, if the blow was *aimed* at the provoker but, by accident, it missed him and killed an innocent person. The doctrine of transferred malice[27] operated and D was guilty of manslaughter only. In *Gross*[28] D, provoked by blows from her husband, fired at him, intending to kill him but missed and killed V. It was held that:

> . . . if the firing at the person intended to be hit would be manslaughter, then, if the bullet strikes a third person not intended to be hit, the killing of that person equally would be manslaughter and not murder.[29]

If D knew it was virtually certain that he would hit V, he would have an independent *mens rea* with respect to V, probably sufficient to fix him with liability for murder[30] at common law; but now the provocation given by the third party would be a defence even for D's acts towards V.

There is, therefore, no limitation to prevent a third party oral account being sufficient to constitute provocation, as where D loses his temper following A's report of V's statement that V had attacked D's daughter.

Acts not directed at D

Before the Homicide Act 1957 it used to be said that the provocation must consist in something done to the defendant[31] but the Act requires the jury to take into account *everything* both done and said according to the effect which, in their opinion, it would have on a reasonable man. Such a broad definition is capable of including acts done to third parties if, in the jury's opinion, they would have provoked a reasonable man in the position of the defendant. In *Pearson*,[32] where two brothers, M and W, killed their violent and tyrannical father, the ill-treatment meted out to M over a period of eight years when the older boy, W, was absent from home was relevant to W's defence, particularly as he had returned home to protect M from violence. The removal of this restriction is significant in the context of domestic killings where, for example an abusive man is attacking his wife and her child is provoked on seeing the attack to kill the man.

(ii) The subjective condition – the loss of self-control

The requirement of the loss of self-control was an attempt to distinguish revenge killings of a premeditated or calculated nature from killings committed in the heat of the moment. It provides an imperfect tool for distinguishing between those two categories of killing. It is unclear whether the main focus in applying the test should be on whether the accused has failed to exercise control, or was incapable of exercising control. Moreover, the test has the potential to operate in a discriminatory way, rendering the defence too readily available to those who are quick to temper (more commonly men), and less accommodating of those who endure the provoking circumstances before responding

27 Above, p 113.

28 (1913) 23 Cox CC 455 (Darling J); and see *Porritt* [1961] 3 All ER 463, [1961] 1 WLR 1372.

29 23 Cox CC at 456.

30 Above, p 436.

31 But see *Fisher* (1837) 8 C & P 182 (Park J, *obiter*) (D coming upon V buggering D's son) and *Harrington* (1866) 10 Cox CC 370 (Cockburn CJ contemplating the possibility of a defence where D found his daughter being violently assaulted by her husband).

32 [1992] Crim LR 193.

with lethal force (often women who kill abusive partners). The acute difficulties arising when the defence of provocation is pleaded in cases of killing in abusive relationships has called into question the appropriateness of this 'sudden and temporary loss of self control' requirement.[33]

Evaluating the evidence of loss of control

In their evaluation of the defence as a whole, the jury should be directed to consider the subjective condition first.[34] In deciding this question of fact they are, naturally, entitled to take into account all the relevant circumstances; the nature of the provocative act and all the relevant conditions in which it took place, the sensitivity or otherwise of D, and the time, if any, which elapsed between the provocation and the act which caused death. D's failure to testify to his loss of self-control is not necessarily fatal to his case.

Provocation is commonly set up as an alternative to the complete defence of self-defence. The admission of loss of self-control would weaken or destroy the alternative defence; and the courts recognize that D has a tactical reason for not expressly asserting what may be the truth.[35] Although D firmly denies that he lost self-control,[36] the judge must direct the jury to consider that possibility, if it is a possibility, should they reject the defences raised.[37] It is the duty of counsel for both sides at the trial to draw the attention of the judge to any evidence of provocation. It is for the judge to decide whether it is sufficient to leave to the jury.[38] The Court of Appeal has shown considerable generosity in discerning evidence of provocation where that defence has not been raised at the trial and even where the defence raised was inconsistent with provocation[39] and D's counsel has given the judge his opinion that it would not be appropriate for him to raise the issue.[40] Arguably, reform should be made to allow D (after legal advice) to waive the right to have the defence left to the jury.

Question is entirely subjective

If D is of an unusually phlegmatic temperament and it appears that he did not lose his self-control, the fact that a reasonable man in like circumstances would have done so will not assist D in the least. A traditional example of extreme provocation is finding a spouse in the act of adultery;[41] but if D, on so finding his wife, were to read her a lecture on the enormity of her sin and then methodically to load a gun and shoot her, it is probable (for

33 The issue has generated an immense literature, see generally K. O'Donovan, 'Defences for Battered Women Who Kill?' (1991) 18 J Law and Soc 219; C. Wells, 'Battered Women Syndrome and Defences to Homicide: Where Now' (1994) 14 LS 266; and n 131 herein.

34 *Brown* [1972] 2 All ER 1328 at 1333.

35 *Bullard v R* [1957] AC 635, [1961] 3 All ER 470n; *Rolle v R* [1965] 3 All ER 582; *Lee Chun-Chuen v R* [1963] AC 220, [1963] 1 All ER 73.

36 The loss need not amount to automatism – *Richens* [1993] Crim LR 384.

37 *Scott* [1997] Crim LR 597, where the defences were accident and self-defence.

38 *Cox* [1995] Crim LR 741.

39 *Cambridge* [1994] 2 All ER 760, [1994] Crim LR 690. See S. Doran, 'Alternative Defences' [1991] Crim LR 878. Arguably there is no inconsistency in pleading provocation and alibi – effectively D is saying it was not me, but whoever it was would have been provoked by V's conduct.

40 *Burgess and McLean* [1995] Crim LR 425.

41 Killing, in such a case 'is of the lowest degree of [manslaughter]; and therefore . . . the court directed the burning in the hand to be gently inflicted, because there could not be a greater provocation': Blackstone, *Commentaries*, iv, 192. See also the leading case of *Manning* (1671) T Raym 212. For a recent case of exactly these facts see *Christie* [2004] EWCA Crim 1338, D was convicted of murder.

it remains a question of fact) either that the judge would rule that there was no evidence that D lost his self-control or that the jury would find that he did not. In that case, D would be guilty of murder and it would be irrelevant that the jury may think that a reasonable man in like circumstances would lose his self-control.

Loss of self control must be sudden and temporary

Although in *Camplin* the House of Lords stated that the 1957 Act 'abolishes all previous rules as to what can or cannot amount to provocation'[42] it appears that the subjective condition is unchanged. In the more recent decisions of *Ibrams*,[43] *Thornton*[44] and *Ahluwalia*[45] the Court of Appeal has reaffirmed that there must be a 'sudden and temporary loss of self-control', as Devlin J put it in *Duffy*,[46] and approved that judge's further words:

> Indeed, circumstances which induce a desire for revenge are inconsistent with provocation, since the conscious formulation of a desire for revenge means that a person has had time to think, to reflect, and that would negative a sudden temporary loss of self-control, which is of the essence of provocation.[47]

In *Thornton*[48] the court rejected an argument that the words 'sudden and temporary' are no longer appropriate. Provocation is not ruled out as a *matter of law* either because the provocative conduct has extended over a long period or because there was a delayed ('slow burn') reaction.[49]

It seems that the words, 'sudden and temporary,' imply only that the act must not be premeditated or calculated. It is the loss of control which must be 'sudden,' which does not mean 'immediate.' However, in *Ahluwalia* the Lord Chief Justice confirmed that 'the longer the delay and the stronger the evidence of deliberation on the part of the defendant, the more likely it will be that the prosecution will negative provocation'.[50] The prolonged nature of the provocation (say in an abusive relationship) may explain why an incident, trivial when considered in isolation, caused a loss of self-control. The jury are bound by the Act to take into account *everything* both done and said according to the effect which in their opinion it would have on a reasonable man; and a jury may well think provocative behaviour over a long period would have a cumulative effect on a reasonable man and had such an effect on the defendant. In *Davies*[51] the Court of Appeal criticized the judge's direction as too generous in allowing the jury to take account of 'the whole course of conduct of [V] right through that turbulent year of 1972'. The Court of

42 *Camplin* [1978] AC 705, 67 Cr App R 14 at 19.
43 (1981) 74 Cr App R 154.
44 [1992] 1 All ER 306, [1992] Crim LR 54. For a further appeal, see [1996] 2 Cr App R 108, [1996] Crim LR 597.
45 [1992] 4 All ER 889, [1993] Crim LR 63. On which see D. Nicholson and R. Sanghvi, 'Battered Women and Provocation: The Implications of *R v Ahluwalia*' [1993] Crim LR 728.
46 [1949] 1 All ER 932n.
47 The test provided by Lord Devlin suggests that the longer the period to cool off and calm down the more likely the killing is not a revenge killing. But this assumption is not borne out by psychological/physiological evidence see P. Brett, 'The Physiology of Provocation' [1970] Crim LR 634. The requirement of suddenness is criticized for restricting the defence and removing from its ambit the cases of outraged retaliation: Horder, above at 69–71.
48 Above, n 45.
49 *Ahluwalia*, supra.
50 Per Lord Taylor C J at 139.
51 (1975) 60 Cr App R 253 at 259.

Appeal's position is hard to justify. The whole course of conduct should only be ignored if no reasonable jury could have thought it had an effect on the accused at the flashpoint. 'Everything both done and said' must be limited to what is relevant; but everything which may in fact have contributed to the accused's loss of self-control is relevant. If a matter so contributed, it is not open to the judge to rule that it would not have affected a reasonable man.

The 'temporary' nature of the loss of self-control seems irrelevant, provided only that it extended to the fatal act. D should not be deprived of defence because he continued berserk for days thereafter – but sudden losses of self-control are in practice temporary. The term 'loss of control' is of course not one founded on medical or psychological learning; it is a legal invention which lacks precision.

Delay and cooling off

Since the sudden and temporariness requirement was designed to exclude from the ambit of the defence cases of premeditated killing, evidence that D had an opportunity to regain control and kill in a calculated fashion is important. In *Ibrams*,[52] D had received gross provocation but the last act occurred on 7 October. The attack was carefully planned on 10 October and carried out on 12 October. It was held that the judge was right to rule that there was no evidence of loss of self-control. The case should be approached with care. The question of delay and potential cooling period is *evidence* relating to the substantive law question whether D had lost his self control at the time.

Recent cases have given a generous interpretation to the element of the defence. There was held to be sufficient evidence to go to the jury in *Thornton*[53] where a wife had previously declared an intention to kill her brutally abusive husband, and after a fresh provocation she went to the kitchen, took and sharpened a carving knife and returned to another room where she fatally stabbed him; in *Pearson*,[54] although the two defendants had armed themselves in advance with the fatal weapon and the killing was a joint enterprise; and *Baillie*[55] where D, being greatly enraged, fetched a gun from an attic and drove his car to V's house (stopping for petrol on the way) before shooting him. 'Cooling time' no longer seems to play the vital role it once did in negating the defence.

Loss of self-control in doing what?

The section does not say what act D must have performed when his self control was lost for the defence to apply, but it seems obvious that it must be the act which causes death. The question is whether D's responsibility for homicide – that is, causing death – should be mitigated.[56] If D has lost control in doing the act which caused death, it is quite immaterial, it is submitted, that he regains it immediately afterwards. In *Clarke*[57] D, under some provocation, head-butted and strangled V, and, then, panicking, placed live wires

52 (1981) 74 Cr App R 154.

53 Above, p 45. The jury rejected the defence, presumably being satisfied that there was no 'sudden and temporary' loss of self-control.

54 [1992] Crim LR 193, above, p 446. See a valuable article, M. Wasik, 'Cumulative Provocation and Domestic Killing' [1982] Crim LR 29, discussing, *inter alia*, some cases and practices which are difficult to reconcile with *Duffy* and *Ibrams*.

55 [1995] Crim LR 739.

56 On the question of whether provocation can properly be regarded as a partial defence or a partial justification, see: Horder, above, ch 1; the Law Commission Report, Part III.

57 [1991] Crim LR 383 and commentary.

into her mouth electrocuting her. She may, however, have been dead before the electrocution. It was held that the judge had rightly declined to tell the jury to ignore the circumstances of the electrocution in considering provocation. The jury must take into account the whole course of D's conduct, 'although some factors (for example, disposal of the body) might be too remote'. But if V was already dead when D put the wires in her mouth, the fact that he had now regained his self-control was surely irrelevant. The only possible relevance of acts done after death (or after the infliction of a fatal injury) could be to show that self-control had not been lost when the earlier acts causing death were done – for example, suggesting that the whole course of conduct was premeditated; but there was no hint of relevance of that kind in *Clarke*. Of course, if the electrocution was a contributory cause of V's death and was done after D had regained his self-control, he was guilty of murder; but the onus was on the Crown to prove this.

One qualification to this might arise where D, under provocation, causes potentially fatal injury to V but, while V is still alive, regains his self-control and deliberately omits to take steps which he knows might save or prolong her life. D would have a duty to act[58] and, if his omission, being unprovoked, resulted in V's death, he might be convicted of murder.

(iii) The response – would the reasonable man have done as D did?

The objective condition at common law[59]

In the older cases, the courts laid down as a matter of law what was, and what was not, capable of amounting to provocation.[60] It usually consisted of a violent act against the defendant, though two other instances were well recognized, that where a husband discovered his wife in the act of adultery and killed either or both of the guilty pair and that where a father found and promptly killed a man committing sodomy with his son.[61] In *Holmes v DPP*[62] the House of Lords held that, as a matter of law, a confession of adultery was insufficient provocation where a husband killed his wife; and added that 'in no case could words alone, save in circumstances of a most extreme and exceptional character', reduce the crime to manslaughter. The reasonable man did not make his appearance until *Welsh*[63] in 1869. Thereafter even when an act was recognized as capable of amounting to provocation, it probably had to pass the reasonable man test.

The test was applied by the Court of Criminal Appeal in *Lesbini*.[64] The girl in charge of a firing range in an amusement arcade made some impertinent personal remarks about D. He asked for a revolver, ostensibly to shoot at the range, and shot her dead. At his trial for murder, his defences of accident and insanity were rejected by the jury. On appeal, it was argued that the jury should have been directed on provocation and *Welsh* did not

58 Above, p 75.

59 See G. Williams, 'Provocation and the Reasonable Man' [1954] Crim LR 740; J. Ll. Edwards, 'Another View' [1954] Crim LR 898.

60 See, eg, Hawkins, I PC c. 13, s 36; East, I PC 233. For a comprehensive review of the historical development of the defence, see J. Horder, *Provocation and Responsibility* (1992).

61 *Fisher* (1837) 8 C & P 182.

62 [1946] AC 588, [1946] 2 All ER 124.

63 (1869) 11 Cox CC 336. See the Law Commission Report No 290, paras 77, 78. The early case law seems a little confused on this point, vacillating between subjective/objective language we would now find to be conflicting.

64 [1914] 3 KB 1116.

apply where, as in the present case, D suffered from defective control and want of mental balance. Avory J interjected that it would seem to follow from this that a bad-tempered man would be entitled to a verdict of manslaughter where a good-tempered one would be liable to be convicted of murder[65] and the court held that, to afford a defence, the provocation must be such as would affect the mind of a reasonable man, which was manifestly not so in the present case.

Before the Homicide Act the judges took it upon themselves to instruct the jury as to the characteristics of the reasonable man. The defendant might be mentally deficient[66] but the jury still had to consider the effects of the provocation on a normal person. Moreover, he (or she) was normal in body as well as mind. The fact the defendant was seven months' pregnant was irrelevant to the application of the objective test.[67] In *Bedder v DPP*,[68] D, a youth of 18 who was sexually impotent killed V, a prostitute, after attempting in vain to have sexual intercourse with her. The court found she had jeered at him and attempted to get away. He tried to hold her and she slapped him in the face, punched him in the stomach and kicked him in the genitals. D knew of his impotence and had allowed it to prey on his mind. The House of Lords held that the jury had been correctly directed to consider what effect V's acts would have had on an ordinary person, not a man who is sexually impotent. Mental and physical characteristics were, in the view of the House of Lords, inseparable.

The objective condition under s 3 of the 1957 Act

The Homicide Act, s 3 made three changes in the law:

(1) It made it clear that 'things said' alone may be sufficient provocation, if the jury should be of the opinion that they would have provoked a reasonable man, thus reversing *Holmes v DPP*.[69]

(2) It took away the power of the judge to withdraw the defence from the jury on the ground that there was no evidence on which the jury could find that a reasonable man would have been provoked to do as D did, reversing *Mancini*.[70]

(3) It took away the power of the judge to dictate to the jury what were to be the characteristics of the reasonable man, reversing *Bedder*.

It was not until the decision of the House of Lords in *Camplin*,[71] more than 20 years after the Act, that the second and third effects were fully recognized. The Court of Appeal in that case was of the opinion that *Bedder* was binding on them. However, the House of Lords decided that the effect of s 3 is to overrule *Bedder* and all other cases which defined any characteristic of the reasonable man except for his power of self-control and the fact that he is sober.

In *Camplin*, D, a 15-year-old boy, killed the victim with a chapatti pan. D's story was that V had buggered him against his will and then laughed at him when he was overcome by shame, whereupon he lost his self-control and made the fatal attack. The trial judge declined the invitation of D's counsel to instruct the jury to consider the effect of the

65 For a discussion of this argument, see the 4th edition of this work at 304–306.
66 *Alexander* (1913) 9 Cr App R 139.
67 *Smith* (1915) 11 Cr App R 81.
68 [1954] 2 All ER 801, [1954] 1 WLR 1119.
69 [1946] AC 588, [1946] 2 All ER 124.
70 [1942] AC 1, [1941] 3 All ER 272.
71 [1978] AC 705, [1978] 2 All ER 168.

provocation on a boy of 15. He directed that the test was the effect of the provocation, not on a reasonable boy, but on a reasonable man. The Court of Appeal held that this was a misdirection and distinguished *Bedder* on the grounds that youth, and the immaturity which naturally accompanies youth, are not deviations from the norm, but norms through which everyone must pass. Youth is not a personal idiosyncrasy and certainly not a physical infirmity or disability like Bedder's impotence.[72] In *Camplin* the House of Lords dismissed the prosecution's appeal on the broader ground that *Bedder* is, in effect, overruled by s 3 of the 1957 Act. Their lordships were much influenced by the fact that, under the Act, words alone may be a sufficient provocation. This accentuates the anomalies, inconveniences and injustices which would flow from continued application of the *Bedder* principle, for the gravity of verbal provocation will frequently depend on the particular characteristics or circumstances[73] of the person to whom a taunt or insult is addressed. In a case of provocation by words, personal characteristics could not be ignored without absurdity. If the alleged provocation was the shout 'go away shorty', it would be impossible to evaluate the reasonableness of the response without taking account of D's stature. To allow such characteristics to be taken into account where the provocation was verbal so undermined the *Bedder* principle that it should no longer be followed, whatever the nature of the provocation.

This conclusion, it is submitted, is well justified by the words of the Act. Section 3 is to be given its natural meaning[74] and tells us that the question for the jury is 'whether the provocation was enough to make a reasonable man do as [D] did'. What is 'the provocation'? It seems obviously to be the things done or things said – which may or may not have been a sufficient provocation at common law – which the jury have found to have provoked the accused. The section goes on to direct that the jury –

> shall take into account *everything* both done and said according to the effect which, *in their opinion*, it would have on a reasonable man.

The words italicized are inconsistent with the continuance of *Bedder* as a rule of law. 'Everything' includes a taunt of impotence where that in fact provoked the accused and the effect of it on a reasonable man is a question for the opinion of the jury.

The relevant 'characteristics'

In *Camplin*, Lord Diplock stated how a jury should be directed:[75]

> The judge should state what the question is using the very terms of the section. He should then explain to them that the reasonable man referred to in the question is a person having the power of self-control to be expected of an ordinary person of the sex and age of the accused, but in other respects sharing such of the accused's characteristics as they think would affect the gravity of the provocation to him; and that the question is not merely whether such a person would in like circumstances be provoked to lose his self-control but also would react to the provocation as the accused did.

It will be noted that age and sex – characteristics which everyone possesses – are to be taken into account in determining the degree of self-restraint required of D; but his other characteristics are said to be relevant only in so far as they affect the gravity of the

72 [1978] 1 All ER at 1241.

73 Such as D's emotional attachment to a person attacked by V: *Horrex* [1999] Crim LR 500.

74 *Davies* [1975] QB 691, [1975] 1 All ER 890.

75 Per Lord Diplock at 175.

provocation, not in their impact on the ability of D to exercise self-control. This line of reasoning accords with the argument made earlier by Ashworth in a seminal article:

The proper distinction is that individual peculiarities which bear on the gravity of the provocation should be taken into account, whereas individual peculiarities bearing on the accused's level of self-control should not.[76]

The same distinction appears in s 169(2) of the New Zealand Crimes Act with which, as Lord Simon pointed out, English law was brought into line by *Camplin*:

Anything done or said may be provocation if –

(a) in the circumstances of the case it was sufficient to deprive a person having the power of self-control of an ordinary person, but otherwise having the characteristics of the offender, of the power of self-control; and
(b) it did in fact deprive the offender of the power of self-control and thereby induced him to commit the act of homicide.

Plainly, the characteristics of the accused were not to be taken into account in assessing the 'ordinary person's' power of self-control. On the contrary, as Lord Simon said, the judge may tell the jury that a man is not entitled to rely on 'his exceptional excitability (whether idiosyncratic or by cultural environment or ethnic origin) or pugnacity or ill-temper or on his drunkenness'.[77]

This distinction was also central to the decision of the House in *Morhall*[78] where it was held that a characteristic of the defendant affecting the gravity of the provocation is material even though it is discreditable. D, a drug addict, was taunted with his addiction. The Court of Appeal held that the reasonable man is not a drug addict and this was a characteristic which could not be taken into account. However, the term 'reasonable man' in s 3 of the Homicide Act is only concerned with reasonable self-restraint. The House held that the addiction should have been taken into account. If a paedophile is taunted with his proclivity, the jury must consider the provocative effect of such taunts on a person with that characteristic. As Lord Goff agreed, if an old lag, now trying to go straight, were taunted with being 'a jailbird', it would not make much sense to tell the jury to consider the effect of such provocation on a man of good character.

In line with these three decisions of the House was that of the Privy Council in *Luc Thiet Thuan v R*,[79] holding that D's mental abnormality, unless it formed the subject of the taunts, is not a relevant characteristic for the purposes of the objective test. D, charged with murder in Hong Kong, unsuccessfully raised defences of diminished responsibility and provocation. There was medical evidence that he had suffered organic brain damage of a kind which often results in difficulty controlling impulses. The judge directed the

[76] 'The Doctrine of Provocation' [1976] CLJ 292. Cf the distinction made between provocativeness and provocability made in the commentary on *Morhall* [1995] Crim LR 890. For consideration of whether the questions can be kept separate see A. Norrie, 'From Criminal law to Legal Theory: The Mysterious Case of the Reasonable Glue Sniffer' (2002) 65 MLR 538, 547.

[77] Lord Simon did not think this list necessarily exhaustive. *McCarthy* [1954] 2 QB 105, [1954] 2 All ER 262 (D's intoxication is to be ignored) remains good law.

[78] [1995] 3 All ER 659, HL, [1995] Crim LR 890. A unanimous decision of the House which was virtually ignored in *Smith* [2001] AC 146.

[79] [1996] 2 All ER 1033 (Lord Goff, Sir Brian Hutton and Sir Michael Hardie Boys, and Lord Steyn). Noted, [1996] Crim LR 433.

jury that this evidence was relevant to diminished responsibility but did not refer to it when dealing with provocation. D was convicted of murder. The Court of Appeal of Hong Kong dismissed D's appeal. The condition went to D's power of self-control, not to the gravity of the provocation. The Privy Council, Lord Steyn dissenting, dismissed D's appeal.

Against this view, there stood a series of Court of Appeal cases which took a more generous approach, accepting that the reasonable man might be endowed with the defendant's mental characteristics. In *Ahluwalia*[80] (where the appeal was allowed on the ground of fresh evidence of diminished responsibility) the court said, *obiter*, that post-traumatic stress disorder or battered woman syndrome might be a relevant characteristic for the purpose of the objective test in provocation. In *Dryden*[81] and in *Humphreys*[82] where the defence was provocation, the courts held that 'eccentric and obsessional personality traits', and abnormal immaturity and attention-seeking by wrist slashing were mental characteristics which ought to have been left specifically to the jury. These cases were disapproved by the majority in *Luc* but found favour with the dissentient Lord Steyn. After *Luc*, the Court of Appeal continued to adopt the broader approach.[83]

The resolution of the division of opinion came in the House of Lords in *Smith (Morgan)*.[84] The House held, Lords Hobhouse and Millett dissenting, that the jury may take into account, in addition to age and sex, other characteristics of the defendant which affect powers of self-control, whether or not they are also relevant to the gravity of the provocation. Smith and his friend, V, both alcoholics, had a petty row. Smith who was suffering from a serious clinical depression, took a kitchen knife and stabbed V to death. Pleas of no *mens rea*, diminished responsibility and provocation were all rejected by the jury. The majority of the House held that the jury ought to have been told that the question was whether the provocation was sufficient to make a man, suffering from that depression, lose his self-control. The same characteristic which is relevant to diminished responsibility is now relevant to provocation. However, where in diminished responsibility the onus of proof is on the defendant, in provocation it remains on the prosecution – a difficult, if not impossible, task for the jury and one which can hardly have been intended by the authors of the Homicide Act 1957, ss 2 and 3. The overlap with s 2 is considered further in the next part of this chapter.[85]

Notwithstanding the clear words of s 3 of that Act, the reasonable man seems to have been virtually eliminated from the law. According to Lord Hoffmann,[86] the judge should:

[80] [1992] 4 All ER 889. See also *Thornton (No 2)* [1996] 2 Cr App R 108, [1996] Crim LR 597.

[81] [1995] 4 All ER 987.

[82] [1995] 4 All ER 1008.

[83] In *Parker* [1997] Crim LR 760 and *Cambell (No 2)* [1997] Crim LR 227.

[84] [2000] 4 All ER 289, [2000] Crim LR 1004, HL. For critical comment see, *inter alia*, T. Macklem and J. Gardner, 'Compassion without Respect: Nine Fallacies in *R v Smith*' [2001] Crim LR 623; Provocation and Pluralism' [2001] MLR 815.

[85] On the merits of such overlap and a potential merging of the defences, see R. Mackay and B. Mitchell, 'Provoking Diminished Responsibility: Two Pleas Merging into One?' [2003] Crim LR 745; J. Chalmers, 'Merging Provocation and Diminished Responsibility: Some Reasons for Scepticism' [2004] Crim LR 198; J. Gardner and T. Macklem, 'No Provocation Without Responsibility: A Reply to Mackay and Mitchell' [2004] Crim LR 213; R. Mackay and B. Mitchell, 'Replacing Provocation: More on a Combined Plea' [2004] Crim LR 219.

[86] [2000] 4 All ER para 10. For support for this approach see J. Stannard, 'Towards a Normative Defence of Provocation in England and Ireland' (2002) J Crim L 528.

be able simply to tell the jury that the question of whether [D's] behaviour fell below the standard which should reasonably have been expected of him was entirely a matter for them.

This appears to throw out the whole of the previous law relating to provocation.[87] Moreover, Lord Hoffmann continued:

[the judge] should not be obliged to let the jury imagine that the law now regards anything whatever which caused loss of self-control (whether an external event or a personal characteristic of the accused) as necessarily being an acceptable reason for loss of self-control.

He had already asserted that 'male possessiveness and jealousy should not today be an acceptable reason'.[88] 'A tendency to violent rages or childish tantrums is a defect in character rather than an excuse'. But a tendency to violent rages seems to have been exactly what Smith was afflicted with.[89] If this was an encouragement to judges to begin to assert what is and what is not 'acceptable', even if they cannot require juries to obey their instructions, it would lead to the redevelopment of law, such as that which Parliament abolished in 1957, to replace the reasonable man. The decision destroys the objective criterion inserted by Parliament to provide a benchmark against which the defendant's failure to exercise control could be judged.

Smith should not be heralded as a great step forward in removing the gender discrimination in the operation of the defence. By relaxing the objective criterion it will more readily allow for the mental characteristics resulting from physical and emotional abuse to be considered by the jury. This is a positive consequence for victims of domestic abuse who kill. However, the relaxation applies equally to the mental characteristics often found in domestic abusers who kill – obsessiveness and jealousy, and it seems from the post-*Smith* cases that the courts have abandoned efforts to keep such characteristics out of the jury's evaluation of the accused's response to the provocation.[90]

Post–Smith developments.[91] *Smith* has the potential to create great confusion for the lower courts in applying the defence. Trial judges are faced with the prospect of directing juries with practically no guidance as to which characteristics, if any, ought not to be drawn to the attention of the jury. A practice very soon developed of judges discussing the proposed direction with counsel, and this approach has been approved by the Court of Appeal.[92]

As for which characteristics the judge ought not to leave for the jury to consider in evaluating whether the ordinary person in D's position would have responded as he did, the Court of Appeal initially adopted an approach of 'anything goes'. In *Weller*[93] it

87 The fact that the minority thought the decision of the majority inconsistent with the recent decision of the House in *Morhall* could have interesting repercussions. The Privy Council will have to face this problem in *Holley v A-G for Jersey* to be heard in Mar 2005.

88 At 309, approving of *Stingel* (1990) 171 CLR 312 where the High Court of Australia withdrew that issue from the jury – a power which the English court lacks.

89 For a view that the question is now one involving the psychology of D, not the moral judgment of the objective test, see Norrie, above.

90 See Part 2 of Law Com Paper No 173, especially paras 21–22.

91 In the subsequent Privy Council Case of *Paria*, the Board declined to choose between the approaches in *Luc* and *Smith*. The Privy Council is soon to hear an appeal which may force a choice between the decision in *Smith* and *Morhall: Holley v A-G for Jersey* [2001] JLR 606 is set for argument in March.

92 *Lowe* [2003] EWCA Crim 677.

93 [2004] 1 Cr App R 1; see also *R (Farnell) v CCRC* [2003] EWHC 835.

was held that the trial judge's failure to direct the jury to consider W's 'unduly possessive and jealous nature' did not render the conviction for murder unsafe provided the characteristics were not specifically removed from the jury's consideration. The trial judge had directed simply that the jury should consider 'what society expects of a man like this defendant in his position'. The Court of Appeal suggested that the:

'question whether the defendant should reasonably have controlled himself is to be answered by the jury taking *all matters* into account. That includes matters relating to the defendant, the kind of man he is and his mental state, as well as the circumstances in which the death occurred. The judge should not tell the jury that they should, as a matter of law, ignore any aspect. He may give them some guidance as to the weight to be given to some aspects, provided he makes it clear that the question is one which, as the law provides, they are to answer, and not him' (emphasis added).

This creates, Professor Ashworth noted, an 'evaluative free for all.'[94] In *Rowland*[95] the Court of Appeal referred to *Weller*[96] and the anxiety about the apparently unlimited characteristics that could now be considered by the jury. The court recognized that the 'reasonable man' was now to be regarded as 'an archetype best left lurking in the statutory undergrowth'.[97] The court endorsed the Judicial Studies Board specimen direction, accepting that:

there may be difficult borderline cases, particularly as between mere bad temper or excitability on the one hand and identifiable mental conditions and personality traits on the other. In such cases, after prior discussion with counsel, the trial judge should be careful to include all potentially relevant factors at the appropriate point in his summing-up to the jury.

The relevant paragraph of the JSB direction endorsed by the court in *Rowland* provides:

It is then for you [the jury] to decide whether or not D's loss of self-control was sufficiently excusable to reduce the gravity of the offence from murder to manslaughter. When deciding this, bear in mind that the law expects people to exercise control over their emotions. If a person has an unusually volatile, excitable or violent nature he cannot rely on that as an excuse. Otherwise, however, it is entirely for you, as representatives of the community, to decide what are appropriate standards of behaviour, what degree of control society could reasonably have expected of D, and what is the just outcome of this case. You should make allowances for human nature and the power of emotions. You should also take into account [here deal with any characteristics of D which may have a bearing on the issue].

In some cases it will be unnecessary to draw any specific characteristics to the jury's attention since the accused will be an 'ordinary' person.[98] In many instances it will be sufficient for the judge simply to instruct the jury to consider an ordinary person 'in [D's] shoes', or 'in [D's] position'.[99] Following *Rowland* the trial judge at least has some guidance, but the principled criticisms levelled at the majority's decision in *Smith* remain as cogent as ever. The objective check designed by Parliament has been completely undermined and juries are left to apply their own moral judgements on whether the particular defendant's conduct was excusable. The increased risks of inconsistency and arbitrariness are obvious.

94 Commenting at [2003] Crim LR 724.
95 [2003] EWCA Crim 3636.
96 [2003] EWCA Crim 815.
97 Para 41.
98 *Christie* [2004] EWCA Crim 1338.
99 *Keaveney* [2004] EWCA Crim 1091.

Intoxication as a characteristic. D's intoxication may be one reason why he lost his self-control but it seems still to be universally agreed that voluntary intoxication must be ignored in applying the objective test. This is one reason for loss of self-control which is certainly not 'acceptable'. Post-*Smith* case law seems to support this position. In *Keaveney*,[100] K had taken methadone and Temazepam before fatally stabbing her allegedly abusive partner. The Court of Appeal upheld her murder conviction, acknowledging that it was not suggested that K's drug problems or her intoxication at the time could have been relevant characteristics. Similarly, in *Rowland*, 'it was stated that self-induced intoxication is no excuse. . . . there was no intention on the part of any of their Lordships in *Smith (Morgan)* to alter the position as expressed in *McCarthy*[101] and *Morhall*'.[102]

Morhall establishes that D's alcoholism may be relevant to the gravity of the provocation if he is taunted with his affliction; but the jury must be directed to consider the effect of this provocation on a sober alcoholic. Suppose that D, an alcoholic, is taunted by V with his addiction and instantly responds with a fatal blow. However drunk D may have been at the time, the jury must be instructed to consider the effect of the taunts on an alcoholic of (if relevant) D's age, sex, etc, who, at the time, is sober. Similarly with a drug addict, 'high' on drugs; the question is whether a drug addict, for the time being free of the effect of the drugs, would have reacted as D did. Suppose that V taunts D, a prominent member of a temperance society, with being 'pissed as a newt' and threatens to report him to his brethren. This is obviously provocative – and the more so if D is indeed in the condition described. If to be taunted with being an alcoholic is relevant, so, surely, is this. It seems that the jury must be told to consider the effect of the provocation on a tipsy temperance society member, displaying the self-control to be expected of a sober person who is otherwise in D's position.

In *McCarthy*[103] the New Zealand Court of Appeal treated the effect of alcohol, 'being transitory and not a characteristic,' as a unique exception to the characteristics to be considered. In *Morhall* Lord Goff doubted whether the transitory nature of intoxication is the explanation for any special treatment which it receives, pointing out that a physical condition like eczema may be transitory but should be taken into account if the subject of taunts. Lord Goff suggests that intoxication is exceptional because it is the policy of the law that drunkenness should not be an excuse of crime. While this is certainly a factor in the decisions, there may also be a distinction in principle. Alcohol tends to reduce inhibitions and restraints and to make a person more volatile when drunk than when sober, whatever the nature of the provocation. Lord Goff observes that a physical condition such as eczema can surely be taken into consideration if it is the subject of taunts. But let it be supposed that the irritation caused by eczema results in general irascibility in the sufferer; and that on being taunted with the dismal performance of the football club of which he is a fanatical supporter he kills his tormentor. Under *Morhall* principles, his affliction could not be taken into account in applying the objective test. The taunts are no more provocative to the eczema sufferer than to the equally ardent fan who has a perfect skin. But, according to *Smith*, the condition will now be relevant for this purpose also. If we have to distinguish between acceptable and unacceptable reasons for loss of

100 [2004] EWCA Crim 1091, [2004] All ER (D) 204 (Apr).

101 [1954] 2 QB 105.

102 [1996] AC 90.

103 [1992] 2 NZLR 550 at 558.

self-control, (although the Court of Appeal seems now to avoid any such line drawing) eczema must be on the acceptable side.

The relationship between the provocation and the mode of resentment

In *Mancini v DPP*[104] D was charged with the murder of V who had been stabbed to death by an instrument with a two-edged blade, a sharp point and sharp sides, at least five inches long. D's story was that V was attacking him with an open pen-knife and MacNaughten J told the jury that, if they believed this story, they should return a verdict of not guilty (on the ground of self-defence.) He did not direct them that, if they rejected the defence of self-defence, they still might find D guilty of manslaughter on the ground of provocation. D appealed on the ground that he ought to have done so. His conviction was affirmed. By their verdict, the jury had rejected his story of the attack with the pen-knife; and the case had, therefore, to be treated as one in which, at the most, V made an unarmed attack on D. If there had been evidence of provocation, it would have been the judge's duty to direct the jury on it, even though the defence had not been argued;[105] but here there was no evidence. An attack by hand or fist 'would not constitute provocation of a kind which could extenuate the sudden introduction and use of a lethal weapon like this dagger, and there was, therefore, ... no adequate material to raise the issue of provocation'.[106]

The House stated the law in general terms as follows:[107]

> ... it is of particular importance ... to take into account the instrument with which the homicide was effected, for to retort, in the heat of passion induced by provocation, by a simple blow, is a very different thing from making use of a deadly instrument like a concealed dagger. In short, the mode of resentment must bear a reasonable relationship to the provocation if the offence is to be reduced to manslaughter.

Clearly such a case could not be decided in this way today. If there was evidence that D was provoked to lose his self-control, the judge could not decline to leave the defence to the jury because the resentment did not bear a reasonable relationship to the provocation. It was in this respect, no doubt, that Lord Diplock in *Camplin* said that *Mancini* is no longer to be treated as an authority on the law of provocation.[108] It would now be wrong to tell the jury, 'fists might be answered with fists but not with a deadly weapon',[109] because if fists were answered with a deadly weapon, such a direction would take out of the jury's hands a question which is exclusively for them and on which their opinion is decisive. So it has been said that the 'reasonable relationship rule' is not a rule of law and that it is wrong for the judge, who has directed them on the subjective and objective conditions, to go on to tell them that there is a third condition, viz that the retaliation must be proportionate to the provocation.[110] Yet in a sense, the reasonable relationship

104 [1942] AC 1, [1941] 3 All ER 272, HL.

105 Above, p 444.

106 [1942] AC at 10, [1941] 3 All ER at 278.

107 [1942] AC at 9, [1941] 3 All ER at 277, per Lord Simon.

108 (1977) 67 Cr App R at 21. See commentary on *Brown* [1972] Crim LR 506.

109 Per Devlin in *Duffy* [1949] 1 All ER 932n.

110 *Brown* [1972] 2 QB 229, [1972] 2 All ER 1328. For discussion see S. Gough, 'Taking the Heat Out of Provocation' (1999) 19 OJLS 481. On the particular problem regarding the proportionality of killing in response to an unsolicited homosexual advance (the Portsmouth defence) see S. Oliver, 'Provocation and Non-violent Homosexual Advances' (1999) J Crim L 586.

rule still is a rule of law because the defence is made out only if the provocation was enough to make the reasonable man 'do as he did'. Thus, it would be right for the judge to direct the jury: 'If you are satisfied that a reasonable man, though he might have answered with fists, would not have answered with the deadly weapon used by D, then you *must* reject the defence of provocation.' This is no more than the application of the words of the section to the facts. The difference, since the Act, is that it is for the jury, not the judge, to decide whether the answer with a deadly weapon was the act of a reasonable man.

It will be noted that, under s 3 of the Homicide Act, the subjective and objective tests differ. The questions are: (i) did D *lose his self-control?* and (ii) was the provocation enough to make the ordinary person in D's shoes *do as D did?* It can hardly have been intended, however, that the jury should consider whether a reasonable man in full control of himself would have done what D did for the logical effect of that would be to eliminate the defence from the law. The objective test must be construed as it was in *Phillips v R*:[111]

> ... the question ... is not merely whether in their opinion the provocation would have made a reasonable man lose his self-control but also whether, having lost his self-control, he would have retaliated in the same way as the person charged in fact did.

This assumed that a person who has lost his self-control acts with more or less ferocity according to the degree of provocation which caused the loss of self-control. The Privy Council has rejected the argument:

> ... that loss of self-control is not a matter of degree but is absolute; there is no intermediate stage between icy detachment and going berserk. This premise, unless the argument is purely semantic, must be based upon human experience and is, in their Lordships' view, false. The average man reacts to provocation according to its degree with angry words, with a blow of the hand, possibly, if the provocation is gross and there is a dangerous weapon to hand, with that weapon.[112]

Whatever scientific opinion may be,[113] this certainly seems to be the view of human conduct on which the section is based; and the objective condition requires affirmative answers to two questions: (i) would the ordinary person in D's position have lost his self-control? and (ii) would he then have retaliated as D did?

Provocation arising from a mistake of fact

The authorities suggest that, where D is provoked partly as the result of a mistake of fact he is entitled to be treated as if the facts were as he mistakenly supposed them to be. This line of reasoning accords with the approach to other defences. The view seems to be further reinforced by the decisions in *B (A Child)* and *K*,[114] confirming the subjective nature of mistake.

In *Brown*[115] D, a soldier, wrongly, but apparently reasonably, supposed that V was a member of a gang who were attacking him and his comrade. He struck V with a sword and killed him. The judges were clearly of the opinion that this was only manslaughter. In the other cases the mistake arose from drunkenness. In *Letenock*[116] the Court of Criminal Appeal substituted a verdict of manslaughter in the case of a solider who had stabbed

111 [1969] 2 AC 130 at 137, PC.

112 Ibid, 137. See White, 'A Note on Provocation' [1970] Crim LR 446.

113 P. Brett, 'The Physiology of Provocation' [1970] Crim LR 634.

114 See above, p 125.

115 (1776) 1 Leach 148.

116 (1917) 12 Cr App R 221, CCA. Cf p 283, above.

a corporal, where the 'only element of doubt in the case is whether or not there was anything which might have caused the applicant, *in his drunken condition*, to believe that he was going to be struck'.[117]

This decision is unaffected by *McCarthy*[118] which was not concerned with a mistake of fact but with the effect of the alcohol on D's self-restraint.

It is established that a drunken mistake may negative the *mens rea* of murder[119] and it is consistent that such a mistake should be relevant in determining whether the killing should be reduced to manslaughter on the ground of provocation. A drunken mistake is almost inevitably an unreasonable one; and it seems clear that it is immaterial whether the mistake is reasonable or not for this purpose. The jury must look at the reactions of the sober reasonable person in the circumstances which the drunken one supposed to exist.

Self-induced provocation

The jury must be told to take into account everything both done and said according to the effect which, in their opinion, it would have on a reasonable man, even where that which was done and said was a predictable result of D's own conduct. It was so held in *Johnson*,[120] not following *dicta* of the Privy Council in *Edwards v R.*[121] D's unpleasant behaviour in a nightclub resulted in an attack on him in response to which he killed. He was not precluded from relying on provocation even if the attack was a predictable result of his behaviour. This might be regarded as a generous approach to the defendant.

It has been suggested[122] that such a decision might open a defence for one who *deliberately* induces provocation – D provokes V to do a provocative act so that D may kill him and rely on the defence of provocation. Such a situation seems far-fetched. If it did occur, it should, it is submitted, be decided on the same lines as *Attorney-General for Northern Ireland v Gallagher*[123] – D should be held liable for the acts which, when unprovoked, he intended to do under provocation. The judge should find there is no evidence that D was provoked.

Provocation by a lawful act

It has been argued that, 'The law would be self-contradictory if a lawful act could amount to provocation',[124] but it is submitted that this proposition will not bear examination.[125] To taunt a man with his impotence or his wife's adultery may be cruel and immoral, but it is not unlawful and it may, surely, amount to provocation. So, we now know, may the crying of a baby.[126] Where V's act is one which he is not merely at liberty to do but which is positively praiseworthy, it is scarcely conceivable that a jury would find that it would provoke a reasonable man to lose his self-control; but under the terms of s 3 it must be a question for the jury in each case. It is impossible, as a matter of law, to divide acts which V is at liberty to do into classes of 'good' and 'bad'.

117 Ibid, at 224.

118 [1954] 2 QB 105, [1954] 2 All ER 262.

119 Above, p 279.

120 [1989] Crim LR 738.

121 [1973] AC 648, [1973] 1 All ER 152, PC.

122 By A. Ashworth [1973] Crim LR 483.

123 Above, p 284.

124 S. Howard, *Australian Criminal Law* (2nd edn) at 93.

125 See *Browne* [1973] NI 96 at 108, per Lowry LCJ: 'I should prefer to say that provocation is something *unwarranted* which is likely to make a reasonable man angry or indignant'.

126 *Doughty* (1986) 83 Cr App R 319, above, p 444.

(iv) Reform

There is considerable confusion as to the scope of the present law and the reform options. It remains unclear in theoretical terms whether the defence is properly regarded as one of partial justification (D has gone beyond what would be an acceptable response to the provoking conduct, or that the deceased deserved it) or of partial excuse (D's loss of self control is uncharacteristic, the bad character exhibited exceeds that to be expected in the circumstances).[127] In practical terms, when applying the defence courts have faced increasing difficulty with each of its elements, and the House of Lords has been radical in reinterpreting the terms of the statute in an attempt to do justice in hard cases made harder still by the mandatory sentence for murder. As for reform, key issues of principle remain unresolved, including whether it is even necessary or desirable to retain the defence if the mandatory sentence were to be abolished.[128] Is the purpose of the defence to unshackle the judge from imposing the mandatory sentence?[129] Is the purpose to label distinctly those killers whose conduct might be regarded as morally different, despite their malice aforethought, owing to some mitigating feature of the killing? The unique stigmas and heightened emotions aroused by the stark fact of death generate strong views on these issues. Many other jurisdictions have faced similar difficulties with the defence and reform proposals have been widely canvassed.[130]

Battered woman syndrome[131]

One of the most compelling influences for reform has been the realization that the defence operates in a discriminatory fashion, which is hardly surprising given its historical origins.[132] Women who kill abusive partners are disadvantaged if they do not act in a state which can legally be described as one of 'sudden and temporary loss of control'. In addition, until relatively recently, the cumulative effect of years of abuse was not considered. Further, until *Smith (Morgan)* the mental characteristics arising from an abusive relationship (including what has become recognized as Battered Woman Syndrome)[133] could only be taken into account if relevant to the gravity of the provocation, but not D's ability to exercise self control. The abused woman is unlikely as a matter of

[127] J. Horder, above, chs 6–9, in particular at 130–135. See further, J. Dressler, 'Provocation: Partial Justification or Partial Excuse' (1988) 51 MLR 467; F. McAuley, 'Anticipating the Past: The Defences of Provocation in Irish Law' (1987) 50 MLR 133; V. Tadros, 'The Characters of Excuses' (2001) 21 OJLS 495. See also the discussion in the Law Commission's Report No 290, para 3.22 et seq and the Irish Law Reform Commission, LRC Consultation Paper No 27, *Homicide: The Plea of Provocation* (2003).

[128] See Law Commission Report No 290, ch 2 and para 3.35 et seq and the responses discussed to the Consultation Paper No 173. Horder considers the arguments for abolition in ch 9, above.

[129] See C. Wells, 'The Death Penalty for Provocation' [1978] Crim LR 662.

[130] See eg, New South Wales Law Reform Commission, *Partial Defences to Murder: Provocation and Infanticide* (1997) No 83; Irish Law Reform Commission, LRC Consultation Paper No 27 (2003), above and Law Commission Paper No 173 for a valuable summary of the position in a number of jurisdictions. For comparative material generally see S. Yeo, *Unrestrained Killings and the Law: Provocation and Excessive Self Defence in India, England and Australia* (1998). See the latest proposals in New South Wales, 'Law Reform Defences to Murder' [2005] Crim LR 256.

[131] S. Edwards, *Sex and Gender in the Legal Process* (1996), ch 6; K. O'Donovan, 'Defences for Battered Women Who Kill' (1991) 18 J Law and Soc 219; C. Wells, 'Battered Women's Syndrome, and Defences to Homicide: Where Now?' (1994) LS 266; A. McColgan, 'In Defence of Battered Women who Kill' (1993) J Law and Soc 508. For a valuable summary see Law Com Consultation Paper No 173, ch 10.

[132] See Horder, above.

[133] See L. Walker, *Battered Women Syndrome* (1st edn, 1984); (2nd edn, 2000).

fact, to kill in self-defence (as that term is understood in law). Owing to relative limited physical strength, it is uncommon for women to respond lethally when facing an immediate attack by an abusive male partner.[134] Women are therefore forced to rely on the defence of diminished responsibility, which aside from requiring expert evidence and imposing a burden of proof on the accused, stigmatizes them. Not surprisingly this has led many to call for the abolition of the defence of provocation and wholesale review of the partial defences to murder.[135]

Adopting a more subjective test

There have been recommendations for the defence to be put on an excusatory basis, focused on the more subjective question of D's loss of control. The CLRC recommended that the question for the jury should be whether, on the facts as they appeared to the defendant, the provocation can reasonably be regarded as a sufficient ground for the loss of self-control leading the defendant to react against the victim with murderous intent,[136] and that, in answering this question, the defendant should be judged with due regard to all the circumstances, including any disability, physical or mental, from which he suffered.[137] This proposal would remove the objective test and, with it, much unnecessary technicality from the law. It is close to the opinion of the majority in the House of Lords in *Smith (Morgan)* with the vital difference that it assumes the abolition of s 3 of the Homicide Act and all the baggage which goes with it.

Extreme emotional disturbance defences

A second alternative, considered recently by the Law Commission and again reflecting the shift in *Smith* towards a broad excusatory defence, would be to adopt a defence similar to that in the US Model Penal Code, s 210(3)(1)(b). This defence merges diminished responsibility and provocation and also accommodates other defendants who kill in circumstances of extreme emotional pressure. It provides that a 'homicide which would otherwise be murder [is manslaughter when it] is committed under the influence of extreme mental or emotional disturbance for which there is reasonable explanation or excuse. The reasonableness of such explanation or excuse shall be determined from the viewpoint of a person in the actor's situation under the circumstances as he believes them to be'.[138] The defence has not been universally welcomed in the USA[139] and has been cogently criticized by academics.[140]

134 On the availability of the defence see A. McColgan, 'In Defence of Battered Women who Kill' (1993) OJLS 508, C. Wells, 'Where Now' above, J. Dressler, 'Battered Women Who Kill Their Sleeping Tormentors' and J. Horder, 'Killing the Passive Abuser: A Theoretical Defence' both in S. Shute and A. Simester (eds), *Criminal Law Theory* (2002).

135 See C. Wells, 'Provocation the Case for Abolition' in A. Ashworth and B. Mitchell (eds), *Rethinking English Homicide Law* (2000).

136 CLRC/OAP/R, para 81.

137 Ibid, para 83.

138 For further consideration see R. D. Mackay and B. Mitchell, 'Provoking Diminished Responsibility: The Two Pleas Merging into One' [2003] Crim LR 745; 'Replacing Provocation: More on A Combined Plea' [2004] Crim LR 219.

139 See the report of Professor Kadish published as an Appendix to the Law Commission Report No 290 (2004); and J. Chalmers, 'Merging Provocation and Diminished Responsibility: Some Reasons for Scepticism' [2004] Crim LR 198.

140 See J. Gardner and T. Macklem, 'No Provocation without Responsibility: A Reply to Mackay and Mitchell' [2004] Crim LR 213.

The Law Commission's latest proposals

The Law Commission's most recent proposals were drafted against a reform agenda dealing not just with provocation but with partial defences to murder more generally.[141] The final proposals represent a radical shift away from the decision in *Smith* to a defence which also incorporates a partial defence to murder for excessive self-defence.[142] The trial judge would regain a power to remove the defence from the jury if no reasonable jury properly directed could conclude that the conduct was provocative: the crying of a baby would not trigger the defence, nor would the innocent conduct of a black man which angers a racist.

The proposal is in short:

(1) Unlawful homicide that would otherwise be murder should instead be manslaughter if the defendant acted in response to:

  (a) gross provocation (meaning words or conduct or a combination of words and conduct which caused the defendant to have a justifiable sense of being seriously wronged); or

  (b) fear of serious violence towards the defendant or another; or

  (c) combination of (a) and (b).

(2) A person of the defendant's age and of ordinary temperament, that is, ordinary tolerance and self-restraint, in the circumstances of the defendant might have reacted in the same or a similar way.

(3) In deciding whether a person of ordinary temperament in the circumstances of the defendant might have acted in the same or a similar way, the court should take into account the defendant's age and all the circumstances of the defendant other than matters whose only relevance to the defendant's conduct is that they bear simply on his or her general capacity for self-control.

(3) The partial defence should not apply where:

  (a) the provocation was incited by the defendant for the purpose of providing an excuse to use violence, or

  (b) the defendant acted in considered desire for revenge.

(4) A person should not be treated as having acted in considered desire for revenge if he or she acted in fear of serious violence merely because he or she was also angry towards the deceased for the conduct which engendered that fear.

(5) The partial defence should not apply to a defendant who kills or takes part in the killing of another person under duress of threats by a third person.

(6) A judge should not be required to leave the defence to the jury unless there is evidence on which a reasonable jury, properly directed, could conclude that it might apply.

141 See Law Comm Consultation Paper No 173 (2003).

142 For criticism see R. D. Mackay and B. Mitchell, 'But is this Provocation? Some Thoughts on Law Commission Report No 290' [2005] Crim LR 44.

(b) Diminished responsibility[143]

The Homicide Act 1957, s 2, introduced into law a new defence to murder, known as 'diminished responsibility', which entitles the accused not to be acquitted altogether, but to be found guilty only of manslaughter.[144] By s 2(2) the Act expressly puts the burden of proof on the defendant and it has been held that, as in the case of insanity, the standard of proof required is not beyond reasonable doubt but on a balance of probabilities.[145] It is not a general defence, but applies only to murder. It is not available as a defence to attempted murder,[146] nor can it be raised on a finding of unfitness to plead.[147] Most defendants would prefer a conviction for manslaughter on the ground of diminished responsibility to an acquittal by reason of insanity, so the importance of the M'Naghten Rules has been greatly reduced since 1957 (see Ch 11 above).

Professor Mackay conducted empirical research for the Law Commission[148] in which of the 157 cases studied, the prosecution accepted a diminished responsibility plea in 77.1% of cases.[149] Statistics reveal that in 2001/2002 for the first time the total number of successful diminished responsibility pleas fell below 20 (the figure for 2000/2001).[150] In 2001/2002 there were 15 successful pleas. The same table also shows that for 2002/2003 the number of convictions for manslaughter under s 2 of the Homicide Act 1957 was as low as five.[151]

(i) Procedural relationship with insanity

Where D, being charged with murder, raises the defence of diminished responsibility and the Crown have evidence that he is insane within the M'Naghten Rules, they may adduce or elicit evidence tending to show that this is so. This is now settled by the 1964 Criminal Procedure (Insanity and Unfitness To Plead) Act, s 6 – resolving a conflict in the cases.

143 R. D. Mackay, 'Diminished Responsibility and Mentally Disordered Killers', in A. Ashworth and B. Mitchell (eds), *Rethinking English Homicide Law* (2000); E. Tennant, *The Future of the Diminished Responsibility Defence to Murder*' (2001); S. Dell, *Murder into Manslaughter: the Diminished Responsibility Defence in Practice* (1984); G. Williams, 'Diminished Responsibility' (1960–1961) 1 Med Sci & L 41; B. Wootton, 'Diminished Responsibility – A Layman's View' (1960) 76 LQR 224; R. Sparks, 'Diminished Responsibility in Theory and Practice' (1964) 27 MLR 9; N. Walker, *Crime and Insanity in England* (1968) 138–164; E. J. Griew, 'The Future of Diminished Responsibility' [1988] Crim LR 75.

144 The defence is borrowed from the law of Scotland, where it was a judicial creation, originating in the decision of Lord Deas in *HM Advocate v Dingwall* (1867) 5 Irv 466. See T. B. Smith, 'Diminished Responsibility' [1957] Crim LR 354 and Lord Keith, 'Some Observations on Diminished Responsibility' [1959] Jur Rev 109. The Scots version has recently been redefined in *Galbraith v HM Advocate (No 2)* 2002 JC 1. The Scottish Law Commission has proposed putting the definition from that case on a statutory footing. See Law Comm Report No 195, *Insanity and Diminished Responsibility* (2004). Available from www.scotlawcom.gov.uk/downloads/nr_insanity_report.195.pdf.

145 *Dunbar* [1958] 1 QB 1, [1957] 2 All ER 737. This rule is not affected by the Human Rights Act 1998: *Ali and Jordan* [2001] 1 All ER 1014, CA. Where the medical evidence of diminished responsibility is based on certain facts, it is for the defence to prove those facts by admissible evidence: *Ahmed Din* (1962) 46 Cr App R 269; *Bradshaw* (1985) 82 Cr App R 79, [1985] Crim LR 733 and commentary.

146 *Campbell* [1997] Crim LR 495, Sedley J.

147 *Antoine* [2001] AC 340.

148 Law Comm Report No 290.

149 Para 5.34. available from www.lawcom.gov.uk/files/lc290.pdf.

150 Home Office Statistical Bulletin 01/04 cited in the Sentencing Advisory Panel Consultation Paper, Sentencing of Manslaughter by Reason of Provocation, 11 Mar 2004. Available from http://cjsonline.org.uk/library/word/Manslaughter_ConsultationPaper.doc.

151 See Law Comm Report No 290, *Partial Defences to Murder* (2004). See above for web address.

The Act also provides for the converse situation. Where D sets up insanity, the prosecution may contend that he was suffering only from diminished responsibility.[152] The roles of the prosecution and defence may be strangely reversed, according to which of them is contending that the defendant is insane. It seems clear in principle that the Crown must establish whichever contention it puts forward beyond reasonable doubt.[153] It must follow that D rebuts the Crown's case if he can raise a doubt. Where D relies on some other defence, such as provocation, and evidence of diminished responsibility emerges, it seems that the most the judge should do is to draw the attention of D's counsel to it.[154] Diminished responsibility is an 'optional defence'. Since the excessively broad interpretation of provocation adopted in *Morgan Smith* (discussed above), the defences of provocation and diminished responsibility overlap to a significant extent.[155] This could lead to a complex decision regarding trial tactics since the defences carry differing burdens. Similarly a jury will have to be directed carefully on the respective burdens.

The Act does not deal with the situation where D's abnormality of mind is put in issue otherwise than by pleading insanity or diminished responsibility – for example, by raising the defence of automatism. However, the CLRC[156] did not think that the limited provision in the Act should throw any doubt on the right of the prosecution to call evidence in cases such as *Kemp*.[157] The prosecution may not, however, lead evidence of D's insanity where the defence have not put the abnormality of D's mind in issue,[158] even though this course is desired by the defence. The position would seem to be that, where the defence rely on the abnormality of mind of any kind, it is open to the prosecution to allege, and to call evidence to prove, that the abnormality amounts to insanity or diminished responsibility. The prosecution should supply the defence with a copy of any statement or report which a prison medical officer may have made on that crime and should make him available as a defence witness.[159]

(ii) The nature of the defence

The Homicide Act 1957, s 2, enacts:

> (1) Where a person kills or is a party to the killing of another, he shall not be convicted of murder if he was suffering from such abnormality of mind (whether arising from a condition of arrested or retarded development of mind or any inherent causes or induced by disease or injury) as substantially impaired his mental responsibility for his acts and omissions in doing or being a party to the killing.
>
> (2) . . .

152 It had been so held at common law by Elwes J in *Nott* (1958) 43 Cr App R 8.

153 *Grant* [1960] Crim LR 424, per Paull J.

154 *Campbell* (1986) 84 Cr App R 255 at 259–260; *Kooken* (1981) 74 Cr App R 30.

155 On the merits of such overlap and a potential merging of the defences, see R. Mackay and B. Mitchell, 'Provoking Diminished Responsibility: Two Pleas Merging into One?' [2003] Crim LR 745; J. Chalmers, 'Merging Provocation and Diminished Responsibility: Some Reasons for Scepticism' [2004] Crim LR 198; J. Gardner and T. Macklem, 'No Provocation Without Responsibility: A Reply to Mackay and Mitchell' [2004] Crim LR 213; R. Mackay and B. Mitchell, 'Replacing Provocation: More on a Combined Plea' [2004] Crim LR 219.

156 Cmnd 2149, para 41.

157 Above, p 259.

158 *Dixon* [1961] 3 All ER 460n, [1961] 1 WLR 337, per Jones J.

159 *Casey* (1947) 32 Cr App R 91, CCA. See A. Samuels, 'Can the Prosecution allege that the Accused is Insane?' [1960] Crim LR 453, [1961] Crim LR 308.

(3) A person who but for this section would be liable, whether as principal or as accessory, to be convicted of murder shall be liable instead to be convicted of manslaughter.

In early cases where the defence was raised, it was held that it was the duty of the judge, in summing up, simply to read the section to the jury and invite them to apply the tests stated therein without further explanation; it was not for the judge to re-define the definition which had been laid down by Parliament.[160] However, it is now clear that it is the duty of the judge to direct the jury as to the meaning to be attached to s 2.

Abnormality of mind[161]

In *Byrne*[162] the trial judge directed the jury as to the meaning of s 2, telling them that difficulty or even inability of an accused person to exercise will-power to control his physical acts could not amount to such abnormality of mind as substantially impaired his mental responsibilities. The Court of Criminal Appeal held that this was a wrong direction and that Byrne's conviction of murder must be quashed. Subsequently in *Terry*[163] the court expressly stated that:

> . . . in the light of [the interpretation that this court put on the section in *Byrne*] it seems to this court that it would no longer be proper merely to put the section before the jury but that a proper explanation of the terms of the section as interpreted in *Byrne* ought to be put before the jury.[164]

The facts of *Byrne* were that D strangled a young woman in a YWCA hostel and, after her death, committed horrifying mutilations on her body. Evidence was tendered to the effect that D, from an early age, had been subject to perverted violent desires; that the impulse or urge of those desires was stronger than the normal impulse or urge of sex, that D found it very difficult or, perhaps, impossible in some cases to resist putting the desire into practice and that the act of killing the girl was done under such an impulse or urge. The court held that it was wrong to say that these facts did not constitute evidence which would bring a case within the section. Lord Parker CJ said:[165]

> 'Abnormality of mind', which has to be contrasted with the time-honoured expression in the M'Naghten Rules, 'defect of reason', means a state of mind so different from that of ordinary human beings that the reasonable man would term it abnormal. It appears to us to be wide enough to cover the mind's activities in all its aspects, not only the perception of physical acts and matters and the ability to form a rational judgment whether an act is right or wrong, but also the ability to exercise will-power to control physical acts in accordance with that rational judgment.

Thus, the defence of irresistible impulse was at last admitted into the law (but only of murder) by way of diminished responsibility. The difficulties of proof, which deterred the judges from allowing the defence under the M'Naghten Rules, remain:

> . . . the step between 'he did not resist his impulse' and 'he could not resist his impulse' is, as the evidence in this case shows, one which is incapable of scientific proof. A fortiori, there is no scientific measurement of the degree of difficulty which an abnormal person finds in controlling his impulses.

160 See *Spriggs* [1958] 1 QB 270, [1958] 1 All ER 300.
161 See R. Mackay, 'The Abnormality of Mind Factor in Diminished Responsibility' [1999] Crim LR 117.
162 [1960] 2 QB 396, [1960] 3 All ER 1.
163 [1961] 2 QB 314, [1961] 2 All ER 569.
164 [1961] 2 All ER at 574.
165 [1960] 2 QB 396 at 403, [1960] 3 All ER 1 at 4.

The only way to deal with the problem is for the jury to approach it 'in a broad common-sense way'.[166] They are entitled to take into account not only the medical evidence but also the acts or statements of the accused and his demeanour and other relevant material. Even when they are satisfied that D was suffering from abnormality of mind there remains the question whether the abnormality was such as substantially to impair his mental responsibility – a question of degree and essentially one for the jury. The jury may address these questions in any order.[167]

It seems that the courts are complicit in the conspiracy with medical and legal practitioners to avoid defining any of the key terms with precision thereby allowing maximum flexibility in the defence so that it allows the broadest opportunity to avoid the mandatory sentence in deserving cases. The Law Commission has recently recommended defining abnormality of mind to mean whether the defendant's capacity to understand, judge and control himself was substantially impaired.[168]

Substantial impairment of mental responsibility

It is not necessary that the impulse on which D acted should be found by the jury to be *irresistible*; it is sufficient that the difficulty which D experienced in controlling it (or, rather, *failing* to control it) was *substantially* greater than would be experienced in like circumstances by an ordinary person, not suffering from mental abnormality.[169] The impairment need not be total, but it must be more than trivial or minimal.[170] Where a doctor testified that an epileptic defendant could be 'vulnerable to an impulsive tendency and therefore occasional impulsive acts', it was held that there was no evidence of diminished responsibility because (*inter alia*) the witness had not said that the impulse would *substantially* impair responsibility.[171] The test appears to be one of moral responsibility. A person whose impulse is irresistible bears *no* moral responsibility for his act, for he has no choice; a person whose impulse is much more difficult to resist than that of an ordinary person bears a diminished degree of moral responsibility for his act. It is focus on morality that provides the opportunity to apply the defence in cases of mercy killing, etc. The Law Commission recently recommended replacing this aspect of the defence with an explicit test focused on whether D's substantially impaired capacity to understand, etc was a significant cause of the defendant's act in carrying out or taking part in the killing.[172]

Test not borderline insanity

The court has from time to time approved directions following those given in Scottish cases and which, in effect, tell the jury what must be proved is a mental state 'bordering on, though not amounting to insanity'[173] or 'not quite mad but a border-line case'.[174]

166 [1960] 2 QB at 404, [1960] 3 All ER 1 at 5, per Lord Parker CJ; *Walton v R* [1978] AC 788, [1978] 1 All ER 542, PC.

167 *Mitchell* [1995] Crim LR 506.

168 Following the recommendation of the New South Wales Law Reform Commission, Report No 83, *Partial Defences to Murder: Provocation and Infanticide* (1997). See now [2005] Crim LR 256.

169 *Byrne*, above; *Simcox* [1964] Crim LR 402; *Lloyd* [1967] 1 QB 175, [1966] 1 All ER 107n. But cf Sparks, above at 16–19.

170 *Lloyd* [1967] 1 QB 175, [1966] 1 All ER 107n.

171 *Campbell* (1986) 84 Cr App R 255 at 259.

172 Law Com No 290, para 5.95.

173 *HM Advocate v Braithwaite* 1945 JC 55, per Lord Cooper.

174 *Spriggs* [1958] 1 QB 270 at 276, [1958] 1 All ER 300 at 304, per Lord Goddard CJ.

Care must be taken in giving such a direction to avoid any suggestion that 'insanity' in this context bears the very narrow meaning of that form of insanity which is a defence under the M'Naghten Rules. If the word is used at all it must be used in 'its broad popular sense'.[175] A depressive illness may found diminished responsibility, although it is by no means on the borderline of insanity. To tell the jury in such a case that D must be on that border-line is a material misdirection.[176] In such a case, reference to insanity is best avoided altogether.

Under English law, persons who are actually insane in the 'broad popular sense' may well be outside the scope of the M'Naghten Rules and have to rely on diminished responsibility.

Role of experts

As with insanity,[177] the decision is to be made by the jury, not the medical experts. They may reject unanimous medical evidence that D is suffering from diminished responsibility if there is anything in the circumstances of the case to justify them in doing so.[178] There is no statutory requirement of medical evidence, such as is now a condition of an insanity verdict, but it has been held that the jury may not find that the defendant is suffering from diminished responsibility unless there is medical evidence of an abnormality arising from one of the causes specified in the parentheses in s 2(1) of the Act.[179] An abnormality arising from some other cause will not suffice. So the words 'disease' and 'injury' are important. Battered women's syndrome, having been included in 1992 in the standard British classification of mental diseases, is – and presumably always was, though not previously recognized as such – a relevant condition.[180] Alcoholism is enough if it injures the brain, causing gross impairment of judgement and emotional responses, or causes the drinking to be involuntary;[181] but the transient effect of alcohol or other drugs is not an 'injury' under the section.[182] Alcoholism only rarely falls within the defence since it must be at such a level that the defendant's brain has been injured by the repeated drinking such that the drinking was involuntary because the defendant lost the ability to resist the impulse to drink.

Medical evidence is 'a practical necessity if the defence is to begin to run at all'.[183] Where no medical evidence is called, there will always be the suspicion that medical opinion has been sought and found unfavourable. It was recognized by the Law Commission that the psychiatric experts were unhappy with the mismatch between law and medicine regarding these central elements of the defence on which they were called to testify.[184]

175 *Rose v R* [1961] AC 496, [1961] 1 All ER 859.

176 *Seers* (1984) 79 Cr App R 261, CA, following the remarks of the Privy Council in *Rose v R* [1961] AC 496, [1961] 1 All ER 859.

177 Above, p 258.

178 Eg *Salmon* [2005] EWCA Crim 70; *Eifinger* [2001] EWCA Crim 1855; cf the position if there is uncontradicted expert evidence and no other live issue: *Sanders* [1991] Crim LR 781.

179 Above, p 465. *Byrne* [1960] 2 QB 396 at 402; *Dix* (1981) 74 Cr App R 306 at 311.

180 *Hobson* [1998] 1 Cr App R 31.

181 *Tandy* (1987) 87 Cr App R 45. See G. R. Sullivan, 'Intoxicants and Diminished Responsibility' [1994] Crim LR 156; J. Tolmie, 'Alcoholism and Criminal Liability' (2001) MLR 688; F. Bowland, 'Intoxication and Criminal Liability' (1986) J Crim Law 100.

182 *O'Connell* [1997] Crim LR 683.

183 *Dix*, above, n 179, at 311.

184 Law Com No 290, para 5.29. See also A. Norrie, *Crime Reason and History* (2nd edn, 2000), ch 9, for a powerful critique of the conflict between the two discourses.

Disease or injury

It seems that 'disease or injury' probably refers to organic or physical injury or disease of the body, including the brain, and 'any inherent cause' covers functional mental illness.[185] The elements have never been satisfactorily defined and the Law Commission recently proposed substituting a test of 'underlying condition' in the sense of a recognized mental condition.

Intoxication and diminished responsibility

In cases where D's intoxication was one cause of the substantial impairment it had been held[186] that D could successfully rely on diminished responsibility only if he could satisfy the jury that the killing would still have occurred even if he had *not* taken the drink or drugs. This approach was rejected by the House of Lords in *Dietschmann*.[187] D killed the victim while he (D) was heavily intoxicated. He was also suffering from a mental abnormality which all the medical witnesses described as an adjustment disorder arising from a 'depressed grief reaction' to the death of his aunt with whom he had a close physical and emotional relationship. Lord Hutton stressed that this case did not involve alcohol dependence syndrome. As such, his Lordship was confident that:

> the meaning to be given to the subsection would appear on first consideration to be reasonably clear. . . . [I]f the defendant satisfies the jury that, notwithstanding the alcohol he had consumed and its effect on him, his abnormality of mind substantially impaired his mental responsibility for his acts in doing the killing, the jury should find him . . . guilty of manslaughter. I take this view because I think that in referring to substantial impairment of mental responsibility, the subsection does not require the abnormality of mind to be the sole cause of the defendant's acts in doing the killing. In my opinion, even if the defendant would not have killed if he had not taken drink, the causative effect of the drink does not necessarily prevent an abnormality of mind suffered by the defendant from substantially impairing his mental responsibility for his fatal acts.

Lord Hutton addressed the policy arguments against this interpretation, and concluded that a brain-damaged person who is intoxicated and who kills is not in the same position as a person who is intoxicated, but not brain-damaged, and who kills. The test is now appropriately focused on the overriding question whether the defendant would have killed and had a substantial impairment of his mental responsibility at that time. The test has been readily applied,[188] but cannot be easy for a jury.

If an alcoholic's craving for drink is proved to be irresistible, the resulting abnormality at the time of the killing may be a defence.[189]

[185] *Sanderson* (1993) 98 Cr App R 325.

[186] *Atkinson* [1985] Crim LR 314 and *Egan* (1992) 95 Cr App R 278.

[187] [2003] 1 AC 1209, [2003] Crim LR 550.

[188] See *Roberts* [2005] EWCA Crim 155; *McNally* [2004] EWCA Crim 2501.

[189] *Tandy* (1987) 87 Cr App R 45, *Inseal* [1992] Crim LR 35, *Egan* [1993] Crim LR 131. See G. R. Sullivan, 'Intoxicants and Diminished Responsibility' [1994] Crim LR 156; J. Tolmie, 'Alcoholism and Criminal Liability' (2001) 64 MLR 688; F. Bowland, 'Intoxication and Criminal Liability' (1986) J Crim Law 100.

(iii) Reform

Numerous proposals have been put forward over the years. The Butler Report recommended that:

> Where a person kills or is party to the killing of another, he shall not be convicted of murder if there is medical or other evidence that he was suffering from a form of mental disorder as defined in [section 1 of the Mental Health Act 1983, that is, 'mental illness, arrested or incomplete development of mind, psychopathic disorder and any other disorder or disability of mind'] and if, in the opinion of the jury, the mental disorder was such as to be an extenuating circumstance which ought to reduce the offence to manslaughter.

Most recently, the Law Commission in its Report No 290 on *Partial Defences to Murder* concluded that[190] there was 'overwhelming support from those consultees who addressed the issue for the retention of a partial defence of diminished responsibility for as long as there is the mandatory life sentence for murder'.

The Commission identified the principal rationale for retention of the diminished defence as being 'fair and just labelling'.[191] Other justifications for a defence of diminished responsibility included the 'out-dated nature of the insanity defence' and its unsatisfactory scope and operation; the stigmatization of the label 'insanity'; the need to prevent jurors being faced with only the option of murder or acquittal lest they perversely acquit; allowing the central issue of culpability to be determined by a jury and not by the judge as part of the sentencing process; the need to ensure public confidence in sentencing which is more likely on a diminished verdict than on murder; the need for a jury, to evaluate the expert evidence; the need to retain the defence for abused women 'driven to kill'; and the opportunity for the defence to provide a merciful but just disposition of mercy killing cases.

If the mandatory life sentence were to be abolished, there would be a strong argument for abolition of the defence. The key arguments identified for abolition in such circumstances were that '*logically*, as diminished responsibility reduces the defendant's *responsibility* for the killing, it ought to be viewed as a mitigating factor rather than a partial defence in a case where, by definition, the defendant's level of *culpability* is established by reference to the traditional concepts of conduct and *mens rea*'; the issues addressed by the defence are matters of mitigation, which go to sentence; abolition is the only appropriate response to the 'insuperable definitional problems'. The present law was regarded by many as 'chaotic' and a rational sentencing exercise would be a better response meeting the needs of the mentally ill defendants; finally, it was noted that the defence is ' "grossly abused" and whether a defendant finds a psychiatrist who will be prepared to testify that, for example, depression was responsible for his behaviour is "a lottery" '.

The Law Commission's final recommendation was for a defence drafted as follows:[192]

> A person, who would otherwise be guilty of murder, is not guilty of murder but of manslaughter if, at the time of the act or omission causing death,

[190] Law Com No 290, para 5.10 and see the Scottish Law Commission, *Insanity and Diminished Responsibility Report*, No 195 (2004).

[191] Ibid, para 5.18.

[192] Ibid, para 5.97.

(1) that person's capacity to:

(a) understand events; or
(b) judge whether his actions were right or wrong; or
(c) control himself,

was substantially impaired by an abnormality of mental functioning arising from an underlying condition and

(2) the abnormality was a significant cause of the defendant's conduct in carrying out or taking part in the killing.

'Underlying condition' means a pre-existing mental or physiological condition other than of a transitory kind.

2. Involuntary manslaughter

This category includes all varieties of homicide which are unlawful at common law but committed without malice aforethought. It is not surprising, therefore, that the fault required takes more than one form. And, as the limits of malice aforethought are uncertain, it follows inevitably that there is a corresponding uncertainty at the boundary between murder and manslaughter. The difficulties do not end there, for there is another vague borderline between manslaughter and accidental death. Indeed, Lord Atkin said[193] that:

> ... of all crimes manslaughter appears to afford most difficulties of definition, for it concerns homicide in so many and so varying conditions ... the law ... recognizes murder on the one hand based mainly, though not exclusively,[194] on an intention to kill, and manslaughter on the other hand, based mainly, though not exclusively,[195] on the absence of intent to kill, but with the presence of an element of 'unlawfulness' which is the elusive factor.

The element of 'unlawfulness' is little less elusive today than when Lord Atkin spoke. This is unfortunate since the offence is one of the most serious in the criminal calendar and carries a maximum life sentence. The outer limits of the offence remain obscure, and there is little internal coherence between the three forms of manslaughter currently recognized – other than the fact that D causes a death. Lumping together the many different types of behaviour that give rise to an unintentional unlawful killing under one label is unsatisfactory in principle, and can engender disparities in sentencing.[196] The three versions of the offence overlap considerably.

There are three broad categories of involuntary manslaughter:

(1) manslaughter by an unlawful and dangerous act;

(2) manslaughter by gross negligence;

(3) manslaughter by subjective recklessness.

The constituents of each of these categories require some degree of analysis.

193 In *Andrews v DPP* [1937] AC 576 at 581, [1937] 2 All ER 552 at 554–555.
194 See above, p 437.
195 See above, pp 443–471.
196 See M. Wasik, 'Form and Function in the Law of Involuntary Manslaughter' [1994] Crim LR 883.

(a) Manslaughter by an unlawful and dangerous act

Coke laid it down that an intention to commit any unlawful act was a sufficient *mens rea* for murder[197] so that if D shot at V's hen with intent to kill it and accidentally killed V, this was murder, 'for the act was unlawful'. This savage doctrine was criticized by Holt CJ[198] and by the time Foster wrote his *Crown Law*,[199] it appears to have been modified by the proviso that the unlawful act must be a felony (and not merely a misdemeanour or civil law wrong such as a tort). Thus, if D shot at the hen intending to steal it, the killing of V was murder. This was the doctrine of constructive murder which survived until the Homicide Act 1957. Alongside this doctrine of constructive murder, from Foster's time there existed a parallel doctrine of constructive manslaughter: any death caused while in the course of committing an unlawful act, other than a felony, was manslaughter. An act was unlawful for this purpose even if it was only a tort, so that the only *mens rea* which needed to be proved was an intention to commit the tort.

The present law is that D is guilty of manslaughter if he kills by an unlawful and dangerous act. The only *mens rea* required is an intention to do that act and any fault required to render it unlawful. It is irrelevant that D is unaware that it is unlawful or that it is dangerous,[200] and that he is unaware of the circumstances which make it dangerous, if a reasonable and sober person would have been aware of them.[201] The offence is heavily and cogently criticized because of this constructive element by which D's liability for manslaughter turns on the consequence of death which will often be unforeseen by D and indeed be regarded as a matter of 'bad luck' beyond his control.[202] The offender is labelled as a manslaughterer when he might only have foreseen, if at all, a risk of *some minor harm* being caused.[203]

The crime comprises:[204]

(i) an unlawful act, intentionally performed;

(ii) in circumstances rendering it dangerous;

(iii) causing death.

Several elements require further examination.

(i) The unlawfulness

Issues requiring elaboration are whether the unlawful act must (a) be criminal, (b) involve a completed crime, (c) be a crime of *mens rea*, (d) be one dependent on proof of

197 3 Inst 56. See Turner, MACL, 195 at 212 et seq for a discussion of the historical development.

198 *Keate* (1697) Comb 406 at 409.

199 (1762) – see p 189, n 160.

200 *Newbury* [1977] AC 500, [1976] 2 All ER 365, *Ball* [1989] Crim LR 730.

201 *Watson* [1989] 2 All ER 865, [1989] Crim LR 733.

202 See generally on liability for consequences A. Ashworth, 'Taking the Consequences', in S. Shute, J. Gardner, and J. Horder (eds), *Action and Value in Criminal Law* (1993).

203 On the issue generally see G. Williams, 'Convictions and Fair Labelling' [1983] CLJ 85; B. Mitchell, 'In Defence of a Principle of Correspondence' [1999] Crim LR 195; cf J. Horder, 'A Critique of the Correspondence Principle in Criminal Law' [1995] Crim LR 759, and 'Questioning the Correspondence Principle: A Reply' [1999] Crim LR 206.

204 Per Lord Hope *A-G's Reference (No 3 of 1994)* [1998] AC 830.

an act, or whether an omission will suffice, (e) be a crime involving an offence against the person.

A crime

At one time it was thought that the act was sufficiently unlawful if it was a civil wrong, a tort. Thus in *Fenton*[205] where D threw stones down a mine and broke some scaffolding which caused a corf to overturn with fatal results, Tindal CJ told the jury that D's act was a trespass and the only question was whether it caused V's death. Even in the 19th century this doctrine was not accepted without reservation by the judges. A notable refusal to follow it is the direction of Field J in *Franklin.*[206] D, walking on Brighton pier, took up 'a good sized box' from a refreshment stall and threw it into the sea where it struck a swimmer, V, and killed him. The prosecution argued that, apart from any question of negligence, it was manslaughter if the commission of the tort of trespass against the stall-keeper had caused death. Field J, after consulting Mathew J who agreed, held that the case must go to the jury 'on the broad ground of negligence'. Expressing his 'great abhorrence of constructive crime', Field J asserted that 'The mere fact of a civil wrong committed by one person against another ought not to be used as an incident which is a necessary step to a criminal case'.

The act must be a crime.

In *Lamb*[207] D pointed a loaded gun at his friend, V, in jest. He did not intend to injure or alarm V and V was not alarmed. Because they did not understand how a revolver works, both thought there was no danger in pulling the trigger; but, when D did so, he shot V dead. D was not guilty of a criminal assault or battery because he did not foresee that V would be alarmed or injured. It was therefore a misdirection to tell the jury that this was 'an unlawful and dangerous act'. It was not, said Sachs LJ, 'unlawful in the criminal sense of the word'; and, referring to *Franklin*, 'it is not in point to consider whether an act is unlawful merely from the angle of civil liabilities'. This was confirmed by *Scarlett.*[208] D, a licensee, caused death by using excessive force while lawfully expelling a trespasser from his pub. His conviction for manslaughter was quashed because the judge had directed that D was guilty if he had used unnecessary and unreasonable force – which would have been the tort of battery. It was necessary to prove that the force used was excessive in the circumstances which D believed to exist[209] – that is, not merely that he had committed the tort but that he had the *mens rea* of the *crime* of battery.

Some doubt might appear to be cast on these cases by the House of Lords in *DPP v Newbury*[210] in which their lordships failed to identify any crime rendering the act unlawful. The 'unlawful' act was throwing a piece of paving stone from the parapet of a bridge as a train approached. This certainly has every appearance of a criminal act which is

205 (1830) 1 Lew CC 179.

206 (1883) 15 Cox CC 163.

207 [1967] 2 QB 981, [1967] 2 All ER 1282. The case is a controversial one. Glanville Williams wrote that 'Lamb was a fool but there is no need to punish fools to that degree. There is no need to punish Lamb at all. He had killed his friend and that was punishment enough' – 'Recklessness Redefined' [1982] CLJ 252, 281.

208 [1993] 4 All ER 629. The case must be read in the light of *Owino* [1995] Crim LR 743, above, p 330. See also *Jennings* [1990] Crim LR 588.

209 *Williams (Gladstone)*, above, p 284.

210 [1977] AC 500, [1976] 2 All ER 365.

perhaps why it was not and, the House thought, could not be, argued that the act was lawful.[211] But the question for the House was whether D could properly be convicted if he did not foresee that his act might cause harm to another. So, despite appearances, the act could not be regarded as an assault or any of the usual offences against the person, all of which require *mens rea.* Unless resort is to be had to the tort of trespass, this leaves as possibilities the offence of endangering passengers contrary to s 34 of the Offences Against the Person Act 1861 or an offence of criminal damage – but an offence against property seems almost as objectionable a basis for convicting of manslaughter as a tort (see below).

The better view, it is submitted, is that in *Lamb* and *Scarlett,* that is, that a criminal act must be identified and proved. The ambiguity of the concept of an 'unlawful' act has, on some occasions led the courts to gloss over the requirement for proof of a criminal offence. In *Cato*[212] D caused V's death by injecting him with heroin with his consent. The court accepted that this was not an offence under the Misuse of Drugs Act and assumed for this purpose that it was not an offence under s 23 of the Offences Against the Person Act 1861[213] but said 'the unlawful act would be described as injecting the deceased with a mixture of heroin and water which at the time of the injection and for the purposes of the injection Cato had unlawfully taken into his possession'. The act was thus closely associated with other acts which are offences but it is submitted that neither this nor any moral condemnation attaching to that act should be enough to found liability for manslaughter.

The 'base' crime must be proved in full

The requirement of a criminal offence prompts a further question: whether it is necessary for the prosecution to establish all of the elements of the crime that would have been charged had no one died – that is, the 'base' crime on which the unlawful act manslaughter charge is constructed. In principled terms the element of 'unlawfulness' should require the prosecution to prove *all* the elements (*mens rea* and *actus reus* with no defence) of the base offence. Unfortunately this apparently obvious interpretation of 'unlawful' has not been put completely beyond doubt by the case law.

It seems clear that the prosecution must prove the full *mens rea* of the base offence. In *Lamb,* the trial judge, Glyn-Jones J had directed the jury that it is an unlawful act 'whether or not it falls within any recognized category of crime'. The Court of Appeal found this to be a misdirection because '*mens rea* is now an essential element of the offence'.[214] The courts all too often gloss over this aspect, using language that implies that a mere voluntary act might suffice, as, for example in *Attorney-General's Reference (No 3 of 1994)*[215] where Lord Hope referred to the requirement merely that D 'did what he did intentionally'.[216] Confusion was also caused by Lord Denning's *dictum* in the civil case of *Gray v Barr*[217] which was criticized by Lord Salmon in *Newbury.*[218] Lord Denning said: 'the accused

211 '... no question arose whether [Newbury's] actions were or were not unlawful': *Scarlett* [1993] 4 All ER at 635, per Beldam LJ.

212 [1976] 1 All ER 260.

213 Below, p 563. In fact D was convicted of the s 23 offence so the remarks discussed in the text may be *obiter.*

214 At 986. See also *Reid* (1975) 62 Cr App R 109 (fright by threat to use firearm was sufficient).

215 [1998] AC 245.

216 Per Lord Hope, at 274.

217 [1971] 2 QB 554 at 568, above, p 50. Lord Denning's italics.

218 [1977] AC 500. Cf Blackstone, at 109.

must do a dangerous act with the *intention* of frightening or harming someone or with *realisation* that it is likely to frighten or harm someone'. This is simply to require the *mens rea* of assault or battery as in *Scarlett*. However, an act which is intended or known to be likely to frighten is not necessarily a 'dangerous' act; and whether it is dangerous, as appears below, is a question to be answered by an objective test. The *dictum* is correct if it is confined to the case where the unlawful act relied on is assault or battery.

The proof of *mens rea* of the base offence is a necessary but not sufficient condition of unlawful act manslaughter. Where D, as on facts similar to *Lamb* thinks that the revolver is loaded and dangerous and he intends to cause V to be frightened (only), but V does not apprehend violence because he does not believe the gun to be loaded, there is no complete assault. D has the *mens rea*, but the *actus reus* is not satisfied.[219] Again, it is submitted that a charge of unlawful act manslaughter cannot be maintained.[220] Lamb's conduct did not constitute an assault *both* because he lacked the *mens rea* (he had no intention to frighten, nor because of his common lack of understanding of the operation of the firearm was he reckless as to causing apprehension in his victim), and there was no *actus reus* because his friend, believing that the whole thing was a joke, had no apprehension of immediate unlawful violence.[221] The court was categorical that '*mens rea* is now an essential element of the offence, and also accepted that counsel had put forward the correct view that for the act to be unlawful it must constitute at least what he then termed a technical assault'. Support also derives from *Arobieke*.[222] D pursued V onto railway 'looking for him'. V was killed. There was no evidence that D had actually threatened V, so no *actus reus* of assault could be established. The conviction was quashed.

In addition to proving the *mens rea* and *actus reus* of the base offence, the prosecution must disprove any excuses or justifications to the base offence raised by D.[223] If the defence itself is clearly defined, there is little difficulty in applying it in the unlawful act manslaughter context. Two particular problems fall for further discussion.

Problems of consent and unlawful act manslaughter

Whether the factual consent of an individual which leads to conduct, where harm is intended or foreseen will be legally recognized is to be decided as a matter of policy: *Brown*.[224] Pleas that V consented to the base crime will be accepted where the conduct falls within an established category for example, boxing, surgery or horseplay, and these will operate to preclude unlawful act manslaughter liability.[225] Similarly, where D has not intended that a consensual assault would lead to any greater degree of harm than the mere assault consented to by V there is no base offence and can be no manslaughter conviction: *Slingsby*.[226]

219 It may be possible to charge a battery. There is no crime of attempted assault since it is a summary only offence.

220 If these fractional crimes are sufficient to form the basis for a UAM charge, that may tell us something about the underlying purpose of UAM. It would be clear that the punishment is based on the 'dangerousness' of the activity rather than on the technical 'unlawfulness'.

221 *Bruce* (1847) Erle J supports this – on the facts no assault as no apprehension by V nor intent by D.

222 [1988] Crim LR 314.

223 *Jennings* [1990] Crim LR 588; *Scarlett* (1994) 98 Cr App R 290.

224 [1994] AC 212; *A-G's Reference (No 6 of 1980)* [1981] Q B 715.

225 Eg *Bruce* (1847) Cox CC 262 (no assault where D span boy round in jest and killed V), and see Lord Mustill's speech in *Brown* [1994] AC 212, 264.

226 [1995] Crim LR 570.

Problems of intoxication and the unlawful act

Where the prosecution rely on an unlawful act which does not require a specific intent and D was intoxicated at the time, it is immaterial that he lacked the *mens rea* of the crime in question and even that he was unconscious: *Lipman*.[227] In this memorable case D killed V by cramming a sheet into her mouth and striking her while he was on an LSD 'trip' and believed he was in the centre of the earth being attacked by serpents. Though the jury convicted on the grounds that D was reckless or grossly negligent when, quite consciously, he took the drugs, the Court of Appeal upheld the conviction by applying the *Church* doctrine. The unlawful act – the base crime – was the battery committed on V while D was unconscious. That battery required only the *mens rea* of recklessness, it was therefore a crime of basic intent, and D's self-induced intoxication provided no excuse.

A crime of *mens rea*?

It is implicit in the rule in *Church*[228] that the base crime must be one of more than mere negligence. An act which all sober and reasonable people would realize entailed the risk (*sc*, an unjustifiable risk) of harm to others almost certainly becomes the tort of negligence when harm results and therefore the reference to 'an unlawful act' would be otiose if it did not mean unlawful in some other respect. This is in accordance with the well-established rule that negligence sufficient to found civil liability is not necessarily enough for criminal guilt and that death caused in the course of committing the tort of negligence is not necessarily manslaughter. But the limitation goes further than this: there are degrees of negligence which are *criminally* punishable which are yet not sufficient to found a charge of manslaughter. If, then, the unlawfulness, whether civil or criminal, of the act arises *solely* from the negligent manner in which it is performed, death caused by the act will not necessarily be manslaughter. This follows from the decision of the House of Lords in *Andrews v DPP*.[229]

In that case Du Parcq J told the jury that if D killed V in the course of dangerous driving contrary to s 11 of the Road Traffic Act 1930 he was guilty of manslaughter. Lord Atkin (who clearly regarded dangerous driving in the 1930 Act as a crime of negligence)[230] said that, if the summing up had rested there, there would have been misdirection:

> There can be no doubt that this section covers driving with such a high degree of negligence as that, if death were caused, the offender would have committed manslaughter. But the converse is not true, and it is perfectly possible that a man may drive at a speed or in a manner dangerous to the public, and cause death, and yet not be guilty of manslaughter.[231]

[227] [1970] 1 QB 152, [1969] 3 All ER 410. The case was heavily criticized. See commentary by I. Hooker [1969] Crim LR 547; G. Orchard, 'Drunkenness, Drugs and Manslaughter' [1970] Crim LR 132; P. Glazebrook, 'Constructive Manslaughter and The Threshold Tort' [1970] CLJ 21; R. Buxton [1970] *Annual Survey of Commonwealth Law*, 128 and 134. It was not followed in Australia: *Haywood* [1971] VR 755 (Crockett J) but was affirmed by the House of Lords in *Majewski* (above, p 276).

[228] Below, p 480.

[229] [1937] AC 576, [1937] 2 All ER 552.

[230] See above, p 471. The offence of dangerous driving was abolished by the Criminal Law Act 1977 but restored in a new form by the Road Traffic Act 1991, s 2. Below, p 1012.

[231] [1937] AC at 584, [1937] 2 All ER at 556, 557.

Lord Atkin expressly distinguished[232] between acts which are unlawful because of the negligent manner in which they are performed and acts which are unlawful for some other reason:

There is an obvious difference in the law of manslaughter between doing an unlawful act and doing a lawful act with a degree of carelessness which the legislature makes criminal.

His Lordship's next sentence implies that killing in the course of unlawful acts generally *was* manslaughter:

If it were otherwise a man who killed another while driving without due care and attention would *ex necessitate* commit manslaughter.

This passage has been severely criticized[233] and it is certainly unhappily phrased: '... doing a lawful act with a degree of carelessness which the legislature makes criminal' is a contradiction in terms, for the act so done is plainly not a lawful act. But the distinction evidently intended, viz, between acts which are unlawful because of negligent performance and acts which are unlawful for some other reason, is at least intelligible and, in view of the established distinction between civil and criminal negligence, a necessary limitation.

There is a further issue which arises. If it is insufficient to construct a manslaughter charge on a base crime of mere negligence, presumably it is even less acceptable to construct such a charge on a base crime of strict liability. The natural reading of Lord Atkin's opinion is that the distinction is between acts which are unlawful because of negligent performance and acts which are unlawful for some other reason. An alternative, strained but more attractive, reading is that only crimes of more than mere negligence will suffice to ground an unlawful act manslaughter conviction. This is supported by the comments of Sachs LJ in *Lamb*: '*mens rea* being now an essential ingredient in manslaughter'.[234] As a matter of principle, the offence should be read restrictively and should be based on offences that require *mens rea* proper. Gross negligence manslaughter is more than broad enough to prevent deserving cases going unprosecuted. The issue has not been directly addressed by the courts. In *Andrews*,[235] D gave V, with her consent, an injection of insulin in order to give her a 'rush'. V who was also voluntarily intoxicated at the time died as a result of the injection of insulin. D appealed against his conviction on the basis that the judge was wrong to rule that he would direct the jury that V's consent to the injection did not render D's act lawful. The Court of Appeal upheld the conviction, holding that ss 58(2)(b) and 67 of the Medicines Act 1968 made D's act unlawful because no consent could be pleaded to that offence. The fact that these offences are of strict liability was not challenged.

Omissions as 'unlawful acts'

In *Lowe*,[236] the Court of Appeal held that D is not guilty of manslaughter simply on the ground that he has committed the offence under s 1(1) of the Children and Young

232 [1937] AC at 585, [1937] 2 All ER at 557.

233 Turner, MACL, at 238. Referred to by Devlin as 'the only obscure speech the great Lord Atkin ever made': 'Criminal Responsibility and Punishment: Function of Judge and Jury' [1954] Crim LR 661, 672.

234 [1967] 2 QB 981 at 988.

235 [2002] EWCA Crim 3021.

236 [1973] QB 702, [1973] 1 All ER 805. See generally I. H. Dennis, 'Manslaughter by Omission' (1980) CLP 255.

Persons Act 1933 of neglecting his child so as to cause unnecessary suffering or injury to its health, and that neglect has caused death. The court disapproved *Senior*[237] which, on similar facts, held that this was manslaughter. *Lowe* has now been overruled on its interpretation of the 1933 Act and *Senior* to some extent rehabilitated by *Sheppard*[238] – but not on this point, on which, it is thought, *Lowe* and not *Senior* represents the law. Death had certainly been caused by unlawful and dangerous conduct, but the court distinguished between omission and commission.

> . . . if I strike a child in a manner likely to cause harm it is right that if that child dies I may be charged with manslaughter. If, however, I omit to do something with the result that it suffers injury to its health which results in its death, we think that a charge of manslaughter should not be an inevitable consequence even if the omission is deliberate.

If the omission is no more than an act of negligence then it is right that the doctrine of the unlawful and dangerous act does not apply and D is not guilty in the absence of gross negligence; but if the omission is truly *wilful* – a deliberate omission to summon medical aid, knowing it to be necessary, there seems to be no valid ground for the distinction.[239]

Other limitations of the category of unlawfulness

It has been questioned whether the base crime must be one involving an offence to the person, and whether an inchoate offence might suffice.

As for inchoate offences, attempted offences of violence would be the most obvious scenarios in which such an issue might arise. Consider D who thinks he is adding poison to V's tea, but he has made a mistake and is simply adding a very concentrated sweetener. V is a diabetic and dies. There is probably no full crime under s 23 of the OAPA, but there is a possible attempted poisoning.[240] The issue does not appear to have arisen in any reported case. In *Willoughby*[241] D had poured petrol around a building which he owned and which he planned to burn down to collect the insurance money. D claimed that he was absent from the premises when a spark ignited the petrol, his associate who was assisting in spreading the petrol was killed. The conviction for manslaughter was upheld by the court, with the conclusion that the base offence was one of causing criminal damage to property being reckless as to whether life was endangered thereby as the jury found. It is unclear whether the question was raised whether D pouring petrol was a completed act of criminal damage, or one that was merely preparatory.[242]

As far as offences other than those against the person, convictions have been upheld where D's unlawful act constituted criminal damage (for example, *Goodfellow*)[243] and burglary (eg, *Watson* (below) and *Kennedy*).[244] In *Ball*[245] (below) the court distinguished

237 [1899] 1 QB 283.

238 [1981] AC 394, [1980] 3 All ER 899 (1980), 72 Cr App R 82, HL.

239 See editorial comment in [1976] Crim LR 529, where Andrew Ashworth is heavily critical.

240 Arguably D would not be liable not because of the unlawfulness element, but because there would be no objective risk of injury from the act.

241 [2004] EWCA Crim 3365.

242 In such cases, a gross negligence charge might be difficult to substantiate.

243 (1986) 83 Cr App R 23.

244 (1994) 15 Cr App R (S) 141 (burglar dropped a match used to illuminate search of house).

245 The point of law certified for the House of Lords postulated 'an act [not directed against V] which is the substantial cause of the death' and the court left open the question whether D was guilty of manslaughter by gross negligence which it could scarcely have done if it was deciding that D did not cause death.

some examples posed by D's counsel on the ground that, unlike the case before the court, they were of acts 'not directed at V' (but that is irrelevant). The court therefore expressed no opinion on 'the example of a person storing goods known to be stolen; if unknown to him the goods contain unstable explosive which explodes killing another, is that manslaughter?' The answer must surely be no, unless the sober and reasonable observer would have known of the danger. Applying *Goodfellow* and *Watson*, he would be guilty. There is something to be said in favour of imposing some limitation to the offence if it is to be retained. It does not seem appropriate that a person's guilt of homicide should depend on whether he was handling stolen goods or committing criminal damage or burglary. Cases of this sort would be better left to the next category of killing by gross negligence.[246]

No requirement that the unlawful act be 'directed at' the victim?

In *Dalby*[247] Waller LJ said that, 'where the charge of manslaughter is based on an unlawful and dangerous act, it must be an act directed at the victim and likely to cause immediate injury however slight'.

D and V were drug addicts. D, who was lawfully in possession of diconal tablets, supplied some to V who took them in a highly dangerous form and quantity and died. D's conviction was quashed apparently on the ground that the supply was not an act directed against the person of V and did not cause direct injury to him. But in *Goodfellow*[248] D's argument that he was not guilty of manslaughter because his act was not directed against V was rejected. D, wanting to move from his council house and seeing no prospect of exchanging it, set it on fire, attempting to make it appear that the cause was a petrol bomb. V died in the fire. The court said that in *Dalby* Waller LJ was 'intending to say that there must be no fresh intervening cause between the act and the death'. It is true that that case could, and probably should,[249] have been decided on this ground, but it does not seem to have been the *ratio decidendi*.[250] It is also true that the act of burglary which causes the death of the obviously frail householder is not directed at him, but it is accepted in *Watson* that it may be manslaughter.[251]

(ii) Dangerousness

Until 1966 it was possible to argue that any unlawful act, other than a merely negligent act, causing death was manslaughter; but in that year in *Church* the Court of Criminal Appeal rejected that view. Edmund Davies J said:

246 For a suggestion that the offence ought to be restricted to cases of 'attack' on another person, see C. Clarkson, 'Context and Culpability in Involuntary Manslaughter: Principle or Instinct' in A. Ashworth and B. Mitchell (eds), *Rethinking English Homicide Law* (2000). The basis for this suggestion is that there is no wrong done by convicting D of a constructive crime of manslaughter because by attacking V, D has shifted his moral stance vis-à-vis V. Since the concept of 'attack' has no foundation in English law, the proposal may generate uncertainty. As Ashworth and Mitchell observe asking whether it is enough to say that choosing to engage in violence means you make your own luck begs the question (at 13).

247 [1982] 1 All ER 916.

248 (1986) 83 Cr App R 23. The conviction was upheld on the grounds of both unlawful act and reckless manslaughter.

249 *Kennedy* [1999] 1 Cr App R 54, above, p 60. In *Kennedy No 2* [2005] EWCA Crim 685, it was accepted that there was no requirement that the act be 'aimed' at V.

250 Above, n 247.

251 [1989] Crim LR 730, CA.

For such a verdict inexorably to follow, the unlawful act must be such as all sober and reasonable people would inevitably recognize must[[252]] subject the other person to, at least, the risk of some harm resulting therefrom, albeit not serious harm.[253]

The test of dangerousness is objective. In *Newbury* Lord Salmon stressed, '. . . the test is not did the accused recognize that it was dangerous but would all sober and reasonable people recognize its danger'.

The test describes the kind of act which gives rise to liability for manslaughter, not the intention or foresight, real or assumed, of the accused. Hence the enactment of s 8 of the Criminal Justice Act 1967[254] had no effect on the law as stated in *Church*. The question is whether the sober and reasonable man would have appreciated that the act was dangerous in the light, not only of the circumstances actually known to the accused, but also of any additional circumstances of which that hypothetical person would have been aware. There is of course a risk that in practice the fact that a death has occurred will be treated by the jury as conclusive evidence of the fact that the activity was dangerous. Such *ex post facto* reasoning ought to be discouraged.

A peculiarity of the victim is relevant if it would have been known to the sober and reasonable observer of the event, even if it was not known to the accused. This principle can be explained by comparing two cases. The burglary of a house in which resides V, a frail 87-year-old man, becomes a 'dangerous' act as soon as V's frailty and great age would be apparent to the reasonable observer. The unlawful act continues through the 'whole of the burglarious intrusion' so that if V dies of a heart attack caused by D's continuing in the burglary after it has become a dangerous, as well as unlawful, act he will be guilty of manslaughter.[255] In contrast, where a petrol station attendant with a weak heart died in consequence of a robbery this was not manslaughter because the observer would not have known of his peculiar susceptibility – the act was not 'dangerous'.[256]

It is worth underlining three aspects of the *Church* doctrine. First, that there must be a 'likelihood' of harm. This suggests more than a mere possibility, but not perhaps that it is more probable than not. Secondly, that the type of harm involved is only 'some' harm, not serious harm. This contrasts with the requirement in gross negligence manslaughter of a risk of death. Thirdly, that there is no requirement that the accused himself foresee any risk of harm. Historically, unlawful act manslaughter was limited to cases in which

252 The degree of risk entailed is not further elaborated. See R. Sparks, 'The Elusive Element of Unlawfulness' (1965) 28 MLR 601.

253 [1966] 1 QB 59 at 70. Cf R. Buxton, 'By Any Unlawful Act' (1966) 82 LQR 174 suggesting that the law could return to a position whereby unlawful act manslaughter is restricted to cases where D intends to cause *serious* injury.

254 Above, p 128.

255 *Watson* [1989] 2 All ER 865, [1989] Crim LR 733. D's conviction was quashed because causation was not established. V's death may have been caused by the arrival of the emergency services. But did this predictable event break the chain of causation? Cf commentary, [1989] Crim LR 734. If V has sustained a fatal shock before D has any opportunity to observe his frailty, D's liability seems to depend on whether his acts after he had that opportunity (now 'dangerous' acts) contributed to the death.

256 *Dawson* (1985) 81 Cr App R 150. Yet before the Homicide Act 1957 this would have been murder (killing in the course or furtherance of a violent felony) and, according to one theory, Parliament's provision that it was not murder left it manslaughter. See 1st edition of this work, at 19–20. The theory has not taken root.

the accused had at least foreseen injury of his victim resulting from his crime.[257] The *Fourth Report of HM Commissioners on Criminal Law*[258] described the offence in terms of 'death result[ing] from any unlawful act or omission done or omitted with intent to hurt the person'.[259] The decision in *Church* may have marked a significant deviation from the historical position. Buxton, writing extra-judicially, described it as a 'staggeringly severe ruling, and one which turns its back on the major part of the 19th century development of the law'.[260] There have been many suggestions to limit the offence to cases where D has committed an unlawful act likely to cause at least serious personal injury, and to restrict it further, by a requirement that D intend or be reckless as to such.[261]

Fright, shock and harm as dangerous acts?

Psychiatric injury is now acknowledged to be actual bodily harm[262] but it would be hard to prove that the risk of such harm would inevitably be recognized by all sober and reasonable people, especially as the law requires expert evidence to prove it. Fright and shock do not amount to 'actual bodily harm' but it does not necessarily follow that they are not 'harm' for the purposes of constructive manslaughter. In *Reid*[263] Lawton LJ, upholding a conviction for manslaughter, said that 'the very least kind of harm is causing fright by threats' – in that case, by the use of firearms – but he was discussing the mental element of an accessory rather than the nature of the act, which is our present concern. The act was, in the opinion of the court, likely to cause death or serious injury and therefore was certainly 'dangerous'. In *Dawson*[264] the court assumed without deciding that in the context of manslaughter 'harm' includes 'injury to the person through the operation of shock emanating from fright'. So it seems that it is not enough that the act is likely to frighten. It must be likely to cause such shock as to result in injury.[265]

(iii) Causing death

The principles of causation discussed above are applicable. The unlawful and dangerous act must cause death. Particular attention is drawn to the discussion on the drug administration cases (pp 60–63) in which the Court of Appeal took a revolutionary approach by holding that where D supplies the syringe for V, a sane adult, to self-inject, D remains liable for V's death if V dies as a result of the injection. In *Kennedy No 2*,[266] the Court of Appeal held that where D provides V with a syringe for immediate injection it is open to a jury to find that D was 'jointly engaged' in the administration of the substance. The court offered little guidance on what would be sufficient evidence of joint engagement. In one statement the court suggests that there was joint engagement because both the D's and V's acts were necessary, it is doubtful whether necessity is a strict prerequisite to holding that D is a joint principal.

As for the further element of the offence of unlawful act manslaughter that D causes V's death, the court said simply that since 'the deceased and the appellant were acting in

[257] The case law bears examples including *Sullivan* (1836) 7 C & P 641, where removing the trap-stick from a cart was sufficient to ground liability as D foresaw the risk of some harm arising.

[258] (1839) see Russell, 588.

[259] Ibid, at 589.

[260] Above, n 254, at p 192.

[261] See also the Draft Scots Criminal Code, cl 38.

[262] *Chan-Fook*, below, p 552.

[263] (1975) 62 Cr App R 109 at 112.

[264] (1985) 81 Cr App R at 155.

[265] See M. Stallworthy, 'Can Death by Shock be Manslaughter' (1986) 136 NLJ 51; A. Busuttill and A. McCall Smith, 'Fright, Stress and Homicide' (1990) 54 J Crim L 257.

[266] *Kennedy No 2* [2005] EWCA Crim 685.

concert in administering the heroin, it seems to us inevitable that the unlawful act contrary to s 23 of the 1861 Act, was causative of the deceased's death.[267]

(b) Gross negligence manslaughter

For many years the courts have used the terms 'recklessness' and 'gross negligence' to describe the fault required for involuntary manslaughter, other than constructive manslaughter, without any clear definition of either term. It was not clear whether these terms were merely two ways of describing the same thing, or whether they represented two distinct conditions of fault.

All previous cases must now be read in the light of *Prentice, Adomako* and *Holloway*[268] in the Court of Appeal, and *Adomako*[269] in the House of Lords. The background to the decisions is that the House of Lords decided in *Seymour*[270] that the law governing involuntary manslaughter, other than unlawful act manslaughter, was the same as that of the statutory offence (now repealed) of causing death by reckless driving, that is, that the fault required was *Lawrence* recklessness, as set out above[271] subject to the omission of any reference to a risk of causing damage to property. There had to be a risk of physical injury to some other person.[272] According to this controversial decision of the House of Lords in *Seymour*, the *Lawrence* direction was 'comprehensive and of general application' and the courts were no longer to apply the common law test of gross negligence propounded by Lord Hewart CJ in *Bateman* –

> ... in the opinion of the jury, the negligence of the accused went beyond a mere matter of compensation between subjects and showed such disregard for the life and safety of others, as to amount to a crime against the state and conduct deserving of punishment.[273]

(i) *Prentice, Holloway* and *Adomako* in the Court of Appeal[274]

In the three appeals considered together in *Prentice*, the Court of Appeal, not wanting to apply the *Lawrence* test but being bound by *Seymour*, held that *Seymour* case applied only to 'motor manslaughter', cases of causing death by driving a motor vehicle. The three appeals before the court, none of which was a motor manslaughter case, were still governed by a gross negligence test. Prentice and Holloway's appeals were allowed. Adomako's appeal was dismissed by the Court of Appeal and by the House of Lords.

In *Prentice* doctors had administered an injection which created an obvious risk of causing death and in fact did so. The jury were directed in accordance with *Lawrence* that the doctors were guilty if they never gave thought to the possibility of there being any such risk. The question should have been whether their failure to ascertain and use the correct method of administering the drug was 'grossly negligent to the point of criminal-

267 Ibid, [31]. 268 [1993] 4 All ER 935, discussed [1994] Crim LR 292.

269 [1994] 3 All ER 79, [1994] Crim LR 757. 270 [1983] 2 AC 493.

271 P 104. See P. A. Ashall, 'Manslaughter the Impact of *Caldwell*' [1984] Crim LR 467; A. Briggs, 'In Defence of Manslaughter' [1983] Crim LR 764; G. Syrota, '*Mens Rea* in Gross Negligence Manslaughter' [1983] Crim LR 776.

272 See the potential qualification in *Kong Cheuck Kwan* (1986) 82 Cr App R 18, discussed by J. M. Brabyn, 'A Sequel to *Seymour* Made in Hong Kong' [1987] Crim LR 84.

273 (1925) 19 Cr App R 8 at 11.

274 See G. Williams, 'Misadventures of Manslaughter' [1993] 153 NLJ 1413.

ity.' In *Holloway* D, an electrician, had given no thought to the obvious risk of death created by the way he installed the electric element of a central heating system, so, in the opinion of the court, he would have been rightly convicted if *Lawrence* provided the right test. It did not: the further question should have been asked, whether it was grossly negligent to have such a state of mind.

In *Adomako* D, an anaesthetist, failed to notice that the tube supplying oxygen to a patient had become detached. According to expert evidence, any competent anaesthetist would have recognized this immediately. The judge directed the jury that a high degree of negligence was required. The Court of Appeal upheld the conviction as this was the appropriate test to apply, and the appellant appealed to the House of Lords.

(ii) The House of Lords decision in *Adomako*[275]

The House held that:

(i) There is no separate offence of motor manslaughter. As Lord Atkin said in *Andrews*, 'The principle to be observed is that cases of manslaughter in driving motor cars are but instances of a general rule applicable to all charges of homicide by negligence'.[276]

(ii) There is no manslaughter by *Lawrence* recklessness, in effect, though not formally, overruling *Seymour.* It would now be wrong to direct a jury on any charge of manslaughter in terms of *Lawrence* recklessness. (Since the decision in *G* overruling *Caldwell*, it would be unthinkable to apply that test.)[277]

(iii) There is now a single, 'simple' test of gross negligence. D must have been in breach of a duty of care under the ordinary principles of negligence; the negligence must have caused death; and it must, in the opinion of the jury, amount to *gross* negligence. The question, 'supremely a jury question', is:

> having regard to the risk of death involved, [was] the conduct of the defendant . . . so bad in all the circumstances as to amount in [the jury's judgment] to a criminal act or omission?

Several aspects of the test require further examination.

A duty of care

The most obvious categories of duty in which liability might arise are those involving doctor and patient,[278] transport carrier and passenger,[279] employment,[280] etc, but the

[275] See commentary at [1994] Crim LR 757 and S. Gardner, 'Manslaughter by Gross Negligence' (1995) 111 LQR 22.

[276] See generally I. D. Brownlee and M. Seneviratne, 'Killing with Cars After *Adomako*: Time for Some Alternatives' [1995] Crim LR 389. See also *Brown* [2005] UKPC p 18.

[277] For a clear review of the development of fault in manslaughter from gross negligence through forms of recklessness and back to gross negligence see J. Stannard, 'From *Andrews* to *Seymour* and Back Again' [1996] 47 NILQ 1.

[278] See *Adomako* itself, *Misra* [2004] EWCA Crim 2375, [2005] Crim LR 234 and R. Ferner, 'Medication errors that led to manslaughter charges' (2000) 321 BMJ 1212; M. Childs, 'Medical Manslaughter and Corporate Libaility' (1999) LS 316.

[279] See *Litchfield* [1998] Crim LR 508 (schooner), *Barker* [2003] 2 Cr App R (S) 110.

[280] *R v DPP, ex p Jones* [2000] IRLR 373; *Dean* [2002] EWCA Crim 2410; *Clothier* [2004] EWCA Crim 2629; *Crow* [2001] EWCA Crim 2968.

categories are limitless and involve duties arising in the course of hazardous activity (for example, smuggling illegal immigrants,[281] taking heroin),[282] or duties arising from relationships (for example, failing to seek medical assistance for a spouse).[283] It is impossible to catalogue all circumstances in which a duty will arise, rather, the approach is to apply the 'ordinary principles of negligence' to determine whether the defendant owed a duty to the victim.

In cases of positive act it is relatively easy to identify whether there was a duty based on whether the acts created a risk of death which was obvious to the ordinary prudent individual. In cases of omission much greater case needs to be exercised as there will be situations in which a risk of death would be obvious, but where D has no duty – as with D witnessing a blind stranger walking towards a cliff. No doubt the courts will be comfortable in many cases to recognize a duty arising from a combination of circumstances.[284] In *Willoughby*[285] for example, D had with V spread petrol around D's property with the intention of burning it down to claim the insurance. V died when the petrol ignited. The Court of Appeal concluded that D's ownership *per se* did not give rise to a duty, but because D engaged the deceased to participate in spreading petrol, and with a view to setting fire to the appellant's premises for the appellant's benefit a duty existed.

Lord MacKay's reference to the 'ordinary principles of negligence' should not be regarded as incorporating all of the technicalities of the tort of negligence into the gross negligence offence. Thus, in *Wacker*[286] it was held that where D had smuggled 60 illegal immigrants into the UK and 58 had died of suffocation owing to his having shut the air vent in their container, he could not displace the duty by relying on the victims' being jointly engaged with him in a criminal enterprise – *ex turpi causa.* The court referred to Lord MacKay's speech in *Adomako* and concluded that his reference to 'ordinary principles of the law of negligence' was:

> not intended to decide that the rules relating to *ex turpi causa* were part of those ordinary principles, he was doing no more than holding that in an 'ordinary' case of negligence the question whether there was a duty of care was to be governed by whether there was a duty of care in the law of negligence.

The courts are clearly anxious to retain a degree of simplicity over this element of the offence which must be put before the jury. Confusion arose over whether the duty question involved a pure question of law to be determined by the judge,[287] or whether the judge was to rule on whether there was evidence capable of establishing a duty in which case that was to be left to be determined by the jury.[288] The matter has finally been resolved in *Willoughby*,[289] in which the Court of Appeal held 'that whether a duty of care

281 *Wacker* [2002] EWCA Crim 1944.

282 *Ruffell* [2003] Cr App R (S) 330; *Parfeni* [2003] EWCA Crim 159 (although this must surely have been a case of unlawful act manslaughter by D injecting V with heroin in order to steal from him).

283 *Hood* [2004] 2 Cr App R (S).

284 As in the cases of omission discussed above p 82 especially in *Stone and Dobinson* [1977] QB 354 in which the duty arose from the cohabitation, blood relationship and voluntary assumption of responsibility.

285 [2005] Crim LR 393.

286 [2003] QB 1203, [2003] Crim LR 108 and commentary. Cf Scots Law, *Transco plc v HM Advocate* [2004] SLT 41.

287 *Singh* [1999] Crim LR 582.

288 *Khan* [1998] Crim LR 830; *Sinclair* (1998) unreported.

289 [2004] EWCA Crim 3365, [2005] Crim LR 393.

exists is a matter for the jury once the judge has decided that there is evidence capable of establishing a duty'.

Breach of duty

The breach can be by positive act or by omission.[290]

Risk of death

The proposition in *Adomako* refers to a risk of *death*, a point emphasized in *Gurphal Singh*.[291] If we are to have an offence of homicide by gross negligence at all, it seems right that it should be so limited.[292] The circumstances must be such that a reasonably prudent person would have foreseen a serious risk, not merely of injury, even serious injury, but of death. The Court of Appeal has confirmed this narrower interpretation in *Misra*.[293] As a matter of policy the CPS will not prosecute on evidence of anything less.

Gross negligence

The test is objective – the question is whether the risk would have been obvious to the reasonably prudent and skilful doctor, anaesthetist, electrician, motorist, or person on the Clapham omnibus (or driver on the North Circular Road as now seems to reflect the modern view), as the circumstances require.

Relationship with recklessness[294]

It is, at first sight, surprising that the gross negligence test should be more favourable to the defendant than a recklessness test – even *Lawrence* recklessness. The difference is that that recklessness test did not include the requirement that the jury must be satisfied that the defendant's conduct was bad enough to be a crime. A direction in *Lawrence* terms deprived D of the chance of acquittal on that ground. In *Prentice*, for example, there were many strongly mitigating factors in the doctors' conduct, which were irrelevant if the jury were concerned only with what was foreseeable, but highly relevant to question whether their behaviour was bad enough to deserve condemnation as manslaughter. Ever since *Bateman* the courts have asserted that the test is whether the negligence goes beyond a mere matter of compensation and is bad enough to amount to a crime; but this is incomplete, if not plainly wrong. Careless driving amounts to a crime and deserves punishment but, manifestly, it does not on that ground alone amount to manslaughter, if it happens to cause death. Even dangerous driving causing death is not necessarily manslaughter. There are degrees of *criminal* negligence, and manslaughter requires a very high degree. Should not the jury be asked whether the negligence is bad enough to be condemned, not merely as a crime, but as the very grave crime of manslaughter?[295]

290 See on omissions eg *Watts* [1998] Crim LR 833; *Litchfield* [1998] Crim LR 507.

291 *Gurphal Singh* [1999] Crim LR 582.

292 Cf the view of L. H. Leigh, 'Liability for Inadvertence a Lordly Legacy' (1995) 58 MLR 457, 459.

293 [2004] EWCA Crim 2375.

294 See Leigh, above, and A. Norrie, *Crime Reason and History* (2000), at 66–69.

295 Cf *Litchfield* [1998] Crim LR 507 and commentary. Whether evidence was sufficient to satisfy a jury, and whether evidence of subjective recklessness is admissible on a charge of manslaughter by gross negligence, is considered in *DPP, ex p Jones* [2000] Crim LR 858 and commentary.

In *Misra*[296] the defendants argued that gross negligence should be replaced with an offence of reckless manslaughter, relying on the fundamental rejection of objectivism in *G*, and the *dicta* in that case that all serious offences require proof of a blameworthy *state of mind.* The Court of Appeal concluded that such arguments had been duly considered and rejected in *Adomako*, and saw nothing in *G*[297] to cause them to regard *Adomako* as no longer binding.[298]

Relevance of D's state of mind

Since the test of gross negligence is therefore purely objective, it might be thought that the state of mind of the particular accused is irrelevant to the inquiry. However, the courts have held that proof of the defendant's state of mind and in particular his foresight of the risk of harm or death is 'not a prerequisite to a conviction' whilst recognising also that there may be cases in which the defendant's state of mind is 'relevant to the jury's consideration when assessing the grossness and criminality of his conduct'.[299] This approach has been endorsed on a number of occasions, and it has been recognized that it may operate in the accused's favour.[300]

Circularity of test

As Lord MacKay acknowledged, the test involves a degree of circularity. It may also be criticized, as was its predecessor, the 'Bateman test', on the ground that it leaves a question of law to the jury. It has always been held that the negligence which suffices for civil liability is not necessarily enough for manslaughter, so someone has to decide whether the particular negligence is bad enough to amount to a crime, indeed this very grave crime. It is not necessary for the judge to refer to the distinction between civil and criminal liability which might tend to confuse the jury.[301]

The jury appear to be left with the task of deciding the scope of the offence – unlike in applying the definition of say intention which has been supplied by the judge, in gross negligence, they determine what constitutes this serious crime. This seems objectionable in principle.

In rejecting a challenge that the offence was insufficiently certain to be compatible with Article 7 of the ECHR, the Court of Appeal in *Misra* held that the jury's function in gross negligence cases is not to decide a point of law, but one of fact:

> The decision whether the conduct was criminal is described [in *Adomako*] not as 'the' test, but as 'a' test as to how far the conduct in question must depart from accepted standards to be 'characterized as criminal'. On proper analysis, therefore, the jury is not deciding whether the particular defendant ought to be convicted on some unprincipled basis. The question for the jury is not whether the defendant's negligence was gross, and whether, additionally, it was a crime, but whether his behaviour was grossly negligent and consequently criminal. This is not a question of law, but one of fact, for decision in the individual case.[302]

With respect, it is doubtful whether this meets the criticisms that the test is circular, and that it requires the jury to determine the scope of the criminal law.

296 [2004] EWCA Crim 2375.
297 [2004] 1 AC 1034.
298 See also the same conclusion in *Mark* [2004] EWCA Crim 2490, All ER (D) 35 (Oct).
299 *A-G's Reference (No 2 of 1999)* [2000] Crim LR 475 (the Southall Rail crash case).
300 *R v DPP, ex p Jones* [2000] IRLR 373, DC; *R (Rowley) v DPP* [2003] EWHC 693. Whether the two are consistent on this is debatable.
301 *Becker*, No 199905228/Y5, 19 June 2000, CA.
302 Para 62.

ECHR compatibility

The Court of Appeal in *Misra* concluded that gross negligence manslaughter was sufficiently clear and did not offend the requirement of legal certainty imposed by Article 7 or the common law. The court referred to the writings of Bacon and Blackstone to support its view that Article 7 merely confirmed the common law position on the principle of legal certainty. Thus, the court felt confident that the House of Lords, when framing the offence in *Adomako*, was not 'indifferent to or unaware of the need for the criminal law in particular to be predictable and certain'.[303] The court observed that Article 7 does not require absolute certainty but that offences are defined '. . . with sufficient precision to enable the citizen to regulate his conduct: he must be able – if need be with appropriate advice – to foresee to a degree that is reasonable in the circumstances, the consequences which any given action may entail'.[304] Even applying the stricter interpretation of the test in *Hashman and Harrup v UK*[305] the offence would be likely to satisfy Article 7 since gross negligence manslaughter depends on jury evaluation of conduct by reference to its consequences, and in gross negligence manslaughter the jury must be satisfied as to the 'risk of death' and of causation.

(c) Reckless manslaughter

Gross negligence is a sufficient, but not necessarily the only, fault for manslaughter. To some extent manslaughter by advertent recklessness, conscious risk-taking still survives. Where D kills by an act (not unlawful apart from the fact that it is done recklessly) knowing that it is highly probable that he will cause serious bodily harm, this was murder (*Hyam*) before the decision in *Moloney*[306] so it must still be manslaughter. Where death is so caused, the jury do not have to decide whether it is bad enough to amount to a crime. That question is appropriate only when we are concerned with degrees of negligence, there being no other way of determining the criminal degree. The jury are not asked this question in non-fatal offences against the person which may be committed recklessly so it would be quite inconsistent if it applied when death is caused.

The main concern with this least controversial from of manslaughter is to distinguish 'subjective recklessness' (manslaughter) from 'oblique intention' (murder).[307] The leading case is *Lidar*[308] in which V died when run over by D's car to which he had been hanging on when pursuing D in the course of a fight. Although the trial judge directed that D's fault element would be satisfied by proof of recklessness (ie D's personal foresight) as to mere injury, the Court of Appeal held that this was not fatal to the safety of the conviction. Subjective reckless manslaughter requires proof that D foresaw a serious (significant) risk that V would suffer serious injury (or death) and took the risk unjustifiably.

303 Para 34; cf commentary in *Misra* [2005] Crim LR 234.
304 *Sunday Times v United Kingdom* [1979] 2 EHRR 245.
305 [2000] Crim LR 185.
306 Above, p 94.
307 Above, p 94.
308 [2000] 4 Archbold News 3.

(d) Reform[309]

(i) Unlawful act manslaughter (UAM)

In view of the sustained principled criticism of the offence, it is no surprise that there have been calls for reform and indeed abolition. In the Law Commission's Consultation Paper No 135 on *Involuntary Manslaughter*, it was observed that there was 'no prospect' of being able to devise any clear principled statement of the law based on concepts of unlawful act manslaughter'.[310] In its Consultation Paper No 135 the Law Commission provisionally proposed abolition of UAM without replacement.[311] By the time of the Report three years later, its opinion had been changed. The Law Commission's final proposal was that a person is guilty of a careless killing (GCK) offence if he has intended to cause injury, or is aware of the risk of injury and unreasonably takes the risk where the conduct causing or intended to cause the injury constitutes an offence. Keating[312] is critical of the failure to secure correspondence between the fault (foresight of injury) and the harm caused, regarding it as 'unfortunate' for the Law Commission to include a version of unlawful act manslaughter. The Home Office subsequently questioned whether some version of the offence based on ought to be retained.[313] It was unconvinced by the merits of the Law Commission proposal that it was wrong in principle to convict of an offence of death where the offender was aware only of a risk of injury. The example given by the Home Office is an extreme one of a person causing a minor wound to the victim who is a haemophiliac.[314] The Home Office proposal creates liability where the accused intended some injury, in the course of the commission of a violent crime, and the death was not foreseen. As with the Law Commission proposal, there is no full correspondence between the fault (foresight of injury) and the harm (death) for which the defendant is punished. The Home Office offers no justification for basing liability on an accidental outcome rather than intention or foresight.

(ii) Gross negligence manslaughter

The Law Commission[315] proposes the reform, rather than abolition, of the gross negligence offence. The new offence would consist in killing by conduct creating a risk of death or serious injury, which he is capable of appreciating at the material time and which would be obvious to a reasonable person in his position, when *either* his conduct falls far below what can reasonably be expected of him in the circumstances *or* he intends by his conduct to cause some injury, or is aware of and unreasonably takes the risk that it may do so. The Report also proposes a separate offence of corporate killing (discussed above Ch 10).[316]

309 For a compelling review of the defects with the present law see Law Com Report No 237, *Involuntary Manslaughter* (1996), Part III.

310 Para 5.4. On earlier reform propsoals including those of the CLRC, Fourteenth Report on *Offences Against the Person* (1980), Cmnd 7844; see S. Prevezer, 'Criminal Homicides Other Than Murder' [1980] Crim LR 530.

311 See M. Wasik, 'Form and Function in the Law of Involuntary Manslaughter' [1994] Crim LR 883.

312 See H. Keating, 'The Restoration of a Serious Crime' [1996] Crim LR 535.

313 Consultation Paper, *Reforming the Law of Involuntary Manslaughter* (2000), para 2.11.

314 This seemingly fanciful scenario has occurred: see *State v Frazier* 98 SW 2d 707 (1936) Mo.

315 *Legislating the Criminal Code: Involuntary Manslaughter*, Law Com No 237 (1996).

316 Above, 245. See Keating above, and C. Wells, 'The Corporate Manslaughter Proposals: Pragmatism, Paradox and Peninsularity' [1996] Crim LR 545.

15

Offences related to homicide

1. Offences ancillary to murder

Parliament was not content to leave to the common law the punishment of acts preliminary to murder. The Offences Against the Person Act 1861 created offences of conspiracy, solicitation, attempt and threats to murder. The offences of attempt were particularly complicated[1] and were repealed by the Criminal Law Act 1967. Attempts to commit murder are now governed by the Criminal Attempts Act 1981.[2] The conspiracy provision was repealed by the Criminal Law Act 1977 and conspiracy to murder is governed by that Act.

(a) Solicitation

By s 4 of the Offences against the Person Act 1861 (as amended by the Criminal Law Act 1977) it is an offence punishable with life imprisonment to 'solicit, encourage, persuade or endeavour to persuade or . . . propose to any person, to murder any other person'.

The offence is relied on commonly to deal with those who hire 'contract killers' (who turn out to be undercover officers).

A child in the womb is not a person, so solicitation to kill it while in the womb is not this offence[3] but in *Shephard*[4] D's conviction was upheld when he wrote to a pregnant woman, 'When the kiddie is born you must lie on it . . . Don't let it live . . .'. The decision seems reasonable on the facts – D *was* soliciting murder – but the court put it on the strange ground that the child was in fact born alive. The implication, that the solicitation was committed only when the child was born alive or would have been undone if the child had been born dead, seems untenable.

This provision adds nothing to the common law of incitement except perhaps on a jurisdictional point. It is expressly provided that the person to be murdered need not be a British subject or within the jurisdiction; but this would generally not be necessary at common law either, since murder by a British citizen is indictable here though committed abroad.[5] The section, however, would catch an alien who, within the jurisdiction, incited

[1] See the 1st edition of this book, at 250–253. [2] Above, p 400.

[3] Nor is it the offence of incitement to cause grievous bodily harm to the mother, since the foetus is not part of the mother; above, p 431.

[4] [1919] 2 KB 125, a case found 'very hard to follow' in *Tait*, below, p 491.

[5] Above, p 429. Cf Greaves's note on the subject in Russell, 612, n2.

the commission of murder abroad and who might otherwise be immune under the rule in *Board of Trade v Owen*.[6] In *El-faisal*[7] the solicitation was to murder all 'Hindus, Jews and non-believers' (in Islam) and it was contemplated that the killings incited might be in any part of the world.

The offence may be committed by the publication of an article in a newspaper and it is immaterial that the readers of the newspapers are not identified.[8] It seems, however, that the offence is not committed unless the mind of the person solicited, etc is reached. Lord Alverstone CJ so held in *Krause*,[9] applying this limitation even to 'endeavour to persuade' which might be thought to cover an unsuccessful attempt to communicate. He held, however, that there was a common law attempt to commit the statutory offence where it was not proved that the offending letters, though sent, had ever reached the addressee.[10] If it is proved that the letter or other publication did reach the addressee, it is not necessary to prove that his mind was in any way affected by it.[11]

In deciding whether the words amount to a solicitation, etc, the jury will take account of (i) the language used; (ii) the occasion on which it was used; (iii) the persons to whom the words were used; and (iv) the circumstances surrounding their use. A soliciting to kill, not merely to do serious harm, must be proved.[12] In *Diamond*,[13] where Coleridge J so directed in leaving to the jury an article extolling the virtues of the assassins of tyrants, the occasion was just after an attempt on the life of the Viceroy of India, and the persons addressed were not 'a debating society of philosophers or divines' but 'anybody whom the paper would reach in this country or in Ireland'.

The proposed victims need not be named, provided that they are a sufficiently well-defined class. Where the indictment used the words 'sovereigns and rulers of Europe' Phillimore J thought 'rulers' a somewhat vague word, but there were some 18 or 20 sovereigns in Europe and that was a sufficiently well-defined class.[14] In *El-Faisal* the incitement was to kill all Jews, Christians, Americans, Hindus and non-believers, but it does not appear from the report to have been challenged as an insufficiently defined class.

There is no scope for an argument that the offence restricts the right to freedom of expression under Article 10 of the ECHR, since the limitation will, most obviously, be justified as necessary and proportionate for the protection of others.

(b) Threats to kill

Section 16 of the Offences Against the Person Act 1861 created an offence of making written threats to murder.[15] The Criminal Law Act 1977, Sch 12, replaces that provision with a new and broader s 16.

6 [1957] AC 602, [1957] 1 All ER 411.

7 [2004] EWCA Crim 343. See the discussion above p 356 relating to the application of a defence of self-defence.

8 *Most* (1881) 7 QBD 244.

9 (1902) 66 JP 121. Contrast *Horton v Mead* [1913] 1 KB 154.

10 See also *Banks* (1873) 12 Cox CC 393 at 399, per Quain J.

11 *Diamond* (1920) 84 JP 211; *Most*, above; *Krause*, above.

12 *Bainbridge* (1991) No 504/24/90, [1991] Crim LR 535 (not reported on this point).

13 Above, n 11.

14 *Antonelli and Barberi* (1905) 70 JP 4.

15 See the 3rd edition of this book, at 266.

A person who without lawful excuse makes to another a threat, intending that that other would fear that it would be carried out, to kill that other or a third person shall be guilty of an offence and liable on conviction on indictment to imprisonment for a term not exceeding ten years.

A foetus is not 'a third person' and so a threat to a mother to kill the foetus in her womb is not this offence.[16] If the threat had been to kill the child after it was born the court's inclination would have been to hold that it was still not an offence – if that were an offence, they asked, why should it not be an offence to threaten a non-pregnant woman to kill any child she might have in the future? – and this, the court thought, 'seems to stretch the meaning of "any third person" altogether too far'. Perhaps so, but this was a threat to kill a particular person, already existing in embryo at least, which is altogether a different threat in terms of its impact on the mother – or anyone else. The actual decision in *Shephard*,[17] ignoring the strange and unsupportable *dictum*, surely suggests that this would have been the offence – how could it be soliciting to kill a person and not threatening to kill a person? Moreover, it *is* a threat to kill a person, which the foetus will by then have become.

The offence is triable either way.[18] It follows closely the pattern of s 2 of the Criminal Damage Act 1971[19] which relates to threats to destroy or damage property. The threat may take any form[20] and presumably may be implied as well as express.[21] In principle, it is thought that a threat should be 'made to another' only when communicated; but, since it has been held that a 'demand' is 'made' within s 21(1) of the Theft Act 1968 when and where a letter containing it is posted,[22] it is at least possible that the same might be decided in the case of a threat. The inclusion of the words 'to another' in this section makes no difference, since the demand under s 21 must impliedly be made to another. Threats to kill in England and Wales made by emails from abroad have been sufficient to found the offence.[23]

(i) Lawful excuses

There would be a lawful excuse for making the threat if, in the circumstances known to D, the killing would be excusable if the threat were carried out, as where D makes the threat in self-defence.[24] A threat to kill may, however, be excusable where actual killing would not. To cause fear of death might be reasonable to prevent crime or arrest an offender whereas actually to kill would be quite unreasonable.[25] In many cases it will be desirable to tell the jury this.[26] Where there is some evidence of a lawful excuse, the onus is on the Crown to prove its absence and the question is always one for the jury.[27]

16 *Tait* [1990] 1 QB 290, [1989] Crim LR 834.
17 [1919] 2 KB 125, above, p 489.
18 Criminal Law Act 1977, Sch 2.
19 Below.
20 Below, p 918. See *Kennedy* [1998] Crim LR 739.
21 Cf *Solanke* [1969] 3 All ER 1383, [1970] 1 WLR 1.
22 *Treacy v DPP* [1971] AC 537, HL; below, p 801.
23 *M* [2003] EWCA Crim 3067.
24 See above, p 329.
25 The two preceding sentences were approved by the Court of Appeal in *Cousins* [1982] 2 All ER 115 at 117.
26 *Cousins*, above.
27 *Cousins*, above.

(c) Concealment of birth

This offence when first created by statute in 1623[28] was limited to (i) an illegitimate child who (ii) was born alive and whose body was disposed of so as to conceal its death (iii) by its mother. The current statute, the Offences Against the Person Act 1861, s 60, is subject to none of these limitations; it applies to any child, legitimate or not and whether born alive or not, whose body is disposed of so as to conceal its birth, by anyone. The section provides:

If any woman shall be delivered of a child, every person who shall, by any secret disposition of the dead body of the said child, whether such child died before, at, or after its birth, endeavour to conceal the birth thereof, shall be guilty of [an offence triable either way] and being convicted thereof shall be liable, at the discretion of the court, to be imprisoned for any term not exceeding two years . . .

The expressed object of the original statute was to catch those women who would otherwise escape on a charge of murder through the difficulty of proving live-birth and it was provided, indeed, that the woman should suffer death as in the case of murder. Under a later Act,[29] which repealed the 1623 provision, conviction of the new offence thereby created was possible only after an acquittal on an indictment for murder, but the current offence is an independent substantive crime for which an indictment will lie in the first instance. It was formerly the law that a person acquitted of murder, infanticide or child destruction might be convicted, on the same indictment, of concealment of birth; but this rule was abolished by the Criminal Law Act 1967, Sch 2.[30]

The test of a 'secret disposition' seems to be whether there was a likelihood that the body would be found. So, said Bovill CJ, it would be a secret disposition, 'if the body were placed in the middle of a moor in the winter, or on the top of a mountain, or in any other secluded place, where the body would not be likely to be found'[31].

If a body were thrown from a cliff top to the sea-shore, it might be a secret disposition if the place were secluded, but not if it were much frequented.[32] So where the body was left in a closed but unlocked box in D's bedroom in such a way as to attract the attention of those who daily entered the room, it was held that there was no secret disposition.[33]

The accused must be proved to have done some act[34] of disposition after the child has died. If the living body of the child is concealed and thereafter dies in the place of concealment, this offence is not committed,[35] though it is probable that murder or manslaughter is.

According to Erle J in *Berriman*[36] the child must have 'arrived at that stage of maturity at the time of birth that it might have been a living child'; so that the concealment of a foetus but a few months old would be no offence.[37]

28 21 Jac 1 c 27.

29 43 Geo 3 c 58.

30 On its historical application see M. B. Emmerichs, 'Trials of women for homicide in nineteenth century England' (1993) 5 Women and Criminal Justice 99.

31 *Brown* (1870) LR 1 CCR 244.

32 Ibid.

33 *George* (1868) 11 Cox CC 41. Cf *Sleep* (1864) 9 Cox CC 559; *Rosenberg* (1906) 70 JP 264.

34 *Derham* (1843) 1 Cox CC 56 (leaving body in privy where born not act of concealment).

35 *Coxhead* (1845) 1 Car & Kir 623 (decided under 9 Geo 4 c 31, but the principle is the same); *May* (1867) 10 Cox CC 448.

36 (1854) 6 Cox CC 388 at 390.

37 *Colmer* (1864) 9 Cox CC 506 is to the contrary but is doubted by Russell, 611, n 69.

(d) Other offences

It is a common law misdemeanour to dispose of or destroy a dead body with intent to prevent an inquest from being held.[38] There is a common law offence of preventing the decent and lawful burial of a body. It is an offence under the Perjury Act 1911 wilfully to make a false statement relating to births or deaths, or the live birth of a child.[39] And it is a summary offence under the Births and Deaths Registration Act 1953, s 36, to fail to give information concerning births and deaths when under a duty, as defined in the Act, to do so.

2. Complicity in suicide and suicide pacts[40]

(a) Position at common law

It was felony at common law for a sane person of the age of responsibility to kill himself either intentionally or in the course of trying to kill another.[41] Such a suicide was regarded as self-murder. Though the offender was, in the nature of things, personally beyond the reach of the law, his guilt was not without important consequences at common law, since it resulted in the forfeiture of his property. The results were more important, however, where the attempt failed, for then:

(i) since D had attempted to commit a felony he was guilty, under ordinary common law principles, of the misdemeanour of attempted suicide;

(ii) if D, in the course of trying to kill himself, killed another, he was guilty of murder under the doctrine of transferred malice.[42]

Though suicide was regarded as 'not a very serious crime',[43] an intention to commit it was the *mens rea* of murder. Moreover, one who was an accessory or principal in the second degree to the suicide of another was likewise guilty of murder as a secondary party. It followed that the survivor of a suicide pact was also guilty of murder, for, even if he did not actually kill, he was an aider and abettor, or at least an accessory before the fact to the other party's self-murder.

(b) Suicide Act 1961

Suicide has now ceased to be a crime by virtue of the Suicide Act 1961 which simply provides that: 'The rule of law whereby it is a crime for a person to commit suicide is hereby abrogated'.

38 Cf *Hunter* [1972] Crim LR 369. See M. Hirst, 'Preventing the Lawful Burial of a Body' [1996] Crim LR 96.

39 Perjury Act 1911, s 4(1).

40 For general discussions, see G. Williams, *The Sanctity of Life* (1957), ch 7; St John Stevas, *Life, Death and the Law* (1961), ch 6; Second Report of the Criminal Law Revision Committee (1960), Cmnd 1187. For a comprehensive review of more recent developments see K. Wheat, 'The Law's Treatment of the Suicidal' [2000] Med LR 182.

41 Hawkins, 1 PC 77.

42 *Hopwood* (1913) 8 Cr App R 143; *Spence* (1957) 41 Cr App R 80. Above, p 113.

43 *French* (1955) 39 Cr App R 192, per Lord Goddard CJ.

It inevitably followed that (i) attempted suicide ceased to be criminal; and (ii) there is no room for the doctrine of transferred malice where D kills V in the course of trying to kill himself, for there is no 'malice' to transfer.

In the latter case, D's liability depends on the general principles of murder and manslaughter. Thus, if the death of V was utterly unforeseeable, it would be accidental death; if there was gross negligence as to causing death or recklessness as to whether death or serious bodily harm was caused, it may be manslaughter; and if D foresaw death or serious bodily harm as virtually certain, it may be murder.[44]

There were very sound reasons for the abolition of the felony of suicide. The felon was beyond the reach of punishment; the legal sanction was not an effective deterrent – there were some 5,000 suicides a year; and the effect was merely to add to the distress and pain of the bereaved relatives. The most important practical effect of the Act, however, was its repeal by implication of the crime of attempted suicide. This also recognized the realities of the situation for it had been the practice for many years to institute proceedings only where it was necessary for the accused's protection, for example, because no relatives and friends were willing to give help. Thus, in 1959, of a total of 4,980 suicide attempts known to the police (and an estimated total of 25,000 actual concealed from the police) only 518 prosecutions were brought. The protection of the attempter may now be secured under the Mental Health Act 1983.

(i) Complicity in another's suicide

Section 2 of the Suicide Act created a new offence:

> A person who aids, abets, counsels or procures the suicide of another or an attempt by another to commit suicide, shall be liable on conviction on indictment to imprisonment for a term not exceeding fourteen years.

The words 'aids, abets, counsels or procures', are those used to define secondary participation in crime[45] but here they are used to define the principal offence. The interpretation of the words should be the same.[46] As in the law of secondary participation the words imply that the deed has been done or attempted.[47] Advising another to commit suicide does not amount to abetting or counselling unless and until that other does commit suicide. Since the aiding, etc is the principal offence, an indictment will lie for an attempt to aid, etc so that unsuccessful advice or encouragement is punishable as an attempt.[48] In *S*,[49] it was held that an attempt to aid and abet suicide was an appropriate charge where the principal had no intention to commit suicide. The distribution of a booklet giving advice to any person who wishes to commit suicide on how to do so efficiently and painlessly is not necessarily an offence under the section. In *Attorney-General v Able*,[50] Woolf J, as he then was, refused to grant a declaration that the

44 See above, p 436.

45 Cf the Accessories and Abettors Act 1861, ss 2, 8 and the Magistrates' Courts Act 1980, s 44; above, Ch 8.

46 See *Reed* [1982] Crim LR 819, CA; *A-G v Able*, below, n 50.

47 Above, p 170.

48 *McShane* [1977] Crim LR 737, CA, discussed by J. C. Smith in *Crime, Proof and Punishment* (1981), 21 at 32–33.

49 [2005] All ER (D) 339 (Mar).

50 [1984] QB 795, [1984] 1 All ER 277, QBD. See K. J. M. Smith, 'Assisting Suicide – The Attorney-General and the Voluntary Euthanasia Society' [1983] Crim LR 579.

distribution was unlawful, holding that an offence would be committed only if the distributor intended that the booklet would be used by someone contemplating suicide and that he would be (and in fact was) assisted or encouraged to do so. This is in accordance with the ordinary principles of the law of secondary participation.[51]

The crime of complicity in suicide is one which covers a variety of situations varying almost infinitely in moral culpability; from D who encourages V to commit suicide for the purpose of inheriting his property, to that of D who merely supplies a deadly drug to a suffering and dying V who is anxious to accelerate the end.[52] In order to achieve consistency in the bringing of prosecutions, this was made one of those crimes in which the consent of the Director of Public Prosecutions is required.[53] The Director has no power to give an undertaking that he will not prosecute the spouse of a person who suffers from an incurable disease which prevents her from committing suicide unaided, if he supplies her with the means of doing so when she requests it.[54] In *Pretty v UK*,[55] the European Court of Human Rights accepted that Article 2's protection provides a right to life, not a right to death. It was accepted that Articles 2, 3 and 9 were not engaged by the claim of a right to assisted death, Article 8 was engaged in such circumstances, but the UK's criminal prohibition was within Article 8(2).[56]

There has been much speculation as to the law's response to spouses and carers who, wishing to assist their terminally-ill loved ones to commit suicide, escort them to suicide clinics abroad (usually in Switzerland). Although prosecutions have been contemplated against those who have done so,[57] none appears to have been brought. Difficulties would arise, not only in establishing the relevant assistance but also in overcoming the jurisdictional problem arising from the death occurring overseas. In *Re Z*,[58] the Family

51 Above, Ch 8.

52 Although under the definition currently adopted, the causation in drug supply cases may give rise to conviction for manslaughter or even murder: *Finlay* [2003] EWCA Crim 3868, above, p 29. The Court of Appeal in *Kennedy No 2* [2005] EWCA Crim 685, concluded that the jury may be entitled to find that D who hands V a syringe which V uses to inject himself is liable for V's Death. D would be liable if he is 'jointly engaged in administering' the substance. As the CCRC pointed out in argument to the Court, this has the potential for D to be liable for murder where he hands V a syringe to self inject where D's intention is to help V in his declared suicide attempt. D ought not to be liable for murder but for assisted suicide. Parliament specifically provided for such circumstances and the common law ought not readily to undermine that explicit Parliamentary intent. The Court of Appeal's suggestion that 'it would be an abuse to prosecute someone assisting another to commit suicide for murder', [32] might not be regarded by all as a sufficient answer to the issue of substantive law, nor its comment that 'in practice it would not happen' [33].

53 *R (On the Application of Pretty) v DPP* [2002] 1 All ER 1, HL. See also on prosecution policy *Dunbar v Plant* [1997] 3 WLR 1261.

54 *R (Pretty) v DPP* [2002] 1 All ER 1, HL. The case decides that the Convention on Human Rights does not oblige a state to legalize assisted suicide. For comment see R. Tur, 'Legislative Techniques and Human Rights – The Sad Case of Assisted Suicide' [2003] Crim LR 3, calling for reform of the law or publication of prosecution guidance from the DPP. Cf D. Calvert Smith and S. O'Doherty, 'Legislative Technique and Human Rights – A response' [2003] Crim LR 384.

55 [2002] 35 EHRR 1.

56 For analysis, see M. Freeman, 'Death, Dying and the Human Rights Act 1998' (1999) 52 CLP 218; 'Denying Death its Dominion' (2002) 10 Med LR 245; Lady Hale, 'A Pretty Pass – When is there a Right to Die?' [2003] 32 Common Law World Review 1.

57 See eg, the widow of R. Crew as discussed in News reports for 22 Jan 2003.

58 [2004] EWHC 2817 (Fam).

Division court ruled that once it was determined that the terminally ill person was competent, her local authority had no power to seek to maintain an injunction to restrain her spouse from complying with the wife's wishes to take her to Switzerland so that she could receive medical assistance there in committing suicide. Hedley J concluded that the court should not of its own motion continue the injunction preventing her from travelling to the death clinic.

English law admits of no defence of mercy killing or euthanasia, nor is there a defence of physician assisted suicide.[59] Medical practitioners' obligations regarding the withdrawal of life sustaining treatment are considered in Chapter 4 above.[60] A competent but paralysed adult is entitled to refuse to continue medical treatment. This is not suicide and the health care professionals are not assisting such.[61] There is no breach of Article 2 of the ECHR by the withdrawal of treatment in such cases.

(ii) Reform

The European Court in *Pretty v UK* declined to express a view on whether an assisted suicide provision would be compliant with Article 2. At the time of writing (March 2005) there is before Parliament a Private Members Bill for the Assisted Dying of the Terminally Ill. This would enable a competent adult who is suffering as a result of a terminal illness to receive medical assistance to die at his own request; and to make provision for a person suffering from a terminal illness to receive pain relief medication. Clause 1 renders it lawful for a physician to assist a qualifying patient who had made a declaration to die. Clauses 2–5 specify the qualifying conditions (physician and consulting physician satisfied of request from patient to be assisted to die, competence of patient, terminal illness of patient, unbearable suffering as a result of illness, etc). The Bill sets out the form of the advance declaration that must be made (witnessed by two individuals including a practising solicitor).

(c) Suicide pacts

A party to a suicide pact who aids, abets, counsels or procures the other party to commit suicide is of course guilty of the offence under s 2 of the Suicide Act.[62]

The survivor of such a pact may, however, have either himself killed the deceased or have procured a third party to do it. Such cases do not fall within the Suicide Act, but within the Homicide Act 1957, s 4(1), which, as amended by the Suicide Act, provides:

> It shall be manslaughter and shall not be murder for a person acting in pursuance of a suicide pact between him and another to kill the other[63] or be party to the other being killed by a third person.

59 Cf Netherlands on which see J. Griffiths, 'Assisted Suicide in the Netherlands' (1995) 58 MLR 232.

60 See especially the detailed analysis in *R (Burke) v GMC* [2004] EWHC 1879 (Admin).

61 *B (Consent to Treatment)* [2002] 2 All ER 449.

62 Until the enactment of the Suicide Act, this was manslaughter under the Homicide Act 1957, s 4. The public interest does not normally call for the prosecution of the survivor of a suicide pact: *Dunbar v Plant* [1997] 3 WLR 1261, CA (Civ Div) per Phillips LJ at 1285.

63 If, otherwise than in pursuance of a suicide pact, D kills V at V's request, D is of course guilty of murder. Cf *Robinson*, above, p 159.

'Suicide pact' is defined by s 4(3) of the Homicide Act as:

a common agreement between two or more persons having for its object the death of all of them, whether or not each is to take his own life, but nothing done by a person who enters into a suicide pact shall be treated as done by him in pursuance of the pact unless it is done while he has the settled intention of dying in pursuance of the pact.

The onus on a charge of murder of establishing the defence of suicide pact is put by s 4(2) on the accused and the standard of proof required is the balance of probabilities. This is not incompatible with Article 6(2) of the ECHR.[64]

The distinction between complicity in suicide and manslaughter by suicide pact is not entirely satisfactory.[65] The latter, being punishable with life imprisonment, is evidently the more serious crime; yet, since the person guilty of it always intends to die himself, it is difficult to see how it can compare in moral heinousness with the case of D who incites V to die in order that he may live and enjoy V's property.

The distinction between the two crimes may be very fine. If D and V agree to gas themselves and D alone survives, it appears that he will be liable under the Homicide Act if he turned on the tap[66] and under the Suicide Act if V did. It may frequently be difficult to establish who did such an act and this is recognized by the provision in s 2(2) of the Suicide Act that, on the trial of an indictment for murder or manslaughter, the jury may find the accused guilty of complicity in suicide if that is proved. If D is charged with murder and he establishes on a balance of probabilities that V committed suicide in pursuance of a suicide pact he is entitled to be acquitted of murder and may presumably be convicted of complicity in suicide since he has, in effect, admitted his guilt. If, however, D was charged with complicity and it appeared that he had killed V, he would have to be acquitted.

There is considerable pressure for reform of the law. Individuals prosecuted for manslaughter of their nearest and dearest may well receive low sentences, and the pain and anguish of their bereavement is exacerbated by the criminal process.[67] Supporters of the law point to the significant protection it affords the vulnerable who face pressure to commit suicide when they perceive themselves to be a burden on carers.

3. Infanticide[68]

The Infanticide Act 1938, s 1(1), provides:

64 *A-G's Reference (No 1 of 2004)* [2004] 1 WLR 2111 [130]–[132].

65 It is regrettable that the Law Commission was not able to consider suicide in its most recent review of Partial Defences to Murder (Law Com No 290, 2004).

66 But if D pours out a glass of poison and V takes it, he will be liable under the Suicide Act 1961.

67 See *Blackburn* (2005) 14 Jan, CCC, suspended sentence for killing terminally ill wife in suicide pact, and see the news reports for 15 Jan 2005.

68 See D. Seaborne Davies, 'Child-Killing in English Law' (1937) 1 MLR 203; MACL 301; G. Williams, *The Sanctity of Life* (1957), 25–45; K. O'Donovan, 'The Medicalisation of Infanticide' [1984] Crim LR 259; R. D. Mackay, 'The consequences of killing very young children' [1993] Crim LR 21; A. Wilczynski and A. Morris, 'Parents who kill their children' [1993] Crim LR 31; D. Maeir-Katkin and R. Ogle, 'A Rationale for Infanticide Laws' [1993] Crim LR 903; M. Jackson, 'Infanticide: Historical Perspectives' (1996) 146 NLJ 416. The Court of Appeal recently called for its urgent reform: *Kai-Whitewind* [2005] All ER (D) 14 (May).

Where a woman by any wilful act or omission causes the death of her child being a child under the age of twelve months, but at the time of the act or omission the balance of her mind was disturbed by reason of her not having fully recovered from the effect of giving birth to the child or by reason of the effect of lactation consequent upon the birth of the child, then, notwithstanding that the circumstances were such that but for this Act the offence would have amounted to murder, she shall be guilty of [an offence], to wit of infanticide, and may for such offence be dealt with and punished as if she had been guilty of the offence of manslaughter of the child.

This enactment replaces a statute of 1922 which confined the defence to a 'newly-born' child, a term which the Court of Criminal Appeal had held to be inapplicable to a child of 35 days, so that the mother was convicted of murder.[69] The 1922 Act was itself the result of an agitation over very many years during which it was practically impossible to get convictions of murder by mothers of their young children because of the disapproval by public and professional opinion of a law which regarded such killings as ordinary murders. Where a conviction was obtained, the judge had to pronounce a sentence of death which everyone, except perhaps the offender, knew would not be carried out. A number of reasons were advanced why infanticide should be considered less reprehensible than other killings: (i) the injury done to the child was less, for it was incapable of the kind of suffering which might be undergone by the adult victim of a murder; (ii) the loss of its family was less great; (iii) the crime did not create the sense of insecurity in society which other murders caused; (iv) generally, the heinousness of the crime was less, the motive very frequently being the concealment of the shame of the birth of an illegitimate child; and (v) where the killing is done by the mother, her responsibility may be reduced by the disturbance of her mind caused by the stress of the birth. It is, of course, the last of these considerations which is the governing one in the present legislation.[70] The killing of an infant by persons other than the mother, or by the mother if the balance of her mind is not disturbed, remains murder.

This section provides both a charge of infanticide, and also a partial defence to murder: by s 1(2) that a woman indicted for the murder of her child under the age of 12 months may be acquitted of murder and convicted of infanticide if the conditions of s 1(1) are satisfied.

Where the charge is murder, an evidential burden on the issue of disturbance will fall on D; but the onus of *proof* remains with the Crown. Where the charge is infanticide, the onus of proving disturbance appears to be on the Crown; but this, of course, is unlikely to be contested.

It appears that the principles on which the Infanticide Act was based may be no longer accepted and that mental illness is not now considered to be a significant cause of infanticide. In most cases the relationship of incomplete recovery from the effects of childbirth or lactation to the child-killing is remote.[71] If the true trigger for the killing is a range of other social factors associated with caring for a young child the offence/defence ought to be available to carers of either sex. Moreover, when the Infanticide Act was

69 *O'Donoghue* (1927) 20 Cr App R 132.

70 The validity of this psychiatric basis for the offence has been doubted see N. Walker, *Crime and Insanity in England* (1968), vol 1, 87–104, cf D. Maier-Katkin and R. Ogle, above.

71 Butler Report, Cmnd 6244 at paras 19.23–19.24.

passed, there was no defence of diminished responsibility to murder.[72] The Butler Committee thought that that defence would now probably cover all cases and recommended the abolition of the separate offence of infanticide.[73] The CLRC disagreed, at first on the ground that, so long as the prosecution are unable to charge manslaughter by reason of diminished responsibility, infanticide has the advantage that it avoids the necessity of charging the mother with murder;[74] and later on the ground that diminished responsibility might not cover all the circumstances which in practice may be held to justify an infanticide verdict.[75] According to the Royal College of Psychiatrists, these circumstances include:

> (1) overwhelming stress from the social environment being highlighted by the birth of a baby, with the emphasis on the unsuitability of the accommodation etc; (2) overwhelming stress from an additional member to a household struggling with poverty; (3) psychological injury, and pressures and stress from a husband or other member of a family from the mother's incapacity to arrange the demands of the extra member of the family; (4) failure of bonding between mother and child through illness or disability which impairs the development of the mother's capacity to care for the infant.

In order to bring the law into line with its practical operation, and because of the difficulty of establishing a direct connection between giving birth and the imbalance of the woman's mind, the CLRC recommend that the test should be whether the balance of her mind was disturbed by reason of the effect of giving birth to the child *or circumstances consequent upon that birth*.[76] A dissentient view was that the effect would be to make adverse social conditions a defence to child killing.[77] Because of the decision to recommend the broadening of the offence in this way (in law, if not in practice)[78] the CLRC abandoned its earlier tentative recommendation that the killing of older children of the family should be infanticide and not murder;[79] and recommended that the maximum penalty should be five years' imprisonment and not two, as they had previously been disposed to think.[80] It is regrettable that the Law Commission was not invited to include Infanticide in its recent review of Partial Defences to Murder.[81]

The CLRC thought that, because of the way in which the offence is drafted, it is not possible to charge a person with attempting to commit infanticide[82] but McCowan J has held that such an indictment will lie.[83]

[72] For comparison of the defence and offence see R. D. Mackay, above, n 68.

[73] Ibid. For criticism see D. Maier-Katkin and R. Ogle, above. It has the advantage of applying to carers of either sex.

[74] CLRC/OAP/WP 26. The Committee tentatively suggested that a person apparently suffering from diminished responsibility should be indictable for manslaughter but later withdrew this proposal: CLRC/OAP/R, para 95.

[75] Research reveals that half of women who plead or are convicted are not suffering any mental disorder. See A. Wilczynski and A. Korris, above.

[76] CLRC/OAP/R, paras 103–106.

[77] See Annexes 7 and 8 to the Report.

[78] On the use of the offence in modern times see R. D. Mackay above and A. Wilczynski and A. Morris, above.

[79] Para 106. [80] Para 108.

[81] Law Commission, *Partial Defences to Murder* (Law Com No 290, 2004). See *Whitewind* (above), n 68.

[82] CLRC/OAP/R para 113.

[83] *K A Smith* [1983] Crim LR 739 and commentary.

4. The Domestic Violence, Crime and Victims Act 2004

Insurmountable problems arose in prosecutions for the non-accidental serious injury or death of a young child when the only individuals who had access to the child at the time of the incident (usually the two primary carers) denied responsibility. Although clear that at least one of the carers was guilty of a serious crime, it was often impossible to prove beyond reasonable doubt that the ill-treatment was at the hand of one (or both) rather than the other. The death or injury may have occurred while one carer was absent. Further, it was also often impossible to prove whether the carer not directly responsible was guilty as an accomplice. Prior to the 2004 Act, if all that could be proved is that the offence was committed either by D1 or by D2, both had to be acquitted. Only if it could be proved that the one who did not commit the crime must have aided and abetted it could both be convicted. This was as true where carers were charged with injury to their child as it was in the case of any other defendants. The only difference was that one carer may have a duty to intervene to prevent the ill-treatment of their child by the other when a stranger would have no such duty. It was for the prosecution to prove that the carer who did not inflict the injuries must have aided and abetted the infliction by failure to fulfill that duty or otherwise.

In a series of cases the Court of Appeal reluctantly accepted that trials in such circumstances would not normally proceed beyond a defence submission of no case to answer.[84] The result proved too much for some courts, and strained attempts to circumvent the problem were adopted. These were unsatisfactory.[85] The problem was a substantial one. Research revealed that in the UK no fewer than three children under the age of 10 died or suffered serious injury each week, and only 27% of cases led to a conviction.[86] The difficulties had exercised great academic minds, but no consensus was reached as to the optimal solution.[87] Was it better to create a new offence to catch A, who *ought to have* been aware of the wrongdoing of the other carer, B, who caused the injury? Alternatively (or additionally) was it appropriate to alter the procedure in such cases to upset the traditional burden of proof and presumption of innocence, or to admit pre-trial incriminating statements made by A against B, or to provide a statutory obligation to account for the death or injury?[88]

Following detailed consideration by the Law Commission, proposals for new offences and procedural changes were made, and provisions based on, though differing significantly from those recommendations were implemented in the Domestic Violence, Crime

84 *Russell and Russell* [1987] Crim LR 494; *Lane and Lane* (1985) 82 Cr App R 5. For a valuable direction where one of two interrogating police officers has caused injury, see *Forman* [1988] Crim LR 677 (Judge Woods).

85 *Gibson and Gibson* (1984) 80 Cr App R 24. See commentary [1984] Crim LR 615.

86 See the Law Commission, *Children: Their Non-Accidental Death or Serious Injury (Criminal Trials)* (Law Com No 282, 2003), Part II.

87 See generally, G.Williams, 'Which of you did it?' (1989) 52 MLR 179; E. Griew, 'It Must Have Been One of Them' [1989] Crim LR 129.

88 See Law Com No 282, 2003, Part V.

and Victims Act 2004.[89] Section 6 of that Act introduces controversial procedural changes whereby inferences can be drawn from a defendant's silence even where no case to answer would otherwise be established. Section 5 introduces the new offence.

Section 5 provides:

(1) A person ('D') is guilty of an offence if –

(a) a child or vulnerable adult ('V') dies as a result of the unlawful act of a person who –

(i) was a member of the same household as V, and

(ii) had frequent contact with him,

(b) D was such a person at the time of that act,

(c) at that time there was a significant risk of serious physical harm being caused to V by the unlawful act of such a person, and

(d) either D was the person whose act caused V's death or –

(i) D was, or ought to have been, aware of the risk mentioned in paragraph (c),

(ii) D failed to take such steps as he could reasonably have been expected to take to protect V from the risk, and

(iii) the act occurred in circumstances of the kind that D foresaw or ought to have foreseen.

(2) The prosecution does not have to prove whether it is the first alternative in subsection (1)(d) or the second (sub-paragraphs (i) to (iii)) that applies.

(3) If D was not the mother or father of V –

(a) D may not be charged with an offence under this section if he was under the age of 16 at the time of the act that caused V's death;

(b) for the purposes of subsection (1)(d)(ii) D could not have been expected to take any such step as is referred to there before attaining that age.

(4) For the purposes of this section –

(a) a person is to be regarded as a 'member' of a particular household, even if he does not live in that household, if he visits it so often and for such periods of time that it is reasonable to regard him as a member of it;

(b) where V lived in different households at different times, 'the same household as V' refers to the household in which V was living at the time of the act that caused V's death.

(5) For the purposes of this section an 'unlawful' act is one that –

(a) constitutes an offence, or

(b) would constitute an offence but for being the act of –

(i) a person under the age of ten, or

(ii) a person entitled to rely on a defence of insanity.

Paragraph (b) does not apply to an act of D.

[89] In particular the Law Commission had proposed a new offence of aggravated child cruelty under s 1 of the Children and Young Person Act 1933, and had produced an offence which dealt with both serious injury and death in relation to children only. For comment on the Law Commission proposals, see P. Glazebrook, 'Insufficient Child Protection' [2003] Crim LR 541, proposing an extremely wide offence which it is submitted would extend the ambit of the criminal law too far.

The offence carries a maximum sentence of imprisonment for 14 years. The offence is limited to cases in which the child or vulnerable adult dies. Despite the attempts to define the key elements, numerous issues will fall for judicial consideration. In some respects the offence is unsatisfactorily wide. It is effectively a crime of negligence since the fault on D's part if he is not the direct cause of the death is a question of whether he *ought to have been* aware of the risk. The only limitation to this is in s(1)(ii) since D's failure is to be assessed against the steps he could be reasonably expected to make. If D is a child or has a learning disability this will be relevant to determining what he could be expected to do. What of the person who is petrified of D? In addition, the core element of 'household' might be regarded as inadequately defined for an offence of this seriousness. Moreover, the conduct which caused death is not limited to that which would form specific crimes provided it was unlawful. However, the offence is heavily qualified: the risk of which D ought to have been aware is a 'significant' one of 'serious injury' and the death must have occurred in the circumstances that D ought to have foreseen. D who is aware that X has previously shaken their baby, V, violently might not be guilty if X caused V's death by, for example, dipping its dummy in methadone to stop its incessant crying. In addition, in assessing the reasonableness of the steps that ought to have been taken by D, the question for the jury is, seemingly, whether the steps are reasonable for this particular defendant to take. Thus, juries might hesitate before convicting D who lives in an abusive and violent relationship with X, and is aware that X batters their child as he does D. Furthermore, it is odd that some categories of carer who have regular contact – for example, nannies – are not caught by the Act.

Where D's unlawful act is the cause of the death, it is unclear why this section would be used in preference to manslaughter or murder, other than in circumstances in which there are two or more in defendants from the household and all are charged under this section.

5. Child destruction and abortion[90]

It has already been observed that it is not murder to kill a child in the womb or while in the process of being born. Nor is it, in itself, an offence against the person of the mother, since the foetus is not part of the mother.[91] Though the killing of the child in the womb after quickening was a misdemeanour at common law, the present law on the subject is statutory. Section 58 of the Offences Against the Person Act 1861 (subject to the Abortion Act 1967)[92] prohibits attempts to procure miscarriage from any time after the conception of the child until its birth; and s 1 of the Infant Life (Preservation) Act 1929 prohibits the killing of any child which is capable of being born alive. The two offences thus overlap. Procuring a miscarriage so as to kill a child capable of being born alive may amount to both offences. Killing a child in the process of being born is not procuring a miscarriage and can amount only to child destruction.

90 See I. Kennedy and A. Grubb, *Medical Law: Texts and Materials (2000)* Part III and G. Williams, *The Sanctity of Life and the Criminal Law*, (1957), 139–223 and 'The Legalization of Medical Abortion' (1964) The Eugenics Review; B. M. Dickens, *Abortion and the Law* (1966); B. Bennett, *Abortion* (2004).

91 *A-G's Reference (No 3 of 1994)*, above, p 432.

92 See below, p 508.

(a) Child destruction[93]

Section 1 of the Infant Life (Preservation) Act 1929 provides:

(1) Subject as hereinafter in this subsection provided, any person who, with intent to destroy the life of a child capable of being born alive, by any wilful act causes a child to die before it has an existence independent of its mother, shall be guilty of an offence, to wit, of child destruction, and shall be liable on conviction thereof on indictment to imprisonment for life: Provided that no person shall be found guilty of an offence under this section unless it is proved that the act which caused the death of the child was not done in good faith for the purpose only of preserving the life of the mother.

(2) For the purposes of this Act, evidence that a woman had at any material time been pregnant for a period of twenty-eight weeks or more shall be prima facie proof that she was at that time pregnant of a child capable of being born alive.

While the actual physical condition in which a foetus would be following birth is a matter for expert medical evidence, whether a foetus at that stage of development can properly be described as 'a child capable of being born alive' is a question of law for the court. Differing interpretations have been proffered including that the expression is limited to the child in the process of being born, that it extended to any viable foetus, and widest of all, that it extended to any foetus capable of being born alive, however short lived its existence.[94]

In *C v S*,[95] the medical experts disagreed as to whether a foetus at the stage it will normally have reached by the 18th to the 21st week would be so described. The court held, in the light of the evidence that it would never be capable of breathing that it could not.[96] In *Rance v Mid-Downs Health Authority*,[97] a civil action, Brooke J thought the meaning of the phrase was clear and that a child is 'born alive' if 'after birth, it exists as a live child, that is to say breathing and living by reason of its breathing through its own lungs alone, without deriving any of its living or power of living by or through any connection with its mother'.

It is not necessary that the child be capable of survival into old age or even for a period of days. Applying this test, Brooke J was satisfied to 'a very high standard of proof' that the particular child was capable of being born alive after 26 weeks of pregnancy and therefore to kill him would have been the offence of child destruction.

The Abortion Act 1967 uses the phrase 'protecting the life of the viable foetus' in respect of the provisions of the 1929 Act; but, rejecting the view that 'viable' has a different and more restrictive meaning, Brooke J held that it was merely used as convenient shorthand for 'capable of being born alive' and its use in 1967 had no effect on the meaning of the 1929 Act.

93 See J. Keown, 'The Scope of the Offence of Child Destruction' [1988] 104 LQR 120.

94 See J. Keown for discussion of the merits of each interpretation. See also D. Price, 'How viable is the present scope of the offence of child destruction' (1987) 16 Anglo Am LR 220.

95 [1988] QB 135, [1987] 1 All ER 1230, CA.

96 Ibid, at 1238–1239 (Heilbron J). Cf G. Wright 'Capable of Being Born Alive?' (1981) 131 NLJ 188; 'The Legality of Abortion by Prostaglandin' [1984] Crim LR 347; *Tunkel and Wright* [1985] Crim LR 133.

97 [1991] 1 QB 587, [1991] 1 All ER 801, QBD.

The European Court has declined to decide whether the protection of Article 2 extends to the unborn child. It was acknowledged in *Vo v France*[98] that the Convention institutions have not 'ruled out the possibility that in certain circumstances safeguards may be extended to the unborn child'.[99] The Court noted that 'the unborn child is not regarded as a person directly protected by Article 2 of the Convention and that if the unborn do have a right to life it is implicitly limited by the mother's rights and interests'.[100]

The jury may convict of this offence on an indictment for murder, manslaughter, infanticide or an offence under s 58 of the Offences Against the Person Act 1861; and on an indictment for child destruction, they may convict of an offence under s 58 of the Offences Against the Person Act 1861.[101]

(i) Interrelationship with the Abortion Act 1967

The Abortion Act 1967 legalizes abortion in certain circumstances and subject to certain formalities. It originally provided that it should not affect the offence of child destruction but, as amended by the Human Fertilisation and Embryology Act 1990,[102] s 5(1) of the 1967 Act states that:

> No offence under [the 1929 Act] shall be committed by a registered medical practitioner who terminates a pregnancy in accordance with the provisions of [the Abortion Act 1967].

Since this amendment came into effect it is not an offence for a doctor, complying with the terms of the 1967 Act, to cause the death of a child capable of being born alive. If the death of such a child is caused by a doctor who is not complying with the provisions of the 1967 Act, or if it is caused by any other person, then it is *prima facie* child destruction. If, however, the act is done for the purpose only of preserving the life of the mother, that will be a defence to a charge of child destruction under the 1929 Act but not to a charge under the 1861 Act unless the *Bourne* defence of necessity has survived the 1967 Act – a matter of some doubt, considered below.[103]

A wide meaning was given to the words 'for the purpose only of preserving the life of the mother' by MacNaghten J in *Bourne*.[104] This was *obiter*, so far as the Infant Life (Preservation) Act 1929 was concerned, since the charge was brought under the Offences Against the Person Act 1861; but MacNaghten J took the view that those words represented the common law and were implicit in the 1861 Act by virtue of the word 'unlawfully'. He said:

> As I have said, I think those words ['for the purpose of preserving the life of the mother'] ought to be construed in a reasonable sense, and if the doctor is of opinion, on reasonable grounds and with adequate knowledge, that the probable consequence of the continuance of the pregnancy will be to make the woman a physical or mental wreck, the jury are quite entitled to take the view that the doctor who under these circumstances and in the honest belief, operates, is operating for the purpose of preserving the life of the mother.[105]

98 [2004] 2 FCR 577. 99 Para 82. 100 Para 80.

101 For an example of a conviction where D used violence against the pregnant woman with the intention of causing the death of the child see *Virgo* (1988) Cr App R (S) 427.

102 On which see A. Grubb, 'The New Law on Abortion: Clarification or Ambiguity' [1991] Crim LR 659.

103 Below, p 512.

104 [1939] 1 KB 687, [1938] 3 All ER 615. 105 [1939] 1 KB at 693, 694, [1938] 3 All ER at 619.

Both before and after this, however, the judge stressed that the test was whether the operation was performed in good faith for the purpose of preserving the *life* of the mother and the passage may be intended to refer only to such enquiries to health as will shorten life because the judge had said '. . . life depends upon health and health may be so gravely impaired that death results'.[106]

Informed medical opinion construed the judgment in the wider sense[107] and this appears to have been vindicated. In *Bergmann and Ferguson*[108] Morris J is reported to have said that the court will not look too narrowly into the question of danger to life where danger to health is anticipated. Then in *Newton and Stungo*[109] Ashworth J stated in his direction to the jury, 'Such use of an instrument is unlawful unless the use is made in good faith for the purposes of preserving the life *or health* of the woman', adding that this included mental as well as physical health. Newton was acquitted of manslaughter by criminal negligence, but convicted of manslaughter by unlawfully using an instrument and of the offence under s 58. He did not appeal (obviously the direction was favourable to him); but it is thought likely that Ashworth J's view would be accepted by the appellate courts.

The criterion of the defence as it has been applied by the courts is a subjective one; that is, the question is not whether the operation is in fact necessary to preserve the life of the mother but whether D believes it to be necessary.[110] In answering this question the court will take account of the size of the fee, a large fee being evidence of bad faith;[111] and whether D followed accepted medical practice.[112] What is the position if the operation was in fact necessary, but was performed by D in bad faith, to oblige, as he thought, the mere convenience of the woman and for a high fee? One view might be that there is no *actus reus* here,[113] but it is thought more likely that the defence will be limited to the case of a *bona fide* belief.[114] Thus, in *Newton*, it does not seem to have been decided that an operation was unnecessary; only that Newton did not *bona fide* believe it to be necessary.[115]

These cases all relate to s 58 of the 1861 Act, where they are probably no longer in point.[116] Since they purport to be an interpretation of the proviso in the 1929 Act, however, they cannot be ignored in considering child destruction. On the other hand it is quite possible that the court, when actually confronted with the interpretation of the proviso, might take a stricter and narrower view of what constitutes the preservation of the life of the mother.

106 [1939] 1 KB at 692, [1938] 3 All ER at 617.

107 J. Havard, 'Therapeutic Abortion' [1958] Crim LR 600 at 605.

108 (1948) unreported; *The Sanctity of Life* (1957), 154; 1 BMJ 1008.

109 [1958] Crim LR 469, fully considered by J. Havard in 'Therapeutic Abortion' [1958] Crim LR 600.

110 *Bergmann and Ferguson* cited in *The Sanctity of Life*, 165.

111 A significant difference between the case of *Newton* and that of *Stungo* (who was acquitted) seems to have been that Stungo took a very small fee, Newton a high one.

112 See J. Havard [1958] Crim LR at 607, 608.

113 Cf the discussion of *Dadson*, above, p 42.

114 Cf G. Williams, *The Sanctity of Life*, 166, who would agree with this conclusion on the ground that the crime is in the nature of an attempt. But it is just as much a substantive crime as burglary.

115 But even if it was necessary to carry out the operation, it was probably not necessary to carry it out in the way it was done – in a consulting room, the patient being sent back to a hotel in a taxi afterwards.

116 Below.

(b) Attempting to procure miscarriage

The common law misdemeanour of abortion applied only after the child had quickened in the womb. To procure an abortion before this occurred was no crime. A statute of 1803[117] enacted that it should be a felony punishable by death to administer a poison with intent to procure the miscarriage of a woman quick[118] with child and a felony punishable with imprisonment or transportation for 14 years to administer poison with a like intent to a woman who was not proved to be quick with child. The distinction between quick and non-quick women gave rise to complications and it disappeared in the re-enactment of the law by the Offences Against the Person Act 1837[119] which established the law substantially in its modern form. The current statute is the Offences Against the Person Act 1861, which provides by s 58:

> Every woman being with child who, with intent to procure her own miscarriage, shall unlawfully administer to herself any poison or other noxious thing, or shall unlawfully use any instrument or other means whatsoever with the like intent, and whosoever, with intent to procure the miscarriage of any woman, whether she be or be not with child, shall unlawfully administer to her or cause to be taken by her any poison or other noxious thing, or shall unlawfully use any instrument or other means whatsoever with the like intent, shall be guilty of an offence, and being convicted thereof shall be liable. . . to imprisonment for life . . .

The extension of the law was of great practical importance, since most self-induced abortions occur before quickening. Prescription, supply, administration or use of the contraceptive pill, mini-pill and morning-after pill does not contravene s 58 of the OAPA 1861 because the pill is not an abortifacient.[120]

The statute makes it clear beyond all doubt that the offence may be committed by the woman herself as well as by others, the only distinction being that if the woman herself is charged, it must be proved that she is in fact pregnant, whereas this is not necessary if the accused is someone other than the mother herself.

The Act is not confined to the use of a 'poison or other noxious thing' or 'any instrument'; the 'other means' include manual interference, even though no instrument is employed and the medical evidence is that the act could not, in the circumstances, cause a miscarriage.[121] The *actus reus* consists simply in the *administration* of the poison or other noxious thing or the *use* of the instrument or other means.

The Act distinguishes between 'poison' and 'noxious thing' and it has been held that in the case of something other than a 'recognized poison' the thing must be administered in such quantity as to be in fact harmful though not necessarily abortifacient.[122] A sleeping pill has been held not to be noxious;[123] and the administration in harmless quantities of

[117] 43 Geo 3 c 58.

[118] 'Quickening' was an ambiguous term but was generally accepted to mean the time at which the mother felt the motion of the child. It was commonly treated as being around the 15th/16th week.

[119] 7 Will & 1 Vic c 85.

[120] *R (On the Application of Smeaton) v Secretary of State for Health* [2002] All ER (D) 115 (Apr); [2002] Crim LR 664.

[121] *Spicer* [1955] Crim LR 772.

[122] *Marlow* (1964) 49 Cr App R 49 (Brabin J); *Douglas* [1966] NZLR 45. Cf *Marcus* [1981] 2 All ER 833, below, p 564.

[123] *Weatherall* [1968] Crim LR 115 (Judge Brodrick) below, p 566.

oil of juniper was no *actus reus*;[124] but Denman J said that it would be otherwise if a thing, innocuous when administered in small quantities, were to be administered in such quantities as to be noxious. Field and Stephen JJ thought that if the thing were a 'recognized poison' the offence might be committed even though the quantity given was so small as to be incapable of doing harm. The distinction is hardly a logical one for 'recognized poisons' may be beneficial when taken in small quantities and in such a case the thing taken is no more poisonous than the oil of juniper was noxious.

It has been observed that the section makes a distinction between the case where the woman administers, etc the thing to herself and that where it is administered to her by another. In the former case the woman must be proved to be with child, in the latter case, she need not. The importance of this distinction has been diminished by the decision in *Whitchurch*[125] that a woman who is not pregnant may be convicted of conspiring with another to procure her own abortion and by the decision in *Sockett* that such a woman[126] may be convicted of aiding and abetting in the offence of the other, if it is complete. Thus, in effect, the woman will be excused on the ground that she is not with child only in cases where she is not acting in concert with another. While one view is that this interpretation has 'set at naught' the intention of Parliament,[127] it has been argued elsewhere[128] that it would have been perfectly reasonable for Parliament to discriminate between the non-pregnant woman who calls in the back-street or professional abortionist and the non-pregnant woman who administers to herself an abortifacient in the solitude of her own bedroom. The point is perhaps not of great practical importance as it appears that it is not the practice to prosecute the mother today.[129]

(c) Knowingly supplying or procuring poison, etc

Section 59 of the Offences Against the Person Act makes a substantive crime of certain preparatory acts, some of which might amount to counselling or abetting the offence under s 58. It provides:

> Whosoever shall unlawfully supply or procure any poison or other noxious thing, or any instrument or thing whatsoever, knowing that the same is intended to be unlawfully used or employed with intent to procure the miscarriage of any woman, whether she be or be not with child, shall be guilty of a misdemeanour, and being convicted thereof shall be liable . . . to imprisonment . . . for any term not exceeding five years . . .

The word 'procure', on the first occasion on which it is used in the section, means 'get possession of something of which you have not got possession already';[130] so D's conviction was quashed when there was no evidence as to how or when he had come into the possession of the instruments and the judge had misdirected the jury that the word was 'wide enough to include getting instruments or getting them together or preparing them for use'.[131]

124 *Cramp* (1880) 5 QBD 307.
125 (1890) 24 QBD 420; above, p 395.
126 (1908) 72 JP 428; above, p 395.
127 Williams, CLGP, 673.
128 B. Hogan, 'Victims as Parties to Crime' [1962] Crim LR 683 at 690.
129 Cf *The Sanctity of Life* at 146; *Peake* (1932) 97 JPN 353.
130 *Mills* [1963] 1 QB 522, [1963] 1 All ER 202, following *Scully* (1903) 23 NZLR 380.
131 [1963] 1 QB at 524.

This leaves a gap in the legislation. As Crown counsel said:[132]

. . . if a defendant went to a chemist and bought an instrument to abort A, he would have committed an offence, but if he then put the instrument away in a cupboard and later, for the purpose of aborting B went to the cupboard and took the instrument he would not have committed an offence.

The words, 'knowing that the same is intended to be unlawfully used' have been construed in an extraordinarily wide sense and one highly unfavourable to the accused. Their natural meaning is surely that some person other than the accused must intend the unlawful user and that the accused must know of that intention. But it has been held that it is enough if the accused *believes* that the poison, etc is to be so used, so that it is no defence for him to show that the person supplied did not intend to use it[133] or that the person supplied was a policeman who had obtained the thing by false representations about a purely fictitious woman.[134] This construction was defended by Erle CJ, the rest of the court concurring, on the extraordinary ground that, 'The defendant knew what his own intention was, and that was that the substance procured by him should be employed with intent to procure miscarriage'.[135]

This attitude contrasts strikingly with the strict construction of the word 'procure'; and these two cases, which have been dissented from in Victoria,[136] though followed elsewhere in the Commonwealth,[137] deserve reconsideration.

(d) The Abortion Act 1967[138]

The law relating to abortion is modified in important respects by the Abortion Act 1967. In the Act:

'the law relating to abortion' means ss 58 and 59 of the Offences Against the Person Act 1861, and any rule of law relating to the procurement of abortion.

Section 1 of the Act, as amended by the Human Fertilisation and Embryology Act 1990, s 37, provides:[139]

(1) Subject to the provisions of this section, a person shall not be guilty of an offence under the law relating to abortion when a pregnancy is terminated by a registered medical practitioner if two registered medical practitioners are of the opinion, formed in good faith –

[132] Ibid at 526. [133] *Hillman* (1863) 9 Cox CC 386, CCR.

[134] *Titley* (1880) 14 Cox CC 502 (Stephen J). [135] (1863) 9 Cox CC at 387.

[136] *Hyland* (1898) 24 VLR 101.

[137] *Scully* (1903) 23 NZLR 380; *Nosworthy* (1907) 26 NZLR 536; *Neil* [1909] St R Qd 225; *Freestone* [1913] TPD 758; *Irwin v R* (1968) 68 DLR (2d) 485.

[138] See J. Hoggett, 'The Abortion Act 1967' [1968] Crim LR 247: *A Guide to the Abortion Act 1967* (Abortion Law Reform Association). On the changes introduced by the Act see H. L. A. Hart, 'Abortion Law Reform: The English Experience' (1972) 8 MULR 389; M. Simms, 'Abortion Law Reform: Has the Controversy Changed' [1970] Crim LR 567, 573 and 'The Abortion Act: A Reply' [1971] Crim LR 86; J. M. Finnis, 'The Abortion Act: What Has Changed? [1971] Crim LR 3.

[139] See the valuable discussion of the amended Act by A. Grubb, 'The New Law of Abortion: clarification or ambiguity?' [1991] Crim LR 659 and generally S. Sheldon, *Beyond Control* (1977).

(a) that the pregnancy has not exceeded its twenty-fourth week and that the continuance of the pregnancy would involve risk, greater than if the pregnancy were terminated, of injury to the physical or mental health of the pregnant woman or any existing children of her family; or

(b) that the termination is necessary to prevent grave permanent injury to the physical or mental health of the pregnant woman; or

(c) that the continuance of the pregnancy would involve risk to the life of the pregnant woman, greater than if the pregnancy were terminated; or

(d) that there is a substantial risk that if the child were born it would suffer from such physical or mental abnormalities as to be seriously handicapped.

(2) In determining whether the continuance of a pregnancy would involve such risk of injury to health as is mentioned in paragraph (a) or (b) of subsection (1) of this section, account may be taken of the pregnant woman's actual or reasonably foreseeable environment.

(3) Except as provided by subsection (4) of this section, any treatment for the termination of pregnancy must be carried out in a hospital vested in the Minister of Health or the Secretary of State under the National Health Service Acts, or in a place for the time being approved for the purposes of this section by the said Minister or the Secretary of State.

(3A) The power under subsection (3) of this section to approve a place includes power, in relation to treatment consisting primarily in the use of such medicines as may be specified in the approval and carried out in such manner as may be so specified, to approve a class of places.

(4) Subsection (3) of this section, and so much of subsection (1) as relates to the opinion of two registered medical practitioners, shall not apply to the termination of a pregnancy by a registered medical practitioner in a case where he is of the opinion, formed in good faith, that the termination is immediately necessary to save the life or to prevent grave permanent injury to the physical or mental health of the pregnant woman.

Where the pregnancy has not exceeded its 24th week[140] the doctor must balance risks involved in an abortion against the risks to the woman or the existing child involved in the continuance of the pregnancy and may perform the abortion only if it is his opinion that the latter are greater than the former.

Where the pregnancy has exceeded 24 weeks the risks to the existing child are no longer a ground for abortion. The abortion can now be justified only on the grounds of risk of grave permanent injury to the woman or her death, or of the birth of a seriously[141] handicapped child. Where the life of the woman is at risk, the doctor must engage in another balancing exercise and may terminate the pregnancy if he is of the opinion that this gives her a better chance of survival: 51/49 is enough. But where the risk is not to her life but of 'grave permanent injury' the pregnancy may be terminated only if abortion is 'necessary' to prevent this. If the doctor is of the opinion that the woman will certainly suffer grave permanent injury if the pregnancy is not terminated, then termination is, undoubtedly, necessary. It must be assumed, however, that Parliament, in distinguishing between grave permanent injury and death, intended that a higher degree of risk of grave permanent injury than of death is required to justify abortion. If so, termination is not

140 It is uncertain when time starts to run. See the discussion by Grubb, above.

141 See *Jepson v Chief Constable of Mercia Police* [2003] EWHC 3318 where D sought judicial review of the refusal to prosecute doctors who performed an abortion where the foetus had a cleft palate. The court concluded that the doctor had acted in good faith.

'necessary' simply because the doctor is of the opinion that grave permanent injury is more likely than not, that is, 51/49 is not enough. Whether necessity can be established somewhere between the balance of probabilities and virtual certainty is not clear. These balancing exercises do not pose problems under Article 2 of the ECHR.

The European Court has recognized that 'if the unborn do have a 'right to life' it is implicitly limited by the mother's rights and interests.[142]

There is a similar problem of determining what is a 'substantial' risk of abnormality resulting in 'serious' handicap to the child – but these uncertainties have been with us since 1967 without troubling the courts (but note *Jepson* above), however much they may have troubled the doctors. Clearly something a good deal less than certainty may amount to a substantial risk and it is thought that most people would regard something well below a 50 per cent chance as substantial in this context.

Section 1(1)(a), on a literal reading, could justify the termination of most pregnancies in their early stages, since some risk is necessarily involved in child-bearing whereas the risks involved in an abortion operation at this stage are very slight.[143] The 1967 Act allowed the interests of the existing children of the woman's family to be taken into account for the first time. These expressions are not defined in the Act, but it has been argued[144] that 'family' means the sociological and not the legal unit, so as to include illegitimate children and perhaps children who have been accepted as members of the family. The view has been expressed[145] that a person over 21 could be a child of the family for this purpose if, for example, he were severely disabled.

(i) Abortion and multiple pregnancies

Multiple pregnancies may be reduced by killing one or more of the foetuses. The Human Fertilisation and Embryology Act 1990 amended s 5(2) of the Abortion Act 1967 to deal with the matter as follows:

> (2) For the purposes of the law relating to abortion, anything done with intent to procure a woman's miscarriage (or, in the case of a woman carrying more than one foetus, her miscarriage of any foetus) is unlawfully done unless authorized by section 1 of this Act and, in the case of a woman carrying more than one foetus, anything done with intent to procure her miscarriage of any foetus is authorized by that section if –
>
> (a) the ground for termination of the pregnancy specified in subsection (1)(d) of that section applies in relation to any foetus and the thing is done for the purpose of procuring the miscarriage of that foetus, or
>
> (b) any other grounds for termination of the pregnancy specified in that section applies.

So if one or more of several foetuses is identified as being substantially at risk of becoming a child suffering from such a mental or physical abnormality as would lead to its being seriously handicapped, that foetus, or those foetuses, may be aborted. Where no foetus is

142 *Vo v France* [2004] 2 FCR 577, para 80.

143 '. . . it follows that a pregnancy may lawfully be terminated in order to secure a relatively small improvement in the woman's medical condition': *A Guide to the Abortion Act 1967*, at 11. The Act is not, however, interpreted in this way by the medical profession and administrators: *Hart* (1972) 8 MULR at 393–394.

144 Hoggett, above at 249; *A Guide to the Abortion Act 1967*, at 6.

145 Ibid.

so identified, but the continuance of the multiple pregnancy would satisfy one of the other conditions in s 1, the doctor may reduce the number of foetuses in order to eliminate or reduce the risk. In this situation, the doctor must select which of a number of healthy foetuses is to die.

(ii) Good faith of medical opinion

The Secretary of State for Health has exercised the powers given to him by s 2 to require the opinion of medical practitioners to be certified in a particular form and notice of the termination of pregnancy and other information to be given. The question of the good faith of the doctors is essentially one for the jury. A verdict of bad faith where there is no evidence as to professional practice and medical probabilities is often likely to be regarded by the Court of Appeal as unsafe; but this depends on the nature of the other evidence.

> An opinion may be absurd professionally and yet formed in good faith; conversely an opinion may be one which a doctor could have entertained and yet in the particular circumstances of a case may be found either to have been formed in bad faith or not to have been formed at all.[146]

If one or both of the doctors has expressed an opinion in bad faith but the operation is performed by a third, D, who is unaware of the bad faith, the conditions of the Act are not satisfied but it is submitted that D has a defence. He lacks *mens rea* for, on the facts as he believes them to be, his act is a lawful one. The doctor in bad faith might, however, be convicted under the doctrine of *Cogan and Leak* or *Millward*.[147]

(iii) Termination 'by a registered medical practitioner'

The defences provided by the Act are available 'when a pregnancy is terminated by a registered medical practitioner'. When the conditions in the Act are satisfied and the pregnancy is terminated by the doctor, there is no *actus reus*. Those who assist him are therefore guilty of no offence. The Act obviously did not contemplate that every action in the steps leading to an abortion would be done personally by the doctor. If, however, the doctor were to delegate more and more of the process to others, there would come a point when it could no longer be said that the pregnancy had been terminated 'by a registered medical practitioner' – and at that point it would become unlawful. In *Royal College of Nursing of the United Kingdom v Department of Health and Social Security*,[148] the House of Lords by a majority of three to two, reversing a unanimous Court of Appeal judgment and restoring the judgment of Woolf J, held that a particular process for the extra-amniotic method of termination of pregnancies was lawful, notwithstanding the substantial part played by nurses in that process. According to Lord Diplock, what the 1967 Act requires is that:

> . . . a registered medical practitioner . . . should accept responsibility for all stages of the treatment for the termination of the pregnancy. The particular method to be used should be decided by the doctor in charge of the treatment for the termination of the pregnancy; he should carry out any physical acts, forming part of the treatment, that in accordance with accepted medical practice are done only by qualified medical practitioners, and should give specific instructions as to the carrying out of such parts of the treatment as in accordance with accepted medical practice

146 *Smith* [1974] 1 All ER 376 at 381, and [1994] Crim LR 527.

147 [1976] QB 217, [1975] 2 All ER 1059, above, p 206.

148 [1981] AC 800, [1981] 1 All ER 545.

are carried out by nurses or other members of the hospital staff without medical qualifications. To each of them, the doctor, or his substitute, should be available to be consulted or called on for assistance from beginning to end of the treatment.

Thus if the doctor were to direct the whole procedure by correspondence, over the telephone, or by webcam the operation would presumably be unlawful.

Treatment to terminate a pregnancy, which, if the treatment were successful, would be lawfully terminated, is lawful treatment,[149] notwithstanding (as apparently happens in one or two per cent of cases) an ultimate failure to terminate the pregnancy. If the conditions of the 1967 Act are otherwise fulfilled and known to be fulfilled, the steps taken to procure abortion are taken without *mens rea* – there is no intent *unlawfully* to administer anything or *unlawfully* to use any instrument. There is moreover no *actus reus* for the legalisation of an abortion must include the steps which are taken towards it.

(iv) Necessity at common law

The provision in s 5(2) of the 1967 Act that, 'For the purposes of the law relating to abortion, anything done with intent to procure a woman's miscarriage . . . is unlawfully done unless authorized by section 1 of this Act . . .' appears to be intended entirely to supersede the law as stated in *Bourne*.[150]

Abortions, and the steps to procure them which are proscribed, are unlawful unless they can be justified by the Act. It is submitted, however, that this provision cannot have been intended entirely to eliminate the operation of general defences to crime. To take extreme examples, a child under the age of 10 or a person within the M'Naghten rules could surely not be convicted of committing or (slightly more likely) abetting an abortion. If this is conceded, then duress by threats ought equally to operate so why not duress of circumstances or necessity? And so we are back to admitting *Bourne's* case into the law. A possible interpretation of the Act would be to allow general defences, other than necessity. Construing s 5(2) in the light of the previous law, a court might conclude that its obvious purpose was to overrule *Bourne*; and that it would be unreasonable to extend its operation beyond that.

A limited defence of necessity would seem desirable in principle. The defence would necessarily be limited in scope by the fact that, in the great majority of cases where it is necessary to procure an abortion, this is lawful by statute so that there is no room for the operation of any broader defence. But suppose that a qualified doctor who is not a registered medical practitioner and so does not come within the terms of s 1(4) above, forms the opinion in good faith that immediate termination of a pregnancy is necessary in order to save the life of the mother who is in a remote place and beyond the help of any registered medical practitioner. Is it the law that he must let the woman die when he could save her by terminating the pregnancy?

In *Bourne* MacNaghten J took the view that there was not only a right but a duty to perform the operation where a woman's life could be saved only by the doctor procuring an abortion:

[149] Per Lord Edmund-Davies, citing the 4th edition of this book at 346, [1981] 1 All ER at 573.

[150] Above, p 317. Cf the Canadian case of *Morgentaler* [1976] 1 SCR 616, 20 CCC (2d) 449 discussed by L. H. Leigh in [1978] Crim LR 151 and *Davidson* [1969] VR 667 (Menhennit J).

. . . if a case arose where the life of a woman could be saved by performing the operation and the doctor refused to perform it because of his religious opinions and the woman died, he would be in grave peril of being brought before this court on a charge of manslaughter by negligence. He would have no better defence than a person who, again from some religious reason, refused to call in a doctor to attend his sick child, where a doctor could have been called in and the life of the child could have been saved.[151]

Section 4 of the Abortion Act now provides:

(1) Subject to subsection (2) of this section, no person shall be under any duty, whether by contract or by any statutory or other legal requirements, to participate in any treatment authorized by this Act to which he has a conscientious objection:
Provided that in any legal proceedings the burden of proof of conscientious objection shall rest on the person claiming to rely on it.

(2) Nothing in subsection (1) of this section shall affect any duty to participate in treatment which is necessary to save the life or to prevent grave permanent injury to the physical or mental health of a pregnant woman.

The same people whose acts are rendered lawful by s 1 are given by s 4 the right in conscience to object to performing those same acts. A person can only claim that right in respect of an act which would have amounted to an offence before the Abortion Act came into force. So a secretary was not entitled, by s 4, to refuse to type a letter arranging an abortion rendered lawful by s 1. It was held that she would not, under the old law, have been guilty of the abortion as a secondary party; her intention would have been merely to carry out her contract of employment, not to counsel or procure.[152]

Section 4(2) does not create any duty, but it does appear to recognize at least the possibility of a duty at common law. The only authority for this appears to be *Bourne*. It will be noted that MacNaghten J dealt only with the case where the woman died, whereas the Act refers to grave permanent injury to physical or mental health. MacNaghten J appeared to regard the doctor's liability as one arising from gross negligence; and this, if a ground of liability at all, is indeed confined to cases where death is caused.[153] There is no general criminal liability for causing grievous bodily harm by gross negligence as distinct from recklessness. If, however, the doctor is under a duty to act, and he knows all the circumstances giving rise to that duty and foresees the consequences of not fulfilling it, it would seem that he has the *mens rea* necessary to found a conviction for causing grievous bodily harm contrary to s 18 of the Offences Against the Person Act 1861.[154] The only doubtful link in this argument appears to be the existence of the duty; but the Act strengthens the case for its existence. Clearly, a doctor with conscientious objections[155] could fulfil his duty by referring the patient to another doctor who does not have such objections; and it is submitted that the doctor has a duty to do this where an abortion is necessary to save the woman from death or grave permanent injury. The question of a duty to participate in the operation can arise only where there is no effective substitute

151 [1939] 1 KB at 693, [1938] 3 All ER at 618.

152 *Salford Area Health Authority, ex p Janaway* [1989] AC 537, [1988] 2 WLR 442, CA.

153 Above, p 485. 154 Below, p 559.

155 See for arguments that the ECHR might impact on this claim L. Hammer, 'Abortion Objection in the UK within the Framework of the ECHR' [1999] EHRLR 564.

for the doctor concerned. Where the patient has conscientious objections there can be no duty to perform the operation since, clearly, it can only be lawfully performed with consent.

Abortion in compliance with the 1967 Act does not contravene Article 2 of the ECHR: *Paton v UK.*[156]

6. Genocide, crimes against humanity and war crimes

The Genocide Act 1969 gave effect to the Genocide Convention, Article II, and rendered it a domestic offence to commit genocide. That offence, and indeed the Genocide Act was repealed by the International Criminal Court Act 2001. Under s 51 of the 2001 Act, from 1 September 2001:[157]

> (1) It is an offence against the law of England and Wales for a person to commit genocide, a crime against humanity or a war crime.
>
> (2) This section applies to acts committed –
>
> (a) in England or Wales, or
>
> (b) outside the United Kingdom by a United Kingdom national, a United Kingdom resident or a person subject to UK service jurisdiction.

The offences can be prosecuted only with the consent of the Attorney-General.[158] They are triable only on indictment and carry a maximum 30-year sentence, except that offences involving murder must be dealt with as such.[159]

In interpreting definitions of genocide, crimes against humanity and war crimes the domestic court must take into account any relevant elements of crimes, and must have regard to any relevant judgment or decision of the International Criminal Court.

(a) Genocide

Genocide is defined to mean any of the following acts committed 'with intent to destroy, in whole or in part, a national, ethnical, racial or religious group', as such: (1) killing members of the group; (2) causing serious bodily or mental harm to members of the group; (3) deliberately inflicting on the group conditions of life calculated to bring about its physical destruction in whole or in part; (4) imposing measures intended to prevent births within the group; (5) forcibly transferring children of the group to another group.[160]

(b) Crime against humanity

Crime against humanity means any of the following acts when committed as part of a widespread or systematic attack directed against any civilian population, with knowledge of the attack:

156 [1980] 3 EHRR 408.

157 On the jurisdiction of the International Criminal Court see generally, R. Dixon and K. Khan, Archbold, *International Criminal Courts: Practice, Procedure And Evidence.* See also D. McGoldrick, 'The Permanent ICC – An End to the Culture of Impunity' [1999] Crim LR 627; N. Stewart, 'The New ICC' (2001) 151 NLJ 1381.

158 Section 53(3).

159 Section 53(5).

160 Schedule 8.

(i) murder; (ii) extermination; (iii) deportation or forcible transfer of population; (iv) imprisonment or other severe deprivation of physical liberty in violation of fundamental rules of international law; (v) torture; (vi) rape, sexual slavery, enforced prostitution, forced pregnancy; (vii) persecution against any identifiable group or collectivity on political, racial, national, ethnic, cultural, religious, gender as defined in paragraph 3, or other grounds that are universally recognized as impermissible under international law, in connection with any act referred to in this paragraph or any crime within the jurisdiction of the Court; (viii) enforced disappearance of persons; (viiii) the crime of apartheid; (x) other inhumane acts of a similar character intentionally causing great suffering, or serious injury to body or to mental or physical health.[161]

(c) War crime

'War crime' is defined in Schedule 8 to mean:

(1) grave breaches of the Geneva Conventions 1949, namely, any of the following acts against persons or property protected under the provisions of the relevant Geneva Convention (a) wilful killing; (b) torture or inhuman treatment, including biological experiments; (c) wilfully causing great suffering, or serious injury to body or health; (d) extensive destruction and appropriation of property, not justified by military necessity and carried out unlawfully and wantonly; (e) compelling a prisoner of war or other protected person to serve in the forces of a hostile power; (f) wilfully depriving a prisoner of war or other protected person of the rights of fair and regular trial; (g) unlawful deportation or transfer or unlawful confinement; (h) taking of hostages;

(2) other serious violations [as specified] of the laws and customs applicable in international armed conflict, within the established framework of international law . . .

(3) in the case of an armed conflict not of an international character, serious violations of any of the specified acts committed against persons taking no active part in the hostilities, including members of armed forces who have laid down their arms and those placed hors de combat by sickness, wounds, detention or any other cause.

7. War Crimes Act 1991[162]

The War Crimes Act 1991 provides that proceedings for murder, manslaughter or culpable homicide may be brought against a person who committed that crime during the period of the Second World War in part of Germany or a place under German occupation and the act constituted a violation of the laws and customs of war. The proceedings may be brought irrespective of the nationality of the accused at the time of the alleged offence.[163]

161 International Criminal Court Act 2001 s 50(6), Sch 8.

162 See T. Richardson, 'Crimes without Frontiers? The War Crimes Act 1991' in I. Loveland (ed), *Frontiers of Criminality* (1995).

163 For the only successful prosecution, see *Sawoniuk* [2000] 2 Cr App R 220.

16

Non-fatal offences against the person[1]

The 'person' who may be the victim of any of the offences discussed in this chapter is a human being. The context excludes associations, whether corporate or unincorporated as victims, though these bodies might be guilty of committing some of the offences as a principal or as an accessory. If a corporation may be guilty of manslaughter[2] there is no reason why it should not be guilty of lesser offences against the person. The meaning of 'person' as a victim has been discussed almost exclusively in relation only to murder but it seems clear that the same principles must apply to non-fatal offences. The Draft Code accordingly provides by cl 53(1) that, for the purposes of the Chapter on Offences Against the Person:

'another' [that is, the victim] means a person who has been born and has an existence independent of his mother and, unless the context otherwise requires, 'death' and 'personal harm' mean the death of, or personal harm to, such a person.[3]

It seems that this probably represents the common law[4] so that a foetus or a child in the process of being born could not be the victim of an assault or any other offence against the person.[5] The act might be an offence against the mother where it affected her person, as distinct from the foetus which is not part of her. Statutory offences are probably to be construed in accordance with the common law.

1. Assault and battery

Assault and battery were two distinct crimes at common law and their separate existence (though now, it has been held, as statutory offences) is confirmed by s 39 of the Criminal Justice Act 1988:

[1] P. Carter and R. Harrison, *Offences of Violence* (1987).

[2] Above, p 241. In *R (On the Application of Gladstone plc) v Manchester City Magistrates' Court* [2004] All ER (D) 296 (Nov) it was held that a private prosecution for assault may be brought by a registered company (the victim being the Chief Executive who was kneed in the groin at the AGM). The company's memorandum of association included power to lay an information in respect of the assault.

[3] For further reform see below p 562.

[4] Cf *Tait*, above, p 491.

[5] In *A-G's Reference (No 3 of 1994)*, above, p 432, the Court of Appeal held that the foetus is part of the mother; but the House of Lords decided that it is not: [1997] 3 All ER 936, 943. 'The mother and the foetus were two distinct organisms living symbiotically, not a single organism with two aspects', per Lord Mustill.

Common assault and battery shall be summary offences and a person guilty of either of them shall be liable to a fine not exceeding level 5 on the standard scale, to imprisonment for a term not exceeding six months, or to both.

Common assault and battery were indictable offences at common law and under s 47 of the Offences Against the Person Act (hereafter in this chapter 'OAPA') 1861; but this provision of that section was repealed by the 1988 Act, together with ss 42 and 43 which provided for summary trial – s 42 where the complaint was made by the party aggrieved, a provision intended for minor offences where the police saw no need to intervene, and s 43 where the offence was too serious to be sufficiently punished under s 42. The replacement of all these provisions by s 39, above, represents a valuable simplification of the law.

As assault is any act by which D, intentionally or recklessly,[6] causes V to apprehend immediate and unlawful personal violence.[7] A battery is any act by which D, intentionally or recklessly, inflicts unlawful personal violence upon V.[8] But 'violence' here includes any unlawful touching of another, however slight, for, as Blackstone wrote:[9]

the law cannot draw the line between different degrees of violence, and therefore prohibits the first and lowest stage of it; every man's person being sacred, and no other having a right to meddle with it, in any the slightest manner.

This reflects the fact that the offences against the person protect the individual's personal autonomy by providing at least the opportunity for criminal punishment for the slightest unjustified infringement. This is supported by the protection offered by the ECHR, in Article 8.[10]

In modern times, Lord Lane CJ described the offence in equally expansive terms:

An assault (sc meaning 'battery') is an intentional touching of another person without the consent of that person and without lawful excuse. It need not necessarily be hostile, or rude, or aggressive, as some of the cases seem to indicate.[11]

However, in *Brown*,[12] the majority of the House of Lords seem to have thought that hostility is an element in assault – and then so interpreted 'hostile' as to deprive the word of all meaning. The case concerned sado-masochistic acts, done for the mutual enjoyment of all concerned, so that they could not conceivably be assaults if hostility, in any ordinary meaning of the word, were required; yet the convictions were upheld. Lord

6 *Venna* [1976] QB 421, [1975] 3 All ER 788, CA (a case of battery but the same principle surely applies to assault); *Savage* [1992] 1 AC 699, 740.

7 In *Ireland* [1997] 4 All ER 225, 236, 239 the House of Lords applied this definition, originating in the 1st edition of this work at 262, adopted in *Fagan v Metropolitan Police Comr* [1969] 1 QB 439, [1968] 3 All ER 442 at 445, below, p 521 and approved in *Savage* [1992] AC 699, 740.

8 *Rolfe* (1952) 36 Cr App R 4.

9 *Commentaries*, iii, 120, cited by Goff LJ in *Collins v Wilcock* [1984] 3 All ER 374 at 378.

10 For more serious infringements the protection lies in Article 3 – freedom from torture, inhuman and degrading treatment and Article 5 – freedom from unlawful deprivation of liberty.

11 *Faulkner v Talbot* [1981] 3 All ER 468 at 471, applied in *Thomas* (1985) 81 Cr App R 331 at 334; and see *Collins v Wilcock* [1984] 3 All ER 374 at 379, DC; *Wilson v Pringle* [1987] QB 237, [1986] 2 All ER 440, CA (Civ Div), criticized by Wood J in *T v T* [1988] 2 WLR 189 at 200, 203, Fam Div; *Brown* [1992] 2 WLR 441 at 446, CA.

12 [1993] 2 All ER 75, [1993] Crim LR 583.

Jauncey said, 'If the appellants' activities in relation to the receivers [of the painful acts] were unlawful they were also hostile and a necessary ingredient of assault was present'. But the acts were only unlawful if they amounted to assaults. The reasoning appears to be circular. Notwithstanding the opinions of their Lordships, it is submitted that the actual decision confirms the view that hostility is not an essential ingredient.

Presumably the same applies to assault in the strict sense – it is enough that V apprehends some unwanted touching.[13] It is however neither an assault nor a battery for D to pull himself free from V who is detaining him, even though D uses force.[14]

Assault and battery form the basis of many aggravated offences – for example, assaulting a police officer, assault with intent to resist arrest, etc.[15] It should be noted that assault and battery are also torts; and many, though not all, of the principles appear to be equally applicable in both branches of the law. Consequently, some of the cases cited below are civil actions.

The CPS Charging Standards advise that the appropriate charge is assault or battery (rather than aggravated assaults) where the injuries sustained amount to no more than: grazes; scratches; abrasions; minor bruising; swellings; reddening of the skin; superficial cuts; or a 'black eye'.[16]

(a) The relationship between assault and battery

The separateness of assault and battery at common law was not universally recognized.[17] There is a terminological problem in that there is no acceptable verb corresponding to the noun, battery, so that 'assaulted' is almost invariably used to mean 'committed a battery against'. Sometimes the term 'assault' is used in statutes to mean 'assault or battery' but on other occasions both words are used. There is a deplorable inconsistency in the statutory terminology. Even the Criminal Justice Act 1988, having made it crystal clear in s 39 that there are two offences, goes on in s 40(3)(a) to use 'common assault' in a context in which it can only sensibly mean – and has now been held[18] to mean – 'common assault or battery'.

There are, however, grave problems of substance as well as terminology which have long been ignored but will have to be faced if we are at last to take seriously the proposition that there are two distinct offences. In *DPP v Little*[19] an information alleging that '. . . did unlawfully assault and batter J' was held to charge two offences and so to be bad for duplicity.[20] Consider the surviving offence under OAPA 1861, s 47: 'Whosoever

13 Note that the concept of touching may achieve a greater significance since it forms the core of a number of offences under the Sexual Offences Act 2003, replacing indecent assault, etc. See below, Ch 17.

14 *Sheriff* [1969] Crim LR 260.

15 The Home Office identified over 70 such offences. *Violence. Reforming the Offences Against the Person Act 1861* (1998), para 3.5.

16 See also C. Clarkson, A. Cretney, G. Davis and J. Shepherd, 'Assaults: The Relationship between Seriousness, Criminalisation and Punishment' [1994] Crim LR 4.

17 The CLRC Fourteenth Report, para 148, treated them as a single offence which may be committed in two ways and the Draft Code, cl 75, follows the CLRC's recommendation.

18 *Lynsey* [1995] 3 All ER 654.

19 [1992] 1 All ER 299, [1991] Crim LR 900, DC.

20 It was by no means the first case to decide that a charge of assault and/or battery in a single count or information is bad. See *Jones v Sherwood* [1942] 1 KB 127, DC and *Mansfield Justices, ex p Sharkey* [1985] QB 613, [1985] 1 All ER 193, DC. But a blind eye appears to have been turned in *Notman* [1994] Crim LR 518.

shall be convicted of an assault occasioning actual bodily harm shall be liable to [imprisonment for five years]'.

In *DPP v Little* the Divisional Court was in no doubt that this offence included both an assault occasioning actual bodily harm and, much more commonly, a battery occasioning such harm – and this is surely right. It is true that in *Savage*[21] Lord Ackner said in respect of this offence, 'It is common ground that the mental element of assault is an intention to cause the victim to apprehend immediate and unlawful violence or recklessness whether such apprehension be caused'; but it is incredible that D, who takes care to ensure that V apprehends nothing and hits him on the back of the head, is not guilty of an 'assault occasioning actual bodily'. If the word 'assault' in the section embraces two offences, it must have the same meaning when used in an indictment or information, alleging an offence under the section. It follows that the standard form of indictment –

'AB . . . assaulted JN, thereby occasioning him actual bodily harm'

alleges two offences and is bad for duplicity. The same considerations apply to aggravated assaults. The effect is that thousands of people have been convicted on defective indictments ever since 1861 – but this in no way detracts from the inescapable logic of the argument. Prosecutors would be well advised to draft particulars of an indictment or information so as to make clear that it charges either an assault or a battery, but not both.

There were further procedural problems since an indictment alleging assault occasioning actual bodily harm required a separate count for s 39 assault because it was not an included offence for an alternative verdict.[22] The Domestic Violence, Crime and Victims Act 2004 remedies this.

(b) Common law or statutory offences?

An aggravated assault or battery – that is, where Parliament has provided for a higher penalty where a specified aggravating circumstance is proved in addition to the assault or battery – is a separate offence under the principle of *Courtie*[23] and is necessarily a statutory offence. This applies to an assault or battery occasioning actual bodily harm, contrary to OAPA 1861, s 47, though until recently the standard form of indictment for the offence made no reference to the Act, treating it as an offence at common law, as indeed was universally supposed before *Courtie*. The *Courtie* principle does not apply to common assault or battery – they are 'common' precisely because there is no aggravating ingredient – and s 39 of the 1988 Act does not on its face create any offence but assumes the existence of offences of common assault and battery, merely prescribing the mode of trial and penalty. Nevertheless in *DPP v Little*[24] it was held that common assault and battery have been statutory offences since the enactment of s 47 of the OAPA 1861. The better view is that s 47 merely prescribed the penalty for the common law offences of common assault – as statutes do for other common law offences, for example, murder,

[21] [1991] 4 All ER 698 at 711.

[22] *Mearns* [1990] 3 All ER 989; *Disalvo* [2004] All ER (D) 316 (Jul). Arguably these were wrongly decided in the first place.

[23] [1984] AC 463, [1984] 1 All ER 740, HL, above, p 40.

[24] Above, p 518.

manslaughter and conspiracy to defraud.[25] These all continue as offences at common law. Although Laws LJ has asserted unequivocally that 'in truth, common assault by beating remains a common law offence',[26] the prosecutor is probably well advised, pending review by a higher court, to follow *DPP v Little* and to charge common assault or battery as a statutory offence, contrary to s 39.

(c) *Actus reus* of assault

The typical case of an assault as distinct from a battery is that where D, by some physical movement, causes V to apprehend that he is about to be struck. D rides or drives at V, or acts so as to appear to V to be on the point of striking, stabbing or shooting him. Assault was once regarded as attempted battery. D had embarked on an act which, if not suspended or evaded, would immediately result in an impact of some kind on V. Many attempted batteries are assaults, but this is not necessarily so. D's acts may be unobserved by V, as where D approaches V from behind, or V is asleep, or insensible, or too young to appreciate what D appears likely to do. And there may be an assault where D has no intention to commit a battery but only to cause V to apprehend one.[27] The requirement is for apprehension, not fear.

(i) Immediacy

There is a tendency to enlarge the concept of assault by taking a generous view of 'immediacy' and including threats where the impending impact is more remote than in the typical assaults instanced above. In more recent cases this approach was precipitated by the courts' desire to provide protection for those suffering harassment at a time before the Protection from Harassment Act 1997 was in force.[28]

In *Lewis*[29] D was held guilty of maliciously inflicting grievous bodily harm and therefore impliedly of an assault,[30] although D was uttering threats from another room. In *Logdon v DPP*[31] it was held that D committed an assault by showing V a pistol in a drawer and declaring that he would hold her hostage. In *Ireland*[32] the House of Lords held that words alone, or even silent telephone calls, are not incapable of amounting to an assault; but they found it unnecessary to decide whether they did so in that case. If the caller said, 'There is bomb under your house which I am about to detonate', that would seem a clear case. Lord Steyn said that the caller *may* be guilty of assault if. he said, 'I will be at your door in a minute or two'. It seems to be a question of fact. Did the call in fact cause V to apprehend immediate unlawful violence? In *Constanza*,[33] V, who had for some time been

25 See [1991] Crim LR 900; Archbold (2005), 19–178. The court in *Lynsey*, above, n 18, noted the criticisms that have been made of *Little* but found it unnecessary to express any opinion.

26 *Haystead v Chief Constable of Derbyshire* (2000) 164 JP 396, [2000] Crim LR 758, DC. The defendant was in fact charged under s 39.

27 *Logdon v DPP* [1976] Crim LR 121, DC.

28 See C. Wells, 'Stalking: the Criminal Law's Response' [1997] Crim LR 463.

29 [1970] Crim LR 647, CA.

30 But see now *Wilson* [1984] AC 242, [1983] 3 All ER 448, below, p 556.

31 Above.

32 Above. See G. Virgo, 'Offences Against the Person – Do-It-Yourself Law Reform' [1997] CLJ 251. J. Horder, 'Reconsidering Psychic Assault' [1998] Crim LR 392, regards this dilution of the immediacy requirement as a welcome shift to an offence based on causing fear. On the merits of general threat offences see P. Alldridge, 'Threat Offences the Case for Reform' [1994] Crim LR 176.

33 [1997] Crim LR 576. The House refused leave to appeal, but that does not imply approval of the decision.

harassed by D, received two letters from him on 4 and 12 June respectively which she interpreted as clear threats. It was held that they amounted to an assault, occasioning actual bodily harm. Was this two assaults or one continuing assault? It is easy to see that the letters might have caused her *immediate apprehension*, but less easy to suppose that, as she read them, she apprehended *immediate violence.*

In *Smith v Chief Superintendent of Woking Police Station*[34] (assault by looking through the window of a bed-sitting room at V in her night clothes with intent to frighten her) Kerr LJ limited his decision to a case where D 'is immediately adjacent, albeit on the other side of a window' and distinguished, without dissenting from, the opinion in the fourth edition of this book that 'there can be no assault if it is obvious to V that D is unable to carry out his threat, as where D shakes his fist at V who is safely locked inside his car'. There may of course be an assault although D has no means of carrying out the threat.[35] The question is whether D intends to cause V to believe that he can and will carry it out immediately and whether V does so believe. The question arises most obviously where D points an unloaded or imitation gun at V. If V knows the gun is unloaded or an imitation, there is no assault, for then he could not apprehend being shot.[36] If V believes it is, or may be a real, loaded gun, there is an *actus reus*, for now he suffers the apprehension which is an essential element of the crime.[37]

(ii) Assault by words alone

As long ago as 1865 it was asserted in *Russell on Crime* that 'it is now quite settled, though many ancient opinions were to the contrary, that no words whatsoever, be they ever so provoking, can amount to an assault'. But the authorities cited were by no means conclusive and the point was always disputed by some writers.[38] *Ireland* has now settled that an assault can be committed by words alone. Obviously, as a matter of fact, words, no less than a gesture, are capable of causing an apprehension of immediate violence.

It has generally been assumed that an act of some kind – even if it is only making a telephone call and remaining silent – is an essential ingredient of assault; but one case[39] seems to be substantially an assault by omission rather than by the 'continuing act' which the court thought it could discern. Where D inadvertently causes V to apprehend immediate violence (D is checking the sights on his gun when V walks into the room) and subsequently wilfully declines to withdraw the threat (by lowering the gun), his omission might constitute an assault.

(iii) Attempt to assault

There can be no conviction for attempt to commit a common assault since common assault is now a summary offence, but there is no reason why there should not be attempt to commit an aggravated assault; as where D points an unloaded gun at V, intending to frighten him in order to resist lawful arrest, but V, knowing the gun is unloaded, is unperturbed.[40]

34 (1983) 76 Cr App R 234. 35 *Pace* Tindal CJ in *Stephens v Myers* (1830) 4 C & P 349.

36 *Lamb*, above, p 473. 37 *Logdon v DPP*, above.

38 See generally G. Williams, 'Assault and Words' [1957] Crim LR 219.

39 *Fagan v Metropolitan Police Comr* [1969] 1 QB 439, [1968] 3 All ER 442.

40 'Is Criminal Assault a Separate Substantive Crime or is it an Attempted Battery?' (1945) 33 Ky LJ 189; *State v Wilson* (1955) 218 Ore 575, 346 P (2d) 115. See also D. White, 'Attempts: Initiatives in the Common Law Caribbean' [1980] Crim LR 780.

(d) *Actus reus* of battery

This consists in the infliction of unlawful personal violence by D upon V. It used to be said that every battery involves an assault; but this is plainly not so, for in battery there need be no apprehension of the impending violence. A blow from behind is not any less a battery because V was unaware that it was coming. It is generally said that D must have done some act and that it is not enough that he stood still and obstructed V's passage[41] like an inanimate object. But suppose D is sitting at the corner of a corridor with his legs stretched across it. He hears V running down the corridor and deliberately remains still with the intention that V, on turning the corner, shall fall over his legs. Why should not this be a battery? It would be if D had put out his legs with the intention of tripping up V. It would not be too difficult to conclude that D has a duty to V from the creation of the dangerous situation, applying the general principle recognized in *Miller*.[42] Further support for this proposition derives from *Santana-Bermudez*[43] where D, an intravenous drug user, assured a police officer who was about to search him that he was carrying no 'sharps' and the officer stabbed her finger on a syringe D was carrying in his pocket. The court upheld the conviction, applying *Miller*:[44]

> where someone (by act or word or a combination of the two) creates a danger and thereby exposes another to a reasonably foreseeable risk of injury which materializes, there is an evidential basis for the *actus reus* of an assault occasioning actual bodily harm. It remains necessary for the prosecution to prove an intention to assault or appropriate recklessness.[45]

By having the needles in his pocket and assuring the police officer about the contents of his pockets, D created a situation of danger.

There is certainly no battery where D has no control over the incident, as where his horse unexpectedly runs away with him;[46] but this might be put on the ground of lack of *mens rea*. It might be otherwise if D foresaw, when he mounted the animal, that there was an unacceptable risk that this might happen. There may also be a battery where D inadvertently applies force to V and then wrongfully refuses to withdraw it. In *Fagan*,[47] where D accidentally drove his mini-car on to a constable's foot and then intentionally left it there, the court held that there was a continuing act, not a mere omission.

(i) Battery with or via an instrument

Most batteries are directly inflicted, as by D's striking V with his fist or an instrument, or by a missile thrown by him, or by spitting upon V. But this is not essential. Where D punched W causing her to drop her baby, V, he was guilty of battery on V. It was found as a fact that D was reckless whether he injured V.[48]

Stephen and Wills JJ thought there would be a battery where D digs a pit for V to fall into, or, as in *Martin*,[49] he causes V to rush into an obstruction. In *DPP v K*[50] D was held

41 *Innes v Wylie* (1844) 1 Car & Kir 257. 42 [1983] AC 161.
43 [2004] Crim LR 471, [2003] EWHC 2908 (Admin). 44 [1983] AC 161.
45 [10]. 46 *Gibbons v Pepper* (1695) 2 Salk 637. 47 [1969] 1 QB 439, [1968] 3 All ER 442.
48 *Haystead v Chief Constable of Derbyshire* (2000) 164 JP 396, [2000] Crim LR 758, DC, citing this work. D could, alternatively, have been held guilty of an intentional assault by reason of transferred malice: above, p 113.
49 Below, p 556.
50 [1990] 1 All ER 331, [1990] Crim LR 321, DC, overruled on other grounds by *Spratt* [1991] 2 All ER 210, CA.

guilty of an assault where he poured acid into a drier in a toilet so that the next user sprayed himself with it. It has been argued[51] that these authorities are inconsistent with the decision of the House of Lords in *MPC v Wilson*[52] but all that case decided was that, though the word 'inflict' does not necessarily imply an assault, an allegation of inflicting harm may do so, and assault is therefore an 'included offence'. We now know that bodily (psychiatric) harm may be inflicted without any impact on V's body by harassment over the phone. That certainly does not involve a battery.[53] Where, however, D has caused an impact on V, indirectly but with no fully voluntary intervening act, it is not obvious why D should not be guilty of battery. The criminal law is not governed by the ancient forms of action at common law.

It is submitted that it would undoubtedly be a battery to set a dog on another.[54] If D beat O's horse causing it to run down V, this would be battery by D.[55] No doubt the famous civil case of *Scott v Shepherd*[56] is equally good for the criminal law. D throws a squib (a firework) into a market house. First E and then F fling the squib away in order to save themselves from injury. It explodes and injures V. The acts of E and F are not 'fully voluntary' intervening acts which break the chain of causation. This is battery by D. If there is no violence at all, there is no battery; as where D puts harmful matter into a drink which is consumed by V.[57]

(e) *Mens rea* of assault and battery

It is convenient to consider the *mens rea* of the two offences together. They are inextricably confused in some of the leading cases but need to be kept distinct if the separateness of the two offences is to be taken seriously. It was established by *Venna*[58] in 1975 that assault and battery may be committed recklessly as well as intentionally. *Venna* was a case of battery occasioning actual bodily harm but *dicta* concerning assault were relied on and it is safe to assume that the same principles apply to both offences. The *mens rea* of assault is an intention to cause V to apprehend immediate and unlawful violence, or recklessness whether such apprehension be caused.[59] The *mens rea* of battery is an intention to apply force to the body of another or recklessness whether force be so applied. Technically there is an argument that D should be shown to have intended or been reckless not only as to V's apprehension, but that V's apprehension would be of *immediate* violence.

(i) Subjective recklessness

The recklessness proved in *Venna* was subjective, *Cunningham* style, recklessness and the assumption then was that this was what the law required. Despite some attempts to apply the *Caldwell* formulation of recklessness in *DPP v K*,[60] that decision was quickly overruled by the Court of Appeal in *Spratt*[61] which was followed by that court in *Parmenter*.[62] The

51 M. Hirst, 'Assault, Battery and Indirect Violence' [1999] Crim LR 557.

52 [1984] AC 242, below, p 556.

53 Cf D. Ormerod and M. Gunn, 'In Defence of Ireland' [1996] 3 Web Jnl CLI.

54 *Murgatroyd v Chief Constable of West Yorkshire* (2000) All ER (D) 1742. But note the caution of the court in *Dume* (1986) The Times, 16 Oct, CA.

55 *Gibbon v Pepper* (1695) 2 Salk 637 (*obiter*).

56 (1773) 2 Wm Bl 892.

57 *Hanson* (1849) 2 Car & Kir 912; but see below, p 563.

58 [1976] QB 421, [1975] 3 All ER 788.

59 Cf *Savage* [1991] 4 All ER 698 at 711, HL.

60 [1990] 1 All ER 331, [1990] Crim LR 321, DC.

61 [1991] 2 All ER 210, [1990] Crim LR 797.

62 [1992] 1 AC 699, [1991] 2 All ER 225.

House of Lords was not asked to decide the point but *dicta*[63] assume that *Cunningham* recklessness is required; and with the overruling of *Caldwell* in *G*, the point is surely unarguable. D must actually foresee the risk of causing apprehension of immediate violence, or the application of it, as the case may be.

(ii) Is the *mens rea* interchangeable?

Is it an offence to cause the *actus reus* of battery with the *mens rea* only of assault or the *actus reus* of assault with the *mens rea* only of battery? In principle, the answer is no.[64] D waves his fist, intending to alarm (assault) V but not to strike him and not foreseeing any risk of doing so; but V does not see D, moves, and is hit. D creeps up behind V intending to hit him over the head without attracting his attention (battery), but V unexpectedly turns round and moves to avoid the blow. Taking the distinction seriously, in the former case D does not commit a battery but is attempting to commit an assault; and in the latter he does not commit an assault but is attempting to commit a battery; and these attempts to commit summary offences are not offences. It remains to be seen how seriously the courts will take the separateness of the offences.

(iii) Assault and battery by an intoxicated person

Assault and battery are classified as offences of 'basic intent' so that it is no defence that D had no *mens rea* because of voluntary intoxication. The reason appears to be that the offences may be committed by recklessness. If, then, an indictment or information specifically alleges an intentional assault or battery, it may be that the offence will be considered to require a 'specific intent' and its absence through intoxication will be a defence.[65] Given the link between alcohol and offences of violence, the courts might find this unpalatable.

2. Defences to assault and battery

(a) Consent[66]

It is clear that consent is an answer to a charge of common assault or battery (though not to the offence of assault occasioning actual bodily harm); but a fundamental question as to why it is an answer is not settled. Is it because the *absence of consent* is an essential

[63] 'Where the defendant neither intends nor adverts to the possibility that there will be any physical contact at all, then the offence under s 47 would not be made out. This is because there would have been no assault, let alone an assault occasioning actual bodily harm' ([1991] 4 All ER at 707): Lord Ackner of course means 'no battery'. Other *dicta* show that he recognized that an assault in the strict sense suffices for an offence under s 47 if it occasions actual bodily harm.

[64] Above, p 519.

[65] Cf *Caldwell* [1981] 1 All ER 961 at 964.

[66] See Law Com Consultation Paper No 134, 'Consent and Offences against the Person' (1994), on which see D. Ormerod, 'Consent and Offences Against the Person: LCCP No 134' (1994) 57 MLR 928; and Law Com Consultation Paper No 139, 'Consent in Criminal Law' (1995), on which see D. Ormerod and M. Gunn, 'Consent – A Second Bash' [1996] Crim LR 694; S. Shute, 'Something Old, Something New, Something Borrowed – Three Aspects of the Consent Project' [1996] Crim LR 684. For a review of the moral arguments see P. Roberts, 'The Philosophical Foundations of Consent in the Criminal Law' (1997) 17 OJLS 389.

element in the offence, as in rape;[67] or is *consent* a defence to the charge? In *Brown*, Lord Jauncey, with whose reasoning Lord Lowry agreed, said that, if it had been necessary to answer this question, which it was not, he would have held consent to be a defence. Lord Templeman treated consent as a defence. Lord Mustill, on the other hand, regarded it as one factor negativing an *actus reus*; while Lord Slynn emphatically agreed with Glanville Williams that 'It is . . . inherent in the concept of assault and battery that the victim does not consent.'[68] This, it is submitted, is the better view. The importance of the question is evidenced by the fact that Lords Mustill and Slynn dissented from the decision of the majority that the defendants were guilty of assaults occasioning actual bodily harm on, and unlawful wounding of, one another, notwithstanding their enthusiastic submission to, and the pleasure which they all derived from, the sado-masochistic 'assaults'. 'Does the public interest require the invention of a new defence?' – the question for the majority – is quite different from 'Does the public interest require the offence to be construed to include sado-masochistic conduct?' – which was the question the minority were answering; and it is not surprising that they led to different conclusions.[69]

While, however, the distinction is fundamental in theory and in judicial law-making, in the practical functioning of the law it is probably not very important.[70] It affects the evidential burden – if the absence of consent is an element of the offence, the prosecution must set out to prove it; if it is a defence, it is for the defendant to introduce evidence of it; but, in either case, the ultimate burden of proof is on the prosecution.

Whether or not consent is properly regarded as a defence or as an element of offences of assault and battery (and therefore as an element of the aggravated assaults discussed below) it is convenient to consider its meaning here. The Law Commission has regarded it as a defence.[71] Perhaps little should be read into Lord Woolf's recent statement that 'it is a requirement of *the offence* that the conduct itself should be unlawful'.[72]

In recent years the courts have been forced to deal with difficult issues including defining what constitutes effective 'consent' (that is, whether frauds or pressure vitiate consent) and, if such factual consent is present, in what circumstances it is appropriate for the State to apply the criminal sanction to punish conduct voluntarily engaged in by sane adults. There are three distinct questions to address:

(1) Was there implied or express consent?

(2) Did the 'victim'[73] give effective consent to the act?' and

(3) Was the act one to which he could in law validly consent?

67 *Larter* [1995] Crim LR 75, below, Ch 17.

68 G. Williams, 'Consent and Public Policy' [1962] Crim LR 74, 75.

69 Cf *Wilson*, below, p 55, where the court asked, 'Does public policy or the public interest demand that the appellant's activities [branding of wife's buttocks at her request] be visited by the sanctions of the criminal law?' and, unsurprisingly, answered, 'No.'

70 The Criminal Injuries Compensation Appeal Panel takes the view that the victim's consent is not determinative of whether an offence of violence has been committed *R(E) v CICA* [2003] EWCA Civ 234.

71 For criticism see S. Shute, above.

72 *Barnes* [2005] Crim LR 381, para 16.

73 The use of the term 'victim' is adopted throughout this chapter, although it acknowledged that if V has truly consented, it is illogical to view him as such.

(i) Implied consent

Since the merest touching without consent is a criminal offence, the exigencies of everyday life demand that there be an implied consent to that degree of contact which is necessary or customary in the ordinary course.

> Generally speaking, consent is a defence to battery; and most of the physical contacts of ordinary life are not actionable because they are impliedly consented to by all who move in society and so expose themselves to the risk of bodily contact. So nobody can complain of the jostling which is inevitable from his presence in, for example, a supermarket, an underground station or a busy street; nor can a person who attends a party complain if his hand is seized in friendship, or even if his back is (within reason) slapped. Although such cases are regarded as examples of implied consent, it is more common nowadays to treat them as falling within a general exception embracing all physical contact which is generally acceptable in the ordinary conduct of daily life.[74]

Touching a person for the purpose of engaging his attention has been held to be acceptable[75] but physical restraint is not. A police officer who catches hold of a boy, not for the purpose of arresting him but in order to detain him for questioning, is acting unlawfully.[76] So is a constable who takes hold of the arm of a woman found soliciting in order to caution her. The fact that the practice of cautioning prostitutes is recognized by statute does not imply any power to stop and detain.[77] But to 'detain' without any actual touching cannot be a battery. If the detention is effected by the threat of force, then it may be false imprisonment.[78] Article 5 of the ECHR has potential significance, but has been interpreted to protect against a 'deprivation of liberty not mere restriction on freedom of movement'.[79]

For this purpose the person of the victim includes the clothes he is wearing; Parke B ruled that there was a common assault where D slashed V's clothes with a knife:

> surely it is an assault on a man's person to inflict injury to the clothes on his back. In the ordinary case of a blow on the back, there is clearly an assault, though the blow is received by the coat on the person.[80]

It is apparently not necessary that V should be able to feel the impact through the clothes. In *Thomas*[81] where D touched the bottom of V's skirt and rubbed it, the court said, *obiter*, 'There could be no dispute that if you touch a person's clothes while he is wearing them that is equivalent to touching him'. It is noteworthy that s 79 of the Sexual Offences Act

74 *Collins v Wilcock* [1984] 3 All ER 374 at 378, per Robert Goff LJ. In *F v West Berkshire Health Authority* [1989] 2 All ER 545 at 563, HL, Lord Goff was more emphatic that the consent rationalization is 'artificial', pointing out that it is difficult to impute consent to those who through youth or mental disorder are unable to give it. See *Mepstead v DPP* [1996] Crim LR 111, DC. In *Wainwright v Home Office* [2003] UKHL 53, Goff LJ was described as having 'redefined' the concept: para 9.

75 *Wiffin v Kincard* (1807) 2 Bos & PNR 471; *Coward v Baddeley* (1859) 4 H & N 478. *Donnelly v Jackman* [1970] 1 All ER 987, [1970] 1 WLR 562, where a police officer was held to be acting in the execution of his duty although he persisted in tapping V on the shoulder when V had made it clear that he had no intention of stopping to speak, is 'an extreme case': [1984] 3 All ER 374 at 379.

76 *Kenlin v Gardiner* [1967] 2 QB 510, [1966] 3 All ER 931.

77 *Collins v Wilcock*, above, n 74.

78 See below, p 567.

79 B. Emmerson and A. Ashworth, 'Human Rights and Criminal Justice' (2002), para 5–02; *Guzzardi v Italy* (1981) 3 EHRR 333, para 92.

80 *Day* (1845) 1 Cox CC 207.

81 (1985) 81 Cr App R 331 at 334, CA.

2003 defines touching as including with any part of the body, with anything else or through anything, and in *H*[82] the Court of Appeal confirmed that touching clothes constituted a 'touching'.

(ii) Effective consent

The principal problems to address in this context are: what capacity V must have to be capable of issuing effective consent, what degree of knowledge V must have to be capable of making a valid consent, what effect on V's apparent consent a fraud by D will have, and whether duress or pressure from D or another will vitiate consent by V.

Capacity[83]

Those with mental disorder or learning difficulty may lack sufficient capacity to issue consent,[84] as may someone who is temporarily incapacitated by intoxication or otherwise. Youth is clearly also a potential impediment to the giving of effective consent.[85] In *Burrell v Harmer*[86] consent was held to be no defence to a charge of assault occasioning actual bodily harm, where D tattooed boys aged 12 and 13, causing their arms to become inflamed and painful. The court took the view that the boys were unable to understand the nature of the act. But in what sense did they not understand it? The case highlights the relative superficiality of the English criminal courts' approach to such fundamental questions underlying the issue of consent.

Informed consent

In principle, V cannot consent to some form of conduct without adequate knowledge of its nature, and the degree of knowledge should depend on the degree of harm to which V is exposing himself. In offences against the person this issue seems to have received little attention. In sexual offences, it is implicit in the statutory formulation that V must have capacity and have 'freely agreed', that there must have been adequate information to render consent effective.[87] In *Konzani*,[88] the Court of Appeal confirmed that if V engages in unprotected sexual intercourse with D, D will only have a defence to gbh if he recklessly infects her with HIV if V had made an informed consent to the risk of infection. It remains unclear to what extent V must have knowledge of the purpose of the conduct even if he is aware of its nature. The issue usually arises in the context of fraud. Again, the courts have not grappled in detail with the relationship between fraud and informed consent. Discussion of whether V made a 'mistake' about an issue[89] and whether D defrauded V as to an issue appears to be used interchangeably in many instances.

[82] [2005] EWCA Crim 732; [2005] All ER(D) 16 (Feb), [2005] Crim LR (Sept).

[83] Law Com Consultation Paper 139, Part V; Law Commission, *Mental Capacity* (Law Com No 231, 1995); see I. Kennedy and A. Grubb, *Medical Law* (3rd edn, 2000), ch. 5.

[84] See *Re MB (An Adult)(Medical Treatment)* [1997] 2 FCR 541. Medical treatment in defiance of the sane adult patient's wishes or in the case of a child in defiance of those of a parent will infringe Article 8: *Glass v UK* (2000) App No 61827/00.

[85] See generally *Gillick v West Norfolk and Wisbech AHA* [1986] AC 112.

[86] [1967] Crim LR 169 and commentary thereon. It is now an offence to tattoo a person under the age of 18, except tattooing by a doctor for medical reasons: Tattooing of Minors Act 1969.

[87] See below, Ch 17.

[88] [2005] EWCA Crim 706.

[89] In which case the issue would be whether D was aware of V's absence of informed consent.

Consent procured by fraud[90]

In offences against the person, fraud does not necessarily negative consent. It does so only if it deceives V as to the identity of the person or the nature of the act.[91] The common law approach to frauds vitiating consent remains unsatisfactorily complex and confused.

If V agrees to X touching her in a manner amounting to a mere battery, her consent is *prima facie* vitiated if D impersonates X and touches her. V's autonomy includes a right (generally) to choose *who* touches her. In *Richardson*,[92] D, a registered dental practitioner who was suspended from practice, carried out dentistry on patients who said they would not have consented had they known that D was suspended. D was convicted of assault occasioning actual bodily harm, the trial judge ruling that the mistake vitiated consent, being equivalent to a mistake of identity, the Court of Appeal disagreed; so to hold would be to strain and distort the everyday meaning of 'identity'. There is to date no recognition of a principle whereby a fraud as to an attribute (for example, being medically qualified) suffices to vitiate consent. It could be argued that there are some situations in which the status or attribute of the individual is inextricably bound up with his or her identity for the purposes of the specific activity in question. It could be that the attribute is actually *more* important than the identity. For example, would a patient visiting a general practitioner and being told that a new doctor is taking the surgery be more concerned as to the 'status' of the person or his 'identity'? The same argument might apply to the attribute of being a police officer.[93]

The courts have had greater difficulty dealing with the effect of frauds as to the nature of the act. The difficulty lies in distinguishing frauds as to issues that affect the nature of the act and frauds that relate to a collateral issue. It would be undesirable for the law to treat all frauds as vitiating consent; otherwise the most trivial lies could give rise to liability.[94] In *Bolduc and Bird*, where D1, a doctor, by falsely pretending that D2 was a medical student, obtained V's consent to D2's presence at a vaginal examination of V, it was held that there was no assault because the fraud was not as to the nature and quality of what was to be done.[95] Similarly, such was the case where a woman consented to the introduction of an instrument into her vagina for diagnostic purposes when the operator was acting only for sexual gratification.[96]

One of the leading cases in this area and one which gave rise to considerable controversy was *Clarence*.[97] D was charged with causing grievous bodily harm to his wife, V, by

90 Law Com Consultation Paper No 139, Part VI.

91 But cf the rule in trespass to land and, therefore, in burglary, below, p 814.

92 [1998] 2 Cr App R 200. *Richardson* now has to be read with *Tabassum* [2000] 2 Cr App R 328, below, p 530.

93 See *Wellard* [1978] 1 WLR 921. It could be argued that there are circumstances in which the attribute or status of the actor is so crucial as to alter the nature of the act performed, as perhaps in a medical context. This would require the court to adopt a much wider reading of 'nature' than the orthodox interpretation which restricts the meaning to the mechanical acts see eg *Williams* [1923] 1 KB 340. There is some Canadian authority supporting a wider test. See *Maurantonio* (1967) 65 DLR (2d) 674; *Harms* [1944] 2 DLR 61.

94 In appropriate cases the law lowers the threshold of what constitutes a sufficient fraud or threat, as where the victim is mentally disordered – see Sexual Offences Act 2003, ss 33–44 below, p 639.

95 *Bolduc and Bird* (1967) 63 DLR (2d) 82 (Sup Ct of Canada, Spence J diss), reversing British Columbia CA 61 DLR (2d) 494. Cf *Rosinski* (1824) 1 Mood CC 19.

96 *Mobilio* [1991] 1 VR 339. See D. Ormerod, 'A Victim's Mistaken Consent in Rape' (1992) J Crim L 407.

97 (1888) 22 QBD 23; below, p 555.

having sex with her knowing that he was suffering from a sexually transmitted disease. It was held that V had consented to intercourse with D and, although she would not have consented to the act of intercourse had she been aware of the disease from which D knew he was suffering, this was no assault. The court concluded that she had not been defrauded as to the nature of the act of intercourse (that is, the mechanics of it)[98] but as to the associated risk of disease. The flaw in this approach was that in focusing on V's awareness of the nature of the act of intercourse, the court ignored V's awareness of the harm which D was charged with causing – that of the infection (it was not a rape case). The crucial issue was whether V had been defrauded as to the risk of infection – it was her awareness of the nature of that risk that ought to have been investigated.

In the important case of *Dica*,[99] where D had infected two sexual partners with HIV, *Clarence* was regarded by the Court of Appeal as being no longer of useful application.[100] Where V was unaware of D's infected state, by consenting to the act of unprotected sexual intercourse she could not be said to have impliedly consented to the risk of infection from that intercourse. In *Dica* the court focused, appropriately it is submitted, on the question whether the fraud related to the infection – which represents the harm alleged – rather than the intercourse. The welcome conclusion was therefore that the victims had been defrauded as to the risk of infection and hence had not consented to bodily harm, but had not been defrauded as to the nature of the act of sexual intercourse and hence had not been raped. HIV infected intercourse is still intercourse.

In the Court of Appeal's subsequent decision on criminal HIV infection in *Konzani*[101] the court emphasized that 'there is a critical distinction between taking a risk of the various, potentially adverse and possibly problematic consequences of sexual intercourse and giving an informed consent to the risk of infection with a fatal disease.'[102] As the court also made clear,

> If an individual who knows that he is suffering from the HIV virus conceals this stark fact from his sexual partner, the principle of her personal autonomy is not enhanced if he is exculpated when he recklessly transmits the HIV virus to her through consensual sexual intercourse. On any view, the concealment of this fact from her almost inevitably means that she is deceived. Her consent is not properly informed, and she cannot give an informed consent to something of which she is ignorant. Equally, her personal autonomy is not normally protected by allowing a defendant who knows that he is suffering from the HIV virus which he deliberately conceals, to assert an honest belief in his partner's informed consent to the risk of the transmission of the HIV virus. Silence in these circumstances is incongruous with honesty, or with a genuine belief that there is an informed consent. Accordingly, in such circumstances the issue either of informed

98 Cf *Williams* [1923] KB 340.

99 [2004] EWCA Crim 1103, [2004] Crim LR 944 and commentary. See for criticism of the case M. Weait, 'Criminal Law and the Transmission of HIV: *R v Dica*' (2005) MLR 121; M. Weait, '*Dica*: Knowledge, consent and the transmission of HIV' (2004) NLJ 826, cf for a positive view of the case J. R. Spencer, 'Retrial for Reckless Infection' (2004) NLJ 762. For detailed examination of the appropriate uses of the criminal law to tackle HIV transmission see S. Bronnit, 'Spreading Disease and the Criminal Law' [1994] Crim LR 21; D. Ormerod and M. Gunn, 'Criminal Liability for the Transmission of HIV' [1996] Web Jnl Current Legal Issues; D. Ormerod, 'Criminalizing HIV Transmission – Still No Effective Solutions' [2001] Common Law World Review 135.

100 The various aspects of that decision had been eroded by the courts over recent years, with *R* [1992] 1 AC 599 dispensing with the marital rape exemption, and *Ireland and Burstow* [1998] AC 147 accepting that 'infliction' need not involve an assault or direct contact.

101 [2005] EWCA Crim 706.

102 [22].

consent, or honest belief in it will only rarely arise: in reality, in most cases, the contention would be wholly artificial.[103]

Following *Tabassum* it became unclear whether a fraud as to the 'quality' of the act (rather than its nature) would always vitiate consent. In that case D had persuaded three women to allow him to examine their breasts by falsely informing them that he was medically qualified and that he was doing research work for a cancer charity. D's conviction for indecent assault was upheld. The court accepted that the women had been aware of the nature of the act of touching their breasts, but defrauded as to the quality of the act – they believed it to be for a medical purpose – and that vitiated their consent. This was recognized to have profound repercussions. Where D has sexual intercourse with V knowing that he is HIV positive D's fraud as to the infection could be regarded as a fraud as to the quality of the act which could render V's consent to the intercourse invalid and D would be a rapist.[104] There is no guidance in *Tabassum* on what might constitute the 'quality' of a particular act.

Duress

Apparently valid consent may also be negatived by duress. A threat to imprison V unless he submitted to a beating would probably invalidate V's consent to the beating. Possibly a threat to dismiss from employment[105] or to bring a prosecution[106] would have a similar effect. It is submitted that non-criminal threats and even threats of lawful action should be sufficient. It is unclear whether the test involves an evaluation of whether the person of reasonable firmness would have succumbed, or whether the law goes further and recognizes that consent should be invalid if, alternatively, D knew of the particular vulnerabilities of the victim although they might not have caused a reasonable person to acquiesce. If the test is whether the threat would be sufficient to overcome the will of a reasonably firm person, the outcome must depend to some extent on the relationship between the gravity of the threat and the act to which V is asked to submit.

Duress may be implied from the relationship between the parties – for example where D is acting as a schoolmaster, and V is a 13-year-old pupil.[107] As in sexual offences,[108] submission is not consent. But an unfounded belief in V's consent is a defence, whether the belief is based on reasonable grounds or not, provided only that it is honestly held. '*Cunningham* recklessness' whether V consents is a sufficient *mens rea*.[109] This is subject to the caveat that D's belief must be as to consent from V which would be recognized by law as a valid consent.[110]

103 [23].

104 Note that under the Sexual Offences Act 2003, s 76 a fraud as to the 'nature or purpose' (not quality) of the act is conclusively presumed to vitiate consent.

105 *McCoy* 1953 (2) SA 4 (AD) (threat to ground air hostess negativing her consent to being caned).

106 *State v Volschenk* 1968 (2) PH H283 (threat to prosecute held *not* to negative consent on rape charge).

107 *Nichol* (1807) Russ & Ry 130.

108 Below, p 600.

109 *Morgan* [1976] AC 182, [1975] 2 All ER 347, HL; above, p 454; *Albert v Lavin* [1981] 1 All ER 628, DC. Absence of consent is 'a definitional element' of assault. Above, p 524.

110 *Konzani* [2005] EWCA Crim 706.

(iii) Legal limits on the validity of consent

Fundamental questions of morality are raised by the extent to which the State ought to use the criminal sanction to restrict a sane adult in his consent to the infliction of harm on his person.[111] English law restricts the validity of consent by reference to the level of harm and the circumstances in which it is inflicted. Consent to mere assault or battery is valid in law. Factual consent to acts intended or likely to cause actual bodily harm or more serious levels of harm (wounding, serious harm, death) is not legally recognized unless the activity involved is one which the courts or Parliament has recognized to be in the public interest. Thus, as a matter of public policy, consent to being killed is ineffective. It is no defence to a charge of murder for D to say that V asked to be killed. On the other hand, V's consent to D's taking a high degree of risk of killing him is effective where it is justified by the purpose of the act, as it may be in the case of a surgical operation. Where the act has some social purpose, recognized by the law as valid, it is a question of balancing the degree of harm which will or may be caused against the value of that purpose.

Three issues require elucidation: what level of harm is caused, what level of harm was foreseen or intended, and whether the activity is one of the exceptional categories in which consent is recognized. Unfortunately, since this is an area in which the decisions of the appellate courts are based so heavily on public policy, it is not always easy to identify clear principles.

The level of harm

If D has caused actual bodily harm – injury of more than a merely transient or trifling nature – the consent of the victim will not be valid unless the conduct falls within one of the recognized exceptional categories below. It is arguable that this is far too low a threshold at which the law should cease to recognize consent as a general defence. The Law Commission propose raising the level of harm to which a person is entitled to consent in general circumstances to harm falling below a new concept of 'serious disabling injury'.[112]

The role of intention and foresight of harms

A problem arises as to the relevance of D's intention or recklessness as to whether the harm is caused. The law has been thrown into doubt by an overbroad statement in the *Attorney-General's Reference (No 6 of 1980)*[113] where two youths of 18 and 17 settled an argument by a fist fight and one sustained a bleeding nose and bruises to his face it was held that the other was guilty of assault occasioning actual bodily harm.

> . . . it is not in the public interest that people should try to cause or should cause each other actual bodily harm for no good reason. Minor struggles are another matter. So, in our judgment, it is

[111] See G. Williams, 'Consent and Public Policy' [1962] Crim LR 74 and 154; Law Com Consultation Paper, Part II, Appendix C and P. Roberts, above, n 66; J. Feinberg, '*The Moral Limits of the Criminal Law*' *Vol 1 Harm to Others* (1984).

[112] See Law Com Consultation Paper No 139. For criticisms of the definition and its incoherence with the offences against the person see D. Ormerod and M. Gunn, above. Many jurisdictions adopt a much higher threshold: see Law Com Consultation Paper No 139, Appendix B.

[113] [1981] QB 715, [1981] 2 All ER 1057.

immaterial whether the act occurs in private or in public; it is an assault if actual bodily harm is intended and/or caused. This means that most fights will be unlawful regardless of consent.[114]

This passage was quoted with approval by all three of the majority in the leading case of *Brown* (below). It is submitted, however, that it goes too far. The difficulty is the words 'or should cause' and 'and/or' which imply that an act done to another with the other's consent is an assault/battery, although it is not intended to cause bodily harm, if it in fact does so. The passage does not suggest that the harm must be foreseen or even foreseeable. That seems a wholly unreasonable result. Subsequent case law is difficult to reconcile with the position.

It is submitted that the following positions fall for consideration.

(1) D intends to cause actual bodily harm and causes such to V with consent. D is liable for actual bodily harm. V's consent is invalid unless one of the exceptional categories below (p 534) pertains.

(2) D is reckless only as to causing actual bodily harm and has V's consent to the risk of causing that level of injury. It is less clear whether V's consent is invalid in all cases irrespective of whether they fall within an exceptional category. Dicta in *Brown* and some decisions such as *Dica* suggest that the law treats V's factual consent as invalid only in respect of intentionally inflicted harms. However, recent cases have also upheld convictions for reckless causing of actual bodily harm with consent as in *Emmett* (sadomasochism).

(3) D intends[115] only to assault V with his consent. In fact, D causes actual bodily harm. According to the dictum in *Attorney General's Reference* D is guilty. It is sufficient that actual bodily harm is caused. D has committed the *actus reus* of actual bodily harm. He has the *mens rea* for actual bodily harm (it being the same as for assault/battery). But the assault/battery for which he has full consent is the foundational element of the actual bodily harm. If D has V's factual consent to the greater harm that was caused – actual bodily harm – that will be invalid unless the conduct is in an exceptional category below. In *Slingsby*[116] D and V engaged in sexual activity – 'vigorous', including D inserting his hand into V's vagina and rectum, but activity to which V could lawfully, and did, consent. D was wearing a signet ring which caused injury to V resulting in her death. D was charged with manslaughter by an unlawful and dangerous act. Judge J ruled that it would be contrary to principle to treat as criminal, activity which would not otherwise amount to an assault merely because an injury was caused. It is submitted that this is right, but inconsistent with the above *dictum*.

(4) D intended actual bodily harm with V's consent but caused only a battery. D ought not to be convicted of any offence. Consent is a valid defence to assault/battery; D has not caused actual bodily harm.[117] Applying the *dictum* above, D would be liable; it is enough that there was an intention to cause actual bodily harm. In *Barnes*[118] Lord Woolf asserted that 'When no bodily harm is caused, the

[114] *A-G's Reference (No 6 of 1980)* [1981] 2 All ER 1057 at 1059.

[115] Arguably the same position applies if D is reckless as to the actual bodily harm.

[116] [1995] Crim LR 570.

[117] Cf the view in *Donovan* [1934] 2 KB 498, CCA.

[118] [2005] Crim LR 381.

consent of the victim to what happened is *always* a defence to a charge.'[119] It is submitted that this is a more desirable approach.

(5) A modification on the previous categories is where D lacks *mens rea* as to the causing of the harm. In *Boyea*,[120] where D's act was similar to that of Slingsby but caused actual bodily harm, it was held that there was an assault because the act was 'likely' to cause harm. D was guilty of an indecent assault even if he did not intend or foresee that harm was likely to be caused.

(6) D is reckless as to causing actual bodily harm with V's consent as to that risk, but causes only a battery. Arguably this falls outside the *dictum*. Since D has caused only a battery and has consent to that level of harm he ought to be acquitted.

It need hardly be said if this analysis is correct, that the law is in a dreadfully confused and unsatisfactory state.

Type of activity involved

In *Brown*, sadomasochists who had engaged in consensual beatings and genital torture but which had not resulted in any participant receiving medical attention, were convicted of offences of assault occasioning actual bodily harm. The House of Lords, by a majority of 3:2 upheld the convictions, and in doing so recognized categories of activity in which the law would recognize factual consent to injury as valid.[121]

In *Barnes*[122] Lord Woolf makes an honest declaration – categorization is a matter of public policy. This 'renders it unnecessary to find a separate jurisprudential basis for the application of the defence in various different factual contexts an which an offence could be committed'. This will do little to satisfy those advocating the need for a clear moral foundation to the law's approach, but is not a great surprise. This policy based approach allows the courts to maintain the incoherent list of exceptions and to add or subtract from that list based on its perception of the social utility of particular conduct. Thus, the courts may continue to allow buttock branding as akin to tattooing (*Wilson*)[123] but not sadomasochistic injury of similar severity (*Brown*).

The differentiation on grounds of perceived public utility can be illustrated by comparing the case of a fist fight and a boxing match, both of which are intended or likely to cause actual bodily harm or worse. Boxing under the Queensberry rules is lawful. A boxer, trying to knock out his opponent, certainly has an intention to cause harm, possibly even serious harm, which is a sufficient *mens rea* for murder, but no prosecutions have been brought against fighters operating under the professional rules and in *Brown* all of their lordships accepted that boxing is lawful. According to Lord Mustill, boxing is best regarded as a special case which, 'for the time being stands outside the ordinary law of violence because society chooses to tolerate it'.[124] Where, however, two youths decided to

119 Para 7, emphasis added.

120 (1992) 156 JP 505, [1992] Crim LR 574.

121 On this, one of the most controversial decisions of the House of Lords in the last few decades, see Law Com Consultation Paper No 139. D. Kell, 'Social Disutility and Consent' (1994) OJLS 121; M. Giles, 'Consensual Harm and the Public Interest' (1994) 57 MLR 101; M. Allen, 'Consent and Assault' (1994) 58 J Crim Law 183; N. Bamforth, 'Sadomasochism and Consent' [1994] Crim LR 661.

122 [2005] Crim LR 381.

123 [1996] 2 Cr App R 241.

124 For a full discussion, see M. Gunn and D. Ormerod, 'The Legality of Boxing' (1995) 15 LS 181, and Law Com Consultation Paper No 139, XII. See also S. Greenfield and G. Osborn (eds), *Law and Sport in Contemporary Society* (2000).

settle an argument by a fight with fists[125] (presumably bare) and one sustains a bleeding nose and bruises to his face the other is guilty of assault occasioning actual bodily harm.

The court in *Attorney General's Reference* sought to catalogue the types of activity to which V will be entitled to consent in law:

> Nothing which we have said is intended to cast doubt on the accepted legality of properly conducted games and sports, lawful chastisement or correction, reasonable surgical interference, dangerous exhibitions etc. These apparent exceptions can be justified as involving the exercise of a legal right, in the case of chastisement or correction, or as needed in the public interest, in the other cases.

Exceptional categories in which consent to (intentionally inflicted)[126] harm is valid

Sports.[127] The law has long recognized the social utility of sport in enhancing the fitness of the population. A number of principles seem to have developed. First, although by playing the sport V consents to whatever the rules permit, if the rules permit an unacceptably dangerous act, the law need not recognize the validity of V's consent. That is a matter of public policy. However, boxing continues to be lawful despite the life-threatening injury and participants' intention to cause grievous bodily harm. Secondly, where unlike boxing and martial arts, playing within the rules of the particular sport does not *necessarily* involve D causing actual bodily harm, but D intentionally inflicts injury, V's consent is irrelevant and D commits the offence: *Bradshaw*.[128] Thirdly, and most difficult in practical terms to apply, if in playing such a sport D was reckless only as to the causing of the injury the question will be whether V impliedly consented to the level of injury in the context in which it was inflicted.

The question of whether the conduct was within the rules of the game is not the sole determinant of liability.[129] It would be too simplistic to suggest that V's consent is only valid to that which the rules of the game permit. V may well, as a matter of fact, impliedly consent to the *risk* of injury occurring in conduct outside the rules as in a late tackle in football, or an illegitimate bouncer in cricket.[130] It is therefore necessary to look to a broader range of factors. In *Barnes*, the Court of Appeal confirmed that it is appropriate to make objective evaluation of these circumstances as in Canada[131] and advocated by the Law Commission.[132] Relevant circumstances include the type of sport, the level at which it was being played, the nature of the act, the degree of force used, the extent of the risk of injury and the state of mind of the defendant. Criminal prosecution is usually reserved for sufficiently grave conduct deserving to be regarded as criminal, having regard to the fact that most organized sports have their own disciplinary procedures and to the availability of civil remedies. What was accepted in one sport might not be covered by

125 A 'prize-fight' in public is unlawful at common law as a breach of the peace tending to public disorder. *Brown* [1993] 2 All ER 75 at 79, 86, 106, 119, HL. Because the whole enterprise is unlawful, consent is not a defence even to a charge of common assault against the contestants: *Coney* (1882) 8 QBD 534.

126 See above. Arguably the consent defence is only invalid where D has intentionally caused harm.

127 See Law Com Consultation Paper No 139, Part XII and M. Cutcheon, 'Sports, Violence and the Criminal Law' [1994] 45 NILQ 267.

128 (1878) Cox CC 83.

129 Ibid.

130 See *Moore* (1898) 14 TLR 229.

131 See *Cicarelli* (1989) 54 CCC (3d) 121.

132 Law Com Consultation Paper No 134. That approach was criticized by S. Gardner, 'The Law and the Sportsfield' [1994] Crim LR 513, but received generally favourable responses: Law Com Consultation Paper No 139, paras 12.6–12.23.

the implied consent in another. In highly competitive sports, conduct 'outside the rules' might be expected to occur in the heat of the moment, but even if such conduct justified not only being penalized but, for example, sending off, it might not reach the threshold required for it to be criminal.

Horseplay.[133] The exception is not confined to organized games. Consent by children to rough and undisciplined play may be a defence to a charge of inflicting grievous bodily harm if there is no intention to cause injury. Consent, or a genuine belief in consent, even an unreasonable belief, apparently negatives recklessness: *Jones*[134] where boys were injured by being tossed in the air by schoolmates. The decision recognizes that children have always indulged in rough and undisciplined play among themselves and probably always will; but the non-consenting child is rightly protected by the criminal law. The 'horseplay' exception seems to have been taken to extreme lengths in *Aitken*[135] where the 'robust games' of Royal Air Force officers at a celebration in the mess included setting fire to one another's fire resistant clothing. Two such incidents apparently caused no harm but then V sustained severe burns. It was held that a ruling that it was not open to the court martial to find that the 'activities' were lawful was wrong. If V consented to them, or if D believed, reasonably or not, that V consented to them, it was open to the trial court to find that there was no offence.

Surgery.[136] Consent to a surgical operation for a purpose recognized as valid by the law is effective[137] and this includes a sex-change operation[138] and, presumably, cosmetic surgery and organ transplants. Where a sane adult refuses consent to medical treatment a failure to respect that decision will render the doctor liable for criminal offences, even in circumstances in which the treatment will be life preserving.[139]

Body modification.[140] Ritual[141] circumcision of males,[142] ear-piercing and tattooing of adults are generally assumed to be lawful. Presumably the same is true of more exotic body-piercing of adults.[143] In *Wilson,*[144] D's branding of his initials on his wife's buttocks, at her request, in lieu of tattooing, was held to be equally lawful. The only distinction from *Donovan*[145] appears to be that Donovan's motive was sexual gratification whereas Wilson's was to bestow on his wife an adornment which she desired. Where the

133 See Law Com Consultation Paper No 139.

134 [1987] Crim LR 123, CA.

135 [1992] 1 WLR 1006, 1011 (C-MAC).

136 See Law Com Consultation Paper No 139, Part VIII.

137 Stephen, *Digest*, art 310. See P. Skegg, 'Medical Procedures and the Crime of Battery' [1974] Crim LR 693 and (1973) 36 MLR 370.

138 *Corbett v Corbett* [1971] P 83 at 99.

139 *St George's Health Care v S* [1998] 3 All ER 673.

140 See Law Com Consultation Paper No 139, Part IX.

141 Ie that performed otherwise than for medical reasons. See further, Law Com Consultation Paper No 139. See *Brown* [1994] 1 AC 212 and *Re J* [2000] 1 FCR 307, CA Civ. Prof Feldman advised the Law Commission that non-therapeutic circumcision might be in breach of Article 3 of the ECHR, para 3.25, see also L. Vickers, 'Circumcision – The Unkindest Cut of All?' (2000) 150 NLJ 1694.

142 See Female Genital Mutilation Act 2003 replacing the Prohibition of Female Circumcision Act 1985 with extended offences to catch those in the UK who aid and abet circumcision performed abroad.

143 See *Oversby* (1990) unreported, cited in Law Com Consultation Paper No 139, para 9.7.

144 [1996] Crim LR 573, CA.

145 [1934] 2 KB 498.

purpose of the act is one which the law condemns, consent may be no answer to the charge.[146]

Coke tells us that in 1604, 'a young strong and lustie rogue, to make himself impotent, thereby to have the more colour to begge or to be relieved without putting himself to any labour, caused his companion to strike off his left hand': and that both of them were convicted of mayhem.[147] Maiming, even with consent, was unlawful because it deprived the king of a fighting man. In early Victorian times when soldiers, as part of their drill, had to bite cartridges, a soldier got a dentist to pull out his front teeth to avoid the drill. Stephen J thought that both were guilty of a crime.[148] Denning LJ followed these instances in discussing, *obiter*, the legality of a sterilization operation.[149] His opinion, that the operation is unlawful if done only to enable the man to have the pleasure of intercourse without the responsibility, is no longer tenable,[150] but it illustrates the continuing and changing influence of public policy.

In circumstances where the body modification is for religious reasons, reliance on Article 9 of the ECHR guaranteeing respect for religious freedom would support the validity of consent. However, the courts have been unwilling to accommodate foreign cultural practices involving children such as incision of cheeks.[151] In view of the recognition that ritual male circumcision practiced by Jews and Muslims is lawful, the law's approach appears incoherent.

Sado-masochism.[152] Public policy is also at the root of the decision in *Brown*. In the opinion of the majority, policy requires the conviction of men participating in consensual sado-masochistic homosexual encounters, resulting in actual bodily harm and wounding, to protect society against a cult of violence with the danger of the corruption and proselytization of young men and the potential for the infliction of serious injury: this, notwithstanding that there was in fact no permanent injury, no infection and no evidence of medical attention being required. The majority's reasoning that this was violence rather than sexual activity led to the conclusion that the activity should be unlawful.

Public policy was invoked to justify conviction for a relatively slight degree of harm in *Donovan*.[153] D, for his sexual gratification, beat a 17-year-old girl with a cane in circumstances of indecency. He was convicted of both indecent assault and common assault. The judge failed to direct the jury that the onus of negativing consent was on the Crown, but the Court of Criminal Appeal held that, if the blows were likely or intended to cause

146 The court was also influenced by the fact that W was married to his victim, but this must be an irrelevance. If the criminal law governing consensual injury is applied differently to homosexuals and heterosexuals (or to men and women) or on the basis of marriage this would almost certainly involve a violation of Articles 8 and 14 of the ECHR taken together.

147 1 Co Inst 127a and b.

148 *Digest* (3rd edn) 142.

149 *Bravery v Bravery* [1954] 3 All ER 59 at 67, 68.

150 The National Health Service (Family Planning) Amendment Act 1972 first authorized the provision of voluntary vasectomy services.

151 *Adesanya* (1974) The Times, 16 July. See S. Poulter, 'Foreign Customs and the English Criminal Law' (1975) 24 ICLQ 136.

152 See Law Com Consultation Paper No 139, Part X.

153 [1934] Law Com Consultation Paper No 2 KB 498. See L. Leigh, 'Sado-Masochism, Consent and the Reform of the Criminal Law' (1976) 39 MLR 130.

bodily harm, this omission was immaterial because D was guilty whether V consented or not. The conviction was quashed because the question whether the blows were likely or intended to cause bodily harm was not put to the jury.

In *Brown* the whole House agreed that consent is a complete defence to the two offences – common and indecent assault – with which Donovan was charged. The Court of Criminal Appeal's opinion in *Brown* that he could have been convicted of these offences because he was guilty of assault occasioning actual bodily harm, an offence with which he was not charged, was unacceptable to both Lord Lowry[154] of the majority and Lord Mustill[155] of the minority. Subsequent cases nevertheless seem to treat the *dicta* in *Donovan* as correct. The only ground on which the *dicta* could be distinguished from *Wilson*[156] (buttock branding) is that Donovan was seeking sexual gratification, whereas Wilson was not – his conduct was like that of a professional tattooist who embellishes intimate parts at the request of their owner. In *Laskey* the European Court distinguished *Wilson* because the injuries were not at all 'comparable in seriousness' with those in *Brown* even though they amounted to assault occasioning actual bodily harm.

The decision in *Wilson* was distinguished, and *Brown* followed in a further case of sadomasochism: *Emmett.*[157] D's conviction for recklessly occasioning actual bodily harm to V by, *inter alia*, setting fire to lighter fuel on her breasts, with her consent was upheld by the Court of Appeal. The court described the conduct as going 'beyond that which was established in *Wilson*'. But the charge was the same – assault occasioning actual bodily harm. Are the courts to start evaluating the validity of consent on the basis of some undeclared judicial barometer of the severity of harm?

Religious flagellation. In *Brown*, Lord Mustill accepted this as a recognized, though rarely practised exception. The protection of religious freedoms under Article 9 of the ECHR would support such a conclusion.[158]

The risk of sexually transmitted disease. The decision of the Court of Appeal in *Dica*[159] is that an adult is entitled to give valid consent to the risk of being infected with a potentially lethal sexually transmitted disease such as HIV. The court distinguished between consensual acts of sexual intercourse where there might be a known risk to the health of one or other participants (consent defence available) and those cases where participants were intent on spreading, or becoming infected with, disease (no consent defence available). The court took the view that criminalization of consensual taking of risks would involve an 'impracticality of enforcement' and would undermine the general understanding of the community that sexual relationships were 'pre-eminently private'. Such arguments did not persuade the House of Lords in *Brown*. The decision might be seen as against the trend of post – *Brown* cases that treat consent even to a risk of harm as invalid. An example of this can be illustrated in *Emmett.*[160] Many will find unconvincing the court's distinction between 'sexual' and 'violent' acts, with cases such as *Emmett* and *Boyea* treated as having 'sexual overtones' but being really concerned with 'violent crime'.

154 'If the jury, properly directed, had found that consent was not disproved, they must have acquitted the appellant of the only charges brought against him' [1993] 2 All ER at 97.

155 'There is something amiss here' [1993] 2 All ER at 112.

156 [1996] Crim LR 573.

157 (1999) The Times, 15 Oct.

158 See Law Com Consultation Paper No 139, paras 10–2–10.7.

159 [2004] EWCA 1103; [2004] Crim LR 944 and commentary.

160 (1999) The Times, 15 Oct.

In *Konzani*[161] the court confirmed that the consent will only be valid if V is informed of the risk of infection.

ECHR compatibility[162]

The case of *Brown* was considered by the European Court of Human Rights in *Laskey v United Kingdom*[163] with the Court unanimously holding that that the prosecution, conviction and sentence did not contravene Article 8 of the Convention. It should be noted that the Court doubted whether the activities even fell within the protection of Article 8. On the assumption that they did, the Court concluded that the prosecution was necessary and proportionate to the legitimate aim of the protection of health (and possibly also the protection of morals). The Court recognized that the margin of appreciation provided national courts, the scope to prescribe the level of physical harm to which the law should permit an adult to consent.

(b) Lawful chastisement

It was always the common law rule that punishment was unlawful:

> If it be administered for the gratification of passion or rage or if it be immoderate or excessive in its nature or degree, or if it be protracted beyond the child's powers of endurance or with an instrument unfitted for the purpose and calculated to produce danger to life and limb. . . .[164]

The rule of the common law entitling parents to inflict moderate and reasonable physical chastisement on their children was held to offend Article 3 of the ECHR, prohibiting torture and inhuman or degrading treatment or punishment: *A v UK*,[165] where a jury had acquitted a step-father who had caned a 9-year-old child. It was accepted that the law needed reform but there was considerable disagreement as to the appropriate form that should take. The English courts continued to acknowledge the parental right: *H.*[166] The judge had to give detailed directions to the jury to take account of the nature, context and duration of D's behaviour, the physical and mental effect on the child the reasons for the punishment, and so on. Immigrant parents must conform to English standards.[167] Reliance on Article 9 of the ECHR by parents claiming a right to inflict corporal punishment as an aspect of their religion will not preclude prosecution.[168]

(i) The Children Act 2004

Section 58 of the Children Act 2004 now provides:

161 [2005] EWCA Crim 706.

162 Law Com Consultation Paper No 139, Part III.

163 (1997) 24 EHRR 39; L. Moran, 'Learning the Limits of Privacy' (1998) 61 MLR 77.

164 *Hopley* (1860) 2 F & F 202 at 206, per Cockburn CJ. Cf *Smith* [1985] Crim LR 42, CA.

165 [1998] TLR 578, (1999) 27 EHRR 611. See also *Costello-Roberts v UK* (1993) 19 EHRR 112 (7-yr-old slippered at public school); *Y v UK* (1992) 17 EHRR 238 (16-yr-old caned at school). See generally, B. Phillips, 'The Case for Corporal Punishment in the UK – Beaten into Submission in Europe' (1994) 43 ICLQ 153.

166 [2002] 1 Cr App R 59. J. Rogers, 'A Criminal Lawyer's Response to Chastisement in European Court' [2002] Crim LR 98.

167 *Derriviere* (1969) 53 Cr App R 637, CA.

168 *R (On the Application of Williamson) v Secretary of State for Education and Employment* [2002] EWCA Civ 1820. Confirmed in *R (Williamson) v Secretary of State for Education* [2005] UKHL 15. See also App No 8811/79, *Seven Individuals v Sweden* 29 DR 104, EComHR.

(1) In relation to any offence specified in subsection (2), battery of a child cannot be justified on the ground that it constituted reasonable punishment.

(2) The offences referred to in subsection (1) are –

(a) an offence under section 18 or 20 of the Offences against the Person Act 1861 (wounding and causing grievous bodily harm);

(b) an offence under section 47 of that Act (assault occasioning actual bodily harm);

(c) an offence under section 1 of the Children and Young Persons Act 1933 (cruelty to persons under 16).

(3) Battery of a child causing actual bodily harm to the child cannot be justified in any civil proceedings on the ground that it constituted reasonable punishment.

(4) For the purposes of subsection (3) 'actual bodily harm' has the same meaning as it has for the purposes of section 47 of the Offences against the Person Act 1861.

The effect is that reasonable and proportionate punishment amounting only to an assault or battery (that does not involve cruelty) is still protected by the defence of lawful chastisement. There is no longer a defence of lawful chastisement for punishment that involves a touching of the child and which constitutes the higher level of harm – actual bodily harm or cruelty. Given the ambiguity of the boundary between assault and actual bodily harm, neither parents nor children have gained a clear position of their rights.

(ii) Corporal punishment in schools

At common law, school teachers were in the same position as parents with regard to the conduct of the child at, or on his or her way to or from school.[169] A 'member of staff' of a school, as defined in s 549(4) of the Education Act 1996 now has no right, by virtue of his position as such, to administer corporal punishment to a 'pupil' as defined in s 548(3) of that Act.[170] Staff may use reasonable force to restrain pupils who are violent or disruptive (s 550A) or to avert an immediate danger of personal injury or damage to property (s 548(5)).

(c) Necessity

As noted above, necessity may negative what would otherwise be an assault, as where D pushes V out of the path of a vehicle which is about to run him down. The fireman, the paramedic, the surgeon and nurses may all do things to a person rendered unconscious in an accident, or by a stroke, which would ordinarily be battery (or, in the case of the surgeon, wounding or grievous bodily harm) if done without consent; but they commit no offence if they are only doing what is necessary to save life or ensure improvement, or prevent deterioration, in health.[171]

Perhaps this is based on the presumption that V would consent if he knew of the circumstances, a principle which excuses conduct in other parts of the criminal law.[172] This is consistent with the view[173] that intervention cannot be justified if it is against V's

169 *Cleary v Booth* [1893] 1 QB 465; *Newport (Salop) Justices* [1929] 2 KB 416; *Mansell v Griffin* [1908] 1 KB 160.

170 As substituted by the School Standards and Framework Act 1998.

171 *F v West Berkshire Health Authority* [1989] 2 All ER 545 at 564, 566, HL, per Lord Goff.

172 Eg the Theft Act 1968, ss 2(1)(b), 12(6), Criminal Damage Act 1971, s 5(2)(b).

173 *F v West Berks*, above, at 566, per Lord Goff.

known wishes. So it seems that a passer-by who prevents V, a sane person, from committing suicide by dragging him from the parapet of a bridge is guilty of battery.[174]

3. Aggravated assaults

Assault forms the basis for a number of more serious offences. Three introductory points should be noted about this. First, a person cannot be convicted of an aggravated assault unless he is guilty of assault. Subject to what was said above relating to consents and assault, if D has a defence to the charge of assault, he is not guilty of the aggravated assault. This apparently self-evident proposition is not always as obvious as it appears. In *Blackburn v Bowering*[175] D was convicted of assaulting V, an officer of the court in the execution of his duty, contrary to the County Courts Act 1984, s 14(1)(b). His defence was that he did not believe V was a bailiff – he thought he was using reasonable force against a trespasser. The trial judge ruled correctly that s 14, like s 51 of the Police Act 1964,[176] created an offence of strict liability, following *Forbes and Webb.*[177] He held that D's mistaken belief was no defence, remarking on the 'extraordinary situation' that it could have been a defence to common assault. D's conviction was quashed. If D was not guilty of assault, he could not be guilty of the aggravated assault. The judge's error appears to have arisen from the inaccurate proposition that an offence of strict liability requires no *mens rea* whatsoever.[178] The reality is that liability will be strict in relation to only one (or more) elements of the *actus reus*: in this case the status of the officer. If the assault had been proved – for example, if D had used force which was excessive even against a trespasser, it would have been no defence that he believed (even on reasonable grounds) that V was not an officer but a thug.

Secondly, this range of aggravated offences do not form a coherent scheme, let alone a nicely structured ladder of offences, rather they are a motley collection which has evolved over time. Many of the offences are found within the Offences Against the Person Act 1861. Some of these were, no doubt, intended to deal with matters causing public concern at the time, and appear rather curious today. Thus, obstructing or assaulting a clergyman in the discharge of his duties in a place of worship or burial place, or who is on his way to or from such duties is an offence triable either way, punishable on indictment with two years' imprisonment under s 36! Assaulting a magistrate or other person in the exercise of his duty concerning the preservation of a vessel in distress or a wreck is an offence punishable on indictment with seven years' imprisonment under s 37. Such provisions are rarely invoked in the modern day and need not be considered further, save to note that for some, the explicit labelling and differentiation between the offences by reference

[174] Cf Williams, TBCL, 616. Otherwise, perhaps, if V is in police custody: *Kirkham v Chief Constable of the Greater Manchester Police* [1990] 2 QB 283, [1990] 3 All ER 246, CA.

[175] [1994] 3 All ER 380, CA (Civ Div). The appeal came to the Civil Division because the offence was in the nature of a contempt of court.

[176] Now replaced by s 89 of the Police Act 1996, below, p 542.

[177] (1865) 10 Cox CC 362 (assaulting constable).

[178] Above, p, 139. This offence is an example of 'constructive crime' because the *mens rea* of a lesser offence, common assault, must be proved.

to the manner and circumstances in which they were caused reflects important moral distinctions that ought to be retained.[179]

Thirdly, these aggravated offences, including those which will be considered, represent some of the starkest examples of crimes which do not respect the correspondence principle – that is D may be convicted of an offence comprising *actus reus* elements A and B even though he has *mens rea* relating only to element A.[180]

(a) Assault with intent to resist arrest

By s 38 of the OAPA 1861:

Whosoever shall assault any person with intent to resist or prevent the lawful apprehension or detainer of himself or of any other person for any offence

is guilty of an offence triable either way and punishable with two years' imprisonment.

It may be assumed that the section creates two offences, assault with intent and battery with intent. For each version, D must be shown to have committed all the elements of the assault/battery *and* that he intended to resist, etc. Thus, threatening the arrester (V) with a weapon to make him let go of the arrestee would be the assault, poking him with it would be battery. Dragging the arrestee from V's grasp, being reckless whether this causes V to fall to the ground will be a reckless battery with intent if V does fall. D has an intention to prevent 'apprehension' when he tries to prevent the arrest taking place, and an intention to prevent the 'detainer' when he tries to bring the arrest to an end. The section applies only where the arrest is 'for any offence'; so it does not apply to an arrest in civil process or for a breach of the peace not amounting to crime. It is immaterial whether the arrest is by a police officer or a citizen; but D's claim that he did not know the arrester was a plain-clothes officer may be crucial where his defence is that he believed he was being attacked by thugs.[181]

The intent must be to resist 'lawful' arrest.[182] It is important to distinguish between D's mistakes of fact and law. If D knows of the factual circumstances which make the arrest lawful, he probably has a sufficient intent even though he believes, on the circumstances known to him, the arrest to be unlawful: for example, having read in an out-of-date law book that conspiracy is not an arrestable offence, he resists arrest for conspiracy. The law of arrest is treated as part of the criminal law for this purpose[183] and his mistake or ignorance of criminal law is no defence.[184] D's honest and, indeed, true belief that he is not, in fact, guilty of any offence is not *per se* a defence: the arrest may be lawful because the arrester has reasonable grounds for suspicion. But, if D makes a mistake of fact he should be judged on the circumstances as he believed them to be – in accordance with

179 See J. Gardner, 'Rationality and the Rule of Law in Offences Against the Person' [1994] CLJ 520.

180 J. Horder, 'A Critique of the Correspondence Principle in Criminal Law' [1995] Crim LR 759; above. Cf B. Mitchell, 'In Defence of the Correspondence Principle' [1999] Crim LR 195.

181 *Brightling* [1991] Crim LR 364, CA, *Blackburn v Bowering*, above, p 540.

182 *Lee* [2001] 1 Cr App R 293, CA, and see commentary at [2001] Crim LR 991.

183 Cf cl 25(2)(b) of the Code Team's Draft Code (Law Commission No 143), a provision not included in the Law Commission's draft (Law Commission No 177).

184 Talfourd J put his decision on this ground in *Bentley* (1850) 4 Cox CC 406. See recently *Hewitt v DPP* [2002] EWHC.

general principle. Thus, if D believes the arrester has, and D believes that the arrester knows he has, no reasonable grounds to suspect that D is guilty – matters of fact – D should be acquitted if he resists. Whatever the true facts, D does not *intend* to resist *lawful* arrest. It may be that the principle of *Fennell*[185] leaves D liable for common assault or battery but it would be wrong in principle to convict him of the aggravated offence when *mens rea* with respect to the aggravating factor is not proved.

(b) Assault on, resistance to, or obstruction of constables

By s 89 of the Police Act 1996:

(1) Any person who assaults a constable in the execution of his duty, or a person assisting a constable in the execution of his duty, shall be guilty of an offence and liable on summary conviction to a fine not exceeding level 5 on the standard scale or to imprisonment for a term not exceeding six months or to both,

(2) Subsection (2) of section 17 of the Firearms Act 1968, shall apply to offences under subsection (1) of this section.

(3) Any person who resists or wilfully obstructs a constable in the execution of his duty, or a person assisting a constable in the execution of his duty, shall be guilty of an offence and liable on summary conviction to imprisonment for a term not exceeding one month or to a fine not exceeding level 3 on the standard scale, or to both.

Though the section is headed 'Assaults on Constables', it contains three crimes, only one of which necessarily amounts to an assault. Resistance to a constable may occur without an assault, as where D has been arrested by V and D tears himself from V's grasp and escapes.[186] Obstruction, as appears below, embraces many situations which do not amount to an assault. On the other hand, both resistance and obstruction clearly may include assaults. The nature of assault and resistance require no further consideration but obstruction presents problems and is examined in some detail below.

Common to all three crimes is the requirement that the constable[187] is acting in the course of his duty. But the *mens rea* of assault and resistance, on the one hand, and obstruction on the other require separate consideration.

(i) A constable acting in the execution of his duty[188]

Identifying whether a police officer is acting in the course of duty is a question which can give rise to difficult problems. There are numerous examples of an officer's action falling on the wrong side of the line. A constable directing a motorist to leave the road to take

[185] [1971] 1 QB 428, [1970] 3 All ER 215. Cf *Ball* (1989) 90 Cr App R 378; [1978] Crim LR 580. See the quashing of the conviction in *McKoy* [2002] EWCA Crim 1628.

[186] *Sheriff* [1969] Crim LR 260.

[187] Ie, a person holding the *office*, not the rank of constable. A prison officer acting as such is a constable for this purpose: Prison Act 1952, s 8, see also the extended power in S 8A. It is also an offence to assault a member of a joint international investigation team, Police Reform Act 2001, s 104. See also the offences under the Traffic Management Act 2004, s 10 in respect of traffic officers.

[188] On the duties of the police, see the discussion in S. Bailey, D. Harris and D. Ormerod, *Civil Liberties, Cases and Material* (5th edn, 2001), at 157–165. See also *Metropolitan Police Comr, ex p Blackburn* [1968] 2 QB 118, [1968] 1 All ER 763, CA, and *(No 3)* [1973] QB 241, [1973] 1 All ER 324, CA; K. Lidstone, 'A Policeman's Duty Not to Take Liberties' [1976] Crim LR 617; U. Ross, 'Two Cases on Obstructing a Constable' [1977] Crim LR 187.

part in a traffic census, before there was a statutory power to do so[189] was not acting in the execution of his duty since his right at common law to regulate traffic derives only from his duty to protect life and property.[190] A constable who restrained D under the mistaken belief that D had been lawfully arrested by another officer was held not to be acting in the execution of his duty.[191]

There are many things which a constable on duty may do which he is probably not under any 'duty' in the strict sense to do; that is, he would commit no crime or tort or even breach of police regulations by not doing it. It might be rescuing a stranded cat or helping to deliver a baby. Older cases[192] suggested that a constable was not in the execution of his duty for the purposes of this section unless he was doing something that he was obliged to do, but in *Coffin v Smith*[193] the Divisional Court rejected an argument on these lines and doubted those authorities. Officers, who had been summoned to a club to ensure that certain people left, were assaulted. It was held that the officers were there in fulfilment of their duty to keep the peace and were plainly acting in the execution of their duty. In one of the doubted cases, *Prebble*,[194] where a constable, at the request of a landlord, turned some persons out of a pub and was held not to be acting in the execution of his duty, the court found there was no nuisance or danger of breach of the peace, and it may possibly be distinguishable as a case where the officer was doing no more than assist a citizen in the enforcement of private rights.

A constable may be acting in the execution of his duty by being present, and by intervening when a breach of the peace occurs or is imminent, but acting outside his duty if he takes it upon himself to expel a trespasser.[195] In a leading case, *Waterfield*,[196] the Court of Criminal Appeal said:

In the judgment of this court it would be difficult, and in the present case it is unnecessary, to reduce within specific limits the general terms in which the duties of police constables have been expressed. In most cases it is probably more convenient to consider what the police constable was actually doing and in particular whether such conduct was prima facie an unlawful interference with a person's liberty or property. If so, it is then relevant to consider whether (a) such conduct falls within the general scope of any duty imposed by statute or recognized at common law and (b) whether such conduct, albeit within the general scope of such a duty, involved an unjustifiable use of powers associated with the duty.

189 See now the Road Traffic Act 1988, s 35 as amended.

190 *Hoffman v Thomas* [1974] 2 All ER 233, DC. In the pursuance of that duty, a constable may require a motorist to disobey a traffic regulation: *Johnson v Phillips* [1975] 3 All ER 682, DC; and remove a vehicle to the police station when the driver is arrested; *Liepins v Spearman* [1985] Crim LR 229. Cf *Saunders* [1978] Crim LR 98 (Judge Heald) and commentary.

191 *Kerr v DPP* [1995] Crim LR 394.

192 *Prebble* (1858) 1 F & F 325 and *Roxburgh* (1871) 12 Cox CC 8. See also *Betts v Stevens* [1910] 1 KB 1 and 4th edition of this book at 361–372.

193 (1980) 71 Cr App R 221. Cf the approval of Sedley LJ in *Porter v MPC* (1999) unrep 20 Nov CA(Civ).

194 Above, n 192.

195 In *Chief Constable of Devon and Cornwall, ex p Central Electricity Generating Board* [1982] QB 458, [1981] 3 All ER 826, 835 the Chief Constable appeared to take the view that he had no right to intervene to expel trespassers, even where they were committing a criminal obstruction, unless a breach of the peace was imminent. Lawton LJ said the CEGB had No right to call on the police to supply 'muscle-power' to remove the obstructors; and if the obstructors allowed themselves to be removed without struggling or causing uproar, 'the police will have no reason for taking action, *nor should they*': at 836–837. (Authors' italics.)

196 [1964] 1 QB 164 at 170, [1963] 3 All ER 659 at 661.

If the police officer's conduct falls within the general scope of the 'duty' to prevent crime and to bring offenders to justice, then it would seem to be within the protection of the statute, if it was lawful. If, in the course of carrying out his duty to prevent crime and to bring offenders to justice, the officer exceeds his powers, then he is no longer acting in the execution of his duty for this purpose.[197] Where D is arrested or detained by an officer unlawfully, for example, where the officer has not used words of arrest or told D the grounds therefore, the officer is not acting in the execution of his duty. Likewise is the case, where he searches D without giving reasons.[198] Similarly where an officer enters premises, otherwise than in accordance with the power given by PACE,[199] or acts beyond the powers incidental to the search when on the premises.[200]

In *McArdle v Wallace*,[201] V was held to be acting in the execution of his duty as a constable when he entered a café to make enquiries regarding some property which he thought might have been stolen. He was told to leave but did not do so and was then assaulted. At the time of the assault he was no longer acting in the execution of his duty since he became a trespasser when he refused to leave: for a constable can hardly have a duty to break the law. A constable who is not acting in the execution of his duty because he is a trespasser begins so to act as soon as circumstances justifying his presence arise – as where he reasonably apprehends a breach of the peace. He does not have to leave the premises and re-enter.[202]

(ii) Trivial touchings by officers

A police officer investigating crime is entitled to speak to any person from whom he thinks useful information can be obtained, even though that person declares that he is unwilling to reply;[203] but the officer has no power to detain for questioning so the use of reasonable force to escape from such detention is not an assault;[204] and the use of excessive force, while a common assault (or wounding, etc) would not be an offence under s 89. Where, however, V tapped D on the shoulder, not intending to detain him but in order to speak to him, it was held that V was acting in the course of his duties, though it seems clear that D did not consent to this contact. The court thought that '. . . it is not

197 *Ludlow v Burgess* [1971] Crim LR 238, CA; *Pedro v Diss* [1981] 2 All ER 59, 72 Cr App R 193.

198 *McBean v Parker* [1983] Crim LR 399; *Brazil v Chief Constable of Surrey* (1983) 77 Cr App R 237, DC; *Osman v DPP* [1999] 163 JP 725; *Linehan v DPP* [2000] Crim LR 816; *Bonner v DPP* [2004] All ER (D) 74 (Oct).

199 Cf *McLorie v Oxford* [1982] 3 All ER 480, [1982] Crim LR 603; *O'Loughlin v Chief Constable of Essex* [1998] 1 WLR 374; cf *Hobson v CC Cheshire* [2003] All ER (D) 264 (Nov); *Odewale v DPP* [2001] 2 Archbold News 2.

200 See however the novel power to detain and segregate in *DPP v Meaden* [2004] Crim LR 587 criticized in the commentary.

201 [1964] Crim LR 467; cf *Davis v Lisle* [1936] 2 KB 434, [1936] 2 All ER 213; *Robson v Hallett* [1967] 2 All ER 407; *McGowan v Chief Constable of Kingston-upon-Hull* [1967] Crim LR 34; *Kay v Hibbert* [1977] Crim LR 226, DC; *Jones and Jones v Lloyd* [1981] Crim LR 340, DC.

202 *Lamb* [1990] Crim LR 58, DC.

203 Code of Practice A (2004), code issued under the Police and Criminal Evidence Act (1984); *Weight v Long* [1986] Crim LR 746.

204 *Kenlin v Gardner* [1967] 2 QB 510, [1966] 3 All ER 931; *Ludlow v Burgess* [1971] Crim LR 238; *Lemsatef* [1977] 1 WLR 812. Cf *Daniel v Morrison* (1980) 70 Cr App R 142, DC.

every trivial interference with a citizen's liberty that amounts to a course of conduct sufficient to take the officer out of the course of his duties'.[205]

That the commission of a crime or tort can ever be part of the duty of a constable is an unacceptable proposition; and the case is an 'extreme' one,[206] explicable only on the ground that the trespass committed by the constable was a momentary and trivial incident in an otherwise lawful course of conduct. In *Bentley v Brudzinski*,[207] on very similar facts, a different result was reached. Where the question is whether something is trivial or *de minimis*, it is perhaps to be expected that assessments will differ. In *C v DPP*,[208] the officer's taking hold of a 14-year-old girl's arm to escort her home when she was reported missing by her parents was not in the exercise of his duty and hence her boyfriend was not guilty of assaulting the officer in the execution of his duty.

Waterfield[209] is a difficult case. V, a constable, had been informed that a car had been involved in a serious offence. Evidently acting on the instructions of a superior officer, he attempted to prevent D, the owner of the car, from removing it from the place on the road where it was parked. D drove the car at V, thus assaulting him, in order to remove it. The court held that V was not 'entitled' to prevent removal of the car[210] and therefore was not acting in the execution of his duty. The difficulty is that the judgment nowhere specifies in what respect V's act was unlawful. He simply stood in front of the car. It has been pertinently asked, why, if it was not an unlawful act, was it not one that V might properly do in fulfilment of the general duty to bring offenders to justice?[211] It may be, however, that the answer is that V was guilty of obstructing the highway under the Highways Act 1959;[212] but there was no finding that the road was a highway.

Officer preventing breach of peace

Probably the most important application of the provision is in the context of the constable's duty to prevent breaches of the peace which he reasonably apprehends.[213] If it appears (i) that facts existed from which a constable could reasonably have anticipated a breach, as a real and not merely as a remote possibility; and (ii) that he did so anticipate, then he is under a duty to take such steps, whether by arrest or otherwise,[214] as he

205 *Donnelly v Jackman* [1970] 1 All ER 987, criticized in J. C. Smith 'Assault: *Donnelly v Jackman*' [1970] Crim LR 219 at 220 and 'Police Power to Stop Without Arrest' [1970] 33 MLR 438; and followed in *Pounder v Police* [1971] NZLR 1080 (constable committing 'a trivial trespass'). Cf *Squires v Botwright* [1972] RTR 462, DC; *Inwood* [1973] 2 All ER 645, CA; *Mepstead v DPP* (1995) 160 JP 475, [1996] Crim LR 111, DC. See D. Lanham, 'Arrest, Detention and Compulsion' [1974] Crim LR 288.

206 *Collins v Wilcock* [1984] 3 All ER 374 at 378, above.

207 [1982] Crim LR 825, DC and commentary.

208 [2003] All ER (D) 37 (Nov).

209 [1964] 1 QB 164, [1963] 3 All ER 659.

210 The case has since been doubted on this point: *Ghani v Jones* [1970] 1 QB 693 at 707, CA. Where a constable in uniform requires a vehicle to stop under s 163 of the Road Traffic Act 1988, the driver commits an offence if he fails to do so. He has a duty to remain at rest for a reasonable period; but it seems that the constable has no right under the section physically to stop or to detain the driver or vehicle: *Lodwick v Sanders* [1985] 1 All ER 577 at 582–584, [1985] Crim LR 210, per Webster J. But if the constable reasonably suspects the vehicle to be stolen by the driver he is entitled to seize and detain it and arrest the driver: ibid; *Sanders v DPP* [1988] Crim LR 605, DC. Similarly if he has reasonable suspicion to search it: *Smith v DPP* [2002] EWHC 113 (Admin).

211 See P. J. Fitzgerald, 'The Arrest of a Motor-Car' [1965] Crim LR 23.

212 Now s 137 of the Highways Act 1980.

213 *Duncan v Jones* [1936] 1 KB 218.

214 *King v Hodges* [1974] Crim LR 424; *Blench v DPP* [2004] All ER (D) 86 (Nov). The requirement for an 'imminent' breach of the peace was interpreted very widely in *Wragg v DPP* [2005] EWHC (Admin).

reasonably thinks are necessary.[215] Even where no breach of the peace is anticipated, a constable may be under a duty to give instructions to members of the public – for example, to remove an obstruction from the highway – and a deliberate refusal to obey such an instruction may amount to an obstruction of the police. It is in the course of a constable's duty to require pickets to move where they would otherwise obstruct lawful passage on the highway by others.[216]

A constable who makes a lawful arrest is acting in the execution of his duty even though the arrest subsequently becomes unlawful when he fails to communicate the ground to the arrestee.[217]

(iii) *Mens rea* in cases of assault and resistance

The only *mens rea* required is that of assault,[218] or an intention to resist, as the case may be. It is no defence that D was reasonably unaware that V was a constable, still less that he was on duty. Liability in relation to the status of the arrester and whether the officer was in the execution of his duty is strict. It was so held by a recorder in a direction to a jury in *Forbes*[219] *and Webb* which six judges in *Prince*[220] accepted as correct; and in *Maxwell*[221] and *Clanchy* the Court of Criminal Appeal, holding that there was evidence to support a jury's finding that D knew V was a policeman, said, *obiter*, that they wished to cast no doubt on *Forbes*; it was followed in *Mark*;[222] and in *Reynhoudt*[223] a majority of the High Court of Australia (Taylor, Menzies and Owen JJ, Dixon CJ and Kitto J dissenting) arrived at a similar result on the construction of the equivalent provision in Victorian legislation. It is submitted that the better view is that of the dissenting judges in *Reynhoudt* – that at least the chance of V's being a peace officer in the execution of his duty must be foreseen by D when he makes the assault.[224] Such a view avoids any difficulty arising from the fact that s 36[225] of the 1861 Act used the words 'to the knowledge of the offender', whereas no such words were used in s 38 or its successors.

Nevertheless, the present English law is that laid down in *Forbes*. This is implicit in *McBride v Turnock*,[226] where D struck at O, who was not a constable, and hit V, who was. Although he had no intention of assaulting V, the Divisional Court held he was guilty of assaulting a constable in the execution of his duty. The *mens rea* for this crime being only that of a common assault, D's 'malice' was transferable.[227] No better illustration could be given of the unsatisfactory nature of the rule in *Forbes*.

215 *Piddington v Bates* [1960] 3 All ER 660.

216 *Kavanagh v Hiscock* [1974] QB 600, [1974] 2 All ER 177, CA, applying *Broome v DPP* [1974] AC 587, [1974] 1 All ER 314, HL. See also *Austin v MPC* [2005] EWHC 480 (QB) on the Article 5 issues.

217 *DPP v Hawkins* [1988] 3 All ER 673, [1988] Crim LR 741.

218 Including recklessness as to unlawful force: *D v DPP* [2005] EWHC 967.

219 (1865) 10 Cox CC 362, applying s 38 of the OAPA 1861.

220 (1875) LR 2 CCR 154.

221 (1909) 73 JP 176, (1909) 2 Cr App R 26. See also *Blackburn v Bowering*, above, p 540. See F. Fairweather and S. Levy, 'Assaults on the Police: A Case of Mistaken Identity' [1994] Crim LR 817.

222 [1961] Crim LR 173 (Judge Maxwell Turner).

223 (1962) 36 ALJR 26.

224 This was the view of the majority of the court in *Galvin (No 2)* [1961] VR 740, overruling *Galvin (No 1)* [1961] VR 733. Barry J thought actual knowledge necessary. Scholl J adhered to his view in *Galvin (No 1)* that the offence was one of strict liability. See also *McLeod* (1954) 111 CCC 106.

225 Above, p 540.

226 [1964] Crim LR 456, DC. This was also assumed to be the law in *Blackburn v Bowering*, above, p 540.

227 Above, p 113.

If D is unaware (whether reasonably or not) that V is a constable and believes in the existence of circumstances of justification or excuse, he should now have a defence.[228] If, however, D knows that V is a constable, it seems that even an honest and reasonable belief that the constable is acting outside the course of his duty will not always be a defence, if the belief is mistaken. In *Fennell*[229] the court assumed that a father might lawfully use reasonable force to free his son from unlawful arrest by the police; but he acted at his peril and, if the arrest proved to be lawful, he was guilty. The court thought it would be otherwise if D mistakenly believed that a relative or friend was in imminent danger of injury and used reasonable force to prevent that.

(iv) Wilful obstruction[230]

The meaning of obstruction

There must be obstruction in fact. An act done with intent to obstruct but which fails to do so is not the offence – and it cannot be an attempt.[231] A wide interpretation of 'obstruction' has been accepted in England. It is not necessary that there should be any interference with the officer himself by physical force or threats. To give a warning to a person who has committed a crime so as to enable him to escape detection by police is enough. Thus in *Betts v Stevens*,[232] D committed the offence by warning drivers who were exceeding the speed limit that there was a police trap ahead. In the earlier case of *Bastable v Little*[233] it had been held that D was not guilty of the offence when he warned a driver, who was not proved to be committing an offence, of the speed trap. This distinction did not persuade the Divisional Court in *Green v Moore*[234] which thought *Bastable v Little* 'a very curious decision based on a highly eccentric view of the facts' and one which 'should be strictly confined to the facts as the court found them'. The court conceded that, if the warning was addressed to motorists who had not exceeded the speed limit and was intended to discourage them from *ever* doing so, the decision was right. But they thought that a more realistic view of the facts was that D intended to warn the drivers to slow down until they had passed through the speed trap, after which they might race away with impunity. So the distinction is between advising a person to *suspend* his criminal activity, so that he will not be found out by the police, which is an offence; and advising him to give it up altogether – in which case he will not be found out by the police – which is not an offence.[235]

In *Green v Moore*, D was a probationer constable who 'tipped off' a landlord of his local pub that a police 'support group' were waiting to catch him in the dastardly act of selling

[228] *Gladstone Williams* [1987] 3 All ER 411, 78 Cr App R 276, above, p 306. *Mark*, supra, requiring reasonable grounds for the belief, can no longer be regarded as good law.

[229] [1971] 1 QB 428, [1970] 3 All ER 215, [1970] Crim LR 581 and commentary, CA; and cf *Ball* (1989) 90 Cr App R 378, [1989] Crim LR 579 and commentary.

[230] See J. Coutts, 'Obstructing the Police' (1956) 19 MLR 411.

[231] Because it is triable only summarily. Cf *Bennett v Bale* [1986] Crim LR 404, DC and commentary.

[232] [1910] 1 KB 1.

[233] [1907] 1 KB 59.

[234] [1982] QB 1044, [1982] 1 All ER 428. Cf *Moore v Green* [1983] 1 All ER 663, DC.

[235] What then of the maps published of all speed camera sites in London, or the devices which warn motorists as they approach a speed trap?

liquor out of hours! Thereafter, naturally, the landlord kept strictly within the letter of the law. D was aware that 'the landlord did not give a high priority to the strict observance of licensing hours', and the court construed his warning as one that the sale of liquor out of hours had better be *suspended* until the support group moved on to deal with some other nefarious activity. If he had said, 'Fred, the sale of liquor out of hours simply isn't on – give it up, once and for all' – the efforts of the support group would have been equally frustrated but that would have been no offence. The 'suspension theory' can only operate where the person 'tipped off' is known or believed to be engaged in a continuing criminal activity or system. If he is dissuaded from persisting in what is or appears to be a 'one-off' offence, which he is about to commit, there is no room for the suspension theory. In *Green v Moore*, D knew of the landlord's illegal practice.

Where the police tell an offender to desist from an offence his deliberate refusal may amount to an obstruction, as where D is obstructing the highway and refuses to obey the instructions of a constable to move.[236] It is not necessary that the constable should anticipate a breach of the peace. But a constable has no power to arrest D for obstructing him, unless the obstruction was such that it actually caused, or was likely to cause, a breach of the peace.[237]

Presumably it must be proved that some named officer was obstructed;[238] it would hardly be enough that D warned E in general terms that if he did not stop committing an offence he would be found out; or if he advised E to get a television licence because the detector van was visiting his street next week – apart from the fact that the operators of the van would not be constables.

Hinchliffe v Sheldon[239] might be thought to go further than *Betts v Stevens*[240] in that it was only suspected, and not proved, that an offence was being committed; but there the warning was tantamount to a physical obstruction.[241] D, a publican's son, shouted a warning to his parents that the police were outside the public house. It was 11.17 pm and the lights were on in the bar, so presumably the police suspected that liquor was being consumed after hours. There was a delay of eight minutes before the police were admitted and no offence was detected. *Bastable v Little*[242] was distinguished on the ground that the police had a right to enter the licensed premises under the Licensing Act 1953.[243] Whether an offence was being committed or not, an entry under this statutory right was in execution of their duty; and their *entry* was obstructed.

Lord Goddard CJ defined 'obstructing' as 'Making it more difficult for the police to carry out their duties'.[244] This is far wider than was necessary for the decision.

Obstructing by not assisting

Lord Goddard's *dictum* has been applied in New Zealand in a case where D, a bystander, merely advised E not to answer any questions put to him by V, a police officer,

236 *Tynan v Balmer* [1967] 1 QB 91, [1966] 2 All ER 133; *Donaldson v Police* [1968] NZLR 32.

237 *Wershof v Metropolitan Police Comr* [1978] 3 All ER 540 (May J); *Gelberg v Miller* [1961] 1 All ER 291, [1961] 1 WLR 153; *Riley v DPP* [1990] Crim LR 422, DC.

238 *Syce v Harrison* [1981] Crim LR 110n.

239 [1955] 3 All ER 406, [1955] 1 WLR 1207.

240 Above, p 547.

241 See Coutts, above.

242 Above, p 547.

243 See now Licensing Act 1964, s 186(1). The police must have reasonable grounds for suspecting that an offence is being or is about to be committed: *Valentine v Jackson* [1972] 1 All ER 90, [1972] 1 WLR 528.

244 [1955] 3 All ER at 408.

investigating a suspected offence.[245] E was perfectly entitled to remain silent but his doing so undoubtedly made it more difficult for V to carry out his duty of investigating crime. An earlier decision[246] in the Supreme Court of Victoria is to the contrary and is to be preferred. Surely a solicitor who advises his client to say nothing cannot be guilty of an offence, though he undoubtedly makes things more difficult for the police; and why should a solicitor be in a different situation from anyone else?

In England, it has been held that refusal to answer a constable's question, though it undoubtedly makes it more difficult for the police to carry out their duties, does not amount to wilful obstruction: *Rice v Connolly*.[247] The fact that the refusal is expressed in abusive and obscene terms should in principle make no difference.[248] If D's language amounts to some other offence, such as that under the Public Order Act 1986, s 4,[249] he should be charged with that. *Ricketts v Cox*[250] seems a doubtful decision. The court accepted the finding of the justices that the 'totality of [the defendants'] behaviour and attitude at this stage amounted to an obstruction . . .', but all that could be added to the total was the abusive, obscene and hostile attitude of the defendants, reprehensible, no doubt, and galling to the officers but still the assertion of an actual right.[251] While the report does refer to some unspecified threat by D, the court attached no particular significance to it and the decision seems to be based on the generally 'obstructive' nature of D's behaviour.

Telling the police a false story is quite different from merely remaining silent and clearly an obstruction.[252] Refusing to reveal the whereabouts of a prohibited drug is not an obstruction; but burying it to hide it from an officer searching for it might be, when the officer's task is made more difficult.[253] These difficulties would not arise if the Act had been held to be limited to physical interference; and it has been held[254] to be so limited in Scotland where 'obstruct' has been construed *ejusdem generis* with 'assault' and 'resist'.[255] D was held not guilty when he told lies to the police to conceal an offence of which he was guilty. There is much to be said in favour of the Scottish view.[256]

Lawful acts as obstruction?

One who is guilty of obstruction is, *ex hypothesi*, in breach of a legal duty; but it is not necessary that the act relied on as an obstruction should be unlawful independently of its operation as an obstruction of the police.[257] It appears that the conferment of powers and imposition of duties on the police, may, impliedly, impose duties on others not to impede

245 *Steele v Kingsbeer* [1957] NZLR 552; distinguished in *Dash v Police* [1970] NZLR 273 (solicited advice, disinterestedly given, to a motorist not to take a breath test, which he was not bound to take; held, not 'wilful' obstruction).

246 *Hogben v Chandler* [1940] VLR 285.

247 [1966] 2 QB 414, [1966] 2 All ER 649, DC.

248 See Marshall J in *Rice v Connolly* at 420.

249 Below, pp 977–978.

250 (1981) 74 Cr App R 298, DC.

251 See commentary at [1982] Crim LR 184. The partial retraction at [1982] Crim LR 484 seems unnecessary.

252 *Rice v Connolly* (above); *Mathews v Dwan* [1949] NZLR 1037.

253 See note on *Syce v Harrison* [1981] Crim LR 110n.

254 *Curlett v M'Kechnie* (1938) JC 176.

255 The re-arrangement of these offences by the Police Act precludes the application of the *ejusdem generis* rule; but it could have been applied when they were contained in the Offences Against the Person Act 1861.

256 See Coutts, above.

257 *Dibble v Ingleton* [1972] 1 QB 480, [1972] 1 All ER 275. See G. Williams, 'Criminal Law – The Duty Not To Obstruct Your Own Conviction' [1972] CLJ 193.

the exercise by the police of these powers and duties. The right of a constable to enter licensed premises when he reasonably suspects an offence is being committed implies a duty on the licensee and others to let him in.[258] The right of a constable to require a driver in certain circumstances to provide a specimen of breath[259] implies a duty on the motorist (though he has not been arrested) to remain 'there or nearby' until the constable has had a reasonable opportunity to carry out the test.[260] If, when D is found to have consumed an excess of alcohol, it is the duty of a constable to remove D's car from the highway, there is an implied duty on D to hand over the keys of the car.[261]

Whether a duty thus to co-operate with the police is to be implied depends on whether this is a compelling inference from the nature of the police duty or right. To some extent it is a question of policy – witness the ruling that there is no duty to answer police questions but there is a duty not to give misleading answers.[262] In *Dibble v Ingleton*[263] the court distinguished between 'positive acts' which will amount to obstruction and omissions which will not. Of course, here as elsewhere,[264] the law penalizes acts more readily than omissions but this is only one factor and omissions may amount to obstruction even when the omission is not an offence independently of s 51.[265]

Mens rea for obstruction

Unlike 'assault' and 'resist', obstruction must be 'wilful'. D must intend to behave in such a way as to make it more difficult for the police to carry out their duties. His conduct need be neither hostile to, nor aimed at, the police, as some cases[266] have suggested: *Lewis v Cox*[267] where D persisted in opening the door of a van in which Q, who had been arrested, was about to be driven away. D's purpose was not to obstruct the police but to find out where Q was being taken, but, since he must have known that he was preventing the police officer from driving off, the justices were bound to find that he intended to make it more difficult for them to carry out their duty.[268] Similarly in *Hills v Ellis*[269] where D laid his hand on a constable's arm to draw his attention to the fact that, as D believed, he was arresting the wrong man. The courts appear to alternate between looking to D's primary purpose and any additional ones. *Forbes* is inapplicable to a charge of obstruction. In *Ostler v Elliott*[270] it was held that D's reasonable belief that the police officers were robbers was a defence to wilful obstruction. Since *Gladstone Williams*[271] the only question would be whether the belief was truly held, reasonably or not.

In *Rice v Connolly*[272] it was said that 'wilfully' means not only 'intentionally' but also 'without lawful excuse'. This is difficult to follow. 'Wilfully' must surely refer to the state

[258] *Hinchliffe v Sheldon*, above, p 248. [259] Road Traffic Act 1988, s 7.
[260] *DPP v Carey* [1970] AC 1072 at 1097, [1969] 3 All ER 1662 at 1680.
[261] *Stunt v Bolton* [1972] RTR 435, [1972] Crim LR 561.
[262] *Rice v Connolly*, above. [263] Above. [264] Above, Ch 4.
[265] For example, *Stunt v Bolton*, above.
[266] *Willmott v Atack* [1977] QB 498, [1976] 3 All ER 794; *Hills v Ellis* [1983] QB 680, [1983] 1 All ER 667.
[267] [1985] QB 509, [1984] 3 All ER 672.
[268] Cf the discussion of intention, above, 546. [269] Above, n 266.
[270] [1980] Crim LR 584. Note that, if he had assaulted the officers, his reasonable belief that they were not officers would not, in itself, have been a defence to a charge of assaulting them in the execution of their duty. See commentary at [1980] Crim LR 585.
[271] [1987] 3 All ER 411, 78 Cr App R 276, CA, above, p 306. [272] Above, p 549.

of mind of the defendant. But whether he has a lawful excuse for what he does generally depends on D's conduct and the circumstances in which he acts.[273] In that case, D would have been no more 'wilful' if he had told a false story. The difference seems to lie in the conduct which the court considers to be permissible. 'Wilfully' may of course import the absence of any *belief* on D's part of circumstances of lawful excuse. If the story told by D were in fact false, but D believed it to be true, the constable might be obstructed, but he would not be 'wilfully' obstructed.

4. Assault occasioning actual bodily harm

By s 47 of the OAPA 1861, 'whosoever shall be convicted on indictment of any assault occasioning actual bodily harm shall be liable to imprisonment for not more than five years'.

The offence is triable either way.

(a) *Actus reus*

(i) Assault or battery

On its face, the section does not appear to create an offence but merely to provide a higher penalty for an assault at common law where actual bodily harm is occasioned. Consequently the offence was treated as a common law offence until the decision in *Courtie*,[274] – and indeed for a period thereafter because it took some time for 'the penny to drop'. We now know that s 47 created a separate statutory offence[275] or, more accurately, two offences, assault and battery. Lord Ackner in *Savage*[276] at one point describes the *mens rea* of the offence exclusively in terms of the battery and, at another, exclusively in terms of the assault. It is safe to assume that there are two offences and that their constituents, so far as the word 'assault' goes, are precisely the same as those of common assault and battery.

(ii) Occasioning

Once that assault or battery is proved, it remains only to prove that it occasioned actual bodily harm, a question of causation,[277] not requiring proof of any further *mens rea* or fault. This was established in *Roberts*[278] where D in a moving car 'assaulted' V by trying to take off her coat (a battery), whereupon she jumped out and sustained injury. It was held that the only question was whether the 'assault' caused V's action – only if it was something that no reasonable man could be expected to foresee would the chain of causation be broken.[279] It is now firmly established that this is the law, after a remarkable series of

273 See comment at [1966] Crim LR 390.

274 [1984] AC 463, [1984] 1 All ER 740, HL, above, p 40.

275 *Harrow Justices, ex p Osaseri* [1986] QB 589, [1985] 3 All ER 185, DC.

276 [1991] 4 All ER 698 at 707 and 711.

277 Cf the view of J. Gardner, 'Rationality and the Rule of Law in Offences Against the Person' [1994] CLJ, 502 at 509.

278 (1971) 56 Cr App R 95, [1972] Crim LR 27.

279 Cf *William, Davis*, above, p 68.

cases had thrown the matter into doubt. In *Spratt*[280] the court, very properly overruling *DPP v K*,[281] held that only *Cunningham*, not *Caldwell*, recklessness would suffice to establish the assault but then went on, not referring to *Roberts*, to hold there must be recklessness as to the occasioning of actual bodily harm. *Savage*,[282] decided on the same day, applied the law as stated in *Roberts* but without reference to that case. In *Parmenter*[283] the court, confronted with this conflict, preferred *Spratt*, again without reference to *Roberts*. Hearing appeals in *Savage* and *Parmenter*, the House of Lords held that the law was correctly stated in *Roberts*, reversing *Parmenter* and overruling *Spratt* on this point.[284]

The offence may be committed in circumstances of omission as in the case of *Santana-Bermudez v DPP*.[285]

(iii) Bodily harm

'Bodily harm', according to the House of Lords in *DPP v Smith*[286] 'needs no explanation'. Since 'Grievous means no more and no less than really serious' it seems to follow that, under s 47, the harm need not be really serious. In *Miller*[287] it was described as any hurt or injury calculated to interfere with the health or comfort of the victim. This is a very low threshold for an offence carrying a five-year maximum sentence. It includes a temporary loss of consciousness.[288] It would seem sufficient that the harm was more than merely transient and trifling.[289]

Actual bodily harm is not limited to physical injury. It includes psychiatric injury. This represents a significant judicial extension of the offence. Neurotic disorders are included because they affect the central nervous system of the body but emotions such as fear and anxiety ('brain functions') are not. While physical injury is within the ordinary experience of a jury, psychiatric injury is not; so, if the prosecution wish to rely on it, they must call expert evidence to prove that the alleged condition amounts to psychiatric injury.[290] Even where the victim can give evidence of physical and mental symptoms of psychiatric injury expert evidence is necessary to prove causation.[291]

(b) *Mens rea*

The only *mens rea* that needs to be proved is that necessary for the assault or battery.

The absence of any requirement that D foresees the additional harm for which he is punished over and above an assault or battery demonstrates the lack of correspondence of *actus reus* and *mens rea* in the offence and the conflict with the general principles of subjectivism.[292]

280 [1991] 2 All ER 210, [1990] 1 WLR 1073.
281 [1990] 1 All ER 331, 91 Cr App R 23.
282 [1991] 2 All ER 220.
283 [1992] 1 AC 699, [1991] 2 All ER 225, CA.
284 [1991] 4 All ER 698.
285 [2003] Crim LR 471 discussed above.
286 [1961] AC 290 at 334, [1960] 3 All ER 161 at 171; above, 437.
287 [1954] 2 QB 282.
288 *T v DPP* [2003] Crim LR 622.
289 Ibid.
290 *Ireland* [1997] 4 All ER 225 at 23–233, HL, approving *Chan-Fook* [1994] 2 All ER 552, [1994] Crim LR 432.
291 *Morris* [1998] 1 Cr App R 386.
292 It has been defended on the basis that D has 'altered his normative position' towards V by choosing to assault V, and therefore must take the consequences of the further harm. See J. Gardner, 'Rationality and the Rule of Law in Offences Against the Person' [1994] CLJ 520; J. Horder [1995] Crim LR 759; above n 181. Cf B. Mitchell, 'In Defence of a Principle of Correspondence' [1999] Crim LR 195; I. Hare, 'A Compelling Case for the Code' (1993) 56 MLR 74.

5. Wounding and grievous bodily harm – OAPA 1861, s 20

Section 20 of the Offences Against the Person Act 1861 creates offences of wounding and inflicting grievous bodily harm. By s 20:

Whosoever shall unlawfully and maliciously wound or inflict any grievous bodily harm upon any other person, either with or without any weapon or instrument shall be guilty of [an offence triable either way] and being convicted thereof shall be liable to imprisonment for five years.

Under s 20 there are two offences (i) malicious wounding, and (ii) maliciously inflicting grievous bodily harm.

The element of unlawfulness should not be overlooked and should always be drawn to the jury's attention.[293]

(a) Malicious wounding

(i) To wound

In order to constitute a wound, the continuity of the whole skin must be broken.[294] Where a pellet fired by an air pistol hit V in the eye but caused only an internal rupturing of blood vessels and not a break in the skin, there was no wound.[295] It is not enough that the cuticle or outer skin be broken if the inner skin remains intact.[296] Where V was treated with such violence that his collarbone was broken, it was held that there was no wound if his skin was intact.[297] It was held to be a wound, however, where the lining membrane of the urethra was ruptured and bled, evidence being given that the membrane is precisely the same in character as that which lines the cheek and the external and internal skin of the lip.[298] It is wrong to direct a jury that 'the surface of the skin' must be broken. On that direction a scratch would suffice which is clearly inadequate.[299]

It was held that there was no wounding under the 1837 Act[300] where V, in warding off D's attempt to cut his throat, struck his hands against a knife held by D and cut them;[301] and where V was knocked down by D and wounded by falling on iron trams.[302] That Act did not contain the words 'by any means whatsoever', and it is probable that these cases would now be decided differently. Even under the earlier law, D was guilty where he struck V on the hat with a gun and the hard rim of the hat caused a wound.[303] It is unclear whether there can be a wounding by omission. It was formerly held that wounding must be the result of a battery but it is probably now sufficient that the wound be directly inflicted whether by a battery or not.[304]

293 *Stokes* [2003] EWCA Crim 2977.
294 *Moriarty v Brooks* (1834) 6 C & P 684.
295 *C (A Minor) v Eisenhower* [1984] QB 331, 78 Cr App R 48, DC.
296 *M'Loughlin* (1838) 8 C & P 635.
297 *Wood* (1830) 1 Mood CC 278.
298 *Waltham* (1849) 3 Cox CC 442. Contrast *Jones* (1849) 3 Cox CC 441.
299 *Morris* [2005] EWCA Crim 609.
300 7 Will. 4 & 1 Vic c 85, s 4.
301 *Beckett* (1836) 1 Mood & R 526 (Parke B); *Day* (1845) 1 Cox CC 207. Cf *Coleman* (1920) 84 JP 112.
302 *Spooner* (1853) 6 Cox CC 392.
303 *Sheard* (1837) 2 Mood CC 13.
304 *Wilson*, below, n 329. Cf *Taylor* (1869) LR 1 CCR 194; *Austin* (1973) 58 Cr App R 163, CA.

It is doubtful whether this specific form of injury (or indeed others in the OAPA such as choking and throwing acid) warrants a separate offence in a modern Code of offences. Some suggest that the specificity of label and the distinctions between the harms and the manner in which they are inflicted are important in moral terms.[305]

(ii) Malice

It is settled that this word means 'intentionally or recklessly' and 'reckless' is used in the *Cunningham*, not the *Caldwell*, sense of course.[306] The next question is, what is 'the particular kind of harm' that must be intended or foreseen? As a matter of general principle, the answer might be expected to be that it is necessary that D has *mens rea* as to all the elements of the *actus reus* – including the wounding or grievous bodily harm.[307] The law has developed differently. It is enough that D foresaw that some bodily harm, not necessarily amounting to grievous bodily harm or wounding, might occur.[308] This constructive element to the crimes is undesirable for the reasons considered above. Diplock LJ said in *Mowatt*:[309]

> . . . the word 'maliciously' does import upon the part of the person who unlawfully inflicts the wound or other grievous bodily harm an awareness that his act may have the consequence of causing some physical harm to some other person. That is what is meant by 'the particular kind of harm' in the citation from Professor Kenny.[310] It is quite unnecessary that the accused should have foreseen that his unlawful act might cause physical harm of the gravity described in [s 20], ie, a wound or serious physical injury. It is enough that he should have foreseen that some physical harm to some person, albeit of a minor character, might result.

It is sufficient to prove that D foresaw that some harm *might* result. To require proof that he foresaw that it *would* result is too generous to the defendant.[311] It is not enough, however, that D intended to frighten (unless he foresaw that the fright might result in psychiatric injury), whether the charge is one of wounding or inflicting grievous bodily harm.[312]

(b) Maliciously inflicting grievous bodily harm

'Grievous bodily harm' was formerly interpreted to include any harm which seriously interferes with health or comfort;[313] but in *Smith*[314] the House of Lords said that there was no warrant for giving the words a meaning other than that which they convey in their

305 See J. Gardner, above.

306 Above, p 104. *Savage* and *Parmenter* [1991] 4 All ER at 721 HL, affirming *Mowatt* [1968] 1 QB 421, [1967] 3 All ER 47.

307 Cf above, p 110.

308 Above, n 305.

309 [1968] 1 QB 421 at 426, [1967] 3 All ER 47 at 50. See also *Dakou* [2002] EWCA Crim 3156, over-simplifying the issue of malice in s 18.

310 *Outlines of Criminal Law* (19th edn), 211. The citation is the passage approved by the Court of Criminal Appeal in *Cunningham* [1957] 2 QB 396, [1957] 2 All ER 412; above, p 103; below, p 566.

311 *Rushworth* (1992) 95 Cr App R 252 at 255, cited in *Pearson* [1994] Crim LR 534 which nevertheless left this point in the air. Earlier *dicta* by Lords Diplock and Ackner are ambiguous.

312 *Flack v Hunt* (1979) 70 Cr App R 51; *Sullivan* [1981] Crim LR 46, CA.

313 *Ashman* (1858) 1 F & F 88.

314 [1961] AC 290, [1960] 3 All ER 161; above, p 437; followed in *Metharam* [1961] 3 All ER 200.

ordinary and natural meaning. It is not always necessary for the jury to be told to look for 'really' serious harm,[315] and it is not clear precisely what that word means when it is included. The jury may take into consideration the totality of the injuries.[316] Although the determination of whether the injury constitutes grievous bodily harm is to be assessed objectively, and not merely on the basis of the victim's perception,[317] the characteristics of the victim may be taken into account – what is grievous bodily harm to a child might not be for an adult.[318] There is no need for the injury to be permanent or life threatening.[319] Grievous bodily harm may cover cases where there is no wounding as, for instance, the broken collarbone in *Wood*.[320] Conversely, there might be a technical 'wounding' which could not be said to amount to grievous bodily harm. The absence of any clear definition of the term and the associated risk of inconsistent applications and a lack of predictability in verdicts is lamentable.

It is settled that *serious* psychiatric injury amounts to grievous bodily harm.[321] This results in the possibility of causing or inflicting grievous bodily harm by telephone – for example a series of obscene phone calls.[322] There is no legal difficulty with the *actus reus* – that is established simply by proving that D inflicted the serious psychiatric injury. It would not be easy to prove the *mens rea* for s 20 since it is not enough that D foresaw that he might cause fear or hysteria to prove that he was reckless for the purposes of s 20. Is it realistic to suppose that the caller realizes that he may cause the kind of result which a psychiatrist subsequently testifies to amount to a psychiatric injury? That is a question of fact. The principal legal difficulty which had to be overcome was with the *actus reus*.

(i) Inflict

In a series of cases[323] from 1861 until 1983 it was held or assumed that the words 'inflict' and 'wound' both imply an 'assault'. D could be convicted of an offence under s 20 only if it was proved that he wounded or caused grievous bodily harm by committing an assault. The leading case was *Clarence*.[324] D, knowing that he was suffering from gonorrhoea, had intercourse with his wife, V, and infected her. He had certainly caused her grievous bodily harm but the majority of the court held that he had not 'inflicted' it because he had not committed an assault. V consented to the intercourse and her consent was not vitiated by the fact that she was unaware of D's condition. It followed that, when D was charged with an offence under s 20, he could be convicted on that indictment of common assault, because that was an 'included offence'. But there was a second line of cases[325] where the alleged requirement of an assault was simply ignored and convictions were upheld although it was very difficult, if not impossible, to discern an assault on the facts. It was

315 *Janua* [1999] 1 Cr App R 91.

316 *Grundy* [1977] Crim LR 543; *Birmingham* [2002] EWCA Crim 2608.

317 *Brown* [1998] Crim LR 484. 318 *Bollom* [2004] 2 Cr App R 50. 319 Ibid.

320 Above, p 553. 321 *Ireland*, above, p 552.

322 *Gelder* (1994) The Times, 25 May (news item).

323 *Yeadon and Birch* (1861) 9 Cox CC 91; *Taylor* (1869) LR 1 CCR 194; *Clarence* (1888) 22 QBD 23; *Snewing* [1972] Crim LR 267; *Carpenter* (1979) 76 Cr App R 320n, cited [1983] 1 All ER 1004.

324 (1888) 22 QBD 23.

325 *Halliday* (1889) 61 LT 701; *Lewis* [1970] Crim LR 647, CA; *Mackie* [1973] Crim LR 54; *Boswell* [1973] Crim LR 307 and *Cartledge v Allen* [1973] Crim LR 530, DC.

held that D committed an offence under s 20 where he so frightened V that he jumped through a window[326] or accidentally injured himself by putting his hand through a glass door under a 'well-grounded apprehension of violence.'[327] In *Martin*[328] where, shortly before the end of a performance in a theatre, D put out the lights and placed an iron bar across the doorway, he was convicted of inflicting grievous bodily harm on those injured in the panic.

In 1983 the House of Lords in *Wilson*[329] resolved the matter by deciding, following the Australian case of *Salisbury*,[330] that 'inflict' does not, after all, imply an assault.[331] Arguably, the case decided no more than that; but Lord Roskill cited the opinion of the Australian court that 'inflict' has a narrower meaning than 'cause' (as used in s 18 below) and requires 'force being violently applied to the body of the victim.' In *Burstow*[332] the House of Lords decided that 'inflict' does not bear this narrow meaning and that grievous bodily harm might be inflicted by telephonic or other harassment, not involving the use of violence to the body or an assault. It remains necessary, as noticed above, to prove that D foresaw that he might cause a condition amounting to psychiatric injury, not necessarily serious psychiatric injury.

The distinction between 'cause' and 'inflict' seems to have been substantially eliminated. The House thought that, while the words are not synonymous, there is 'no radical divergence' of meaning. Perhaps this is to be read to mean no 'material' difference. Lord Hope, however, said[333] that 'inflict' implies that the consequence of the act is something that the victim is likely find unpleasant or harmful whereas 'cause' may embrace pleasure as well as pain. In a modern statute, the use of different words in adjacent sections might compel the conclusion that different meanings were intended; but no such inference can be drawn in the 1861 Act because it was never intended, and does not purport, to be a consistent whole.[334] *Clarence* can no longer be justified on the ground that there was no assault or violent application of force or that V consented.[335] It was not overruled but it appears to have been wrongly decided.[336]

[326] *Halliday* (1889) 61 LT 701.

[327] *Cartledge v Allen* [1973] Crim LR 530.

[328] (1881) 8 QBD 54, CCR.

[329] [1984] AC 242 at 260, [1983] 3 All ER 448 at 455.

[330] [1976] VR 452 at 461.

[331] The House nevertheless contrived to hold that a person charged under s 20 could be convicted on that indictment of a common assault by virtue of s 6(3) of the Criminal Law Act 1967 – a much criticized decision but approved by the House in *Savage* [1991] 4 All ER 698 at 711. See Glanville Williams, 'Alternative Elements and Included Offences' [1984] CLJ 290 and commentary at [1984] Crim LR 37.

[332] Heard and decided together with *Ireland* [1997] 4 All ER 225. Arguably the case is restricted to those cases involving the infliction of psychiatric injury. This would create an undesirable confusion in the law.

[333] But, if that is so, the sado-masochists in *Brown* [1994] 1 AC 212, above, p 517, could not have been held to have been guilty of *inflicting* grievous bodily harm, contrary to s 20, because everyone was having a jolly good time. This would be surprising, as they were guilty of wounding, contrary to the same subsection on the ground that consent was no defence.

[334] C. S. Greaves, *The Criminal Law Consolidation and Amendment Acts* (2nd edn, 1862), at 3–4, cited by Lord Steyn at 234.

[335] Cf above, p 529.

[336] The draft Bill in the Home Office Consultation Paper of February 1998 expressly excludes from the proposed offences recklessly (but not intentionally) causing anything by disease and asks for opinions on this, obviously sensitive, matter. See now *Dica* [2004] EWCA Crim 1103 above, p 529.

(ii) Co-existence of s 20 and s 47

The co-existence of s 47 with that of maliciously inflicting grievous bodily harm contrary to s 20 of the same Act, also punishable with a maximum of five years, makes no sense.[337] The prosecutor's task is slightly easier under s 47 since he does not need to prove even that foresight of slight bodily harm which is necessary under s 20. He does have to prove an assault or battery which is not necessary under s 20; and s 20 no longer requires proof of a direct application of force. Section 20 is regarded in practice as the more serious offence. In *Parmenter*[338] the Court of Appeal said that:

> although the sentences imposed in practice for the worst s 47 offences will overlap those imposed at the lower end of s 20, nobody could doubt that the two offences are seen in quite different terms, whether by defendants and their advisers contemplating pleas of guilty, or by judges passing sentence under s 47 on defendants whose pleas of guilty have been accepted by the prosecution, or by subsequent sentencers casting an eye down lists of previous convictions.

This is reflected in the CPS charging standard which recommends charging s 47 where there is a loss or breakage of teeth, loss of consciousness, extensive or multiple bruising, displaced broken nose, minor fractures, minor non-superficial cuts or psychiatric injury. By comparison, examples of what would usually amount to s 20 include: injury resulting in permanent disability or permanent loss of sensory function; injury which results in more than minor permanent, visible disfigurement; broken or displaced limbs or bones, including fractured skull; compound fractures, broken cheek bone, jaw, ribs, etc; injuries which cause substantial loss of blood, usually necessitating a transfusion; injuries resulting in lengthy treatment or incapacity; psychiatric injury.[339]

6. Racially or religiously aggravated assaults[340]

The Crime and Disorder Act 1998 created a new category of racially aggravated crimes and in the wake of 9/11, the Anti-Terrorism Crime and Security Act 2001 extended these to include religiously aggravated offences.[341] Racist crime is increasing alarmingly.[342]

Section 28(1) of the Crime and Disorder Act provides two offences. Subsection (1)(a) applies where at the time of committing the offence or immediately[343] before or after doing so, the offender demonstrates towards the victim[344] of the offence racial or religious hostility based on the victim's membership of a racial or religious group. Subsection

337 Cf the view of J. Gardner, above.

338 [1991] 2 All ER at 233.

339 See CPS Charging Standard www.cps.gov.uk/legal/section5/chapter_c.html#10.

340 See E. Burney, 'Using the Law of Racially Aggravated Offences' [2003] Crim LR 28.

341 See generally, M. Malik, 'Racist Crime: Racially Aggravated Offences in the Crime and Disorder Act 1998' (1999) 62 MLR 409; M. Idriss, 'Religion and the Anti-Terrorism Crime and Security Act 2001' [2002] Crim LR 890; A. Tomkins, 'Legislating Against Terror: The Anti-terrorism Crime and Security Act 2001' [2002] PL 205.

342 See T. Fowles and D. Wilson, 'Racist and Religious Crime Data' (2004) 43 Howard Jnl of Crim Justice 441. See CPS Charging Standard, www.cps.gov.uk/legal/section6/index.html.

343 This qualifies both acts before and after – a 20 minute delay after the act before D made the racist remark demonstrating hostility was too long: *Parry v DPP* [2004] EWHC 3112 (Admin).

344 Who need not be present: *Parry v DPP* [2004] EWHC 3112 (Admin).

(1)(b) applies where the offence is motivated wholly or partly by hostility towards members of a racial or religious group based on their membership of that group.

A person commits an offence under s 29 if he commits (i) an offence under s 20 of the OAPA 1861 (malicious wounding or grievous bodily harm) or (ii) an offence under s 47 of that Act (above, p 551) or (iii) a common assault, which is 'racially aggravated' for the purposes of s 29. Offences (i) and (ii), above, are punishable on indictment with seven year' imprisonment (compared with five years for the basic, non-aggravated offence) and offence (iii) with two years, the basic offence being triable only summarily. In cases where offences (i) or (ii) are charged, a jury could convict[345] of the basic offence if they were satisfied that it had been committed, but were not satisfied that aggravation was proved. A jury could not, however, convict of a common assault because that is triable only summarily.[346]

'Race' is widely defined to include colour, nationality (including citizenship) or ethnic or national origins. It has been held[347] that 'African' does not denote an ethnic, but does denote a racial group. It has been said, *obiter*, that a racially aggravated assault might be committed by one white person on another if the former were, for example, to call the latter 'nigger lover'.[348] It is submitted that this is an appropriate interpretation of the Act. The offences apply where the conduct is between members of the same racial group. The courts have taken an extremely wide view of what constitutes a race and racial group. It has been accepted that the terms will be satisfied by non-inclusive expressions if eg D demonstrates hostility to V by calling him 'non white' or 'foreign'.[349]

'Religious group' means a group of persons defined by reference to religious belief or lack of religious belief. The Act gives no further guidance. Given the broad interpretation in Article 9 of the ECHR, it would seem likely that the domestic courts will interpret the offence as affording protection to a religion as widely understood.[350] By analogy with the interpretation of race, non-inclusive terms will suffice, for example, 'gentile'.[351]

(a) Assault and contemporaneous demonstration of hostility

The courts have now made clear that the offence under subs (1)(a) does not apply *only* in those cases in which D is motivated solely or even mainly by racial malevolence. It is designed to extend to cases which may have a racially neutral gravaman but in the course of which there is demonstrated towards the victim hostility based on V's race.[352] As a matter of statutory interpretation, the key term in the section is that the hostility is 'based on' V's race. This might at first appear to suggest that the sole basis for the hostility is racial, but several aspects of s 28 militate against such a reading. First, subs (1)(a) stands alongside (1)(b) in which the hostility is motivated by race. Parliament would be unlikely to duplicate offences. Secondly, s 28(3) provides that 'it is immaterial whether or

345 Criminal Law Act 1967, s 6(3).

346 *Clifford* [2003] EWCA Crim 3630.

347 *White* [2001] Crim LR 576, but see commentary on difficulties this creates.

348 *DPP v Pal* [2000] Crim LR 756 per Simon Brown LJ.

349 *DPP v M* [2004] EWHC 1453, [2005] Crim LR 392. See also *A-G's Reference (No 4 of 2004)* [2005] EWCA Crim 889.

350 See *Pendragon v UK* (1999) 27 EHRR CD 179.

351 *DPP v M* [2004] EWHC 1453, [2005] Crim LR 392.

352 Per Maurice Kay J in *Woods* [2002] EWHC 85 (Admin) para 11. See also *DPP v Green* [2004] All ER (D) 70 (May); *DPP v MacFarlane* [2002] All ER (D) 78 (Mar); *DPP v M* [2004] EWHC 1453, [2005] Crim LR 392.

not the offender's hostility is also [that is otherwise than racially] based to any extent on (b) any other factor'. This qualification cuts both ways. It supports the broad interpretation of s 28(1)(a) now accepted by the courts, by implicitly acknowledging that the offence applies where other bases for hostility exist. But, because these other bases for hostility are 'immaterial', it also serves to emphasize that the prosecution must prove that there is *some* racial basis for the hostility. Finally, reference to the Parliamentary debates shows that this broad interpretation was intended, since it was felt that proving a sole racial motive for the offence would be too difficult a task for the prosecution.[353]

Section 28(1)(a) is extremely broad, leading to racially neutral minor incidents such as a scuffle over car-parking being elevated into a more serious offence in terms of trial venue, sentence and stigma, because of the use of an adjective when a party is throwing insults at his opponent. Lord Monson in the debates on the Crime and Disorder Act anticipated this problem and described the section as Orwellian in that it seeks to police people's emotions.[354] At present at least, only insults relating to religion and race are criminalized in this way. This highlights the arbitrariness of the legislation – as Maurice Kay J noted calling someone a 'fat bastard' is not criminal (yet). In terms of broader social objectives of the legislation, the section may well be regarded as a success if it deters individuals from using racist language in any context. Whether this will be the effect or whether those convicted will bear such resentment at the stigma as to become more racist is debatable.[355]

(b) Racially/religiously motivated assaults

The (1)(b) offence is much narrower and less controversial, being one focused on the defendant's state of mind and one of his motivations for the crime being one of racial or religious hostility, although not necessarily against the victim in person. It provides an interesting example of an offence in which the motivations rather than intentions of the defendant become crucial in substantive law.

7. Section 18 of the Offences Against the Person Act 1861

By s 18, as amended by the Criminal Law Act 1967:

Whosoever shall unlawfully and maliciously by any means whatsoever wound or cause any grievous bodily harm to any person with intent to do some grievous bodily harm to any person or with intent to resist or prevent the lawful apprehension or detainer of any person, shall be guilty

353 In *Pal* [2000] Crim LR 756 the Divisional Court accepted that the racial statement 'whiteman's arse licker' was not in itself sufficient to prove hostility based on racial grounds. Simon Brown LJ stated that he did 'not regard the fact that D would not have used such a term but for V's race as a *sine qua non* of the racial hostility'. His lordship did note that the use of racially abusive insults will 'ordinarily no doubt be found sufficient'. *Pal* has since been described as turning on its own facts. It is unclear precisely which of its facts render it so unique. It cannot be because the expression was based partly from resentment towards V. Presumably it must be because both parties were of the same race.

354 HL, col 1266, 12 Feb 1998.

355 See generally E. Burnley and G. Rose, 'Racially Aggravated Offences: How is the Law Working?' (2002) HORS 244.

of [an offence triable only on indictment], and being convicted thereof shall be liable to imprisonment of life.[356]

The elements of the *actus reus* have been considered in relation to s 20 above.

(a) *Mens rea*

The concept of malice has been considered above. Where, under s 18, the charge is of causing grievous bodily harm with intent to do grievous bodily harm, the word 'maliciously' obviously has no part to play. Any *mens rea* which it might import is comprehended within the ulterior intent. Even if 'wounding' is not foreseen, it is 'malicious'. Where the charge is of wounding or causing grievous bodily harm with intent to resist lawful apprehension, there is no difficulty in giving meaning to 'maliciously' and it is submitted that meaning should be given to that word.[357] A mere intent to resist lawful apprehension should not found liability for a charge of wounding or causing grievous bodily harm. It is submitted that the Court of Appeal went too far in *Mowatt*[358] in saying that 'In section 18 the word "maliciously" adds nothing.'

It is clear that there must be proof that the accused actually foresaw the specified result. Any doubt there may have been about this was dispelled by the Criminal Justice Act 1967, s 8.[359] *Mowatt* was decided before the Act came into force, and certain observations in the case are therefore suspect. It was said[360] that where the act:

> ... was a direct assault which any ordinary person would be bound to realize was likely to cause some physical harm to the other person ... and the defence put forward on behalf of the accused is not that the assault was accidental or that he did not realize that it might cause some physical harm to the victim, but is some other defence such as that he did not do the alleged act or that he did it in self-defence, it is unnecessary to deal specifically in the summing up with what is meant by the word 'maliciously' in the section.

This suggests that the jury need not be directed on the issue because they are bound to infer that D foresaw the result, by reason of its being a natural and probable consequence of his actions. This is directly contrary to the words of s 8. Under s 10 of the Criminal Justice Act 1967, formal admissions may be made; but, if D has not admitted his malice, then it is submitted that it must be proved like every other element in the crime. The fact that the evidence appears to the judge to be overwhelming is not a good reason for not leaving it to the jury.

356 There are numerous forms of the s 18 offence other than that commonly relied upon – grievous bodily harm with intent to do grievous bodily harm – dealing with the causing of injury with ulterior intents to resist arrest, etc wounding with intention to do some grievous bodily harm; wounding with intent to resist lawful apprehension; wounding with intent to prevent lawful apprehension; wounding with intent to resist lawful detainer; wounding with intent to prevent lawful detainer; causing grievous bodily harm with intent to resist lawful apprehension; causing grievous bodily harm with intent to prevent lawful apprehension; causing grievous bodily harm with intent to resist lawful detainer; causing grievous bodily harm with intent to prevent lawful detainer.

357 *Morrison* (1989) Cr App R 17. D seized by a WPC as she was arresting him. D dived through a window pane and WPC was dragged with him suffering serious facial injury. D clearly *intended* to resist arrest, CA held he must also be subjectively (*Cunningham*) reckless as to the grievous bodily harm.

358 [1968] 1 QB 421, [1967] 3 All ER 47. See R. Buxton, 'Negligence and Constructive Crime' [1969] Crim LR 112. See also *Ward* (1872) LR 1 CCR 356.

359 Above, p 125.

360 [1968] 1 QB 421 at 426–427, [1967] 3 All ER 47 at 50.

(i) The ulterior intent

Section 18 requires an ulterior intent which may be either intent to do grievous bodily harm or intent to resist or prevent the lawful apprehension or detainer of any person. Recklessness is not enough.[361] A count is not bad for duplicity because it specifies the ulterior intent in the alternative; the intents specified 'are variations of method rather than creations of separate offences in themselves', according to *Naismith*[362] – though it is difficult to see how an ulterior intent can be equated with a 'method'.

The intent specified in the indictment must be proved. It is not enough to prove another variety of intent described in the section. So D had to be acquitted where the various counts of the indictment charged intent to murder, to disable, or to do some grievous bodily harm and the jury found that the acts were done to resist and prevent D's apprehension *and for no other purpose.*[363] But if D intends to prevent his apprehension and, in order to do so, intends to cause grievous bodily harm, he may be convicted under an indictment charging only the latter intent. It is immaterial which is the principal and which the subordinate intent.[364]

Intention has the same meaning as in the law of murder[365] the prosecution must prove either (i) that it was D's purpose to cause grievous bodily harm or, if it was not his purpose, (ii) that he knew that grievous bodily harm was a virtually certain consequence of his act. In case (ii), the jury may then find that he had the requisite intent.[366] The jury need not be directed on the oblique intention definition except in rare cases.[367]

If D intends to cause grievous bodily harm to O and, striking at O, he by accident wounds another person V, he may be indicted for wounding V with intent to cause grievous bodily harm to O.[368] If D intends to cause grievous bodily harm to O, and strikes the person he aims at who is in fact V, he may be convicted of wounding V with intent to cause grievous bodily harm to V.[369]

(b) Alternative verdicts

A charge of causing grievous bodily harm with intent contrary to s 18 has been held to include a charge of inflicting grievous bodily harm contrary to s 20[370] which in turn includes a charge of assault occasioning actual bodily harm contrary to s 47.[371] The effect is that, on an indictment for the s 18 offence, the jury may find D guilty of an offence under s 20, or under s 47; and, on an indictment for the s 20 offence, of an offence under s 47. Whether to direct the jury that, if they acquit of the offence charged they may convict of a lesser included offence is a matter for the discretion of the judge; but he must

361 *Re Knight's Appeal* (1968) FLR 81.

362 [1961] 2 All ER 735, [1961] 1 WLR 952, C-MAC.

363 *Duffin and Marshall* (1818) Russ & Ry 365; cf *Boyce* (1824) 1 Mood CC 29.

364 *Gillow* (1825) 1 Mood CC 85.

365 *Bryson* [1985] Crim LR 669; cf *Belfon* [1976] 3 All ER 46, CA.

366 Above, p 94.

367 See *Phillips* [2004] EWCA Crim 112.

368 *Monger* [1973] Crim LR 301, per Mocatta J holding that D could not be convicted where the indictment alleged intent to harm V. This is in accord with *Ryan* (1839) 2 Mood & R 213 and *Hewlett* (1858) 1 F & F 91 but contrary to *Hunt* (1825) 1 Mood CC 93 and *Jarvis, Langdon and Stear* (1837) 2 Mood & R 40. Cf the doctrine of transferred malice, above, p 113 and comment on *Monger* in [1973] Crim LR 301.

369 *Smith* (1855) Dears CC 559 at 560; *Stopford* (1870) 11 Cox CC 643.

370 *Mandair* (1994) 99 Cr App R 250, [1994] Crim LR 666, HL.

371 *Wilson* [1984] AC 242, [1984] Crim LR 36, HL, below, p 556.

consider whether there is a real risk that, if he does not leave the lesser offence to the jury, they will convict of the greater, although they are not satisfied that D committed it, because they are not willing to see a person who has behaved disgracefully go 'scot' free. If there is such a risk the judge must leave the lesser offence to the jury.[372]

8. Reform

The case for reform of these offences against the person (assault, battery, s 47, s 20, s 18) is compelling.[373] The Law Commission commented that the law 'was defective on grounds both of effectiveness and of justice'.[374] The Home Office *Consultation Paper on Violence*[375] proposes a structured hierarchy of offences as follows:

The Draft Bill provides

1.—(1) A person is guilty of an offence if he intentionally causes serious injury to another.

(2) A person is guilty of an offence if he omits to do an act which he has a duty to do at common law, the omission results in serious injury to another, and he intends the omission to have that result. . . .

(4) A person guilty of an offence under this section is liable on conviction on indictment to imprisonment for life.

2.—(1) A person is guilty of an offence if he recklessly causes serious injury to another. . . .

(3) A person guilty of an offence under this section is liable–

(a) on conviction on indictment, to imprisonment for a term not exceeding 7 years;

(b) on summary conviction, to imprisonment for a term not exceeding 6 months or a fine not exceeding the statutory maximum or both.

3.—(1) A person is guilty of an offence if he intentionally or recklessly causes injury to another. . . .

(3) A person guilty of an offence under this section is liable–

(a) on conviction on indictment, to imprisonment for a term not exceeding 5 years;

(b) on summary conviction, to imprisonment for a term not exceeding 6 months or a fine not exceeding the statutory maximum or both.

4.—(1) A person is guilty of an offence if–

(a) he intentionally or recklessly applies force to or causes an impact on the body of another, or

(b) he intentionally or recklessly causes the other to believe that any such force or impact is imminent.

372 *Maxwell* [1994] Crim LR 848, applying *Maxwell* (1990) 91 Cr App R 61, HL.

373 E. Genders, 'Reform of the Offences Against the Person Act : Lessons from the Law in Action' [1999] Crim LR 689.

374 Law Com Consultation Paper No 122, *Legislating the Criminal Code: Offences Against the Person and General Principles* (1992), on which see S. Gardner, 'Reiterating the Criminal Code' (1992) MLR 839; A. T. H. Smith, 'Legislating the Criminal Code' [1992] Crim LR 396. See also Law Commission Proposals in Report No 218, *Offences Against the Person and General Principles* (1993).

375 (1998) on which see J. C. Smith, 'Offences Against The Person: The Home Office Consultation Paper' [1998] Crim LR 317.

(2) No such offence is committed if the force or impact, not being intended or likely to cause injury, is in the circumstances such as is generally acceptable in the ordinary conduct of daily life and the defendant does not know or believe that it is in fact unacceptable to the other person.

(3) A person guilty of an offence under this section is liable on summary conviction to imprisonment for a term not exceeding 6 months or a fine not exceeding level 5 on the standard scale or both.

15.—(1) In this Act 'injury' means–

(a) physical injury, or

(b) mental injury.

(2) Physical injury does not include anything caused by disease but (subject to that) it includes pain, unconsciousness and any other impairment of a person's physical condition.

(3) Mental injury does not include anything caused by disease but (subject to that) it includes any impairment of a person's mental health.

(4) In its application to section 1 this section applies without the exceptions relating to things caused by disease.

9. Administering poison

(a) *Actus reus*

Sections 23 and 24 of the Offences Against the Person Act 1861 create offences, punishable with 10 and five years' imprisonment respectively, with a similar *actus reus*. In each case, the definition includes the words '. . . unlawfully . . . administer to or cause to be administered to or taken by any other person any poison or other destructive or noxious thing . . . .'[376]

But under s 23, the *actus reus* includes a further element: '. . . so as thereby to endanger the life of such person, or so as thereby to inflict upon such person any grievous bodily harm . . .'.

Section 24 might be seen as an inchoate offence, with the focus on the conduct whereas s 23 is a result oriented crime.[377]

(i) Administer

The words 'administer' and 'take' are to be construed by the court and not left as a question of fact to the jury.[378] The words are disjunctive and 'takes' postulates some 'ingestion' by the victim. 'Administer' includes 'conduct which not being the direct application of force to V nevertheless brings the noxious thing into contact with his body', as by spraying CS gas into his face.[379] Section 23 criminalizes not just

376 The meaning of poison, etc is considered above, p 507.

377 See A. Ashworth, 'Defining Criminal Offences without Harm', in *Essays in Honour of J. C. Smith* (1987), at 13

378 *Gillard* (1988) 87 Cr App R 189 at 194.

379 *Gillard*, above. See also *Cronin-Simpson* [2000] 1 Cr App R (S) 54, D surreptitiously pouring petrol into neighbours house through loft pipe.

'administering' *per se*, but also 'causing to be administered' and 'causing to be taken'. There is no requirement that the 'administration' under s 23 involves surreptitious conduct.

In *Kennedy*[380] D handed to V a syringe containing heroin with which V injected himself and, in consequence, died. The court said, *obiter*, that it could see no reason why D should not have been convicted of an offence under s 23. There seems to be a very good reason, simply that D did not administer the thing to V or cause V to take it. V, a person of full age and capacity, not labouring under any mistake, administered it to himself. Such an act breaks the chain of causation. After seemingly returning to orthodoxy in *Dias*, the Court of Appeal has returned to the revolutionary approach to causation in *Rogers*,[381] and *Finlay*.[382] In *Kennedy (No 2)*,[383] the Court of Appeal held that where D hands V a syringe with which V injects himself, the jury are entitled to find that D is jointly responsible for the death and D is jointly engaged in administering the heroin. Since V is not committing a crime of self administration, it seems that D is jointly engaged with V in the offence which only he can commit.[384]

In *Kennedy (No 2)*, the court regards the Court of Appeal in *Finlay* as adopting the *Empress* approach to causation only as regards whether D caused to be taken by V a noxious substance, but not to the separate question of causation as to death. This was regarded as an 'unnecessary sophistication'. Since V has voluntarily taken the decision to inject himself, it is difficult to see how his free informed act does not break the chain of causation. It is different if D secretly puts the noxious thing into V's drink and V consumes it. V's consumption is then not a fully voluntary act – he believes he is drinking nothing but, say, coffee and has no intention to take the noxious thing. D has then 'administered' it to him or caused him to take it.[385]

It seems that the thing is not 'administered' until it is taken into the body.[386] To leave the poison, intending it to be taken by an unwitting victim, is an attempt to administer it, as Wightman J sensibly instructed a jury,[387] but today the judge would have to leave the question to them.[388]

(ii) Noxious

In *Marcus*,[389] a case under s 24, 'noxious' was broadly interpreted. A substance which may be harmless if taken in small quantities is noxious if administered in sufficient quantity to injure, aggrieve or annoy.[390] The meaning is taken to be coloured by the purpose which D may have in view. It is not necessary that the substance should be injurious to bodily

380 [1999] Crim LR 65, above, p 60. Cf *Khan* [1998] Crim LR 830.

381 [2003] Crim LR 555.

382 [2003] EWCA Crim 3868.

383 [2005] EWCA Crim 685.

384 See Ch 4 above for detailed comment.

385 *Harley* (1830) 4 C & P 369; *Dale* (1852) 6 Cox CC 14. D would have been more appropriately be charged with 'causing . . . to be taken'.

386 *Cadman* (1825) *Carrington's Supplement* 237. The report to the contrary in Ryan and Moody 114 is said to be inaccurate: *Harley* (above) per Parke J: and 6 Cox CC 16 n (c). But see *Walford* (1899) 34 L Jo 116, per Wills J.

387 *Dale* (1852) 6 Cox CC 14.

388 Above, p 408.

389 [1981] 2 All ER 833, [1981] 1 WLR 774, CA.

390 Following *Hennah* (1877) 13 Cox CC 547 and *Cramp* (1880) 5 QBD 307. Cf *Marlow* (1964) 49 Cr App R 49 (Brabin J).

health: 'by "noxious" is meant something different in quality from and of less importance than poison or other destructive things'. The court quoted the *Shorter Oxford Dictionary* meaning, 'injurious, hurtful, harmful, unwholesome', and opined that the insertion of the celebrated snail in the ginger beer bottle in *Donoghue v Stevenson*[391] with intent to annoy would have amounted to the offence. It was held that the insertion of sedative and sleeping tablets into a bottle of milk was an attempt to commit an offence under s 24. While the tablets would cause no more than sedation or possibly sleep, they might be a danger to a person doing such normal but potentially hazardous acts as driving or crossing the street.

The court 'explained' *Cato*,[392] a case under s 23, where it was said that a thing could not be noxious merely because it was harmful if taken in large quantities. That observation was not 'explicable' but wrong. The actual decision, however, that heroin is a noxious thing even where it is administered to a person with a high tolerance to whom it is unlikely to do any particular harm, is presumably right. Heroin is noxious because 'it is liable to cause injury in common use'.[393] It was no answer that V was experienced in taking heroin and had a high tolerance. Ecstasy has been held to be a noxious substance for these purposes.[394] It has been argued that HIV could be regarded as a noxious substance capable of being administered in the course of sexual activity.[395] Charges under s 20 (above) are more likely.

An argument that V can consent to the administration of a noxious substance that might cause grievous bodily harm or endanger life is unlikely to succeed in light of the policy towards consent adopted in *Brown*.[396] The courts have repeatedly asserted that factual consent will not provide a legal defence to a charge under s 23.[397] It is arguable that V ought to be able to provide valid consent to the administration of a substance under s 24. However, the level of harm likely is that of injury, which seems to be on a par with the threshold at which consent is generally treated as invalid in *Brown*.[398]

Because the interpretation of 'noxious' in s 24 was coloured by the words, 'injure, aggrieve or annoy', it is arguable that in s 23 the word must be read in the light of the fact that the substance must endanger life or inflict grievous bodily harm, and it is indeed difficult to see how a substance with a potential only to aggrieve or annoy could result in the *actus reus* for the s 23 offence.

(iii) 'Thereby'

The use of the term 'thereby' in s 23 could represent a significant restriction on the offence if it is interpreted in as narrow a fashion as for example in relation to the life endangering offences under the Criminal Damage Act 1971. If the life endangerment arises from consequences other than the noxious substance itself, it is arguable that the

391 [1932] AC 562.

392 [1976] 1 All ER 260, [1976] 1 WLR 110; cf *Dalby* [1982] 1 All ER 916, [1982] 1 WLR 425, CA.

393 [1976] 1 All ER at 268.

394 See *Gantz* [2003] EWCA Crim 2862.

395 See D. Ormerod and M. Gunn, 'Criminal Liability for the Transmission of HIV' [1996] 1 Web Jnl; S. Bronnit, 'Spreading Disease and the Criminal Law' [1994] Crim LR 21.

396 [1994] AC 212.

397 *Cato; McShane* (1977) 66 Cr App R 97. Cf the CLRC 14th Report, Cmnd 7844, para 190.

398 Cf the remarks in sentencing in *Sky* [2000] 2 Cr App R (S) 260, para 6.

offence is not committed. As where V's life is endangered by the manner of his driving which was affected by the noxious substance which induced drowsiness.[399]

The *mens rea*

Section 23

Under s 23 the only *mens rea* required is intention or recklessness as to the administration of a noxious thing. This, at least, is plainly required by the use in the section of the word 'maliciously'; and, of course, it has been so held in the leading case of *Cunningham.*[400] The contrast between 'so as thereby to' in s 23 and 'with intent to' in s 24; suggests that no *mens rea* is required as to the second part of the *actus* in s 23 – so as to endanger life or inflict grievous bodily harm; and it was so held in *Cato.* The requirement of 'malice' was satisfied by the deliberate injection of heroin into V's body. No foresight of danger to life or the infliction of grievous bodily harm was required.

In *Cunningham*, the court thought the jury should have been told that D must have foreseen that the coal gas might cause injury to someone. They did not say he must have foreseen that life would be endangered. This is an extraordinary result, in that a less culpable state of mind is required for the more serious offence than the less.

Section 24

This offence requires an ulterior intent: 'with intent to injure aggrieve or annoy such person'.

When a drug is given to V with intent to keep him awake it seems that whether this amounts to an intention to injure depends on whether D has a malevolent or a benevolent purpose. If D, a paedophile, gives the drug to V, a small boy, with the motive of ingratiating himself with V or rendering him susceptible to sexual offences, he has an intention to injure: *Hill.*[401] It would probably be otherwise if D's intention was to enable V to stay awake to enjoy the fireworks or greet his father on return from work. The administration of a drug to the pilot of an aircraft to keep him awake is probably not an offence. The administration of the same drug for the purpose of carrying out a prolonged interrogation may be.[402] This casts doubt on *Weatherall.*[403] D put a sleeping tablet in V's tea to enable him to search her handbag for letters proving that she was committing adultery. It was held that there was insufficient evidence of intent to injure, aggrieve or annoy: but there was surely evidence of a 'malevolent' purpose, as there would be if D gave V a sleeping tablet with intent to rape her. The test of malevolence is presumably objective. The paedophile's belief that the drugged child will enjoy and profit from the sexual experience is unlikely to be regarded as capable of being a 'benevolent' purpose. The question of intention comes perilously close to being one of motive, and at least on orthodox approaches to mens rea, these are irrelevant.

399 Cf *Steer* [1988] AC 111.

400 [1957] 2 QB 396, [1957] 2 All ER 412; D tore the gas meter from the wall of an unoccupied house to steal money from it. The gas seeped into the neighbouring houses and was taken by V, whose life was endangered. D's conviction under s 23 was quashed because the judge directed the jury only that 'malicious' meant 'wicked'. See now Criminal Damage Act 1971, s 1(2), below, ch 24.

401 (1986) 83 Cr App Rep 386, HL.

402 Examples taken from *Hill*, above.

403 [1968] Crim LR 115 (Judge Broderick).

By s 25, a person charged under s 23 may be convicted of an offence under s 24. But a person charged under s 24 may not be convicted of an offence under s 23.[404]

(b) Other poisoning offences

(i) Administering substances in relation to sexual offences

Two important changes are made by the Sexual Offences Act 2003. First, s 61 introduces an offence of intentional administration of a substance/causing it to be taken by V without consent with intent to stupefy/overpower to enable any person to engage in sex with V. This is a further response to the growing problem of drug assisted rape. In addition, there is a presumption of an absence of consent where V has been caused to take a stupefying substance s 75(2)(f) below.[405] These are dealt with in Chapter 17.

(ii) Terrorist related poisonings

The Public Order Act 1986, s 38 creates an offence of food terrorism, and the Anti-Terrorism, Crime and Security Act 2001, ss 113 and 114 create very broad offences of using or threatening to use a noxious substance or thing to cause harm and intimidate.[406]

10. False imprisonment

False imprisonment, like assault and battery, is both a misdemeanour at common law and a tort.[407] The civil remedy is commonly invoked and most of the restored cases on this subject are civil actions but it features as a count in many indictments. As will appear, there are some important distinctions between the crime and the tort.

False imprisonment is committed where D unlawfully and intentionally or recklessly restrains V's freedom of movement from a particular place without lawful justification. 'Imprisonment' is probably a wider term than, and includes, 'arrest'.[408]

Article 5 of the ECHR provides a guarantee against arbitrary deprivation of liberty, but that has been interpreted more narrowly than restricting movement. 'Article 5 is concerned with the *deprivation* of liberty and not with mere *restrictions* on freedom of movement'.[409] The distinction is not always easy to identify since the difference is 'merely one of degrees or intensity, and not one of nature or substance'.[410]

[404] Cf *Stokes* (1925) 19 Cr App R 71.

[405] Cf the offences of poisoning under ss 23 and 24 of the OAPA 1861.

[406] See C. Walker, *The Anti-Terrorism Legislation* (2001), at 167–169.

[407] See W. V. H. Rogers, *Winfield and Jolowicz on Tort* (16th edn, 2002) at 68–94; R. Clayton and H. Tomlinson, *Civil Actions Against the Police* (3rd edn, 2003) at 147 et seq.

[408] *Rahman* (1985) 81 Cr App R 349 at 353, CA. *Brown* [1977] Crim LR 291, CA, and commentary thereon and articles by D. Telling, 'Arrest and Detention – The Conceptual Maze' [1978] Crim LR 320 and K. Lidstone, 'A Maze in Law!' [1978] Crim LR 332.

[409] *Engel v Netherlands* (1976) 1 EHRR 647, para 58; *Guzzardi v Italy* (1980) 3 EHRR 333, para 92; *Raimondo v Italy* (1994) 18 EHRR 237, para 39; *HM v Switzerland*, 26 Feb 2002, App No 39187/98. Lesser restrictions on freedom of movement are governed by Article 2 of the 4th protocol, to which the UK is not a party. See the narrow interpretation in *Austin v MPC* [2005] EWHC Crim 480 (QB) and in *R (Laporte) v CC of Gloucestershire* [2005] 1 All ER 473.

[410] *Guzzardi v Italy* (1980) 3 EHRR 333, para 92; *Ashingdane v United Kingdom* (1985) 7 EHRR 528, para 41; *Engel v Netherlands* (1976) 1 EHRR 647, paras 58–589. See also *Blume v Spain* (2000) 30 EHRR 632.

(a) *Actus reus*

(i) 'Imprisonment'

The 'imprisonment' may consist in confining V in a prison,[411] a house,[412] even V's own house,[413] a mine[414] or a vehicle;[415] or simply in detaining V in a public street[416] or any other place. It is not necessary that he be physically detained. There may be an arrest by words alone, but only if V submits. If V is not physically detained and does not realize he is under constraint he is not imprisoned.[417] If V agrees to go to a police station voluntarily, he has not been arrested though the constable would have arrested him if he had refused to go.[418] If it is then made clear to V that he will not be allowed to leave until he provides a laboratory specimen, it has been suggested that, though he has never been 'arrested', he is 'under arrest'.[419] If the distinction is valid it would seem to be enough for false imprisonment that V is 'under arrest'. It is enough that D orders V to accompany him to another place, and V goes because he feels constrained to do so. V is not imprisoned if, on hearing D use words of arrest, he runs away or makes his escape by a trick.[420] An invitation by D to V to accompany him cannot be an imprisonment if it is made clear to V that he is entitled to refuse to go. Thus Lord Lyndhurst CB thought there was no imprisonment where D asked a policeman to take V into custody, and the policeman objected, but said that if D and V 'would be so good as to go with him', he would take the advice of his superior.[421] The distinction between a command, amounting to an imprisonment, and a request not doing so, is a difficult one.[422] Probably Alderson B went too far in *Peters v Stanway*[423] in holding that V was imprisoned if she went to the police station with a constable voluntarily but nevertheless in consequence of a charge against her.

Though some of the older authorities[424] speak of false imprisonment as a species of assault it is quite clear that no assault need be proved.[425] In *Linsberg*,[426] the Common Sergeant held that V, a doctor, was falsely imprisoned where D locked the door to prevent him leaving a confinement. The restraint need be only momentary, so that the offence would be complete if D tapped V on the shoulder and said, 'You are my prisoner.'[427] But a

[411] *Cobbett v Grey* (1849) 4 Exch 729; *R v Govenor of Brockhill Prison, ex p Evans No 2* [2001] 2 AC 19.

[412] *Warner v Riddiford* (1858) 4 CBNS 180.

[413] *Termes de la Ley*, approved by Warrington and Atkin LJJ (1920) 122 LT at 51 and 53.

[414] *Herd v Weardale Steel, Coal and Coke Co Ltd* [1915] AC 67.

[415] By driving at such a speed that V dare not alight: *McDaniel v State* 15 Tex Crim 115 (1942); *Burton v Davies* [1953] QSR 26. See also *Bowell* [2003] EWCA Crim 3896, single count of false imprisonment split where D detained V in the car, and redetained when she escaped and injured herself.

[416] Blackstone, *Commentaries*, iii, 127; *Ludlow v Burgess* [1971] Crim LR 238; *Austin v MPC* above.

[417] *Alderson v Booth* [1969] 2 QB 216, [1969] 2 All ER 271.

[418] *Campbell v Tormey* [1969] 1 All ER 961, [1969] 1 WLR 189.

[419] Ibid, per Ashworth J.

[420] *Russen v Lucas* (1824) 1 C & P 153.

[421] *Cant v Parsons* (1834) 6 C & P 504.

[422] G. Williams in *Police Power and Individual Freedom* at 43.

[423] (1835) 6 C & P 737, followed in *Conn v David Spencer Ltd* [1930] 1 DLR 805.

[424] Eg, Hawkins, I PC, c. 60, s 7; *Pocock v Moore* (1825) Ry & M 321.

[425] *Grainger v Hill* (1838) 4 Bing NC 212; *Warner v Riddiford* (1858) 4 CBNS 180.

[426] (1905) 69 JP 107.

[427] *Simpson v Hill* (1795) 1 Esp 431, per Eyre CJ; *Sandon v Jervis* (1859) EB & E 942, '. . . a mere touch constitutes an arrest, though the party be not actually taken'; per Crowder J.

battery is not necessarily an imprisonment. In *Bird v Jones*[428] V was involved in 'a struggle during which no momentary detention of his person took place'. It is not an imprisonment wrongfully to prevent V from going in a particular direction, if he is free to go in other directions. This was decided in *Bird v Jones*,[429] where Coleridge J said: 'A prison may have its boundary large or narrow, visible and tangible, or, though real, still in the conception only;[430] it may itself be moveable or fixed: but a boundary it must have . . .'. It would be otherwise if V could move off in other directions only by taking an unreasonable risk;[431] it could hardly be said that a man locked in a second-floor room was not imprisoned because he could have climbed down the drainpipe.

There is little authority on the question how large the area of confinement may be. It has been suggested that it would be tortious to confine V to a large country estate or the Isle of Man;[432] but it could hardly be false imprisonment to prevent V from leaving Great Britain, still less to prevent him from entering. But a person who has actually landed and is not allowed to leave an airport building is imprisoned.[433] Is V also imprisoned, then, if he is not allowed to leave the ship which has docked in a British port?

Merely deciding to restrain a person if he attempts to leave does not amount to imprisonment.[434] But if steps are taken to prevent his leaving, as by placing a policeman at the door, he is imprisoned although he is not aware of it: *Meering v Grahame-White Aviation Co Ltd*[435] where Atkin LJ said:

> It appears to me that a person could be imprisoned without his knowing it. I think a person can be imprisoned while he is asleep, while he is in a state of drunkenness, while he is unconscious, and while he is a lunatic . . . though the imprisonment began and ceased while he was in that state.

A contrary decision of the Court of Exchequer[436] was not cited and the case has been heavily criticized,[437] although cited by the House of Lords with approval in *Murray v Minister of Defence*;[438] but the arguments advanced against awarding damages in this situation are not applicable to the crime. D's conduct may not be damaging to V if V knows nothing about it, but it is not necessarily any less blameworthy for, in most cases, the fact that V remains in ignorance must be a matter of mere chance.

Like other crimes, false imprisonment can be committed through an innocent agent. So D is responsible for the *actus reus* if, at his direction or request, a policeman takes V

428 Below. 429 (1845) 7 QB 742 (Denman CJ dissenting).

430 For example, V is forbidden to move more than ten yards from the village pump.

431 *Street on Torts* (11th edn, 2003) at 32.

432 Ibid. But 'Napoleon was certainly imprisoned on St Helena': *Winfield and Jorowicz on Torts* (15th edn, 1998) at 71. In *Re Mwenya* [1960] 1 QB 241, [1959] 3 All ER 525, a writ of *habeas corpus* was sought for V who was confined to an area of some 1,500 square miles but he was released before it became necessary to decide whether he was imprisoned for the purpose of *habeas corpus*.

433 *Kuchenmeister v Home Office* [1958] 1 QB 496, [1958] 1 All ER 485.

434 *Bournewood Community and Mental Health NHS Trust, ex p L* [1998] 3 All ER 289 at 298, HL; but Lord Steyn, dissenting, more realistically thought (at 306): 'The suggestion that L was free to go is a fairy tale'. Note the European Court's finding of a breach of Article 5 in *HL v UK*, App No 45508/99.

435 (1919) 122 LT 44, Duke LJ dissenting, where two policemen were stationed outside the door of a room to prevent V leaving. He was as effectively imprisoned as if the door had been locked. *Meering* was approved in *Murray v Ministry of Defence* [1988] 2 All ER 521 at 529, HL.

436 *Herring v Boyle* (1834) 1 Cr M & R 377.

437 G. Williams in *Police Power and Individual Freedom* at 45–46; *Street on Torts* (11th edn, 2003), ch 3.

438 [1998] 1 WLR 692.

into custody,[439] or he signs the charge-sheet when the police have said they will not take the responsibility of detaining V unless he does;[440] but merely to give information to a constable, in consequence of which he decides to make an arrest has been held not to be actionable, at all events if D is *bona fide*.[441] *A fortiori*, it should not be *criminal*, for lack of *mens rea*; but why should D not be guilty if he deliberately supplies false information to a constable who, acting on his own authority but relying exclusively on D's information, arrests V?[442] D has surely caused the *actus reus* with *mens rea* and may be liable for the ministerial act of the constable as distinct from the judicial act of the magistrate.[443] Where D is initially liable for false imprisonment his liability ceases on the intervention of some judicial act[444] authorizing the detention or on any other event, breaking the chain of causation.[445]

Whatever may be the position in the law of tort,[446] it is thought that it would be immaterial in the criminal law that the imprisonment was not 'directly' caused by D; and that it would be sufficient that he caused it with *mens rea* – as by digging a pit into which V falls and is trapped.[447]

Another question in the law of tort is whether it is possible falsely to imprison by mere omission in view of the requirement of a trespass. In *Herd v Weardale Steel Coal and Coke Co Ltd*[448] V voluntarily descended into D's mine and, in breach of contract, stopped work and asked to be brought to the surface before the end of the shift. D's refusal to accede to this request was not a false imprisonment: he was under no duty to provide facilities for V to leave in breach of contract. Clearly, the result would be different if D were to take positive steps to prevent V from leaving in breach of contract,[449] as by locking him in a factory. Buckley and Hamilton LJJ[450] thought that mere omission could not have been false imprisonment, even if it occurred when the shift was over. V's only civil remedy would have been in contract; but the House of Lords expressed no opinion on this point.

In *Mee v Cruickshank*,[451] Wills J held that a prison governor was under a duty to take steps to ensure that his officers did not detain a prisoner who had been acquitted. In that case there were acts of imprisonment by the prison officers but they were not the servants of D, the governor, and it seems to have been D's omission which rendered him liable in

439 *Gosden v Elphick and Bennett* (1849) 4 Exch 445.

440 *Austin v Dowling* (1870) LR 5 CP 534. It is otherwise if D signs the charge sheet as a matter of form, when the police are detaining V on their own responsibility: *Grinham v Willey* (1859) 4 H & N 496.

441 *Gosden v Elphick and Bennett*, above; *Grinham v Willey*, above; 'We ought to take care that people are not put in peril for making complaint when a crime has been committed,' per Pollock CB. Cf *O'Hara v Chief Constable of RUC* [1997] AC 286.

442 See *Hough v Chief Constable of Staffordshire* [2001] EWCA Civ 39.

443 See *Austin v Dowling* (1870) LR 5 C & P 534 at 540.

444 *Lock v Ashton* (1848) 12 QB 871. Cf *Marrinan v Vibart* [1963] 1 QB 528, [1962] 3 All ER 380.

445 *Harnett v Bond* [1925] AC 669. D's report caused V to be taken to an asylum; D was not liable for the imprisonment after the doctor at the asylum had examined V and decided to detain him. Cf *Pike v Waldrum* [1952] 1 Lloyd's Rep 431.

446 R. Clayton and H. Tomlinson, para 4–046.

447 Cf *Clarence* (1888) 22 QBD 23 at 36, per Wills J.

448 [1915] AC 67, HL.

449 Unless, perhaps, the contract was that V should be entitled to leave only on the fulfilment of some reasonable condition: *Robinson v Balmain New Ferry Co Ltd* [1910] AC 295, PC. *Sed quaere* whether one is entitled to restrain another from leaving even if it is a breach of contract for him to do so? The contract can hardly be specifically enforceable.

450 [1913] 3 KB at 787 and 793.

451 (1902) 20 Cox CC 210.

tort. As the House of Lords accepted in *Ex p Evans* the failure to release a prisoner on the due date gives rise to an action in false imprisonment, even if the failure was in good faith. And it ought to make no difference that D's duty to release V arises out of a contract:

> If a man gets into an express train and the doors are locked pending its arrival at its destination, he is not entitled, merely because the train has been stopped by signal, to call for the doors to be opened to let him out.[452]

But if he is kept locked in for a day at his destination this surely ought to be false imprisonment. And if the technicalities of the forms of action preclude a remedy in tort this is no reason why the omission should not be held to be criminal. The CLRC were of the opinion that the crime of false imprisonment is, and ought to be, capable of commission by omission.[453]

(ii) Unlawful restraint

The imprisonment must be 'false', that is unlawful. A convicted person sentenced to imprisonment may be lawfully confined in any prison and, as against prison officers so confining him in good faith, he has no 'residual liberty'. If he is subjected to intolerable conditions he may have other remedies but he cannot sue (or, it may be assumed, prosecute) the officers for false imprisonment.[454] It might, however, be false imprisonment for a fellow prisoner, or an officer acting in bad faith outside the scope of his duty, to lock him in a confined space, such as a hut, within the prison. A parent may lawfully exercise restraint over a child, so long as he remains within the bounds of reasonable parental discipline and does not act in contravention of a court order,[455] or the Children Act 2004, s 58. Where a girl of 14 or 15 was fostered out by her father with the consent and assistance of the local authority and he abducted her against her will and with intent to take her to her country of origin, it was for the jury to say whether they were satisfied that this was outside the bounds of legitimate parental discipline and correction.[456] A defendant charged with false imprisonment may rely on other justifications such as the prevention of crime.[457]

The question of false imprisonment most commonly arises in connection with the exercise of powers of arrest. If such powers are exceeded, there is a false imprisonment. The principal powers are as follows.

Arrest by a constable under a valid warrant

Where the justice lacks jurisdiction to issue the warrant, the constable is statutorily protected[458] from any action if he acts in obedience to it. As the term 'action' is

452 *Herd v Weardale Steel Coal and Coke Co Ltd* [1915] AC 67 at 71, per Lord Haldane. See M. Amos, 'A Note on contractual restraint of liberty' (1928) 44 LQR 464; K. F. Tan, 'A Misconceived Issue in the Tort of False Imprisonment' (1981) 44 MLR 166.

453 CLRC/OAP/R, paras 253, 254.

454 *Hague v Deputy Governor of Parkhurst Prison* [1991] 3 All ER 733, HL. What if the conditions are so intolerable as to found a defence of necessity to a charge of escape (above, Ch 11)? Is it false imprisonment to prevent such a prisoner from leaving the prison?

455 *Rahman* (1985) 81 Cr App R 349, CA. Cf *D* [1984] AC 778, [1984] 1 All ER 574, below, p 575.

456 *Rahman*, above, at p 567. In fact, D pleaded guilty, and his appeal was dismissed.

457 D acting to prevent theft relied on s 3 of the Criminal Law Act 1967: *Bowden* [2002] EWCA Civ 1279.

458 The Constables Protection Act 1750. See *O'Connor v Isaacs* [1956] 2 QB 288.

inappropriate to a criminal proceeding, a constable could not rely on the Act as a defence to criminal prosecution; but he would probably have a good defence on the ground of lack of *mens rea.*[459] An arrest under warrant for a civil matter is unlawful if the arresting officer does not have the warrant in his possession.[460]

Arrest by a constable or other person for an arrestable offence

The Police and Criminal Evidence Act 1984, s 24 provides:[461]

> (4) Any person may arrest without a warrant –
>
> (a) anyone who is in the act of committing an arrestable offence;
>
> (b) anyone whom he has reasonable grounds for suspecting to be committing such an offence.
>
> (5) Where an arrestable offence has been committed, any person may arrest without a warrant –
>
> (a) anyone who is guilty of the offence;
>
> (b) anyone whom he has reasonable grounds for suspecting to be guilty of it.
>
> (6) Where a constable has reasonable grounds for suspecting that an arrestable offence has been committed, he may arrest without a warrant anyone whom he has reasonable grounds for suspecting to be guilty of the offence.
>
> (7) A constable may arrest without a warrant –
>
> (a) anyone who is about to commit an arrestable offence;
>
> (b) anyone whom he has reasonable grounds for suspecting to be about to commit an arrestable offence.

Section 24(3) provides that the above subsections apply to conspiring, attempting, inciting, aiding, abetting, counselling or procuring an arrestable offence and that these acts are also arrestable offences.

It will be noted that arrest is always lawful where D reasonably suspects[462] V to be in the act of committing the arrestable offence, even though in fact V is not doing so: but that where D reasonably suspects that V *has committed* an arrestable offence, the arrest is unlawful if that offence has not been committed by anyone, unless D happens to be a constable.[463] This, in effect, re-enacts the rule laid down for arrest for felony in *Walters v W. H. Smith & Son Ltd.*[464] D suspected on reasonable grounds that V had stolen a number of books from his book stall. He arrested him on a charge of stealing a particular book. Though other books had certainly been stolen, this one had not been stolen by V or anyone else. Because the offence for which the arrest was made had not been committed, D was held liable in damages. The Criminal Law Revision Committee thought it right to preserve the rule, although they pointed out that it may be:

> a trap to a private person who is careful instead of precipitate about deciding whether to arrest a person. If, for example, a store detective saw a person apparently shoplifting, he could arrest him

459 Below, p 575. 460 *De Costa Small v Kirkpatrick* (1978) 68 Cr App R 186, [1979] Crim LR 41.

461 Note that the Serious Organised Crime and Police Act 2005 s 1.10 will replace s 24. Once it comes into force this chapter will be updated on the updates website.

462 See *O'Hara v CC RUC* [1997] AC 268; *O'Hara v UK* [2002] 34 EHRR 32; *Fox Campbell and Hartley v UK* [1991] 13 EHRR 784.

463 *Self* [1992] 3 All ER 476, [1992] Crim LR 572.

464 [1914] 1 KB 595. The case does not decide that D committed the *crime* of false imprisonment.

under clause 2 (2) [now s 24(4)(b) of PACE] on the ground that he had reasonable cause to suspect him of being in the act of committing an arrestable offence, and he would not be liable for unlawful arrest even if it turned out that he was wrong; but if he preferred out of caution to invite the other to the office to give him an opportunity of clearing himself, and then arrested him on being satisfied that he was guilty, the detective would be liable if this turned out to be wrong.[465]

The justification for the rule is that an increase in the powers of arrest of private persons would not be acceptable to public opinion and that it is desirable, where it is at all doubtful whether an offence has been committed, for a private person to put the matter in the hands of the police.[466] This hardly allows, however, for the case where the citizen has no opportunity to inform the police and must either let the suspected person escape or make an arrest himself.

The powers of arrest of a constable are wider under s 24 than those of other persons in three respects. An arrest by a constable of a person reasonably suspected of having committed an arrestable offence is not unlawful even though the offence in question has never been committed. Secondly, a constable may arrest a person reasonably suspected to be *about to commit* an arrestable offence, whereas other persons must wait until he is *in the act* of committing the offence. Thirdly, a constable who has made an arrest may do what is reasonable to investigate the matter and discover whether his reasonable suspicions are well founded; but a private person must hand the arrested person over to a constable or magistrate as soon as possible.[467] A constable may rely on the powers of arrest available to 'any person' as may any other citizen.[468]

Where a constable or other person arrests for breach of the peace

If the breach of the peace is committed in his presence, or where he reasonably believes that such a breach will be committed in the immediate future by a person unless he is arrested, or where a breach has been committed and he reasonably believes that a renewal of it is threatened.[469] There is a breach of the peace whenever harm is actually done or is likely to be done to a person, or in his presence to his property, or a person is in fear of being so harmed through an assault, an affray, a riot, or other disturbance.[470] Public alarm, excitement or disturbance is not of itself a breach of the peace, unless it arises from actual or threatened violence.

Arrest by a constable under the 'general arrest conditions'

By s 25(1) of the Police and Criminal Evidence Act, a constable who has reasonable grounds for suspecting that any offence which is not an arrestable offence has been

465 Cmnd 2659, para 14.

466 Ibid, para 15, or what would now be one of the civilian members of the extended police family.

467 *Dallison v Caffrey* [1965] 1 QB 348, [1964] 2 All ER 610 at 616–617, CA, per Lord Denning. It is lawful for a private detective to take a suspected shoplifter to his employer for a decision whether to prosecute; *John Lewis & Co Ltd v Tims* [1952] AC 676, [1952] 1 All ER 1203, HL, but it is not, apparently, lawful for the private arrester of a child to take the child to his father to deal with; *Brewin* [1976] Crim LR 742 (Recorder Jowitt) and commentary.

468 *Gapper v Chief Constable of Avon and Somerset* [2000] QB 29.

469 *Howell* (1981) 73 Cr App R 31 at 36; *Kelbie* [1996] Crim LR 862 and commentary; *Jarrett v CC West Midlands Police* [2003] EWCA Civ 397.

470 Ibid at 37. Lord Denning has said that even the lawful use of force is a breach of the peace: *Chief Constable of Devon and Cornwall, ex p Central Electricity Generating Board* [1981] 3 All ER 826 at 832; but this can hardly subject the person using such force to arrest.

committed or attempted, or is being committed or attempted, by X, may arrest X if it appears to him that the service of a summons is impracticable or inappropriate because of the 'general arrest conditions' specified in the section. The conditions are, broadly, (i) the constable is unable to ascertain X's true name and address or a satisfactory address for service of a summons; or (ii) the constable has reasonable grounds for believing that the arrest is necessary to prevent X from causing or sustaining physical injury to himself, causing physical injury to others, causing loss of or damage to property, committing an offence against public decency, causing an unlawful obstruction of the highway; or to protect a child or other vulnerable person from X.[471]

Arrest under the powers preserved by Schedule 2 to the Police and Criminal Evidence Act 1984

Numerous statutory powers of arrest without warrant were abolished by s 26 of the 1984 Act which, however, preserved the powers specified in Schedule 2.[472]

Arrest unlawful, unless information given

Where a person is arrested, otherwise than by being informed he is under arrest, he must be so informed as soon as practicable afterwards: s 28(3).[473] Article 5(2) of the ECHR provides the right of 'everyone arrested to be informed promptly in a language he understands of the reason for his arrest'.

No arrest is lawful unless the person arrested is informed of the ground of the arrest at the time or as soon as is practicable thereafter; and, where the arrest is by a constable, this is so even where the ground for the arrest is obvious. If the arrested person escapes before it is reasonably practicable for him to be informed that he is under arrest, or the ground for the arrest, the arrest is not rendered unlawful.[474] The arrester must have a valid ground for the arrest in mind when he makes it.[475] The existence of a valid ground cannot justify an arrest when it was not actually exercised by the arrester.[476]

Detention by a community support officer

Under the Police Reform Act 2002, a community support officer has the power to 'detain' a person for up to 30 minutes pending the arrival of a police officer where the suspect fails to provide an accurate name and address. This is tantamount to an arrest despite its euphemistic label.[477]

471 Does this provision imply that any person other than a constable, acting on the same necessity, does so unlawfully? Above, Ch 11.

472 Archbold, 15–172. N.B.: the redefinition in s 110 of the SOCPA 2005, as above.

473 See *Taylor v Chief Constable of Thames Valley* [2004] EWCA Civ 858.

474 These rules, in s 28 of the 1984 Act, replace the common law as stated in *Christie v Leachinsky* [1947] AC 573, [1947] 1 All ER 567. See *DPP v Hawkins* [1988] 3 All ER 673, [1988] Crim LR 741; *Brosch* [1988] Crim LR 743 and (especially) commentary.

475 *Edwards v DPP* (1993) 97 Cr App R 301, 306–307, DC, above, p 43.

476 *Redman* [1994] Crim LR 914.

477 For criticism and suggestions as to how this might be challenged see D. Ormerod and A. Roberts, 'The Police Reform Act 2002 – Increasing Centralisation, Maintaining Confidence and Contracting out Crime Control' [2003] Crim LR 141.

(b) *Mens rea*

Since the great majority of the reported cases are civil actions, there is little authority on the nature of the *mens rea* required for false imprisonment but in *Rahman*[478] the court stated that 'false imprisonment consists in the unlawful and intentional or reckless restraint of a victim's freedom of movement from a particular place'. This was confirmed by *Hutchins*[479] which held that the offence is one of 'basic intent' so that a belief caused by self-induced intoxication that the victim is consenting is no defence. The courts did not specify what kind of recklessness they had in mind; but a common law offence would naturally require *Cunningham* recklessness. This may be taken to be established now that it is settled that assault requires *Cunningham* recklessness.[480] Assault and false imprisonment are both common law offences and are so closely related that it is inconceivable that they should be governed by different principles of *mens rea*. As suggested above, D would not have been criminally liable in *Walters v W. H. Smith & Son Ltd* because he believed on reasonable grounds that the felony for which he arrested V had been committed; and, today, it should make no difference that there were no reasonable grounds for his belief, so long as it was honestly held. This makes no difference, of course, to the position in the civil law and D remains liable to pay damages to V in the circumstances of that case.

11. Kidnapping

Kidnapping is an aggravated form of false imprisonment[481] so the rules of lawful excuse are, no doubt, the same. Since both offences are common law misdemeanours, punishable with imprisonment or fine at the discretion of the court, the significance of the element of aggravation is that it enables the kidnapper to be labelled as such and given an appropriate penalty.

In *R v D*[482] the House of Lords gave an authoritative account of the law of kidnapping.

First, the nature of the offence is an attack on, and infringement of, the personal liberty of an individual. Second, the offence contains four ingredients as follows: (1) the taking or carrying away of one person by another, (2) by force or by fraud, (3) without the consent of the person so taken or carried away and (4) without lawful excuse. Third, until the comparatively recent abolition by statute of the division of criminal offences into the two categories of felonies and misdemeanours (see s 1 of the Criminal Law Act 1967), the offence of kidnapping was categorized by the common law as a misdemeanour only. Fourth, despite that, kidnapping was always regarded, by reason of its nature, as a grave and (to use the language of an earlier age) heinous offence. Fifth, in earlier days the offence contained a further ingredient, namely that the taking or carrying away should be from a place within the jurisdiction to another place outside it; this further ingredient has, however, long been obsolete and forms no necessary part of the offence today. Sixth, the offence was in former days

[478] (1985) 81 Cr App R 349 at 353, CA, above, p 567. [479] [1988] Crim LR 379.

[480] Above, p 103. [481] East, 1 PC, 429.

[482] [1984] AC 778, [1984] 2 All ER 449, [1984] Crim LR 558. Kidnapping has never been satisfactorily defined: see D. Napier, 'Detention Offences at Common Law' in P. Glazebrook (ed), *Reshaping the Criminal Law* (1978), 198, The Law Commission Draft Criminal Code cl. 81 proposes radical amendment to the offence by restricting it to cases of carrying away for ulterior purposes – eg to commit an arrestable offence.

described not merely as taking or carrying away a person but further or alternatively as secreting him; this element of secretion has, however, also become obsolete, so that, although it may be present in a particular case, it adds nothing to the basic ingredient of taking or carrying away.

In defining the offence in that way, Lord Brandon's attempts to consolidate earlier interpretations resulted in a considerable degree of overlap. His lordship's approach creates problems in relation to the issues of frauds, force and consent. Each of the four elements deserves examination.

(a) Taking and carrying away

The crime is complete when V is deprived of his liberty and carried away from the place where he wished to be.[483] The requirements of carrying away and the use of force or fraud seem to be the only factors distinguishing kidnapping from false imprisonment. It seems that every kidnapping is also a false imprisonment but a detention without any taking away or force or fraud (D merely turns the key locking V in the room) is only the latter offence. Where D has carried V away by force or fraud, he may be convicted of both offences.[484]

(b) 'Force or fraud' and/or consent?

The question arises whether 'force or fraud' and 'without consent' are disjunctive and whether they are necessary conditions for the offence. Clearly where D forces V by violence or threats of violence there will be no true consent on her part, but it may be that lesser threats or trivial force will not invalidate consent and yet ought to be sufficient for kidnapping. Similarly, where D deceives V into accompanying him by telling a lie, in some instances this lie will be so fundamental as to vitiate V's consent, but in other circumstances the lie will be so insignificant as to have no effect on V's consent. Conversely, are there circumstances in which D uses no force or fraud and yet it is possible to say that V has not consented to being taken away? Perhaps the most obvious example of such circumstance is where V is incapable of understanding the nature and purpose of D's act: most commonly where V is a child. D may persuade V to accompany him without using force or fraud, and in such circumstances D ought to be liable for an offence.

This leads to a number of possible interpretations:

(a) There must be force or fraud *and* an absence of consent in all cases.

(b) It is sufficient that there is 'force or fraud' *or* an absence of consent.

(c) There must be proof of an absence of consent, and the force or fraud must have caused that absence of consent.

Some of the difficulties in interpretation are demonstrated by the facts of *Cort.*[485] D had on a number of occasions stopped his car at bus stops, falsely stating to women in the queue that the bus they awaited had broken down and offered them a lift. On two

483 *Wellard* [1978] 3 All ER 161, [1978] 1 WLR 921.

484 *Brown* [1985] Crim LR 398, CA (five years' imprisonment concurrent on both counts upheld).

485 [2003] EWCA Crim 2149, [2004] Crim LR 64.

occasions women got into the car. One changed her mind and asked to be let out of the car and D complied; the other was taken to her destination without being assaulted by D in any way. D was convicted of two counts of kidnapping. The Court of Appeal upheld the conviction, finding that D had defrauded VV as to the nature of the act. In this case it was held that the complainants did not consent to the events, VV only consented to a ride in the car, but that the ride in the car was a 'different thing' from that with which D was charged.

(i) Force or fraud and an absence of consent

If both elements must be proved in all cases several problems arise. First, the offence might be regarded as seriously deficient in protecting children. Although it is possible to say that in the case of a young child[486] who lacks the understanding or intelligence to give consent, the absence of consent is a necessary inference that still leaves the requirement for proof of a force or fraud. In the case of a young child D may not need to use force or fraud (unless those words are very broadly construed) to succeed in taking V away, as where a toddler is persuaded by true statements ('I'll buy you sweets') to accompany D. Arguably such cases need not be kidnapping since they constitute false imprisonment which is equally punishable so, though it looks a little odd if a baby cannot be kidnapped,[487] no great harm is done. Secondly, this interpretation would require the courts to address what types of force or fraud would be sufficient to constitute kidnapping (see below).

(ii) 'Force or fraud' or an absence of consent

This more radical interpretation also poses problems, although of course it would leave the offence available as a charge when the taking and carrying away was of a child and did not involve force or fraud. The principal difficulty would be in establishing what levels of force and what types of fraud were sufficient to constitute kidnapping. Because the element of force or fraud is a *sufficient* condition for liability, the courts would have to provide precise definition. One way of identifying which inflictions of force and which frauds were sufficient to constitute the offence would be to adopt a causation based approach: by asking whether 'but for'[488] the force or fraud V would have been taken and carried away. This would place emphasis on the requirement that the taking is '*by* the force or fraud' in Lord Brandon's definition. In a case like *Cort*, the question would be whether 'but for' D's lie about the buses, V would have agreed to be taken away by D. Would it be sufficient if D lied about the anticipated weather or the comfort of the ride he could offer in order to induce the victims to take the lift? The counter argument to this is that juries would be unlikely to accept that trivial lies were the cause of the victim's agreement to being taken. A further problem with this interpretation is also that it is difficult to square with Lord Brandon's definition, which does not use force or fraud

486 In the case of an older child, it is a question of fact for the jury whether (i) the child has sufficient understanding and, if so, (ii) it in fact consented. Lord Brandon thought that a jury would usually find that a child under 14 lacked sufficient understanding to give consent; but this surely underestimates the capacity of the modern child.

487 See Glanville Williams, 'Can Babies be Kidnapped?' [1989] Crim LR 473.

488 Consistently with established jurisprudence on causation, it should be sufficient that the fraud was a more than *de minimis* cause of the carrying away, but it need not be the sole cause: *Kimsey* [1996] Crim LR 35.

or consent as disjunctive elements. However, in *Cort*, the court suggested, *per curiam*, that there was no room for the 'consent' limb of Lord Brandon's definition in a case of fraud.

(iii) Force or fraud sufficient to vitiate consent

On this composite approach, the elements of force or fraud would represent routes through which the prosecution might establish the absence of consent. Force or fraud would not be a necessary condition for the offence, but a *sufficient* condition if the force or fraud was of such a type as to vitiate consent. On this view consent remains at the core of the wrongdoing. It is an interpretation which resonates with Lord Brandon's emphasis in *D* that, 'the nature of the offence is an attack on, and infringement of, the personal liberty of an individual.' Such an approach begs three important questions. (a) Towards what must the fraud relate in order for it to vitiate consent? (b) What types of fraudulent conduct would suffice? (c) What level of force would vitiate consent?

Fraud as to what?

Applying general principles, the force or fraud should relate to the carrying or taking away. Thus in circumstances such as *Cort*, the question would be whether the fraud was as to the nature (and purpose) of the taking away.[489] On the facts it would be difficult to see any such fraud. D told the women they would get a lift home. That is what they got. It would be different if D had defrauded them as to their destination.

What types of fraud?

Again, adopting general principles to frauds vitiating consent, any fraud as to the identity of the actor should suffice. In this context, it is submitted that there is a stronger claim than in most circumstances for a fraud as to certain attributes of the actor and not just his correct name or identity being sufficient. Thus, as in *Wellard*,[490] the impersonation of a police officer should suffice to negative the consent of the person. Other examples might include impersonation of State officials, ambulance crews, etc.

In addition to frauds as to identity, it is recognized that frauds as to the *nature* of the act will vitiate consent. This is where the most significant difficulties arise, as illustrated by the cases on sexual offences discussed below in Ch 17. There is also the question whether a fraud as to the 'purpose' of the taking will suffice to vitiate consent? Consider D who falsely tells V that her husband is injured and he drives her home (because he enjoys her company). Or consider D, who tells his 17-year-old daughter that they are to travel abroad to visit an ailing relative when his true motive is for her to take part in an arranged marriage. The destination, manner of transport, etc are identical so the nature of the carrying way is not affected by the fraud. But note the decision in *Nnamdi*,[491] in which on the facts the court did not find it necessary to determine, on a charge of conspiracy to kidnap, whether telling V that she should meet D to join his modelling agency would be a sufficient fraud.

[489] However, in *Cort*, the court suggests that the relevant act was the 'taking away *by fraud*' (emphasis added), and the victim has clearly not consented to that. It is submitted that the approach creates great difficulty. Aside from occasional circumstances where eg D lies to V in order to get her to accompany him to a surprise party, the victim is unlikely ever to have consented to being taken by fraud.

[490] [1978] 3 All ER 161.

[491] [2005] EWCA Crim 74.

Level of force vitiating consent

As with other areas, particularly sexual offences, there will be difficulty in identifying the precise threshold for that level of force which would vitiate consent. Unlike some offences there is little opportunity to apply a proportionality based test. D has forced V to accompany him. It is not a question of balancing the level of force or threat against what he has subsequently done to V. As a matter of principle, violence or threats of violence ought to be sufficient.

(c) Without lawful excuse

What is a lawful excuse is left completely at large; and whether a taking by a parent in other circumstances amounts to kidnapping is likely to be resolved in the same way whether the court proceeds by the route of deciding (as the majority would) whether there is a lawful excuse or by deciding (as Lord Bridge would) whether the offence extends to those further circumstances. If a 12-year-old child refuses to return home from a visit to his grandmother's and his father forcibly carries him off, he surely commits no offence. The majority would say, presumably, because the father has a lawful excuse and Lord Bridge, because kidnapping does not extend to those circumstances. The result is the same. The question must be whether the parent has gone beyond what is reasonable in the exercise of parental authority.

Where V is not D's child and D is not acting in pursuance of any statutory authority or power of arrest, 'lawful excuse' is likely to be narrowly confined. In *Henman*[492] D was guilty of attempted kidnapping when he tried to take by force an acquaintance whom he believed to be in moral and spiritual danger from a religious sect to which she belonged. There was no lawful excuse because there was no 'necessity recognized by the law as such' for D's conduct.

(d) Who may be kidnapped

It was held in *Reid*[493] that a husband may be convicted of kidnapping his wife and in *D* that a father may be guilty of kidnapping his child. It was recognized that, until modern times, it may be that an indictment of a father for kidnapping his child would have failed because of the paramount stature of his position in the family; but common law principles adapt and develop in the light of radically changed social conventions and conditions. Lord Bridge held that parental kidnapping includes the case (as in *D*) where the parent acts in contravention of the order of a competent court, leaving open the question whether a parent might be convicted in any other circumstances; but the majority preferred to hold simply that the parent is guilty where he acts 'without lawful excuse'.

12. Other abduction offences

(a) Taking of hostages

The Taking of Hostages Act 1982 creates an offence of exceptional breadth in that it extends to a person of any nationality acting anywhere in the world, or indeed, in outer

[492] [1987] Crim LR 333, CA.

[493] [1973] QB 299, [1972] 2 All ER 1350.

space. It is committed by anyone who detains another and, in order to compel a State, international governmental organization or person to do or abstain from doing any act, threatens to kill, injure or continue to detain the hostage. It is punishable with imprisonment for life. Proceedings may not be instituted except by or with the consent of the Attorney-General.

(b) Abduction of children

The Child Abduction Act 1984, as amended by the Children Act 1989, creates two offences of abduction of a child under the age of 16.

The first offence (s 1) may be committed as a principal[494] only by a person 'connected with' the child who takes or sends the child out of the United Kingdom 'without the appropriate consent'.

A person 'connected with' a child is (i) the child's parent; (ii) in the case of a child whose parents were not married at the time of birth, a man in respect of whom there are reasonable grounds for believing him to be the father; (iii) a guardian; (iv) a person in whose favour 'a residence order'[495] is in force with respect to the child; or (v) a person having custody. The 'appropriate consent' is the consent of *each* of the child's mother, the child's father if he has 'parental responsibility'[496] for him, any guardian, any person in whose favour a residence order is in force with respect to the child *and* any person having custody of him; *or* the leave of the court under the Children Act 1989,[497] or, in the case of any person having custody, the leave of the court which awarded custody.

The offence is not committed where a person in whose favour a residence order is in force takes or sends the child out of the United Kingdom for a period of less than one month unless this is a breach of an order under Part II of the Children Act 1989.

The Act provides defences s 1(5) of which D bears an evidential burden and the prosecution the burden of proof where:

(i) D believes that he has the appropriate consent or that he would have it if the person or persons whose consent is required were aware of all the relevant circumstances; or

(ii) he has taken all reasonable steps to communicate with those persons but has been unsuccessful; or

(iii) the other person has unreasonably refused to consent.

The second offence (s 2) is committed where a person who is not the mother of 'the child in question'[498] or, where the parents were married at the time of the birth, his father or

494 A person who is not 'connected with' the child may be convicted as a secondary party or conspirator: *Sherry and El Yamani* [1993] Crim LR 537.

495 As defined in s 8(1) of the Children Act 1989.

496 As defined in s 3 of the Children Act 1989.

497 Note the amendments under the Adoption and Children Act 2002, s 139(1), not yet in force.

498 This means the child actually taken: *Berry* [1996] 2 Cr App R 226, [1996] Crim LR 574 where D, the father of S1, took S2, believing she was S1. For criticism see the commentary by J. C. Smith in [1996] Crim LR.

guardian, custodian or a person in whose favour a residence order is in force, without lawful authority or reasonable excuse, takes or detains the child –

(i) so as to remove him from the lawful control of any person having lawful control of him; or

(ii) so as to keep him out of the lawful control of any person entitled to lawful control of him.

There are therefore four ways in which the offences can be committed.

'Remove' does not require any 'geographical' removal – it is not the removal of the child but removal of control of the child which is material. 'Lawful control' is not defined in the Act and the courts have declined to define it. The concept varies according to the person said to have control – for example, parent, schoolteacher or nanny. A relevant question is whether the child was deflected by D from doing that to which his lawful controller had consented into some other activity. Has D substituted his authority or will for that of the lawful controller? There was evidence on which a jury could find that D had taken control where he persuaded a 14-year-old boy on his way home from school to go to D's flat,[499] and where he persuaded children to go with him to look for a bicycle which he said had been stolen.[500]

It is immaterial that the child consented to the lawful removal from the lawful control.[501]

The words 'so as to' are ambiguous. Two conflicting decisions have added to the confusion. In *Mousir*, the Court of Appeal held that the words import an element of *actus reus* (that D's conduct had the objective consequence of removing the child from lawful control) but not *mens rea* (that D intended to remove lawful control) but in the extradition case of *Re Owens*[502] the Divisional Court, without being referred to *Mousir*, concluded that proof of *mens rea* was required. The Divisional Court in *Foster*[503] recently favoured the conclusion in *Mousir*.

In *Mousir* the court held that D's conduct had to bring about a sufficient degree of interference with the lawful control of the child,[504] but that the concept of control did not require an assessment of the individual child's maturity. The conclusion that the words import such an element of *actus reus* seems, with respect to be correct in principle. The natural meaning of the term 'so as to' is 'with the effect of' removing the child from lawful control. It introduces a causal element additional to the *actus reus* of 'taking' or 'detaining'.[505] *Owens* does not contradict this. Simon Brown LJ stated that the words 'so as to mean 'with the intention of' rather than *merely* 'with the effect

499 *Mousir* [1987] Crim LR 561.

500 *Leather* (1993) 98 Cr App R 179.

501 *A* [2001] Cr App R 418.

502 [2000] 1 Cr App R 195.

503 [2004] EWHC 2955 (Admin), [2005] Crim LR (July).

504 Where, as in that case, the charge is one of attempt, so the issue is whether the acts are more than merely preparatory to that effect.

505 It is possible that D might remove or detain a child without lawful excuse but without causing him to be removed from lawful custody where D also removed or detained the lawful custodian.

of'.[506] In *Re Owens* the Divisional Court expressly held that D must 'intend' to interfere with another person's lawful control of the child.[507] The court in *Mousir* had accepted counsel's concession that the phrase did not import an element of *mens rea* – that D had knowledge as to the effect of his conduct being removal of the child from lawful control. Since the offence charged in that case was one of attempt, the element of intention would be required separately under the Criminal Attempts Act 1981.

In *Foster*,[508] the court concluded that the emphasis on *mens rea* in *Owens* was unnecessary to reach the result in that case, suggesting that *Owens* should have been treated as a case in which D had a lawful excuse rather than one in which she lacked *mens rea*. The court stated that the *mens rea* for the s 2 offence is:

> an intentional or reckless taking or detention of a child under the age of sixteen, the effect or objective consequence of which is to remove or to keep that child within the meaning of section 2(1)(a) or (b).

Article 8 of the Convention – the right to respect for private life – may impose positive obligations on the State to respect family life. This may include the State's providing safeguards against abduction.[509]

13. Offensive weapons

Legislation regulating the possession and use of firearms and offensive weapons is of major importance in the prevention of offences against the person. In earlier editions of this book (see the 6th edition at 416–422) an account was given of the principal offences under the Firearms Act 1968 and other legislation. This is omitted from the present edition and the reader is referred to *Archbold Crown Court* (2005), chapter 24, and *Blackstone's Criminal Practice*, s B12.[510]

Consideration is, however, given here to an important offence of general interest, that created by the Prevention of Crime Act 1953.

The Prevention of Crime Act 1953 is, according to its long title, 'An Act to prohibit the carrying of offensive weapons in public places, without lawful authority or reasonable excuse'.

The Act provides:

> 1–(1) Any person who without lawful authority or reasonable excuse, the proof whereof shall lie on him, has with him in any public place any offensive weapon shall be guilty of an offence, and shall be liable –

506 Emphasis added, at 201. 507 [2000] 1 Cr App R 195. 508 [2004] EWHC 2955 (Admin).

509 *Iglesias Gil and AIU v Spain*, 29 (2003) (App No 56673/00); *Maire v Portugal*, (2003) (App No 48206/99).

510 R. Shields, *Offensive Weapons* (2nd edn, 1996). The government recently released a wide ranging consultation paper on firearms offences: *Controls on Firearms* (2004) available from www.homeoffice.gov.uk/docs3/controls_on_firearms.pdf. Further up to date information on the prevalence and policing strategies against gun crime from www.homeoffice.gov.uk/crime/guncrime/index.html.

(a) on summary conviction, to imprisonment for a term not exceeding six months or a fine not exceeding [the statutory maximum], or both;

(b) on conviction on indictment, to imprisonment for a term not exceeding four years or a fine, or both.

(2) Where any person is convicted of an offence under subsection (1) of this section the court may make an order for the forfeiture or disposal of any weapon in respect of which the offence was committed.

(a) Offensive weapons

'Offensive weapon' is defined by s 1(4), as amended by the Public Order Act 1986, to mean 'any article made or adapted for use for causing injury to the person, or intended by the person having it with him for such use by him or by some other person'.

It will be noted that this definition is narrower than that of 'weapon of offence' in s 10(1)(b) of the Theft Act 1968. It does not include, as the Theft Act does, articles made, adapted or intended for *incapacitating* a person.[511]

There are three categories of offensive weapon: *Simpson*.[512]

(i) Articles *made for causing injury* would include a service rifle or bayonet, a revolver, a cosh, a truncheon,[513] knuckle-duster,[514] dagger, swordstick[515] or flick knife.[516] It has been held that the fact that rice flails are *used* as weapons is sufficient evidence that they are *made* for that purpose[517] but this seems doubtful. Whether an article is 'made for' causing injury requires the jury to consider whether it is of a kind which is generally speaking made for such use.[518] Categorization is a matter of fact, although judicial notice has been taken of the fact that flick-knives and butterfly knives are offensive *per se*.[519] The judge is entitled to direct the jury that this element of the offence is established, but never to direct a conviction *per se*.[520]

(ii) Articles *adapted for causing injury* would include razor blades inserted in a potato or cap-peak, a bottle broken for the purpose, a chair-leg studded with nails and so on. 'Adapted' probably means altered so as to become suitable.[521] It is not certain

511 Below, p 826. Smith, *Law of Theft* (7th edn, 1993), paras 11.33–11.39.

512 [1983] 1 WLR 1494.

513 *Houghton v Chief Constable of Greater Manchester* (1986) 84 Cr App R 319.

514 '. . . bludgeons, properly so-called, clubs and anything that is not in common use for any other purpose but a weapon are clearly offensive weapons within the meaning of the legislature' (the Smuggling Acts): (1784) 1 Leach 342 n (a).

515 *Butler* [1988] Crim LR 695.

516 An offensive weapon *per se* because judicially noticed as such *Simpson* [1983] 3 All ER 789, [1983] 1 WLR 1494; cf *Gibson v Wales* [1983] 1 All ER 869, [1983] Crim LR 113, DC and commentary; and *DPP v Hynde* [1998] Crim LR 72, DC (butterfly knife).

517 *Copus v DPP* [1989] Crim LR 577 and commentary. It was conceded at the trial in *Malnik* [1989] Crim LR 451 that a rice flail was an offensive weapon.

518 *Warne* [1997] 7 Archbold News 2.

519 See also the Criminal Justice Act 1988 (Offensive Weapons) Order 1988, SI 2019.

520 *Wang* [2005] UKHL 9; *Dhindsa* [2005] EWCA Crim 1198.

521 Cf *Davison v Birmingham Industrial Co-operative Society* (1920) 90 LJKB 206; *Flower Freight Co Ltd v Hammond* [1963] 1 QB 275, [1962] 3 All ER 950; and *Herrmann v Metropolitan Leather Co Ltd* [1942] Ch 248, [1942] 1 All ER 294; *Maddox v Storer* [1963] 1 QB 451, [1962] 1 All ER 831; *Formosa* (1990) 92 Cr App R 11, [1990] Crim LR 868, CA.

whether the intention of the adaptor is relevant.[522] Is an *accidentally* broken milk bottle 'adapted for use for causing injury to the person'? It is submitted that it is not and that if the article was not adapted with intent, it can only be an offensive weapon in the third category.

(iii) It is very important to distinguish the third category of articles which are neither made nor adapted for causing injury, but are carried for that purpose. Whether D carried the article with the necessary purpose is a question of fact.[523] Articles which have been held to be carried with such intent include a sheath-knife,[524] a shot-gun,[525] a razor,[526] a sandbag,[527] a pick-axe handle,[528] a stone,[529] and a drum of pepper.[530] *Any* article is capable of being an offensive weapon; but if it is of such a nature that it is unlikely to cause injury when brought into contact with the person, then the onus of proving the necessary intent will be very heavy.

(i) Articles adapted or intended by the carrier to injure himself

It was held by the Crown Court in *Bryan v Mott*[531] that a bottle broken for the purpose of committing suicide is 'adapted' for causing injury to the person. In *Fleming*,[532] on the other hand, the judge ruled that a large domestic carving knife carried by D to injure himself was not 'intended' for causing injury to the person: though the Act does not say 'another person', that is what it means. The view of the judge in *Fleming* is to be preferred. The question is whether the thing is 'an offensive weapon' and since 'offensive' implies an attack on *another* the injury which the adaptor or carrier must contemplate must be injury to another. The cases may, however, be distinguishable if 'adapt' does not imply any intention on the part of the adaptor. Breaking the milk bottle in fact makes it more suitable for injuring others, even if the adaptor intends injury only to himself. But such a distinction does not seem justified in principle.

(ii) Burdens of proof

In the case of articles 'made or adapted', the prosecution have to prove no more than possession in a public place.[533] D will then be convicted unless he can prove, on a balance of probability, that he had lawful authority or reasonable excuse.[534] But if the article falls into the third category the onus is on the prosecution to show that it was carried with intent to injure.[535] The prosecution must satisfy the jury that the article is either offensive *per se* (made or adapted) or, if it is not, that D had it with him with intent. If some of the jury think it is the one, and some the other, the case, it is submitted, is not made out.[536]

522 *Maddox v Storer* [1963] 1 QB 451, [1962] 1 All ER 831.
523 *Williamson* (1977) 67 Cr App R 35, [1978] Crim LR 229.
524 *Woodward v Koessler* [1958] 3 All ER 557.
525 *Gipson* [1956] Crim LR 281; *Hodgson* [1954] Crim LR 379.
526 *Petrie* [1961] 1 All ER 466; *Gibson v Wales* [1983] 1 All ER 869.
527 Ibid.
528 *Cugullere* [1961] 2 All ER 343.
529 *Harrison v Thornton* (1966) 68 Cr App R 28, [1966] Crim LR 388, DC.
530 120 JP 250. Also, no doubt, a stiletto heel which can be a very dangerous weapon: (1964) The Times, 25 Sept.
531 (1975) 62 Cr App R 71. The point was not decided by the Divisional Court.
532 [1989] Crim LR 71 (Judge Fricker QC).
533 *Davis v Alexander* (1970) 54 Cr App R 398.
534 See *L v DPP* [2003] QB 137.
535 *Petrie* [1961] 1 All ER 466; *Leer* [1982] Crim LR 310.
536 *Flynn* (1985) 82 Cr App R 319, [1986] Crim LR 239 and commentary.

(iii) The requisite intention

The question in *Woodward v Koessler*[537] was whether D intends to 'cause injury to the person' if he intends merely to frighten or intimidate by displaying a knife. It is now established that he does not. If there is no intention to cause physical injury, there must be an intention to cause injury by shock, a psychiatric injury – and only in very exceptional circumstances could evidence of such an intention be found.[538] A conditional intention to use the article is sufficient but it must be an intention to use the article in the future. If D sets out from Berkshire intending, if the occasion arises, to use a domestic knife for causing injury in Cornwall, the knife is an offensive weapon so long as it is carried in a public place and the intention continues. Once D believes that there is no possibility of the knife being used for causing injury – because, for example, his purpose has been accomplished – it ceases to be an offensive weapon.[539] It may, therefore, be no offence to carry the knife – whether or not it had been used – from Cornwall back to Berkshire. Recklessness as to use will not be sufficient *mens rea* for the offence.[540]

(iv) Offences of carrying not using

After some hesitation, the courts have construed the Act in the light of its long title. It is aimed at the *carrying* of offensive weapons *in public places.* It is not aimed at the actual *use* of the weapon, which can invariably be adequately dealt with under some other offence. In *Jura*[541] D was holding an air rifle at a shooting gallery when on a sudden provocation, he shot and wounded a woman. It was held that he had a reasonable excuse for *carrying* the rifle though not, of course, for using it in that way. But he had committed one offence, not two. It was as if a gamekeeper at a shooting party were suddenly to lose his temper and shoot at someone. If, then, D is lawfully in possession of the article, whether it be an offensive weapon *per se* or not, his decision unlawfully to use and immediate use of it does not amount to an offence under the Act. In *Dayle*[542] D took a car jack from the boot of his car and threw it at V in the course of a fight. In *Ohlson v Hylton*[543] D, a carpenter, took a hammer from his tool bag in the course of a fight and struck V. In neither case was D guilty of an offence under the Act.

It seems that if D is not in possession of the article until an occasion for its use arises and he then takes it up for immediate use, he commits no offence under the Act.[544] The law was so stated in *Ohlson v Hylton*:[545]

537 [1958] 3 All ER 557.

538 *Edmonds* [1963] 2 QB 142, [1963] 1 All ER 828; *Rapier* (1979) 70 Cr App R 17; *Snooks* [1997] Crim LR 230.

539 *Allamby* [1974] 3 All ER 126, CA. Cf *Ellames* [1974] 3 All ER 130.

540 See *Byrne* [2003] EWCA Crim 3253, [2004] Crim LR 582 and commentary.

541 [1954] 1 QB 503, [1954] 1 All ER 696, CA.

542 [1973] 3 All ER 1151.

543 [1975] 2 All ER 490, DC. See also *Police v Smith* [1974] 2 NZLR 32 (guest in restaurant using table knife offensively); *Humphreys* [1977] Crim LR 225, CA (penknife).

544 A point seemingly overlooked in *Byrne* [2004] Crim LR 582.

545 [1975] 2 All ER 490 at 496. The requirement that the intention to use the weapon has to be formed before the occasion of its use has been reaffirmed recently in *Veasey* [1999] Crim LR 158 and *C v DPP* [2002] Crim LR 202 with commentaries by J. C. Smith.

To support a conviction under the Act the prosecution must show that the defendant was carrying or otherwise equipped with the weapon, and had the intent to use it offensively before any occasion for its actual use had arisen.[546]

This interpretation avoids the formidable difficulty which would otherwise arise where D picks up an article in the course of a fight, allegedly for self-defence. The onus of proving that this was an unreasonable step for the purposes of self-defence is on the Crown but, if it was capable of being an offence under the Act, it would be for D to prove he had a reasonable excuse.

(v) Duration of offence

An 'occasion' has a beginning and it must also have an end.[547] If D picks up a glass to defend himself in the course of a pub brawl he does not commit an offence under the Act; but suppose, when the fight is over, he declines to put the glass down and insists on carrying it home through two miles of streets? Probably the 'occasion' has come to an end, and the question is whether D has a reasonable excuse.

(b) Lawful authority or reasonable excuse

It may be that the existence of lawful authority is a pure question of law, whereas whether there is a reasonable excuse is a question of fact, subject to the usual judicial control.[548]

'Lawful authority' presents difficulties. Before the Act, it was presumably generally lawful to be in possession of an offensive weapon in a public place – otherwise there would have been no necessity for the Act. Now it is generally unlawful. 'Lawful authority' postulates some legal exception to the general rule of the Act; yet none is provided for and the words themselves are certainly not self-explanatory. In *Bryan v Mott* Lord Widgery CJ said[549] that 'lawful authority' refers to those 'people who from time to time carry an offensive weapon as a matter of duty – the soldier with his rifle and the police officer with his truncheon.' It seems that the 'duty' must be a public one – an employer cannot authorize his employees to carry offensive weapons simply by getting them to contract to do so.

Whether there is a reasonable excuse is said to depend on whether a reasonable man would think it excusable to carry the weapon[550] and in *Butler*[551] D's argument that he had a reasonable excuse because he never considered whether the swordstick he was carrying was an article made or adapted for causing injury was left to the jury; but that may have been too generous. What did he suppose a swordstick was for, if not injuring people? A possible answer is that he thought it was made as a curio or 'collector's item'. Generally the courts have construed the provision strictly and exercised close control over magistrates and juries. It is not enough that D's intentions were entirely lawful.[552]

A belief, however reasonable and honest, that an extendible baton (an offensive weapon) is an aerial or some other innocent article is not a reasonable excuse.[553] It is not

546 *Powell* [1963] Crim LR 511, CCA, and *Harrison v Thornton* [1966] Crim LR 388, DC, appear to be wrongly decided in the light of this principle.

547 Cf *Giles* [1976] Crim LR 253 (Judge Jones).

548 *Peacock* [1973] Crim LR 639; *Leer* [1982] Crim LR 310, CA.

549 (1975) 62 Cr App R 71 at 73, DC.

550 *Bryan v Mott*, above, p 584, n 531.

551 [1988] Crim LR 695.

552 *Bryan v Mott*, above.

553 *Densu* [1998] 1 Cr App R 400, [1998] Crim LR 345.

necessarily a reasonable excuse that the weapon is carried only for self-defence. D must show that there was 'an imminent particular threat affecting the particular circumstances in which the weapon was carried'.[554] One who is under constant threat it is said, must resort to the police. He commits an offence if he regularly goes out armed for self-defence.[555] So there was held to be no excuse for carrying an iron bar though D had reasonable cause to fear and did fear that he would be violently attacked and intended to use the bar for defence only.[556] It is not reasonable for an Edinburgh taxi driver to carry two feet of rubber hose with a piece of metal inserted at one end, though he does so for defence against violent passengers whom taxi drivers sometimes encounter at night.[557] It has been held that possession of a broken milk-bottle (an article adapted for causing injury) is not excused by the fact that D intended to use it to commit suicide.[558] It is an offence for security guards at dance halls to carry a truncheon 'as a deterrent' and as 'part of the uniform'.[559]

Unlawful possession may become lawful if circumstances change so as to give rise to a reasonable excuse. When a person is attacked he may use anything that he can lay his hands on to defend himself, so long as he uses no more force than is reasonable in the circumstances. It may be reasonable to use an offensive weapon that he is unlawfully carrying. When Butler[560] was viciously attacked, his use of the swordstick to defend himself was justified or excused, so possession of it must have become lawful, but that could not undo the offence already committed.[561] The narrow interpretation of reasonable excuse may qualify the important principle that a person cannot be driven off the streets and compelled not to go to a public place where he might lawfully be because he will be confronted by people intending to attack him.[562] If he decides that he cannot go to that place unless armed with an offensive weapon, it seems that he must stay away. He commits an offence if he goes armed.[563]

Where D had an explanation for possession of the weapon for example, by putting it in his work trousers and forgetting 'that he was wearing those trousers' and was found in possession in public, the defence of a reasonable excuse ought still have been to be left to the jury.[564] Forgetfulness alone is not a sufficient good reason, but coupled with other factors may be and should be left to the jury.[565]

The imposition of a burden of proof on the defendant can cause great difficulty where he is charged in a second count with another offence which imposes no such burden. In *Snooks and Sergeant*[566] DD were also charged with possessing an explosive, contrary to OAPA, s 64. They relied on self-defence. For s 64, the onus was on the prosecution, under the 1953 Act the onus is on DD. The jury have an impossible task.

554 *Evans v Hughes* [1972] 3 All ER 412 at 415, DC; *Evans v Wright* [1964] Crim LR 466.

555 For a comparative view see D. Lanham, 'Offensive Weapons and Self Defence' [2005] Crim LR 85.

556 Ibid. See also *Bradley v Moss* [1974] Crim LR 430, DC; *Pittard v Mahoney* [1977] Crim LR 169, DC.

557 *Grieve v MacLeod* (1967) SLT 70.

558 *Bryan v Mott*, above. See also *Bown* [2003] EWCA Crim 1989 [2004] 1 Cr App R 13, decided under the 1988 Act, s 139.

559 *Spanner* [1973] Crim LR 704.

560 Above, n 551.

561 Smith, *Justification and Excuse* (1989), at 117–123.

562 *Field* [1972] Crim LR 435.

563 *Malnik v DPP* [1989] Crim LR 451, DC.

564 *Bird* [2004] EWCA Crim 964.

565 *Jolie* [2004] EWCA Crim 1543.

566 [1997] Crim LR 230.

(c) A 'public place'

Section 1(4) of the Prevention of Crime Act 1953 provides:

'public place' includes any highway and any other premises or place to which at the material time the public have or are permitted to have access whether on payment or otherwise.

This is very similar to the interpretation which has been placed upon s 192 of the Road Traffic Act 1988 and to the definition of public place, etc in other Acts. It should always be borne in mind that the same term may bear different meanings according to the context in which it is found and that whether a place is public is a question of fact.[567]

A public place could not include land adjoining that to which the public had access even if D could have inflicted harm from such land.[568] A householder impliedly invites persons having legitimate business to walk up his garden path to the door, but this does not render the garden a 'public place'. The class of persons invited to enter is too restricted for them to constitute 'the public'.[569] On the other hand, the communal landing of a block of flats has been held to be a public place on the ground that the public had access in fact, whether or not they were permitted to have it.[570] In the absence of a notice restricting entry, there was evidence on which justices could find that the unrestricted access of the public to a council estate extended to the stairways and landings of the flats.[571] The jury are, of course, entitled to draw reasonable inferences; so that where D produced an air pistol in a private dwelling-house which he was visiting, it was open to them to infer that he brought it to or took it away from the house through the public street.[572]

(d) Possession and *mens rea*

In order to prove that D 'has with him' the article, the prosecution must prove that minimum mental element which is necessary to constitute possession, as well as that 'closer contact' than mere possession which the phrase implies.[573] The question then is whether the offence is one of strict liability or whether any *mens rea* is required. In *Cugullere*[574] it was held that the phrase means 'knowingly has with him' and, while it is certainly arguable that the court was concerned only with the question of possession, this was held in a reserved judgment in *Russell*[575] to mean that the court was 'applying the general principle of responsibility which makes it incumbent on the prosecution to prove full *mens rea*'. This decision was misunderstood in *Martindale*,[576] followed in *McCalla*,[577] which treated *Russell* as simply a decision, and therefore a wrong decision, on the meaning of possession. The prevailing view, therefore, is that the offence is one of strict liability; but the better opinion is that *Russell*, though treated as overruled, should be

567 *Theodolou* [1963] Crim LR 573.

568 *Roberts* [2004] 1 Cr App R 16; [2003] EWCA Crim 2753 (garden 1m wide).

569 *Edwards and Roberts* (1978) 67 Cr App R 228, [1978] Crim LR 564 (a case under s 5 of the Public Order Act 1936).

570 *Knox v Anderton* (1982) 76 Cr App R 156, [1983] Crim LR 114, DC, and commentary. But, a place is not a public place simply because the public are not excluded: *Harriott v DPP* [2005] EWHC 965 (Admin).

571 See also *Hanrahan* [2004] All ER (D) 144 (Nov), rehabilitation centre to which access gained through intercom.

572 *Mehmed* [1963] Crim LR 780.

573 *McCalla* (1988) 87 Cr App R 372 at 378.

574 [1961] 2 All ER 343.

575 (1984) 81 Cr App R 315.

576 (1986) 84 Cr App R 31.

577 Above, n 18.

regarded as the binding authority.[578] In the recent case of *Jolie*[579] D was found in possession of a knife in a car he was driving and claimed that he had forgotten it was there although he admitted putting it there as he had used it to start the broken ignition. Kennedy LJ suggested that in the cases of *McCalla, Martindale* and *Buswell* it had been clear that the article had remained under D's control. His lordship suggested that the jury should be directed that they may find possession if either D was aware of the presence of the weapon or he was responsible for putting it where it was mislaid. The court offered two examples of facts on which there might be a valid good reason based on forgetfulness: a parent who, having bought a kitchen knife, put it in the glove compartment of a car out of the reach of a child (reason 1), forgetting (reason 2) later to retrieve it. Similarly as in *Glidewell*[580] where a taxi driver discovered weapons left by a passenger (reason 1), and forgot to remove because he was busy (reason 2).

As regards the relevant *mens rea* as to the offensiveness of the weapon, in *Densu*[581] counsel abandoned an argument before the Court of Appeal that the ruling of the trial judge was wrong in so far as it suggested that the proof that D has with him is satisfied on proof that D knew that he had the weapon (a baton) with him but did not know that it was a weapon. The prevailing view is that liability is strict.

(e) Articles with blades or points

The Prevention of Crime Act is supplemented by an offence triable either way punishable on summary conviction by six months', and, on indictment, by two years' imprisonment under the Criminal Justice Act 1988, s 139, of having with one in a public place an article 'which has a blade[582] or is sharply pointed except a folding pocket knife[583] [with a cutting edge not exceeding three inches]'. The article need not be made or adapted for causing injury, nor intended by D for such use. The fact that a blade might be used for other functions than as a weapon (for example, Swiss Army knife) does not mean that it is not *prima facie* a bladed article within s 139.[584] Otherwise, the constituents of the offence are similar to those required by the 1953 Act. It is a defence for D to prove that he had *good reason* or lawful authority for having the article with him. In *Jolie* the court regarded the words 'good reason' in the 1988 Act as intended to be narrower than 'reasonable excuse' 1953 Act. The court concluded that the words 'good reason' do not generally require a judicial gloss in directing the jury.

Self-defence against an anticipated imminent attack may be a good reason.[585] In *Davis*,[586] the court thought that the section imposed 'a very significant limitation on the citizen's freedom. It should not be assumed that it has been achieved except by the use of

578 See commentary on *Wright* [1992] Crim LR 596.

579 [2003] EWCA Crim 1543, [2003] Crim LR 730.

580 (1999) 163 JP 557.

581 [1998] 1 Cr App R 400.

582 This probably means a blade which has a cutting edge. A screwdriver, even if it may be properly described as having a blade, is not within the section: *Davis* [1998] Crim LR 564.

583 Which means a knife which is 'readily and indeed immediately foldable at all times, simply by the folding process': *Fehmi v DPP* (1993) 96 Cr App R 235, DC, so that a pocket knife which locks into position is not 'folding': *Deegan* [1998] 2 Cr App R 121, [1998] Crim LR 562.

584 *Giles* [2003] All ER (D) 68 (Feb).

585 *Emmanuel* [1998] Crim LR 347.

586 [1998] Crim LR 564. Contrast the attitude of the court in *Deegan*, above, n 583.

clear words.' It is specifically provided that it is a defence for D to prove that he had the article with him for use at work,[587] religious reasons,[588] or as part of national costume. It is necessary to prove that he had it with him for a specific reason *in public* on this occasion.[589]

A new s 139A was inserted by the Offensive Weapons Act 1996, creating offences of having on school premises (i) an article to which s 139 applies (punishable on indictment with two years' imprisonment) and (ii) an offensive weapon within the meaning of the Prevention of Crime Act 1953 (punishable on indictment with four years' imprisonment). It is a defence to both offences to prove 'good reason or lawful authority'.

14. Hoax offences

(a) Bomb hoaxes: Criminal Law Act 1977[590]

The bomb hoax, always irritating and sometimes frightening, was dealt with in a variety of ways before 1977. If a demand were made by the hoaxer, it might be treated as blackmail.[591] If, as is usually the case, it involved a threat to damage property, s 2 of the Criminal Damage Act 1971[592] might be invoked. In other cases, the hoax amounted to the offence of wasting the time of the police.[593] On one occasion at least, the clumsy weapon of public nuisance was used.[594] The Criminal Law Act 1977, s 51, now provides a special offence.

> 51–(1) A person who –
>
> (a) places any article in any place whatever; or
>
> (b) dispatches any article by post, rail or any other means whatever of sending things from one place to another, with the intention (in either case) of inducing in some other person a belief that it is likely to explode or ignite and thereby cause personal injury or damage to property is guilty of an offence.
>
> In this subsection 'article' includes substance.
>
> (2) A person who communicated any information which he knows or believes to be false to another person with the intention of inducing in him or any other person a false belief that a bomb or other thing liable to explode or ignite is present in any place or location whatever is guilty of an offence.
>
> (3) For a person to be guilty of an offence under subsection (1) or (2) above it is not necessary for him to have any particular person in mind as the person in whom he intends to induce the belief mentioned in that subsection.

587 A question of fact for the jury: *Manning* [1998] Crim LR 198 (knife carried to do repairs to D's own car).

588 Which must be the dominant reason: *Wang* [2003] EWCA Crim 3228. D must show that the religion was the reason for his possession on this occasion, ie that he was to use it in some religious connection. The court acknowledged, *per curiam*, that Article 9 of the ECHR might require the State authorities to allow persons to carry bladed instruments in public in pursuit of their religious beliefs.

589 *Giles*, above.

590 See C. Walker, *The Prevention of Terrorism in British Law* (2nd edn, 1992), ch 12.

591 Below, 802. *King* [1976] Crim LR 200.

592 Below, 000. *Farrell* [1976] Crim LR 318.

593 Criminal Law Act 1967, s 5(2). *Bikram* [1974] Crim LR 55.

594 *Madden* [1975] 3 All ER 155, CA; below, p 994.

(4) A person guilty of an offence under this section shall be liable –

(a) on summary conviction, to imprisonment for a term not exceeding six months or to a fine not exceeding the prescribed sum, or both;

(b) on conviction on indictment, to imprisonment for a term not exceeding five years.

The gist of the offences is the *mens rea*. The *actus reus* of s 51(1)(a) is an act which everyone does every day. Under s 51(2) the information communicated may in fact be true; it is sufficient that D believes it to be false. If he believes that the information is, or may possibly be, true, then it obviously cannot be an offence to pass it on.

(b) Hoaxes relating to biological weapons[595]

Section 51 does not deal with hoaxes involving things that do not 'ignite or explode', such as sending powders or liquids through the post and claiming that they are harmful. Section 114 of the Anti-Terrorism, Crime and Security Act 2001 fills that gap. It is an offence to place anywhere or send any substance or article intending to make others believe that that it is likely to be or contain a noxious substance or thing which could endanger human life or health. A further offence is provided by subs (2) for a person to falsely communicate any information to another that a noxious substance or thing is or will be in a place and so likely to cause harm to endanger human life or health. The offences are triable either way. On summary conviction the maximum sentence is six months, or a fine up to the statutory maximum or both. On conviction on indictment a person may be imprisoned for up to seven years, or fined or both.

Section 113 of the Anti-Terrorism Crime and Security Act 2001 makes it an offence for a person to use or threaten to use a biological, chemical, radioactive or other noxious substance to cause various kinds of serious harm in a manner designed to influence the government or to intimidate the public. The maximum sentence is 14 years' imprisonment.

595 See C. Walker, *The Anti-Terrorism Legislation* (2002), at 165–169.

17

Sexual offences[1]

1. Introduction

The Sexual Offences Act 2003 Act came into force on 1 May 2004.[2] The Act represents the most comprehensive and radical overhaul of the law relating to sexual offences ever undertaken in England and Wales. Previously, most of the relevant law was contained in the Sexual Offences Act 1956, but that was itself merely a consolidation of various statutes dating back to the late nineteenth century, and the 1956 Act had been amended incrementally to meet numerous specific problems.[3] The 2003 Act redefines many of the offences found in the old legislation, but introduces scores of new offences. It is not however a complete codification of sexual offences; some regulation remains elsewhere – for example that relating to prostitution[4] and indecent photographs.[5]

(a) The need for new law

There had been a growing level of concern over the effectiveness of the 1956 Act. It was described by one commentator as 'cumbersome and inadequate',[6] and by Lord Falconer when introducing the Bill as 'archaic, incoherent and discriminatory'.[7] This was a widely, though not universally held view. Despite the sometimes dramatic incremental development, both at common law[8] and by legislation,[9] the protection offered against

[1] See generally on the Act: P. Rook and R. Ward, *Sexual Offences: Law and Practice* (2004); R. Card, *Sexual Offences: The New Law* (2004); K. Stevenson, A. Davies and M. Gunn, *Blackstone's Guide to the Sexual Offences Act 2003* (2004).

[2] Where the prosecution has not demonstrated whether the events constituting the charge occurred before or after this date, it has been held that the prosecution cannot continue: *R v Newbon* [2005] Crim LR (Sept). (HHJ Glenn). This may pose problems for a few historic sexual abuse cases.

[3] For a statement of the previous law see the 10th edition, ch 16.

[4] See especially ss 33–36 of the Sexual Offences Act 1956. The Home Office has begun a consultation process on prostitution – *Paying the Price* (2004).

[5] See the Protection of Children Act 1978.

[6] J. Temkin, 'Getting it right: sexual offences law reform' (2000) 150 NLJ 1169, and see J. Temkin, *Rape and the Legal Process* (2nd edn, 2002).

[7] HL, vol 644, col 771.

[8] For example the House of Lords in *R v R* [1992] 1 AC 599 declaring that the historical exception whereby a man could not be found guilty of raping his wife was finally abolished. For a detailed history see J. Temkin, *Rape and Legal Process* (2nd edn, 2002), 72–89; M. Giles, 'Judicial Law-Making in the Criminal Courts: The Case of Marital Rape' [1992] Crim LR 407.

[9] Eg rape was extended to include non-consensual anal intercourse with a person of either sex by the Criminal Justice and Public Order Act 1994, s 142; the jurisdictional reaches of the English criminal law were extended by the Sexual Offences (Conspiracy and Incitement) Act 1996 to criminalize sex tourism (on which see P. Alldridge, 'The Sexual Offences (Conspiracy and Incitement) Act 1986' [1997] Crim LR 30.) Other significant statutory involvement included the Sexual Offences (Amendment) Act 2000, on which see J. Burnside, 'The Sexual Offences (Amendment) Act 2000: The head of a "kiddy-libber" and the torso of a "child-saver"?' [2001] Crim LR 425.

sexual offences remained unsatisfactory. One consequence of the continued incremental development of the law was its incoherence. In more general terms, it was recognized that the 1956 Act failed adequately to reflect the morality and prevalent sexual attitudes and practices of the twenty-first century. It provided inadequate protection for the vulnerable whilst also failing to respect the sexual autonomy of those capable of making informed choices about their sexual behaviour.[10] Moreover, the language used throughout the legislation was archaic and in some instances offensively inappropriate as, for example, with the references to 'defectives' rather than people with learning disabilities and mental disorder. Many essential terms such as 'consent' and 'capacity' remained ill-defined, and in addition, some elements of the previous law were so discriminatory as to be incompatible with ECHR obligations: for example, criminalizing consensual homosexual intercourse. Other offences such as gross indecency between males breached Article 8,[11] and there is the broader ECHR obligation for the State to provide adequate and effective rape legislation.[12]

Recognition of the unsatisfactory nature of the law extended beyond the legal community. Greater public awareness of the nature and effect of sexual assaults on victims coupled with the increase in reporting of sexual crimes rendered awareness of the Act's failings increasingly acute. Research into the process of prosecuting rapes and the decreasing conviction rates[13] had generated considerable public unease.[14] It was felt that this failing was in part a consequence of the inadequacies of the substantive law as well as of the shortcomings of the law of evidence and procedure.[15]

(b) The reform process

Previous reform proposals including the *Fifteenth Report* of the CLRC had been largely ignored.[16] The 2003 Act began with a more fundamental review: the Home Office Review of sex offences, *Setting the Boundaries*;[17] and the *Review of Part 1 of the Sex Offenders Act 1997*.[18] Following consultation, these led to a Government White Paper, *Protecting the Public: strengthening protection against sex offenders and reforming the law on sexual offences*.[19] The Review drew upon a wide range of expertise including non-legal advice from relevant agencies (NSPCC, Dept of Health, Victim Support, etc) and on the

10 There is a growing jurisprudential literature on sexual behaviour and the significance of consent. See in particular, N. Lacey, *Unspeakable Subjects* (1998); S. Schulhofer, *Unwanted Sex: the culture of intimidation and the failure of law* (1998); J. Horder and S. Shute, 'The Wrongness of Rape', in J. Horder, *Oxford Essays in Jurisprudence* (2000); M. Childs, 'Sexual Autonomy and the Law' (2001) 64 MLR 309 and references therein.

11 See *ADT v UK* (2000) 31 EHRR 803.

12 *MC v Bulgaria* [2003] ECHR 39272/98.

13 Setting the Boundaries; *Reforming the law on sexual offences* (July 2000), Home Office, paras 2.3, and 2.8.5. See Temkin, above, 1–3 and 60–67.

14 The conviction rates fell from 1/3 to 1/13 between 1997 and 1999. See *Report of the Joint Investigation into the Investigation and Prosecution of Cases Involving Allegations of Rape* (2002) HMCPSI. See also A. Myhill and J. Allen, *Rape and Sexual Assault on Women: The Extent and Nature of the Problem – findings from the British Crime Survey* (2002) HORS No 237.

15 As addressed in the Youth Justice and Criminal Evidence Act 1999.

16 CLRC, *Fifteenth Report, Sexual Offences* (1984), Cmnd 9213; B. Hogan, 'On Modernising the Law of Sexual Offences', in P. Glazebrook (ed), *Reshaping the Criminal Law* 174; J. Temkin, 'Towards a Modern Law of Rape' (1982) MLR 399.

17 (2000). See N. Lacey, 'Beset by Boundaries' [2001] Crim LR 3; J. Temkin, *Rape and the Legal Process*, at 60–67.

18 (2001).

19 Cm 5668 2002.

extensive research into offending patterns, the impact of offending on victims, etc. It produced 62 recommendations, with its main themes being to refocus the law on the critical issues: (a) consent and protection of sexual autonomy and (b) providing special protection for vulnerable individuals and children. Although very wide ranging, some regarded the Review as inadequate for its failure to address issues such as prostitution and pornography generally. The government, in its subsequent legislative proposals in *Protecting the Public*,[20] adopted many proposals but took a stricter approach to sentencing and was prepared to place burdens on the defence in relation to serious offences.

Since enactment in November 2003, a further string of consultation papers on the Act have been published.[21] Despite the legislative and subsequent attempts to define the minutiae of each offence there remains considerable work for the courts in clarifying fundamental issues – not least the scope of the definition of consent and the relevant *mens rea* in rape.

(c) The Sexual Offences Act 2003

The Act divides into three Parts, only the first of which deals with substantive criminal law. That Part alone creates numerous new offences, and it is impossible to deal with all of those in any detail. The laudable aims of the Review cannot be criticized. Unfortunately whilst achieving some of those aims, such as a measure of gender neutrality[22] and modernization of the language, the Act creates numerous difficulties, many of a significant and substantial nature.

The Act takes 80 sections to set out the many new offences, and these often contain numerous sub-categories of offence. For example, many involve aggravated versions for penetrative acts, and since these are indictable only and carry a different sentence, following *Courtie*[23] each represents a separate offence.

Although it might be argued that it is better to have too many offences than too few in an area of law as serious as this, it is questionable whether tighter drafting and structure could have achieved adequate protection. This is not just a criticism levelled at the length of the Act; substantive problems arise when there are too many charging options. It produces confusion and inhibits optimal development of case law, with no guarantee that similar conduct will be treated consistently by the CPS and by courts. The CPS guidelines[24] state that:

> Prosecutors should choose the most appropriate charge to fit the circumstances of the case, taking account of the courts' sentencing powers. As a general rule, where the circumstances of a case match a particular offence specified in the Act, this offence should be charged, for example s 25 (familial child sex offence) where the victim is 14 should be charged rather than s 9 (sexual activity with a child), so long as all the elements can be proved.

In some instances, it would appear that the objective in including a new crime is to trigger the availability of possible sexual offender orders under Part 2 of the Act. This reliance on so many offences is especially ironic given that the Sexual Offences Review was described

[20] Described by Lord Ackner in the Debates as a 'pamphlet': HL, col 846, 13 Feb 2003.

[21] *Sexual Offences Bill: Government Proposals on the Issue of Sex Offenders who Travel Abroad* (Home Office, 2003), www.homeoffice.gov.uk/docs/travel_abroad.pdf. See also the HO Circular 21/2004 on Part 1 of the Act.

[22] Cf the Gender Recognition Act 2004 relating to gender specific offences.

[23] [1984] AC 463.

[24] www.cps.gov.uk/legal/section7/sexoffencesact2003.html.

as seeking to 'focus the law more sharply' and 'to abolish the unnecessary and useless offences which have accumulated over the years'.[25]

There are many examples of the Act providing overbroad offences. One simple example is s 62 'committing an offence with intent to commit a sexual offence'. This contains no limitation to the types of offence and no requirement that the preliminary offence is directed at the person who will be the victim of the sex offence.[26]

The Act makes use of strict liability in many contexts – most notably the offences committed against children under 13. There is a clear and legitimate objective in providing protection against sexual exploitation for young people. However, the use of strict liability, to render irrelevant an offender's belief in consent or the age of his 'victim', *may* be problematic both as a matter of justice, and as an issue under Article 6 of the ECHR. These problems may be exacerbated by the failure in the Act to distinguish between young and other offenders. Lord Millett's recent observations in the House of Lords in *R v K* go unheeded: 'the age of consent has long ceased to reflect ordinary life, and in this respect Parliament has signally failed to discharge its responsibility for keeping the criminal law in touch with the needs of society.'[27]

The government claimed that it was not seeking to prosecute consensual conduct between youths that was not previously prosecuted. Given the much wider range of conduct that gives rise to the potential for prosecution this is doubtful. Under the old law the main protection for under-16s derived from the offences of indecent assault and unlawful sexual intercourse. The 2003 Act criminalizes a broader range of consensual sexual activities (such as watching sexual activity). Moreover, even if the new offences were no broader and not prosecuted more frequently, this is not an adequate justification for creation of offences criminalizing consensual sexual activity (short of penetration) between minors and carrying a maximum of 14 years. The Act is supposed to modernize the law and to reflect the sexual mores of the twenty-first century.[28]

Implementing broad offences in the context of sexual conduct also poses a danger in the message it sends to society. Criminalization sends conflicting messages to young members of society. In general, the new Act seeks to encourage and re-educate people about the significance of respecting the autonomy of individuals by obtaining their consent.[29] But with children under 16 that message may be undermined by a starker one – even if you do act responsibly, seek and gain consent, you will commit a serious offence.

The clarity and complexity of the Act is not always assisted by the innovative drafting style – 'it is an offence for a person (A) to behave in a specified way to a person (B)' which achieves gender neutrality but is not used consistently throughout the Act.[30]

25 J. Temkin (2000) 150 NLJ 1169.

26 A, 18, criminally damaging the condom machine to gain condoms to have consensual sex with B, 15, commits the offence.

27 [2001] UKHL 41, [44]. On the House of Lords' approach to strict liability and age in sexual offences see J. Horder, 'How Culpability Can and Can't be Denied in Under Age Sex Crimes' [2001] Crim LR 15.

28 The Sentencing Advisory Panel recommends that sexual touching of a child by a person under 18 should receive a supervision order for a first offence of touching the breasts or buttocks over the 'victim's' clothes.

29 On the criminal law's role in facilitating conditions in which autonomy can be promoted, see N. Lacey, *Unspeakable Subjects* (1998), p 151.

30 On the importance of gender neutrality see P. Rumney and M. Morgan–Taylor, 'Recognising the Male Victim: Gender Neutrality and the Law of Rape' (1997) 26 Anglo American Law Review 198. Throughout this chapter 'A' will be used to denote the principal defendant and 'B' the complainant.

Many of the provisions attempt to describe in tremendous detail the relevant elements of offences. This obsession with detail and with the manner in which the offence is committed rather than with the harm caused shows commendable respect for the principles of fair labelling and maximum certainty, but it creates confusion and density[31] in the legislation which renders it less accessible than it ought to be.[32]

An example of this detail can be seen for example in s 67 (voyeurism) – A, for the purpose of obtaining sexual gratification, observes or records or enables another to observe (with equipment or otherwise) B doing a 'private act' knowing B does not consent to observation for that purpose. By s 68 'private acts' are those 'in a private structure in which one would expect privacy and B's genitals, buttocks or breasts are exposed or covered only with underwear, or B is using the lavatory, or B is doing a sexual act not of a kind ordinarily done in public! This obsession with exhaustive definition is sadly lacking in some of the key definitions of fundamental issues such as 'consent'.

Parliament received repeated Ministerial assurances that the volume, strictness and breadth of the offences would not lead to over-criminalization in practice because the CPS would exercise their discretion not to prosecute.[33] Aside from the fact that the Act leaves some very hard decisions to be made (will a prosecution for 'rape' of a child under 13 be dropped – perhaps where B was consenting to oral sex with her 12-year-old boyfriend?), in terms of principle, it is undesirable that such significant issues are a matter of discretion not law. As the Joint Parliamentary Committee on Human Rights observed in the *Twelfth Report*,

> Creating catch all offences and then relying on the prosecutor's discretion to sort things out satisfactorily undermines [the rule of law]. It leaves prosecutors to do the job that Parliament should be doing, and gives them discretion to prosecute (or not to prosecute) people who ought never to have been within the scope of criminal liability in the first place.[34]

The exercise of discretion will arise not just with child offences but in many situations involving serious offences including for example consenting sexual penetration between adult relatives and cases of mentally disordered individuals who engage consensually in sexual practices together.

In ECHR terms the Act is only a partial success. Although the Act succeeds in removing several incompatible offences (gross indecency, buggery, etc), it creates new problems of ECHR incompatibility. One of the most obvious and heavily criticized examples, is the criminalization of sexual conduct between consenting children, particularly those aged 13–16. It is possible that a child who was a willing participant to sexual conduct (which includes activity as limited as kissing) with another could claim an infringement of his/her Article 8 rights to respect for private life. There is surely no question that Article 8 is engaged when the law seeks to regulate a person's sexual behaviour.[35] Moreover, the fact

31 See the definition of foster siblings at s 27 for an example.

32 Other memorable examples include the degree of detail in defining offences such as intercourse with an animal, where the Act goes so far as to extend the definition to the 'vagina or anus' to include references 'to any similar part' in animals – eg those functionally equivalent body parts in amphibians and crustaceans.

33 The CPS policy is available from www.cps.gov.uk/legal/section7/sexoffencesact2003.htm.

34 Para 2.11.

35 *Laskey v UK* (1997) 24 EHRR 39; *Sutherland v UK* (1997) 24 EHRR CD22; but cf *E v DPP* (2005) WL 62315, in which the Divisional Court saw no infringement of Article 8 by the offence under s 6 of the Sexual Offences Act 1956 – unlawful sexual intercourse with a girl under 16.

that a person is exposed to the risk of prosecution is sufficient to constitute an interference with Article 8 (any CPS policy against prosecution may be inadequate to save the offence from ECHR challenge).[36] Although the offence may be sufficiently clearly prescribed in the statute, it is doubtful whether it is 'necessary' and 'proportionate' to a legitimate aim such as the protection of health or morals, or the protection of the rights and freedoms of others. Necessity is a strict requirement, based on whether there is a pressing social need.[37] The Parliamentary Joint Committee on Human Rights[38] suggested that some sections of the Act were overbroad in criminalizing all sexual touching of children.

Article 6 also poses a possible problem. Although the orthodox interpretation[39] of Article 6 is that it is restricted to process and not substantive law, it is arguable that the removal of the element of consent from the offences creates an implicit presumption of non-consent. Arguably this is an 'evidential' issue, and not one of (mere) 'substantive' law, and Article 6 thus applies.

Another unfortunate feature of the Act is that it perpetuates the growing trend of creating 'quasi crimes' – civil orders that are backed by a criminal sanction for breach. These have become a common feature – ASBO, Football Banning Order, exclusion order, etc – and they pose many problems.[40] The 2003 Act introduces new orders including FTO (Foreign Travel Orders), SOPO (Sexual Offence Prevention Orders), and RSHO (Risk of Sexual Harm Orders).[41]

There is a danger that the Act will be seen as a panacea for the problems of investigating and prosecuting sexual offences, and for the high attrition rates. There are deeper underlying causes for the prevalence of sex offences, the reluctance to report, and the problems of proof at trial.[42] Redefining rape to include non-consensual oral sex and all penile penetration of under-13s irrespective of consent will in one way increase the number of rape convictions. Similarly, in relation to child pornography, by raising to 18 the age of those who must not be photographed in circumstances of indecency, the defence will be much less likely to succeed in claiming that they believed the pubescent child was above that age.

The volume of offences and the minute definition of many elements produce some glaring examples of incoherence. One of the most blatant is that although a person can engage in sexual activity at 16, it is still illegal to have a relationship with her/his carer until over 18, or to engage in sexual conduct with certain members of the extended family even though s/he could marry them. Similarly, whilst it is legal to have sexual intercourse

36 *Norris v Ireland* (1991) 13 EHRR 186.

37 *Dudgeon v UK* (1981) 4 EHRR 149.

38 *Twelfth Report 2002–3 Scrutiny of Bills: Further Progress Report* 2003 (HL 119; HC 765).

39 *Barnfather v London Borough of Islington Education Authority, Secretary of State for Education and Skills* [2003] EWHC 418, [2003] 1 WLR 2318. For discussion, see B. Fitzpatrick, 'Strict liability and Article 6(2) of the European Convention on Human Rights: School Non-Attendance Offence (2004) 68 *Journal of Criminal Law* 16–24.

40 See generally A. Ashworth, 'Social Control and Anti-Social Behaviour: the Subversion of Human Rights?' (2004) 120 LQR 263.

41 See S. Shute, 'New Civil Preventative Orders: Sexual Offences Prevention Orders; Foreign Travel Orders; Risk of Sexual Harm Orders' [2004] Crim LR 417.

42 See J. Harris and S. Grace, 'A Question of Evidence? Investigating and Prosecuting Rapes in the 1990s' (1999) HORS No 196; J. Gregory and S. Lees, *Policing Sexual Assault* (1999) 60–66; Temkin, above 11–30.

with B aged 16, consensually taking or possessing her nude photo will not be legal unless A is married to her, or living with her in an enduring family relationship.

Throughout the Act sentences are generally harsher than for offences under the previous law. For example, sexual intercourse with a person under 16 with consent now carries a 14-year sentence. There is one summary only offence in the entire Act – sex in a public lavatory.[43]

2. Recurring fundamental concepts in the 2003 Act

(a) Consent

At the core of the most serious offences in the 2003 Act is the concept of consent. One of the principal aims of the Act was to clarify the meaning of this fundamental issue.

It has long been recognized that determining the consent of the complainant is not restricted to ascertaining whether there has been the use or threat of force,[44] nor whether the sexual acts were 'against her will'.[45] However, beyond these negative observations the law has struggled to define, in positive terms, the scope of consent.[46] This was widely acknowledged to be one of the major difficulties with the 1956 Act.[47] The leading authority of *Olugboja*[48] did little more than leave the question to the jury to apply their common sense, giving consent its 'ordinary meaning'. This approach prompted stringent academic criticism: Glanville Williams regarded it as 'one more manifestation of the deplorable tendency of the criminal courts to leave important questions of legal policy to the jury.'[49]

One very obvious consequence of this approach was that it increased the likelihood of inconsistent decisions.[50] Remedying this shortcoming was one of the most important objectives of the law reform. *Setting the Boundaries* emphasized the need for clarity in 'the most private and difficult area of sexual relationships . . . so that the boundaries of what is acceptable, and of criminally culpable behaviour, are all well understood.'[51] It was stressed that this is particularly important because in sexual activity consent often involves 'verbal and non-verbal messages [which] can be mistaken and where assumptions about what is and is not appropriate can lead to significant misunderstanding.'[52]

43 Section 71. Below p 644. The Sentencing Advisory Panel proposes a £50 fine for a first offence.

44 Until relatively recently courts continued erroneously to direct juries that the use of force by the defendant and resistance by the complainant were essential ingredients of the offence of rape. See *Dimes* 7 Cr App R 43, *Harling* [1938] 1 All ER 307, and *Howard* [1965] 3 All ER 684.

45 *Camplin* (1845) 1 Cox CC 220 Tindal CJ and Parke B were of the view that rape was ravishing a woman 'where she did not consent' and not ravishing her 'against her will'.

46 See generally, the discussion in the Law Commission Policy Paper appended to *Setting the Boundaries*. For more philosophical analysis see eg H. Hurd, 'The Moral Magic of Consent' (1996) 2 Legal Theory 168; J. McGregor, 'Why when she says no she doesn't mean maybe and doesn't mean yes' (1996) 2 Legal Theory 175.

47 For a review of circumstances in which consent was held to be absent under the old law see *Setting the Boundaries*, para 2.2.2.

48 [1981] 3 All ER 443.

49 G. Williams, TBCL (2nd edn, 1983) at 551.

50 Although see S. Gardner, 'Appreciating *Olugboja*' (1996) 16 LS 275 for a defence of this approach emphasizing that it focused correctly on the issue of the victim's autonomy.

51 Ibid, para 2.7.2; para 2.10.1.

52 Ibid. See also P. Rumney, 'The Review of Sex Offences and Rape Law Reform: Another False Dawn' (2001) 64 MLR 890 emphasizing that consent should involve a dialogue between the parties.

Given such determination to clarify the law of consent, echoed as forcefully as it was by Ministerial statements,[53] the provisions in the 2003 Act are rather disappointing. Although there is greater clarity than under *Olugboja*, the jury are still left with considerable discretion since the definitions are not as clear or as comprehensive as they could be. In particular, it is doubtful whether the Act succeeds in providing any solution to some of the more frequently encountered difficulties such as the complainant who was, at the time of the sexual act, voluntarily and heavily intoxicated or who succumbed to threats or pressure short of violence.

(i) Definition of consent

Three sections in the Act seek to clarify the concept. Under s 76, where the defendant, A, deceives the complainant, B, as to the nature or purpose of the act or his identity, it is conclusively presumed that there is a lack of consent and that A has no reasonable belief in consent. Under s 75, six specified circumstances give rise to a rebuttable presumption that there was no consent and that A did not have a reasonable belief in B's consent. Finally, s 74 provides a general definition of consent which may be relevant in combination with ss 75 and 76 in appropriate cases, and independently governs all other situations. It is unclear whether the three tiered approach to consent reflects a hierarchy of circumstances in which consent is absent.[54]

These definitions apply throughout Part I of the Act (in particular for the non-consensual offences of rape, assault by penetration, sexual assault, and causing a person to engage in sexual activity without consent). One very significant omission is to extend the application of ss 75 and 76 beyond the substantive offences, to inchoates.

Section 74

Section 74 provides that 'a person consents if he agrees by choice, and has the freedom and capacity to make that choice'. This definition, based on 'free agreement', is intended to emphasize that the absence of the complainant's protest, resistance or injury does not necessarily signify his consent.

Although the Act is silent as to the precise moment at which B's consent or agreement must be present, it is clear that the relevant time is that of the alleged sexual wrongdoing. This may present problems where, for example B has indicated to A his willingness to engage in sexual activity later that evening, but then becomes so heavily intoxicated that at the time of the sexual act B is incapable of making any coherent decision.[55] *A fortiori* where B initially indicates his disinclination to engage in sexual activity but later does so when voluntarily intoxicated.

'Freedom', it is submitted, is too loose a word to use in defining this crucial element of such serious offences. Freedom is a term which is heavily context dependent and always implies 'freedom from' something.[56] The jury will have to address the existence and

[53] See Lord Falconer speaking of the need for 'crystal clarity', HL Debates, col 772, 13 Feb 2003. See also *Protecting the Public*, para 30.

[54] See J. Temkin and A. Ashworth, 'Rape, Sexual Assaults and the Problems of Consent' [2004] Crim LR 328.

[55] See also the Law Commission's Policy Paper para 4.54. See generally, Temkin, 90–116.

[56] As Temkin and Ashworth point out above n 54, freedom is only used to rule out the suggestion of some or all of its antitheses. See p 336, citing J. L. Austin, 'A Plea for Excuses', in H. Morris (ed), *Freedom and Responsibility* (1961), 8.

weight of this 'other' pressure from which B might have been acting freely. It may therefore be desirable for the jury to address the question of freedom by reference to proportionality. The greater the pressure facing B the less 'freedom' he has to make his choice to engage in sexual activity. This may involve the jury in a difficult assessment of a wide range of factors when the degree of freedom is inhibited by, for example, A's threat to terminate B's employment unless he has sex. This may lead into further difficulties such as the source of the pressures, particularly where the defendant is not directly responsible for bringing them to bear. It is submitted that the term is ill-suited in this legislative context. It remains to be seen how the courts will grapple with this and whether they will draw on analogous familiar concepts from the criminal law such as the freedom of the defendant to resist pressure as in the defence of duress.[57]

Beyond freedom from physical pressure, it is unclear what degree of freedom is envisaged to validate consent. In particular, issues will arise as to B's economic freedom, as where B, an underprivileged employee of a wealthy businessman agrees to his sexual advances to retain his position. Similarly, issues might arise in relation to B's religious freedom as where a dependent young member of a strict religion agrees to sexual activity with an elder whom in all other respects he has been taught never to question.

This question of defining freedom also raises the difficult relationship between consent and submission. Under the 1956 Act, in *Olugboja*[58] the court placed considerable emphasis on the difference between consent and submission, but never fully identified what the distinction was. Thus, B may reluctantly submit to sexual intercourse only because her fiancé threatens that he will break off their engagement if she does not. Such a case is very far removed from rape but it seems to be one of submission. At the other extreme, B may submit because the man is holding a knife at her throat. This is plainly rape (this would indeed now give rise to a presumption of non-consent under s 75(2)(a)). In both cases B yields because a threat is made; it is not easy to distinguish them on the basis of submission or consent. The confusion in addressing these terms was in part a result of the dictum of Coleridge J in *Day*:[59] 'every consent involves a submission; but it by no means follows that a mere submission involves consent'. It is submitted that this is wrong. B who joyously embraces her reluctant lover undoubtedly consents to the acts that follow but it would seem inappropriate, to put it mildly, to say that B 'submits' to that which she ardently desires and provokes. On the other hand, B who 'gives in' to threats from her fiancé does in fact agree, although not freely.

'Choice' presupposes that B has options from which to choose and that in turn surely presupposes B is possessed of adequate information about each to make an 'informed' choice between them. Again, the section fails to offer any guidance as to the degree of information about the activity (such as penetration) that B is to engage in. Does B have free choice where, for example, A is HIV positive and has not informed B of that fact?[60] The Court of Appeal has confirmed that a complainant's consent to the risk of contracting HIV has to be an informed consent.[61]

57 See above, Ch 11. 58 (1981) 73 Cr App R 344. 59 (1841) 9 C & P 722 at 724.

60 See D. Ormerod and M. Gunn, 'Criminal Liability for the Transmission of HIV' [1996] 1 Web Jnl Current Legal Issues; D. Ormerod, 'Criminalising HIV Transmission – Still No Effective Solutions' [2001] Common Law World Review 135–168; J. R. Spencer, 'Liability for Reckless Infection' (2004) 154 NLJ 384–385 (part 1) and 448–471 (part 2).

61 *Konzani* [2005] EWCA Crim 706.

'Capacity' is not further defined. In this context is clearly intended to mean mental capacity. It is submitted that the crucial issue should be whether B has the capacity to choose to perform the specified act with A on the occasion in question. It is unclear to what extent B must have the capacity to understand the consequences of the action as well as its nature. For example, must B understand the risks of disease and pregnancy from unprotected intercourse in case of penile penetration? If the essence of the test is that B must have the capacity in the form of knowledge and understanding this may be problematic. What, for example, of B who has a learning disability and has sound anatomical knowledge but lacks any ability to comprehend the broader consequences of the activity – for example to understand the risks of disease and pregnancy from unprotected intercourse and the social consequences of having sexual intercourse?

Some further statutory light ought to be shed on the meaning of capacity by cross-referring to the offences protecting those with a mental disorder. Some of those offences refer to the victim's 'inability to refuse' which is based on each individual's circumstances. Thus, s 30(2) provides:

B is unable to refuse if –

(a) he lacks the capacity to choose whether to agree to the [activity] (whether because he lacks sufficient understanding of the nature or reasonably foreseeable consequences of what is being done, or for any other reason), or

(b) he is unable to communicate such a choice to A.

In explaining the concept of inability to refuse, Lord Falconer described the issue as:

whether at that time they were able to understand enough of what was proposed to refuse if they did not want to engage in sexual activity. The clauses as drafted define the criminal behaviour in terms of it being committed against someone who is unable to refuse being subjected to it. That clearly defines the vulnerability of the victim in these cases and does so in straightforward language.[62]

The definition of 'inability to refuse' includes cases where B lacks capacity: in such cases there is clearly no consent. This deals with cases such as that of *Jenkins*[63] under the 1956 Act where B with a learning disability was held to have consented to the sexual activity by her 'animal' instincts. Inability to refuse includes, in the alternative, an inability to communicate a choice to this defendant. That begs the question whether complainants who are unable to refuse through their inability to communicate are also not consenting. It is submitted that this begs a further question – why is B unable to communicate these issues to this defendant? There is also a further complication because the concept of 'inability to refuse' is normally treated as being a category of incapacity following the Law Commission's Report No 231, *Mental Incapacity*.[64] As such, does it follow that *all* those whose

[62] HL, col 397, 10 Apr 2003, Lord Falconer of Thoroton. The criminal courts might benefit from reference to the civil courts constructions of capacity in eg *Re T (Adult Refusal of Treatment)* [1992] 2 FLR 458; *Re C (Refusal of Medical Treatment)* [1994] 1 FLR 31.

[63] (2000) *Guardian*, 24 Jan.

[64] Cf K. Stevenson, A. Davies and M. Gunn, *Blackstone's Guide to the Sexual Offences Act* (2004) 'a person who is unable to refuse is a person who does not have the capacity to make the choice' 14.

communication skills are so limited are denied the opportunity to a legally consensual sexual relationship?[65]

In short, there appear to be the following categories:

- B lacks mental capacity to make the choice – no consent;
- B lacks ability to refuse because of mental disorder – unable to refuse; if the inability also amounts to inability to choose no consent;
- B lacks ability to refuse for reasons unrelated to mental disorder – if inability amounts to inability to choose no consent;
- B has mental capacity to choose, but *mentally* (not physically)[66] incapable of communicating choice to this defendant – unable to refuse; arguably[67] also lacking consent.

So much for the 'crystal clarity' of this fundamental issue promised by the Review and the government ministers.

Section 75 – Evidential presumptions

If A is proved to have performed the relevant act (for example, penetration),[68] and it is proved that any of the circumstances listed in subs (2) exists and A knows it exists, B is taken not to have consented and A not to have a reasonable belief in B's consent unless sufficient evidence is adduced to raise the issue.

The circumstances in subs (2) are:

(a) any person was, at the time of the relevant act or immediately before it began, using violence against the complainant or causing the complainant to fear that immediate violence would be used against him;

(b) any person was, at the time of the relevant act or immediately before it began, causing the complainant to fear that violence was being used, or that immediate violence would be used, against another person;

(c) the complainant was, and the defendant was not, unlawfully detained at the time of the relevant act;

(d) the complainant was asleep or otherwise unconscious at the time of the relevant act;

(e) because of the complainant's physical disability, the complainant would not have been able at the time of the relevant act to communicate to the defendant whether the complainant consented;

(f) any person had administered to or caused to be taken by the complainant, without the complainant's consent, a substance which, having regard to when it was administered or taken, was capable of causing or enabling the complainant to be stupefied or overpowered at the time of the relevant act.

65 The position is further complicated by the fact that in cases in which B is unable to communicate to this defendant by reason of physical disability, there is, presumptively, no consent. See s 75(2)(e).

66 B lacks physical ability to communicate consent to this defendant – presumptively no consent (s 75).

67 Stevenson *et al.*, above regard these as all non-consensual cases.

68 See s 77.

Although A has to know that '*those* circumstances existed',[69] the requirement is in fact only that his knowledge of any *one* circumstance is proved.[70] The Act is silent on whether this must be proof by the prosecution.[71] There is no requirement that the existence of the circumstances listed in (a)–(f) *caused* B's lack of consent.[72] The absence of consent is simply presumed.

Controversially, s 75 relates to both the issue of consent and the issue of A's belief in consent. If the trial judge decides that A has raised 'sufficient evidence' to raise an issue as to whether B consented/whether A believed reasonably that B had consented, it will then be left to the jury. If sufficient evidence has not been raised in either of the above circumstances and there is no other defence available to A the jury will be bound to find A guilty. Mere assertion by A that there was consent or that he believed there was will be insufficient to rebut this presumption.

Section 75 creates a rather odd set of presumptions since A can raise evidence sufficient to rebut the presumption without challenging the actual circumstance on which the presumption arises. Thus, where the prosecution allege that B was asleep, A can raise evidence which will rebut this without denying the fact that B was asleep. A can claim that he believed, reasonably, that B was consenting (based on their previous sexual practices). A is obliged not to rebut the fact of the presumption, but the legal consequences of that presumption. This can cause problems. If the prosecution proves the three elements – the relevant act, A's awareness and the circumstance giving rise to the presumption – A is obliged to raise sufficient evidence to rebut the issue. This can be done by calling evidence, testifying, or by cross-examination of a Crown witness.[73] If A has raised such evidence, the question is how the judge should then direct the jury. Are the jury to be told to have regard to s 75 and the relevant circumstance? It is submitted that the jury ought not to be permitted to convict on the basis of the proof of the three elements once A has raised sufficient evidence to rebut.[74] They should be directed to deal with the issue of consent under the general guidance in s 74.

The obligation on A to satisfy the judge, from the evidence, that there is a real issue about consent that is worth putting to the jury is more likely to withstand ECHR challenge[75] than the original version in the Bill which incorporated reverse burdens for A's belief in consent.[76] Creating such presumptions has an important symbolic value,[77] and was widely welcomed in principle.[78] Whilst it is not clear how demanding the evidential burden will be, in Parliament Baroness Scotland of Asthal stated:

> In order for these presumptions not to apply, the defendant will need to satisfy the judge from the evidence that there is a real issue about consent that is worth putting to the jury. The evidence

[69] Section 75(1)(c). [70] Section 75(1)(b).

[71] What if D2 seeks to prove the existence of the circumstance in the course of showing that he lacked knowledge of it but D1 did not?

[72] Cf the proposals in *Setting the Boundaries*, 2.10.9.

[73] Note that earlier version of Bill specifically stated cross examination of the victim would not be sufficient to raise issue as to V's consent unless let to the equivalent of an admission of consent.

[74] Cf *Card*, above 42. Surely this would render s 75 an irrebuttable presumption? Thanks are due to Peter Rook QC for discussions on this issue.

[75] Cf the views expressed in Stevenson *et al.*, para 2.4.3.

[76] HL, cols 1062–1063, 2 June 2003. Lord Thomas of Gresford.

[77] See Beverley Hughes, HC Standing Committee B, 15 Oct, col 26.

[78] See Home Affairs Committee Fifth Report 2002–3 HC 639.

relied on may be, for example, evidence that the defendant himself gives in the witness box, or evidence given on his behalf by a defence witness, or evidence given by the complainant during cross-examination. If the judge is satisfied that there is sufficient evidence to justify putting the issue of consent to the jury, then the issues will have to be proved by the prosecution in the normal way. If the judge does not think the evidence relied on by the defendant meets the threshold, he will direct the jury to find the defendant guilty.[79]

The Canadian courts have interpreted similar provisions as requiring that any claims by the defence have an 'air of reality'.[80] It is submitted that even if such an interpretation were adopted in the English courts, that should not render it necessary for the defence to produce corroborative independent evidence, in the formal sense, to rebut the presumption.[81]

Section 75 will clearly have an impact on the process of the trial. In practical terms it will render it more likely that A will testify.[82] In addition, it will have a significant impact on the way that sexual offences are investigated and on the manner of police interviews. If the complainant alleges that one of the s 75(2) circumstances was present, the suspect will be under considerable pressure to offer an explanation in interview and advance his defence at an earlier stage.

Aside from these general concerns about creating presumptions, the individual circumstances listed in s 75(2) also pose problems.

Threats of violence

The use/threats of immediate violence need not emanate from A before they are treated, presumptively, as vitiating B's consent. This is a welcome extension of the law. S 75(2)(a) will operate in circumstances such as those in *Dagnall*[83] where A had grabbed B and dragged her off the road telling her he would rape her. Under threat, B told A that he could 'do what he liked as long as he did not harm her'. A was apprehended before penetrating B and convicted under the old law of attempted rape.[84] The fact that B had explicitly assented to sexual acts did not in these circumstances mean that she was consenting.

However, there are other difficulties with the provision. It is unclear why the requirement is one of 'immediate' violence. Arguably, it should be sufficient that A threatens B that he will 'make her suffer one day' unless she has sex with him at once. It may be that the concept of 'immediacy' is interpreted expansively by the courts.[85] Of course, even without the presumption, in a case of threats of a non-immediate nature, B's consent might still be absent applying the general test of free agreement under s 74.

[79] HL, col 670, 17 June 2003.

[80] A striking example cited by P. Rook and R. Ward is of *Filice* (1999) Carswell Ont 1262 where evidence that she had (as was her custom) taken out her false teeth was sufficient to give the claim an air of reality. See further *Pappajohn* [1980] 2 SCR. 120 discussed by Lord Steyn in *R v A (No 2)* [2002] 1 AC 67. For discussion on this see: J. Temkin, '*Rape and the Legal Process*' (2nd edn, 2002), 132.

[81] *Osolin* [1993] 4 SCR 595; *Park* [1995] 2 SCR 836.

[82] See Explanatory Notes Sexual Offences Act 2003 ch 42, which makes it clear that evidence given by the defendant himself may constitute 'sufficient evidence'.

[83] [2003] EWCA Crim 2441.

[84] See also *Low* [1997] Crim LR 692 where V performed oral sex on D after persuading him not to rape her vaginally as she was pregnant. Note that there is a potential problem with applying the s 75 presumption to attempts. See HH D. Rodwell QC, 'Problems with the Sexual Offences Act 2003' [2005] Crim LR 290.

[85] See the interpretation of 'immediate' in assault, p 520.

Although it might appear sensible for a threat of violence to give rise to a conclusive presumption of non-consent, it is clear that in some circumstances even the most explicit threats of violence to B might not vitiate consent as, for example, where A and B are sadomasochists.[86] The rebuttability of the presumption provides for this scenario.

'Violence' is not defined. It is clear from the Parliamentary debates that it was intended to be limited only to violence to the person, but regrettably that does not appear on the face of the statute. Where A threatens to damage B's property unless she engages in sexual activity, s 75 does not apply and the jury are left to determine the question of B's consent by reference to the criteria in s 74.

This raises a further interesting point. It is lamentable that the 2003 Act provided no replacement for the offence under s 2 of the 1956 Act, despite contrary recommendations in *Setting The Boundaries*. Section 2 provided an offence of procuring sexual intercourse by threats. A broader gender-neutral version of causing sexual activity by threats would have provided a useful backstop offence for cases in which the threats fall short of violence but might be regarded by the jury as insufficient to have prevented the victim from agreeing freely. For example, in *Olugboja*[87] reference was made to an unreported case in which Winn J held that a constable had no case to answer where he induced B to consent to sexual intercourse by threatening to report her for an offence; whereas in *Wellard*[88] A was said to have a previous conviction for rape (for which he was sentenced to six years' imprisonment) by masquerading as a security officer and inducing a girl to consent by threatening to report to her parents and the police that she had been seen having intercourse in a public place. Other examples are easy to envisage: A threatens that, if B does not consent, he will (i) tell the police of a theft she has committed; (ii) tell her father of her previous immorality; (iii) dismiss her from her present employment; (iv) not give her a rise in salary; (v) never take her to the pictures again.[89] Clearly, a line must be drawn somewhere, but the boundary of consent in such cases is difficult to draw and the new Act ought to have provided more guidance.

Section 75(2)(b) also relates to threats of violence, applying where B is caused to fear that violence was being used, or that immediate violence would be used against another person. This is an extremely broad presumption, but it has been welcomed as 'clarifying the common law regarding the fear of violence to third parties'.[90] There is no requirement that A is in any way involved in the causing of the complainant's fear. Thus, A who is aware that B, an immigrant, has heard on the TV of ongoing violent atrocities against the population of her homeland, who then performs a relevant sexual act with B is presumed to have done so without consent. Although this may seem like a fanciful example which is unlikely to present problems in practice, because of the ease with which the presumption could be rebutted, it demonstrates the unsatisfactory nature of the overbroad drafting.

86 See N. Bamforth, 'Sado-masochism and consent' [1994] Crim LR 661.

87 [1982] QB 320 at 347–348.

88 Above, p 528 (1978) 67 Cr App R 364 at 368. The court made no comment on the propriety or otherwise of the conviction.

89 Note that in the case of mentally disordered complainants ss 34–37 provides offences based on 'inducement threat or deception' where the degree of threat is not limited – it could include a threat to break friends with the complainant.

90 Temkin and Ashworth, above, n 54.

Unlawful detention

Section 75(2)(c) seems to be an uncontroversial provision. Where, for example, B has been kidnapped, and A is aware of B's detained status, it is legitimate to presume that B is not consenting to sexual activity. Although there are instances of hostages forming a sexual bond with their kidnappers, it is unlikely that A will be able easily to rebut this presumption. The section does highlight a practical problem. Where B alleges that she was raped by A who had detained her, if B is believed, the presumption will operate, but the question whether B is to believed as to the detention is a matter of fact for the jury. How can the judge decide whether the trigger of unlawful detention is satisfied and thereby create the presumption against A without usurping the jury's role?

Unconsciousness

The presumption in s 75(2)(d) requires proof that A is aware that B is unconscious.[91] At common law, it was held that unconsciousness (including lack of consciousness through sleep) was sufficient to vitiate consent.[92] There are numerous cases of sexual activity when the complainant was asleep resulting in a conviction.[93] Arguably the presumption in s 75(2)(d) provides less protection than had been afforded at common law in these cases in which the consent was vitiated *per se*. It is arguable therefore that this circumstance of 'unconsciousness' ought to give rise to a conclusive presumption of non-consent by B.[94] However, if B is unconscious and A is aware of that fact there may be circumstances in which A will be readily capable of rebutting a presumption of non-consent. For example, A, who performs a relevant sexual act (note that the presumption applies to offences of touching and not just penetrative acts) on his sleeping partner as a gesture of intimacy to wake her ought not to be conclusively presumed guilty.

There is no stipulation as to the cause of the lack of consciousness; it could arise from self-induced intoxication. In *Protecting the Public*, the government rejected a broader suggestion for a provision that 'someone who is inebriated could claim they were unable to give consent – as opposed to someone who was unconscious for whatever reason, including because of alcohol' on the ground that it would give rise to 'mischievous accusations'. At common law, if a complainant, through alcohol or drugs, was not capable of exercising a judgement on consent, she was not consenting.[95] Such circumstances now only give rise to *a presumption* of a lack of consent. It is clear that the Sexual Offences Review envisaged that consent would be lacking in such a case.[96]

Inability to communicate owing to physical disability

At common law, and under the 1956 Act, there was no requirement that the absence of consent has to be demonstrated or communicated to A.[97] As a matter of logic it is unclear why the physical inability to *communicate* should be seen as presumptive of a lack of consent. The statutory formula seems to presuppose that B has the capacity to make the

91 Cf the view expressed in Stevenson, Davies and Gunn, above n 1, para 2.4.1.3.
92 See *Larter and Castleton* [1995] Crim LR 75; *Howard* [1966] 1 WLR 13.
93 See recently *Johnston* [2003] All ER (D) 266 Jun.
94 See eg Temkin and Ashworth above n 54.
95 *Malone* [1998] 2 Cr App R 454.
96 See *Setting The Boundaries* p 18, para 2.10.7 ff.
97 *Malone* [1998] 2 Cr App R 447, [1998] Crim LR 834.

choice of free agreement, but merely lacks the physical ability to communicate to this defendant. The inclusion of this presumptive category renders even more complex the relationship between consent generally and the capacity of those with mental disorders. It is unclear whether by limiting the category of presumptive non-consent to 'physical' disability it is intended that all cases of mental inability to communicate should be prosecuted not under the non-consensual provisions (ss 1–4) but under the specific provisions (ss 30–44).

It is notable that the presumption only applies if B's physical disability inhibits his communication with *this* defendant. This may be significant if B has a particular speech or sign pattern that can be understood by some individuals.

Causing to be taken by the complainant, without consent, a substance capable of causing or enabling the complainant to be stupefied or overpowered at the time of the relevant act

This provision was introduced late in the Bill's progress as a response to the growing concern over 'drug assisted rape'.[98] The Act seeks to combat this problem by the presumption in this section and the introduction of the new offence in s 61.[99] Under the old law there was a much narrower offence under s 4(1) of 1956 Act applicable to administering drugs only to women with intent to stupefy or overpower in order only to facilitate intercourse. The new presumption of non-consent applies to both sexes and to sexual acts other than intercourse.

Although targeted at drugs which induce states of incapacity such as Rohypnol and GHB, (gamma hydroxyl butyrate acid) there is no statutory limitation on the type of substance which will trigger the presumption. Alcohol is certainly capable of satisfying the definition,[100] so A who surreptitiously laces B's soft drink with spirits will be caught. Similarly, there is no limitation on the manner of the administration. Unless it is established that A knew or believed that the substance was capable of rendering B stupified or overpowered the presumption will not apply. This will depend on the type of drug involved.

The presumption will also apply where A 'caused [the substance] to be taken by the complainant' this includes deceiving B into self-administration of the substance as where the substance is mixed with an innocuous one (laced drinks). If B's consumption is purely voluntary and fully informed the presumption does not bite. In cases of complainants who have become voluntarily intoxicated through drink or drugs, the question of their consent will fall to be decided under the general provisions of capacity and free choice under s 74.[101]

The section makes clear that it is irrelevant who administers or causes B to take the substance, only that one is administered and that B is therefore presumed not to consent. The presumption would therefore apply where X administers, then B gets in a taxi home and the taxi driver, A, performs a sexual act on B.

98 For comprehensive analysis see E. Finch and V. Munro, 'Intoxicated Consent and the Boundaries of Drug Assisted Rape' [2003] Crim LR 773; 'The Sexual Offences Act 2003: Intoxicated Consent and Drug Assisted Rape Revisited' [2004] Crim LR 789.

99 See below p 642.

100 See Beverely Hughes HC Standing Committee B, 14 October, col 54.

101 See recently *Abbess* [2004] EWCA Crim 1813 where there was no trace of GHB found.

In those cases in which the presumption applies, A can argue that although he administered the drug being aware of its effects, B nevertheless consented to the sexual acts that finally ensued. If, for example, B indicated at the beginning of the date that he would not have sex with A, and A surreptitiously laces B's drink with potent alcohol, it may be that B later willingly engages in sexual activity with him (not being unconscious nor stupified); his inhibitions having been lowered.

Section 75(2)(f) will increase the pressure on A to testify and strengthen the hand of the police in interview since they can inquire why A thought that B was consenting given the circumstance of his administering the substance. It will also render prosecution far easier in some circumstances, as for example in *Minas*,[102] where the complainant (aged 13) had become intoxicated by alcohol voluntarily but was also found to have valium in her blood, the prosecution's case was put on the basis that she was rendered incapable. The complainant had said in interview that she could not remember her actions, but would not have had sex with A but for the intoxication and peer pressure.

Section 76 – conclusive presumptions

If it is proved that A performed the relevant act[103] and any one of the circumstances specified in s 76(2) existed, it is to be *conclusively presumed* that the complainant did not consent to the relevant act, and that A did not believe that the complainant consented. It is questionable whether since these are conclusive presumptions they represent the worst forms of non-consent. It seems doubtful that they outrank the violent attack, but some would argue that the element of deception renders the position more serious because of the potential guilt felt by the complainant in being tricked.[104]

The circumstances giving rise to a conclusive presumption are:

(a) the defendant intentionally deceived the complainant as to the *nature or purpose* of the relevant act;

(b) the defendant intentionally induced the complainant to consent to the relevant act by *impersonating a person known personally* to the complainant.

It is sufficient that any *one* of the deceptions is proved. These provisions aim to replicate the common law as regards deceptions as to the nature of the act[105] and the identity of the actor. In both instances the section goes further. The provisions are immediately open to challenge on the basis that as a matter of logic, it is unclear why these are conclusive of anything beyond D's absence of a belief in consent.[106] These are also arguably objectionably wide as *conclusive* presumptions especially since they apply in relation to offences other than one of penetration, for example, touching. It is arguable that the breadth of such a conclusive presumption might be incompatible with Article 6 of the ECHR.

102 [2003] EWCA Crim 135.

103 Section 77.

104 Similar arguments led the Sexual Offences Review to conclude that stranger rape was not worse *per se* than acquaintance rape where the complainant may feel an element of guilt in misjudging her attacker. Temkin and Ashworth (above) 337, cf the debate on theft below regarding the relative seriousness of being deceived into acting as opposed to actions being performed against the will.

105 *Williams* [1923] 1 KB 340.

106 Cf Stevenson *et al.*, who regard this as unarguable above, n 1, para 2.4.2.

Nature or purpose

At common law, a fraud as to the nature of the act vitiated consent.[107] Thus, there was no consent where B was unaware that she was submitting to sexual intercourse because, for example, she had been persuaded by A, as in *Flattery*[108] that he was performing a surgical operation, or as in *Williams*[109] that he was acting to improve her singing voice. Section 76 creates a conclusive presumption in such circumstances.

A need not have caused the lack of consent, indeed there is no need to establish that there was no consent; it is sufficient that he has deceived B about the nature of the act. Deceptions as to the nature of non-penile penetration will be covered. Deceptions as to the nature of the act might also arise in relation to the act of sexual intercourse, although in an age of national sexual education this is unlikely, at least for adults of normal mental capacity.

In *Dica*[110] knowing that he was HIV positive, D had engaged in consensual unprotected sexual intercourse with the two complainants, thereby infecting each of them with the disease. He was convicted of inflicting grievous bodily harm, contrary to s 20 of the Offences Against the Person Act 1868. It was the Crown's case that he had been reckless as to whether the complainants might become infected with the disease; and that, had the complainants known of his condition, they would not have consented to sexual intercourse. The trial judge had ruled that *Clarence*[111] had been thoroughly undermined, and that the decision in *Brown*[112] deprived the complainants of the legal capacity to consent to such serious harm. The Court of Appeal allowed the defendant's appeal and ordered a retrial since it was unclear whether the complainants had been aware of the risks. Since the alleged concealment by D was not as to the nature of the sexual act itself, but as to the risk of infection he was not guilty of rape.[113]

Under the old law, it was unclear whether a deception as to 'quality' as opposed to the 'nature' of the act would be sufficient to vitiate consent. In *Tabassum*[114] A, who was not medically qualified, persuaded women to allow him to measure their breasts by representing (perhaps truthfully) that he was doing so for the purpose of a database he was preparing for doctors. His convictions for indecent assault were upheld, although the women were fully aware of the nature of the acts to be done because (i) they would not have consented to these acts if they had not believed that he had medical qualifications and (ii) the defendant knew that this was so. Thus, following *Tabassum*, though the complainant is aware of the nature of the act, her consent may be negatived if she is

107 See *Flattery* (1877) 2 QBD 410; *Williams* [1923] 1 KB 340.

108 (1877) 2 QBD 410, CCCR.

109 [1923] 1 KB 340, CCA. Williams, TBCL, 561–562 thinks *Williams* 'clearly wrong' because it was not proved that B did not know the facts of life and may merely have been persuaded that sexual intercourse improves breathing. If that were all, it was not rape; but Hewart LCJ said that the girl never consented to sexual intercourse but only a necessary operation.

110 [2004] EWCA Crim 1103; [2004] Crim LR 944 and commentary. See the full discussion above, p 529. See also *Konzani* [2005] EWCA Crim 706.

111 (1888) 22 QBD 23 (where an immediate connection between an assault and the onset of its consequences was necessary to make out a conviction for inflicting grievous bodily harm; with the result that a defendant was not liable under s 20 where he had infected his wife with gonorrhoea through consensual sexual intercourse).

112 [1994] 1 AC 2123.

113 See *Tabassum* [2002] 2 Cr App R 328 and *Cort* [2003] 3 WLR 1300.

114 [2000] 2 Cr App R 328, [2000] Crim LR 686, CA.

mistaken as to its *quality*. This appeared to be a new distinction for which there was no authority.[115] The concept of a deception as to 'quality' has not been included in the Act, but the inclusion of '*purpose*' in s 76(2)(a) confirms that the legislation is designed to extend the protection of the law.

Deceptions as to the 'purpose' of the act are most likely to arise in relation to sexual touching and non-penile penetration, although it is possible that a deception as to the purpose of the act of intercourse will arise. The presumptions apply in respect of male and female victims. They would operate for example in cases such as *Green*,[116] where a doctor had conducted bogus medical examinations of young men, including wiring them to monitors while they masturbated, allegedly so that he could assess their potential to be impotent.

Difficulties with extending the law to include deceptions as to the 'purpose' of the defendant will arise where A acts with more than one purpose. It is possible for A to have multiple purposes, only some of which are legitimate and about which the accused has been honest with B. What for example, where A, a doctor performs a *necessary* intimate medical examination of B, with the additional aim of allowing his friend, X, to watch for his sexual gratification?[117] It is submitted that these facts represent a deception as to the 'purpose'.

The extension to include deceptions as to purpose might represent a much more significant extension of the law than Parliament intended. Circumstances such as those in *Linekar* might now raise a conclusive presumption of non-consent. In *Linekar*[118] A procured a prostitute to have intercourse with him by promising to pay her £25. He never intended to pay. It was held under the 1956 Act that this was not rape. The deception did not go to the nature of the act, since the prostitute knew the nature of the conduct of intercourse. Under the 2003 Act, it might be argued that the deception as to payment alters the 'nature and *purpose*' of the act for the prostitute. On this interpretation, A would as a result of a conclusive presumption, be classified as a rapist. This would be an unwelcome extension of the offence. The pressure to treat such conduct as rape is increased because the Act fails to include any provision analogous to s 3 of the 1956 Act, criminalizing procuring sexual intercourse by false pretences (short of those which would vitiate consent).

Deceptions by A as to purely peripheral circumstances which did not relate to the nature or purpose of the sexual act did not vitiate consent at common law, and the 2003 Act does not alter that position. False promises to give the complainant a part in a film,[119] or to marry her do not bring A's ignoble conduct within the conclusive presumptions.

Finally, it should be noted that the section deals with deceptions practised by A, and not with mistakes unilaterally formed by B. It is doubtful whether in such circumstances there is any legal obligation on A to disabuse B of his misconception, although if A admits

[115] *Setting the Boundaries* gave the example of a false representation of a medical examination, para 2.10.9 at 19.

[116] [2002] EWCA Crim 1501.

[117] Cf *Bolduc and Bird* (1967) 63 DLR (2d) 82.

[118] [1995] 2 Cr App R 49, [1995] Crim LR 320. See A. Reed, 'Analysis of Fraud Vitiating Consent in Rape Cases' (1995) 59 J Crim LR 310.

[119] As occurred in *Melliti* [2001] EWCA Crim 1563.

to being aware of B's confusion, this may assist the prosecution in proving his *mens rea* – that he did not reasonably believe in B's consent to that sexual act.[120]

Section 76(2)(b) – identity fraud

By virtue of s 142(3) of the Criminal Justice and Public Order Act 1994, it was rape for a man to induce a woman to have intercourse with him by impersonating her husband. At common law, this was extended to include impersonation of long term (heterosexual) partnerships.[121] Section 76(2)(b) extends the law beyond any particular category or duration of relationship, it also extends beyond the offence of rape to other acts of penetration and sexual activity. This is a welcome extension.

The conclusive presumption in s 76(2)(b) is more limited than that in para (a) since it is not sufficient for A to have lied about his identity, or even to have lied successfully and deceived B, it must be *by that* impersonation that B is induced to consent. The prosecution must prove this causal link.

The section poses other difficulties in interpretation, particularly regarding the limitation expressed in the formula 'known personally to' the accused. This is clearly intended to prevent the presumption arising when A claims to be a celebrity with whom B has no personal acquaintance, but for whom B may be expected to hold an attraction. Are all people B has ever met 'known personally to' him? Is it only those with whom B has had some greater degree of intimacy? Can a person be known personally to B by email correspondence? Consider the couple who arrange to meet after internet dating. X gets cold feet and decides he cannot face meeting B. A, his friend steps in. Is there a conclusive presumption that B was not consenting to any sexual acts which follow?

Disappointingly, despite Law Commission recommendations to the contrary,[122] the Act does not deal expressly with the problem of deception as to the defendant's attributes (medical qualification, being a police officer, etc) or other personal authority to perform the act.[123] Thus, the position in cases such as *Richardson*[124] remains unchanged. In that case the defendant had continued to practice as a dentist although suspended. Patients claimed that they would not have allowed her to treat them if they had known of her suspension. She pleaded guilty to assault after the trial judge ruled that her deception had vitiated consent. The defence submission that the patients had consented to treatment despite their ignorance as to the circumstances was rejected. The Court of Appeal refused to accept the prosecutor's argument that the concept of the identity of a person extended to cover the qualifications or attributes of the dentist on the basis that the patients only consented to treatment by a qualified and not a suspended one. The court felt that this would be straining and distorting the definition of identity.

[120] Cf Peter Alldridge's proposal that consent should be vitiated if without mistake, consent would not have been given and the person to whom it was given knew: 'Sex Lies and the Criminal Law' (1993) 44 NILQ 250.

[121] *Elbekkay* [1995] Crim LR 163.

[122] The Law Commission Report *Consent in Sex Offences* submitted to the Home Office, *Sex Offences Review* (2000) para 5.25. The Commission concluded 'that it should be open to a jury to decide that, for the purposes of a particular act, the 'identity' of the actor included the possession of a professional qualification or other authority to do the act in question, and that if the defendant had no such authority then he or she did it without consent.'

[123] See *Richardson* [1999] Crim LR 62.

[124] [1998] 2 Cr App R 200.

(b) Sexual – s 78

Most offences in the Act involve proof of 'sexual' activity of one kind or another. The concept of 'sexual' is therefore of great significance, and the Act seeks to define it in a fashion similar to that propounded in the House of Lords in *Court*:[125]

[P]enetration, touching or any other activity is sexual if a **reasonable person** would consider that –

(a) whatever its circumstances or any person's purpose in relation to it, it is because of its nature sexual, or

(b) because of its nature it may be sexual and because of its circumstances or the purpose of any person in relation to it (or both) it is sexual.

The first limb requires consideration only of the nature of the act divorced from its circumstances. Where the nature of the activity is unambiguously sexual,[126] (for example, penile penetration, oral sex, etc) the activity is sexual irrespective of the defendant's purpose.

The second limb deals with cases where the nature of an activity is ambiguous. Such actions are only 'sexual' if the circumstances or the defendant's purpose render them such. According to the Court of Appeal in *H*[127] the judge should identify two distinct questions for the jury (i) whether they as 12 reasonable people considered that the conduct in the particular circumstances before them because of its nature might be sexual and (ii) whether they, as reasonable people considered that the conduct in view of the circumstances or the purpose of the person in relation to it or both was in fact sexual. In relation to the first question, evidence as to the circumstances before or after the conduct was irrelevant.

The facts of *Court* provide an illustration. A, an assistant in a shop, pulled a girl aged 12 who was in the shop across his knee and spanked her on her clothed bottom. When asked why he did it, he said 'Buttock fetish'. The House held (Lord Goff dissenting) that because the act was ambiguous, it was necessary to prove an indecent intention. Under the 2003 Act, A's acts would, presumably, fall within s 78(b) and the jury would be left to determine his purpose (on the facts it would clearly be sexual). The test is far from satisfactory, it would appear to be both over and under-inclusive. If, on facts such as those in *Court*, A had pulled down B's shorts, the case may well fall immediately into s 78(1)(a), with the nature of the act rendering it unambiguously sexual. What, however, if in pulling down B's shorts, A had a merely (admittedly odd) disciplinary motive? Arguably there should be an opportunity for A's explanation, but that only arises if the case is decided under s 78(b).

Other examples of the operation of s 78(b) might include A inducing B to remove clothing, or an intimate examination involving digital penetration of the vagina or anus. If performed by a doctor for a medical purpose, and in appropriate medical circum-

125 [1989] AC 28. See on this G. Williams, 'The Meaning of Indecency' (1990) LS 20; G. R. Sullivan, 'The Need for A Crime of Sexual Assault' [1989] Crim LR 331.

126 The unambiguous nature of the indecency is relevant to whether a proved assault is indecent. It is not relevant to the question whether there is an assault in the first place. *Tabassum* [2000] 2 Cr App R 328, above, p 609, is surely wrong in this respect.

127 [2005] EWCA Crim 732, [2005] Crim LR (Sept) and commentary.

stances, these would be non-sexual. This can give rise to difficult cases such as *Pratt*[128] where A made two young boys strip and point a torch at each other while he watched. A claimed that he was looking for cannabis. Under s 78, if the jury believe that this non-sexual purpose, and provided they do not conclude that the act is sexual *per se* (category (a)) A will be acquitted.

Section 78 also creates difficulties with odd sexual fetishes. In *George*[129] A attempted to remove a girl's shoe from her foot because this gave him sexual gratification. Streathfield J, rejecting an argument that A's indecent motive made this an indecent assault, held that there were no circumstances of indecency. This decision was not followed under the 2003 Act in *H*. Assuming a reasonable person would consider that this 'may be' sexual (78(b)), A's purpose would render it such. The less overtly sexual the fetish, the less likely the reasonable jury might regard it as being sexual and the less likely it will be caught by the section.

The significant shift throughout the Act from 'indecent' to 'sexual' fails to address other difficulties. For example, in the recent case of *CW*[130] it was questioned whether A's touching of a 13-year-old's 'belly bar piercing' was 'indecent' under the 1956 Act. It is no clearer whether this is sexual under the 2003 Act than whether it was indecent under the old law. More commonly occurring questions might be whether a kiss is inherently sexual in which case its categorization depends on the circumstances and purpose of the kisser (thus, not where a hairy old aunt issues a slobbering greeting to a reluctant nephew). Distinguishing on the basis of whether the kissing involved is 'deep'[131] (presumably meaning whether tongues are involved) or otherwise is not an accurate basis of distinction.

In more general terms, the fact that the jury remain sole arbiters of what is 'sexual' is not conducive to the creation of a consistent jurisprudence of such a fundamental concept. There is a substantial danger that the fact of the complaint by B will induce the jury to regard the conduct as sexual (viewed retrospectively and against that background of complaint) when they would not in prospect have viewed it as such.

(c) Touching – s 79(8)

Under the old law the offences other than those of intercourse centred predominantly on acts involving 'assault'. The law relating to indecent assault was stated by the Crown in the Court of Appeal in *Court*:[132]

> The offence . . . included both a battery, or touching, and psychic assault without touching. If there was touching, it was not necessary to prove that the victim was aware of the assault or of the circumstances of indecency. If there was no touching, then to constitute an indecent assault the victim must be shown to have been aware of the assault and of the circumstances of indecency.

The 2003 Act creates offences based on 'touching' which includes touching –

128 [1984] Crim LR 51.

129 [1956] Crim LR 52. Such cases are not uncommon: see *Price* (2004) 1 Cr App R 12, [2003] EWCA Crim 2405, CA (Crim Div) where D stoked V's leg and boot and admitted it was because he had a shoe fetish.

130 *R v CW* [2004] EWCA Crim 340, CA (Crim Div).

131 See Williams, above (1990) LS 29.

132 [1987] 1 All ER 120 at 122.

(a) with any part of the body,[133]
(b) with anything else,
(c) through anything,[134]

and in particular includes touching amounting to penetration.

As elsewhere, there is no attempt to define further any of the terms, and this may lead to a regrettable inconsistency in the application of the law. The shift from 'assault' to 'touching' is significant. Although assault did not require any element of hostility,[135] a touching might appear to be broader than even a non-hostile assault. It is submitted that as with the old law, there is no room for any '*de minimis*' exception.[136] In other circumstances it seems that the law has been narrowed. Thus, sexual words do not constitute a touching but might well have been assaults. Similarly, where D walks towards someone with his penis exposed,[137] this could have been an assault: the old law did not require any apprehension of indecent touching: *Sargeant*.[138] Similarly, it is unclear whether under the definition in s 79 A has to make physical contact with B. It is questionable whether A ejaculating over B would constitute a touching. This would certainly have amounted to a battery and hence to an indecent assault. Similarly, would soaking B's T-shirt be a touching?

It is also unclear whether there can be a touching by omission. What, for example, of cases such as *Speck*,[139] where A's failure to remove B's hand which she had voluntarily placed on his penis, caused it to become erect? Does this constitute a touching? Is it a sexual touching if the sexual element derives from B and not A.

The Court of Appeal has confirmed that there can be a touching by contact with clothing.[140]

3. Non-consensual offences

(a) Rape

Rape was an offence at common law. Although placed on a statutory basis in the Sexual Offences Act 1956, s 1, there was no statutory definition of the offence, and this position continued until the Sexual Offences (Amendment) Act 1976[141] introduced a partial

133 Note that under s 79(3) surgically reconstructed body parts are included as parts of the 'body' with which touching can occur.

134 This covers D who engages in frottaging (rubbing his genitals against a fellow passenger on public transport): see eg *Tanylidiz* [1998] Crim LR 228.

135 Although cf the House of Lords in *Brown* and above p 609.

136 *Ananthanarayanan* (1994) 98 Cr App R 1, 5 per Laws J. See recently *Mills* [2003] EWCA Crim 3723, two-second touching of barmaid's breasts by customer.

137 *Rolfe* (1952) 36 Cr App R 4.

138 (1996) 161 JP 127, [1997] Crim LR 50, where the assault was a threat with a knife and the circumstance of indecency was A's demand that B masturbate into a condom in a public place.

139 [1977] Crim LR 689. See also *B* [2004] EWCA Crim 319 where A had allowed B to touch his genitals and where she had placed A's hand on her genitals.

140 *H* [2005] Crim LR (Sept) above.

141 Section 1(1) of the Sexual Offences Act 1956 simply provided 'It is a felony for a man to rape a woman', whilst s 1(2) provided 'A man who induces a married woman to have sexual intercourse with him by impersonating her husband commits rape.'

definition of the *mens rea* requirement and the Criminal Justice and Public Order Act 1994 extended the offence to include anal rape. There had been sustained calls for reform of the offence, particularly the mental element and the opportunity for an acquittal on the basis of a mere honest belief in the complainant's consent since the controversial decision in *Morgan*.[142] The need for this issue to be addressed and for clearer definition of this most serious sexual offence were significant catalysts for reform, as was the low conviction rate for rape: by 1999 only one in 13 rapes reported led to conviction.[143]

The reform process prompted several radical suggestions for rape to be subdivided into different categories of offence. One suggestion was to distinguish between cases on the basis of whether there was a previous relationship between the accused and complainant (acquaintance rape) and the more stereo-typical but less common stranger rape. This was rejected. There is no doubt that rape by an acquaintance, including as it does an abuse of trust, can be as traumatic as stranger rape.[144] The Court of Appeal has accepted that, in sentencing terms, there is in general no difference between a stranger rape and an acquaintance rape.[145] The 2003 Act also rejected the possibility of structuring different offences of rape based on the extent of mental fault.[146]

Despite the rejection of these more radical proposals, the new rape offence represents a significant change from the 1956 Act. It provides:

(1) A person (A) commits an offence if –

  (a) he intentionally penetrates the vagina, anus or mouth of another person (B) with the penis,

  (b) B does not consent to the penetration, and

  (c) A does not reasonably believe B consents.

(2) Whether a belief is reasonable is to be determined having regard to all the circumstances, including any steps A has taken to ascertain whether B consents.

(i) *Actus reus*

Penile

The Sexual Offences Review team were eager for the offence of rape to resonate with the general public understanding of the term, and concluded that, although it would perpetuate gender inequality, penile penetration should nevertheless remain an essential element of the offence.[147] The Review considered that penile penetration was a distinctive act, carrying as it can risks of pregnancy and disease transmission, and that it should, therefore, be treated separately from other penetrative assaults. This strong commitment

142 [1976] AC 182 see below, p 618.

143 *Rape and Sexual Assault of Women*, Findings from the BCS (2002) Home Office .

144 Statistics reveal that 45% of rapes are by partners, 16% are by acquaintances: Home Office Research Study No 237, *Rape and Sexual Assault of Women: the extent and nature of the problem* (March 2002). See www.homeoffice.gov.uk/rds/pdfs2/hors237.pdf.

145 See also the Sentencing Advisory Panel's advice to the Court of Appeal, Forword by the Chairman, 1 May 2002, paras 32–35. On the court's controversial qualification of this see P. Rumney, 'Progress at a Price: The Construction of Non-Stranger Rape in the *Millbery* Sentencing Guidelines' (2003) 66 MLR 870.

146 See J. Temkin, (2nd edn, 2002), ch 3 above, n 80; H. Power, 'Towards a redefinition of the *Mens rea* of Rape' (2003) 23 OJLS 379, a view also considered by the Heilbron Committee para 79–80.

147 Whether this principle has been adhered to by the inclusion of oral sex is debatable.

to the principle of fair labelling is especially important in sexual offences where the stigma of conviction is most acute. If jurors are to apply the offences appropriately it is also important that the offences reflect society's general understanding of the wrongdoing involved. By restricting rape to penile penetration,[148] s 1 reflects this attitude.

Because the offence requires penetration by a penis, rape remains one of the few sexual offences capable of being committed by a male only (as a principal offender).[149] However, in a welcome extension of the offence, a post-operative transsexual can commit rape with her reconstructed penis[150] (hence, presumably, the drafting in terms of 'a person' rather than 'a man').[151] A female can aid and abet the offence[152] as where she encourages or assists a man, A, to penetrate B without consent. It may be possible for the woman aider and abettor to be convicted even though A is acquitted of rape on the basis of his lack of *mens rea.*[153] In such circumstances, a female can also now be charged with an offence under s 4 – causing a person to engage in sexual activity – and it is submitted that this is the more appropriate charge (see below).

The conclusive presumption that boys under 14 were incapable of sexual intercourse was abolished by the Sexual Offences Act 1993, s 1, for acts done after 20 September 1993. It has been held that a boy under 10 years old cannot commit an offence and so cannot be procured to commit rape,[154] but this reasoning seems flawed.[155]

Penetration

Penetration is not defined in the Act, although s 79(2) provides that it is a continuing act, thus putting on a statutory footing the decisions of the Privy Council in *Kaitamaki*[156] and the Court of Appeal in *Cooper and Schaub.*[157] Penetration continues until withdrawal,[158] and A can be convicted of rape where having initially penetrated B with consent, B subsequently withdraws that consent and A, being aware of that retraction of consent, does not remove his penis.[159] Presumably, D will not commit the offence until he either knows or could reasonably be expected to know that consent had been withdrawn.

The Act does not provide any clarification of the degree of penetration necessary. Presumably the common law rule applies so that the slightest degree of penetration will suffice. In relation to vaginal rape, this will include any penetration of the vulva,[160] and thus, the common law rule that it is not necessary to show that the hymen was ruptured

148 *Setting the Boundaries*, ch 2, para 2.8.4.

149 The Sexual Offences Act 1993 removed the common law presumption that boys under the age of 14 are incapable of vaginal or anal intercourse. In a prosecution for historic offences pre 20/09/93 a defendant cannot be guilty of charges involving acts of sexual intercourse perpetrated when he was aged under 14. See *R v W* [2003] 10 Archbold News 2 and D. Ormerod, 'A Presumption of Intercourse' (2003) Archbold News 2.

150 Under s 79(3).

151 Section 79(3). See *Setting the Boundaries* recommendation at para 2.8.4.

152 *Ram* (1893) 17 Cox CC 609; *Lord Baltimore's case* (1768) 1 Black, W. 648.

153 *Cogan and Leak* [1975] 2 All ER 1059.

154 *DPP v K and C* [1997] 1 Cr App R 36 at 42.

155 See commentary in [1997] Crim LR 121, and above, p 207.

156 [1985] AC 147.

157 [1994] Crim LR 531.

158 For criticism of *Kaitamaki* see previous editions, where it was emphasized that the offence requires penetration without consent as an essential part of the *actus reus* of rape and this act of penetration must be accompanied by the *mens rea.*

159 See also *Tarmohammed* [1997] Crim LR 458; *Greaves* [1999] 1 Cr App R (S) 319.

160 Section 79(3).

remains.[161] In the recent case of *F*,[162] 'vagina' was held to be used in the general sense of the female genitals not in its strict anatomical sense[163] There is no express provision making clear that rape is complete upon penetration *without the emission of seed*,[164] but this must surely still represent the law. The fact that the Act creates numerous other offences of non-penile penetration supports this view.

If the prosecution fails to establish that there was penetration by a penis, a verdict of attempted rape may be returned if A's conduct amounted to more than mere preparation to penile penetration. It was held under the old law that digital penetration of the vagina might be sufficient to found an attempted rape conviction. In such circumstances a conviction under s 2 (non-penile penetration), would also be available, as would a conviction under s 3 (sexual assault). If the prosecution fails to establish that there was any penetration at all, it may still be the case that the conduct is more than merely preparatory to the commission of the full offence of rape. In addition, the offence of sexual assault under s 3 (below) may be available.

Of the vagina, anus or mouth

'Vagina' is to be interpreted as including the vulva.[165] At common law rape protected only against penetration of the vagina, indeed historically it was an offence protecting virginity.[166] The Criminal Justice and Public Order Act 1994 s 142, introduced the offence of anal rape, and the Court of Appeal has held that in sentencing terms anal rape and vaginal rape should not generally be distinguished. The 2003 Act extends the offence yet further by including non-consensual penile penetration of the mouth. The Sexual Offences Review acknowledged that non-consensual oral sex is as 'abhorrent, demeaning and traumatizing' as vaginal and anal penetration by the penis.[167] There is no doubt that this form of conduct deserves appropriate condemnation by the law in terms of labelling and sentence, but it is arguable that it would have been more appropriately dealt with as non-consensual penetration under s 2 (which also carries a life sentence). Jurors' willingness to convict of 'rape' for this conduct remains to be seen. There may of course be greater forensic difficulties in establishing oral sex as opposed to vaginal or anal penetration, although that in itself should not militate against it being classified as rape.[168]

The Court of Appeal has confirmed that sentencing should not distinguish between the orifice penetrated.[169]

Section 79 of the Act provides further relevant definition, including welcome confirmation that surgically reconstructed penises can penetrate, and surgically reconstructed vaginas be penetrated.[170]

[161] *Hughes* (1841) 9 C & P 752; *Lines* (1844) 1 C & K 393; *Allen (Henry)* (1839) 9 C & P 31; *M'Rue* (1838) 8 C & P 641.

[162] [2002] EWCA Crim 2936.

[163] Cf *Holland* (1993) 117 ALR 193, Aus High Ct.

[164] Cf s 44 of the SOA 1956.

[165] Section 79(9).

[166] J. Temkin, *Rape and the Legal Process* (2nd edn), 57.

[167] *Setting the Boundaries*, para 2.8.5. See the Government response to the *Home Affairs Committee Fifth Report*.

[168] The Sentencing Advisory Panel proposes that which orifice is penetrated should not affect the starting point for sentencing, 15.

[169] *Ismail* [2005] EWCA Crim 397.

[170] Section 79(3) of the SOA 2003. This puts on a statutory footing the ruling in *Matthews* (unreported) Oct 1996. See also M. Hicks and G. Branston, 'Transexual Rape – A Loophole Closed?' [1997] Crim LR 526.

Without consent

The critical element of rape remains the absence of consent. Without that, penile penetration is not merely not criminal, it is an explicit expression of intimacy. The Act's approach to consent is discussed above.

(ii) *Mens rea*

Intentional penetration

The requirement that the defendant *intentionally* penetrate the relevant orifice should not give rise to difficulty in practice. One circumstance in which A might realistically claim that penile penetration was 'accidental' might include those where A intended to penetrate B's vagina with her consent, but accidentally penetrated her anus, for which act he knew he did not have consent, or to which he could not reasonably believe that he had consent (whether from previous knowledge or from B's expression of non-consent once A penetrated her anally).[171]

Since this element of the offence is expressed in terms of intention, it would seem that a mistake of this nature induced by voluntary intoxication can be relied upon.[172]

Mens rea as to consent

One of the most dramatic changes to the offence relates to the defendant's mental element. Under s 1(1) of the Act the prosecution has to prove intentional penetration of the vagina, anus or mouth of the complainant, and an absence of a *reasonable* belief that the complainant was consenting. 'Reckless rape' as it was previously understood has been abolished.

It will be recalled that in *Morgan* it was held that rape was not proved if the man may have honestly believed that the woman was consenting, even if that belief was unreasonable. Lord Hailsham in *Morgan* required an 'intention of having intercourse, willy-nilly, not caring whether the victim consents or not'.[173] Another way of putting this was to ask, 'Was D's attitude one of "I could not care less whether she is consenting or not, I am going to have intercourse with her regardless".'[174] Thus, the *mens rea* under the old law was an intention to have sexual intercourse with V, (i) knowing that V does not consent, or (ii) being aware that there is a possibility that she does not consent.

Following widespread public concern with this approach the Heilbron committee[175] reviewed the position and, while endorsing *Morgan*, recommended some statutory clarification. The Sexual Offences (Amendment) Act 1976 provides in s 1(2): 'It is hereby declared that if at a trial for a rape offence the jury has to consider whether a man believed that a woman or man was consenting to sexual intercourse, the presence or absence of reasonable grounds for such a belief is a matter to which the jury is to have regard, in conjunction with any other relevant matters, in considering whether he so believed.' This was largely a public relations provision explaining the jury's role in evaluating a defendant's mistaken beliefs of facts; it did not enact any rule peculiar to rape.

171 See eg *Pigg* (above) and discussion by S. White, 'Three Points on *Pigg*' [1989] Crim LR 539.

172 Cf *Woods* (1981) 74 Cr App R 132.

173 [1976] AC 182 at 215. See also the Heilbron, Report of the Advisory Group on the Law of Rape (1975) Cmnd 6352, para 77.

174 *Taylor* (1984) 80 Cr App R 327; *Haughian* (1985) 80 Cr App R 334.

175 Cmnd 6352 (1975). See [1976] Crim LR 97.

There was little categorical evidence that *Morgan* defences were successfully run, so jurors were presumably not readily believing defendants' spurious claims. Even if largely unsuccessful, the plea was easy to run and difficult to disprove, and sent an undesirable message to society – that it is acceptable to take unreasonable risks as to your partner's consent to sexual conduct.[176] Unsurprisingly, many submissions to the Sexual Offences Review were highly critical of the doctrine. *Setting the Boundaries* regarded this 'defence' as in direct conflict with the ordinary perceptions of contemporary society. A more objective approach to the issue of *mens rea* as to consent was desirable, or even necessary, but further difficulty lay in determining the appropriate degree of objectivity.

One key issue of the reform agenda became whether the *mens rea* (for rape in particular) ought to be rendered wholly objective (would a reasonable person have realized that B was not consenting?). Although the general trend of English criminal law has been increasingly favouring subjective approaches to *mens rea* – even in serious sexual offences[177] – there are powerful arguments against adopting a purely subjective approach in this context. When the conduct in question is of a sexual nature, the ease with which the defendant can ascertain the consent of his partner coupled with the catastrophic consequences for the victim if the defendant acts without consent militate strongly against the purely subjective approach. The generosity the law extends to accepting a defendant's genuine but unreasonable mistakes in, for example, matters of self-defence need not be replicated in sexual cases because the conduct in question calls for a qualitatively different degree of vigilance on his part.[178]

The government took a strong stance on this aspect of the reform.[179] In early versions of the Sexual Offences Bill, it was proposed that the defendant would bear a *legal* burden (on the balance of probabilities) to show that he did believe that the complainant consented. This may well have been in breach of Article 6(2) of the ECHR. The final version is less objective, and although to be welcomed for extending the *mens rea*, the Act is far from clear, and still leaves the opportunity for *Morgan*-type pleas to be run (although they will be even less likely to succeed).

The *mens rea* in rape and the other non-consensual offences (ss 1–4) comprises two elements:

(i) A does not reasonably believe B consents.

(ii) Whether a belief is reasonable is to be determined having regard to all the circumstances, including any steps A has taken to ascertain whether B consents.

The new provisions do not render the test wholly objective.[180] The defendant's personal characteristics and beliefs remain important, but both the concluded belief as to consent and the manner by which A reached it are to be assessed by reference to some objective criteria.

176 See the Law Commission's Policy Paper in *Setting the Boundaries* (2000) (vol 2).

177 See *R v K* [2001] UKHL 41; *DPP v B* [2000] 2WLR 452.

178 See generally J. Horder, 'Cognition, Emotion and Criminal Culpability' (1990) 106 LQR 469, 477; T. Pickard, 'Culpable Mistakes' (1980) 30 U Toronto J 75; C. Wells, 'Swatting the Subjectivist Bug' [1982] Crim LR 209.

179 See HL, col 1089, 31 Mar 2003, Lord Falconer.

180 Cf *Card*, above para 2.13.

A does 'not reasonably believe'

This encompasses cases in which (i) A's purpose is to act without B's consent; (ii) A is aware that B might not be consenting; (iii) A has no belief whether B is consenting or not; (iv) A holds a belief that B is consenting but that is an unreasonable belief. What remains unclear is whether in (iv) the question is as to (a) A's purely subjective belief about consent measured against a standard of reasonableness applied by the jury or magistrate, or (b) A's assessment that his own belief as to consent was reasonable. It is submitted that the correct interpretation is that in (a).[181] The dilution of the purely objective test originally proposed to accommodate those with limited capacity has not been that substantial. A with a learning disability, who believes B is consenting will have the *mens rea* if the reasonable juror concludes that belief was an unreasonable one, irrespective of the fact that the basis for belief is understandable given A's limited capacity.

Importantly, the issue of the reasonableness of belief will now be worth pursuing in interview with the suspect.

Reasonable having regard to all the circumstances including the steps taken

The reasonableness test does not oblige the defendant to have taken any specific steps to ascertain consent; the government was keen to emphasize that there would be no need to have blank consent forms by the bedside. However, where steps have been taken they must be taken into account by the jury in deciding whether the defendant's claimed belief in consent was reasonable.[182]

Ministerial statements[183] suggest that the expression 'all the circumstances' in subs (2) will allow juries when determining the reasonableness of the belief, to take account of any *relevant* characteristics of the defendant. Ministers rejected the idea that the very narrow interpretation of similar provisions in New Zealand might be followed creating a purely objective test.[184] It is clear then that the defendant's age; general sexual experience; sexual experience with this complainant;[185] learning disability; and any other factor that could have affected his ability to understand the nature and consequences of his actions may be relevant depending on the circumstance of the particular case. What weight will attach to these characteristics will be a matter for judicial direction.

Several difficulties flow from the breadth of this provision. First, there is the question as to which characteristics of the defendant might be *excluded* from the jury's deliberation. Should the jury be able to take into account the defendant's self-induced intoxication by drink or drugs? On the basis of the long-established position that rape is a crime of basic intent, it would seem not.[186] What of other characteristics, such as those which are inherently unreasonable in the context of sexual conduct? For example, what of A who claims that women who invite him for coffee are automatically agreeing to sex? Or that dressing in a short skirt is an invitation to be touched in a sexual manner? Ministers reassured Parliament that the jury would not be asked to take into account such

[181] HC, col 639 refers ambiguously to the 'focus on the defendant's belief' para 23.

[182] HC, 3rd reading, col 669, 17 June 2003.

[183] HC, col 1073, Lord Falconer of Thoroton, 2 June 2003; HC, col 674, Baroness Scotland of Asthal, 17 June 2003.

[184] HC, col 674, Baroness Scotland of Asthal, 17 June 2003.

[185] *McAllister* [1997] Crim LR 233.

[186] *Fotheringham* (1988) 88 Cr App R 206.

characteristics.[187] The crucial question for the courts will lie in defining the limits on which less-strikingly unreasonable characteristics are legally relevant. This has created difficulty elsewhere in the law, particularly with provocation.[188] Careful judicial direction will be critical. Once again it is disappointing that such an important issue is not resolved in the Act.

Secondly, and related to this point, the statute does not expressly preclude the most objectionable of the *Morgan*-type pleas from being advanced. A could claim that he had taken reasonable steps to ascertain the consent of the complainant by asking her friends, or by seeking the confirmation of her husband (as in *Morgan*). A could also claim that it was reasonable for him to ignore B's explicit 'no' since he believes that all women sometimes say 'no' and mean 'yes'. Such pleas will be extremely unlikely to be considered to be 'reasonable' by any right thinking jury. Nevertheless, the new provisions allows for the plea to be run and thus for the complainant to face questioning on such a basis. It should be noted that *Setting The Boundaries* recommended a significantly wider list of circumstances presumptively vitiating consent including where a person has agreement given for them by a third party.[189] This was rejected because of concerns that a person with a learning disability, A, might be easily deceived by X and have sex with B believing her to be consenting on the basis of X's false statement.[190]

(iii) Procedural matters

Rape is triable only on indictment (except for certain cases where there is provision for trial in the Youth Court).[191] The maximum penalty is life imprisonment.[192] Rapes abroad may be tried in England if the victim of the rape was under 16 and the offender is a British citizen or resident in the UK, provided the act is an offence under the law in the country in which it took place.[193]

(iv) Prosecutions for historic marital rape

The rule of the common law from the time of Hale was that, with few exceptions, a husband could not be convicted of raping his wife. The rule was based on a fiction that a wife could not retract the consent to intercourse which she gave upon marriage – a proposition which family law had long since rejected. In 1991, in *R*, the House of Lords decided that there was no rule that a husband cannot be guilty of rape of his wife and that

187 Lord Falconer of Thoroton stated 'Introducing a requirement that all of the personal characteristics of the defendant should be taken into account would mean that the jury would be asked to take into account characteristics that should not absolve him from his guilt: for example, the fact that he has a quick temper or that the sight of a girl in a mini-skirt will always turn him on and make him unable to resist her. That cannot be the intention'. HL, 17 June 2003.

188 See especially in relation to provocation *Smith (Morgan)* and note that the House of Lords expressly rejected this hybrid approach, preferring to overrule *Caldwell* than find a middle ground: *R v G* [2003] UKHL 50.

189 Ibid 20, para 2.10.9.

190 See Temkin and Ashworth, above n 54, 339.

191 Magistrates' Court Act 1980, s 24, as amended by the Powers of Criminal Courts (Sentencing) Act 2000, s 165(1) and Sch 9, para 64.

192 Sexual Offences Act 2003, s 1(4). Attempted rape formerly carried a maximum of seven years' imprisonment: Sexual Offences Act 1956, s 37 and Sch 2. The maximum was increased to life by the Sexual Offences Act 1985, s 3(2).

193 Section 72 of the Act.

the word, 'unlawful' in s 1 of the 1976 Act was 'surplusage'. It is arguable that this decision flouted the will of Parliament but the result was highly desirable.

A husband can even be guilty of raping his wife if the non-consensual sexual intercourse took place before the House of Lords' abolition of the exemption in *R v R* in 1991. The ECtHR expressly held that this will not violate Article 7.1 of the Convention,[194] rejecting this claim in *SW v United Kingdom, CR v United Kingdom*.[195] The Court held that Article 7.1 did not prohibit the gradual evolution and clarification of the common law rules of criminal liability through judicial interpretation, provided that the developments were consistent with the essence of the offence and could reasonably be anticipated. Since the House of Lords in *R* had continued a discernible trend of developing case law incrementally removing the husband's immunity, and this was a foreseeable development there was no violation.

In *Crooks*,[196] the Court of Appeal upheld the defendant's 2002 conviction for raping his wife in 1970. The court was confident that a solicitor would have told his client in 1970 that the courts had developed and continued to develop exceptions to the marital exemption, and that if the appellate courts reconsidered the issue they might abolish it. With respect, this is doubtful. At the time, the only exceptions to the application of the marital rape exemption appeared to be for an agreement to separate and a *decree nisi*.[197] This also ignores the fact that the House of Commons had expressly rejected a motion to change the law 15 years before *R v R*; the Law Commission had in its exhaustive treatment of the issue in 1990 listed the exceptions,[198] and noted that they extended only to specified judicial orders of separation, and not even to cases where judicial proceedings had been initiated.[199]

(b) Assault by penetration – s 2

A person, A, commits an offence if he intentionally penetrates the vagina or anus of another person (B), sexually, with a part of his body or anything else, where B does not consent to the penetration, and A does not reasonably believe that B consents.

This is a completely new offence carrying a maximum life sentence.[200] It is designed to reflect the seriousness of non-consensual penetration with objects other than the penis. Acts of penetration with bottles, knives, fingers, etc are caught by s 2. Such acts would have been charged as indecent assault under the old law, and thus lacked a sufficiently

194 'No one shall be guilty of any criminal offence on account of any act or omission which did not constitute a criminal offence under national or international law at the time when it was committed.'

195 [1996] 1 FLR 434.

196 [2005] Crim LR 238 and commentary by Ashworth.

197 See *Miller* [1954] 2 QB 282. See also the explanation in the 1st edition of this work, p 291; *O'Brien* [1974] 3 All ER 663; *Steele* [1977] Crim LR 290.

198 See Law Com Working Paper No 116 (1990), paras 2.12–2.16. See further Law Com Report No 205, *Rape within Marriage* (1992).

199 Cf the decision in *Laskey* [2003] All ER (D) 69 (May), where D was convicted of the rape in marriage between 1988–1995. At this point in time it would have been clear to any lawyer that the exemption was on the brink of being abolished.

200 The Sentencing Advisory Panel recommends that it shares the same sentencing starting point as rape but in *A-G's Reference (No 104 of 2004)* [2004] EWCA Crim 2672, the Court of Appeal suggested a statutory point of four years.

accurate or stigmatizing label and sentencing power.[201] The Court of Appeal has made clear that a life sentence may be appropriate for some acts of digital penetration.[202]

(i) *Actus reus*

Penetration is discussed above. Unlike rape the penetration need not be by a penis; where it is, the charge ought to be under s 1. Where there is doubt as to with what the complainant was penetrated the charge should be under s 2. The offence can be committed by a person of either sex on a person of either sex. The act of penetration is regarded as continuing until withdrawal. Since the degree of penetration need only be slight, and 'vagina' includes 'vulva',[203] oral sex performed on a woman is caught by s 2. The requirement that the penetration is 'sexual' (as discussed above) excludes medical examinations, intimate body searches, etc. If the prosecution cannot establish the 'sexual' element, there is no *actus reus*, and the offence is not committed even if the complainant is not-consenting to the penetration. Such acts should be charged as offences against the person.

(ii) *Mens rea*

The penetration must be intentional; there is no crime of reckless sexual penetration. This is significant since it provides an excuse for the voluntarily intoxicated defendant who relies on his intoxicated state to support his claim that his penetration of V with an object/part of his body was not intentional, but 'accidental'. Such circumstances are however unlikely to be commonplace.

The *mens rea* regarding consent is determined in accordance with the principles discussed above pp 619–621. Sections 75 and 76 relating to presumptions on consent apply.

It remains unclear whether there is an element of *mens rea* as to the 'sexual' nature of the penetration. As a matter of principle, each element of the *actus reus* ought to have a corresponding element of *mens rea*. The fact that this element of *actus reus* (sexual) is to be determined by the jury does not of itself preclude a corresponding requirement of *mens rea*.[204] If this additional *mens rea* element is required, a defendant might claim, for example, that his penetration of V's vagina with an object such as a bottle was motivated solely by a desire to cause injury, being performed with a violent and not a sexual intent. It is doubtful that such a plea would be successful, and the defendant would, in any event, have thereby admitted an offence against the person.[205] There are bizarre instances of penetrative conduct that would appear to be motivated by such non-sexual motives.[206] It may be that penetrative acts by state agents would be dealt with, additionally, as offences against the person where performed as acts of violence or torture.[207]

[201] A maximum 10 years. [202] *Corran* [2005] EWCA Crim 192. [203] Section 79.

[204] The definition of grievous bodily harm is left to the jury but D must still be proved to have intended it for a s 18 charge under the OAPA 1861.

[205] Section 18 of the OAPA 1861. See Stevenson, *et al.* above, p 41.

[206] In *C* [2001] 1 Cr App R (S) 533 D paid a prostitute to fellate him and surreptitiously inserted live maggots into her vagina.

[207] In *Aydin v Turkey* (1997) 25 EHRR 251 it was recognized that rape by a State official could constitute torture.

(c) Sexual assault – s 3

Under the law prior to the 2003 Act there were two offences of 'indecent assault', one protecting men and the other women.[208] For the want of anything more specific, these offences dealt with all non-consensual conduct: non-penile penetrations of the vagina and anus, oral sex; the merest touching in an indecent manner; and even psychic assaults in circumstances of indecency. The label on conviction did not differentiate between the vastly different forms of conduct and their disparate gravity.[209] Many of the activities dealt with previously as indecent assaults would now be rape (oral sex) or s 2 (most commonly digital penetration).

The 2003 Act introduces a very much wider offence with greater ambiguity stemming from the broad definition of the central elements of 'sexual' and 'touching'.

A commits an offence if he intentionally touches another person (B), sexually, and B does not consent to the touching, and A does not reasonably believe that B consents. The maximum sentence is 10 years on indictment; and 6 months summarily.[210]

(i) *Actus reus*

The elements of 'sexual' and 'touching' have been discussed above. In combination the terms render the offence very broad indeed. There is no element of hostility required; a kiss could be sufficient provided it is regarded as sexual, as could stroking clothing without the victim's awareness. Although described as 'sexual assault' there is no need for a technical assault or battery; a touching is what is needed. As such, conduct that would constitute a psychic assault would not satisfy the *actus reus*.[211]

If the touching is in non-sexual circumstances there is no offence – for example, where a police officer pats down a suspect, or a rugby player grabs the testicles of an opponent in the scrum. If the complainant is not consenting to such touching the conduct should be charged, if at all, as an offence against the person.

The sexual touching must be proved to be without consent. The presumptions in ss 75 and 76 (discussed above) apply. Given the breadth of the activity covered, there is a potential for problems with the conclusive presumptions. What, for example, of the Dr A who tells B, accurately, that a breast examination is necessary, but who also nurses a secret sexual purpose? This would probably be regarded as sufficient to trigger the conclusive presumption, if it could be proved.

(ii) *Mens rea*

The touching must be intentional. The crime is one of specific intent. The voluntarily intoxicated defendant who claims that his touch was 'accidental' may rely on his intoxicated state to displace the *mens rea*. This is likely to be a much more commonly occurring plea than one of intoxicated penetration. The voluntarily intoxicated defendant who is

208 Sections 14 and 15 of the Act.

209 J. Temkin, (2000) 150 NLJ 1169, 1170 described them as 'mindless' (by which presumably is meant that they did not describe the essence of the wrongdoing, particularly in serious cases).

210 The Sentencing Advisory Panel distinguishes 13 categories of sexual touching, decreasing in seriousness from penetration to rubbing against another's clothed body with one's own clothed body (frottage), 18.

211 Cf *Rolfe* (1952) Cr App R 4 (above).

charged with having 'groped' a person at a party may claim that the touching was unintentional and that he was merely flailing around (in what nowadays passes for dancing) or holding his hands out to steady himself in his stupor.

The defendant must be shown to have *mens rea* as to consent (above pp 619–621).

A claim that the touching was not intended to be 'sexual', but rather was one of pure violence could in some circumstances form the basis of a plausible plea, certainly more so than in circumstances of penetration under s 2 discussed above. It remains unclear whether the courts will entertain such a plea.

(d) Intentionally causing someone to engage in sexual activity – s 4

A commits an offence if he intentionally causes another person (B) to engage in an activity, the activity is sexual, B does not consent to engaging in the activity, and A does not reasonably believe that B consents.

This is an entirely new and potentially very useful offence, which has as one of its purposes criminalizing the actions of women who force men to penetrate them. Under the old law this conduct would have been prosecuted as indecent assault only. Examples of other types of conduct caught by this offence would include requiring a person to masturbate him/herself[212] or to masturbate another person. It is an extremely broad offence and could also include A, who for example, causes B to act as a prostitute.

Aggravated versions of the offence (which attract a maximum of life imprisonment rather than the standard maximum 10 years on indictment/6 months summarily) are created by subs (4). These involve penetration of B's anus or vagina; penetration of B's mouth with a person's penis; penetration of a person's anus or vagina by B with his body or otherwise; or penetration of a person's mouth with B's penis. Applying *Courtie*,[213] there are separate offences created and this must be reflected in the indictment.[214]

(i) *Actus reus*

The offence can be committed by words alone, and there is no explicit requirement that A is present when B engages in the activity nor that A participate in the activity. The offence could also involve a third party, who might also be a victim if neither the third party nor B consent. However, this is not a preliminary offence: the sexual activity must take place for A to be guilty. Although A must 'cause' the action, following orthodox principles of causation[215] it appears to be sufficient for A to be 'a' cause of the sexual activity without being the 'sole' cause. It is doubtful that an omission to prevent sexual activity occurring is a sufficient *actus reus*.[216]

The presumptions regarding consent in ss 75 and 76 (discussed above) apply.

(ii) *Mens rea*

As with rape, discussed above, the reasonableness of belief is determined by reference to 'all the circumstances' including 'any steps A has taken to ascertain B's consent'.

212 As in *Sargeant* [1997] Crim LR 50.

213 [1984] AC 463.

214 Where penetration is involved the Sentencing Advisory Panel suggests the same starting point as rape should apply: 17.

215 Discussed in Ch 4.

216 See *Clarkson and Carroll* [1971] 3 All ER 344. Card, above, n 1.

There is a requirement of 'intention', which in this context would apparently include oblique intention – foresight by A that B's engaging in the sexual activity is a virtually certain consequence of A's action, even though it might not be his 'direct intention'.[217]

The requirement of intention to cause B to engage in the activity, creates a specific intent offence. A who in a voluntarily intoxicated state jokingly encourages B to strip might claim that there was no such intent, but drunken intent is still intent.

4. Offences against children under 13 (ss 5–8)[218]

The offences in ss 5–8 are very similar to those in ss 1–4, except that they relate only to offences against children under 13, and there is no requirement to prove the absence of consent. Under the old law a child under 16 could not consent to indecent assault, but could consent to sexual intercourse.[219] Determining whether a child consented to sexual intercourse involved an assessment of her understanding of the activity.[220] Consent is no longer an issue. This shift proved to be very controversial as the legislation progressed through Parliament. The commendable underlying policy of the offences is to protect the child from the 'predatory' older offender, and to guard against exploitation of young people, but the breadth of the offences raises a number of problems.

First, the legislation makes no attempt to distinguish between exploitative sexual activity against a child under 13 (whether by older individual or not) and that of fully informed consensual sexual experimentation between children under that age.

Secondly, denying the relevance of the factual consent of the under-13-year-old clashes with the law's willingness to accept their capacity to consent to, for example, invasive medical procedures. Elsewhere the law recognizes a child's capacity to consent. The Home Secretary has stated in a press release on the Act receiving Royal Assent that there would be no prosecution for sexual activity between children under the age of 16 where the activity is genuinely consensual. This rather begs the question why the Act is not drafted so as to include a requirement of an absence of consent.

Thirdly, this poses potential problems under the ECHR. It is possible that a child aged 12 who was a willing participant to sexual conduct (which includes activity as limited as kissing) could claim an infringement of his/her Article 8 rights to respect for private life.[221] There is no additional restraint on prosecution such as a requirement of the DPP's consent.

The final general point to note is that the breadth of the new offences means that in cases of consensual sexual activity between 12-year-olds they will both commit an offence – for example, as penetrator (s 5) and penetrated (s 9). In this context, the drafting undermines the principle in *Tyrell*[222] whereby a child 'victim' could not be convicted as a participant in the offence.

217 See above Ch 5.

218 See generally F. Bennion, 'Criminalizing Children under the Sexual Offences Bill' (2003) 167 JP 784; J. R. Spencer, 'Child and Family Offences' [2004] Crim LR 347. For sentencing guidance see *Corran* [2005] EWCA Crim 192.

219 It was arguable that since all acts of intercourse must include an indecent assault, the law was irremediably incoherent.

220 *Howard* [1966] 1 WLR 13.

221 See the discussion above.

222 [1894] 1 QB 710.

Note the degree of overlap of ss 9–10 and s 13 with ss 5–8. For example, a person guilty of s 5 could be guilty of s 9 or s 13 also ('touching' including penetration). The sections have considerable sentencing discrepancy – s 5 is a maximum of life, s 9 (over 18s) maximum 14 years, s 13 (under 18s) maximum 5 years/6 months.

CPS guidance

In relation to an adult defendant committing offences under ss 5–8, the CPS guidance[223] is that 'a prosecution will usually take place unless there are public interest factors tending against prosecution which clearly outweigh those tending in favour.' The Crown Prosecution Service emphasizes that the 'overriding public concern is to protect children. It was not Parliament's intention to punish children unnecessarily or for the criminal law to intervene where it is wholly inappropriate.' The CPS view is that the 2003 Act does 'not change the principles or the decision making process in deciding whether or not to prosecute youths for sexual offences.'[224] Prosecutors are to have regard to:

- the age and understanding of the offender. This may include whether the offender has been subjected to any exploitation, coercion, threat, deception, grooming or manipulation by another which has lead him or her to commit the offence;
- the relevant ages of the parties, that is, the same or no significant disparity in age;
- whether the complainant entered into sexual activity willingly, that is, did the complainant understand the nature of his or her actions and that (s)he was able to communicate his or her willingness freely;
- parity between the parties in regard to sexual, physical, emotional and educational development;
- the relationship between the parties, its nature and duration and whether this represents a genuine transitory phase of adolescent development;
- whether there is any element of exploitation, coercion, threat, deception, grooming or manipulation in the relationship;
- the nature of the activity eg penetrative or non-penetrative activity;
- what is in the best interests and welfare of the complainant; and
- what is in the best interests and welfare of the defendant.

It is recognized that 'it is **not** in the public interest to prosecute children who are of the same or similar age and understanding that engage in sexual activity, where the activity is truly consensual for both parties and there are no aggravating features, such as coercion or corruption'.

(a) Rape of an child under 13 – s 5

There had been much discussion of the merits of a 'statutory rape' offence, commonly found in the USA, and s 5 introduces one: a person commits an offence if he

223 See www.cps.gov.uk/legal/section7/sexoffencesact2003.html.

224 The Guidance emphasizes the need to gather as much information as possible from sources, such as the police, Youth Offending Teams (YOTs), and any professionals assisting those agencies about the defendant's home circumstances and the circumstances surrounding the alleged offence, as well as any information known about the victim.

intentionally penetrates the vagina, anus or mouth of another person with his penis, and the other person is under 13.

As noted above, the Sexual Offences Review was anxious for the offence of rape to continue to reflect everyday conceptions of that term, hence the requirement of penile penetration. In this instance, the unique stigma of 'rape' has been applied to conduct which seems to be lacking the most important aspect of the everyday conception of the offence – an absence of consent. The maximum sentence is one of life imprisonment.[225] It remains to be seen whether prosecutorial discretion is exercised so as to prevent this offence from being prosecuted inappropriately. Given that it is rape, it will be more difficult for the CPS to declare that it is not in the public interest to prosecute, particularly in the face of pressure from the complainant's parents.[226]

(i) *Actus reus*

Each element of the *actus reus* – penetration, with a penis, of the vagina, anus or mouth – has already been discussed in the section on rape. It has already been noted that this is a very broad offence: B, aged 12, who willingly performs oral sex on her 12-year-old boyfriend thereby renders him a rapist (and she commits offences under ss 7 and 9). The absence of any requirement of consent means that it is less likely that the complainant will face the ordeal of giving evidence. The additional element of the *actus reus* is that B is aged under 13. Given the significance of B's age, it is crucial that this element is proved strictly via the usual mechanisms. The defendant may be of any age, although criminal liability as a principal offender arises at the age of 10.[227]

(ii) *Mens rea*

Penetration must be intentional, as discussed above. There is no opportunity for a plea of consent, and thus no plea of mistaken belief as to consent, however reasonable. Similarly there is no scope for a plea of mistake, however reasonable, as to the age of the complainant.

(iii) Defences for secondary liability

Concern was expressed in Parliament as to the potential for such broad offences to criminalize the actions of teachers and health care workers who advise young people about sex education and safe sexual practices in general. For example, there was concern that the doctor who provided contraceptives to the 12-year-old girl to protect her in her consensual sexual acts with her partner would be aiding and abetting her 'rape'. To meet this difficulty, s 14 of the Act provides that there is no liability for aiding and abetting or counselling if the purpose of the actor is to protect the child from sexually transmitted diseases or pregnancy or to protect physical safety or promote emotional well being, unless the actor's purpose is to gain sexual gratification or to cause or encourage the relevant sexual act.[228]

225 The Sentencing Advisory Panel propose that the starting point for sentencing is as with rape.

226 See Mr Malins, HC Standing Committee B, col 107, 11 Sept 2003.

227 See above, Ch 11 on defences.

228 Section 73.

(b) Assault of a child under 13 by penetration – s 6

It is an offence for a person intentionally to penetrate the vagina or anus of a person under 13 with a part of the body or anything else where that penetration is sexual.

This is an entirely new offence, identical to that in s 2, except that there is no requirement that the complainant is not consenting. Again there is no scope for a plea of mistaken belief in consent or mistaken reasonable beliefs as to the age of the victim. This is a very broad offence which criminalizes consensual sexual (for example, digital) penetration between 12 year-olds. As with the offence under s 5, there is no liability for aiding and abetting or counselling if the purpose of the assistance is to protect the child unless the actor's purpose is to gain sexual gratification or to cause or encourage the relevant sexual act.[229] Section 6 is triable on indictment only and carries a maximum sentence of life imprisonment.

(c) Sexual assault of a child – s 7

It is an offence intentionally to touch a person under 13, where that touching is sexual. This new offence is identical to that in s 3 (above), except that there is no requirement that the complainant is not consenting. There is no scope for a plea of mistaken belief in consent or mistaken reasonable belief as to the age of the victim. This is an excessively broad offence which criminalises consensual kissing between 12-year-olds.[230] The defence applicable to abetting or counselling applies as under ss 5 and 6.[231]

(d) Causing or inciting a child under 13 to engage in sexual activity – s 8

It is an offence intentionally to cause a person under 13 to engage in an activity, which is sexual. It is also an offence intentionally to incite a person under 13 to engage in a sexual activity. These are entirely new offences, broader than the offence under s 4 above. Separate offences carrying a maximum of life imprisonment (rather than the standard 14 years on indictment/ six months summarily) are created under subs (4) if the activity involves causing or inciting:

(a) penetration of B's anus or vagina,
(b) penetration of B's mouth with a person's penis,
(c) penetration of a person's anus or vagina by B, or
(d) penetration of a person's mouth with B's penis.

(i) *Actus reus*

One offence can be committed by causing B to engage in sexual activity in which case it is identical to that under s 4 above except that there is no requirement that B is not consenting. A who persuades his 12-year-old girlfriend to masturbate herself commits the *actus reus* of this offence.

229 Section 73.

230 Section 7 is triable either way. The maximum sentence is 14 years on indictment; six months summarily.

231 Section 73.

In addition, there is an offence of 'incitement' of B. It is submitted that the word incitement should carry its technical legal meaning.[232] The inclusion of a specific offence of incitement enables a prosecution where the child incited would not herself commit an offence, thereby precluding liability under a common law charge of incitement. This version of the offence is much broader and does not require that any sexual activity occurs. It covers the case where A, the friend of B, aged 12, encourages B to have oral sex with B's boyfriend C.

Unlike ss 5–7 there is no defence for 'abetting or counselling' to protect the child.[233] Thus, teacher, A, approached by B, 12, who asks whether she should engage in full sex with her boyfriend X as he would like, commits the offence if he, A, incites her by suggesting that since she and X are only 12 they should stick to other intimate activities short of sex (even perhaps just kissing).

5. Sexual offences against children aged 13–16

The legal age of consent remains at 16.[234] Under the old law the protection afforded to children under 16 years included specific offences of unlawful sexual intercourse with a girl under 16 (s 6); buggery of a person under 16 (s 12); indecent assault against boys and girls under 16 irrespective of their consent (ss 14 and 15) and offences under the Indecency with Children Act 1960. These offences had been incrementally amended and lacked coherence.

The 2003 Act creates a series of specific offences targeting a wider range of sexual activity with children under 16. These reflect the Act's policy of protecting children from sexual exploitation. There is no time limit on prosecution as there was under some of the 1956 Act offences, which reflects the growing awareness of frequent delays in disclosing childhood sexual abuse.

The creation of such broad ranging offences raises a number of difficulties. In particular, a successful challenge under Article 8 of the ECHR might be mounted by consenting 15-year-olds.[235] Widespread public concern that the Act criminalized consensual sexual activity between children produced only Ministerial assurances that the use of these offences in prosecuting children will be limited.

> there are no convictions at present [for kissing]. The guidelines [for the CPS] will be strong and I do not think that there will be prosecutions in the future for less serious consensual activity between children.[236]

Parliament expressly rejected the approach in other jurisdictions whereby liability for consensual sexual activity with those under 16 would be criminal only where one of the

232 See Ch 12 above. 233 Section 73.

234 *Setting the Boundaries*, recommended that age of consent remain at 16 – para 3.5.7 (recommendation no 17) the age of consent is lower in most other European countries – para 3.9.9.

235 Cf the view in *E v DPP* [2005] EWHC 147 (Admin), in which it was held that Article 8 was not infringed by s 6 of the 1956 Act.

236 See Paul Goggins, HC, col 622, 3 Nov 2003.

parties was older than the other by a specified amount – for example, two years as in Canada.[237] One of the principal reasons for rejection was the recognition that many offences against children are committed by children.[238]

(a) Sexual activity with a child – s 9

It is an offence intentionally to touch a person, B, where that touching is sexual and either –

(i) B is under 16 and A does not reasonably believe that B is 16 or over, or

(ii) B is under 13.

The offence under s 9 can be committed by a person aged 18 or over. The maximum sentence is 14 years. Sexual touching in these circumstances committed by offenders below that age is criminalized in identical terms by s 13.[239]

A separate offence[240] is created by subs (2) where the touching involves penetration (a) penetration of B's anus or vagina, (b) penetration of B's mouth with a person's penis, (c) penetration of a person's anus or vagina by B, or (d) penetration of a person's mouth with B's penis. This offence carries a maximum penalty of 14 years and is triable on indictment only.

(i) *Actus reus*

The elements of 'touching and 'sexual' are discussed above. There is no requirement that B is not consenting. A, 18, kissing/touching his consenting 15-year-old girlfriend is guilty if his conduct is 'sexual touching' which is to be decided by the jury.

(ii) *Mens rea*

The touching must be intentional as discussed above in relation to s 3. If B is under 13 there is no other element of *mens rea.* A's pleas of honest (and reasonable) beliefs in consent or age are irrelevant. Liability is strict.[241] If B is aged between 13 and 16, A must also be proved not to have had a reasonable belief that B was aged over 16. This is a more generous defence than the young man's defence under the 1956 Act which was limited to cases where D faced his first charge of this nature and was under 24.[242] Beliefs in consent remain irrelevant in such a case.

(iii) Defences

As with ss 5–8 above, the defence under s 73 applies to aiding and abetting or counselling for the child's protection. A marriage defence was deleted in the final stages of the Bill.

237 Criminal Code 1985, s 150.1.

238 E. Lovell, *Children and Young People who Display Sexually Harmful Behaviour* (2002) NSPCC.

239 The sentence is one of six months summarily, five years on indictment: s 13.

240 See above.

241 This represents a direct reversal of the House of Lords' decisions in *DPP v B* [2000] 2 WLR 452 and *R v K* [2001] UKHL 41.

242 See *Kirk and Russell* [2002] EWCA Crim 1580.

(b) Causing or inciting a child to engage in sexual activity – s 10

It is an offence intentionally to cause or to incite a person under 16, B, to engage in a sexual activity, if either – B is under 16 and A does not reasonably believe that B is 16 or over, or B is under 13. A separate offence is created by subs (2) for penetrative touching (as in s 9 above). That offence carries a maximum penalty of 14 years and is triable on indictment only. These offences can be committed by a person under the age of 18, in which case the sentence is one of six months summarily, five years on indictment: s 13. This is an extremely broad offence, technically capable of criminalizing much schoolyard banter.

(i) *Actus reus*

There are two versions of the offence: an act 'causing' B to engage, or conduct 'inciting' B to engage in the activity. The relevant elements are discussed above in relation to s 8. The offence is very broad. A, 18, who begs his 15-year-old girlfriend to strip for him commits the offence whether she declines or willingly assents. Examples of inciting sexual activity might include the conduct in *DPP v B* where the defendant invited the girl to give him 'a shiner' (perform oral sex on him). It includes A causing/inciting B to engage in sexual activity with a third party.

The breadth of the *actus reus* in terms of causing or inciting leaves no room for the application of the defence under s 73.

(ii) *Mens rea*

A must 'intend' to cause or incite. It is submitted that in this context intention extends to oblique intention in this context. There is no scope for a plea of consent. If B is under 13 there is no other element of *mens rea.* A's pleas of honest (and reasonable) beliefs in consent or age are irrelevant. Liability is strict. If B is aged between 13 and 16, A must also be proved not to have had a reasonable belief that B was aged over 16. Beliefs in consent remain irrelevant in such a case.

(c) Engaging in sexual activity in the presence of a child – s 11

It is an offence intentionally to engage in a sexual activity, when a person under 16, B, is present or is in a place from which the defendant can be observed, where for the purpose of obtaining sexual gratification the defendant engages in it knowing or believing that B is aware, or intending that B should be aware that he is engaging in it, and either B is under 16 and A does not reasonably believe that B is 16 or over, or B is under 13.[243]

This is another entirely novel offence. It will cover much of the activity that might previously have been charged as gross indecency. It is triable either way. The maximum sentence is 10 years on indictment/ six months summarily. The offence can also be committed by a person under 18, for which the sentence is one of six months summarily, five years on indictment: s 13.

243 See eg *Chevron* [2005] All ER (D) 91 (Feb), masturbating in sight of 12-year-old on beach.

(i) *Actus reus*

A must engage in a sexual[244] activity. B's position is far from clear. There is no requirement that B is actually witnessing the act, merely that B is present or in a position from which A can be observed. Since observation includes viewing directly or viewing an image,[245] the offence can be committed via a web-cam. To that extent it is unclear what degree of physical proximity B must have to A. There is also no guidance as to whether the observation has to be in real time. There is no requirement that B is aware of the sexual activity, but B must actually be under 16; an undercover officer witnessing the event will not suffice. B's consent to being present or witnessing the events is irrelevant.

The offence is directed primarily at the defendant who masturbates in front of a child but it has the potential to criminalize a much wider range of conduct. Sexual thrill seekers ('doggers' as they are called) who have sex in public places might commit the offence by having sex in a park visible from the nearby play area.

(ii) *Mens rea*

There are four elements of *mens rea*: (i) A must intentionally engage in the sexual activity; (ii) A must have as his 'purpose' (which is presumably narrrower than his intention and is restricted to 'direct' intention) to derive sexual[246] gratification from B's presence. It remains unclear whether A's *sole* purpose must be to derive sexual pleasure from B's watching? A and C will not commit the offence if their child, B, walks in on their sexual activity in the parental bedroom; (iii) A must 'know or believe' that B is aware or 'intend' that B should be aware of the activity; (iv) In the case of B being between 13 and 16, A must be shown not to have had a reasonable belief that B is 16 or over.

(d) Causing a child to watch a sexual act – s 12

It is an offence intentionally to cause another person under 16, B, to watch a third person engaging in an activity, or to look at an image of any person engaging in a sexual activity, where the defendant acts for the purpose of obtaining sexual gratification, and is aware that B is under 16 and does not reasonably believe that B is 16 or over, or B is under 13.

This offence was included to supplement that in relation to grooming below. Research suggests that paedophiles often diminish the sexual inhibitions of children by exposing them to explicit pornography to facilitate subsequent sexual acts. The offence under s 12 is wider than that under s 11 because the activity/image B is watching is not restricted to one involving A. It is a very wide offence: A aged 18 who shows his willing 15-year-old girlfriend a pornographic film for their mutual sexual enjoyment commits the offence.

The offence is triable either way and carries a maximum 10-year sentence on indictment. By s 13 it can be committed by a child under the age of 18, in which case the maximum sentence is five years.

(i) *Actus reus*

A must cause B to watch the activity/image. Ordinary principles of causation apply here as elsewhere. Omitting to prevent B from watching the activity/image will not

244 As defined in s 78 and discussed above, p 612.

245 Section 79(4) and (5).

246 Section 78 (above).

ground liability, as where a parent A turns a blind eye to B watching a pornographic film. In such a case A would also lack the *mens rea* of acting for the purpose of sexual gratification.

'Image' is widely defined to include moving or still images however produced and 3D images.[247] The broadest definition possible was created to include, for example, cartoons and 'etchings' as well as video and computer generated pseudo-images. The image must be sexual as defined in s 78.

B must watch the activity or image. This involves using the visual sense. It must be proved that B was under 16, again, an undercover officer being caused to watch an act will not suffice.

(ii) *Mens rea*

The elements of *mens rea* are that A must (i) intend to cause B to watch, (ii) act for the 'purpose' of sexual gratification. As in s 11 'purpose' is to be narrowly construed. If A has a dual purpose, for example, to explain sexual matters to B, but also to derive some sexual gratification from the activity it is submitted that A commits the offence.

Although there is no explicit element of *mens rea* in relation to the 'sexual' nature of the activity in s 12(1)(b), the courts might imply a requirement of knowledge. This could create problems. Since what is 'sexual' is to be defined retrospectively by the jury, A might claim that he did not realize it was sexual when he caused B to watch the image. In particular this argument might be advanced when the images are regarded as 'art'.

(e) Arranging or facilitating commission of a child sex offence – s 14

It is an offence for A intentionally to arrange or facilitate something that A intends to do, intends another person to do, or believes that another person will do, in any part of the world, and doing it will involve the commission of an offence under any of ss 9 to 13 (above).

This is a controversial 'sweeper' provision. It is a form of inchoate offence and can be committed in a number of ways. Its breadth in the original Bill caused consternation among youth and health care workers (and teenage magazine advice columnists) anxious that by giving legitimate advice to teenagers about safe sexual practices they would expose themselves to prosecution. As a result, the offence is markedly narrower than its original draft.

(i) *Actus reus*

The element of 'arranging' is not defined. The Home Office provides as an example the case where A approaches an agency and requests a 15-year-old girl for sex. This is a preliminary offence in the sense that no offence under ss 9–13 need arise, but it is unclear whether 'arrangement' requires the details of the proposed activity to be concluded. The courts might draw upon the case law relating to the completion of an agreement in conspiracy. The offence is extremely broad. A, 18, who agrees with his willing 15-year-old girlfriend to meet later for sex commits the offence. It is particularly wide since it

[247] Section 79(4).

governs arranging or facilitating acts anywhere in the world, it seems that A who arranges to marry B, 14, in her native country in which the age of consent is 14 commits the offence.

'Facilitating' is not defined. It is intended to cover the case where A lets his room to C so that C can have sex with B aged 15. This is also an overbroad offence. It applies also to suppliers of pornography which might be used in ss 11 and 12. A, the father of a 15-year-old girl who would rather she had sex with boyfriend at home than elsewhere appears to facilitate that action (although he may have a defence under subs (3)(b) below).

(ii) *Mens rea*

A must intend the activity. In this context it would seem that oblique intention would be sufficient. However, the offence is limited in the sense that A must intend that an offence under ss 9–13 *will* be committed.

(iii) The exceptions

In view of the overbroad terms of the offence, the statutory exceptions provided in the section are extremely important. These provide:

> (2) A person does not commit an offence under this section if –
>
> (a) he arranges or facilitates something that he believes another person will do, but that he does not intend to do or intend another person to do, and
>
> (b) any offence within subs (1)(b) would be an offence against a child for whose protection he acts.
>
> (3) For the purposes of subs (2), a person acts for the protection of a child if he acts for the purpose of –
>
> (a) protecting the child from sexually transmitted infection,
>
> (b) protecting the physical safety of the child,
>
> (c) preventing the child from becoming pregnant, or
>
> (d) promoting the child's emotional well-being by the giving of advice, and not for the purpose of obtaining sexual gratification or for the purpose of causing or encouraging the activity constituting the offence within subs (1)(b) or the child's participation in it.

These are designed to safeguard the health care worker who provides condoms and sex education and the teacher who advises children under 16 on sexual matters. Although well-intentioned, major ambiguities remain, in particular in defining 'emotional well-being' in (3)(d). The courts will be left to flesh out these issues.

(f) Meeting a child following sexual grooming, etc – s 15

Paedophiles' use of the internet, in particular 'chatrooms' to contact and 'groom' children before meeting them with a view to committing sexual acts has become a widespread problem.[248] Under the old law the principal offences available were those of

248 On the scale of this type of activity see A. Gillespie, 'Child protection on the internet – challenges for criminal law' (2002) CFLQ 411.

attempt which required the investigating authorities to wait until confident that the offender had gone beyond acts of mere preparation to the substantive sexual offence.[249] This was unsatisfactory since it exposed the child to a risk of harm. In response, the government created the much publicized grooming offence. The seriousness with which this risk is considered by the government is evidenced by the maximum sentence of 10 years on indictment/six months summarily.

(1) A person aged 18 or over (A) commits an offence if –

(a) having met or communicated with another person (B) on at least two earlier occasions, he –

(i) intentionally meets B, or

(ii) travels with the intention of meeting B in any part of the world,

(b) at the time, he intends to do anything to or in respect of B, during or after the meeting and in any part of the world, which if done will involve the commission by A of a relevant offence,

(c) B is under 16, and

(d) A does not reasonably believe that B is 16 or over.

(2) In subsection (1) –

(a) the reference to A having met or communicated with B is a reference to A having met B in any part of the world or having communicated with B by any means from, to or in any part of the world.

(i) *Actus reus*

There must be two communications. There is no restriction on the manner of communication, nor on the period of time between them. It is unclear whether two messages in the course of one dialogue in an internet chatroom will suffice. There is no requirement that the messages are sexual in nature. This reflects the fact that paedophiles will secure the confidence of their targets by discussing innocuous issues in early communications. Moreover, there is no clear limit on the period of time between the previous meeting/communication and the planned meeting. This raises the problem at what point must A believe B to be over 16 – in the course of communication or at the time of the proposed meeting? What if B turns 16 in the interim?

Despite its laudable aims, anxieties must be raised by the breadth of the offence. A, 18, writes two love letters to B, 15, arranging to meet at the local disco. A might commit the offence depending on his *mens rea*.[250]

Arguably, however, the offence is too narrow. A, 58, a paedophile, posts internet messages to B, believing her to be 15. She is X, an undercover woman police officer aged over 16. No offence is committed. A might be liable for an attempt, but such a charge is pushing the boundaries of the criminal law: there is an attempt to commit a statutorily created inchoate offence.

249 For a comprehensive analysis of the old law and its failings see A. Gillespie, 'Children, Chatrooms and the Law' [2001] Crim LR 435.

250 Ie if he hopes that the evening may involve sexual conduct with B, he commits the offence when he travels to the disco.

(ii) *Mens rea*

There is a requirement of intention. It is submitted that given the lack of any requirement for manifest wrongdoing in communicating and setting out to meet B, this element should be very strictly construed by the courts. In lobbying Parliament during the passage of the Bill, the offence was likened to a 'thought-crime' because of the absence of any tangible harm.[251]

6. Offences of abuse of trust

The Sexual Offences (Amendment) Act 2000[252] created new offences of abuse of a position of trust.[253] The 2003 Act replaces them with four offences where A (aged over 18) in a position of trust to B (under 18): sexually touches B (s 16); causes or incites B to engage in sexual activity (s 17); engages in sexual activity in B's presence for the purpose of sexual gratification (s 18); or causes B to watch a sexual image or activity for the purpose of obtaining sexual gratification.

The most notable feature of the offences is that they criminalize consensual conduct with those under 18. Although 16–18-year-olds may consent to sexual activity in other circumstances, they cannot do so with those who regularly 'look after' them.[254] This reflects the Act's theme of preventing exploitation. The category of those in positions of trust is widely defined and includes, for example, pupils and students, but is not all embracing; there is no specific inclusion of categories such as clergy and non-professional carers such as scout leaders. Individuals in these positions may fall within the terms of the offence depending on the circumstances of their responsibility for B.

The offences place a burden on A where his position of trust arises in an institutional setting, to present evidence that he did not know nor could he reasonably be expected to know that he was in a position of trust towards B. This may well be a difficult plea to raise unless A and B are in a large institution.

No offence is committed where A has a reasonable belief that B is aged over 18 (unless B is under 13). There is a defence for A to prove that he was lawfully married to B (aged 16+) or that immediately before the position of trust arose there existed a lawful sexual relationship between them. This covers cases where, for example, A and B had a sexual relationship before A became a trainee teacher at B's school.

7. Family offences

The 2003 Act creates two sets of offences to deal with offences within the family. In relation to children, ss 25 and 26 criminalize the same forms of activity as ss 9 and 12

[251] See Liberty and Criminal Bar Association responses to the Government's White Paper, *Protecting the Public*.

[252] See J. Burnside, 'The Sexual Offences (Ammendment) Act 2000: The Head of a "kiddy libber" and the torso of a "child-saver"?' [2001] Crim LR 425.

[253] See the 10th edition, p 478.

[254] As defined in ss 21 and 22. The requirement of regularity may be unduly restrictive. Does it catch the supply teacher? Guidance for Care Workers on the SOA 2003 can be found at www.homeoffice.gov.uk/docs3/care_workers.pdf.

(above): sexual touching and causing a child to engage in sexual activity. These are welcome extensions, protecting vulnerable individuals against acts other than sexual intercourse. Sections 25 and 26 differ from ss 9 and 12 in two important respects: B must be under 18 and A must be a family member. Family membership is defined in very broad terms in the Act, extending well beyond blood relationships to reflect the diverse structures of modern families. Family members, include adoptive relationships,[255] wider family members who live, or have lived, in the same household as the child or who are, or have been, regularly involved in caring for, training or supervising or being in sole charge of the child[256] and others who are living in the same household as the child and who hold a position of trust or authority in relation to the child at the time of the alleged offence.[257] The breadth of the extended family[258] caught by the Act reflects the shift in emphasis in the legislation from a blood relationship based offence of heterosexual intercourse (incest)[259] to one based on gender neutral exploitation of sexual vulnerability in the home environment.

There are defences in s 28 where A is lawfully married to B[260] at the time of engaging in the sexual activity, and under s 29 where A proves that a lawful sexual relationship existed between A and B immediately before the familial relationship arose.[261]

The 2003 Act also creates controversial sexual offences involving consenting adult relatives. Section 64 makes it an offence for A aged 16 or over to intentionally penetrate sexually (anally vaginally or orally) a relative B who is aged 18 or over if he knows or could reasonably have been expected to know that B is his relative. The converse offence is provided for in s 65: A aged 16 or over commits an offence by consenting to being penetrated sexually by a relative B aged 18 or over if he knows or could reasonably have been expected to know that B is his relative. The concept of a 'relative' is broadly defined.[262] Where the prosecution establishes that A is related to B, A will be taken to have known or to have reasonably been expected to know that they were related in that way unless A raises sufficient evidence as to whether he knew or could reasonably have been expected to know. These are broad, gender-neutral offences. They have been heavily

[255] Parents, current or former foster parents, grandparents, brothers, sisters, half-brothers, half-sisters, aunts and uncles.

[256] Stepparents, cousins, stepbrothers and stepsisters, current or former foster siblings.

[257] This offence will not be committed if A has a lawful sexual relationship with the child after the familial relationship has ceased, even where the child is under 18.

[258] This is so wide that it has been argued that sports coaches will be caught: C. Brackenridge and Y. Williams, 'Incest in the "family" of sport' (2004) 154 NLJ 179. See DCMS and Home Office Consultation on the scope and implementation of the SOA 2003 in relation to sports coaches: www.culture.gov.uk/global/consultations/default.htm.

[259] Founded historically in part at least on eugenics arguments: V. Bailey and S. Blackburn, 'The Punishment of Incest Act 1908: A Case Study in Law Creation' [1979] Crim LR 708; S. Wolfram, 'Eugenics and the Punishment of Incest Act 1908' [1983] Crim LR 308; J. Temkin, 'Do we need a crime of incest?' (1988) CLP 185.

[260] Note the amended definition in the Civil Partnerships Act 2004.

[261] Eg two 16-year-olds are in a sexual relationship and the girl's father and boy's mother subsequently marry.

[262] Parent, grandparent, child, grandchild, brother, sister, half brother, half sister; and blood relationships of uncle, aunt, nephew or niece.

criticized.[263] Both offences are triable summarily or on indictment and have a maximum penalty of two years' imprisonment. Together ss 64 and 65 make both parties to sexual activity guilty, so who is the law trying to protect? Will this be found to be compatible with Article 8 of the ECHR for consenting adults?

8. Offences involving mental disorder

The Act provides three specific groups of offences to protect those with a mental disorder. In each category the types of behaviour criminalized are roughly the same as those in relation to children. In short the activities prohibited are:

- sexual touching of B;
- causing or inciting sexual activity by B;
- engaging in sexual activity in B's presence;
- causing B to watch sexual activity.

In the offences dealing with children, the Act has decreed that it is sufficient to prove that one of these activities is intentionally performed; liability as to the factor of vulnerability, age, is strict, but such an approach would be too harsh in the present context.[264] Thus, only when these activities arise in an exploitative context are they criminalized. The three prohibited contexts for such activity are:

- sections 30–33 where B is mentally disordered and '**unable to refuse**';
- sections 34–37 where B is mentally disordered and the activity is caused by '**threats or deception or inducement**' which need not vitiate consent under s 74;
- sections 38–41 where B is mentally disordered and A is '**in a relationship as a carer**'.

There are numerous general improvements in the new scheme. Creating specific offences produces much fairer labelling – defendants are convicted of offences that better describe their actions. The language has been modernized, and gender specificity has been removed. This is not mere window dressing: for example, one result is that mentally disordered men are protected against heterosexual abuse. The offensive terminology of the 1956 Act has been replaced by the appropriate (but technical) language of the Mental Health Acts. 'Mental disorder' is defined[265] as 'mental illness is a state of arrested or incomplete development of mind, psychopathic disorder[266] and any other disease or disability of the mind.'

[263] See J. R. Spencer above, n 218 who doubts that they could ever be properly used. But what of the situation where, for example, X aged 17 penetrates his 19-year-old sister, Y, having secured her agreement with a threat which is not sufficient to vitiate consent under s 74. This constitutes an offence under s 64, but not any other serious offence, and it may well be proper to prosecute it. X commits the s 64 offence (X being over 16 and Y being over 18), but not the child offences (Y is over 16), nor the family offences (Y being over 18).

[264] *Setting the Boundaries*, para 4.6.4.

[265] Section 79(6) refers to s 1 of the Mental Health Act 1983.

[266] 'Psychopathic disorder' is itself defined in s 1(2) of the MHA 1983 – 'persistent disorder or disability of mind (whether or not including significant impairment of intelligence) which results in abnormally aggressive or seriously irresponsible conduct.' Note that s 1(3) provides that this definition shall not be construed as implying that a person may be dealt with under the Act as suffering from a mental disorder by reason of 'promiscuity or other immoral conduct, sexual deviancy or dependence on alcohol or drugs.'

This produces greater coherence, and extends protection beyond those with severe mental disorder, to those with a learning disability.[267] Some have questioned the merits of amalgamating both groups under the protection of one set of offences,[268] particularly as other recent reforms have acknowledged them as separate – for example, Youth Justice and Criminal Evidence Act 1999, s 16(2).[269] However, the alternative would have produced even greater proliferation of offences with yet more distinctions.

As with the Act in general, there is tremendous complexity. Many of the definitions are internally complex and their interrelationship with other provisions in the Act exacerbates this problem. For example, the relationship between the s 30 offence of sexual touching with a person with mental disorder impeding the ability to refuse and the general offence of non-consensual sexual touching in s 3 is confusing.

As elsewhere, there is the potential for significant overlap with other offences. If the activity is seemingly non-consensual (or at least B is unable to refuse), and involves a child complainant and a carer who is in a family relationship with B, the possible range of offences committed is vast.

It is arguable that too much discretion lies in the hands of the CPS who will face an especially difficult task in deciding whether to prosecute in cases where, for example, A and B are both mentally disordered, or where a carer claims that the actions were performed for the appropriate sex education of an individual with learning disability. In many instances it will still be necessary to determine the capacity of the complainant and this will involve her giving evidence – albeit under the Youth Justice and Criminal Evidence Act 1999 regime.

Symbolically it was very important for the Act to criminalize exploitative behaviour, but the message is confused when it overcriminalizes and potentially inhibits the appropriate sexual behaviour of those with a learning disability.[270]

9. Other sexual offences

(a) Prostitution and pornography

The Act provides specific protection against the sexual exploitation of children in pornography and prostitution. Section 47 provides an offence of paying (as widely defined) for the sexual services of a child and s 48 provides wider supporting offences of causing or inciting child prostitution or pornography, being designed to catch those who recruit vulnerable children into such activities.

Further broadly defined offences provide protection against controlling a child prostitute or a child involved in pornography[271] and arranging or facilitating child prostitution or pornography.[272]

[267] Estimates are of 200,000 people with learning disability: *Setting the Boundaries*, para 4.1.5.

[268] HL Debates, col 400,10 Apr 2003; Card, above, n 1, p 109.

[269] See also *Valuing People: A New Strategy for the 21st Century* (2001), Cm 5086.

[270] The *Twelfth Report of the Parliamentary Joint Committee on Human Rights* (2003) (HL 199; HC 765) concluded that the provisions were probably compatible with ECHR obligations under Article 8.

[271] Section 49. [272] Section 50.

Provisions to deal with adult sexual exploitation are strengthened with a range of offences introduced to deal with causing or inciting[273] or controlling prostitution for gain.[274] The rise in trafficking for prostitution is combated by offences of trafficking into, within and outwith the UK.[275] Section 56 and Schedule 1 also extend the offences under the Street Offences Act 1959, rendering them gender-neutral in effect.

(b) Indecent photographs of children[276]

There are offences of taking, making, permitting to take, distributing, showing, possessing with intent to distribute, and advertising indecent photographs or pseudo-photographs of children under 18. There is a defence if the child is aged over 16 and A proves that he and the child were married or living together as partners in an enduring family relationship, that the child consented to the image being taken and that the image shows no one other than B (and A).[277] This is an area of considerable controversy.

The strictness of the offences has given rise to concern in some cases, particularly as regards the definition of creation, which can occur by the act of downloading an image to view it on the screen of a computer and then immediately deleting it without consciously saving it. Other difficulties arise because of the strictness of liability in relation to age where D downloads images of teenagers claiming that he was led by the website to believe the models to be older. There are also broader concerns about freedom of expression.[278]

(c) Preliminary offences

(i) Administering drugs

The Act introduces three important new preliminary sex offences. Section 61 introduces an offence of intentional administration of a substance/causing it to be taken by B without consent with intent to stupefy/overpower to enable any person to engage in sex with B. This is a further response to the growing problem of drug assisted rape (see also s 75(2)(f) above).[279] The offence is much wider than that in s 4 of the 1956 Act, being gender-neutral and relating to all sexual activity rather than just sexual intercourse. The offence covers A spiking B's drinks as well as administering drugs such as GhB and Rohypnol. It does not extend to A encouraging B to get drunk so that A could more readily persuade B to have sex.

Section 61 applies where A himself administers the substance to B, and where A causes the substance to be taken by B, by for example persuading C to administer it to B. There is no requirement that the intended sexual activity involve A. It is a preliminary offence in the sense that there is no requirement that B actually is involved in any sexual activity. It is

273 Section 52. 274 Section 53. 275 Sections 57, 58, 59.

276 On the prevalence of this activity see B. Gallagher, K. Christmann, C. Fraser and B. Hodgson, 'International and internet child sexual abuse and exploitation – issues emerging from research' (2003) CFLQ 353.

277 On the complexity and unsatisfactory nature of the offences see A. Gillespie, 'The Sexual Offences Act 2003: (3) Tinkering With "Child Pornography" ' [2004] Crim LR 361.

278 See I. Cram, 'Criminalising Child Pornography – A Canadian Study in Freedom of Expression and Charter-led Judicial Review of Legislative Policy Making' (2002) J of Criminal Law 359 on the decision of the Canadian Supreme Court in *R v Sharpe* [2001] 1 SCR 45.

279 Cf the offences of poisoning under ss 23 and 24 of the OAPA 1861.

unclear whether those who manufacture or supply the drugs will be liable as aiders and abettors or for inchoate offences under s 61.

(ii) Committing an offence with intent to commit a sexual offence

Section 62 introduces an offence of 'committing an offence with intent to commit a sexual offence.' The offence was designed primarily to tackle cases where A kidnaps B so that he can rape her or assaults B to subdue her.[280] The offence as drafted is much wider: there is no requirement that the preliminary offence is directed at B, the person against whom the substantive sexual offence is committed. A, 18, speeding in his car to B, 15, to have consensual sex with her commits the offence. Stalking under the Protection from Harassment Act 1997 will suffice as the preliminary crime.[281]

At common law it remains uncertain whether the offence of assault with intent to rape exists.[282] There is no doubt that an indictment for assault with intent to rape would lie at common law but it is not certain whether it was a specific offence or an example of a wider common law offence of assault with intent to commit a felony. If the latter, it ceased to exist with the abolition of felonies by the Criminal Law Act 1967 and the repeal of the words in s 38 of the OAPA 1861 which provided that assault with intent to commit a felony was punishable with two years' imprisonment. The better view is that there was no general offence of assault with intent to commit a felony at common law, and that assault with intent to rape was, and is, a specific offence which was not abolished by the 1861 Act or by the repeal of the general statutory offence. Most significantly, it was treated by the draftsman of the 1861 legislation, C. S. Greaves, as continuing to exist after the 1861 Act.[283] Most cases of assault with intent to rape will amount to attempted rape under the Criminal Attempts Act 1981 but there will be instances where the assault is a 'merely preparatory' act.[284] In such cases the most obvious charge is that under s 62.

(iii) Trespass with intent to commit a sexual offence

The third preliminary offence is that under s 63: 'trespass with intent to commit a sexual offence'. This is committed where A commits a sexual offence whilst he is on any premises as a trespasser, either knowing or being reckless[285] as to whether he is trespassing. A person is a trespasser if he is on any premises without the owner's or occupier's consent, or other lawful excuse. This replaces the offence under the Theft Act 1968, s 9 in relation to burglary with intent to rape. It is clearly wider since it involves any trespass and includes sexual offences beyond rape.[286]

280 See the first sentencing case on the offence *Wisniewshi* [2004] EWCA Crim 3361.

281 Where the preparatory offence is kidnapping or false imprisonment, the offence is triable on indictment only, and has a maximum penalty of life imprisonment. In all other cases, the offence is triable summarily or on indictment and has a maximum penalty of 10 years of an indictment.

282 In *J* (Crown Court at Stafford, 9 June 1986) Turner J held that it does exist and in *P* [1990] Crim LR 323, Pill J held that it does not. In *Lionel* (1982) 4 Cr App R (S) 291 an appeal against sentence was dismissed, the assumption that the offence exists not being challenged. See S. Spencer, 'Assault with Intent to Rape – Dead or Alive' [1986] Crim LR 110.

283 *Russell on Crime* (4th edn, 1865, by C. S. Greaves) 927.

284 Above Ch 11.

285 This is one of the few offences that includes a reckless *mens rea* element.

286 The offence is triable summarily or on indictment and has a maximum penalty of 10 years.

(d) Miscellaneous sexual offences

(i) Exposure

Section 66 creates an offence if A intentionally exposes his or her genitals with the intention that another person will see them and be caused alarm or distress. This extends the previous law to include female exposure, although that is a particularly rare phenomenon. It is not necessary that anyone should have seen the genitals or have been caused alarm or distress. There was much controversy over the offence when originally introduced since it was feared that it would criminalize naturism. As finally enacted, the offence would not apply to a naturist unless the exposure is with intention to cause alarm or distress. Similarly, it is unlikely that 'streakers' at sports events will be prosecuted. The distress they cause for most is by holding up play not by exposing their genitals.[287]

(ii) Voyeurism

Section 67 creates an offence, where A, for the purposes of sexual gratification, observes another person doing a 'private act' in the knowledge that the other person does not consent to being observed for that purpose. The offence extends beyond simple peeping toms looking through keyholes. Subsection (2) creates an offence of A 'operating equipment' with the intention of enabling another person, C, for their sexual gratification, to observe B doing a 'private act' in the knowledge that B has not consented to this being done for another person's sexual gratification. This provision was enacted in response to the numerous instances reported in the news of people setting up illicit cameras. In *Vigon v DPP*[288] surreptitious viewing of customers changing into swimwear in a market stall cubicle was held capable of being 'insulting behaviour' for the purposes of the Public Order Act 1986, s 5.[289] The common law offence of outraging public decency was also prayed in aid when a defendant secretly filmed women urinating in a supermarket toilet. 'Disgusting conduct' was held to be that which fills an onlooker with loathing or extreme distaste or causes the onlooker extreme annoyance: *Choi*.[290]

Similarly, s 67(3) makes it an offence for a person A to record B doing a 'private act' with the intention that A or a third person will, for the purposes of sexual gratification look at the recorded image, when it is known that B does not consent to being recorded for that purpose. Finally, s 67(4) creates an offence for a person to install equipment, or to construct or adapt a structure,[291] with the intention of enabling himself, or another person, to commit an offence under subs (1).[292]

For each of these offences a 'private act' is defined in s 68 as 'an act done in a place and in circumstances where the person would reasonably expect privacy and either the person's genitals, buttocks or breasts are exposed or covered only by underwear, or the

287 The offence is triable summarily, or on indictment with a maximum penalty of two years' imprisonment.

288 [1998] Crim LR 289, DC.

289 It is sufficient that the defendant is aware that his conduct may be insulting, so there is no need to prove that he intended to insult the customer – it is no defence that he concealed the camera.

290 [1999] 8 Archbold News 3.

291 'Structure' includes 'a tent, vehicle or vessel or other temporary or movable structure'.

292 The offence is triable summarily or on indictment with a maximum penalty of two years' imprisonment.

person is using a lavatory or the person is doing a sexual act that is not of a kind ordinarily done in public.' There is much scope for judicial interpretation.[293]

(iii) Bestiality

Section 69 creates an offence for A to intentionally penetrate the vagina[294] or anus of a living animal with his penis where he knows or is reckless as to whether that is what he is penetrating. It also creates an offence for A intentionally to cause or allow her vagina or his or her anus to be penetrated by the penis of a living animal where he or she knows or is reckless as to whether it is the penis of a live animal that is penetrating him/her.[295]

(iv) Necrophilia

Section 70 makes it an offence for A intentionally to penetrate sexually[296] any part of the body of a dead person B with A's penis, any other body part or any other object, knowing or being reckless as to whether A is penetrating any part of a dead body. A commits no offence if B dies during intercourse unless A realizes and continues to penetrate B.[297] The penetration must be sexual but it remains unclear whether D must have any *mens rea* in relation to that element of the *actus reus*. As a matter of principle that would be desirable.

(v) Sexual activity in a public lavatory

Section 71 creates an offence for A to engage in sexual activity[298] in a public lavatory.[299] There is no requirement that any person is alarmed or distressed by the activity. This is the only offence in the Act which is triable summarily only.[300] Section 320 of the CJA 2003 has made the common law offence of 'outraging public decency' triable summarily as well as on indictment. The offence under s 71 is wider since there is no need for the act to have shocked, disgusted or revolted a member of the public.

293 *P* [2004] All ER(D) 31 (Oct).

294 The reference to vagina or anus in this context is further explained at subss (9) and (10) of s 79. References to 'vagina' include vulva and in relation to an animal, references to the vagina or anus include references to any similar part.

295 The offence is triable summarily or on indictment and has a maximum penalty of two years.

296 Hence pathology staff will not commit the offence by penetrating the corpse for medical purposes.

297 The offence is triable summarily or on indictment and has a maximum penalty of two years.

298 An activity is sexual if a reasonable person would, in all the circumstances but regardless of any person's purpose, consider it to be sexual.

299 'Public lavatory' is defined as a lavatory to which the public or a section of the public has or is permitted to have access, whether on payment or otherwise.

300 It has a maximum penalty of six months' imprisonment or a fine.

18

Theft and related offences

1. Interpreting the Theft Acts

The law of theft and related offences is to be found in the Theft Acts 1968, 1978 and the Theft (Amendment) Act 1996.[1] These Acts are not a re-statement of the common law and its numerous statutory additions. They provide a code of the most important offences of dishonest dealing with property, (with the notable exception of forgery, and the common law offence of conspiracy to defraud), based on a fundamental reconsideration of the principles by the Criminal Law Revision Committee (CLRC)[2].

Since the Acts represent a code they must be interpreted unencumbered from the old law and must be 'within [their] field the authoritative, comprehensive and exclusive source of that law'.[3] If a code is not so regarded it is in danger of failing to develop or reform the law.[4] Only in very limited circumstances is reference to authorities on the former law of larceny appropriate. One instance is where the Theft Acts use expressions taken from the earlier legislation that have acquired a settled meaning. In blackmail, for example, the CLRC decided to retain 'menaces' rather than to substitute 'threats' because 'menaces' had acquired a settled meaning, which the CLRC thought to be correct. Strictly, the earlier authorities are no longer binding but they are persuasive and generally followed.

The law of theft is concerned with invasions of the proprietary interests of others but the law of property is not to be found explained in any detailed fashion in the Theft Acts. It is a matter of civil law. The Theft Acts assume its existence. The criminal courts, including the appellate courts, have sometimes shown impatience with arguments based on 'the finer distinctions in civil law'[5] but, many of the fundamental issues of criminal liability turn on these civil law concepts. For example, whether property 'belongs to another' for the purposes of theft 'is a question to which the criminal law offers no answer and which can only be answered by reference to civil law principles'.[6] Equally the Acts provide no

[1] See J. C. Smith, *The Law of Theft* (8th edn, 1997) (hereinafter Smith, *Theft*); E. J. Griew, *The Theft Acts 1968 and 1978* (7th edn, 1995) (hereinafter Griew, *Theft*); Smith, *Property Offences* (hereinafter Smith, *Property Offences*).

[2] Cmnd 2977, para 7. See Eighth Report, *Theft and Related Offences* (1966) Cmnd 2977, HMSO (hereinafter referred to as Cmnd 2977) and Thirteenth Report (1977), Cmnd 6733 (hereinafter referred to as Cmnd 6733).

[3] Scarman, *Codification and Judge-Made Law* (1966) at 7.

[4] Ibid, 8.

[5] *Baxter* [1971] 2 All ER 359 at 363, CA: *Morris* [1983] 3 All ER 288 at 294, HL.

[6] *Dobson v General Accident Fire and Life Assurance Corpn plc* [1989] 3 All ER 927 at 937, CA, per Bingham LJ.

definition of what constitutes 'a proprietary right or interest' for the purposes of s 5 of the 1968 Act, nor who is a 'trustee or personal representative' for the purposes of s 4 of the 1968 Act. Theft offences sometimes necessarily involve consideration of 'the finer distinctions in civil law'.[7] It follows of course that changes in the civil law may affect the scope of the criminal law.[8]

In interpreting the Acts, the courts have usually aimed to give words and expressions their ordinary meaning so as to avoid undue technicality and subtlety. This is a sensible approach, but it has led to the practice of leaving the interpretation of 'ordinary' words and expressions to the jury and not only in the context of the Theft Acts.[9] There is House of Lords authority concerning this approach to the interpretation of statutes, but it is now less fashionable than it once was.[10] The interpretation even of ordinary words must sometimes be a matter for the court if consistency in the application of the law is to be achieved. This is necessary to maintain respect for the rule of law and to ensure certainty, consistency and clarity in the definition and interpretation of the law. To leave interpretation in the hands of the juries (or more frequently the magistrates) is to risk their taking different views on indistinguishable facts. Even such ordinary words in the Theft Act as 'dishonesty', 'force', 'building', etc may involve definitional problems on which a jury may require guidance if like is to be treated as like. This poses potential problems of compatibility with Article 7 of the ECHR which protects against retrospective criminalization, and includes a requirement that crimes are defined with sufficient certainty and predictability.

Unfortunately the interpretation of the Theft Acts has produced a great deal of complex case law. Whether this is due to inherent defects in the Acts or failures on the part of the judges and lawyers to apply and construe them properly is debatable.[11] At all events, the law of theft is once again being reconsidered by the Law Commission[12] who cite the opinion of Beldam LJ, a former chairman of the Commission, that it is 'in urgent need of simplification and modernisation, so that a jury of 12 ordinary citizens do not have to grapple with concepts couched in the antiquated "franglais" of "choses in action", and scarce public resources are not devoted to hours of semantic argument divorced from

[7] See *Shadrokh-Cigari* [1988] Crim LR 465, CA, below, p 680; *Wheeler* (1990) 92 Cr App R 279, CA, below, p 666. See also J. C. Smith, 'Civil Law Concepts in the Criminal Law' [1972B] CLJ 197; G. R. Williams, 'Theft, Consent and Illegality' [1977] Crim LR 127 and 205; G. Trietel, 'Contract and Crime' in C. Tapper (ed), *Crime, Proof and Punishment: Essays in Memory of Sir Rupert Cross* (1981), 81.

[8] See discussion of *Floyd v DPP*, below, p 682.

[9] See G. Williams, 'Law and Fact' [1976] Crim LR 472; D. W. Elliott, 'Law and Fact in Theft Act Cases' [1976] Crim LR 707.

[10] *Brutus v Cozens* [1973] AC 854, [1972] 2 All ER 1297. But in *Chandler v DPP* [1964] AC 763, [1962] 3 All ER 142, HL, Lord Radcliffe said, at 149, 'The Act of Parliament [the Official Secrets Act 1911] in this case has introduced the idea of purpose as a determining element in the identification of the offence charged *and lawyers therefore, whose function it is to attribute meaning to words and to observe relevant distinctions between different words, cannot escape from this duty* merely by saying that "purpose" is a word which has no sharply defined context. They must do the best they can to find what its content is in the context of this Act' – italics supplied. See D. W. Elliott, '*Brutus v Cozens*, Decline and Fall' [1989] Crim LR 323.

[11] See J. C. Smith, 'The Sad Fate of the Theft Act 1968', in W. Swadling and G. Jones, *The Search for Principle, Essays in Honour of Lord Goff of Chieveley* (1999), 97.

[12] Law Com No 228 (1994). See in particular, Consultation Paper No 155, *Fraud* (1999); Law Com Report No 276, *Fraud* (2001).

the true merits of the case.'[13] In fact, the Act does not use the expression 'chose in action' or any other franglais. If juries are being confused by the use of such terms, that is the fault of the judges (and/or advocates). The law cannot avoid the use of the *concept* of a 'thing in action' because that is a variety of intangible property that is frequently the subject of theft; and the law must make clear that it is capable of being stolen. It is the duty of the judge to explain this and other legal concepts to the jury in terms intelligible to them.

One view is that there is not very much wrong with the Theft Acts if they are properly handled.[14] An alternative view is that the Acts are now in need of some radical reappraisal having been repeatedly patched up to deal with specific problems that have arisen and in some instances the Acts have been overtaken by technological advances. This has led to a rather pragmatic patchwork: an unprincipled and unstructured range of overlapping and technical offences. Although the adoption of numerous specific offences may be attractive in some respects (supporting principles of fair labelling, legality, etc) it also has less attractive features: the greater the number of offences the greater the overlap, complexity, risk of incorrect charging, and incomprehensibility for jurors dealing with alternative counts.

One final aspect of the interpretation of the Theft Acts should also be noted. The appellate courts have demonstrated a distinct willingness to uphold the convictions of those who have been found to have acted dishonestly, even though there are fundamental errors with the conviction in other respects.[15] This has not generated the level of clarity and certainty of principle in the law that is desirable. In addition, such an approach places a degree of emphasis on the concept of dishonesty, which as we shall see, it is ill suited to bear.

2. Theft

By s 1(1) of the Theft Act 1968:

A person is guilty of theft if he dishonestly appropriates property belonging to another with the intention of permanently depriving the other of it; and 'thief' and 'steal' shall be construed accordingly.

The offence was originally punishable by 10 years' imprisonment (s 7) but the maximum was reduced to seven years by s 26 of the Criminal Justice Act 1991.[16]

There is much about this definition that is self-explanatory and the vast majority of thefts can be dealt with without further elaboration. This is worth noting before turning to detailed consideration of the offence.

13 *Hallam* (1994), CA, No 92/4388/W3.

14 J. C. Smith, 'Conspiracy to Defraud: Some Comments on the Law Commission's Report' [1995] Crim LR 210 (a view shared by the Model Criminal Code Committee of the Attorney-General's Department, Australia, Final Report (1995), ch 3, 6) and J. C. Smith (1996) 28 Bracton Law Journal 27. See also D. W. Elliott, 'Dialogues on the Theft Act', in P. Glazebrook (ed), *Reshaping the Criminal Law: Essays in Honour of Glanville Williams* (1978), 287.

15 See eg Lord Steyn in *Hinks*, at 844, discussed below, p 653.

16 Under the Penalties for Disorderly Behaviour (Amount of Penalty)(Amendment No 2) Order 2004, SI 2468, made under the Criminal Justice and Police Act 2001, s 3(1), a fixed penalty may be awarded.

(a) *Actus reus*

The *actus reus* of theft consists (1) in the appropriation of (2) property (3) belonging to another.

(i) Appropriation[17]

By s 3 of the Theft Act 1968:

> (1) Any assumption by a person of the rights of an owner amounts to an appropriation, and this includes, where he has come by the property (innocently or not) without stealing it, any later assumption of a right to it by keeping or dealing with it as owner.
>
> (2) Where property, or a right or interest in property is or purports to be transferred for value to a person acting in good faith, no later assumption by him of rights which he believed himself to be acquiring shall, by reason of any defect in the transferor's title, amount to theft of the property.

Section 3(1), said the CLRC,[18] is a 'partial definition . . . which is included partly to indicate that this is the familiar concept of conversion . . .'. 'Conversion' is the name of a tort about which there is a great deal of complicated law.[19] It may be 'familiar' to lawyers but it is certainly not familiar to laymen (jurors and magistrates) in its legal sense of usurping rights of property belonging to another.

The CLRC thought that 'appropriation' and 'conversion' had the same meaning but preferred appropriation because it more aptly describes the kind of acts it is intended to cover. The term was intended to be broad enough adequately to describe various types of conduct that had been separate offences under the previous law: 'taking and carrying away' – which was required for simple larceny; 'conversion' by a bailee; embezzlement[20] and fraudulent conversion.[21]

Three basic problems of interpretation have arisen, each of which has had a significant impact on the overall scope of the offence

- Is it sufficient that D assumes *a right* of the owner, not *all* the rights of that owner?
- Can D 'assume' rights when the alleged assumption is an act done with the consent of the owner?
- Can there be an appropriation when the effect is that the entire proprietary interest in the thing then belongs indefeasibly to the alleged thief?

Controversially, all three questions have been answered in the affirmative by the House of Lords: the first two in *Gomez*,[22] and the third in *Hinks*.[23]

[17] For early comment on this element of the offence see L. Koffman, 'The Nature of Appropriation' [1982] Crim LR 331; D. Stuart, 'Reform of the Law of Theft' (1967) 30 MLR 609.

[18] Cmnd 2977, para 34.

[19] See W. V. H. Rogers, *Winfield and Jolowicz on Tort* (16th edn, 2002), 595 et seq.

[20] A statutory offence involving the misappropriation by a servant of any property delivered to him on account of his employer.

[21] A statutory offence of conversion by a trustee or fiduciary of property entrusted to him.

[22] [1993] AC 442, HL, [1993] Crim LR 304 and commentary. On which see also M. Davies, 'Consent after the House of Lords: taking and leading astray the House of Lords' (1993) 13 LS 308; S. Cooper and M. Allen, 'Appropriation After *Gomez*' (1993) 57 J Crim Law 186.

[23] [2000] 4 All ER 833, [2001] Crim LR 162. On which see also: A. T. H. Smith, 'Theft or Sharp Practice: Who Cares Now' [2001] CLJ 21; J. Beatson and A. Simester, 'Stealing One's Own Property' (1999) 115 LQR 372; S. Shute, 'Appropriation and the Law of Theft' [2002] Crim LR 445.

Assumption of a right

An assumption of 'the rights of an owner' as the section puts it seems *prima facie* to mean all the rights, not one, or some, of the rights of the owner in question. But in *Morris* Lord Roskill, having conceded that there was force in that view, nevertheless said, 'But the later words, "any assumption of a right" in sub-s (1) and the words in sub-s (2) "no later assumption by him of rights" seem to me to militate strongly against [that view]'.

Remarkably, this citation from subs (1) omits the subsequent and important words, 'to it'. Surely, if D assumes *a right to* the thing, he treats it as *his*, something in which he owns *all* the rights. As for the reference to subs (2), it is hard to see how a reference to 'rights' can point to a conclusion that the assumption of 'a right' is sufficient. Though some may think Lord Roskill's conclusion was obviously wrong, it was an element in the *ratio decidendi* of *Morris*, and in *Gomez*, where the House reconsidered *Morris*, Lord Keith said, without giving reasons, that it was obviously right; so, for better or worse, we must take it that the law is settled. Any assumption of *any of* the rights of an owner amounts to an appropriation. It is obvious that this extends the scope of the overall offence so that acts which might naturally be regarded as mere preparation or attempts would, because they involve the assumption of a single right, constitute the *actus reus* of the full offence.

Morris was concerned with the then common case where D switches the labels on two articles displayed on the shelves of a supermarket with the intention of buying the more expensive article for the price of the less expensive one. The right to label the goods is a right of the owner, so the label switching amounted to an appropriation and theft. D, of course, intended to deceive the cashier and to obtain the goods by deception, an offence under s 15 of the 1968 Act. So far as s 15 is concerned, the label switching is probably a merely preparatory act, not amounting even to an attempt to obtain by deception; but, no matter, it is theft contrary to s 1. This would be so even if D then abandoned the enterprise, leaving the goods with the switched labels safely on the shelf. Even if he re-switched the labels and left the articles exactly as he found them, that could not undo the theft he had committed. It is important to remember that in this case D must be shown to have *mens rea* – the intention to permanently deprive and dishonesty, thus there would not necessarily be a completed theft where D moves articles in a supermarket as a prank.

Appropriation with consent

It should be noted that s 3 is not drafted in terms of requiring a 'misappropriation'. In *Morris* Lord Roskill, with whom all their lordships agreed, said, 'In the context of s 3(1), the concept of appropriation involves not an act expressly or impliedly authorized by the owner but an act by way of adverse interference with or usurpation of those rights'.[24] This, however, was *obiter*, because the label switching was plainly unauthorized by the store and there was no need for the court to say anything about authorized acts. In *Gomez*, the House held that the *dictum* was wrong, following the earlier decision of the House in *Lawrence*. In that celebrated case V, an Italian with little English, showed D, a

24 [1983] 3 All ER at 292. See L. H. Leigh, 'Some remarks on appropriation in the law of theft after *Morris*' (1985) 48 MLR 167.

taxi driver, a paper on which was written an address and tendered £1. The authorized fare was about 50p but D indicated that £1 was not enough and took from V's still open wallet a £1 and a £5 note. V permitted him to do so. D's appeal against his conviction for theft on the ground that he took the money with V's consent was dismissed. One of the questions certified for the decision of the House was whether the Theft Act was to be construed as if it contained the words 'without the consent of the owner'. The answer was, rightly, an emphatic 'no'. Those words, which were part of the definition of old offence of simple larceny, were deliberately left out by the CLRC in their draft Bill. It did not follow, however, that it was intended by Parliament that an act done with consent should be capable of amounting to appropriation. The model for the definition of theft was the definition in the Larceny Act 1916 of the offences of fraudulent conversion and larceny by a bailee. These offences did not include the phrase, 'without the consent of the owner'; but it was never suggested that a bailee who acted with the consent of the bailor could be guilty of theft. A bailee who acted with consent would not 'fraudulently convert to his own use' the property in question. It would have been inept for the draftsman of the Larceny Act to write 'converts to his own use without the consent of the owner'. If, as the CLRC intended, 'appropriates' means the same as converts, it would have been equally inept to qualify that word in such a way in the Theft Act.

Gomez, the assistant manager of a shop, persuaded the manager to sell goods to the value of £17,000 to his accomplice, X, and to accept payment by two cheques. The cheques, as Gomez and X knew, were stolen and worthless. If they had been charged with obtaining the goods by deception, contrary to s 15 of the 1968 Act, the case would never have been heard of; but, for some reason, they were charged with theft. The Court of Appeal, following *Morris*, quashed their convictions. The contract of sale was voidable for fraud but not void, ownership of the electrical goods passed to X, and the contract not having been avoided, he was entitled to take possession and he did so with the consent and express authority of the owner. The court declined to follow *Dobson v General Accident Fire and Life Assurance Corpn plc*,[25] a decision of the Civil Division of the Court of Appeal, which applied *Lawrence*. In *Dobson* the plaintiff claimed from his insurers the value of a watch and ring that a rogue, R, had induced him to sell for a worthless cheque. The policy covered only loss by theft. It was not enough for Dobson to prove (this being a civil case) that his property had been obtained by deception (as it undoubtedly had), contrary to s 15. The insurers argued that the ownership passed when a contract of sale was made over the telephone two days before delivery so that R, when he collected the goods, was taking delivery of his own property. Parker LJ said that, if that were so, the making of the contract constituted the act of appropriation, being an assumption of ownership by R.[26]

The House in *Gomez*, relying heavily on the judgment of Parker LJ in *Dobson*, restored the convictions holding that, on the issue of the effect of consent, *Lawrence* and *Morris* were irreconcilable. The proposition in *Lawrence* was *ratio decidendi*, that in *Morris* an *obiter dictum*. That was good enough for the majority: *Lawrence* prevailed.

25 [1990] 1 QB 274.

26 On the insurance implications of the definition of theft generally see M. Wasik, 'Definitions of Crimes in Insurance Contracts' [1986] J Bus Law 45.

The background to *Gomez*

Gomez involves an issue that has troubled the courts for centuries. The common law recognized a form of stealing known as 'larceny by a trick' which was committed where D, dishonestly intending permanently to deprive V of property, used a trick or false pretence to induce V to transfer to D possession, but not ownership, of that property.[27] In the leading case, *Pear*,[28] D obtained the hire of a horse by saying that he wanted it to ride to Sutton when, all along, he intended to ride the horse to Smithfield market and sell it. He was guilty of larceny when he obtained possession of the horse by this 'trick'. V of course, intended to part, and parted, only with possession, not ownership, of the horse. This is a clear illustration of the importance of civil law concepts of property – ownership and possession – in the criminal law.

Larceny was never extended at common law to the case where D induced V to transfer to him ownership as well as possession of the property. Parliament had to intervene, creating the separate offence of obtaining by false pretences to cover the case where ownership was obtained. The two offences were generally thought to be mutually exclusive. The distinction was one of some subtlety and produced much case law. If, for example, D used some deception to induce delivery of property under a contract of hire-purchase from V, that might be larceny by a trick because D obtained only possession of the property, ownership remaining with V; but if the same deception induced delivery of property under a contract of credit sale, that could only be obtaining by false pretences, because D obtained possession *and* ownership – the entire proprietary interest in the property.

The CLRC considered whether theft could be defined to incorporate the offence of obtaining by false pretences so as to obviate this difficult distinction. They came to the conclusion, rightly or wrongly, that this could not be done satisfactorily. Their preferred solution was to create the new offence of obtaining property by deception. This is embodied in s 15 of the 1968 Act, and is defined widely – 'a person is to be treated as obtaining property if he obtains ownership, possession or control of it' – so it clearly includes everything that would have been larceny by a trick or false pretences. The prosecutor could not go wrong if he charged s 15 whenever D had obtained any interest in property by any kind of trick or false pretence. Cases amounting to the former larceny by trick, of course, continued also to be theft – in *Pear*, for example, D had obtained possession of the horse with consent but he had not obtained ownership, so his assumption of ownership – he intended throughout to sell the horse – would be theft.[29] The offences were intended to overlap – Pear would now be guilty of both.

CLRC's scheme misunderstood

Unfortunately some prosecutors and judges failed to grasp the structure of the 1968 Act and its proposed solution to the problem. Lawrence, the dishonest taxi driver, obviously, obtained the ownership of the excessive fare by deception since V permitted him to take the money only because D had told him, falsely, that £1 was not enough. There should have been no answer to a charge of obtaining property by deception under s 15, but, if the Act were applied as the CLRC intended, that was not theft. The issues were not, however,

[27] See G. Ferris, 'The Origins of Larceny by Trick and Constructive Possession' [1998] Crim LR 17.
[28] (1779) 1 Leach 212, CCR.
[29] Cf Smith, *Property Offences*, para 5–17.

properly presented to the House of Lords in that case;[30] and there is a significant reluctance on the part of the judges to allow those found by a jury to be dishonest to escape, if they can find a way of preventing it. The effect, however may well be to make bad law.

In *Gomez* the House was invited to discover the true intention of Parliament by looking at the Report of the CLRC whose draft clauses were enacted with no material change. The majority thought it would 'serve no useful purpose' to do so. However, Lord Lowry, demonstrated convincingly in his dissent that reference to the Report would have shown it was the *dictum* in *Morris*, not the decision in *Lawrence*, which implemented the intention of Parliament; and that Gomez was wrongly convicted of theft. Some may think that would have been 'a useful purpose'.

Theft where consent is given without deception by D

The point of law of general importance certified for the decision of the House in *Gomez* was whether there is an appropriation where 'consent has been obtained by a false representation', as occurred in that case. It was not necessary for the House to go beyond that; and there was powerful, though, it is submitted, mistaken, academic support for answering that question in the affirmative.[31] The House of Lords however did not confine themselves to the case where there has been a false representation. Indeed, the fact that there had been deception on the facts of that case played no part in the decision. The House explicitly confirmed that there could be an appropriation even where D has practised no deception on V, as illustrated by their example of the label switcher in the supermarket. Their lordships were in no doubt that he appropriates property when he touches the article, although he has, as yet, practiced no deception.

A further illustration of their Lordships' confirmation that an appropriation can occur with the owner's consent, irrespective of that consent being induced by deception, lies in the overruling of *Fritschy*.[32] Fritschy was instructed by the owner of some krugerrands to collect them from bullion dealers in England and take them to Switzerland. He did exactly what he was told to do until he arrived in Switzerland and then, as he had intended from the beginning, he disposed of the property for his own benefit. The court in *Fritschy*, following *Morris*, held that, as everything he did in England was done with the consent and authority of the owner, he committed no theft within the jurisdiction of the court. However, according to the House of Lords in *Gomez*, Fritschy committed theft no later than the moment he got his hands on the property with intent to steal it, although there was no finding of any deception.

So controversial was this aspect of the decision in *Gomez* that some argued[33] that it remained open to the House of Lords, without using its power to overrule its own decisions under the 1966 Practice Statement to renounce the decision as erroneous in so far as it extends to cases involving no deception; but after *Hinks*, that argument seems hopeless.

30 For an opinion as to the questions which the House ought to have been asked, see [1971] Crim LR 53, 54.

31 See G. Williams, 'Theft and Voidable Title' [1981] Crim LR 666, and see the reply by J. C. Smith at [1981] Crim LR 677. See also a letter by G. V. Hart [1982] Crim LR 391.

32 [1985] Crim LR 745. A charge of obtaining property by deception was withdrawn from the jury.

33 Griew, *Theft*, 2–85.

The effect of *Gomez*

The effect is to render theft an extraordinarily wide offence, embracing many acts which would more naturally be regarded as merely preparatory acts, not even amounting to an attempt, to steal or obtain by deception. The general principle of the civil law is that only the owner of property has the right to do *anything* to or with it; so, logically, the exercise of any such right is an appropriation.

Anyone doing anything whatever to property belonging to another, with or without his consent, appropriates it; and, if he does so dishonestly and with intent by that, or any subsequent act, permanently to deprive, he commits theft.

Prosecutors may find it easier to secure convictions for theft in most cases, but the interpretation may cause acute problems identifying the precise time and place of the act which constitutes the appropriation.

By placing additional emphasis on dishonesty and reducing the *actus reus* almost to vanishing point the offence becomes (too) dependent on *mens rea*, and loses what Fletcher would describe as its 'manifest criminality'.[34] It should be noted that a minority of academics welcomed this shift. For example, Gardner, regarded the decision in *Gomez* as 'unimpeachable' in following the decision in *Lawrence*, and 'desirable from first principles . . . [since] the quality of the dishonest conduct is not necessarily altered by the victim's consent'.[35]

The effect of *Hinks*

It was argued that despite the incredible breadth of the concept of appropriation following *Gomez*, there was one necessary limitation to that concept. In all the decided cases, any proprietary right acquired by D was voidable: the owner was entitled to rescind the transaction and get his property back. Following *Gomez* this could constitute theft. In contrast, where D gets an absolute, indefeasible right to the property, he has the right to retain the property. It was thought by some to be unacceptable – impossible even – for a criminal court to hold that the transaction which resulted in D obtaining such a right amounted to a theft of the property by him. If D has a right to retain the property, or even to recover it from the alleged victim, it could hardly be held to be theft for him to take and keep it. If it were theft, the civil law would be, by providing protection through the law relating to conversion, assisting D to enjoy, or to recover, the fruits of his crime! This argument underestimated the determination of some judges including, as it happened, a majority of a particular committee of the House, to convict those deemed by a jury to be dishonest.

In each of a series of three cases, D received a substantial gift from V, a person of a vulnerable mental state, over whom D had acquired some influence. In each case V was of sufficient mental capacity in law to make a gift. The gift might, in civil law, have been voidable because of the exercise of undue influence by D, but the juries were not asked to consider that question, so we must take it that it was not. In the first case, *Mazo*,[36] it was

34 G. Fletcher, *Rethinking Criminal Law*, 82 See M. Giles and S. Uglow, 'Appropriation and Manifest Criminality in Theft' (1992) 56 J Crim L 179, and N. Lacey, C. Wells and O. Quick, *Reconstructing Criminal Law* (3rd edn, 2003), ch 4.

35 S. Gardner, 'Appropriation in Theft: The Last Word' (1993) 109 LQR 194.

36 [1996] Crim LR 435.

'common ground that the receiver of a valid gift *inter vivos* could not be the subject of a conviction for theft' – D's conviction was quashed. But in *Hopkins and Kendrick*[37] the Court of Appeal upheld the conviction of the recipients of the gifts. The court distinguished *Mazo*, but expressly doubted the validity of the 'common ground' premise on which *Mazo* was decided. In the third case, *Hinks*,[38] the Court of Appeal confronted the problem directly and held that it was immaterial whether there was a valid gift: *Mazo* was based on a mistaken premise. The only question was whether the D, the donee of the gift, was dishonest – and jury had found that she was. The House, Lords Hutton and Hobhouse dissenting, upheld the conviction.

The conduct of the accused in all three cases was despicable. They were, as the jury must have found, dishonestly taking an unfair advantage of a person with failing powers. If the donors were incapable of making a valid gift owing to their diminished mental capacity, the cases were unanswerable. But we must take it that they were capable and had done so. It should be noted that the offence of theft was drafted with the purpose of protecting property rights, not protecting against exploitation *per se*.[39]

The result of the decision of the House of Lords in *Hinks* is therefore that the recipient of a valid gift may now be guilty of stealing it – provided only that a jury is satisfied that his mind was dishonest in the sense to be considered below. Aside from creating an astonishingly broad offence of theft, this creates numerous problems. First, although there is a theft there are never any stolen goods because the donor, *ex hypothesi*, never has any right to restitution:[40] the property belongs absolutely to D for ever.

Secondly, there is the problem of the relationship between civil and criminal law.[41] There are very strong arguments of principle for the criminal law not extending beyond the civil law, in particular in the area of theft where the criminal law is necessarily developed on the foundations of civil law concepts of property, ownership, etc. The majority of the House in *Hinks* acknowledge, with surprising equanimity, that their decision does create a conflict between the civil and the criminal law. D who has V's consent to appropriate the property will commit no civil law wrong and, indeed, will be able to rely on the civil law to enforce the transfer of property, but will be exposed to prosecution for theft. In *Hinks*, Lord Steyn states however that '. . . it would be wrong to assume on *a priori* grounds that the criminal law rather than the civil law is defective' in creating this conflict. If we were constructing a new code of civil and criminal law, it

37 [1997] 2 Cr App R 524, [1997] Crim LR 359.

38 [1998] Crim LR 904. The court derived 'some comfort' from Simon Gardner's article, 'Property and Theft' [1998] Crim LR 35.

39 Cf A. L. Bogg and J. Stanton-Ife, 'Protecting the Vulnerable: Legality, Harm and Theft' (2003) 23 LS 402.

40 See s 24(3) of the Theft Act 1968, below, p 839. Assuming a valid gift, the goods were never out of lawful custody or possession and the donor never had a right to restitution. Hinks was ordered to pay £19,000 compensation to Dolphin. Compensation for what? For keeping a gift which she was legally entitled to keep? The jury's verdict did not decide that she did not have an *indefeasible* title to the property. Was the judge entitled to decide that her title was defeasible? – for misrepresentation, undue influence, or what? Could Hinks have an argument that the order was contrary to her right to peaceful enjoyment of her possessions under Article 1, protocol 1 of the ECHR?

41 See on this more generally: J. C. Smith, 'Civil Law Concepts in the Criminal Law' [1972B] CLJ 197; G. Williams, 'Theft, Consent and Illegality' [1977] Crim LR 127 and 205.

would certainly be open to the legislator to prefer a principle of the criminal law to one of the civil law, but that is not the position. The Theft Acts assume the existence of the civil law of property rights and the criminal courts are, or should be, bound to take it as they find it.

Suppose that V, becoming very excited on seeing D's painting of Salisbury Cathedral and, thinking he is about to get a bargain, offers D £100,000 for it. D realizes that V thinks the painting is by Constable but D knows that it was painted by his sister and is worth no more than £100. He accepts V's offer. D has made an enforceable contract and he is entitled to recover and to retain the money.[42] Similarly, if a buyer knew that a picture was in fact by Constable and bought it for a very small sum from a seller, who, as the buyer was aware, did not know this, a jury might well regard D's conduct in these examples as dishonest – and, of course, V would not have consented, had he known the true facts. The effect of *Hinks* is that, if the jury is satisfied that these defendants were dishonest they are guilty of stealing the property – property to which they are absolutely entitled in civil law.

Thirdly, in the trilogy of cases *Mazo, Hopkins and Kedrick* and *Hinks*, the property belonged to the donor, V, until the instant when the dishonest act of receiving the gift was done. D's acquisition of the entire proprietary interest and the appropriation were simultaneous. If, however, D acquires the entire interest first and then, after an interval, does the act alleged to be an appropriation, it seems he cannot, even after *Hinks*, be guilty: he has not then appropriated property belonging to another – it is already his.[43] V, a poor person infatuated by a wealthy man, D, sends a valuable gift to D's house where it comes into his possession during his absence abroad. When he comes home, he treats it as his own – which it is. However dishonest a jury might think him, this cannot be theft.

Further consideration of *Gomez*

(i) The impact on s 15 – The effect of *Gomez* is that virtually[44] all offences of obtaining property by deception contrary to s 15 are also theft, except obtaining land, which, the Act provides, cannot be stolen. The creation of this degree of overlap is capable of making life much easier for prosecutors.[45] Proving an operative deception for the purposes of s 15 can be difficult, and it is unnecessary if theft is the charge. But some prosecutors have not grasped, or are perhaps unwilling to take advantage of this new freedom, for obtaining property by deception continues to be charged where theft would do.[46] Perhaps this stems from prosecutors' anxieties that in some instances a jury would be bemused by the

[42] Cf *Smith v Hughes* (1871) LR 6 QB 597 (sale of oats enforceable by seller although he knew that the buyer thought they were old oats, new oats being useless to him, and that the oats were in fact new). The question was not 'what a man of scrupulous morality or nice honour would do in such circumstances'. Another example may be the case where a finder has in law a better right to the thing found than the landowner: below, 678, n 170. However dishonest the finder may be, he should not be guilty of theft by appropriating that which the law says he may appropriate.

[43] See Lord Hobhouse at [2000] 4 All ER 855f–g.

[44] R. Heaton, 'Deceiving without Thieving' [2001] Crim LR 712, describes some cases where the obtaining of goods may still not amount to theft, including eg goods delivered under a mail order contract.

[45] It is striking that, in the recent case of *Briggs* (below) the Court of Appeal resisted a wide reading of appropriation, by relying on an argument that to do otherwise would mean that there was too great an overlap between theft and deception. This is precisely the reasoning that has on three occasions failed to persuade the House of Lords against creating an almost total overlap between the offences.

[46] See, eg, *Talbott* [1995] Crim LR 396.

allegation of theft rather than deception, and might reflect their mistrust of the prosecution by returning a perverse verdict. In addition, it should be noted that s 15 is now the more serious offence and, in some cases, the prosecutor may well feel that it more properly reflects the conduct alleged.

It has been argued that the overlap between s 15 and theft is not problematic, in the same way that the existence of the offence of robbery (which necessarily includes theft) is not regarded as problematic.[47] There is, however a significant difference: the Act was drafted with the intention that all robberies require proof of theft, but with the express intention that s 15 and theft dealt with distinct forms of conduct, overlapping only in cases that had formerly been obtaining possession by a trick. The important distinction in terms of labelling, with 'theft' and 'deception' reflecting separate moral wrongs, also suggests that there ought not, as a matter of principle, to be such extensive overlap between the two offences.[48] The judicial blurring of such distinctions undermines the coherence of the scheme of offences under the Theft Acts.

(ii) The Court of Appeal's reaction – The initial reaction of the Court of Appeal to *Gomez* seems to have been one of incredulity. In *Gallasso*,[49] an appeal heard on the very day that judgment was given in *Gomez*, the court said that although a taking with consent may be an appropriation, 'there must still be a taking'. That would have imposed drastic limitations on theft, but it is an untenable opinion. It is certain that 'appropriation' includes what we formerly knew as conversion, as well as taking. In *Gallasso*, D, a nurse, received cheques on behalf of a mentally handicapped patient, V, and, instead of paying them into one of two existing accounts in V's name, opened a new account, also in V's name, and paid the cheques into that account. It was alleged that D's purpose was to make unauthorized withdrawals. The court held that, even if D was acting dishonestly and with intent permanently to deprive V, this was not theft because there was no taking and therefore no appropriation. But D was certainly exercising a right of the owner and, according to *Gomez*, it was immaterial that she was doing so with consent, provided that she was acting dishonestly and with intent to deprive. The case appears indistinguishable from *Fritschy*.

The House of Lords' decision in *Gomez* was applied, but with great reluctance, by the Court of Appeal in *Atakpu*.[50] D and E hired cars in Germany and Belgium and drove them to England, intending to sell them to *bona fide* purchasers. They were detained in Dover and charged with conspiracy to steal. The trial judge, applying the Court of Appeal's decision in *Gomez*, held that there was no theft outside the jurisdiction of the court (that is, England and Wales) because everything that was done there (Germany and Belgium) was done with the consent of the owner. The judge went on to hold that theft

[47] S. Gardner, 'Appropriation in Theft: The Last Word' (1993) 109 LQR 194.

[48] See in particular, S. Shute and J. Horder, 'Thieving and Deceiving: What is the Difference' (1993) 56 MLR 548, 'the thief makes war on a social practice from the outside, the deceiver is the traitor within'; C. Clarkson, 'Theft and Fair Labelling' (1993) 56 MLR 554. See for a more pragmatic view P. Glazebrook, 'Thief or Swindler: Who Cares?' [1991] CLJ 389, and P. Glazebrook, 'Revising the Theft Acts' [1993] CLJ 191. Shute and Horder suggest that the true distinction lies in the voluntariness of the transfer. This test, it is submitted, carries its own substantial difficulties, some of which are addressed by Clarkson.

[49] [1993] Crim LR 459. See also [1993] Crim LR at 307. Griew, *Theft*, 2–89 thinks the 'strange judgment' may 'defy rationalisation'; and Smith, *Property Offences*, para 5–56, concludes that it is 'simply wrong'.

[50] [1994] QB 69, [1993] 4 All ER 215.

would have been committed in England when the goods were retained after the expiration of the hire with the dishonest intention of permanently depriving the owners. It was *Fritschy* in reverse. D and E were guilty of conspiracy to steal in England. However, by the time *Atakpu* reached the Court of Appeal, the House of Lords had allowed the appeal in *Gomez.* The Court of Appeal felt bound to conclude that theft was committed outside the jurisdiction when the cars were obtained irrespective of the consent of the owner which D and E had induced by their deception. The court concluded that while theft may continue as long as the thief is 'on the job', and that this is a question for a jury, no jury could reasonably decide that these thefts were continuing days after the appellants had first obtained the cars. Theft is a finite act and this theft ended outside the jurisdiction of the English courts. There was a conspiracy in England to steal in Germany and Belgium, but not *in England.*[51] That conspiracy would now be indictable under s 1A of the Criminal Law Act 1977.[52]

Sullivan and Warbrick,[53] argue that the court was misled by the phrase 'theft abroad is not triable in England' and that so-called 'theft abroad' is not theft under English law; D and E had come by the cars without stealing them[54] so their later assumption of a right to the cars in England would have amounted to an appropriation; the cars were to be stolen in English law for the first time when appropriated in England. The court relied on s 24(1) of the Theft Act 1968 which provides that: 'The provisions of this Act relating to goods which have been stolen shall apply whether the stealing occurred in England or Wales or elsewhere, and whether it occurred before or after the commencement of this Act, provided that the stealing (if not an offence under this Act) amounted to an offence where and at the time when the goods were stolen . . .'. Sullivan and Warbrick argue that this points to the opposite conclusion – the subsection provides an extended definition of 'stolen goods' for the purposes of the offence of handling and it acknowledges that stealing goods outside England and Wales is 'not an offence [sc theft] under this Act'. It can be argued to the contrary, that the words in parentheses imply that some stealing outside England and Wales *will be* an offence under the Act. In some jurisdictions, for example, Canada, taking with intent *temporarily* to deprive is theft. Are these words intended to cover cases such as the handling in England of goods stolen in Canada under Canadian law, whether or not there was an intent permanently to deprive? Should such conduct be an offence under English law?[55]

The Court of Appeal's apparent disbelief at the breadth of the offence of theft in the wake of *Gomez* and *Hinks* continues to manifest itself. In *Ashcroft*[56] D, a haulier, was alleged to have conspired to steal items from sealed containers in transit. The court regarded as 'some way removed from reality' D's argument that the theft occurred when D originally took possession of the goods in his lorries (in Scotland). Having referred to *Atakpu,* the court commented that in this case 'there never was in any ordinary sense of the word an "appropriation" of the stolen goods until the conspirators removed them

[51] G. Sullivan and C. Warbrick, 'Territoriality, Theft and *Atakpu*' [1994] Crim LR 650, 659.

[52] Above, p 373. See further, M. Hirst, *Jurisdiction and the Ambit of the Criminal Law* (2003), 24–26.

[53] [1994] Crim LR 650, 659.

[54] See s 3(1), above, p 648.

[55] The words in parentheses cannot be intended to apply to stealing in England and Wales before the commencement of the Act, because that could never be an offence under the Act.

[56] [2003] EWCA Crim 2365.

from the containers . . .'.[57] True enough, but since *Gomez*, the word appropriation does not bear the 'ordinary' meaning that its drafters had intended.[58] It is difficult to distinguish the case from *Skipp* or *Fritschy*, neither of which was cited by the court.

Cases overruled by *Gomez*

The only case other than *Fritschy*, which was expressly overruled in *Gomez* was *Skipp*.[59] There D, 'posing as a genuine haulage contractor' (presumably that was itself an operative deception), collected three loads from different places in London with instructions to deliver them in Leicester. D deviated from the route to Leicester and transferred the goods to an accomplice as he had planned all along. It was unsuccessfully argued that a single count for theft of the entire load was bad for duplicity because it alleged three separate appropriations and therefore three thefts. The court held that though D may have had a dishonest intention permanently to deprive at the time he received each of the three loads, he had done nothing inconsistent with the rights of the owners until he diverted the goods from their proper destination. Since *Gomez* it is now clear that he committed three thefts – each theft being also an offence of obtaining property by deception.

Other cases are impliedly overruled. *Eddy v Niman*[60] decided that a person who takes goods from the shelves of a self-service store and puts them into the wire basket provided with intent to steal does not commit theft because everything he has done was with the store's implied consent. There is an obvious difficulty in proving intent in such a case but, if that can be done, this is now theft.[61] It is probably the same where a motorist at a self-service station fills his tank, intending to drive off without paying.[62] This is unlike the supermarket case in that the ownership in the petrol probably passes to the motorist when he puts it into his tank; but after *Hinks* it is no answer that he had acquired an absolute, indefeasible right to the property. Even now, however, it should be an answer that he did not form the dishonest intent until after he had acquired the entire proprietary interest. The prosecutor might, therefore, be well advised to charge making off without payment, contrary to s 3 of the Theft Act 1978.[63]

In *Hircock*,[64] D, by deception, obtained possession of a car under a hire-purchase agreement. Fourteen days later he dishonestly sold the car. It was held that he was guilty of an offence under s 15 when he obtained the car and of theft when he sold it. Applying

57 Para 45.

58 For an early discussion of the two senses of the word 'appropriation' see A. Halpin, 'The Appropriate Appropriation' [1991] Crim LR 426, A. Halpin, *Definitions in the Criminal Law* (2004), 166–181.

59 [1975] Crim LR 114.

60 (1981) 73 Cr App R 237, [1981] Crim LR 502, DC. Parker LJ, in his judgment in *Dobson*, which was approved in *Gomez*, discussed the question and held that *Eddy v Niman* was inconsistent with the decision of the Court of Appeal in *McPherson* [1973] Crim LR 191. The latter case did not depend on the fact that the goods were concealed in a shopping bag – the offence was committed as soon as they were taken from the shelves.

61 This is another case where the goods are stolen but are not 'stolen goods' for the purposes of the Act as they remain in the possession and ownership of the shop. But, unlike the situation in *Hinks*, the shopper has set out to do something – take the goods out of the possession of the owner – which would render them stolen. It is submitted that here the law of theft intervenes too early, whereas in *Hinks*, it should never interfere at all.

62 In *McHugh* (1976) 64 Cr App R 92 it was assumed, without argument, that this was theft. If it was theft before *Gomez*, it is so still. Cf *Edwards v Ddin* [1976] 3 All ER 705, DC.

63 Below, p 731.

64 (1978) 67 Cr App R 278, [1979] Crim LR 184.

Gomez, he was guilty of theft (and obtaining) when he got possession of the car and, as in *Atakpu*, that theft had finished before he sold the car (he was no longer 'on the job' of stealing). Once stolen by him, he could not steal it again.

In *Dip Kaur v Chief Constable for Hampshire*[65] D found in a rack of shoes which she knew to be properly priced £6.99, a pair, one of which was labelled £6.99 and the other £4.99. She took the pair to the cashier, and, as she hoped, the cashier saw the lower and not the higher price. She paid £4.99 and left the shop with the shoes. Her conviction for theft was quashed on the ground that the cashier had authority to accept D's offer to buy at the lower price and the ownership passed to D. It now seems clear that D was guilty of theft as soon as she did anything with the shoes with a dishonest intent – probably when she picked them up and noticed the price discrepancy, certainly not later than when she tendered them to the cashier.

Appropriation and the civil law

Glanville Williams argued that no act should amount to theft unless it is contrary to the civil law. Nearly all thefts do amount to the civil wrongs of trespass, conversion or breach of trust but it does not follow that civil unlawfulness is a necessary constituent of the offence.[66] The definition of theft does not use the word 'unlawfully' nor does it say '*mis*appropriate'. It has been argued[67] that a requirement of unlawfulness can be read into the concept of dishonesty. Thus, it has been suggested that the word 'dishonestly' has an objective as well as a subjective meaning and that actions that are lawful at civil law are not the dishonest conduct which the section requires.

The courts are extremely reluctant to admit consideration of civil law into criminal cases, even where it is inevitable, and these arguments have not been judicially accepted.[68] After *Gomez*, and *Hinks*,[69] the arguments appear untenable. The removal of goods from the shelves of a supermarket is not a civil wrong merely because the act is done with a secret dishonest intent but it is now theft. Fritschy committed no civil wrong by carrying out his employer's instructions to take the krugerrands to Switzerland but we are now told he was a thief.

In *Hinks*, the House of Lords recognized that the decision led to a conflict, but took comfort from Gardner's argument that the criminal law can 'float free' of the civil law in this context. It is submitted that this ignores the underlying purpose of the offence of

65 [1981] 2 All ER 430, DC. D was probably guilty of obtaining by deception by representing that the authorized price was £4.99 when she knew it was £6.99. The transaction at the cash desk seems to be the same whether D has swapped labels herself, seen them swapped by a mischievous child or the article has been mislabelled by a careless assistant. If D knows she is presenting a 'false' price label to the cashier, she is obtaining by deception.

66 '. . . the aims and purposes of the civil law are not co-extensive with the criminal.' Smith, *Property Offences*, para 5–06; but see also paras 5–11–5–52.

67 A. Arlidge and J. Parry on *Fraud in the Criminal Law* (1st edn), para 1.10.

68 A partner has been held guilty of theft of the partnership property, even though his act did not amount to the tort of conversion. The court did not think it necessary to look for any other civil wrong – in fact the act must have been a breach of contract: *Bonner* [1970] 2 All ER 97n.

69 See Lord Hobhouse at [2000] 4 All ER 865b.

theft and others in the Theft Acts being designed to protect property – a civil law concept.[70] Shute suggests an alternative argument; dishonest conduct such as that in *Hinks*, might not constitute a civil law wrong, it 'may nonetheless have a *tendency* to undermine property rights either directly by attacking the interests that they protect, or indirectly by weakening an established system of property rights and so threatening the public good that the system represents.'[71] It is submitted that such vague concepts of harm do not form a sufficiently clear or solid foundation for an offence that is serious, commonplace, and for which a clear rationale – protecting property rights – has existed since its inception. The consequence of accepting the arguments supporting the *Hinks* proposition is of course that the offence becomes almost entirely dependent on the concept of dishonesty.

Appropriation by 'keeping' and 'dealing'

It is difficult to conceive of D being held to be 'dealing' with the property where he has done nothing at all in relation to the goods, even though he has made up his mind to steal them.[72] Arguably however, 'keeping' goes somewhat further.

Suppose that D, having borrowed V's cycle for a week, resolves on the expiry of that period to keep it. It would clearly be an appropriation, at the expiry of the period, to refuse to return it on demand,[73] or to deny V access to it, or for D to claim it as his own. Such conduct shows that he is keeping it as owner. It would also constitute appropriation if D were to use the cycle after the expiry of the loan because this is an assumption of one of the owner's rights. But what if D, on the expiry of the loan, merely leaves the cycle where it is in his garage hoping that V will forget about it and intending to keep it? Literally the case falls within the section since D is 'keeping . . . it as owner' and there would appear to be no warrant for giving the words other than their plain meaning. Of course it would be very difficult to prove D's *mens rea* in the form of the intention permanently to deprive, but he satisfies the appropriation requirement of keeping as owner.

As the court has recently underlined in *Gresham*[74] 'keeping' as owner in relation to a bank account may be difficult to prove in a case where [D] does no more than refrain from bringing the mistake to the attention of the bank'.[75] Some positive act such as drawing a cheque on the account may be necessary.

Appropriation – requirement of a positive act?

In general terms, the concept of appropriation, being defined in terms of an 'assumption' of the rights of another would seem clearly to require conduct on D's part demonstrating such an assumption. What of cases in which D induces V to hand over property to him? Can there be an appropriation before the point in time at which D has physical contact, possession or control of the property?

70 See also J. Beatson and A. Simester, 'Stealing One's Own Property' (1999) 115 LQR 372.
71 S. Shute, 'Appropriation and the Law of Theft' [2002] Crim LR 445, 455.
72 But see *A-G's Reference (No 1 of 1983)* [1985] QB 182, [1984] 3 All ER 369, CA, below, p 686.
73 Cf *Wakeman* (1912) 8 Cr App R 18.
74 [2003] EWCA Crim 2070.
75 Approving the statements in *Ngan* [1998] 1 Cr App R 331, at 336, *Gresham*, para 22.

In *Hilton*,[76] where D, who had direct control of a bank account belonging to a charity, gave instructions for the transfer of the charity's funds to settle his personal debts, it was held that he stole the thing in action (the charity's right to payment of that sum from its bank) belonging to the charity. *Hilton* might be regarded as a straightforward case since D always had control of the bank account and instructed his agent (the bank) to act in relation to the property.

It was argued in previous editions that it is different where D, by deception, induces, V, the owner and controller of the bank account to transfer funds from it because although V's credit balance, or part of it, has gone, D did not 'appropriate' it.[77] The Court of Appeal recently affirmed this view in *Briggs*[78] where D had, by deception, induced her elderly relatives to transfer to her proceeds of their house sale. The Court of Appeal quashed a conviction for theft of the credit balance representing the proceeds of the sale (there was some confusion as to what D was alleged to have stolen). The court held that the word 'appropriation' connoted a physical act rather than a more remote action triggering the payment that gave rise to the charge.[79] The court relied heavily on Sir John Smith's commentary on *Caresena:*

> It is true that D procures the whole course of events resulting in V's account being debited; but the telegraphic transfer is initiated by V and his voluntary intervening acts break the chain of causation. It is the same as if V is induced by deception to take money out of his safe to pay to D. D does not at that moment 'appropriate' it – V is not acting as his agent. D commits theft only if and when the money is put into his hands.

It is submitted that while *Gomez* and *Hinks* do not expressly preclude this approach they do make it very much harder to draw any clear distinction between (i) D's direct acts towards V's property, with V's fraudulently obtained consent, and (ii) D's acts causing V to transfer his property (or extinguish his chose in action) with V's fraudulently obtained consent. Arguably they are distinguishable on the basis that V's act of transfer in (ii) breaks the chain of causation since V will not be acting in a free informed manner (having been deceived). However, if D used an innocent agent, E, to effect the transfer of V's property, or to extinguish it, there would be no difficulty in establishing a theft charge at the moment that E assumes any right in relation to V's property. Why are things different when D causes V to act towards his own property in a way that will lead to its being destroyed or transferred to D? Both the agent and V appear to have been deceived. The fact that V has the authority to act in this way by transferring the property and consenting is, according to *Gomez* and *Hinks*, irrelevant. D's setting in motion of the transaction could be regarded as the commencement of the continuing act of appropriation. It is therefore arguable that where D, by deceit of V, causes a transfer of property that act is itself an appropriation. This possibility flows from the shift in emphasis in interpreting the concept of appropriation generally.

76 [1997] 2 Cr App R 445, [1997] Crim LR 761 and commentary.

77 Reliance was placed on *Caresana* [1996] Crim LR 667, *Naviede* [1997] Crim LR 662. See also J. C. Smith, Archbold News, Issue 9, 14 Nov 1996.

78 [2004] EWCA Crim 3662, [2004] Crim LR 455.

79 Despite the court's approving reference to the *Oxford English Dictionary* definition of appropriation involving a 'taking', it is submitted that a physical 'taking' or 'touching' is only a sufficient but not a necessary element of the offence, otherwise there would be no protection for intangible property.

It remains true that theft requires proof of an 'act' by D towards the property that belongs to another, subject to what was said above about keeping and dealing. 'Appropriation' is quite different from 'obtaining' in this respect. Whereas appropriation requires an act by D, in s 15 the element of 'obtaining' can be satisfied by passivity on D's part: the crucial element of criminal conduct for that offence is D's deception.

Dishonest sale by a buyer on sale or return

In earlier editions of this book[80] it was argued that D, a buyer of goods from V on sale or return, who sold the goods to E, dishonestly intending never to pay V for them, was not guilty of theft of the goods or the proceeds of sale. He was doing only what V had authorized him to do. He had concluded a contract to buy the goods and he owed V the price; he was merely a debtor. After *Gomez*, and *Hinks* this argument may no longer be tenable. It is true that, by selling the goods, D was exercising a right that he had already acquired honestly but the dishonest exercise of a right may now amount to an appropriation. This is a further illustration of the extension of the scope of the offence. As regards the proceeds of the sale, *Gomez* cannot affect the civil law under which, notwithstanding D's secret dishonest intention not to pay V, the ownership of the goods will pass to E; but if, as *Hinks* decides, the dishonest receipt of a valid gift may amount to theft, so too might the dishonest receipt of a price properly paid.

Theft without loss

In *Chan Man-sin v Attorney-General of Hong Kong*[81] it was held that a company accountant, who drew a forged cheque on the company's bank account, stole from the company the thing in action consisting in its credit balance, or its contractual right to overdraw, even though it was settled law that the honouring of the forged cheque and debiting of the company's account was a nullity and the company, on discovering the unauthorized debit, was entitled to have it reversed. In law, D's actions were wholly ineffective, the company was never a penny the worse off; but it was held that there was an appropriation – because D assumed the rights of an owner over the credit balance – and an intent permanently to deprive – because he intended to treat the thing as his own to dispose of regardless of the company's rights.[82]

That case concerned things in action but presumably the same principles apply to tangible property. In the old law of larceny, a bailee of a tape recorder was held guilty of stealing when he dishonestly offered to sell it.[83] In *Bloxham*,[84] D, not being a bailee or in possession of the property, dishonestly and without authority, contracted to sell to X a refrigerator belonging to D's employer, V. He was held to be not guilty of attempted larceny because he never made any attempt to take and carry away the thing. He probably never intended to deliver it; and it would have been better to charge him with obtaining the price from the buyer by false pretences (now, deception). On a charge of theft, however, the question would now be whether he appropriated the fridge. It appears that

80 7th edn, 525–526.

81 [1988] 1 All ER 1.

82 See below, p 704.

83 *Rogers v Arnott* [1960] 2 QB 244, [1960] 2 All ER 417, DC. A bailee could commit larceny by 'converting' (in effect, appropriating) the bailed property but, for an accused who was not a bailee, a taking and carrying away had to be proved.

84 (1943) 29 Cr App R 37.

he probably did. It has been argued[85] that the purported sale was not an assumption of a right of another because:

> . . . whereas the owner has a right against others that they shall not deliver his property to third persons (because that involves a tortious interference) he has no general right that they shall not contract to sell it, or purport to pass ownership in it.

The owner certainly has a right (unless he has surrendered it) to sell his own property, so the argument appears to be that the third party has not assumed the owner's right because he has his own right to sell the property – everyone has the right to sell anyone else's property – which seems a trifle bizarre. Certainly you may lawfully *contract* to sell my property at some future date in the expectation or the hope that, in the meantime, you will be able to buy it from me and fulfil your contract;[86] but a purported present sale to a *bona fide* purchaser seems quite different.

The switch brought about by the 1968 Act from larceny, 'an offence against possession', to theft, 'an offence against ownership', is significant here. The thief does indeed generally deprive his victim of possession but only in very exceptional circumstances does he deprive him of ownership in its strict sense. The stolen goods nearly always continue to belong to the original owner, so theft generally has no effect on the owners' rights, as such. The thief may in fact acquire possession but he can only purport to be the owner.

Pitham – a doubtful decision

Even in the light of *Gomez*, the earlier case of *Pitham* remains difficult to justify. D, knowing that V was in prison, took Pitham to V's house and offered to sell V's property to Pitham. It was held that the offer amounted to a completed theft of V's property, so that when the goods were delivered to Pitham he received them 'otherwise than in the course of the stealing'[87] and was therefore guilty of handling stolen goods. But in this case, unlike *Rogers v Arnott*[88] or *Bloxham*, the buyer, Pitham, knew that D had no authority to sell V's property and D knew that the 'buyer' knew that. D did not purport to be the owner or have the owner's authority to sell the property. It was not really an offer to sell at all but a proposal for a joint theft of the property.[89]

Continuing appropriation[90]

An offence that is complete at a particular moment may nevertheless continue being committed for some time thereafter. It is often important to know how long a particular theft continued. A person may be guilty of a theft by aiding and abetting it while it is being committed by another, but he cannot aid and abet once the theft is over. A person may be guilty of robbery if he uses force while theft is being committed but not by using force when the theft is at an end. A person may be guilty of the offence of handling stolen

85 Smith, *Property Offences*, 5–49.

86 Cf Sale of Goods Act 1979, s 5. 87 See below, p 848. 88 n 83, above.

89 The jury acquitted Pitham of theft although 'The evidence that they had bought property knowing that it was stolen, arose from the fact that they said they had bought considerably under price', 65 Cr App R at 47. How can a buyer knowing that the seller, by selling the property, is stealing it, not be guilty of theft? See also Williams, TBCL (2nd edn, 1983), 764; Smith, *Theft*, para 2–30.

90 G. Williams, 'Appropriation: A Single or Continuous Act' [1978] Crim LR 69.

goods only if he does a proscribed act 'otherwise than in the course of the stealing'. A person may use reasonable force in preventing a crime while it is being committed.[91]

Theft may certainly be committed in an instant, so that D could be convicted of the offence even if he was immediately arrested. It does not follow that the offence is over in an instant, though that seems to have been the opinion of the court in *Pitham*.[92] In *Atakpu*,[93] after a careful review of the pre-*Gomez* authorities, Ward J summarized the law as follows:[94]

> (1) theft can occur in an instant by a single appropriation but it can also involve a course of dealing with property lasting longer and involving several appropriations before the transaction is complete; (2) theft is a finite act – it has a beginning and it has an end; (3) at what point the transaction is complete is a matter for the jury to decide upon the facts of each case; (4) though there may be several appropriations in the course of a single theft or several appropriations of different goods each constituting a separate theft as in *R v Skipp*, no case suggests that there can be successive thefts of the same property. . . .

The court thought that, on a strict construction, *Gomez* left 'little room for a continuous course of action'; but they would not wish that to be the law and preferred the view that appropriation continues so long as the thief can sensibly be regarded as in the act of stealing, or in more understandable words, so long as he is 'on the job' as it was put in the 7th edition of this book at page 513. In *Atakpu* it was not necessary for the court to decide the matter, because no jury could have reasonably concluded that the theft of the cars in Frankfurt or Brussels in that case, was continuing when the cars were brought, days later, into England. It is thought that this is the better view and that to treat appropriation simply as an instantaneous act would be inconsistent with the provisions of the Act relating to robbery and handling, which presuppose that there can be a course of stealing.

Appropriation – when and where?

Where the thief and the property are in different places does the theft take place where and when he acts, or where and when his act affects the property? The problem usually arises in relation to the theft of things in action – intangible property – but it is equally possible with tangible property. D, in England, may dishonestly assume V's rights of ownership over goods in a warehouse in Scotland by selling, or purporting to sell, them to E.[95] In *Tomsett*[96] the Court of Appeal accepted without argument that the theft occurred at the location of the property in question. The V Bank transferred US$7m to a New York bank to earn overnight interest. D, a telex operator employed by V, dishonestly and without authority, sent a telex from London diverting the $7m plus interest to another bank in New York for an account at its Geneva branch which V's accomplice had opened. D's conviction for conspiracy to steal was quashed:[97] the planned theft took place, not in

[91] See *Bowden* [2002] EWCA Crim 1279, where D claimed a defence under s 3 of the Criminal Law Act 1967 when detaining youths whom he believed to have stolen car keys. The Court of Appeal held that the judge was right to leave to the jury the issue of whether the youths' crime of theft of the keys was still continuing at the time of D's actions.

[92] Above, p 663.

[93] Above, p 656.

[94] [1993] 4 All ER 215 at 223.

[95] See Smith, *Theft*, para 2–108.

[96] [1985] Crim LR 369.

[97] This would not be so today. See Criminal Law Act 1977, s 1A, above, p 373.

London, but in Geneva or New York, outside the jurisdiction of the English court. Similarly, in *Kohn*[98] where D dishonestly drew cheques on a company's account, Lane LJ said, *obiter*, that the theft did not take place until the account was debited. However in *Ex p Osman*,[99] an extradition case, a Divisional Court comprised of Lloyd LJ and French J, both members of the court in *Tomsett*, refused to follow that case. Osman, in Hong Kong, sent a telex assuming the rights of the owner of a bank account in New York. It was held that this could be theft in Hong Kong. In *Ex p Levin*,[100] another extradition case, the court thought that the fact that a computer operator was physically in Russia was of far less significance than the fact that he was looking at and operating on magnetic discs in USA: he had committed theft in USA and could be extradited to that country.

In *Ngan*[101] a large sum intended for V had been mistakenly paid into D's bank account in England. By virtue of s 5(4) of the 1968 Act (discussed below) this property was to be regarded as belonging to V. D dishonestly drew blank cheques on the account and sent them to her sister in Scotland who presented them there for payment. The court, equating the presentation of the cheque with the sending of the telex in *Osman*, held that the theft took place in Scotland. The signing and issuing of the cheques were preparatory acts to the theft.

These problems are less likely to arise since the bringing into force of Part 1 of the Criminal Justice Act 1993 and s 1A of the Criminal Law Act 1977 but they are still significant and require resolution. In the light of the broad notion of appropriation followed since *Gomez*, it may be that the theft is committed where and when D does some act which only the owner could properly do; but that it continues to the time when and place where it affects the property.

The exception in favour of *bona fide* purchasers: s 3(2)

Where property or a right or interest in property is or purports to be transferred for value to a person acting in good faith, no later assumption by him of rights which he believed himself to be acquiring shall, by reason of any defect in the transferor's title, amount to theft.

The CLRC explained this exception as follows:[102]

A person may buy something in good faith, but may find out afterwards that the seller had no title to it, perhaps because the seller or somebody else stole it. If the buyer nevertheless keeps the thing or otherwise deals with it as owner, he could . . . be guilty of theft. It is arguable that this would be right; but on the whole it seems to us that, whatever view is taken of the buyer's moral duty, the law would be too strict if it made him guilty of theft.

The exception operates in favour only of a person acquiring his interest in good faith and for value – a 'BFPFV'. It would extend to a pledgee or a person acquiring a lien as well as a buyer of property; but if a pledgee, having discovered the pledgor's lack of title, were to,

98 (1979) 69 Cr App R 395, below, p 667.

99 *Governor of Pentonville Prison, ex p Osman* [1989] 3 All ER 701, DC. This issue was not discussed in the House of Lords: [1997] AC 741, [1997] 3 All ER 289.

100 *Governor of Brixton Prison, ex p Levin* [1997] QB 65, [1997] 3 All ER 289, DC.

101 [1998] 1 Cr App R 331.

102 Cmnd 2977, para 37. But this exception may now be neutralized by the money laundering legislation, below, pp 861–863.

say, destroy the property he might be guilty of theft because he is assuming rights greater than those that he believed he had acquired. The BFPFV who discovers that the property is stolen is not guilty of handling if he disposes of it to an innocent person.[103] But the property in the hands of the BFPFV continues to belong to the owner from whom it was stolen, and if the BFPFV, by representing himself as having title to the property, induces V to buy it, he may be guilty of obtaining the price by deception.[104]

(ii) Property

Those types of property which may be stolen are defined in s 4 of the Theft Act 1968, and the broad effect of this section is that all property may be stolen subject to certain exceptions in relation to land, things growing wild and wild creatures. It is important to note that the offence is founded on orthodox civil law concepts of property. Legal conceptions of property are constantly evolving to reflect developments in society, and in recent years the particular concern has been for the law to reflect the rapid developments in information technology and the way in which data are stored and accessed. There have been calls to expand the definition of property to provide protection in this area.[105] More radically, there is pressure for the law to recognize a diverse range of rights and interests as species of property (for example, environmental rights and welfare rights).[106] Irrespective of the validity of this reconceptualisation of property, it is submitted that the law of theft is certainly not the most appropriate mechanism for securing protection of these rights under the criminal law.

Under the Act, the definition of property is extremely broad, and coupled with the breadth of the definition of appropriation renders the *actus reus* minimal. The breadth of the definition of property illustrates that the structure of the Act avoids defining offences by distinctions based on the type of property involved, and focuses instead on the manner of the harm being caused. Section 4(1) provides the general definition:

> 'Property' includes money and all other property, real or personal, including things in action and other intangible property.

There are specified exceptions relating to land, animals and plants to be discussed below.

Things in action

The one limitation on the generality of this definition, apart from the specified exceptions, is that the property must be capable of appropriation. Intangible property may be appropriated by any assumption of any of the rights of an owner over it.[107] This is best illustrated by reference to bank accounts. Where a bank account is in credit, the relationship between banker and customer is that of a debtor and creditor. In law, the customer, V, does not have 'money in the bank';[108] there is no specific pile of money that is

103 Below, p 852.

104 See *Wheeler* (1990) 92 Cr App R 279, CA. D did not obtain by deception in selling stolen goods to V but only because the sale, though not the delivery, took place before D became aware that they were stolen.

105 See eg J. Lipton, 'A revised property concept for the New Millenium' (1999) Int Jnl of Law and IT 171.

106 See N. Lacey, C. Wells and O. Quick, *Reconstructing Criminal Law* (3rd edn, 2003), 380.

107 See *Storrow and Poole* [1983] Crim LR 332.

108 'Although we talk about people having money in the bank, the only person who has money in the bank is the banker', *Davenport* [1954] 1 All ER 602, 603, per Goddard LCJ.

designated as his. The property that he has is a 'thing in action', a right to payment by the bank of the sum of money it owes him. Thus, if D dishonestly causes a bank to debit V's account, D does not appropriate V's money, he appropriates a thing in action belonging to V (V's right to payment of that sum from the bank) and may be guilty of theft of that property.[109] D has reduced or extinguished V's right to that payment from the bank. Where V has an overdraft with the bank, V has a right to payment from the bank of the sum up to the limit of that agreed overdraft, and that is property – a thing in action – that D may steal by dishonestly causing the Bank to debit V's account. The operation of this aspect of the law of theft is illustrated by *Kohn*.[110] D, an accountant, employed by a company to draw cheques to pay the company's debts, drew cheques on the company's account to meet his personal liabilities and was held guilty of theft of the thing in action.

Care must always be taken to ascertain the state of V's account at the time of the alleged theft by D. If V is overdrawn and has no overdraft facility, D's drawing of a cheque on V's account cannot amount to theft because there is no property to steal – V has no contractual right to any payment from the bank. D's action might amount to attempted theft, like an attempt to steal from an empty pocket.

In *Hilton*,[111] where D, who had direct control of a bank account belonging to a charity, gave instructions for the transfer of the charity's funds to settle his personal debts, it was held that he stole the thing in action belonging to the charity. On the other hand, D does not steal from his *own* bank where he uses his banker's card to make a purchase, knowing that his own account is overdrawn and that his authority to use the card has terminated.[112] The bank is obliged to meet the cheque and its own funds will be thereby diminished. D has caused the bank to become indebted but he has not assumed a right over any specific property of the bank.

Stealing or obtaining cheques[113]

Where a cheque is alleged to have been stolen or obtained by deception a different problem arises. A cheque is piece of paper which, if given for consideration, creates a thing in action – a right in the person in whose favour it is drawn to sue the drawer for the sum stated. So, where V writes a cheque payable to D, as well as obtaining the piece of paper into his physical possession, D also obtains a thing in action – a right to sue V's bank for the sum specified on the cheque. However, it is crucial to note that the particular thing in action obtained by D *is not* an item of property that previously belonged to V; the thing in action D obtains is *his* right to sue V's bank. This is a new item of property,

[109] *Chan Man-sin v A-G for Hong Kong* [1988] 1 All ER 1, PC, p 662 above; *Ex p Osman* [1989] 3 All ER 701, DC, above, p 665; *Williams* [2001] 1 Cr App R 362.

[110] (1979) 69 Cr App R 395, CA. See further E. J. Griew, 'Stealing and Obtaining Bank Credits' [1986] Crim LR 356.

[111] [1997] 2 Cr App R 445, [1997] Crim LR 761 and commentary. As discussed above, p 661 it may be different where D, by deception, induces, V, the owner and controller of the bank account to transfer funds from it. V's credit balance, or part of it, has gone, but arguably D did not 'appropriate' it until he took control/possession of the property: *Caresana* [1996] Crim LR 667; *Naviede* [1997] Crim LR 662; *Briggs* [2004] Crim LR 455.

[112] *Navvabi* [1986] 3 All ER 102, [1986] 1 WLR 1311, CA.

[113] See J. C. Smith, 'Obtaining Cheques by Deception or Theft,' [1997] Crim LR 396, 'Stealing Tickets' [1998] Crim LR 723 and commentaries on *Horsman* [1998] Crim LR 128 and *Aston* [1998] Crim LR 498.

distinct from that which V owned before he wrote the cheque to D; the previous item of property was *V's* right to sue his bank.

It is worth explaining the background to this difficulty. Before 1968, stealing or obtaining a thing in action, an intangible thing, was impossible because there had to be a taking and carrying away of the property, but the courts had no difficulty in holding that a person could steal a cheque or obtain it by false pretences.[114] After 1968 courts and commentators tended to consider the question of obtaining cheques as if it were exclusively one of obtaining a thing in action. This trend began with *Duru*[115] in 1973 and continued up to, and beyond the decision of the House of Lords in *Preddy*.[116] In that case, the House at last rejected the erroneous notion, given currency by *Duru*, that D obtains a thing in action belonging to V when he induces him to draw a cheque in his favour. *Preddy* confirms that D does not do so because the thing in action he does obtain belonged from the instant of its creation to him. It never belonged, or could belong, to V. He could not sue himself.

What offences are committed by D's subsequent conduct with the cheque? Where D dishonestly induces V to draw a cheque in his favour, and D attempts to cash the cheque he will be guilty of attempting to obtain by deception from the bank contrary to s 15 of the 1968 Act. If however D presents the cheque for the credit of his own account, he commits no offence under that section because D's increased credit balance (a thing in action belonging to D – his right to sue his bank) was never 'property belonging to another'.[117] But he is at that point guilty of theft of a different thing in action which does belong to V, namely V's credit balance (or right to overdraw if such a facility exists), at his bank.[118] On presenting the cheque,[119] D has assumed V's right to destroy that part of V's property.

As noted, there is also the question of D obtaining the cheque itself, the physical thing in the form of the piece of paper. The House was not required in *Preddy* to decide whether D might be guilty of obtaining this item of property. Lord Goff noted that it does belong to V but said that D would not be guilty because he had no intention permanently to deprive – he knew that the cheque form would, after presentation, be returned to V via his bank (or at least be available for V's collection).[120] It is submitted that this was *obiter* (as well as wrong) but the Court of Appeal in *Graham*[121] treated it as ratio and in *Clark*[122] held that it was bound by that decision. So at present a cheque form cannot be stolen or obtained.

However, though D does not obtain a thing in action from V, and does not steal the cheque form, he obtains something more than a valueless piece of paper from him. A cheque is a 'valuable security'. It is a tangible thing that, as s 20 of the 1968 Act recognizes can be 'executed'. It is not a mere piece of paper, any more than a key is just a piece of metal or a swipe card is a piece of plastic. The physical thing is one that has special

114 *Pople* [1951] 1 KB 53, sub nom *Smith* [1950] 2 All ER 679, CCA. See also *Essex* (1857) 7 Cox CC 384, CCR (conviction quashed on other grounds) and *Hudson* [1943] KB 458, CCA.

115 [1973] 3 All ER 715.

116 [1996] AC 815, [1996] 3 All ER 481, below, p 686.

117 *Burke* [2000] Crim LR 413, applying *Preddy*.

118 *Burke*, above, and *Williams (Roy)* [2001] 1 Cr App R 362, [2001] Crim LR 253.

119 *Ngan* [1998] 1 Cr App R 331.

120 This assumes they will all be retained for V.

121 [1997] 1 Cr App R 302.

122 [2001] Crim LR 572, [2001] EWCA Crim 884.

properties.[123] It is not just any piece of paper which will cause, say, a bank clerk to hand over £1,000; but a cheque will do that. Of course the cheque *is* (i) a piece of paper which (ii) *creates* a thing in action but it is also (iii) a valuable security. The Theft Act 1968 does not specifically refer to 'valuable securities' as property which may be stolen or obtained, any more than it refers to title deeds to land, or dogs, or other things which the Larceny Acts had to mention expressly because they could not be stolen at common law. There is no longer any need to refer to any of these, because they are all 'property', as widely defined for the purposes of theft and obtaining by s 4(1) of the 1968 Act. Just as a dog or title deeds may now be stolen, or obtained, so may a valuable security; and that means, not the thing in action, nor a mere piece of paper, but the instrument, the physical thing with certain writing on it.[124] The Court of Appeal in *Clark*, like the Supreme Court of Victoria in *Parsons*,[125] found this argument 'highly persuasive' but, unlike the Victorian court, was unable to follow it. They certified a point of law of general importance, but it is understood that the House refused leave on the ground that the new offence of obtaining a money transfer by deception and other offences are adequate. It appears that this is not so[126] and it is submitted that there is no binding decision, so the matter remains open to argument.

It is convenient to dispose also of the issue of intention permanently to deprive. D intends to return the piece of paper, but he does not intend to return the valuable security. This was well established before 1968 and there is nothing in the Theft Act to change the position.[127]

A cheque creates a thing in action *only if it is given for valuable consideration* – that is, any consideration sufficient to support a simple contract or an antecedent debt or liability.[128] If D induces V to make him a gift of a cheque for £50, that cheque does not create any thing in action – but it is still a cheque and, it is submitted, a valuable security. Unless V stops it, the cheque will enable D to deprive V of £50. When D gets his hands on it, he has a valuable, tangible, thing in his possession. It is submitted that such a cheque is a valuable security capable of being stolen or obtained by deception.

Other intangible property

The reach of the law of theft is extended yet further by s 4(1) beyond things in action to include 'other intangible property'. An illustration is provided by *Attorney-General of Hong Kong v Chan Nai-Keung*,[129] the law of theft in Hong Kong being identical in this

123 'A cheque is not a piece of paper and no more. . . . It is a piece of paper with certain special characteristics', *Kohn* (1979) 69 Cr App R 395 at 409, per Lord Lane CJ.

124 *Arnold* [1997] 4 All ER 1, [1997] Crim LR 833. D was convicted of stealing a valuable security, a bill of exchange, signed by V, creating a thing in action which V could never own, but was nevertheless, property belonging to him. But cf *Horsman*, below, p 762.

125 [1998] 2 VR 478; affd 73 ALJR 27, High Ct of Aus.

126 In *Marshall*, the ticket case considered below, p 674, it was argued that, if a cheque cannot be stolen from the drawer, a ticket cannot be stolen from the company issuing it. The court dismissed this argument as impossible, but it is submitted that it is right. The cheque and the ticket are both papers which create and embody a thing in action against the issuer. In neither case can the thing in action be stolen or obtained from the issuer – it cannot belong to him – but that is no reason why the paper, which does belong to him and which is a valuable thing, cannot be stolen from him.

127 Kenny, *Outlines*, 280; Russell, 1167. See *Duru* [1973] 3 All ER 715 at 720e–f.

128 Bills of Exchange Act 1882, s 27(1).

129 [1987] 1 WLR 1339, [1988] Crim LR 125, PC.

particular to the law of England. The export of textiles from Hong Kong was prohibited except under licence, and exports were regulated by a quota system. An exporter who, in a given year, could not meet his quotas could sell his surplus export quotas to an exporter who could meet them, and there was a flourishing market in these quotas. D, a director of the A exporting company, without the authorisation of the A company, sold surplus quotas at a gross undervalue to the B exporting company in which D had an interest as a director. It was held that the quotas, though they were not things in action, were nevertheless 'other intangible property' – the quotas were things of value which could be bought and sold and by knowingly selling them at an undervalue D had appropriated them.[130]

Electricity

On the face of it all property is capable of appropriation but there were formerly doubts whether electricity was capable of appropriation. The dishonest use, wasting or diverting of electricity was a separate offence under the Larceny Acts and the position was preserved by s 13 of the Theft Act. The CLRC observed that, 'This has to be a separate offence because owing to its nature electricity is excluded from the definition of stealing in . . . [s] 1(1) of the [Act].'[131]

The Committee's view was endorsed in *Low v Blease*[132] where it was held that, electricity not being property capable of appropriation, D could not be convicted of burglary in entering premises and making a telephone call from them.[133] Heat is a thing of value, as anyone paying the bills well knows, but it seems that it would not be theft to assume the right to heat belonging to V, by diverting V's hot water so as to warm D's premises.[134] The heat is energy (as is electricity) but is not property.

Confidential information

It has been held[135] that confidential information, though it has a value and can be sold, is not property within s 4(1). Accordingly an undergraduate was not guilty of theft where he unlawfully acquired an examination paper and returned that original piece of paper after he had read its contents.[136] While the 'theft' of information is a serious problem, particularly in the form of industrial espionage, for which the civil law may not provide adequate remedies, it seems, as Griew observes,[137] that the Theft Act is not the appropriate instrument to deal with this specialized kind of mischief. The Law Commission has reviewed the possibility of introducing a specific offence of the misuse of

130 *Pilgram v Rice-Smith* [1977] 2 All ER 658, DC; *Bhachu* (1976) 65 Cr App R 261, CA.

131 Cmnd 2977, para 85.

132 [1975] Crim LR 513, DC.

133 See *P* (2000) 11 Aug, CA, No 0003586 Y5, where D entered his neighbour's property as a trespasser and made phone calls to premium rate sex chat lines.

134 *Clinton v Cahill* [1998] NI 200. Nor is it theft of the hot water, unless all, or substantially all, of the heat is exhausted, so as to deprive the water of its 'virtue'.

135 *Oxford v Moss* (1978) 68 Cr App R 183, [1979] Crim LR 119.

136 But see commentary at [1979] Crim LR 119.

137 Griew, *Theft*, para 2–25. See further R. Hammond, 'Theft of Information' (1984) 100 LQR 252; J. T. Cross, 'Protecting Confidential Information under the Criminal Law of Theft and Fraud' (1991) OJLS 264; A. Coleman, *Intellectual Property Law* (1994). See also L. Weinreib, 'Information and Property' (1988) 38 UTLJ 117, and the Canadian Supreme Court in *Stewart* (1988) 50 DLR 1.

trade secrets,[138] and in view of the significance and prevalence of the problem, legislation would seem desirable. The Law Commission's proposal was to criminalise non-consensual use or disclosure of another's trade secrets.

Services

Services do not constitute property, so it is not theft for D dishonestly to walk off without paying for his haircut. Specific offences are created under the 1978 Act to deal with such problems.[139]

Limitations on the theft of land

It would have been technically possible to make land generally stealable, since rights over land are just as capable of appropriation as rights in goods. But limitations have been imposed for reasons of policy. If D dishonestly moves the boundary fence between his and V's property and thus annexes some of V's land there is no technical reason why this should not be theft of the land. D has appropriated land belonging to V with intent to deprive him permanently of it. The CLRC considered that there were numerous reasons[140] for not treating this action as theft, including: that appropriating land by encroachment was not so widespread or socially evil that civil remedies were insufficient;[141] and that the civil law might give D a good title by occupation for twelve years and it would be odd if he remained even theoretically guilty of theft for ever afterwards. Section 4(2) therefore gives effect to this view, and provides:

A person cannot steal land, or things forming part of land and severed from it by him or by his directions, except in the following cases, that is to say –

(a) when he is a trustee or personal representative, or is authorized by power of attorney, or as liquidator of a company, or otherwise, to sell or dispose of land belonging to another, and he appropriates the land or anything forming part of it by dealing with it in breach of the confidence reposed in him; or

(b) when he is not in possession of the land and appropriates anything forming part of the land by severing it or causing it to be severed, or after it has been severed; or

(c) when, being in possession of the land under a tenancy, he appropriates the whole or part of any fixture or structure let to be used with the land.

For purposes of this subsection 'land' does not include incorporeal hereditaments; 'tenancy' means a tenancy for years or any less period and includes an agreement for such a tenancy, but a person who after the end of a tenancy remains in possession as statutory

[138] See Law Com Consultation Paper No 150, *Legislating the Criminal Code: Misuses of Trade Secrets* (1997), and the review by J. Hull, 'Stealing Secrets: A Review of the Law Commission Consultation Paper' [1998] Crim LR 246. For a recent review of the criminal law's general protection for intellectual property see C. Davies, 'Protection of Intellectual Property – A Myth?' [2004] J Crim Law 398.

[139] It is worth noting however that the Court of Appeal has demonstrated an unusual willingness to substitute convictions for obtaining 'services' by deception when the defendant's conviction for obtaining 'property' by deception is unsafe: *Nathan* [1997] Crim LR 835; *Smith (No 4)* [2004] Crim LR 951 and commentaries.

[140] Cmnd 2977, paras 40–44. Cf Smith, *Property Offences*, paras 3.32 to 3.33, 3.38.

[141] But the Committee observed (ibid, para 42) that moving boundaries was a 'real problem, especially in crowded housing estates'. Cf the offence under s 11 (below, p 715) which seems to owe its origin to *three* known instances of its occurrence.

tenant or otherwise is to be treated as having possession under the tenancy, and 'let' shall be construed accordingly.

(i) *Appropriation by trustees etc.*[142] The rule here is that land, or things forming part of the land, are capable of being stolen. Thus a trustee may appropriate land held in trust by an unauthorized disposition. Of course an unauthorized dealing is not of itself theft since the other elements of the offence must be present. If, for example, a trustee is authorized to sell the land only to A and he sells it to B because B is offering a much better price, the unauthorized sale by the trustee may not be dishonest.

(ii) *Appropriation by persons not in possession.* Here, as has been shown, the rule is that land as such cannot be stolen by a person not in possession. However a person not in possession can steal anything forming part of the land by severing it or by appropriating it after it has been severed. Thus it may be theft where D helps himself to the topsoil in V's garden, or to a gate, or to rose bushes, or even to growing grass.[143] In each case the appropriation is complete upon severance,[144] but where the thing is already severed, as where the gate is lying in V's yard for repair, the appropriation would be complete, at the latest, when D takes control of it.

(iii) *Appropriation by tenants of fixtures.* A tenant cannot steal the land which he possesses by virtue of the tenancy nor of things forming part of the land. If D, a tenant, removes topsoil from the premises, say to sell it to a neighbour, he is appropriating property of another (the landlord) but he is not guilty of theft. But if D's son, who is living with D, removes the topsoil for the same purpose the son would be guilty of theft because he is not 'in possession' of the land although he happens to live there.

A tenant may be guilty of theft, however, where he appropriates (and here severance is not required) any fixture or structure let to be used with the land. A fixture here means something annexed to land for use or ornament, such as a washbasin, cupboards or fireplace, and a structure seems to mean some structure of a moveable or temporary character, such as a garden shed or a greenhouse. A house would not be a structure in this sense.

Limitations on the theft of things growing wild

There is a long standing cultural tradition in Britain of picking fruits from the land for consumption.[145]

Section 4(3) of the Act provides:

142 See M. Brazier, 'Criminal Trustees?' (1975) 39 Conv (NS) 29.

143 By human hand or by grazing cattle: *McGill v Shepherd* (unreported), M. Williams and C. Weinberg, *The Australian Law of Theft* (3rd edn), 116. In 1972 a man was prosecuted at Leeds Crown Court for stealing Cleckheaton railway station by dismantling and removing it. He was acquitted on the merits, the jury accepting that on this bold enterprise he was acting under a claim of right. But railway stations are stealable by severance.

144 Note that if D is caught in the act of severing he is guilty only of an attempt. By attempting to sever D is of course assuming the rights of an owner and in other circumstances, (above, p 657), this alone constitutes a complete appropriation. But in this case the effect of the subsection is to insist upon severance to complete the theft.

145 See M. Welstead, 'Season of Mists and Mellow Fruitfulness' (1995) 150 NLJ 1499.

A person who picks mushrooms growing wild on any land, or who picks flowers, fruit or foliage from a plant growing wild on any land, does not (although not in possession of the land) steal what he picks, unless he does it for reward or for sale or other commercial purpose.

For purposes of this subsection 'mushroom' includes any fungus, and 'plant' includes any shrub or tree.

In some ways it might be thought that s 4(3) is a rather unnecessary provision. It exempts from liability for theft someone who picks wild mushrooms, or one who picks flowers, fruit or foliage '*from* a plant' (thus a person who takes the whole plant may be convicted of theft)[146] growing wild on land unless done for sale or other commercial purpose. Picking holly branches round about Christmas time for the purpose of sale may amount to theft as may picking elderberries for making wine if the purpose is to sell the wine. The whole matter might have been left to the common sense of the prosecutor who would hardly institute proceedings where the appropriation was trivial. Of course this would leave the aggrieved landowner free to take proceedings in such trivial cases, but generally under the criminal law the person aggrieved is free to take proceedings in the most trivial case and this does not apparently lead to any serious abuse. However, the CLRC thought that, 'a provision could reasonably be criticized which made it even technically theft in all cases to pick wild flowers against the will of the landowner'.[147]

In some instances liability might also arise under the Criminal Damage Act 1971.

Limitations on the theft of wild creatures

Section 4(4) of the Act provides:

Wild creatures, tamed or untamed, shall be regarded as property; but a person cannot steal a wild creature not tamed nor ordinarily kept in captivity, or the carcase of any such creature, unless either it has been reduced into possession by or on behalf of another person and possession of it has not since been lost or abandoned, or another person is in course of reducing it into possession.

Wild animals while at large are not owned by anyone, nor does a landowner have a proprietary interest in such animals even where they constitute game. The landowner has, however, the right to take wild animals and once a wild animal is caught or killed it immediately becomes the property of the landowner where this takes place.

The taker (that is, the killer, trapper, etc) would be guilty of theft but for the protection afforded by s 4(4). He is guilty of a minor offence of poaching.[148] The CLRC recommended[149] that poaching should be theft when done 'for reward or for sale or other commercial purpose' but this was not acceptable to Parliament and the provision was deleted. Poaching is unlawful but it was felt that it would be going too far, even in such cases, to turn this traditional country pastime into theft.

It is, however, possible to steal wild creatures where these have been tamed or are ordinarily kept in captivity. A tiger may be stolen from a zoo, and if it has escaped it may

[146] This raises interesting possibilities in the case of GM protestors who remove seedlings.

[147] Cmnd 2977, para 47. The Wildlife and Countryside Act 1981 makes it an offence to kill, possess or sell certain creatures; and to pick, uproot or destroy certain wild plants.

[148] See *Halsbury's Laws of England*, vol 11, para 570. See K. Cook, *Wildlife Law: Conservation and Biodiversity* (2004).

[149] Cmnd 2977, para 52.

be stolen while at large because it is 'ordinarily' kept in captivity. Wild animals may also be stolen when they are in process of being reduced into possession by or on behalf of another. A lazy poacher who picks up the pheasants shot from the skies by V is a thief, as is a gamekeeper who keeps for himself a pheasant which he shot for his employer. And if V, having shot a pheasant, cannot find it in the brush and gives up the search, a subsequent appropriation by D makes him a thief from the landowner.[150]

(iii) Belonging to another

The third element of the *actus reus* is that the property which D appropriates must belong to another.

The general rule

Section 5(1) of the Theft Act 1968 provides:

> Property shall be regarded as belonging to any person[151] having possession or control of it, or having in it any proprietary right or interest (not being an equitable interest arising only from an agreement to transfer or grant an interest).

The onus is on the prosecution to prove that the property in question belonged to V. Frequently this is self-evident and not a live issue, but not always. In *Marshall*[152] D obtained part-used underground tickets and travelcards from members of the public passing through railway barriers and resold them to other potential customers, so depriving London Underground Ltd (LUL) of the revenue it would have gained from the potential customers. D was convicted of theft of the part-used tickets from LUL. The court assumed that those tickets, though in the possession of the passengers, continued to belong to LUL because there was a term to that effect on the reverse of each ticket. That issue was not contested, but the existence of the term is not conclusive. The term was operative only if it was proved that reasonable steps had been taken by LUL to bring that condition to the notice of the 'buyer,' as the passenger probably thought himself to be.[153] If he had been given sufficient notice, he was not a buyer but a mere bailee of the ticket[154] – he was in possession of a ticket belonging to LUL. If sufficient notice was not given, the ticket belonged only to the passenger who had originally purchased it, LUL had no proprietary interest in it, and D could not properly be convicted of stealing from LUL.

150 As to abandonment, see below, p 691.

151 The person to whom the property belongs will usually be known and identified in the indictment, but if the owner is unknown D may be charged with stealing the property of a person unknown provided that this does not result in D being unable to ascertain the nature of the case he has to meet. Cf *Gregory* [1972] 2 All ER 861 at 866, CA (handling property of person unknown); and see *Anglim and Cooke v Thomas* [1974] VR 363 at 374 (SC of Victoria). In *Costello v Chief Constable of Derbyshire* [2001] 3 All ER 150, CA, a car was seized by the police from C. The car had been stolen and C knew it, but the owner was unknown. It was held that C was entitled to recover the car from the police. As possessor, he had a better right to it than anyone but the true owner.

152 [1998] 2 Cr App R 282, discussed by J. C. Smith, 'Stealing Tickets' [1998] Crim LR 723. For consideration of the case and offences that may have been committed see also K. Reid and J. MacLeod, 'Ticket touts or theft of tickets and related offences' (1999) 63(6) J Crim Law 593.

153 A question posed by the law of contract, to be answered by the jury, as it would formerly have been in the civil law: *Parker v South Eastern Rly Co* (1877) 2 CPD 416, CA.

154 He was a buyer of the right to travel on the railway, a thing in action.

In the ordinary case property is stolen from one who both owns and possesses it, by one who has no interest in the property whatever, as where V's wallet is stolen by a stranger, D. Section 5(1) covers this case of course but it goes much further. Two partners both own the whole of the partnership property; but, if one of them dishonestly makes off with it to the exclusion of the other, he steals it from the other.[155] As a further example of the breadth of s 5(1), suppose that V lends a book to X and that X is showing the book to Z when D snatches the book from Z's hands and makes off with it. Here D has stolen the book from Z (who has control of it), and X (who has possession of it), and V (who also has a proprietary interest – ownership – in it).

Moreover, under s 5(1), it does not matter that the property happens to belong to D in one of these senses (that is, possession, control) if at the same time it also belongs to V and it is D's intention dishonestly to deprive V permanently of his interest. Thus in the above illustration if Z were dishonestly to appropriate the book he would steal it from both V and X,[156] and if X were dishonestly to appropriate the book he would steal it from V.

Conversely an owner may steal his book from the bailee of it. If A owns a book, and lends it to B, while the book is in B's possession it belongs to B for the purposes of s 5(1). When A appropriates it, there is 'another' who has a proprietary interest: B. It is important to note that s 5 does not place any limitations on the class of persons who may steal. Thus, there is nothing to say that a person cannot steal where he has a better proprietary claim than the victim, as in our example where an owner, D, steals his property from someone in mere possession of it.

Of course the circumstances in which D's appropriation of his own property will amount not just to an appropriation but to a complete theft will not be common since D will be unlikely to possess *mens rea*: he may easily be able to show a claim of right,[157] or be unlikely to be found dishonest generally. But consider *Turner (No 2)*.[158] D had left his car with V for repair, promising to pay for the repairs when he returned to collect the car the following day. D, however, returned a few hours later and surreptitiously took back his car using the spare keys. Although D claimed that he was entitled to do as he did, it was clear from the circumstances that he was acting dishonestly, and his conviction for stealing the car from V was affirmed. At first sight this seems obviously right because D was out to cheat V of his right to retain the property until the debt for the work was satisfied (technically his 'lien'). V had a proprietary right or interest in the property and, even as against the owner, D, the car could be properly regarded as belonging to V so long as he had his lien. Unfortunately the trial judge told the jury to disregard the question of the lien. Thus, the case is authority for a much broader proposition: that D may steal from V when V's status regarding the property is as D's 'bailee at will', (that is, where D is entitled to terminate the bailment *at any time*). It is obvious that such a person, so long as he remains in possession of D's property has a 'proprietary right or interest' as against third parties. Should X have come along and taken Turner's car while it was in V's possession,

155 *Bonner* [1970] 2 All ER 97n, [1970] 1 WLR 838.

156 Cf *Thompson* (1862) Le & Ca 225. D made off with a sovereign which V handed him to buy a ticket for her because she was unable to make her way through the crowd before a ticket office. This would be theft by D. Cf *Rose v Matt* [1951] 1 KB 810, [1951] 1 All ER 361, DC.

157 Below, p 693.

158 [1971] 2 All ER 441, CA.

there would be no difficulty in saying X stole it from V. But it seems odd to regard V as having a 'proprietary interest' as against D, the bailor, when D decided, whether by notice or otherwise, to determine the bailment and take back his property as he is entitled to do.

Turner is difficult to justify.[159] A better decision is that of Judge Da Cunha in *Meredith*.[160] D surreptitiously removed his car from a police pound where it had been lawfully placed by the police for causing an obstruction. It was held that D could not be convicted of stealing the car. The police were lawfully in possession of it so that a third party could have stolen it from them but as against D they had no right to retain it though they did have a right to enforce the statutory charge for its removal from the compound. The police, unlike the repairer in *Turner (No 2)*, were not bailees of the car (they came into possession by a statutory power to take the car). However, the repairer in *Turner (No 2)*, disregarding the repairer's lien, seems to have been in a position indistinguishable from that of the police in *Meredith*.

Possession or control

Possession and control may overlap, and it is not important to pursue any possible distinction between them because property is treated as belonging to V if he has *either* possession or control. It is the limits of these concepts which are important, not the difference between them.

Possession requires both an intention to possess and some degree of control in fact. If V and D both see a wallet on the pavement, both may have the same intent to possess it, but until one of them seizes it neither has possession. Once V seizes it he has both possession and control. If he hands it to D just to show D what he has got, it would normally be said that V retains possession while D has control.

Possession and control are not, however, always as clear cut as in this illustration. There V's intent existed in respect of a specific article and he reduced it into his actual control – he had it in his hands. But it is not necessary to have, or ever to have had, control of a thing in this sense in order to have possession. A drinks vending-machine supplier may have possession of the coins inserted in the machine without knowing at any given moment how many coins, if any, are in the machine.[161] Similarly, a householder normally has possession of the whole contents of his house even though he cannot itemize all his goods. He may consign unwanted articles to his attic or cellar and forget about them, but he still retains possession.

It is not, then, essential that V's intent to possess should exist in respect of a specific thing: it may be enough for V's intent to exist in respect of all the goods situated about his premises. In *Woodman*[162] V sold all the scrap metal on certain disused business premises to X; X removed most of it but left some as being too inaccessible to be worth the expense

159 In so far as *Turner* decided that V's possession need not be lawful, it is obviously right and was approved on this point in *Kelly* [1998] 3 All ER 741 at 750. It may be theft to take the stolen property from a thief; the law protects his possession. But the point in *Turner* is that D (in the absence of a lien) had every right to take his own property back. If the owner takes his property from a thief who is unlawfully detaining it, does he steal it if he mistakenly thinks it is someone else's property?

160 [1973] Crim LR 253.

161 Cf *Martin v Marsh* [1955] Crim LR 781 (electricity meters). But see [1956] Crim LR 74.

162 [1974] QB 754, [1974] 2 All ER 955, CA. See also *Hibbert v McKiernan* [1948] 2 KB 142, [1948] 1 All ER 860, DC (theft of golf balls 'lost' on club premises); *Williams v Phillips* (1957) 41 Cr App R 5, DC (theft of refuse from dustbins).

of removal. D then entered the premises to take some of this scrap and was held to have been rightly convicted of theft from V. V continued to control the site and his conduct in erecting fences and posting notices showed that he intended to exclude others from it; that was enough to give him control of the scrap which V did not wish to remove.

This principle was exemplified in the recent case involving the theft of golf balls from lakes and water features on courses with a view to the balls being resold (reportedly producing a £15,000–30,000 annual turnover). In *Rostron*,[163] the Court of Appeal confirmed that the issue was whether there was evidence that golf balls hit into a lake were property belonging to another – the club owning the course.[164] It remains necessary for the prosecution to prove that the golf ball retrievers were acting dishonestly in order to sustain a theft conviction, and that may be no easy task.

Proprietary interests and treasure trove At common law any article of gold or silver hidden by its owner with a view to its subsequent recovery was 'treasure trove'. In the absence of its original owner and his successors in title, treasure trove belonged to the Crown. The Crown did not have possession or control of the treasure if it was found on someone else's land, but it did have a proprietary interest in it. It was therefore capable of being stolen from the Crown by any person including the owner or possessor of the land in or on which it was found. In *Hancock*[165] D was charged with stealing from the Crown Celtic silver coins which he had found using a metal detector on another person's land. It was not established that the coins were treasure trove but it was argued that the Crown's right to have their doubtful status determined was itself a 'proprietary interest'. If a finder conceals his find from the Crown, the Crown has lost something of value – the chance that, on investigation, the find would prove to be treasure trove. It was held, however, that such a chance is not a proprietary interest. If A and B each claims to be the sole owner of certain property, and the dispute is eventually resolved in favour of A, it would be odd to hold that B had a proprietary interest in the property up to the moment when it was determined that he had never had any interest in it. Another way of looking at this is to treat the 'chance' not as a property right in the disputed treasure, but as a freestanding item of property derived from the existence of the treasure.

The Treasure Act 1996 abolished the law relating to 'treasure trove', replacing it by a wide concept of 'treasure' including, as well as any object which would previously have been treasure trove, other specified objects at least 300, or in some cases 200, years old.[166] As previously with treasure trove, when 'treasure' is found it vests in the Crown (or the Crown's franchisee). The finder of treasure who takes it for himself commits the *actus reus* of theft: he has appropriated property belonging to the Crown. To prove theft, it has to be shown that he knew the Crown was, or at least might be,[167] the owner – that is, that the property had the factual characteristics of treasure – for example, that a bracelet is at least 300 years old and is made of at least 10 per cent by weight of precious metal. But a

163 [2003] All ER (D) 269 (Jul), [2003] EWCA Crim 2206.

164 See L. Toczek, 'Never Plead Guilty!' (2002) 146 SJ 455.

165 (1989) 90 Cr App R 422, [1990] Crim LR 125.

166 See generally J. Marston and L. Ross, 'Treasure and Portable Antiquities in the 1990s still chained to the Ghosts of the Past: The Treasure Act 1996' [1997] Conv 273, criticising the Act for offering only piecemeal protection.

167 'Might be' because the finder may be aware that 'reasonable steps' might reveal that the find was of silver and that it had been concealed, not lost: Theft Act 1968, s 2(1)(c), below, p 694.

defendant might know that the property had the factual characteristics of treasure and still be unaware of the Crown's proprietary interest because of his understandable ignorance of the law of treasure.[168] So proving theft may be very difficult. The court in *Hancock* was sceptical about the alternative of charging the finder with theft from the owner of the land. The law has been clarified by *Waverley Borough Council v Fletcher.*[169] F, using a metal detector in a public park belonging to the council, found a mediaeval gold brooch. A coroner's inquest decided that it was not treasure trove and returned it to F. It was held that the council was entitled to a declaration that the brooch was its property. Auld LJ stated two principles.

(1) Where an article is found in or attached to land, the owner or possessor of the land has a better title than the finder.

(2) Where an article is found unattached on land, the owner or possessor of the land has a better title than the finder only if he exercised such manifest control over the land as to indicate an intention to control the land and anything that might be found on it.[170]

In the *Waverley* case it was immaterial that the land was held by the council as a public open space to be used for various sports and recreations. Digging in the land was an act of trespass. A digger who dishonestly intended to keep anything he found for himself would be guilty of attempted theft and of stealing from the council anything he found and kept for himself.[171] The owner of the land in which articles are buried has a proprietary interest in those articles because they are in his possession or control. The property may also, if it is treasure, belong to the Crown. The proprietary interest of the owner of the land is much easier to prove than that of the Crown. Under the doctrine of 'transferred malice',[172] the finder's intention dishonestly to deprive the landowner of the property may be treated as an intention dishonestly to deprive the Crown. If the property turns out to be treasure, the finder may be guilty of stealing it both from the landowner and from the Crown.

168 Ignorance of the civil law may negative *mens rea*: above, p 122.

169 [1995] 4 All ER 756.

170 In *Bridges v Hawksworth* (1851) 21 LJQB 75 the plaintiff, the finder of banknotes, apparently lost by someone on the floor of a shop, was held to have a better right to the money than the owner of the shop: 'The notes were never in the custody of the defendant nor within the protection of his house, before they were found, as they would have been if they had been intentionally deposited there'. In *Parker v British Airways Board* [1982] QB 1004 a passenger who found a gold bracelet in a British Airways executive lounge was held to have a better right to it than British Airways. On the other hand in *Hibbert v McKiernan* [1948] 2 KB 142 a trespasser on a golf course was held guilty of larceny of balls lost by golfers from the secretary and members of the golf club. He was aware of the intent of the club to exclude him as a 'pilferer' of lost balls, so the case is distinguishable cf *Rostron* [2003] EWCA Crim 2206.

171 In *Rowe* (1859) 8 Cox CC 139 R was convicted of larceny from a canal company of iron found in the bed of a canal when it was drained. The true owner of the iron was unknown but the canal company had a sufficient proprietary interest in it. *Rowe* was followed by Chitty J in *Elwes v Brigg Gas Co* (1886) 33 Ch D 562 where an ancient boat, buried in land belonging to the plaintiff was discovered by his lessee, the defendant, excavating the site for a gasholder. The boat was held to belong to the plaintiff. In *South Staffordshire Water Co v Sharman* [1896] 2 QB 44 two gold rings were found in the mud in the Minster Pool in Lichfield by one of a number of labourers employed to clean it out. It was held by Lord Russell of Killowen CJ that the owner of the pool had a better right than the finder. And cf *Woodman* (1974) 59 Cr App R 200, CA above, p 676.

172 Above, p 113.

Any proprietary right or interest

Property is also to be regarded as belonging to any person having in it 'any proprietary right or interest'. Obviously, then, property may be stolen from the owner although at the time of the appropriation the owner is not in possession or control, as where V lends his library book to X and D steals the book from X. Furthermore, property may be stolen from the owner even though he may never have been in possession or control. If X sells goods to V (ownership passing to V) and X remains in possession of them, a dishonest appropriation of the goods by D will be theft from both X and V.[173] Moreover on those facts, a dishonest appropriation of the property by X after he has sold the goods to V may constitute theft of the property by X from V though X has never been out of possession of the property; X has usurped V's proprietary right in the property. Similarly V, by a dishonest removal of *his* property from X's premises (it may be assumed that V intends to avoid paying for the property) steals from X because he usurp's X's remaining interest in the property.[174]

D may appropriate property which belongs to V in any of the senses described in s 5(1). It does not matter that V's interest is precarious or that it may be short-lived; wild birds reared by V may belong to V although they may 'betake themselves to the woods and fields' as soon as they are old enough to fly,[175] and flowers left on a grave remain the property of the leaver.[176] Nor does it matter that someone exists who has a better right to the property than V: a thief may steal from a thief.[177] This is a well-established principle. It does not matter that it is impossible for the victim (the original thief) to assert his title in a civil court: public policy which prevents the wrongdoer from enforcing a property right should have no application to criminal proceedings brought in the name of the Crown. The criminal law is concerned with keeping the Queen's peace, not vindicating individual property rights.

Equitable interests

'Any proprietary right or interest' extends to both legal and equitable proprietary interests. Where property is subject to a trust it belongs to both the trustee (legal interest) and beneficiary (equitable interest) and it may be stolen from either.[178] The question whether V has an equitable interest in property alleged to have been stolen from him may involve difficult issues of civil law.

In *Clowes (No 2)*[179] the question was whether investors, who had subscribed money for investment in gilts by a company controlled by D, had an equitable interest in certain

[173] Frequently the thief will have no idea of the identity of the owner, or owners, of the property; it suffices that he knows the property belongs to *another*.

[174] Cf *Rose v Matt* [1951] 1 KB 810, [1951] 1 All ER 361, DC (pledgor of clock dishonestly retook it from pledgee).

[175] Cf *Shickle* (1868) LR 1 CCR 158.

[176] According to *Bustler v State* 184 SE 2d 24 (1944) (SC of Tennessee). Cf *Edwards and Stacey* (1877) 13 Cox CC 384.

[177] Cf *Clarke*, referred to at [1956] Crim LR 369–70; *Meech* [1974] QB 549, [1973] 3 All ER 939, CA.

[178] See further s 5(2), below p 680.

[179] [1994] 2 All ER 316. See also M. C. Davies, 'After *R v Clowes No 2*: An Act of Theft Empowered – A Jury Impoverished' (1997) J Crim Law 99 commenting that with a trial based on complex legal issues the effect is to reduce the issues that fall to be determined by the jury, potentially displacing the importance of eg s 2(1)(a) of Theft Act 1968. See also the *Fraud Trials Protocol* (2005).

assets of the company. In deciding that they did, the court found it necessary to consider various Chancery decisions and to rely on the principle, *inter alia*, that where a trustee mixes trust money with his own the beneficiaries have a first charge on, and therefore an equitable interest in, the mixed fund. A person dishonestly withdrawing money from such a fund may therefore be guilty of stealing it from the beneficiaries.

Changes in the civil law may affect the reach of the law of theft. So a decision that the payer of money retains an equitable interest in money paid under a mistake of fact and is not, as was previously thought, a mere creditor is significant for the law of theft. The result is that the dishonest appropriation of the money mistakenly paid by V may be theft according to general principles: V retains a proprietary interest in that property.[180] This removes the need for the prosecution to rely on the tortuous provisions of s 5(4) discussed below.[181]

Section 5(1) places a limitation on equitable interests constituting property belonging to another. Property is not to be regarded as belonging to a person who has an equitable interest arising only from an agreement to transfer or grant an interest. A specifically enforceable contract to sell property may give the intending buyer an equitable interest in the property[182] and the provision makes it clear that the seller cannot commit theft by reselling the property to another, however dishonest this may be thought to be.

Trust property[183]

Section 5(2) of the Theft Act 1968 provides:

> Where property is subject to a trust, the persons to whom it belongs shall be regarded as including any person having a right to enforce the trust, and an intention to defeat the trust shall be regarded accordingly as an intention to deprive of the property any person having that right.

In the ordinary case, appropriation of trust property by a trustee is covered not only by this subsection but also by s 5(1) because the beneficiary ordinarily has a proprietary interest and accordingly the trust property belongs to another – the beneficiary – within s 5(1). But in some exceptional circumstances there may be no ascertained beneficiary. This occurs in the case of 'purpose' trusts whether charitable[184] or private,[185] where the object is to affect some purpose rather than to benefit ascertainable individuals. To meet such cases s 5(2) goes further than s 5(1) by providing that the property is to be treated as belonging to anyone who has a right to enforce the trust.[186] As far as charitable trusts are concerned, the trustees are the legal owners of the charity's funds but, if they misappropriate the money, they steal not from the donors to that charity, but from the Attorney-General who has the right to enforce the trust.[187]

180 *Chase Manhattan Bank NA v Israel–British Bank (London) Ltd* [1981] Ch 105.

181 Below, p 685. 182 See Smith, *Theft*, paras 66–67.

183 M. Brazier, 'Criminal Trustees?' (1975) 39 Conv (NS) 29.

184 Eg, where money is given to D in trust for the improvement of schools in a particular locality.

185 Eg, where money is given to D in trust for the maintenance of a tomb, or for the upkeep of animals.

186 In the foregoing examples this would be, respectively, the Attorney-General and the person entitled to the residue of the estate.

187 *Dyke and Munro* [2002] Crim LR 153, [2002] 1 Cr App R 404.

Property received for a particular purpose

Section 5(3) of the 1968 Act provides that:

> When a person receives property from or on account of another, and is under an obligation to the other to retain and deal with that property or its proceeds in a particular way, the property or proceeds shall be regarded (as against him) as belonging to the other.

If there is no legal obligation on D to retain and deal with the property in a particular way, it is his to do as he likes with, and it cannot be theft for him to do what he is entitled to do. But where there is such an obligation, it seems right that the property should be capable of being stolen by D.

Breadth of application

Subsection (3) covers a very wide range of cases. Every bailment seems to be included. So does every trust. So where D has received property from or on account of V in the circumstances described in the subsection, V will usually have a legal or equitable interest in the property or proceeds.[188] Should D dishonestly appropriate the property, he will be stealing it from V who has retained a proprietary right or interest. The case then is covered by s 5(1) and subs (3) is unnecessary. Even where that is so, s 5(3) is useful because it allows the prosecution to make out its case more easily, without the need to resort to the technical question whether V retains an equitable interest.

The subsection may, however, go beyond this and apply to cases of mere breach of contract not covered by s 5(1). For example, D who buys a non-transferable ticket may become the owner of the ticket, but be under a contractual obligation to 'retain and deal with it in a particular manner' in the sense of 'not dealing' with it.[189] In the case of a rail ticket, such as that in *Marshall*, his ownership of the ticket involved his contractual obligation not to assign it to another. But note that the property must be 'received'. Where D enters into a contract to deal with his own property in his own possession the subsection does not apply.[190]

'From or on account of another'

The section applies only where the property is 'received from or on account of another'. This creates a difficulty where the property is credited to D's account by a bank transfer.[191] *Preddy* decides that, since the credit is new property, a thing in action which belongs to D and has never belonged to anyone else, D cannot be guilty of obtaining property *belonging to another* by deception. The property has only ever been D's. This is

188 In *Klineberg and Marsden* [1999] Crim LR 419 the court said that this sentence did not anticipate the unreported case of *Smith (Paul Adrian)*, 14 May 1997, 'in which, when cheques from investors were paid into Intercity's [Smith's] bank account, the person on whose account the money was received (GRE) did not have a legal or equitable interest in the credit balance but it was nevertheless to be regarded under s 5(3) as belonging to GRE'. Since Smith was under a contractual obligation to GRE to forward all the monies received, it was unnecessary to decide, and the court does not appear to have decided, whether GRE had an equitable interest. The case is an excellent illustration of the utility of the subsection as described above. *Klineberg* seems, in this respect, straightforward, since the money was paid to D on the understanding that it would be 'safeguarded by trusteeship'.

189 Cf J. C. Smith, 'Stealing Tickets' [1998] Crim LR 723 at 726. It is pointed out that this is not theft of the thing in action, but whether it is theft of the thing in possession (the ticket) is not considered.

190 It may however create an equitable interest. Cf commentary on *Arnold* [1997] Crim LR at 834.

191 Though it is commonly called a bank transfer, in law it is not a 'transfer' at all.

significant for the offence of theft, since it seems necessarily to follow that D has not 'received' the property from another or on account of another. The property of the other, V, was the thing in action – V's right to sue his bank – and that was extinguished when D's new item of property was created. It would seem then that, s 5(3) does not apply and D can be guilty of theft only if the person whose bank account has been debited retains an equitable interest in the new property owned by D. Although in *Klineberg*,[192] the court did not distinguish between funds provided by cash, cheque, or bank transfer, it is clear that the first two are property 'received' from another, the third is not.

'Obligation'

It is settled that 'obligation' in s 5(3) (and (4) to be discussed below) means a legal, not a merely moral or social, obligation. That much is straightforward, determining whether there is such an obligation is far less so. Where the relevant transaction which allegedly creates the obligation is wholly in writing, it is for the judge to decide as a matter of law whether it does create the legal obligation and to direct the jury accordingly.[193] Where the obligation is alleged to have been created wholly or partly by word of mouth, or by conduct, the judge should direct the jury that, if they find the necessary facts (which he must refer them to specifically) proved, there *is* an obligation – not that it is 'open to them' to find that there is an obligation.[194]

Aside from the correct procedure for determining whether a legal obligation existed, the substance of that question will often involve complex issues of civil law.[195]

Obligation owed to V It is plain that the obligation must be owed by D to his victim, V. It is not enough that D is under an obligation to a third party to deal with the property for the benefit of V. The case of *Floyd v DPP*[196] is difficult to square with this principle. D collected money in weekly premiums from colleagues who had ordered goods from a Christmas hamper company – V Ltd. She failed to pay the money to V Ltd and her conviction for stealing it from V Ltd was upheld in reliance on s 5(3). The court said it was unnecessary to show that V Ltd had any legal or equitable interest in the money. The only remaining source of an obligation seems to be a contract; but D had made no contract with V Ltd that she would collect and hand over the money. There was probably a contract between D and her colleagues that she would 'retain and deal' with the money they gave her for the benefit of V Ltd but V Ltd was not privy to that contract and acquired no rights at common law. Since the Contracts (Rights of Third Parties) Act 1999 came into force[197] the position may be different.

Examples of the section in operation

If D is under no legal obligation to retain and deal with property which has been delivered to him, he can lawfully do what he likes with it and it is incapable of being stolen, as are its proceeds. This is ordinarily the position where money is lent. Assuming

192 [1999] Crim LR 417.

193 *Clowes (No 2)* [1994] 2 All ER 316, holding that a brochure inviting the payment of money for investment in gilts was a contractual document creating a trust.

194 *Dubar* [1995] 1 All ER 781, following *Mainwaring* (1981) 74 Cr App R 99 and disapproving *dicta* in *Hall* [1972] 2 All ER 1009 at 1012 and *Hayes* (1976) 64 Cr App R 82 at 85 and 87.

195 See eg *Breaks and Huggan* [1998] Crim LR 349 (contractual obligations of insurance brokers placing insurance with Lloyds).

196 [2000] Crim LR 411, DC.

197 Applying to contracts made on or after 11 May 2000.

that when V lent money to D, he received the money honestly, D's subsequent decision to dispose of the money and never to repay it, however, dishonest, cannot be theft. It is not always easy to determine whether D was under an obligation to retain and deal or at liberty to dispose of the property entirely as he wished. It is, to underline the point, a question of civil law.

Advance payments If D agrees to do certain work for V and V makes an advance payment of £100, D's failure to do the work or return the £100 will be a breach of contract but no criminal offence. Of course, if D never intended to do the work, he would be guilty of obtaining the money by deception and, since *Gomez*, of theft of it. But if he was acting honestly at the time he received the money, once he had received it he was the absolute owner of it and there was nothing belonging to another for him to steal. The position would be different if V had given D the money *for a specified purpose*, such as to buy materials for the job. That would create the obligation on D to retain and deal, so that D's dishonest disposal of the money for some other purpose would be theft.

Deposits If V were to pay a deposit to D, a trader, for goods to be supplied under a contract of sale, such a transaction would normally imply that D is under no obligation to deal with that deposit in a particular way. D might well pay the deposit into his trading account but he could draw on that account as he wished and would not be obliged to keep in existence a discrete fund representing V's deposit. If, on the other hand, V were to give D, his secretary, £100 with instructions to go to a travel agency and purchase a ticket for a flight, the normal inference would be that D is under an obligation to deal with the £100 in a particular way.

The difficulties in application are well illustrated by *Hall*.[198] D, a partner in a firm of travel agents, had received money from V and others as deposits for air trips to America. The flights never materialized and the deposits, which had been paid into the firm's general trading account, were never returned to V and other customers. The Court of Appeal had no difficulty in accepting the jury's verdict that D had acted dishonestly in spending this money, but quashed D's conviction for theft on the ground that D had not received the money under an obligation to deal with it in a particular way. The court reached this conclusion with obvious reluctance (as ever when there has been a finding of dishonesty):

> Nevertheless, when a client goes to a firm carrying on the business of travel agents and pays them money, he expects that in return he will, in due course, receive the tickets and other documents necessary for him to accomplish the trip for which he is paying, and the firm are 'under an obligation' to perform their part to fulfil his expectation and are liable to pay him damages if they do not. But, in our judgment, what was not here established was that these clients expected them 'to retain and deal with that property or its proceeds in a particular way', and that an 'obligation' to do so was undertaken by [D]. We must make clear, however, that each case turns on its own facts. Cases could, we suppose, conceivably arise where by some special arrangement (preferably evidenced by documents), the client could impose on the travel agent an 'obligation' falling within s 5(3).[199]

[198] [1972] 2 All ER 1009, CA, and see *Hayes* (1976) 64 Cr App R 82.

[199] [1972] 2 All ER 1009 at 1011. See *Re Kumar* [2000] Crim LR 504, DC, where there was such an obligation.

The case shows that if D owes a debt to V and he dishonestly disposes of his assets so that when the time comes for payment to V he has no funds from which to meet his debts, he will not be under an obligation for the purposes of s 5(3). Moreover, it makes no difference, so far as the law of theft is concerned, that D has acted in this way in order to defeat his creditors. A liability to pay V is accordingly not enough under s 5(3) unless D is obliged to keep in existence a fund representing that property.

Charity sponsorship A common occasion for the application of s 5(3) is where D receives property from C for onward transmission to, or for the benefit of, E. The required obligation may be imposed on D either by D's relationship with C, or his relationship with E, or both. In *Lewis v Lethbridge*[200] D obtained sponsorships in favour of a charity (E) and received £54 from sponsors (C). He failed to deliver the money. His conviction of theft was quashed because the magistrates had made no finding of any rule of the charity requiring D to hand over the actual cash received or to maintain a separate fund; there was no evidence that he was anything other than a debtor to the charity. No consideration was given to the question whether any obligation was imposed by the sponsors. They might have been surprised to learn that they were giving the money to D to do as he liked with. In *Wain*[201] the Court of Appeal disapproved *Lethbridge*, holding that the approach was unduly narrow and that, on similar facts, the defendant was under such an obligation and, accordingly, guilty of theft.

Obligations imposed by statute It is possible for the obligation to be imposed on D by statute. No doubt when the State pays housing benefit to D to enable D to pay his rent the expectation is that D will use that money to pay his landlord, but it was held in *Huskinson*[202] that D was not guilty of theft where he spent some of the money received as housing benefit on himself. There was nothing in the relevant legislation suggesting that D was bound to pay *that* money or its proceeds to the landlord. D could have met his legal obligation to pay the rent from any source, such as an unexpected win on the lottery and spent the benefit as he chose.

Obligations and agency An obligation to deal with property in a specified way may be imposed on D in civil law through the acts of his agents. However, if D is unaware of the facts giving rise to that obligation, the prosecution cannot rely on s 5(3).[203] Moreover, if D knew the facts but owing to his mistake of civil law believed that there was no obligation and that the money was his to do as he liked with, he would not be dishonest and should be acquitted on that ground.

If an agent receives a bribe in contravention of his duty to his principal, the principal may recover the amount of the bribe in a civil action; but whether the agent can steal the amount of the bribe depends on whether he is a mere debtor to the principal or holds the

200 [1987] Crim LR 59, DC.

201 [1995] 2 Cr App R 660, following *Davidge v Bunnett* [1984] Crim LR 297, DC, where, in pursuance of an agreement by flatmates to share the costs of gas, etc D received money from the others for the gas bill and spent it on Christmas presents. Domestic arrangements are commonly not intended to give rise to legal relationships but here the parties were not members of the same family and presumably intended their agreement to be legally binding. More doubtful is the case where a woman was held guilty of stealing money entrusted to her by her lover to buy food, etc for their household: *Cullen* (No 968/C74 of 1974, unreported).

202 [1988] Crim LR 620, DC.

203 *Wills* (1990) 92 Cr App R 297.

bribe on trust for the principal. This is a question of civil law. According to the Court of Appeal in *Lister & Co v Stubbs*,[204] the agent is a mere debtor, and therefore no sufficient obligation would arise. But the Privy Council in *Attorney-General for Hong Kong v Reid*[205] has held that in such circumstances D is a trustee of the bribe. If the Hong Kong case is followed by English courts, the scope of the law of theft has been extended by this change in the civil law.

It is not necessary that the fiduciary duty should arise out of the transaction between D and the person delivering the property to him; it is enough that D's fiduciary duty arises out of a relationship with a person other than the deliveror.

Where D, a broker, is engaged to collect premiums on behalf of V, D may steal the premiums if the agreement provides that they vest in V[206] but not if the agreement merely makes D a debtor to V for the amount of the premiums paid.[207] In both cases the broker has been dishonest and in both V is the loser but in the first case the broker is a thief and in the second he is not; a distinction which may be effected by a few strokes of the pen in the agreement between V and D.[208]

Property got by mistake

Section 5(4) of the Theft Act provides:

> Where a person gets property by another's mistake, and is under an obligation to make restoration (in whole or in part) of the property or its proceeds or of the value thereof, then to the extent of that obligation the property or proceeds shall be regarded (as against him) as belonging to the person entitled to restoration, and an intention not to make restoration shall be regarded accordingly as an intention to deprive that person of the property or proceeds.

This provision was enacted to deal with the problem encountered in the case of *Moynes v Coopper*.[209] D, a labourer employed by V, was given an advance of pay by the site agent amounting to £6 19*s*. 6½*d*. Unaware that this advance had been made, V's wages clerk paid D the full weekly wage of £7 3*s*. 4*d*. and D dishonestly kept all of the money.

The difficulty in treating this as theft by D is that in law the whole of the £7 3*s*. 4*d*. belongs to D. The wages clerk made a mistake of course, but his mistake was not such as would prevent ownership of all the money passing to D. Had the clerk known of the advance that D had received he would have paid D only 3*s*. 9½*d*; nevertheless the clerk did intend to pay the full amount, and he was authorized as V's wages clerk to pay wages. The case is now covered by s 5(4) and D steals the excess payment if he dishonestly appropriates it; although D becomes the owner of the money he is under a legal obligation, at the very least, to repay the value of the excess payment.

But why, it may be asked, is all this trouble taken to deal with this particular kind of debtor? In terms of moral turpitude only the finest shading separates a character such as *Moynes* from the ordinary debtor who dishonestly decides not to repay his loan. Under the former law *Moynes* was in fact acquitted, but in view of the criticism which his acquittal attracted it was no doubt felt necessary to bring such conduct within the net of the criminal law.

204 (1890) 45 Ch D 1.

205 [1994] 1 AC 324. See J. C. Smith '*Lister v Stubbs* and the Criminal Law' (1994) 110 LQR 180.

206 *Brewster* (1979) 69 Cr App R 375, CA.

207 *Robertson* [1977] Crim LR 629 (Judge Rubin QC).

208 See also *Breaks and Huggan* [1998] Crim LR 349.

209 [1956] 1 QB 439, [1956] 1 All ER 450.

Section 5(4) was applied in these circumstances in *Attorney-General's Reference (No 1 of 1983)*.[210] D's salary was paid into her bank account by direct debit and on one occasion her employers mistakenly overpaid her by £74.74. The question for the court was: assuming that she dishonestly decided not to repay that sum would she have been guilty of theft? In law she became the owner of the money and, as Lord Lane CJ pointed out, had no special provision been made for the case that would have been an end to the matter. But s 5(4) provided for the case. The 'money in the bank' was entirely hers to do as she liked with, but she was under an obligation to repay an equivalent sum (the value) to her employers. On these facts, subject to proof of dishonesty, her failure to do so meant she was guilty of theft.

V's position in circumstances of making a mistaken payment is well settled: if owing to a mistake of fact V believes that he is legally obliged to make a payment and he does so, he is entitled in civil law to recover the equivalent of the sum he mistakenly paid.[211] More difficult is D's civil law position once he has received a payment made in error. The issue whether D was under a legal obligation to repay the value was resolved in the *Attorney-General's (Ref No 1)* without difficulty, but it will be appreciated that it will not always be so straightforward. The law of unjust enrichment[212] is one of considerable subtlety. This may mean that D's liability for theft may turn upon a consideration of fine points of civil law remote from the central question of D's dishonesty.

There was no evidence in the *Attorney-General's Reference* that D had spent the money that was overpaid or that she had done any act in relation to it. To meet a possible argument that in doing nothing D cannot intend permanently to deprive the owner, s 5(4) further provides that an intention not to make restoration shall be regarded as an intention permanently to deprive.[213]

A further difficulty with cases such as this follows from the decision in *Preddy* and the need to identify which item of property is in issue. In *Gresham* (below), D's mother had been in receipt of pension payments from her former employer which were made by automatic transfers to her bank account. D failed to inform her employer (the Department of Education) and the bank of his mother's death. The payments continued to be credited for 10 years after her death and D, having had the power of attorney to act for her when she was alive, continued to use this power to cash cheques drawn on her account. The cheques drawn by D reduced the credit balance in his mother's account. D was convicted of theft and obtaining a money transfer by deception (contrary to s 15A of the 1968 Act.) The credit balance that D diminished by drawing cheques was not an item of property that belonged to the Dept of Education within the terms of s 5(1). The prosecution relied instead on the fact that the payments had been by mistake and that s 5(4) applied. The court upheld convictions for theft on this basis, rejecting an argument that s 5(4) has no application where D has induced V's mistake by deception as 'eccentric'.

Is s 5(4) superfluous?

The foregoing discussion of s 5(4) assumes, as seemingly did the CLRC, that the entire proprietary interest in the money passes to D who is no more than a debtor. No doubt

210 [1985] QB 182, [1984] 3 All ER 369, CA.

211 *Norwich Union Fire Insurance Society Ltd v William H Price Ltd* [1934] AC 455.

212 See R. Goff and G. Jones, *The Law of Restitution* (6th edn, 2002).

213 'Keeping' is a sufficient appropriation. See above, p 660.

this is so at *law* but the position now appears to be different in *equity*. In *Chase Manhattan Bank NA v Israel–British Bank (London) Ltd*[214] the X bank by mistake paid $2 million to the Y bank for the account of the Z bank which subsequently went into liquidation. The X bank was of course entitled to a dividend in the liquidation but it sought to recover the whole of its loss. It was held by Goulding J that V who pays money (or, presumably, delivers any property) to D under a mistake of fact retains an equitable interest[215] in the money and the conscience of the defendant is subject to a fiduciary duty to respect V's proprietary right.[216]

If this decision is correct, and it appears to have met with approval, s 5(4) seems strictly unnecessary. In *Moynes v Coopper* V retained an equitable interest in the money overpaid and D, on these facts, could now be convicted of theft even if s 5(4) had not been enacted.

The *Chase Manhattan* principle was relied on by the Court of Appeal (Criminal Division) in *Shadrokh–Cigari*.[217] The O bank had in error credited a child's account at the V bank with £286,000 instead of £286! D, the child's guardian, got the child to sign authority for the V bank to issue banker's drafts, and when D was arrested only £21,000 of the £286,000 remained in the account. Upholding D's conviction for theft from the V bank, the court said that the drafts belonged to the bank and although legal ownership passed to D by delivery, the bank retained an equitable interest by virtue of the *Chase Manhattan* principle and D had appropriated property belonging to another (V) within the broad terms of s 5(1). It was accordingly not necessary to rely on s 5(4) though that subsection provided an alternative route to conviction.[218]

Identifying the property got by mistake

Section 5(4), or the *Chase Manhattan* principle, applies though only part of the property is got by mistake. In *Moynes v Coopper*[219] D appropriated only the amount by which he was overpaid. In such a case it would be impossible to identify the coins which represented the overpayment but the prosecution is not required to do so because the relevant property is sufficiently identified if it is proved to be part of an identifiable whole. This principle was applied in *Davis*.[220] By a computer error D was sent two cheques a month in respect of housing benefit when he was entitled to only one. It was held that where D had cashed these cheques he could be convicted of stealing the proceeds (the cash) of one of the cheques and it was not necessary for the prosecution to establish which proceeds he had stolen and which he had not.

214 [1981] Ch 105, [1979] 3 All ER 1025 – doubted, but not so as to affect its application in criminal cases, by Lord Browne-Wilkinson in *Westdeutsche Landesbank Girozentrale v Islington LBC* [1996] AC 669, 715. See further J. C. Smith, *Theft*, para 2–84.

215 Section 5(1) extends to equitable interests, see above, p 679.

216 Accordingly the X bank was entitled to the restoration of the whole of the money mistakenly paid and was not relegated to claiming a dividend in the liquidation.

217 [1988] Crim LR 465, CA. See further G. MacCormack 'Mistaken payments and Proprietary Claims' [1996] Conv 86.

218 See also the statements in *Gresham* [2003] EWCA Crim 2070.

219 Above, p 685.

220 (1988) 88 Cr App R 347, CA.

Requirement of legal obligation

It will be evident from the foregoing discussion that 'obligation' in s 5(4) can only refer to a legal obligation imposed by the civil law. This is confirmed by *Gilks*[221] though the case has its complications. V, a bookmaker, mistakenly believing that D had backed a winning horse, overpaid D on the bets he had placed and D, aware of the error, dishonestly decided not to return the overpayment. Since V had made no mistake either as to the amount or the recipient ownership of the money passed to D. The court was clear that s 5(4) was inapplicable. As this was a betting transaction, as a matter of civil law, V had no right of restitution in respect of the overpayment, so D could be under no legal obligation to make restoration. But the court went on, relying upon an antique and questionable authority under the law of larceny,[222] to uphold D's conviction on the grounds that since V would not have made the overpayment but for his mistake, ownership in the money did not pass to D. This is at odds with the civil law and the holding needs to be reconsidered. It is a further example of the courts striving to uphold the convictions of those found to be dishonest, at the expense of clarity and principle in the definition of the Theft Act offences.

Property of corporations

A corporation such as a limited company or the University of Leeds is, in law, a person distinct from its members. It can own property and be the victim of theft and other offences under the Theft Acts. A member of the corporation can be guilty of stealing the property of the corporation – it is property belonging to another: the company. If a director, D, of a limited company misappropriates the company's property the injury is suffered by the company's shareholders or, if it is insolvent, its creditors; but the property D has appropriated does not belong to the directors and D is guilty of theft, not from them, but from the company.[223] This is straightforward where D is misappropriating the property because he is acting without authority. The matter is more difficult if the alleged theft from the company is, say, an act authorized by the board of directors at a properly constituted meeting. Although it exists as a separate legal person, a company can act only through its human controlling officers and, in some contexts at least, they are identified with the company – their acts are the company's acts.[224] If company directors resolve to use the company's assets for their personal advantage instead of for the company's proper purposes, and if this act is the company's act (ie the company authorizes it (albeit by the directors' decision), it is hard to see how it can be theft; no one can steal from himself. It is different if the act is ultra vires the company because then it is not the company's act at all; but the courts seem to have regarded the question of ultra vires as irrelevant.

The problem is most acute where the directors, say, D and E, are also the sole shareholders. If D and E, as the controlling mind of the company, C, agree that C shall pay them money for their personal use, have they stolen the money from C? Judicial opinion, before *Gomez*, was divided about this situation. One view was that this was

221 [1972] 3 All ER 280, [1972] 1 WLR 1341, CA.

222 *Middleton* (1873) LR 2 CCR 38.

223 *R (On the Applicaton of A) v Snaresbrook Crown Court* (2001) 165 JPN 495.

224 Above, p 234.

theft from the company.[225] The other was that of the Court of Appeal in *McHugh and Tringhamm*:[226]

(4) An act done with the authority of the company cannot in general amount to an appropriation. Such authority may be – (a) express, or (b) implied. (5) Where the actor is beneficially entitled to the entire issued share capital (or at least the entire voting share capital) of the company it may be that his act is not an appropriation because – (a) his act is equivalent to an act of the company, and his intent is the intent of the company, so there can be no circumstances in which any of his acts is unauthorized; and/or (b) since he has the irresistible power to determine what policies the company shall pursue, there is nothing which he himself may do in the company's name which could in practice be unauthorized.

In so far as this opinion depended on the fact that the payment to D and E was done with the company's consent, given by the only persons able to consent on its behalf, namely D and E, it is no longer tenable after *Gomez*. A dishonest appropriation is now theft, even if the owner consents. In *Gomez*, Lord Browne-Wilkinson (with whom three judges, including Lord Lowry who dissented on the main issue, agreed) said that their lordships' decision rendered 'the whole question of consent by the company irrelevant'. It might be objected that D and E were not merely acting with the consent of the company: they *were* the company. If I give away all my property with the intention of defrauding my creditors, it is impossible to hold that I have committed theft because I have not appropriated something belonging to another. However, Lord Browne-Wilkinson also said:[227]

In my judgment [the approach in *McHugh*, above] was wrong in law even if the dictum in *Morris* [requiring an appropriation to be an act without authorisation or consent] had been correct. Where a company is accused of a crime the acts and intentions of those who are the directing minds and will of the company are to be attributed to the company. That is not the law where the charge is that those who are the directing minds and will have themselves committed a crime against the company.

It must now be conceded, following *Gomez*, that in these cases D appropriates property belong to another, but there is still difficulty in seeing how it can be a *dishonest* appropriation.[228] The act is not dishonest vis-à-vis the shareholders because they are the appropriators and therefore it is unreal to say that it is dishonest with respect to the company, which exists for the benefit of the shareholders. It may well be dishonest with respect to the company's creditors – but the property does not belong to them. The illogicality of the position is demonstrated further when comparison is made with the position of partnership property. If D and E were not the directors of a company but the sole members of a partnership, they could not be guilty of theft of the partnership's assets, even if they disposed of them in riotous living with intent to defeat their creditors. There does not seem to be any difference in substance. It has been argued[229] that the interests of

225 *A-G's Reference (No 2 of 1982)* [1984] QB 624; *Phillipou* (1989) 89 Cr App R 290.

226 (1988) 88 Cr App R 385, CA at 393. See also *Roffel* [1985] VR 511, discussed by J. C. Smith (1985) Crim Law Jnl 320.

227 [1993] 1 All ER at 40.

228 D. W. Elliott, 'Directors' Thefts and Dishonesty,' [1991] Crim LR 732; Griew, *Theft*, paras 2.86–2.87.

229 G. R. Sullivan, Letters to the Editor [1991] Crim LR 929.

the creditors of an insolvent or doubtfully solvent company are the interests of the company, and as such D and E are rightly guilty of theft in such circumstances. But it is not clear that this is an established principle or that it is the foundation of the cases holding the sole director may steal the company's property.

Ownerless property

A person cannot be guilty of stealing property that is not owned by another at the time of the appropriation. If there is no person to whom the property belongs in any of the senses set out in s 5, that property cannot be stolen. Property that is capable of belonging to another may be ownerless because it has never been made the subject of ownership. D can commit no offence where, for example, he takes a swarm of bees not presently owned by another.

Corpses[230]

The common law rule that there is no property in a corpse or part of corpse still prevails. Executors or administrators or others with a legal duty to inter a body have a right to custody and possession of it until it is buried; but it seems the corpse is incapable of being stolen from them. In *Doodeward v Spence*,[231] a decision of the High Court of New South Wales where the English authorities are examined, it was held that a proprietary interest could be acquired by one who expended work and skill on the corpse with a view to its preservation on scientific or other grounds. This decision was applied in *Kelly*[232] where parts of bodies preserved as anatomical specimens and taken from the Royal College of Surgeons were held to have been stolen. The Human Tissue Act 2004[233] provides a framework for issues of donation, storage and use of body parts, organs and tissue. The Act is a response to the concerns raised by events at Alder Hay and Bristol Royal Infirmary.[234]

Property of the deceased

In *Sullivan and Ballion*,[235] the defendants had appropriated the £50,000 they found on their friend who had died of natural causes in their company the night before. The deceased was a drug dealer and the money represented his takings. Dismissing the charge of theft of the money, the trial judge ruled that the property did not 'belong to another'

230 See A. T. H. Smith, 'Stealing the Body and its Parts' [1976] Crim LR 622 and *Property Offences*, paras 3.03 to 3.06; P. Skegg, 'Criminal liability for the unauthorized use of corpses for medical education and research' (1992) 32 Med Sci Law 51; M. Pawlowski, 'Dead Bodies as Property' (1996) 146 NLJ 1828; A Maclean, 'Resurrection of the Body Snatchers' (2000) 150 NLJ 174.

231 (1908) 95 R (NSW) 107.

232 [1998] 3 All ER 741. Cf *Dobson v North Tyneside Health Authority* [1996] 4 All ER 474, CA (Civ Div).

233 The Human Tissue Act 2004 provides safeguards and penalties in relation to improper retention of tissue and organs without consent. The Act sets up an overarching authority which will rationalize existing regulation and will introduce regulation of post mortems and the retention of tissue for purposes like education and research and provides for the Human Tissue Authority to issue Codes of practice giving practical guidance on the conduct of activities within its remit: Department of Health Guidelines www.dh.gov.uk/PolicyAndGuidance/HealthAndSocialCareTopics/Tissue/fs/en. See also I. Kennedy and A. Grubb, *Medical Law: Text and Materials* (3rd edn, 2000), ch 18.

234 See Department of Health guidelines: *The removal, retention and use of human organs and tissue from post-mortem examination* (2001).

235 [2002] Crim LR 758.

when it was taken.[236] As pointed out in the commentary to the case, the property must have belonged to someone other than the thieves (who had no rights to it). Since there may be a conviction of theft of property of a person unknown, it follows that it is enough to show that the property must have belonged to someone and that the defendants knew it belonged to someone other than themselves. The money did not belong to those who had purchased drugs from the deceased (in this case a group known as 'The Firm') because, as the judge held, they had parted with their entire proprietary interest in the money; but the proprietary interest can hardly have vanished into thin air-it passed to the deceased or, if he was acting as an agent, his principal. At the time of the alleged theft, the money must have belonged either to D's principal, if any; or to those entitled under his (or their) will or intestacy; or, if they did not exist, to the Crown as *bona vacantia*.[237] There remains the difficulty in establishing the defendants' *mens rea*. If the defendants supposed, or may have supposed, that the property belonged to no one and could be taken by the first person to come across it, then they are not guilty. But if they knew it must belong to someone other than themselves, it is immaterial that they did not know who that person was.

Abandonment

Property which has at one time been owned may become ownerless by abandonment. But abandonment is not something to be lightly inferred: property is abandoned only when the owner is indifferent to any future appropriation of the property by others. It is not enough that V had no further use for the goods. A farmer who buries diseased animals has no further use for them but he would clearly intend that others should not make use of them and retains ownership of the carcases.[238] More importantly, a householder who puts rubbish in his dustbin has no further use for the rubbish but he puts it there to be collected by the authorized refuse collectors and not as an invitation to all comers to help themselves.[239] Nor is property abandoned because the owner has lost it and has given up the search.[240] A husband may have lost his wedding ring and long since given up the search but will not have abandoned it.

[236] Hale, *Pleas of the Crown* (1736) vol 1, 514: 'If A dies intestate, and the goods of the intestate are stolen before administration committed, it is felony, and the goods shall be supposed to be bona episcopi de D. ordinary of the diocese, and if he made B his executor the goods shall be supposed bona B tho he hath not proved the will, and they need not show specifically their title as ordinary or executor because it is of their own possession, in which case a general indictment as well as a general action of trespass lies without naming themselves as executor or ordinary, and so for an administrator'. East, *Pleas of the Crown*, ii, 652 and *Russell on Crime* (2nd edn, 1843), ii, 99 state the law in similar terms.

[237] A suggested direction for such cases is 'Before you can convict the defendants of theft, you must be sure (i) that the deceased died in possession of the money; (ii) that D took it for their own use; (iii) knowing that the money was not theirs to take; and that it must have belonged to someone other than themselves; (iv) intending to deprive whoever was entitled to the money permanently of it; and (v) that they did so dishonestly'. See commentary, n 235 above.

[238] Cf *Edwards and Stacey* (1877) 36 LT 30.

[239] Cf *Williams v Phillips* (1957) 121 JP 163. The availability of theft charges in such circumstances is important in dealing with those who rummage through the refuse of celebrities for information to sell to tabloid newspapers, and those who appropriate confidential industrial or financial information from refuse. For Home Office initiatives on identity theft see www.identity-theft.org.uk/HTML/whatisbeingdone.html.

[240] *Hibbert v McKiernan* [1948] 1 All ER 860, DC, discussed in [1972B] CLJ at 213–215 (lost golf balls not abandoned).

(b) *Mens rea*

The changes made by the 1968 Act to the *mens rea* of theft were less fundamental than the reform of the *actus reus*. The law of larceny required an intention to take or to convert property belonging to another and theft requires an intention to appropriate property belonging to another.[241] Larceny required that the act be done 'fraudulently and without a claim of right made in good faith' and with intent permanently to deprive the owner. It need not, however, be done *lucri causa*, that is, it was unnecessary to prove that D intended to make any kind of profit for himself or another. These characteristics are broadly preserved by the 1968 Act.

(i) View to gain immaterial

Section 1(2) of the 1968 Act provides, 'It is immaterial whether the appropriation is made with a view to gain, or is made for the thief's own benefit.'

This section is designed to defeat claims such as that which might be made by D, a shop worker who charged his friend, E, for only some of the goods in his trolley. The fact that the gain was for E does not prevent D being a thief. Similarly, the section renders prosecution easier in cases of D causing only loss to V, without a corresponding gain. Thus, to take examples from the old law, if D takes V's letters and puts them down a lavatory or backs V's horse down a mine shaft he is guilty of theft notwithstanding the fact that he intends only to cause loss to V and not gain for himself or anyone else. It might be thought that these instances could safely and more appropriately have been left to other branches of the criminal law – criminal damage to property for instance. But there are cases where there is no such damage or destruction of the property which would be sufficient to found a charge under another Act. For example, D takes V's diamond and flings it into a deep pond. The diamond lies unharmed in the pond and a prosecution for criminal damage would fail. It seems clearly right that D should be guilty of theft.[242]

(ii) Dishonesty[243]

The CLRC thought that 'dishonesty' could probably be left undefined and they did not define it but merely sought to clarify its meaning in certain respects. By s 2 of the Act:

> (1) A person's appropriation of property belonging to another is not to be regarded as dishonest –
>
> (a) if he appropriates the property in the belief that he has in law the right to deprive the other of it, on behalf of himself or of a third person; or
>
> (b) if he appropriates the property in the belief that he would have the other's consent if the other knew of the appropriation and the circumstances of it; or
>
> (c) (except where the property came to him as trustee or personal representative) if he appropriates the property in the belief that the person to whom the property belongs cannot be discovered by taking reasonable steps.

241 *Ingram* [1975] Crim LR 457, CA (absent-minded taking a defence to charge of shop-lifting). *Small* [1987] Crim LR 777, CA (D, who believes, reasonably or not, that property has been abandoned, does not intend to appropriate property belonging to another (or, *ex hypothesi*, permanently to deprive)).

242 An alternative solution would be to consider creating an offence of unlawfully depriving the owner of the use of his property: see below, p 892.

243 See also Smith, *Property Offences*, ch 7; *Arlidge and Parry on Fraud*, ch 1; Law Com Report No 276, *Fraud* (2002), Part V.

(2) A person's appropriation of property belonging to another may be dishonest notwithstanding that he is willing to pay for the property.[244]

It will be noticed that this section specifies three situations in which an appropriation of property belonging to another is *not* to be regarded as dishonest and one in which it may be. By this negative approach, the section assists somewhat in defining the meaning of dishonesty, but the section does not specify any state of mind that *must* be regarded as dishonest. The negative approach to defining dishonesty raises interesting questions about the role that the element has to play in the offence of theft generally. Dishonesty operates both as a peg on which to hang claims of an exculpatory nature – that is, as equivalent to an element of unlawfulness or lack of blameworthiness – and also as a positive element of *mens rea*, requiring proof of D's state of mind. Horder describes dishonesty as a concealed excuse, 'taking the form of a morally open textured mental element'.[245] This overlap between 'dishonesty' as a state of mind (requiring a factual inquiry from the jury) and as a concept describing the wrong done (requiring a moral evaluation by the jury) is perpetuated by the case law. A further complexity with the element of dishonesty (beyond the law of theft *per se*) has been described by the Law Commission:

In some crimes, such as conspiracy to defraud, the other elements of the offence are not prima facie unlawful, so dishonesty renders criminal otherwise lawful conduct. However, in deception offences the other elements of the offence, if proved, would normally be unlawful in themselves. If someone has practised a deception in order to gain a benefit their conduct is prima facie wrongful. Therefore dishonesty can be raised to rebut the inference that conduct was in fact wrongful . . . The former type of crime [can be described] as having a *positive* requirement of dishonesty, and the latter as having a *negative* requirement.[246]

It is regrettable that there is no statutory definition of dishonesty, particularly since the common law definition which supplements s 2 is so vague, and as noted above, dishonesty has assumed an elevated importance following the excessively broad interpretations of the *actus reus* elements of the offence.[247]

Belief in the right to deprive

D is not dishonest if he believes, whether reasonably or not, that he has the legal right[248] to do the act which is alleged to constitute an appropriation of the property of another. In spite of the courts' general insistence, historically, on reasonableness when defences of 'mistake' were raised, it never seems to have been doubted that a claim of right afforded a defence, even though it was manifestly unreasonable. The prosecution must disprove any

[244] Care must be taken when considering the concept of dishonesty since s 2 is not applicable to all of the offences under the Theft Acts.

[245] *Excusing Crime*, 49.

[246] Law Com No 276, above, para 5.12. For criticism of this as unhelpful see P. Kiernan and G. Scanlon, 'Fraud and the Law Commission: The Future of Dishonesty' (2003) 24 Comp Law 4.

[247] Cf the Law Commission's current view which is that no definition is possible: Law Com No 276, *Fraud*, above, Part V.

[248] It is irrelevant that no such right exists in law. A *dictum* to the contrary in *Gott v Measures* [1948] 1 KB 234, [1947] 2 All ER 609, is irreconcilable with the decision in *Bernhard* [1938] 2 KB 264. The belief need not relate to a 'property' right: *Wood* [1999] Crim LR 564 and commentary.

belief in such a right that D claims to have held. The Act refers specifically to a belief in a right *in law* as inconsistent with dishonesty. This does not *necessarily* mean that a belief in a merely moral right will be insufficient to negative dishonesty.[249] The common law, that taking another's property is not justifiable, even where it is necessary to avoid starvation, suggests that even the strongest moral claim to deprive another is not enough; but, if it is now a jury question, there is no law to this effect and a jury would be likely to find that a truly starving person was not dishonest.

D's belief in the legal right of another, X, will negative D's dishonesty. Thus, in *Close*[250] an employee, paying his employer's debt in kind by taking his employer's property without consent, was apparently held not to be dishonest by a jury. Where D specifically pleads a belief in a claim of right, the jury ought, it is submitted, to be directed in relation to s 2 and not left to deal with the issue under the general test in *Ghosh* (below).[251]

Since a belief in a claim of right should negate *mens rea* in all cases, it is arguable that this element of s 2 should have been made generally applicable throughout rather than being restricted to cases of theft.

Belief that the owner would consent

It is sufficient that D holds a mistaken though genuine belief that the person to whom the property belonged would have consented had he known of the circumstances. Thus, D will not be dishonest where he helps himself to his flatmates' milk from the fridge if he holds a belief that this would be consented to. Numerous appropriations of this nature occur every day and a specific provision dealing with the matter precludes silly prosecutions. Following *Hinks*, the issue of mistaken beliefs will be of particular importance in cases in which D claims that he was acting with the owner's consent.[252]

Belief that the person to whom the property belongs cannot be discovered by taking reasonable steps

Though the Act makes no reference to 'finding', this provision is obviously intended to preserve the substance of the common law rule relating to finding. The finder who appropriates property commits the *actus reus* of theft (assuming that the property does belong to another and has not been abandoned) but is not dishonest unless he believes the owner *can* be discovered by taking reasonable steps. There is no requirement that D's belief is reasonable; merely that his belief relates to the reasonableness of the steps necessary to trace V. This will depend on the nature of the property in question.[253]

249 A belief in a moral right was not a defence to larceny: *Harris v Harrison* [1963] Crim LR 497, DC. Cf Williams, CLGP, 322.

250 [1977] Crim LR 107.

251 The Court of Appeal has taken a contrary view approving a general *Ghosh* direction in *Rostron* [2003] EWCA Crim 2206, where D believed that he had a legal right to collect 'lost' golf balls. Cf *Smith (Paul Adrian)* [1997] 7 Arch News 4, CA. On charges to which s 2 does not apply *Ghosh* must perform the function: *Woods* [1999] 5 Arch News 2, CA.

252 See above, p 654. See especially Lord Hutton's dissent focusing on dishonesty and the question of whether D can be convicted if he has a claim of right – consent, but not if he has a mere belief in a claim of right – under s 2(1)(a).

253 See eg the implausible defence in *Sylvester* (1985) CO/559/84 where D alleged that the car he was stripping of parts in a car park was abandoned and therefore s 2(1)(c) applied.

If D's initial appropriation of lost property is innocent (either because he does not believe that the owner can be discovered by taking reasonable steps or because he intends to return the thing to the owner when he takes it) a dishonest later assumption of a right to it by keeping or dealing with it as owner will (contrary to the former common law) be theft by virtue of s 3(1).[254] While this provision was intended primarily for the case of finding, it is not confined to that case and there are other instances where it would apply. Suppose that V arranges with D that D shall gratuitously store V's furniture in D's house. V leaves the town and D loses touch with him. Some years later D needing the space in his house and being unable to locate V sells the furniture.[255] This is undoubtedly an appropriation of the property of another and D is civilly liable to V in conversion; but he appears to be saved from any possibility of conviction of theft by s 2(1)(c). Though the purchase money probably belongs to V, D's immunity under the Act for lack of dishonesty must extend to the proceeds of sale.

Where the property came to D as a trustee or personal representative and he appropriates it, he may be dishonest even though he believes that the person to whom the property belongs cannot be discovered by taking reasonable steps. This seems to provide a particularly strict approach, with the intention being that the trustee or personal representative can never be personally entitled to the property (unless it is specifically so provided by the trust instrument or the will) for, if the beneficiaries are extinct or undiscoverable, the Crown will be entitled to the beneficial interest as *bona vacantia*. However, if the trustee or personal representative appropriates the property for his own use, honestly believing that he is entitled to do so, then it is submitted that he must be acquitted. But if he knows that he has no right to do this and that the property in the last resort belongs to the Crown, he commits theft from the beneficiaries, if they are in existence and, if not, from the Crown.

Dishonest appropriation, notwithstanding payment

Section 2(2) is intended to deal with the kind of situation where D takes bottles of milk from V's doorstep but leaves in its place the full price. Certainly D has no claim of right and he intends to deprive V permanently of his property. Doubts had, however, arisen as to whether this was dishonest. This subsection resolves them. The mere fact of payment does not negative dishonesty but the jury are entitled to take into account all the circumstances and these may be such that even an intention to pay for property, let alone actual payment, may negative dishonesty. The fact of payment, or intention to pay, may be cogent evidence where D's defence is that he believed V would have consented, as where D takes milk bottles from V's unattended float and leaves the price, claiming that he assumed that V would have been very happy to sell him the milk had he been there, but that he had not time to wait for V to return. If D is believed – and the fact of repayment would be persuasive evidence – it would seem that he has no dishonest intent. The section is important in emphasising that D's willingness to pay the market value for appropriated property will not negate dishonesty, otherwise there would be no theft where D took V's original work of art that he had long coveted, leaving its listed valuation price.

[254] Above, p 660.

[255] Cf *Sachs v Miklos* [1948] 2 KB 23, [1948] 1 All ER 67; *Munro v Wilmott* [1949] 1 KB 295, [1948] 2 All ER 983.

Dishonesty as an element of the offence

The commentators on the Larceny Act 1916 had difficulty in finding any function whatever for the word 'fraudulently' (which was the precursor to 'dishonesty'). The great expert on larceny, Dr Turner,[256] went so far as to say that the word added nothing to 'without a claim of right' (now found in s 2(1)(a)). It was surplusage. Others thought it had the limited function of exculpating (i) the taker who believed the owner would have consented if it had been possible to ask him[257] – a case now expressly covered by s 2(1)(b) of the 1968 Act; and (ii) the taker of money or other 'fungibles'[258] who intended to, and had no doubt that he could, return, not the identical thing, but an equivalent[259] – a case which is not expressly provided for in the 1968 Act. The CLRC seem, surprisingly, to have overlooked the limited role played by 'fraudulently' and to have proceeded in their *Eighth Report*[260] on the assumption that the word had some large though unspecified role to play. They used 'dishonesty' rather than 'fraudulently', not because the meaning was any different but because they thought it to be more easily understood:

> 'Dishonestly' seems to us a better word than 'fraudulently'. The question 'Was this "dishonest"?' is easier for a jury to answer than the question 'Was this "fraudulent"?' 'Dishonesty' is something which laymen can easily recognize when they see it, whereas 'fraud' may seem to involve technicalities which have to be explained by a lawyer.

This passage suggests that it is for jurors to decide whether 'this' (D's conduct) is dishonest. Of course, it is for jurors to decide all questions of fact, including the state of mind of the defendant – what was his intention and belief, including his belief as to his legal rights. But, under the Larceny Act, it was probably for the judge to say whether that state of mind, when ascertained, was to be characterized in law as 'fraudulent'.[261] The substitution of 'dishonestly' for 'fraudulently' has led to an important change in the law. Possibly influenced by this misleading passage in the CLRC Report, the Court of Appeal in *Feely*[262] held that it is for the jury in each case to decide, not only what the defendant's state of mind was, but also, subject to s 2, whether that state of mind is to be categorized as dishonest.

> Jurors, when deciding whether an appropriation was dishonest can be reasonably expected to, and should, apply the current standards of ordinary decent people. In their own lives they have to decide what is and what is not dishonest. We can see no reason why, when in a jury box, they should require the help of a judge to tell them what amounts to dishonesty.

Only a moment's comparison with the approach to other *mens rea* requirements is needed to illustrate how much of a departure from the old law and from orthodoxy this is. For example, in a case involving recklessness, the judge defines that concept and directs the jury to determine whether, on the facts as they find them to be, D's state of

256 Writing as editor of *Russell on Crime* (12th edn), 996.

257 Wing-Commander Lowe, 'The Fraudulent Intent in Larceny' [1956] Crim LR 78.

258 Ie, something that is exchangeable or substitutable.

259 J. C. Smith, 'The Fraudulent Intent to Larceny: Another View' [1956] Crim LR 238.

260 Para 39. On the CLRC intentions see also D. W. Elliott, 'Dishonesty in Theft: A Dispensable Concept' [1982] Crim LR 395 at 405.

261 *Williams* [1953] 1 QB 660, CCA; *Cockburn* [1968] 1 All ER 466, CA.

262 [1973] QB 530, [1973] 1 All ER 341, [1973] Crim LR 193 and commentary.

mind is within that legal definition. The jury are not invited to define recklessness themselves.

The court in *Feely* was certainly much influenced by the opinion of the House of Lords in *Brutus v Cozens*[263] that the meaning of an ordinary word of the English language is not a question of law for the judge but one of fact for the jury. 'Dishonestly' is such a word and so it was for the jury to attribute to it such meaning as they thought proper. A major difficulty about this view is that juries – and magistrates – are likely to give different answers on facts which are indistinguishable. This creates very obvious injustices that bring the criminal law into disrepute. It also raises the potential for challenges to the law under Article 7 of the ECHR on the basis of lack of certainty.

Feely did at least provide a standard – that of 'ordinary decent people', as understood by the jury – against which the defendant's intentions and beliefs were to be tested. Other cases, however, went further. In *Gilks*,[264] D agreed that it would be dishonest if his grocer gave him too much change and he kept it but he said bookmakers are 'a race apart' and there was nothing dishonest about keeping the overpayment in that case. The judge invited the jury to 'try and place yourselves in [D's] position at that time and answer the question whether in your view he thought he was acting dishonestly'. The Court of Appeal thought this was a proper and sufficient direction, agreeing apparently that, if D may have held the belief he claimed, the prosecution had not established dishonesty. This applied, not the standards of ordinary decent people, but the defendant's own standards, however deplorable they might be. In *Boggeln v Williams*,[265] the court expressly rejected an argument that D's belief as to his own honesty was irrelevant and held that, on the contrary, it was crucial. D, whose electricity had been cut off, reconnected the supply through the meter. He knew that the electricity board did not consent to his doing so, but he notified them and believed, not unreasonably, that he would be able to pay at the due time. It was held that the question was whether he believed that what he did was honest. A further complexity was introduced in *McIvor*,[266] where the Court of Appeal said that the test of dishonesty in conspiracy to defraud was different from that to be applied in theft.

The leading case is now *Ghosh*.[267] In that case, the Court of Appeal significantly improved the position by rejecting any distinction between the test of dishonesty in different offences. *Ghosh* itself was a case of obtaining by deception contrary to s 15 of the 1968 Act; and it is now reasonably clear that the same principle applies throughout the Theft Acts and the common law of conspiracy to defraud as well as other statutory offences such as fraudulent trading under the Companies Act 1985. There is one test of dishonesty in English criminal law.[268]

263 [1973] AC 854, [1972] 2 All ER 1297.

264 Above, p 688; [1972] 3 All ER 280 at 283. On the very early cases see D. W. Elliott, 'Dishonesty Under the Theft Act' [1972] Crim LR 625.

265 [1978] 2 All ER 1061, [1978] Crim LR 242 and commentary.

266 [1982] 1 All ER 491.

267 [1982] QB 1053, [1982] 2 All ER 689.

268 In some circumstances the *Ghosh* test is applicable in civil cases: *Aktieselskabet Dansk Skibsfinansiering v Brothers* [2001] BCLC 324; *Royal Brunei Airlines Sdn Bhd v Tan* [1995] 2 AC 378 and see the discussion in *Twinsectra Ltd v Yardley* [2002] 2 WLR 802, [2002] UKHL 12, particularly at paras 27–33 and 115–134, on which see M. Thompson, 'Criminal Law and Property Law: An Unhappy Combination' (2002) 66 Conv 387. R. Thornton, 'Dishonest Assistance: Guilty Conduct or a Guilty Mind' [2002] 61 CLJ 524.

The court also provided a new and more elaborate explanation of the approach to be taken in determining D's dishonesty. The test to be applied by the trier of fact is twofold.

(i) Was what was done dishonest according to the ordinary standards of reasonable and honest people? If no, D is not guilty. If yes –

(ii) Did the defendant realize that reasonable and honest people regard what he did as dishonest? If yes, he is guilty; if no, he is not.

The Court of Appeal has frequently stressed that it is not necessary to give this *Ghosh* direction to the jury in every case.[269] Thus, it is unnecessary where D's claim is a lack of dishonesty owing to forgetfulness,[270] or where the question relates solely to the genuineness of D's belief rather than D's claim that the ordinary person would not regard it as dishonest.[271] If there is any evidence to suggest that D's attitude was, 'Whatever others may think, *I* did not consider this dishonest', the direction must be given. Where there is no such evidence it is probably unnecessary. Where this direction is necessary, the exact form of words ought to be used.[272]

Several effects of this test need to be noted. First, it gets away from the extreme and unacceptable subjectivism of *Gilks* and *Boggeln v Williams.* D is no longer to be judged by his own standards of honesty. Secondly, *Ghosh* attempts a compromise between a purely objective *Feely* type test which might be regarded as too harsh and a purely subjective test such as that in *Gilks* which would create a thief's charter. However, in seeking to achieve this compromise it introduces an unnecessary confusion in the form of the second limb. Campbell[273] cogently argues that this additional limb is superfluous if under the first limb the jury is properly directed to take account of all the circumstances. Taking the example of D who fails to pay a travel fare because he is new to the country and is accustomed to free public transport, it should not be necessary to rely on the second limb to conclude that D is not dishonest. A properly directed jury would so conclude under the first limb.

Thirdly, the attempted compromise may fail in its intended purpose – to prevent the 'Robin Hood defence', that is, where D claims that the activity was not dishonest – but it is not clear that it does so. The defendant would have to be acquitted 'if the jury think *either* (a) that what Robin Hood did (rob the rich to feed the poor) was not dishonest *or* (b) that Robin Hood thought the reasonable and honest man would not consider what he did as dishonest'.[274] The same might be said of a more modern hypothetical example;

269 See in particular *Roberts* (1985) 84 Cr App R 177; *Price* [1990] Crim LR 200. Cf A. Halpin, 'The Test for Dishonesty' [1996] Crim LR 289, at 291.

270 *Atkinson* [2004] Crim LR 226.

271 *Wood* [2002] EWCA Crim 832, CA where D claimed that his trespassing into empty premises to remove the entire stock of curtain fabric, was not dishonest since he believed it to be abandoned. Cf *Rostron* [2003] EWCA Crim 2266, where the Court of Appeal seem to restrict *Ghosh* to cases where D would have a claim of right under s 2(1)(a).

272 *Hyam* [1997] Crim LR 439.

273 K. Campbell, 'The Test of Dishonesty in *Ghosh*' [1994] 43 CLJ 349, Campbell suggests that if the aim is to provide this hybrid test it should be: whether a reasonable jury, applying ordinary standards of honesty, is prepared to excuse D's failure to recognize that his own behaviour would be regarded as dishonest by the standards of ordinary people.

274 Such examples contradict the view of some commentators that apart from 'morons and lunatics' the only people likely to rely on a claim that they did not realize that ordinary honest people would regard their conduct as dishonest are business people who assert that their activities are the norm in that context. Arlidge and Parry, para 1–027.

a member of an animal welfare association who liberates beagles from a research laboratory because he knows they are being used in experiments and is charged with theft. He would certainly not regard his own conduct as dishonest and so would have escaped under the rule as stated in *Gilks*. He might still escape under *Ghosh*.[275] A jury of animal lovers would be likely to agree with him; and it might be difficult for the prosecution to satisfy any jury that the defendant did not believe that all right thinking people would agree with him. Members of animal welfare organizations probably do so believe. But this surely *should* be theft. One who deliberately deprives another of his property should not be able to escape liability because of his disapproval, however profound and morally justified, of the lawful use to which that property was being put by its owner. In deciding whether a certain state of mind should be regarded as dishonest it is not irrelevant to consider how the matter will be regarded by the ordinary decent citizen who is the victim of the offence. The owners of the beagles will certainly consider that their property has been stolen, even though they are fully aware of the state of mind of the takers. The law fails in one of its purposes if it does not afford protection to a person against what he quite reasonably regards as a straightforward case of theft.

Critique and reform

Ghosh has generated much criticism and some valuable proposals for reform.[276]

Criticism

Perhaps the most trenchant critic of the *Ghosh* test was Professor Griew,[277] who catalogued its numerous deficiencies. Griew suggested that the test confuses the state of mind with the concept of dishonesty;[278] leaves a question of law to the jury[279] which may lead to inconsistent decisions with the potential for different juries to reach different verdicts on identical facts thus presenting acute problems in respect of Article 7 of the ECHR;[280] leads

275 This is an instance in which it appears motive, which is generally regarded as irrelevant to *mens rea* in practice, assumes an importance.

276 E. J. Griew, 'Dishonesty – the Objections to *Feely* and *Ghosh*' [1985] Crim LR 341; D. W. Elliott, 'Dishonesty in Theft: A Dispensable Concept' [1982] Crim LR 395 at 398. Elliott's solution is to dispense with the word 'dishonestly' altogether but to add a new subs (3) to s 2: 'No appropriation of property belonging to another which is not detrimental to the interests of the other in a significant practical way shall amount to theft of the property'.

277 Author of *The Theft Acts 1968 and 1978* (7th edn, 1995) and 'Objections to *Feely* and *Ghosh*' [1985] Crim LR 341.

278 See also K. Campbell, 'The Test of Dishonesty in *Ghosh*' [1994] 43 CLJ 349, 354 criticizing *Ghosh* for confusing the state of mind and the defendant's standards of honesty.

279 For an argument in support of leaving such issues to the jury see R. Tur, 'Dishonesty and the Jury Question' in A. Phillips Griffiths (ed), *Philosophy and Practice* (1985). The Law Commission provisionally concluded that 'the circumstances in which such conduct may be found to be non-dishonest cannot be circumscribed by legal definition. Where dishonesty is a positive element, it *must* be open to the fact-finders to find that particular conduct is not dishonest, even if the legislation does not say so'. Law Comm Paper No 155 (1999), para 5.6.

280 Article 7 guarantees not only against retrospective criminalization in strict terms, but also that 'legal provisions which interfere with individual rights must be adequately accessible, and formulated with sufficient precision to enable the citizen to regulate his conduct', *G v Federal Republic of Germany* 60 DR 252, 262 (1989). So vague are the elements of dishonesty under *Ghosh* that the Law Commission Paper No 155 provisionally took the view that a Home Secretary could not safely be advised to make a statement of compatibility in relation to a Bill creating a general dishonesty offence. Subsequently, the Law Commission

to more trials as defendants have little to lose by pleading not guilty and hoping that the dishonesty element is not made out; leads to longer trials as the dishonesty issue is a 'live' one in all cases; assumes a community norm within the jury in that they must agree on the ordinary standards of honesty; assumes that jurors are honest, or at least that they can apply ordinary standards of honesty even if they do not adhere to them in their personal lives; and, is unsuitable in specialized cases such as complex commercial frauds where the 'ordinary' person is unlikely to understand the honesty or otherwise of the activities.[281] The CLRC view of dishonesty relied on the common sense of members of society and a consensus about the appropriate benchmarks for protecting private property. As Norrie[282] points out, this view of private property might not be an accurate reflection of current values, particularly in relation to specific types of misappropriation – for example, petty pilfering from the workplace and omissions from tax returns.

Nevertheless, in terms of principle, these criticisms are rendered all the more cogent for several reasons. First, the test applies in a great volume of cases in English courts – all those involving an element of dishonesty, which includes all Theft Act and common law conspiracy to defraud cases and many other offences under specific legislation, (although it seems that dishonesty does not create enormous problems in practice).[283] Secondly, broad interpretations of the elements of *actus reus* have left dishonesty as the principal determinant of criminality in theft. As the Law Commission commented recently, 'where the conduct elements of an offence are morally neutral [as, for example, appropriation], the element of dishonesty has to do more than simply exclude specific types of conduct which, though *prima facie* wrongful, do not deserve to be criminal'.[284]

Ghosh has not been universally accepted in other jurisdictions. Before *Ghosh*, the Supreme Court of Victoria had refused to follow *Feely*, when construing the identical provision in Victorian legislation. In *Salvo*,[285] Fullagar J, with whom Murphy J seems to have agreed in substance, held that it was the duty of the judge to explain to the jury what 'dishonestly' meant; and he should tell them that it means 'with disposition to defraud, that is with disposition to withhold from a person what is his right'. There are, however, two difficulties about this interpretation. The first is that it seems to add nothing to what is expressly stated in s 2(1)(a) – that is, a person who has a claim of legal right is not dishonest – and leaves no function for the word 'dishonestly'.[286] Secondly, it seems too narrow as a matter of policy.[287] Such an approach leads to the conviction of D who, knowing that he has no right to do so, takes V's money with intent to spend it but with

concluded in Report No 276, *Fraud* (2002), para 5.33, that the test might be compatible. It has been held at first instance that dishonesty under *Ghosh* is not itself incompatible with Article 7: *Pattni* [2001] Crim LR 570. And see D. Ormerod, 'Cheating the Public Revenue' [1998] Crim LR 627 and D. Ormerod, 'A Bit of a Con – The Law Commission's Proposals on Fraud' [1999] Crim LR 789.

281 On the suitability of dishonesty in these cases see also D. W. Elliott, 'Directors' Thefts and Dishonesty' [1991] Crim LR arguing that insufficient attention has been paid to the issue of dishonesty in cases of sole traders committing theft from the company.

282 P 42, See also N. Lacey, C. Wells and O. Quick, *Reconstructing Criminal Law* (3rd edn, 2004), 363.

283 See eg Magistrates' Association response to the LCCP 155, reported in Law Com No 276, para 5.14. And see the Commission's conclusion at para 5.18.

284 Law Com No 155, para 5.6. 285 [1980] VR 401.

286 Williams, TBCL (2nd edn, 1983), 730.

287 See D. W. Elliott, 'Dishonesty in Theft: A Dispensable Concept' [1982] Crim LR at 406.

the certainty (in his own mind) that he will be able to replace it before it is missed, so that V will never know anything about it and suffer no detriment whatever.[288]

Reform

The Law Commission recently commented that it found the criticisms of the present law 'compelling'.[289] In light of the volume and strength of such criticisms, it is not surprising therefore that numerous reform proposals have been advanced. Professor Elliott went so far as to suggest the removal of the element of dishonesty from the definition of theft. His proposal was to leave s 2 to deal with the bulk of cases and to add a further exculpatory element to the definition of the offence for conduct 'not detrimental to the interests of the owner in a significant practical way'.[290] It is unclear that such a proposal would offer any greater degree of certainty and promote any greater degree of consistency that the present law. There have been many other proposals, each with its strengths and defects.[291]

One attractive solution would be a provision that a person appropriating property belonging to another *is* to be regarded as dishonest unless one of the three existing exemptions (in s 2) apply or, fourthly –

> he intends to replace the property with an equivalent and believes that no detriment whatever will be caused to the owner by the appropriation.

This would excuse the employee who 'borrows' £5 from the till when closing the shop on Saturday afternoon, having no doubt that he will be able to replace it when he opens up on Monday morning, only to be robbed and rendered penniless on his way home from the pub on Saturday night.[292] His actions would be unlawful (in civil law) although not dishonest. It probably would not save the postmaster who 'borrows' from the post office till to keep his ailing grocery business going, in the hope that business will improve.

This test might however be thought too severe, leaving no escape route for hard cases such as the parents taking food for their starving children. But perhaps the concept of dishonesty is not the right vehicle for such cases. Suppose that the person breaks a window to get at the food and is charged with criminal damage. The definition of criminal damage does not require dishonesty. It would not make much sense to acquit the parent of theft and convict instead of criminal damage. They should stand or fall

288 In Australia the *Salvo* approach has been followed in *Love* (1989) 17 NSWLR 608, and *Condon* (1995) 83 A Crim R 335. In *Peters v The Queen* (1998) 192 CLR 493 the majority of the High Court distinguished *Salvo*, but declined to adopt the *Ghosh* test, preferring that the jury be directed by the standards of ordinary decent people – a test seemingly akin to *Feely*. See also *Spies* (2000) 201 CLR 603, Aus High Ct.

289 Law Com Consultation Paper No 155, para 5.32.

290 See D. W. Elliott, 'Dishonesty in Theft: A Dispensable Concept' [1982] Crim LR 395. See also D. W. Elliott, 'Directors' Theft and Dishonesty' [1991] Crim LR 732. Cf G. Williams, 'Innocuously Dipping into trust funds' (1983) LS 183.

291 See *inter alia*, P. Glazebrook, 'Revising the Theft Acts' [1993] CLJ 191 who provides a list of excepted circumstances that are not dishonest. This approach is developed by A. Halpin, 'The Test for Dishonesty' [1996] Crim LR 283, 294 – '1. The treatment by a person of the property of another is to be regarded as dishonest where it is done without a belief that the other would consent to that treatment if he knew of all the circumstances, unless the person believes that the law permits that treatment of the property. 2. The treatment by a person of the property of another is not to be regarded as dishonest if done (otherwise than by a trustee or personal representative) in the belief that the person to whom the property belongs is unlikely to be discovered by taking reasonable steps'. See further, A. Haplin, *Definition in the Criminal Law* (2004), 162–166.

292 This proposal goes back substantially to the explanation offered many years ago for the meaning of 'fraudulently' in the Larceny Act 1916 and to that made by J. C. Smith in the first two editions of *Law of Theft*.

together. The parent might claim he had a 'lawful excuse' for the doing the damage – that is, necessity or duress of circumstances, general defences – and this is the right approach for theft. If dishonesty were defined appropriately as a state of mind, exculpatory claims would be dealt with under the general defences which are applicable equally to theft and criminal damage. It is important of course to distinguish elements of unlawfulness and dishonesty. D may be acting unlawfully (and aware that he is), and yet not aware that he is acting dishonestly.

(iii) Intention permanently to deprive

The Theft Act preserves the rule of the common law and of the Larceny Act 1916 that appropriating the property of another with the intention of depriving him only temporarily of it is not stealing. There is no general offence in English law of stealing the use or enjoyment of a chattel or other property. The taking of motor vehicles and of articles from public places are exceptions, considered below. Apart from those cases, the 1968 Act left the law substantially unchanged; so that, if D takes V's horse without authority and rides it for an afternoon, a week or a month, he commits no offence under the 1968 Act if he has an intention to return the horse at the end of this period.[293]

Deprivation of persons with limited interests

As we have seen, theft may be committed against a person having possession or control of property or having any proprietary right or interest in it. The element of permanence relates to the deprivation of V, not to the proposed benefit to D. Where V has an interest less than full ownership, it appears that an intention by D to deprive him of the whole of that interest, whatever it might be, is sufficient.[294] Thus, if as D knows, V has hired a car from X for a month, and D takes it, intending to return it to X after the month has expired, this appears to be theft from V, who is permanently deprived of his whole interest in the property, but it is not theft from X. The question is one of intention; so, if in the above example, D, when he took the car, believed V to be the owner, he would apparently not commit theft from V (because he intended to return it) even though V was, in fact, deprived of his whole interest.

Section 6 and the common law

The draft Bill proposed by the CLRC contained no definition or elaboration of the phrase 'intention of permanently depriving'. The Committee were well aware of the existing case law and must have assumed that it would continue to be applied. The government had other ideas and introduced a clause which, after much amendment, became s 6.[295] At common law and under the Larceny Acts the phrase was held to include the cases where –

(i) D took V's property with intention that V should have it back only by paying for it – for example, he took V's property so that, pretending that it was his own, he could sell it to V[296] ('Ransom' cases).

293 *Neal v Gribble* [1978] RTR 409, below, p 725.

294 Cf Smith, *Property Offences*, para 6–05.

295 See J. R. Spencer, 'The Metamorphosis of Section 6 of the Theft Act' [1977] Crim LR 653.

296 *Hall* (1849) 1 Den 381.

(ii) D took V's property intending to return it to V only when he had completely changed its substance – for example, D, being employed by V, to melt pig iron, took an axle belonging to V and melted it down in order to increase his output and consequently his earnings;[297] or D wrongfully fed V's oats to V's own horses;[298] or took V's horse intending to kill it and to return the carcase.[299]

(iii) D took V's property and pawned it, intending to redeem and restore it to V one day but with no reasonable prospects of being able to do so.[300]

Section 6 was apparently intended to cover these cases and no more. Inevitably, the cases at common law all concerned tangible property. The extension under the Theft Act of the meaning of property capable of being stolen to include intangible property has created some unforeseen problems. Section 6 is expressed to apply only to the offence of theft, but obtaining by deception contrary to s 15 also requires an intention permanently to deprive. Section 15(3) provides that s 6 shall apply for the purposes of s 15, with the necessary adaptation of the reference to appropriating, as it applies for the purposes of s 1. As virtually all cases under s 15 are, *prima facie*, also cases of theft, it would be highly unsatisfactory if different tests were applicable.

As Spencer has written,[301] and the Court of Appeal was inclined to agree,[302] s 6 'sprouts obscurities at every phrase'. Section 6(1) provides:

> A person appropriating property belonging to another without meaning the other permanently to lose the thing itself is nevertheless to be regarded as having the intention of permanently depriving the other of it if his intention is to treat the thing as his own to dispose of regardless of the other's rights, and a borrowing or lending of it may amount to so treating it if, but only if, the borrowing or lending is for a period and in circumstances making it equivalent to an outright taking or disposal.

In *Lloyd*,[303] the Court of Appeal approved academic opinions that s 6 only need be referred to in exceptional cases and then the question for the jury should not be 'worded in terms of the generalities' of the section but be related to the particular facts. The court cited the opinion of Edmund Davies LJ,[304] that 'Section 6 . . . gives illustrations, as it were, of what can amount to the dishonest intention demanded by s 1(1). But it is a misconception to interpret it as watering down s 1', and concluded, 'we would try to interpret the section in such a way as to ensure that nothing is construed as an intention permanently to deprive which would not prior to the 1968 Act have been so construed'. But, before and since *Lloyd*, courts have given the words of the section their wider ordinary meaning.

In *Downes*,[305] the Court of Appeal held that D committed theft when, being in possession of vouchers belonging to the Inland Revenue and made out in his name, he sold them to others who, as he knew, would submit them to the Revenue so as to obtain tax advantages. The primary reason for the decision was that the document when returned to

297 *Richards* (1844) 1 Car & Kir 532.
298 *Morfit* (1816) Russ & Ry 307.
299 Cf *Cabbage* (1815) Russ & Ry 292.
300 *Phetheon* (1840) 9 C & P 552; *Medland* (1851) 5 Cox CC 292. Cf *Trebilcock* (1858) Dears & B 453 and *Wynn* (1887) 16 Cox CC 231 which are inconclusive on the point.
301 Spencer, n 295, above.
302 *Lloyd* [1985] QB 829 at 834.
303 [1985] QB 829, [1985] 2 All ER 661.
304 *Warner* (1970) 55 Cr App R 93 at 97.
305 (1983) 77 Cr App R 260, [1983] Crim LR 819 and commentary.

the Revenue would be in substance a different thing; but the court also held that s 6 was to be given its ordinary meaning – D intended to treat the vouchers as his own to dispose of regardless of the Revenue's rights. Subsequently, in *Chan Man-sin*[306] the Privy Council held that, where a company accountant drew a forged cheque on the company's account, there was 'ample evidence' of intention permanently to deprive the company of its credit balance, even on the assumption that D contemplated that the fraud would be discovered and the company would lose nothing. He intended to treat the balance as his own to dispose of regardless of the company's rights. *Re Osman*,[307] another case of 'theft without loss', is similar. In *Bagshaw*,[308] the Court of Appeal said that the restrictive view taken in *Lloyd* was *obiter* and that 'there may be other occasions on which s 6 applies'.

Thus, the current opinion seems to be that s 6 is to be given its ordinary meaning (whatever that may be) and is not necessarily restricted to the scope of the common law meaning of the concept. The concept certainly has to be applied to situations which did not arise at common law like the theft or obtaining of a thing in action. Subject to that, it is submitted that, in view of the acknowledged obscurity of s 6, the better opinion is that it should be treated as a restatement of the common law, equally applicable to both s 1 and s 15.[309]

Conditional intention to deprive

Consider a case where D takes V's bag, intending to take anything of value which he finds in it. Is such a 'conditional' intention sufficient? In *Easom*,[310] the Court of Appeal held, controversially, that 'a conditional appropriation will not do'. A difficulty with this proposition is that all intention is conditional, even though the condition is unexpressed and not present to the mind of the person at that time. In that case D picked up a woman's handbag in a cinema, rummaged through the contents and put it back having taken nothing. The handbag was attached by a thread to a policewoman's wrist. D's conviction for stealing the handbag and the specified contents – tissues, cosmetics, etc – was quashed because D never had any intention of permanently depriving V of any of those things. It followed that he was not guilty of attempting to steal any of them. No doubt he intended to steal things which were not there – presumably money – and might have been convicted of attempting to steal on a suitably worded indictment.[311] D had no intention permanently to deprive, and consequently, he was not guilty of attempting to steal the handbag, or the specified contents either.

In *Husseyn*,[312] DD opened the door of a van in which there was a holdall containing valuable sub-aqua equipment. They were charged with attempted theft of the equipment. The judge directed the jury that they could convict if DD were about to look into the holdall and, if its contents were valuable, to steal it. The Court of Appeal, following *Easom*, held that this was a misdirection: 'it cannot be said that one who has it in mind to steal only if what he finds is worth stealing has a present intention to steal'. In *Re*

306 [1988] 1 All ER 1, [1988] Crim LR 319, PC.
307 [1988] Crim LR 611.
308 [1988] Crim LR 321.
309 Cf Griew, *Theft*, para 2–103.
310 [1971] 2 QB 315 at 319, [1971] 2 All ER 945 at 947.
311 Below.
312 (1977) 67 Cr App R 131n, [1978] Crim LR 219 and commentary; discussed at [1978] Crim LR 444 and 644.

Attorney-General's References (Nos 1 and 2 of 1979),[313] the Court of Appeal held that these words were applicable only to an indictment which alleged an intention to steal a specific object, such as sub-aqua equipment. If the indictment had charged an attempt to steal 'some or all of the contents of the holdall' or, in *Easom*, of the handbag, there would be no problem. Yet, in *Husseyn*, the sub-aqua equipment *was* the contents of the holdall – there were no other contents; so, according to the court, D was not guilty of attempting to steal the equipment if it was described as such, but he was guilty if it was described as the 'contents of the holdall'. At that time it was clear law that there could be no conviction for attempting to steal a thing that was not there – it was the sub-aqua equipment or nothing. Since the Criminal Attempts Act 1981,[314] this is no longer so. A person looking for money in an empty handbag might now be convicted of attempting to steal money.

The real problem in cases of this kind is the form of the indictment. The formula approved in the *Attorney-General's References* is not satisfactory because, in these cases, the defendant did not intend (or it was not proved that he intended) to steal any of the contents. But he undoubtedly intended to steal something – something which was *not* 'all or any of the contents'.[315] The indictment would be accurate if it alleged simply that D attempted to steal from the handbag, or holdall.[316] This is so whether or not there is anything there that D would have stolen. D's intention to steal anything he finds which he thinks worth stealing is a present intention to steal, at least so far as the law of attempts is concerned. The failure to specify any subject matter cannot be an objection since the Criminal Attempts Act 1981.[317]

It is submitted that the better view is that an assumption of ownership, which is conditional because there is an intention to deprive only in a certain event, is theft. For example, D takes V's ring intending to keep it if the stone is a diamond, but otherwise to return it. He takes it to a jeweller who says the stone is paste. D returns the ring to V. It is submitted that he committed theft when he took the ring. The fact that he returned it is relevant only to mitigation in sentence. A similar problem may arise where D takes the property of V, say a ring, intending to claim a reward from V for finding it. If he intends to return the ring in any event and hopes to receive the reward, he is not guilty of stealing the ring though he is about to attempt to obtain by deception – and so to steal – the reward. But if he intends to retain the ring unless he receives the reward, he seems to be in substantially the same situation as the taker who sells the property back to the owner. It might be said, however, that in this example, the taker is not treating the property as his own. There are two possible answers to this: the assertion of a better right to possession might be regarded as treating the property as one's own; or, s 6 not providing an exclusive definition, this might be regarded as an analogous case falling within the general principle.

[313] [1980] QB 180, [1979] 3 All ER 143, [1979] Crim LR 585 and commentary.

[314] Above, p 400.

[315] Cf *Bayley and Easterbrook* [1980] Crim LR 503 and commentary.

[316] Cf *Smith and Smith* [1986] Crim LR 166 and commentary.

[317] As with the law of burglary, this is an instance in which it appears motive, which is generally regarded as irrelevant in *mens rea* in practice, assumes an importance below, p 822. It may be different where the charge is theft. A lorry driver was held (in a civil action) not guilty of theft of the goods loaded on his lorry when he drove off intending to steal the load 'if and when the circumstances were favourable': *Grundy (Teddington) Ltd v Fulton* [1983] 1 Lloyd's Rep 16, CA; but he had assumed a right of the owner (cf *Gomez*) and the only question is whether the conditional intention was enough: *Archbold* 21–76.

Disposal of the property as one's own

The attribution of an ordinary meaning to the language of s 6 presents some difficulties. It is submitted that an intention merely to use the thing as one's own is not enough and that 'dispose of' is not used in the sense in which a commander might 'dispose of' his infantry but rather in the meaning given by the *Shorter Oxford Dictionary*: 'To deal with definitely; to get rid of; to get done with, finish. To make over by way of sale or bargain, sell.'[318] In *DPP v Lavender*,[319] however, the Divisional Court seems to have held D's intention to treat the thing as his own, regardless of the owner's rights, as crucial and to have minimized the importance of 'to dispose of'. D, a council tenant, without authority, removed two doors from another property belonging to the council to replace doors in the council property he occupied. Did he not in fact treat the doors as the property of the council, like the rest of the premises he occupied? If a secretary surreptitiously swaps his typewriter for the similar model operated by a colleague (because he believes it works better), does he steal the typewriter from his employer? He may well steal it from his colleague whom he does intend to deprive permanently of his limited interest.

It is submitted that, on a similar basis, there is no reason why there should not be a conviction for theft (rather than having to rely on s 11) in a case like that of the taker of the Goya from the National Gallery: 'I will return the picture when £X is paid to charity.' Substantially, the taker is offering to sell the thing back and his case is, in principle, the same as those contemplated by s 6(1). Nor should it make any difference that the price demanded is something other than money. 'I will return the picture when E (who is imprisoned) is given a free pardon' – this should be sufficient evidence of an intention permanently to deprive. The general principle might be that it is sufficient that there is an intention that V shall not have the property back unless some consideration is supplied by him or another; or, more generally still, unless some condition is satisfied.

Borrowing or lending

Where money or anything which is consumed by use – like petrol – is 'borrowed', the dishonest 'borrower' has an intention permanently to deprive even though he intends to replace the money or the article with another which is just as good. He intends to deprive the owner of the specific thing he has appropriated.[320] In the case of a true borrowing it appears that there can be no theft, however dishonest the borrower may be, because, by definition, he does intend to return the specific thing taken. Yet by s 6(1), if the borrowing 'is for a period and in circumstances making it equivalent to an outright taking . . .' the borrower may be regarded as having the intention of depriving the owner permanently. This is a rather puzzling provision, because it would seem, *prima facie*, that borrowing cannot be an 'outright taking'. Clearly, however, this part of the subsection is intended to do something and, therefore, certain borrowings are to be treated as the equivalent of outright takings. Once this is accepted, it is not difficult to divine the kind of borrowings which are intended to be covered: they are those where the taker intends not to return the thing until the virtue is gone out of it: D takes V's non-rechargeable battery, intending to return it to V when it is exhausted; or V's season ticket, intending to return it to V when

318 This passage was cited in *Cahill* [1993] Crim LR 141.
319 [1994] Crim LR 297.
320 *Velumyl* [1989] Crim LR 299.

the season is over. Similar in principle are those cases where D intends to return the thing only when it is completely changed in substance.[321]

Where property belonging to another has been entirely deprived of an essential characteristic, which has been described as its 'virtue', the matter seems reasonably clear. A person stealing a cheque from the drawer, V, may know that, when he has cashed it, the piece of paper will be returned to V; but he intends to deprive V permanently of the valuable security because it will have ceased to be one (it will now be a worthless piece of paper only). Similarly with the theft of a ticket which will be returned only after it has been used. What if the virtue has not been entirely eliminated – but very nearly? D takes V's season ticket for Arsenal's matches intending to return it to him in time for the last match of the season. Is this an 'outright taking' so as to amount to theft of the ticket? If it is, is it theft if D intends to return the ticket in time for two matches? – or three, four, five or six – where should the line be drawn? The difficulty of drawing a line suggests that it should not be theft of the ticket unless D intends to keep it until it has lost *all* (or, at least, substantially all) its virtue.[322] The difficulty might satisfactorily be overcome in this particular case by holding that the right to see each match is a separate thing in action, of which V is permanently deprived once that match is over. This means, of course, that if D takes V's car and keeps it for 10 years, he will not be guilty of theft if, when, as he intended all along, he returns it to V, it is still a roadworthy vehicle, though the proportion of its original value which it retains is very small. If it can no longer be described as a car, but is scrap metal, then, if D intended to return it in this state, he has stolen it.[323]

The provision regarding lending appears to contemplate the situation where D is in possession or control of the property and he lends it to another. If D knows that the effect is that V will never get the property back again, he clearly has an intent permanently to deprive. Similarly if D knows that, when V gets the property back again, the virtue will have gone out of it, this is equivalent to an outright disposal. The examples of the non-rechargeable battery, season ticket, etc are applicable here, though they seem less likely to arise in the context of lending than of borrowing.

Parting with property under a condition as to its return

Section 6(2) provides:

> Without prejudice to the generality of subsection (1) above, where a person, having possession or control (lawfully or not) of property belonging to another, parts with the property under a condition as to its return which he *may not* be able to perform, this (if done for purposes of his own and without the other's authority) amounts to treating the property as his own to dispose of regardless of the other's rights.

This is clearly intended to deal with the kind of case which gave difficulty under the old law, where D, being in possession or control of V's goods, pawns them. If D had no intention of ever redeeming the goods, there was no problem – he was guilty of larceny and he would now clearly be guilty of theft, apart from s 6(2). But what if D does intend to redeem? The answer now is that if he knows that he may not be able to do so, he is

[321] See cases cited above. *Dicta* in *Bagshaw* [1988] Crim LR 321 concerning the 'virtue' test seem inappropriate to the facts of that case.

[322] Cf *Chan Wai Lam v R* [1981] Crim LR 497.

[323] Cf *DPP v J* [2002] EWHC 291, holding that the magistrates were wrong to accept a submission of no case where D had taken V's headphones, snapped them and returned them.

guilty of theft. The subsection does not seem to allow any distinction to be drawn between the case where D knows that the chances of his being able to redeem are slight and the case where he believes the chances are high; in either case, the condition is one which he knows he may not be able to perform.

The common law cases suggested that it was theft, notwithstanding an intention to redeem the goods, if the person pawning them had no reasonable prospects of being able to redeem them.[324] It is submitted, however, that the question under the Theft Act is a purely subjective one: D must *intend* to dispose of the property regardless of the other's rights, and s 6(2) merely describes what he must intend. If then D is in fact *convinced*, however unreasonably, that he will be able to redeem the property, he does not come within the terms of s 6(2) because he intends *to dispose of it under a condition which he will be able to perform.*

This is not necessarily conclusive, however, for subs (2) is without prejudice to the generality of subs (1); and it might reasonably be argued that even the person who is convinced when pawning the goods of his power to redeem them intends to treat the goods as his own to dispose of, regardless of the other's rights. This would be equally true if the person pawning the goods in fact had power to redeem; and, since pawning is not 'lending', there is no need to prove that it was equivalent to an outright disposal. The difficulty about this interpretation is that it makes it very difficult to see why s 6(2) is there at all; if D's disposition of property under a condition which he is able to perform is theft under subs (1), why refer specifically to the case of a condition which he may not be able to perform?

On the whole it would seem that the better approach is to hold that one who is certain of his ability to redeem does not have an intention permanently to deprive. Such a person, in some circumstances, may well be found by the jury not to be dishonest. For example D, a tenant for a year of a furnished house, being temporarily short of money, pawns the landlord's clock, knowing that he will certainly be able and intending to redeem it before the year expires. A prosecution for theft of the clock should fail on the grounds both that he is not dishonest and that he has no intent permanently to deprive.

Abandonment of property

Early nineteenth century cases on the taking of horses decided that there was no intention permanently to deprive, even though D turned the horse loose some considerable distance from the place where he took it. In the conditions of those times it might be supposed that D must have known that there was a substantial risk that V would not get his horse back. This lenient attitude may be contrasted with that adopted in the pawning cases, and the right course would seem to be to attach no importance to these old decisions in the interpretation of the Theft Act.

The case where the property is abandoned is not within s 6(2) for D does not part with the property under a condition. He might, however, be regarded as having an intention to treat the thing as his own to dispose of regardless of the other's rights. If D borrows the thing and then leaves it where he knows the owner or someone on his behalf will certainly

324 *Phetheon* (1840) 9 C & P 552; *Medland* (1851) 5 Cox CC 292. *Trebilcock* (1858) Dears & B 453 and *Wynn* (1887) 16 Cox CC 231 are inconclusive.

find it, he clearly does not have an intention permanently to deprive. But if he abandons the thing in circumstances such that he knows that it is quite uncertain whether the owner will ever get it back or not, then it would not be unreasonable to hold that he has an intention to treat the thing as his own to dispose of regardless of the other's rights.

By analogy to the pawning case discussed above, it would seem that it should be immaterial whether D believes that the chances of V's getting the property back are large or small; it is sufficient that he intends to risk the loss of V's property. In *Fernandes*,[325] Auld LJ concluded that 'section 6 may apply to a person in possession or control of another's property who dishonestly and for his own purpose deals with that property in such a manner that he knows he is risking its loss'.[326] Suppose, for example, that D, being caught in the rain when leaving a restaurant in London, takes an umbrella to shelter him on his way to the station and abandons it in the train on his arrival at Leeds. He should be guilty of theft.[327]

Other things to be returned – but for a price

A problem arises with the theft of a railway ticket or any other ticket which entitles the holder to services or goods when he returns it.[328] If D takes the ticket from another passenger, V, there is no difficulty. D intends to deprive V permanently not only of the piece of paper but also of the thing in action (the contractual right to travel) which it represents; but if he takes the ticket from the rail company intending to use it, he may well intend to give it up at the end of the journey.[329] The rail company own the piece of paper but they cannot own the contractual right to travel. As with a cheque,[330] it may be said that D intends to return a different thing, a cancelled ticket with a hole punched in it; it has lost its virtue.

An alternative explanation is that D intends that the rail company shall have the ticket only by paying for it – through the provision of a ride on their train. That should be enough. This explanation has the advantage that it extends to things which are intended to be returned (but only for value) in an unchanged form. For example, D takes tokens from a coffee shop intending to return them in exchange for his espresso; or gaming chips from the proprietor of a gaming club, intending to return them in exchange for the right to play.[331] In all these cases there is probably a conditional intention permanently to deprive in the literal sense. The ticket, tokens and chips will probably

[325] [1996] 1 Cr App R 175. [326] P 188.

[327] Cf the position in Scotland where temporary deprivation may suffice, and note the Scottish Draft Code proposing that recklessness as to permanent deprivation should be an alternative *mens rea*. See further the discussion by P. Ferguson, 'Codifying Criminal Law (1): A Critique of Scots Common Law' [2004] Crim LR 49 and also P. Ferguson, 'Codifying Criminal Law (2): The Scots and the English Draft Codes Compared' [2004] Crim LR 105.

[328] Cf *Marshall* [1998] 2 Cr App R 282, above, p 674.

[329] At one time everyone knew that all tickets had to be given to the collector at the end of the journey, but, in these days of 'open stations', this is not necessarily so. If I am travelling to King's Cross (an open station) I expect (and intend) to retain my ticket; but if I am travelling to Leeds (a closed station), I expect (and intend) to give it up.

[330] Above, p 669.

[331] Cf correspondence in [1976] Crim LR 329 and commentary on *Pick* [1982] Crim LR 238 which should be read in the light of the Gaming Act 1968, s 16 which was overlooked.

not be returned at all if the taker realizes that he is not going to receive the value they represent.

(c) Reform

Over the last century the central focus of acquisitive crimes has shifted from protecting the possession of tangible goods against transportation to the protection of ownership of property (as broadly construed) against misuse. Those interests being protected and which form essential elements of the *actus reus* – property and ownership – have expanded. The constant concept has been that of *mens rea* – fraud or dishonesty. So it seems that it will be in the future. It may be that the *actus reus* of the offences will disappear almost to vanishing point as the interests the law seeks to protect become more diffuse, diverse and indefinable.

There is also a growing pressure to use the criminal law to protect other 'interests' from misuse – trade secrets being a strong example. The law may need to be more forward-thinking by protecting 'rights' and 'interests' such as the 'use' and 'value' derived from 'having access' to facilities. As these interests are harder to define the mental element of dishonesty offences will become ever more important.

3. Robbery[332]

By s 8 of the Theft Act 1968:

> (1) A person is guilty of robbery if he steals, and immediately before or at the time of doing so, and in order to do so, he uses force on any person or puts or seeks to put any person in fear of being then and there subjected to force.
>
> (2) A person guilty of robbery, or of an assault with intent to rob, shall on conviction on indictment be liable to imprisonment for life.

Robbery is an extremely serious offence, carrying a maximum life sentence, and attracting substantial sentences in practice. It is triable only on indictment. In recent years there has been a steady increase in its incidence, and enhanced media attention focused on street 'muggings' (especially for mobile phones),[333] car jacking, and robberies of those using ATM (cash point) machines.[334]

The offence is very broad, applying to theft in any circumstances ranging from the work of sophisticated gangs[335] and armed bank robbers,[336] to extreme forms of playground bullying.[337] There have been cogent calls for reform to subdivide the offence

332 See generally A. Ashworth, 'Robbery Reassessed' [2002] Crim LR 851; J. Andrews, 'Robbery' [1966] Crim LR 524; Griew, *Theft*, ch. 3; Smith, *Property Offences*, ch 14.

333 See *A-G's Reference Nos. 4 and 7* 'Q' [2002] 2 Cr App R (S) 345.

334 For a recent review of police data see J. Smith, *The Nature of Personal Robbery* (2003).

335 See M. Gill, *Commercial Robbery* (2000).

336 Armed robbery attracts very high sentences. See generally on armed robbery I. O'Donnell and S. Morrison, 'Armed and Dangerous: the use of firearms in robbery (1997) 36(3) Howard Jnl 305. A relevant firearms offence ought to be added to the indictment: *Murphy* [2002] Crim LR 674.

337 See *F A and Others* [2003] 2 Cr App R (S) 503.

based on the gravity of the threat or use of violence involved.[338] This would provide offences which would have more appropriate labelling and sentencing. Since the offence necessarily includes theft,[339] and will usually also involve an offence against the person, it might be argued that the offence is otiose and that the combination of the two charges would cater adequately in terms of labelling and sentencing powers. Despite the overlap, it is submitted that a specifically labelled offence of robbery is desirable, not least because in cases of a threat, unless the threat is to kill, the offence against the person likely to have been committed will only be that of assault.[340]

(a) Requirement of theft

As defined, robbery is essentially an aggravated form of theft; and if there is no theft, or attempted theft, there can be no robbery or attempted robbery. All of the elements of theft must be proved. So it would not be robbery where D by force takes a car from V in the belief that he has the legal right to it (no dishonesty);[341] or where D by force takes a car from V not intending to deprive V permanently of it. In the first case D may be guilty of an assault,[342] and in the latter of both an assault and an offence under s 12 of the Theft Act, but in neither case is he guilty of robbery. It is not necessary that D keeps the property, rather only that he has the intention permanently to deprive V, as where D takes V's headphones by force, snaps and returns them in 'useless' form.[343]

The offence of robbery is complete when the theft is complete, that is when the appropriation is complete. Following recent interpretations of that concept, a robbery can be completed much earlier than at common law, and than the drafters of the Theft Act intended. So in *Corcoran v Anderton*[344] where D and E sought to take V's handbag by force, it was held that the theft was complete when D snatched the handbag from V's grasp though it then fell from D's hands and the defendants made off without it. It is now arguable that the theft in such a case is complete when D first touches the handbag, for by that conduct he is assuming a right of an owner.

In the case of robbery the appropriation must normally be by 'taking' since it is difficult to imagine realistic situations in which robbery might be affected by other modes of appropriation.[345] One possibility is where a bailee refuses to return property to the owner, and backs this refusal with a threat of force. It is unclear whether D can be said to have completed the robbery where, he issues a threat to V and demands that V hand over his property and V is in the process of doing so, but D has not yet touched it.[346] A safer course is to charge an attempted robbery in such circumstances.

338 See A. Ashworth, 'Robbery Reassessed' [2002] Crim LR 851, Ashworth, POCL, 390.

339 *Guy* (1990) 93 Cr App R 108, CA.

340 Ashworth, above, 863.

341 Cf *Skivington* [1968] 1 QB 166, [1967] 1 All ER 483; *Robinson* [1977] Crim LR 173, CA; *Forrester* [1992] Crim LR 793, CA.

342 D's claim that he believes himself to be entitled to the property appropriated does not of itself legitimate his use of force: see above, p 399.

343 Magistrates wrong to accept submission of no case: *DPP v J* [2002] EWHC Admin 291.

344 (1980) 71 Cr App R 104, [1980] Crim LR 385.

345 See Andrews, above, n 332, for possible instances.

346 Cf *Briggs* [2004] Crim LR 495. Cf *Farrell* (1787) 1 Leach 332n. D apprehended before V handed over the property.

(b) Use or threat of force

Any use or threat of 'force' against the person suffices.[347] D may threaten a use of force and satisfy the requirement of the offence of robbery although V is not made to apprehend the immediate infliction of force on him which is necessary to constitute an assault.[348] 'Force' is wider than the concept of 'violence' used at common law, and might be regarded as a more neutral word. It remains undefined and in the prevailing climate of judicial opinion it can come as no surprise that it has been identified as an ordinary English word the meaning of which is to be determined by the jury.[349] It is submitted that no jury could reasonably find that the slight physical contact that might be involved where D picks V's pocket would amount to a use of force.[350] However, very little may be required to turn a case of theft into one of robbery and to push or nudge the victim so as to cause him to lose his balance is capable of being a use of force.[351]

A threat of force may be implied as well as express. So long as D intends V to understand, and V does so understand, that force will be used against him if he seeks to prevent the theft, the theft is accomplished by the threat of force.[352]

Where D threatens V with force unless V complies with D's demands (eg to accompany him) and at a later stage D takes property from an unprotesting V, D may be convicted of robbery if he intends, and V understands, the threat to continue, even though D's original threats were not made for the purpose of taking V's property.[353] This might be a common occurrence where D threatens V and subsequently V escorts D to V's bank ATM and withdraws cash to hand over to D.

(i) Force to the person

Under the former law, robbery was thought of as stealing accomplished by force against the person, the force being used to overpower V's resistance and not merely to seize the property.[354] The CLRC appeared to have the same distinction in mind for they said that they would 'not regard mere snatching of property, such as a handbag, from an unresisting owner as using force for the purpose of the definition'.[355] That requirement that the force be administered directly to a person and not the property being stolen was meant to be retained by the words in s 8: '. . . if he steals . . . and in order to do so, he uses force *on any person* or seeks to put any person in fear of being then and there subjected to force'. But in *Clouden*[356] the distinction was rejected and D's conviction for robbery was upheld where he wrenched a shopping basket from V's hand and ran off with it. In the view of the court the former distinction could not stand with the words of the section and it was open to a jury to find on these facts that force had been used on V with intent

347 Whether it is actually used will be significant for sentencing purposes: PCC(S)A 2000, s 161(3).

348 *Tennant* [1976] Crim LR 133, CC.

349 *Dawson and James* (1976) 64 Cr App R 170, CA.

350 See eg *Monaghan and Monaghan* [2000] 1 Cr App R (S) 6 where 'jostling' to pick V's pockets was charged as theft.

351 *Dawson*, n 2. See Williams, TBCL (2nd edn, 1983), 825, suggesting a distinction based on 'gentle force' used to take by stealth as opposed to force used to overcome resistance. See also Griew, para 3–05; Smith, *Property Offences*, para 14–10.

352 See eg *Grant v CPS* [2000] QBD unreported, 10 Mar.

353 *Donaghy and Marshall* [1981] Crim LR 644 (Judge Chavasse).

354 *Gnosil* (1824) 1 C & P 304; *Harman's Case* (1620) 2 Roll Rep 154.

355 Cmnd 2977, para 65.

356 [1987] Crim LR 56, CA. Griew believes the case to be wrongly decided: para 3–05.

to steal. *A fortiori* it will be robbery where, for example, a struggle, even a fleeting one, takes place for possession of a handbag,[357] or where an earring is snatched tearing the lobe of the ear.[358] The decision in *Clouden* is an interesting illustration of the ambiguity over the true foundation of robbery: it is a hybrid offence protecting property and personal safety, and the courts refuse to narrow down the offence more specifically by defining its concepts in an unduly technical fashion.

(ii) In order to steal

If D assaults V and, having disabled him without any intention of stealing from him, opportunistically takes V's wallet there is no robbery. There are offences of violence and theft.[359]

(c) On *any* person

In most cases of robbery, D will use or threaten force against the person in possession of the property. But the offence is not so limited. Provided the force is used or threatened *in order* to steal, it will be robbery.

> If, for example, the only force used at the time of the [Great Train Robbery] in 1963 had been on a signalman, this would under the [Act] have been sufficient.[360]

It does not matter that the person against whom the force is used or threatened has no interest whatever in the property; it would be robbery to overpower the same signalman because his signal-box overlooks a factory from which the thieves wish to steal and they fear that he will notice them and raise the alarm.

It does not amount to robbery where D threatens to use force on X (who has no knowledge of the threat) in order to overcome V's reluctance to part with his money, as where D hands V, a bank teller, a note which reads 'I have a gun pointed at a customer'.[361] If D reads the note aloud, that is sufficient for robbery since the customer, X, is in fear. There is no glaring failing in the law since all cases of this type could be treated as blackmail under s 21 of the 1968 Act.

(d) Immediately before or at the time of stealing

Strictly interpreted this expression might suggest that force used only a second after the theft is technically complete would not suffice for robbery, a view which may be said to receive further support from the requirement that the force be used 'in order to steal'. The argument was advanced in *Hale*.[362] D and E entered V's house and while D was upstairs stealing a jewellery box, E was downstairs tying up V. The Court of Appeal declined to quash their convictions for robbery though the appropriation of the jewellery box might have been completed before the force was used. The appropriation, said the court, should

357 *Corcoran v Anderton* (1980) 71 Cr App R 104, [1980] Crim LR 385, DC.

358 Cf *Lapier* (1784) 1 Leach 320.

359 *Harris* (1998) The Times, 4 Mar; *James* [1997] Crim LR 598.

360 Cmnd 2977, para 65. Cf *Smith v Desmond and Hall* [1965] AC 960, [1965] 1 All ER 976.

361 *Taylor* [1996] 10 Archbold News 2, CA. Cf *Reane* (1794) 2 Leach 616.

362 (1978) 68 Cr App R 415, [1979] Crim LR 596, CA. Confirmed post-*Gomez* in *Lockley* [1995] Crim LR 656. Cf *Gregory* (1981) 74 Cr App R 154, [1982] Crim LR 229, CA. Cf *Atakpu*, above, p 656.

be regarded as a 'continuing act' and it was open to the jury on these facts to conclude that it continued while V was tied up. The matter needs to be looked at in a common sense way; while the force must be used at the time of the theft and *in order to steal*,[363] the theft needs to be looked at in its entirety.

There is, arguably, an ever greater need for the courts to adopt a pragmatic approach to this issue following the extension of the concept of appropriation. Technically, where D first touches V's handbag he has appropriated it, but it would render the offence of robbery useless if the theft was deemed complete at that time and D applied force a second later. Thus, where D has already gained access to V's car, and locked himself in, and V is only threatened by D's driving at him to escape, the theft might be said to be continuing and a robbery committed.[364] But, a line has to be drawn somewhere. If, having taken property from V without using or threatening force, D is subsequently stopped by a police officer in the street outside and knocks him down in order to avoid arrest this would not amount to robbery. Force used to retain possession of property not obtained by force would not ordinarily be thought of as robbery.[365] Even on a broad view the use of force is neither at the time of, nor in order to commit, the theft.[366] There may be merit in extending the offence to include force or the threat of force 'immediately after' a theft.[367] This would resonate with the existing underlying approach which is that robbery is protecting against the use of force in the acquisition of property.

'Immediately before' must add something to 'at the time of' the theft. The approach taken in some Australian decisions – 'no intervening space or lapse of time or event of any significance'[368] – may be too restrictive. Clearly if a gang overpower V, the security guard at the main gate of a factory, this would be a use of force immediately before the theft, although some minutes must elapse before the gang reaches the part of the factory where the safe is housed.[369] And it can make no difference that V is not present in the factory at all; it would be robbery where some members of the gang by force detain V at his home while their confederates open the safe in the factory. It does not seem to be possible to put any particular temporal limit on 'immediately'. All the circumstances have to be considered including the time when, and the place where, the force was used or threatened in relation to the theft. Force converts theft into robbery only when its use or threat is in a real sense directly part of the theft, and is used in order to accomplish the theft.

It is not enough that D gets V to part with property by threatening to use force on a separate and future, occasion. This may well amount to blackmail but the fact that V is intimidated or frightened is not in itself enough for robbery unless he is put in fear of being 'then and there' subject to force. But suppose a gang by threats of force persuade V, the factory security guard, to stay away from work the following evening, and on that

363 Failure to direct the jury on this point renders the conviction unsafe: *West* (1999) 14 Sept, CA, unreported.

364 *Hayward v Norwich Union Insurance Ltd* [2000] Lloyd's Rep IR 382. Whether the offence is one of theft or robbery may be of special significance for V's insurance claim: see generally M. Wasik, 'Definitions of Crime in Insurance Contracts' [1986] J Bus Law 45.

365 *Harman's Case* (1620) 2 Roll Rep 154.

366 Cf Cmnd 2977, para 65.

367 Griew, para 3–08.

368 *Stanichewski* [2001] NTSC 86.

369 It would surely be open to the jury so to find. Cf *Hale* (1978) 68 Cr App R 415, [1979] Crim LR 596, above n 362.

evening they steal from the factory uninterrupted. At the time of the theft the threat of force still operates on V's mind; he stays at home because he is afraid of what will happen if he goes to work. But this does not seem to amount to robbery. At the time of the theft V is not put in fear of being 'then and there' subjected to force.

(e) *Mens rea*

Obviously robbery requires at least an intention to steal, which in this context will usually be a purposive, direct intent.[370] But it seems to require more than this. What of the *mens rea* requirement in relation to the use or threat of force? It could be argued that liability in respect of the force is strict and that if D intends to steal it will be robbery if in fact there is some use of force, or if in fact he puts someone in fear, whether he intends to do so or not. But in principle this would not be a desirable interpretation. It seems clear that D must use or threaten force *in order* to steal, and a merely accidental use of force would not be done in order to steal.[371] Moreover, it should be proved that D intended to use the force in relation to a person, and not merely to property.[372]

It is enough that D seeks to put another in fear of being subjected to force. Fear here means to apprehend, and it would be no less a robbery because V was not afraid. Even if V does not apprehend that he will be subjected to force (because, perhaps, plain-clothes policemen are present and D has walked into a trap), it will be robbery if D intended to make him fear. But it would not be enough that V is in fact put in fear unless D intended to put V in fear. A timorous witness to a smash and grab raid might well fear that the thieves will turn on him, but if the thieves do not intend to put him in fear of being there and then subjected to force the offence cannot amount to robbery.

4. Offences of temporary deprivation[373]

In general it is not an offence dishonestly to use the property of another unless there is an intention to deprive the other permanently of the property. There is a case to be made out for creating a general offence (which need not necessarily be termed theft) of dishonest use or unauthorized use of another's property.[374] Arguably, the case for such an offence is growing stronger as so much property derives its particular value to an individual or company from its availability for immediate use.

At the time of drafting the 1968 Act, the Criminal Law Revision Committee decided against any such offence and their view, though subject to vigorous assault in Parliament, was accepted. The Committee were of the opinion that such a considerable extension of the criminal law was not called for at that time by any existing serious evil.[375] But it was recognized that there were particular cases in which temporary deprivation of property is a serious evil. The taking of vehicles (which was first made an offence by s 28 of the Road Traffic Act 1930) is one obvious instance; and the taking of vessels (which was first made

370 See above, p 94. 371 Cf *Edwards* (1843) 1 Cox CC 32.

372 Intention here might include oblique intention, above, p 94.

373 See generally Smith, *Theft* ch 7; Griew, ch 5; Smith, *Property Offences*, ch 8.

374 See especially G. Williams, 'Temporary Appropriation should be Theft' [1981] Crim LR 129.

375 Cmnd 2977, para 56.

an offence by s 1 of the Vessels Protection Act 1967)[376] is another. These offences are now dealt with in s 12 of the Theft Act 1968 that extends the offence to a much wider range of conveyances.

In addition, the Theft Act 1968 added a further and entirely new offence of temporary deprivation; that of removing articles from places open to the public. Before the Act there had been a number of notorious 'removals' such as the removal from the National Gallery of Goya's portrait of the Duke of Wellington, and the Committee thought the problem 'serious enough to justify the creation of a special offence'.[377]

(a) Removal of articles from places open to the public

Section 11 of the Theft Act 1968 provides:

(1) Subject to subsections (2) and (3) below, where the public have access to a building in order to view the building or part of it, or a collection or part of a collection housed in it, any person who without lawful authority removes from the building or its grounds the whole or part of any article displayed or kept for display to the public in the building or that part of it or in its grounds shall be guilty of an offence. For this purpose 'collection' includes a collection got together for a temporary purpose, but references in this section to a collection do not apply to a collection made or exhibited for the purpose of effecting sales or other commercial dealings.

(2) It is immaterial for purposes of subsection (1) above, that the public's access to a building is limited to a particular period or particular occasion; but where anything removed from a building or its grounds is there otherwise than as forming part of, or being on loan for exhibition with, a collection intended for permanent exhibition to the public, the person removing it does not thereby commit an offence under this section unless he removes it on a day when the public have access to the building as mentioned in subsection (1) above.

(3) A person does not commit an offence under this section if he believes that he has lawful authority for the removal of the thing in question or that he would have it if the person entitled to give it knew of the removal and the circumstances of it.

(4) A person guilty of an offence under this section shall, on conviction on indictment, be liable to imprisonment for a term not exceeding five years.

It is questionable why special protection should be provided for the temporary deprivation of this category of items in such specific circumstances when the temporary removal of non-exhibited property of individuals or companies will commonly be a cause of much greater concern, and pose the risk of much greater financial hardship to the victim.

(i) *Actus reus*

On the face of it the offence under s 11 is one of considerable complexity; the draftsman's intention was to deal with the specific mischief discussed and care has been taken to confine the operation of the section to that mischief. The following points arise for consideration.

376 As repealed by the Theft Act 1968.

377 CLRC, para 57 (ii).

Public access to a building

The public must have access to the building not merely the grounds. Access must be *public* access; access limited to a particular section of the public will not suffice.[378] It does not matter that the public are required to pay for the privilege of access, nor whether the purpose of imposing the charge is merely to cover expenses or to make a profit.[379] But the access must be to a building or part thereof. So if D removes a statuette displayed in the open in a municipal park this would not be within the section.[380] If, however, the park consists of a building and its grounds, and the public have access to the building in order to view, D's removal of the statuette would be within this section.

Normally, no doubt, D will have entered the building in consequence of the owner's invitation[381] to the public to view. But, so long as the public have access to view, D may commit the offence although he entered as a trespasser or although he is the owner's guest and is temporarily residing in the building.

In order to view

The access to the building must be *in order* to view the building (or part of the building) or a collection (or part of a collection) housed in it. It has been held that the question whether access is 'in order to view' is to be determined by reference to the occupiers' intention in allowing access.[382] The public might have access to a building (a shopping precinct or arcade for example) where collections are from time to time exhibited in the lanes connecting the shops; but in such circumstances access exists in order to shop and access to view the collection is only incidental to that shopping purpose. If, however, the collection is housed in a cordoned off part of the precinct and access is given to that part specifically so that the collection may be viewed, it would be within the protection of s 11.

Articles displayed or kept for display

The offence proscribes the removal of *any* articles displayed or kept for display, and is not confined to works of art. The coronation stone in Westminster Abbey (something which the CLRC expressly considered)[383] is clearly for this purpose an article displayed to the public though it is not a work of art. The criterion is only whether the article, which may be priceless in either sense of the term, is displayed or kept for display to the public.

'Display' here is presumably used in the sense of 'exhibit' and not merely in the sense of able to be seen; the article must be displayed or exhibited *to the public*.[384] Consequently the removal of a fire extinguisher from a building housing exhibits would not be within the section even though it can be seen by members of the public, but it would be within the section if the fire extinguisher was itself exhibited, perhaps as an example of an early type of extinguisher, or as an example of unique design, or even nowadays if it was acclaimed as a work of modern 'art'.[385]

378 But the exclusion of a particular class, for example, the exclusion of children from an exhibition considered unsuitable for them, would not prevent access being public access.

379 But see below, p 718.

380 Cf the discussion in relation to burglary, below p 892.

381 *Barr* [1978] Crim LR 244 (Deputy Judge Lowry) and commentary.

382 Ibid.

383 Cmnd 2977. Cp *Barr* [1978] Crim LR 244, CA.

384 So linked in *Barr*.

385 Without even being laid in an unmade bed or pickled!

It is enough that the article, though not displayed, is 'kept' for display, as where a painting is kept in the gallery's store-room.[386]

Removal

To complete the *actus reus* of the offence the article must be removed from the building *or* from its grounds. Thus, removal from the building to the grounds or vice versa will suffice. The removal, as s 11(2) makes clear, need not be during the times at which the public have access. If the collection is permanently[387] exhibited (which would be the case, for example, with municipal galleries and museums) removal at any time, even on a holiday when the building is closed to the public, may amount to an offence. But if the exhibition is temporary only, the removal must take place on a day when the public have access to the building in order to view. This serves to illustrate how unduly complex the provision is as a result of its being tailored to meet such a particular mischief. It underlines the fact that the offence is driven in part by a desire to criminalise the abuse of trust of those given access to public exhibitions.[388]

Commercial exhibitions

This limitation to the offence creates considerable ambiguity. As has been seen,[389] s 11 applies notwithstanding that the owner charges the public for admission, and even though he admits the public only to make profit. But, whether the owner charges for admission or not, the section does not apply where the owner admits the public only to view a collection,[390] where the collection is 'made or exhibited for the purpose of effecting sales or other commercial dealings'.

It seems odd that the law draws this distinction between exhibitions for commercial and non-commercial purposes. The reason for this restriction upon the offence was to avoid creating an unduly wide offence, involving a very substantial exception to the general principle that temporary deprivation should not be criminal.[391] It would have meant, for example, that a removal from the premises of an ordinary commercial bookseller would have been an offence. In addition, since the section protects things at risk because they are on display to the public, it is reasonable for that risk to be borne by the commercial exhibitor.

As it stands the limitation applies only where the collection is made or exhibited for *the purpose*[392] of sale or other commercial dealings. If then a commercial bookseller, for the purpose of encouraging local art, arranges exhibitions in a room of his bookshop to which the public are admitted, the removal by D of the paintings, or of any other article displayed or kept for display in his premises, would fall within the section whether or not it was available for sale.

386 Cf *Durkin* [1973] QB 786, [1973] 2 All ER 872, CA.

387 In this context 'permanently' means for an indefinite period: *Durkin* [1973] QB 786, [1973] 2 All ER 872, CA.

388 See Griew, para 5.08.

389 Above, p 716.

390 Note that if the owner admits the public to view the building as well as the collection D may commit the offence by removing anything displayed (including articles forming part of the collection) although the collection is exhibited for commercial purposes. Cf Smith, *Theft*, paras 7–12.

391 The clause as originally drafted would have excluded not only the case where the public was invited to view the contents for a commercial object, but also where the public was invited to view the building for a commercial object. The latter limitation was removed; cf n 390.

392 Presumably it is the dominant one that matters.

(ii) *Mens rea*

D must intend to remove the article from the building *or* its grounds. Dishonesty is not required but D would not be guilty of an offence if he removed an article in the belief (and clearly the test of D's belief is here subjective) that he had lawful authority or that the person entitled to give consent would have done so. Strictly it would be an offence for D to remove a statuette from the house to the garden because he thinks the setting better, provided D believes the person entitled to give consent would not have done so.

(b) Taking conveyances[393]

Because of the ease of tracing intact vehicles via their identification numbers, it is often difficult to establish that D intended permanently to deprive V when taking V's vehicle.[394] Thus, a specific offence criminalizing temporary deprivation of conveyances was created.[395] Section 12 of the Theft Act 1968 (as amended) now provides:

(1) Subject to subsections (5) and (6) below, a person shall be guilty of an offence if, without having the consent of the owner or other lawful authority, he takes any conveyance for his own or another's use or, knowing that any conveyance has been taken without such authority, drives it or allows himself to be carried in or on it.

(2) A person guilty of an offence under subsection (1) above shall . . . [be liable on summary conviction to a fine not exceeding level 5 on the standard scale, to imprisonment for a term not exceeding six months, or to both].

(3) [Repealed]

(4) If on the trial of an indictment for theft the jury are not satisfied that the accused committed theft, but it is proved that the accused committed an offence under subsection (1) above, the jury may find him guilty of the offence under subsection (1) [and if he is found guilty of it, he shall be liable as he would have been liable under subsection (2) above on summary conviction].

[Subs 4 deals with procedural issues for commencement of prosecution]

(5) Subsection (1) above shall not apply in relation to pedal cycles; but, subject to subsection (6) below, a person who, without having the consent of the owner or other lawful authority, takes a pedal cycle for his own or another's use, or rides a pedal cycle knowing it to have been taken without such authority, shall on summary conviction be liable to a fine not exceeding [level 3 on the standard scale].

(6) A person does not commit an offence under this section by anything done in the belief that he has lawful authority to do it or that he would have the owner's consent if the owner knew of his doing it and the circumstances of it.

(7) For purposes of this section –

393 See further in connection with the offences under s 12; below, p 726. For a practical view see *Wilkinson's Road Traffic Encyclopaedia* (21st edn, 2003) ch 15; and for a more broad-ranging socio-legal review of car crime see C. Corbett, *Car Crime* (2003).

394 See S. White, 'Taking the Joy out of Joy-Riding' [1980] Crim LR 609; Smith, *Theft*, ch 8; Griew, *Theft*, ch 6; Smith, *Property Offences*, ch 9.

395 Technically, charges of theft of the fuel might be brought.

(a) 'conveyance' means any conveyance constructed or adapted for the carriage of a person or persons whether by land, water or air, except that it does not include a conveyance constructed or adapted for use only under the control of a person not carried in or on it, and 'drive' shall be construed accordingly; and

(b) 'owner', in relation to a conveyance which is the subject of a hiring agreement or hire-purchase agreement, means the person in possession of the conveyance under that agreement.

(i) Taking for own or another's use

Taking

The offence is committed where D 'takes any conveyance for his own or another's use.' D 'takes' when he (i) assumes possession or control *and* (ii) moves the conveyance, or causes it to be moved. Where possession is assumed, abandoned and resumed there is a second taking.[396] It is not enough that D uses the conveyance for some purpose (say to sleep or shelter in it) since he must also take it. The offence can be completed only by some movement, however slight, of the conveyance.[397] The taking must be intentional.[398] In the case of a motor vehicle the taking will be most frequently accomplished by driving but the taking may be accomplished in some other way, as by pushing or towing or even by removing the conveyance on a transporter. In *Pearce*[399] D's conviction was upheld when he took an inflatable dinghy and drove off with it on his trailer; the court rejecting an argument that the offence could be committed only where D took the conveyance by moving it in its own medium. Nor was there a need for D to have been conveyed on the boat.

Although the offence is commonly regarded as one relating to temporary deprivation of use, the requirement of a physical taking demonstrates that the offence does not protect against deprivation generally. Thus, where D intentionally hides V's car keys, depriving V of the use of the vehicle, he does not commit the offence under s 12.[400]

For his own or another's use

The essence of the offence was thought by the Criminal Law Revision Committee to be 'stealing a ride'.[401] Strictly, however, D may steal a ride without committing this offence. A hitch-hiker who jumps on to the back of a passing lorry literally steals a ride but does not commit the offence since in no sense has he *taken* the vehicle for his own or another's use. So too if D, releases the handbrake of a car so that it runs down an incline (without his being on board), or releases a boat from its moorings so that it is carried away by the tide,

396 *DPP v Spriggs* [1994] RTR 1, [1993] Crim LR 622.

397 *Bogacki* [1973] QB 832, [1973] 2 All ER 864, CA. Cf *Miller* [1976] Crim LR 147, CA (boarding boat anticipating journey but no movement in fact), and *Diggin* (1980) 72 Cr App R 204, [1980] Crim LR 565, CA. Because the offence is now summary only there is no attempt charge, but the Criminal Attempt Act 1981, s 9 creates a specific offence of interference with a motor vehicle with the intention that an offence under s 12(1) shall be committed.

398 The offence was not committed where D accidentally put his foot on the accelerator in an automatic car: *Blayney v Knight* [1975] Crim LR 237.

399 [1973] Crim LR 321, CA.

400 The *actus reus* of theft does not of course require a physical moving of the vehicle. See also the discussion in relation to criminal damage below, p 892.

401 Cmnd 2977, para 84.

this would not fall within the section.[402] In neither case is the conveyance taken by D for his own or another's use.

Considering these last two examples the Court of Appeal in *Bow*[403] expressed the firm view that the reason why D was not guilty of an offence was that although the conveyance had been moved, it would not have been 'used' as a conveyance. In other words 'use' means, and means only, use as a conveyance. No doubt in the vast majority of cases D's purpose in taking the conveyance is to transport himself from one place to another, but it is not entirely clear that the offence is, or ought to be, confined to takings with that purpose. In *Pearce* it does not clearly appear why D took the dinghy but in *Marchant and McCallister*[404] the Court of Appeal assumed that the conviction was based on D's intended use of the dinghy as a conveyance and confirmed that taking a conveyance with intent to use it on some future occasion as a conveyance sufficed.[405] *Bow* suggests, and *Marchant* appears clearly to confirm, that if D in *Pearce* had some use other than as a conveyance in mind (for example, to use the dinghy as a paddling pool for his children) he could not be convicted under s 12. *Stokes*[406] is to the same effect. There it was held that D did not commit the offence where he pushed V's car around the corner to make V think it had been stolen.[407]

The courts have interpreted s 12(1) as though the words 'as a conveyance' had been inserted after 'use'. But on the face of the provision 'use' is capable of extending to uses other than use as a conveyance.[408] It should be recalled that this is provision was inserted to deal with the problem of temporary deprivations. The mischief aimed at is surely that the use of the conveyance is denied to V and it should not be significant to what use D puts it when he takes it.

Even if use is restricted to use as a conveyance any such use suffices. It is enough that D releases a boat from its moorings so that he can be carried downstream in it. So in *Bow*,[409] where D released the handbrake of V's car and coasted some 200 yards down a narrow road in order to enable him to remove his own obstructed car, it was conceded that no distinction could be drawn between driving the motor and allowing it to freewheel. But it was argued that D had not used the car as a conveyance, merely to move it as an obstruction. The court accepted that to push an obstructing vehicle a yard or two to get it out of the way would not involve the use of the vehicle as a conveyance,[410] but where the vehicle was necessarily used as a conveyance, the taker cannot be heard to say that it was not for that use. Yet D did not use V's car in order to convey himself from one end of the lane to the other. It so happened, that to remove it as an obstruction required its removal not for two yards but for 200. It is not easy to see why the distance involved should make all that difference if all D is doing is to remove a conveyance as an obstruction.[411]

402 Even though the owner temporarily loses the use of his car or boat and is equally inconvenienced.

403 (1977) 64 Cr App R 54, [1977] Crim LR 176 and commentary.

404 (1985) 80 Cr App R 361.

405 Equally a conditional intent (eg, an intent to use should it prove suitable) will suffice.

406 [1983] RTR 59, CA.

407 The outcome of the case may have been different had D got into the car and steered it round the corner.

408 See White, above, 611. 409 (1977) 64 Cr App R 54.

410 In such circumstances D might in any case have lawful authority for the removal, see below, p 724.

411 In *Bow* D was probably engaged in a poaching expedition and V's car had been deliberately placed to block D's egress. But if D finds a vehicle blocking the highway he is presumably entitled to remove it whether he is on his way to or from a crime.

Taking by unauthorized use

Thus far it has been assumed that D is not in possession or control of the conveyance but it may happen that D already has lawful possession or control and the question arises whether D can be said to 'take' the conveyance by using it in an unauthorized way. Suppose, for example, that D, authorized to use V's van in the course of V's business, uses the van to take his family to the seaside. It seems clear that under this section he may commit the offence for he now 'takes [the van] for his own . . . use'. D does not have the consent of V for the taking for his, D's, own use. This was the view taken by the Court of Appeal in *McGill*,[412] a case decided under s 217 of the Road Traffic Act 1960. D, given permission to use V's car to drive E to the station and on condition that he returned it immediately, subsequently drove it elsewhere and did not return it for some days. D's conviction for taking the car without the consent of the owner, in relation to his use after the trip to the station, was upheld. The same result must follow under this provision of the Theft Act even though there is no requirement for driving away and where the emphasis is squarely placed on taking 'for his own or another's use'. So in *McKnight v Davies*[413] the conviction of a lorry driver was upheld when instead of returning the lorry to the depot at the end of the working day he used it for his own purposes and did not return it till the early hours of the following morning. It would seem that an unauthorized use in terms of either the destination involved or time of taking,[414] or duration will constitute the offence.

McGill and *McKnight v Davies* were cases where the use by D was plainly outside the scope of the terms of the bailment or the terms of the employment so there was no difficulty in finding a taking for D's own use. It is thought, however, that not every deviation by a bailee from the terms of the bailment, or of an employee from the terms of his employment, would constitute a taking for his own use. There must be a use that is sufficiently at variance with the terms of the contract to demonstrate that D has replaced use on behalf of another by use on his own behalf.[415] But there is an exception in the case of a hirer under a hire-purchase agreement. His unauthorized use cannot amount to an offence because by s 12(7) he is treated as owner for the purposes of the section.

(ii) Without owner's consent or lawful authority

The ordinary run of cases where D takes V's vehicle without reference to V presents no problem. It follows from the discussion in the previous paragraph that where D has obtained V's permission to use the vehicle for a particular purpose and for a given time, D may be convicted of the offence if he uses it beyond that time for a different purpose: *McGill*.[416] There is no difficulty in such a case in saying that D has taken the vehicle for his own use, and that particular use is clearly one to which V has not consented.

412 [1970] RTR 209, CA. 413 [1974] RTR 4, DC.

414 *Wibberley* [1966] 2 QB 214, [1965] 3 All ER 718, CCA.

415 'Not every brief, unauthorized diversion from his proper route by an employee in the course of his working day will necessarily involve a "taking" of the vehicle for his own use', *McKnight v Davies* [1974] RTR 4 at 8, per Lord Widgery CJ. See also *Wibberley* [1966] 2 QB 214, [1965] 3 All ER 718, CCA; *Phipps* [1970] RTR 209, CA. In determining whether an employee has taken his employers' vehicle it would seem proper to consider whether for civil purposes D is acting in the course of his employment.

416 [1970] RTR 209, CA; above.

Consent by fraud

McGill is a clear case. Suppose, however, that D made some false representation to induce V to allow him to take the car. The falsity might relate to (i) some attribute of D (for example, his being licensed to drive); (ii) some fundamental issue such as D's identity; or, (iii) D's purpose in taking the vehicle.

Taking the first of these issues, what if D had falsely represented that he was licensed to drive in order to borrow V's car for the trip to the station? There is perhaps no compelling reason why D should not be guilty of the offence since he knows perfectly well that V has 'consented' only because he has been misled. But on a strict interpretation of the section all that is required is that V should have consented to D taking the car for the trip to the station (the taking for D's own use) and to this V may be said to have consented even though he would never have consented had he known that D was unlicensed. The point arose in *Whittaker v Campbell.*[417] D and E required a vehicle to transport goods but D was not licensed to drive and E had only a provisional licence. Somehow they came into possession of T's licence and D, representing himself as T, hired a vehicle from V. Their convictions for taking a vehicle without consent were quashed. The court thought that while there might be a taking without consent where the owner is by force compelled to part with possession,[418] where he is induced to do so by fraud it could not be said 'in commonsense terms' that he had not consented to the taking. Distinguishing between agreements induced by force and fraud in this manner is at odds with the general approach of the criminal law and undermines the principle that consent necessarily involves an agreement made freely, and which is based on adequate accurate information. On the other hand, the broad commonsense approach to consent is less problematic in this context given the mischief at which the section is aimed.

The court in *Whitaker v Campbell* also considered the second issue – whether the offence would be committed where the fraud is such as to induce a 'fundamental mistake'. The court thought that it would not make sense, having regard to the mischief at which the offence was aimed, to have D's liability turn upon whether the transaction was voidable for fraud or void for mistake. That distinction is one that presents complexity in civil law. Moreover, it does not sit easily with the criminal law's approach to the concept of consent. Suppose that D telephones V and impersonates V's brother, thereby inducing V to agree the loan of his car to his brother and to leave the keys in an accessible spot while V is out of town. If D then avails himself of this trick to take possession of the car while V is away, it would be an astonishing conclusion to say that V had consented to D taking his car. It is submitted that the issue of consent by fraud under s 12 deserves reconsideration.[419]

As for the third problem of falsity, in *Whittaker v Campbell* there was no suggestion of any misrepresentation as to the use to which D and E proposed to put the vehicle and their actual use was within the terms of the hire.[420] Suppose, however, that D obtains

417 [1984] QB 318, [1983] 3 All ER 582, DC.

418 See *Hogdan* [1962] Crim LR 563.

419 Cf Smith, *Property Offences*, paras 9–23.

420 In *Singh v Rathour (Northern Star Insurance Co Ltd, third party)* [1988] 2 All ER 16, CA, a civil case where the issue was whether D was insured under his policy which covered him when driving any vehicle 'provided he had the consent of the owner', it was held that D did not have the consent of the owner where he was aware that the consent given did not extend to the use to which he put the vehicle. See J. Birds, 'Consent of the Owner under a Motor Policy' [1998] J Bus Law 421.

possession by describing to V a use that he knows V will consent to while proposing to use the vehicle for a use to which he knows V would not consent. D might, for example, secure V's consent to the use of his vehicle for the transportation of goods from Leeds to London knowing that V would not consent had he known that the goods were stolen. The case is essentially indistinguishable from *Whittaker v Campbell.* V has consented to the use of his vehicle for that journey though he would not have agreed to incur criminal liability as a handler of stolen goods.

Suppose, though, that D's purpose is not to drive to London and back but to take the vehicle on a fortnight's holiday to the south of France. The point arose in *Peart.*[421] D persuaded V to lend him a van by pretending that he needed it for an urgent appointment in Alnwick and that he would return it by 7.30 pm. In fact D wanted the van for a journey to Burnley where he was found with the van by the police at 9.00 pm, and he knew all along that V would not have consented to this use. It was held, quashing D's conviction, that V's consent was not vitiated by the deception since V had merely been deceived as to *the purpose* for which the car was to be used and reliance was placed on this decision by the court in *Whittaker v Campbell.*

But there are difficulties with *Peart.* By reason of the direction given to the jury by the trial judge, the Court of Appeal had to consider the position at the time when the van was borrowed in the afternoon:

> There was no issue left to [the jury] whether, in this particular case, there could have been a fresh taking . . . at some time after it was originally taken away at 2.30 pm The consent which has to be considered is thus a consent at the time of taking possession of the van with licence to drive and use it.[422]

It seems then that even if he did not commit an offence at the time of the taking he would, like the defendants in *McGill* and *McKnight v Davies,*[423] have done so as soon as he departed from the Alnwick road and set course for Burnley.

There is, however, a difference. In *McGill* and *McKnight v Davies* there was no evidence that the defendants had the unauthorized use in mind when they obtained possession but that proof was not lacking in *Peart* – D frankly admitted it – and it is submitted the case ought to be reconsidered. Given the use for a journey to which V had consented, D *took* it for a journey for which no consent was given. As a practical matter of evidence it will often be necessary to prove a departure from the stated use in order to prove that D intended to use the vehicle in other than the authorized way but this cannot affect the substantive criminal law.

Lawful authority

D commits no offence where he takes a vehicle, even without the consent of the owner, when acting under 'other lawful authority'. This is appropriate to cover the growing number of cases where local authorities or the police are authorized under various statutory powers to remove vehicles. No doubt D would be acting lawfully in moving V's

421 [1970] 2 QB 672, [1970] 2 All ER 823, CA.

422 [1970] 2 All ER 823 at 824. It seems surprising that the proviso which was then available to the Court of Appeal was not applied.

423 Above, p 722.

vehicle a few yards so that he can obtain access to the highway for his own vehicle, even though he may know that V does not consent to the removal.[424]

It may fairly be assumed that general defences such as self-defence and duress are available on a charge of this offence.

(iii) Conveyance

'Conveyance' as defined by s 12(7)(a) has been interpreted to mean a mechanical contrivance of some kind. While it includes conveyances such as cars and motor-cycles, it does not include horses;[425] horses are clearly not constructed, though they may be suitable, for the carriage of persons, and the argument that they might be 'adapted' by the use of halter and bridle was rejected.

Because the essence of the offence was thought to be stealing a ride,[426] conveyance is defined, in effect, to exclude conveyances that are not meant for riding.[427] Thus, though it would be an offence to take an aircraft, hovercraft or railway engine, it is not an offence within this section to take a handcart or certain kinds of lawnmower which, though power driven, are operated by a person who is not carried in or on it.

(iv) Driving or being carried

Section 12 creates a second version of the offence to deal with the person who allows himself to be carried or who himself drives a vehicle which has already been taken, but who might not be caught by ordinary principles of accessorial liability since he might not have been a party to the taking.

Where D takes a conveyance without consent or other lawful authority, it is an offence for E, knowing the conveyance has been so taken, to drive it or allow himself to be carried in or on it. A hitch-hiker would therefore not be guilty of an offence where, unknown to him, the driver is using his employer's van, contrary to his instructions, to go to Blackpool for the day. If the driver tells the hitch-hiker that he is so using the van then the hitch-hiker will be liable if he allows himself to be carried further.[428] E's mere presence in or on the conveyance, knowing that it has been taken without consent or authority, does not suffice unless he allows himself to be 'carried' in or on it and this requires some movement of the conveyance.[429]

It could happen that D believes he has authority to take the conveyance but E knows he has not. In such a case E would be guilty of an offence since he knows it was taken without authority. And no doubt E knows the conveyance has been taken without authority, and may be convicted under this provision, though he knows that D has in fact stolen the conveyance.[430]

424 But see *Bow* (1977) 64 Cr App R 54, CA, above, p 721.

425 *Neal v Gribble* (1978) 68 Cr App R 9, [1978] RTR 409.

426 Cf Cmnd 2977, para 84. Earlier (para 82) the Committee seemed to have viewed the mischief of the offence as the danger, loss and inconvenience which often result from it. See HL, vol 290, col 141.

427 But on this see above, p 721.

428 *Boldizsar v Knight* [1980] Crim LR 653, DC. For more detailed analysis see Smith, *Theft*, paras 8–13. There are problems of proof where the prosecution seek to rely on D informing E that the vehicle has been taken: *Francis* [1982] Crim LR 694.

429 *Miller* [1976] Crim LR 147, CA; *Diggin* (1980) 72 Cr App R 204, [1981] RTR 83, CA.

430 Cf *Tolley v Giddings* [1964] 2 QB 354, [1964] 1 All ER 201, DC.

(v) Pedal cycles

Section 12(5) creates an offence of taking pedal cycles, which has broadly similar elements to the offence under s 12(1). A small difference is that the offence under s 12(5) is not committed by one who allows himself to be carried on the cycle knowing that it has been taken without authority. And, of course, the offence is summary only.[431]

(vi) *Mens rea*

Section 12(6) provides that a person does not commit an offence by anything done in the belief that he has lawful authority to do it or that the owner would have consented. The test of belief appears to be subjective. If D honestly believes that V has consented to his use of V's car, it is not relevant to enquire whether V did in fact consent or whether V would have consented had he known of the circumstances – for example, that D was uninsured,[432] or even that D was unlicensed to drive. If D takes a vehicle 'without having the consent of the owner' and does not believe that the owner would have consented had he known of the taking, he may be convicted though the owner subsequently says that he would have consented;[433] the offence is constituted not by taking a conveyance without the owner's consent, but in taking it without *having* the consent of the owner.

If D takes a conveyance not caring whether the owner would or would not have consented, it would seem that he may be convicted for, in such a case, he does not *believe* that the owner would have consented.[434] But where E is charged with driving or allowing himself to be carried in a conveyance taken by D, it must be shown that E *knew* that D had taken the conveyance without authority; presumably wilful blindness on E's part will suffice but it may be[435] that nothing short of actual knowledge will suffice. Hence E would be acquitted where he thinks it quite possible that D might have taken the vehicle without authority but makes no enquiries to ascertain whether this is so or not.

Taking a conveyance has been held to be a crime of basic intent so that evidence of intoxication is not relevant as tending to show that D lacked *mens rea*.[436] Arguably, where D's belief as to the consent of the owner is based on a mistake induced by voluntary intoxication he can rely on that mistake.[437]

(c) Aggravated vehicle taking[438]

The so-called 'joyrider' (or 'twocker') under s 12 is liable to relatively limited punishments. The taker is additionally liable for any offence involved in taking the vehicle (most obviously criminal damage caused in making access to the conveyance and in interfering with the locks and the electrics in order to get it started) and the driver, whether or not he

[431] Thus there can be no attempt charge.

[432] *Clotworthy* [1981] RTR 477, CA.

[433] *Ambler* [1979] RTR 217, CA.

[434] Cf the discussion of recklessness above, Ch 5.

[435] Cf *Tolley v Giddings* [1964] 2 QB 354, [1964] 1 All ER 201. Cf the offence of handling; below, Ch 22.

[436] *MacPherson* [1973] RTR 157, CA; *Gannon* (1988) 87 Cr App R 254, CA. For a contrary view see White, above.

[437] By analogy with the decision in *Jaggard v Dickinson* [1981] QB 527, DC, decided under s 5(2) of the Criminal Damage Act 1971 which uses similar terms. See Griew, para 6.20. G. Williams is heavily critical of *Gannon*, 'Two Nocturnal Blunders' (1990) 140 NLJ 1564.

[438] See J. N. Spencer, 'The Aggravated Vehicle Taking Act 1992' [1992] Crim LR 69.

is the original taker, is liable for any offence committed whilst driving the vehicle (for example, driving whilst uninsured, careless driving, dangerous driving). And, of course, a person who allows himself to be carried in or on a conveyance may be liable as a secondary party to these further offences under the principles which govern aiding and abetting.[439]

It might be thought therefore that s 12 was entirely adequate to deal with the taker, those who subsequently drive the taken conveyance and those who allow themselves to be carried in or on it. In the normal case the fine of £5,000 and/or six months' imprisonment would seem adequate. In the abnormal case where the driver drives dangerously, or kills whilst driving dangerously, a count can be added for that and again the punishment (imprisonment in this case) would seem to be adequate. But the abnormal case became not so abnormal in the early 1990s. The taking of motor vehicles increased to an extent that it was described as epidemic. As the activity increased, so did the risks. Youngsters (usually male) use the vehicles they have taken to demonstrate their driving 'skills' or become involved in high-speed chases when pursued by the police. The hazards of either are obvious. Even in the face of this epidemic, it might be argued that s 12 and the range of driving offences and ordinary criminal charges for damage and injury inflicted were adequate in the sense that the activity would always be capable of being punished and the penalties provided seemed appropriate.[440]

There was an additional problem, in many cases the taking was performed by a group, and the vehicle was then damaged or injury inflicted, but it was difficult to prove whether it was D or E or F who damaged the vehicle or caused the injury, One or more of them was able to claim that the damage was done before he joined the enterprise. And where, as not infrequently happens, the vehicle is found burned out, all three would say that this must have been done by someone else after they had abandoned the vehicle.

It was to deal with all of these problems, and what was seen as a rapidly growing social menace, that s 12A of the Theft Act 1968, was inserted by the Aggravated Vehicle-Taking Act 1992. It provides:

> 12A. – (1) Subject to subsection (3) below, a person is guilty of aggravated taking of a vehicle if –
>
> (a) he commits an offence under section 12 (1) above (in this section referred to as a 'basic offence') in relation to a mechanically propelled vehicle; and
>
> (b) it is proved that, at any time after the vehicle was unlawfully taken (whether by him or another) and before it was recovered, the vehicle was driven, or injury or damage was caused, in one or more of the circumstances set out in paragraphs (a) to (d) of subsection (2) below.
>
> (2) The circumstances referred to in subsection (1)(b) above are –
>
> (a) that the vehicle was driven dangerously on a road or other public place;
>
> (b) that, owing to the driving of the vehicle, an accident occurred by which injury was caused to any person;
>
> (c) that, owing to the driving of the vehicle, an accident occurred by which damage was caused to any property, other than the vehicle;

439 Above, Ch 8.

440 It is not suggested that the answer or solution lies in the penalty, merely that the penalty is adequate in relation to the crime. The answer lies in foolproof (or is it expert-proof?) immobilizing devices.

(d) that damage was caused to the vehicle.

(3) A person is not guilty of an offence under this section if he proves that, as regards any such proven driving, injury or damage as is referred to in subsection (1)(b) above, either –

(a) the driving, accident or damage referred to in subsection (2) above occurred before he committed the basic offence; or

(b) he was neither in nor on nor in the immediate vicinity of the vehicle when that driving, accident or damage occurred.

(4) A person guilty of an offence under this section shall be liable on conviction on indictment to imprisonment for a term not exceeding two years or, if it is proved that, in circumstances falling within subsection (2)(b) above, the accident caused the death of the person concerned, fourteen years.[441]

(5) If a person who is charged with an offence under this section is found not guilty of that offence but it is proved that he committed a basic offence, he may be convicted of the basic offence.

Since there is a different maximum sentence for those cases in which death results there are technically two offences created by the section.[442] The offences are draconian, and have features that depart markedly from the principles that ordinarily govern liability at least for serious crimes.

The prosecution must first prove that D has committed the basic offence (that is, the offence under s 12(1) of the 1968 Act which is described above) in relation to a mechanically propelled vehicle – the offence does not apply to conveyances generally.

Secondly, the prosecution must prove that at any time after the vehicle was unlawfully taken (proof of the identity of the taker is not required) and before it was recovered (that is, restored to the owner or other lawful custody: s 12A(8)) the vehicle was driven or injury or damage was caused in one or more of the circumstances specified in s 12A(2). These circumstances, apart from dangerous driving which requires a measure of fault,[443] require no proof of fault on the part of D, or D and others involved in the enterprise, merely that either injury to the person or damage to property was owing to the driving,[444] or that damage was caused to the vehicle taken, whether by driving or not.[445] There is therefore strict liability in respect of all these consequences. D's driving might be impeccable, but he will not escape liability if the injury damage or death arises. Moreover, each of the participants in the enterprise commits the offence though he was not driving the vehicle. The section creates an offence of guilt by association.

So if D and E commit the basic offence (s 12) each of them is liable if either one of them causes injury or damage when driving the vehicle. More remarkably, if during the enterprise D chooses to damage the vehicle by slashing the seats, E commits the offence under s 12A though he does not abet D in slashing the seats or even if E tries to dissuade

441 Criminal Justice Act 2003, s 285(1).

442 Such should therefore be charged separately: *Courtie* [1984] AC 463; *Sherwood* [1995] RTR 60.

443 See below, Ch 28.

444 The Court of Appeal in *Marsh* [1997] 1 Cr App R 67 held that the words 'owing to the driving of the vehicle' were plain and simple and no gloss ought to be provided by referring the jury to the manner of the driving. See [1997] Crim LR 205 and comment. If D has used the car as a weapon, he will still be caught by the section: accident includes deliberate causing of injury. *B* [2005] Crim LR (July).

445 *Dawes v DPP* [1995] 1 Cr App R 65 at 72, 73.

D from so doing.[446] This highlights the draconian nature of the provision. Even if E is no longer in the vehicle, he may be walking away from it when D decides to set fire to it. E is liable provided he is still 'in the immediate vicinity' of the vehicle. Not only does the offence create guilt by association but guilt by approximation.

Section 12A(3) deals with the problem of proof identified above. The prosecution may prove, or D may admit, that D committed the basic offence but D may claim that he had left the enterprise before the injury or damage was done or that he joined the enterprise after the injury or damage had been done. In such circumstances it is for D to prove on the balance of probability that the dangerous driving or the accident or the damage took place before he committed the basic offence; or that, having committed the basic offence, he was no longer in nor on nor in the immediate vicinity of the vehicle when one of those events took place.

The increasingly prevalent activity known as 'car jacking' – where D causes V to stop his car and D then forcibly ejects V from the car and drives V's vehicle away – is more appropriately prosecuted by offences of theft, robbery, offences against the person, etc. In particular, in cases where V is caused to stop by D's minor collision with V's vehicle, aggravated vehicle taking will not be a suitable charge because the damage will have occurred prior to the taking.

It is unclear whether an attempt to commit aggravated vehicle taking is an offence. The s 12A offence requires proof of the basic offence under s 12 which is triable summarily only (and therefore can not be the subject of an attempt charge), but the s 12A offence itself is triable either way. It is submitted that in an appropriate case a charge of attempt would be available, as where D is apprehended trying to break into a high powered vehicle and admits that his intention was to take it for an evenings 'racing' against his friends' car.

5. Abstracting electricity

It has been shown[447] why the CLRC thought it necessary to make special provision for electricity and the view that electricity is not property capable of being appropriated has been confirmed by the courts.[448] Section 13 of the Theft Act 1968 accordingly provides:

> A person who dishonestly uses without due authority, or dishonestly causes to be wasted or diverted, any electricity shall on conviction on indictment be liable to imprisonment for a term not exceeding five years.

This provision will ordinarily be applied to the case where D dishonestly[449] uses some

446 'A passenger may be liable even though the passenger has protested at the driving which has caused damage to the vehicle': *Dawes v DPP* [1995] 1 Cr App R 65 at 72 per Kennedy LJ. See also *Wiggins* [2001] RTR 37 on the sentencing implications in such cases.

447 Above, p 670. See further Griew, paras 2.162–2.165; Williams, TBCL (2nd edn, 1983), 736–737; Smith, *Theft*, ch 9.

448 *Low v Blease* [1975] Crim LR 513, DC. Cf *Flack v Baldry* [1988] 1 All ER 412, [1988] 1 WLR 214, treating electricity as a 'noxious thing' for the purposes of Firearms Act 1968, s 5(1)(b).

449 See *Boggeln v Williams* [1978] 2 All ER 1061, [1978] Crim LR 242, DC, above, p 697. Care must be taken when the offence alleged is against a number of occupants of a property in which the meter has been bypassed – *Hoar and Hoar* [1992] Crim LR 606; *Collins and Fox v Chief Constable of Merseyside* [1988] Crim LR 247.

device to by-pass his electricity meter, but beyond that it is capable of some curious applications.[450] Strictly there might be an offence under this section where D borrows an electrically driven vehicle such as a milk float, golf buggy or disabled- person's scooter, though there would be no theft of the vehicle nor an offence of taking a conveyance under s 12.[451] But proceedings under s 13 in such a case are perhaps very unlikely; there might be some reluctance to prosecute when the substance of what D does is not criminal even though there is technically some incidental offence.[452] Moreover, in this sort of situation, it may be that D does not advert to the fact that he is causing the electricity to be used, and thus lacks the necessary *mens rea*.

It was perhaps for these reasons that the law was amended by the Theft Act 1968[453] to create a specific offence of dishonestly using a communication system with intent to avoid payment.[454] This gets at the substance of the mischief and avoids any difficulty of D claiming that he had not realized that use of the device would involve abstracting electricity. It also provides an appropriately labelled charge and avoids the prosecution appearing strained.

The partial definition of dishonesty in s 2 of the Act does not apply. The test of dishonesty in *Ghosh* does.[455] Although it has been held in cases of electricity meter tampering that the defendant must be shown to have an intention not to pay, this is too generous to the defence; it is one factor to be considered in the overall question of dishonesty.[456]

It is enough under s 13 that D dishonestly causes electricity to be wasted or diverted; he need not be shown to have made any use of the electricity for himself. An employee who out of spite for his employer puts on all the lighting and heating appliances in the office would commit the offence, but a fellow employee, or even a stranger, who, knowing what D has done, chooses to stay in the office to enjoy the warmth, would not: 'use' implies some consumption of electricity which would not occur but for the accused's acts.[457]

The offence extends only to the abstraction of electricity, whether from the mains or battery source. Gas and water if dishonestly appropriated can form the subject of a theft charge. Despite the upsurge in using more environmentally friendly energy sources (solar

450 Cf Smith, *Theft*, paras 9–01 to 9–04. It has been prosecuted where, eg, D has wired his house up to the nearby street lamp to run appliances free, and where D has entered premises as a trespasser and called a premium rate sex chat line: *P* (2000) 11 Aug, CA, No 0003586 Y5.

451 See above.

452 Prosecutions have been brought for stealing the petrol consumed where D has borrowed a motor vehicle, but this was never regarded as satisfactory and the offence of taking motor vehicles was introduced. Cf *Low v Blease*, above, n 450, where it was apparently assumed that a dishonest user of a telephone may commit the offence under s 13.

453 Sch 2, Part 1, para 8, see now Communications Act 2003, s 125: dishonestly obtaining an electronic communications service with intent to avoid payment of a charge applicable to that service. But this does not cover 999 calls since no payment is involved; it is, however, an offence under s 5(2) of the Criminal Law Act 1967 to cause any wasteful employment of the police.

454 Punishable, on summary conviction, by six months' imprisonment and/or a fine not exceeding the statutory maximum; and, on indictment, by two years' imprisonment. As to the intent, cf *Corbyn v Saunders* [1978] Crim LR 169, DC.

455 *R v Melwani* [1989] Crim LR 565, CA.

456 See *Collins and Fox v Chief Constable of Merseyside* [1988] Crim LR 247; Griew, para 2.164.

457 This sentence was approved in *McReadie and Tume* (1992) 96 Cr App R 143,CA, [1992] Crim LR 872.

and wind, etc) the s 13 offence only protects against the dishonest abstraction of these forms of power once converted. There are strong policy arguments for saying that if D prevents V's solar panels from working by blocking the sun over his property or deprives V's turbines of wind, V's remedy should be through the civil law, and not the criminal law.

Parliament has created specific offences to deal with dishonesty in relation to particular conduct involving electronic equipment including, for example, receiving programmes broadcast via satellite and cable,[458] and reprogramming mobile phone SIM cards.[459]

6. Making off without payment[460]

By s 3 of the Theft Act 1978:

(1) Subject to subsection (3) below, a person who, knowing that payment on the spot for any goods supplied or service done is required or expected from him, dishonestly makes off without having paid as required or expected and with intent to avoid payment of the amount due shall be guilty of an offence.

(2) For purposes of this section 'payment on the spot' includes payment at the time of collecting goods on which work has been done or in respect of which service has been provided.

(3) Subsection (1) above shall not apply where the supply of the goods or the doing of the service is contrary to law, or where the service done is such that payment is not legally enforceable.

(4) Any person may arrest without warrant anyone who is, or whom he, with reasonable cause, suspects to be, committing or attempting to commit an offence under this section.

By s 4 the offence, which is triable either way, is punishable on summary conviction by imprisonment and/or a fine not exceeding the prescribed maximum (presently £5,000), and on indictment by imprisonment for a term not exceeding two years and/or a fine.

This offence aims to deal in a simple and straightforward way with conduct that was commonly called 'bilking'. It deals with the person who, having consumed a meal in a restaurant, or filled the tank of the car with petrol, or reached their destination in a taxi, decamps without paying. For all their factual simplicity, as we will see,[461] these cases create considerable difficulties if prosecuted as theft or deception. There are no such difficulties under s 3. There is no requirement whatever under this section that D's conduct should amount to theft or deception or even that he has practiced any deception at all. There is no requirement to prove that D was dishonest when he ordered

[458] See the Copyright Designs and Patents Act 1988, s 297(1) and s 297A inserted by the Conditional Access (Unauthorized Decoders) Regs 2000, SI 1175.

[459] Mobile Telephones (Re-programming) Act 2000.

[460] See J. Spencer, 'The Theft Act 1978' [1979] Crim LR 24, 35; G. Syrota, 'Annotations to Theft Act 1978' in *Current Law Statutes* 1978; (1978) 42 MLR 301, 304. Smith, *Theft*, ch 5; Griew, ch 13; Smith, *Property Offences*, ch 20.

[461] See, eg, *DPP v Ray* [1974] AC 370, [1973] 3 All ER 131, HL, below, p 746; *Edwards v Ddin* [1976] 3 All ER 705, [1976] 1 WLR 942.

the meal or began to fill his car; it is sufficient if the dishonesty occurs at the point of making off.

It might be noted that the offence creates an exception to the general principle that it is not an offence dishonestly to avoid the payment of a debt.[462] This might be thought to pose a potential problem of over criminalizing. The exception is, however, limited and understandable. In the ordinary case a dishonest debtor (who can be traced) can be coerced into payment via civil remedies without resort to criminal sanctions; where bilking is involved it is usually a matter of enforcement on the spot or never since the person becomes difficult if not impossible to trace. Hence also by s 3(4) a power of arrest is conferred.[463] Without this, the enforcement of the law would be jeopardized.

(a) Makes off

The term 'makes off' might be thought of as having a pejorative connotation implying some requirement of stealth in the manner of the person making off. Certainly the offence extends to such cases (the diner who waits till the manager leaves the room or decamps via the cloakroom window) but it cannot be confined to such cases. A motorist who brazenly drives off after filling his tank with petrol at the filling station is properly said to make off though his act is done openly and without stealth; so too, a heavyweight boxer whose departure cannot be prevented by a timorous restaurant owner.[464]

'Makes off' appears to mean simply that D leaves one place (the place where the payment is required) for another place. Nor does the offence necessarily require that D should have 'made off' from V's premises; the spot from which D makes off is simply the place where payment is required[465] and this may be a newsvendor's stand or an ice-cream van on the highway. In the case of a taxi ride it will be the agreed destination. If D has not left the first place he has not made off but if he is in the process of leaving there may be an attempt.[466] Presumably, this element of the *actus reus* continues for such time as D can be said to be in the process of 'making off'.[467]

If D leaves with V's consent it may be more difficult to say that D has made off. Suppose that D, having determined never to pay, gives his correct name and address to V and is allowed to go. It would be a strained reading of the section to say that D had made off; D has left without paying but the offence requires something more than that. A more difficult case is that where E, who also intends never to pay, gives a false name and address to V and is allowed to go. The two cases differ in that D can be traced and coerced into payment under the civil law while E cannot be traced at all. If D leaves with V's consent it may be more difficult to say that D has made off. Spencer[468] argues that the difference between these cases is material. The mischief aimed at by this section, he argues, is the

462 See further G. H. Treitel, 'Contract and Crime', in P. Glazebrook (ed), *Reshaping the Criminal Law* (1978), 89.

463 The offence carries only a maximum two-year sentence and is not automatically arrestable.

464 See F. Bennion, 'Letter to the Editor' [1980] Crim LR 670.

465 Payment may be legitimately required at more than one spot: *Moberly v Allsop* [1992] COD 190, 156 JP 514, DC. See also *Aziz* [1993] Crim LR 708.

466 *Brooks and Brooks* (1982) 76 Cr App R 66, [1983] Crim LR 188, CA; making off, said the court, 'may be an exercise accompanied by the sound of trumpets or a silent stealing away after the folding of tents'.

467 This point will be important for the purposes of determining the lawfulness of arrests: *Drameh* [1983] Crim LR 322.

468 [1983] Crim LR 573.

bilking customer who cannot be traced and he supports this by reference to the power of arrest afforded V; it would be highly undesirable if V could arrest a customer of whose identity he is aware, that power being required for the unidentifiable bilker.

Spencer's argument that the applicability of the offence turns on the traceability of the bilker has force, but is not easy to square with the language of s 3. It can lead to some illogical results. For example, assume that F is V's best customer of many years' standing. One day F determines not to pay and decamps from the premises via the toilet window. All the elements of the offence appear to be present unless it is to be said that F did not make off. It may puzzle us all to wonder why F should have thought that he could get away with his conduct but he seems clearly to have made off. A customer in a wheelchair would surely make off if he decamps without paying though he does not at all fancy his chances of outpacing the restaurateur.[469] If the untraceability of D was the touchstone of the offence, it is arguable that the offence would then fail to protect the proprietor (for example, the restaurant owner) who knows who D is, but is unlikely to pursue D's small debt via the civil courts.[470] The CLRC,[471] regarded the purpose of the offence as to protect legitimate business.

Section 3 does not, on a natural interpretation, mean that D does not make off if he gives a correct identification but E does make off it he gives a false one. Suppose in the latter case that V orders a taxi for E and bids him a cheery farewell from the hotel lobby. Can it really be said that E has made off?[472]

If, however, V permits D to leave the spot where payment is required for a purely temporary purpose (for example to answer a telephone call or to collect his wallet from his overcoat which he has deposited in the cloakroom) expecting him to return to settle up, it is submitted that D commits the offence if he then decamps. In such cases V has not consented to D leaving without paying, quite the contrary, he has consented to D facilitating payment. So where V, a taxi driver, permits D to leave so that D, as he claims, may go into his house to get the fare it would appear that D, if he then decamps, has made off within the meaning of this section.

The Home Office has recently rejected a reform proposal which would have extended the offence to include cases where D acts with intent to defer payment.

(b) Goods supplied or service done

The offence requires that the goods[473] be *supplied* or that a service be *done*. Most obviously goods are supplied where V delivers them to D but the offence cannot be limited only to cases of delivery by V. Petrol is clearly supplied to D at a self-service filling station though D supplies himself and, by the same token, goods taken from the shelves in a self-service store are supplied.[474] Supplied in this context connotes goods proffered by V and accordingly taken by D. Hence it would not be an offence under this section (though

[469] For further views on this difficult aspect of the offence see Williams, TBCL, 878; F. Bennion, Letter, 'The Drafting of Section 3 of the Theft Act 1978' [1980] Crim LR 670; Letters [1983] Crim LR 205, 574; Griew, paras 13–16.

[470] See Griew, paras 13–16. [471] Cmnd 6733, para 19.

[472] Cf *Hammond* [1982] Crim LR 611, below, p 735.

[473] As defined in s 34 of the 1968 Act, applicable to the 1978 Act by s 5(2).

[474] *Contra* A. T. H. Smith, 'Shoplifting and the Theft Acts' [1981] Crim LR 586. Cf Griew, para 13.07; Smith, *Theft*, para 5.03.

it may be theft) for D to take goods in a shop which is not self-service; such goods are not proffered until tendered by V or his assistant. It is thought that goods may be supplied though D has a dishonest intent from the outset and accordingly steals the goods; it can hardly have been intended that theft and making off should be mutually exclusive since the effect of that would create difficulties for prosecutors.

Where 'service' is concerned the service must be 'done'. Obvious examples of a service done are the provision of hotel accommodation or a meal in a restaurant but it will also apply to the collection of goods, such as clothes, shoes or cars, on which work (repair etc) has been done. A service may be done (as goods may be supplied) though nothing is physically done by V other than proffering the service of which D takes advantage, as where D is permitted to park his car on V's lot.

There is no definition of 'service' in s 3 as there is of 'services' in s 2 of the 1978 Act but it is not easy to see that any difference of significance was intended and reference may be made to the discussion below.

(c) Unenforceable debts

The offence under s 3, unlike the offence under s 1 of the 1978 Act, cannot be committed where the supply of the goods or the doing of the service is contrary to law; or where the service done is such that payment is not legally enforceable. The reason for the distinction is that while the aim of s 1 is to punish fraud, the aim of s 3, as noted is to protect legitimate business. Thus it is no offence for D to make off from a brothel without paying.

Whether a supply of goods or services is contrary to law or whether payment for a service is not legally enforceable involves a consideration of the general law and cannot be detailed here.[475] But the distinction that s 3 makes may be illustrated by reference to transactions entered into by a minor.[476] If a landlord supplies 'intoxicating liquor' to a minor the transaction is contrary to law and the minor commits no offence in making off without payment. If the minor has a service provided which is not a 'necessary' one (say flying lessons) he commits no offence in making off since payment for that service is not legally enforceable. If the minor is supplied with non-necessary goods (say 11 fancy waistcoats) and makes off he commits the offence; while payment for the waistcoats is not legally enforceable, the supply of these *goods* is not contrary to law.

The courts do not seem to have been troubled by defence claims that although performance of the contract was not contrary to law, some collateral aspect of V's conduct in the supply of the goods or services was contrary to law and therefore unprotected by s 3. It was anticipated by some that this would give rise to problems in cases such as D bilking on the unlicensed taxi driver.[477]

(d) Without having paid as required or expected

It is implicit in the section that V requires or expects payment on the spot and that the payment is due in fact and law. If a taxi driver, in the course of a journey, commits a

[475] For a general review of the relationship and consideration of s 3 see G. Trietel, 'Contract and Crime', in C. Tapper (ed), *Crime Proof and Punishment: Essays in Memory of Sir Rupert Cross* (1981), 81.

[476] Cf P. Rowlands, 'Minors: Can they make off without payment' (1981) JP 410: cf Smith, *Property Offences*, para 20–69.

[477] See Griew, para 13–10.

breach of contract entitling his passenger to rescind the contract, the passenger does not commit an offence by making off.[478] Where the money is due, does a person who gives a worthless cheque in 'payment' of the debt commit the offence? Since s 2(3) applies only to the offence under s 2(1)(b) it is arguable that, for the purposes of other offences under the 1978 Act, a person who takes a cheque by way of conditional satisfaction of a pre-existing liability is to be treated as being paid.[479] As D would in such circumstances be guilty of the more serious offence under s 2(1)(b), the question may not be of great importance. In the one reported case (although only at first instance)[480] in which the matter has arisen the judge ruled that the offence was not committed because a worthless cheque was not the same as counterfeit money and that D was not making off because he departed with V's consent. The true answer may well be that D is guilty because he has not paid 'as required or expected'. V requires and expects payment in legal tender or by a good cheque. Payment by a worthless cheque no more satisfies his requirement or expectation than payment in counterfeit money. If, however, the cheque is backed by a cheque guarantee card, then, depending on the conditions of its issue, D may have paid as required or expected although his authority to use the card has been withdrawn or even if it has been stolen.[481] Similarly with payment by credit card.[482] If the bank is bound to honour the cheque or card, a question of civil law, V has been paid. The offence is not committed if the supplier consents to D's leaving without payment, even if the consent was obtained by fraud, as where D deceives V into accepting postponement of payment.[483] Payment in such a case is not required or expected at *that* time.

(e) *Mens rea*

The offence requires that D should make off (i) dishonestly; (ii) knowing that payment on the spot is required or expected from him; and (iii) with intent to avoid payment.

(i) Dishonesty

Reference may be made to the general discussion of dishonesty. It does not matter at what stage D decides to act dishonestly so long as he is dishonest when he makes off. While dishonesty is a question for the jury D would not be dishonest in refusing to pay for goods or a service genuinely believed by him to be deficient.

(ii) Knowing that payment on the spot is required or expected of him

The offence is concerned only with cases where payment on the spot is required. Such transactions are difficult to define in abstract terms but usually easy enough to identify[484]

478 *Troughton v Metropolitan Police* [1987] Crim LR 138, DC.

479 See G. Syrota, 'Are Cheque Frauds covered by Section 3 of the Theft Act 1978' [1980] Crim LR 413.

480 *Hammond* [1982] Crim LR 611 (Judge Morrison).

481 Cf *First Sport Ltd v Barclays Bank plc* [1993] 3 All ER 789, CA (Civ Div).

482 Cf *Re Charge Card Services Ltd* [1988] 3 All ER 702, [1988] 3 WLR 764, CA (Civ Div).

483 *Vincent* [2001] Crim LR 488, [2001] 2 Cr App R 150, [2001] EWCA Crim 295, CA. A charge under s 2(1)(b) would be appropriate. See also *Evans v Lane* (1984) CO/137/84, CA.

484 Section 3(2) provides that it includes 'payment at the time of collecting goods on which work has been done or in respect of which service has been provided'. But this seems to have been added *ex abundanti cautela* and adds nothing. See Smith, *Theft*, para 5–04.

by reference to normal trading practices, although these may in particular instances be modified by the course of dealing between the parties.[485] If D honestly believes that the transaction is on credit terms, he cannot be convicted of this offence for he is not acting dishonestly and he does not *know* the transaction to be a spot transaction. And where D believes that payment is to be made by another (for example, where he believes that E will pay for the meal) he does not commit the offence because he neither acts dishonestly nor does he know that payment is to be required of him.[486]

(iii) Intention to avoid payment

Unlike s 2(1)(b) of the 1978 Act with which s 3 invites comparison, the latter does not in terms require an intention to make permanent default and commentators tended to favour the view that a dishonest intention temporarily to avoid payment would suffice. However, *Allen*[487] holds that the offence requires an intention to make permanent default. D had left an hotel without settling his bill and the trial judge directed the jury that all that was required was an intention to make default at the time payment was required. The Court of Appeal held, however, that an intention to make permanent default was required because s 3 required both (i) a making off without paying on the spot; and (ii) an intent to avoid payment. In view of the requirement in (i), (ii) made sense only if permanent default was intended. The House of Lords endorsed this view and drew further support for it by reference to the fact that the CLRC had intended permanent default to be necessary.[488]

7. Stealing by spouses and corporations

(a) Spouses and civil partners[489]

For many purposes husband and wife and, since the Civil Partnership Act 2004 those in a 'civil partnership', occupy a special position under the law and have special rules relating to themselves. Section 30 of the Theft Act 1968, reversing the position under the previous law provides:

> (1) This Act shall apply in relation to the parties to a marriage, and to property belonging to the wife or husband whether or not by reason of an interest derived from the marriage, as it would apply if they were not married and any such interest subsisted independently of the marriage.
>
> (2) Subject to subsection (4) below, a person shall have the same right to bring proceedings against that person's wife or husband for any offence (whether under this Act or otherwise) as if they were not married, and a person bringing any such proceedings shall be competent to give evidence for the prosecution at every stage of the proceedings.[490]

485 It cannot be enough that V requires a payment to be made on the spot, eg seeing D who owes him £10 lent a month ago, V demands payment on the spot. The reference is to those transactions where payment customarily follows immediately upon the provision of the goods or service.

486 *Brooks and Brooks* (1982) 76 Cr App R 66, [1983] Crim LR 188, CA.

487 [1985] AC 1029, [1985] 2 All ER 641, [1985] Crim LR 739.

488 Cmnd 6733, para 18.

489 See Smith, *Theft* ch 14.4; Griew, ch 1.

490 As amended by the Youth Justice and Criminal Evidence Act 1999, s 67(3), Sch 6.

(3) [Repealed]

(4) Proceedings shall not be instituted against a person for any offence of stealing or doing unlawful damage to property which at the time of the offence belongs to that person's wife or husband [or civil partner], or for any attempt, incitement or conspiracy to commit such an offence, unless the proceedings are instituted by or with the consent of the Director of Public Prosecutions:

Provided that –

(a) this subsection shall not apply to proceedings against a person for an offence –

(i) if that person is charged with committing the offence jointly with the wife or husband [or civil partner]; or

(ii) if by virtue of any judicial decree or order (wherever made) that person and the wife or husband are at the time of the offence under no obligation to cohabit;[491] or

[(iii) an order (whenever made) is in force providing for the separation of that person and his or her civil partner]

[(5) Notwithstanding [section 6 of the Prosecution of Offences Act 1979] subsection (4) of this section shall apply –

(a) to an arrest (if without warrant) made by the wife or husband [or civil partner], and

(b) to a warrant of arrest issued on an information laid by the wife or husband [or civil partner]].

The substantial effect of s 30(1) is to make spouses and civil partners liable in respect of offences against each other's property as though they were not married. Consequently either spouse/partner may, for example, steal property belonging to the other. It may just be worth pointing out here that while it is clear that a spouse may steal property belonging exclusively to the other, it is equally clear that a spouse/partner may steal property jointly owned with the other spouse/partner since one co-owner may steal from another.[492]

By s 30(2) one spouse may prosecute the other, subject to s 30(4), for *any* criminal offence whether that offence is committed by a spouse on the person or property of the other, or whether by a spouse against a third party. A wife might, for example, prosecute her husband for stealing property belonging to a child of the marriage or for assaulting his mother-in-law.

While it is desirable that a spouse should have the general protection of the criminal law from depredations by the other, it will be appreciated that an over-readiness to institute proceedings by the one against the other,[493] can only be divisive, and is not conducive to the continuation of a satisfactory domestic relationship. It is for this reason that s 30(4) provides that proceedings may not be instituted except by or with the consent of the Director of Public Prosecutions.[494] But note that the Director's consent need only be sought where the offence consists of 'stealing or doing unlawful damage to property which at the time of the offence belongs to that person's wife or husband or civil partner'. Neither a wife nor a police officer, then, would need the Director's leave to institute

491 Criminal Jurisdiction Act 1975, s 14(5), Sch 6, Part I.

492 See above, p 675.

493 Or by a third party against one spouse for an offence on the other spouse.

494 By the Prosecution of Offences Act 1985 s 1(7). The consent may be given by a Crown Prosecutor.

proceedings for an assault on the wife by the husband, nor to prosecute the husband in respect of *any* offence committed by him on a third party.

Moreover, the Director's leave is not required in the two cases excepted by s 30(4)(a). The idea behind these exceptions is that in neither case does the risk of vexatious or divisive proceedings – which is the basis for the Director's control – exist. Thus a husband may, without the Director's leave, bring proceedings in respect of an appropriation of his property at a time when he was no longer bound to cohabit.[495] And a third party may similarly bring proceedings where the spouses are jointly charged in respect of an offence relating to property belonging to one of them; an example of this might be where H sets fire to his house in order to endanger the life of another and W aids him in the enterprise.

(b) Corporations and their officers

So far as offences under the Theft Acts generally are concerned, the liability of corporations for them falls to be determined in accordance with the general principles applicable to the liability of corporations for crime.[496] Where a corporation commits a crime it must be the case that the crime has been committed by a person, or persons, in control of the corporation's affairs.[497] Such persons are of course liable in accordance with the ordinary principles governing liability for crime. In this particular s 18 contains a special provision relating to the offences of obtaining property by deception, obtaining a pecuniary advantage by deception, and false accounting. The section provides:

> (1) Where an offence committed by a body corporate under section 15, 16 or 17 of this Act is proved to have been committed with the consent or connivance of any director, manager, secretary or other similar officer[[498]] of the body corporate, or any person who was purporting to act in any such capacity, he as well as the body corporate shall be guilty of that offence, and shall be liable to be proceeded against and punished accordingly.
>
> (2) Where the affairs of a body corporate are managed by its members, this section shall apply in relation to the acts and defaults of a member in connection with his functions of management as if he were a director of the body corporate.

The Theft Act 1978 extended its application to offences under sections 1 and 2 of that Act.[499] This provision was explained by the Criminal Law Revision Committee as follows:[500]

> The [section] follows a form of provision commonly included in statutes,[501] where an offence is of a kind to be committed by bodies corporate and where it is desired to put the management[502] under a positive obligation to prevent irregularities, if aware of them. Passive acquiescence does

495 Mere separation will not negative a requirement for the DPP'S leave: *Withers* [1975] Crim LR 647; but a judicial order in the form of an injunction will: *Woodley v Woodley (Criminal Damage: Married Couple)* [1978] 8 Fam Law 207, [1978] Crim LR 629.

496 See above, p 234.

497 A corporation may of course be vicariously liable for crimes even though the crime is not committed by a person in control of its affairs: see above, p 228. But vicarious liability would not apply in connection with offences under the Theft Act 1968.

498 See *Boal* [1992] 3 All ER 177, limiting this to those in positions of real power.

499 See Theft Act 1978, s 5.

500 Cmnd 2977, para 104.

501 See further, above, p 242.

502 Note that s 18 imposes criminal liability only on the management; this may include (s 18(2)) any member who is in fact in control even though he may not formally hold a managerial post.

not, under the general law, make a person liable as a party to the offence, but there are clearly cases (of which we think this is one) where the director's responsibilities for his company require him to intervene to prevent fraud and where consent or connivance amount to guilt.

The inference from this seems to be that, but for some such provision, the director might not in some circumstances, be liable under the general principles governing liability for crime. The circumstances in which the director does not incur liability as a joint perpetrator or accessory will be relatively few. Suppose, for example, that D, a director, learns that E, a fellow director, proposes to raise an overdraft from a bank by stating that it is required to enable the company to purchase plant when it is required to pay off creditors, but that D does nothing about it and the overdraft is authorized by the bank. The effect of s 18 appears to be that D incurs criminal liability in respect of the obtaining of the pecuniary advantage by deception because the offence has been committed with his consent. There would be no need to show that D communicated to E his approval of the deception. Possibly, however, D would be liable under general principles for he has a clear duty to control the actions of E in this situation and his deliberate failure to perform his duty, coupled with his guilty knowledge may make him an abettor.[503]

(c) Restitution

Section 28 of the Theft Act 1968 provided a power permitting the court to provide restitution of property stolen. The power is now found in s 148 of the Powers of Criminal Courts (Sentencing) Act 2000. A 'restitution' order can be made in favour of any person with a pre-existing entitlement to recover the stolen goods. The statutory provisions relating to the restitution of stolen property lie beyond the scope of this work.[504]

503 See above, p 177; *Tamm* [1973] Crim LR 115, CA.

504 See 6th edn, 639–644; Griew, ch 18; Smith, *Theft*, paras 220–229.

19

Offences involving deception and fraud

1. Introduction

The early common lawyers seem to have had an unsympathetic attitude to the victims of deception. In 1704, Holt CJ held that D did not commit larceny by obtaining £20 from V by pretending that he was authorized by X to collect it and asked, 'Shall we indict one man for making a fool of another'?[1] Parliament acted to create an offence of obtaining property by false pretences in 1757.

The present law takes a very different attitude as it offers a wide range of specific offences[2] backed by the overarching availability where two or more are involved of a charge for conspiracy to defraud. The protection offered by the substantive law is unstructured, less clear than it ought to be, dependent on numerous technicalities, particularly in the 1978 Act with lacunae frequently exposed, and in principled terms rests on shaky foundations.[3] It will come as no surprise to hear that radical proposals for reform are under consideration, and these are discussed in the next chapter. The most important aspect of the proposed shift is that the focus of the offences shifts from a series of discretely defined but often overlapping and overparticularized deception offences, to a broad general offence of fraud.[4] The eight deception offences would be replaced but not the offence of conspiracy to defraud. In view of the significance of the proposed reform, it is worth examining briefly, the interrelationship of the concepts of deception and fraud in the present law.

(a) Definitions of deception and 'fraud'[5]

An accepted definition of the concept of 'fraud' in English law remains elusive. Fraud has evolved in diverse legal contexts, not all of which relate to acquisitive crime (the issue arises in relation to sex offences and offences against the person such as kidnap). In

1 *Jones* (1704) 2 Ld Raym 1013.

2 Principally the 1968 Act, ss 15, 15A, 16, 20(2) and the 1978 Act, ss 1, 2(1)(a), 2(1)(b) and 2(1)(c).

3 There is also inconsistency and incoherence in the approaches to investigation and prosecution of frauds – unsurprisingly given the wide range of circumstance in which they arise and the diversity of agencies and policies involved.

4 See Law Com Report No 276, *Fraud*, paras 7.49–7.54.

5 See generally A. Arlidge and J. Parry, ch 4; L. Dobbs and R. Sutton (eds), *Fraud: Law, Practice and Procedure* (2004), ch 2; J. C. Smith, *The Law of Theft* (8th edn, 1997), ch 4 (hereafter in this chapter, Smith, *Theft*); E. J. Griew, *The Theft Acts* (7th edn, 1995), chs 8–11 (hereafter Griew, *Theft*); Smith, *Property Offences* (1st edn, 1994), chs 17–18 (hereafter in this chapter, Smith, *Property Offences*).

addition, there is no clear demarcation of the relationship between 'fraud' and concepts such as 'deception', 'dishonesty' and 'with intent to defraud'. The traditional English approach to fraud is perhaps encapsulated by Sir Rupert Cross who described it as 'one of those irritating words that seems more technical than it really is'.[6] This attitude has, of course not encouraged detailed examination. At one level, fraud could be seen as nothing more than a convenient layperson's label to describe dishonesty or deceit. Alternatively, it may constitute a legal term of art denoting a collection of states of *mens rea* applying throughout the criminal law. A third possibility is that it represents a more specific legal term of art that appears miraculously to have avoided precise definition despite being in common use for several centuries. If so, there remain fundamental questions to address, for example, is the purpose of criminalizing fraud: to protect economic loss, or to protect commercial autonomy? If D, a car dealer, dishonestly and deceptively tells V that he has cut 10 per cent off the price of a vehicle, and this induces V to buy it, should D be guilty of an offence if V has paid no more than he would have paid elsewhere? If the law seeks to protect economic interests and property, this behaviour would not merit criminal sanction. If on the other hand the law seeks to protect the victim's commercial autonomy, D's conduct has clearly infringed V's interests.

The concept of fraud has evolved over the centuries rather than being a product of statutory design. The classic definition remains valuable despite its ambiguities:

> Whenever the words 'fraud' or 'intent to defraud' or 'fraudulently' occur in the definition of a crime two elements at least are essential to the commission of the crime: namely, first, deceit or an intention to deceive or in some cases mere secrecy; and, secondly, either actual injury or possible injury or an intent to expose some person either to actual injury or to a risk of possible injury by means of that deceit or secrecy.[7]

The definition is far from ideal since it contains no explicit requirement of dishonesty, despite that being commonly regarded as lying at the core of fraud.

Stephen's definition does not suggest that fraud is synonymous with deception, and it is clear that fraud has along been acknowledged by Parliament to be a wider concept. For example, stealing contrary to s 1 of the Larceny Act 1916 was committed 'fraudulently' but without the need for proof of deceit. The distinction has been expressly acknowledged judicially, as Buckley J made clear:

> To deceive is, I apprehend, to induce a man to believe that a thing is true which is false, and which the person practising the deceit knows or believes to be false. To defraud is to deprive by deceit: it is by deceit to induce a man to act to his injury. More tersely it may be put, that to deceive is by falsehood to induce a state of mind; to defraud is by deceit to induce a course of action.[8]

One of the fundamental differences that proposed reform would bring is that the focus of the offence will be on D's fault *per se* rather than on the impact that this has on the mind of the victim.[9]

[6] R. Cross, 'The Theft Bill 1: Theft and Deception' [1966] Crim LR 415.

[7] J. Stephen, *History of the Criminal Law* (1883) vol 2, 121.

[8] *Re: London and Globe Finance Corporation Ltd* [1903] 1 Ch 728, 732–3.

[9] On the theoretical implications of an offence without harm see A. Ashworth, 'Defining Criminal Offences Without Harm', in P. Smith (ed), *Criminal Law Essays in Honour of J. C. Smith* (1987), p 8.

2. The common elements in offences of obtaining by deception

The current protection against deception takes the form of eight specific offences. Many share common features – obtaining, causation, deception and dishonesty – which are considered before a detailed examination of the offences themselves.

(a) The meaning of deception

The first common element of the deception offences is that they require proof of a deception. By the 1968 Act, s 15(4):

> For purposes of this section 'deception' means any deception (whether deliberate or reckless) by words or conduct as to fact or as to law, including a deception as to the present intentions of the person using the deception or any other person.

The definition in the 1968 Act, s 15(4) applies to offences under the 1968 Act, ss 15, 16 and 20(2) and to the 1978 Act, ss 1 and 2. It will be noted in considering the construction of the term deception that, as in other aspects of the Theft Acts, it is important that the criminal law remains in harmony with civil law obligations relating to misrepresentation, etc in commercial dealings. The Home Office proposals for a new fraud offence are, notably, based on the concept of 'false representations'.

(i) Proof of falsity

For any deception it must be proved that D made a false statement. If his statement was true he cannot be guilty of the offence (though he may now be guilty of an attempt), even though he believed it to be false and was dishonest. Where this rule requires the prosecution to prove a negative, there may be an onus on D if it is within his knowledge, not to prove anything, but at least to introduce some evidence of the affirmative fact that, if it exists, will establish the truth of the statement. For example, in *Mandry and Wooster*,[10] street traders selling scent for 25 pence said, 'You can go down the road and buy it for 2 guineas in the big stores'. The police checked on certain stores but it was admitted in cross-examination that they had not been to Selfridges. It was held that it was not improper for the judge to point out that it was impossible for the police to go to every shop in London and that 'if the defence knew of their own knowledge of anywhere it could be bought at that price . . . they were perfectly entitled to call evidence'. Since no evidence was called to show that the perfume was on sale at Selfridges or anywhere else, the convictions were upheld.

(ii) Deliberate or reckless

A deception is deliberate if D knows his statement is false and will or may be accepted as true. It is sufficient that the deception is reckless. A deception is reckless if D is aware that it may be false and will or may be accepted as true; or if he is aware that it is ambiguous

[10] [1973] 3 All ER 996; cf *Silverman* (1987) 86 Cr App R 213.

and may be understood in the false sense.[11] Recklessness is of course distinct from mere awareness, since recklessness requires an unjustifiable taking of a risk of which D is aware. Carelessness or negligence is not enough in these offences.[12] If D believes his statement to be true, he is not reckless, however unreasonable his belief may be; but the more unreasonable D's alleged belief, the more likely is it that the court or jury will be satisfied that the belief was not really held. The now redundant *Caldwell* test of recklessness, though it was at one time stated to be of general application, has not been applied in the context of reckless statements.[13]

(iii) By words or conduct

By s 15(4) of the 1968 Act (which is also applicable to s 16 and to deception offences under the 1978 Act), deception means any deception by words or conduct. The case law provides many memorable examples of this in operation. In *Barnard*,[14] D went into an Oxford shop wearing a 'fellow commoner's' cap and gown (as was commonly worn by members of that University at the time). He induced the shopkeeper to sell him goods on credit by an express oral representation that he was a fellow commoner; but Bolland B said, *obiter*, that he would have been guilty even if he had said nothing. In an Australian case,[15] the wearing of a badge was held to be a false pretence when it indicated that the wearer was entitled to take bets on a racecourse.

Where D knows that V is, or may be, under a misapprehension, anything whatever done by D to confirm V in his error, is capable of amounting to a deception. Positive steps taken by a seller to conceal from a buyer defects in the goods may amount to fraud in the civil law and are capable of being deception under the Theft Acts. If V inspects the goods and, because of the concealment, fails to detect the fault, the offence would be complete. It has been held to be fraud in the civil law for the seller of a ship to remove her from a position where it might be seen that the bottom was eaten and her keel broken, and to keep her afloat so that these defects were concealed under water.[16] This would seem to amount to deception. Suppose, however, that the ship was already in the water before any sale was in prospect. Would it be an offence for the seller to leave her there when viewed by the buyer and say nothing about the defects? It would seem not; there are no 'words or conduct' here and presumably the seller would not even be civilly liable in such a case. Note however the proposed reform of the fraud offences which will extend liability in this context.[17]

(iv) Conduct and omissions

In a commercial transaction, D is under a duty not to act so as to confirm any misunderstanding by V, but has no duty to correct a misunderstanding even though he is fully

[11] *Dip Kaur v Chief Constable for Hampshire* [1981] 2 All ER 430, above, p 659.

[12] *Staines* (1974) 60 Cr App R 160, CA.

[13] *Large v Mainprize* [1989] Crim LR 213, DC. Cf *Goldman* [1997] Crim LR 884 and commentary (a case on fraudulent trading). See also M. Gale, S. Gale and G. Scanlon, 'Fraud and the Sale of Shares' [2001] Comp Law 98, arguing that *Caldwell* recklessness applies to s 47 of the Financial Services Act 1986.

[14] (1837) 7 C & P 784. [15] *Robinson* (1884) 10 VLR 131.

[16] *Schneider v Heath* (1813) 3 Camp 506, approved by the Court of Appeal in *Ward v Hobbs* (1877) 3 QBD 150 at 162.

[17] See below, p 796.

aware of it. 'The passive acquiescence of the seller in the self-deception of the buyer does not entitle the buyer to avoid the contract'.[18] *A fortiori*, it cannot amount to a criminal offence. It may be different, however, if D is under a duty to speak. In *Firth*,[19] a consultant was held to have deceived a hospital, contrary to 1978, s 2(1), by failing to inform the hospital that certain patients were private patients, knowing that the effect would be that they would be treated as NHS patients and exempted from liability to make a payment. The court made no reference to the statutory definition, presumably regarding the defendant's omission in breach of his duty as 'conduct' for these purposes. The proposed offence of fraud will extend to failure to disclose information in specified circumstances.

(v) Deception by implied statement

A difficult question is to determine in what circumstances statements are implied in words or conduct. It is well-established that D who enters a restaurant and orders a meal impliedly represents by his conduct that he intends to pay for the meal before leaving[20] and probably also represents, in the absence of an agreement for credit, that he has the money to pay.[21] A person who registers as a guest in a hotel represents that he intends to pay the bill at the end of his stay.[22] A wine waiter employed at a hotel impliedly represents that the wine he offers is his employer's, not his own.[23] A motor trader who states that the mileage shown on the odometer of a second-hand car 'may not be correct' represents that he does not know it to be incorrect.[24] A bookmaker, it is submitted, represents, when he takes a bet, that he intends to pay if the horse backed wins.[25] A passenger who takes a taxi represents that he intends to pay, and has the means of paying, at the end of the ride.[26] A customer in a supermarket who tenders goods to the cashier represents that the price label on the goods proffered is that which he believes to be authorized by the management,[27] so that there is a deception if he knows that the label has been 'switched' by himself or another. These are all representations of present fact.

Where there has been an express representation, there will usually be ample evidence that the representee actually had the misrepresented fact in mind. In the case of implied representations, this may not be so. When a customer in a restaurant orders food, it is unlikely that the waiter actually thinks, 'He is saying that he has the means to pay for this meal'. The buyer of a car may not consciously reflect that the seller is asserting that he is the owner, or that he has the right to sell the car. In each case, it is something that goes without saying. The waiter would not take the order if he knew that the customer had no means of paying for it. Moreover in each of these cases it *matters* to the representee[28]

[18] *Smith v Hughes* (1871) LR 6 QB 597, above, p 655.

[19] (1989) 91 Cr App R 217, [1990] Crim LR 326, CA, and commentary, criticized in *Archbold*, 21–275. Cf *Shama* [1990] 2 All ER 602.

[20] *DPP v Ray* [1974] AC 370 at 379, 382, 385, 388, 391.

[21] Ibid, at 379, 382.

[22] *Harris* (1975) 62 Cr App R 28.

[23] *Doukas* [1978] 1 All ER 1061, [1978] Crim LR 177. The decision is to be preferred to *Rashid* [1977] 2 All ER 237.

[24] *King* [1979] Crim LR 122.

[25] Cf *Buckmaster* (1887) 20 QBD 182.

[26] *Waterfall* [1970] 1 QB 148, [1969] 3 All ER 1048.

[27] Cf *Morris*, above, p 649.

[28] Unlike the representees in *Charles* and *Lambie* (below). The representees in *Charles* and *Lambie* were quite content to deal with their customers, whether they had authority to use their bank cards or not (so long as they did not *know* the customers had no authority). Unlike the waiter, they knew they would be paid anyway.

that the representation is true. The waiter, for example, is not content to deal with the customer whether he has the means to pay or not.

(vi) Representations implied by cheques

From *Hazelton* (1874)[29] until *Charles* (1976)[30] it was thought to be settled law that a person tendering a cheque impliedly makes three representations: (i) that he has an account on which the cheque is drawn; (ii) that he has authority to draw on the bank for that amount; and (iii) that the cheque as drawn is a valid order for that amount. In *Charles*, the House of Lords cast doubt on the second of these representations, saying that in substance there is only one representation – that the facts are such that, as far as can reasonably be foreseen, the cheque will be honoured on being presented. Lord Edmund-Davies quoted with approval the words of Pollock B in *Hazelton* that the representation is that 'the existing state of facts is such that in the ordinary course the cheque will be met'. In *Gilmartin*,[31] the Court of Appeal thought that 'this terse but neat epitome of the representation . . . should properly be regarded as an authoritative statement of the law'. It is the same where the cheque is post-dated as where it is not. Such a representation is complete only if the facts include a certain intention and belief of the drawer. As the court points out, whether the cheque is post-dated or not, it may be the drawer's intention to pay in sufficient funds to meet it before presentation. Alternatively, the drawer of the cheque may believe that a third party is going to pay in such funds – as where he draws a cheque, knowing that his account is overdrawn but confidently expecting that he will have an ample credit balance tomorrow when his monthly pay is paid into his account by his employer. There being no express representation, the drawer must be taken to be saying that either, (a) there are sufficient funds in the account to meet the cheque; or, (b) he intends to pay in sufficient funds; or, (c) he believes that a third party will do so. Each is a representation of fact, not a mere promise, and so, if none is true, drawing the cheque is a misrepresentation.[32]

In *Greenstein*[33] DD made a practice (known as 'stagging') of applying for very large quantities of shares, sending an accompanying cheque for an amount far in excess of the money in their bank accounts. They had no authority to overdraw their accounts but they expected to be allotted a relatively small number of shares (not the amount they had applied for) and to receive a 'return cheque' for the difference between the prices of the shares applied for and the shares allotted. By paying the return cheques into their accounts they enabled the cheques drawn by them to be honoured, on most occasions, on first presentation, on other occasions after a very short interval, on second presentation. It

[29] (1874) LR 2 CCR 134, the source of the proposition in Kenny, *Outlines*, 359, adopted in *Page* [1971] 2 QB 330n at 333.

[30] [1977] AC 177, [1976] 3 All ER 112.

[31] (1983) 76 Cr App R 238 at 244.

[32] In *Charles* [1976] 3 All ER 112 at 116, Viscount Dilhorne said, 'Until the enactment of the Theft Act 1968 it was necessary in order to obtain a conviction for false pretences to establish that there had been a false pretence of an existing fact.' This is misleading. It is still necessary to prove a representation of an existing fact or of law: *Beckett v Cohen* [1973] 1 All ER 120, DC; *British Airways Board v Taylor* [1976] 1 All ER 65, HL. All that the 1968 Act did was to make clear that certain statements of fact – ie present intentions – were for the future to be treated as such. The implication of Viscount Dilhorne's statement was not accepted by Lord Diplock (at 113) or Lord Edmund-Davies (at 121) or by the court in *Gilmartin* [1983] 76 Cr App R 238, [1983] Crim LR 330.

[33] [1976] 1 All ER 1.

was alleged that DD had obtained shares by '*Hazelton*' representations[34] that they had authority to draw the cheques and that they were good and valid orders. In some cases, where DD had given an undertaking required by the issuing houses that 'the cheque sent herewith will be paid on first presentation', there was an allegation of a further representation to that effect. Since all the cheques were met on first or subsequent presentation, no one lost a penny but some other applicants who might have got shares if DD had made more modest applications did not get them because, as DD anticipated, there were not enough to go round.[35] It was held that DD had no authority, either from banking practice or the particular facts proved, to draw the inflated cheques; and that they were not valid orders because they could be met only by paying in the return cheques. There was, therefore, a deception. The deception was effective because the share issuing houses would not have entertained the application had they known that their own return cheques were going to be used to fund it. The jury's verdict implied that DD was reckless whether their cheques would be honoured on first presentation; and, on the facts, the jury 'were entitled if not bound to infer that the deception was deliberately dishonest'.

(v) Omission to undeceive as a deception

Where D's statement is true at the time it is made but later to his knowledge it becomes false, he may be guilty of obtaining by deception if V acts on the false statement. In *DPP v Ray*,[36] the statement was D's implied representation that he intended to pay for his meal. This statement was true when made and continued true until the end of the meal, but when D changed his mind it became false. It was held that the waiter acted on D's false statement by leaving the room, when he would not have done so had he known the truth, that D intended to leave without paying. If D had changed his mind during the meal, it is clear that any part of the meal served and any service performed by the waiter thereafter would have been obtained by deception. It is essential to prove that there is an operative deception – that V acted on the false representation and that the result of V's so acting was that D obtained the property or the service as the case may be. In *Rai*[37] D obtained a grant from the city council to provide a bathroom for his disabled mother. Before it was installed, she died. D did not disclose this fact and allowed the work to proceed. He was convicted of obtaining services by deception.

The same result must follow in the case where the statement is false when made but believed by D at that time to be true, if D subsequently discovers that the statement is false and thereafter accepts property or a service from V who, as D knows, is acting on the false statement. In these situations there is in effect a duty on D to correct V's false belief or, at least, to decline any property or service deriving from that belief. This is not to argue that criminal liability should be imposed in all cases where the civil law imposes a duty to speak. In some of these cases it would not be obvious to the layman that to remain silent would be tantamount to deception and it would be wrong to impute to him an intention to deceive. The point is that criminal liability should not be imposed where the civil law imposes no duty to speak. Where it does impose a duty then the omission is

34 The case being decided before *Charles* [1976], above.

35 This might have been sufficient for a charge of conspiracy to defraud the other applicants.

36 [1974] AC 370, [1973] 3 All ER 131, above, p 744; *Nordeng* (1975) 62 Cr App R 123 at 129.

37 [2000] 1 Cr App R 242, [2000] Crim LR 192. The case rejects the idea that *Firth* is a general authority for a proposition that mere silence constitutes deception.

capable of being a deception. As has emphasized throughout the chapters on property offences it is desirable for the criminal law to respect the civil law foundations on which the offences are created.

(vi) As to fact or law

The Act settles any doubt there may have been whether a misrepresentation of law can amount to deception. It can. If D deliberately misrepresents the legal effect (a question of law) of a document, intending, for example, to lead V to believe that D has some right over V's land so as to induce V to pay money for the release of that right, this would be obtaining by deception. It does not follow that any statement of law that turns out to be false is a deception. The law is often uncertain (as we are all too aware!) and assertions as to the state of the law made between parties at arms' length are unlikely to amount to deception. The following proposition originally formulated by Street[38] for the law of the tort of deceit is probably equally true of deception under s 15:

> If the representations refer to legal principles as distinct from the facts on which those principles operate and the parties are on an equal footing, those representations are only expressions of belief and of the same effect as expressions of opinion between parties on an equal footing. In other cases where the defendant professes legal information beyond that of the [claimant] the ordinary rules of liability for deceit apply.

(vii) Deception as to intention

The definition of deception under the Theft Acts includes a deception as to the present intentions of the person using the deception or any other person. A representation as to present intention may be expressed or implied. Several examples of implied representations have already been considered above. If the statement is a promise, it must be proved that D had no intention of carrying out his promise at the time he made it, or at the time it was acted on. If he intended to carry out his promise at those times but later changed his mind he may be guilty of a breach of contract but of no criminal offence. It has long been recognized that a misrepresentation as to present state of mind will found a civil action for deceit and there is no difference in principle in the criminal law – though the standard of proof is higher. Evidence as to the circumstances in which the promise was made, or as to a systematic course of conduct by D or, of course, as to a confession, are examples of ways in which a jury might be convinced that D was deceiving V as to his present intentions.

An example of a deception as to the intention of another is an agent, D, obtaining property for his principal, X, by representing to V that X intends to render services, knowing that X has no such intention.

(viii) Statements of opinion

A statement of opinion was not a sufficient false pretence under the old law[39] – a doctrine that was sometimes carried to extreme lengths.[40] In principle, a deception as to a person's

[38] *Torts* (11th edn, 2003), 123. [39] Section 32 of the Larceny Act 1916.

[40] *Bryan* (1857) Dears & B 265, Willes J *dissentiente* and Bramwell B *dubitante*. Even D's own counsel conceded: 'I cannot contend that the prisoner did not tell a wilful lie'; yet D was acquitted.

opinion or belief is not distinguishable from a deception as to his intention. The latter case, however is expressly declared to be a 'deception' by s 15(4) of the 1968 Act, whereas the former is not. This should not and, it is submitted, does not inhibit the courts from holding that a person's statement of an opinion that he does not actually hold is a misrepresentation of fact. The difficulty is one of proof. How, for example, can it be proved that a representation that property is 'worth £X' is, and is known to be, a misrepresentation?[41] In *Jeff and Bassett*[42] DD said 'that they [had] effected necessary repairs to a roof [which repairs were specified] that they had done the work in a proper and workmanlike manner and that [a specified sum] was a fair and reasonable sum to charge for the work involved'. The evidence showed that nothing needed to be done to the roof, what had been done served no useful purpose and it could have been done for £5, whereas £35 was charged. This was held to be a misrepresentation of fact. Even an excessive quotation for work to be done may be a sufficient deception where a situation of mutual trust has been built up between D and his customer so that D must be taken to be saying dishonestly that he is going to make no more than a modest profit, when he knows that the profit, if the quotation is accepted, will be very large.[43]

(b) Obtaining

The second common element of deception offences is that of obtaining. Though the Acts use four verbs, 'obtain', 'procure', 'secure' and 'induce', the word 'obtain' is used throughout this discussion to include the other three verbs because it is thought they all have the same meaning in this context. None of the terms appear to have given rise to particular problems in interpretation.

(c) 'By' deception

The obtaining must be *by* deception.[44] There is a requirement of causation. It must be proved that D's false representation actually deceived V and caused him to do whatever act is appropriate to the offence charged – transfer property, provide services, execute a valuable security, etc.

Several preliminary, but fundamental points need to be made. First, the deception must precede the relevant act. If D, a motorist, has had his petrol tank filled and *after* the entire proprietary interest in the petrol has passed to him, he falsely represents that it will be paid for by his employer, he does not obtain the petrol by deception.[45] He may be guilty of evading his liability to pay the price by deception contrary to s 2(1)(b) of the 1978 Act.

41 Cf *Mirror Group Newspapers v Northants County Council* [1997] Crim LR 882 (Consumer Protection Act 1987).

42 (1966) 51 Cr App R 28. Cf *Hawkins v Smith* [1978] Crim LR 578 ('Showroom condition throughout' a false trade description of a car which has interior and mechanical defects).

43 *Silverman* (1987) 86 Cr App R 213, [1987] Crim LR 574. Note the proposed Doorstop Selling (Property Repairs) Bill 2004 which would have criminalized unsolicited household visits to sell repairs.

44 See, generally, A. T. H. Smith, 'The Idea of Criminal Deception' [1982] Crim LR 721.

45 *Collis-Smith* [1971] Crim LR 716, *Coady* [1996] Crim LR 518. If D borrows goods from V without any deception and then, while in possession, induces V by deception to sell him the goods, he commits the offence under s 15 of the 1968 Act by obtaining ownership.

Secondly, someone must be deceived. Part of the *actus reus* of the offences comprises the state of mind of another. If V knows that D's statement is false,[46] but for example, transfers the property anyway, he has not been caused to do so by D's deception. Similarly, if, though V believes D's false statement to be true, V would have acted in the same way even if he had known it was false (perhaps because he feels sorry for D's plight)[47] V has not been caused to act by the deception.[48] Equally, if V does not rely on the false statement but arrives at the same erroneous conclusion from his own observation or some other source[49] he has not been caused to act *by D's* deception – rather it is by his own failing. And, if V does not read or hear the false statement, so it has no opportunity to make an impact on V's mind and cause him to do anything, V has not been deceived. In each of these cases, however, D may be convicted of an attempt to obtain by deception.[50] His deceptive conduct is morally reprehensible even though on this occasion it failed in some respect or other.

The onus is on the prosecution to prove that the representation operated on the person's mind. The normal way of proving that a deception was operative is by calling V who will testify that he was deceived. This is not always as easy as it sounds. In some instances the victim will be unfit (a particular problem with the vulnerable and elderly who are more at risk of deception offences) and in some cases, even if the victim knows in his own mind that he has been deceived,[51] his pride or commercial reputation might inhibit his willingness to testify openly to that fact. This is one reason why prosecutors often prefer to bring charges of theft where no such practical difficulties can arise. Like any other allegation, however, the element of deception that operated on V's mind may be proved by inference from other facts without direct evidence.

Whether a representation was made and, if so, whether it was false, are questions for the jury, even where the statement is made in a document.[52] In *Laverty*,[53] a case under s 15 (obtaining property by deception), D changed the registration number plates and chassis number plate of a car and sold it to V. It was held that this constituted a representation by D's conduct that the car was the original car to which these numbers had been assigned; but D's conviction for obtaining the price of the car by deception from V was quashed on the ground that it was not proved that the deception operated on V's mind. There was no direct evidence to that effect – V said he bought the car because he thought D was the owner – and it was not a necessary inference that he also relied on the validity of the

46 *Ady* (1835) 7 C & P 140; *Mills* (1857) Dears & B 205; *Hensler* (1870) 11 Cox CC 570; *Light* (1915) 11 Cr App R 111.

47 *Edwards* [1978] Crim LR 49 and commentary.

48 But for D's deception would V have behaved as he did?

49 *Roebuck* (1856) Dears & B 24. Cf the similar principle which applies to misrepresentation in relation to the law of contract: *Attwood v Small* (1838) 6 Cl & Fin 232; *Smith v Chadwick* (1884) 9 App Cas 187. The principle that the deception must be the cause of the obtaining seems to have been stretched in *Miller* [1992] Crim LR 744.

50 *Hensler* (1870) 11 Cox CC 570.

51 Cf *Charles* and *Lambie* above.

52 *Adams* [1993] Crim LR 525 and commentary.

53 [1970] 3 All ER 432.

plates.[54] It is a fundamental principle that V must have been caused to act as a result of D's deception. The case emphasizes the importance of securing clear testimony from the complainant at trial, and of the obligation on the prosecution to particularize which representation is alleged to be the operative deception. It also highlights the fact that individuals seldom make decisions, even about purchases of expensive items, on the basis of a single representation.

In *Etim v Hatfield*,[55] where D presented to a post office clerk a false declaration that he was entitled to a welfare benefit payment and was granted £10.60, but no post office employee gave evidence, it was held, distinguishing *Laverty*, that D was rightly convicted because there was no conceivable reason for the payment other than the false statement: post office clerks do not give £10.60 to customers at random. *Etim* may be defensible as a case where it was a *necessary* inference that V acted on the representation.

A case of some significance and one that is very difficult to reconcile with principle that V must be deceived is *DPP v Ray*.[56] D, having consumed a meal in a restaurant, dishonestly decided to leave without paying, waited until the waiter went out of the room and then ran off. The House of Lords, Lords Reid and Hodson dissenting, held that the waiter was induced to leave the room by D's implied and continuing representation that he was an honest customer intending to pay his bill. It does not appear that the waiter was ever called in evidence; and it would seem, on the facts, very far indeed from being a necessary inference that the waiter acted on the alleged representation. This is a doubtful application of the fundamental principle, but even a doubtful application by the House of Lords, does not impair the validity of the principle itself; and it remains necessary in every case to prove that V was deceived by and acted on the representation.

Where more than one false representation is alleged, it is sufficient to prove that one of them was operative; but the jury must, subject to the majority verdict provisions, be agreed on the operative one. It is not sufficient that some members of the jury are satisfied only as to one representation and the remainder only as to another.[57]

(i) Particular problems with proving an operative deception

Obtaining by using a cheque card or credit card

The principle that V must be caused to act by D's deception has created problems where something is obtained by D using a cheque backed by a cheque card, or a credit card.

First, a word is necessary about the operation of cheque cards. The cheque card contains an undertaking by the issuing bank that, if the conditions on the card are satisfied

[54] If the only flaw in the prosecution's case was that the representation did not influence V, it would have been in order for the court to substitute a conviction for an attempt. They did not do so, possibly because there was also insufficient evidence that D intended to deceive V into buying the car by this representation. The purpose of changing the plates may well have been not to deceive the buyer, but to deceive the police, the true owner and anyone else who might identify the vehicle. It would seem that the prosecution would have been on stronger ground had they alleged that D had made a representation by conduct that he had a right to sell the car.

[55] [1975] Crim LR 234.

[56] [1974] AC 370, [1973] 3 All ER 131, [1974] Crim LR 181. The prosecution was brought under 1968, s 16(2)(a) which has now been repealed, but the case remains an authority on this point. See for discussion S. White, 'Continuing Representations in the Criminal Law' (1986) 37 NILQ 255.

[57] *Brown* (1983) 79 Cr App R 115. J. C. Smith, 'Satisfying the Jury' [1988] Crim LR 335. This is a significant problem in many trials and is all too commonly overlooked.

(the signature matches the cheque, etc), the cheque will be honoured. The position with credit cards is similar. The bank issuing the card enters into contracts with traders, agreeing to pay the trader the sum shown on a voucher signed by the customer when making a purchase, provided that the conditions are satisfied. The trader is guaranteed to receive payment from the bank for the value of the transaction, and this is a useful safeguard for traders for which they are prepared to pay consideration to the bank. There is one difference between credit cards and cheque cards: in the case of credit cards, the contract between the bank and the trader precedes the purchase by the customer, whereas in the case of the cheque card that contract is made when the trader accepts the customer's cheque, relying on the card which is produced. This distinction is not material for present purposes.

The conditions on both types of card may be satisfied although the holder is exceeding his authority – for example, the cheque card holder's bank account is overdrawn without authority or even where the account has been closed, or the credit card holder is exceeding the credit limit which the bank has allowed him. A trader accepting either type of card will usually do so simply because the conditions on the card are satisfied. He will neither know nor care whether the customer is exceeding his authority and using the card in breach of contract with the bank. The trader will get his money from the bank in any event – and that is all he will be concerned with. This is not unreasonable. The whole object of these cards is to save the trader from concerning himself in any way with the relationship between the card-holder and his bank. The trader is perfectly entitled to take advantage of the facility which the banks offer him (and in the case of credit cards at least for which it charges him). The 'chip and pin' system that is now being introduced requires the customer to type in his pin code when presenting his debit or credit card to the trader. The system provides a better safeguard against fraudulent use by someone forging the signature on a stolen card. When the pin number is typed into the device it confirms that the pin number typed matches that stored on the magnetic strip on the card. It seems that no electronic communication with the bank is made, and therefore there is no greater likelihood that the bank will prevent the use of cards in excess of authority.

So much for the way the cards operate, how does this create a problem? When D presents a card, knowing that in doing so he is exceeding the bank's authority, he is making a false representation. Following D's presentation of the card and compliance with the procedures (providing a matching signature, etc), T (the trader) will transfer something to D (perhaps property, or services). But, if T does not care whether D is using the card in excess of his credit limit, etc because T knows the bank (V) will pay up, how can T be said to have been deceived?

In *Charles*,[58] D obtained gaming chips at a gaming club by the use of cheques and a cheque card, knowing that his account was overdrawn and that he had no authority to overdraw. The conditions on the card were satisfied so that the representation that is usually implied on the drawing of a cheque,[59] that is, that the facts are such that the cheque will be met, was true. The representation alleged, however, was that he was entitled and authorized to use the cheque card. That representation would have been untrue and known by D to be untrue. He was convicted of obtaining a pecuniary

58 *Metropolitan Police Comr v Charles* [1977] AC 177, [1976] 3 All ER 112.

59 Above, p 745.

advantage, namely increased borrowing by way of overdraft (discussed below), by the deception that he was entitled and authorized to use the card. The manager of the casino, T, said, 'If there is a cheque card we make no enquiries as to [D's] credit-worthiness, or as to the state of his account with the bank. All this is irrelevant unless the club has knowledge that he has no funds, or the club has knowledge that he has no authority to overdraw.'[60] Notwithstanding this forthright statement (and others) given in evidence at trial the House of Lords held that there was evidence that T had been induced to give the gaming chips by D's implied representation that he was entitled and authorized to use the cheque card.[61]

In the light of T's evidence, this finding seems perverse; but *Charles* was followed in *Lambie*.[62] D was the holder of a Barclaycard. She had exceeded her credit limit and been asked to return the card but had not done so. She bought goods in a shop and tendered the card to pay. The assistant, T, having checked that the conditions were satisfied, allowed her to take the goods. D was convicted of obtaining a pecuniary advantage from the bank (being allowed to borrow) by the false representation that she was entitled to use the card. Her conviction was quashed by the Court of Appeal, which thought, wrongly, that there was a material distinction between cheque cards and credit cards. The House of Lords restored the conviction. T, the trader, was as emphatic as T in *Charles* that she was totally uninterested in the state of account between the customer and her bank. 'From my experience I or my shop is not any more worried about accepting a Barclaycard as accepting the same number of pound notes . . . we will honour the card if the conditions are satisfied whether the bearer has authority to use it or not'. It seems to have been recognized on all hands that the state of the card holder's account with her bank is a matter of complete indifference to the trader. Since the authority to use the card depends on the state of the account, it is difficult to see how the trader can be indifferent to the one (the state of account) without being equally indifferent to the other (authority). Apparently in the teeth of her own testimony, the House of Lords held that there was evidence that T had been induced to accept the card by D's false representation that she was entitled to use it. It need hardly be said that these are further extreme examples of the appellate courts being prepared to go to great lengths to uphold the convictions of those who have been found to have acted dishonestly.

It is clear that if the traders in *Charles* and *Lambie* had been aware that the bearer of the card had no authority to use it, neither would have entered into the transaction. Had they done so they would have been parties to a fraud on the bank. They were honest people. They did not care whether D had authority or not – the bank had, in effect, told them they need not bother their heads about that – but they would have cared if they had

[60] See [1976] 1 All ER at 663–664.

[61] The holding that there is an implied representation of authority to use the card is suspect. If the relationship between D and his bank is irrelevant, as it surely is, why should D be taken to be saying anything about his authority? If T actually asks him, D can answer, 'It is none of your business – you are only concerned with the conditions on the card'. Representations, like terms in contracts, should only be implied under the compulsion of necessity; and that means, only where *any* reasonable person would infer the statement from D's conduct.

[62] [1982] AC 449, [1981] 2 All ER 776, [1981] Crim LR 712, HL, and commentary. Since the repeal of s 16(2)(a) of the 1968 Act, Lambie's conduct could not constitute obtaining a pecuniary advantage; but it is probably obtaining services, contrary to 1978 Act, s 1, below at p 773.

known he had no authority. In both cases the House attached great importance to this fact. It seems irrelevant. The traders declared that as far as they were concerned it was immaterial whether D had authority or not. The House of Lords is in effect creating an offence of constructive deception, with all of the unattractive features that constructive crimes possess. But, however dubious the House of Lords' reasoning, these decisions establish, for all practical purposes, that one who dishonestly uses a cheque or credit card in excess of his authority is guilty of obtaining a pecuniary advantage, or services, from the bank. Under the proposed reforms the difficulties will disappear since the offence is complete on D making a false representation.

Notwithstanding *Charles* and *Lambie*, it appears that prosecutors have had difficulties in obtaining convictions in similar cases where the trader has admitted that the deception did not operate on his mind. For example, it seems that this was the reason why the prosecution resorted unsuccessfully in *Navvabi*[63] to a charge of theft, though the facts were strikingly similar to those of *Charles*. In *Kassim*,[64] the difficulty was said to be the reason for preferring a proliferation of charges of procuring the execution of a valuable security, contrary to s 20(2) of the 1968 Act. It is not at all surprising that the honest trader should say in testifying, 'I didn't care whether D had authority to use the card or not' but it is surprising that he would also say, 'And I would still have accepted the card even if I had known he had no authority to use it'. Unless he is prepared to go so far, *Charles* and *Lambie* assert that he has been deceived. But if the indictment alleges that the trader was induced to accept the card by D's false statement that he had authority to use it and the truth is that it did not matter to him whether D had authority or not, D should be acquitted. It may be that prosecutor's anxiety is borne of a recognition that juries would refuse to convict, preferring the truth to legal fiction, even fiction written by the House of Lords.

Since it is the trader who is 'deemed' to have been deceived, it follows that the goods or services are obtained from him by the same 'deceptions'. In *Lambie*, the House criticized the justices for dismissing a charge of obtaining goods from the shop, contrary to s 15 of the 1968 Act. It may be, however, that the justices observed that D caused no loss to the trader, who got his money from the bank, and it may be that D neither intended nor foresaw any loss to the trader. They may, therefore, have held that, so far as the trader of the goods was concerned, as opposed to the bank, that there was no evidence of dishonesty.[65]

In *Nabina*[66] D obtained credit cards by deceiving the bank as to his attributes (thus rendering the transaction with the bank voidable). D then used the cards to obtain property from various retail outlets. His conviction for obtaining that property by deception was quashed for misdirection; but the court doubted whether a properly directed jury would have been entitled to convict. The court acknowledged that there was 'room

63 [1986] 3 All ER 102, above, p 667.

64 [1988] Crim LR 372, CA; revsd [1991] 3 All ER 713. See especially Lord Ackner at 721.

65 Note that the trader will clearly not lose out, and the bank is unlikely to lose since D has a contract with them and will be compelled to repay at unfavourable rates of interest and with penalties for unauthorized use. Is there a need to criminalize such conduct? Some would argue that it is inappropriate to punish D for overspending resulting in no loss when the banks do their utmost to induce more borrowing on credit.

66 [2000] Crim LR 481. The court rejected an argument that it was not bound to apply the rules of civil law (voidable contracts). Following *Hinks* (above, p 653) *Nabina* might be convicted of stealing the property.

for doubt' whether a supplier of goods is interested (i) in how a buyer got his credit card from the bank in the first place, and (ii) whether D represented any more than that he had authority to bind the bank (which, apparently, he had, because although the issue of the card was voidable it had not been avoided at the time of the transactions) and that the transaction would be honoured by the bank (which was true).

Obtaining from a corporation

A second difficulty in applying the principle that someone must be caused to act by an operative deception arises in respect of corporations. The difficulties stem from the manner in which criminal law approaches the question of the corporation's 'mind'.[67] It was held in *Rozeik*[68] that where it is alleged that D obtained a cheque from a limited company, it must be proved that a person whose state of mind was that of the company was deceived. In *Rozeik* the managers who signed the cheques were the persons authorized to do so within the company and they were not deceived because they knew that D's representations were false, but – surprisingly – they were not parties to the fraud. The managers were the company for the purpose of issuing the cheques, they were not deceived, and therefore since they were the mind of the company, so it was not deceived either. Once again, the proposed new offences of fraud discussed below avoid this problem since there is no element of deception, merely a requirement that D made a false representation.

In determining whether a deception has been operative when practised on a company, the question seems to be whether the employee who is deceived into supplying that which has been obtained had the authority of the company to do so. In the case of obtaining cheques by deception there is an important distinction to note. If the cheques are treated as things in action, only those authorized in the company have authority to issue them. If however, the cheques are regarded as pieces of paper it seems to be different. If D deceives the company's messenger, whose duty it is to deliver cheques, into handing signed cheques (pieces of paper) to him, D has obtained the cheques, in this sense, from the company, just as he would have obtained any other item of tangible property he acquired in this way. If D deceives the waiter at the Savoy into supplying him with a meal he has obtained it by deception from the owner of the hotel, whether company or individual, because the waiter is the person with the authority of the company to take D's order and deliver his meal.

Deception and machines

As noted, it has long been established that 'to deceive is . . . to induce a man to believe that a thing is true which is false, and which the person practising the deceit knows or believes to be false'.[69] Deceit can therefore be practiced only on a human mind.[70] Where D obtains property or a pecuniary advantage as the result of some dishonest practice on a machine, without the intervention of a human mind, he cannot be guilty of an obtaining offence. It was held to be larceny (and, implicitly, not obtaining by false pretences) to get cigarettes

67 Cf above, Ch 10 on corporate responsibility.

68 [1996] 1 Cr App R 260, [1996] Crim LR 271.

69 *Re London and Globe Finance Corpn* [1903] 1 Ch 728 at 732.

70 *Davies v Flackett* [1973] RTR 8, DC. See the discussion by M. Chapman, 'Can a Computer be Deceived' (2000) J Crim Law 89.

from a machine by using a brass disc instead of a coin.[71] The owner of the machine intends to pass ownership *and* possession of the goods only to a person who inserts the proper coin. D would nowadays be convicted of theft. There is no difference, so far as the law of theft is concerned, between operating the machine by the use of a foreign coin or worthless disc and causing it to disgorge its contents by the use of a screwdriver.

There is a similar problem where the machine does not produce goods but provides a service. If the service is dishonestly obtained without deceiving a human being, there can be no obtaining offence. If D, by using a foreign coin, operates the washing machine in V's launderette, he is not guilty of obtaining the service by deception but may be convicted of the offence of abstracting electricity and possibly of making off without payment contrary to the Theft Act 1978, s 3(1).

In *Holmes*[72] the court observed that *Davies v Flackett* is not a binding authority for the proposition that deception of a machine or computer is not a deception, but accepted that the prevailing view is that it is not possible to deceive a machine. The court regarded this as regrettable, and urged a new offence of theft or some cognate offence to deal with the problem.

The problem has become an acute one in recent years, as businesses become increasingly automated with, for example, facilities to pay by credit card via an automated telephone system or via the internet. As a result, the Law Commission gave detailed consideration to the issue in its recommendations on fraud. The Commission's proposal is that it should be an offence to obtain a service dishonestly – whether by deceiving a person, giving false information to a machine, manipulating a machine without giving it false information, or by any other dishonest means. This offence would be more analogous to theft than to deception, because it could be committed by (helping oneself) to the service rather than dishonestly inducing another person to provide it.[73] The offence will be capable of being committed by D causing the machine to respond in the manner required, and where a machine is 'designed or programmed to perform a task *automatically* whenever certain criteria are satisfied at any future date' by D causing 'the machine to perform that task on a particular occasion . . . even though those responsible for designing or programming the machine may not be personally aware that the necessary criteria have been satisfied on that occasion'.[74]

Obtaining too remote from deception

As with all issues of causation, there are potential problems of remoteness and intervening causes. Under the former law of false pretences it was held that, if D induces V by deception to accept bets on credit and D backs a winning horse, the money paid by V to D is not obtained by the deception: the effective cause of the obtaining is not the deception but the fact that D backed a winner. Similarly it was held that D who obtained employment as a teacher by deception did not obtain the salary paid at the end of the month by deception: the salary was paid for the work done, not in consequence of the

71 *Hands* (1887) 16 Cox CC 188. Cf *Cooper and Miles* [1979] Crim LR 42 (Judge Woods), *Goodwin* [1996] Crim LR 262.

72 [2004] EWCA Crim 2020.

73 Law Com Report No 276, para 8.8.

74 Ibid, para 8.9.

deception. Both of these cases are now expressly provided for in the 1968 Act, s 16(2)(c) and constitute an offence of obtaining a pecuniary advantage by deception.[75]

The issue continues to present difficulties. In the important case of *King and Stockwell*,[76] convictions for attempting to obtain property by deception were upheld where DD persuaded V to employ them to cut down V's trees by falsely stating that the trees were dangerous. The court rejected the argument that, if the money had been paid, it would have been paid because the work had been done, not because of the deception. The question whether the deception would have been an operative cause of the obtaining of the money was one of fact for the jury. In the case of many contracts of service, however, it is obvious that there does come a point when the salary or wage is paid *solely* because the work has been done and any deception by which the employment was obtained has become inoperative. It would be absurd to suggest that D, who obtained his job by deception 30 years ago, obtained last month's salary in that post by that deception. Even in that case, however, D might be convicted under s 15 where he is paid a higher salary if his employer still believes the false representation he made on appointment that he holds a particular qualification that entitles him to be on a higher salary scale. The deception then appears to be the direct and continuing cause of his obtaining the additional money.[77]

(d) Dishonesty[78]

The final common element of these offences is that of dishonesty. This is a separate element of the offences from that of deception. As the CLRC wrote of the clause which became s 15 of the 1968 Act:

> Owing to the words 'dishonestly obtains' a person who uses deception in order to obtain property to which he believes himself entitled will not be guilty; for though the deception may be dishonest, the obtaining is not.[79]

The provisions relating to dishonesty in s 2(1)[80] of the 1968 Act are not expressly made applicable to obtaining offences – some of them would be inappropriate to obtaining – and the CLRC thought it unnecessary and undesirable to complicate the Act by a separate definition. Dishonesty is substantially undefined for theft, no less than for obtaining and it seems clear that it should bear the same meaning throughout the Theft Acts. This view is reinforced by the effect of *Gomez*, that practically all obtaining of property other than land is also theft. A claim of right which negatives dishonesty for the purposes of theft must surely do the same for obtaining property by deception and, it is submitted, the other obtaining offences in the Acts which require dishonesty.

75 Below, p 765. 76 [1987] QB 547, [1987] 1 All ER 547, [1987] Crim LR 398 and commentary.

77 Cf *Levene v Pearcey* [1976] Crim LR 63 and commentary (taxi driver obtaining excessive fare by telling passenger normal route blocked).

78 See Law Com Report No 276, Part V.

79 Cmnd 2977, para 88. In *Parker* (1910) 74 JP 208 Ridley J held that a claim of right was no answer to a charge of demanding money upon a forged document with intent to defraud. In *Woolven*, the court thought that case was not a decisive authority against a claim of right defence under s 15; and *Parker* has been overruled by the Forgery and Counterfeiting Act 1981, s 10(2).

80 Above, p 692.

D may deceive deliberately or recklessly, yet be found not to be acting dishonestly. *Ghosh*, itself, was a case under s 15. D, a surgeon, claimed a fee for an operation that he said he had carried out. The prosecution alleged that someone else had carried it out. The jury believed the prosecution which, as the court said, rendered the finding of dishonesty inevitable, whichever test was applied. Having considered the cases on both theft and obtaining offences, the court stated the test set out above.[81]

Two further issues relating to dishonesty deserve attention.

(i) Dishonesty where there is or may be a claim of right

In *Woolven*[82] the Court of Appeal thought that the *Ghosh* direction was wide enough to embrace those occasions on which D might have a claim of right. If this is true for obtaining, it is equally true for theft; and s 2(1)(a) of the Act is in effect redundant. If every jury would inevitably find that a person with a claim of right is not dishonest under the *Ghosh* test, there is no need for a judge to give a separate claim of right direction. But in the case of obtaining offences it may be desirable to do so. Dishonesty here comes into question only where D has made a deliberate or reckless deception. There is a risk that a jury might think that a person who had practiced a deliberate deception in order to obtain must have obtained dishonestly even when he did so to get something to which he thought (perhaps rightly) that he was entitled. In *Talbott*[83] D, in order to conceal from her landlord that she was obtaining housing benefit, obtained a lease in her stage name and applied to the local authority for benefit in her real name, pretending that her stage name was that of her landlady. The authority's officers testified that they would not have paid had they known the truth. That was apparently regarded as conclusive of her guilt. But D seems to have believed, and perhaps she was right, that she was entitled to the benefit, whatever the identity of her landlord. If so, though she may have practiced a dishonest deception, she had not obtained the benefit dishonestly[84] and should not have been convicted.

(ii) Dishonesty where there is no claim of right

Prior to *Feely*[85] the courts decided as a matter of law that certain obtainings were dishonest. In *McCall*,[86] obtaining a loan by deception was held to be dishonest, notwithstanding D's intention to repay. D's submission that such conduct 'is not necessarily tainted with dishonesty' was rejected. There was 'an unanswerable case' against him. In *Halstead v Patel*,[87] D knowingly overdrew on a Giro account, intending to repay at some future date when a strike was over. It was held, relying on decisions that were not followed in *Feely*, that the 'pious hope' of repaying at some future date was no defence; the justices

81 See p 697. 82 (1983) 77 Cr App R 231, [1983] Crim LR 623, CA.

83 [1995] Crim LR 396.

84 She might possibly have obtained *the lease* dishonestly – obtaining a service, contrary to Theft Act 1978, s 1.

85 Above, p 696.

86 (1970) 55 Cr App R 175. In *Melwani* [1989] Crim LR 565, CA, it was said that *McCall* 'cannot really survive the decisions in *Feely* and *Ghosh*'; and this may be true of the other cases cited in this paragraph.

87 [1972] 2 All ER 147. The judgment is clearly wrong in so far as it refers to a 'belief based on reasonable grounds'. See [1972] Crim LR 236; *Lewis* [1976] Crim LR 383, CA.

were bound to convict. In *Potger*,[88] where D induced V to subscribe for magazines by the false representation that he was a student taking part in a points competition, it was no answer that magazines worth the money paid for them would have been delivered in due course. In none of these cases was there any evidence of a claim of right to that which was obtained.

In *Feely*, Lawton LJ contrasted the case of the person who takes money from a till intending to repay (presumably before it is missed); and the person who obtains cash by passing a cheque on an account with no funds, intending to pay funds in to meet the cheque when it is presented, as 'the [person] who passes the cheque is deemed in law not to act dishonestly if he genuinely believes on reasonable grounds that when it is presented to the paying bank there will be funds to meet it'.

Lawton LJ commented, 'Lawyers may be able to appreciate why one [person] should be adjudged to be a criminal and the other not; but we doubt whether anyone else would'.

This misses the point that the person passing the cheque would be acquitted of an obtaining offence on the ground that he does not intend to deceive, so the question of dishonesty would be unlikely to arise. After *Gomez* he might now be charged with theft; and, if he were it would be a matter for the judgement of the jury in accordance with *Ghosh*. Moreover, the cases are distinguishable on the basis that the raider of the till intends to commit a legal wrong – a trespass against, or a breach of contract with, the owner – whereas the passer of the cheque has no such intention.

3. Obtaining property by deception: s 15

Section 15(1) of the 1968 Act provides:

> (1) A person who by any deception dishonestly obtains property belonging to another, with the intention of permanently depriving the other of it, shall on conviction on indictment be liable to imprisonment for a term not exceeding ten years.

Although all obtaining property (except land and possibly other exceptional cases)[89] by deception is, after *Gomez*, theft, the offence under s 15 is by no means redundant. It is, theoretically, the more serious offence since the maximum for theft has been reduced to seven years. More significantly, it is often the charge more appropriate to the facts which better describes the blameworthy conduct of the accused and labels him appropriately on conviction as a fraudster not a thief. On the other hand, the prosecutor who relies on s 15 may be undertaking an additional and by no means negligible burden: he has to prove an operative deception, which is not necessary to establish theft. Even with the degree of overlap with the offence of theft, if there is no operative deception the appropriate charge is theft; s 15 will fail.[90] In *Talbott*,[91] for example, the prosecutor's path might have been eased if he had charged theft of the housing benefit. The difficulty of proving dishonesty is the same, whichever charge is brought.

88 (1970) 55 Cr App R 42.

89 Noted by R. Heaton, 'Deceiving without Thieving' [2001] Crim LR 712.

90 See *Davies* [2003] EWCA Crim 1482.

91 Above, p 757.

(a) Property belonging to another

The offence may be committed in respect of any 'property belonging to another'. By s 34(1) of the Theft Act 1968, s 4(1)[92] and s 5(1)[93] – which contain the primary definitions of 'property' and 'belonging to another' – are applied generally for the purposes of the Act.

Consequently 'money and all other property, real or personal, including things in action and other intangible property' may be obtained by deception. So far as things in action are concerned D might commit the offence where, for example, by deception he induces V to transfer or assign a debt, a copyright or patent, or other intangible property. The categories of property that, by s 4, may not be stolen (land, wild animals and flora, etc) may be obtained by deception. So far as land is concerned the most obvious case is that of an impostor claiming trust property or a deceased person's estate,[94] but it would extend to any case where D by deception obtains the whole of another's interest in land.

Since 'property belonging to another' is to be given the same meaning it has for theft under s 5(1),[95] it follows that D may commit an offence under s 15 where by deception he obtains property of which he is the owner. If, for example, having pawned his clock, D recovers possession from the pawnbroker by deception, he may be guilty of the offence under s 15.

(b) Ownership, possession or control

Section 15(2) provides:

> For the purposes of this section a person is to be treated as obtaining property if he obtains ownership, possession or control of it, and 'obtain' includes obtaining for another or enabling another to obtain or retain.

Usually D obtains ownership, possession and control simultaneously but the obtaining of any one of these suffices. The offence appears to be committed when and where any of them is obtained. If D, in England, becomes the owner, the offence is committed in England, though he acquires possession, then or later, abroad. The offence may be committed in more than one place but, presumably, on one occasion only.[96]

Most often D will obtain the goods for himself but the offence is also committed where D obtains for another or enables another to obtain or retain. Thus the offence might be committed where, for example, D by deception induces V to transfer the ownership in property to E; or where by deception D induces V, who has lent goods to E, to not enforce his right to recover goods from E. In such cases E may be a confederate but D may commit the offence whether E is a confederate or not.

But D would commit no offence under s 15 where, for example, owing V £10, he dishonestly tells V that he has paid him and that V must have forgotten about it. Here D does not obtain any property belonging to V.[97] Nor would D commit this offence where he enables himself to retain property belonging to V, as where he falsely tells V that he has lost a book that V lent him.[98] He might commit the offence under s 15 by falsely

[92] Above, p 666. [93] Above, p 674. [94] Cmnd 2977, para 91. [95] Above, p 674.

[96] Cf the position in theft, pp 664–665 above.

[97] But D commits an offence under s 2 of the 1978 Act; below, p 776.

[98] But D would be guilty of stealing the book.

telling V that E has lost the book which V lent to E, for this might enable E to retain the book; but not by falsely telling V that E has repaid a loan of money which V made to E because this does not enable E to retain property belonging to V.

(c) Something belonging to V must be transferred to D

The offence is not committed unless something which belongs to V before the deception is transferred to D in consequence of it. In the landmark case of *Preddy*,[99] the House of Lords, reversing the Court of Appeal, held that where D dishonestly and by deception procures a transaction whereby V's bank account is debited by £x and, consequently, D's bank account is credited by £x, D is not guilty of obtaining property 'belonging to' V. The effect is exactly the same as if D had obtained £x belonging to V but, in law, nothing which formerly belonged to V now belongs to D. A thing in action belonging to V[100] (the indebtedness of V's bank to V) has been diminished (or perhaps extinguished) and a different thing in action (the indebtedness of D's bank to D) has been enlarged (or perhaps created). This is the effect when funds are transferred between bank accounts, as is now common, by telegraphic transfer or CHAPS (Clearing House Automatic Payment System), or a similar order. The decision caused consternation because of the many frauds, particularly 'mortgage frauds,' which had been and were being prosecuted, it now appeared wrongly, under s 15. The Law Commission speedily produced a Report and draft Bill,[101] which rapidly became the Theft (Amendment) Act 1996, filling the lacuna exposed by *Preddy* with a new s 15A of the 1968 Act creating an offence of obtaining a money transfer by deception.[102]

(d) *Mens rea*

There are four elements of *mens rea* under s 15: (i) a deliberate or reckless deception; (ii) dishonesty; (iii) an intention permanently to deprive; and (iv) an intention to obtain the property.

Those elements of *mens rea* which are common to the offences under ss 15 15A, 16, and ss 1 and 2 of the 1978 Act, viz the making of a deliberate or reckless deception and dishonesty. Section 15(3) provides that as regard an intention permanently to deprive s 6 applies with the necessary adaptation of the reference to appropriating and reference may be made to the discussion elsewhere.

There must, lastly, be an intention to obtain the property for oneself or another by the deception. If, for example, during the course of negotiations for the purchase of goods on credit D tells V what he thinks to be an inconsequential lie (say that he was on active service during the war) he would not commit this offence though V is in fact induced to let him have the goods on credit because he is an ex-serviceman. D did not intend by the deception to obtain the goods. Nor would it be enough that D intends to cause loss to V unless he intends to obtain the property for himself or another.[103]

99 [1996] AC 815, [1996] 3 All ER 481.

100 Cf above, p 666.

101 Law Com No 243, *Offences of Dishonesty: Money Transfers* (1996).

102 See below, p 764.

103 See Smith, *Theft*, para 4–63. Cf *Balcombe v Desimoni* [1972] ALR 513.

(e) Some special cases

There are some types of obtaining property that present peculiar difficulties and require special consideration.

(i) Obtaining (or stealing) cheques

Obtaining from V a negotiable cheque drawn by X in favour of V

It is generally assumed that, where D, by deception, causes V to negotiate to him a negotiable cheque drawn by X in favour of V,[104] a thing in action belonging to V – V's right to sue X on the cheque – has passed to D. D has obtained property belonging to V by deception and he intends to deprive V permanently of it by presenting the cheque, thus extinguishing the thing in action. Since *Preddy*,[105] it is arguable that what has happened is that the thing in action belonging to V was destroyed when the cheque was negotiated and that D acquired a new, different thing in action. If that is right, D has not obtained anything belonging to V. He is guilty of theft of V's thing in action (by destroying it), but not of obtaining it.

But this view is questionable. It depends on the nature of the concept of negotiability. One opinion is that the delivery of the document transfers the obligation locked in it[106] – the same, continuing obligation, to honour the cheque. If that is right, D has obtained the thing in action that formerly belonged to V. Even if this is not so, as is submitted, above, D has clearly obtained property in the form of, the physical instrument itself which is a valuable security giving access to X's bank account; but in *Clark*[107] the Court of Appeal reluctantly decided otherwise. The essence of a bill of exchange (of which an 'uncrossed' cheque is one) is that the drawer acknowledges the right of any subsequent lawful presenter to sue him on the bill. This right to sue can be transferred by the original payee by endorsement of the bill but the chose in action remains the same.

Where D takes the cheque from V without deception, it is clear that there is only one thing in action which belongs to V and D steals it by assuming V's rights, probably when he presents the cheque for payment[108] and, at the latest, when the cheque is cleared.

Where D induces V to draw a cheque in favour of D

In this situation D acquires a thing in action – the right to sue V on the cheque – but this thing was clearly never 'property belonging to another.' It could not be obtained from V, contrary to s 15, because it never belonged, or could belong to him: he could not sue himself! A cheque, however, has two aspects; it is a thing in action and it is also a piece of paper. The piece of paper certainly belonged to V; but there is a difficulty in finding an intention permanently to deprive V of the paper. When, as he presumably intends, D cashes the cheque, it will probably be returned in due course to V's bank. How then, it is argued can D (if he understands banking practice) be said to intend permanently to deprive V of the paper? This can hardly be regarded as a case of 'borrowing' so as to be 'equivalent to an outright taking or disposal' under s 6.

104 Surely this is a rarity in era of crossed cheques?

105 [1996] AC 815, above, p 760.

106 Goode, *Commercial Law* (3rd edn, 2004), 274.

107 [2002] 1 Cr App R 141, [2001] Crim LR 572.

108 Cf *Ngan*, above, p 665.

The answer given in *Duru*[109] was twofold: (i) that V was permanently deprived of the thing in action represented by the cheque; and (ii) that the cheque, as a piece of paper, changed its character completely once it was paid, 'because then it receives a rubber stamp on it saying it has been paid and it ceases to be a thing in action, or at any rate it ceases to be, in its substance, the same thing as it was before: that is, an instrument on which payment falls to be made'. It has now been decided by the House of Lords in *Preddy*,[110] overruling *Duru* on this point, that the first reason is misconceived: the thing in action never was property belonging to V so there was nothing of which he could be deprived, permanently or otherwise.[111] This was decided in *Danger*,[112] as long ago as 1857 but that case was overlooked or ignored by the courts before *Preddy*.

Preddy decides that there can be no obtaining (or, by implication, theft) of the thing in action. That is clearly right, but the decision has been taken as authority for the wider proposition that there can be no theft of *the cheque* – which is a tangible thing, not a thing in action.[113] As noted above, this must be accepted as the law for the present, but it remains open to challenge. The difficulties may all be avoided by using s 20(2) of the Act, below, instead of s 15. Section 20(2) is tailor-made for the purpose, being the successor of the provision passed to fill the gap revealed by *Danger*.

In *Lee (Lucky Boy Charlie)*,[114] D obtained a cheque for £4,700 from a 92-year-old woman for one hour's work cutting her hedge. The cheque was stopped by an alert bank clerk. The conviction for obtaining property by deception was held to be flawed since the cheque would have been returned to V and there was no intention permanently to deprive. The Court of Appeal substituted a conviction for attempting to obtain a money order by deception under s 15A (below), but it is submitted that a charge under s 20 would have been appropriate.

Alternatively, if D has presented the cheque, he might be charged with theft, not of the cheque but of V's bank balance. D has assumed the rights of an owner over V's credit balance, or right to overdraw as the case may be and intends permanently to deprive V of that. It is as if he had obtained the key to open V's safe and extract the money. He is guilty of theft.[115] Since *Gomez* it is no longer an objection that D's dealing with the cheque signed by V was authorized by V.

(ii) Procuring transfers of funds by electronic means

A related problem arises where D by deception procures a CHAPS order or a telegraphic or electronic transfer of funds by V. The result is that V's bank account is debited by £x

109 [1973] 3 All ER 715, [1973] Crim LR 701 (sub nom *Asghar*) and commentary. *Mitchell* [1993] Crim LR 788, CA, was also overruled.

110 [1996] 3 All ER 481.

111 The first reason might be good if the cheque were drawn by a third party in favour of V but this was not so in *Duru*.

112 (1857) 7 Cox CC 303.

113 In *Horsman* [1997] 3 All ER 385, [1998] Crim LR 128 and commentary, it was 'common ground' that, because there could be no obtaining of the thing in action, there could be no obtaining of the cheque. It is submitted that this is inconsistent with *Arnold* [1997] 4 All ER 1, where D was convicted of stealing a valuable security, a bill of exchange, signed by V, and received from V by D, with an obligation to retain and deal with it in a particular way. The thing in action embodied in the bill could not belong to V, but it is implicit in the decision that the bill did.

114 (1999) 98/78031/25.

115 *Hallam and Blackburn* [1995] Crim LR 323, CA.

and D's account is simultaneously credited with £x. This was held by the Court of Appeal in *Preddy*[116] to be an obtaining by D from V. The ruling in the Court of Appeal was that this situation had the same effect as if something belonging to V had been transferred to D. However, the House of Lords decided that, both in fact and in law, nothing has transferred; D has not obtained 'property belonging to another'. For the House of Lords that concluded the matter: s 15 was 'being invoked for a purpose for which it was never designed and for which it does not legislate'. The matter is now dealt with by the new s 15A.[117] The problem remains that some such transactions are entirely automated and the new s 15A offence still requires the element of deception which on an orthodox interpretation cannot be committed against a machine.

(iii) How far does *Preddy* go?

If V has a £50 note, theoretically, he possesses a thing in action as well as the piece of paper. The thing in action is the right to demand the sum from the Bank of England (each note bears the legend 'I promise to pay the bearer . . .'). If D deceives V into transferring that piece of paper (the £50 note) to him, has D obtained more than the piece of paper? Can it be argued that the thing in action D obtains – D's right to demand from the Bank of England – is a new piece of property, and quite distinct from that which V owned.[118] Surely this oversimplifies the position of negotiable instruments?

(iv) Obtaining a leasehold

Suppose that D, by deception, induces V, the owner of freehold land, to grant him a lease of the land for two years. Clearly D does not intend to deprive V permanently, or indeed at all, of the property which belongs to him – that is, his freehold interest. Nor, if he intends to vacate the property after two years, does he intend to deprive V permanently of possession of the land. The position would be the same if V were himself a lessee whose lease had three years to run and he granted D a sub-lease for two years. These cases look much the same as that of the owner of a ship who charters it for two years. If the charterer has induced the charter by deception but intends to return the ship he does not commit the offence, because of his lack of intention permanently to deprive. Moreover, the leasehold estate never 'belonged to', or could belong to V, the owner of the freehold.[119] The leasehold interest does not exist until the lease is granted – and then it belongs to D. This case would best be dealt with as an obtaining of services contrary to 1978, s 1.

116 [1995] Crim LR 564; revsd [1996] 3 All ER 481, HL. 117 Infra.

118 See on transfers D. Fox, 'The Transfer of Legal Title to Money' [1996] Restitution LR 60.

119 *Chan Wai Lam v R* [1981] Crim LR 497 (Court of Appeal of Hong Kong) and commentary. In *Chan Wai Lam v R*, D was held to have no intent permanently to deprive where he obtained from the Hong Kong government a lease which would have expired three days before the end of the lease of the New Territories held by the government. Had the lease obtained been three days longer, it is submitted that there would have been evidence that D would have obtained possession with intent permanently to deprive. Otherwise he might have been held liable on the *de minimis* principle – but the courts are properly reluctant to invoke that principle in criminal cases.

4. Obtaining a money transfer by deception[120]

Section 15A of the 1968 Act (enacted bt the Theft (Amendment) Act 1996) provides:

> (1) A person is guilty of an offence if by any deception he dishonestly obtains a money transfer for himself or another.
>
> (2) A money transfer occurs when –
>
> (a) a debit is made to one account,
>
> (b) a credit is made to another, and
>
> (c) the credit results from the debit or the debit results from the credit.
>
> (3) References to a credit and to a debit are to a credit of an amount of money and to a debit of an amount of money.

This very specific provision describes what *Preddy* did and enacts that it is an offence.[121] There is a statutory 'transfer' although *Preddy* decides that there is no transfer of property in law or fact. The Law Commission rejected the option of amending s 15, finding that this could be done only by an undesirable amount of 'deeming'. The more direct approach in s 15A is preferred, although it does illustrate how the deception offences have been enacted incrementally to tackle perceived lacunae rather than implemented as a more structured and coherent package of offences.

The new offence under s 15A seems to fill the *Preddy* lacuna very effectively but it is not, of course, retrospective, so only money transfers obtained after 18 December 1996 may be prosecuted under s 15A.[122] Subsection (3) limits the offence to 'money', (which is not limited to sterling) meaning an obligation to pay money, notably the obligation of a banker to his customer. It would not therefore apply to transfers of other things in action, such as bonds and securities.[123]

There has been little judicial consideration of the terms of the offence. In *Holmes*,[124] D faced extradition for his conduct when working as an official in a German bank. He used a co-worker's password to credit an account under his control in a Dutch bank. The banking practice, of which the court took judicial notice, was such that the transfer was not complete until the Dutch bank received confirmation from the German bank. The Administrative Court held that 'credit' in s 15A is to be construed as an 'unconditional credit' so that

120 For criticism of the Act see J. C. Smith, *Current Law Statutes Annotated* (1996); C. Osborn, 'Fraud Fudge' [1996] 93(41) Law Soc Gaz 24; the SFO was reported as seeing s 15A as a 'sticking plaster solution', *Financial Times*, 16 Oct 1996.

121 On *Preddy* problems around the world see G. J. Lugar-Mawson, 'The Preddy Problem' (Letter to the Editor) [1996] Crim LR 845. The decision in *Wilkinson* (31 Oct 1998) in New Zealand followed that in *Preddy* and prompted the NZLRC response. Although the Commission considered adopting the English 1996 Act, it was rejected as being too confined and insufficiently flexible for future problems. The preferred solution was to extend the ambit of existing offences by inserting into its offence of obtaining by false pretences, a more general formula criminalising D who with intent to defraud by any false pretence . . . 'obtains for himself or for any other person any privilege, benefit, pecuniary advantage, or valuable consideration'.

122 See *O'Neill* [2003] EWCA Crim 411.

123 This limitation was criticized by Lord Donaldson of Lymington, whose amendments designed to broaden the ambit of the offence were not accepted: HL, vol 576, col. 796.

124 [2004] EWHC Admin 2020; [2005] Crim LR 229 and commentary.

for the purposes of the offence the credit only occurred once the Dutch bank received confirmation. In other respects the court took a broad approach to interpretation, holding that it was not necessary to identify which account had been debited or whether it was in credit at the time. The court did not find it necessary to resolve whether s 15A could be committed where the transaction is entirely automated and no mind had been 'deceived'. The court did find it regrettable that obtaining by means of computer operation where the accused knew that he had no right to do so was not a substantive offence.

Subsection (4) anticipates and excludes possible unmeritorious defences. It is not material that the amount credited is different from the amount debited; that delay occurs in the process of transfer; that intermediate credits are made in the course of the transfer from V to D; or that either account is overdrawn before or after the transfer. This is not an exclusive list, as the words 'in particular', are intended to make clear. There are many matters which a court may properly hold to be immaterial, though they are not listed in the subsection.

(a) Obtaining a money transfer by cheque

As noted above, *Preddy* also settled[125] that where D induces V to draw and deliver a cheque in favour of D, D is not guilty under s 15 of the 1968 Act of obtaining by deception the thing in action represented by the cheque. That thing in action was never 'property belonging to' V. From the moment it came into existence, it belonged to D. When D presents the cheque and it is honoured a debit is made to V's account and a corresponding credit to D's, so a money transfer as defined in s 15A(1) occurs. Arguably, in such a case, the so-called *transfer* has not been obtained by deception but by D's presentation of the cheque (as where a key is obtained by deception and used to open a safe and steal: the money taken from the safe has been stolen, not obtained by deception). Subsection (4)(b) appears to assume that the transfer has been obtained by deception and, for practical purposes, probably puts the matter beyond all doubt. Even so, the new offence will not be committed until the cheque is honoured. D will, however, be guilty of an attempt to commit that offence when he presents, or attempts to present, the cheque.[126] Until he does so, he has probably not done any act that is more than merely preparatory to the commission of the s 15A offence. Nor will D be guilty of obtaining a transfer of funds if he negotiates the cheque to E for cash. V's account has not yet been debited and no account has been credited. The offence will be committed only when E, or some subsequent holder of the cheque presents it, and it is honoured. It is therefore almost as important as it was before the Theft (Amendment) Act 1996 to know whether D has obtained the cheque, as a valuable security, contrary to s 15.[127]

5. Obtaining a pecuniary advantage by deception: s 16[128]

The offence of obtaining a pecuniary advantage under s 16(2)(a) was found to create such formidable difficulties of interpretation (being described as 'a nightmare') that it was repealed and replaced by new offences under ss 1 and 2 of the 1978 Act. Otherwise

125 Following *Danger* (1857) 7 Cox CC 303, CCR and overruling *Duru* [1973] 3 All ER 715.
126 *See Lee* (1999) above. 127 See above.
128 See Smith, *Theft*, para 4–65 et seq; Griew, *Theft*, ch 11.

the offence of obtaining a pecuniary advantage is retained but it may be committed only in the ways specified in paragraphs (b) and (c).[129]

Section 16 provides:

> (1) A person who by any deception dishonestly obtains for himself or another any pecuniary advantage shall on conviction on indictment be liable to imprisonment for a term not exceeding five years.
>
> (2) The cases in which a pecuniary advantage within the meaning of this section is to be regarded as obtained for a person are cases where – . . .
>
> (b) he is allowed to borrow by way of overdraft, or to take out any policy of insurance or annuity contract, or obtains an improvement of the terms on which he is allowed to do so; or
>
> (c) he is given the opportunity to earn remuneration or greater remuneration in an office or employment, or to win money by betting.
>
> (3) For the purposes of this section 'deception' has the same meaning as in section 15 of this Act.

Only those types of pecuniary advantage listed in s 16(2) are protected: the definition of pecuniary advantage in s 16(2) is exhaustive. Proof that some pecuniary advantage was obtained by D will not suffice unless it falls within the definition; and if the case falls within the definition it is irrelevant that D in fact obtained no pecuniary advantage since the section states that D is *deemed* to have obtained the advantage if its terms are met.[130] Under the proposed reform below, the offence would occur where D made false representations, irrespective of their causal impact.

(a) Overdrafts

D may commit an offence, by virtue of s 16(2)(b), where by deception he is allowed to borrow by way of overdraft; as where he tells his banker that he requires the credit to enable him to sell goods abroad when in reality he intends to purchase a new car. An overdraft, as if it needed explanation at least for student readers, is ordinarily regarded as a facility whereby a person may, if he so wishes, overdraw his account to a stated limit.[131] It has been held that D commits an offence under this section by being 'allowed' to borrow by way of overdraft where he *uses* the cheque guarantee card issued to him by the bank and creates an unauthorized overdraft or exceeds his overdraft. In such circumstances, the bank is bound to honour cheques issued by D even where they exceed the amount by which his account is in credit.[132] Even though D is acting in express

129 But only one offence is created: *Bale v Rosier* [1977] 2 All ER 160, [1977] 1 WLR 263. The charge must specify the pecuniary advantage which D is alleged to have obtained: *Aston and Hadley* [1970] 3 All ER 1045, [1970] 1 WLR 1584, CA.

130 *DPP v Turner* [1973] 3 All ER 124 at 126, per Lord Reid. Cf T. Waters, 'Obtaining a Pecuniary Advantage' (1974) 37 MLR 562.

131 So the offence is complete when D obtains the facility to overdraw; it is not necessary that D should have used the facility: *Watkins* [1976] 1 All ER 578 (Crown Court).

132 *Waites* [1982] Crim LR 369, CA. This seems a surprising decision as it would surely astonish bankers to learn that by issuing such cards they are *allowing* their customers to borrow by way of overdraft to an unspecified amount. But *Waites* was followed in *Bevan* (1986) 84 Cr App R 143, [1987] Crim LR 129, CA. See also E. J. Griew, 'Unauthorized Overdrawing by Use of Cheque Card Abroad' [1987] 2 JIBL 116.

contravention of the bank's authorization, the courts treat him as being 'allowed' to borrow. A bank loan is not an overdraft. It is effected by crediting the customer's account and debiting a separate loan account.

(b) Insurance policies

Section 16(2)(b) also applies to insurance policies and annuity contracts obtained by deception,[133] as where D secures a policy, or a policy on better terms, by falsely stating for example that he is a non-smoker where this is material to the issue of the policy or its terms on a health insurance form or life insurance contract. Another straightforward illustration would be where D claims, falsely, to have more no claims entitlement when applying for motor insurance.

(c) Opportunity to earn by employment or win by betting

As has been shown the offence of obtaining by deception contrary to s 15 is not committed unless the deception is an effective cause of the obtaining of the property. Consequently there are doubts whether D commits the s 15 offence when his bookmaker pays up, having been deceived into taking the bet on credit: D's backing a winner may be regarded as the effective cause of the obtaining, not D's deception as to his credit.[134] The case is now expressly covered by s 16(2)(c) and the offence may be committed whether D is allowed to bet on credit or cash terms.

Section 16(2)(c) similarly gets over the ruling in *Lewis*[135] that, where D obtains a job by deception, he cannot be convicted of obtaining his salary by deception because his salary is paid in respect of work he does, not the deception that got him the job. This ruling has been doubted[136] and it may well be that the case is covered by s 15. Section 16(2)(c) provides a more certain sanction.

Paragraph (c) refers to 'office or employment'. An office can be held by one who is employed and if that office carries additional remuneration this offence may be committed if it is obtained by deception. But an office may exist without any contract of service, as where D is appointed chairman of a voluntary society and if that office is remunerated, as by an honorarium, it would be an offence to obtain the opportunity to earn that remuneration by deception. D commits the offence by obtaining the office by deception or by obtaining a promotion (higher remuneration) by deception. In *McNiff*[137] it was held that the tenancy of a public house was not an office. Nor had the tenant obtained the opportunity to earn remuneration in employment because the tenant of a pub earns the opportunity to earn money by his own efforts and is not remunerated by the brewery. Since an office may exist without a contract of service[138] there would seem to be no reason for confining 'employment' to cases where there is a contract of service. Giving

133 The offence may be committed although, as a result of the deception, D could not enforce the contract against V, *Alexander* [1981] Crim LR 183, CA.

134 Cf *Clucas* [1949] 2 KB 226, [1949] 2 All ER 40; above, p 000. But *King*, below, n 136 and above, p 756 casts doubt on this.

135 (1922) Russell 1186 (Rowlatt J).

136 In *King* [1987] QB 547, [1987] 1 All ER 547, CA.

137 [1986] Crim LR 57, CA.

138 On the crucial difference between contract of service and contract for services, see J. Bowers, *A Practical Approach to Employment Law* (7th edn, 2005), ch 3.

'employment' its ordinary meaning it would seem to extend to contracts for services and it was so held in *Callender*.[139]

(d) *Mens rea*

Those elements of *mens rea* which are common to the offences under both s 15 and s 16, viz the making of a deliberate or reckless deception and dishonesty, have been discussed above. Here it must be noted that, where D tells lies in order to get a job but maintains that he was not dishonest because he intended to give his employer full value for money, the question must be left to the jury.[140] In addition to the common elements, the offence under s 16 requires an intention to obtain the pecuniary advantage for oneself or another. It is not enough that D obtains a pecuniary advantage in fact unless his deception was made in order to gain it; nor is it enough that D's deception inflicts some pecuniary loss on V unless it was made in order to obtain for D or another the pecuniary advantage.

6. Procuring the execution of a valuable security

By s 20 of the Theft Act 1968:

> (2) A person who dishonestly, with a view to gain for himself or another or with intent to cause loss to another, by any deception procures the execution of a valuable security shall on conviction on indictment be liable to imprisonment for a term not exceeding seven years; and this subsection shall apply in relation to the making, acceptance, endorsement, alteration, cancellation or destruction in whole or in part of a valuable security, and in relation to the signing or sealing of any paper or other material in order that it may be made or converted into, or used or dealt with as, a valuable security, as if that were the execution of a valuable security.
>
> (3) For purposes of this section 'deception' has the same meaning as in section 15 of this Act, and 'valuable security' means any document creating, transferring, surrendering or releasing any right to in or over property, or authorising the payment of money or delivery of any property, or evidencing the creation, transfer, surrender or release of any such right, or the payment of money or delivery of any property or the satisfaction of any obligation.

This is an unhappily worded provision. The typical instance of the offence is that where D, by deception, procures V to draw a cheque in D's favour. The offence is complete on the cheque being drawn. It avoids all the problems involved in attempting to bring the case within s 1 or s 15 of the 1968 Act. In many cases it will be available in respect of conduct that would only constitute an attempt to commit obtaining or theft.

The history of s 20(2) begins in 1857 with *Danger*.[141] D produced to V a bill of exchange payable to himself and, by deception, induced V to accept the bill by writing his

139 [1993] QB 303, [1992] 3 All ER 51. On the impact of the commission of an offence under s 16 on D's ability to recover damages for loss sustained in the course of employment see *Hewison v Meridian Shipping Services Ltd* [2002] EWCA Civ 1821.

140 *Clarke (Victor)* [1996] Crim LR 824.

141 (1857) 7 Cox CC 303. See commentary on the decision of the Court of Appeal in *Kassim* [1988] Crim LR 372. See further J. C. Smith, 'Obtaining Cheques by Deception or Theft' [1997] Crim LR 396.

name across it. It was held that D was not guilty of obtaining a valuable security by false pretences: to be the subject of obtaining by false pretences, a valuable security had to be the property of someone other than D. V had no property in the document. The thing in action, and even the paper on which it was written, belonged to D.[142] In response to this decision an Act of 1858[143] made it an offence to obtain by any false pretence the signature of any person to a bill of exchange, promissory note, or any valuable security. Section 20(2) is directly descended from that Act.[144] In *Kassim*[145] the House of Lords confirmed that the 1968 Act was not intended to make any change in the law.

In *King*,[146] it was suggested that the court should approach s 20 by asking first what the relevant document does, secondly, in the light of that asking whether the document falls within any part of the definition of valuable security, and finally, whether it has been executed.

(a) Valuable security

Valuable security is widely defined and includes a crossed cheque.[147] In *Benstead and Taylor*,[148] it was held that an irrevocable letter of credit was a 'valuable security' within the meaning of the subsection, apparently on the ground that it was a document creating a right in property. This is a questionable interpretation of the provision. The words, 'any right to, in or over property', seem to assume some existing property, a right to, in or over which is created, transferred, surrendered or released. In the case of a letter of credit there is no existing property to, in or over which a right is created. The letter of credit creates a right, but it is not a right to, in or over property. It is no answer to say that the thing in action created by the letter of credit is itself property because the subsection does not include a document creating property.[149] If the decision is taken to its logical conclusion, any written contract is a valuable security because, being an enforceable contract, it creates a thing in action. In *King*, the court thought that, whether or not this criticism was justified, it did not affect that case because there was property in existence and the document evidenced both the creation and the transfer of a right.[150]

Documents 'authorising the payment of money' which would include cheques and bills (and probably a letter of credit) are expressly included. But promissory notes (which were expressly mentioned in the 1858 Act) neither create any right in existing property nor 'authorize' the payment of money. Clearly promissory notes ought to be valuable securities but this badly drafted subsection seems to exclude them.

142 See above, p 760. 143 21 & 22 Vict, c 47.

144 It was replaced by a more elaborate provision in s 90 of the Larceny Act 1861, which was re-enacted without substantial change in the Larceny Act 1916, s 32(2). The CLRC gave little consideration to the matter (Eighth Report, para 107), concluding that the subsection of the clause in their draft Bill which became s 20(2) reproduced the substance of 1916, s 32(3).

145 [1991] 3 All ER 713, HL. 146 [1991] 3 All ER 705.

147 *Cooke* [1997] Crim LR 436. Probably also a 'payable order' issued by a government department: *Graham* [1997] 1 Cr App R 302 at 325–326.

148 (1982) 75 Cr App R 276, [1982] Crim LR 456, CA, and commentary.

149 Cf Smith, *Property Offences*, 24–17. 150 Cf *Crick* (1993) The Times, 18 Aug.

(b) Execution

Woolf LJ said in the Court of Appeal in *Kassim* that 'a valuable security is "executed", properly speaking, only by its making'.[151] That court was obliged to give the terms a wider meaning but it now seems clear that they are to be interpreted in the proper sense. 'Execute, make, accept, endorse' apply only to writing on a document or doing some other act which makes the document the 'valuable security' in question. The words have the same meaning as in the law relating to bills of exchange – a classic illustration of the dependence of the criminal law in this area on (often extremely complex) civil law. The offence is committed by D who procures V to write a cheque payable to D, or endorse a cheque making it payable in D's favour. Similarly, V might act through an agent as where a building society cashier signs documents on behalf and under the direct authority of an elderly customer.[152]

The offence does not extend to carrying out the terms of, or giving effect to a valuable security which has already been executed. Thus, s 20 should not be charged when D seeks to cash the cheque. In this respect it is now clear that *Beck*[153] was wrongly decided. D acquired travellers' cheque forms which had been stolen in transit between the printer and an English bank. He forged the cheques and cashed them in France. The bank knew that the cheques were forged but felt obliged to honour them. It was held, wrongly, that the act of honouring the cheques constituted the execution of a valuable security in England. Note that the offence is now governed by the Criminal Justice Act 1993.

It was held in *King*[154] that a 'CHAPS' (Clearing House Automated Payment System) order was a valuable security, even though the primary 'executor' was the defendant himself, because it was also signed by bank officials and their signatures were obtained by deception. This was decided before the House of Lords decision in *Kassim* and, though their lordships accepted it as right, it is not clear that this conclusion is correct. The bank officials might be compared to the witnesses to a promisor's signature on a promissory note. Such witnesses do not 'execute' the note. Perhaps the counter-signature of the bank officials had a more substantive effect on the validity of the CHAPS order, rendering them more than mere witnesses.

In *Bolton*,[155] the judge's direction that a telegraphic transfer of funds was capable of being a valuable security was held to be wrong in the absence of any evidence of how such a transfer works. In *Manjdadria*,[156] it was held that neither the telegraphic transfer nor the computerized ledger account of the solicitors making it was a valuable security. There was no document authorising a money transfer.[157] The court was somewhat sceptical about *King*, which was described as 'a case in which perhaps the extreme boundaries of a

[151] Cf *Nolan* [2003] EWHC 2709 (Admin), making does not equal an execution since that would mean that mere creation would constitute execution.

[152] *Cawley* (1999) 29 April, No 9805371/W3.

[153] [1985] 1 All ER 571, [1985] 1 WLR 22, (1984) 80 Cr App R 355.

[154] [1992] QB 20, [1991] 3 All ER 705.

[155] (1991) 94 Cr App R 74.

[156] [1993] Crim LR 73.

[157] *Peter Weiss v Government of Germany* [2000] Crim LR 484, DC, explaining *Manjdadria*.

valuable security were canvassed.'[158] Transfers of money by electronic means should normally be charged under s 15A.[159]

(c) 'Procures'

The execution of the valuable security must be 'procured' by deception. In *Beck*, it was argued that the execution by the bank was not procured by a deception because the bank, knowing that the travellers' cheques were forged, paid out on them when they knew they were not legally bound to do so. The court rejected the argument, holding that, by deceiving the trader in France, D had brought about a situation in which for 'legal and/or commercial reasons' the bank had no alternative but to pay. The court appears to have approved the trial judge's direction that 'procured' is only another word for 'caused'. The deception of the trader in France caused the bank to pay out in England. On those facts, after *Kassim*, the question no longer arises, but it would arise where V signed a cheque, being aware of the deception by D, but feeling bound to sign for legal or commercial reasons.

Where D seeks by deception to procure the payment of a sum of money and is aware that it may be paid by, *inter alia*, the execution and delivery of a valuable security, for example, a cheque, and it is so paid, he commits the offence.[160] If the payment had been made by telegraphic transfer, as in *Manjdadria*, he would not commit the offence – nor, it seems, would he be guilty of an attempt to commit it. He acted, being reckless whether he caused the execution of a valuable security, but could hardly be said to have intended to do so. The position would be otherwise if D had requested payment by cheque.

(d) *Mens rea*

It must be proved that D knew or was reckless[161] whether the effect of a successful deception would be to cause the execution of a valuable security. It is immaterial that the valuable security which was executed was of a different type from that which D anticipated.[162] It must also be proved that D had a view to gain or an intent to cause loss. These concepts are considered below.[163] D must be shown to have acted dishonestly, and the discussion of that concept above applies here.[164]

7. Obtaining services by deception[165]

The central focus of the Theft Act 1968 lies in protecting against infringements of property rights, but the law would be seriously inadequate if it were limited to protecting

[158] In *Nolan* [2003] EWHC 2709, having regard to these cases, the court accepted that a print out of a transfer to the defendant's account was a valuable security.

[159] See *Mensah-Lartey* [1996] 1 Cr App R 143, [1996] Crim LR 203.

[160] *Aston and N'Wadiche* [1998] Crim LR 498.

[161] *Ashton and N'Wandiche*, last note.

[162] See 'Transferred malice', above, p 113 and *Mensah Lartey* [1996] 1 Cr App R 143, [1996] Crim LR 203.

[163] p 789.

[164] See also *Wood* [1999] Crim LR 564 on pleas of claim of right under s 20.

[165] Smith, *Property Offences*, ch 18; Griew, ch 9; Arlidge and Perry, ch 4; Smith, *Theft*, pp 128–135.

victims against only harm to those interests. The 1978 Act[166] replaces the disastrously complex 'nightmare'[167] provisions of the 1968 Act which dealt with some specific circumstances of obtaining a 'pecuniary advantage'. It adds broad and overlapping offences to protect against deceptive conduct to secure services, and to avoid liabilities. The provisions arouse some degree of controversy since they expose deceitful debtors to criminal prosecution. As discussed below, the proposed reform of deception offences would involve replacing the 1978 Act ss 1 and 2 with an offence of obtaining services dishonestly (without deception).

The offences under the 1978 Act are Group A offences for the purposes of the Criminal Justice Act 1993, so that the commission of an element of the offence within England and Wales will provide the English courts with jurisdiction.

Section 1 of the Theft Act 1978 provides:

(1) A person who by any deception dishonestly obtains services from another shall be guilty of an offence.

(2) It is an obtaining of services where the other is induced to confer a benefit by doing some act, or causing or permitting some act to be done, on the understanding that the benefit has been or will be paid for.

(3) Without prejudice to the generality of subsection (2) above, it is an obtaining of services where the other is induced to make a loan, or to cause or permit a loan to be made, on the understanding that any payment (whether by way of interest or otherwise) will be or has been made in respect of the loan.[168]

By s 4 the offence is triable either way; on summary conviction it is punishable by imprisonment for a term not exceeding six months and/or a fine not exceeding the prescribed maximum (£5,000), and on indictment by imprisonment for a term not exceeding five years and/or a fine.

Where D employs a deception to induce V to render a valuable service, the mischief is much the same as where V's property is obtained by deception. It is as clear today as ever it was that not only property should be regarded as of 'value' and an interest worthy of protection, and it is therefore appropriate to criminalize obtaining the services of another by deception.

(a) Deception

Section 5(1) provides that 'deception' has the same meaning as in s 15 (above). Two further points may be noted. First, the deception must cause V to provide the services on the understanding that they will be paid for. It is not an offence for D by deception to cause V to provide services without charge, irrespective of whether the service is one for which payment would be normally be expected. The consequence of this limitation is that if D gets V to mow his lawn by pretending that he has sprained his ankle he commits

166 J. R. Spencer, 'The Theft Act 1978' [1979] Crim LR 24. On the need for the offences see A. T. H. Smith, 'Reforming Section 16 of the Theft Act' [1977] Crim LR 259.

167 *Royle* (1971) 56 Cr App R 51, per Edmund Davies LJ.

168 Subsection (3): inserted by the Theft (Amendment) Act 1996, s 4(1).

no offence. But if D at the same time offers V £10 for the job, the offence will be committed when V mows the lawn if he is in part induced to do so because he believes the story of the sprained ankle. This seems odd, since V's effort is no less expended as a result of D's deception when V acts for free as where he acts for payment. One reason for the limitation on the offence might be that in such a case V could be said to have suffered no economic loss because no price has been put on his services. But this is not wholly convincing since the offence may be committed in other circumstances notwithstanding that V suffers no economic loss. Furthermore, as with the offence under s 15 of the 1968 Act,[169] a person's conduct may be dishonest notwithstanding that he intends to pay for the service. No doubt a jury would be reluctant to find D's conduct dishonest where no economic loss is in fact caused and the deception plays only a minor part in influencing V to act but a conviction in such circumstances can be supported.

Section 1 applies where the deception is as to something other than the prospect of payment.[170] Significantly therefore, the offence can be committed where D pays in full and V loses nothing; which is rather paradoxical since, as discussed, D commits no offence if the service is gratuitous. This has posed problems in the provision of financial services since it is common to find that opening a bank account incurs no charge.[171]

Secondly, the service must be obtained by deceiving V. It is not enough that the service is obtained by stealth and that a charge for the service is avoided. D does not commit this offence where he secretly enters a cinema or cricket ground or where he induces a taxi driver to carry him by threats: no one is deceived in such a case.

(b) Services

'Services' is widely defined.[172] Typical services are the provision of hotel accommodation, social or sporting amenities or entertainment, repairing and decorating and the letting of goods on hire. All the section requires is the inducement by deception of 'some act' – apparently any act – which 'confers a benefit' and is understood to be paid for.

This aspect of the offence gave rise to considerable difficulty following the aberrant decision in *Halai*[173] that a mortgage advance does not constitute a 'service', apparently because it is a lending of money for property, which would be an offence under s 15 of the 1968 Act. *Halai* was heavily criticized and was distinguished in *Widdowson* where the court said that an agreement to let on hire purchase would be a service. The effect of *Halai* is reversed by the new subs (3), enacted by the Theft (Amendment) Act 1996.[174] That subsection does not apply to anything done before 18 December 1996. However, in *Cooke*[175] the Court of Appeal held that *Halai* was wrongly decided and had never been the law. But, later, in *Naviede*,[176] *Halai* was merely distinguished, implying that it remains law

[169] See *Potger* (1970) 55 Cr App R 42, CA, above, p 758.

[170] *Naviede* [1997] Crim LR 662.

[171] In the case of opening a bank account which includes an automatic overdraft facility, the offence under Theft Act 1968, s 16(2)(b) (obtaining pecuniary advantage by deception) might be committed even though the opening of the account incurs no charge.

[172] The CLRC initially had in mind a narrower offence involving deception as to the prospect of payment (see Working Paper, paras 26–29 and 31–34) but this was rejected by Parliament and the Committee's redraft took account of Parliament's expressed preference for an offence of obtaining services, widely defined.

[173] [1983] Crim LR 624, CA, criticized, Griew, *Theft*, 171–172, Smith, *Theft*, 4–70.

[174] Above, p 681. [175] [1997] Crim LR 436. [176] [1997] Crim LR 662.

for events before 18 December 1996. It is submitted that the better view is that it was wrongly decided. The result is that the s 1 offence as amended heavily overlaps other Theft Acts offences, but that is the effect of the section properly construed.

In *Preddy*[177] Lord Goff had expressed concerns that treating financial services such as opening bank accounts as 'services' within s 1 would render the offence too wide. This view was rejected implicitly by the extension of the offence to cases of loans (s 1(3) as inserted by the 1996 Act) and the Court of Appeal expressly rejected this approach in *Sofroniou*,[178] where D had used false names to open bank accounts. The court was not prepared to distinguish between opening the accounts and their subsequent use. Following that case, it is clear that the offence can be committed by D obtaining by deception 'services' which include: opening bank accounts; issuing credit cards; arranging overdraft facilities, etc. It is submitted that this is a welcome decision. Having a bank account provides the customer with a range of facilities that allow him to conduct his financial affairs with greater ease. There are many actual (for example, interest, cheque facilities) and potential (cash-back, improved credit ratings, etc) benefits that flow from having the facility. Imposing criminal liability for dishonestly obtaining such facilities by deception reflects the fact that society increasingly recognizes the value in conferment of 'use' or 'access' to a facility as an economic commodity.

One important limitation on the offence is that V must be induced to do some *act*; a mere omission will not suffice. But this limitation is not likely to be of any great practical significance since the offence extends to inducing V to cause or permit some act to be done. Permission may be given by passive acquiescence as where V allows D to park a car in V's lot or allows D to take a boat which is offered for hire. Where D induces an act which confers a benefit the offence is complete when V does the act. Where D induces V to permit an act it is arguable that the offence is complete when the permission is given but it is submitted that a preferable view is that the offence is complete only when an act is done pursuant to that permission. The latter view seems more consistent with the wording of s 1(2): 'causing or permitting some act to be done'.

The benefit

There are at least three different views about the significance of the word 'benefit'. One is that it is simply a drafting device to avoid a clumsiness of saying '. . . on the understanding that [the act, or the causing or permitting of the act] has been or will be paid for'.[179] 'Benefit' comprehends the bracketed words. According to that view, the word adds nothing to the meaning of the section. A second view[180] is that it has a limiting effect on the words that follow, possibly restricting them to the conferment of something of economic value. But as the act is, *ex hypothesi*, to be paid for, it must have an economic value to D, so it is not easy to think of any example where, under this construction 'benefit' would add anything.[181] A third view[182] is that the word might serve a valuable purpose in excluding cases where the act amounts to a criminal offence that has the object of protecting D (or

177 [1996] AC 81. 178 [2004] Crim LR 381. 179 Griew, *Theft*, para 9–06.

180 J. R. Spencer, 'The Theft Act 1978' [1979] Crim LR 24 at 27.

181 D promises V £100 if V will walk to York. It is well recognized in the law of contract that V's walking to York is such a 'benefit' to D as to amount to a sufficient consideration to make D's promise enforceable.

182 Smith, *Theft*, 4–84 et seq.

the third party on whom the alleged benefit is conferred) against the act in question. If D, aged 17, induces V to tattoo him by falsely representing that he intends to pay, V is *prima facie* guilty of an offence under the Tattooing of Minors Act 1969. V could not, of course, recover the price of the tattooing from D but that is not in itself enough to rule out an offence under s 1: unenforceable transactions conferring a benefit are caught. Since, however, the law regards this as an evil to be prevented it is arguable that as a matter of principle, it cannot also regard it as 'a benefit'. A counter to this argument is that other offences under the Acts protect the interests of those who might be acting illegally (for example, there can be a theft from a thief). Section 1 might be regarded as different: property is still property in need of protection even if it is of illicit provenance, but the law does not protect all forms of conduct – as where the victim's provision of services is illegal.

It does not matter for the purposes of s 1 that D's deception is to obtain a service for or confer a benefit on another.[183]

(d) The understanding

The understanding is that someone, not necessarily V, has been or will be paid. Where D induces V by deception to render for nothing a service for which he would normally charge – by a lie he persuades a taxi driver to give him a free ride – D commits no offence against s 1.[184] The understanding may be that the payment will be made not by D but by a third party, as for example where D represents that his firm will pay his hotel bill.

In the important recent case of *Sofroniou*, the court interpreted 'understanding' as intended to cover situations where nothing explicitly was said between the parties about payment, but where there was a common understanding that the services would not be provided gratuitously. There need not be a formal agreement. In a subjective sense the understanding will be unlikely to be 'mutual' since D will commonly have no intention or understanding that he will pay.[185] It is sufficient that there was a 'putative objective mutual understanding as to payment on the assumption that the inducement was not dishonest'. In addition, the court held that there must be a sufficient understanding that an *identifiable payment* had been or would be made by or on behalf of the person receiving the services to the person providing them (or another). Where there was evidence that a defendant obtained the services of a bank account that he dishonestly intended to overdraw, it was open to the jury to infer that the banks would charge interest on the overdrawn amount. Such an inference would be a sufficient putative objective mutual understanding as to payment for the purposes of the offence. The offence is a continuing one.

Sections 2 and 3 of the 1978 Act are both confined to cases in which there is an enforceable liability. No such limitation is expressed in s 1 and there is no ground for implying it. The prostitute cannot sue for the price of her services but they may be

[183] *Nathan* [1997] Crim LR 835.

[184] D is, however, probably guilty of the offence of obtaining exemption from liability to make a payment, contrary to 1978, s 2(1)(c).

[185] Although of course he might have such an understanding where the deception relates to an issue other than payment.

obtained from her by deception. Suppose similarly that D, a minor, by falsely representing that he intends to pay the fee of £100, induces V to give him flying lessons. V will probably be unable to sue successfully for the fee because as a matter of contract law it is most unlikely that flying lessons will be held to be necessary for a minor. V has, however, undoubtedly conferred a benefit on D and D is guilty of an offence of obtaining services by deception.

(e) Payment

In the ordinary run of cases the understanding will be that the service will be paid for in monetary form (cash, cheque or credit card). Suppose, however, that D by deception induces V to provide services in return for services or foods, for example, that if V digs D's garden then D will paint V's house or will provide V with a power drill. 'Paid for' presumably has the same meaning as 'payment' and it does not strain the ordinary meaning of the word to extend it to recompense in forms other than money. Payment may be said to describe any of the ways in which an obligation may be discharged.[186] On this view D in the examples given would commit the offence.

In *Sofroniou* above the court, rightly it is submitted, rejected the sophisticated argument that 'inferred indirect commercial advantages to the bank' might be understood to be payments. Although it is possible to characterize the financial benefit to the bank from D's operation of the account or credit card as a 'gain' and to identify a 'cost' to D incurred by holding the account, these charges are of such a oblique nature that they would not be usually be 'understood' to be 'payments'.

(f) Dishonesty

The offence requires dishonesty and reference may be made to the discussion of this matter above.[187] As emphasized above, the elements of dishonesty and deception are quite separate.

8. Evasion of liability by deception

Section 2 of the Theft Act 1978 provides:

(1) Subject to subsection (2) below, where a person by any deception –

(a) dishonestly secures the remission of the whole or part of any existing liability to make a payment, whether his own liability or another's; or

(b) with intent to make permanent default in whole or in part on any existing liability to make a payment, or with intent to let another do so, dishonestly induces the creditor or any person claiming payment on behalf of the creditor to wait for payment (whether or not the due date for payment is deferred) or to forgo payment; or

(c) dishonestly obtains an exemption from or abatement of liability to make a payment;

he shall be guilty of an offence.

186 [2004] Crim LR 381; cf *White v Elmdene Estates Ltd* [1959] 2 All ER 605 at 610, per Lord Evershed MR.

187 At pp 696–702.

(2) For purposes of this section 'liability' means legally enforceable liability; and subsection (1) shall not apply in relation to a liability that has not been accepted or established to pay compensation for a wrongful act or omission.

(3) For purposes of subsection (1)(b) a person induced to take in payment a cheque or other security for money by way of conditional satisfaction of a pre-existing liability is to be treated not as being paid but as being induced to wait for payment.

(4) For purposes of subsection (1)(c) 'obtains' includes obtaining for another or enabling another to obtain.

An offence under this section is triable and punishable in the same way as an offence under s 1. The section probably creates three separate offences.[188] There are material differences in both *mens rea* and *actus reus* between the three paragraphs, (a), (b) and (c), and the section lacks the common unifying element of s 16 of the 1968 Act which it replaced.[189] In short, the offences apply in the following manner.

- Section 2(1)(a) is focused on remission of liability – that is, where V accepts that the liability ceases to exist. An example might be where D, having taken a taxi home, falsely tells the driver on arrival that he must have had his wallet stolen and that he has no money to pay. If the driver believes him and agrees to let him off the fare, D commits the para (1)(a) offence.
- Section 2(1)(b) deals with forgoing or waiting for payment – that is, where V stops his present demands for payment of the liability, but the liability continues to exist. In the above example, if D had deceived the cabbie by explaining that his wallet was stolen but that he would pay at the cab office the next day, secretly intending never to pay he would commit the offence.
- Section 2(1)(c) – this is significantly different since it deals with prospective liability.

The three offences are not mutually exclusive;[190] they overlap but it must be assumed that they are not coincident and that no one of them includes the whole of another. D who secures the remission of a liability contrary to para (a) and who has an intent to make permanent default is almost certainly also guilty of inducing his creditor to forgo payment contrary to para (b). If D has no intention to make permanent default, he may be guilty under (a) but not under (b). If D induces V merely to forgo payment (as distinct from remitting the liability – whatever that distinction may be) with intent to make permanent default, he is guilty under (b) but not under (a).

The elements of dishonesty and deception have been examined above, each of the other elements of the offences presents problems. It is unclear whether 'payment' in s 2 is restricted to payment in money or whether it extends to payment in kind.

(a) Securing remission of a liability – s 2(1)(a)

This offence has been heavily criticized, not merely for the complexity of the drafting, but for the fact that it appears to be unnecessary. It results in the possibility of conviction for

[188] In *Holt* [1981] 2 All ER 854, CA, the court referred to 'the three offences' in s 2(1). Smith, *Property Offences*, 20.15.

[189] *Bale v Rosier* [1977] 2 All ER 160, above, p 766.

[190] *Holt* (above); *Jackson* [1983] Crim LR 617.

D who causes V to wipe out a debt that D owed. In civil law, V can resurrect the debt. V's position after the offence is that he has a right to sue D for the money owed, which is exactly what V's position was before the offence.[191] However, the provision has been defended as filling a 'loophole left open to dishonest and unscrupulous debtors by contract principles.'[192]

(i) An existing liability

There must be an existing liability though it may have been created only seconds beforehand. For example, where D fills his car with petrol at a self service station and then secures remission of his liability to pay for it, by telling the attendant that he is a friend of the manager and does not have to pay. But s 1(a) does not apply where D by deception induces V to agree – before V performs the service and creates D's liability – to render the service free (or at a reduced price). Thus, had D deceived V before getting the petrol by telling him that he was the manager's friend and need not pay, the offence would be under s 2(1)(c).

Several other points are worth noting. First, V must be aware that there is an existing liability. If D deceives V by telling him that he has already paid, V is not deceived into remitting a liability, V is deceived into believing that there never was a liability. Secondly, the liability may be an existing one for a period before the payment of money actually becomes due, eg where the contract is agreed but with payment contingent on the occurrence of an event.[193] Thirdly the 'existing liability' referred to may be the liability of D or another.

(ii) An enforceable liability

Section 2(1)(a) applies only to legally enforceable liability, not to a 'debt' which is unenforceable because V is a third party to the contract creating it[194] or because it arises out of an illegal transaction (for example, prostitution), or, like a wagering debt is void.

(iii) No need for permanent default

Section 2(1)(a) does not require any intention to make permanent default. This interpretation is put beyond doubt when the words, 'secures the remission of . . . any existing liability', are read in contrast to the separate offence under para (b) of inducing a creditor to forgo payment with intent to make permanent default.

(iv) Remission

A 'remission' of liability suggests that V knowingly accepts that the liability ceases to exist (or is reduced if the allegation is of remission in part). If D's deception causes V to believe that no liability existed (for example, the goods from V never arrived) there is no 'remission' since V does not believe that there is a liability to remit.

191 See Spencer, above, p 774.

192 G. H. Treitel, 'Contract and Crime', in Tapper (ed), *Crime, Proof and Punishment Essays in Memory of Sir Rupert Cross* (1981) 92.

193 See *Modupe* [1991] Crim LR 530, CA.

194 *Gee* [1999] Crim LR 397. Note the Contract (Rights of Third Parties) Act 1999.

The section is usefully compared with the neighbouring provisions. Plainly a difference is intended between 'remitting' liability (s 2(1)(a)) and 'forgoing' payment (s 2(1)(b)), otherwise the same word would have been used. The obvious difference seems to be that if V forgoes payment, he does not regard D's liability as being discharged although V desists from demanding payment. If V remits D's liability it comes to an end. Similarly para (c) seems to be concerned with a deception that affects the legal relationship between two persons, whereas, quite clearly, para (b) does not.[195] This interpretation – that remission involves a change in legal duties – explains the absence of the words 'with intent to make permanent default' in (a) and in (c). If a person intends that something shall cease to exist, he intends to deprive the owner of it forever. By securing remission, D deprives V permanently of his right; and that is sufficient to constitute the offence even though D may not intend to 'make permanent default' in that he intends to pay the appropriate sum one day.[196]

There is a technical argument that renders the application of s 2(1)(a) extremely narrow, although the argument has not received judicial approval. Take the example of the CLRC of the commission of the offence:

> An example would be where a man borrows £100 from a neighbour and when repayment is due, tells a false story of some family tragedy which makes it impossible for him to find the money; this deception persuades the neighbour to tell him that he need never repay.

This is, it is submitted, flawed. Since the neighbour has been deceived into waiving the debt he has not in civil law extinguished it. How then can the man have 'secured the remission' of the liability to pay £100 when that liability continues unimpaired throughout?[197] What if D won the lottery the following week, would not the neighbour expect his money? On the other hand, there is no doubt that the neighbour has been induced to forgo payment (of the existing, unremitted debt). The effect of this construction would be that, contrary to the expectations of the CLRC, para (b) would have a much wider sphere of operation than para (a). As a matter of principle, criminal sanctions should be imposed on defaulting debtors sparingly. But it is not inappropriate to criminalize defaulting where D causes V actually to give up his legal right or where he has an intent to make permanent default.[198]

If this construction were applied to para (c) it would render it almost useless because (c) is the only provision which extends to prospective as well as existing liability. In order to salvage (c), it may be argued that the right interpretation is to construe 'secure the

195 In *Holt* [1981] 2 All ER 854 the court said that it found great difficulty in introducing these concepts into the construction of the subsection. They added, 'Thus the differences between the offences relate principally to the different situations in which the debtor–creditor relationship has arisen.' This is difficult to follow. Both paras (a) and (b) with which the court was concerned simply assume an 'existing liability' which, apparently, may have arisen in any way whatsoever. The differences relate to the manner in which the parties treat the existing liability, not to the way in which it arose.

196 Smith, *Property Offences*, 20–35, argues that this argument gives insufficient weight to the fact that every remission contemplated by para (a) is vitiated by the debtor's fraud. But a voidable remission is a remission until it is avoided. The 'remission' in the CLRC's example is wholly ineffective – void.

197 *Jorden v Money* (1854) 5 HL Cas 185, HL; *D & C Builders Ltd v Rees* [1966] 2 QB 617, [1965] 3 All ER 837, CA.

198 Cf Smith, *Property Offences*, paras 20–29, rejecting the argument that by impeding V in his private law rights D is 'obstructing justice'.

remission' in (a) to mean 'secure an agreement to remit' and to accept that the words 'or to forgo payment' in (b) are inoperative. Others[199] think that the paragraph has a wider operation.

The Court of Appeal had the opportunity to consider these problems in *Dawson*[200] where D had secured the agreement of his creditors by entering into an individual voluntary agreement (IVA).[201] It was argued that the creditors' agreement to the IVA when it was proposed by D had removed any existing liability so that by the time Vs were finally induced to agree to it in its final form (by D's deception), there was no enforceable liability. The court sidestepped the issue by concluding that by reference to the obligations imposed under the Insolvency Act, ss 264 and 276, an existing liability remained at the time of the final IVA and that a charge under s 2(1)(b) was appropriate.

Where D, the holder of a credit card, dishonestly and by deception induces his creditor, V, to accept 'payment' by credit card he secures the remission of an existing liability because *his* liability to V is extinguished.[202] In *Jackson*,[203] the card was tendered in payment not by the holder but by a thief. It was held that D had secured the remission of his liability. The trader who accepted the card in payment would not look to D for payment, but to the credit card company and, if the conditions on the card were satisfied, the company would be bound to pay and the trader could not recover the debt twice. There is, on the technical analysis above, a potential problem with this interpretation, since it is not so clear that D's liability would be totally extinguished. If the credit card company defaulted, it would seem unlikely that D could rely on his use of the stolen card to resist an action by the trader to recover the debt. Even on this view, D's liability might fairly be regarded as having been remitted, though it could revive in specific but very unlikely, circumstances.

(b) Inducing creditor to wait for or forgo payment

The operation of s 2(1)(b) may be illustrated by reference to the facts of *DPP v Turner*.[204] D, who owed V £38 for work done and was being pressed for payment, told V that he had no ready cash and persuaded V to accept a cheque. D knew that he had insufficient funds and that the cheque would be dishonoured. Such conduct falls within s 2(1)(b) if, and only if, D intends to make *permanent* default on the debt. If, as seemed likely in *Turner* itself, D simply wanted to rid himself temporarily of the demands of his creditor in order to give himself a breathing space, and was bent on settling the debt at a later stage, he would not commit an offence.

The effect of D's deception must be to make the creditor 'wait for . . . or forgo' payment. 'Forgo' appears to require that V in some way no longer pursues payment. It would be apt to cover the case where V, a waiter in a restaurant, is falsely told by D, a diner, that X, another waiter, has taken payment for the meal.[205] 'Wait' is more apt to

199 G. Syrota, *Current Law Statutes* (1978); Griew, 9–10.

200 [2001] EWCA Crim 155.

201 Insolvency Act 1986.

202 *Re Charge Card Services Ltd* [1987] Ch 150, [1986] 3 All ER 289 (Millett J); affd [1989] Ch 497, [1988] 3 All ER 702, CA. Payment by credit card, unlike payment by cheque, even where the cheque is backed by a cheque card, is an absolute and not merely conditional payment.

203 [1983] Crim LR 617, CA.

204 [1974] AC 357, [1973] 3 All ER 124, HL.

205 *Holt* [1981] 2 All ER 854, [1981] 1 WLR 1000.

cover the case where by a deceitful stratagem (for example sending his son to the door to say 'Daddy's out', or returning bills marked 'not known at this address') D delays his creditor. The creditor in such cases does not forgo payment but is made to wait for it. Note that under this section there must be an existing liability, as discussed above.[206] This represents a further illustration of the potential over-criminalization by this section – V has been stalled by D who seeks time to pay, but his manner of doing so and his intention never to pay exposes him to serious criminal penalty. But of course V is in no worse a position in civil law than he was before. The offence is no doubt committed many hundreds of times each day.

The offence is committed only where the person deceived is the creditor or someone acting on his behalf. In *Gee*[207] D contracted with E that he will pay money to V, V, not being a party to the contract, was not able to sue on it.[208] Conversely, the offence can be committed only where the liability is that of the person who makes default.[209]

One of the main targets of s 2(1)(b) is to criminalize writing dud cheques.[210] Section 2(3) provides specifically that where V is induced to accept a worthless cheque in payment, as happened in *Turner*, he is to be treated as not being paid and being induced to wait for payment. Strictly speaking the acceptance of a cheque as payment merely suspends the creditor's remedies to recover the debt until the cheque is either honoured or dishonoured; this provision, however, provides that for the purpose of s 2(1)(b) the creditor is induced to wait for payment. It has been accepted in the Crown Court that s 2(3) only operates in circumstances where V is induced to accept the payment by cheque rather than cash,[211] and not where cheque payments are acceptable in the course of dealings between D and V. Arguably, with the increased use of electronic payments and the decrease in the use of cheques this will be of less significance.

(c) Obtaining an exemption from or an abatement of liability

Section 2(1)(c) differs from s 2(1)(a) and (b). Whereas paras (a) and (b) assume an existing liability and a subsequent deception, para (c) is concerned with a deception which induces V to confer an exemption from or abatement of a *prospective* liability.[212] It covers the straightforward case of D who falsely tells a taxi driver, V, that he has had his wallet stolen. If the taxi driver agrees to give him a ride home for free, D has obtained an exemption from the liability that would have arisen. If D, in order to secure a discounted entry price informs the cinema ticket operator, V, that he is a student, D has obtained an abatement of liability by his deception. The argument for criminalisation is at its strongest in this subsection.

The provision was explained by the CLRC:[213]

[206] See especially *Dawson* [2001] EWCA Crim 1554.

[207] *Gee* [1999] Crim LR 397.

[208] The decision was before the Contract (Rights of Third Parties) Act 1999.

[209] *Attewell-Hughes* [1991] 4 All ER 810, [1991] Crim LR 437, CA.

[210] For comparative analyses of the problem see A. Campbell and N. Kibble, 'Dishonoured Cheques: A Comparative Analysis' [2001] JIBL 77; C. Anyangwe, 'Dealing with the Problem of Bad Cheques in France' [1978] Crim LR 31.

[211] *Andrews and Hedges* [1981] Crim LR 106.

[212] *Firth* (1990) 91 Cr App R 217, [1990] Crim LR 326, CA.

[213] Cmnd 6733, para 15.

The ratepayer who makes a false statement in order to obtain a rebate to which he is not entitled is acting dishonestly and is practising a deception in order to obtain an abatement of his liability to pay rates and, accordingly, would be guilty of an offence under clause 2(1)(c). The wording of this provision, 'where a person by any deception . . . dishonestly obtains any exemption from or abatement of liability to make a payment' is intended to cover cases where the deception has induced the victim to believe that there is nothing due to him or that the amount due to him is less than would be the case if he knew the true facts. Another example of the application of this part of clause 2 is the case where a person by deception obtains services at a reduced rate (for example, air travel at a special rate for students when the traveller is not a student).

There is, however, a difficulty with the operation of para (c) (similar to that which it has been suggested[214] applies to para (a)). Suppose D, a council tax payer, makes false statements in order to secure a reduction in his tax and the local authority accordingly assess his tax category at £200 per annum rather than the proper level which is £300. As a matter of civil law D does not thereby obtain an 'abatement of liability' because his liability to pay £300 continues undiminished. (Of course at some stage the authority will make a demand for £200 and at that stage they will, as a result of the continuing deception by D, be induced to forgo part of the existing liability to pay £300 and the case would then fall within paragraph (b).) Strictly, and though this was not the result intended by the CLRC, the case does not fall within paragraph (c) which is, on this view, likely to be of only limited application. Again the gap is not a serious one because at a later stage D will normally commit an offence under paragraph (b) and, indeed, by submitting the false claim to the local authority he would appear to be guilty of an attempt.

In *Sibartie*,[215] however, it was held that D was guilty of an attempt to commit the offence under paragraph (c) where, on passing a ticket inspector, he flashed (that is, held it up so briefly that the inspector could not read it) an invalid season ticket. The court said the proper approach to paragraph (c) was to consider its 'ordinary meaning' and ask whether D's conduct came within that. D could be taken as representing that he was the holder of a valid ticket, that he was not under a liability to pay, and was thus trying to obtain an exemption from his liability to pay the fare. So he was but, assuming he successfully deceives the inspector, he has not persuaded the inspector to remit the liability but rather to believe there is no liability. And whatever liability D has is not in law remitted (this is not therefore within para (a)). What D has done is to persuade the inspector to forgo a payment that is due and the case falls within para (b).

As with the cases under the 1968 Act, this provides a further stark example that the courts are prepared to uphold convictions where there has been a finding of dishonesty, even where to do so involves them adopting an unsatisfactorily broad brush approach to interpretation. In the courts' defence the impenetrable drafting found in s 2 has not assisted their task.

(d) Excluded liabilities

By s 2(2) an offence under s 2(1) may be committed only where the liability is legally enforceable.[216] The section thus has no application to a 'liability' which is unenforceable

214 See above, p 779. 215 [1983] Crim LR 470, CA.

216 There is an existing liability notwithstanding that a court order is required before it can be enforced: *Modupe* [1991] Crim LR 530, CA.

because it is illegal or against public policy or is for any other reason unenforceable; a minor cannot commit an offence under this section if the transaction to which it relates is one that is unenforceable in civil law against him.

Nor does s 2(1) apply in relation to a liability that has not been accepted or established to pay compensation for a wrongful act or omission. 'Without this provision', said the CLRC,[217]

> there would be room for argument that subsection (1)(a) of the clause applies where, for example, a person lies about the circumstances of an accident in order to avoid the bringing of civil proceedings for negligence against him. We think that the dividing line is reached where liability is not disputed even though the amount of that liability is. On this basis it would be an offence under clause 2(1)(a) for an antique dealer to lie about the age and value of jewellery sent to him for valuation which had been lost as a result of his admitted negligence, but not for him to lie about the circumstances of the loss in disputing an allegation of negligence. We see no justification for extending the criminal law to cases where the existence of any liability is disputed: the claimant can launch civil proceedings if he thinks he had been deceived when he absolved the other party from liability.

The 'dividing line' is a fine one. The dealer commits an offence under the section if by deception he induces V to settle on the basis that the jewellery is worth £100 when it is worth £500, but not if by deception he induces V to believe that he has not been negligent so that V drops his claim altogether. It is not clear that the section succeeds in achieving the aim of the CLRC since the offence would not apply where D has accepted liability but is in the course of agreeing quantum, and D deceives V into accepting £500 when the true measure of damages is £1000. There is in such cases no existing liability to pay £1,000.[218]

9. False accounting

Section 17 of the Theft Act 1968 provides:

> (1) Where a person dishonestly, with a view to gain for himself or another or with intent to cause loss to another, –
>
> (a) destroys, defaces, conceals or falsifies any account or any record or document made or required for any accounting purpose; or
>
> (b) in furnishing information for any purpose produces or makes use of any account, or any such record or document as aforesaid, which to his knowledge is or may be misleading, false or deceptive in a material particular;
>
> he shall, on conviction on indictment, be liable to imprisonment for a term not exceeding seven years.

It has been suggested that the section creates six offences, although the court acknowledged that 'false accounting' is the appropriate way to refer to the offence no matter how committed.[219] The offences overlap with a number of others; for example, where D

217 Cmnd 6733, para 16.

218 See Smith, *Theft*, 4–90.

219 *Bow Street Magistrates, ex p Hill* (1999) 29 Nov, unreported, DC.

falsifies any document or record made for an accounting purpose he might, also commit forgery or attempt to commit an offence under s 2 of the 1978 Act. But the offence under s 17 is wider than forgery or evading liability in some respects. One advantage in charging this offence is that it is designed not only to deal with schemes that were fraudulent from the outset but also with those that became so when, for example, a business got into financial difficulties. In addition, charges of false accounting can accurately reflect the scale of the wrongdoing without the need to deal with the increasingly complex issues of when and where property transfers (whether as bank credits or otherwise) occurred.

(a) Section 17(1)(a)

(i) *Actus reus*

The offence may be committed by any person who falsifies, etc any document 'made or required' for an accounting purpose. It is immaterial that no one accepts or acts on the falsified document; this is a conduct offence, not an offence of deception requiring a result caused by D's conduct. The falsification, etc is a sufficient manifestation of the criminal intent to warrant criminalisation, irrespective of whether it causes loss or results in gain for the accused.

The account or record

Account is an ordinary English word. 'Any account or any record' is wide enough to include a mechanical accounting device such as a computer, a taximeter,[220] or a turnstile which records paying customers.[221] The admission of two persons through one movement of the turnstile amounts to falsification by the omission of a material particular. A completely false set of accounts is also an account for the purposes of this section.[222]

'Made or required for'

These are disjunctive elements of the offence.[223] The terms are not to be read restrictively, and should be given their ordinary meaning in the context and potential purpose for which the document was required, not being treated as technical terms of 'forensic accounting'.[224] Nevertheless, difficulties do arise from the inclusion of these words which were designed to limit the scope of the offence so that it does not apply to all documents or records. An account is *prima facie* made for an accounting purpose. Any other record or document is 'made for' an accounting purpose where that is the purpose of the document. It has been held that a document may be 'required' for an accounting purpose even though that is not its principal purpose, so long as it is required in part for an accounting purpose.[225] This is a controversial extension of the

220 Cf *Solomons* [1909] 2 KB 980.

221 *Edwards v Toombs* [1983] Crim LR 43, DC.

222 *Scot-Simonds* [1994] Crim LR 933.

223 *Baxter v Gov of HM Prison Brixton* [2002] EWHC 300 (Admin).

224 Ibid, Auld LJ para 22.

225 *A-G's Reference (No 1 of 1980)* [1981] 1 All ER 366, [1981] 1 WLR 34, CA (personal loan proposal forms addressed to finance company).

offence.[226] It has been persuasively suggested that 'made for' refers to the purposes of the maker of the document and 'required for' to the purposes of the recipient.[227]

In terms of establishing their purpose, it appears that documents fall into two categories: (i) Those from the inspection of which a jury, with such experience and knowledge of the world as jurors may be expected to have, could be satisfied that the document was required for an accounting purpose and (ii) those from which no such inference could safely be drawn. In the second category, the prosecution must adduce evidence of the purpose of the document. The court or jury may infer from the circumstances that the document is so required[228] but only if sufficient evidence exists for this conclusion to be drawn. One of the difficulties with the offence is that jurors must not be assumed to know about accounting practice,[229] and the type of document that might be required for an accounting purpose is extremely wide ranging.

Unfortunately, the courts have failed to adopt a consistent approach to this aspect of the offence. In *Cummings-John*[230] it was held that a 'Report on Title' was required by a building society 'for an accounting purpose'. The document was clearly required by the society in order to decide whether to grant a mortgage advance. It is not so clear that it was required for an accounting purpose. In *Okanta*[231] the court was not satisfied that a letter containing false information which induced a mortgage advance was so required. The distinction is not obvious. In *Manning*[232] it was held that it would be open to a jury to conclude that an insurer's cover note was 'required' in the terms of this section simply by looking at the document because it set out what the client owed – but it was borderline case. An insurance claim form was held to fall on the wrong side of the line.[233] A form claiming entitlement to housing benefit is a 'document made or required for' any accounting purpose: *Osinuga v DPP*.[234] Significantly, for the purposes of prosecuting high yield investment frauds and pyramid frauds, application forms sent to a potential investor which included false statements as to the rate of return on investments may constitute a document made or required for any accounting purpose since they would be retained by the investor: 'it was the sort of document he would put in a wall safe not a waste paper basket'.[235]

'Any accounting purpose'

The section further extends its reach to any document, so long as it is made or required for *any* accounting purpose, though the document itself is not in the nature of an account and though the falsification does not relate to figures. So if D enters in a hire-purchase

226 See the cogent criticism of Arlidge and Parry, para 5–060.

227 Some support for this view is implicit in Auld LJ's judgment in *Baxter*.

228 *Osinuga v DPP* [1998] Crim LR 216, DC; *Baxter* (above).

229 *Sundhers* [1998] Crim LR 497.

230 [1997] Crim LR 660.

231 [1997] Crim LR 451.

232 [1998] 2 Cr App R 461, [1999] Crim LR 151.

233 *Sundhers* [1998] Crim LR 497.

234 [1998] Crim LR 216, cf the at first instance HH Judge Jackson in *S* [1997] 4 Arch News 1, which must be regarded as wrongly decided. NB the specific offence under the Social Security Administration Act 1992, s 111A, inserted by the Social Security Administration (Fraud) Act 1997, s 13.

235 *Baxter v Gov of HM Prison Brixton* [2002] EWHC 300 (Admin).

proposal form false particulars relating to a company director, the case would fall within the plain words of s 17(1)(a).[236]

Destruction, etc

Some account or record must be destroyed, defaced, concealed or falsified by D or as a result of information provided by D. It is not enough that D is cheating V, as by selling his own property as V's, if that transaction is not recorded in any account.[237]

The courts do not seem to have provided any detailed consideration of the terms destruction, defacement or concealment. Destruction and defacement should present few if any problems. 'Concealment' raises the interesting question whether it is necessary for D to be hiding some record etc being aware that he is under a duty to disclose it, or whether it is sufficient simply that D conceals it. The issue will commonly be rolled up with that of dishonesty since knowing concealment commonly implies a lack of honesty.

Falsification

The more important issues arise in relation to falsification. Under s 17(1)(a) the offence is committed by falsification of the account etc whereas under s 17(1)(b) it is committed by *use* of a falsified account, etc. Section 17(2) provides an extended though non-exhaustive definition of falsity:

> For purposes of this section a person who makes or concurs in making in an account or other document an entry which is or may be misleading, false or deceptive in a material particular, or who omits or concurs in omitting a material particular from an account or other document, is to be treated as falsifying the account or document.

The extended meaning attaches only to documents and accounts, not records.[238] Clearly falsification may be by omission, but the case law has extended the scope of the *actus reus* much further than that simple proposition. In *Shama*[239] D, an international telephone operator, was required to fill in for each call a 'charge ticket', which was then used for an accounting purpose. He connected certain favoured subscribers without filling in a charge ticket, so they were not charged. The prosecution was unable to produce any falsified document. Upholding D's conviction, the court said that 'failure to complete a charge ticket by omitting material particulars from a document required for an accounting purpose' constituted the offence. But how can the omission to make a document at all be the omission of material particulars from it? The omission of material particulars seems necessarily to imply the existence of a document from which those particulars are omitted.[240] The offence applies irrespective of whether D is under a formal duty to account, but if D is acting under such

236 *A-G's Reference (No 1 of 2001)* [2002] Crim LR 844.

237 *Cooke* [1986] AC 909, [1986] 2 All ER 985, HL.

238 Cf Arlidge and Parry, para 5–062.

239 [1990] 2 All ER 602, [1990] Crim LR 411, CA.

240 Presumably, D, at the end of his shift returned a bundle of charge tickets to his employers. Effectively it was his work record for the shift and was required for an accounting purpose. The 'record' might be regarded as a single document though it records each transaction on a separate page; on this view the document would be false by omitting to record some of the transactions.

a duty that will prescribe the scope of his obligation to include material in the documents.[241]

Material particular

Where the allegation is of falsification, that must relate to a material particular.[242] This aspect of the offence has also been interpreted broadly. Information is so material if it is something that matters to V in making up his mind about action to be taken on the document.[243] It need not be material to the accounting purpose directly. In *Mallett* the Court of Appeal approved the trial judge's description of a material particular as 'an important matter; a thing that mattered'. It was not specified to whom it must be shown to have been important. The particulars may be material precisely for the purpose of auditing and detecting fraud. Thus, omitting the name of an account holder to whom unauthorized payments were to be made is a material particular since the name would have revealed instantly that the payment was unauthorized.[244] In cases of omission, it will only be possible to evaluate the materiality of the omitted particular in the context of the account as a whole.

(ii) *Mens rea*

The *mens rea* of the s 17(1)(a) offence requires that D:

(i) intentionally destroys, defaces, conceals or falsifies the document, and

(ii) does so dishonestly, and

(iii) acts with a view to gain for himself or another, or with intent to cause loss to another.

In principled terms, the need for specificity and clarity in each element of *mens rea* is especially important in this offence given the breadth of the *actus reus* as discussed above. However, the courts have relied heavily on the general element of dishonesty as the gravamen, avoiding unduly technical separation of the issues of knowledge and falsity.[245]

Intentionally making the statement in the account or record

Problems can arise where D is submitting large quantities of records, and is aware that only some of them *may* be false in a material particular. In *Atkinson* the defendant, a pharmacist, completed prescription forms to the pricing authority to secure repayment of prescription costs. She admitted to filling in the forms while watching TV and playing with her children. Some were false in a material particular. The trial judge directed the jury to concentrate on her dishonesty and that it was sufficient if the jury were sure that she knew it was *likely* that some of the forms were false in a material particular. The Court of Appeal regarded this as a dilution of the element of intention, coming close to mere recklessness. There must be a view to gain or intent cause loss

241 *Keatley* [1980] Crim LR 505 (Judge Mendl).

242 If it is of destruction, etc it is the whole document or record or, presumably a relevant part.

243 *Mallett* [1978] 3 All ER 10, [1978] 1 WLR 820, CA.

244 *Taylor* (2003) EWCA Crim 30 April, D authorizing £73,000 payments from employer to parents.

245 In *Atkinson* [2004] Crim LR 226 the court's suggestion that 'only lawyers would think of breaking [the *mens rea*] into component parts' is rather odd. Is this not one element of the art of statutory construction?

(below), which would not be satisfied by proof that the defendant saw the falsity of a statement as 'likely'.[246] There is, therefore, a distinct requirement that D 'deliberately and intentionally' makes the statement in the account or document. It is important to keep this element separate from the question of intention to gain since there are cases in which D will act with knowledge of falsity but with no ulterior intent to gain or cause loss.[247] This is an important element of the offence since the nature of completing records and accounts is such that there is great potential for recklessness or negligence in the recording of data. Such failings should not give rise to liability under this offence.

Knowledge as to falsity

Since s 17(2) extends the offence to cover cases in which the statement 'is or may be' misleading, false or deceptive, it is arguable that D may be guilty if he intentionally makes statements in the account or record, knowing that they *may be false* and acts with a view to gain or intent to cause loss. The learned authors of Arlidge and Parry[248] suggest that 'it can hardly be intended that the subsection should apply where it is uncertain whether the proposition in question is true or false'. The conclusion is that the expression 'or may be' must relate *only* to the s 17(1)(b) offence which includes the terms 'deception' and 'misleading'.[249]

'Dishonesty'

The term should be interpreted, as far as possible, consistently with its application in other sections. The concept of a claim of right includes a claim to the payment of a debt, and it is unclear whether the concept has any relevance here, as it does in ss 1 and 15.[250] On one hand it can be argued that such a claim should not exclude liability for false accounting any more than it excludes liability for robbery where violence is used to get payment. The legitimacy of the end, or the belief in the legitimacy of the end should not justify an illegality in the means of securing that end. This is a powerful argument when the means involve a free standing offence such as assault (as in robbery). Similarly, in the case of false accounting, it can be argued that irrespective of D's claim of right as to the end he seeks to achieve, the nature of the offence is such as to impose a separate obligation of honesty as to the means by which D seeks to secure that gain. If D has a genuine belief in the claim of right to the money to which he acts with a view to gain, there is no reason for his use of a false means (evidencing his dishonesty) in his attempt to attain that money. In the *Attorney-General's Reference (No 1 of 2001)*[251] X had been charged with an offence in the USA, which attracted high-profile media coverage. A fund was established with payments from well-wishers and an appeal committee placed monies received in an account, irrespective of whether the donors expressly stated it was for X and her parents (G and S) or for the fund. G and S

[246] It is acceptable to say that D intends result A (causing loss/making gain) if he does an act B (making false statement) which is likely to bring about the result A, *provided* D also has an *intention* to perform act B.

[247] See further Smith, *Theft*, para 6–07 and cases cited therein.

[248] *On Fraud* (2nd edn, 1996).

[249] See Arlidge and Parry, para 5–068.

[250] *Wood* [1999] Crim LR 564. Williams, TBCL, 890.

[251] [2002] Crim LR 844.

submitted false invoices in respect of expenses incurred in travelling to attend their daughter's trial. The judge accepted the submission that because some of the money transferred to the trust was money originally donated to G and S to use as they chose the prosecution could not prove that the amount of money that was obtained on the invoice was not the money of G and S. No claim of a belief in a claim of legal entitlement was made. It is easy to see how even though G and S had a 'view to gain' in the sense of acquiring the property, a jury might have found that they were not dishonest in submitting the false invoices if they believed they had a legal right to acquire the property.

Gain and loss

'Gain' and 'loss' are defined in s 34(2)(a) which is discussed elsewhere.[252] There might be a view to gain or an intention to cause loss in falsifying the account although the gain or loss has already taken place. 'Gain' includes a gain by keeping what one has, so D commits an offence under s 17 where, having already appropriated property of V's, he destroys, defaces, conceals of falsifies an account so that he will not be found out, or to put off the evil day when he will be called to account: *Eden*.[253] But *Golechha*[254] appears to decide that D's intention to cause his creditor to forbear from enforcing the debt does not involve a view to gain or an intention to cause loss on D's part. It is submitted that it involves both. It is not easy to reconcile this decision with *Eden*. By putting off the evil day when D will be called to account, that is to pay tomorrow that which he would otherwise have to pay today, would seem clearly to constitute a 'gain' to D. *Golechha* has been described as a case turning very much on its own facts.[255] A 'deed of postponement', postponing the priority of a registered charge in favour of another obligation does 'cause loss'.[256]

Where D falsifies accounts to exaggerate the profit which his department is making in order to induce his employer to continue his employment there may be no appropriation, or intended appropriation, of any money or goods belonging to the employer and thus no theft; but clearly D is acting dishonestly, and it seems he has both a view to gain (he does this to keep his job and his salary) and an intent to cause loss (in so far as it causes him to continue to operate an uneconomic department).[257] In *Masterson*[258] the defendant's falsification of invoices in an attempt to 'improve relations with his co-directors' who were unhappy with the acquisitions he had recently made was not sufficient to constitute the necessary 'view to gain'. D knew that there was no question of losing his position and could not therefore be said even to be falsifying them with a view to retaining that 'which he had'.

As for the intention to cause loss, it is unclear whether the intent must be direct or whether an oblique intention (where D sees a loss as virtually certain barring some unforeseen intervention) will suffice. The motives for intending to cause the loss are irrelevant. Thus, in *Leedham*[259] D so disliked the government ban on handguns (imposed

252 See below, p 807. Cf *Lee Cheung Wing v R*, infra, n 261.
253 [1971] Crim LR 416, CA.
254 [1989] 3 All ER 908, [1990] Crim LR 865 (sub nom *Choraria and Golechha*), CA.
255 *Masterson* (1996), unreported, 30 Apr, 1996, CA.
256 *Cummings-John* [1997] Crim LR 660.
257 Cf *Wines* [1953] 2 All ER 1497, CCA.
258 (1996) CA 94/2221/X5.
259 No 200200135/Y3.

after the Dunblane shootings) that he completed compensation forms falsely and dishonestly to cause loss to the Home Department by allowing claims for ineligible items owned by others.

In the *Attorney-General's Reference (No 1 of 2001)*[260] discussed above, G and S accepted that there was evidence that the invoice was false in the respects alleged but contended that because some of the money transferred to the trust was money originally donated to G and S to use as they chose, the prosecution could not prove that the amount of money that was obtained via the false invoice was not the money of G and S and that they had not 'gained' anything within the meaning of s 34(2)(a) because the trustees had incorporated into the trust money which in fact belonged to G and S. The judge accepted that submission and ruled that G and S should be acquitted. The Court of Appeal rejected this argument, holding that where the accused has provided false information with a view to obtaining money or other property it is not necessary for the prosecution to prove that the accused had no legal entitlement to the money or other property in question.

In *Lee Cheung Wing*[261] D was an employee of a company offering facilities for dealing in futures. Employees were not allowed to use these facilities. D, in breach of his contract of employment, opened an account in the name of a friend, X. The transactions were profitable and D signed withdrawal slips in X's name. The question was whether the slips were made 'with a view to gain'. D said he was withdrawing money to which he was entitled. Since a person has a view to gain even if he is entitled to the property demanded[262] Lee's conviction might perhaps have been upheld on that ground. The Privy Council, however, held that D was not entitled to the money because he would have been bound to account to his employer for a profit made by improper use of his position as an employee,[263] adding that, anyway, action by D to recover the profits would probably have been met by a plea of *ex turpi causa non oritur actio*.

Strict liability as to accounting purpose

As discussed above, there are two additional elements of *actus reus* – that the document is made or required for an accounting purpose and that the falsity, etc relates to a material particular – as a matter of principle, these ought to attract elements of *mens rea*. It has been held[264] however, that there is no *mens rea* requirement of D's awareness of the purpose for which the document is required. A person may be guilty of false accounting although he has no idea, perhaps reasonably so, that this is what he is doing – as for example where the document is one which requires expert evidence to show that it is required for an accounting purpose. This amounts to the imposition of strict liability as to an essential element of a serious offence, which seems objectionable.

260 [2002] Crim LR 844.
261 (1991) 94 Cr App R 355, [1992] Crim LR 440, PC.
262 *A-G's Reference (No 2 of 2001)* [2002] Crim LR 844.
263 *Reading v A-G* [1951] AC 507, 516, 517.
264 *Graham* [1997] 1 Cr App R 302 at 314.

Awareness of materiality?

The further element of *actus reus* is that if the allegation is one of falsifying the document, etc the falsity must relate to a material particular. The question of D's knowledge or awareness of the materiality of the particular has not been the subject of detailed judicial scrutiny. In *R v Bowie and McVicar*[265] HH Judge Atherton ruled that it was necessary for the prosecution to establish that additional element of *mens rea*. The charges arose from the sale of the defendants' portfolio of properties, which had been let to various tenants. The details of the properties were in some cases inaccurate in recording that the rents were paid from housing benefit rather than privately by the tenants. These were false statements, and arguably material since they would affect the security of future payments. The defendants denied that they had acted 'intentionally' or 'recklessly' either as to the falsehood or the materiality of that falsehood, but were convicted.

In most cases this issue will be subsumed within the question of dishonesty. If, for example, D makes an application for insurance and in doing so he makes a false statement as to his sexual orientation – perhaps out of embarrassment – he knows that it is false, but is arguably unaware of the materiality of that status in enhancing the insurance rate he will be offered. Arguably, the lack of awareness or recklessness as to the materiality can be adequately addressed in the broader question of whether D is dishonest and is acting with a view to gain. The overlap is so substantial that it is difficult to envisage circumstances in which D will be able to plead simultaneously that he accepts that he was dishonest but that he lacked *mens rea* as to the materiality and should therefore be acquitted.[266]

(b) Section 17(1)(b)

(i) *Actus reus*

The offence under s 17(1)(b) involves using rather than destroying, falsifying, etc the account. This is an extremely broad offence since it applies where D uses the document etc for any purpose. A document may be misleading or false within the subsection by its failure to include material particulars even though it is accurate in the sense that each statement which is contained is true.[267] It is notable that the prosecution need to show only that information in the account may be (not is) misleading or deceptive. Difficulties may arise in establishing the misleading, false or deceptive particular, and expert accounting evidence may be necessary. The elements relating to accounts and records or documents made or required for any accounting purpose are as in relation to s 17(1)(a), as are the requirements relating to falsity.

(ii) *Mens rea*

The *mens rea* for the s 17(1)(b) offence comprises: (i) intentionally using a document; (ii) knowing[268] it is false; (iii) dishonestly; and (iv) with a view to gain for himself or another,

265 Manchester Crown Court, 19 Feb 2003.

266 Cf Smith, *Property Offences*, 24–07a.

267 See *Kylsant* [1932] 1 KB 442.

268 Which may include a wilful blindness as to falsity.

or with intent to cause loss to another. It is important to note that the *mens rea* differs here in one important respect from the elements as discussed in relation to s 17(1)(a). D may commit the offence in furnishing information not only where he knows that the material particular is false, but also where he knows that the document *may* be false or misleading in a material particular; evidently wilful blindness suffices.

10. False statements by company directors

Section 19 of the Act provides:

(1) Where an officer of a body corporate or unincorporated association (or person purporting to act as such), with intent to deceive members or creditors of the body corporate or association about its affairs, publishes or concurs in publishing a written statement or account which to his knowledge is or may be misleading, false or deceptive in a material particular, he shall on conviction on indictment be liable to imprisonment for a term not exceeding seven years.

(2) For purposes of this section a person who has entered into a security for the benefit of a body corporate or association is to be treated as a creditor of it.

(3) Where the affairs of a body corporate or association are managed by its members, this section shall apply to any statement which a member publishes or concurs in publishing in connection with his functions of management as if he were an officer of the body corporate or association.

The offence is designed to deal with cases of directors publishing false prospectuses in an attempt to induce investment. It is one of a range of legislative provisions seeking to protect investors.[269] In two senses the offence is a narrow one. First, it may be committed only by an officer[270] of a body corporate or unincorporated association. Secondly, it may be committed only where the intention is to deceive[271] members or creditors of the corporation or association and not the public at large about its affairs. But in another sense the offence is a wide one for it extends to the publication of any *written* statement of account that *may be* misleading in a material particular. Recklessness suffices. It is not necessary to show that there is any view to gain or intention to cause loss in publishing the statement or account, though no doubt either or both will often be present. There is no requirement that D acted dishonestly, although it has been suggested that there is no practical difference between defining the *mens rea* as an intent to deceive or dishonesty.[272] The prosecution will depend in many cases on the expert accountancy evidence as to whether the accounts were misleading. The offence might be committed where an officer, in order to inspire confidence in the company, falsely publishes that a well-known person has been appointed to the board. Possibly the offence might be committed where

269 See generally, J. Fisher, J. Bewsey, M. Waters and E. Ovey, *The Law of Investor Protection* (2nd edn, 1996); Arlidge and Parry, ch 8; M. Gale, 'Fraud and the Sale of Shares' (2001) Company Lawyer 98. Investor protection has taken on a greater significance as increasing numbers of the general public have personal investment portfolios.

270 The officers of a body corporate are frequently defined in the articles or bye-laws of a corporation. Under the Companies Act 1985, s 74(4), 'officer' includes a director, manager or secretary. An auditor may be an officer: *Shacter* [1960] 2 QB 252.

271 As to intent to deceive, see *Welham v DPP* [1961] AC 103, [1960] 1 All ER 805, HL.

272 See *Shuck* [1992] Crim LR 209.

an officer publishes in the accounts a payment as having been made to the Conservative Party where it has in fact been paid to the Labour Party.

11. Suppression of documents

By s 20:

(1) A person who dishonestly, with a view to gain for himself or another or with intent to cause loss to another, destroys, defaces or conceals any valuable security, any will or other testamentary document or any original document of or belonging to, or filed or deposited in, any court of justice or any government department shall on conviction on indictment be liable to imprisonment for a term not exceeding seven years.

This provision is not likely to be of great practical importance; it was included because:

It seemed to us that it might provide the only way of dealing with a person who, for example, suppressed a public document as a first step towards committing a fraud but did not get so far as attempting to commit the fraud. In accordance with the scheme of the [Act] the offence is limited to something done dishonestly and with a view to gain or with intent to cause loss to another.[273]

12. Cheating[274]

Cheating was a misdemeanour at common law and was developed most vigorously during the eighteenth century. The authorities suggest an incredibly broad definition. Hawkins[275] defined cheating as '. . . deceitful practices, in defrauding or endeavouring to defraud another of his own right by means of some artful device, contrary to the plain rules of common honesty'.

The common law offence of cheating still retains significant importance because, though s 32(1) of the Act abolishes cheating (along with common law offences against property), it does so only 'except as regards offences relating to the public revenue'. The punishment is imprisonment and/or a fine without limit.

As a practical matter the offence of cheating has been used, on any scale at all, only in connection with frauds against the public revenue. Given the available sentence and the breadth of the offence it is not surprising that it is popular with the Inland Revenue and Customs and Excise and is frequently prosecuted in preference to specific offences under the Theft Acts or the Taxes Management Act.

In *Hudson*[276] the Court of Criminal Appeal upheld D's conviction on a charge of making false statements to the prejudice of the Crown and the public revenue with intent to defraud where it appeared that D had falsely stated to the Inland Revenue the profits of his business. It was argued that the indictment disclosed no offence known to the law,

273 Cmnd 2977, para 106.

274 D. Ormerod, 'Cheating the Public Revenue' [1998] Crim LR 627; D. Ormerod, 'Summary Evasion of Income Tax' [2002] Crim LR 3.

275 1 PC 318.

276 [1956] 2 QB 252, [1956] 1 All ER 814, discussed by 'Watchful' [1956] BTR 119.

but the court, relying on *dicta* of Lord Mansfield CJ in *Bembridge*,[277] and statements by Hawkins[278] and East,[279] held that it was an offence for a private individual, as well as a public officer, to defraud the Crown and public. The argument that there was no such offence was raised again in *Mulligan*[280] and was just as forthrightly rejected by the Court of Appeal.

The CLRC was minded to abolish the offence and its retention was the result of special pleading by the revenue authorities who wished to retain it for serious revenue frauds where penalties under other provisions were seen by them as inadequate. Perhaps, too, the Revenue was attracted by the expansive terminology of Hawkins' definition. At all events the Revenue's fondest hopes for cheating must have been realized by *Mavji*.[281] D had dishonestly evaded value added tax to the tune of over £1,000,000. Charged, as he might have been, under what was then s 38(1) of the Finance Act 1972 with the fraudulent evasion of tax he would have been liable to a maximum of two years' imprisonment and/or a fine of £1,000 or three times the tax whichever was the greater. Convicted, as he was, of cheating he was sentenced to six years' imprisonment and made criminally bankrupt in the sum of £690,000. The Court of Appeal, affirming D's conviction and sentence, rejected counsel's submission that cheating required a positive act such as a deception and not merely an omission to make a VAT return. The court held that D was under a duty to make such a return and his failure to do so with intent to cheat the revenue of money to which it was entitled constituted the offence.[282] So to hold was, with respect, a novel extension of the offence. *Hudson*,[283] which was treated in *Mavji* as the leading case, appears to assume that cheating requires the use of a false representation or false device. Even the expansive language of *Hawkins* is conditioned by the requirement 'by means of some artful device'. What artful device was employed by D in *Mavji*?

The *actus reus* of the offence has become so wide that the definition is almost best stated in negative terms. There need not be a dishonest act; an omission will suffice. The act or omission must be intended to prejudice the Inland Revenue, Customs and Excise[284] or Department of Social Security. The offence cannot be committed in respect of a local authority,[285] nor it is submitted, against the EC.[286] There is no requirement of an operative deception,[287] nor of a need to prove actual loss to the revenue,[288] or to any other. It is not necessary to prove that the accused's conduct resulted in any gain to himself,[289] nor for the defendant to be a government official.[290] The types of behaviour caught include: failing to account for VAT,[291] withholding PAYE and National Insur-

277 (1783) 22 State Tr 1 at 156. 278 1 PC 322. 279 2 PC 821.

280 [1990] Crim LR 427, CA.

281 [1987] 2 All ER 758, [1987] 1 WLR 1388, CA. *Mavji* was followed in *Redford* (1988) 89 Cr App R 1, CA.

282 Cheating is a 'conduct offence' and it is not necessary to prove that D caused any loss: *Hunt* [1994] Crim LR 747.

283 Above. 284 *R v Blake* (1844) 6 QB 126; *R v Tonner* [1985] 1 WLR 344.

285 *Lush v Coles* [1967] 1 WLR 685.

286 On fraud in the European Union, see L. Kuhl, 'The Criminal Law Protection of the Communities' Financial Interests against Fraud' [1998] Crim LR 259 and 323, especially at 264–266, and 330.

287 *R v Mavji* [1987] 1 WLR 1388.

288 *R v Hunt* [1994] STC 819 at 827, per Stuart-Smith LJ. Hence its use in VAT carousel frauds.

289 *R v Hunt* [1994] STC 819, [1994] Crim LR 747. 290 *R v Mulligan* [1990] Crim LR 427.

291 *R v Ryan* [1994] STC 446, [1994] Crim LR 858.

ance,[292] failing to register for VAT,[293] or simply failing to disclose income.[294] It is a particularly useful offence in cases of carousel frauds where there is no duty to pay VAT arising. It is difficult to see how the offence could be stated in more expansive terms. The breadth of the offence means that often the only live issue at trial will be dishonesty.

The jury's difficulty in applying the dishonesty test in commercial settings has been considered above. In relation to carefully planned tax schemes the problems appear obvious: it seems ludicrous to ask jurors to apply the test of whether a reasonable and honest person would see it as dishonest when they (probably) have little or no understanding of the very complex civil law tax position or commercial background. To ask them further whether they believe that the accused realized that the activity would be regarded as dishonest by the standards of reasonable people is expecting rather a lot. The activity engaged in might have been what the defendant genuinely, and on expert advice, regarded as mere tax avoidance (acceptable in civil and criminal law), but which the jury considers to be dishonest and therefore to constitute a cheat. This is tantamount to retrospective criminalization and may well offend the protection in Article 7 of the ECHR.[295]

Notwithstanding the criticism of the cheating offence the Revenue introduced a new statutory version of the offence which is triable either way. Section 144 of the Finance Act 2000 criminalizes 'being knowingly concerned in the evasion of income tax'. This is an ill-defined and extremely broad offence, but for numerous reasons may prove less successful than the Revenue anticipated.[296]

13. Fraud reform proposals

In response to increasing concern about the ill-defined and incoherently structured deception offences, the Law Commission recently drafted a Consultation Paper on *Fraud and Deception*[297] and subsequent Report on *Fraud*.[298] Aside from the prevalence of fraud – reported to cost £14bn per annum[299] – a driving pressure for reform of the offences has been the need to keep pace with technology as it allows for instantaneous and ever more sophisticated methods of transfer of diverse types of property interest, often between jurisdictions.[300] Interestingly, the terrorist attacks of 9/11 have provided a further impetus

292 *R v Less* (1993), The Times, 30 Mar.

293 *R v Redford* [1988] STC 845, [1989] Crim LR 152.

294 *Anderson* (1992) 13 Cr App R (S) 564.

295 Cf *Pattni* [2000] Crim LR 570 at first instance. See Law Com Consultation Paper No 155, *Legislating the Criminal Code: Fraud and Deception* (1999), para 3.23.

296 See D. Ormerod, above n 275.

297 Law Com Consultation Paper No 155 (1999) above. See D. Ormerod, 'A Bit of A Con' [1999] Crim LR 789. See also T. Palfrey, 'Is Fraud Dishonest?' (2000) J Crim L 518.

298 Law Com No 276. See G. Sullivan, 'Fraud the Latest Law Commission Proposals' (2003) 67 J Crim L 139; P. Kiernan and G. Scanlan, 'Fraud and the Law Commission: The Future of Dishonesty' (2003) Comp Law 4.

299 On the difficulty in identifying the precise scope of the problem see M. Levi, 'The costs of transnational and other financial crime: making sense of the worldwide data' (2001) 1 Int Jnl of Comp Criminology 8.

300 Aside from any legal shortcomings, pressure for reform derives from the commercial sector, where there is widespread anxiety over the inability of the present offences to protect the increasingly sophisticated methods of transacting business in electronic form.

for reform as the government seeks broader powers to criminalise the use of illicit money. Thus, the package of measures being implemented include those in the Proceeds of Crime Act 2002, and safeguards against Identity Fraud.[301]

The main issue of contention in reform has been whether there ought to be further incremental reform of the deception based offences, or replacement with a general fraud offence.[302] This would replace the numerous over particularized deception offences in the 1968, 1978 and 1996 Acts. After initial hesitation, the Law Commission has favoured the latter approach and this has the support of the Home Office, which observed recently that:

> It is not a realistic solution to continue plugging loopholes in fraud law by the addition of more specific offences. Not only does this piecemeal law reform lead to further complexities and potential for charging defendants wrongly, but it means that the law will always be lagging behind any developments in technology or new methods of committing fraud.

General fraud offences have operated successfully in other jurisdictions,[303] and it is no surprise that under pressure from strong lobbying voices including the CPS and SFO, a proposal for such an offence, based on the Law Commission Report, is now being taken forward.[304] The merits of the general fraud offence are considered fully in the Law Commission Report.[305] Amongst the many *practical* advantages that might flow from such an offence are the clearer expression of large scale criminality in one charge; the ability to render complex schemes more readily understood by jurors; the avoidance of fragmenting factual chronologies to meet technical requirements of specific counts on the indictment; the removal of the risk of duplicity or of overloading the indictment; and the ease of cross-admissibility of evidence. These practical advantages must not however, be allowed to produce a general offence that is overbroad, based too heavily on the ill-defined concept of dishonesty, too vague to meet the obligation under Article 7 of the ECHR, and otherwise deficient in principle.

As noted, the main shift in emphasis is from offences based on an operative deception effective on a victim, to offences focused on the defendant's blameworthy and dishonest conduct *per se*. This produces an overarching concern that the proposals are too heavily reliant on dishonesty. It is notable that the Law Commission and Home Office criticism of the common law offence of conspiracy to defraud – that 'dishonesty is left to do all the work' – could equally be levelled at the proposals.

(a) The latest proposals

The Law Commission's proposed offences of 'Fraud' which have the general endorsement of the Home Office are reproduced here in full draft Bill form since the Bill or a version thereof is likely to be enacted in the near future.

301 See *Entitlement Cards and Identity Fraud* (2002), Home Office; *Legislation on Identity Cards* (2004) Home Office.

302 On the merits see generally, G. R. Sullivan, 'Fraud and Efficacy in the Criminal Law: A Proposal for a Wide Residual Offence' [1985] Crim LR 616.

303 As for example under s 380 of the Canadian Criminal Code and *Olan* (1978) 5 CR (3d) 1.

304 See *Fraud Law Reform: Consultation on Proposals for Legislation* (2004), Home Office. On which, see P. Binning, 'When Dishonesty is Not Enough' (2004) 154 NLJ 1042.

305 Cf the views of the CLRC in the *Eighth Report*, paras 97–100.

(i) False representation

(1) A person is in breach of this section if he –

(a) dishonestly makes a false representation, and

(b) intends, by making the representation –

(i) to make a gain for himself or another, or

(ii) to cause loss to another or to expose another to a risk of loss.

(2) A representation is false if –

(a) it is untrue or misleading, and

(b) the person making it knows that it is, or might be, untrue or misleading.

(3) 'Representation' means any representation by words or conduct as to fact or law, including a representation as to the state of mind of –

(a) the person making the representation, or

(b) any other person.

A number of advantages flow from adopting an offence of this form, not least from its generality and simplicity. The concept of 'false representation' is, it seems, well established in law, but is it a suitably clear foundation for the creation of an offence? The criminal offence will never be wider than the potential civil liability of a person who makes a false representation. The new section will create a 'conduct' crime rather than a 'result' crime, and it will not be necessary for the prosecution to prove that the deception was operative on the victim, if indeed there is an identifiable victim. In particular, the offence is a means of avoiding the tortuous interpretations of the House of Lords in cases such as *Lambie*[306] and *Charles.*[307] It would also cover cases of 'phishing' (that is, sending requests for bank details via the internet). The offence is very wide. It may criminalize conduct which at present some might see as sharp practice. In particular, D will be liable where his representation 'might be' misleading. It comes close to an offence of 'lying'. The opportunities to prosecute this offence against dishonest traders is obvious.

(ii) Fraud by failing to disclose information

(1) A person is in breach of this section if he –

(a) dishonestly fails to disclose information to another person, which he is under a legal duty to disclose

(b) intends, by failing to do so –

(i) to make a gain for himself or another, or

(ii) to cause loss to another or to expose another to a risk of loss.

The offence gives rise to less concern. Arguably, all those cases in which there is a legal duty might be regarded as capable of prosecution under the false representation offence.[308] It is questionable whether the offence provides sufficient certainty and fair

[306] [1982] AC 449. [307] [1997] AC 17.

[308] Provided the failure to disclose when under such a duty can be seen as synonymous with a false representation by omission.

warning if the defendant's criminal liability is to turn on his civil law obligations to disclose. Problems may arise since D might always claim that he was not dishonest since he lacked awareness of the obligation to disclose. Will the concept of a 'legal' duty to disclose be a sufficiently clear basis for the offence? Will it involve the courts in complex civil law questions?

(iii) Fraud by abuse of position

(1) A person is in breach of this section if he –

(a) occupies a position in which he is expected to safeguard, or not to act against, the financial interests of another person,
(b) dishonestly abuses that position, and
(c) intends, by means of the abuse of that position –

(i) to make a gain for himself or another, or

(ii) to cause loss to another or to expose another to a risk of loss.

(3) A person may be regarded as abusing his position even though the conduct alleged to amount to the abuse consists of an omission rather than an act.

Although in principle an offence of this nature has many attractions[309] the categories of relationship which should qualify will be difficult to define with sufficient precision. The suggestion in the Home Office paper is that relationships might extend to those in the family or in the context of voluntary work! Criminalizing financial disputes in such relationships seems to be an overreaction.

(iv) Obtaining services dishonestly

The Commission's further proposal is for an offence of obtaining services dishonestly, but without deception.

(1) A person is guilty of an offence under this section if he obtains services for himself or another –

(a) by a dishonest act, and
(b) in breach of subsection (2).

(2) A person obtains services in breach of this subsection if –

(a) they are made available on the basis that payment has been, is being or will be made for or in respect of them,
(b) he obtains them without any payment having been made for or in respect of them or without payment having been made in full, and
(c) when he obtains them, he –

(i) knows that they are made available on the basis described in paragraph (a), or

(ii) knows that they might be,

but intends that payment will not be made, or will not be made in full.

309 It would tackle the problems encountered in cases such as *Tarling v Govt of Singapore* (1978) 70 Cr App R 77; *Adams v The Queen* [1995] 1 WLR 52.

This avoids the difficulty of the person who 'deceives' a machine and cannot under the present orthodox interpretation[310] of the deception be guilty of an offence under s 1 of the 1978 Act.

(v) Conspiracy to defraud

The Home Office concluded disappointingly but not surprisingly that the offence of conspiracy to defraud ought to be retained, at least until it was clear how the new offences operated.

310 Cf *Holmes* [2005] Crim LR 229, above.

20

Blackmail and related offences

1. Blackmail[1]

Originally the word blackmail was used to describe the tribute paid to Scottish chieftains by landowners in the border counties in order to secure immunity from raids on their lands. In the early stages of its development the crime of blackmail seems to have been pretty well coextensive with robbery and attempted robbery,[2] but over the years the definition has been extended to embrace more subtle methods of extortion. The law is now set out in s 21 of the Theft Act 1968:[3]

> (1) A person is guilty of blackmail if, with a view to gain for himself or another or with intent to cause loss to another, he makes any unwarranted demand with menaces; and for this purpose a demand with menaces is unwarranted unless the person making it does so in the belief –
>
> (a) that he has reasonable grounds for making the demand; and
>
> (b) that the use of the menaces is a proper means of reinforcing the demand.
>
> (2) The nature of the act or omission demanded is immaterial, and it is also immaterial whether the menaces do or do not relate to action to be taken by the person making the demand.
>
> (3) A person guilty of blackmail shall on conviction on indictment be liable to imprisonment for a term not exceeding fourteen years.

This rather complicated provision when unravelled comprises an *actus reus* of an unwarranted demand with menaces, and *mens rea* requirements of an intention to make the unwarranted demand with menaces, with a view to gain or intention to cause loss, in the belief that there are reasonable grounds for making the demand and that the menacing is a proper means of enforcing the demand.

There are relatively few reported appellate court decisions on the substance of the offence; those that are reported relate to sentencing, and it should be noted in that regard that the offence is one of the most serious in the criminal calendar attracting long term

[1] J. C. Smith, *Theft*, ch 10, Griew, ch 14; CLRC *Eighth Report* (1966) Cmnd 2977, paras 108–125.

[2] W. Winder, 'The Development of Blackmail' (1941) 5 MLR 21; G. Williams, 'Blackmail' [1954] Crim LR 7; J. Lindgren, 'The Theory, History, and Practice of the Bribery-Extortion Distinction' (1993) 141(5) U Pa L Rev 1695. M. Hepworth, 'The British Conception of Blackmail' (1975) Int J of Criminology and Penology 1.

[3] B. MacKenna, 'Blackmail' [1966] Crim LR 467; B. Hogan, 'Blackmail' [1966] Crim LR 474; C. R. Williams, 'Demanding with Menaces: A Survey of the Australian Law of Blackmail' (1975) 10 Melb LR 118, especially at 136–144.

imprisonment.[4] The ease with which demands can be communicated via email and mobile phones, and the ease with which private information can be accumulated and accessed by others renders the opportunity for blackmail ever greater.[5]

Although the offence appears in the Theft Act 1968 and its requirement of an act with a view to loss or gain demonstrates that it serves to protect property, in many cases it is more appropriately viewed as an offence against privacy.[6] Identifying the harm or interest being protected by the offence of blackmail has generated a wealth of academic literature.[7]

(a) The demand

A demand may take any form, and may be implicit as well as explicit. It extends well beyond the obvious '£1,000 or I will publish the photographs exposing your adultery'. The demand could be oral, in writing, by gestures or by D's demeanour provided, objectively viewed it, is a demand. The essence of the matter is that D's communication to V, however phrased, conveys to V the message that a menace will materialize unless V complies with the demand. D may be guilty of blackmail where, for example, he apprehends V in the act of stealing and, without any formal demand, makes it clear to V that if he pays D money he will hear no more of the matter.[8] D's humblest form of request may be a demand.[9] But, whether express or implied, there must actually be a demand. If, having caught V in the act of stealing, D receives and accepts an unsolicited offer to buy his silence, D would not be guilty of blackmail (but might commit the offence of withholding for gain information relating to an arrestable offence).

A demand may be made through an intermediary.[10] It may be complete though it has not been communicated to V because, say, V is deaf. A demand by letter is made where and when it is posted.[11] Presumably the same is true of email communications, with the demand being complete once sent. The offence is, of course, complete irrespective of V's compliance with the demands or otherwise. It has been argued that the wide

4 See eg *Hadjou* [1989] Crim LR 390.

5 See eg the increasingly common practice of hackers threatening to corrupt a company's website by posting pornography, etc or to disable a company's website unless payment is made. See M. Griffiths, 'Internet Corporate Blackmail: a growing problem' (2004) 168 JP 632.

6 See P. Alldridge, 'Attempted Murder of the Soul: Blackmail, Privacy and Secrets' (1993) 13 OJLS 368. For a sociological view of the activity, see M. Hepworth, *Blackmail, Publicity and Secrecy in Everyday Life* (1975).

7 See *inter alia*, 'Blackmail – A Symposium' (1993) 141(5) U Pa L Rev and L. Katz, *Ill-gotten gains: evasion, blackmail, fraud, and kindred puzzles of the law* (1996). For recent English literature see W. Block, 'The logic of the argument of legalising blackmail' [2001] Bracton LJ 61; W. Block and R. McGee, 'Blackmail as a Victimless Crime' [1999] Bracton LJ 24.

8 Cf *Collister and Warhurst* (1955) 39 Cr App R 100, CCA: 'the demeanour of the accused' was sufficient.

9 Cf *Robinson* (1796) 2 East PC 1110, where the words 'Remember, Sir, I am now only making an appeal to your benevolence' were held in the circumstances capable of importing a demand. In *Miah* [2003] 1 Cr App R (S) 379, D sent videos of child pornography to Vs with return address and then contacted Vs informing them that their fingerprints were on the videos and 'urging' them or 'inviting' them to call a telephone number. D pleaded guilty and no issue arose as to whether these invitations to call the number were a 'demand'.

10 *Thumber* (1999) No 199900691, 29 November, CA.

11 *Treacy v DPP* [1971] AC 537, [1971] 1 All ER 110, HL. See P. J. Pace, 'Demanding with Menaces' (1971) 121 NLJ 242.

interpretation of demand means that there is no room for a crime of attempted blackmail,[12] although there are hypothetical scenarios of D being intercepted on his way to the post etc. Treating the full offence as committed before the demand has been communicated, emphasizes that the gravamen of the offence is the making of unwarranted demands *per se*.

Normally D will demand money or other property but s 21(2) provides that 'the nature of the act or omission demanded is immaterial'. At first sight, this seems to undermine a foundation of the offence as one protecting property, but it is not as far reaching as may appear because the offence can be committed only if D also has a view to gain or an intention to cause loss, and this refers to gain or loss in money or other property.[13] The purpose of s 21(2) seems to have been[14] to forestall a possible argument that D cannot be guilty unless his demand is for some property. If D demands with menaces that he be given paid employment or demands that V append his signature to a promissory note provided by D,[15] he may be guilty of blackmail if he acts with a view to gain although he does not demand any property of V. Demands for sexual intercourse or other acts of a sexual nature are not within the scope of the offence and are dealt with under the Sexual Offences Act 2003.[16]

(b) Menaces

The word 'menace' is an ordinary English word which in most cases will be understood by a jury without the need for elaboration.[17] On one view it might suggest only threats of violence to persons or property, but under the former law[18] 'menace' was given a much wider meaning. It seems clear that the CLRC intended to retain the former law; the Committee was of course well aware of the meaning 'menace' had acquired and deliberately chose to use this word when they might have chosen some other.[19] It extends to threats to damage property and to make damaging allegations whether truthful or not. In *Thorne v Motor Trade Association*,[20] Lord Wright said[21] that a menace was a threat of 'any action detrimental to or unpleasant to the person addressed'. This is of course a very wide definition. The CLRC chose menaces in preference to threats because, 'notwithstanding the wide meaning given to "menaces" in *Thorne's case* . . . we regard that word as stronger than "threats", and the consequent slight restriction on the scope of the offence seems to us right'. In view of Lord Wright's definition of menaces it might be thought that any distinction between menaces and threats is wholly illusory in practice, although

12 See *Moran* (1952) 36 Cr App R 10, 12, cf J. Ll. Edwards, 'Criminal Attempts' (1952) 15 MLR 345.

13 Theft Act 1968, s 34; below, p 807.

14 Cf Cmnd 2977, Annex 2.

15 Cf *Phipoe* (1795) 2 Leach 673, where Mrs Phipoe armed with a carving knife 'in the French language threatened, amidst the most opprobrious expressions, to take away [V's] life' unless he signed a promissory note on paper and with materials provided by her.

16 See above, Ch 17. Note that the offence of procuring a woman to have sexual intercourse by threats contrary to s 2 of the Sexual Offences Act 1956 has not been replicated in the 2003 Act. There are reported instances of convictions for blackmail in these circumstances (eg *Downer* (2000) 17 Oct CA), but these must be erroneous.

17 *Lawrence and Pomroy* (1971) 57 Cr App R 64, CA.

18 Although not called blackmail, see ss 29–31 of the Larceny Act 1916.

19 Cmnd 2977, para 123.

20 [1937] AC 797, [1937] 3 All ER 157, HL.

21 [1937] AC at 817, [1937] 3 All ER at 167.

existing in theory.[22] But it does perhaps serve to emphasize that there is a limit, below which conduct will not be regarded as a menace.

Three situations need to be distinguished.

(1) Where D has in fact made a demand with a 'menace' that would cause a person of ordinary firmness to succumb, V's *subsequent* refusal to accede to the demand cannot relieve D of liability. There can be a menace even if V is not intimidated. Thus, D may be guilty of blackmail where he threatens to assault V unless V pays him money, though V is in no way frightened and squares up to D with the result that D runs away.[23]

(2) The law will not treat as a menace words or conduct which would not intimidate or influence anyone to respond to the demand. So in *Harry*[24] where the organizers of a student Rag had written to shopkeepers offering them immunity from any 'inconvenience' resulting from Rag activities, the trial judge ruled that there was not sufficient evidence of a menace. Some shopkeepers had complained of the veiled threat in the letter but this menace was not, to use the words of Sellers LJ in *Clear*,[25] 'of such a nature and extent that the mind of an ordinary person of normal stability and courage might be influenced or made apprehensive so as to accede unwillingly to the demand.'

(3) However, D's conduct may amount to a menace even though a person of ordinary firmness would not accede to the demand where, *to D's knowledge*, the particular victim, owing to such factors as infirmity, youth, timidity or even plain cowardice, will accede to the demand.[26] Indeed, the blackmailer will often select his victim precisely because he is aware of the victim's vulnerability.[27] If D intends that his menace should operate on the mind of V and knows of circumstances that will make V unwillingly accede to the demand, D may properly be convicted of blackmail. Since the offence is completed irrespective of the demand being successfully communicated to V, there is some tension with this aspect of the offence being interpreted by reference to the victim's susceptibilities.[28]

(c) Unwarranted demand

Not every demand accompanied by a menace will amount to blackmail. It will be appreciated at once that it ought not to be blackmail to demand payment of a debt from V and to threaten civil proceedings in the event of his failure to comply. There is a menace (a threat of action detrimental to or unpleasant to the person addressed) but it is in the

[22] See nn 32–38 and L. Katz, p 157.

[23] Cf *Moran* [1952] 1 All ER 803n, CCA. For theoretical consideration of the justifications for punishing the harm threatened or that inflicted see L. Katz, 'Blackmail and Other Forms of Arm-Twisting' (1993) U Pa L Rev 1567.

[24] [1974] Crim LR 32 (Judge Petre).

[25] [1968] 1 All ER 74 at 80, CA.

[26] *Clear* [1968] 1 All ER 74 at 80, CA; *Garwood* [1987] 1 All ER 1032, [1987] 1 WLR 319, CA.

[27] Cf *Tomlinson* [1895] 1 QB 706, CCR. A recent illustration is of businessmen being charged extortionate prices for champagne ordered in Soho clubs and threatened with violence if they fail to pay. The perpetrators are rarely charged since the businessmen are unwilling to admit their presence in the clubs: *The Observer*, 29 Feb 2004.

[28] See Smith, *Property Offences*, 15–18.

circumstances a perfectly lawful demand accompanied by a justifiable threat. At the other extreme a demand by D for property to which he is not legally entitled accompanied by a threat to kill V would be thought of as an obvious instance of blackmail.

(i) The paradox of blackmail

But between these two extremes, less clear-cut cases emerge. D may threaten to publicize V as a defaulter unless he pays a gaming debt;[29] D may threaten to publish memoirs which expose V's discreditable conduct unless V buys them from her;[30] or D may threaten to expose V's immoral relationship with her unless V pays money which he had promised her.[31] Whether the conduct in any or all of these cases *ought* to be blackmail might give rise to a good deal of argument. In particular, there is a paradox in that while it is lawful for D to make a demand for payment of a debt owed by V and it is lawful for D to expose, or threaten to expose V's immorality, it is an offence of blackmail to perform the two in combination. This has given rise to an extensive academic literature, and a diverse range of theories has been employed in an attempt to justify the inclusion of the offence of blackmail in a coherent and principled code of criminal law.[32] These include: analyses of the offence in terms of its economic efficiency;[33] claims that blackmail is outlawed as a means of avoiding private law enforcement,[34] and the growth of an industry trading on confidential material which generate fear and inhibit normal lifestyles;[35] that the offence prevents D being unjustly enriched by using another's interests (V's confidential information and the public's 'right to know' about that information in some cases).[36] Some of the most cogent theoretical explanations for the offence are focused on the coercion and exploitation it involves, even in the paradox cases.[37] Far from seeing the paradox as creating an anomaly, some respected American academics have treated blackmail as a paradigmatic crime with its core being D's creation of subordination of V.[38]

(ii) Subjective approach

The Theft Act's pragmatic solution to defining the type of menace that will be lawful is provided in s 21(1). D's demand will be unwarranted unless made in the belief (a) that there are reasonable grounds for making it, *and* (b) that the use of the menaces is a proper means of enforcing the demand. The test is essentially a subjective one: what matters are D's beliefs about the reasonable grounds for making the demand and the propriety of using a menace to enforce the demand. D's belief in the reasonableness of the demand

29 Cf *Norreys v Zeffert* [1939] 2 All ER 187, KBD.

30 Cf the case discussed in Lord Denning's *Report*, Cmnd 2152, paras 31–36.

31 Cf *Bernhard* [1938] 2 KB 264, [1938] 2 All ER 140, CCA.

32 A very interesting review of many of the theories can be found in J. Isenbergh, 'Blackmail from A to C' (1993) U Pa L Rev 1905.

33 See further: D. H. Ginsburg and P. Shechtman, 'Blackmail : An economic analysis of the law' (1993) U Pa L Rev 1849; R. Posner, 'Blackmail, Privacy and Freedom of Contract' (1993) U Pa L Rev 1817.

34 J. G. Brown, 'Blackmail as Private Justice' (1993) U Pa L Rev 1935.

35 R. Epstein, 'Blackmail Inc.' (1983) 50 U Chi L R. 553.

36 See further on this J. Lindgren, 'Unravelling the Paradox of Blackmail' (1984) 84 Col L Rev 670.

37 See further, S. Altmann, 'A Patchwork Theory of Blackmail' (1993) U Pa L Rev 1639; G. Lamond, 'Coercion, Threats and the Puzzle of Blackmail', in A. Simester and A. T. H. Smith (eds), *Harm and Culpability* (1996).

38 See G. Fletcher, 'Blackmail: The Paradigmatic Crime' (1993) U Pa L Rev 1617 and L. Katz, 'Blackmail and Other Forms of Arm-Twisting' (1993) U Pa L Rev 1567.

may stem from the fact that V owes him money, or that D believes he has a legal claim against V, or some other basis.[39] D's belief that the use of menaces is a proper way of enforcing that demand may stem from D's upbringing, his relationship and past dealings with V, etc.[40]

Suppose that D has had a sexual relationship with V and V promises that he will pay D £100 for the sexual favours which he has received; V fails to keep his promise whereupon D threatens to expose the relationship to V's regular sexual partner unless he pays.[41] D's liability would now turn upon whether she believed that she had reasonable grounds for demanding the £100, *and* believed that her threat to expose V's immorality was a proper way of enforcing the demand. All the circumstances have to be taken into account in so far as they are relevant as tending to show or negative that D's beliefs were genuine. D might have believed (wrongly) that she was legally entitled to the £100 (reasonable grounds) and that it was lawful for her to threaten to expose V to get it (proper means of enforcement). D might have believed she was morally entitled to enforce payment in this way, and this would be enough provided she believed in fact that this was reasonable and proper. One person (a lawyer for example) might feel that he was morally entitled to something and yet recognize that his moral claim would not afford him reasonable grounds for making the demand. Another person might genuinely think that his moral right affords him reasonable grounds. In practice, it may be thought, D does not think precisely in terms of the legality or morality of his conduct, but more in terms whether it is, in a broad way, reasonable.

In *Harvey, Ulyett and Plummer*[42] D and his associates paid V £20,000 for what V claimed was a consignment of cannabis but which turned out to be 'a load of rubbish'. Incensed by this swindle, the defendants kidnapped V's wife and child and made threats of serious bodily harm to them and to V unless the money was returned. No doubt a lawyer (or even a reasonably well informed layman) would have appreciated that in these circumstances the money was not recoverable since it was paid in pursuance of an illegal contract. Such a person might have difficulty in forming a belief that there were reasonable grounds for the demand. But in *Harvey* the particular defendants no doubt felt that they had been swindled ('ripped off to the tune of £20,000' as the trial judge put it) and it was for the jury to determine whether as a matter of fact they believed that their demand was reasonable.

It has been argued[43] that this goes too far, and that it is not right that D's own moral standards should determine the rightness or wrongness of his conduct; that the law should give 'efficacy to the defendant's moral judgments whatever they may be'.[44] The criticism is that the *mens rea* turns not merely on D's subjective beliefs about the

[39] See eg in *Kewell* [2000] 2 Cr App R (S) 38 V owed a debt to D but there was little difficulty in establishing that D knew it was improper to threaten to reveal embarrassing but consensually taken photos of V from their period of cohabitation. Similarly, in *St Q* [2002] 1 Cr App R (2) 440, where D's threat was to distribute videos of consensual sex to encourage his wife to agree a divorce settlement.

[40] Car clampers do not commit the offence provided they believe that clamping is a proper means of enforcing the demand for payment: *Arthur v Anker* [1997] QB 564, 577.

[41] Cf *Bernhard* [1938] 2 KB 264.

[42] (1981) 72 Cr App R 139, CA.

[43] By MacKenna J, 'Blackmail' [1966] Crim LR 467, 469.

[44] See *Lambert* [1972] Crim LR 422 (Newcastle Crown Court); where Judge John Arnold appears to have accepted that this is the effect of the section.

circumstances in which he is acting (as in recklessness etc), but on D's beliefs about appropriate moral standards. There are a number of responses to this. First, as a practical matter most people do act according to generally accepted legal and moral standards, and the cases must be rare where D can *genuinely* rely on his own moral standards where these are seriously at odds with accepted standards. Secondly, it is important to note that it is not enough that D feels that his conduct is justified or that it is in some way right for him; 'proper' in this context involves a consideration of what D believes would be generally thought of as proper. The test of D's belief is of course a subjective one but that belief refers to an external standard – that of propriety; D cannot, therefore, take refuge in his own standards when he knows that these are not thought proper by members of society generally.[45] In this respect the test reflects that found in the *Ghosh*[46] formula of dishonesty. Thirdly, there is a further limitation on the opportunity for D to claim that his own standards apply in evaluating what is a proper means of enforcing a demand. It has been held that if D knows that the threat he makes is to commit a crime, he cannot maintain that he believes such a threat to be proper.[47] This is a questionable limitation. The focus must surely remain on the question of D's belief as to the propriety, and the fact that D is aware that his menace is a crime may be strong evidence that he did not believe it to be a proper means of enforcing the demand, but is not conclusive.

One consequence of this subjective approach is that D may be guilty of blackmail where he personally believes that he has no reasonable grounds for his demand or that the use of the menaces is improper, even though, viewed objectively, his demand is perfectly reasonable and his threat perfectly proper. Concentrating to this extent on D's state of mind as the criterion of criminality represents something of an innovation in English criminal law, but cases where the matter arises must inevitably be rare.

Finally, it should be noted that s 21(2) provides that it is immaterial whether the menaces relate to action to be taken by the person making the demand. Consequently if D makes a demand of V and threatens that E will assault V if he does not comply, this may amount to blackmail. Perhaps this was clear enough without express provision for it, but the provision was included to prevent any possible argument.[48]

(d) View to gain or intent to cause loss

It has been noted above[49] that the requirement of a view to gain or intent to cause loss operates as a limiting factor on the offence of blackmail. It anchors it, rather precariously, in the scheme of offences protecting property interests.[50] Many might regard as blackmail

45 Cf Griew, 14–30. In *Harrison* [2001] EWCA Crim 1314, where D had been demanding money to which he believed himself to be entitled as compensation for his being sacked by V, the judge directed the jury that 'proper was a word of wide meaning – wider than lawful, but no act which was not believed to be lawful could be believed to be proper within the subsection. The test is not what the defendant regarded as justified but what he believed to be proper . . .' The Court of Appeal commented that the directions contain a rogue sentence 'proper in that sense . . . meant a suitable and apt way, not threats of unlawful or criminal actions.'

46 [1982] QB 1053.

47 *Harvey, Ulyett and Plummer* (1980) 72 Cr App R 139, CA.

48 Cmnd 2977, Annex 2.

49 At p 802.

50 There is a view to gain where D at gun-point demands that a doctor give him an injection of morphine (morphine is property) to relieve pain: *Bevans* (1987) 87 Cr App R 64, [1988] Crim LR 236, CA. It is not uncommon for blackmail charges to be laid where one drug gang has demanded drugs from another, backed by threats of violence, eg *Hart and Bullen* [1999] 2 Cr App R (S) 233.

a threat by D to prosecute V for a theft she has committed unless she has sexual intercourse with him, but this, though it may constitute some other offence,[51] would not amount to blackmail under s 21(1) of the Act. The Theft Act is concerned with invasions of economic interests, and gain and loss are defined accordingly in s 34(2)(a):

. . . 'gain' and 'loss' are to be construed as extending only to gain or loss in money or other property, but as extending to any such gain or loss whether temporary or permanent; and –

(i) 'gain' includes a gain by keeping what one has, as well as a gain by getting what one has not; and

(ii) 'loss' includes a loss by not getting what one might get, as well as a loss by parting with what one has.

In the ordinary case of blackmail D will have both a view to gain (for himself) and an intention to cause loss (to V), but either suffices. D may commit the offence where he intends to cause loss to V without making a gain for himself; as where, by threats, he demands that Q destroy property belonging to V. And in such a case, D clearly intends to cause loss to 'another' though the person threatened is not the person to whom the loss is caused. Conversely D may act with a view to gain although there is no intention to cause loss. D might demand that V appoint him as a paid director in V's company; here D has a view to gain for himself but it may well be that, far from intending to cause V loss, he intends to bring him increased profits.

Most often D's view to gain will be transparently obvious since a blackmailer's prime objective is normally to get money or other property from V. And, normally, D will intend to deprive V permanently of the property. Section 34(2)(a) makes it clear, however, that there is no need for the intended gain or loss to be permanent. D might be guilty of blackmail, for example, where by menaces he demands that V make a loan of property. This again reflects the fact that the gravamen of the offence is that an unwarranted demand has been made. But will any view to gain – no matter how remote – suffice?[52] Clearly there may be a view to gain although the gain is not to materialize for a period of time, or even though the gain may never materialize. D might by threats cause his sister to destroy their grandmother's will on the assumption that this will be to D's financial advantage; it can make no difference that granny is on her death bed or is in the best of health, or that she has made another will revoking the one destroyed. The essence of blackmail is the demand with menaces and the offence is then complete whether D succeeds thereafter in making a gain or not.[53]

The interpretation of the concept of 'view to gain' has not been fully explored in the case law under s 21. What seems to be important is that D should have the view of gain in his mind when he makes the demand; the fact that it has crossed his mind at some stage that there may be a gain involved might not be enough. While it is probably not necessary to show that D's primary purpose in making the demand was to make a gain for himself or another, it must be one of his objectives. Equally where it has to be shown that D *intended* to cause loss to another, it would not be enough that D foresaw some likelihood of loss unless he also intended to cause the loss. Arguably it should be sufficient that D

[51] See above, Ch 17. [52] See Smith, *Theft*, paras 10–22.
[53] Cf *Moran* [1952] 1 All ER 803n, CCA.

demands something and in doing so realizes that it is virtually certain to result in his causing loss to V.

Subparagraphs (i) and (ii) of s 34(2)(a) were introduced to meet a possible argument that D would not be acting with a view to gain, or with intent to cause loss, where the gain or loss had already taken place. For example, D, who owes V £10, might by threats demand that V forgo his claim; it is now quite clear[54] that D is acting with a view to gain.

A further difficulty under this section is whether D can be said to have a view to gain or intent to cause loss where he acts under a supposed legal claim of right to the property demanded (the paradox position above). Suppose that D, who is in fact owed £100 by V, threatens to expose to V's employers the fact that V is a paedophile unless V pays the debt. Obviously D can satisfy the requirement that he believes he has reasonable grounds for making the demand, but it may be supposed (as must almost invariably be the case) that D does not believe that the use of the menace is a proper means of reinforcing the demand. It was clearly intended by the CLRC that D might be guilty of blackmail if he failed to meet *either* of the criteria in paragraphs (a) and (b) of s 21(1), and irrespective of whether D acted under a legal claim of right to the property demanded:

> The essential feature of the offence will be that the accused demands something with menaces when he knows either that he has no right to make the demand or that the use of the menaces is improper. This, we believe, will limit the offence to what would ordinarily be thought should be included in blackmail. The true blackmailer will know that he has no reasonable grounds for demanding money as the price of keeping his victim's secret: *the person with a genuine claim will be guilty unless he believes that it is proper to use the menaces to enforce his claim.*[55]

The offence of blackmail is, however, governed in all cases by the requirement of view to gain or intent to cause loss, and it can be argued[56] that where D demands property to which he is *legally* entitled (or believes himself to be legally entitled), he has no view to make a gain for himself or to cause loss to another; D makes no gain in getting what he is legally entitled to, and V sustains no loss in paying his lawful debts. In other statutory contexts gain is sometimes treated as economic gain or profit, but it has also been said to mean 'acquisition' and is not necessarily to be equated with 'profit'.[57] To give it the latter meaning in the context of the Theft Act would certainly be consistent with the CLRC's intentions.[58] In *Lawrence and Pomroy*,[59] where D and E were convicted of blackmail in making threats to recover a debt, it appears to have been assumed by the Court of Appeal, though the point was not directly argued,[60] that D and E had a view to gain. This accords

54 Or is it? See *Golechha* [1989] 3 All ER 908, [1990] Crim LR 865, CA, above, p 789.

55 Cmnd 2977, para 121, italics supplied.

56 B. Hogan, 'Blackmail' [1966] Crim LR 474, 476. Cf Smith, *Theft*, paras 10.15–10.17; cf Griew, *Theft*, 14.25–14.28.

57 Cf Smith, *Theft*, para 10.17 and authorities there cited. Cf *Blazina* [1925] NZLR 407 on the meaning of 'extort or gain' in the New Zealand Crimes Act 1908.

58 As expressed in the passage cited at n 55, above. But the Committee also characterized blackmail as an offence of dishonesty (cf paras 118 and 122) and one who demands that to which he believes he is legally entitled is not acting dishonestly: cf *Skivington* [1968] 1 QB 166, [1967] 1 All ER 483, CA, and *Robinson* [1977] Crim LR 173, above, p 711.

59 (1971) 57 Cr App R 64, CA.

60 But the point was argued in *Parkes* [1973] Crim LR 358 (Judge Dean); where it was ruled that a person demanding money undoubtedly owed to him did have a view to gain.

with s 21(2) (above) which emphasizes that the 'nature of the act or omission demanded is immaterial', which on a literal interpretation should mean that a demand for a debt legally owed will suffice for the offence.[61]

By the same token, if D intends V to lose a particular item even where D is prepared to replace it with one of identical value, the offence may be committed.[62]

2. Unlawful harassment of debtors

Section 40 of the Administration of Justice Act 1970 creates an offence of unlawful harassment of debtors, which, because it may overlap blackmail, may be noted at this point. The offence, which is summary only and is punishable by fine,[63] is committed by one who, with the object of coercing another person to pay money claimed as a debt under a contract,

(a) harasses the debtor by demands which by reason of their frequency or manner of making are calculated to subject the debtor or members of his household to alarm, distress or humiliation; or
(b) falsely represents that criminal proceedings lie for non-payment; or
(c) falsely represents that he is authorized in some official capacity to enforce payment; or
(d) utters a document falsely represented to have an official character.

Whatever may be the position in relation to the offence of blackmail, it is clearly no defence to a charge under this provision that the debt was owed. The offence was created to curb the growing practice of enforcing the payment of debts in a fashion that is unreasonable, unfair or improper; such as where a creditor calls at the debtor's house to make a demand and is accompanied by a brace of large, fierce and hungry-looking rottweilers. The offence is wider than blackmail in that it may cover conduct that the creditor believes to be proper as a means of enforcing the debt. Under para (a) it is enough that the demands are 'calculated to' cause distress, and this will probably be interpreted to import an objective standard (calculated in the eyes of reasonable people) so that it will be no defence that D himself did not calculate to cause distress.

3. Other offences based on threats

There are numerous other offences based on threats including: threats to kill,[64] assaults,[65] robbery,[66] threats to damage property,[67] threats of food terrorism,[68] threats of violence for the purpose of securing entry to premises,[69] sending malicious communications,[70] and

[61] Considered in *A-G's Reference (No 1 of 2001)* [2002] EWCA Crim 1768; [2003] 1 Cr App R 131 in the context of false accounting.

[62] See Smith, *Theft* 10–18.

[63] Level 5 on the standard scale.

[64] OAPA 1861, s 16.

[65] Criminal Justice Act 1988, s 39.

[66] Theft Act 1968, s 8.

[67] Criminal Damage Act 1971, s 2.

[68] Public Order Act 1986, s 38.

[69] Criminal Law Act 1977, s 6(1)

[70] Malicious Communications Act 1988, s 1, as extended by the Criminal Justice and Police Act 2001, s 43.

demanding payment for unsolicited goods with threats.[71] There is little coherence in English Law's approach to threat offences.[72]

[71] Unsolicited Goods and Services Act 1972, s 2(2).
[72] See P. Alldridge, 'Threats Offences: A Case for Reform' [1994] Crim LR 176.

21

Burglary and related offences

Burglary is an offence under the Theft Act 1968. The offence is much broader than the common (mis)understanding of a breaking and entering to steal.

1. Burglary[1]

Section 9 of the Theft Act 1968 provides:

(1) A person is guilty of burglary if –

(a) he enters any building or part of a building as a trespasser and with intent to commit any such offence as is mentioned in subsection (2) below; or

(b) having entered any building or part of a building as a trespasser he steals or attempts to steal anything in the building or that part of it or inflicts or attempts to inflict on any person therein any grievous bodily harm.

(2) The offences referred to in subsection (1)(a) above are offences of stealing anything in the building or part of a building in question, of inflicting on any person therein any grievous bodily harm [. . .][2] therein, and of doing unlawful damage to the building or anything therein.

(3) A person guilty of burglary shall on conviction on indictment be liable to imprisonment for a term not exceeding –

(a) where the offence was committed in respect of a building or part of a building which is a dwelling, fourteen years;

(b) in any other case, ten years.[3]

(4) References in subsections (1) and (2) above to a building, and the reference in subsection (3) above to a building which is a dwelling, shall apply also to an inhabited vehicle or vessel, and shall apply to any such vehicle or vessel at times when the person having a habitation in it is not there as well as at times when he is.[4]

[1] For further analysis of the offence see J. C. Smith, *The Law of Theft* (8th edn, 1997), ch 11; E. J. Griew, *The Theft Acts* (7th edn, 1995), ch 4, hereafter in this chapter Griew; Smith, *Property Offences* (1994), ch 28.

[2] The offence of entering a building with intent to commit rape was repealed by the Sexual Offences Act 2003, Sch 7, para 1. Section 63 of that Act creates a much broader offence of trespass with intent to commit a sexual offence (see above, Ch 17).

[3] For the current pattern in sentencing for burglary, see *McInerney* [2003] EWCA Crim 3003, [2003] Crim LR 207. The sentencing of burglary is one of great controversy, arousing strong public emotion and commonplace misunderstanding of sentencing practice. See M. Davies, 'Filling in the Gaps' [2003] Crim LR 243.

[4] Subsections (3) and (4) are as substituted by the Criminal Justice Act 1991, as amended by the PCC(S)A 2000.

Paragraphs (a) and (b) of s 9(1) create numerous offences. Under 9(1)(a) there are three separate offences (entering with intent to steal, commit grievous bodily harm or unlawful damage), and each of these offences can be committed by entry into either a dwelling (a 'domestic burglary')[5] or other building. Because there are separate sentencing provisions depending on whether the building in question is a dwelling, there are in fact six separate offences created by s 9(1)(a). It should be noted that these offences are committed once D has entered as a trespasser with the necessary intent,[6] irrespective of whether D succeeds in his ulterior intent, theft, grievous bodily harm, etc.[7] Section 9(1)(b) creates four separate offences (attempting to steal, stealing, attempting to inflict grievous bodily harm and inflicting grievous bodily harm). Again, these can be committed as domestic burglaries or otherwise, with separate sentencing regimes for each.

It has been decided[8] that a person charged with an offence under s 9(1)(b) may be convicted of an offence under s 9(1)(a) because (however contrary to the facts this may seem to be) the allegation of an offence under s 9(1)(b) is held to include an allegation of an offence under 9(1)(a).

The law may seem to be unduly technical but this is in part a result of the need to refer to the civil law in respect of fundamental elements such as on 'trespass'. There is a dissonance with the layman's conception of burglary and the offence does not define the principal harm against which it offers protection – it can be seen as invasion/intrusion onto private space, the risk of violent confrontation or aggravated forms of theft.[9] There are powerful arguments that the offence involves so many qualitatively different types of wrongdoing within one label that it deserves reformulation.[10]

(a) *Actus reus*

(i) Enters

At common law, the insertion of any part of the body, however small, into the building or structure was a sufficient entry. So where D pushed in a window-pane and the forepart of his finger was observed to be inside the building that was enough.[11] The Act gives no express guidance on this issue and it seems to have been assumed in Parliament that the common law rules would apply.[12] In the celebrated case of *Collins*,[13] D, naked but for his socks, had climbed up a ladder on to a bedroom window-sill, as a trespasser and with intent to rape, when the woman in the bedroom invited him in. It was not clear whether

[5] Under s 111 of the PCC(S)A 2000. Note that burglary comprising the commission of, or an intention to commit, an offence triable only on indictment and a burglary in a dwelling where any person in the dwelling was subjected to violence or the threat of violence are triable on indictment only: Magistrates' Courts Act 1980, Sch 1, para 28; *MacGrath* [2003] EWCA Crim 2062, [2004] Crim LR 142; *Practice Direction (Criminal Proceedings: Consolidation)* [2002] 1 WLR 2870, para 51.

[6] *Watson* [1989] Crim LR 733; *Toothill* [1998] Crim LR 876.

[7] If he does he can still be charged under s 9(1)(a): *Taylor* [1979] Crim LR 649.

[8] *Whiting* (1987) 85 Cr App R 78, applying *Wilson and Jenkins* [1984] AC 242, [1983] 3 All ER 448, HL. *Whiting* is criticized at [1987] Crim LR 473. See also the CLRC *Eighth Report*, para 76.

[9] See Ashworth, POCL, 395.

[10] B. Mitchell, 'Multiple Wrongdoing and Offence Structure' (2001) 64 MLR 393.

[11] *Davis* (1823) Russ & Ry 499.

[12] HL Deb, vol 290, cols 85–86.

[13] [1973] QB 100 at 106, [1972] 2 All ER 1105 at 1111.

he was on the sill outside the window or on the inner sill at the moment when he ceased to be a trespasser and became an invitee. Generations of students have pondered whether any part of D might have been inside the building at that point in time. Edmund Davies LJ said that there must be 'an effective and substantial entry' as a trespasser to constitute burglary. Later cases, however, do not support this opinion. In *Brown*,[14] there was a sufficient entry where D's feet were on the ground outside a shop and the top half of his body was inside the broken shop window, as if he was rummaging for goods displayed there. The court said that the word 'substantial' did not materially assist but the entry must be 'effective' and here it was: D was presumably in a position to steal. But in *Ryan*[15] D became trapped by the neck with only his head and right arm inside the window. His argument that his conduct was not capable of constituting an entry because he could not have stolen anything was rejected.

It is submitted that it cannot have been intended that D must have got so far into the building as to be able to accomplish his unlawful purpose. D who intends to inflict grievous bodily harm is guilty of burglary when he enters through the ground floor window though his victim is on the fourth floor. Thus it seems that the act of entry need not be either an 'effective' or a 'substantial' entry. But *Ryan* decided only that there was evidence on which a jury could find that D had entered. It is in principle unsatisfactory that such a crucial element of the *actus reus* of a serious offence should be left for a jury to determine. The best course would be to accept the continued existence of the common law rule.

At common law burglary might be committed by an innocent agent, as where D sends a child under the age of 10 into the building to steal.[16] It is not certain whether this rule has survived the 1968 Act, but probably it has.[17] Suppose that, instead of a child, D sends in a monkey. It is hard to see that this should not equally be an entry by D. But if that point were conceded, it is admitted that the insertion of an animate instrument is an entry; and are we to distinguish between animate and inanimate instruments? Unless we are, the insertion of the telescopic poles or hooks, etc must also be an entry.

At common law, if an instrument was inserted into the building for the purpose of committing the ulterior offence, there was an entry even though no part of the body was introduced into the building. So it was enough that hooks were inserted into the premises to drag out the carpets, or that the barrel of a gun was introduced with a view to shooting someone inside. But the insertion of an instrument merely for the purpose of gaining entry and not for the purpose of committing the ulterior offence was not an entry if no part of the body entered. If D bored a hole in a door with a drill for the purpose of gaining entry, the emergence of the point of the drill bit on the inside of the door was not an entry. Even if the courts are willing to follow the common law in holding that the intrusion of any part of the body is an entry, they may be reluctant to preserve these technical rules regarding instruments, for they seem to lead to outlandish results – that there is an entry if a stick of dynamite is thrown into the building or if a bullet is fired from outside the building into it, or a time bomb is sent by parcel post. Has D 'entered', even though he is not on the scene at all – perhaps even abroad and outside the jurisdiction? This is hardly an 'entry' in the 'simple language as used and understood by ordinary

14 [1985] Crim LR 212, CA.

15 [1996] Crim LR 320, (1996) 160 JP 610, CA.

16 Hale I PC, 555.

17 Cf *Wheelhouse* [1994] Crim LR 756, above, p 206.

literate men and women' in which the Act is said to be written. Perhaps D must at least be present at the scene, or 'on the job'. Arguably, a distinction should be drawn between cases where D causes an instrument to enter V's building (for example, by throwing it), and those where the instrument entering V's building represents an extension of D's body (as where he uses a telescopic pole).[18] These issues do not seem to have given rise to difficulty under the Act, perhaps due to the sensible use of more suitable charges.

(ii) As a trespasser

Trespass is a legal concept and resort must be made to the law of tort in order to ascertain its meaning.[19] It would appear that as a matter of civil law any intentional, reckless or (possibly) negligent entry into a building is a trespass if the building is in fact in the possession of another who does not consent to the entry. In all cases of burglary it must be shown that D entered the building as a trespasser, although evidence from the occupier in person is unnecessary.[20] In *Collins*,[21] it was held that, whatever the position in the law of tort, an invitation by the occupier's daughter for D to enter her bedroom and have intercourse with her, without the knowledge or consent of the occupier, precluded a finding of trespass against D for the purpose of burglary. Suppose, however, that she had invited her lover, D, into her father's house to steal her father's property. This surely ought to be burglary if D realized that she had no right to invite him in for this purpose. Where the invitation to enter is issued by a member of the household, it is submitted that the crucial question will often be that of D's *mens rea* – whether D knew that, or was reckless whether, the invitation from that person was issued without the relevant authority. This highlights a problem stemming from the fact that burglary protects against a number of harms – the trespass, and the ulterior harms – and the interests being protected may be those of different individuals.[22]

In *Jones and Smith*,[23] where the occupier's son, D, had a general permission to enter the house, his entry with E for the purpose of stealing constituted burglary. D had knowingly exceeded the permission granted to him by his father. It is perhaps noteworthy that it was a case 'where [D and E] took elaborate precautions, going there at dead of night'; and that, even if D's entry was covered by his father's general permission, this would scarcely extend to the entry of his accomplice. If E's entry was unlawful, D abetted it. Williams[24] argued that *Jones and Smith* is wrongly decided, being inconsistent with *Collins*,[25] because Collins also exceeded the permission since he entered intending to use force if necessary.

[18] Cf Griew, *Theft Acts*, para 4.21. The offence has been used successfully where eg D has used a mechanical digger to steal a cash dispenser by ripping it from the wall of a bank: *Richardson and Brown* [1998] 2 Cr App R (S) 87.

[19] See especially W. V. H. Rogers, *Winfield and Jolowicz on Tort* (16th edn, 2003), ch 13.

[20] *Maccuish* [1999] 6 Archbold News 2, CA.

[21] [1973] QB 100 at 107, [1972] 2 All ER 1105 at 1111. Cf *Robson v Hallett* [1967] 2 QB 939, [1967] 2 All ER 407 (invitation by occupier's son effective until withdrawn by occupier). See S. Bailey, D. Harris and D. Ormerod, *Civil Liberties, Cases and Materials* (5th edn, 2001), 254–255.

[22] Burglary does not require that the ulterior offence should concern the occupier. If D and E, squatters, occupy V's house, it would strictly amount to burglary were D to steal E's wallet or to inflict on E grievous bodily harm.

[23] [1976] 3 All ER 54, CA.

[24] TBCL (2nd edn, 1983), 846–850.

[25] Cf Mason J in *Barker v R* (1983) 7 ALJR 426 at 429: '. . . The foundation for this conclusion [sc, that of Williams] is too frail.'

But as the girl saw him to be 'a naked male with an erect penis' it seems that she invited him in expressly for the purpose of sexual intercourse, that he knew he was so invited and that any intention to rape must have lapsed by the time of entry.

In *Collins*, the invitation to enter was issued under a mistake as to the man's identity. It is submitted that, if he had known of the mistake, he would have intentionally entered as a trespasser. Mistake as to identity, where identity is material, generally vitiates consent.[26] Mistake by the person entering is no defence to an action in tort; so that, if D on a very dark night were to enter the house next door in mistake for his own, this would be regarded as an intentional entry and a trespass. This would apparently be so even if D's mistake was a reasonable one, *a fortiori* if it were negligent as, for example, if he made the mistake because he was drunk. It is established that it is not sufficient (though it is necessary) for burglary that D is a trespasser in the civil law. The criminal law requires *mens rea*. If D is charged under s 9(1)(a), it need not be proved that D knew *in law* that he was a trespasser. It must however be proved that, when he entered, he knew *the facts* which caused him to be a trespasser or at least that he was reckless whether those facts existed.[27] A merely negligent entry, as where D enters another's house, honestly but unreasonably believing it to be his own, is not enough. A belief in a right would also negative *mens rea*. Suppose that D, being separated from his wife, wrongly supposes that he has a right to enter the matrimonial home of which she is the owner-occupier and does enter with intent to inflict grievous bodily harm upon her. Even if he is in law a trespasser, he is not a burglar.[28]

If D's entry is involuntary, he does not enter as a trespasser. So if, having been dragged against his will into V's house and left there by drunken companions, he steals V's vase and leaves, this is not burglary. If, however, D had intentionally entered the building, believing it to be his own house and committed theft on discovering the truth, he would have committed theft after entering as a trespasser and thus committed the *actus reus* of burglary with the *mens rea* required by s 9(1)(b): the offence is committed, not at the time of entry, but when the ulterior crime is committed; and at that time, he knows that he has entered as a trespasser.[29]

Trespass by exceeding a permission

Where D gains entry by deception he enters as a trespasser. There is no need to distinguish between entry under a licence that is void and one that is merely voidable, because entry under either is a trespass. For example, D gains admission to V's house by falsely pretending that he has been sent by the BBC to examine the radio in order to trace disturbances in transmission. The old law went so far as to hold that this was a constructive 'breaking' (as in 'breaking and entering'), but that is not an element of the offence of burglary. There can, however, be no doubt that such conduct constitutes a

[26] See above, Ch 17 in relation to sexual offences.

[27] *Collins* [1973] QB 100 at 104–105, [1972] 2 All ER 1105 at 1109–1110. 'Reckless' is used in *Cunningham* ([1957] 2 QB 396) and *R v G* [2003] UKHL 50. See above, pp 106–107. D need not know the civil law of trespass.

[28] There are of course other offences with which he could be charged.

[29] The common law doctrine of trespass *ab initio* was held not to apply to burglary under the Theft Act: *Collins* [1973] QB 100 at 107, [1972] 2 All ER 1105 at 1111. See J. C. Smith, *The Law of Theft* (2nd edn) at paras 377–378 and (4th edn), paras 338–339.

trespassory entry. The authorities, however, go farther, and this has serious consequences for the offence of burglary.

A person who has a limited authority to enter for a particular purpose enters as a trespasser though he practices no deception, if he has an unlawful purpose outside the scope of that limited authority. Thus, in *Taylor v Jackson*,[30] D had express permission to go on V's land and hunt for rabbits. He went there to hunt for hares and the Divisional Court held that this was evidence of trespass in pursuit of game, contrary to the Game Act 1831, s 30. In *Hillen and Pettigrew v ICI (Alkali) Ltd*,[31] members of a stevedore's gang employed to unload a barge (thus having permission to enter for a limited purpose) were held to be trespassers when they placed kegs on the hatch covers, knowing that this was a wrong and dangerous thing to do. They were, therefore, not entitled to damages when the hatch covers collapsed and were injured. Lord Atkin said:

> As Scrutton LJ has pointedly said: 'When you invite a person into your house to use the staircase you do not invite him to slide down the banisters.'[32] So far as he sets foot on so much of the premises as lie outside the invitation or uses them for purposes which are alien to the invitation he is not an invitee but a trespasser, and his rights must be determined accordingly.

In *Farrington v Thomson and Bridgland*,[33] an Australian court held that a police officer who entered a hotel for the purpose of committing a tort was a trespasser. The tacit or implied invitation to the public to enter the hotel did not extend to persons entering for the purpose of committing a tort or a criminal offence. In *Barker v R*,[34] the High Court of Australia (Murphy J dissenting) held that D committed burglary where, having been asked by his neighbour, V, to keep an eye on V's house while V was on holiday and told the whereabouts of a concealed key in case he needed to enter, D entered in order to steal. 'If a person enters for a purpose outside the scope of his authority then he stands in no better position than a person who enters with no authority at all.'[35] One decision goes against this view. In *Byrne v Kinematograph Renters Society Ltd*,[36] Harman J held that it was not trespass to gain entry to a cinema by buying tickets with the purpose, not of seeing the film, but of counting the patrons. It is submitted that this decision is against the weight of authority and should not be followed.

It seems therefore that a person who enters a shop for the *sole* purpose of shoplifting is a burglar, though two of the majority in *Barker* thought otherwise. In their view, where the permission to enter is not limited by reference to purpose, a person with permission to enter is not a trespasser merely because he enters with a secret unlawful intent. It was argued that the shopkeeper's invitation to the public is not limited by reference to a specific purpose: '. . . the mere presence of the prospective customer upon the premises is itself likely to be an object of the invitation and a person will be within the invitation if he

30 (1898) 78 LT 555. 31 [1936] AC 65. 32 *The Carlgarth* [1927] P 93 at 110.

33 [1959] VR 286 (Smith J). See also *Gross v Wright* [1923] 2 DLR 171.

34 (1983) 7 ALJR 426. 35 Per Mason J at 429.

36 [1958] 2 All ER 579 at 593; distinguished in *Jones*, above, p 814 and by Mason J in *Barker v R* (1983) 7 ALJR 426 at 429 on the ground that 'the invitation by the lessee of the cinema to the public to enter the cinema was in very general terms and could on no view be said to be limited in the way in which was contended'.

enters for no particular purpose at all'.[37] It is doubtful, however, if the shopkeeper's invitation can be said to extend to those who enter for the *sole* purpose of shoplifting.

It is only in the exceptional case that it will be possible to prove this particular intent at the time of entry – as where there is evidence of a previous conspiracy, or system, or preparatory acts such as the wearing of a jacket with special pockets. Such an entry may be no more than a merely preparatory act to stealing and so not attempted theft; but it ought to be possible, where there is clear evidence, to make an arrest. Few would object to the conviction of burglary of bank robbers who enter the bank flourishing pistols, for they are clearly outside the invitation extended by the bank to the public. A person who enters a shop for the sole purpose of murdering the manager is surely a trespasser; and the case of the intending thief is no different in principle.

This extension of the law beyond what was intended by the CLRC[38] is significant in terms of the number of people potentially at risk of prosecution for burglary. The interpretation in *Jones and Smith* echoes the view expressed by Fletcher that the emphasis in burglary has shifted from an act of manifest illegality – 'breaking' and entering – to an illicit entry where the principal element of blameworthiness lies in the criminal intent.[39] The cumulative effect of the extension in *Jones* with that of recent decisions in theft must also be considered. Consider D, an antiques dealer who calls on a gullible old lady with the intention of tricking her into selling him her priceless heirloom for a gross undervalue (obtaining property by deception, but seemingly also now theft) D could be guilty of burglary.

The decision in *Jones and Smith* does, however, have the advantage of focusing on *mens rea* and reducing the reliance within the criminal law on the technicalities of the civil law of trespass.[40] It has been suggested that to keep the *Jones and Smith* extension within desirable limits a distinction might be drawn between buildings that are open to the public and others,[41] but such a distinction might create an unnecessary layer of technicality. Buildings are increasingly commonly quasi-public[42] (as for example in large shopping centres) and this might produce further doubts on the ability of the tort of trespass to provide a sufficiently clear foundation for the offence in this context.

(iii) The victim of the burglary

Trespass is an interference with possession. Burglary is therefore committed against the person in possession of the building entered. Thus, where the premises are let, the burglary is committed against the tenant and not against the landlord. The landlord could commit burglary of the premises, the tenant could not. On the other hand, a guest in a hotel will not ordinarily have sufficient possession of his room in law to enable him to sue

[37] Brennan and Deane JJ (1983) 7 ALJR at 436. See also Williams, TBCL (2nd edn, 1983), 'a person who has a licence in fact to enter does not become a trespasser by reason of his criminal intent', 846. See further 846–849; P. J. Pace, 'Burglarious Trespass' [1985] Crim LR 716; A. T. H. Smith, 'Shoplifting and the Theft Acts' [1981] Crim LR 586. In terms of sentencing, a burglarious shoplifter should be sentenced in accordance with shoplifting sentencing guidelines rather than burglary guidelines: *Creed* [2005] EWCA Crim 215.

[38] See *Eighth Report*, para 35.

[39] See Fletcher, *Rethinking Criminal Law* (1977), 128.

[40] Ashworth, POCL, 395.

[41] Smith, *Property Offences*, paras 28–14, referring to the American Model Penal Code, s 221.1.

[42] See K. Gray and S. Gray, 'Civil rights, civil wrongs and quasi-public space' [1999] 1 EHRLR 46, discussed in the breach of the peace case, *Porter v MPC* (1999) 20 Oct, CA Civ Div, unreported.

in trespass.[43] It has been held that, where an employee occupies premises belonging to his employer for the more convenient performance of his duties, he cannot maintain an action for trespass against his employer.[44] In such a case it is, of course, necessary to look at the precise terms of the arrangement between the parties; if the employee has been given exclusive possession, he and not the employer is the victim of a trespass. And it does not necessarily follow that, because the employee in a particular case may not maintain trespass against his employer, he cannot do so against third parties.[45] The position of a lodger depends on the precise terms of his contract. If he has exclusive possession so that he can refuse entry to the landlord then, no doubt, he may maintain trespass. Many lodgers, however, do not have such possession and in such cases an unauthorized entry by a third party is a trespass against the landlord.

It seems to follow that burglary is not committed where an hotelier enters the room of a guest, even though the entry is without the guest's consent and with intent to steal; and that, depending on the terms of the contract, the same may be true in the case of an employer entering premises occupied by his employee for the purposes of his employment and a landlord entering the rooms of his lodger. There is no glaring deficiency in the law, since charges of attempted or actual theft will lie in each of these cases.

It seems that an indictment will lie although it does not allege that the building was the property of anyone. Whereas the Larceny Act 1916 required that the breaking and entering be of the dwelling house *of another*, there is no such expression in the Theft Act.[46] The requirement of trespass means that evidence must be offered that someone other than the accused was in possession. If that is all that is necessary, evidence that A or B was in possession should suffice – it is equally a trespass in either event. But if a statement of ownership is required in the indictment, 'A or B' will hardly do. It is submitted, therefore, that it should be sufficient that the indictment alleges that D trespassed in a building without alleging who is the owner of the building.

(iv) Any building or part of a building

The meaning of 'building' in various statutes has frequently been considered by the courts.[47] Clearly the meaning of the term varies according to the context and many things that have been held to be buildings for other purposes will not be buildings for the purpose of the Theft Act – for example, a garden wall, a railway embankment or a tunnel under the road. According to Lord Esher MR, its 'ordinary and usual meaning is, a block of brick or stone work, covered in by a roof'.[48] It seems clear, however, that it is not necessary that the structure be of brick or stone to be a building within this Act. Clearly all dwellings are protected and yet these may be built of wood; while 'the inhabited vehicle or vessel' which is expressly included is likely to be built of metal or of wood.

43 J. Murphy (ed), *Street on Torts* (11th edn, 2003), pp 74–76.

44 *Mayhew v Suttle* (1854) 4 E & B 347; *White v Bayley* (1861) 10 CBNS 227.

45 Though in *White v Bayley* (above, n 44) Byles J thought, *obiter*, that an action could not have been maintained by the servant against a stranger (10 CBNS at 235).

46 See J. N. Adams, 'Trespass under the Theft and Firearms Act' (1969) 119 NLJ 655.

47 An early examples is *Manning and Rogers* (1871) LR 1 CCR 338.

48 *Moir v Williams* [1892] 1 QB 264. Cf Byles J in *Stevens v Gourley* (1859) 7 CBNS 99 at 112 – 'a structure of considerable size and intended to be permanent or at least to endure for a considerable time'.

To be a building the structure must have some degree of permanence.[49] But moveable structures, which are intended for permanent use as offices, workshops and stores (portakabins) may fairly be regarded as buildings though their intended use on a given site is only temporary. It has been generally assumed that a tent cannot be a building,[50] notwithstanding that it is occupied on a particular site indefinitely, but a structure may be a building even though its construction is flimsy.

To constitute a building the structure does not need to be one occupied by people. Farm outbuildings, such as stables, barns or silos, though they are used only to house animals or products are buildings for the purposes of burglary, as are factory buildings and stores. Similarly the detached garage, toolshed or greenhouse standing in the grounds of a dwelling.

At what point in the process of erection does a structure become a building? In *Manning and Rogers*,[51] Lush J said, '. . . it is sufficient that it should be a connected and entire structure. I do not think four walls erected a foot high would be a building.'

In that case all the walls were built and the roof was on, so it was obvious that the structure was a building. It is possible that a structure with a roof and no walls, such as a bandstand, is a building. So too with a structure which is intended to have a roof – a house where the walls are complete but not yet roofed or a house which has lost its roof in a hurricane. It has been held in a different context that 'a mere structure or superstructure composed of a steel and concrete frame [as yet] having no roof' could constitute a building.[52]

Lines must be drawn and it will not always be easy to draw these lines.[53] The probability is that a court would hold, following *Brutus v Cozens*,[54] that 'building' is an ordinary word the meaning of which is 'a matter of fact and degree' to be determined by the trier of fact. The judge must at least rule whether there is evidence on which a reasonable jury could find the structure to be a building. As with the concept of entry, one of the essential elements of the offence is left to be determined by the trier of fact.

The extent of a 'building'

Under the unduly complex pre-1968 law, the entry had to be into a particular dwelling house, office, shop, garage, etc. A single structure might contain many dwelling houses – for example a block of flats – many offices, shops or garages. If D got through the window of Flat 1 with intent to pass through it, go upstairs and steal in Flat 45, the breaking and

49 There is authority that a structure is capable of being a 'building' notwithstanding that it is 'implanted within another building': *Royal Exchange Theatre Trust v The Commissioners* [1978] VATTR 139.

50 See CLRC *Eighth Report*, para 78. This is certainly questionable in the case of, for example a substantial marquee housing many facilities. Cf *Storn* (1865) 5 SCR (NSW) 26.

51 (1871) LR 1 CCR 338.

52 *R v Ealing London Borough Council, ex parte Zainuddain* [1994] 2 PLR 1, 4 per Tucker LJ.

53 Contrast *B and S v Leathley* [1979] Crim LR 314 (Carlisle CC) and *Norfolk Constabulary v Seekings and Gould* [1986] Crim LR 167 (Norfolk CC). In the former it was held that a freezer container detached from its chassis, resting on railway sleepers and used to store frozen food, was a building; while in the latter it was held that two similar containers, still on their wheeled chassis, remained vehicles though they were, as in the first case, being used by a supermarket to provide temporary storage space. Cf *King* [1978] 19 SASR 118 (walk-in freezer could be a building).

54 [1973] AC 854, [1972] 2 All ER 1297, HL.

entering of Flat 1 was neither burglary nor housebreaking because D did not intend to commit a felony therein.[55]

Under the Theft Act everything depends on what is the extent of a 'building'.[56] In its ordinary natural meaning, this term could certainly include a block of flats. Adopting that meaning, D's entry of the window of Flat 1 as a trespasser with intent to pass through it, to go upstairs and steal in Flat 45 is an entry of a building as a trespasser with intent to steal therein – it is burglary. The effect is to criminalize as burglary what was previously, at most, an attempt, and probably only an act of preparation. There seems no good reason, however, why the law should not be extended in this way. On the contrary, there is everything to be said for enabling the police to intervene at the earliest possible moment to prevent such offences; and for forestalling unmeritorious defences such as 'I had no intention to steal in the flat – I was only using it as a passage to another flat which I never reached'. It is submitted therefore that the word 'building' should be given its natural meaning.

Part of a building

It is sufficient if the trespass takes place in part of a building so that one lodger may commit burglary by entering the room of another lodger within the same house, or by entering the part of the house occupied by the landlord. A guest in a hotel may commit burglary by entering the room of another guest. A customer in a shop who goes behind the counter and takes money from the till during a short absence of the shopkeeper would be guilty of burglary, having entered that part as a trespasser, even though he entered the shop (the building) with the shopkeeper's permission. The permission did not extend to his going behind the counter.[57]

What is 'a part' of the building may be a difficult and important question. Take a case put by the CLRC.[58] D enters a shop lawfully[59] but conceals himself on the premises until closing time and then emerges with intent to steal. When concealing himself he may or may not have entered a part of the building to which customers are not permitted to go; but even if he did commit a trespass at this stage, he may not have done so with intent to commit an offence in that part of the building into which he has trespassed. For example, he hides in the broom cupboard of a supermarket, intending to emerge and steal tins of food. Entering the broom cupboard, though a trespass committed with intent to steal, is not burglary, for he has no intent to steal in the part of the building that he has entered as a trespasser. When he emerges from the broom cupboard after the shop has closed, he is a

55 Cf *Wrigley* [1957] Crim LR 57. It was probably not even an attempt, not being sufficiently proximate to the intended crime.

56 In *Hedley v Webb* [1901] 2 Ch 126, Cozens-Hardy J held that two semi-detached houses were a single building for the purpose of determining whether there was a sewer within the meaning of the Public Health Act 1875, s 4. In *Birch v Wigan Corpn* [1953] 1 QB 136, [1952] 2 All ER 893, the Court of Appeal (Denning LJ dissenting) held that one house in a terrace of six was a 'house' within the meaning of s 11(1) and (4) of the Housing Act 1936 and not 'part of a building' within s 12 of that Act. But, since the sections were mutually exclusive, the house could not be both a 'house' and 'part of a building' for the purpose of the Act. Otherwise, Denning LJ would have been disposed to say that the house was both and Romer LJ also thought that 'for some purposes and in other contexts two "houses" may constitute one building'. Cf J. C. Smith, *The Law of Theft* (8th edn, 1997), paras 11–21.

57 *Walkington* [1979] 2 All ER 716, [1979] 1 WLR 1169, CA.

58 Cmnd 2977, para 75.

59 Ie, without intent to steal; above, p 816.

trespasser and it is submitted that he has entered a part of the building with intent to steal. He is just as much a trespasser as if he had been told in express terms to go, for he knows perfectly well that his licence to remain on the premises terminated when the shop closed.[60] Suppose, however, having entered lawfully, he merely remained concealed behind a pile of tins of soup in the main hall of the supermarket. This was not a trespass because he had a right to be there. When he emerged and proceeded to steal, still in the main hall of the supermarket, was he entering another part of the building? It is submitted that every step he took was 'as a trespasser', but it is difficult to see that he entered any part of the building as a trespasser; the whole transaction took place in a single part of the building which he had lawfully entered.[61] It is illogical to treat these two cases differently.

The word 'part' has no precise meaning in relation to buildings. Its significance for the purpose of the section is that a person may lawfully enter one part of a building, yet be a trespasser on setting foot in another. This was the view taken in *Walkington*.[62] D, having entered a department store, entered an area bounded by a moveable three-sided counter where he opened a till. It was held that there was evidence on which the jury could find that the counter area was a 'part' of the building from which the public were excluded and that if D knew that, he entered it as a trespasser. Buildings, it now seems clear, fall into two parts: those parts where D is entitled to be and those where he is not.

If D is lawfully in Flat 1 and, without leaving the building, he enters Flat 2 as a trespasser with intent to pass through it into Flat 3 and steal therein, his entry into Flat 2 does not constitute burglary if each flat is regarded as a separate part. He has not entered *Flat 2*, with intent to steal *therein*. Yet, as we have seen, if he had entered Flat 2 from outside the building as a trespasser, there would have been no problem; he would have entered the *building* as a trespasser with intent to steal *therein*.[63] Perhaps it may fairly be said, however, that the building is in two parts: one part comprising the flat, where D is lawfully present, and the other part comprising *all* the remaining flats, where D may not lawfully go. On this view D would commit burglary by entering as a trespasser that part (ie the remainder of the building) with the appropriate intent.

Inhabited vehicle or vessel[64]

Whilst all 'buildings' are protected by the law of burglary, vehicles and vessels are protected only where they are 'inhabited'. The obvious cases which are brought within the protection of burglary by this provision are a caravan or a houseboat which is someone's home. There seems to be no reason whatever why a home should lack the ordinary protection of the law because it is mobile and this extension is welcome.[65] Its limits should be noted. 'Inhabited' implies, not that there is someone present inside the vehicle at the moment of the entry as a trespasser, but that someone lives there. My saloon car is not an inhabited vehicle because I happen to be sitting in it when D enters against my

[60] The CLRC thought 'The case is not important, because the offender is likely to go into a part of the building where he has no right to be, and this will be a trespassory entry into that part'. But he has no right to be in any part of the building after closing time and the only question, it is submitted, is whether he went into *another* part.

[61] Cf *Laing* [1995] Crim LR 395.

[62] [1979] 2 All ER 716, [1979] 1 WLR 1169, CA.

[63] Cf S. White, 'Lurkers, Draggers and Kidnappers' (1986) 150 JP 37, 56.

[64] Section 9(3).

[65] Arguably, on this rationale, the offence should also extend to protect tent dwellers.

will. The caravan or houseboat that is a person's home is, however, expressly protected, whether or not the occupier is there at the time of the burglary. He may, for example, be away on holiday.

Owners of 'dormobiles' or motorized caravans use them for the ordinary purposes of a car during most of the year but on occasions they live in them, generally while on holiday. While the vehicle is being lived in, it is undoubtedly an inhabited vehicle.[66] When it is being used for the ordinary purposes of a motor car it is submitted that it is not. The exact moment at which the dormobile becomes an inhabited vehicle may be difficult to ascertain.[67]

Applying ordinary principles of construction, D should not be convicted unless he knew of the facts which make the thing entered 'a building' in law, just as *Collins*[68] shows that D must know (or be reckless as to) the facts which constitute him a trespasser. Suppose D enters a dormobile parked by the side of the road. If he knew that V was living in the vehicle, there is no problem. But what if he did not know? It would now seem that he must be acquitted of burglary, unless it can be shown that he was at least reckless whether anyone was living there or not; and this involves showing that the possibility was present to his mind.

'Dwelling'

Since the Criminal Justice Act 1991, it has become crucial to identify whether the building entered is a dwelling, rendering the offence a 'domestic burglary' for sentencing purposes. This issue is discussed below.

(b) *Mens rea*

(i) Intention to enter as a trespasser

Collins[69] shows that it must be proved on a charge of burglary that D knew (or was reckless as to) the facts that, in law, make his entry trespassory. It would follow that if D sets up an honest belief in a right to enter, it would be for the Crown to prove that D's belief was not held.

(ii) The ulterior offence

It must be proved that D, *either*

(i) entered with intent[70] to commit one of the following offences:

(a) stealing,

(b) inflicting grievous bodily harm,

(c) unlawful damage to the building or anything therein;[71]

or

66 Query the unoccupied boat or caravan, which is visited and lived in only during holidays; see Smith, *Property Offences*, paras 28–39 (no); Williams, TBCL (2nd edn, 1983), 841, (yes); Griew, *The Theft Acts*, paras 4–27 (no).

67 J. C. Smith, *The Law of Theft* (8th edn, 1997), paras 11–23. Cf *Bundy* [1977] 2 All ER 382, [1977] 1 WLR 914, CA, below, pp 831–832.

68 [1973] QB 100, [1972] 2 All ER 1105; above, p 812.

69 [1973] QB 100, [1972] 2 All ER 1105.

70 The crime is one of specific intent: *Durante* [1972] 1 WLR 1612, above, p 279.

71 The further alternative of intending rape was repealed by the Sexual Offences Act 2003.

(ii) entered and committed *or* attempted to commit one of the following offences:
  (a) stealing,
  (b) inflicting grievous bodily harm.

Where the charge is one of entering with intent, it follows that an actual intent at the time of entry to cause the harm in question must be proved. In many such cases D's intent may be conditional at the time of entry, in the sense that he intends to steal if there is anything worth stealing, or intends to cause grievous bodily harm if V, his enemy, happens to be in the building. That there is nothing in the building worth stealing or that V is out of town is no bar to D's conviction.[72] If D intends to steal a specific item only (should it be present), it seems that the 9(1)(a) offence is not committed.[73]

Intention must be proved, it is not sufficient that D is shown to have been reckless at the time of entry as to whether the ulterior offence would be committed.[74] Although intention in this context will usually be direct or purposive intent, it is possible that D will have an oblique intention, as where he intends to remove from V's premises an item of property that is his, but foresees that in doing so he is virtually certain to cause criminal damage to V's property.

The offences in 9(1)(a) may be accurately described as inchoate versions of the three ulterior offences. Since the trespassory intrusion represents a freestanding harm to V's interests, it is generally accepted that it is appropriate in principle to criminalize these actions by a specific offence – burglary.

Stealing

This clearly means theft, contrary to s 1.[75] Following *Gomez* this includes obtaining of property other than land by deception.[76] The rogue who enters V's house intending to deceive him, for example, by obtaining goods in exchange for a worthless cheque is guilty of burglary as well as theft.[77]

Grievous bodily harm

The intention to inflict grievous bodily harm in s 9(1)(a) must be an intention to commit an offence, that is, to inflict that harm unlawfully. The offence in question would be causing grievous bodily harm with intent to do so, contrary to s 18 of the Offences Against the Person Act 1861. If there is no evidence of the intent at the time of entry, the charge under 9(1)(a) should not be left to the jury even if the occupiers have been assaulted.[78]

[72] *A-G's References (Nos 1 and 2 of 1979)* [1979] 3 All ER 143, CA. See the discussion above, p 406. This interpretation of intention illustrates the flexibility of that concept: A. Ashworth, 'The elasticity of *mens rea*', in *Crime Proof and Punishment: Essays in Memory of Sir Rupert Cross*, 45, 49.

[73] See J. C. Smith, *The Law of Theft* (8th edn, 1997), paras 11–27.

[74] *A v DPP* [2003] All ER (D) 393 (Jun).

[75] Electricity is not property for the purposes of theft and cannot therefore found a burglary charge as where D enters property and makes a telephone call: *Low v Blease* [1975] Crim LR 513.

[76] Above, p 650.

[77] *Dobson v General Accident Fire and Life Assurance Corpn plc* [1990] 1 QB 274, [1989] 3 All ER 927, CA, above, p 650.

[78] *O'Neill, McMullen and Kelly* (1986) The Times, 17 Oct.

Section 9(1)(b), however, does not use the word 'offence' but simply requires that D inflicts or attempts to inflict on any person in the building any grievous bodily harm. The omission of the word 'offence' is in fact a legislative accident;[79] but in *Jenkins*[80] the Court of Appeal held that the infliction need not amount to an offence of any kind. The court gave this example:

An intruder gains access to the house without breaking in (where there is an open window for instance).[81] He is on the premises as a trespasser and his intrusion is observed by someone in the house of whom he may not even be aware, and as a result that person suffers a severe shock, with a resulting stroke . . . Should such an event fall outside the provisions of s 9 when causing some damage to property falls fairly within it?

This is a question (in its context) plainly expecting the answer, 'no'. It is submitted that the right answer is an emphatic 'yes'. Otherwise a person may become guilty of burglary in consequence of a wholly unforeseen and unforeseeable event. The analogy with damage to property is misplaced. Causing damage to property does not fall within the provisions of s 9(1)(b). There must be an actual intention to cause damage at the time of the trespassory entry to constitute the offence under 9(1)(a). This requires a *mens rea* which is wholly absent in the example put by the court. The House of Lords allowed the appeal[82] in *Jenkins* but on a different point and no allusion was made to the interpretation by the Court of Appeal of s 9(1)(b). The case, therefore, stands as an authority – but, it is submitted, a bad one. When para (b) is read in the context of s 9(1) and (2) it is reasonably clear that the infliction of bodily harm required must be an offence – in effect, under s 18 or 20 of the Offences Against the Person Act 1861.

What if D enters with intent to murder? It would be very strange if an entry with intent to inflict grievous bodily harm amounted to burglary, and an entry with intent to murder did not. It is submitted that the greater includes the lesser and that an intention to kill by inflicting physical injuries is enough.

Unlawful damage to the building or anything therein

Again the causing of the damage must amount to an offence, that is, be unlawful. It might be any of the offences of causing damage created by the Criminal Damage Act 1971. In the case of every one of the offences which is likely to be invoked under this provision, the *actus reus* must be committed intentionally or recklessly.

It might be questioned why the offence of burglary is limited to the ulterior intent to commit such a limited number of specified offences and the commission of an even smaller number. There have been suggestions to criminalize trespass with intent to commit any indictable offence, but these would create considerable overlap with offences of inchoate liability, and would not appear to be necessary.

79 See J. C. Smith, 'Burglary under the Theft Bill' [1968] Crim LR 367 and commentary on *Jenkins* [1983] 1 All ER 1000, [1983] Crim LR 386, CA.

80 [1983] 1 All ER 1000, at 1002. Cf *Watson* (1989) 89 Cr App R 211 (death caused after entry is caused in the course of committing an offence under s 9(1)(a)).

81 The relevance of the absence of breaking is obscure.

82 [1983] 3 All ER 448, [1984] Crim LR 36 and commentary.

2. Burglary in respect of a dwelling

As noticed above[83] burglary in respect of a dwelling, whether contrary to s 9(1)(a) or s 9(1)(b) of the Act, is, since the Criminal Justice Act 1991, a separate offence – a new aggravated form of burglary. Arguably, this represents a return to the origins of the offence being a crime against 'habitation,'[84] and has significance in labelling the conduct appropriately. The only constituent of the offence that requires consideration is 'dwelling'; but it must be looked at in respect of both *actus reus* and *mens rea.*

(a) *Actus reus*

'Dwelling' is not defined but it presumably means substantially the same as 'dwelling house' in the former offence of burglary at common law and under the Larceny Acts.[85] The single word better describes many forms of accommodation that would not qualify as a 'house'. A person dwells in that place where he sleeps, not that where he spends his waking hours where those places are different. A building, such as a block of flats, may contain many dwellings. Entering the 'public' parts of the block may be burglary but perhaps not burglary in 'a dwelling.' A hotel room is probably not a dwelling unless the particular inhabitant does live there as his home. Premises that have become a dwelling will not cease to be such because of the temporary absence of the inhabitants, provided that at least one of them intends to return. A person may have more than one dwelling as where he has a flat in London and a house in the country, sleeping sometimes in one and sometimes the other. The dormobile considered above will probably be a dwelling while the family is living in it, but will cease to be a dwelling when they stop doing so.

(b) *Mens rea*

As 'dwelling' is an aggravating element in the offence warranting a higher maximum sentence of imprisonment, it should, in principle, import a requirement of *mens rea.* A person who commits burglary in a dwelling should be convicted only of simple burglary if he believed that no one lived there. But, in principle and by analogy to the construction of 'as a trespasser' in *Collins,*[86] recklessness should be enough. If D entered knowing that someone might be living there, and someone was, he should be guilty of burglary in respect of a dwelling.

83 Above, p 812. See *Courtie*, above, Ch 1.

84 Blackstone, *Commentaries on the Laws of England*, vol 4, 220. For statistical data on the incidence see T. Budd, *Burglary of Domestic Dwellings: Findings from the British Crime Survey* (1999).

85 See the first edition of this book (1965), 399; *Russell on Crime* (12th edn, 1964) 826. Cf Public Order Act 1986, s 8: '"dwelling" means any structure or part of a structure occupied as a person's home or as other living accommodation (whether the occupation is separate or shared with others) but does not include any part not so occupied, and for this purpose "structure" includes a tent, caravan, vehicle, vessel or other temporary or movable structure.' Cf Terrorism Act 2000, s 121: '"dwelling" means a building or part of a building used as a dwelling, and a vehicle which is habitually stationary and which is used as a dwelling . . .'

86 P 812, above.

3. Aggravated burglary

By s 10 of the Theft Act:

(1) A person is guilty of aggravated burglary if he commits any burglary and at the time has with him any firearm or imitation firearm, any weapon of offence, or any explosive; and for this purpose –

(a) 'firearm' includes an airgun or air pistol, and 'imitation firearm' means anything which has the appearance of being a firearm, whether capable of being discharged or not; and

(b) 'weapon of offence' means any article made or adapted for use for causing injury to or incapacitating a person, or intended by the person having it with him for such use; and

(c) 'explosive' means any article manufactured for the purpose of producing a practical effect by explosion, or intended by the person having it with him for that purpose.

(2) A person guilty of aggravated burglary shall on conviction on indictment be liable to imprisonment for life.

The reason given by the CLRC for the creation of this additional offence is that 'burglary when in possession of the articles mentioned . . . is so serious that it should in our opinion be punishable with imprisonment for life. The offence is comparable with robbery (which will be so punishable). It must be extremely frightening to those in the building, and it might well lead to loss of life.'[87] The offence can be committed in dwellings or other buildings.

(a) The articles of aggravation

'Firearm' is not defined in the Act, except to the extent that it includes an airgun or air pistol. The term is given a very wide meaning by the Firearms Act 1968,[88] but since that statutory definition has not been incorporated in the Theft Act it is submitted that the word should not be given a meaning any wider than that which it naturally bears; and that, therefore, the term 'imitation firearm' be similarly limited.[89]

The definition of 'weapon of offence' is marginally wider than that of 'offensive weapon' in s 1(4) of the Prevention of Crime Act 1953,[90] in that it includes (as well as everything within the 1953 Act) any article made for *incapacitating* a person, any article adapted for *incapacitating* a person, and any article which D has with him for that purpose. Articles *made* for incapacitating a person might include a pair of handcuffs; articles *adapted* for incapacitating might include a pair of socks made into a gag, and articles *intended* for incapacitating a person might include sleeping pills to put in the

87 Cmnd 2977, para 80.

88 See s 57 and *Grace v DPP* (1989) 153 JP 491. Note that the possession of a firearm with intent to commit an indictable offence (including burglary) is an offence carrying a maximum life imprisonment: s 18, Firearms Act 1968.

89 The term has been widely construed under the Firearms Act 1968. A jury can not conclude that D pointing a finger inside his coat at V is sufficient: *Bentham* [2005] UKHL 18.

90 Above, p 588. Note that the defences of lawful authority or reasonable excuse available under the 1953 Act do not apply here.

night-watchman's tea, a rope to tie him up, a sack to put over his head, pepper to throw in his face, and so on.

The definition of 'explosive' closely follows that in s 3(1) of the Explosives Act 1875 which, after enumerating various explosives, adds: '. . . and every other substance, whether similar to those above mentioned or not, used or manufactured with a view to produce a practical effect by explosion or by a pyrotechnic effect . . .'.

It will be observed that the definition in the Theft Act is narrower. The Explosive Substances Act 1883, if read literally, is wide enough to include a box of matches – these produce a 'pyrotechnic effect'; but it seems clear that a box of matches would not be an 'explosive' under the Theft Act. The main difficulty about the definition – and this is unlikely to be important in practice – lies in determining the meaning of 'practical effect'. Perhaps it serves to exclude fireworks which, so it has been said in connection with another Act, are 'things that are made for amusement'.[91]

(b) 'At the time' of commission of burglary

It must be proved that D had the article of aggravation with him *at the time* of committing the burglary. Where the charge is one of entry with intent (9(1)(a)) this is clearly at the time of entry. Where the charge is one of committing a specified offence, having entered (9(1)(b)), it is at the time of commission of the specified offence.

Burglary is not aggravated merely because a weapon is used against the occupier outside the building or is held by an accomplice in a getaway car.[92] Nor it is enough to prove an armed entry by D as a trespasser unless that entry is accompanied by one of the specified intents. If, then, D, having no such intent at the time of entry, discards his weapon and thereafter commits one of the specified offences he is not guilty of aggravated burglary[93] though he would be so guilty if he re-armed himself for this purpose.[94] Whether D who arms himself only to escape, having already completed the burglary (for example, by stealing), is guilty of the aggravated offence is debatable.[95] By analogy with the courts approach in *Watson*,[96] and the courts' willingness to treat theft act offences as continuing[97] it is likely that the offence would be held to have been committed.

(c) 'Has with him'

The expression 'has with him' appears in the Prevention of Crime Act 1953 and reference should be made to the discussion of that Act,[98] particularly as regards the controversial issues of D claiming to have forgotten that he has with him the forbidden article.[99]

[91] *Bliss v Lilley* (1862) 32 LJMC 3, per Cockburn CJ, and Blackburn J; but Wightman J thought that a fog-signal was a 'firework'. Cf *Bouch* [1982] 3 All ER 918, CA; *Howard* [1993] Crim LR 213, CA.

[92] *Klass* [1998] 1 Cr App R 453.

[93] *Francis* [1982] Crim LR 363, CA.

[94] *O'Leary* (1986) 82 Cr App R 34, CA.

[95] See Smith, *Property Offences*, paras 28–61

[96] *Watson* (1989) 89 Cr App R 211.

[97] *Ataakpu* (1994) 98 Cr App R 254, CA above, p 656.

[98] Above, p 588. See also *Pawlicki and Swindell* (1992) 95 Cr App R 246, [1992] Crim LR 584 ('have with him' under Firearms Act 1968, s 18(1)), and see recently *North* [2001] EWCA Crim 544. In respect of the Firearms Act offence, it has been held that the question of propinquity is to be approached in a common sense way. A person could not therefore be said to 'have with him' a firearm two or three miles away: *Bradish* (2004) 148 SJ 474, CA.

[99] See especially *Jolie* [2003] above, p 589.

When the prosecution have proved that the article was made or adapted for causing injury or incapacitating, they need not prove that D intended to use the weapon in the course of the burglary. Where the article was not so made or adapted, but the prosecution prove D had it with him for such use it is not necessary to show that he intended so to use it *in the course of the burglary*. D's conviction was accordingly upheld in *Stones*[100] where at the time of the burglary he had with him an ordinary kitchen knife that, he claimed, he was carrying to use in self-defence in case he was attacked by a gang. The mischief at which the section is aimed, said the court, is that if a burglar has a weapon which he intends to use to injure some person unconnected with the premises burgled, he might nevertheless be tempted so to use it if challenged during the course of the burglary. And clearly a conditional intent to use a weapon suffices for the offence.

It will be recalled that it has been decided that, under the Prevention of Crime Act, a person carrying an inoffensive article for an innocent purpose does not become guilty of having an offensive weapon with him merely because he uses that article for an offensive purpose. The 1953 Act is directed against the *carrying* of articles intended to be used as weapons, not against the *use* of an article as a weapon. It was to be expected that the same construction would be put upon the similar words of s 10 of the Theft Act, but in *Kelly*[101] it was held that D, who had used a screwdriver to effect an entry, became guilty of aggravated burglary when he used it to prod V in the stomach. The court purported to apply the ordinary meaning of the words of the subsection; but they seem indistinguishable in this respect from the words of the Prevention of Crime Act; and the same considerations of policy seem applicable to the two provisions. *Kelly* seems a dubious decision.

It has also been held under the 1953 Act that no offence is committed where a person arms himself with a weapon for instant attack on his victim;[102] but, if *Kelly* is right, it seems that that decision can hardly apply to s 10. So if D is interrupted in the course of stealing after a trespassory entry and picks up a paperweight (or any object) and throws it with intent to cause injury, he will thereby become guilty of aggravated burglary. He could be adequately dealt with by a second count charging whatever offence against the person he has committed; and it is submitted that this is the proper course. On the other hand, if D picked up a stone outside the house to use as a weapon if he should be disturbed after entry, the subsequent burglary would properly be held to be aggravated. Here D has armed himself before an occasion to use violence has arisen; and the stone is a weapon of offence. In *O'Leary*[103] D, having entered V's house as a trespasser, took up a kitchen knife and proceeded upstairs where by use of the knife he forced V to hand over property. It was held that he was rightly convicted of aggravated burglary. Burglary is committed under s 9(1)(b) at the time when the ulterior offence is committed, and before its commission in this case, D had armed himself for use in connection with it.

100 [1989] 1 WLR 156, 89 Cr App R 26, CA. See N. J. Reville, 'Mischief of Aggravated Burglary' (1989) 139 NLJ 835.

101 (1992) 97 Cr App R 245, [1993] Crim LR 763 and commentary.

102 *Ohlson v Hylton* [1975] 2 All ER 490; *Giles* [1976] Crim LR 253; *Bates v Bulman* (1979) 68 Cr App R 21, and see recently *Byrne* [2004] Crim LR 582.

103 (1986) 82 Cr App R 341, CA.

4. Trespass with intent to commit a sexual offence

Section 63 of the Sexual Offences Act 2003 introduces a new offence to replace burglary with intent to rape.

(1) A person commits an offence if –

(a) he is a trespasser on any premises,

(b) he intends to commit a relevant sexual offence on the premises, and

(c) he knows that, or is reckless as to whether, he is a trespasser.

(2) In this section –

'premises' includes a structure or part of a structure;

'relevant sexual offence' [is all those in that Part of the Act];

'structure' includes a tent, vehicle or vessel or other temporary or movable structure.

The offence is significantly wider than burglary. (i) Any trespass is sufficient and there is no need to prove a trespassory *entry*. The trespass may arise as a result of D exceeding permission as regards the purpose for which entry was granted or exceeding permission in terms of the areas or parts of promises entered. (ii) The trespass relates to 'premises', which is wider than the concept of a building or part of a building. It is a term used in many statutes, including criminal ones, and is usually widely construed.[104] Technically it could extend to all areas of land which could be the subject of a lease. This will include open spaces (fields and parks). (iii) The concept of 'structure' is widely defined, it will include a car or van.[105] (iv) As with s 9(1)(a) there is no need for the ulterior (sexual) offence to occur, indeed, there is no need for any intended victim to be on the premises; (v) the list of ulterior offences to which this section applies is much wider than purely rape, as under the old law; it extends to all those in Part 1 of the 2003 Act.

The *mens rea* of the offence requires proof that D intended to perform the relevant sexual offence, and knowledge or subjective recklessness as to the facts that render him a trespasser.

5. Going equipped

By s 25(1) and (2) of the Theft Act:

(1) A person shall be guilty of an offence if, when not at his place of abode, he has with him any article for use in the course of or in connection with any burglary, theft or cheat.

[104] For example, in the Criminal Law Act 1977, 'premises' means any building, any part of a building under separate occupation, any land ancillary to a building, the site comprising any building or buildings together with any land ancillary thereto: s 12(1)(a).

[105] 'Structure' is a term used in numerous statutes, but its interpretation is heavily dependent on context. A recent example is the Criminal Justice and Police Act 2001, where s 66 provides: 'premises' includes any vehicle, stall or moveable structure (including an offshore installation) and any other place whatever, whether or not occupied as land'. Section 48 of the RIPA 2000 similarly provides that 'premises' includes any vehicle or moveable structure and any other place whatever, whether or not occupied as land. This suggests that structure is wider than building.

(2) A person guilty of an offence under this section shall on conviction on indictment be liable to imprisonment for a term not exceeding three years.[106]

This useful inchoate offence is expressed to be directed against acts preparatory to:

(i) burglary contrary to s 9;

(ii) theft contrary to s 1;

(iii) criminal deception contrary to s 15;[107]

(iv) taking and driving away a conveyance, contrary to s 12.[108]

(a) *Actus reus*

The cross heading in the statute, 'Possession of house-breaking implements, etc', and the side note, 'Going equipped for stealing, etc', indicate that the offence, like s 28 of the Larceny Act 1916 which it replaced, is aimed primarily at a person who sets out on an expedition equipped with jemmy, skeleton keys and such like. However, in *Re McAngus*,[109] an extradition case, it was held that there was evidence of the offence when undercover agents said that D had agreed to sell them counterfeit clothing and shown them shirts, wrongly bearing an American brand name, in a bonded warehouse. D was certainly 'equipped' for criminal deception and, when visiting the warehouse, he was not at his place of abode. If he had been hawking the shirts from door to door it would have been a straightforward case but D did not 'go' anywhere with the articles. The side-note is not part of the section but might now be considered as a legitimate aid to statutory construction[110] and it might be taken to show that 'going' is the essence of the offence.[111] Presumably it would have made no difference if the shirts had been kept in D's own warehouse, which does not seem substantially different from keeping them at home.

D must have with him 'any article'. Clearly the article need not be made or adapted for use in committing one of the specified offences. It is sufficient that the *mens rea* is proved in respect of the article, that is, that the accused intended to use it in the course of, or in connection with, one of the specified offences. Thus the article may be a tin of treacle intended for use in removing a pane of glass, a diving suit to allow D to steal balls from a lake on a golf course,[112] a pair of gloves to be worn to avoid leaving fingerprints, and it is implicit in numerous decisions that it may be a sliced loaf and a bag of tomatoes[113] or bottles of wine[114] which D intends to pass off as the property of his employer.[115]

106 See generally, J. K. Bentil (1979) 143 JP 47; Williams, TBCL (2nd edn, 1983), 853–857; Griew, ch 16; ATHS, *Property Offences*, 31.1.

107 By s 25(5), 'cheat' means an offence under s 15.

108 By s 25(5), 'theft' in this section includes an offence under s 12(1).

109 [1994] Crim LR 602, DC, and commentary.

110 *M* [2004] UKHL 50, [2005] Crim LR 479.

111 As the long title showed that 'carrying' was the essence of the offence under the Prevention of Crime Act 1953, above, p 585.

112 *Rostron* (2003) All ER (D) 269 (Jul).

113 *Rashid* [1977] 2 All ER 237, 64 Cr App R 201, CA; cf *Cooke* [1986] AC 909, applied in relation to s 25 in *Whiteside* [1989] Crim LR 436.

114 *Doukas* [1978] 1 All ER 1061, [1978] 1 WLR 372, CA.

115 This series of cases place unwarranted emphasis on the question of whether the intended victim would be deceived, when the true issue is, it is submitted, whether D intends to obtain property by deception. See J. C. Smith, *The Law of Theft* (8th edn, 1997) para 12–07; Griew, paras 16–11 – 16–13.

D can hardly be committing an offence by wearing his shoes or any other item of everyday apparel. Yet it was argued above that gloves for the avoidance of fingerprints would entail liability.[116] This suggests that the article must be one that D would not be carrying with him but for the contemplated offence. If it is something that he would carry with him on a normal, innocent outing, it should not fall within this section. So there might be a difference between a pair of rubber gloves and a pair of fur-lined gloves that D was wearing to keep his hands warm on a freezing night, even though he did intend to keep them on so as to avoid leaving fingerprints. The latter pair of gloves is hardly distinguishable, for this purpose, from D's overcoat, which seems to fall into the same category as his shoes. If D is carrying a pair of plimsolls in his car to facilitate his cat-burgling, this seems a plain enough case; but what if he has simply selected his ordinary crepe-sole shoes for wear because they are less noisy than his hobnail boots? The offence is extremely broad and in some instances the *actus reus* might be regarded as negligible. The emphasis is, as with most inchoate offences, on the proof of *mens rea*, and for that reason, care must be taken to avoid overly broad application.

The expression 'has with him'[117] is the same as in s 10(1)(b) of the Act. Questions as to D's knowledge of the nature of the thing can hardly arise here, since it must be proved that he intended to use it in the course of or (more broadly) in connection with one of the specified offences. If a number of defendants are charged jointly with going equipped it must be proved that all the members of the enterprise knew of the existence of the articles and had the common purpose to use those articles in the specified offence[118]

No doubt D has an article with him if it is in his immediate possession or control; so that he will be guilty if the article is only a short distance away and he can take it up as he needs it; as where a ladder has been left in a garden by an accomplice and D enters the garden intending to use the ladder to make an entry. If the article is found in D's car some distance from the scene of the crime this will be evidence that D was in possession of the article when driving the car. The tenor of decisions on the interpretation of 'has with him' indicates that mere momentary possession will not suffice,[119] as where D is apprehended on picking up a stone which he intends to use to break a window in order to commit burglary. But in *Minor v DPP*[120] it seems to have been decided that D may be convicted of going equipped (in this case to steal petrol from cars) though he did not take the equipment (petrol cans and a hose) with him and somehow came across it while he was removing the cap from the petrol tank of a car. It appears to have been regarded as enough that the theft 'was to be posterior to the acquisition of the articles'. On this view the burglar who picks up a nearby stone to break a window would commit the offence of going equipped but it is respectfully submitted that 'has with him' requires more than that the acquisition of the article should precede the theft.

'Place of abode' connotes a place, that is a site, where D lives.[121] Clearly no offence is committed when D has articles for housebreaking etc in his own home, but place of abode is apt to cover the whole of the premises where D lives so that D does not commit the offence by having the articles in his garage or even in his car while that is on his premises. Once D steps into the street with the articles or drives off with them in his car

[116] Cf *Ellames* [1974] 3 All ER 130, CA; below, p 832, where gloves were included in the charge.

[117] See above, p 827. [118] *Reader, Connor and Hart* [1998] 7 April 1998, CA.

[119] Above, p 830. [120] (1987) 152 JP 30, DC.

[121] *Bundy* [1977] 2 All ER 382, CA; *Kelt* [1977] 3 All ER 1099, [1977] Crim LR 556 and commentary.

the offence may be committed. The ambit of the exemption is presumably based on a respect for D's privacy. Though a car or a caravan may constitute a place of abode while stationary at some site, they can never constitute a *place* of abode while D is in transit and if he then has the articles with him he may commit the offence.[122]

(b) *Mens rea*

The *mens rea* for the offence would appear to consist in:

(i) knowledge that one possesses the article; and

(ii) an intention to use the article in the course of or in connection with any of the specified crimes.

It was held in *Ellames*[123] that the intent to use must necessarily relate to use in the future so that D was not guilty of this offence where the evidence showed only that he was in possession of certain articles (masks, guns, gloves, etc) after a robbery and was trying to get rid of them. But given an intent to use the article in the future the expression 'in the course of or in connection with' any burglary, theft or cheat is wide enough to cover not only articles intended for use in the perpetration of the crime but also articles intended for use before or after its commission. The string used by D in *Robinson*[124] to tie himself up as part of his preparation to defraud his insurers could properly be said to be intended for use 'in connection with' the commission of the crime of deception. Equally a car intended for use to make an escape after the commission of a robbery falls within the offence. But the article must be intended for some direct use in connection with the crime and it has been held that D's possession of a stolen driving licence so that he could obtain a job which would give him an opportunity to steal is not within the offence.[125]

In *Ellames*[126] it was said that D could commit the offence where he possessed the articles for future use by another, so that D would have been guilty in that case had he been hiding away the guns, etc for their future use by others. And it was also the view of the court that it was not necessary to show that D intended the article to be used in connection with a particular theft or cheat; the section requires only intended use in connection with *any* burglary, theft or cheat. No doubt a conditional intent (for example, possessing a jemmy to use if necessary) suffices but D must have made up his mind, even if only contingently, to use the article. If D had not so determined he does not commit the offence.[127]

Section 25 (3) provides:

> Where a person is charged with an offence under this section, proof that he had with him any article made or adapted for use in committing a burglary, theft or cheat shall be evidence that he had it with him for such use.

This is probably no more than enactment of the general rules regarding proof of intent.[128] It puts upon D an evidential burden. If he offers no explanation then the jury

122 *Bundy* [1977] 2 All ER 382, CA.
123 [1974] 3 All ER 130, CA.
124 [1915] 2 KB 342; above, p 412.
125 *Mansfield* [1975] Crim LR 101, CA.
126 [1974] 3 All ER 130, [1974] 1 WLR 1391, CA.
127 So in *Hargreaves* [1985] Crim LR 243, CA, the jury were misdirected when told they could convict if satisfied that D might have used the article.
128 Cf Criminal Justice Act 1967, s 8; above, p 125.

may be told that there is evidence upon which they may find that he had the necessary intent; but it is submitted that they should be told so to find only if satisfied beyond reasonable doubt that he in fact had that intent.[129] If D does offer an explanation then the jury should be told to acquit if they think it may reasonably be true and to convict only if satisfied beyond reasonable doubt that the explanation is untrue. The provision does not reverse the burden of proof and poses no difficulty under Article 6(2) of the ECHR.[130]

Where the article in question is not made or adapted for use in any specified offence, mere proof of possession without more will not amount to *prima facie* evidence – that is, the case will have to be withdrawn from the jury.[131] It is a question of law for the judge, at what point proof of other incriminating circumstances amounts to a case fit for submission to the jury.

The Home Office propose the introduction of a new offence akin to s 25, rendering it an offence to possess equipment to commit frauds whether at home or elsewhere. The proposal is that the new offence will criminalise the possession of articles (defined so as to include computer software and pro forma blank utility bills) irrespective of whether these are at D's abode, 'for use in the course of or in connection with' the commission or facilitation of a fraud, with a defence to show that there was lawful authority or reasonable excuse. It is also proposed to create an offence of manufacturing, selling or supplying equipment designed for the commission of frauds.[132] These are potentially wide reaching offences with the emphasis shifted from 'going out' to commit a specific dishonesty offence to the mere possession with intent.

129 Cf the case where the alleged receiver is proved to have been in possession of recently stolen property and offers no explanation: *Abramovitch* (1914) 11 Cr App R 45, CCA.

130 *Whiteside* [1989] Crim LR 436. See also A. Ashworth and M. Blake, 'The Presumption of Innocence in English Criminal Law' [1996] Crim LR 306.

131 Cf *Harrison* [1970] Crim LR 415, CA.

132 See Home Office, *Fraud Law Reform* (2004), Ch 19 above.

22

Handling and related offences

1. Handling stolen goods[1]

By s 22 of the Theft Act 1968:

(1) A person handles stolen goods if (otherwise than in the course of the stealing) knowing or believing them to be stolen goods he dishonestly receives the goods, or dishonestly undertakes or assists in their retention, removal, disposal or realisation by or for the benefit of another person, or if he arranges to do so.

(2) A person guilty of handling stolen goods shall on conviction on indictment be liable to imprisonment for a term not exceeding fourteen years.

It will be noted that the maximum sentence is twice that available for theft.[2] This reflects the desire to deter the professional 'fence' so that the market for stolen goods will thereby diminish and the incidence of theft will decrease.[3] It is this same philosophy that lies behind the far reaching and draconian Proceeds of Crime Act 2002 under which dealing with the proceeds of criminal activity, not just stolen goods, becomes criminal. In practical terms the substantial differences between the sentencing of large scale professional fencing and, for example, receipt of low value goods for personal use[4] raises questions about whether the handling offence ought to be subdivided so as to better reflect the type of criminality involved. This over-generalization and failure to provide adequate differentiation in the offence has long been the subject of criticism.[5]

It is notable that English law provides a specific offence of handling and has, since the nineteenth century, treated this conduct as an independent crime rather than one of

[1] See generally, Smith, *The Law of Theft* (8th edn, 1997), ch 13; Griew, *The Theft Acts* (7th edn, 1995), ch 15; Smith, *Property Offences* (1994), ch 30; CLRC *Eighth Report* (1966) paras 127–132. The present law is subjected to telling criticism by D. W. Elliott, 'Theft and Related Problems – England, Australia and the USA Compared' (1977) 26 ICLQ 110, 135–144.

[2] Sentencing guidelines were provided in *Webbe* [2001] EWCA Crim 1217.

[3] *Shelton* (1986) 83 Cr App R 379; *Tokeley-Parry* [1999] Crim LR 578 (deterring removal of antiquities from Egypt). See also M. Sutton, K. Johnston and H. Lockwood, *Handling Stolen Goods and Theft: a market reduction approach* (1998). M. Sutton, 'Supply by theft: does the market for second-hand goods play a role in keeping crime figures high?' (1995) 35 Brit Jnl Criminology 400.

[4] See generally the Sentencing Advisory Panel, *Handling Stolen Goods* (2001) and *Archbold* (2005) 21–279a. Low monetary value goods received for handler's own use will attract a modest fine or conditional discharge. For analysis of the activities of the professional handler see C. B. Klockars, *The Professional Fence* (1975).

[5] See D. A. Thomas, 'Form and Function in Criminal Law', in P. Glazebrook (ed), *Reshaping the Criminal Law* (1978) 23–24.

being an 'accessory after the fact' to theft.[6] The diversity of the activities it is sought to criminalise results in a broad and complex offence – Glanville Williams memorably described s 22 as a 'draftsman's omelette'.[7]

(a) *Actus reus*

The *actus reus* is drafted in extremely broad terms, resulting in an offence that can be committed in many different ways.[8] It is immediately obvious from the section that there is no requirement that the handler ever comes into physical possession of the stolen goods, and that the concept of stolen goods itself carries an extended meaning.

The questions that require consideration are: what are 'goods'? when are they 'stolen'? and what is 'handling' that is, undertaking or assisting in retention, removal, disposal or realization?

(i) Stolen goods

By s 34(2)(b), '. . . "goods", except in so far as the context otherwise requires, includes money and every other description of property except land, and includes things severed from the land by stealing'.

It will be noted that this definition differs from the definition of 'property' for the purposes of theft contrary to s 1(1). Since, however, land generally is excluded from theft by s 4(2), the effect seems to be that, subject to small exceptions discussed below, property which can be stolen can be the subject of a handling charge.

Things in action

Things in action are expressly mentioned in s 4(1) of the Theft Act 1968 as capable of being the subject of theft but are not mentioned in s 34(2)(b). They must however be included in the all-encompassing words 'every other description of property except land' within that section. Having established that things in action may constitute stolen goods, a further question is then whether they can be handled. Some forms of the *actus reus* in s 22 – for example, 'realisation' and 'disposal' – would on a natural interpretation extend to D's dealings with things in action. This is uncontroversial. Whether things in action can be the subject of a charge of 'receiving' is less clear. If 'receiving' in s 22 is given the same meaning as it bore under the former pre-Theft Act law (where it referred to taking control of a physical thing), it would not be apt to apply to things in action. But if 'receiving' is given its ordinary meaning unfettered by connotations drawn from the earlier law (and there would seem to be no good reason for so fettering it) there is no reason why D cannot receive a thing in action. Thus, if D opens a bank account into which he pays stolen money and subsequently assigns the balance to E, it does not seem to be an abuse of language to say that E receives that balance.[9]

[6] J. Hall, *Theft Law and Society* (2nd edn, 1952), 55–58, cf Hale 618. G. Fletcher, *Rethinking Criminal Law* (1978), 645–646, regards this as an illustration of the gradual replacement of the offence of being an accessory after the fact.

[7] Williams, TBCL (2nd edn, 1983), 858.

[8] *Nicklin* [1977] 1 WLR 403.

[9] This it is submitted forestalls any argument that because only some forms of the conduct (realization, disposal, etc) specified in s 22 (but not receiving) are applicable to things in action, they can never be handled.

The Court of Appeal was prepared to take the broad view of the section in *Attorney-General's Reference (No 4 of 1979)*[10] where it was said:

[I]t is clear that a balance in a bank account, being a debt, is itself a thing in action which falls within the definition of goods and may therefore be goods which directly or indirectly represent stolen goods for the purposes of s 24(2)(a).

It is submitted that this view is in accord with the interpretation of the Act and makes good sense. In *Forsyth*[11] the court had no doubt that there could be an offence of handling of a thing in action.

Land

A 'thing', attached to or forming part of the land, can be stolen by virtue of s 4(2)(b),[12] and can therefore always be the subject of handling since the stealing necessarily involves severance of the thing in question. Under s 4(2)(c) of the Theft Act, on the other hand, a fixture or structure can be stolen with or without being severed from the land. Only if it is severed can it be the subject of handling. Thus, if E, an outgoing tenant, dishonestly sells to D, the incoming tenant, a fixture belonging to V, the landlord, D cannot be guilty of handling (whether or not his act is in the course of stealing) if the fixture is not severed. Nor, of course, is F guilty of handling if, knowing all the facts, he takes over the premises, including the fixture, from D; although F has knowingly taken possession of a stolen fixture.

Land which is stolen contrary to s 4(2)(a) (by trustees or personal representatives) will rarely be capable of being handled since the kind of conduct contemplated by s 4(2)(a) will not normally involve severance.

Land may be the subject of both obtaining by deception and blackmail, both of which create 'stolen' goods for the purposes of handling.[13] Again, severance may or may not take place and handling is possible only if it does so.

Meaning of 'stolen'

By s 24(4):

For purposes of the provisions of this Act relating to goods which have been stolen (including subsections (1) to (3) above), goods obtained in England or Wales or elsewhere either by blackmail or in circumstances described in section 15(1) of this Act shall be regarded as stolen; and 'steal', 'theft' and 'thief' shall be construed accordingly.

By s 24A(8):

References to stolen goods include money which is withdrawn from an account to which a wrongful credit[14] has been made, but only to the extent that the money derives from the credit.

10 [1981] 1 All ER 1193 at 1198, [1981] Crim LR 51 and commentary. See now *Preddy* [1996] AC 815 and discussion above, p 760.

11 [1997] 2 Cr App R 299, [1997] Crim LR 581, below, 842. Though the conviction was quashed on other grounds.

12 Above, 671. 13 Below.

14 Inserted by the Theft Amendment Act 1996. See s 15A (obtaining a money transfer by deception) above, 764 and s 24A (dishonestly retaining a wrongful credit) below, 858.

And by s 24(1):

The provisions of this Act relating to goods which have been stolen shall apply whether the stealing occurred in England or Wales or elsewhere, and whether it occurred before or after the commencement of this Act, provided that the stealing (if not an offence under this Act) amounted to an offence where and at the time when the goods were stolen; and references to stolen goods shall be construed accordingly.

These five categories demonstrate the extended meaning of the concept of stolen goods and underline the breadth of the offence. The effect of these provisions is that goods are 'stolen' for the purposes of the Act if they:

(i) have been stolen contrary to s 1;[15]

(ii) have been obtained by blackmail contrary to s 21;

(iii) have been obtained by deception contrary to s 15(1);

(iv) consist of money dishonestly withdrawn from a wrongful credit; or

(v) have been the subject of an act done in a foreign country which was (a) a crime by the law of that country and which (b), had it been done in England, would have been theft, blackmail or obtaining by deception contrary to s 1 or s 21 or s 15(1) or, s 15A respectively.[16] In terms of the jurisdictional scope of the offence, it is now the case that if T steals property in, for example, Greece by performing an act that is theft in Greek law[17] but would not be theft if performed in England, and D, in England, handles that property with *mens rea*, D can be convicted of handling under s 22.[18]

If the information or indictment specifies that the goods were stolen from a specific entity, the prosecution is obliged to prove that issue, if the ownership by the entity is integral to the case.[19]

The 'thief' must be guilty

Though s 22 does not say so expressly, the goods must have been stolen in fact.[20] It is not sufficient for the prosecution to prove that D believed them to be 'stolen' if they were not. If, because of a mistake of fact (or of civil law) D wrongly believed the goods to be stolen he might be guilty of theft or, since the Criminal Attempts Act 1981, of an attempt to handle. If D says he knew the goods were stolen because E told him so, this is evidence of

[15] This will include goods obtained by offences of robbery and burglary which involve theft. See eg *Pitham and Hehl* (1976) 65 Cr App R 45.

[16] Handling is a Group A offence for the purposes of the Criminal Justice Act 1993. See generally, M. Hirst, *Jurisdiction and the Ambit of the Criminal Law* (2003), 180 *et seq.*

[17] This will have to be proved and cannot be presumed: *Ofori and Tackie (No 2)* (1994) 99 Cr App R 223; *Okolie* [2000] All ER (D) 661, The Times, 15 May. Note also the Administration of Justice Act 1920, s 15.

[18] The question whether D commits theft in England if he performs acts in eg Greece amounting to theft under Greek law and transports the goods to England, is considered above, p 656; *Atakpu* [1994] QB 69; and G. Sullivan and C. Warbrick, 'Territoriality, Theft and *Atakpu*' [1994] Crim LR 650. D who commits theft abroad and returns to England with it commits an offence of money laundering offence contrary to s 329 of the Proceeds of Crime Act 2002.

[19] *Iqbal v DPP* (2004) All ER (D) 314 (Oct).

[20] *Haughton v Smith* [1973] 3 All ER 1109 at 1112, 1119 and 1124.

D's *mens rea* but it is not evidence that the goods were stolen in fact.[21] An admission based on hearsay[22] is of no more value than the hearsay itself. It is a misdirection to tell the jury that they are entitled to take such an admission into account, except as evidence of *mens rea.*[23] In contrast, D's admission of facts that he himself perceived (by for example, seeing E steal the goods) is evidence of those facts from which a jury could infer that the goods were stolen. Thus, in a more likely scenario, D's admission that he bought goods in a pub at a ridiculously low price is *prima facie* evidence that those goods were stolen; similarly, where a television set is bought in a betting shop or where a publican buys cases of whisky from a lorry driver.[24]

The conduct of a person, E, who offers a bag of jewellery to a stranger, D, for £2,000 and then accepts £100 for it, suggests strongly, as a matter of common sense, that the jewellery is stolen.[25] However, the seller's conduct in this and similar cases goes to show only that he believed the goods to be stolen. At common law, as a matter of evidence, in the same way as E's express statement to that effect would be inadmissible as hearsay, so too his implied assertion that the goods were stolen would be inadmissible: *Kearley.*[26] Under the new hearsay regime introduced by the Criminal Justice Act 2003, such conduct will only be inadmissible hearsay if (one of) E's purpose(s) was to cause D to believe the matter relied upon – the stolen provenance of the jewellery.[27]

If the alleged thief is not guilty, the handler cannot be convicted for there are no stolen goods for him to handle. So, for example, if the alleged thief turns out to have been under the age of 10 at the time of the alleged theft, then the goods appropriated cannot be stolen goods and there can be no conviction for handling them.[28] If he believed the 'thief' was 10 or above, he might be convicted of an attempt to handle.[29] Whatever his belief as to the 'thief's' age, the more appropriate charge would be theft of the goods. In considering the liability of the handler and the question of whether there has been a theft, the courts have not drawn any distinctions between cases in which the alleged thief is acquitted on the basis of a justification – for example, consent – and an excuse – for example, insanity.

If the appropriator of the goods is guilty of theft (or the deceiver of obtaining or the blackmailer of receipt, etc), it is submitted that the goods appropriated may be the subject of handling although the appropriator is immune from prosecution by reason, for example, of diplomatic immunity.[30] The thief could be prosecuted for the theft if diplomatic immunity were waived. The handler may be convicted whether that immunity is waived or not – unless, of course, he too is entitled to diplomatic immunity.

It must be proved, as against an alleged handler, that another person (T) was guilty of stealing the goods. If the thief, T, and handler, D, are tried together, the acquittal of T is

[21] *Porter* [1976] Crim LR 58; *Marshall* [1977] Crim LR 106; *Lang v Evans (Inspector of Police)* [1977] Crim LR 286; *Hack* [1978] Crim LR 359; *Overington* [1978] Crim LR 692, CA.

[22] An out of court assertion relied on for the truth of its content; see now the impenetrable Criminal Justice Act 2003, s 115.

[23] *Hulbert* (1979) 69 Cr App R 243, CA.

[24] An example put by Lawton LJ in *McDonald* (1980) 70 Cr App R 288, CA. See also *Barnes* [1991] Crim LR 132.

[25] *Korniak* (1983) 76 Cr App R 145, CA.

[26] [1992] 2 All ER 345, HL.

[27] Section 115.

[28] *Walters v Lunt* [1951] 2 All ER 645, thus remains good law.

[29] See *Toye* [1984] Crim LR 555.

[30] Cf *Dickinson v Del Solar* [1930] 1 KB 376; *AB* [1941] 1 KB 454; *Madan* (1961) 45 Cr App R 80.

not necessarily an inconsistent verdict with one convicting D; evidence admissible against D may have been inadmissible against T. In separate trials, the fact that T has been acquitted of stealing the goods is no bar to the prosecution of the handler and is, indeed, inadmissible in evidence. But the fact that T has been convicted of stealing the goods is now admissible at D's trial for handling and, when it is admitted, T must be taken to have committed the theft unless the contrary is proved.[31] Under this controversial evidential provision, if D claims that T did not steal the goods – that T was wrongly convicted – it is for D to prove it on a balance of probabilities.

(ii) When goods cease to be stolen

It is obvious that goods that have once been stolen cannot continue to be regarded as 'stolen' so long as they continue to exist thereafter. A line must be drawn somewhere, and the Act draws it in the same place as did the common law. By s 24(3) of the Act:

> But no goods shall be regarded as having continued to be stolen goods after they have been restored to the person from whom they were stolen or to other lawful possession or custody, or after that person and any other person claiming through him have otherwise ceased as regards those goods to have any right to restitution in respect of the theft.

So if the stolen goods are taken from the thief by the owner or someone acting on his behalf, or by the police,[32] and subsequently returned to the thief so that he may hand them over to a receiver, D (in a police sting operation), will not then be guilty of handling because the goods he subsequently receives are no longer stolen goods.[33] A charge of attempted handling is available, and one of theft may also be possible. It is also possible that D could be convicted of handling if his acts of arranging occurred during the period after the theft but before the goods had been restored.

Difficult questions may arise over whether goods have in fact been 'restored to the person from whom they were stolen or to other lawful possession or custody'. It cannot be enough that V (the owner or his agent) knows that D has stolen the goods and follows D to his destination so that the handler can be caught red-handed;[34] nor that V marks the goods after the theft for the purpose of their identification in the hands of the handler.[35]

A more difficult case in this context is *King*.[36] A parcel containing the stolen goods (a fur coat) was handled by T, the thief, to a policeman who was in the act of examining the contents when the telephone rang. The caller was D, the proposed receiver. The policeman discontinued his examination, D was told to come along as arranged, he did so and received the coat. It was held that D was guilty of receiving stolen goods on the ground that the coat had not been reduced into the possession of the police – though it was admitted that there was no doubt that, in a very few minutes, it would have been so reduced, if the telephone had not rung. The case has, however, been criticized. It is easy to

[31] See s 74 of PACE 1984, *O'Connor* (1986) 85 Cr App R 298, 302, and *Cross and Tapper on Evidence* (10th edn, 2004), 126–128.

[32] *Re A-G's Reference (No 1 of 1974)* [1974] QB 744, [1974] 2 All ER 899, CA.

[33] Cf *Dolan* (1855) Dears CC 436; *Schmidt* (1866) LR 1 CCR 15; *Villensky* [1892] 2 QB 597.

[34] In *Haughton v Smith* [1975] AC 476, [1973] 3 All ER 1109, where the police accompanied the driver of a van containing stolen goods to its destination in order to trap the handler, Lords Hailsham and Dilhorne questioned whether the prosecution was right to concede that the goods had been restored to lawful custody.

[35] *Greater London Metropolitan Police Comr v Streeter* (1980) 71 Cr App R 113, DC.

[36] [1938] 2 All ER 662, CCA.

appreciate that if the police are examining a parcel to see whether it contains stolen goods, they do not take possession of the contents until they decide that this is what they are looking for.[37] In *King*, however, T had admitted the theft of the coat and produced the parcel. One might have expected, therefore, that the policeman had in fact made up his mind to take charge of it before the telephone rang. The decision presumably proceeds on the assumption that the police officer had not done so.

On that assumption the decision would, it seems be the same under the Theft Act[38] for it was held in *Re A-G's Reference (No 1 of 1974)*[39] that whether the police officer has taken possession depends primarily on the intentions of the police officer. In that case a police officer, correctly suspecting that goods in the back of a car were stolen, immobilized the car by removing the rotor arm from the engine and kept watch until D returned to the car. He questioned D and in view of the unsatisfactory nature of D's replies arrested him. It was held that the jury ought to have been asked to consider whether the officer had decided before D's appearance to take possession of the goods or whether he was of an entirely open mind, intending to decide after he had questioned D. Possession[40] requires both an intention to possess and some act of possession. To immobilize a car does not necessarily involve an intention to possess it or its contents but, along with other circumstances, it may afford evidence of such an intention. This approach is hardly conducive to certainty and consistency in the law.

It is clear that the goods cease to be stolen in the case where the police take control acting without the authority of the owner, for they are clearly in 'other lawful possession or custody of the goods'. Indeed, it would seem to be enough that the goods fall into the possession of any person provided that person intends to restore them to the person from whom they were stolen.

Section 24(3) also provides that the goods lose their character of being 'stolen goods' if the person from whom they were stolen has ceased to have any *right to restitution* in respect of them. Whether a 'right to restitution' exists is a complex question of civil law. A person whose goods have been wrongfully converted (under the Torts (Interference with Goods) Act 1977) does not have a *right* to have those goods restored to him. He has a right to damages to compensate him for the conversion, but it is in the discretion of the court whether to order the goods to be delivered to him.[41] It is quite clear that s 24(3) is not intended to be limited to only those cases in which a court would exercise its discretion to order the goods to be returned to V. In the criminal proceedings, it would be impossible to identify such cases and it is submitted that the subsection is applicable to all cases in which V *could* succeed in a civil action based on his proprietary interest in the thing, whether in conversion or for the protection of an equitable interest.

As drafted, the provision seems to have been intended to bear a still wider meaning. The CLRC explained it as follows:[42]

37 Cf *Warner v Metropolitan Police Comr* [1969] 2 AC 256, [1968] 2 All ER 356, HL.

38 In *Re A-G's Reference (No 1 of 1974)* [1974] 2 All ER 899 at 904, Lord Widgery CJ said that *King* 'might be thought to be a rather bold decision'.

39 Ibid.

40 For the purposes of s 24(3) possession *or control* suffices. Arguably in both the above cases the police officer had at least control of the goods but control, like possession, must involve an intention to take charge.

41 Torts (Interference with Goods) Act 1977, s 3. See generally, W. V. H. Rogers, *Winfield and Jolowicz on Tort* (16th edn, 2004), para 17–28.

42 Cmnd 2977, para 139.

. . . if the person who owned the goods when they were stolen no longer has any title to them, there will be no reason why the goods should continue to have the taint of being stolen goods. For example, the offence of handling stolen goods will . . . apply also to goods obtained by criminal deception under [s 15]. If the owner of the goods who has been deceived chooses on discovering the deception to ratify his disposal of the goods he will cease to have any title to them.

It is clear that 'title' is here used in a broad sense to include a right to rescind. The Committee clearly had in mind a case where property passes from V to D at the moment when the goods are obtained by deception.[43] In such a case, V, strictly, has no 'title' and his right to recover the goods (or much more likely, their value) will only arise on his rescinding the contract.[44] Such a potential right is, it is submitted, clearly a 'right to restitution' within the Act.

(iii) Goods representing those originally stolen may be stolen goods

By s 24(2) of the Act:

For the purposes of those provisions references to stolen goods shall include, in addition to the goods originally stolen and parts of them (whether in their original state or not), –

(a) any other goods which directly or indirectly represent or have at any time represented the stolen goods in the hands of the thief as being the proceeds of any disposal or realisation of the whole or part of the goods stolen or of goods so representing the stolen goods; and

(b) any other goods which directly or indirectly represent or have at any time represented the stolen goods in the hands of a handler of the stolen goods or any part of them as being the proceeds of any disposal or realisation of the whole or part of the stolen goods handled by him or of goods so representing them.

The CLRC stated[45] of this provision:

It may seem technical; but the effect will be that the goods which the accused is charged with handling must, at the time of the handling or at some previous time, (i) have been in the hands of the thief or of a handler, and (ii) have represented the original stolen goods in the sense of being the proceeds, direct or indirect, of a sale or other realisation of the original goods.

The effect is best explained by example. Suppose D steals an Audi car and subsequently that car passes, by way of sale or exchange or otherwise, through the hands of E, F and G. The Audi remains stolen until such time as it ceases to be stolen by virtue of s 24(3), (that is, until the Audi is restored to the owner or other lawful custody or until the owner ceases to have a right to restitution in respect of it). It follows that until such time any person acquiring the Audi may be convicted of handling it, if he acquires it knowing or believing it to be stolen. It is not necessary for every person in the chain to have been a handler for the Audi to remain stolen. So, where the person acquiring the Audi, say G, acquires it from F, knowing or believing it to be stolen, G handles it even though F's acquisition of the car did not constitute handling by F because he, F, acquired it innocently.

[43] As discussed above, p 655.

[44] Cf Smith, *Theft*, (6th edn), para 89, where it was argued, in relation to s 5(4), that a person holding property under a voidable title is not 'under an obligation to make restoration'; above, p 688.

[45] Cmnd 2977 at 66.

The position with regard to the *proceeds* of stolen goods is different. Assume that D exchanges the stolen Audi with E for a BMW. The BMW is now notionally stolen for the purposes of the offence because it directly represents the proceeds of the stolen Audi *in the hands of the thief*, D. Assume that E was aware that the Audi was stolen and he exchanges it with F for a Citroën. The Citroën is now notionally stolen because it represents the proceeds of the stolen Audi *in the hands of the handler*, E. Assume, then, that D sells the BMW to H who buys in good faith for £5,000. The BMW now ceases to be stolen goods as V has no right to restitution and (unlike with actual stolen goods in the example of the Audi with G and F above) once *notionally* stolen goods cease to be stolen goods they cannot revert to being notionally stolen because they are subsequently acquired by someone who is aware of their provenance.

The £5,000 in D's hands, however, *is* notionally stolen because it indirectly represents the proceeds of the stolen Audi in the hands of the thief and a recipient of all or part of that £5,000 would, if aware of its provenance, be guilty of handling. The position may be a little more complex where D banks the £5,000. If the £5,000 represents all that D has in the account, money which D draws from the account is stolen goods and a receiver of it, having the requisite knowledge, would be guilty of handling. Where, however, D has other innocently acquired money in his account, say a further £5,000, it may be difficult to prove that a cheque drawn for £2,000 that is cashed by E represents the proceeds of the stolen £5,000. It is not enough to establish that the recipient believed that the cheque for £2,000 represented proceeds of the stolen £5,000 – that it represented his share of the ill-gotten £5,000.[46] This will establish the recipient's *mens rea*, which would be enough to convict him of an attempt, but, to establish the full offence it must additionally be proved that D intended the £2,000 to represent the proceeds of the stolen money.

In the difficult case of *Forsyth*[47] T stole funds in a company's bank account and transferred them to a series of other banks in which he had accounts. It was held that 'in the hands of' means 'in the possession or control of' and therefore that the new credit balances remained under T's control. This renders the offence even wider. The balances were new property, distinct from that stolen,[48] but they 'represented' that stolen money and, 'being in the hands of' the thief, were accordingly stolen goods. More difficult to follow is the court's assumption that the actual banknotes withdrawn, on T's instructions, by D from one of the accounts were also stolen, so that D was guilty of handling them when she took physical possession of them. The notes belonged exclusively to the bank and had never been in the hands of a thief or handler until D received them and therefore could not have been stolen under s 24(2). If A pays stolen money into a bank account and, in payment of a debt he owes to B, gives B a cheque drawn on that account, B, if he cashes the cheque, does not receive stolen money. The actual cash in the shape of pound coins in the hands of the bank is not stolen goods. B is not the thief, nor is he receiving stolen goods. He is not guilty of handling. Nor is it permissible to argue that B is a handler and therefore that the goods are stolen because they are in his hands. That is a circular argument.

46 *A-G's Reference (No 4 of 1979)* [1981] 1 All ER 1193, [1981] 1 WLR 667, CA.

47 [1997] 2 Cr App R 299, [1997] Crim LR 589 and additional commentary, 755.

48 *Preddy* [1996] AC 815

In that example, however, B is acting on his own behalf. In *Forsyth* D was acting as agent for T, the original thief. For the reason given above, D (it is submitted) was not *receiving* stolen goods. But, because D, unlike B in the example, was acting as agent for the thief, the cash, though physically in D's hands, was, in law, 'in the hands of' T – that is, it 'indirectly represented the stolen goods in the hands of the thief' (s 24(2)(a)) – and was therefore stolen goods. D was not a receiver of stolen goods – the cash became stolen only when she received it. She then had stolen goods in her hands. That is not an offence; but she then went on to assist in the retention, etc, of the stolen goods for the benefit of T; and that is the offence of handling.

(iv) Forms of handling

Under the old law in s 33(1) of the Larceny Act 1916, the only way of committing the offence was by 'receiving' the stolen goods. Section 22 of the 1968 Act creates a much broader offence in which receiving is only one of several ways in which 'handling' can be committed. These are:

(i) *Receiving* the goods.

(ii) *Undertaking* the retention, removal, disposal or realisation of the goods by or for the benefit of another person.

(iii) *Assisting* in the retention, removal, disposal or realisation of the goods by or for the benefit of another person.

(iv) *Arranging* to do (i), (ii), (iii).

Although in the leading case of *Bloxham*,[49] Lord Bridge said, 'It is, I think, well settled that this subsection creates two distinct offences but no more than two', this must be wrong. It is generally accepted that s 22 creates only one offence[50] which may be committed in a variety of ways. What was well settled before *Bloxham* (and remains so) was that, where the evidence justified it, the proper practice was to have one count for receiving (or perhaps arranging to receive) and a second count for all the other forms of handling.[51] In law, however, the subsection creates only one offence. Thus in *Nicklin*[52] it was held that an indictment alleging unparticularized handling charges only one offence and is not bad for duplicity.

If D is charged specifically with receiving only, he may not be convicted on that indictment of some other form of handling;[53] and vice versa. Since receiving is 'a single finite act' each receipt of stolen goods is a separate offence and, therefore, a single count for receiving a whole quantity of goods found in D's possession will be bad for duplicity if the receipt of various parts of that whole took place on more than one occasion.[54] The forms of handling other than receiving include 'an activity which may be continuing'; so

49 [1983] 1 AC 109, [1982] 1 All ER 582 on which see L. Blake, 'The Erstwhile Innocent Purchaser of Stolen Goods' (1982) J Crim Law 220.

50 *Griffiths v Freeman* [1970] 1 All ER 1117.

51 *Willis and Syme* [1972] 3 All ER 797, CA; *Deakin* [1972] 3 All ER 803, CA.

52 [1977] 2 All ER 444, CA, [1977] Crim LR 221. Particulars should be given so as to enable the accused to understand the ingredients of the charge he has to meet: *Sloggett* [1972] 1 QB 430, [1971] 3 All ER 264. The maximum number of counts for a single instance of handling in the ordinary case is two: *Ikpong* [1972] Crim LR 432, CA.

53 *Nicklin*, above.

54 *Smythe* (1980) 72 Cr App Rep 8, CA. Cf *Skipp*, above, p 658 (overruled, but still relevant on this issue).

that a single count may legitimately encompass a quantity of goods, parts of which have been received on different occasions. The word, 'retention', in particular, would be apt to apply where a large quantity of goods is found in D's possession and has been received by him in portions over a long period of time. In order to obtain a conviction under the single count it would of course be necessary to prove, not merely that D received the goods, but that he was retaining them for the benefit of another person, or that he was assisting another person in retaining them.

Receiving

All forms of handling other than receiving or arranging to receive are subject to the qualification that it must be proved that D was acting 'for the benefit of another person'. If there is no evidence of this – as will frequently be the case – then it must be proved that D received or arranged to receive the goods and evidence of no other form of handling will suffice. The Theft Act does not define receiving in any way and it must be assumed that all the old authorities remain valid.

So, to establish receiving, it must be proved that either:

(i) D took possession or joined with others to share possession (whether actual or constructive), intending to possess the goods, or

(ii) D took control of the stolen property or joined with others to share control of it with intent to do so.

'Receiving' the thief himself who has the goods in his possession does not necessarily amount to receiving the goods. If the thief, T, retains exclusive control, there is no receiving by D.[55] There may, however, be a joint possession in thief and receiver, so it is unnecessary to prove that the thief ever parted with possession – it is sufficient that he shared it with the alleged receiver.

The question is then what joint possession means in these circumstances. In *Smith*[56] it was held that a jury had been correctly directed when told that if they believed that the stolen watch was then in the custody of the thief 'with the cognizance of the [the alleged handler], [the thief] being one over whom the [alleged handler] had absolute control, so that the watch would be forthcoming if [he] ordered it, there was ample evidence to justify them in convicting . . .'. Lord Campbell CJ said that if the thief had been employed by D to commit theft, so that the watch was in D's control, D was guilty of receiving. Under the old law, this posed a rather strange anomaly since D was an accessory before the fact to larceny, and therefore became guilty of both 'theft' and receiving at the same moment. The result is less anomalous under the 1968 Act. D would be guilty of theft and receiving, but since virtually all handling is now theft, it is the general rule that the two offences are committed simultaneously.[57] In the ordinary case, however, the offence is handling because a previous theft has occurred. The principal peculiarity of the problem under the present law is that there has been no *previous* theft so it may be that D becomes a handler only by some act done *after* the theft. It is of course important to identify the point at which D receives the stolen goods since it is at that point that he must have the relevant *mens rea*.[58]

[55] *Wiley* (1850) 2 Den 37.

[56] (1855) Dears CC 494. See also *Gleed* (1916) 12 Cr App R 32, CCA.

[57] *Sainthouse* [1980] Crim LR 506.

[58] *Brook* [1993] Crim LR 455.

As is clear from *Smith*, actual manual possession or physical control by D in person need not be proved. It is enough if the goods are received by his agent with D's authority.[59] There are few other limits on what constitutes receiving: D's receipt may be for a merely temporary purpose such as concealment from the police;[60] and, it is unnecessary that the receiver should receive any profit or advantage from the possession of the goods.[61] However, it is not enough that D took possession by 'finding' goods that were stolen; there must be a receipt from another.[62] If D took possession of goods from the thief without his consent, this appears to be both capable of being both theft and handling, since it is clear that the two offences can be committed by one and the same act.[63]

In all cases of receiving, it continues to be essential for the judge to give a careful direction as to possession or control.[64] If the only evidence against D is that he ran away on being found by the police in a house where stolen property had been left, there would appear to be no case to leave to a jury. Likewise where the evidence is consistent with the view that D went to premises where stolen goods were stored with the intention of assuming possession but had not actually done so,[65] or where the only evidence of receiving for example, a stolen car is that D's fingerprint was found on the rear-view mirror.[66] The mere fact that the stolen goods were found on D's premises is not sufficient evidence to establish receiving. It must be shown that the goods had come either by invitation or arrangement with him or that he had exercised some control over them.[67] It has even been held that D is not necessarily in possession of a stolen safe simply because he assists others in trying to open it.[68]

Arranging to receive

Where it is impossible to prove an actual receipt by D, the evidence may nevertheless show that D has arranged to receive the goods. Where D has merely made preparations to receive and has not yet reached the stage of an attempt to do so, the preparations may constitute a sufficient arrangement. The difficulties in a case like *King*[69] will be overcome if it appears that the arrangement to receive was concluded before there was a possibility of the goods ceasing to be stolen. Presumably it is enough if the proposed receipt is by an agent of D. The arrangement must be made after the theft, since D must know or believe the goods to be stolen when he makes the arrangement.[70]

Though there is no such express requirement, it is difficult to envisage an arrangement that does not involve an agreement with another. Such an agreement will therefore almost

59 *Miller* (1854) 6 Cox CC 353.

60 *Richardson* (1834) 6 C & P 335.

61 *Davis* (1833) 6 C & P 177.

62 *Haider* (1985) unreported, discussed in Griew, *The Theft Acts*, para 13.

63 This was formerly only larceny (from the thief) and not receiving: *Wade* (1844) 1 Car & Kir 739.

64 *Frost and Hale* (1964) 48 Cr App R 284, CCA.

65 *Freedman* (1930) 22 Cr App R 133, CCA. But this might be sufficient evidence of an arrangement to receive.

66 *Court* (1960) 44 Cr App R 242, CCA.

67 *Cavendish* [1961] 2 All ER 856, CCA; *Lloyd* [1992] Crim LR 361.

68 *Tomblin* [1964] Crim LR 780, CCA.

69 Above, p 839. And similarly the difficulties of *Haughton v Smith* [1975] AC 476, [1973] 3 All ER 1109, HL, above, p 407.

70 *Park* (1987) 87 Cr App R 164, CA.

always amount to a conspiracy to receive so the extension of the law effected by this provision is less far-reaching than might appear. Clearly, however, an arrangement made by D with an innocent person is enough (provided D has the relevant *mens rea*), as is an arrangement that does not involve another party at all, if that can be envisaged.

The offence of handling is complete as soon as the proposed receipt is arranged. It is immaterial (except as to sentence) that D repents or does nothing in pursuance of the arrangement. In this respect it is clear that the substantive offence of arranging to receive has developed as a form of inchoate offence, rather than a form of secondary participation.

Undertaking and assisting

The provision of the Act relating to handling by 'undertaking and assisting' extends the law to cover cases which were formerly not criminal at all, not even by way of an attempt. They are far-reaching and overlapping. 'Undertaking' presumably covers the case where D sets out to retain, etc the stolen goods, on his own initiative and appears more apt to describe the activity of the seller of stolen goods rather than that of the buyer. 'Assisting' seems more apt to cover the case where D joins the thief or another handler in doing so.[71]

Retention

In *Pitchley*,[72] the court suggested that retention means 'keep possession of, not lose, continue to have'. It is a continuing activity. The obvious cases of retaining will be where D stores stolen goods for the thief. An example of assisting in retention would be where D's 15-year-old son, T, brings home a bicycle which he has stolen: D assists in its retention if (i) he agrees that T may keep the bicycle in the house, or (ii) he tells the police there is no bicycle in the house, or (iii) he gives T a tin of paint so that he may disguise it.

Merely to *use* goods knowing them to be stolen does not in itself amount to assisting in their retention. D did not commit the offence by using a stolen heater and battery charger in his father's garage,[73] nor by erecting stolen scaffolding in the course of a building operation.[74] Nothing was done with the purpose, or with the effect, of assisting in retention. It must be proved that D assisted in retention by concealing the goods or making them more difficult to identify or some other such conduct. It has been held that it is sufficient that D's passive conduct constitutes such assistance.[75]

According to *Kanwar*,[76] 'something must be done by the offender, and done intentionally and dishonestly, for the purpose of enabling the goods to be retained'. However, it was held to be sufficient in that case that D told lies to protect her husband who had dishonestly brought the stolen goods into the house. She knew that, if the deception succeeded, the effect would be that her husband would be enabled to retain the goods.

Disposal

This would most obviously cover cases of D destroying the stolen goods, or by using stolen money to pay for goods or services.[77] It extends beyond that to cases where D negotiates with E to sell him goods which D knows to have been stolen by T, although D is

[71] But cf *Deakin* [1972] 3 All ER 803, CA.

[72] (1972) 57 Cr App R 30, CA.

[73] *Sanders* (1982) 75 Cr App R 84.

[74] *Thornhill* (unreported; discussed in *Sanders* (1982) 75 Cr App R 84).

[75] *Burroughes* (2000) 29 Nov, unreported, CA.

[76] [1982] 2 All ER 528, 75 Cr App R 87.

[77] Cf Williams, TBCL (2nd edn, 1983), 867, interpreting disposal as being limited to alienation.

never in possession or control of the goods,[78] he would appear to have undertaken or assisted in the disposal of stolen goods.

A person does not 'assist' in the disposition of stolen property merely by accepting any benefit deriving from that disposition. There must be proof that D gave help or encouragement; an omission to act will not generally ground liability. In *Coleman*,[79] D knew that his wife was using stolen money to pay solicitors' fees relating to the purchase of a flat in the couple's joint names. That did not in itself amount to assisting though it was evidence from which a jury might infer that he had assisted by telling his wife to use the stolen money or agreeing that she should do so.

Removal

This would occur where, for example, D assists T to lift from a van a barrel of gin which he knows to have been stolen by T or another. Even if D never has possession or control[80] he has assisted or undertaken the removal of the stolen goods. D who lights the way for T to carry stolen goods from a house to a barn, so that he may negotiate for the purchase of them[81] has assisted in the removal of the goods and even if that were the full extent of his intended dealing with the goods he would still be liable to conviction (though his sentence might be lighter).

Realization

According to the House of Lords in *Bloxham*, this means 'exchanging goods for money or other property'. This form of the offence overlaps with disposal.

Assistance

The undertaking or assisting must relate to the retention, etc of the goods. The assistance can be by words or conduct. It was said in *Kanwar* that, '[t]he requisite assistance need not be successful in its object'. But is it true to say that one who attempts to assist and fails nevertheless 'assists'? This seems to involve reading the section as if it read, 'does an act with the purpose of assisting'. The would-be assister who fails to assist in any way would surely be more properly convicted of an attempt.

In all cases of undertaking it is necessary for the prosecution to prove that D was acting by or for the benefit of another, and in cases of 'assisting in' D must be assisting another.

Arranging to undertake or assist

The extension of the law to undertaking and assisting is far-reaching, but the Act goes further still. The mere arrangement to do any of the acts amounting to undertaking or assisting amounts to the complete offence of handling. The goods must of course be stolen by the time of such an arrangement. It is, presumably, enough that D agreed to negotiate the sale of the stolen goods, to lift down the barrel of stolen gin or to do any act for the purpose of enabling T to retain, remove or dispose of the stolen goods.

(v) Handling by omission

'Receiving', 'undertaking' and 'arranging' all suggest that some positive conduct is required, though as little as a nod or a wink might suffice in particular circumstances.

[78] Cf *Watson* [1916] 2 KB 385. [79] [1986] Crim LR 56, CA.

[80] *Gleed* (1916) 12 Cr App R 32, CCA; *Hobson v Impett* (1957) 41 Cr App R 138, CCA.

[81] *Wiley* (1850) 2 Den 37.

'Assisting', however, may be constituted by inactivity provided it is in circumstances where that inactivity does in fact provide assistance.[82] Take a simple case. D, a wife, could hardly be constituted a handler because T, her husband, each dawn returns to *his* house with the fruits of the night's burglaries. As has been shown above, D would not become a handler even if she used the goods, provided such use did not involve assistance in their retention, etc.

Knowledge of the whereabouts of stolen goods cannot suffice to make D a handler; nor does D become a handler simply by refusing to answer police questions as to the whereabouts of the goods[83] since there is no obligation to help the police with their enquiries.[84] So in *Brown*,[85] where T secreted stolen goods in D's flat and told D he had done so, it was held a misdirection to tell the jury that assisting in the retention of the goods could be inferred from D's refusal to reveal the presence of the stolen goods when questioned by the police about them. The conviction in *Brown* was, however, upheld by applying the proviso then available to the Court of Appeal. D had tacitly, if not expressly, permitted T to hide the goods on his premises and had thereby assisted in their retention. This is not to say that knowledge of the presence of stolen goods on his premises renders the occupier a handler. Obviously D does not assist in the retention of stolen goods where D knows that T is wearing a stolen overcoat and invites T into his premises, even if D puts it in the cloakroom for the duration of T's stay. But if D's premises are used, as they were used in *Brown*, to house the goods and D allows them to remain there he can properly be said to be assisting in their retention just as plainly as if he had initially given permission. What is important here is that D has control of premises and has chosen to allow their use for the storage of stolen goods.

Pitchley[86] is to the same effect. T, D's son, gave D stolen money telling him that he had won it on the horses and D paid it into his bank account. Two days later D became aware that the money was stolen but he did nothing about it until questioned by the police four days later. D's conviction for handling by assisting in the retention of the stolen money[87] was upheld because he had continued to retain possession after he became aware that the money was stolen. D had assumed control of the money and had, with guilty knowledge, retained control for the benefit of E.[88]

(vi) Otherwise than in the course of the stealing[89]

The offence is committed only if the conduct that amounts to handling occurs otherwise than in the course of the original stealing, that is, that causing the goods to be stolen goods in the first place before the alleged handling arose. (Almost every handling is also a second theft – the handler dishonestly appropriates property belonging to another with

[82] See above, p 177.

[83] Though D may become a handler (assist in the retention of the goods) if lies are told to put the police off the scent: *Kanwar* [1982] 2 All ER 528, [1982] 1 WLR 845, above, p 846.

[84] See above, p 549. [85] [1970] 1 QB 105, [1969] 3 All ER 198, CA.

[86] (1972) 57 Cr App R 30, CA. Cf *Tamm* [1973] Crim LR 115.

[87] The decision overlooks the fact that when D acquired his knowledge there was no longer any 'stolen' money to handle (see Smith, *Theft*, paras 13–32, n 3) but this does not affect the point at issue.

[88] Cf theft by 'keeping [goods] as owner', above, p 660.

[89] See generally A. T. H. Smith, 'Theft and/or Handling' [1977] Crim LR 517, and *Property Offences* (1994), paras 30–71–30–82.

the intention permanently to deprive the other of it – but that is not significant for this issue).

If D was a party to the original theft, his participation in that theft cannot also render him liable for the offence of handling stolen goods. This limitation is necessary to keep handling within proper bounds. Without it, virtually every instance of theft by two or more persons would also be handling by one or other or, more likely, both of them. It assists in separating these two distinct forms of conduct that carry vastly different sentences and particular labels to which different stigmas attach.

The courts have emphasized that charging and jury directions should be kept simple where these issues arise.[90] It is often a sensible course for alternative counts of theft and handling to be left to the jury.

The duration of stealing

One crucial issue is identifying when the stealing stops and the handling begins. The duration of 'the course of the stealing' depends on the extent to which appropriation is a continuing act.[91] Following *Gomez*, and the extension of the concept of appropriation, rendering what were previously mere preparatory acts to completed thefts, the issue has become even more complex. As has been observed, one case involving handling, *Pitham and Hehl*,[92] suggested that appropriation is an instantaneous act, concluded at the moment the goods are stolen. If this were right, the words 'in the course of the stealing' would be rendered nugatory. It is submitted that, in the light of *Hale*[93] and *Atakpu*,[94] cases concerned with robbery and theft respectively, *Pitham* must be wrongly decided in this respect.

Atakpu adopts the transaction test – was D still 'on the job'? Although pragmatic, this does not, of course, solve all the problems. A thief is likely to be held to be on the job while he is in a building that he has entered for the purpose of stealing and from which he intends to remove the stolen goods. But is he still in the course of theft as he walks down the garden path with the goods? as he drives home? and as he shows them to his wife at home? Griew[95] suggests that the scope of theft is determined by looking at the 'the total process of the effective appropriation, including the getaway,' but it is doubtful that this is any improvement on the test of the thief being 'on the job'.

It does not necessarily follow that the theft is still in the course of commission because the stolen property has not yet been removed from the premises on which it was stolen. If D and T agree to steal from their employer V and in pursuance of the plan D steals goods which he places in T's locker so that T may remove them from the premises, T is a thief and not a handler even though some time elapses between D's appropriation of the goods and T's removal of them. It is one enterprise for the theft of V's goods. If, however, D steals V's goods and secretes them on the premises, a *subsequent* arrangement with T for

[90] See *Bosson* [1999] Crim LR 596.

[91] Above, p 664. See also G. Williams, 'Appropriation: a single or continuous act'? [1978] Crim LR 69.

[92] (1976) 65 Cr App R 45, above, p 837.

[93] (1978) 68 Cr App R 415, above, p 713. The offence of robbery under s 8 requires theft 'at the time of' whereas s 22 focuses on 'the course of'.

[94] [1994] QB 69, above, p 664.

[95] Paras 15–46

T to remove them from the premises constitutes T being a handler.[96] T is not a party to the original theft.

Proof of handling or theft

It has been held that in an ordinary case, the words, 'otherwise than in the course of the stealing', have little importance and the jury should not even be told about them. But where the evidence is such that a reasonable jury might think it reasonably possible that the alleged handler was a participant in the theft, they should surely be told that, if this was so, he was not guilty of handling – because that is the law. However, in *Cash*,[97] it was held that the words 'otherwise than in the course of stealing' do not constitute an element in the offence that has to be proved in order to establish a *prima facie* case of handling. In *Cash*, stolen goods were found in D's possession on 25 February. The property was stolen (by a burglar) not later than 16 February. It was held that it was not open to the jury to infer that D was the burglar rather than a receiver. Perhaps the evidence was insufficient to satisfy the jury beyond reasonable doubt that D was the burglar but may they not, given the opportunity, have thought that it was reasonably possible, if not probable, that he was the burglar? Is it unheard of for burglars to retain possession of the stolen property for nine days? In *Greaves*,[98] it was held that the judge had properly left it open to the jury to convict of burglary where the time lapse was 17 days. In the recent case of *Wells*[99], it was held that *Cash* applies in any case in which there is no evidence to be left to the jury suggesting that D was a burglar/thief. *Cash* was described as a decision which makes 'entirely good sense'.[100]

There are at least four possible scenarios for D's recent possession in these cases – (i) that he is the thief, (ii) that he took part in the theft and received the goods in the course of it, (iii) that he was implicated in the theft and only received his proceeds later, (iv) that he was not involved in the theft and received the stolen goods at a later date.[101] If all that can be proved by the prosecution beyond a reasonable doubt, is that D was in possession with a dishonest state of mind, how can handling be satisfactorily established?

(vii) For the benefit of another person

Each of the nouns, 'retention', 'removal', 'disposal' and 'realization' is governed by the words 'by or for the benefit of another person'.[102] It must therefore be proved that:

[96] Cf *Atwell and O'Donnell* (1801) 2 East PC 768. D1 and D2 bent on stealing some of their employer's property moved it nearer the warehouse door during the course of the morning. Later that day E1 and E2 arranged to buy the goods from them and all returned later that evening to take away the goods from the warehouse. It was held that E1 and E2 were thieves and not receivers; the theft was a continuing transaction as to those (E1 and E2) who joined the plot before the goods were finally removed from the warehouse. Assuming this case was correctly decided under the former law of larceny, it is arguable that if these facts were to recur that E1 and E2 are handlers and not thieves. The theft (the appropriation) may have been complete before E1 and E2 became aware of it.

[97] [1985] QB 801, [1985] Crim LR 311 and commentary.

[98] (1987) The Times, 11 July, discussed in *Archbold* (2005), para 21–127. *Cash* was also distinguished in *Bruce* [1988] VR 579. Failure to add alternative theft counts can be fatal to the indictment *Suter* [1997] CLY 1339 (Judge Bull Guildford CC).

[99] [2004] EWCA Crim 79.

[100] Para 1.

[101] See M. Hirst, 'Guilty but of what' (2000) 4 E & P 31.

[102] *Sloggett* [1971] 3 All ER 264 at 267.

(a) D undertook or arranged the retention, removal, disposal or realization *for the benefit of another person*; or

(b) D assisted or arranged the retention, removal, disposal or realization *by another person*.[103]

There can hardly ever have been a thief who did not retain, remove, dispose of or realize the stolen goods, so this requirement of conduct being 'for the benefit of another' prevents all thieves from being handlers as well. The italicized words are an essential part of the offence and the indictment must allege that the handling was 'by or for the benefit of another person'.[104] The thief may himself be guilty of handling (by undertaking) if he himself retains, removes, etc the goods for the benefit of another person. It would seem to be immaterial that the other person is guilty of no offence and even unaware of what is going on.

In *Bloxham*[105] it was held that a purchaser, as such, of stolen goods is not 'another person' within the meaning of the section. Thus, where D sells stolen goods to E, D's act is not for the benefit of the buyer, E, it is for D's own benefit. Sellers usually sell for their own benefit, not the benefit of the purchaser; that much is uncontroversial. However, even if the sale could be described as for the purchaser's benefit, it would not, in the opinion of Lord Bridge, be within the ambit of the section. This gives a special meaning to the term 'another person', the limits of which are not clear. Griew lucidly summarizes the interpretation – something will be for the benefit of another when it is 'an act done on behalf of another person; it is an act that the other might do himself'.[106]

In *Bloxham*, D, acting in good faith, purchased a stolen car for £1,300. Eleven months later, suspecting the truth, he sold it for £200 to a person unknown who was prepared to buy it without documents. D was charged with handling by undertaking or assisting in the realisation of the car for the benefit of the buyer. A submission of no case to answer was rejected, whereupon he pleaded guilty. His conviction was upheld by the Court of Appeal who thought that the buyer's use of the car, for which he had paid less than its true value, was a benefit to him. Maybe it was; but it seems a travesty to say that the sale was for his benefit. The House of Lords quashed the conviction. The buyer was not 'another person'. In fact, of course, he was 'another person'; but the sale was certainly not effected 'on his behalf'.

Bloxham was distinguished in *Tokeley-Parry*[107] where D was charged with undertaking or assisting in removal by E, whom he had procured to smuggle stolen antiquities from Egypt. An argument that D and E were one person was firmly rejected. E was 'another person' in fact and in law. Further, *Roberts*[108] decides that, if A and B are jointly charged in

103 Cf L. Blake, 'The Innocent Purchaser and Section 22 of the Theft Act' [1972] Crim LR 494, arguing that there is no need that the third party benefits if he retains, removes, realizes or disposes.

104 *Sloggett* [1972] 1 QB 430, [1971] 3 All ER 264.

105 Above, p 851.

106 Paras 15–22. See also Spencer's suggestion '... the requirement that the act be "for the benefit of another" serves no intelligible purpose unless it limits the offence to those who act on another's behalf': 'The Mishandling of Handling' [1981] Crim LR 682 at 685, commenting on the Court of Appeal decision in *Bloxham*.

107 [1999] Crim LR 578. It is questionable how this was for the benefit of anyone other than D.

108 No 93/0075/Z2 (9 July 1993, unreported), see [1996] Crim LR 495 and see *Gingell* [2000] 1 Cr App R 88.

one count with an act of handling 'by or for the benefit of another,' the other must be some person other than A or B. This seems logical if, indeed, only one act, jointly done by A and B, is alleged.[109] A might, however, arrange the disposition of the goods *by* B; and B might undertake the disposition *for the benefit of* A. In that case both have committed an offence under s 22 and there is no need to show that any third person was involved.

Conspiracy to handle

As s 22 creates only one offence (according to Lord Bridge in *Bloxham*) an indictment for conspiracy to handle contrary to s 22, without particularizing the form of handling, is good: it is not an allegation of conspiracy to commit crime X *or* crime Y.

Notwithstanding *Roberts*, an agreement by A and B that B would, for example, dispose of the goods for the benefit of A is a conspiracy to handle. A and B have agreed that B will commit the offence of handling, and that is enough. If B does dispose of the goods as agreed, he commits the offence under s 22; and, obviously A has counselled or procured him to do so. They are both guilty of the same offence. There seems to be every reason, pace the court in *Roberts*, why A and B should be jointly charged with committing it.[110]

(viii) Innocent receipt and subsequent retention with *mens rea*

If D receives the stolen goods innocently, either, that is, believing them not to be stolen or knowing them to be stolen but intending to return them to the true owner, of course, he commits no offence.[111] Suppose he subsequently discovers the goods to be stolen or decides not to return them to the true owner or disposes of them. He has dishonestly undertaken the retention of, or has disposed of stolen goods knowing them to be stolen. Whether he is guilty of an offence depends on a number of factors.

(1) Where D does not get ownership of the goods (the normal situation where goods are the product of theft):

- (i) D gives value for the goods.
  - (a) D retains or disposes of the goods for his own benefit. This is not theft because of s 3(2);[112] nor is it handling by undertaking, assisting or arranging since it is not for the benefit of another.[113] D might be guilty of handling by aiding and abetting the receiving by the person to whom he disposes of the goods, if that person has *mens rea*.
  - (b) D retains or disposes of the goods for the benefit of another. This is not theft (s 3(2)) but is handling.
- (ii) D does not give value.
  - (a) D retains or disposes of the goods for his own benefit. This is theft but not handling unless it amounts to aiding and abetting receipt by another.
  - (b) D retains or disposes of the goods for the benefit of another. This is theft and handling.

[109] Although why this should only apply if they are jointly charged is less logical, see R. Harrison, 'Handling Stolen Goods for the Benefit of Another' (2000) 64 J Crim L 156.

[110] See *Slater and Suddens* [1996] Crim LR 300.

[111] *Alt* [1972] Crim LR 552, CA.

[112] Above, p 665.

[113] *Bloxham* [1983] 1 AC 109, [1982] 1 All ER 582, HL.

(2) Where D gets ownership of the goods (because the rogue obtained them by deception and acquired a voidable title or because of some exception to the *nemo dat* rule):

(i) D gives value for the goods.

Retention or disposal of the goods cannot be theft since V has no property in the goods. It is not handling since V has lost his right to restitution,[114] his right to rescind being destroyed on the goods coming into the hands of D who was a bona fide purchaser for value.

(ii) D does not give value. Again this cannot be theft, since V has no property in the goods, but it may be handling since V's right to rescind and secure restitution of his property is not extinguished by the goods coming into the hands of one who does not give value. It will be handling if this is so *and* D either aids and abets a guilty receipt by another or disposes of the goods for the benefit of another.

(ix) Handling by the thief[115]

The common law rules regulating the liability of a thief to a charge of receiving goods feloniously stolen by him were complicated. The present position appears to be that any thief may be convicted of handling goods stolen by him by receiving them – if the evidence warrants this conclusion.[116] In the majority of cases the thief can only be guilty of handling by receiving where he is assisting or encouraging the receipt by another because he is already in possession or control and therefore cannot receive as the principal offender. In some circumstances, however, a thief might be convicted of handling the stolen goods by receiving them as the principal offender. For example, D steals goods and, in the course of the theft, delivers them to E. Two days later E returns the goods to D.

(b) *Mens rea*

D's *mens rea* as described below must coincide in time with the relevant conduct constituting the *actus reus* of the offence. In the case of receiving, this is when D first receives the goods or makes the arrangement to receive,[117] and in the case of other forms of handling, since they may be continuing in nature, it is sufficient that the *mens rea* exists at some point in that continuum, for example, where D has taken possession innocently, but has subsequently become aware of the provenance of the goods and then acts for the benefit of another.[118]

(i) Knowledge or belief[119]

It must be proved that the goods were stolen and that D handled them 'knowing or believing them to be stolen goods'. It is of course vital that the belief or knowledge is D's,

[114] Above, p 840. [115] A. T. H. Smith, 'Theft and/or Handling' [1977] Crim LR 517.

[116] *Dolan* (1975) 62 Cr App R 36, CA; *Stapylton v O'Callaghan* [1973] 2 All ER 782, DC.

[117] *Alt* (1972) 56 Cr App R 45. [118] See V. Tunkel (1983) 133 NLJ 844.

[119] See in particular E. Griew, 'Consistency, Communication and Codification – Reflections on Two *Mens Rea* Words', in P. Glazebrook (ed), *Reshaping the Criminal Law* (1978), 57; S. Shute, 'Knowledge and Belief in the Criminal Law', in S. Shute and A. Simester (eds), *Criminal Law Theory: Doctrines of the General Part* (2002), 171; G. Sullivan, 'Knowledge, Belief and Culpability' ibid, 207; A. R. White, *Misleading Cases* (1991) 133.

not merely that of the reasonable man since this is a subjective *mens rea* requirement.[120] The Criminal Law Revision Committee thought that the provision would extend the law:

It is a serious defect of the present law that actual knowledge that the property was stolen must be proved. Often the prosecution cannot prove this. In many cases indeed guilty knowledge does not exist, although the circumstances of the transaction are such that the receiver ought to be guilty of an offence. The man who buys goods at a ridiculously low price from an unknown seller whom he meets in a public house may not *know* that the goods were stolen, and he may take the precaution of asking no questions. Yet it may be clear on the evidence that he believes that the goods were stolen. In such cases the prosecution may fail (rightly, as the law now stands) for want of proof of guilty knowledge.[121]

It seems clear that they intended to include the concept of 'wilful blindness', which is often held by the courts to be included in the word 'knowing' standing alone.[122] But, if this was their intention, it has not been achieved. Wilful blindness postulates that D has a strong suspicion that something is so and consciously decides not to take steps that he could take to confirm or deny that fact. But the courts have repeatedly said that, for the purposes of s 22, suspicion, however strong, is not to be equated with belief.[123] It is a misdirection to tell the jury that it is enough that D, 'suspecting that the goods were stolen deliberately shut his eyes to the consequences'.[124] What, if anything, then, does 'believing' add to 'knowing'? According to *Hall*:[125]

A man may be said to know that goods are stolen when he is told by someone with first-hand knowledge (someone such as the thief or the burglar) that such is the case. Belief, of course, is something short of knowledge. It may be said to be the state of mind of a person who says to himself: 'I cannot say I know for certain that these goods are stolen but there can be no other reasonable conclusion in the light of all the circumstances, in the light of all that I have heard and seen'.

This seems to be merely a distinction between two *sources* of D's state of mind. But s 22 suggests a distinction between two states of mind, not two modes of arriving at the same state of mind. The case suggests that if D had direct evidence, he knows; if he has mere circumstantial evidence, he believes, but, it would surely be more accurate to describe knowledge in terms of the accuracy of the belief, not the directness of the evidence leading to the belief? As Shute has recently suggested, the distinctions between the two concepts are twofold: knowledge constitutes a true belief, and belief includes acceptance of the proposition in question whereas knowledge does not.[126] In *Forsyth*[127] the court said that the judgment in *Hall* is 'potentially confusing'. In *Moys*[128] the court suggested

120 *Bellenie* [1980] Crim LR 43; *Brook* [1993] Crim LR 455.

121 Cmnd 2977, 64. Cf *Woods* [1969] 1 QB 447, [1968] 3 All ER 709, CA. See also G. Williams, 'Handling, Theft and the Purchaser who takes a chance' [1985] Crim LR 432.

122 Above, p 146.

123 *Forsyth* [1997] Crim LR, CA; *Grainge* [1974] 1 All ER 928, CA. Cf *Woods* [1969] 1 QB 447, [1968] 3 All ER 709, CCA; *Ismail* [1977] Crim LR 557 and commentary. Cf Griew, *Theft*, paras 15.30–15.33; Spencer [1985] Crim LR 101. See Shute, above, 192.

124 *Griffiths* (1974) 60 Cr App R 14, CA. *Atwal v Massey* [1971] 3 All ER 881, DC, is definitely misleading on this point and seems to have misled the judge in *Pethick* [1980] Crim LR 242, where it was said that suspicion, 'however strong', does not amount to knowledge.

125 (1985) 81 Cr App R 260 at 264, [1985] Crim LR 377.

126 P 194.

127 Above, p 843. A *Hall* direction is not necessary in every case – *Toor* (1987) 85 Cr App R 116.

128 (1984) 79 Cr App R 72, CA.

simply that the question whether D knew or believed that the goods were stolen is a subjective one and that suspicion, even coupled with the fact that D shut his eyes to the circumstances, is not enough.

In practical terms, D may be left in varying degrees of certainty as to the provenance of the goods whether or not he has been told by the thief, or deduced the fact from his own observation. What matters is that D is caused to be certain that the goods are stolen, there is no significance for these purposes in the source of information.

Although what seems to be implied in *Hall* is that the person with direct information is certain and the person with circumstantial evidence is nearly certain, it would be dangerous in such terms to direct a jury because 'near certainty' is strong suspicion and that is not enough. It is unclear whether it is sufficient that D considers the likelihood that the goods are stolen to be 'virtually certain'; presumably not. It is clearly not enough for D to believe that the goods are 'probably' stolen.[129]

In general, it seems that a judge cannot go wrong by simply directing the jury in accordance with the words of the section and offering no elaboration or explanation of 'believing'.[130] Of course, it may be that the jury will then apply the word as if it included wilful blindness, but no one will ever know. This is another example of the judicial interpretation of definitional elements of crimes which is unsatisfactory but which remain uncorrected because the cloak of jury secrecy avoids the true shortcomings of the interpretation being exposed.

Some have called for a further extension of the offence to include reckless handling.[131] There are of course competing policy arguments: on the one hand there is the need not to stifle trade of honest dealers and on the other the recognition that in most cases dishonest defendants could escape liability by not confirming mere suspicions. In view of the increasing incidence of low level handling by individuals dealing through 'car boot sales' such arguments have persuasive force, and would become compelling if the offence was subdivided to distinguish that activity from professional fencing.

Knowledge of what?

It is sufficient that D knows or believes that the goods, whatever they are, are stolen. His knowledge or belief need not extend to the identity of the thief, or the owner,[132] or the nature of the stolen goods.[133] If D knows he is in possession of a box containing stolen goods, it is no defence that he does not know what the contents are and is shocked to discover that the box contains guns; nor would it be a defence that he believed the box contained stolen watches. Equally, it is enough for D to know or believe that the goods are stolen in the extended meaning that term has under s 34. Thus, it does not matter that D believed the goods to be the product of blackmail when they were in fact the product of a

[129] *Reader* (1977) 66 Cr App R 33, 36 CA. For consideration of whether this ought to be a sufficient *mens rea* see J. Spencer, 'Handling, Theft and the Mala Fide Purchaser' [1985] Crim LR 92 at 95–96; G. Williams, 'Handling, Theft and the Purchaser who takes a chance' [1985] Crim LR 432 at 435; J. Spencer, 'Handling and Taking Risks: A Reply to Professor Williams' [1985] Crim LR 440.

[130] *Reader* (1977) 66 Cr App R 33; *Harris* (1986) 84 Cr App R 75; *Toor* (1986) 85 Cr App R 116, [1987] Crim LR 122, CA.

[131] See J. Spencer [1985] Crim LR 92.

[132] *Fuschillo* [1940] 2 All ER 489; but it may be necessary to name the owner where the property is of a common and indistinctive type: *Gregory* [1972] 2 All ER 861. See recently *Webster* [2002] EWCA Crim 1346.

[133] *McCullum* (1973) 57 Cr App R 645.

theft. As elsewhere, it is not necessary for D to know the criminal law: it is sufficient that D has knowledge or belief as to the facts and conduct of the thief that renders it criminal.

(ii) Dishonesty

Dishonesty was an essential ingredient of the old crime of receiving though it was not expressed in the statute. The inclusion of the word 'dishonestly'[134] thus made no change in the law. D may receive goods knowing or believing them to be stolen and yet not be guilty if, for example, he intends to return them to the true owner or the police.[135] A claim of right will amount to a defence, but it will be difficult to establish such a claim where D knows or believes the goods to be stolen except in the case put above, where he intends to return the goods to the owner.

(iii) Proof of *mens rea*

The general principles of evidence in criminal cases apply to the proof of offences of theft and handling as they apply to other crimes. This is not the place to examine those rules but their application to these offences has created special problems and an exposition of the substantive law that did not examine these matters would be incomplete.

The 'doctrine of recent possession'

Where D is found in possession of, or dealing with, property which has recently been stolen, a jury properly may infer that he is guilty of an offence if he offers no explanation or if they are satisfied beyond reasonable doubt that any explanation he has offered is untrue. They are not bound so to infer and must not do so unless they are sure that D was in fact guilty of the particular offence. The onus of proof remains on the Crown throughout. Whether D offers an explanation or not, the jury must not convict unless they are sure that he committed the offence in question.[136]

These principles are frequently misleadingly referred to as 'the doctrine of recent possession'. The 'doctrine' is nothing more than the application to this constantly recurring situation of the ordinary principles of circumstantial evidence. Sometimes the correct inference will be that D was the thief (or robber or burglar if the goods were stolen in the course of a robbery or burglary), sometimes that he was a handler. If the lead is stolen off the church roof at midnight and D is found dragging it across a field at 1 am, this is very cogent evidence that he stole the lead from the roof. If it is found in his backyard next day and he offers no explanation,[137] or an explanation which is shown to be untrue, as to how he came by it, this is slightly less cogent evidence that he was the thief but very persuasive that he either stole it or received it knowing it to be stolen.

As the time lengthens between the theft and discovery of D's connection with the stolen property, the weight of the evidence diminishes but it will vary according to

134 Cf *Ghosh* [1982] QB 1053, [1982] 2 All ER 689, CA; above, p 698.

135 Cf *Matthews* [1950] 1 All ER 137, CCA.

136 *Abramovitch* (1914) 11 Cr App R 45; *Aves* (1950) 34 Cr App R 159; *Hepworth* [1955] 2 QB 600.

137 Note that inferences at trial might be drawn under ss 34–38 of the Criminal Justice and Public Order Act 1994 for the failure. See generally, C. Tapper, *Cross and Tapper on Evidence* (10th edn, 2004). The court must be careful not to apply the inference in such a way as to reverse the burden of proof: *Camara v DPP* (2003) All ER (D) 264 (Oct).

the nature of the property stolen and other circumstances.[138] One relevant circumstance will be the nature of D's conduct in relation to the goods, but the same principles apply whether D is charged with receiving or with one of the other forms of handling. So in *Ball*,[139] it was held that there was evidence of handling otherwise than by receiving where D assisted the thief in physically handling stolen goods and accompanying him on an expedition to sell the stolen property.

The difficulty which arises is that a jury may be quite certain that D was either the thief or a receiver but not satisfied beyond reasonable doubt that he was the one rather than the other. Indeed, it may be that there is no evidence on which they could possibly be satisfied that he was the one rather than the other. In that case, it appears that neither offence is proved, and the only proper course is a complete acquittal – a conclusion satisfactory to no one but the accused. A solution which has been adopted in some jurisdictions, following *Langmead*,[140] is to direct the jury that, if they are satisfied beyond reasonable doubt that D was *either* the thief *or* a receiver, they may convict of the offence which they think more probable – that is it is enough that they are satisfied on a balance of probabilities that D was the thief, or that he was the receiver. As the jury is unlikely to find that the evidence is exactly evenly balanced, this is a practical solution, and one that should be Article 6(2) compliant.[141] It was, however, rejected by the Privy Council in *Attorney-General of Hong Kong v Yip Kai-foon*.[142] D was charged with robbery and with handling the goods stolen. The Privy Council held that the jury had been rightly directed to consider the robbery charge first. Once they had decided that they were not sure that D was guilty of robbery, he was to be presumed to be innocent of the theft of the goods and it followed that any handling that occurred took place 'otherwise then in the course of the stealing' so there was no need for more than a passing reference to those words. This is a novel use of the presumption of innocence against a defendant. Because the jury are not satisfied beyond reasonable doubt that D was guilty of theft it is apparently to be conclusively presumed that he was not guilty of that offence. If the jury are satisfied that he was guilty of one offence or the other, it follows inevitably that he was guilty of handling. But this is arbitrary. The outcome depends on which offence the jury consider first, and it becomes critical for the jury to be directed carefully as to the order in which they approach the verdicts.[143] More fundamental objections are that the approach treats the acquittal as proof of innocence and may offend Article 6(2) of the ECHR.[144]

Because of the difficulty of proving guilty knowledge, the Larceny Act provided for the admission of certain evidence on a receiving charge that would not be admissible in criminal cases generally. The Theft Act has corresponding provisions. By s 27(3):

> Where a person is being proceeded against for handling stolen goods (but not for any offence other than handling stolen goods),[145] then at any stage of the proceedings, if evidence has been

[138] See eg *Mason* [1981] QB 881 – antique wine coasters in D's possession five months after theft.

[139] (1983) 77 Cr App R 131, [1983] Crim LR 546.

[140] (1864) Le & Ca 427.

[141] If the approach was applied more widely it would pose problems particularly where more than two alternatives are left, leading to possible conviction of an offence of which the jury are not even sure D is probably guilty. See further Hirst, above.

[142] [1988] AC 642, [1988] 1 All ER 153, followed in *Foreman* [1991] Crim LR 702; but see commentary at 704.

[143] *Fernandez* [1997] 1 Cr App R 123.

[144] See M. Hirst, 'Guilty but of what' (2000) 4 E & P 31.

[145] Cf *Anderson* [1978] Crim LR 223 (Judge Stroyan).

given of his having or arranging to have in his possession the goods the subject of the charge, or of his undertaking or assisting in, or arranging to undertake or assist in, their retention, removal, disposal or realisation, the following evidence shall be admissible for the purpose of proving that he knew or believed the goods to be stolen goods:

(a) evidence that he has had in his possession, or has undertaken or assisted in the retention, removal, disposal or realisation of, stolen goods from any theft taking place not more than twelve months before the offence charged;[146] and

(b) (provided that seven days' notice in writing has been given to him of the intention to prove the conviction) evidence that he has within the five years preceding the date of the offence charged been convicted of theft or of handling stolen goods.[147]

The provisions have the potential to operate unjustly by allowing the police repeatedly to round up the 'usual suspects' and for the jury to reason from prejudice to guilt. The careful exercise of the trial judge's discretion in the use of the section is critical, as is the judicial obligation to warn the jury of the uses to which the evidence might legitimately be put. The Law Commission has called for their abolition.[148]

2. Dishonestly retaining a wrongful credit

Section 24A of the Theft Act 1968 (inserted by s 2 of the Theft (Amendment) Act 1996) provides:

(1) A person is guilty of an offence if –

(a) a wrongful credit has been made to an account kept by him or in respect of which he has any right or interest;

(b) he knows or believes that the credit is wrongful; and

(c) he dishonestly fails to take such steps as are reasonable in the circumstances to secure that the credit is cancelled.

(2) References to a credit are to a credit of an amount of money.

(3) A credit to an account is wrongful if it is the credit side of a money transfer obtained contrary to section 15A of this Act.

The offence is punishable under s 24A on indictment with imprisonment for 10 years.

The effect is that D1, a person who has committed an offence under the new s 15A,[149] commits a second offence if he does not take steps within a reasonable time to divest himself of his ill-gotten gains. Section 24A is not, of course, aimed at him but at D2, where D1 has procured the crediting, not of his own account, but of D2's account. If this were done with D2's connivance, D2 would be guilty as a secondary party to D1's offence under s 15A. There would be no need to invoke s 24A.

146 There is no requirement for D to have been convicted on this earlier occasion. As to what detail may be admitted see *Bradley* (1979) 70 Cr App R 200, [1980] Crim LR 173, CA, and commentary.

147 These provisions have attracted both judicial and academic criticism: see *Hacker* [1995] 1 Cr App R 332, HL, overruling *Fowler* (1987) 86 Cr App R 219, [1987] Crim LR 769, CA; R. Munday, 'Handling the Evidential Exception' [1988] Crim LR 345; I. Dennis, *The Law of Evidence* (2nd edn, 2002) 649.

148 See Law Commission *Evidence of Bad Character in Criminal Proceedings* (2001) Cm 5257, paras 4.13–4.23, 11.53–11.55. On the prejudice see generally S. Lloyd-Bostock, 'The effects on juries of hearing about the defendant's previous criminal record: A simulation study' [2000] Crim LR 734.

149 Above, p 764.

Suppose, however, that the credit was made without D2's connivance. One day D2 finds that an unexpected credit has been made to his account. As soon as he knows or believes that the credit has been made in such circumstances as amount to an offence under s 15A he comes under a duty to divest himself of this unforeseen windfall. D2 need not know that the transfer is an offence; his ignorance of the existence of s 15A is no defence. That is ignorance of the criminal law. He must only know, or believe in the existence of the material facts. If D2 then fails to secure the cancellation of the credit within a reasonable time he commits the offence under s 24A. It is an offence of omission,[150] rather like theft where s 5(4) applies. Whereas, however, s 5(4) requires D to intend to 'make restoration' of the property, s 24A(1)(c) merely requires him to cancel the credit. If he withdraws the money to spend for his own benefit, he cancels the credit and might escape liability under s 24A – if the draftsman meant 'make restoration' he should have said so – but, by s 24A(8), the money withdrawn is stolen goods so he will be guilty of receiving stolen goods.

The Act does not stop there. It extends to other conduct which was not an offence even before the decision of the House of Lords in *Preddy*. Section 24A(4) provides:

(4) A credit to an account is also wrongful to the extent that it derives from –

(a) theft;

(b) an offence under section 15A of this Act;

(c) blackmail; or

(d) stolen goods.

So D2 may be guilty of the offence if:

(i) D1 steals money and pays it into D2's account;

(ii) D1 procures a wrongful credit to his own account and then transfers funds from it to D2's account;

(iii) D1 obtains money by blackmail and pays that money into D2's account;

(iv) D1 receives stolen money and pays it into D2's account.

In each of these cases the credit in D2's account is a new item of property – a thing in action belonging to D2 – which has never been 'in the hands' of a thief or handler and so is not 'stolen goods' within s 24(2). D2 is not guilty of handling by retaining it. Now, however, he commits an offence under s 24A(1) if he dishonestly fails to cancel 'the wrongful credit' within a reasonable time. Presumably he can do so and escape liability under s 24A by immediately withdrawing the money. But s 24A(8) provides that any money that is withdrawn from a wrongful credit will be stolen goods and subject to the general law of handling so D2 may commit an offence under s 22.

An incidental effect is that the thief, blackmailer or handler who pays the proceeds of his offence into his own account commits another offence when he fails to take reasonable steps to cancel the credit. This is so because the Law Commission thought 'It would be difficult, if not impossible, to devise a simple way of excluding the case where A dishonestly secures a credit to his own account, while including the case where A

150 The argument of the Law Commission that this is necessary is in Law Com No 243 at 39.

dishonestly secures a credit to B's.'[151] The Commission comforted themselves with the consideration that there was already an enormous degree of overlap in the existing offences under the Theft Acts.

Section 24A(5) provides that it is immaterial whether an account is overdrawn before or after a credit is made. So if D2's account is overdrawn to the tune of £100 when a wrongful credit of £50 arrives, he is under a duty, somehow, to get his overdraft restored to its former level!

There is no provision corresponding to s 24(3)[152] (stolen goods cease to be 'stolen' when they are restored to lawful custody or when the owner and any others claiming through him have ceased to have any right to restitution of the goods). Nor is there any exemption for the bona-fide purchaser such as is to be found in s 3(2).[153] Suppose that D sells his car in good faith to A who pays him with stolen money. After learning that the money was stolen D spends it. He did not commit any offence before the enactment of s 24A. He still commits no offence if A paid him in cash and he spends the cash. But if D paid the cash into his own bank account, or if he was paid by a cheque which he has paid into that account, he has received a wrongful credit and it appears that he will (subject to proof of dishonesty) commit an offence under s 24A when he spends the money, because he has failed to take reasonable steps to disgorge. That would create not only an unsatisfactory anomaly but also a conflict with the civil law. A transferee of stolen currency for value and without notice gets a good title: *Miller v Race.*[154] The money, whether in cash or in the bank, is surely his to dispose of as he chooses? How then can he be guilty of a crime by doing so? It may be that a court will think it necessary to read into s 24A(1)(c) some such qualification as 'except where no person has any right to restitution of the credit,' on the ground that Parliament could not have intended to change, or create a conflict with, such a fundamental rule of the civil law. This would introduce a limitation to the same effect as that relating to stolen goods generally in s 24(4).

3. Advertising for the return of stolen goods

The existence of this offence might come as a surprise given the number of such advertisements that are commonly seen.[155] By s 23 of the Theft Act 1968 it is an offence publicly to advertise for the return of stolen goods indicating that no questions will be asked about how the person returning the goods came by them. The antecedents of this offence go back to 1828[156] and it was retained, after some hesitation on the part of the CLRC, because it was thought that advertisements of this kind might encourage dishonesty.[157] Though such advertisements may encourage dishonesty in other people, dishonesty is not required of the perpetrator. It operates harshly in preventing the advertiser offering to pay the (innocent) *bona fide* purchaser of the advertiser's stolen goods.

151 Law Com No 243, paras 6.16–6.17. 152 Above, p 841. 153 Above, p 665.

154 (1758) 1 Burr 452. See D. Fox, 'Bona Fide Purchase and the Currency of Money' [1996] 55 CLJ 547.

155 Eg 'Laptop stolen from library before exams no questions asked but please place the data on a disc and return to . . .'.

156 See Hall, above, pp 70–76 on its history. See also Smith, *Property Offences*, ch 31B.

157 *Eighth Report*, para 144.

Indeed the offence has been held to be one of strict liability so that the advertising manager of a newspaper in which such an advertisement appeared committed the offence though he was unaware that it had appeared in the paper.[158] In light of the House of Lords' recent stance against interpreting provisions as imposing strict liability, the authority should be treated with caution,[159] although when analysing the offence, Goff LJ in *Denham* regarded the section as creating a 'quasi criminal' offence.

4. Money laundering[160]

In a series of pieces of complex legislation over the last two decades the government has sought to combat serious crime by targeting not just the offenders, but those who assist in the disposal of criminal proceeds. The legislative response to serious and organized crime has involved not only criminal offences but a raft of measures providing for confiscation, assets recovery, civil recovery, and restraint proceedings. In some respects the offences of money laundering share a similar rationale to handling: to target those who render criminal activity profitable rather than the person committing the substantive crime himself. However, the money laundering offences are concerned not just with stolen goods but with criminal proceeds more generally. The legislation has been driven by the international treaty obligations, and these are frequently relied upon by the courts as an aid to interpretation.[161]

The offences under the Criminal Justice Act 1993 and the Drug Trafficking Act 1988 provided a series of offences which criminalized entering into or being concerned in an arrangement involving the retention, acquisition, use possession, etc of criminal proceeds or the proceeds of drug crime.[162] This strict division between laundering 'drug' money and 'other criminal proceeds' created significant practical problems, as when D claimed that he thought that he was involved in something suspicious but was not sure what. Unless the Crown could establish that he knew or suspected it was drug money *or* that he suspected it was proceeds of non-drug crime he would be acquitted. This led to complex indictments alleging that D laundered either drug and/or other property. Even greater complexity arose in prosecutions for conspiracies of these offences.[163] The Proceeds of Crime Act 2002 (POCA) remedies some of these problems but creates offences of a no less draconian nature, often requiring *mens rea* of no more than suspicion or even objective tests of fault. The Act also creates far reaching offences of failing to report[164] (to

158 *Withers* [1975] Crim LR 647; *Denham v Scott* (1983) 77 Cr App R 210 DC.

159 See *DPP v B* [2000] 2 AC 428; *R v K* [2001] AC. See above, p 122.

160 See generally, A. Mitchell, S. Taylor and K. Talbot, *On Confiscation and the Proceeds of Crime* (2002) ch 9; Archbold, *Crown Court* (2005), ch 33; *Blackstone's Criminal Practice* (2005), B.22; and for a more theoretical account see P. Alldridge, *Money Laundering Law* (2003), ch 9.

161 See *M* [2005] Crim LR 479, [2004] UKHL 53.

162 For an excellent review of some of the problems under the old law see J. Fisher and J. Bewsey, 'Laundering the Proceeds of Fiscal Crime' (2000) JIBL 11.

163 See *El Kurd* [2001] Crim LR 234; *Hussain* [2002] Crim LR 407.

164 Sections 330–332.

NCIS)[165] money laundering, and of 'tipping off'[166] individuals that investigations are pending or under way. The net of deterrence from involvement in suspicious financial activity is thereby spread even wider. The legislation is extremely technical and cannot be dealt with in a work of this nature. This section offers only a brief overview of three offences.

(a) The Proceeds of Crime Act 2002[167]

Part 7 of the Act introduces three sections which create at least nine offences replacing the separate categories of offence relating to drug and non-drug crime.

(i) Criminal property

The offences in POCA relate to dealings with 'criminal property'. Section 340 is therefore central to their operation. Section 340(3) provides that:

> . . . property is criminal property if (a) it constitutes a person's benefit from criminal conduct or it represents such a benefit (in whole or part and whether directly or indirectly), and (b) the alleged offender knows or suspects that it constitutes or represents such a benefit.

'Criminal conduct' includes the accused's own criminal conduct and conduct abroad that is not an offence under any UK law but which would be such an offence if committed somewhere in the UK. The offence are very broad and criminalize conduct involving not just money which is the product of criminality, but on dealing, acquiring etc any property related to the criminality. Clearly, there is considerable overlap with the offences of handling stolen goods and dishonestly retaining a wrongful credit.

(ii) Common elements

The *mens rea* requirements are astonishingly wide, being based on suspicion. In *Hussein v Chong Fook Kam*[168] suspicion in its ordinary meaning is a state of conjecture or surmise where proof is lacking. 'I suspect but I cannot prove'. Suspicion arises at or near the starting point of an investigation of which the obtaining of *prima facie* proof is the end.[169] There is no requirement to prove dishonesty. Such a low level of *mens rea* is remarkable for offences of such seriousness. The offences are triable either way, and punishable with up to 14 years' imprisonment.

There is a common defence to each of the offences where a person makes an authorized disclosure to the authorities under s 338 or was intending to do so and had a reasonable excuse for failing to do.

(iii) Section 327

Section 327 creates offences where D conceals, disguises, converts, transfers or removes criminal property from the UK. Subsection (3) defines concealing or disguising criminal property as including 'concealing or disguising its nature, source, location, disposition,

165 See the website www.ncis.co.uk/ukta/2003/threat06.asp. 166 Section 333.

167 See references in n 1 above and E. Rees and A. Hall, *Blackstone's Guide to the Proceeds of Crime Act 2002* (2003).

168 [1970] AC 942. 169 P 948.

movement or ownership or any rights with respect to it.' The broad scope of the offence is obvious. Read strictly, it appears that the section creates five different offences, and on that basis the indictment should specify which to avoid being bad for duplicity. This could create undue complexity, and it may be that the section is treated, as with handling, as creating a single offence that can be committed in one of a number of ways.[170]

(iv) Section 328

Section 328 creates only one offence of entering into or becoming concerned in an arrangement which he 'knows or suspects facilitates (by whatever means) the acquisition, retention, use or control of criminal property by or on behalf of another person.' It is has been held that this extraordinarily broad offence does not cover the ordinary conduct of litigation by professions.[171]

(v) Section 329

Section 329 creates three offences of acquisition, use and possession of criminal property.

Subsection 3 provides that for the purposes of this section –

(a) a person acquires property for inadequate consideration if the value of the consideration is significantly less than the value of the property;

(b) a person uses or has possession of property for inadequate consideration if the value of the consideration is significantly less than the value of the use or possession;

(c) the provision by a person of goods or services which he knows or suspects may help another to carry out criminal conduct is not consideration.

170 Cf *Griffiths v Freeman* [1970] 1 ALL ER 1117.
171 *Bowman v Fels* [2005] EWCA Civ 328.

23

Forgery[1]

Forgery and counterfeiting are now regulated by the Forgery and Counterfeiting Act 1981. This Act is largely based upon the recommendations of the Law Commission,[2] and forms part of the programme for the codification of the criminal law. Earlier legislation, in particular the Forgery Act 1913 and the Coinage Offences Act 1936, was repealed and the offence of forgery at common law was abolished. It follows that decisions under the former law are no longer binding though they may retain some persuasive authority and provide examples for discussion.

Counterfeiting is discussed in the sixth edition of this work, pp 669–676 but is omitted from later editions.

The forging of documents in itself rarely brings any advantage to the forger. The forgery is usually done as a preparatory step to the commission of some other crime, most often a crime involving deception, which will result in some material advantage (most obviously money or other property transferring) to the forger. Since preparatory acts, falling short of attempts, are not as such made criminal by the law, it has been cogently argued[3] that, with the exception of special cases such as banknotes and coins, there is no need for a separate offence of forgery. The Law Commission did not accept this view. In its view:

> There are a number of reasons for not accepting the soundness of this premise. In the many and varied activities of modern society it is necessary to rely to a large extent on the authenticity of documents as authority for the truth of the statements which they contain.[4]

[1] Smith, *Property Offences* (1994), ch 23, A. Arlidge and J. Parry, *Fraud* (2nd edn, 1996) ch 5.

[2] Law Com No 55, *Report on Forgery and Counterfeit Currency* (1973). See also Com Working Paper No 26, *Forgery* (1970).

[3] By E. J. Griew, 'The Law Commission's Working Paper on Forgery: A General Comment' [1970] Crim LR 548 and P. Glazebrook, 'The Law Commission's Working Paper on Forgery: Some Further Comments' [1970] Crim LR 554. Yet many statutes create offences of possessing even apparently innocuous articles with intent to commit crimes. There are proposals to create a new offence of possessing equipment with a dishonest intent to produce credit cards. See Home Office, *Fraud Law Reform: Consultation on Proposals* (2003), para 43. The Bill includes a new offence covering the possession (without lawful authority or reasonable excuse) of articles for use in connection with the commission or facilitation of fraud, for which the maximum penalty would be five years. The Bill will provide a maximum penalty of 10 years for the manufacture, sale or supply of articles made or adapted for use in frauds, and the possession of such articles with intent to commit fraud. See further www.homeoffice.gov.uk/docs3/fraud_law_reform.pdf.

[4] Law Com No 55, para 14. When introducing the Bill to the House of Lords (HL, vol 416, col 605) Viscount Colville declined to enter 'the philosophical . . . or jurisprudential discussions' about the need to have an offence of forgery. To him it was right that forgers 'who, after all, are a special form of criminal that we tend to recognize as such' should have legislation directed against them. The circularity of this reasoning was apparently lost on their lordships. Lord Elwyn-Jones favoured the retention of forgery because it was a fact that 'forgeries do run into thousands each year as crimes'.

While the Commission recognized that it was unnecessary to rely on forgery where property was obtained by the use of forged documents, the necessity for an offence of forgery was strikingly illustrated by the kind of person who has in his possession numbers of forged documents (such as passports,[5] credit cards, railway season tickets, even Cup Final tickets) where it would not be possible to bring home a charge of attempting to commit any offence. Perhaps it might be added, as a reason for retaining forgery, that it has long been regarded as a serious offence; history is on the side of the Law Commission.

1. The subject matter of forgery

A person is guilty of forgery if he makes a false instrument and for this purpose 'instrument' is defined by s 8 –

(1) Subject to subsection (2) below, in this Part of this Act 'instrument' means –

(a) any document, whether of a formal or informal character;

(b) any stamp issued or sold by the Post Office;

(c) any Inland Revenue stamp; and

(d) any disc, tape, sound track or other device on or in which information is recorded or stored by mechanical, electronic or other means.

(2) A currency note within the meaning of Part II of this Act is not an instrument for the purposes of this Part of this Act.

(3) A mark denoting payment of postage which [a postal operator authorizes] to be used instead of an adhesive stamp is to be treated for the purposes of this Part of this Act as if it were a stamp issued by [the postal operator concerned].

(3A) In this section 'postal operator' has the same meaning as in the Postal Services Act 2000.

(4) In this Part of this Act 'Inland Revenue stamp' means a stamp as defined in section 27 of the Stamp Duties Management Act 1891.

The terms 'writing', 'document' and 'instrument' have been traditionally used in the criminal law to denote the subject matter of forgery. At common law the preference was for 'writing', under the Forgery Act 1913 it was for 'document', under the new legislation 'instrument' is given pride of place but this is immediately defined to mean, inter alia, 'any document, whether of a formal or informal character'. The question then is what does 'document' mean?[6]

A document will normally be written on paper but may be written on any material and the writing may consist in letters, figures or any other symbols used for conveying information. 'Instrument' might convey the notion that the document must be of a formal nature (wills, deeds, etc) but since s 8(1)(a) extends to documents of an 'informal' character this notion would clearly be too restrictive. It has been held under earlier legislation that a forged letter purporting to come from an employee and requesting

[5] This is an increasingly common offence, giving rise to concern: see recently *Kolawole* [2004] All ER (D) 439 (Nov).

[6] Arlidge and Parry submit that 'any document' may be the subject matter of forgery: para 5–011. Cf the extensive definition in the context of hearsay evidence in the Civil Evidence Act 1995, Sch 1, para 12: 'document' means anything in which information of any description is recorded.

money from the employer,[7] a telegram which had been ante-dated in order to defraud a bookmaker,[8] a certificate of competency to drive,[9] and a football pools coupon[10] were all documents and there is no reason to suppose that they would not be considered instruments within s 8(1)(a). It may often be relevant to ask, though it is not suggested as an exclusive test, whether the document is of such a kind that the recipient is expected to act on it in some way.[11]

'Document' cannot include all articles which are commonly called forgeries. In common parlance a replica of a Stradivarius may be said to be a forgery but a violin cannot be regarded as a document. Nor is a painting as such a document. On the other hand an authentication certificate, purporting to come from an acknowledged expert and which ascribes that painting to a particular artist, is a document which may be forged,[12] and it is no less a document because it is pasted to the back of, or even directly written on the back of, the canvas. What, then, if D produces a facsimile Constable or Turner and further signs the painting in the style of the artist? In *Closs*[13] it was argued that such a signature was, in effect, a certificate, authenticating the work and as such it would constitute a forgery. The argument was rejected. Cockburn CJ asked, 'If you go beyond writing where are you to stop? Can sculpture be the subject of forgery?'[14]

The court went on to regard the signature as no more than a mark put upon the painting by the artist with a view to identifying it. *Closs* was decided at common law and, on essentially similar facts, a ruling was giving in *Douce*[15] that the signature constituted a document within the 1913 Act because it purported to convey information about the picture. The Law Commission proposed to settle this argument in favour of *Closs* by defining 'instrument' as 'an instrument *in writing*'[16] but the Commission's wording has been modified in the Act.[17] If it were the practice of an artist to write on the back of his paintings the date and place of origin of his paintings and then add his signature, it would seem clear enough that this writing constitutes a document; if so there can only be the finest of lines between this and a signature on the face of the painting.

Glanville Williams suggests a useful test: if the thing is intended to have utility apart from the fact that it conveys information or records a promise, it is not a document.[18] The stamping of the manufacturer's name on a gun, a car or a package (for example, the wrappers of the baking powder in *Smith*)[19] conveys information but does not convert the gun or car or package into a document. Nor does the legend, 'Made in Sheffield' on

[7] *Cade* [1914] 2 KB 209, CCA. [8] *Riley* [1896] 1 QB 309, CCR.

[9] *Potter* [1958] 2 All ER 51, [1958] 1 WLR 638 (Paull J).

[10] *Butler* (1954) 38 Cr App R 57, CCA.

[11] Compare the tests for determining whether documents are accounts for the purposes of false accounting, as discussed above, p 784.

[12] *Pryse-Hughes* (1958) The Times, 14 May.

[13] (1857) Dears & B 460, CCR. The decision was revered by the Fine Arts (Copyright) Act 1862, s 7. See the discussion by C. Fry, 'Forgeries and signatures on paintings' (1993) 143 NLJ 1233.

[14] (1857) Dears & B 460 at 466. [15] [1972] Crim LR 105, QS.

[16] Law Com No 55, para 23, italics supplied.

[17] D. Crystal-Kirk, 'Forgery Reforged' (1986) 49 MLR 608 argues that the painting in *Closs* falls within the 1981 Act.

[18] 'What is a Document' (1948) 11 MLR 150 at 160. [19] Below, p 467.

a pair of scissors made in Korea make the scissors a document. All these articles have a primary purpose other than the conveying of information or a promise.

The meaning of document for the purposes of forgery cannot be considered in isolation from the rule that it must 'tell a lie about itself'.[20] The number plate of a car may be thought to have a purpose of conveying information because it tells us the date of first registration of the car (and, indirectly, the name of the registered owner). Considered simply as a plate, it may be a document; but it does not tell a lie until it is affixed to a car of different (invariably earlier) registration. Then however it is *the car* which tells a lie about itself ('I am an N-reg car') and the car is not a document.[21] If the number on the vehicle excise licence is correspondingly altered, that is forgery of a document because the licence purports to have been issued in respect of a vehicle with a particular number and the sole purpose of the licence is to supply information.

To be the subject of forgery the document, in the view of the Law Commission, must usually contain messages of two distinct kinds:

> The essence of forgery, in our view, is the making of a false document intending that it be used to induce a person to accept and act upon the message contained in it, as if it were contained in a genuine document. In the straightforward case a document usually contains messages of two distinct kinds – first a message about the document itself (such as the message that the document is a cheque or a will) and secondly a message to be found in the words of the document that is to be accepted and acted upon (such as the message that a banker is to pay a specified sum or that property is to be distributed in a particular way). In our view it is only documents which convey not only the first type of message but also the second type that need to be protected by the law of forgery.[22]

On this view it would not be forgery to make a false copy of a celebrity's autograph since the autograph conveys only one message (viz about the genuineness of the signature) and there is no second message about the genuineness of the piece of paper on which the autograph is written. But where a cheque is forged by the insertion of a false signature two messages are conveyed; one that the signature is genuine and the other that the signature validates the order for the payment of money.

In *Smith*[23] D sold baking powder in wrappers substantially resembling the wrappers of one George Borwick, a well-known manufacturer of baking powder. It was held that the wrappers were not forgeries since they were not documents. The same result would appear to follow on the Law Commission view. The wrappers conveyed only one message, that they were George Borwick wrappers, and conveyed no further messages concerning the genuineness of the document. They may have conveyed a second message about the lineage of the baking powder but there was no second message conveying the notion that the *wrapper* was to be accepted and acted upon.

The Law Commission was minded, and so provided in its draft Bill, to exclude from the definition of 'instrument' documents of historical interest only or as collector's items, but this does not form part of the Act. Suppose then that D makes a false copy of Shakespeare's will with a view to selling it as genuine. It is of course clear that if D makes

20 Below, p 871.

21 See however *Clifford v Bloom* [1977] RTR 351, [1977] Crim LR 485, DC, *Clayton* (1980) 72 Cr App R 135, [1981] Crim LR 186, CA.

22 Law Com No 55, para 22.

23 (1858) Dears & B 566, CCR.

a false copy of his father's will with a view to securing the inheritance for himself, this is a forgery. Both wills are made false with a view to dishonest gain but the Shakespeare will differs in one important respect. It is not produced with a view to affecting the devolution of Shakespeare's property and if V buys it he will do so not because the will, *qua* will, is going to affect his or anyone else's interests but merely for the intrinsic value of that piece of paper.

The essence of 'instrument' or 'document' is peculiarly difficult to define. To constitute an instrument for the purposes of forgery, the document must do more than merely convey information; it must be of such a nature that the information contained in it[24] as a document is intended to be acted on in some way, usually, though not necessarily exclusively, by purporting to affect the rights or interests of some person or persons.

By s 8(1)(d) the definition of 'instrument' embraces 'any disc, tape, sound track or other device on or in which information is recorded or stored[25] by mechanical, electronic or other means'. This extension, if extension it be,[26] must be regarded as entirely right in an age when so much documentation is so processed. Under this definition, magnetic strips on credit and debit cards are protected.[27] The extension will of course be subject to the same qualifications as other instruments. If D produces a recording of what purports to be Mr Gladstone's voice, he is not guilty of forgery though he intends to defraud purchasers; the recording is no more than a document for the purposes of the Act than the false Shakespeare will. Nor is D, a bank teller, guilty of forgery merely by causing false entries to be made in the bank's computer any more than he would be guilty of forgery in making false entries in the bank's ledgers.[28] Nor is E guilty of forgery if he obtains access to information stored in a computer by sending electronic signals which cause the computer to accept him as an authorized user.[29] If, however, D and E cause entries to be made which purport to be made or authorized by one who did not make them, they may be guilty of forgery.

(a) The forgery

By s 9 of the Act:

(1) An instrument is false for the purposes of this Part of this Act –

(a) if it purports to have been made in the form in which it is made by a person who did not in fact make it in that form; or

(b) if it purports to have been made in the form in which it is made on the authority of a person who did not in fact authorize its making in that form; or

(c) if it purports to have been made in the terms in which it is made by a person who did not in fact make it in those terms; or

24 A document may be comprised of more than one part, eg a letter may be taken together with its envelope.

25 Cf *Gold and Schifreen* [1988] AC 1063, [1988] 2 All ER 186, HL, below, p 882.

26 It has never been of any account in the law of forgery on what material, or in what symbols or code, the information is recorded.

27 Arlidge and Parry, para 5–012.

28 Cf *Re Windsor* (1865) 6 B & S 522.

29 *Gold and Schifreen* [1987] QB 1116, [1987] 3 All ER 618. See below, p 882. But in these last two cases D will probably commit an offence under the Computer Misuse Act 1990.

(d) if it purports to have been made in the terms in which it is made on the authority of a person who did not in fact authorize its making in those terms; or

(e) if it purports to have been altered in any respect by a person who did not in fact alter it in that respect; or

(f) if it purports to have been altered in any respect on the authority of a person who did not in fact authorize the alteration in that respect; or

(g) if it purports to have been made or altered on a date on which, or at a place at which, or otherwise in circumstances in which, it was not in fact made or altered; or

(h) if it purports to have been made or altered by an existing person but he did not in fact exist.

(2) A person is to be treated for the purposes of this Part of this Act as making a false instrument if he alters an instrument so as to make it false in any respect (whether or not it is false in some other respect apart from that alteration).

(i) Falsity in general

The definition given by s 9 of 'falsity' is exhaustive and the governing notion is that the document must not only tell a lie, it must also tell a lie about itself.[30] Telling a lie does not become a forgery because it is reduced to writing; it is the document which must be false and not merely the information in it.

In its ordinary application the distinction is easy enough to grasp. If an applicant for a job falsely states his qualifications in his letter of application, the letter is not a forgery; but if he writes a reference which purports to come from his employer, the reference is a forgery. The reference is false within s 9(1)(a) because it purports to have been made in the form in which it is made by a person (the employer) who did not make it in that form. A cheque is similarly false if D signs it in the name of P.[31]

The application of s 9(1)(a) is straightforward and no serious difficulties are likely to be encountered in the application of the next three cases instanced in the subsection. Paragraph (b) deals with the case where D makes a document which purports to be made on V's authority (even though it does not purport to be made by V himself) when V's authority has not been given. It can make no difference, incidentally, if D has the same name as V provided that D intends his signature, or his authorization, to be taken for the signature or authorization, of V.

Paragraphs (c) and (d) in effect parallel (a) and (b) in relation to cases where V has in fact made or authorized the instrument in certain terms but D alters those terms. Thus (c) extends to the case where V draws a cheque for £10 and D makes the amount appear as £100; while (d) deals with the case where V, having authorized D to make out the cheque for £10, D in fact enters £100.

Paragraphs (e) and (f) contain further parallel provisions in relation to alterations. Usually the maker of an instrument, V, is at liberty to alter it (he may, for instance, alter the name of the payee or the amount to be paid on a cheque); but where another, D, alters it, the alteration purporting to be made or authorized by the maker, the other, D, makes a

[30] The aphorism appears to have been coined by Kenny, *Outlines*, 375. Professor Edward Griew used to refer to the concept as one of 'automendacity'.

[31] See also the discussion in Smith, *Property Offences*, para 23–19 of cases where D signs a credit card issued to X with D's own name in the hope that the difference will not be detected.

false instrument. In this connection the facts of *Hopkins and Collins*[32] provide a convenient illustration. D and E, the secretary and treasurer of a football supporters' club, received monies raised by members and made payments on behalf of the club. Over a period of time they (i) entered in the books amounts less than were paid in; (ii) entered amounts in excess of what was paid out; and (iii) altered certain of the entries. It is clear that their accounts were inaccurate but, while the making of inaccurate accounts may be the offence of false accounting,[33] it is not a forgery. The accounts tell a lie but to be false within s 9(1)(e) or (f) they must tell a lie about themselves. So far as D and E's acts (i) and (ii) are concerned the accounts merely told a lie; they purported to be the accurate accounts of D and E when they were the inaccurate accounts of D and E. But what of (iii) the alterations? Paragraphs (e) and (f) do not render a document false merely because it has been altered; the alteration is a forgery only if it purports to be made or authorized by one who did not make or authorize it. Thus so long as the alterations were made or authorized by D and E they were not forgeries. Suppose, however, that only D, the secretary, had been acting dishonestly, and suppose further that only E, the treasurer, was authorized to keep the accounts. If D, without E's authority, altered entries so that the alterations appeared to have been made or authorized by E, the accounts would be forged. To constitute a forgery the hand of Jacob must purport to be the hand of Esau.

A document is accordingly not forged merely because it contains false information and has been prepared by D to perpetrate a fraud. If D, with a view to defrauding V, procures E to execute documents which are to be used to convince V that D is a man of substance or of good character, the documents, so long as they purport to be executed by E, are not forged even though the transactions or facts to which they purport to relate are a complete sham.[34]

But a case which is at odds with the foregoing is *Donnelly*.[35] D, a jeweller, at E's request, gave E a written valuation of certain items of jewellery, stating that D had examined the jewellery. In fact there was no jewellery to be valued; the valuation was a sham and part of a plan to defraud insurers. Upholding D's conviction for forgery the Court of Appeal said that it was only concerned to determine whether the valuation certificate was a false instrument by virtue of s 9. The court held that it was, because it fell foul of s 9(1)(g) in that it had been made 'otherwise in circumstances' in which it was not in fact made. 'In our judgment,' said the court[36]:

> the words coming at the end of paragraph (g) 'otherwise in circumstances . . .' expand its ambit beyond dates and places to *any* case in which an instrument purports to be made when it was not in fact made. This valuation purported to be made *after* [D] had examined the items of jewellery . . . He did not make it after examining these items because they did not exist. That which purported to be a valuation after examination of items was nothing of the kind: it was a worthless piece of paper.

Obviously the valuation certificate told a lie, but did it tell a lie about the *circumstances* in which it was made? If it did then a begging letter in which the beggar, or someone on his

32 (1957) 41 Cr App R 231, CCA. 33 Above, p 786.

34 Cf *Dodge and Harris* [1972] 1 QB 416, [1971] 2 All ER 1523, CA.

35 (1984) 79 Cr App R 76. See also the criticism of Smith, *Property Offences* (1994), para 23–16–18; Arlidge and Parry above, para 5–028.

36 Ibid at 78.

behalf, falsely states that he is bedridden or unemployed, is equally a forgery because the circumstances to which the writer alludes do not exist. This would be a remarkable extension of the law of forgery as previously understood but *if* this is the conclusion to which s 9(1)(g) inexorably leads then it would have to be accepted.[37]

It is submitted, however, that it cannot stand with the decision of the House of Lords in *More*,[38] (in which *Donnelly* was not mentioned) where Lord Ackner, in a speech with which all their Lordships agreed, firmly stated that s 9(1) requires the document to tell a lie *about the circumstances of its making* (as distinct from the circumstances which it purports to report). 'It is common ground,' he said:[39]

that the consistent use of the word 'purports' in each of the paragraphs (a) to (h) inclusive of s 9(1) of the Act imports a requirement that for an instrument to be false it must tell a lie about itself, in the sense that it purports to be made by a person who did not make it (or altered by a person who did not alter it) or otherwise purports to be made or altered in circumstances in which it was not made or altered.

Donnelly was followed as a decision binding on the court, and *More* was unconvincingly distinguished, in *Jeraj*[40] where D, a bank manager, signed a document stating that he had received a letter of credit and that he, on behalf of the bank, endorsed it. The letter of credit did not exist. It seems to be a simple case of writing a falsehood. Then in *Warneford and Gibbs*[41] the court, unaware of *Jeraj*, held that *Donnelly* could not stand with *More*.

The situation is further confused by *Attorney-General's Reference (No 1 of 2000)*.[42] D, a coach-driver, tampered with the tachograph in his vehicle so that it falsely recorded in a document that he had taken a break from driving as required by law and that the vehicle had been driven by another driver. The court concluded that *Donnelly* was binding on them; *Warneford* was wrong, but *Donnelly* and *Jeraj* should be restricted 'so that they apply only where *circumstances* need to exist before the document can properly be made or altered'.[43] How this distinguishes the case from a simple lie is not explained. If D writes a letter stating that he has a first-class honours degree from the University of Cambridge when he has never been near that place he is asserting the existence of non-existent examination scripts which have been evaluated and rated first class – circumstances which must exist before he could properly write such a letter. If that is a forgery, then so is any other written lie. Equally baffling is the court's opinion that, while the tachograph record was a forgery, a handwritten statement of the same lie would not have been.

Paragraph (g) of s 9(1) deals with the case where the document purports to be made or altered on a date or at a place or otherwise in circumstances where it was not in fact made or altered. This would deal, for example, with the case where D alters the date on a will or

37 Counsel for the Crown in *Donnelly* conceded that the valuation certificate would not have been a forgery either at common law or under the Forgery Act 1913 but argued that it was now a forgery by virtue of s 9(1)(g).

38 [1987] 3 All ER 825, [1987] 1 WLR 1578 discussed below, p 873.

39 Ibid, at 830.

40 [1994] Crim LR 595. Cf R. Leng, 'Falsity in Forgery' [1989] Crim LR 687, arguing that the document was not merely a false valuation, but purported to be something it was not – a valuation based on an inspection of jewellery.

41 [1994] Crim LR 753.

42 [2001] 1 Cr App R 218, [2001] Crim LR 127 and commentary.

43 At para [24] – the court's italics.

deed to make it appear to antedate another will or deed.[44] Nor is the will or deed any less false because it is D's own will or deed; a will or deed which purports to be executed on the 1st of the month tells a lie about itself if it was in fact executed on the 10th and D, provided he acts with *mens rea*, is guilty of forgery.[45]

(ii) Falsity and non-existing persons

Much the most difficult provision in s 9(1) is para (h). Most frequently false documents purport to be made or authorized by some existing person known to the person intended to be affected by the contents of the document. Sometimes, however, D may find it equally, or better, suits his purpose to invent the name of a person by whom the document purports to be made. Suppose, for instance, that D and E apply for a job and in order to bolster their prospects D falsely makes a reference purporting to come from Sir George X while E falsely makes a reference purporting to come from Sir Peter Y. In fact there is no Sir George X, who is merely D's invention, but there is a Sir Peter Y who was formerly E's employer. E's reference is clearly a forgery and, on the face of it, there is no reason why D's case should be treated any differently; certainly D's case falls within s 9(1)(h).

But consider the facts of *Hassard and Devereux*.[46] D, a company bookkeeper made out cheques to a company creditor, BSA, and after the cheques had been signed by directors, he altered the cheques to B s Andrews and handed them to his confederate, E. Obviously these cheques were forgeries (s 9(1)(b)) and we are not concerned with them. D and E now needed to cash these cheques so they gave them to F who opened an account in the name of B S Andrews, F representing herself as Andrews and giving her correct address. F then drew a cheque on this account. While F's conviction for forgery under the 1913 Act was upheld and was a questionable decision under that Act, the question which now arises is whether this cheque is a forgery by virtue of s 9(1)(h). It might be said that the case falls literally within the paragraph; the cheque purports to be made by an existing person (B S Andrews) who did not in fact exist.[47]

Yet any person may assume an alias. Authors frequently do. If, for example, an author called X chooses to write under the name of Y and has his royalties paid to Y in which style he opens a bank account, is he guilty of forgery if he draws cheques on that account in the name of Y? The answer must be an obvious no. Y is not someone who does not exist; he is someone who does exist, Y being a mere alias for X. Clearly, if the bank knows that X and Y are one and the same person, there can be no question of forgery. It can hardly become forgery because the bank is unaware of the true name of X, knowing him only in the style of Y. Nor can the cheques be regarded as forgeries because X has opened

44 Cf *Wells* [1939] 2 All ER 169, 27 Cr App R 72, CCA; D was convicted of forgery where he altered the date on a settlement so as to ante-date the provisions of an Act of Parliament in order to avoid the payment of tax on the settlement.

45 Under the 1913 Act there was a requirement that a document must be forged in a *material* particular. Arguably on facts such as those in *Wells*, last note, D would not have been guilty of forgery in ante-dating the settlement if he had failed to ante-date it sufficiently to avoid tax. There is now no requirement for materiality and D on facts such as *Wells* may be guilty of forgery even though the alteration does not achieve its intended effect. D may also be guilty of forgery if he alters it to make it false in any respect whether or not it is false in some other respect: s 9(2).

46 [1970] 2 All ER 647, [1970] 1 WLR 1109, CA.

47 A similar problem is presented by the facts of *Martin* (1879) 6 QBD 34, CCR.

a bank account in the name of Y for a dishonest purpose, such as avoiding paying tax on his royalties.

It is suggested, therefore, that the assumption of an alias by D, by which alias he is known to V, falls outside s 9(1)(h), and documents presented by D to V in the style of his alias are not documents which are made by a person who did not in fact exist.

In *Hassard and Devereux* the bank, had it been aware that B S Andrews was not F's real name, would not have honoured the cheque or, at least, would have required a convincing reason why it should. But the bank was not misled by anything which appeared on the face of the cheque into thinking that it was honouring a cheque other than the cheque of the person presenting it for payment whether that person chose to call herself F or B S Andrews. The cheque does not purport to be made by an existing person who does not exist; it purports to be made by an existing person who chooses to assume one name rather than another.

This seems clearly to follow from *More*.[48] D came by a cheque made out to M R Jessell with which he opened an account at a building society in the name of Mark Richard Jessell and later drew on that account by completing a withdrawal form in the name of Mark Richard Jessell. Affirming D's conviction for forgery, the Court of Appeal held that the withdrawal form came within s 9(1)(h) since it purported to have been made by an existing person who did not in fact exist. The House of Lords disagreed and quashed the conviction. As Lord Ackner pointed out:[49]

> [D] was a real person . . . The withdrawal form clearly purported to be signed by the person who originally opened the account and in this respect it was wholly accurate. Thus, in my judgment, it cannot be validly contended that the document told a lie about itself. . . .

This, with respect, is entirely right. It follows that, while there is no mention in *More* of *Hassard and Devereux* (presumably because the latter is a decision under the repealed 1913 Act), if the facts of *Hassard* were to recur, a conviction for forgery under the 1981 Act could not be sustained.

This does not mean that s 9(1)(h) is devoid of effect though the scope for its application is probably not extensive. It would apply where D makes a document purporting to emanate from E (E being purely a fiction in the sense that neither D nor any accomplice of D's is going to assume the alias of E and representing himself as such to V) the case must fall within s 9(1)(h) and D is guilty of forgery.[50] Thus the case instanced at the beginning of this section, where D presents to V a reference purporting to emanate from Sir George X, there being no Sir George X, would be one of forgery. Another case falling within the paragraph might be where D writes begging letters to V apparently emanating from distressed ex-servicemen called X, Y and Z, where X, Y and Z are merely figments of D's imagination.

All in all it would seem that para (h) can apply only in restricted circumstances and it may be that Williams was right in suggesting[51] that we ought to be spared the complexity which arises from the application of the law of forgery to documents in the name of fictitious persons.

48 [1987] 3 All ER 825, [1987] 1 WLR 1578, HL.

49 [1987] 3 All ER 825 at 830.

50 Cf *Gambling* [1975] QB 207, [1974] 3 All ER 479, CA.

51 'Forgery or Falsity' [1974] Crim LR at 71 and 80. Cf Williams, TBCL (2nd edn, 1983), 898. See also R. N. Goodman, 'When is a Document False in the Law of Forgery' (1952) 15 MLR 11.

(iii) Falsity by omission

At first sight it may seem odd to suggest that forgery may be committed by omission since if anything requires positive and painstaking effort it might be said that this is so of the craft[52] of the forger. But appearances can be deceptive. Though such cases may be of rare occurrence, it is possible to predicate cases of forgery by omission. If, for example, V, a blind man, dictates his will to D and D, with a view to gain for himself or another with intent to cause loss to another, omits certain provisions, the will appears to be a forgery. The will purports to be made or authorized in the terms in which it is made by a person (V) who did not in fact make or authorize its making in those terms and thus falls within s 9(1)(c) or (d). In order for an omission to constitute forgery its effect must be to render the document false within s 9(1), that is, it must result in the document telling a lie about itself. If in *Hopkins and Collins*[53] D and E had simply failed to enter in the club's books monies which were paid in by members, the accounts would not be forged. Their accounts would be inaccurate but they would not be false within any of the definitions in s 9(1); they would remain what they purported to be: a statement of accounts prepared by D and E.

(b) *Mens rea*: intent to prejudice

(i) Double requirement of intention

Sections 1–5 of the Act create various offences involving forgery. For purposes of convenience of exposition the *mens rea* of the various offences may be regarded as having two aspects. There is first of all the mental element required in relation to the making, using or possessing the false instrument and this aspect is considered in relation to the specific offences in the next section. The second aspect, which governs the offences under ss 1–4 and certain of the offences under s 5, is the requirement that D should intend that V should be induced, by reason of accepting the false instrument as genuine, to do some act to his own or another's prejudice. It is this aspect which is discussed in this section. As the Court of Appeal in *Attorney-General's Reference (No 1 of 2001)*[54] recently confirmed, it is necessary for the prosecution to show that D had a double intention – (i) an intention to induce somebody to accept the false document as genuine and (ii) an intention that his victim, by reason of accepting the document, would do or not do some act to his own or any other person's prejudice. In *Tobierre*[55] it was accordingly held that D's conviction was to be quashed where the trial judge appeared to have directed the jury that it was enough that D intended a false instrument to be accepted as genuine and did not or did not

52 Regrettably the photocopier, scanner, digital camera, computer and even kitchen cleaners (which can be used to remove signatures from credit and cheque cards) have brought forgery within the reach of the artisan as well as the artist. For reform proposals to deal with cloning and skimming of credit cards see Home Office, Fraud Law Reform, May 2004, available at www.homeoffice.gov.uk/docs3/fraud_law_reform.pdf. See also in Australia, the Model Criminal Code Officers' Committee of the Standing Committee of Attorney General's discussion paper, *Credit Card Skimming Offences*, available at www.law.gov.au/www/agdHome.nsf.

53 (1957) 41 Cr App R 231, CCA, above, p 870.

54 [2002] EWCA Crim 1768, [2002] Crim LR 844, CA.

55 [1986] 1 All ER 346, [1986] 1 WLR 125, [1986] Crim LR 243, CA; *Garciá* (1987) 87 Cr App R 175, [1988] Crim LR 115 CA.

adequately, explain that it must be proved *also* that D intended thereby to induce another to act to his prejudice.

(ii) Induce and prejudice

By s 10 of the Act which *exhaustively* defines 'induce' and 'prejudice':

(1) Subject to subsections (2) and (4) below, for the purposes of this Part of this Act, an act or omission intended to be induced is to a person's prejudice if, and only if, it is one which, if it occurs –

(a) will result –

(i) in his temporary or permanent loss of property; or

(ii) in his being deprived of an opportunity to earn remuneration or greater remuneration; or

(iii) in his being deprived of an opportunity to gain a financial advantage otherwise than by way of remuneration; or

(b) will result in somebody being given an opportunity –

(i) to earn remuneration or greater remuneration from him; or

(ii) to gain a financial advantage from him otherwise than by way of remuneration; or

(c) will be the result of his having accepted a false instrument as genuine, or a copy of a false instrument as a copy of a genuine one, in connection with his performance of any duty.

(2) An act which a person has an enforceable duty to do and an omission to do an act which a person is not entitled to do shall be disregarded for the purposes of this Part of this Act.

(3) In this Part of this Act references to inducing somebody to accept a false instrument as genuine, or a copy of a false instrument as a copy of a genuine one, include references to inducing a machine to respond to the instrument or copy as if it were a genuine instrument or, as the case may be, a copy of the genuine one.

(4) Where subsection (3) above applies, the act or omission intended to be induced by the machine responding to the instrument or copy shall be treated as an act or omission to a person's prejudice.

(5) In this section 'loss' includes not getting what one might get as well as parting with what one has.

Essentially 'prejudice' may be of two kinds, viz the causing of economic loss or the causing of conduct in contravention of a duty.

Economic loss

Usually an instrument is forged with a view to the economic benefit (in terms of money or other property) of the forger and consequential economic loss to the victim. Gain and loss are usually two sides of the same coin but the section treats separately the loss caused and advantage gained.

Most obviously D intends to induce V to act, or omit to act, to his prejudice if as a result V will be deprived, permanently or temporarily, of property (s 10(1)(a)(i)). This is most commonly the forger's intention and is typically instanced by the forgery of cheques, credit cards and other instruments in order to induce another to act to his prejudice. So if D falsifies a cheque guarantee card to induce V to part with money, or falsifies a credit card to induce X to part with goods, he may be convicted of forgery. The fact that X may, as is often the case with credit cards, claim reimbursement from Z (a bank) cannot mean that X has not been induced to act to his prejudice; X has lost, and D intended to induce the loss of, the goods.

In practice most cases will be covered by s 10(1)(a)(i) but the section goes on to deal with other cases of much less frequent occurrence. Section 10(1)(a)(ii) deals with the sort of case where V is seeking, say, employment or promotion in employment, and D writes a letter to the employer purporting to come from someone whose opinion is respected by the employer and which is intended to ensure that V does not get the post or the promotion. Such cases may be of limited occurrence but when they occur an instrument has been made false with a view to V's prejudice and there is no reason why they should not fall within the ambit of forgery.

Section 10(1)(a)(iii) may have been included *ex abundanti cautela.* A case may be supposed where D and E are bidding for a contract to supply vehicle components to V. D might forge a letter purporting to come from someone who has done business with E which asserts that E cannot be relied on to keep delivery dates. If E does not get the contract he has not been deprived of property within s 10(1)(a)(i). Nor might the case fall within s 10(1)(a)(ii) since 'remuneration' ordinarily connotes a payment for services rendered and may not be apt to cover the case where someone loses his profit margins under a contract for the supply of goods. Accordingly subpara (iii) was included to make it clear that such a case falls within the Act.

Section 10(1)(b) is concerned with financial advantage and there is no need to prove loss to any particular victim. The offence is therefore complete and can be charged at a very early stage in the wrongdoing. Usually that advantage will accrue to the forger or an accomplice but an offence may be committed though the beneficiary is unaware of the fraud. If D forges a testimonial with a view to securing the employment, or promotion, of someone in V's firm, it does not matter whether that someone is D himself, or someone who has procured the forged testimonial or someone who is wholly ignorant of D's action. The case falls within s 10(1)(b)(i) since 'somebody' is given an opportunity to earn remuneration or greater remuneration. Nor does it matter that the 'someone' who gets the job, or the promotion, fully justifies the remuneration, or greater remuneration, or, indeed, brings financial gain to V.

Section 10(1)(b)(ii) deals with the case where a financial advantage, otherwise than by way of remuneration, is sought. So if in the bidding for a contract D forges a letter extolling the virtues of his own (or another bidder's) products an offence may be committed. Again, it cannot matter that D's (or the other's) products are in fact the best and the cheapest. The section makes it clear that an act or omission intended to be induced 'is' to another's prejudice if the case falls within the section.

Normally D may falsify an instrument with a view to giving himself (or another) an advantage over other competitors, or seek to disadvantage another competitor, but a case may fall within s 10 though D is the sole applicant for a job or a sole bidder for a contract.

Performance of duty

Under the former law it was unclear how far the *mens rea* of forgery extended beyond an intention to cause economic loss. The argument is now, in a sense, settled by s 10(1)(c) –

a victim is prejudiced if it is intended that he should accept a false instrument as genuine 'in connection with his performance of any duty'.

In formulating this provision the Law Commission sought,[56] on the one hand, to include such cases as forging a security pass to gain access to premises, forging a certificate of competency to drive, and forging documents in such circumstances as *Welham v DPP*[57] where documents were forged not with the intention of causing financial loss but with the intention of avoiding statutory restrictions on borrowing. On the other hand, the Commission wished to exclude cases where the prejudice was trivial or inconsequential.

The Act seeks to achieve this balance by the employment of the concept of 'duty'. 'Duty' here must refer to a legal duty and cannot extend to what might be regarded as a social or moral duty. It will extend, however, to a duty arising under contract as well as a duty imposed by law independently of contract. Thus such cases as *Harris*[58] (where papers were forged to secure the release of a prisoner from jail); *Toshack*[59] (where a seaman forged a certificate of good conduct so that the Trinity House examiners would let him take an examination); *Moah*[60] (where a testimonial was forged to gain admission to the police force); and *Bassey*[61] (where a student forged papers to gain admission to the Inner Temple) would all fall within s 10(1)(c).

But where it is not intended to induce anyone to act in connection with a duty no offence is committed under the Act. The Law Commission gave as an example the case of the bogus invitation to a party with a view to raising a laugh. It is understandable that the heavy hammer of forgery should not be used on so small a nut,[62] even though real inconvenience may be caused.[63]

It is not enough that an instrument is falsified with a view to deceiving V unless there is an intention to induce an act or omission which constitutes 'prejudice' as defined. It would not constitute forgery, for example, to falsify a birth certificate if D's *only* object is to make her friends believe that she was a little younger than she looked. And to constitute forgery D must intend by the false document to prejudice the victim or some other party; it is not enough that acceptance of the false document will result in someone doing, or not doing, something to D's prejudice: literally 'a person's prejudice' in s 10 might be read as including D himself but in *Utting*[64] the Court of Appeal rightly regarded such a submission as absurd.

(iii) Claim of right

It will be recalled that s 10(2) states that 'an act which a person has an enforceable duty to do and an omission to do an act which a person is not entitled to do shall be disregarded for the purposes of this Part of this Act'. What then of the case where although D acts

56 Law Com No 55, paras 28–37.
57 [1961] AC 103, [1960] 1 All ER 805, HL.
58 (1833) 1 Mood CC 393, CCR.
59 (1849) 1 Den 492.
60 (1858) Dears & B 550, CCR.
61 (1931) 22 Cr App R 160, CCA.
62 Yet the heavy hammer would be applicable if the invitation was intended to induce a doorman or butler to admit the bearer to the party.
63 What if the bogus invitation was sent as a means of getting V out of the way while D burgles his premises? Has D, by reason of getting V to accept the invitation as genuine, induced an act which, if it occurs, will result in V's loss of property within s 10(1)(a)(i)?
64 (1988) 86 Cr App R 164, [1987] Crim LR 636.

with the necessary intent, he seeks merely to cause V to do what he has an enforceable duty to do?

Actual claim of right

This issue may be conveniently illustrated by reference to the facts of *Parker*,[65] a decision under the former law. D, who had made a loan of £3 to V and was unable to get payment from V wrote V a letter, purporting to come from the War Office, which asked V to give D's demand his best attention without delay. On these facts D has obviously made a false instrument within s 9 but he is not guilty of forgery by reason of what is now s 10(2). Arguably V suffers no 'prejudice' within s 10(1) if he is merely made to pay that which he already owes[66] but s 10(2) puts the matter beyond doubt. In a case where D does have a legal entitlement to the money or other property in question, the effect of s 10(2) is that an act is not to 'a person's prejudice' if that person has an enforceable duty to do that act. The 'enforceable duty' must of course be one which is imposed by law or arises under contract.

Some confusion is created by the application of the principle in the case of *Attorney-General's Reference (No 1 of 2001)*.[67] DD were the parents of L who was charged with a serious offence abroad. Her conduct attracted media attention and an appeal was launched to meet DD's travelling and other expenses in attending L's trial. Some £250,000 was raised and paid into a trust account. Unbeknown to DD and without their consent, mail addressed to them was delivered by the Post Office to the fund organizers and opened by volunteers who placed all monies received, without consideration being given to the expressed intention of the donors, into the fund's bank account. It was alleged that DD provided the trustees with false invoices relating to accommodation expenses incurred. DD were acquitted on the direction of the trial judge on an indictment alleging, *inter alia*, using a false instrument, contrary to s 3, following a submission that the money was 'theirs to start with in law and becomes theirs as a result of any act done by the trustees then they have not gained because it was always theirs and there was no advantage.' The Court of Appeal held that this submission ought not to have succeeded. The referred question for the Court of Appeal, was whether, on a charge under s 3:

> where the accused has used a false instrument or furnished false information with a view to obtaining money or other property it is necessary for the prosecution to prove that the accused had no legal entitlement to the money or other property in question.[68]

The court accepted that the existence of a claim of right at the time when the false document was used might negative an intention to cause another to act to his prejudice in some cases. If the effect of D's legal entitlement to the property would create in the alleged victim of the offence of forgery a duty to deliver the property as requested, then the prosecution must prove that D had no legal entitlement to it. Otherwise the prosecution need not disprove a legal entitlement. But, even if D has no legal entitlement

65 (1910) 74 JP 208, CCC. Cf. *Winston* [1999] Crim LR 81, in which V was under no duty to pay.

66 Cf the discussion in connection with blackmail, above, p 800.

67 [2002] EWCA Crim 1768, [2002] Crim LR 844, CA and commentary.

68 If all money had belonged to DD it would have continued to belong to them under the principle in *Taylor v Plumer* (1815) 3 M & S 562 (agent converting principal's property into another form, property in changed form belongs to principal).

to the property in the sense of a proprietary interest, the prosecution must disprove any claim of which he offers evidence that the property is due as a debt. On the facts it was held that the prosecution had demonstrated both elements of intention: an intention to induce the trustees to accept the false invoice as genuine, and an intention to cause them by so accepting it to authorize payment, which it was their duty not to do, and it was irrelevant that DD might have intended to deprive the trust only of that sum which they could have obtained if they had pursued their claim in another way.

There are a number of difficulties with the decision and the approach to the trustees' duties. The court placed significant reliance on the fact that DD had no proprietary interest in the money, but, even though DD retained no proprietary interest, they were surely, creditors of the trust fund, and the trustees had a duty to pay the debt, a duty which existed from the moment the money passed into their legal ownership. Moreover, the court took a restricted approach to s 10(2). Whilst acknowledging that s 10(2) was intended to reverse *Parker*, the court relied on statements in *Campbell*[69] which might be read as conflicting with the generally accepted approach that s 10(2) assumes that V's duty, if there is one, continues to exist notwithstanding his being deceived by D's forged instrument.[70]

Belief in claim of right

In *Parker* (and arguably in the *Attorney-General's Reference No 1*) D had a claim of right since V was in debt to him. It is submitted that D's honest belief[71] that V has an enforceable duty to do the act in question suffices, even if the belief is unreasonable. But it is not enough that D genuinely believes that his action is morally justified.[72] D may feel that he has been unfairly overlooked for promotion on previous occasions but if on the next occasion he falsifies a testimonial intending to induce his employer, V, to promote him, all the requirements of forgery are satisfied. The Law Commission explained the problem in the following terms:

> If a person makes a false instrument intending that it be used as genuine to prejudice another by inducing him to act contrary to his duty it is irrelevant that that person may genuinely believe that he is entitled to what he is trying to obtain. However firmly he may believe, for example, that he is entitled to a driving licence, he intends another to act contrary to his duty if he intends to induce him to issue such a licence against a false certificate of competency to drive, as it is the issuing officer's duty to issue a licence only against the presentation of a valid certificate of competence.

Suppose that D forges the acceptance to a bill of exchange in the name of E and claims that when he did so he intended all along to meet the bill and has now paid the bankers who honoured the bill so that no actual loss has been sustained by anyone.[73] The case appears to be an offence under the Act. By the forged signature D has induced the bankers

[69] (1985) 80 Cr App R 47 at 49 (presentation of forged cheque).

[70] If the duty existed before the false instrument was made or used, s 10(2) should apply.

[71] The Law Commission, Law Com No 55, para 35 considered adding 'dishonestly' to the mental element but did not think that it was 'either necessary or helpful'.

[72] Cf *Hagan* [1985] Crim LR 598, CA, holding it irrelevant that D may have made no personal gain from the property obtained and may have applied it to an entirely worthy cause. The case was decided under the 1913 Act but the same result would follow under the 1981 Act.

[73] These are the facts of *Geach* (1840) 9 C & P 499.

to honour the bill and by this D gains a financial advantage.[74] D cannot be relieved of liability by s 10(2) because it cannot be asserted that the bankers have any enforceable duty to honour a forged bill; had the bankers known that they were in the position of accepting a bill without the usual security of an acceptor they would have been duty bound to reject it.

Irrelevance of dishonesty

It follows that while a claim of legal right may negative D's intention to cause another to act to his prejudice, it is not ordinarily relevant to consider whether D was acting dishonestly. It is necessary for the court to ascertain what acts D intended to induce, and that is a subjective question; but whether the act intended to be induced is to the actor's prejudice appears to be an objective question, a question, once the facts are ascertained, of law, for only the judge can decide whether there is an enforceable duty to do a particular act. If there is such a duty then the offence is not committed, even though D was unaware of the existence of the duty.

Some might say that the forger of the acceptance to a bill who all along intends to meet the bill is not acting dishonestly, but this would not affect his liability for forgery since he has intentionally made a false instrument with intent thereby to induce another to do that which it is his duty not to do. This is confirmed by *Campbell*.[75] E, a plausible rogue, told D that she had returned a car to a seller and the only way the seller could repay the purchase price was for E to make out a cheque in a fictitious name. D then obliged E by endorsing the cheque in the fictitious name to herself and paying it into her account, later drawing out the money which she paid to E. It was never doubted that D had been duped and that she thought she was acting honestly in that no one would be the loser. Affirming her conviction for forgery the Court of Appeal said that the trial judge was right to rule that dishonesty was not a necessary element for forgery. Both elements of the *mens rea* were present here; she intended the bank to accept the false signature on the cheque as genuine and by reason thereof to cause the bank to do that which it was its duty not to do. It was thus irrelevant that she intended no permanent or temporary loss to the bank.

(iv) Forgery and machines

D may, with a dishonest intent, make a device with a view to causing a machine to operate to his advantage. It might be merely a metal disc the size of a coin or it might be a card storing information to which the machine will respond. The former cannot be an 'instrument' and so cannot be a forgery but the latter now may be. 'The increasing use of more sophisticated machines', said the Law Commission:[76]

> has led us to include within 'instruments' capable of being forged the discs, tapes and other devices mentioned in paragraph 25, which may cause machines into which they are fed to respond to the information or instructions upon them, and, of course, there are machines which are designed to respond to an instrument in writing. It is necessary, therefore, to make provision to cover in such cases the intention to cause a machine to respond to a false instrument as if it were a genuine instrument. There also has to be provision for treating the act or omission intended to flow from the machine responding to the instrument as an act or omission to a person's prejudice.

74 In effect D obtains credit or time to pay.

75 (1985) 80 Cr App R 47, CA.

76 Paper No 55, para 36.

Section 10(3) and (4) are intended to implement the Commission's recommendation. References to inducing *somebody to accept* a false instrument as genuine include references to inducing *a machine to respond* to the instrument as it if were genuine.

These provisions were intended by the Law Commission (and presumably Parliament) to apply to a person who makes his own cash card with a view to obtaining money from a cash dispenser (ATM), a practice which has been made much easier with the advent of personal computers and the availability of software packages which create such cards.[77] If he carries out his intention he will be guilty of theft of the money,[78] but the preparation of the card is a merely preparatory act, not amounting to attempted theft. There are two difficulties in construing the Act to apply to this case.

(1) The card is certainly an 'instrument' within s 8(1)(d);[79] but it must also be a 'false' instrument within s 9 and it is hard to see that it 'purports' to be anything other than what it is, any more than a copy of a key[80] made by an intending thief.

(2) Section 10(4) and (5)[81] appear to contemplate two successive 'inducements': (i) the machine is induced to respond to the false instrument; and (ii) the response of the machine induces an act or omission. Subsection (3) extends the meaning of accepting a false instrument as genuine but it does not extend the meaning of 'do or not do some act'; and subs (4) appears to confirm that an act or omission is still required. Everywhere else in the Act this undoubtedly means the action or omission of a person; and that is its natural meaning in subs (4).[82]

If that is right, 'prejudice' will result in the bank dispenser case only if and when a bank clerk acts in some way in consequence of the operation of the machine, perhaps by debiting the genuine customer's account or sending him an inaccurate statement of account. Whether or when that will happen depends on the degree of mechanisation of the bank's operations. It might be argued that 'act or omission' is here loosely used to mean the functioning of the machine, but that is not what s 10(4) says; and, while we might swallow the notion that a machine can act or omit, the idea that it can perform a

[77] In the Explanatory Notes to the Draft Bill (Law Com No 55) the Commission said of its provision (which is not reproduced in *identical* terms in the Act) that it 'is required to deal with those cases where the false instrument, whether it be an instrument in writing or a disc, tape, sound track or other device, is made or used to cause a machine to respond to it as if it were a genuine instrument. The use of a false card to cause a bank's cash dispensing machine to pay out money would not be within [section] 3 standing alone as there would be no intention of inducing somebody to accept it as genuine and to act upon it.' And see now the Computer Misuse Act 1990 which in the instances discussed above will usually offer an alternative route to conviction.

[78] Cf *Hands* (1887) 56 LT 370, DC, above, p 755.

[79] Above, p 865.

[80] The key, of course, could not be a document, at least where the key is of the traditional variety and not a card key of the kind nowadays favoured in hotels.

[81] Above, p 875.

[82] The incorporation of the extended meaning of 'inducing to accept' into the definition of forgery in s 1 cannot avoid a reference to a person at some stage. There are two alternatives. The first assumes that a machine can act or omit. The second, preferable, alternative avoids that solecism: (i) 'A person is guilty of forgery if he makes a false instrument with the intention that he or another shall use it to induce a machine to respond to the instrument as if it were a genuine instrument and by reason of so responding to it to [*do or not to do some act to a person's prejudice*]'; (ii) for the bracketed words, substitute: [*cause another person to do or not to do some act to his own or any other person's prejudice*].

duty is surely unacceptable. If D makes his own swipe card with a view to gaining unauthorized access to premises this can be a forgery only if the D intends it to result in the acceptance of the card by someone 'in connection with the performance of any duty.' There is the same question whether the card purports to be what it is not any more than does a password written on a piece of paper and shown to the gatekeeper, but there is also the more formidable difficulty – indeed, it is submitted, impossibility – of treating the electronic device as having a duty to admit only authorized persons.

In all this discussion it is easy to lose sight of the fact that we are talking about the intention of the accused. If prejudice requires a human act or omission, the question is not whether a person would actually act or omit in consequence of the use of the alleged forgery but whether D intended that they would. The difficulty of proving such an intention might incline a court against the view that prejudice requires a human act where a machine has been 'induced to respond'. Nevertheless, it is thought that the proper construction of the Act requires this result. On the other hand, it does not appear to be what Parliament intended. The outcome is not easy to predict. If the court could discern an ambiguity then it could resort to the Law Commission's Report or even Hansard and probably the Law Commission's intention would prevail.

Other difficulties are illustrated by *Gold and Schifreen*.[83] Here D and E, two skilled 'hackers', obtained unauthorized access to V's computer on which information was stored by causing the computer to accept them as authorized users. The House of Lords agreed with the Court of Appeal that their convictions for forgery should be quashed on the ground that the signals which caused the computer to treat them as authorized users were never 'recorded or stored' within s 8(1)(d) of the Act;[84] they appeared only momentarily on a screen and were then immediately expunged. The House did not find it necessary to decide on the further argument, relied on in the Court of Appeal that the extension of forgery to discs, tapes, etc did not alter the need for the requirement that the document must tell a lie about itself. Here, it seems, D and E simply caused the computer to accept *them* as authorized users. In effect they simply told a lie (viz, we are authorized users) and the case might be likened to D writing a password on a piece of paper which tricks the sentry into admitting him to the premises he guards.

The courts in *Gold* were evidently unhappy about what they regarded as a procrustean attempt to use the Act for situations for which it was not designed.[85]

(v) Causation

Forgery extends not only to the case where by reason of accepting the false instrument as genuine V is intended to be induced to act, or fail to act, to his prejudice but also to the case where V is intended to be caused so as to act, or not to act, to the prejudice of any

83 [1988] 2 All ER 186, HL. See the comments by I. Lloyd 'Computer Abuse and the Law' (1988) 104 LQR 202 and Y. I. Cole-Wilson, 'Old Bailey Hacks: Some Reflections on *R v Gold and Schifren*' (1987) 137 NLJ 1118 (on the CA).

84 Above, p 868. This view does not sit easily with the approach in relation to the offences in the Protection of Children Act 1978 of making an indecent image of a child, it seems that such images are 'made' by the internet cache on a machine even though not knowingly stored by D who views them.

85 See the Computer Misuse Act 1990, below, Ch 25, which deals with the problem. The decision of the House of Lords prompted the comment in the Journal of International Business Law ((1987) at 107) that the 'theory and practice of the criminal law are shown to be light years behind technological developments in the commercial sector'.

other person. As has been shown,[86] a false testimonial may be sent by D to V in order to induce V to appoint D or to appoint E or not to appoint F, and all three situations fall within the ambit of forgery. But it is not enough that the false instrument results in prejudice to someone; the prejudice must result from a person (or persons) having accepted the false instrument as genuine and being induced thereby to do or refrain from doing something. Prejudice clearly results to F if as a result of the false reference F is not considered for the job and is denied the opportunity to earn remuneration, but the offence lies, not in F being prejudiced, but in V being induced to act to F's prejudice.

Suppose that D wishes to acquire a vehicle from V, a dealer, and because D does not have the ready money, he is referred by V to X Co, a finance company, to arrange a hire-purchase of the vehicle. D signs the hire-purchase proposal in the name of Z, Z being a creditworthy individual, which D is not. Having satisfied himself that Z is creditworthy, X Co confirms the proposal with V and V delivers the vehicle.[87] Supposing that V is prejudiced by delivering the vehicle to D,[88] it would not be apt to allege in an indictment that D has made a false instrument intending to induce V to act to his prejudice. The victim must be a person who, by reason of being induced to treat the false instrument as genuine, does something (or fails to do something) to his own or another's prejudice. The case presents no problems if D is charged with inducing X Co to act to its own or another's prejudice in that D gains from X Co a financial advantage otherwise than by way of remuneration (s 10(1)(b)(ii)).[89]

2. The offences

(a) Forgery

By s 1 of the Act –

A person is guilty of forgery if he makes a false instrument, with the intention that he or another shall use it to induce somebody to accept it as genuine, and by reason of so accepting it to do or not to do some act to his own or any other person's prejudice.

By s 6 the offence is triable either way; on summary conviction it is punishable by six months' imprisonment and/or a fine not exceeding the statutory maximum and on trial on indictment by 10 years' imprisonment. It is a Group A offence under the Criminal Justice Act 1993.

Forgery is committed at the moment when the instrument is made, or it is not committed at all.[90] To be a forgery, it must be made with the dual intention that (i) somebody shall be induced to accept it as genuine and (ii) by reason of so accepting it, do some

[86] Above, p 867.

[87] These are the facts of *Hurford* [1963] 2 QB 398, [1963] 2 All ER 254, CCA.

[88] It may be that V is not prejudiced since he may be able to claim the whole of the price of the vehicle from X Co.

[89] Hence the Law Commission (Law Com No 55, para 47) saw no need to reproduce the offence under s 7 of the 1913 Act of demanding property under or by virtue of forged instruments.

[90] Creating a draft will for a vulnerable neighbour from whom DD had been receiving large financial 'gifts' and keeping the will in a drawer was not sufficient to establish an attempt to make a false instrument: *Bowles* [2004] EWCA Crim 1608.

prejudicial act. If it is made with that intention, it is immaterial that neither of these events takes place, though the fact that they did take place may be relevant evidence of what the maker intended.[91] It is not enough, therefore, that D makes a copy of an instrument if his intention is to represent it as a copy; were it otherwise the photocopier would have made us a nation of forgers. Nor would it suffice, it is submitted, that, subsequently realizing that the copy is good enough to pass as the original, D decides to pass it as the original. The definition requires that D *makes* the false instrument with the requisite intent at that time of making.

In *Ondhia*,[92] the alleged forgery was of a 'copy bill of lading.' D created the copy bill – he was not merely making a photocopy of an existing bill – so the copy bill was 'false' and a forgery, if, but only if, it was made with appropriate intents. He did not, however, intend to use *that paper* to induce anybody to do anything. It does not appear that he intended to show it to anyone. No one was to be induced to do anything by looking at the alleged forgery. He intended to use it to make a facsimile. After that he had no further use for it. He intended that V should act on the facsimile. So the question appears to be: was D's intention to use the facsimile an intention to induce someone to accept the original copy bill as genuine and, consequently, act to his prejudice? The court's answer is in the affirmative – the appeal was dismissed. If D were to make a false instrument, intending to hold it in front of a TV or web camera so that V could read it and act upon it, that would seem a clear case of forgery. The fax machine comes close to that;[93] but in the camera example, the false instrument must exist (and be intended to exist) when it is read; but D might have intended to destroy the copy bill the moment he had faxed it and before the fax was read. Its existence was not essential to induce the prejudicial act envisaged. These difficulties suggest that it would have been better if Ondhia had been charged under s 2, below.

What then of the case where D creates the document in entirely electronic form and emails it to V?

(b) Copying a false instrument

By s 2 of the Act:

> It is an offence for a person to make a copy of an instrument which is, and which he knows or believes to be, a false instrument, with the intention that he or another shall use it to induce somebody to accept it as a copy of a genuine instrument, and by reason of so accepting it to do or not to do some act to his own or any other person's prejudice.

The offence is triable and punishable in the same way as forgery under s 1.

The commission of this offence requires (a) that the instrument that is copied is in fact a false instrument;[94] and (b) that D 'knows or believes'[95] it to be false. In addition (c) the copy must be made with the intention of inducing someone to accept it as a copy of a genuine instrument.

[91] *Ondhia* [1998] 2 Cr App R 150, [1998] Crim LR 339 and commentary.

[92] Above, n 91.

[93] The court suggested that there is a distinction between faxes and photocopies. See *Ondhia*, above, commentary at 341.

[94] Just as for handling, above, p 836, it must be proved that the goods are in fact stolen. If the instrument is not false but is believed by D to be false there may be an attempt, above, p 400.

[95] As to which see above, p 853.

It is not an offence simply to copy an instrument known or believed to be false if the copy is made to pass as a copy of a false instrument. At a trial for forgery, copies of the allegedly false instrument may be photocopied for the convenience of judge and counsel and it can hardly be supposed that this conduct falls within s 2.

The operation of the section may be illustrated by reference to the facts of *Harris*.[96] D, who owed money to V, had acquired a receipt to which V's signature had been forged. He told V that he had paid the debt and when V questioned this, D photocopied the forged receipt and sent the copy to V. Such conduct clearly falls within s 2. Strictly it is arguable that a photocopy of a false instrument made with the intention of being passed *as a copy* of a false instrument does not tell a lie about itself and courts elsewhere[97] have been disposed to take this view. Only where the copy is made to pass as the original false instrument would the copy tell a lie about itself. The point is, however, no longer of importance in view of s 2; the offence is committed if D *intends* to pass the photocopy as a copy of a genuine instrument. But if D intends to pass off his copy of the false instrument as the false instrument itself this is forgery under s 1 and does not fall within s 2.

(c) Using false instruments and copies

By s 3:

It is an offence for a person to use an instrument which is, and which he knows or believes to be false, with the intention of inducing somebody to accept it as genuine, and by reason of so accepting it to do or not to do some act to his own or any other person's prejudice.

And by s 4:

It is an offence for a person to use a copy of an instrument which is, and which he knows or believes to be, a false instrument, with the intention of inducing somebody to accept it as a copy of a genuine instrument, and by reason of so accepting it to do or not to do some act to his own or any other person's prejudice.

Both offences are triable and punishable in the same way as forgery under s 1.

The offence under s 3 in substance replaces the former offence, under s 6 of the Forgery Act 1913, of uttering. Under s 6 a person who 'uses, offers, publishes, delivers, disposes of, tenders in payment or exchange, exchanges, tenders in evidence or puts off' was guilty of uttering. This extravagance of language is now replaced by the single verb 'uses' but this does not import any restriction on the ambit of the offence. The Law Commission was aware[98] that 'uses' is the paramount verb, was so regarded by the courts,[99] and would do duty for the remaining expressions in the earlier legislation.

Any use of the false instrument will suffice. While the actual making of the false instrument can hardly be regarded as a use of it, its communication to another is clearly a use of it. No doubt it would be enough that it is left in a position where V will see it and it may be enough that it is sent to another.[100]

96 [1966] 1 QB 184, [1965] 3 All ER 206n, CA.

97 *Tait* [1968] NZLR 126 (New Zealand Court of Appeal).

98 Law Com No 55, para 49.

99 Cf *Harris* [1966] 1 QB 184, [1965] 3 All ER 206n, CA.

100 Cf *Harris*, last note. There is clearly a use of a false witness statement when it is sent forward along with other documentation relating to the case. Cf *A-G's Reference (No 2 of 1980)* [1981] 1 All ER 493, [1981] 1 WLR 148, CA.

The use is not restricted to the maker of the false instrument. It is equally an offence for someone who did not make the false instrument to use it with the appropriate intent, whether or not there is any collaboration with the maker.

Whether making a copy of a false instrument, without any further steps taken to communicate it to another, constitutes a use of a false instrument[101] is no longer of importance in view of the fact that it would in any case be an offence under s 2. Strictly, though, the case seems to fall within s 3. While it can hardly be said that D in forging a document purporting to be made by V is 'using' the very document he forges, there is no reason why E, who comes across D's forgery and photocopies it with the appropriate intent, should not be regarded as using D's forged instrument. In the ordinary use of language he has used the instrument which was forged by D. There may thus be a use of a false instrument though it is not communicated to another.

Little needs to be said about s 4 which parallels s 3 in relation to the use of a copy of the false instrument. It is submitted that copying a false instrument does not constitute a use *of the copy* within s 4. As has just been indicated this may constitute a use of the false instrument within s 3; at the stage of copying D may properly be said to have used the original forged instrument but he can hardly be said to be *using* the copy which he makes.

(d) Possession offences

By s 5 of the Act:

(1) It is an offence for a person to have in his custody or under his control an instrument to which this section applies which is, and which he knows or believes to be, false, with the intention that he or another shall use it to induce somebody to accept it as genuine, and by reason of so accepting it to do or not to do some act to his own or any other person's prejudice.

(2) It is an offence for a person to have in his custody or under his control, without lawful authority or excuse, an instrument to which this section applies which is, and which he knows or believes to be, false.

(3) It is an offence for a person to make or to have in his custody or under his control a machine or implement, or paper or any other material, which to his knowledge is or has been specially designed or adapted for the making of an instrument to which this section applies, with the intention that he or another shall make an instrument to which this section applies which is false and that he or another shall use the instrument to induce somebody to accept it as genuine, and by reason of so accepting it to do or not to do some act to his own or any other person's prejudice.

(4) It is an offence for a person to make or to have in his custody or under his control any such machine, implement, paper or material, without lawful authority or excuse.

(5) The instruments to which this section applies are –

(a) money orders;

(b) postal orders;

(c) United Kingdom postage stamps;

(d) Inland Revenue stamps;

101 A point canvassed but left open in *Harris*, last note.

(e) share certificates;

(f) passports and documents which can be used instead of passports;

(fa) immigration documents;[102]

(g) cheques and other bills of exchange;

(h) travellers' cheques;

(ha) bankers' drafts;

(hb) promissory notes;

(j) cheque cards;

(ja) debit cards;

(k) credit cards;

(l) certified copies relating to an entry in a register of births, adoptions, marriages or deaths and issued by the Registrar General, the Registrar General for Northern Ireland, a registration officer or a person lawfully authorized to register marriages; and

(m) certificates relating to entries in such registers.

(6) In subsection (5)(e) above 'share certificate' means an instrument entitling or evidencing the title of a person to a share or interest –

(a) in any public stock, annuity, fund or debt of any government or state, including a state which forms part of another state; or

(b) in any stock, fund or debt of a body (whether corporate or unincorporated) established in the United Kingdom or elsewhere.

The offences under s 5(1) and (3) are triable and punishable in the same way as forgery under s 1. The offences under s 5(2) and (4) are also triable either way and are punishable on summary conviction with the same maxima of six months imprisonment and/or a fine not exceeding the statutory maximum; on trial on indictment, however, these offences carry a maximum of two years' imprisonment.

Section 5 penalizes the possession of the instruments specified in s 5(5). The list is exhaustive so that it is not an offence under this section to possess a false instrument as such (say a false testimonial or will) unless it is one of the instruments specified.

(i) Possession of device for making an instrument

Section 5(3) also penalizes the possession of any 'machine or implement, or paper or any other material, which to [D's] knowledge has been specially designed or adapted[103] for the making of an instrument' to which the section applies. It is accordingly not enough that D possesses implements with which he intends to make an instrument unless the implements are *specially* designed or adapted to make one of the *specified* instruments. It is no offence to possess a pen though D's intention is to use it to make one of the specified instruments; nor is it an offence to possess a household cleanser in order to falsify one of the specified instruments[104] since neither the pen nor the cleanser specially designed, nor need be adapted, for the making of a false instrument. It is of course not possible to

[102] As inserted by the Asylum and Immigration (Treatment of Claimants) Act 2004, s 3.

[103] As to which see the discussion, above, n 52.

[104] Certain household cleansers can be used to remove the holder's signature from credit cards thus enabling D to sign the holder's signature in his own hand which can be easily reproduced by D.

provide an exhaustive list of the machine, implements, paper or other materials which are specially designed or adapted for making instruments to which the section applies; it is for the prosecution to establish that the implement, etc is so designed or adapted and that D knew that. 'Knowledge' in this subsection is not coupled with 'belief' as it is elsewhere in the section and generally in offences under the Act.[105] Clearly 'knowledge' is more restricted than 'knowledge or belief' but the boundary between the two is somewhat speculative.[106]

It is only necessary to show that the implement, etc has been specially designed or adapted to make an instrument to which the section applies, not that the machine, etc has been designed or adapted to make *false* instruments. No doubt it will often be D's intention that he or another should so use it, but it suffices that the implement etc is specially designed or adapted to produce any of the specified instruments. Very commonly cheque books are stolen and may be found in the custody or control of D; if D has one of the relevant states of mind he is guilty of an offence since the paper or other materials used are specially designed for the making of cheques and cheques are included in the specified instruments.

(ii) Custody or control

D must be proved to have 'custody or control' of the false instrument or of the implement etc which is specially designed or adapted for its making. The Law Commission, not entirely unreasonably, is reluctant to plump for 'possession' because of the technicalities which have come to be associated with that concept.[107] The Commission prefers 'custody or control' as it did with criminal damage and reference may be made to the discussion in that context.[108]

While s 5 creates four offences, there are in essence two pairs of offences. All four offences have the common element of custody or control of instruments or implements. The offences under s 5(1) and (3) are more serious than those under s 5(2) and (4) in requiring proof that D has the instrument intending to induce another to accept it as genuine and thereby to do, or not to do, something to his own or another's prejudice, or has the implement with a view to its use to produce an instrument with like intent. This intent has already been discussed.[109] The offences under s 5(2) and (4) differ only, but markedly, in relation to the mental element that needs to be established. Under these provisions it is enough that D has custody or control of a specified instrument which he knows to be false, or a proscribed implement, 'without lawful authority or excuse'. Section 5(1) does not provide any such defence, because its strict *mens rea* requirements of intention render such unnecessary.[110] Aside from undercover police officers possessing counterfeit documents it is difficult to envisage circumstances in which there could co-exist a lawful possession of documents known to be false coupled with an intention to prejudice.

105 See *Dhindsa* [1992] COD 396. 106 See above, p 853. 107 See above, p 151.

108 Below, Ch 24.

109 Above, p 874. It may be that s 5(2) is available as an alternative within s 6(3) of the Criminal Law Act 1967, see *Fitzgerald* [2003] Crim LR 631 and commentary.

110 *Dickson v Gill* [1896] 2 QB 310 suggests that the absence of a lack of intention to defraud does not constitute a lawful excuse for the possession. That is a separate question from whether D's lawful excuse for possession can co-exist with his intention to defraud.

(iii) Lawful authority or excuse

Lawful authority or excuse is not defined in the Act and its use in other contexts[111] affords no grounds for thinking that, so far as D is concerned, it will be generously interpreted. No doubt a police officer who in the course of his duty seizes false documents or implements has lawful authority for his custody, as does a private citizen who gains such custody with a view to delivering them to the police or other proper authority.[112] Lawful authority must extend not only to those authorized by law but also to those who plan to act in accordance with the law. 'Excuse' is more difficult to define. It must extend to cases other than those where D has available to him some general defence to crime (for example, insanity, infancy or duress) for otherwise its inclusion would be meaningless. What is capable of being an excuse must be a matter of law for the judge, but there is little in the decided cases by way of guidance[113] and the issue must turn on what the court believes is reasonable. It is thought unlikely that a court would consider it an excuse that a false instrument or an implement of forgery is kept as a curio.

Where D is charged under s 5 with having control of an implement it would appear to be necessary to prove that D knows it to be specially designed or adapted. Knowledge of falsity is required for the offence under s 5(2) and knowledge that the implement is so designed or adapted is required for the offence under s 5(3); and by s 5(4) the custody of any *such* machine, etc is an offence.

The onus of proving lack of lawful authority or excuse lies on the prosecution. Once the prosecution has proved that D had custody of (a) an instrument he knew to be false, or (b) an implement specially designed or adapted, there would be an evidential burden on D to proffer an explanation. If D does adduce some evidence of lawful authority or excuse it will be for the prosecution in the ordinary way to satisfy the jury that D has no authority or excuse.

111 See above, p 332.

112 Cf *Wuyts* [1969] 2 QB 474, [1969] 2 All ER 799, CA. Cf *Sunman* [1995] Crim LR 569, CA (counterfeiting case where D undecided as to what to do with instrument discovered to be false).

113 Cf *Dickins v Gill* [1896] 2 QB 310, DC, where it was held in a case under the Post Office (Protection) Act 1884, s 7 that the proprietor of a philatelist newspaper had no lawful authority or excuse for possessing a dye which he made in order to produce black and white illustrations of a postage stamp in his newspaper.

24

Offences of damage to property

The principal offences of damage to property are governed by the Criminal Damage Act 1971 which replaced the prolix and complicated provisions of the Malicious Damage Act 1861. Like the Theft Acts of 1968 and 1978 the Criminal Damage Act is a code, and it must be approached and interpreted in the same fashion.[1] The Criminal Damage Act is in the main, the work of the Law Commission and reference to the papers of the Commission is helpful in understanding the underlying policies and in elucidating the provisions of the Act.[2]

The Law Commission wished to keep the policies and concepts of the law of damage to property in line with the law of appropriating property – theft. Complete parity for theft and criminal damage is neither practicable nor desirable, but it is important that there should be no conflict of principle if the criminal code as a whole is to be consistent and harmonious. Thus, while land cannot in general be stolen, there is no need for any similar limitation in relation to offences of criminal damage; on the other hand, it is clearly desirable that if it is not generally an offence to pick another's wild mushrooms, it should not be an offence to destroy or damage them and the Criminal Damage Act so provides.

1. Destroying or damaging property of another

By s 1(1) of the Criminal Damage Act 1971:

> A person who without lawful excuse destroys or damages any property belonging to another intending to destroy or damage any such property or being reckless as to whether any such property would be destroyed or damaged shall be guilty of an offence.

And by s 4 the offence is punishable by imprisonment for 10 years on indictment.[3]

(a) Destroy or damage

The expression 'destroy or damage' was commonly used in the Malicious Damage Act 1861 and previous decisions on the meaning of these words, though no longer binding, retain a persuasive value.

[1] See above, p 645.

[2] See Law Com No 29, *Offences of Damage to Property* (1970). See also Law Commission Working Paper No 23, *Malicious Damage* and D. W. Elliott, 'Criminal Damage' [1988] Crim LR 403.

[3] Although originally the same as theft, this is now more severe than theft (maximum seven years).

In *Roe v Kingerlee*[4] the Divisional Court held that '[w]hat constitutes criminal damage is a matter of fact and degree and it is for the [triers of fact], applying their common sense, to decide whether what occurred was damage or not'. In *Samuels v Stubbs*,[5] Walters J said:

It seems to me that it is difficult to lay down any very general and, at the same time, precise and absolute rule as to what constitutes 'damage'. One must be guided in a great degree by the circumstances of each case, the nature of the article and the mode in which it is affected or treated ... It is my view, however, that the word ... is sufficiently wide in its meaning to embrace injury, mischief or harm done to property, and that in order to constitute 'damage' it is unnecessary to establish such definite or actual damage as renders the property useless, or prevents it from serving its normal function....

Once again the courts have abdicated responsibility for precise legal definition of a key element of an offence in favour of reliance on the ordinary use of the term.

What is contemplated by 'destroy or damage' is actual destruction or damage; that is, some *physical* harm, impairment or deterioration. This will be usually be capable of being perceived by the senses,[6] but it is the property that must be tangible for the purposes of this offence, not the damage.[7] The damage can be by act or omission.[8] It is not enough to show that what has been done amounts to a civil wrong, as for example a trespass to land or goods for neither requires proof of actual damage. It was held in *Eley v Lytle*[9] that D was guilty of no offence when, during a game of football, he ran over V's land and the only evidence of actual damage was that he had committed a trespass. It seems clear that the same result would follow under the Criminal Damage Act. Actual damage, however, need only be slight. Grass can be damaged by trampling it down,[10] and is easily and rapidly damaged by football, cricket, or even bowls.[11] And even sterner stuff is susceptible of damage, as where a stalagmite is broken away.[12]

Greater difficulty arises over whether property is damaged where it is rendered unfit for a use to which it might be put. A thing may be damaged in the sense of being physically harmed though nothing is actually broken or deformed. A car is damaged just as much by uncoupling the brake cable as by cutting it with a pair of pliers. So a machine may be damaged by removing some integral part,[13] or by running it in an improper fashion so that physical impairment will result,[14] or tampering with some part so that it

4 [1986] Crim LR 735. 5 [1972] 4 SASR 200 at 203.

6 But no doubt a non-rechargeable battery is damaged by exhausting the charge. The damage cannot be perceived by the eye but it has been rendered useless. Similarly with the erasure of recordings from audio, video and storage media: it has been held that a card containing a computer program is damaged by erasure of the program: *Cox v Riley* (1986) 83 Cr App R 54, DC. But as to the modification of computers and computer material see now the Computer Misuse Act 1990 below, Ch 25.

7 See below, p 895. 8 *Miller* [1983] 2 AC 161, above, p 83. 9 (1885) 50 JP 308, DC.

10 *Gayford v Chouler* [1898] 1 QB 316, DC.

11 Cf *Laws v Eltringham* (1881) 8 QBD 283, DC, below, p 895, n 39.

12 See (1964) The Times, 12 Sept.

13 Cf *Tacey* (1821) Russ & Ry 452. Charges of criminal damage were brought against the person who sabotaged floodlights at a premiership football game intending to fix bets: The Times, 13 Feb 1999.

14 Cf *Norris* (1840) 9 C & P 241.

will not work although no part is removed or broken.[15] However, in *Lloyd v DPP*[16] the court rejected a submission that the clamping of a car was, by itself, damage to the car and that was followed in *Drake v DPP*[17] where it was held that clamping involved no intrusion into the physical integrity of the vehicle. The clamp renders the vehicle useless for its purpose for the time being, just as the removal of an essential working part does. The distinction appears to be that the clamp renders the vehicle unworkable by being attached rather than by physically harming any integral part.

In *Lloyd* a large yellow sticker was also affixed firmly to the windscreen, rendering it impossible to drive the car until considerable effort had been put into removing it. Brian Hogan contended strenuously, and reasonably, that this must be criminal damage. But did it intrude into 'integrity' of the vehicle any more than the clamp? Affixing with glue can hardly be more intrusive than affixing with steel bolts. The question of damaging by impairing 'usefulness' might arise where the owner is deprived access to a house or car by the theft or borrowing of keys to the front door or ignition keys. It would not be a natural use of language to describe these actions as damaging the house or car (even though the owner may be put to expense before he can put the house or car to their intended uses).[18] The Scottish Law Commission have proposed a new offence to combat this problem. Interference with property or a persons lawful use of property which causes harm or inconvenience would be criminalized. This would catch the wheel-clamper and the borrower of car or house keys.[19]

Similar problems of interpreting the expression arise when the question of 'damage' is made to turn on the property being rendered less 'valuable'. It has been held that property may be damaged though there is no interference with its performance if it is rendered less valuable.[20] A car is damaged if the paintwork is scratched and food is damaged by spoiling, as is milk where watered.[21] In each of those cases there is a physical interference. Smith[22] argues that focusing on the impact of D's conduct on the value of V's property is an erroneous approach since it could lead to the prosecution for criminal damage in wholly unsuitable circumstances.[23] This reinforces the point that the property must be physically interfered with.

15 Cf *Fisher* (1865) LR 1 CCR 7, DC, and see *Getty v Antrim County Council* [1950] NI 114 (dismantling). Though a machine or a structure may be damaged by the removal of a part or by dismantling, it does not necessarily follow that the parts are damaged by the removal or dismantling; if the parts are undamaged D can be charged only with damaging the whole: *Woolcock* [1977] Crim LR 104 and 161; *Morphitis v Salmon* [1990] Crim LR 48, DC. Care must be taken in drafting the charge accurately.

16 [1992] 1 All ER 982, DC.

17 [1994] RTR 411, DC, [1994] Crim LR 855. Cf the position in Scotland discussed by A. Phillips, 'Criminal and Civil Aspects of wheel clamping on private property' (1993) 38 Jnl of the Law Soc of Scotland 187.

18 *Henderson and Battley* (1984), CA unreported but extensively cited in *Cox v Riley* (1986) 83 Cr App R 54, [1986] Crim LR 460, DC.

19 See Draft Criminal Code for Scotland (2003), cl 83.

20 Cf *Foster* (1852) 6 Cox CC 25. Cf *King v Lees* (1948) 65 TLR 21, DC (passenger urinating in taxi held to have caused injury for purposes of the London Hackney Carriage Act 1831, s 41).

21 Cf *Roper v Knott* [1898] 1 QB 868, DC.

22 Smith, *Property Offences*, para 27–16.

23 The example given is that of the taking of the examination paper in *Oxford v Moss* (1978) 68 Cr App R 183, but the offence would surely not be made out in that case because the harm done (whether damage or not) is to the interest in confidentiality which does not constitute property for criminal damage (nor for theft).

In an attempt to avoid difficult decisions of whether damage is *de minimis*, the courts have occasionally been guided by the potential for expense to be incurred by the owner in rectifying the apparent harm.[24] In *Samuels v Stubbs*,[25] it was held that a 'temporary functional derangement' of a policeman's cap resulting from its being jumped upon constituted damage though there was no evidence that the cap might not have been restored to its original state without any real cost or trouble to the owner. By contrast, in *Hardman v Chief Constable of Avon and Somerset Constabulary*[26] it was held that pavement drawings in water soluble paint constituted damage to the pavement where the local authority was involved in expense in removing them with high-pressure water jets. This seems entirely right. No one would maintain that property which has been daubed by slogans or drawings was not damaged simply because the elements would eventually remove all trace of them[27] or because the householder could remove them more quickly with soap and water. *Samuels v Stubbs* is, perhaps, a less clear case. If an article is accidentally trodden upon (and for the purpose of determining whether there has been damage it can make no difference that it is intentionally trodden upon) and the owner finds that it takes a matter of moments to press it back into shape, surely he would say that no damage had been done? In *A (A Juvenile) v R*[28] it was held that spitting on a policeman's raincoat did not damage the raincoat where the spittle could be removed by a wipe with a damp cloth. No doubt it would have been otherwise had the material been capable of being stained by the spittle.[29]

The cases[30] suggest that whether what is done to property amounts to damage is a matter of fact and degree to be determined by the trier of fact in a commonsense way. Under the usual principles, a court or jury must not be allowed to find that the result constitutes damage when no reasonable tribunal could so find; and a magistrates' court may be corrected, as a magistrate was in *Samuels v Stubbs*,[31] if it finds that the result was not damage when, in law, it was. This does not optimize consistency in the law.

The defendant's opinion that what he did was not damage is irrelevant if damage is caused in law and fact. V's wall is damaged by D's graffiti irrespective of whether D regards it as an improvement.[32]

These principles apply to land or interests in land as to chattels. To dump rubbish on another's land, even though there is no tangible hurt to the land beneath the rubbish,

24 The problem arises disproportionately frequently with criminal damage because the activities of protestors commonly involve a symbolic act of minor damage – daubing slogans, decapitating statutes of former Prime Ministers, snipping perimeter fencing of air-force bases, etc.

25 [1972] 4 SASR 200 at 203. 26 [1986] Crim LR 330 (Judge Llewellyn Jones & Justices).

27 For a call for criminal damage prosecutions of dog owners who allow their dogs to foul pavements see P. Alldridge, 'Incontinent Dogs and the Law' (1990) 140 NLJ 1067.

28 [1978] Crim LR 689 (Judge Streeter & Justices).

29 But would the policeman have been unduly fastidious to insist that even a rain-proofed material should be dry-cleaned after it had been spat upon?

30 *Roe v Kingerlee* [1986] Crim LR 735, DC; *Henderson and Battley*, CA, unreported but approved in *Cox v Riley* (1986) 83 Cr App R 54, DC; *Morphitis v Salmon* [1990] Crim LR 48, DC.

31 [1972] 4 SASR 200 at 201.

32 Nor is D's motive (eg painting fig leaves over parts he considers indecent) relevant. Cf *Fancy* [1980] Crim LR 171, CC (whiting out National Front slogans). See also M. Watson, 'Graffiti – Popular Art, Anti Social Behaviour or Criminal Damage' (2004) 168 JP 668.

may be to damage the land if the owner is put to expense in removing the rubbish before the land can be put to his uses.[33]

'Destroy' clearly goes beyond damage and does not contemplate half measures. The word is a useful addition, more accurately describing certain forms of conduct; to destroy of structures means to pull down or demolish, of crops or growing things to lay waste, of machines to break up, and of animals to deprive of life.[34] The courts do not seem to have faced an argument that D who intends or is reckless as to mere damage should not be guilty if charged with having intentionally or recklessly destroyed property.

(b) Property

Section 10(1) of the Criminal Damage Act provides:

In this Act 'property' means property of a tangible nature, whether real or personal, including money and –

(a) including wild creatures which have been tamed or are ordinarily kept in captivity, and any other wild creatures or their carcasses if, but only if, they have been reduced into possession which has not been lost or abandoned or are in the course of being reduced into possession; but

(b) not including mushrooms growing wild on any land or flowers, fruit or foliage of a plant growing wild on any land.

For the purposes of this subsection 'mushroom' includes any fungus and 'plant' includes any shrub or tree.

The exceptions in paragraphs (a) and (b) are of course to keep the law of damage to property in line with the law of theft.[35] But while there is a substantial measure of correspondence in the definitions of property for theft and damage, there are three significant differences.

In the first place land, which in general cannot be stolen, may be the subject of criminal damage. The policies which favour exempting land from the offence of stealing[36] do not apply to the offences of damaging property. The distinction also has the support of history, for while land has always been excepted from definitions of stealing there has never been any such limitation in offences of damage to property. It is, then, still the law that while D cannot steal his neighbour's croquet lawn by annexing it,[37] he may commit criminal damage by turning it over to grow vegetables.

[33] One might question the consistency of this with the decision in *Lloyd* [1991] Crim LR 904, DC, where as noted, the court took the view that a car was not damaged by placing a wheel clamp on it. Criminal damage charges had also proved ineffective in combating the menace of prostitutes' cards being stuck on public telephone boxes hence the new offence under the Criminal Justice and Police Act 2001, s 46 (see Home Office, *New Measures to Control Prostitutes' Cards in Phone Boxes* (1999)).

[34] Cf *Barnet London Borough Council v Eastern Electricity Board* [1973] 2 All ER 319, DC.

[35] But note that the destruction of, or damage to, wild animals and plants may be an offence under other legislation; see for example the Wildlife and Countryside Act 1981 and the Protection of Badgers Act 1992.

[36] See above, p 671.

[37] He might steal by removing the turf. The Warden of a university hall was once surprised to discover that, in his absence, his lawn had been carried away (though not 'dishonestly') by the Vice-Chancellor to make a bowling green.

Secondly, while intangible property has now been brought within the subject matter of theft, it is still excluded from the definition of property for the purposes of criminal damage. 'Offences of criminal damage to property,' said the Law Commission, 'in the context of the present law connote physical damage in their commission, and for that reason we have not included intangible things in the class of property, damage to which should constitute an offence'.[38]

Consequently such intangible property such as easements and profits, patents and copyrights, are excluded for the purposes of criminal damage.[39]

Thirdly, whereas it is theft to pick wild mushrooms, fruit and foliage, etc for commercial purposes, these cannot be the subject of a criminal damage charge irrespective of the ulterior motive of the damager or destroyer.[40] It is important to note that the limitation extends only to fruit or foliage of plants growing on the land. The land itself may be damaged by, for example, environmental protest against GM crops.[41]

A person does not constitute property for the purposes of this offence.[42]

(c) Belonging to another

The offence under s 1(1) may be committed only where D destroys or damages property 'belonging to another'. Here, again, the policy of the law of criminal damage, which must be to protect interests in addition to ownership, is very much the same as that for the law of theft. Consequently s 5 of the Theft Act[43] has a substantially similar counterpart in s 10 of the Criminal Damage Act which provides:

(2) Property shall be treated for the purposes of this Act as belonging to any person –

(a) having the custody or control of it;

(b) having in it any proprietary right or interest (not being an equitable interest arising only from an agreement to transfer or grant an interest); or

(c) having a charge on it.

(3) Where property is subject to a trust, the person to whom it belongs shall be so treated as including any person having a right to enforce the trust.

(4) Property of a corporation sole shall be so treated as belonging to the corporation notwithstanding a vacancy in the corporation.

It is, then, enough that V has some proprietary interest in the property which D damages, and it does not have to be shown that V is the owner of the property; D may, for example, damage property of which V is the lessee or bailee. Further, D may commit an offence where the property belongs to him provided that V also has a proprietary interest in the property. Thus, where D owns a car and loans it to V, but then damages the car during the

38 Law Com No 29, para 34.

39 Cf *Laws v Eltringham* (1881) 8 QBD 283, DC. D and others had been charged with damaging Newcastle Town Moor by playing bowls upon it. It was held that the property could not be laid in the freeman who had merely the (incorporeal) right of herbage; the property ought to have been laid in Newcastle Corporation as the freeholder.

40 On the relationship of the provisions with the Wildlife and Countryside Act 1981, see M. Welstead, 'Seasons of Mists and Mellow Fruitfulness' (1995) 145 NLJ 1499.

41 See M. Stallworthy, 'Damage to Crops' (2000) 150 NLJ 728, 801.

42 *Baker* [1997] Crim LR 497.

43 See above, p 674.

loan period, he damages property 'belonging to another'. In such cases it may be difficult to prove that D acted with *mens rea* or without lawful excuse,[44] but, given that, D may commit criminal damage though he both owns, has custody and control of the property. Just as a co-owner of property may steal it by appropriating the other's share,[45] a co-owner may commit criminal damage by destroying or damaging the property.

But V must have some *proprietary* right or interest in the property.[46] Where property is insured the insurer acquires an interest in the property, but the interest is not a proprietary one.[47] If D destroys his own property which he has insured with V, he does not destroy property belonging to another even though he may have destroyed it with a view to making a dishonest claim against V.[48] In *Appleyard*[49] where D, the managing director of a company, set fire to the company's premises, it was argued that he could not be convicted of arson since he was 'in effect' the owner of the premises. D's conviction for arson was nevertheless upheld apparently on the basis that he was not the owner of the premises and knew he was not.

Property is also treated as belonging to a person who has a charge on it. This expression does not, in terms, appear in s 5 of the Theft Act 1968 and is probably unnecessary in either Act, since a charge is almost certainly a 'proprietary interest'. It was included in the Criminal Damage Act because the Law Commission thought:

> it should be made clear that a person who has a charge on property should be regarded as having a significant interest in the property to entitle him to the protection of the criminal law for damage done to it by the owner who subjected it to the charge.[50]

It will be noted that the definition of property belonging to another in the Criminal Damage Act, s 10, contains no provision equivalent to s 5(4) of the Theft Act – property got by another's mistake. This distinction can be of no practical importance: the getting of property by another's mistake may well excite acquisitive instincts but it is unlikely to excite an outburst of vandalism. There do not seem to have been difficulties over allegations of damaging abandoned property.[51]

Where D is the owner of property in which no other person has any proprietary right or interest, his destroying or damaging it cannot amount to an offence under s 1(1).[52] Nor generally is it an offence to damage one's own property apart from the special case dealt with in s 1(2).[53] It is not an offence for D to destroy a work of art which he owns or to lay waste his plentiful stocks of food at a time of acute shortage. Such acts may be properly described as wanton but they are not criminal because there is at present no compelling policy reason for making them criminal. But where such a reason does exist,

44 See below, p 900. 45 *Bonner* [1970] 2 All ER 97n, [1970] 1 WLR 838, CA, above, Ch 18.

46 See above, p 900.

47 An insurer has an interest in the safety of the insured property but, without more, this does not constitute a proprietary interest. Cf *Lucena v Craufurd* (1806) 2 Bos & PNR 269, HL, per Lawrence J at 302.

48 Cf *Denton* [1982] 1 All ER 65, [1981] 1 WLR 1446, CA, below, p 901. Such offences were included in the Malicious Damage Act 1861, ss 3 and 59.

49 (1985) 81 Cr App R 319, [1985] Crim LR 723, CA, below, p 898.

50 Law Com No 29, para 39.

51 Cf theft of 'abandoned' property: above, p 691.

52 If, in a case like *Hinks*, above, p 653, the donee is given a chattel, he may steal it, but he can then damage or destroy it with impunity. Where the donee's title is voidable, it may be arguable that it is different.

53 Below, p 912.

and cruelty to animals provides an illustration, particular offences can be created which extend to harm by an owner to his own property.[54]

(d) *Mens rea*

Section 1(1) requires that the destruction or damaging of the property should be intentional or reckless, and without lawful excuse.

(i) Intention and recklessness[55]

'In the area of serious crime,' said the Law Commission,

> the elements of intention, knowledge or recklessness, have always been required as a basis of liability . . . We consider, therefore, that the same elements as are required at present should be retained, but they should be expressed with greater simplicity and clarity. In particular, we prefer to avoid the use of such a word as 'maliciously',[56] if only because it gives the impression that the mental element differs from that which is imposed in other offences requiring traditional *mens rea*. It is evident from such cases as *Cunningham*[57] and *Mowatt*[58] that the word can give rise to difficulties of interpretation. Furthermore, the word 'maliciously' conveys the impression that some ill-will is required against the person whose property is damaged.[59]

By 'traditional *mens rea*' it is clear that the Law Commission meant to convey that liability for damage was predicated upon conduct of D which was intended by D to cause the damage in question or was foreseen by D as creating a risk of causing that damage.

This view certainly governs *intentional* damage. It is not enough that D intended to do the act which caused the damage unless he intended to cause the damage itself; proof that D intended to throw a stone is not proof that he intended to break a window.[60] Nor is it enough that D intends to damage property if he does not intend to damage property *of another*. Since D commits no offence under s 1(1) of the Act in damaging or destroying his own property, it follows in principle that he ought to be guilty of no offence where he destroys V's property under the mistaken impression that it is his own. Whether D's mistake is one of fact or law he commits no crime for he lacks *mens rea*, and this view was firmly endorsed by the Court of Appeal in *Smith*.[61] Upon the termination of his tenancy of a flat D had caused £130 worth of damage in removing wiring which he had himself installed and boarded over. In law the landlord became the owner of the wiring and boarding as fixtures, and the trial judge directed the jury that D could have no lawful excuse since he had in law no right to do as he did. D's appeal against conviction was allowed. James LJ said on behalf of the court:[62]

> Applying the ordinary principles of *mens rea*, the intention and recklessness and the absence of lawful excuse required to constitute the offence have reference to property belonging to another. It follows that in our judgment no offence is committed under this section if a person destroys or

54 Protection of Animals Act 1911, s 1. Other examples would include protection of listed buildings.

55 Cf the general discussion of intention and recklessness, above, Ch 5.

56 'Maliciously' was the expression most commonly used in the Malicious Damage Act 1861 to describe *mens rea*.

57 [1957] 2 QB 396, [1957] 2 All ER 412, CA, above, p 103.

58 [1968] 1 QB 421, [1967] 3 All ER 47, HL, above, p 103.

59 Law Com No 29, para 44.

60 Cf *Pembliton* (1874) LR 2 CCR 119.

61 [1974] QB 354, [1974] 1 All ER 632, CA.

62 [1974] 1 All ER 632 at 636.

causes damage to property belonging to another if he does so in the honest though mistaken belief that the property is his own, and provided that the belief is honestly held it is irrelevant to consider whether or not it is a justifiable belief.

The mistake in *Smith* was a mistake as to the civil law; D knew all the facts and drew the wrong conclusion of law from them. The result is the same so far as criminal liability is concerned whether the mistake is one of fact or law so long as the mistake negatives *mens rea*.[63] As such D commits no offence in pulling down a house if he honestly believes the house is his whether his mistake is one of fact or law and however egregious his error may have been.[64] It makes no difference that D's conduct might be described as wanton (as where he destroys a work of art) or that his purpose is a crime of fraud (for example, to defraud insurers). If D does not intend to destroy or damage property of *another*, nothing can render him liable to a charge under s 1(1). In *Appleyard*,[65] above, had D believed that he owned the company's premises then he could not have been convicted whatever his motive (to defraud insurers or creditors, to inflict loss on the shareholders) may have been.

(ii) *Mens rea* as to damage – foresight of consequences?

The Act extends liability not merely to damage which is caused intentionally but also damage which is caused recklessly. That recklessness in this context was meant to connote foresight of consequences is apparent from the Law Commission's Report. This is reinforced by the Law Commission's proposed definition of recklessness[66] which, as Lord Edmund Davies pointed out,[67] was surely in the draftsman's mind when he drafted the Criminal Damage Act. This was not the view taken in *Caldwell*,[68] where the criminal law was plunged into unnecessary confusion and complexity,[69] and the breadth of the offence posed risks of serious unfairness.[70] Fortunately, the House of Lords has now acknowledged that the decision of the majority in *Caldwell* constituted a misinterpretation of the 1971 Act, and for that reason and for sound reasons of policy and principle as discussed above in Chapter 5, the orthodox subjective interpretation of recklessness which the Law Commission intended has been re-established. *Caldwell* is overruled.

In *G*[71] the two defendants aged 11 and 12, when on a camping expedition without their parents' permission, entered the yard of a shop set fire to bundles of newspapers leaving some lit newspaper under a large plastic wheelie-bin. The newspapers set fire to the wheelie-bin and the fire spread causing £1m worth of damage. The boys had expected the

63 See generally above, p 122.

64 Cf *Langford* (1842) Car & M 602.

65 (1985) 81 Cr App R 319, [1985] Crim LR 723, CA.

66 'A person is reckless if, (a) knowing that there is a risk that an event may result from his conduct or that circumstances may exist, he takes that risk, and (b) it is unreasonable for him to take it, having regard to the degree and nature of the risk he knows to be present': Working Paper No 31, *The Mental Element in Crime*. See now Law Com No 89, *Report on the Mental Element in Crime*.

67 *Caldwell* [1981] 1 All ER 961 at 968, HL, [1982] AC 341.

68 [1981] 1 All ER 961, [1982] AC 341.

69 See Lord Steyn in *G* [2004] AC 1034, [2003] 4 All ER 765 at para 57.

70 See per Lord Bingham in *G*, above, at para 33: 'It is neither moral nor just to convict a defendant (least of all a child) on the strength of what someone else would have apprehended if the defendant himself had no such apprehension. Nor, the defendant having been convicted is the problem cured by imposition of a nominal penalty'.

71 [2004] AC 1034, [2003] 4 All ER 765.

fires to extinguish themselves on the concrete floor; neither had appreciated that there was any risk of the fire spreading in the way that it did. They were convicted of arson contrary to ss 1(1) and 1(3) of the Criminal Damage Act. Applying the *Caldwell* formula of recklessness, although the jury acknowledged some difficulty in applying fairly an objective standard to children whose capacity to see risk was limited by their immaturity.

In overruling *Caldwell*, Lord Bingham observed that:

section 1 as enacted followed, subject to an immaterial addition, the draft proposed by the Law Commission. It cannot be supposed that by 'reckless' Parliament meant anything different from the Law Commission. The Law Commission's meaning was made plain both in its Report (Law Com No 29) and in Working Paper No 23 which preceded it. These materials (not, it would seem, placed before the House in *R v Caldwell*) reveal a very plain intention to replace the old-fashioned and misleading expression 'maliciously' by the more familiar expression 'reckless' but to give the latter expression the meaning which *R v Cunningham* . . . and Professor Kenny had given to the former. In treating this authority as irrelevant to the construction of 'reckless' the majority fell into understandable but clearly demonstrable error. No relevant change in the mens rea necessary for proof of the offence was intended, and in holding otherwise the majority misconstrued section 1 of the Act.[72]

The definition of recklessness to be applied in criminal damage is now that found in clause 18(c) of the Draft Criminal Code:

A person acts recklessly within the meaning of section 1 of the Criminal Damage Act 1971 with respect to –

(i) a circumstance when he is aware of a risk that it exists or will exist;

(ii) a result when he is aware of a risk that it will occur;

and it is, in the circumstances known to him, unreasonable to take the risk.

The doctrine of transferred malice[73] applies, so that if D intends, or is reckless as to, damage to property of A, he may be liable where he in fact causes damage, neither intentionally nor recklessly, to property of B.

The intention or the recklessness need not be related to the particular property damaged, provided that it is related to another's property. If, for example, a person throws a stone at a passing motor car intending to damage it, but misses and breaks a shop window, he will have the necessary intention in respect of the damage to the window as he intended to damage the property of another. But if in a fit of anger he throws a stone at his own car he will not have the requisite intention. In the latter case the question of whether he has committed an offence will depend upon whether he was reckless as to whether any property belonging to another would be destroyed or damaged.[74]

Williams suggests[75] that transferred malice would not apply where D, bent on damaging property other than by fire, accidentally starts a fire in circumstances where there is no

72 Ibid, para 29. See also Lord Steyn at para 45; and Lord Rodger at para 64.

73 See above, Ch 5.

74 Law Com No 29, para 45.

75 (1983) 42 CLJ 85, 86. Cf A. Ashworth, 'Transferred Malice and Punishment for Unforeseen Consequences' in P. Glazebrook (ed), *Reshaping the Criminal Law* (1978) 77, 92. The issue is discussed more recently in J. Horder, 'A Critique of the Correspondence Principle in Criminal Law' [1995] Crim LR 759, 769–770. Horder argues that what really matters is 'the representative label: is it right to label D as an arsonist if he did not intend to start a fire . . .'. Cf B. Mitchell, 'In Defence of A Principle of Correspondence' [1999] Crim LR 195.

obvious and serious risk of fire. This, with respect, seems an acceptable conclusion. Arson is a separate offence carrying a higher punishment than damage caused by other means and its *mens rea* requires not merely the intentional or reckless damaging of property but the intentional or reckless damaging of property *by fire. A fortiori,* D would not commit an offence of criminal damage where he throws a stone at V but misses him and breaks a window, unless of course D was subjectively reckless as to the risk of breaking the window.[76]

Obviously *mens rea* cannot be supplied by an afterthought. If D inadvertently breaks V's window he cannot become liable when, having learned that V is a tax inspector, he rejoices in the harm caused. On the other hand, if D inadvertently sets fire to V's property and subsequently becomes aware[77] that he has done so, he may be criminally liable if, intending or being reckless that *further* damage ensue to V's property, he lets the fire takes its course when it lies within his power to prevent or minimize that further damage.[78]

It will be incumbent on the judge to provide careful direction on the issues of intention and recklessness if charged on the same indictment.[79]

(e) Lawful excuse

The Law Commission took the view that in most cases:

> there is a clear distinction between the mental element and the element of unlawfulness, and in the absence of one or other element no offence will be committed, notwithstanding that damage may have been done to another's property. For example, a police officer who, in order to execute a warrant of arrest, has to force open a door of a house is acting with lawful excuse although he intends to damage the door or the lock. On the other hand a person playing tennis on a properly fenced court who inadvertently hits a ball on to a greenhouse roof, breaking a pane of glass, acts without lawful excuse, but will escape liability because he has not the requisite intention.[80]

This distinction drawn by the Law Commission between the 'mental element' and the element of 'unlawfulness' may be a distinction of convenience but it is a distinction generally adopted in this work. It is thought convenient to consider separately, so far as the situation permits, the issue of intention or recklessness as to the damaging of the property and the various grounds of exculpation or justification that may exist for damage deliberately done.

Under the former law, it was not always clear in what circumstances it was justifiable to damage or destroy the property of another. Strictly speaking, the Criminal Damage Act 1971 is to be interpreted without reference to the earlier law, but it is of course impossible to legislate, as it were, in a vacuum; and there is always a risk that policies implicit in the earlier law will continue to flourish unless new policies are clearly articulated. Consequently s 5 of the Act provides a partial definition of 'lawful excuse', which applies these policies and makes a clean break with the earlier law. The section in part provides –

76 Cf *Pembliton* (1874) LR 2 CCR 119.

77 It is not enough that D ought to have been aware, or was not aware because he gave no thought to it: *Miller*, next note.

78 *Miller* [1983] 2 AC 161, [1983] 1 All ER 978, HL. See above p 83.

79 *Mason* [2005] All ER (D) 04 (Feb).

80 Law Com No 29, para 49.

(2) A person charged with an offence to which this section applies[81] shall, whether or not he would be treated for the purposes of this Act as having a lawful excuse apart from this subsection, be treated for those purposes as having a lawful excuse –

(a) if at the time of the act or acts alleged to constitute the offence he believed that the person or persons whom he believed to be entitled to consent to the destruction of or damage to the property in question had so consented, or would have consented to it if he or they had known of the destruction or damage and its circumstances; or

(b) if he destroyed or damaged or threatened to destroy or damage the property in question . . . in order to protect property belonging to himself or another or a right or interest in property which was or which he believed to be vested in himself or another, and at the time of the act or acts alleged to constitute the offence he believed –

(i) that the property, right or interest was in immediate need of protection; and

(ii) that the means of protection adopted or proposed to be adopted were or would be reasonable having regard to all the circumstances.

(3) For the purpose of this section it is immaterial whether a belief is justified or not if it is honestly held.

(4) For the purposes of subsection (2) above a right or interest in property includes any right or privilege in or over land, whether created by grant, licence or otherwise.

(i) Belief in consent

Section 5(2)(a) closely follows the pattern of s 2(1)(b) of the Theft Act 1968,[82] and it is right that it should since the parallel between theft and criminal damage is at this point exact. As appears to be the case with theft, D's belief is judged by the single criterion that it be honestly held; a point which, if it is not clear enough from the wording of s 5(2)(a), is put beyond doubt by s 5(3).

The provision covers a number of mistaken beliefs. First, and most obviously this provision covers the case where D believes that the owner has consented to the destruction or damage. So in *Denton*[83] it was held that D was not guilty of arson in setting fire to his employer's mill where D believed that his employer had encouraged him to do so (even thought this was in order to make a fraudulent claim against the insurers). Secondly, the provision covers the case where D comes across an injured animal and, believing that the owner *would have consented* had he been able to contact him, D kills the animal to put it out of its misery.[84] Thirdly, the provision covers the case where D believes that X is a person entitled to consent to the destruction or damage and he has consented. Thus, for example, an employee destroying or damaging property belonging to the firm would commit no offence where he believed that some person in authority (say a foreman) was entitled to consent, and had consented.[85] Fourthly, the provision applies where D honestly believes that X is the person entitled to consent and that he would have consented to the damage if asked. Mistakes as to the identity of the person entitled to

[81] The section applies to an offence under s 1(1); as to other offences see below.

[82] See above, p 694.

[83] [1982] 1 All ER 65, [1981] 1 WLR 1446, CA.

[84] There is also a specific defence under the Wild Mammals (Protection) Act 1986, s 3, for the attempted killing of a wild mammal as an act of mercy if D shows that the mammal had been so seriously disabled otherwise than by his unlawful act that there was no reasonable chance of its recovering.

[85] Cf *James* (1837) 8 C & P 131.

consent, the status of the person, the presence of consent and the likelihood of conditional consent are all accommodated in this extremely wide defence.

One controversial example of the breadth of the defence is that in *Jaggard v Dickinson*[86] where D had permission to treat the house of a friend, X, as her own. One night when D was heavily intoxicated she took a taxi to the street where X lived. D then attempted to enter what she mistakenly believed to be X's house, smashing a window in the process. The magistrates had rejected the s 5(2)(a) defence since D's belief in consent was brought about by self-induced intoxication. The Divisional Court quashed the conviction because of the explicitly subjective focus of s 5(3): 'a belief can be just as much honestly held if it is induced by intoxication, as if it stems from stupidity, forgetfulness or inattention'.[87] Williams exposes the breadth of the decision by posing the case of D, intoxicated by LSD who believes that the owner of a Rolls Royce has instructed him to roll it over a cliff.

Subjective though the defence is, it seems that a belief that God is entitled to, and does, consent to the damage is no answer.[88]

(ii) Defence of property

A person is entitled to take measures to protect his own property, real or personal, from harm caused by, or by the use of, property belonging to another whether animate (such as trespassing cattle) or inanimate (such as a caravan). If, for example, a dog is attacking sheep it may be shot if this is a necessary measure to protect the sheep.[89] A right of way over land belonging to another, being a 'right or privilege in or over land,' is 'property' and may be defended, in appropriate circumstances, by the demolition of a wall obstructing it.[90] The owner clearly has this right where the risk to his property exists in fact, but the Act goes further. D has a lawful excuse within s 5(2)(b) if (i) he destroyed or damaged the property in question in order to protect property which he *believed* to be vested in himself or another; (ii) he *believed* the property to be in immediate need of protection; and (iii) he *believed* that the means of protection adopted were reasonable having regard to all the circumstances. It is of course for the prosecution to disprove these matters so long as D meets the evidential burden by laying a foundation for his claim to lawful excuse. The obligation is interpreted strictly: it is not for the judge to raise the defence and it has been held that the defendant must raise the defence by testifying.[91]

This provision is in line with general principles of defences in so far as it relates to beliefs in facts or circumstances; however, it goes well beyond that in so far as it provides D's *belief* that the means employed *were reasonable* will excuse. This must be contrasted with the position in self-defence and the prevention of crime where D may use such force as *is found by a jury to be reasonable* in the circumstances which D believed to exist.[92] The

86 [1981] 3 All ER 716.

87 Per Mustill J at 532. See G. Williams, 'Two Nocturnal Blunders' (1990) 140 NLJ 1564.

88 *Blake v DPP* [1993] Crim LR 586, DC, above, p 335 and commentary suggesting difficulties also because God is not a 'person'.

89 Where there is no such justification, injuring the animal may constitute to an offence under the Protection of Animals Act 1911, s 1 (as amended), *Isted v Crown Prosecution Service* (1997) 162 JP 513, DC.

90 *Chamberlain v Lindon* [1998] 2 All ER 538, DC.

91 And not through defence statements or counsel: *Jones* [2003] EWCA Crim 894, Buxton LJ at para 14.

92 Above, p 331. Note that an apparent attempt in *Scarlett* [1993] 4 All ER 629 to introduce a similar subjective standard into the law of self-defence and prevention of crime was rebuffed.

D's belief in the trigger for the defence is assessed on a subjective basis but the response to it is assessed objectively. The disparity between the 1971 Act and the common law was acknowledged in *DPP v Bayer*[93] where Brooke LJ noted that the degree of incoherence provided a further illustration of the urgent need for codification.

The breadth of the defence may be thought to carry subjectivity to excessive lengths. It departs from the general principle of criminal law that standards are set by the law, in practice by the jury or magistrates, not by every person for himself. The effect may be that a person's right to use force to defend his dog, which is property, may be more fully protected by the law than his right to use force to defend his child, who is not property. Section 5(2)(b) does not apply to damage to property in order to protect a person.[94]

'In order to' and *'immediate need'*

This aspect of the provision has caused most difficulty. In a series of cases the courts have said that the words, 'in order to protect property' and 'in immediate need of protection' have an objective meaning. The insistence that the test is objective is difficult to reconcile with the wording of the statute which suggests a purely subjective test.

In *Hunt*[95] D who assisted his wife in her job as warden of a block of old people's flats set fire to some bedding. He said he did so in order to demonstrate that the fire alarm was not working and so to protect the flats from immediate danger by getting it put right. The court asserted that, while this act was done in order to draw attention to the defective state of the fire alarm, it was not done in order to protect property. Roskill LJ was clear that the question whether or not a particular act of destruction or damage or threat of destruction or damage was done or made 'in order to' protect property belonging to another must be an objective test.

In *Ashford and Smith*[96] and *Hill and Hall*[97] the defendants were convicted of possessing articles with intent to damage property, namely the perimeter fences surrounding military bases. They claimed to have a lawful excuse because the bases, being an obvious target for enemy attack, constituted an immediate danger to property in the neighbourhood, and they acted in order to have the bases, and with them, the danger, removed. In both cases the court said that the defence had rightly been withdrawn from the jury: *objectively*, the defendants did not act in order to protect property; and, in *Hill and Hall*, it was added that there was no evidence on which it could be found that D believed the property was in immediate need of protection.

In *Johnson v DPP*[98] D, a squatter, damaged the door frame of a house in order to replace the locks with one of his own. He said that he did so in order to protect his property which he believed to be in immediate need of protection. The court purporting to apply an objective test (but in fact, it seems, simply disbelieving D) said that his purpose was not to protect property but to enable him to use the door; and, in applying a subjective test, that he did not believe his property was in immediate need of protection and that the means of protection were reasonable. It should be noted that a person may act with

93 [2004] 1 Cr App R 38, [2004] Crim LR 663.

94 *Baker & Wilkins* [1997] Crim LR 497.

95 (1977) 66 Cr App R 105, CA. Cf *Phillips v Pringle* [1973] 1 NSWLR 275 (CCA of New South Wales, action pursuant to a UN resolution against racialism not a lawful excuse for damaging goalposts).

96 [1988] Crim LR 682, CA.

97 (1988) 89 Cr App R 74, CA.

98 [1994] Crim LR 673, DC.

more than one purpose, and it is sufficient that one of those purposes was to protect property.[99]

As the court in *Hill and Hall* accepts, there are two distinct matters to be addressed. The first matter to be decided is D's actual state of mind. If D is asked, 'Why did you do this act'? and answers 'In order to protect the flats from fire', or 'to save the houses from damage by enemy attack' or 'to protect my property from thieves', he may be disbelieved but, if his answer is or may be true, if this was, or may have been, his reason for acting, it is impossible to say, rationally, that he did not act 'in order to' protect property. A purpose can exist only in the mind it need not have an objective existence. If A sticks pins into a wax model of Buckingham Palace in order to destroy it, all reasonable people will agree that the act does not imperil the Palace. 'Objectively' the act is quite harmless; but no amount of objectivity can alter the fact that A acts 'in order to' destroy property if that is why he is acting. Similarly if he acts in order to *protect* property. This issue should be assessed on D's subjective belief.

There is, however, justification for the importation of an objective element into the further question of D's alleged belief that the property was 'in immediate need of protection'. Under s 5(2)(b)(i) and (ii) it is irrelevant that the belief was wholly unreasonable if it was, or may have been, actually held. Unreasonableness is only evidence which assists the trier of fact in determining the ultimate question: whether the belief was honestly held or not. But, once D's belief is ascertained, however unreasonable the existence of the belief, the question whether it is a belief of the kind specified in the section is an objective question – a question of law or, perhaps, mixed fact and law. Whether the need, as seen by D, is an 'immediate' need is a question for the court or jury. For example, if Johnson had said that he believed his goods would be in need of protection when he moved them into the premises in a week's time, the court may believe him but not accept that this belief is a belief in an 'immediate' need for protection.

It may be that all three decisions above can be justified without resort to the unacceptable view that 'in order to' bears an objective meaning. The more acceptable basis for the decisions is that in each case the need, even as asserted by the defendants, was not an immediate need.[100]

The courts have followed the approach in *Hill and Hall*, to deny the defence where protestors have caused criminal damage as a symbolic gesture of protest where there is no 'direct and proximate' threat to their property.[101] In *Jones*, D was convicted of causing £65,000 worth of damage to council premises in a protest over planning permission. Buxton LJ, citing the 10th edition of this work with approval, accepted that the objective evaluation of beliefs in the defence was no different from the court deciding whether a defendant's claim that his intent was to break the victim's nose amounted in law to grievous bodily harm.[102] The absence of any 'immediate' need for protection also

99 In *Chamberlain v Lindon* [1998] 1 WLR 1252, [1998] 2 All ER 538, above, it was held that it was immaterial that D may have had a second purpose of avoiding civil litigation. This attitude has not been reflected in other cases, including recently *Mitchell* [2004] Crim LR 139 where the court rejected the common law defence of recaption where D had removed wheel clamps. Self-help is a last resort.

100 In *Chamberlain v Lindon*, above, it was held that D, within the meaning of the Act, believed the right of way was in immediate need of protection because the wall across it was an existing obstruction and delay would be evidence of acquiescence in it.

101 *Jones* [2003] EWCA Crim 894.

102 Ibid, para 19.

precludes reliance on s 5(2)(b) by D who damages a wheel clamp on his car from relying on s 5(2)(b).[103]

Belief in the reasonableness of the action

Once again the subjective terms of s 5(2)(b) need to be emphasized. There is no requirement that D's belief be reasonable, still less that D's conduct must meet some objective standard of reasonableness. But it does mean that D must believe that it was reasonable for him to do as he did. In theory D might justify laying waste an oil refinery because he believes its effluent is damaging his geraniums. However, a jury is unlikely to believe he did think, or could possibly have thought, that this was reasonable.

Hunt might be different. There was some evidence that efforts had been made to get the Council to repair the fire alarm but these had proved unavailing. D may thus have reached the end of his tether and his claim that he believed the action reasonable might carry some credibility.

Prophylactic measures in defence of property

A common case calling for the protection of property is where a dog is worrying livestock. In such a case s 5(2)(b) will ordinarily provide a lawful excuse for the killing of the dog. But the civil law goes further. The Animals Act 1971, s 9(3)(a), provides that D incurs no civil liability in this situation provided that D is a person entitled to act for the protection of the livestock and that he gives notice within 48 hours to the officer in charge of a police station of the killing or injury. But s 9(3)(b) then goes on to provide that D also incurs no civil liability for the killing of the dog where:

> the dog *has been*[104] worrying livestock, has not left the vicinity and is not under the control of any person and there are no practicable means of ascertaining to whom it belongs.

In such a case D's sheep might not, objectively viewed, be strictly in 'immediate' need of protection and the killing might be essentially a prophylactic measure. But it would be odd if D was criminally liable where he may be exempted from civil liability; it would involve D having to incriminate himself in order to take advantage of the civil defence. It is submitted that in these circumstances D would commit no criminal offence.[105] The incoherence of this area of law is exacerbated by the possibility of prosecution under the Protection of Animals Act 1911, s 1 for causing unnecessary suffering to any animal where the animal is injured. In *Isted v CPS*,[106] Brooke LJ urged further reform to reflect differences in policy when damage or destruction is caused to animate property.

D may not destroy or damage property of another because he honestly believes that harm may occur to his property at some time in the future. On the other hand it is not as such unlawful for D to take defensive measures in relation to his own property. It is an offence under s 31 of the Offences Against the Person Act 1861 to set traps so as to endanger life, and it is an offence under s 1(2) of the Criminal Damage Act 1971 to destroy or damage property in order to endanger life,[107] but it is not otherwise an offence merely to take defensive measures (to set broken glass on walls, erect spiked fences, etc)

[103] See *Lloyd v DPP* [1992] 1 All ER 982; *Mitchell* [2004] Crim LR 139.
[104] Italics supplied.
[105] See the discussion of *Workman v Cowper* [1961] 1 All ER 683.
[106] [1998] Crim LR 194.
[107] Below, p 912.

for the purpose of discouraging or preventing incursions by persons or their property.[108] In such cases the question of criminal liability can arise only where some harm is caused to the person or property of another.

So far as harm to another's property is concerned, D will ordinarily have taken his defensive or protective measures at some stage before his property was in 'immediate need of protection', and when the harm occurs D may be absent and unaware of it. It is submitted that where what D has done is a normal method of protecting property, say a barbed wire fence erected by a farmer, he would not be liable though a trespasser tears his best suit in climbing through the fence, notwithstanding that D himself could not have justified ripping open the trespasser's suit as a use of reasonable force to eject him.[109] But where D adopts unusual defensive measures, say traps calculated to maim animals it would normally not be difficult to show that he did not honestly believe this was a reasonable way to protect his property.

A measure frequently adopted for the protection of property is the keeping of a guard dog. The Animals Act 1971 provides that a person is not civilly liable for damage caused if the animal is kept for the protection of persons or property and 'keeping it there for that purpose was not unreasonable'.[110] The Act also provides that no liability is incurred to any person who has 'voluntarily accepted the risk thereof'.[111] The Guard Dogs Act 1975 makes it a summary offence, punishable by a fine at Level 3, to use or permit the use of a guard dog (that is, a dog kept for the purpose of protecting persons or property or a person guarding the same)[112] unless a person capable of controlling the dog, the handler, is present and controlling it, except where the dog is secured and not at liberty to go about the premises.[113] But it is further provided that the Act shall not be construed as conferring any civil right of action, or as derogating from any remedy (whether civil or criminal) in proceedings instituted otherwise than by virtue of the Act.[114]

In *Cummings v Granger*,[115] a civil action, it was held by the Court of Appeal that it was not unreasonable for an owner to keep an unsecured alsatian guard dog on enclosed business premises, and that he was not liable to a trespasser who entered the premises at night having seen the notice 'Beware of the dog' on the gate. The attention of the court was drawn to the provisions of the Guard Dogs Act but Lord Denning MR concluded that they did not affect civil liability and so far as reasonableness was concerned they had no application. If these facts were to recur the owner would now commit an offence under the Guard Dogs Act in permitting the use of an uncontrolled guard dog, but the question remains whether he would be liable for an offence against the person or, if property is damaged, under the Criminal Damage Act. So far as the latter is concerned the issue is whether the owner believed that the keeping of an uncontrolled guard dog was reasonable having regard to all the circumstances. In *Cummings v Granger* the Court of Appeal was firmly of the view that the keeping of an uncontrolled guard dog was not, in the

108 Cf potential civil liability under the Occupiers' Liability Act 1984, on which see W. V. H. Rogers, *Winfield and Jolowicz on Tort* (16th edn, 2003), 324–327.

109 Note the specific powers to remove trespassers under the Criminal Justice and Public Order Act 1994, ss 68 and 69.

110 Section 5(3)(b). 111 Section 5(2). 112 Section 7.

113 Section 1. *Hobson v Gledhill* [1978] 1 All ER 945, [1978] 1 WLR 215, DC.

114 Section 5(2).

115 [1977] QB 397, [1977] 1 All ER 104, CA, followed in *Mirvahedy v Henley* [2003] UKHL 16.

circumstances of that case, unreasonable; and conduct is not necessarily unreasonable even though it involves a breach of the criminal law.[116] No doubt in determining whether D thought the measure was reasonable, regard would be had to D's knowledge of the risk of accidental as opposed to deliberate trespass, of the risk to children not capable of looking properly to their own protection, of the propensities of the particular dog and other similar factors. What is important is that at this point the civil and criminal laws should not set different standards.

Protecting the interests of others

In most cases no doubt D will be the owner of the property which he seeks to protect, but even if D is not the owner he will not incur criminal liability if he honestly believes himself to be the owner and the other circumstances exist. By s 5(4) property is expressly defined to include any right or privilege in or over land. Consequently D may commit no crime where, honestly but mistakenly believing he has a right of way across V's land, he tears down a hut erected by V which, as D thinks, obstructs his imagined right of way.

Moreover, D is in the same position though the right or interest which he believes himself to have in the property which he protects is not a right or interest which is recognized by law since, by s 5(3), it is immaterial whether a belief is justified or not so long as it is honestly held. Suppose, for example, that D has a right to kill and take game on O's land, and D kills V's dog which he sees chasing and destroying game. In such a case there is in law no right or interest in property to protect; until D himself reduces the game into his possession he has no proprietary interest in it whatever. But if D believes he has a right or interest in the game, he would incur no criminal liability in killing V's dog provided the other circumstances exist.[117] In such a case as this, D's belief that he has a right in property to protect is understandable, but even if D's belief is absurd it suffices to provide him with the defence if honestly held.

The position is essentially the same where D claims no right or interest in the property which he protects, but acts to protect the property of another. An employee who caused damage to V's property in defending property belonging to his employer would commit no offence given his belief that the measures were reasonable and were immediately needed. But there need be no nexus whatever between the person intervening to protect the property and the owner of it. An officious bystander who chooses to intervene to protect the property of another will be free from criminal liability if he acts honestly on the same terms.

D must have at least a belief that there is some *property interest* that he is protecting. Thus, the defence was held, correctly to be unavailable where D decapitated a statue of Baroness Thatcher. He explained his motive as being that he held her responsible for developments in world politics with which he disagreed and that he genuinely feared for the future of his son growing up in this world.[118] D had no belief that he was protecting property.

116 Cf *Buckoke v Greater London Council* [1971] 1 Ch 655, [1971] 2 All ER 254, CA, above, p 318.

117 On the facts of *Gott v Measures* [1948] 1 KB 234, [1947] 2 All ER 609, DC, D would now be acquitted.

118 *Kelleher* [2003] EWCA Crim 2486. Bizarrely, at his first trial the prosecution conceded the defence of 'lawful excuse' under s 5(2)(b) was available to D. As an indication of the difficulty if these defences are allowed to go to the jury in cases of protest, it should be noted that in that first trial the jury failed to reach a verdict.

(iii) Cases not falling within the Act

By its terms s 5(2) recognizes that there may be other circumstances which would constitute lawful excuse on a charge of criminal damage, and s 5(5) further provides:

> This section shall not be construed as casting any doubt on any defence recognized by law as a defence to criminal charges.

It is clear that certain general defences (such as infancy, insanity, duress) are available on a charge of criminal damage and these are discussed elsewhere in this work.[119] But some particular matters call for further discussion here.

Self-defence, necessity and duress of circumstance

So far as necessity is concerned the law relating to defence of property is a particular, and well defined, instance where necessity is recognized as a defence, as is the case with defence of the person. The question remains as to how far it is permissible to destroy or damage property on the grounds of necessity in circumstances not involving defence of property. As a starting point it must be obvious that just as harm to the person may be justified on the grounds of self-defence of the person, so too the destruction of or damage to property may be justified in defence of the person.[120]

In so far as the attack involves the commission of a crime, as will be commonly the case, the situation would be covered by s 3 of the Criminal Law Act 1967,[121] which provides that a person may use such force as is reasonable in the circumstances in the prevention of crime. If, then, V sets his dog to attack D, D would not commit an offence of criminal damage if in using reasonable force to defend himself he killed the dog. But s 3 imports an objective requirement of reasonableness,[122] and D could not rely upon this section where the force used is unreasonable even though D himself honestly believed it was reasonable. Thus there appears to be the odd situation that if D is defending his property it is enough (under s 5) that he honestly believed that the force used was reasonable, but if he is defending his person his honest belief will not save him unless the force used was in fact reasonable in the circumstances.[123]

Now suppose that V's dog, quite unknown to V, attacks D. If D, in self-defence, kills or injures the dog, s 3 of the Criminal Law Act can have no application since D is not seeking to prevent the commission of any crime: the dog acting of its own volition commits no crime. D must rely on the common law and the question is not whether he thought his reaction was reasonable but whether it *was* reasonable. The Law Commission knew what they were doing in creating this distinction with the 1971 Act:

> We appreciate that our extended definition of lawful excuse introduces a less stringently framed defence than that of self-defence, where the force used must be reasonable when looked at objectively. There may therefore be the anomaly that different tests will apply to self-defence against bodily injury, but we do not think that this is sufficient reason to dissuade us from the present recommendation in this context.[124]

[119] Ch 11. As to intoxication see above, p 273 et seq.

[120] So if D lawfully repelling an attack by E causes E to fall through F's window, D cannot be convicted of criminal damage to F's window: *Sears v Broome* [1986] Crim LR 461, DC.

[121] See above, 332. [122] See above, 333.

[123] Perhaps, then, D should say that he feared for the safety of his trousers rather than his ankles.

[124] Law Com No 29, para 52.

The policy of greater generosity to those who act in protection of property over those who act in protection of personal safety is unattractive.

It may also be noted that s 5(2)(b) of the Criminal Damage Act provides a wider defence in connection with offences of damage to property than is afforded by the common law defence of duress of circumstances. It appears to be the case at present that duress of circumstances is available only where D faces a threat of death or serious bodily harm or, possibly, imprisonment.[125] But s 5(2)(b), where it applies, permits a purely utilitarian calculation.

Suppose there is a flood affecting the properties of X and Y and the fire brigade are called. Their assessment is that while X's house is not in danger there will be serious damage to Y's house by flooding unless X's fence is knocked down to allow the flood-waters to recede. A few pounds worth of damage needs to be done to the fence in order to prevent damage of several hundred pounds to the house. The firemen ask X for permission to knock down the fence, which he refuses, but the firemen nonetheless knock down the fence.[126] The firemen would have a lawful excuse to a charge of criminal damage if damaging the fence is reasonable in the circumstances. But if, additionally, the firemen have to restrain X because he resists their efforts to knock down the fence they would not be able to avail themselves of the common law defence of duress of circumstances since there is no threat of any harm to the person, let alone death or serious injury. They could rely only on the uncertain common law defence of necessity. If their action were regarded as not merely excused but justified, it may be that X would have no right to use force to defend his property.

Claim of right

It is clear that D cannot commit an offence under s 1(1) of the Act by destroying or damaging property which is, or which he believes to be, his own. The position would appear to be the same where D, though he does not believe he is the owner of the property which he destroys or damages, nevertheless acts under a claim of legal right. In *Twose*,[127] a case decided under the Malicious Damage Act, where it appeared that persons living near a common had occasionally burnt the furze in order to improve the growth of grass, it was accepted that D's belief in a right to burn the furze would be a good defence though there was no such right. Here D's belief was at least understandable, but in *Day*,[128] again under the old law, it was held that D was not guilty of an offence in maiming sheep belonging to V which he had distrained,[129] where he did so in the honest belief that he was entitled to do so upon V's refusal to pay compensation for damage done by the sheep. It would seem clear that cases such as these would be decided in the same way under the Criminal Damage Act where the clear emphasis is upon honest belief in right without any objective qualification.

In similar vein it is thought that a person who destroys or damages property found by him in circumstances where he believes the owner cannot be traced by taking reasonable steps can no more be convicted of criminal damage than he can be of theft by appropriating the property.

125 See above, p 314.

126 The illustration is based on fact except that X readily gave his permission.

127 (1879) 14 Cox CC 327.

128 (1844) 8 JP 186.

129 Taken out of V's possession pending compensation.

Protest defences

While the foregoing discussion deals with the more obvious categories of lawful excuse for damage to property there are certainly other cases. Moreover 'lawful excuse', like 'lawful authority or reasonable excuse,'[130] may have an inbuilt elasticity which enables courts to stretch it to cover new situations so that it is never possible to close the categories that might constitute lawful excuse.

Criminal damage is commonly committed in the course of political protest, as in the cases of *Hill and Hall, Jones* and *Kelleher.* The courts have recently dealt with two new claims of defence to charges under the Act. First, although accepting that an act of criminal damage (such as the snipping of wire fence at a nuclear weapons base) could be regarded as an act of expression for the purposes of Article 10 of the ECHR,[131] the courts have held that the criminalization of such activity is a proportionate response to the legitimate aims in Article 10(2).[132]

Secondly, the courts have so far rejected attempts to argue that the commission of criminal damage is lawfully excused when in response to actions of the State which the defendant believes to be contrary to international law. Thus, in *Hutchinson v Newbury Magistrates' Court*, the defendant relied on the opinion of the International Court of Justice on the legality of the threat or use of Nuclear Weapons and in Article VI of the Treaty on the Non-Proliferation of Nuclear Weapons to suggest that the UK's continued manufacture of such weapons at Aldermaston was contrary to international law. The court rejected the argument, holding that it was very difficult to identify any rule of law from the opinion of the International Court of Justice that was agreed with sufficient certainty to form part of a system of mandatory rules. Even if the UK was in breach of international law, the defendant had committed a crime to stop an unlawful but not criminal act, and could not rely on the UK's unlawfulness alone as an excuse for his own criminal conduct. Similar arguments were advanced in *Pritchard and Others*[133] where the conduct involved possession of articles to cause damage on an RAF base. The defendants pleaded that the action was necessary and lawful to attempt to prevent what they believed was the UK's unlawful act of war against Iraq. Grigson J held that the non-justiciability of the legality of the war did not preclude reliance on s 5 defences. On an interlocutory appeal, the Court of Appeal held that the s 5 defence would be available to D irrespective of the determination as to the legality of the war. D is entitled to defend his property against threats of a non-criminal and even of a lawful nature. The only objective element in the defence in s 5(2)(b) of the Criminal Damage Act 1971 was whether it could be said that, on the facts as the defendant believed them to be, the criminal damage alleged could amount to something done to protect another's property; subject to that the court and the jury were concerned simply with the question of a defendant's honestly held beliefs. The judge was therefore right to rule that no issue arose in relation to this defence which involved consideration of the legality of the war in Iraq. Strictly, the court's conclusion

130 See above, p 900.

131 See *Steele v UK* (1999) 28 EHRR 603.

132 *Hutchinson v Newbury Magistrates' Court* (2000), *The Independent*, 20 Nov.

133 [2004] EWCA Crim 1981.

that the legality of the war is irrelevant to the *availability* of the s 5(2) defence seems correct. But, is the illegality relevant to its *application*? Surely the circumstances – the immediacy, potency, lawfulness, etc – of the action will be important to the jury in its evaluation of D's belief that his conduct is 'reasonable' as the statute requires? The success of the defence on facts such as these nevertheless remains debatable. Is there sufficient immediacy of threat to property, particularly where the charges of conspiracy to damage? Which item of property is D seeking to protect? (The defence does not apply to protect people).[134]

This will certainly not be the last the courts hear of this line of defence.

Authorized damage

At a more mundane level, clear cases arise where there is authority for the destruction or damage.[135] The more general problem is set by the sort of facts that occurred in *Workman v Cowper.*[136] D had shot a fox hound, the owner of which was unknown at the time of the shooting, and which was running wild on common land. There was no evidence that the dog was attacking or likely to attack, sheep, but it was the lambing season and D thought it best, attempts to catch the dog having failed, to shoot it. On such facts as these D's liability is unclear. There was nothing to suggest that the dog had been abandoned so that D could claim that he did not intend to destroy property *belonging* to another. Turning to the defences, since owners of healthy and expensive foxhounds do not readily consent to their destruction and there was no evidence that the dog was going to attack sheep, D would struggle to bring his conduct within s 5(2)(a). D might bring himself within the terms of s 5(2)(b) if he honestly believed that his sheep were in need of *immediate* protection. D could no doubt claim that he was acting honestly and that what he did was reasonable as a prophylactic measure – the dog, after all, might start attacking sheep. It is interesting to note that in the case itself the magistrates thought that D had acted reasonably and the Divisional Court had some sympathy for their conclusion. D was in fact convicted and it is thought that on similar facts he could still be convicted. Although there may be many who think that what he did was reasonable, even prudent, D was not acting in defence of property and it seems a necessary inference from s 5(2)(b) that unless his property is in immediate need of protection (or D honestly believes that it is) there can be no lawful excuse. But if D manages to catch the dog there is a procedure available authorizing its destruction within seven days of capture if efforts to trace the owner fail.[137] There is, in effect, a loophole in lawful excuse through which an agile, friendly and healthy dog may avoid a premature death.

134 *Baker* [1997] Crim LR 497.

135 Eg, statutory provisions for the destruction of dangerous, diseased or injured animals (Halsbury's Statutes, vol 2, tit. Animals); damage to property incidental to arrest, search and seizure (Police and Criminal Evidence Act 1984); where property is lawfully seized under statutory powers it would seem that in certain cases (firearms, offensive weapons, drugs) the police would have lawful excuse for destroying the property although the statute may not give an express power to destroy.

136 [1961] 2 QB 143, [1961] 1 All ER 683, DC.

137 Dogs Act 1906, s 3. (See also Clean Neighbourhoods and Environment Act 2005, s 68, not yet in force.)

2. Destroying or damaging property with intent to endanger life

Section 1(2) of the Criminal Damage Act 1971 provides:

A person who without lawful excuse destroys or damages any property, whether belonging to himself or another –

(a) intending to destroy or damage any property or being reckless as to whether any property would be destroyed or damaged; and

(b) intending by the destruction or damage to endanger the life of another or being reckless as to whether the life of another would be thereby endangered,

shall be guilty of an offence.[138]

By s 4 the offence is punishable by imprisonment for life. The section creates aggravated offences of criminal damage and arson.[139]

This subsection incorporates what is essentially an offence against the person into the Criminal Damage Act. The Law Commission were aware of this anomalous aspect of the offence they were proposing and observed that 'it may be that when the Criminal Law Revision Committee completes its review of the law of offences against the person it will be necessary to look again at this matter'.[140] The CLRC has long since completed its review of offences against the person and the Commission has made its own proposals in the draft Criminal Law Bill but the matter has not been reconsidered. Meanwhile the subsection requires the making of what the Court of Appeal has said 'may seem to many a dismal distinction'.[141]

The *actus reus* is the destruction of or damage to property. The destruction or damage which occurs in fact may be quite different from that envisaged by the defendant. Where there is such a difference, it is the destruction or damage which D intended, or as to which he was reckless, to which we must look in order to determine whether he intended to endanger, or was reckless whether he endangered, the life of another.[142] Thus if D aimed to throw his petrol bomb through the window of an occupied house, but the bomb hits the outer wall causing only trivial damage to the target, it is the intended damage to the interior which is relevant. The question is as to D's state of mind when he did the act and we cannot, at that point, know for certain what, if any, destruction or damage will be caused. The offence is not committed unless D's act caused some destruction or damage – there must be an *actus reus* – but whether the terms of s 2(1)(b) are satisfied has been predetermined. The nature of the destruction or damage actually caused may be very good evidence of what D intended, or of his recklessness, but that is all.

The *actus reus* does not require that any life is in fact endangered. Thus, in *Parker*,[143] D was convicted under s 1(2) of criminal damage, being reckless as to the endangerment of

138 D. W. Elliott, 'Endangering life by destroying or damaging property' [1997] Crim LR 382.

139 The trial of a person accused of arson being reckless as to whether life would be endangered must be heard by a full-time judge: *R v Jones (Stephen)* (1999) The Times, 20 May, CA.

140 Law Com No 29, para 27.

141 *Webster and Warwick* [1995] 2 All ER 168 at 173.

142 *Dudley* [1989] Crim LR 57 and commentary as cited with approval by the Court of Appeal in *Webster and Warwick*.

143 [1993] Crim LR 856.

his neighbours' lives when he started a fire in his semi-detached house. And the fact that the neighbours were absent and therefore never at risk did not preclude conviction.

In *Steer*[144] it was held that the offence requires intention or recklessness as to the endangering of life *by the damaging or destruction of property*, not merely by D's act. D fired rifle shots at the windows of a house occupied by V, against whom he had a grudge. The House of Lords held that the charge under s 1(2) was misconceived. Danger to life was caused by the bullets, not by any damage to the windows or property in the bedroom. The question, as we have seen, is not whether or how life was endangered in fact, but what D intended, or as to what result he was reckless.[145] While there was certainly cogent evidence that D was reckless as to danger to life from the bullets, he did not commit the offence unless he foresaw danger to life from, say, flying broken glass and there was no evidence of that. The contrary interpretation would also produce potential anomalies. Lord Bridge gave an example of A and B firing bullets into the air, being reckless whether life was endangered. It would be absurd if A alone was liable because only his bullet damaged property.

In *Webster* D pushed a heavy coping stone from a bridge onto a passenger train passing below. Only a corner of the stone penetrated the roof but the passengers were showered with glass fibre and other material. The judge failed to direct the jury that D was guilty only if he foresaw danger to life from the damage to the carriage, not merely from the stone, so the conviction had to be quashed. In *Warwick*[146] D drove a stolen car from which E threw bricks at a pursuing police car, smashing a window and showering officers with glass. It was held that there was evidence from which a jury could infer recklessness whether the police driver might lose control through being so showered, thus endangering life. Recklessness whether he might lose control through being hit by the brick would not be enough. The distinction applied in each of these cases is indeed 'dismal' but inevitable on the proper construction of the Act.

The fact that the damage may be to D's own property adds to the anomalous nature of the offence.[147] Suppose that D, the owner of a house, removing unwanted electrical equipment belonging to him, cuts a cable also belonging to him and exposes the live wire in such a way as that he foresees a risk to the life of another. The *actus reus* is the 'damage' to the cable. It is no answer that the cable belongs to D and that he is entitled to cut the cable if he wants to. It seems extraordinary that this should be an offence of damage to property, but that seems to be the implication of *Merrick*.[148] O, a householder, employed D to remove old television cable. D did so, leaving the live cable exposed for six minutes. His conviction was upheld. It would appear that the result would have been the same if O had done the act himself instead of through an agent. It would be understandable if the offence were simply the endangering of life; but the gravamen of the conduct in a case like *Merrick* has nothing to do with damage to property. Why should it be different if the danger arose not from cutting old cable but from the installation of new? The implications of the result are 'absurd and alarming'.[149]

144 [1988] AC 111, [1987] 2 All ER 833, HL.

145 *Dudley* [1989] Crim LR 57.

146 [1995] 1 Cr App R 492.

147 There have been a number of cases in which the charge has been laid where D has set fire to his own property intent on committing suicide, and has been reckless as to the endangerment of neighbours' lives: eg *Brewis* [2004] EWCA Crim 1919.

148 [1996] 1 Cr App R 130, [1995] Crim LR 802.

149 D. W. Elliott, above at 389.

So the offence has features both of an offence against property and an offence against the person. In some circumstances (as where D severs the brake cable of V's car intending V to drive to his death) the offence will overlap with the offence of attempted murder, but it is wider than attempted murder in two respects. One is that it does not require the intent to kill which is necessary on a charge of attempted murder:[150] intention or recklessness as to the endangering of life will suffice. On facts such as those occurring in *Cunningham*,[151] for example, it could be that when D severed the gas pipe he did not intend to asphyxiate V but was reckless whether her life would be endangered; he would not be guilty of attempted murder but he would be guilty of the offence under the Criminal Damage Act.[152] The other is that the offence under the Criminal Damage Act may be committed where the acts done by D are too remote to constitute an attempt[153] to murder. If, for example, D were to sever the brake cable of O's car intending thereafter to induce V to drive the car to his death, D's act of damaging the car might be too remote to support a charge of attempting to murder V but it would support a charge under the Act.

Certain general features of the offence under s 1(2) (such as destruction or damage, property, intention and recklessness) are the same as for the offence under s 1(1) which has already been discussed. The following additional matters need to be discussed in relation to the offence under s 1(2).

(a) Intention and recklessness

Intention and recklessness in relation to destroying or damaging property has been discussed above[154] applies, *mutatis mutandis*, to intention and recklessness in relation to endangering the life of another,[155] and reference may also be made to the general discussion of intention and recklessness elsewhere in this book.[156] It need not be shown that life was in fact endangered by the damage nor that the damage in fact done created any risk to life so long as D, by damaging the property, intended or was reckless as to the endangering of life.[157] Where D starts a fire in an unoccupied building with no one present, he might be reckless whether he endangers the lives of firemen, if he foresees a risk of a life being endangered by the damage. Recklessness, following *G* is subjective: *Cooper*.[158] The Court of Appeal required that the risk be one that was 'obvious and significant' to the defendant. Thus, where D has realized that there is a risk but has dismissed it as negligible, it could not be said that he was taking an obvious and significant risk. This is an unusual interpretation of the subjective form of recklessness. It is submitted that the correct test is whether D has foreseen *a* risk of life being endangered by the damage that he intends or about which he is reckless and that he takes that risk unjustifiably.

150 See above, p 401.

151 [1957] 2 QB 396, [1957] 2 All ER 412, above, p 103.

152 And also, of course, of the offence under s 23 of the Offences Against the Person Act 1861. It might be noted in passing that the toxic elements are now removed from gas used for domestic purposes and natural gas does not contain them; hence domestic gas can cause death only by asphyxiation, and even this risk is almost nil. But there remains a very high risk of explosion which is a serious danger to life.

153 See above, p 405.

154 At p 9.

155 *Hardie* [1984] 3 All ER 848, [1985] 1 WLR 64, CA.

156 Above, Ch 5.

157 *Sangha* [1988] 2 All ER 385, CA; *Dudley* [1989] Crim LR 57, CA. The definition of recklessness applied was that under *Caldwell.*

158 [2004] EWCA Crim 1382.

There must be a causal connection between the destroying or damaging of the property and the endangering of life. If, to extend an example used above, D were to damage the lock in the process of entering V's garage in order to sever the brake cable of V's car, there would be no offence under s 1(2). D intends to damage the lock and he further intends to endanger V's life, but he does not intend '*by the destruction or damage* to endanger the life of' V. It is only when D damages the brake cable that he would commit the offence under s 1(2). So in *Steer*[159] it was held that the offence was not committed where D fired off some shots at V and his wife as they stood at their bedroom window. While D must have foreseen that the shooting would cause damage by smashing the bedroom window and also endanger the lives of V and his wife, D would not have foreseen that that their lives would be endangered *by the damage to the window*, because it was not by that damage that they were, or were likely to be, endangered. On the other hand, it may be that if, having destroyed or damaged property belonging to V (eg having set fire to V's premises), D subsequently realizes that V's life is in danger, D would commit the offence under s 1(2), if, provided it lies within D's power to prevent or minimize the further harm, he then omits to do so, intending that or being reckless whether, V's life should be endangered.[160]

In *Attorney-General's Reference (No 3 of 1992)*[161] it was said that the property which D intends to damage need not be the same as the property which endangers life, instancing the case of a man who cuts the rope (the first property) of a crane, causing its load to crush the roof of a car (the second property) which kills the driver. But this seems to make far too heavy weather of the problem. Cutting the rope damages the crane, of which the rope is part, and the question then is whether D foresaw that the damaged crane might endanger life. It makes no difference whether the danger arises from the falling object or the car roof – it is caused by the damage to the crane.

(b) Lawful excuse

Since the gist of the offence under s 1(2) lies in endangering life by destroying or damaging property, it is understandable that D may commit the offence whether he creates a risk to life by destroying or damaging the property of another or by destroying or damaging his own. The risk is just the same whether D severs the brake cable on V's car, or severs the brake cable on his own car before lending it to V to drive.

It is equally understandable that the partial definition of lawful excuse in s 5(2) should not be applicable to an offence of this nature, and s 5 does not apply to offences under s 1(2). It can be appreciated that it ought not to be a defence to an offence of this nature that, say, D, with the assent of E, severed the brake cable on E's car before lending it to V to drive. Equally, D ought to have no lawful excuse in damaging property, although done for the purpose of protecting other property, where in so doing he knowingly creates a risk to life.

159 [1988] AC 111, [1987] 2 All ER 833, HL.

160 *Miller* [1983] 1 All ER 978, HL, above, p 83. Cf *Fuller* [1974] Crim LR 134, CA. D pleaded guilty to damaging property being reckless whether life would be endangered though warned by his brother of danger arising from a fractured gas pipe only after he had returned home. Appeal was against sentence only.

161 (1993) 98 Cr App R 383, [1994] Crim LR 348. The case was primarily concerned with the law of attempt, above, p 404.

Clearly, then, the intention in framing the offence under s 1(2) was that certain matters (such as destruction by D of his own property, destruction with owner's consent, destruction in defence of property) which constitute lawful excuse where D is charged with an offence under s 1(1) do not constitute lawful excuse where D is charged under s 1(2). This does not mean that there can never be a lawful excuse where D is charged under s 1(2), because s 1(2) expressly states that the offence may be committed only by one 'who *without lawful excuse* destroys or damages any property'. It follows that there may be circumstances, presumably of an exceptional character, where D would have lawful excuse for destroying or damaging property even though he does it realizing that he may endanger life. An exceptional case of this character would be where D damages property in self-defence; if it is legitimate for D to kill in order to prevent himself being killed, D would not commit an offence under s 1(2) because he happened to use, and damage, property belonging to another in killing his attacker.[162] Similarly, the police might have lawful excuse for damaging property where this was done to prevent the commission of a serious crime against the person, even though what was done might endanger the life of the criminal. And if necessity is a defence where D chooses to put one life at risk in order to save many others,[163] it would extend to damaging property to do so.

(i) Endangerment offences

The problems of the s 1(2) offence stem in part from the confusion between its objective in penalizing endangerment, and the requirement for that endangerment to be founded on damage to property. This has called some to question why English law does not adopt a general offence of life endangerment,[164] and this is certainly an issue to which the Law Commission should have regard in the codification programme.[165] To date, English law has created endangerment offences only in relation to specific activities for example, causing explosions[166] or specific circumstances such as behaviour on an aircraft.[167] There is no general property endangerment offence.[168]

3. Arson

The Law Commission took the view that there should be no separate offence of arson, that is, of destroying or damaging property by fire,[169] and simply provided in the Draft Bill that an offence committed under s 1(1) by fire should be punishable on indictment by imprisonment for life. In so far as arsonists may be commonly mentally unbalanced[170]

162 Cf *Sears v Broome* [1986] Crim LR 461, DC.

163 See above, p 315. 164 See Ashworth, POCL, 309.

165 See generally K. J. M. Smith, 'Liability for Endangerment: English Ad Hoc Pragmatism and American Innovation' [1983] Crim LR 127; D. Lanham, 'Danger Down Under' [1999] Crim LR 960.

166 Explosive Substances Act 1883, s 2.

167 Aircraft Security Act 1982, ss 2–3.

168 Cf the Scottish Draft Criminal Code, cl 82 which provides for causing a risk of unlawful damage to property.

169 Paper No 29, paras 28–33.

170 See *Callandine* (1975) The Times, 3 Dec, CA, stating that it would be unwise to sentence for arson in the absence of a psychiatric report.

and in so far as fire-raising creates extra hazardous risks, this seemed a sensible way to meet the case and avoided complication of the substantive law. But this way of meeting the case proved unacceptable to Parliament,[171] and s 1(3) of the Act provides:

An offence committed under this section by destroying or damaging property by fire shall be charged as arson.

And by s 4 it is punishable by imprisonment for life.[172] Arguably, the retention of a separate offence was desirable to provide a more appropriate label and reflect public anxiety about the offence. Arson remains disturbingly prevalent, particularly in certain types of property such as schools.[173]

The provision is a mandatory one – '*shall* be charged as arson'. Where D destroys or damages property by fire the proper course would appear to be to charge him with an offence under s 1(3).[174] Where there is also an allegation of endangerment, there should be separate counts of arson with intent to endanger life and of arson being reckless that life is endangered.[175]

The general features of arson are the same as for the offences under s 1(1) and s 1(2) except that the destruction or damage is to be by fire. For the offence to be complete some property must be destroyed or damaged by fire. The damage may of course be quite insignificant (it would be enough, for example, that wood is charred)[176] but there must be some damage by fire; it would not be enough that property is merely blackened by smoke though there might well be an attempt in such a case. D must intend, or be reckless as to, destruction or damage *by fire*. So if D, abetted by E, throws a bottle which, unknown to E, D filled with petrol in order to set fire to V's house, D may be convicted of arson but E may not.[177] E, however, may be convicted of simple criminal damage in respect of any damage caused by the throwing of the bottle.

4. Racially or religiously aggravated criminal damage

Section 30 of the Crime and Disorder Act 1998 (as amended)[178] provides:

(1) A person is guilty of an offence under this section if he commits an offence under section 1(1) of the Criminal Damage Act 1971 (destroying or damaging property belonging to another) which is racially or religiously aggravated for the purposes of this section.

[171] See HC, vol 817, col 1433 et seq. The reasons given for singling out damage by fire would be equally applicable to singling out damage by explosives; that 'arson' is such a splendidly evocative term cannot have been unimportant in securing its retention.

[172] The Powers of Criminal Courts (Sentencing) Act 2000, s 161(3) classifies arson within the term 'violent offence'.

[173] Each week there are 2,100 arson attacks with one or two deaths. See www.arsonpreventionbureau.org.uk.

[174] *Booth* [1999] Crim LR 144.

[175] In sentencing the court has the more specific verdict of the jury: *Hoof* (1980) 72 Cr App R 126, CA. But cf *Flitter* [2001] Crim LR 328.

[176] Cf *Parker* (1839) 9 C & P 45. No visible flame is necessary: *Stallion* (1833) 1 Mood CC 398.

[177] *Cooper (G) and Cooper (Y)* [1991] Crim LR 524, CA.

[178] By the Anti-terrorism, Crime and Security Act 2001, s 39(5)(b) and (6)(b). The amendment (inserting the words 'or religiously') has no effect in relation to anything done before it came into force (14 Dec 2001): s 42.

Definitions of 'racially aggravated' and 'religiously aggravated' and a discussion of the racial and religious aggravation offences in general are set out above.[179] The offence is punishable on summary conviction by imprisonment for six months or a fine not exceeding the statutory maximum or both, and, on conviction on indictment, by imprisonment for 14 years or a fine or both. The offences are extremely broad and elevate what is sometimes a trivial amount of damage (for example, a broken window caused in the course of a dispute with no racial background) into a racially aggravated offence because the offender uses a racial or religious insult at the time of the offence.[180] The racial hostility must be roughly contemporaneous with the damage being caused.[181]

5. Threats to destroy or damage property

Section 2(1) of the Criminal Damage Act 1971 provides:

A person who without lawful excuse makes to another a threat, intending that that other would fear it would be carried out –

(a) to destroy or damage any property belonging to that other or a third person; or

(b) to destroy or damage his own property in a way which he knows is likely to endanger the life of that other or a third person; shall be guilty of an offence.

The offence is punishable by 10 years' imprisonment: s 4(2).

(a) The conduct threatened

In order to constitute an offence under this section the conduct threatened must be conduct which would be an offence under s 1 of the Act. D would commit the offence where, without lawful excuse, he threatened to destroy or damage the property of another (whether property of the person threatened or of a third party), or where he threatened to destroy or damage his own property in a way which he knows is likely to endanger the life of another (whether the life of a person threatened or the life of a third party).

If D is charged under s 2(1)(a) 'lawful excuse' has the meaning ascribed to it by s 5 so that D would not commit an offence where, for example, he threatens to shoot V's dog should he find it attacking his sheep.[182] But by s 5(1) the partial definition of lawful excuse in the section does not apply to an offence 'involving a threat by the person charged to destroy or damage property in a way which he knows is likely to endanger the life of another . . .'.

This does not mean that there cannot be a lawful excuse for an offence under s 2(1)(b) merely that the partial definition of lawful excuse in s 5 cannot apply.[183] Where D threatens to destroy property of another with intent to endanger life he would have to be charged under s 2(1)(a), and cannot be charged under s 2(1)(b). Curiously, it would seem

[179] See Ch 16.

[180] *DPP v M* [2005] Crim LR 392 and commentary; the offence has of course also been used in circumstances in which it was entirely appropriate as where D spat and urinated on the Stephen Lawrence Memorial in London, *Guardian*, 20 July 1999.

[181] *Parry v DPP* [2004] EWHC 3112 (Admin) (20 min delay between throwing nail varnish on V's door and calling him an Irish so-and-so).

[182] See generally above, p 908.

[183] As to what may therefore constitute a lawful excuse, see above, p 900.

that if D is in such a case charged under s 2(1)(a) there would be a lawful excuse if it appeared that he believed the owner would have consented to the threatened destruction or damage (s 5(2)(a)), but if he is charged under s 2(1)(b) it would not be a lawful excuse that he was threatening to destroy his own property. But the distinction can be of small practical importance: if D threatens to destroy V's property in order to endanger the life of X then it would be difficult to show that D honestly believed that V would have consented to the threatened destruction 'had [V] known of the destruction or damage *and its circumstances*'.[184]

(b) The threat

The threat may take any form. The Law Commission said:

> There seems to be no good ground for limiting threats to written threats, for a telephonic threat, particularly if repeated, can cause more alarm in the recipient than any written threat. If the law is to be extended to cover telephonic threats, then logically there is no reason why it should not be extended to all threats, however made. The only limitation that needs to be imposed is that the threats should be intended to create a fear that what is threatened will be carried out.[185]

This last limitation needs to be imposed because the gist of the offence is the threat and, given that D intends that V should believe that the threat will be carried out, there ought to be no requirement that D himself should have intended to carry his threat into effect.

In *Cakmak*[186] the accused had threatened to set fire to herself as a protest when on the London Eye. The charges were laid under s 2(1)(a), even though the threat was to set fire to herself. The Court of Appeal held that despite this the jury were entitled to find a threat of damage to property of another, because there was an implied threat to damage such property. Whether there is an implied threat is an objective question: would a reasonable person in the particular circumstances regard the words used as a threat to damage the London Eye?

If D intends that V would fear the threat would be carried out, D commits the offence only if, judged objectively, the nature of the threat would have caused V to believe that the threat would be carried out. The actual thoughts and fears of the person threatened are irrelevant (*Cakmak*). It would seem that the threat need not be a threat to do the damage immediately, but immediacy may be a relevant factor, along with other circumstances, in determining whether there is something that can be called a threat.

(c) *Mens rea*

In *Cakmak* the court held that whether an offence under s 2(1)(a) or (b) is charged, the jury must be satisfied that the defendant made a threat to another with the intention (recklessness not being a sufficient *mens rea*) that the other would fear that it would be carried out.

Section 2(1)(a) deals exclusively with the property of a person other than the defendant. It is only in relation to s 2(1)(b) that the prosecution must prove that the defendant knew that the damage or destruction threatened was likely, if carried out, to endanger the life of a person other than the defendant.

184 Section 5(2)(a), italics supplied.
185 Law Com No 29, para 55.
186 [2002] 2 Cr App R 10, CA, [2002] Crim LR 581.

6. Possession offences

By s 3 of the Act:

A person who has anything in his custody or under his control intending without lawful excuse to use it or cause or permit another to use it –

(a) to destroy or damage any property belonging to some other person; or

(b) to destroy or damage his own or the user's property in a way which he knows is likely to endanger the life of some other person;

shall be guilty of an offence.

The offence is punishable by imprisonment for 10 years: s 4(2).

In line with the offence of threatening under s 2, the possession of the thing must be for the purpose of committing an offence under s 1 of the Act. There is of course no need for the commission of an offence of destruction or damage, but there must be an intent to use the thing, or allow another to use it, for the purpose of committing what would be an offence under s 1.[187] Accordingly the same provisions apply, *mutatis mutandis*, in relation to lawful excuse as apply to charges under s 2.[188]

(a) Custody or control

Although it is convenient to talk of this offence as one of possession, the section speaks only of custody or control.

Having regard to the difficulties inherent in the concept of possession, we prefer the idea of custody or control. These words are both to be found in the Statute Book, and together provide a better concept than 'possession', which is a technical term of some difficulty.[189]

It may well have been a wise decision to avoid the term 'possession', but what really helps to simplify the situation is the clear requirement for *mens rea.*

As the Law Commission observed:

Problems which may arise where a substance, such as a stick of gelignite, is slipped into a person's pocket without his knowledge will be wholly academic, because if that person has no knowledge of its presence he cannot have an intention to use it or permit or cause another to use it. If he has no intention to use it or permit or cause it to be used, he does not commit an offence. . . .[190]

But there must be custody or control; a mere intention to use something to commit an offence of criminal damage will not suffice. D may be about to pick up stones from the highway to throw through a shop window, but since at this stage he does not have custody or control of the stones he commits no offence under this provision. D need not of course be the owner of the thing in order to have custody or control of it, but he must have the charge of it. Where D is charged with permitting E to use the thing D must be in a position where, as against E, he might properly have prevented E from using it.

187 *Fancy* [1980] Crim LR 171, CC.
188 Above, p 900.
189 Law Com No 29, para 59.
190 Ibid.

(b) The things used

The section imports no limitation on the things which may be possessed with intent to commit criminal damage – 'anything' may do for the purpose.

The essential feature of the proposed offence is to be found not so much in the nature of the thing – for almost any every-day article, from a box of matches to a hammer or nail, can be used to destroy or damage property – as in the intention with which it is held.

Clearly the nature of the thing may have significance in proving that D possessed the thing with intent to commit criminal damage (the possession of a box of matches may be one thing and the possession of a ton of dynamite quite another) but given that the intent can be proved the nature of the thing is immaterial.

At this point it may be noted that under s 6 of the Act a search warrant may be issued to a constable where it appears there is reasonable cause to believe that a person has anything in his control or custody or on his premises for the purpose of committing an offence under s 1. This power of search was explained by the Law Commission[191] as being parallel to the power to search for stolen goods under s 26 of the Theft Act 1968. On one view the power of search is a wide one since it extends to anything, but it is always limited by the requirement that there must be reasonable cause to believe that the thing has been used or is intended for use in committing an offence of criminal damage. Powers of stop and search have also recently been extended to apply to this offence, in an attempt to combat graffiti.

(c) *Mens rea*

The offence may be committed only where D intends to use, or cause or permit another to use, the thing to destroy or damage property. It is not enough that D realizes that the thing may be so used: he must intend or permit such use. But it is not necessary that D should intend an immediate use of the thing; the offence is aimed at proscribing what is essentially a preparatory act and it is therefore enough that D possesses the thing with the necessary intent even though he contemplates its actual use of the thing at some time in the future. And it would also seem to be clear that a conditional intent (an intention to use the thing to cause damage should it prove necessary) will suffice.[192]

7. Kindred offences

In keeping with the aim of codification[193] the Criminal Damage Act 1971 contains, as near as may be, the whole of the law relating to damage to property. The Act abolished the common law offence of arson, repealed most of the provisions of the Malicious Damage Act 1861, repealed the Dockyards Protection Act 1772, and a large number of statutory provisions containing miscellaneous offences of damage to property.

But the Criminal Damage Act leaves untouched the Explosive Substances Act 1883. The Law Commission had at first planned to repeal s 2 (causing an explosion likely to

191 Paper No 29, Appendix A, notes to cl 6.

192 *Buckingham* (1976) 63 Cr App R 159, CA; cf *Bentham* [1973] QB 357, [1972] 3 All ER 271, CA.

193 See above, p 890.

endanger life or to cause serious injury to property) and s 3 (possessing explosives with intent to endanger life or cause serious injury to property, and doing an act to cause an explosion likely to endanger life or cause serious injury to property) since these might easily have been brought within the scheme of the Criminal Damage Act. But in the end the Law Commission did not do this because it was felt that the Explosive Substances Act belonged to the area of public order offences, and its replacement should be considered in the context of a review of offences relating to public order. This means that on given facts there may be an offence both under the Criminal Damage Act and the Explosive Substances Act, and it should be noted that there are differences in relation to the *mens rea* that has to be established.

The Criminal Damage Act did not repeal the following provisions of the Malicious Damage Act 1861: s 35 (placing wood etc on rail lines or obstructing signals with intent to obstruct or overturn any engine); s 36 (obstructing railway engines); and the retention of these offences made necessary the further retention of general provisions of the Malicious Damage Act relating to malice (s 58) and jurisdiction (s 72). It will be seen that none of these offences would necessarily (or even ordinarily) involve damage to property, though the ultimate aim may be to cause damage to property. Frequently such acts might amount to an attempt to commit criminal damage, but in so far as the acts might be merely preparatory these provisions render the preparatory acts criminal.

Nor does the Act repeal offences of damage arising under other legislation where the liability for the damage may be grounded in negligence or where there is strict liability for the damage. In particular cases there may be thought valid policy reasons for imposing criminal liability for damage to property caused negligently, or even for imposing strict liability for offences of damage to property.[194] These offences are perhaps best considered in relation to a review of criminal liability for negligence and a review of strict liability.

8. Mode of trial and sentence

While the maximum punishments provided by the Act for offences of damage tried on indictment (broadly, 10 years for the simple offence, and life imprisonment for aggravated offences) may seem high, this was done merely to provide for the worst sort of case within each class and it was not intended in any way to alter previous sentencing practice. The Act provides for summary trial of offences under ss 1(1), 2 and 3, and in practice most offences will be so tried.[195] There used to be a complex ruling relating

[194] Eg, s 85(1) of the Postal Services Act 2000 creates an offence to send by post a postal packet which encloses any creature, article or thing of any kind which is likely to injure other postal packets in course of their transmission by post or any person engaged in the business of a postal operator.

[195] As to summary trial of offences of damage when the value does not exceed £5,000, see above, p 8. As to offences of damage triable either way see the Magistrates' Courts Act 1980, Sch 2. The Magistrates' Courts Act 1980, s 22 affects mode of trial but has no effect on the classification of criminal damage as an 'offence triable either way': *Fennell* [2000] 2 Cr App R 318, CA approved in *Alden* [2002] 2 Cr App R (S) 74, CA. It can therefore be charged as an attempt in the magistrates where value is less than £5000. Particular difficulties have arisen over evaluating the 'market' value of eg GM crops *R (On the Application of the DPP) v Prestatyn Magistrates' Court* [2002] All ER (D) 421 (May). If under £5,000, criminal damage is, in practice treated as summary only although it remains triable either way.

to the ouster of the jurisdiction of magistrates in cases of damage involving title to real property, but this rule has now been abolished. In addition, s 130 of the Powers of Criminal Courts (Sentencing) Act 2000 empowers the court to make compensation orders, the magistrates' court may not order more than £5,000 in respect of any offence: s 131(1).

25
Computer misuse offences[1]

The impact of computer technology on society has of course been profound. From simple beginnings in arithmetical calculations it has spawned immense data retrieval systems; systems controlling traffic by land, sea and air; systems indispensable to the functioning of industry, healthcare, education, banking and commerce. All is to the common good or nearly all to the common good because, inevitably, some will use the technology for anti-social purposes. These may range from simple 'nosey-parkering', as where the hacker gains access to computer systems just for the fun of it (perhaps to demonstrate his computing ability), or for industrial espionage, or for perpetrating frauds, or for disrupting systems with viruses, worms or Trojan horses[2] with serious commercial consequences, or for disrupting traffic control systems which may put life at risk.

The law before the Computer Misuse Act 1990 could deal with some of these problems.[3] Appropriating property belonging to another is no less theft[4] because it is done not by picking a pocket but by causing a computer to debit one account and to credit another. Should someone cause death or injury not with a blunt instrument but by interfering with a traffic control system, he would be equally liable to conviction of an offence against the person.

But there were gaps to which the Law Commission addressed itself in a Working Paper published in 1988.[5] At this stage the Law Commission was primarily concerned with unauthorized access to computing systems (hacking) though it noted other problems such as the inapplicability of deception offences to computers.[6] The problem with hacking was that nosey-parkering (gaining unauthorized access to the correspondence, personal details, business records of another) is not generally an offence; invasion of privacy and industrial espionage[7] are not, as such, offences. Is there a special case for making nosey-parkering by way of hacking into a computer system a criminal offence?

[1] M. Wasik, *Crime and the Computer* (1991), and 'The Computer Misuse Act 1990' [1990] Crim LR 767; J. Arlidge and A. Parry, *Fraud* (2nd edn 1996), ch 11; Smith, *Property Offences* (1994), ch 11; I. Lloyd, *Information Technology Law* (4th edn, 2004), ch 13.

[2] For a comparative analysis of legal regulation of viruses see M. Klang, 'A Critical Look at the Regulation of Computer Viruses' (2003) Int J of Law and IT 162.

[3] See C. Tapper, 'Computer Crime: Scotch Mist?' [1987] Crim LR 4.

[4] Cf the problem of deceiving a machine, discussed above, p 755.

[5] Working Paper No 110, *Computer Misuse*. See M. Wasik, 'Law Reform Proposals on Computer Misuse' [1989] Crim LR 257.

[6] Cf the similar problems in relation to forgery, above, p 881, and the discussion in the Deception chapter on proposed reforms in this area.

[7] See Consultation Paper No 150, *Legislating the Criminal Code: Misuse of Trade Secrets* (1997) and see J. Hull, 'Stealing Secrets: A Review of the Law Commission's Consultation Paper on the Misuse of Trade Secrets' [1998] Crim LR 246.

The Law Commission thought that there was and in this it was overwhelmingly supported by commentators on the Working Paper.

The proposal in the Law Commission's Working Paper to criminalize unauthorized access was thus generally applauded. But before the publication of its final Report[8] the Commission conducted further discussions with computer and software manufacturers and with computer users in banking and commerce which convinced the Commission of the need not only for a summary offence of unauthorized access (hacking) but also for two further offences, which may be tried on indictment, of unauthorized access with intent to commit or facilitate the commission of further offences and of unauthorized modification of computer material.

This chapter will focus on the offences created by the Computer Misuse Act 1990. Analysis of the growing problem of what has become known as 'cybercrime' – offences against the person or property or of cyberobscenity and cybertrespass – lies beyond the scope of this work.[9] Similarly, the offences under the Communications Act 2003, and the Data Protection Act 1998 such as that of knowingly or recklessly obtaining or disclosing personal data or procuring its obtaining without the consent of the data controller,[10] are not examined here. Nor are the offences of making, possessing, distributing, etc indecent images of children.

1. Unauthorized access to computer material

By s 1 of the Computer Misuse Act 1990:

(1) A person is guilty of an offence if –
- (a) he causes a computer to perform any function with intent to secure access to any program or data held in any computer;
- (b) the access he intends to secure is unauthorized; and
- (c) he knows at the time when he causes the computer to perform the function that that is the case.

(2) The intent a person has to have to commit an offence under this section need not be directed at –
- (a) any particular program or data;
- (b) a program or data of any particular kind; or
- (c) a program or data held in any particular computer.

The offence is punishable on summary conviction by six months' imprisonment and/or a fine not exceeding level 5 on the standard scale.[11]

This is the most far-reaching of the offences under the Act. The idea, in effect, is to close the door in the hacker's face. The offence is committed though the hacker has

[8] Report No 186, *Computer Misuse* (1989) Cmnd 819.

[9] See in particular the special edition of the Criminal Law Review [1998], edited by D. S. Wall, and R. Essen, 'Cybercrime: a Growing Problem' (2002) J Crim L 269; O. Ward 'Information Technology Watch Out, There's a hacker about', (2000) 150 NLJ 1812. D. Thomas, and B. D. Loader, *Cybercrime* (2000); Y. Akdeniz, 'Cybercrime' in *E-Commerce Law & Regulation Encyclopaedia* (2003).

[10] See s 55 of the Data Protection Act 1998.

[11] The All Party Internet Group (APIG) recommended raising the maximum to two years [para 99], n 61 below.

no sinister purpose and is no more than a nosey-parker. But why should it be an offence to access files held in the office computer and not an offence to access files held in the filing cabinet?[12] The Law Commission thought it best to close the door altogether on the hacker in order to deter the hacker who *might* be contemplating fraud, or who *might* go on to commit some further offence or who *might*, because of his skills, be recruited by others with more sinister motives. With respect, these are not convincing reasons; conduct is not properly penalized because it *might* lead to the commission of an offence. One reason for criminalizing such conduct is that the proprietor of the system which is accessed by an unauthorized user may be put to considerable expense to repair his defences.[13] Of course the proprietor of paper files incurs expense repairing his defences if an intruder breaks into his office to look through the files. There are other differences in that the intruder in the latter case must break into the office; he cannot access the files, as he can in the case of computer held material, from a distant part of the country or as is frequently the case, from the other side of the world.[14] Computer systems are always vulnerable to the determined hacker. In a world that is increasingly dependent on computers, and the integrity of computer systems, it appears entirely right that the criminal law should be employed to discourage the hacker.

(a) *Actus reus*

The *actus reus* consists in causing a computer to perform any function.

(i) Computer

The Act does not define 'computer', the Law Commission taking the view that to have done so would be 'foolish'. Perhaps so but a court, though it might be foolish to attempt a comprehensive definition, may be required to decide whether a particular contrivance is a computer. Most obviously a computer is something that computes but computers have long since done more than merely mathematical calculations and may be used to store other information which can be processed for a wide variety of purposes ranging from legal research (LEXIS and WESTLAW), traffic control or manufacturing purposes. It is tentatively suggested that the defining characteristics of a computer are the abilities of the appliance (i) to store information; (ii) to retrieve the information so stored; and (iii) to process that information. Hence the abacus and the slide-rule are not computers;[15] they can be used to make calculations but they have no 'memory' and they cannot themselves process information.[16]

12 Some regard the Act as overbroad and suggest that s 1 ought to be limited to conduct which breaches a 'security measure': S. Room, 'Criminalising Cybercrime' (2004) 154 NLJ 950.

13 The Law Commission instanced a case where the restoration of a system following unauthorized access required 10,000 hours of the time of skilled staff. This is borne out by the losses incurred in some of the cases prosecuted.

14 On jurisdictional issues see M. Hirst, *Jurisdiction and the Ambit of the Criminal Law* (2003), 193–196.

15 But not because these are mechanical; computers are now electronic but Babbage's computer was no less a computer because it was mechanical.

16 The Convention on Cybercrime uses the term 'computer system'. It defines a computer as a device that runs a 'program' to process 'data' but does not define these other terms. APIG concluded that there had been no difficulties with the (lack of) definition of any of words in the Act. The Home Office reported that they had 'never come across a case' where the courts had failed to use a 'broad definition' [para 15]. It recommended retaining the current approach.

It is submitted that it is insufficient that a machine is programmed to perform a function or number of functions. A washing machine may be programmed to perform several varieties of wash but is not, on this view, a computer; it can only obey instructions and not process them. A computer can select a course of action on the basis of instructions given or information received. A machine which ensures that traffic lights will show red or green at stated intervals is not a computer; a machine which varies the intervals in response to information about traffic density is.

But it may be that some would argue for a wider definition. A computer may be thought of as any machine which responds to signals (now usually electronic) to perform programmed functions. On this view the unauthorized user of the washing machine or microwave oven would commit the offence under s 1. But such machines are not sold as, nor are they considered to be, computers. The appropriate charge for the unauthorized user of a dishwasher or microwave oven would appear to be the dishonest abstraction of electricity contrary to s 13 of the Theft Act 1968 rather than unauthorized access to computer material under s 1 of the Computer Misuse Act.

The offence is committed where D causes *any* computer to perform a function. Although often the offence is committed remotely via another computer, D also commits the offence by causing the target computer to perform a function.[17]

(ii) Performing a function

Given that the machine is a computer, the *actus reus* is complete if it is caused to perform 'any' function. It is accordingly enough to switch on the computer though it may be difficult to prove *mens rea* if this is all that D has done. The strict requirements of proof are reported to present difficulties in prosecution under the Act. It is not enough merely to view data that is already displayed on the monitor, but it is sufficient that D has, for example, accessed the internet by hitting the back key or return key when a computer has been left logged on to a University network by the previous user.[18] Expert evidence will not always be necessary to establish that a computer performed a function.[19]

(b) *Mens rea*

D must cause a computer to perform a function with *intent* to secure access to any program or data held in any computer, *knowing* that the access he intends to secure is unauthorized.

(i) Intent to secure access

Intention should, it is submitted be interpreted consistently with other offences as discussed above.[20] Recklessness is insufficient. By s 17 'access' is widely defined and includes any 'use' of a computer. There is no need to prove an intention in relation to any particular program. In practice it will usually be necessary to establish that D has secured access as so defined in order to establish *mens rea* but the offence is complete on causing a computer to perform any function with intent to secure access.

17 *A-G's Reference (No 1 of 1991)* [1993] QB 94.

18 See *Ellis v DPP* [2001] All ER (D) 190 (May) where D argued unsuccessfully that such conduct was akin to reading a discarded newspaper.

19 Ibid.

20 P 94.

(ii) Knowing it is unauthorized access

D must 'know'[21] that the access he intends to secure is unauthorized. By s 17(5) D's access is unauthorized if:

(i) he is not himself entitled to control access of the kind in question to the program or data; *and*

(ii) he does not have consent to access of the kind in question to the program or data from any person who is so entitled.

A person who is authorized to secure access of the kind in question to the program, does not commit an offence where he does so for some unauthorized purpose. Police computer operators who extracted details of the registration and ownership of cars for their private purposes were not guilty of this offence,[22] though they may have been guilty of an offence under the Data Protection Act 1984.[23] If D believes, however unreasonably, that he is entitled to control access or that his access is authorized by someone entitled to secure access, he cannot know that his access is unauthorized. More difficult is the case where D is unsure whether he is entitled to control access or, much more likely, he is unsure of the extent of his authorization to access a computer, but decides nonetheless to access the computer without checking on his authorization.[24] If, as will usually be the case, D could readily ascertain the nature and extent of his authority but chooses not to do so and decides to take the risk that his access is authorized, and his access is in fact unauthorized, it may be that he does not *know* his access is unauthorized but this is only because he does not want to know. It is submitted that wilful blindness of this kind is enough to constitute knowledge. At the other extreme, the fact that it crosses D's mind that he might possibly be exceeding his authority would not suffice for knowledge.

The offence may be committed where D has authority to use a computer, but not a particular program.[25] It may be committed though D is authorized to access one computer, computer X, if he does so to access another, computer Y, to which he does not have authorized access. Here again proof of the offence would be very difficult without proof that D has accessed computer Y, but the offence is complete when D has accessed computer X with intent to access computer Y.

Equally, the offence may be committed when D has limited authority to access the computer and he exceeds his authorization. An employee of American Express committed the offence when, having authority to access only specified accounts, she accessed other accounts.[26]

The offence requires both (i) that the access intended by D is in fact unauthorized; and (ii) that D knows that his access is unauthorized. If D believes his access is unauthorized when it is in fact authorized he does not commit the offence. Nor is he guilty of an attempt since the offence is summary only.

21 See generally, above, p 146.

22 *DPP v Bignell* [1998] 1 Cr App R 1, [1998] Crim LR 53, DC.

23 See now the Data Protection Act 1998.

24 This gave rise to difficulty in some early high-profile prosecutions: see P. Davies, 'Computer Misuse' (1995) 145 NLJ 1776.

25 See *Ellis v DPP* [2001] EWHC Admin 362.

26 *Bow Street Magistrate, ex p Government of USA* [2000] 2 AC 216, [2000] 1 Cr App R 61, HL, disapproving a *dictum* in *Bignell*, above, see commentary at [1999] Crim LR 971.

The essence of the offence under s 1 is causing a computer to perform a function with intent to secure unauthorized access. No particular computer needs to be targeted by D and it is enough that he is out fishing without a licence. Indeed, it is enough that he sets out to fish without a licence.

2. Unauthorized access with intent to commit or facilitate further offences

By s 2 of the Act:

(1) A person is guilty of an offence under this section if he commits an offence under section 1 above ('the unauthorized access offence') with intent –

(a) to commit an offence to which this section applies; or

(b) to facilitate the commission of such an offence (whether by himself or by any other person);

and the offence he intends to commit or facilitate is referred to below in this section as the further offence.

The section applies to arrestable offences generally and is punishable on indictment with five years' imprisonment. The offence requires proof of the s 1 offence together with an intent to commit an arrestable offence[27] or to facilitate the commission of such an offence by another. By s 2(3) it is immaterial whether the ulterior offence is to be committed at the time of access or on some future occasion.

There is no requirement that the ulterior offences will involve the use of a computer. In practical terms the offences most likely to be intended or facilitated by D will be offences against property involving dishonesty but all arrestable offences are included.[28] As to the former it might have been thought that the Theft Acts were adequate to deal with the case with a possible amendment to deal with deception offences in relation to machines.[29] This was how the Law Commission initially viewed the matter but it had second thoughts and concluded that it would be preferable to extend the criminal law to the hacker before he had committed a substantive offence under the Theft Acts or had reached the stage of an attempt. Like s 1, s 2 is accordingly aimed at preparatory conduct. Thus, to take examples given by the Law Commission, the hacker who, with intent to steal, is searching for the password to enter an account might not be guilty of an attempt to steal, and the hacker who seeks confidential information in order to blackmail would clearly not be guilty of an attempt to blackmail.[30] Both, however, would commit the substantive offence under s 2. It is not just the hacker in the usual sense whom is caught by this offence; the employee who accesses bank data and discloses those to accomplices to enable them to commit frauds commits the offence.[31]

[27] Note the replacement of arrestable offences in the Serious Organised Crime and Police Act 2005, s 110.

[28] A traffic or air traffic control system might be entered with intent to injure or even kill. Hacking with intent to commit treason is, perhaps, somewhat fanciful.

[29] See the recognition of the availability of the charge in the case of *Holmes* [2005] Crim LR 229; and the proposals in the latest Fraud Bill. APIG endorsed the need for a new fraud offence to deal with this problem [para 35] and recommended further reform on the misuse of trade secrets so as to develop a suitable framework to adequately criminalize the unlawful 'theft of data'.

[30] As in *Zezev* [2002] Crim LR 648.

[31] *Delamare* [2003] All ER (D) 127 (Feb).

The Law Commission thought that the s 2 offence bore 'some relation to an attempt'[32] in that the ulterior offence needs only to be intended and not affected and accordingly s 2(4) provides that the offence may be committed though commission of the ulterior offence is impossible. It is submitted, that this provision is unnecessary but it may save argument.

Since the offence under s 2 is a substantive offence there may, in turn, be a conspiracy to commit, or an incitement to commit, or an attempt to commit the offence. These would represent extremely broad offences. Given the preparatory nature of the offence, however, there is little scope for the operation of attempt.[33]

3. Unauthorized modification of computer material

By s 3 of the Act:

(1) A person is guilty of an offence if –

(a) he does any act which causes an unauthorized modification of the contents of any computer; and

(b) at the time when he does the act he has the requisite intent and the requisite knowledge.

(2) For the purposes of subsection (1)(b) above the requisite intent is an intent to cause a modification of the contents of any computer and by so doing –

(a) to impair the operation of any computer;

(b) to prevent or hinder access to any program or data held in any computer; or

(c) to impair the operation of any such program or the reliability of any such data.

(3) The intent need not be directed at –

(a) any particular computer;

(b) any particular program or data or a program or data of any particular kind; or

(c) any particular modification or a modification of any particular kind.

(4) For the purposes of subsection (1)(b) above the requisite knowledge is knowledge that any modification he intends to cause is unauthorized.

(a) Background to the offence[34]

It is, and remains, an offence under the Criminal Damage Act 1971 to destroy or damage a computer or its software as by taking a hammer to them and causing damage that can be perceived by the senses. Difficulties arise, however, where there is no perceptible physical damage but where D, say, interferes with programs to render the computer incapable, or less capable, to carry out the functions the programs are designed to perform. This may be done without causing any physical damage.

If D erases data held on a disc, the disc is rendered less valuable to V but the information lost to V, being *intangible* property, cannot be the subject of a charge under the

32 Paper No 186, para 3.58.

33 Reaching for the switch?

34 See generally, Y. Akdeniz, 'Section 3 of the Computer Misuse Act 1990 – An Antidote for Computer Viruses' [1996] Web Jnl CLI.

Criminal Damage Act. While, however, the property must be 'tangible', the damage need not be – indeed damage is perhaps incapable of being tangible, being a concept. The disc remains unharmed in that it can be re-used to store information, but in another sense it is certainly damaged. If it were not so, D might have escaped liability under the Criminal Damage Act though he had inflicted a loss on V that would take time and expense to repair or may even be irreparable. Opportunities would have been open for mischief-makers to inflict considerable inconvenience on computer users and considerable economic loss on their owners,[35] without fear of any criminal sanction.

In *Cox v Riley*,[36] however, it was held that D was guilty of criminal damage where he erased the program from a plastic circuit card which operated a saw to cut wood to programmed designs. D's counsel argued that the program was not 'property of a tangible nature' within the Criminal Damage Act. In this he was no doubt right but, in the view of the court, it failed to take account of the fact that D was charged not with damaging the program but with damaging the plastic card. And in *Whitely*[37] it was held that D was properly convicted of criminal damage to computer discs where he gained unauthorized access to an academic computer system and by altering their magnetic particles caused them to delete and add files. His counsel's argument that only intangible information on the discs had been damaged was rejected; the discs had been damaged because their usefulness had been impaired.

These decisions might be viewed as bringing computer misuse, because of its obvious potential for harm, within the Criminal Damage Act by procrustean means,[38] but it is submitted that both decisions were defensible under the Act. The plastic circuit card in *Cox v Riley*, though it may not have been rendered useless and could have been reprogrammed to perform its original function, was temporarily unable to perform the function it was designed to perform. Though the disc was not damaged, it was rendered incapable of performing one of its programs and the case seems indistinguishable from *Fisher*.[39] Similarly, in *Whitely*[40] the computer, though not itself damaged, had been rendered inoperable by tampering with its control mechanisms, namely the programs on the discs. That the discs could be restored is irrelevant since temporary impairment suffices.

The Law Commission, however, took the view that the problem of computer misuse should be tackled directly. It might have been possible to deal with the problem by amending the Criminal Damage Act to include interference with data and programs. But the Commission decided on the creation of a new offence for two reasons. One was that 'the theoretical difficulties posed by applying the concept of damage to intangible property such as data or programs'[41] would render the law unacceptably uncertain. The other was that criminal damage may be committed recklessly and the Commission did not think that the new offence should extend to a person who recklessly modified computer material.[42] In addition, as will appear, the Commission sought to clarify the relationship between the modification offence under s 3 of the Computer Misuse Act 1990 and the offence of criminal damage under the Criminal Damage Act.

35 See Wasik, above ch 5.
36 (1986) 83 Cr App R 54, DC.
37 [1991] Crim LR 436, CA.
38 See Wasik above 137–145.
39 (1865) LR 1 CCR 7, above, p 892.
40 [1991] Crim LR 436, CA.
41 Law Com No 186, para 3.62.
42 See below, p 932.

(b) *Actus reus*

Essentially s 3 is concerned with the sabotaging of computer systems by any of the acts specified in s 3(2). The most obvious instances will be by transferring viruses,[43] Trojan horses or worms to computer systems or by corrupting websites.[44] The offence has also proved useful in prosecuting those who create devices to allow unauthorized access to cable TV.[45] Unauthorized use is insufficient unless it results in a modification of the contents of a computer but any such modification will suffice. Causing a computer to debit V's bank account and credit D's[46] is such a modification because the data concerning V's account is now unreliable. The modification need only be temporary.

The offence has been construed very broadly. In *Zevez*,[47] it was held that if a computer is caused to record information (an email) which shows that it comes from one person, when it in fact comes from someone else, that manifestly affects its reliability.[48] This can be seen as a significant extension of the offence, since the reliability of the data is merely that the email tells a lie about itself, it does not affect the reliability of other data on the computer.

(c) *Mens rea*

The offence requires an *intention* to cause a modification, knowledge that such modification is unauthorized and an intention that the modification will have one of the prohibited consequences – impairment of operation, preventing or hindering access, or impairing the operation or reliability of a program.

Intention is required.[49] Recklessness does not suffice. The reason given by the Law Commission[50] for a strict *mens rea* requirement was that it did not wish to extend the offence to the person who inadvertently modified the contents of a computer. It is less clear that the offence should not extend to the person who adverts to the risk of modifying the contents of a computer but the Commission apprehended, no doubt rightly, that recklessness in the context of the Computer Misuse Act would have been given the same (*Caldwell*) meaning it had at that time for criminal damage.[51] The Commission thought that such a person would already be guilty of the basic unauthorized access offence but this will not necessarily be the case; the mere fact that D recklessly modifies the contents of a computer does not involve the conclusion that his access is unauthorized and that he knows it.

43 See eg *Vallor* [2004] 1 Cr App R (S) 54 spreading the third most virulent virus in the world.

44 See eg *Lindesay* [2002] 1 Cr App R (S) 370, disgruntled sacked employee corrupting firm's website.

45 See *Parr-Moore* [2003] 1 Cr App R (S) 425 and *Maxwell-King* [2000] All ER (D) 1957, where the charge was one of incitement to commit the s 3 offence.

46 Cf *Thompson* [1984] 3 All ER 565, [1984] 1 WLR 962, CA.

47 [2002] Crim LR 648.

48 D had placed in the files of a computer a bogus email purporting to come from a person which it had not. This was held to have caused a modification of the computer within s 17(7) 'A modification of the contents of any computer takes place if . . . any . . . data is added to its contents . . .'.

49 This should it is submitted be construed as elsewhere in English criminal law, and not be confused with motives or underlying purposes. Cf the much publicized acquittal of Paul Bedworth (1993) when he claimed to have an addiction to hacking which precluded him forming the necessary intention. See further A. Charlesworth, 'Addiction and Hacking' (1993) 143 NLJ 540.

50 Paper No 186, para 3.62.

51 See above, p 105.

D's intent need not be directed at any particular computer or program. Nor does this offence require that D himself should access, or intend to access, a computer. The Commission gave the example[52] of X who puts into circulation a disc which he knows to be infected[53] which passes through the hands of Y and Z to V whose files and data are corrupted by its use. X would be guilty of the offence if he intends to cause an unauthorized modification of 'any' computer. The same result would of course obtain by the application of the principle of transferred malice.[54] The offence is complete only when the contents of V's computer are modified but by putting the infected disc into circulation X would be guilty of an attempt.

(d) The relationship between section 3 and criminal damage

Assuming that *Cox v Riley* and *Whitely*[55] correctly hold that the modification of the circuit card and the discs by the removal or alteration of electronic particles stored therein constitutes criminal damage there would be an overlap between the offence of criminal damage and the offence under s 3 of the Computer Misuse Act. The Law Commission thought that such an overlap would be unfortunate partly because it would cause confusion and partly because a person might be exposed to different penalties for the same conduct. Section 3(6) accordingly provides:

> For the purposes of the Criminal Damage Act 1971 a modification of the contents of a computer shall not be regarded as damaging any computer or computer storage medium unless its effect on that computer or computer storage medium impairs its physical condition.

This provision is intended to reverse the effect of *Cox v Riley* and no doubt prosecutors will heed s 3(6) and use the Criminal Damage Act only where the 'physical condition' of the computer or computer storage medium is impaired. One reason given by the Law Commission for this is that it would not be right to expose offenders to potentially higher penalties by continuing to use the 1971 Act.[56] Perhaps so, but it seems odd that, the hacker instanced by the Law Commission[57] whose electronic vandalism required 10,000 hours of skilled work to repair, should be liable to five years' imprisonment under the 1990 Act, whereas if he had used a hammer to cause the same loss (or even a penny's worth) he would be liable to 10 years under the 1971 Act. Indeed, it may well be that damage with the hammer causes only loss in terms of the physical property of the computer itself and not the (much more valuable) data it stores. Moreover, the offence under the 1971 Act extends to recklessly caused damage. If the aforesaid hacker had recklessly caused this enormous loss he would have been liable under *Cox v Riley* but now escapes scot free because the 1990 Act does not extend to recklessly caused harm and he has not, presumably, impaired the 'physical condition' of the computer. To some, and especially the proprietors of computer systems, it might seem odd in this case to say, 'Well, there's nothing wrong with the computer. It *looks* exactly the same as it did yesterday. There's only one slight difference. It doesn't work.'

52 Paper No 186, para 3.70.
53 Acknowledged even then to be a 'substantial and serious' problem.
54 Above at p 113.
55 Above at 931.
56 Paper No 186, para 3.78.
57 Above at p 926, n 13.

4. Reform

There has been a growing pressure from some[58] to extend the scope of the Act in particular to deal with 'denial of service attacks'[59] which lead to commercial websites being rendered unavailable to legitimate users.[60] Further pressure for reform derives from the international treaty obligations.[61] The Parliamentary All Party Internet Group have recently reviewed and reported on the Act and made recommendations for reform.[62] The group concluded that many of the perceived problems with the Act actually stemmed from 'widespread ignorance of the current law'.[63]

58 Cf C. Holder, 'Staying one step ahead of the criminals' (2002) 10(3) IT Law 17.

59 A Denial-of-Service (DoS) attack occurs 'when a deliberate attempt is made to stop a machine from performing its usual activities by having another computer create large amounts of specious traffic. The traffic may be valid requests made in an overwhelming volume or specially crafted protocol fragments that cause the serving machine to tie up significant resources to no useful purpose. In a Distributed Denial-of-Service (DDoS) attack a large number of remote computers are orchestrated into attacking a target at the same time.' [APIG, para 56] These are extremely common at over 4,000 reported instances a week. There have been prosecutions, although unsuccessful on the facts. See *R v Caffrey* discussed in the APIG report.

60 A private members' Bill – the Computer Misuse (Amendment) Bill 2000 – sought to introduce a new offence of causing or intending to cause a degradation, failure or other impairment of function of a computerized system. The offence was aimed at protecting computer systems from denial of service attacks.

61 See especially the Convention on Cybercrime, CETS No 185 (2001) discussed by S. Room above, p 950. The Home Office is currently reviewing the need for further legislation, particularly an offence to deal with denial of service attacks. See further Internet crime forum www.internetcrimeforum.org.uk; European Convention www.eurim.org/consult/e-crime/dec03/ECS_WP6_web_031209.htm. UK law does not currently meet the requirement in Article 6 to create a criminal offence, when committed 'intentionally and without right' of the 'production, sale, procurement for use, import, distribution or otherwise making available of [. . .] a computer password, access code or similar data by which the whole or any part of a computer system is capable of being accessed, with intent that it be used for the purpose of committing [CMA type offences]'.

62 See www.apig.org.uk/computer_misuse_act_inquiry.htm. Discussed by G. Fearon, 'All Party Internet (APIG) Report on the Computer Misuse Act' (2004) 15 Comps and Law 36.

63 Para 23.

26

Criminal libels and related offences

The common law recognized four forms of criminal libel – blasphemous, defamatory, obscene and seditious. Lord Scarman regarded them as part of a group of criminal offences designed to safeguard the internal tranquillity of the kingdom; and thought that there was force in the 'lawyer's conceptual argument' that the requirements of *mens rea* should be the same for all of them.[1] Regrettably the courts have not approached the offences consistently. If the purpose of the offences is the protection of internal tranquillity, that object has not always been kept clearly in view and the requirements of *mens rea* differ very significantly. Though all four offences still exist at common law, obscene libels are now in practice governed by the Obscene Publications Acts 1959 and 1964.

1. Blasphemy[2]

It is a common law misdemeanour to publish blasphemous matter.

(a) *Actus reus*

The *actus reus* comprises publishing blasphemous material. Publication may be oral or in writing. Prosecutions have involved theatre productions and film recordings. It is a defence if the publication was without D's authority, consent or knowledge and there was no lack of due care on his part.[3] There are procedural safeguards in that an order from a judge in chambers is required before a prosecution of a newspaper proprietor or editor (but not a journalist)[4] can occur.[5]

[1] *Whitehouse v Gay News Ltd* (1979) 68 Cr App R 381 at 404 and 409, HL.

[2] See generally: G. D. Nokes, *History of the Crime of Blasphemy* (1928); C. S. Kenny, 'The Evolution of the Law of Blasphemy' [1922] 1 CLJ 127; Stephen, II HCL, 469–476; S. Bailey, D. Harris and D. Ormerod, *Civil Liberties Cases and Materials* (5th edn, 2001), 1045 et seq; G. Robertson, *Freedom, the Individual and the Law* (7th edn, 1993), 248–254; L. Blom-Cooper and G. Drewry, *Law and Morality* (1976), 254–260; N. Walter, *Blasphemy Ancient and Modern* (1990); R. Webster, *A Brief History of Blasphemy* (1990); R. Buxton, 'The Case of Blasphemous Libel' [1978] Crim LR 673. For a comprehensive general discussion see Appendix 3 and for a comparative analysis see Appendix 5 of the House of Lords Select Committee on *Religious Offences in England and Wales First Report* (2003), vol I (HL Paper 95-I), www.parliament.the-stationery-office.co.uk/pa/ld200203/ldselect/ldrelof/95/9506.htm.

[3] Libel Act 1843, s 7, *Bradlaugh* (1883) 15 Cox CC 217.

[4] *Gleaves v Insall* [1999] 2 Cr App R 466, DC.

[5] Law of Libel (Amendment) Act 1888, s 8.

(i) Meaning of 'blasphemy'

Matter is blasphemous if it denies the truth of the Christian religion[6] or of the Bible[7] or the Book of Common Prayer,[8] or the existence of God. The earlier cases required no more than this for, as Stephen says, they 'all proceed upon the plain principle that the public importance of the Christian religion is so great that no one is allowed to deny its truth.'[9]

The gist of the offence was said to be 'a supposed tendency to shake the fabric of society generally'.[10] Yet, while the law was stated in these broad terms, there is no recorded instance of a conviction for blasphemy where an element of contumely and ribaldry was absent.[11] In the course of the nineteenth century it came to be held that the act of denying the truth of Christianity, etc would not be held criminal if it was expressed in decent and temperate language and not in such terms as are likely to lead to a breach of the peace. 'If the decencies of controversy are observed, even the fundamentals of religion may be attacked without the writer being guilty of blasphemy.'[12]

Stephen found himself unable to accept this milder view of the law because of the weight of the earlier authorities;[13] but the milder view found favour with the House of Lords in *Bowman v Secular Society Ltd.*[14] In that case it was held that a company formed to promote the secularisation of the state was not unlawful although one of its objects was to deny Christianity. On this view blasphemous words are punishable:

> for their manner, their violence, or ribaldry, or, more fully stated, for their tendency to endanger the peace then and there, to deprave public morality generally, to shake the fabric of society and to be a cause of civil strife.[15]

The application of this test would virtually abolish the crime because it is scarcely conceivable that any utterance regarding Christianity could seriously be expected to produce such drastic results today. In *Whitehouse v Gay News Ltd and Lemon*,[16] the first prosecution for over 60 years, the House of Lords applied a much less strict test. A publication is blasphemous if it is couched in indecent or offensive terms likely to shock and outrage the feelings of the general body of Christian believers in the community. There appears to be no need to prove any tendency to endanger the peace, still less 'to shake the fabric of society'. The publication in question, a poem and illustration vilifying Christ in his life and his crucifixion, was, no doubt, extremely offensive to many people; but there was no indication that it had provoked or was likely to provoke violence and it would be ludicrous to suggest that it was likely to have any effect on the fabric of society.

6 *Taylor* (1676) 1 Vent 293.

7 *Hetherington* (1841) 4 State Tr NS 563.

8 According to Russell, 1519; Archbold (39th edn) §3401.

9 II HCL 475.

10 Per Lord Sumner in *Bowman v Secular Society Ltd* [1917] AC 406 at 459.

11 This was common ground in *Bowman v Secular Society Ltd*, see, eg, per Lord Sumner [1917] AC 406. Stephen says that the placards held to be blasphemous in *Cowan v Milbourn* (1867) LR 2 Exch 230, 'could hardly have been expressed in less offensive language': II HCL at 474; but that was a civil action, and Lord Sumner and the Court of Appeal thought the decision wrong: [1917] AC 463.

12 *Ramsey and Foote* (1883) 15 Cox CC 231 at 238, per Coleridge CJ.

13 2 HCL 474, 475 and *Digest* (4th edn), art. 161.

14 [1917] AC 406.

15 Per Lord Sumner [1917] AC at 466.

16 [1979] AC 617, [1979] 1 All ER 898, [1979] Crim LR 311 and commentary.

Application only to Christianity

In *Chief Metropolitan Stipendiary Magistrate, ex p Choudhury*[17] it was argued for the first time that the offence of blasphemy is applicable to religions other than Christianity. The court held that the law applies only to Christianity, and possibly only to the established church, though the latter point was not decided. The court had no power to extend the law to other religions and would not have exercised it if it had. Judicial decision is not an appropriate means of providing for a matter involving such complex issues of public policy. Accordingly, it was held that the chief magistrate had rightly refused to issue summonses alleging blasphemous libel against the religion of Islam by the author, Salman Rushdie, and the publishers of *The Satanic Verses.*

Whether or not the particular doctrines of Christian religions other than those of the established church are protected as such, an attack on Christianity generally may amount to the offence because that is the religion of the established church.[18] The established church is said to be unique because it is part of the constitution of the country, presumably part of 'the fabric of society' which it is the object of the law to protect.

(b) *Mens rea*

In *Lemon and Gay News* the majority of the House of Lords held that the only *mens rea* that need be proved is an intention to publish the offending words. It is not necessary to prove that the defendant intended to attack Christianity or to shock and insult Christians or even that he knew that the words would or might have that effect. Lords Diplock and Edmund-Davies, dissenting, thought that the prosecution should be obliged to prove that D knew that this was the probable effect of the words. They considered that the decision of the majority turned the offence into one of strict liability, a charge which the majority denied. Presumably, however, it must be shown that D was aware of the presence and understood the meaning of the offending words. If they were in a foreign language and he believed they were a recipe for Christmas pudding, he would surely not be guilty.

(c) ECHR[19]

An argument that the law of blasphemy was inconsistent with Article 10 of the ECHR failed in *Wingrove v United Kingdom.*[20] W had been denied a certificate for his video concerning the life of St Teresa of Avila, entitled 'Visions of Ecstasy'. The British Board of Film Classification and the Video Appeals Committee, concluded that 'a reasonable jury properly directed would find that it infringed the criminal law of blasphemy'. The

[17] [1991] 1 QB 429, [1991] 1 All ER 306, DC. See on this M. Tregilas-Davey, 'An Opportunity Missed' (1991) 54 MLR 294 as to how the law might have been legitimately extended to protect Islam.

[18] *Gathercole* (1838) 2 Lew CC 237 (Alderson B).

[19] There is also protection under Article 20(2) of the International Covenant on Civil and Political Rights which provides that 'Any advocacy of national, racial or religious hatred that constitutes incitement to discrimination, hostility or violence shall be prohibited by law'. However, the United Kingdom has entered a reservation with respect to this Article: 'The Government of the United Kingdom interpret Article 20 consistently with the rights conferred by Articles 19 and 21 of the Covenant and having legislated in matters of practical concern in the interests of public order (ordre public) reserve the right not to introduce any further legislation. The United Kingdom also reserves a similar right in regard to each of its dependent territories'.

[20] (1996) 24 EHRR 1, ECtHR.

European Court held that the law was a necessary and proportionate restriction on the right to freedom of expression for the legitimate aim of protecting the rights of others. Blasphemy was also acknowledged to be sufficiently clearly prescribed by law. The Court held that:

> . . . the English law of blasphemy does not prohibit the expression, in any form, of views hostile to the Christian religion. Nor can it be said that opinions which are offensive to Christians necessarily fall within its ambit. As the English courts have indicated, it is the manner in which views are advocated rather than the views themselves which the law seeks to control. The extent of insult to religious feelings must be significant as is clear from the use by the courts of the adjectives 'contemptuous', 'reviling', 'scurrilous', 'ludicrous' to depict material of a sufficient degree of offensiveness.
>
> The high degree of profanation that must be attained constitutes in itself, a safeguard against arbitrariness. It is against this background that the asserted justification under Article 10(2) in the decisions of the national authorities must be considered.[21]

Thus, it seems unlikely that challenges based on a lack of certainty (Article 7) or based on freedom of expression (Article 10) will succeed. Challenges under Article 9 based on the restriction on freedom of religions other than Christianity and the discrimination against other religions would seem unlikely following the Commission's dismissal of the application in *Choudhury v UK*,[22] although that is a less clear cut issue. Although the parameters of Article 9 are vague, reflecting the lack of consensus on religion within Europe, and the conduct protected is ill-defined[23] the European Court has acknowledged that states must be given a particularly wide margin of appreciation in relation to Article 9 matters.[24] Where there is a potential conflict between Article 9 and Article 10 the Court must conduct a complex balancing exercise. In *Otto-Preminger Institut v Austria* the Court emphasized that:

> Those who choose to exercise the freedom to manifest their religion cannot reasonably expect to be exempt from all criticism. They must tolerate and accept the denial by others of their religious beliefs and even the propagation by others of doctrines hostile to them. However, the manner in which religious beliefs and doctrines are opposed or denied is a matter which may engage the responsibility of the State, notably its responsibility to ensure the peaceful enjoyment of the right guaranteed under Article 9 to holders of those beliefs and doctrines.[25]

21 See generally, S. Gandhi and J. James, 'The English Law of Blasphemy and the ECHR' [1998] EHRLR 430. Some regarded the decision with particular dissatisfaction: I. Loveland commented that 'the English courts and the ECHR pander to the bigoted sensibilities of religious zealots by upholding our archaic blasphemy laws' in 'Back to the Future' (2000) 150 NLJ 1220. For concerns that it suppresses art, see P. Kearns, 'The Uncultured God: Blaphemy Law's Reprieve and the Art Matrix' [2000] EHRLR 512.

22 *Choudhury v UK* (1991) 12 HRLJ 172. The decision does not stand easily with that of the Court in *Otto-Preminger* v *Austria* (1995) 19 EHRR 34.

23 See P. Kearns, 'Religion and the Human Rights Act 1998' (2001) 151 NLJ 498. The European Court has generally taken a liberal approach to the question of what constitutes a religion for the purposes of Article 9. See C. Evans, *Freedom of Religion under the European Convention on Human Rights* (2001), 53. See also B. Emmerson and A. Ashworth, *Human Rights and Criminal Justice* (2000), 238.

24 See on this P. Mahoney, 'Universality and Subsidiarity in the Strasbourg, Caselaw on Free Speech: Explaining some Recent Judgments' [1997] EHRLR 364. See also M. Idriss, 'Religion and the Anti-Terrorism, Crime and Security Act 2001' [2002] Crim LR 890, 902, and S. Stokes, 'Blasphemy and Freedom of Expression Under the ECHR: Two Recent Cases' (1996) 7 Ent LR p 98.

25 (1995) 19 EHRR 34 at p 56. See further, D. Pannick, 'Religious Freedom and the European Court' [1995] PL 7.

It should be noted that the argument that the offence is disproportionate and unnecessary is strengthened by the absence of any defence of the expression being in the public good (as in the Obscene Publications Act 1959 discussed below).[26]

(d) Reform of the law

Prosecutions for blasphemy have been extremely rare for over a hundred years[27] but several attempts to abolish the blasphemy laws have failed.[28] The attempts to enact a new offence of inciting religious hatred have served as a vehicle for discussion on the status of blasphemy.[29] There is a strong case for abolition. It is illogical that scurrilous publications relating to the Christian religion should be punishable because of their tendency to outrage the feelings of believers when similar publications relating to other religions are not. Christians are not alone in their susceptibility to outrage. On the other hand it would be wrong for the protection of the law to be extended to all religious beliefs, however weird. Events in Jonesville in Guyana in 1979, and in Waco Texas in 1993 demonstrated that there may be religions which ought, in the public interest, to be vilified, however outraged their adherents might be. The Home Secretary has rejected the suggestion that the offence be extended in this way.[30]

The rarity of prosecutions indicates that the Christian religion does not need the protection of the blasphemy laws. Other less strongly supported religions are well able to flourish in this country without it.

The conclusion is that the law of blasphemy should be abolished.[31] The Law Commission, by a majority, has so recommended.[32] This would remove any legitimate grievances about the inequality of treatment of religions. The offences in the Public Order Act seem quite adequate to deal with any threat to public order. Moreover, with the advent of religiously aggravated offences there is little doubt that religious activity is adequately protected. The two dissenting Commissioners recommended that the common law

26 For criticism that the offence therefore represses artistic expression see P. Kearns, 'Obscene and Blasphemous Libel: Misunderstanding Art' [2000] Crim LR 652.

27 *Pooley* (1857) 8 State Tr NS 1089; *Ramsey and Foote* (1883) 15 Cox CC 231; *Boulter* (1908) 72 JP 188; *Gott* (1922) 16 Cr App R 87 and *Lemon*, above.

28 R. S. W. Pollard, *Abolish the Blasphemy Laws* (1957), 7. For broader discussion of the issues see also C. Unsworth, 'Blasphemy, Cultural Divergence and Legal Relativism' (1995) 58 MLR 658; S. M. Poulter, 'Towards Legislative Reform of the Blasphemy and Racial Hatred Laws' [1991] PL 371 examining the merits of the incitement to religious hatred offence.

29 See in particular the Select Committee Report, above; on the Report, see A. W. Jeremy, 'Religious Offences' [2003] Ecc LJ 127.

30 HC, col 708 (26 Nov 2001).

31 Lord Lester QC is reported as saying: 'It is all crazy, given that there are only one million Anglicans and two million Muslims in this country . . . The Christian church . . . is strong enough to protect itself. I don't think we should be operating under a medieval system of criminal law', J. Currie, (2002) *The Lawyer*, 22 July, 13. It is notable that the Muslim Council of Britain, in evidence to the Select Committee recommended the retention of the offence for Christianity on the basis that it was better that some religion was protected than none, above, Vol III, 36.

32 Law Commission Paper No 145, *Offences against Religion and Public Worship* (1985). This was preceded by Law Commission Working Paper No 79, *Offences against Religion and Public Worship* (1981) on which see J. R. Spencer, 'Blasphemy: The Law Commission Working Paper' [1981] Crim LR 810; G. Robertson, 'Blasphemy: The Law Commission Working Paper' [1981] PL 295; St J Robilliard, 'Offences Against Religion and Public Worship' (1981) 44 MLR 556.

offence be replaced by a new offence of publishing grossly abusive or insulting material relating to a religion with the purpose of outraging religious feelings.

2. Defamatory libel[33]

The publication of a libel is a common law misdemeanour but by s 5 of the Libel Act 1843, it is now punishable by no more than one year's imprisonment. It is also a tort[34] and the tortious aspect of libel is much more important. Criminal proceedings for libel are rare and are not encouraged by the courts. Kennedly LJ recently referred to the offence being resorted to 'only in comparatively exceptional circumstances'.[35]

(a) *Actus reus*

A libel[36] is traditionally described as a writing[37] which tends to vilify a man and bring him into hatred, contempt and ridicule.[38] This definition has been replaced in the law of tort by the test proposed by Lord Atkin: 'Would the words tend to lower the plaintiff in the estimation of right thinking members of society generally?'[39]

The traditional definition has, however, been accepted as representing the law of criminal libel in relatively recent cases.[40] It was at one time thought that libel amounted to a criminal offence only if it was likely to result in a breach of the peace. It is now clear that this is not so except perhaps where the libel is published only to the person defamed,[41] or where the person defamed is dead. If criminal libel does require some additional constituent, it is that the libel must be 'serious'. This seems to represent a very high threshold, at least as interpreted in recent cases.[42] If it is likely to provoke a breach of the peace or to disturb the peace of the community, then it is certainly serious; but it may be serious although it has no such tendency.[43] 'Deliberate character assassination and the wild dissemination of defamatory matter by cranks' are – and, it is said, ought to be – offences, whether or not the person defamed, or anyone else is likely to resort to unlawful violence.[44] It seems that seriousness is now part of the definition of the offence.[45]

33 See P. Milmo and W. V. H. Rogers (eds), *Gatley on Libel and Slander* (10th edn, 2004) ch 22.

34 See Salmond (21st edn, 1996), ch 8; *Winfield and Jolowicz on Tort* (16th edn, 2002), ch 12.

35 *Gleaves v Insall* [1999] 2 Cr App R 466.

36 See J. R. Spencer, 'Criminal Libel: A Skeleton in the Cupboard' [1977] Crim LR 383 and 465; Archbold (2005), 29–71.

37 Defamatory words published in the course of the performance of a play amount to a criminal libel unless the performance is given on a domestic occasion in a private dwelling: Theatres Act 1968, ss 4 and 6. The publication of words in the course of a 'programme service' is capable of constituting a criminal libel. A programme service includes TV, radio and other broadcast – see Broadcasting Act 1990, s 202(1).

38 *Thorley v Lord Kerry* (1812) 4 Taunt 355.

39 *Sim v Stretch* [1936] 2 All ER 1237 at 1240.

40 *Goldsmith v Pressdram Ltd* [1977] QB 83 at 87, per Wien J; *Gleaves v Deakin* [1980] AC 477 at 487, [1979] 2 All ER 497 at 502, per Viscount Dilhorne.

41 *Adams* (1888) 22 QBD 66, CCR; Law Com Working Paper No 84, para 38.

42 See *Gleaves v Insall* where published allegations that VV were phoney ambulance crew who turned up to accidents to gain sexual gratification was not sufficiently serious.

43 *Wicks* [1936] 1 All ER 384 at 386; *Gleaves v Deakin* [1979] 2 All ER 497, HL.

44 J. R. Spencer, 'The Press and the Reform of Criminal Libel', in P. Glazebrook (ed), *Reshaping the Criminal Law* (1978), 285, quoted by Lord Edmund-Davies [1979] 2 All ER at 505.

45 See, however, somewhat ambiguous remarks of Lord Dilhorne at [1979] 2 All ER at 501. Cf Law Com Working Paper No 84, paras 3.6–3.7, and Gatley, above n 33, p 655.

An examining magistrate would not send for trial unless he was satisfied that the alleged libel is so serious as to justify a prosecution in the public interest presumably this test applies to an application to dismiss in the Crown Court under the Crime and Disorder Act 1998.[46] Evidence of the truth of statements complained of, or of the general bad reputation of V, is not relevant at this stage: *Gleaves v Deakin*.[47] The House thought that the consent of the Attorney-General to the bringing of a prosecution should be required but there are at present no such general restrictions.

(i) Newspaper publication

Where the prosecution is of any person responsible for the publication of a newspaper (but not a journalist)[48] for any alleged libel therein, the leave of a judge is required by s 8 of the Law of Libel Amendment Act 1888. The judge should not exercise his discretion in favour of an application unless he is satisfied that (i) there is a clear *prima facie* case, (ii) the libel is so serious that it is proper for the criminal law to be invoked and (iii) that the public interest *requires* the institution of criminal proceedings. Wien J found these conditions to be satisfied in a case where the applicant occupied important public positions, where his integrity had been impugned and a criminal offence alleged against him and where a campaign of vilification had been carried on for months.[49]

(ii) Distinction from tort of defamation

Defamatory libel is best studied as a branch of the law of tort but it is necessary here to note the differences which exist between the crime and the tort. In the first place, libel is the only form of defamation which is indictable. Slander is not a crime.[50] The crime of libel is wider than the tort in at least two and possibly five respects.

(i) Publication to the person defamed is sufficient in crime but not in tort.[51] In tort, the gist of the matter is the loss of the claimant's reputation and this only occurs through publication to a third party; but a principal reason why libel is indictable is the danger to the public peace[52] and this may obviously be even greater where the publication is to the prosecutor himself than where it is to another.

(ii) The truth of the defamatory statement affords a complete defence (justification) in tort but in crime the defendant must prove[53] not only that the statement is true but that it is for the public benefit that it be published. This is the effect of s 6 of the

46 [1979] 2 All ER 502 and 505. 47 Above, n 42.

48 *Gleaves v Insall* [1999] 2 Cr App R 466.

49 *Goldsmith v Pressdram Ltd* [1977] QB 83, [1977] 2 All ER 557 (Wien J). Cf *Desmond v Thorne* [1982] 3 All ER 268, [1983] 1 WLR 163 (Taylor J).

50 *Burford* (1669) 1 Vent 16; *Langley* (1704) 6 Mod Rep 124. But note that blasphemous or seditious spoken words, or words likely to cause a breach of the peace, are indictable.

51 *Adams* (1888) 22 QBD 66.

52 *Holbrook* (1878) 4 QBD 42 at 46; but cf *Wicks*, above.

53 See above p 24 on the implications of the Human Rights Act 1998 on evidential as opposed to legal burdens. Cf *Worme v Commissioner of Police of Grenada* [2004] UKPC 8, construing the Grenadan provision, the Privy Council held that the legal burden of proof lay on the prosecution once D had raised a defence. At para 22, Lord Rodger distinguishes the English offence where the burden is more clearly placed on the accused.

Libel Act 1843, modifying the common law under which it is probable that truth was not a defence to an indictment. In effect this represents a justificatory defence of lawfulness.

(iii) It is clear that the common law defence of privilege applies equally in crime as in tort[54] but it is not certain that the defence of fair comment on a matter of public interest is available. Wien J left the matter open in *Goldsmith v Pressdram Ltd*[55] and leading works say[56] that the defence may be relied on.[57] The statutory protection afforded to certain newspaper reports by the Defamation Act 1996 does not apply to criminal libel.[58]

(iv) A libel on a class of persons is not actionable in tort unless the class is so small, like a body of trustees or directors, that it might be taken to refer to each member individually,[59] or it is otherwise so worded as to appear to refer to an individual. It is possible, however, that a libel intended to excite public hatred against a class, such as the clergy of Durham or the Justices of the Peace of Middlesex is indictable,[60] though no individual's reputation be harmed.

(v) It is not actionable to defame a dead person, but according to Coke[61] it is indictable, again because of a tendency to cause strife. Later decisions, however, suggest that this is so only if the libel is designed to bring the surviving relations to the deceased person into hatred or contempt[62] – in which case it seems to be a libel on them – or was actually intended to provoke or annoy the surviving relatives.[63]

(b) Vicarious liability

In other respects, the crime is narrower than the tort. In accordance with general principle, a master is liable in tort for libels published by his servant in the course of his employment.[64] It may be that vicarious liability also extended at common law to a criminal charge against the proprietor of a newspaper in respect of libels published by his servant.[65] However that may be, by the Libel Act 1843, s 7, it is a defence to prove that the publication was made without D's authority, consent or knowledge and that the

54 *Perry* (1883) 15 Cox CC 169 and *Rule* [1937] 2 KB 375.

55 [1977] QB 83 at 90. In [1977] 2 All ER 557 he is reported to have said, without citation of authority, that the defence does not apply; but his (one assumes) second thoughts, being stated in the Law Report, must prevail.

56 28 Halsbury's Laws of England (4th edn), para 29–78; Archbold, para 29–75 ('probably'); Russell, 803–805.

57 The Law Commission's provisional recommendation is that there should be no such defence in their proposed offence which would require an intent to defame: Working Paper No 84, 8–49.

58 See Defamation Act 1996, ss 14, 15, 20(2).

59 *Knupffer v London Express Newspapers Ltd* [1944] AC 116, [1944] 1 All ER 495; Gatley (above), p 281.

60 *Williams* (1822) 5 B & Ald 595.

61 *Case de Libellis Famosis* (1605) 5 Co Rep 125a.

62 *Topham* (1791) 4 Term Rep 126.

63 *Ensor* (1887) 3 TLR 366; and see Stephen, *Digest* (4th edn), 208n; *Critchley* (1791) 4 Term Rep 130n; *Hunt* (1824) 2 State Tr NS 69 at 98; *Labouchere* (1884) 12 QBD 320.

64 Above, p 225.

65 *Walter* (1799) 3 Esp 21; *Gutch, Fisher and Alexander* (1829) Mood & M 433. But cf *Holbrook* (1877) 13 Cox CC 650.

publication did not arise from want of due care or caution on his part.[66] It seems to follow from this provision that D is liable for the acts of his servants within the scope of their authority unless the statutory conditions are satisfied.

(c) *Mens rea*

The defendant must have intended to publish the words which are alleged to be libellous. It is not enough that he intentionally published the book or paper in which they were contained.[67] It is not certain what further mental element is required. In *Wicks*[68] Du Parcq J said that the crime was one of strict liability but this was *obiter* and not supported by the authority cited.[69] It is submitted that D must at least know of the existence, or the possibility of the existence, of the facts which render the statement defamatory.[70] Other authorities suggest that there must be an actual intention to defame.[71] As publication to the victim is sufficient, it is difficult to see how this can be so in that type of case since there is no evidence of an intention to injure the victim's reputation. Arguably, that is a special case. Analogy with blasphemous libel, as defined in *Lemon*,[72] would suggest that an intention to defame is not required; analogy with seditious libel would suggest that it is.[73]

As noted above, a person may be held vicariously liable for libel if he fails to prove that the publication did not arise from his negligence; but this is not inconsistent with the opinion expressed above. It is not unknown for vicarious liability to attach to offences requiring *mens rea*[74] and it may be that *mens rea* has to be proved in the agent.

(d) ECHR

The compatibility of the offence with Article 10 of the ECHR (freedom of expression) lies in some doubt.[75] The European Court has accepted that offences of this nature may be compatible, but only if demonstrated to be strictly necessary within the terms of Article 10(2). Prosecutions for expressions of opinion (particularly by journalists)[76] are unlikely to be compatible, but it is otherwise where the publication contains explicitly false allegations.[77] It has been recognized that the criminal sanction may be necessary to protect public officials from 'offensive and abusive verbal attacks' but it is doubtful that an offence as ill-defined and broad as the common law offence of libel is necessary to

66 *Holbrook* (1877) 3 QBD 60; *Holbrook* (1878) 4 QBD 42 at 50–51, 60–61, DC; *Love* (1955) 39 Cr App R 30, CCA.

67 *Munslow* [1895] 1 QB 758 at 765.

68 (1936) 25 Cr App R 168 at 173.

69 *Walter* (1799) 3 Esp 21.

70 So that there would be no criminal liability on the facts of *E. Hulton & Co v Jones* [1910] AC 20; *Cassidy v Daily Mirror Newspapers Ltd* [1929] 2 KB 331 or *Newstead v London Express Newspaper Ltd* [1940] 1 KB 377, [1939] 4 All ER 319.

71 *Lord Abingdon* (1794) 1 Esp 226; *Creevey* (1813) 1 M & S 273; *Evans* (1821) 3 Stark 35; *Ensor* (1887) 3 TLR 366.

72 [1979] AC 617, [1979] 1 All ER 898.

73 Below, p 967.

74 Above, p 226.

75 See also the statements of Lord Diplock in *Gleaves v Deakin* (above).

76 See *Dalban v Romania* [2000] EHRLR 84 and *Lopes Gomes de Silva v Portugal* (2000) 34 EHRR 1376.

77 See eg *Constantiescu v Romania* (2000) 33 EHRR 817, and compare *Lingens and Leitgens v Austria* (1982) 4 EHRR 373 and *Lingens v Austria* (1986) 8 EHRR 407.

provide such protection.[78] The Privy Council[79] has recently upheld the constitutionality of an offence of intentional libel against a challenge based on freedom of expression. The offence under the Grenada Code was found to be 'reasonably required for the purpose of protecting the reputations, rights, and freedoms of other persons'.[80]

(e) Publication of libel known to be false

The publication of a libel *known to be false* is a misdemeanour under s 4 of the Libel Act 1843 punishable with two years' imprisonment. If it is not proved that D knew the libel to be false, or if it is true, D may be convicted of the common law offence and sentenced to not more than one year's imprisonment.[81]

3. Obscene publications[82]

Obscenity was originally an ecclesiastical offence but it was held in *Curl*[83] that the publication of an obscene libel was a common law misdemeanour. The law is now to be found in the Obscene Publications Acts 1959 and 1964.

(a) What is obscenity?

The ordinary meaning of obscene is filthy, lewd, or disgusting. In law, the meaning is in some respects, narrower, in other respects possibly wider.

The 1959 Act, s 1(1), provides the test of obscenity:

> For the purposes of this Act an article[84] shall be deemed to be obscene if its effect or (where the article comprises two or more distinct items) the effect of any one of its items is, if taken as a whole, such as to tend to deprave and corrupt persons who are likely, having regard to all relevant circumstances, to read, see or hear the matter contained or embodied in it.

This retains, in substantially the same form, the test at common law laid down by Cockburn CJ, in *Hicklin*:[85]

> . . . I think the test of obscenity is this, whether the tendency of the matter charged as obscenity is to deprave and corrupt those whose minds are open to such immoral influences, and into whose hands a publication of this sort may fall.

78 See *Janowski v Poland* (1999) 21 Jan, cf *Nikula v Finland* [2001] EHRLR 338.

79 *Worme v Commissioner of Police of Grenada* [2004] UKPC 8 allegations of bribery by PM in election.

80 Ibid, Lord Rodger of Earlsferry, para 16.

81 *Boaler v R* (1888) 21 QBD 284.

82 S. Bailey, D. Harris and D. Ormerod, *Civil Liberties Cases and Materials* (5th edn, 2001), 682–711; D. Feldman, above ch 16; N. St. John Stevas, 'Obscenity and the Law' [1954] Crim LR 817; C. H. Rolph, *The Trial of Lady Chatterley*; G. Robertson, *Freedom, the Individual and the Law* (7th edn, 1993), ch 5; D. G. T. Williams, 'The Control of Obscenity' [1965] Crim LR 471, 522; C. Manchester, 'A History of the Crime of Obscene Libel' [1991] Journal of Legal History 31.

83 (1727) 2 Stra 788; following *Sidley* (1663) 1 Sid 168, sub nom *Sydlyes' Case* 1 Keb 620, a case of an indecent exhibition.

84 For the definition of 'Article', see below, p 953.

85 (1868) LR 3 QB 360 at 371. This was an appeal from a decision of a recorder quashing an order of the justices for the destruction of certain pamphlets under the Obscenity Publications Act 1857; below, p 957.

It has been said that the test was largely ignored at common law and that, if matter was found to be 'obscene' in the ordinary meaning of the word, the tendency to deprave and corrupt was presumed. If that was true, the effect of the statutory enactment of the definition has been to tighten the definition by requiring proof of an actual tendency to deprave and corrupt.[86] In *Anderson*[87] (the case of the 'Oz School Kids' Issue') the conviction was quashed because the judge left the jury with the impression that 'obscene' meant 'repulsive', 'filthy', 'loathsome', or 'lewd'. An article might be all of these and yet not have a tendency to deprave and corrupt. This should, it is submitted be a high threshold. Sexually explicit material is not necessarily obscene.[88]

(i) Aversion argument

The very 'obscenity' (in the popular sense) of a publication may, paradoxically, prevent it from being 'obscene' (in the legal sense). If the article were so revolting that it would put anyone off the kind of depraved activity depicted (the 'aversion argument') then it would have no tendency to deprave.[89] Whether the defence is available seems to depend on the nature of the article and the manner of publication. In *Calder v Boyars* it was – *Last Exit to Brooklyn*, which is 'a most powerfully written book, and, in some eyes is regarded as repulsive and nauseating,' was on general sale. In contrast, the defence could hardly be 'effectively run' in *Elliott*,[90] a video club case, where the material (homosexual activity) was being offered as attractive to members.

It appears that the requirement that the article be 'obscene' in the ordinary meaning of the word may have disappeared and have been replaced with a technical meaning. An article may be obscene within the statute if it has a tendency to deprave and corrupt, (even though it is not filthy, lewd or disgusting), but it may be found not to be obscene because it is so filthy, lewd and disgusting that it would put anyone off.

(ii) Subject matter capable of being obscene

Until 1965 the law of obscenity was only invoked in relation to sexual depravity. The prosecutions invariably concerned publications of an erotic and pornographic kind. The words 'deprave and corrupt' are clearly capable of bearing a wider meaning than this; and it has now been held that depravity and corruption is not confined to sexual depravity and corruption. In *John Calder (Publications) Ltd v Powell*[91] it was held that *Cain's Book* might properly be found obscene on the ground that it:

> . . . highlighted, as it were, the favourable effects of drug-taking, and, so far from condemning it, advocated it, and that there was a real danger that those into whose hands the book came might be tempted at any rate to experiment with drugs and get the favourable sensations highlighted by the book.

The difficulty about extending the notion of obscenity beyond sexual morality is that it is not now apparent where the law is to stop. It seems obvious that an article with a

86 *DPP v Whyte* [1972] 3 All ER 12 at 18, HL, per Lord Wilberforce.
87 [1972] 1 QB 304, [1971] 3 All ER 1152. See T. Palmer, *The Trials of Oz* (1971).
88 *Darbo v DPP* [1992] Crim LR 56.
89 *Calder and Boyars Ltd* [1969] 1 QB 151, [1968] 3 All ER 644; *Anderson*, above.
90 [1996] 1 Cr App R 432 at 436.
91 [1965] 1 QB 509, [1965] 1 All ER 159.

tendency to induce violence is now obscene;[92] and, if taking drugs is depravity, why not drinking, or, since evidence of its harmful effects is beyond doubt, smoking? Whether the conduct to which the article tends amounts to depravity would seem to depend on how violently the judge (in deciding whether there was evidence of obscenity) and the jury (in deciding whether the article was obscene) disapproved of the conduct in question. This is an unsatisfactory state of affairs. It can be argued that the offence is ill-defined and fails adequately to respect the principles of certainty and fair warning. However, challenges to the offence on the basis of its incompatibility with the ECHR requirement that restrictions on freedom of expression be prescribed by law have been rejected in the English courts. In *Perrin*[93] the Court of Appeal held that the offence was sufficiently clearly prescribed within the broad scope of that concept as described by the ECtHR in *Sunday Times v UK (No 1)*:[94]

> Firstly, the law must be adequately accessible: the citizen must be able to have an indication that is adequate in the circumstances of the legal rules applicable to a given case. Secondly, a norm cannot be regarded as a 'law' unless it is formulated with sufficient precision to enable the citizen to regulate his conduct: he must be able – if need be with appropriate advice – to foresee, to a degree that is reasonable in the circumstances, the consequences which a given action may entail.

Indeed, one of the leading cases in Strasbourg jurisprudence on certainty is the obscenity case of *Handyside v UK*, in which the court stated:

> Freedom of expression constitutes one of the essential foundations of a [democratic] society, one of the basic conditions necessary for its progress and for the development of every man. Subject to paragraph 2 of Article 10, it is applicable not only to information and ideas that are favourably received, or regarded as inoffensive, but also to those that offend, shock or disturb the state or any sector of the population. Such are the demands of that pluralism, tolerance and broadmindedness without which there is no democratic society.[95]

(iii) Depravity defined

The core of the offence is the tendency to deprave and corrupt. It is now clear that 'depravity' may be a mental state, not resulting in external action of any kind. On the contrary, the protection of the minds of the people is the primary object of the law. In *DPP v Whyte*[96] it was found that the articles would enable their readers to engage in private fantasies of their own, not involving overt sexual activity of any kind. It was held that they were obscene. That case also settled that an article may be obscene although it is directed only to persons who are already depraved. It is enough that it maintains a state of corruption which might otherwise be escaped. 'The Act is not merely concerned with the once for all corruption of the wholly innocent, it equally protects the less innocent from further corruption, the addict from feeding or increasing his addiction.'[97]

(iv) Proving obscenity

The admissibility of expert evidence usually arises in the context of the public good defence (discussed below). Expert evidence also has a part to play in some cases in

[92] Cf *DPP v A and BC Chewing Gum Ltd* [1968] 1 QB 159, [1967] 2 All ER 504; *Calder and Boyars Ltd* [1969] 1 QB 151 at 172.

[93] [2002] EWCA Crim 747.

[94] [1979] 2 EHRR 245.

[95] (1979–80) 1 EHRR 737, para 49.

[96] Above, n 86.

[97] At 19, per Lord Wilberforce.

proving the tendency to deprave, but this must be approached with caution. Expert opinion is admissible on for example, the medical effects of cocaine and the various ways of taking it because this is a matter which is outside the experience of the ordinary jury member.[98] But whether those effects constitute depravity and corruption – that is, whether the article, whatever it is, is obscene – is exclusively a question for the jury. Expert evidence is not admissible on that issue,[99] except apparently in the case of material directed at very young children, when experts in child psychiatry may be asked what the effect of certain material on the minds of children would be.[100] But that authority is to be regarded as 'highly exceptional and confined to its own circumstances.'[101] The theory seems to be that a jury is as well able as an expert to judge the effect on an adult but not on a child. This does not mean that the jury should be left without guidance on the question. It would seem right that they should be reminded that 'deprave and corrupt' are very strong words; that material which might lead morally astray is not necessarily corrupting;[102] and that they should keep in mind the current standards of ordinary decent people.[103] In the end, they have to make a judgement of what they believe to be the prevailing moral standard. On one view, this represents the deficiency of the offence in terms of the lack of certainty and fair warning, on another view this at least preserves the flexibility of the offence and ensures the opportunity for it to evolve with contemporary moral standards.[104]

In *Reiter*,[105] the jury were asked to look at a large number of other books in order to decide whether the books which were the subject of the charge were obscene. The Court of Criminal Appeal held that this was wrong. It appears that it is still not permissible, under the Act, to prove that other books, which are just as obscene as the one in issue, are freely circulating:[106] 'What is permitted elsewhere in the world is neither here nor there.'[107]

(v) Jury directions

Where so much power to define the scope of the wrongdoing lies with the jury, much will depend not only on the content, but also the tone of the judge's direction. In the case of *Martin Secker Warburg*,[108] concerning the publication of *The Philanderer*, Stable J gave a direction to a jury which was acclaimed in the press for its enlightened attitude and was

98 *Skirving* [1985] QB 819, [1985] 2 All ER 705, CA, criticized by R. T. H. Stone, 'Obscene Publications: The Problems Persist' [1986] Crim LR 139 at 142.

99 *Calder and Boyars Ltd* [1969] 1 QB 151, [1968] 3 All ER 644; *Anderson* [1972] 1 QB 304, [1971] 3 All ER 1152; *DPP v Jordan* [1977] AC 699, [1976] 3 All ER 775. For an argument that the limited availability of the expert evidence may contravene Article 6 and Articles 10 and 14 of the ECHR see C. Nowlin, 'Expert Evidence in English Obscenity Law: Implications of the Human Rights Act 1998' (2001) Common Law World Review 94. See generally on expert evidence in obscenity trials F. Bates, 'Pornography and the Expert Witness' (1978) 20 Crim LQ 250.

100 *DPP v A and BC Chewing Gum Ltd* [1968] 1 QB 159, [1967] 2 All ER 504.

101 *Anderson* [1972] 1 QB 304 at 313.

102 *Knuller (Publishing, Printing and Promotions) Ltd v DPP* [1972] 2 All ER 898 at 932, 936.

103 Ibid, at 904.

104 Cf *Muller v Switzerland* [1991] 13 EHRR 212.

105 [1954] 2 QB 16, [1954] 1 All ER 741.

106 *Penguin Books* (1961) Rolph, above, 127.

107 The judge was held to have correctly so directed the jury in *Elliott* [1996] 1 Cr App R 432 at 435, [1996] Crim LR 264, applying *Reiter*.

108 [1954] 2 All ER 683, [1954] 1 WLR 1138.

thought to be reassuring to those who fear that the criminal law as applied by the judges is out of touch with public opinion.[109] The learned judge told the jury:[110]

. . . the charge is a charge that the tendency of the book is to corrupt and deprave. The charge is not that the tendency of the book is either to shock or to disgust. That is not a criminal offence. The charge is that the tendency of the book is to corrupt and deprave. Then you say: 'Well, corrupt and deprave whom?' to which the answer is: those whose minds are open to such immoral influences and into whose hands a publication of this sort may fall. What, exactly, does that mean? are we to take our literary standards as being the level of something that is suitable for the decently brought up young female aged fourteen? Or do we go even further back than that and are we to be reduced to the sort of books that one reads as a child in the nursery? The answer to that is: Of course not. A mass of literature, great literature, from many angles, is wholly unsuitable for reading by the adolescent, but that does not mean that a publisher is guilty of a criminal offence for making those works available to the general public.

Dealing with the particular book, he said:[111]

. . . the book does deal with candour or, if you prefer it, crudity with the realities of human love and of human intercourse. There is no getting away from that, and the Crown say: 'Well, that is sheer filth.' Is it? Is the act of sexual passion sheer filth? It may be an error of taste to write about it. It may be a matter in which, perhaps, old-fashioned people would mourn the reticence that was observed in these matters yesterday, but is it sheer filth? That is a matter which you have to consider and ultimately to decide.

Other directions to juries in recent times, however, have been a good deal less liberal and it has been suggested that Stable J's is not the typical judicial attitude.[112]

It is now made perfectly clear by the Act that an 'item' alleged to be obscene must be 'taken as a whole' so that where an article consists of a single item,[113] like a novel the article must be judged as a whole. Where an article, like a magazine, comprises a number of distinct items, each item must be tested individually; and if one item is found to be obscene, the whole article is obscene.[114] In *Goring*[115] this approach was extended to films. There is a danger with this approach that juries will be more likely to focus on individual 'purple passages', which will be given an unwarranted significance in the assessment of the overall work. The normal practice is for no more than six articles to form the basis of the indictment – that being sufficient to highlight the different types of activities portrayed or described.

(vi) Who must be at risk of being depraved?

It remains unclear whether the law requires us to take our standards from 'the decently brought up young female aged fourteen'. An article is obscene if it has a tendency to deprave 'persons who are likely . . . to read, see or hear the matter contained or embodied in it'. Only if the number of readers likely to be corrupted is 'so small as to be negligible'

109 See S. Prevezer, Note (1954) 17 MLR 571.

110 [1954] 2 All ER at 686. 111 Ibid, at 687, 688.

112 H. Street, *Freedom, the Individual and the Law* (5th edn, 1984), 122. For rather extreme arguments that the offence is too liberal see S. Edwards, 'A Plea for Censorship' (1991) 141 NLJ 1478.

113 This is a question of law for the judge: *Gorring* [1999] Crim LR 670, CA.

114 *Anderson* [1972] 1 QB 304 at 312, above, p 945. 115 [1999] Crim LR 670 and commentary.

is the article not obscene.[116] It is certainly obscene if it has a tendency to deprave 'a significant proportion' of those likely to read it.[117] It would not be obscene simply on the ground that it might tend to deprave 'a minute lunatic fringe of readers'.[118] If, however, a significant, though comparatively small, number of the likely readers were decently brought up 14-year-old children, then whether the book was obscene would turn on whether it was likely to deprave them. A direction on the number of viewers/readers is not a prerequisite in all cases since there is a danger that it will confuse the jury where for example, the publication is of a novel on general sale. This is a significant issue since in ECHR terms it may assist in the determination of whether the use of the offence was proportionate within Article 10(2).

It has been suggested that the ambiguity of this aspect of the law renders the law ineffective since it offers an opportunity for cases to be diverted from the criminal courts.[119] In cases that do go to trial, the questions for the jury are of a highly speculative nature. How, for example, is the jury to say whether a significant proportion of the readers will be 14-year-olds? The answer seems to depend on all kinds of matters of which the jury can, at best, have imperfect knowledge. The same article may or may not be obscene depending on the manner of publication. If it has a tendency to deprave 14-year-olds, a bookseller who sells a copy to a club for 14-year-olds is obviously publishing an obscene article; but if he sells the same book to the Conservative Club or a working men's club, this may not be so. The fact that the publisher (in the sense of the producer) of the book is acquitted of publishing an obscene libel, does not mean, then, that other subsequent 'publishers' of the book do not commit an offence.

This issue raises particular problem in terms of the publication of material on the internet. Since any file on the internet is theoretically available to any person of computer literate age in the world, the likelihood of material being read or viewed by a particular group in terms of age, religion, culture, etc is impossible to predict.

(vii) No requirement of intention to corrupt

The actual intention of the author is irrelevant. If the article has a tendency to deprave a significant proportion of the readership, it does not matter how pure and noble the author's intent may have been,[120] the article is obscene. In *Martin Secker Warburg* Stable J told the jury:[121]

> You will have to consider whether the author was pursuing an honest purpose and an honest thread of thought, or whether that was all just a bit of camouflage. . . .

This was too favourable to the defence, unless the jury were to take account of the author's intention, as it appeared in the book itself, as a factor which would have a bearing on whether people would be depraved.

[116] *DPP v Whyte* [1972] 3 All ER 12 at 21 and 25, per Lords Pearson and Cross. See also *O'Sullivan* [1995] 1 Cr App R 455. Cf the obligations of the BBFC when classifying videos under s 4A of the Video Recordings Act 1984, discussed in *R v Video Appeals Committee of the BBFC, ex p BBFC* [2000] EMLR 850.

[117] *Calder and Boyars Ltd* [1969] 1 QB 151 at 168.

[118] Ibid, at 984.

[119] S. Edwards, 'On the Contemporary Application of the Obscene Publications Act 1959' [1998] Crim LR 843, arguing that it renders official statistics valueless.

[120] *Calder and Boyars Ltd* [1969] 1 QB 151 at 168–169. Cf *Lemon*, above, p 936.

[121] [1954] 2 All ER 683 at 688.

(viii) Freedom of expression

A prosecution will engage the right to freedom of expression under Article 10 of the ECHR, but will be justified for the prevention of crime or the protection of morals within Article 10(2) provided it is necessary and proportionate. In *Perrin*,[122] the Court of Appeal accepted that the offence was necessary and proportionate within the meaning in Article 10(2). A potential difficulty arises over how the proportionality is to be fairly assessed given that the likely audience may well be unknown. For example, in *Hoare v UK*[123] it was held that prosecution was not disproportionate when videotapes were sent to the intended purchaser by post because there were insufficient safeguards to ensure that only the intended purchasers would gain access to the material. It would be otherwise where the publication is to a group voluntarily assembled with restricted access as in *Scherer v Switzerland*,[124] which involved showing a pornographic film in a private room in a sex shop.[125]

(b) Offences

It is an offence if D:

(i) publishes an obscene article for gain or not;[126] or

(ii) 'has' an obscene article for publication for gain (whether gain to himself or gain to another).[127]

Making an obscene article is not an offence, as such; but those who participate in its manufacture may be liable as secondary parties to the publication, or the 'having', which is a continuing offence.[128] If the article created involves an image or pseudo image of a child, liability will lie under the Protection of Children Act 1978.

(i) Publication

Section 1 of the Obscene Publications Act 1959,[129] provides:

> (3) For the purposes of this Act a person publishes an article who –
>
> (a) distributes, circulates, sells, lets on hire, gives, or lends it, or who offers it for sale or for letting on hire; or
>
> (b) in the case of an article containing or embodying matter to be looked at or a record, shows, plays or projects it or, where the matter is data stored electronically, transmits that data. –
>
> (4) For the purpose of this Act a person also publishes an article to the extent that any matter recorded on it is included by him in a programme included in a programme service.

[122] [2002] EWCA Crim 747. [123] [1997] EHRLR 678.

[124] 18 EHRR 276; see also *X and Y v Switzerland* (1991) 16564/90.

[125] Cf *Muller v Switzerland* [1991] 13 EHRR 212 which involved displays of sexually explicit paintings in a public gallery without warnings.

[126] Obscene Publications Act 1959, s 2(1). [127] Ibid, s 2(1) as amended by the 1964 Act, s 1(1).

[128] *Barton* [1976] Crim LR 514, CA.

[129] As amended by the Broadcasting Act 1990, s 162(1)(b) and by the Criminal Justice and Public Order Act 1994, s 168(1) and Sch 9.

(5) Where the inclusion of any matter in a programme so included would, if that matter were recorded matter, constitute the publication of an obscene article for the purposes of this Act by virtue of subsection (4) above, this Act shall have effect in relation to the inclusion of that matter in that programme as if it were recorded matter.

(6) In this section 'programme' and 'programme service' have the same meaning as in the Broadcasting Act 1990.

If the charge alleges publication to a named person, it must be proved that the article had a tendency to deprave and corrupt that person.[130] If the article does not have a tendency to deprave the person to whom it is published, it will be obscene only if either –

(1)(a) there are 'persons who are likely, having regard to all the relevant circumstances, to read, see or hear matter contained or embodied in it' (whether they have done so or not) *and*

(b) it will have a tendency to deprave and corrupt those persons;[131]

or

(2) it has in fact been published to a person whom it is likely to deprave and corrupt, and this publication could reasonably have been expected to follow from publication by D.[132]

If D is appropriately charged, he may then be convicted of publishing an obscene article to those persons.

In *Barker*,[133] where D published certain photographs to V and the judge told the jury that the fact that V kept them under lock and key was unimportant, the conviction was quashed. If the jury had been told that they were to consider the tendency of the article to deprave and corrupt only V, the direction would seem to be unobjectionable. If, however, they were directed or left to suppose that they should consider its tendency to deprave and corrupt others, then the direction was clearly wrong. The fact that V kept the articles under lock and key was not *conclusive*, for he may have intended to produce them at some future time; but it was certainly *relevant* to the answer to proposition 1(a) above.

Internet publications

It is clear that 'transmitting data electronically' constitutes a publication. Uploading and downloading material to and from webpages has been held to be sufficient.[134] Thus, if D makes available articles of an obscene nature via a website there is a publication. D will also be held to have 'shown' obscene material by providing others with a password to access such material.[135] The publication of material on the internet raises a difficult jurisdictional question which was, it is submitted, not adequately addressed in the leading case of *Perrin*.[136] In that case D had published material on a website in the USA (sewersex.com) which depicted coprophilia and coprophagia. X, a police officer had

130 *DPP v Whyte* [1972] 3 All ER 12 at 29, per Lord Salmon.

131 Obscene Publications Act 1959, s 1(1).

132 Ibid, s 2(6).

133 [1962] 1 All ER 748, [1962] 1 WLR 349.

134 *Perrin* [2002] EWCA Crim 747.

135 See *Fellows and Arnold* [1997] 2 All ER 548, CA, drawing analogy with the individual who offers the key to his library containing obscene works.

136 For discussion of this problem see M. Hirst, *Jurisdiction and the Ambit of the Criminal Law* (2003), 188–190.

accessed the site in England and had viewed a 'preview page' on the site offering a sample of the material available on subscription. That viewing in England (that is, downloading) was held, without any detailed consideration, to constitute a publication by D in England. Reliance was placed on the decision in *Waddon*,[137] but the matter appears to have been conceded by counsel in that case. Indeed, the court in *Waddon* declined to rule upon what the position might be in relation to 'jurisdiction if a person storing material on a website outside England intended that no transmission of that material should take place back to this country'. The result is that D can be convicted of publishing obscene material in England by uploading it to a website in another jurisdiction in which such publication was legal. It is submitted that this is an extremely harsh result.

In broader terms, there is a danger that the internet will produce undesirably tight restrictions on obscenity. Since it will be impossible for a publisher to comply with the requirements of every jurisdiction, for safety's sake he may have to comply with the most restrictive.

Publication to whom?

Two issues have arisen in the context of the relevant recipient: does the publication have to be to a third party? And can there be a tendency to corrupt and deprave a police officer?

The Act does not require publication to a third party. Thus, the Court of Appeal held in *Taylor*[138] that there was a publication where X a photographic developer developed and printed obscene photographs which were then returned to the customer, D.[139] As regards publication to police officers, if the article has no tendency to deprave and corrupt the person to whom it is published and neither of the conditions specified above is satisfied, then D must be acquitted. So in *Clayton and Halsey*[140] where V was an experienced police officer who testified that he was not susceptible to depravity or corruption and there was no evidence of publication, or likelihood of publication, to a third party, the Court of Criminal Appeal held that the case should have been withdrawn from the jury.[141] Lord Parker CJ said:[142]

> . . . while it is no doubt theoretically possible that a jury could take the view that even a most experienced officer, despite his protestations, was susceptible to the influence of the article yet, bearing in mind the onus and degree of proof in a criminal case, it would, we think, be unsafe and therefore wrong to leave that question to the jury.

In *Perrin*, the Court of Appeal distinguished that case from the publication of a single webpage offering a preview of material on offer from the site for those willing to subscribe. The court held that the trial judge had been correct to direct the jury that it was for them to determine who was likely to see the material, and the fact that the only evidence of anyone having actually seen it was that of the police officer investigating it, did not bring the case within the exception acknowledged in *Clayton and Halsey*. Its

137 [2000] All ER (D) 502. 138 [1995] 1 Cr App R 131, CA,

139 There is a resonance with the concept of supply in drugs see above, p 153.

140 [1963] 1 QB 163, [1962] 3 All ER 500.

141 D, of course, did not know that he was dealing with an incorruptible police officer. He had *mens rea* and might now be guilty of an attempt under the Criminal Attempts Act 1981, above, p 400.

142 [1963] 1 QB at 168, [1962] 3 All ER at 502.

availability on the internet meant that there were persons who are likely, having regard to all the relevant circumstances, to read or see the matter *and* the jury concluded that it would have a tendency to deprave and corrupt those persons.

(ii) Having an obscene article for publication for gain

This second type of offence was introduced by amendments made by the 1964 Act and was intended to deal with the difficulties arising from *Clayton and Halsey*. In fact the accused in that case were convicted of *conspiracy*[143] to publish the articles, because the buyers they had in view were not incorruptible police officers. But the implications of the case were serious; for, where there was no evidence that D had conspired with another, it made it virtually impossible to get a conviction on the evidence of a police officer that the articles had been sold to him. Under the amendment it is now possible to charge D with *having* the article for publication for gain; and the incorruptibility of the particular officer who purchases it will be irrelevant. The jury is unlikely to suppose that D kept these articles solely for sale to police officers; and they need only be satisfied that, having regard to all the relevant circumstances, (i) D contemplated publication to such a person as the article would have a tendency to deprave and corrupt, or (ii) that he contemplated publication from which a further publication to susceptible persons could reasonably be expected to follow (whether D in fact contemplated that further publication or not). By s 1(3)(b) of the 1964 Act:

> the question whether the article is obscene shall be determined by reference to such publication for gain of the article as in the circumstances it may reasonably be inferred he had in contemplation and to any further publication that could reasonably be expected to follow from it, but not to any other publication.

The prosecution must prove more than mere possession of the articles. The reference to 'such publication' is to that which is for gain, and this must be proved.[144]

Ownership possession or control

The meaning of 'having' an article is elucidated by s 1(2) of the 1964 Act:

> . . . a person shall be deemed to have an article for publication for gain if with a view to such publication he has the article in his ownership, possession or control.

Thus the owner of the shop in which the article is stocked may be convicted as the owner of the article, as well as his agent or employee who has possession or control of it. The van driver who takes it from wholesaler to retailer may be in possession or control with a view to eventual publication for gain to another. Where articles were alleged to be held for distribution to sex shops and there bought by customers, it was necessary to prove that D contemplated that these steps would be taken. The jury had to be sure that the contemplated publication would tend to deprave and corrupt a significant proportion of the readers or viewers.[145]

143 The Law Officers have given an assurance that conspiracy will not be used as a charge so as to circumvent the public good defence below.

144 *Levy* [2004] All ER (D) 321 (Apr).

145 *O'Sullivan* [1995] 1 Cr App R 455, at 460.

'Offers' for sale

This provision overcomes another difficulty which arose under the 1959 Act. It was held[146] that a person who displays an obscene article in a shop window is not guilty of publishing it. Of the various ways of publishing referred to in s 1(3), the only one which could conceivably have been applicable was 'offering for sale'; and it was held that 'offer' must be construed in accordance with the law of contract,[147] under which the display of goods in a shop window is an 'invitation to treat' and not an offer.[148] This decision, of course, remains good law; but now a charge might successfully be brought of having the obscene article for publication for gain, whether it had been displayed or not.

Film exhibitions

The proviso to s 1(3)(b) formerly extended to film exhibitions taking place otherwise than in a private house. The effect of the amendment to the proviso by s 53 of the Criminal Law Act 1977 is that the exhibition of a film anywhere is a publication for the purposes of the Obscene Publications Act; but no prosecution under s 2 may be brought without the consent of the Director of Public Prosecutions, where the article is a moving picture film not less than 16 mm wide and publication of it took place or could reasonably be expected to take place only in the course of a film exhibition.[149]

'Film exhibition' in s 2[150] means any exhibition of moving pictures which is produced otherwise than by the simultaneous reception and exhibition of programmes included in a programme service within the meaning of the Broadcasting Act 1990.

If the film were such as to outrage public decency then its public showing was a common law offence. A local authority which, in performing its licensing duties, authorized the showing of an outrageously indecent film might have been guilty of aiding and abetting the offence.[151] A local authority has no duty to censor films, except in relation to children; but if it chooses to act, through its licensing powers, as a censor for adults, it must act in accordance with the law and not expressly permit the commission of an offence. Since the Criminal Law Act 1977, however, no proceedings may be brought for an offence at common law (including conspiracy) in respect of a film exhibition alleged to be obscene, indecent, offensive, disgusting or injurious to morality.[152] An indictment for statutory conspiracy, contrary to s 1 of the Criminal Law Act 1977,[153] would lie in appropriate circumstances.

(c) Defences

(i) No reasonable cause to believe article obscene

By s 2(5) of the 1959 Act and s 1(3)(a) of the 1964 Act, it is a defence for D to prove[154] that he (i) had not examined the article and (ii) had no reasonable cause to suspect that it

[146] *Mella v Monahan* [1961] Crim LR 175, following *Fisher v Bell* [1961] 1 QB 394, [1960] 3 All ER 731.

[147] For a criticism of this ruling, see [1961] Crim LR at 181; cf *Partridge v Crittenden* [1968] 2 All ER 421, [1968] 1 WLR 1204.

[148] *Pharmaceutical Society of Great Britain v Boots Cash Chemists (Southern) Ltd* [1953] 1 QB 401, [1953] 1 All ER 482.

[149] Obscene Publications Act 1959, s 2(3A).

[150] As amended by the Cinemas Act 1985, Sch 2.

[151] *Greater London Council, ex p Blackburn* [1976] 3 All ER 184.

[152] Obscene Publications Act 1959, s 2(4A).

[153] Above, p 362.

[154] On the compatibility of reverse burdens of proof with Article 6(2) of the ECHR see p 24 above.

was such that his publication of it, or his having it, as the case may be, would make him liable to be convicted of an offence against s 2. Both conditions must be satisfied; so if D has examined the article, his failure to appreciate its tendency to deprave and corrupt is no defence under these sections.[155]

(ii) Public good

Section 4 of the 1959 Act (as amended by the Criminal Law Act 1977) provides a defence of 'public good':

> (1) Subject to subsection (1A) of this section a person shall not be convicted of an offence against section 2 of this Act . . . if it is proved that publication of the article in question is justified as being for the public good on the ground that it is in the interests of science, literature, art or learning, or of other objects of general concern.
>
> (2) It is hereby declared that the opinion of experts as to the literary, artistic, scientific or other merits of an article may be admitted in any proceedings under this Act either to establish or negative the said ground.

The defence becomes relevant only when the jury has decided that the book is obscene – that it has a tendency to deprave a significant proportion of those likely to read it. The Act assumes that this harm to a section of the community might be outweighed by the other considerations referred to in the section. The jury should be directed to consider first whether an article is obscene within s 1. If not satisfied of that beyond reasonable doubt, they must acquit. If so satisfied, they should go on to consider whether, on a balance of probabilities, the publication of the article, though obscene, is for the public good.[156] The jury's task is then to:

> . . . consider, on the one hand, the number of readers they believe would tend to be depraved and corrupted by the book, the strength of the tendency to deprave and corrupt, and the nature of the depravity or corruption; on the other hand, they should assess the strength of the literary, sociological or ethical merit which they consider the book to possess. They should then weigh up all these factors and decide whether on balance the publication is proved to be justified as being for the public good.[157]

Expert evidence is not admissible in support of a defence under s 4 to the effect that pornographic material is psychologically beneficial to persons who are sexually repressed, perverted or deviant, in that it relieves their sexual tensions and may divert them from anti-social activities. The House of Lords so held in *DPP v Jordan.*[158] The other 'objects of general concern' must fall within the same area as those specifically mentioned. The effect on sexual behaviour and attitudes was a totally different area, covered in s 1. The Court of Appeal[159] had reached the same conclusion on the ground that the same qualities relied on by the Crown to show that the article was obscene were being relied on by the defence to show that it was for the public good. To admit such evidence would be to allow every jury to decide for itself as a matter of public policy whether obscene material should be

155 In the case of a broadcast or transmission in a programme service under the Broadcasting Act 1990, D must show he had no knowledge or grounds to suspect that the programme included obscene content.

156 *DPP v Jordan* [1976] 3 All ER 775. Cf *Sumner* [1977] Crim LR 362 (Judge Davies).

157 *Calder and Boyars Ltd* [1969] 1 QB 151 at 172.

158 Above.

159 Sub nom *Staniforth* [1976] 2 All ER 714, [1976] 2 WLR 849.

prohibited. Parliament has decided that it should – unless it possesses certain merits; and whatever doubt there may be as to the range of those merits, they clearly cannot include obscenity itself. 'Merits' must mean qualities which show that the publication of the article is for the public good in that it tends to the advancement of an object of general concern. In *Penguin Books*, Byrne J said that merits from a sociological, an ethical and an educational point of view were included.[160] This decision must now be read in the light of *Jordan*.

'Learning' was described in *Attorney-General's Reference (No 3 of 1977)*[161] as a noun, being the product of scholarship, something with inherent excellence gained by the work of a scholar. The judge had wrongly permitted the defence to adduce expert evidence to establish that magazines had value in terms of sex education.

The 'other objects of general concern' must not only be such as to be conducive to the public good but must also be of 'concern' to members of the public in general. The Court of Appeal in *Jordan*[162] appears to have assumed judicial knowledge that the public generally are not 'concerned' with, or about, the relief of the sexually repressed. It is not clear whether 'concerned' is interpreted to mean 'interest in' or 'activity in'. According to the court, 'The disposal of sewage is no doubt for the public good but it is not a matter with which the generality of the public is concerned'. The general public is certainly interested in the disposal of sewage, at least in the sense that if it were not efficiently done, they would have a great deal to say about it. On the other hand, it is difficult to suppose that the general public could ever be active in the disposal of sewage. It is submitted, however, that 'concern' ought to be interpreted to mean 'interest'. The general public are not active in literature, art or science, but the Act assumes, rightly, it is submitted, that these are objects of public concern.

As noted above, it is not permissible to prove that other books, which are just as obscene are freely circulating,[163] but evidence relating to other books may be admitted to establish the 'climate of literature' in order to assess the literary merit of the book.[164]

In *Penguin Books*,[165] Crown counsel conceded in argument that the intention of the author in writing the book is relevant to the question of literary merit. If this is right, it must again[166] refer only to the intention as it appears in the book itself.

The onus of establishing the defence is on the accused and the standard of proof required is proof on a balance of probabilities.[167] The defence is not available on a charge of conspiracy to corrupt public morals; but Parliament has been assured that such a charge will not be brought so as to circumvent the defence.[168]

Subsection (1) does not apply where the article is a moving picture film or moving picture soundtrack or television or sound programme.[169] In the case of these articles a

160 See 'The Trial of Lady Chatterley' by C. H. Rolph, at 234; *Calder and Boyars Ltd* [1969] 1 QB 151 at 172; *John Calder (Publications) Ltd v Powell* [1965] 1 All ER 159 at 161.

161 [1978) 67 Cr App R 393, CA.

162 [1976] 2 All ER 714 at 719, CA.

163 *Penguin Books* (1961) Rolph, above, 127.

164 Ibid.

165 Rolph, above, 87 and 123.

166 As with the question whether the book is obscene. Above, p 944.

167 *Calder and Boyars Ltd*, above, at 171.

168 'That should be known by all who are concerned with the operation of the criminal law', per Lord Morris in *Knuller v DPP* [1972] 2 All ER 898 at 912. See Lord Diplock's doubts as to the efficacy of the assurance (924) and Lord Reid's opinion that it does not apply to conspiracy to outrage public decency (906).

169 'Moving picture soundtrack' means 'any sound record designed for playing with a moving picture film, whether incorporated with the film or not', s 4(3).

similar defence of public good is provided except that the interests which may justify publication are those of drama, opera, ballet or any other art, or of literature or learning.[170]

(d) *Mens rea*

(i) At common law

In *Hicklin*[171] it was held that it was not necessary to establish that D's motive was to deprave and corrupt; and that, if he knowingly published that which had a tendency to deprave and corrupt, it was no defence that he had an honest and laudable intention in publishing the work in question. D, a member of the Protestant Electoral Union, sold[172] copies of *The Confessional Unmasked.* He argued that he did so with the intention, not of prejudicing good morals, but of exposing what he deemed to be the errors of the Church of Rome and, particularly, the immorality of the confessional. To this Cockburn CJ answered:

> Be it so. The question then presents itself in this simple form: May you commit an offence against the law in order that thereby you may effect some ulterior object which you have in view, which may be an honest and even a laudable one? My answer is, emphatically, no.[173]

The case did not decide, as is sometimes supposed, that no *mens rea* is required. The argument was not that D did not know the nature of the thing published nor even that he did not know that its natural consequence was to tend to deprave and corrupt; but that the publication was justified by his predominant intention of exposing the errors of the Church of Rome. Cockburn CJ indeed assumed that D *did* know what the effect of the publication would be:

> . . . it is impossible to suppose that the man who published it must not have known and seen that the effect upon the minds of many of those into whose hands it would come would be of a mischievous and demoralising character.[174]

A person who knows that a certain result will follow may properly be said to intend[175] it or, at the very least, to be reckless. Blackburn J relied particularly upon *Vantandillo*,[176] which lays down that it is a misdemeanour to carry a person with a contagious disease through the street, though no intent to infect anyone be alleged; but in that case the court insisted that D should have 'full knowedge'[177] of the fact of the contagious disease. *Hicklin*,[178] then, need not be taken to have decided more than that, if D publishes that which he knows will have a tendency to deprave and corrupt, it is no defence that he did so with the best of motives.

No case before the Act of 1959 decided anything to the contrary. In *Thomson*[179] the Common Sergeant admitted evidence of other books found on D's premises as tending to

[170] Section 4(1A). Cf Theatres Act 1968, s 3; below, p 964; Broadcasting Act 1990, Sch 15.
[171] (1868) LR 3 QB 360.
[172] For the price he paid for them and not 'for gain'. [173] (1868) LR 3 QB at 371, 372.
[174] Ibid, at 372. If the law requires knowledge, this is now clearly a question for the jury: Criminal Justice Act 1967, s 8; above, p 125.
[175] Above, p 94. [176] (1815) 4 M & S 73. [177] Ibid, at 77.
[178] Above. [179] (1900) 64 JP 456 at 457.

show that 'she sold this book with the intention alleged in the indictment [to corrupt morals], and not accidentally'.

In *Barraclough*,[180] it was held unnecessary (but desirable) that the indictment should contain an allegation of intent, because the intent was implicit in the allegation of publishing obscenity.[181] In *De Montalk*,[182] D handed to a printer some poems he had written, intending to circulate about 100 copies, mostly to young people of both sexes ('literary people'). The printer sent the poems to the police and D was convicted. His appeal on the ground that there was no sufficient direction on intent was dismissed; but the headnote goes farther than the judgment in asserting that the jury should not be directed that they must find an intention to corrupt public morals. Crown counsel (later Byrne J) submitted merely that intention *was to be inferred* from the act of publication and that no affirmative evidence of intention need be given; and the court dismissed the appeal, saying that the law was accurately stated in *Barraclough*.[183] But in *Penguin Books*,[184] Byrne J held that, if D publishes an article which is obscene, the inference that he intends to deprave and corrupt is irrebuttable. Such an approach today would seem to be inconsistent with s 8 of the Criminal Justice Act 1967;[185] but, though Byrne J used the language of proof, he was probably saying, in substance, that intent to deprave was not a constituent of the offence.[186] He conceded that the judgment in *De Montalk* was not very clear, but stated that the court came to the conclusion that there was nothing in the argument that the presumption was rebuttable, and that he was bound by that decision.

(ii) Under the Obscene Publications Act

In *Shaw v DPP*[187] D was charged with publishing an obscene article in the form of the *Ladies Directory* (a catalogue of prostitutes and the services offered). His appeal to the Court of Criminal Appeal[188] on the ground that the judge did not direct the jury to take into account D's 'honesty of purpose' was dismissed. Ashworth J said:[189]

> If these proceedings had been brought before the passing of the Obscene Publications Act 1959, in the form of a prosecution at common law for publishing an obscene libel, it would no doubt have been necessary to establish an intention to corrupt. But the Act of 1959 contains no such requirement and the test of obscenity laid down in s 1(1) of the Act is whether the effect of the article is such as to tend to deprave and corrupt persons who are likely to read it. In other words obscenity depends on the article and not on the author.[190]

This, of course, is inconsistent with the view of Byrne J who, in *Penguin Books*,[191] conceived that he was applying the common law rule. According to the Court of Criminal Appeal's view, he was wrong about the common law, but reached the right result by

180 [1906] 1 KB 201, at CCR.

181 '. . . intent . . . is still part of the charge or the publication would not have been lawful': per Darling J, ibid, at 212.

182 (1932) 23 Cr App R 182. 183 Above. 184 Above, p 956. 185 Above, p 125.

186 See the discussion of s 8; above, pp 125 and 437.

187 [1962] AC 220, [1961] 2 All ER 446; above, p 390.

188 He was refused leave to appeal to the House of Lords on this count.

189 [1962] AC at 227, [1961] 1 All ER at 333, CCA.

190 The reference to the author is puzzling. Presumably 'the publisher' is meant. They were one and the same in *Shaw*.

191 Above.

accident, the common law having been revised by the Act! As a matter of fact, it seems that this was not the intention of Parliament.[192]

It was not necessary to the decision to hold that no *mens rea* was required. To rule that 'honesty of purpose' is irrelevant is one thing and no more than was done in *Hicklin*; to decide that no *mens rea* with reference to depravity and corruption is necessary, is another. D's motive of benevolence towards the prostitutes whom he was assisting to ply their trade may have been wholly admirable but if he knew (as he must have done!) that the inevitable result would be what the law regards[193] as depravity and corruption, he intended that result. Moreover, the test laid down in s 1(1) is not decisive, for this merely defines the *actus reus* and says nothing about *mens rea*. It is difficult, however, to dispute the conclusion of the Court of Criminal Appeal in the light of the defence provided by s 2(5).[194] If *mens rea* in the sense described above were required, this provision would be quite unnecessary. But the clear implication of s 2(5) is that D would be guilty (i) although he had examined the article and concluded that it had no tendency to deprave and corrupt if there were reasonable grounds on which he might have suspected that it would; (ii) although the jury thought it as likely as not that he did not suspect the article's tendency;[195] and (iii) although he had examined the article and failed to appreciate its tendency. Thus it appears likely that the Act, perhaps inadvertently, has restricted the requirement of *mens rea*.

In *Anderson*,[196] the court thought it quite obvious that the jury had acquitted of conspiracy to corrupt public morals because they were not satisfied that there was the required intent to corrupt. But the court did not consider this fatal to the charge under the Obscene Publications Act and, indeed, considered whether they should uphold the conviction under the proviso in s 2 of the Criminal Appeal Act 1968 (as it existed at the time) on the ground that no actual miscarriage of justice had occurred[197] – something they could hardly have done if the jury had negated the intent necessary for the crime.

(e) Forfeiture of obscene articles

The Obscene Publications Act 1857 provided a summary procedure for the forfeiture of obscene articles. That Act is replaced by s 3 of the Obscene Publications Act 1959. The procedure is that information on oath must be laid before a magistrate that there is reasonable ground for suspecting that obscene articles are *kept* in any premises, stall or vehicle in the justice's area *for publication for gain*.[198] The justice may then issue a warrant authorising a constable to search for and seize any articles which he has reason to believe to be obscene and to be kept for publication for gain. Such a warrant authorizes only a single entry and a second entry in reliance on the warrant will be unlawful; but, in the absence of evidence of 'oppression', the court has no discretion to exclude any evidence unlawfully obtained.[199]

192 H. Street, *Freedom, the Individual and the Law* (3rd edn), 141.

193 Whether he knew the law so regarded it, is irrelevant. Cf *Sancoff v Halford* [1973] Qd R 25.

194 Above, p 954.

195 The onus of proof on a balance of probabilities is on D.

196 Above, p 945.

197 [1971] 3 All ER 1152 at 1161.

198 *Hicklin's* case might thus now fall outside the Act. He sold the pamphlets for the price he paid for them and this was evidently considered not to be selling for gain: (1868) LR 3 QB at 368 and 374. But cf n 85, above.

199 *Adams* [1980] QB 575, [1980] 1 All ER 473, CA.

Any articles seized must be brought before a justice for the same area. If the justice, after looking at the articles, decides they are not obscene, then the matter drops and the articles[200] are, no doubt, returned.[201] But if he thinks they may be obscene (and he need not come to a decided opinion at this stage) he may issue a summons to the occupier of the premises, etc to appear before the court and show cause why the articles should not be forfeited. If the court is satisfied[202] that the articles, at the time they were seized, were obscene articles kept for publication for gain, it must order the articles to be forfeited. The power does not apply to any article which is returned to the person from whom it was seized.[203] The section applies to material destined for publication abroad.[204] The magistrates may thus be required to form an opinion as to the likely effect of the material on foreigners with different attitudes and customs but, in practice, they are likely to rely on their knowledge of human nature and unlikely to hold an article to be obscene where it is destined for country X and not obscene where it is destined for country Y. As with the discussion of obscenity on the internet, there is a danger that this leads to the lowest common threshold.

The owner, author or maker of the articles, or any other person through whose hands they had passed before being seized, is entitled to appear and show cause why they should not be forfeited; and any person who appeared or was entitled to appear to show cause against the making of the order has a right of appeal to the Crown Court.

The defence of 'public good' is available in proceedings for forfeiture;[205] but the decision is, of course, now in the hands of the justices and not in the hands of a jury. Thus, if proceedings for forfeiture are brought instead of an indictment, the author or publisher of a book can, in substance, be deprived of a right to jury trial.

There is not necessarily any uniformity of decision. One bench may pass a magazine or picture, while another condemns it.[206] In practice, it seems that the advice of the Director of Public Prosecutions is usually taken by the police before applying for a warrant. His advice is not *necessary* for it is thought undesirable that he should be in the position of a literary or moral censor.

Where, however, the article is a moving picture film in respect of which a prosecution under s 2 of the 1959 Act could not be instituted without the consent of the Director,[207]

200 It is not necessary for each justice to read all the material, provided the whole is discussed and considered by them: *Olympia Press Ltd v Hollis* [1974] 1 All ER 108. On an appeal to the Crown Court, the judge may take a number of articles at random to sample, showing them to the defence as an indication of the basis on which he has reached his decision: *Crown Court at Snaresbrook, ex p Metropolitan Police Comr* (1984) 79 Cr App R 184, DC. Cf R. T. H. Stone, 'Obscene Publications the Problems Persist' [1986] Crim LR 139.

201 *Thomson v Chain Libraries Ltd* [1954] 2 All ER 616, [1954] 1 WLR 999.

202 In *Thomson v Chain Libraries Ltd* [1954] 2 All ER 616 at 618, Hilbery J said that the onus of proof is on the person who appears to show cause. *Sed quaere*: the magistrate must be *satisfied* that the article is obscene.

203 Criminal Law Act 1977, Sch 12.

204 *Gold Star Publications Ltd v DPP* [1981] 2 All ER 257, HL.

205 Obscene Publications Act 1959, s 4(1).

206 The same thing could of course occur in relation to proceedings on indictment. If another publisher were to be prosecuted for publishing *Lady Chatterley*, the decision in *Penguin Books* (above, p 956) would not be relevant in evidence, let alone an estoppel; and another jury, hearing different expert evidence, might well arrive at a different conclusion.

207 See above, p 954.

no order for forfeiture may be made unless the warrant under which the article was seized was issued on an information laid by or on behalf of the Director.[208]

(i) European matters

An argument that forfeiture is incompatible with the right to peaceful enjoyment of possessions (Article 1, protocol 1) will be unlikely to succeed.[209] If the forfeiture denied D the opportunity to have the material shown in circumstances in which there was no likelihood of corruption (for example, by taking it off general sale and making it available in a private outlet) the argument might have more substance.

As far as the Treaty of Rome and free movement of goods with the EU is concerned, the Divisional Court has held that once goods were within the definition of obscenity in s 1 of the 1959 Act, there was no difficulty in applying Article 30 (formerly Article 36) of the Treaty to permit restriction on importation and forfeiture.[210]

(ii) Reform

The law relating to obscenity was not reviewed in the recent Sexual Offences Review. It remains in a state of incoherence and ambiguity and is in desperate need of reform. Suggestions have been made to reform the central test of corrupting and depraving, replacing them with schedules of prohibited material (for example, torture, coprophilia, child pornography, etc).[211] As an example of the types of conduct currently liable to be prosecuted, the CPS charging practice notes that the following categories are those most common: sexual acts with children; sexual assaults upon children; portrayal of incest; buggery with an animal; rape; drug taking; flagellation; torture with instruments; bondage (especially where gags are used); dismemberment or graphic mutilation; cannibalism; activities involving perversion or degradation (such as drinking urine or smearing excreta on a person's body)'.[212]

(f) The common law of obscene libel

The 1959 Act did not, in terms, abolish the common law misdemeanour of obscene libel,[213] but provided in s 2(4):

> A person publishing an article shall not be proceeded against for an offence at common law consisting of the publication of any matter contained or embodied in the article where it is of the essence of the offence that the matter is obscene.

It might be thought that the intention was that, in future, all proceedings in respect of obscene publications should be brought under the Act. The subsection has not been so interpreted. In *Shaw v DPP*[214] it was relied on by the defence in relation to the first count alleging a common law conspiracy to corrupt public morals by the publication of the

208 Obscene Publications Act 1959, s 3(3A). 209 *X Co v UK* (1983) 32 DR 231.

210 See *R v Bow Street Magistrates Court, ex p Noncyp Ltd* [1990] 1 QB 123; *Wright v Commissioners of Customs and Excise* [1999] 1 Cr App R 69. See for detailed discussion S. Weatherill and P. Beaumont, *EU Law* (3rd edn, 1999), ch 16; P. Craig and G. de Búrca, *EU Law: Text, Cases and Materials* (3rd edn, 2003), ch 15.

211 See generally on reform the Williams Committee (1979), Cmnd 7772.

212 See www.cps.gov.uk/legal/section12/chapter_e.html.

213 1 Hawk, c. 73, s 9; *Wilkes* (1770) 4 Burr 2527 at 2574. 214 [1962] AC 220.

Ladies' Directory; that is, as was held, the publication of an obscene article. The answer to this argument, accepted by the Court of Criminal Appeal[215] and the House of Lords,[216] was that the conspiracy did not 'consist of the publication' of the booklet; it consisted in the agreement to corrupt public morals by publishing it.

It thus appears that it would still be possible to bring a prosecution for conspiracy to publish an obscene libel (and possibly an incitement or attempt to do so). Such a prosecution should not be brought to evade the statutory defence of public good.[217]

(g) What is an article?

The 1959 Act provides by s 1(2):

> In this Act 'article' means any description of article containing or embodying matter to be read or looked at or both, any sound record, and any film or other record of a picture or pictures.

This includes a video cassette[218] and a computer disk.[219] In *Straker v DPP*[220] it was held that while a negative *might* be within this definition,[221] it was not kept for 'publication' as described in s 3(1) since it was not to be shown, played or projected,[222] but to be used for making prints. It could not, therefore, be forfeited under s 3. This gap is closed by s 2 of the 1964 Act which provides:

> (1) The Obscene Publications Act 1959 (as amended by this Act) shall apply in relation to anything which is intended to be used, either alone or as one of a set, for the reproduction or manufacture therefrom of articles containing or embodying matter to be read, looked at or listened to, as if it were an article containing or embodying that matter so far as that matter is to be derived from it or from the set.

By s 2(2) of the 1964 Act an article is had or kept for publication 'if it is had or kept for the reproduction or manufacture therefrom of articles for publication'.

The negatives in *Straker* clearly fall within this provision.

In *Conegate Ltd v Customs and Excise Comrs*[223] it was conceded that inflatable life-size dolls, though obscene, were not 'articles'. It has been suggested that the concession was wrong because the dolls, having faces painted on them, were to be 'looked at'. However the gist of the obscenity seems to lie in the use to which the dolls were intended to be put, rather than in their appearance.

(h) Posting indecent or obscene matter

(i) Offence

The Postal Services Act 2000, s 85 provides:

> (3) A person commits an offence if he sends by post a postal packet which encloses –

215 [1962] AC at 235, 236. 216 [1962] AC at 268, 269, 290 and 291. 217 Above, p 955.

218 *A-G's Reference (No 5 of 1980)* [1980] 3 All ER 816, [1981] 1 WLR 88.

219 *Fellows and Arnold* [1997] 1 Cr App R 244, [1997] Crim LR 524 and commentary.

220 [1963] 1 QB 926, [1963] 1 All ER 697, DC.

221 Widgery LCJ had little doubt that this was so; *Derrick v Customs and Excise Comrs* [1972] 2 WLR 359 at 361.

222 Section 1(3)(b), above, p 950.

223 [1987] QB 254, [1986] 2 All ER 688, [1986] Crim LR 562, ECJ.

(a) any indecent or obscene print, painting, photograph, lithograph, engraving, cinematograph film or other record of a picture or pictures, book, card or written communication, or

(b) any other indecent or obscene article (whether or not of a similar kind to those mentioned in paragraph (a)).

(4) A person commits an offence if he sends by post a postal packet which has on the packet, or on the cover of the packet, any words, marks or designs which are of an indecent or obscene character.

(5) A person who commits an offence under this section shall be liable –

(a) on summary conviction, to a fine not exceeding the statutory maximum,

(b) on conviction on indictment, to a fine or to imprisonment for a term not exceeding twelve months or to both.

The offence follows closely that under the Post Office Act 1953 which it replaces, and the authorities on that section retain significance.

(ii) Meaning of indecent or obscene

Under the predecessor offence (s 11 of the 1953 Act) it was held in *Stanley*[224] that the words 'indecent or obscene':

> convey one idea, namely offending against the recognized standards of propriety, indecent being at the lower end of the scale and obscene at the upper end of the scale . . .
> . . . an indecent article is not necessarily obscene, whereas an obscene article must almost certainly be indecent.

Therefore the verdict of a jury holding that certain cinematograph films were not obscene (for the purposes of the Obscene Publications Act) but were indecent (for the purposes of the Post Office Act) was upheld. If 'indecent' comprehends everything which is obscene and more the word 'obscene' in the section is redundant.

Under the 1953 Act it was held that 'obscene' bears its ordinary meaning[225] and so may not extend to material simply because it advocates drug-taking or violence[226] which would not ordinarily be described as 'indecent'.[227] On the other hand, such articles might well be said to offend against 'recognized standards of propriety'; and, for the purposes of other legislation, abusive language and shouts in church alleging hypocrisy against the reader of the lesson[228] have been held to be 'indecent'. It is possible therefore that 'indecent' is not confined to sexual indecency, but extends to other improper matter.

The test of indecency is objective and the character of the addressee is immaterial.[229] Indeed, the object of the section looked at as a whole seems to be the protection of Post Office employees against dangerous, deleterious or indecent articles.[230] It is evidently not limited to employees, however, since it is only in rare cases that they will have access to

224 [1965] 2 QB 327, [1965] 1 All ER 1035.

225 *Anderson* [1971] 3 All ER 1152 at 1162. The judge's direction (above, p 945) was thus correct so far as the 'Post Office count' was concerned. *Stamford* [1972] 2 QB 391, [1972] 2 All ER 427.

226 Above, p 946.

227 *Lees v Parr* [1967] 3 All ER 181n (bye-law).

228 *Abrahams v Cavey* [1968] 1 QB 479, [1967] 3 All ER 179 (Ecclesiastical Courts Jurisdiction Act 1860, s 2); *Farrant* [1973] Crim LR 240.

229 *Straker* [1965] Crim LR 239, CCA; *Kosmos Publications Ltd v DPP* [1975] Crim LR 345.

230 *Stamford* [1972] 2 All ER 427 at 429.

matter 'enclosed' as para (b) requires. Evidence is not admissible by any person to say what the effect of the article was on him. The jury do not need assistance. They are themselves 'the custodians of the standards for the time being'.[231]

(g) Other communications offences

Sending unsolicited matter describing human sexual techniques, or unsolicited advertisement of such matter, is an offence[232] under s 4 of the Unsolicited Goods and Services Act 1971. Under the Communications Act 2003, s 127 a person is guilty of an offence if he (a) sends by means of a public electronic communications network a message or other matter that is grossly offensive or of an indecent, obscene or menacing character; or (b) causes any such message or matter to be so sent. On summary conviction, an offender is liable to six months' imprisonment or a fine not exceeding level 5 on the standard scale, or to both.[233]

(h) Obscenity in the theatre

The Theatres Act 1968 which abolished censorship of the theatre, makes it an offence, punishable under s 2, summarily with six months, and on indictment with three years' imprisonment, to present[234] or direct an obscene performance of a play. The definition of obscenity is the same as in s 1(1) of the Obscene Publications Act 1959,[235] except that attention is directed to the effect of the performance on the persons who are likely to *attend* it instead of 'read, see or hear it'. A defence of 'public good' is provided by s 3 which is the same as that under s 4 of the 1959 Act,[236] except that the interests which may justify the performance are, as in the case of films, those of 'drama, opera, ballet or any other art or of literature or learning'.

A performance given 'on a domestic occasion in a private dwelling' is excepted by s 7 from the provisions of s 2; and, by s 8, proceedings may not be instituted except by or with the consent of the Attorney-General.

If proceedings are to be brought in respect of the alleged obscenity of the performance of a play, they must be brought under the Act; for, by s 2(4), it precludes proceedings at common law (including conspiracy). A prosecution on indictment under s 2 must be commenced within two years of the commission of the offence: s 2(3).

(i) Indecent displays

The Indecent Displays (Control) Act 1981 makes it an offence to make, cause or permit the public display of any indecent matter. Matter displayed in, or so as to be visible from, any public place is publicly displayed. A public place is one to which the public have or are permitted to have access, whether on payment or otherwise, except (a) where the payment is or includes payment for the display, or (b) the place is a shop or part of a shop to which the public can gain access only by passing an adequate warning notice, as specified

231 Ibid, at 432.

232 *DPP v Beate Uhse (UK) Ltd* [1974] QB 158, [1974] 1 All ER 753.

233 The Penalties for Disorderly Behaviour (Amount of Penalty) Order 2002, SI 1837 provides that an offence under s 127 may be the subject of a fixed penalty with the amount payable being £40.

234 Cf *Grade v DPP* [1942] 2 All ER 118; above, p 231, n 52.

235 Above, p 944.

236 Above, p 955.

in the Act (s 1(6)). The Act is aimed at displays that people cannot avoid seeing as they go about their business – bookshop and sex shop window displays, cinema club posters, and so on. It does not apply to television broadcasts as defined in the Broadcasting Act 1990, displays visible only from within an art gallery or museum, the performance of a play within the Theatres Act 1968 or a film exhibition as defined in the Cinemas Act 1985. 'Matter' is anything capable of being displayed except an actual human body or part of it. Thus 'lap dancing' or 'stripping' is not caught. 'Indecent' is not defined. Whether matter is indecent will no doubt be considered a matter of fact to be determined by applying the ordinary meaning of the word.[237]

(j) Other statutes

There are a number of other statutes under which summary proceedings may be, and are, instituted, where the safeguards of the Obscene Publications Acts do not apply. These include the Metropolitan Police Act 1839, s 54[238] and the Children and Young Persons (Harmful Publications) Act 1955. No doubt there are also many local Acts and bye-laws which may be invoked.[239]

(k) Outraging public decency[240]

It is now clear that the common law offence of outraging public decency survives. The offence is now triable either way.[241] An article outraging public decency is not necessarily obscene. It may well outrage and disgust without having any tendency to deprave and corrupt. In such a case, a prosecution for the common law offence is not barred by s 2(4) of the Obscene Publications Act.[242] It was so held in *Gibson*[243] where in a commercial art gallery D exhibited 'Human Earrings', earrings made out of freeze-dried human foetuses. It was not suggested that anyone was likely to be corrupted by the exhibition but, as the jury had found, the public would be outraged by it.

The defence of 'public good' under s 4(1) of the 1959 Act does not apply to the common law offence. An article may have a tendency both to corrupt and to cause outrage. It seems to follow that, in such a case the protection of the Act can be avoided by charging the common law offence. It can hardly be said that the 'essence of the offence' charged is that the article is obscene because the prosecution do not have to prove obscenity in order to establish it; and, if obscenity is not of the essence of the offence charged, the prosecution is not barred by s 2(4). The less grave conduct of outraging public decency therefore attracts no defence when the more serious one of corrupting and depraving does.

237 Below, p 979.

238 'Every person who shall sell or distribute or offer for sale or distribution, or exhibit to public view, any profane, . . . book, paper, print, drawing, painting or representation, or sing any profane, indecent, or obscene song or ballad, . . . or use any profane, indecent or obscene language to the annoyance of the inhabitants or passengers'.

239 See, generally, *Report of the Home Office Working Party on Vagrancy and Street Offences* (1974).

240 See P. Rook and R. Ward, *Sexual Offences Law and Practice* (2004), ch 14.

241 Criminal Justice Act 2003 (Commencement No 2 and Saving Provisions) Order 2004, SI 81.

242 Above, p 961.

243 [1991] 1 All ER 439, [1990] Crim LR 738. See above, p 140. See also M. Childs, 'Outraging Public Decency: The Offence of Offensiveness' [1991] PL 20.

(i) *Actus reus*

An act outraging public decency must be proved. If no such act is done, the offence is not committed, however outrageous D's intentions or fantasies, as revealed, for example, in his private diaries.[244] It might be different where the observers of ambiguous conduct are aware of the actor's purpose. They might then be outraged by acts which, if not known to be done with that purpose, would not be outrageously indecent.

The act must be done in a place where at least two members of the public *might* see it.[245] It is insufficient that the act is witnessed by two people in a private dwelling,[246] or in public where only one person would see the conduct.[247] In *Lunderbech*[248] where D, masturbating in a children's playground, was seen only by two police officers who did not testify that they were outraged, the court said that where the act is plainly indecent and likely to disgust and annoy, 'the jury are entitled to infer such disgust and annoyance without affirmative evidence that anyone was disgusted and annoyed'. The so-called 'inference' is plainly fictitious. In *May*[249] (schoolmaster 'behaving in an indecent manner with a desk' in the presence of two boys) it was held to be irrelevant that the two boys may have enjoyed the performance.[250] The effect seems to be that the offence is committed if the jury think the conduct outrageously indecent because it would disgust and annoy them, and therefore the ordinary members of the public whom they represent, if they witnessed it. 'Disgusting' is that which is capable of filling the onlooker with loathing or extreme distaste or of causing the onlooker extreme annoyance.[251]

In principled terms, the offence lacks the degree of precision and certainty in definition that is desirable.

(ii) *Mens rea*

To the extent that the House of Lords in *Lemon* declared blasphemy to be an offence of strict liability, *Gibson* does the same for outraging public decency. D must presumably be aware of the nature of the act he is doing. If Gibson had not known that the earrings were made from human foetuses he would presumably not have been guilty. But the case decides that it was not necessary to prove that he intended or foresaw that the effect of the exhibition would be to outrage public decency.[252] As the court said, the practical effect of this ruling is not great. It is difficult to imagine a jury not being satisfied that D knew very well what the effect of his act would certainly be. But this does not justify dispensing with *mens rea*. Rather, it demonstrates that there is not that necessity which is sometimes urged as a justification for strict liability – ie, that no one would be convicted if *mens rea* were required.

244 *Rowley* [1991] 4 All ER 649, [1991] Crim LR 785.

245 *Curran* (1998) unreported, CA, 29 Oct (copulation and oral sex on bonnet of car in short stay car park at Heathrow sufficient).

246 *W* (1995) 159 JP 509 (D masturbating in front of his daughter and 10-year-old friend).

247 See eg *Davies* (1999) No 98/5489/Y4 (D masturbating in car in remote country lane in presence of only his driving pupil).

248 [1991] Crim LR 784.

249 (1989) 91 Cr App R 157, [1990] Crim LR 415.

250 See also *Choi* [1999] EWCA Crim 1279 (filming ladies' lavatory in supermarket).

251 *Choi* [1999] EWCA Crim 1279, see also *Cuthbertson* [2003] EWCA Crim 3915 (filming under cubicles in swimming baths with a mobile phone camera).

252 See eg *Tinley* [2004] EWCA Crim 3032, D with paraphilia for looking up women's skirts surreptitiously using video camera.

The court remarked that one reason why the early authorities are of little assistance is the existence before the enactment of s 8 of the Criminal Justice Act 1967 of the presumption that a person intends the natural and probable consequences of his actions. The court failed to draw the inevitable conclusion from this premise. If, before 1967, intention need not be proved only because it was conclusively presumed, it is no longer presumed and must be proved.

Coupled with the ambiguity of *actus reus*, such a strict *mens rea* renders the offence doubly unsatisfactory.

(iii) ECHR

The European Commission dismissed as inadmissible an application challenging the offence in *S and G v UK*.[253] It is difficult to see how the offence can be said to be sufficiently certain to be prescribed by law within Article 10, nor how it is necessary and proportionate within Article 10(2).

(I) Seditious words and libels

Sedition is closely related to the form of treason consisting in 'levying war' against the Queen in her realm and may be a preliminary step towards that crime. There is probably no offence properly described as 'sedition' in English law,[254] but the oral or written publication of words with a seditious intention is a common law misdemeanour and an agreement to further a seditious intention by doing an act is a conspiracy. The question then is what is seditious intention? Stephen[255] defined it as:

> . . . an intention to bring into hatred or contempt, or to excite disaffection against the person of Her Majesty, her heirs or successors, or the government and constitution of the United Kingdom, as by law established, or either House of Parliament, or the administration of justice, or to excite Her Majesty's subjects to attempt, otherwise than by lawful means, the alteration of any matter in Church or State by law established, or to raise discontent or disaffection amongst Her Majesty's subjects, or to promote feelings of ill-will and hostility between different classes of such subjects.
>
> An intention to shew that Her Majesty has been misled or mistaken in her measures, or to point out errors or defects in the government or constitution as by law established, with a view to their reformation, or to excite Her Majesty's subjects to attempt by lawful means the alteration of any matter in Church or State by law established,[256] or to point out, in order to their removal, matters which are producing, or have a tendency to produce, feelings of hatred and ill-will between classes of Her Majesty's subjects, is not a seditious intention.

This definition was approved by the criminal code Commissioners and followed by Cave J in his direction to the jury in *Burns*.[257]

(i) *Mens rea*

In *Chief Metropolitan Stipendiary Magistrate, ex p Choudhury*[258] the Divisional Court, following the Supreme Court of Canada in *Boucher v R*,[259] held that:

[253] Appn 17634/91 (the *Gibson* case).

[254] Stephen, II HCL, 298.

[255] *Digest* (3rd edn), art. 93. See now 9th edn, art. 114.

[256] In the 4th edition, Stephen inserted at this point '. . . or to incite any person to commit any crime in disturbance of the peace . . .'.

[257] (1886) 16 Cox CC 355 at 360.

[258] [1991] 1 All ER 306 at 322–323, [1990] Crim LR 711, DC.

[259] [1951] 2 DLR 369.

. . . the seditious intention on which a prosecution for seditious libel must be founded is an intention to incite to violence or to create public disturbance or disorder against His Majesty or the institutions of government. Proof of an intention to promote feelings of ill-will and hostility between different classes of subjects does not alone establish a seditious intention. Not only must there be proof of an incitement to violence in this connection but it must be violence or resistance or defiance for the purpose of disturbing constituted authority.

The court therefore upheld the decision of the magistrate that Salman Rushdie's *The Satanic Verses* was not a seditious libel because there was no evidence that it was an attack on the institutions of government. The earlier authorities were inconsistent,[260] one view being that an objective test was applicable, another that intention or recklessness would suffice. None of these authorities was binding on the Divisional Court and the above proposition represents the law. The strict requirement of *mens rea* is in marked contrast to the principles applicable to other varieties of common law libel.

(ii) *Actus reus*

It cannot be enough that the words are used with a seditious intention. There must also be an *actus reus.* That is, the words must have a tendency to incite public disorder. In deciding whether the words have this tendency, it is proper to look at all the relevant surrounding circumstances – the state of public feeling, the place, the mode of publication, and so on. Most important of all, the jury is entitled:

. . . to look at the audience addressed, because language which would be innocuous practically speaking, if used to an assembly of professors or divines, might produce a different result if used before an excited audience of young and uneducated men.[261]

On the other hand if the tendency of the words is to incite ordinary people to violence, it is no defence that the audience addressed was unaffected by the incitement:

A man cannot escape from the consequences of uttering words with intent to excite people to violence solely because the persons to whom they are addressed may be too wise or too temperate to be seduced into that violence.[262]

Thus words are seditious (i) if they are likely to incite ordinary people whether likely to incite the audience actually addressed or not; or (ii) if, though not likely to incite ordinary people, they are likely to incite the audience actually addressed.

D need not have himself written the libel. The crime may consist in the publication of the words of another with the appropriate intent. If the publisher has *mens rea* it is immaterial that the writer of the libel did not.[263]

Whether publication is necessary is not settled. In *Burdett*,[264] Holroyd J and Abbott CJ thought that the mere composition of the libel without publishing it was an offence.

260 See the 6th edition of this book, pp 834–835.

261 *Aldred* (1909) 22 Cox CC 1 at 3, per Coleridge J.

262 *Burns* (1886) 16 Cox CC 355 at 365, per Cave J. In *Cohen* (1916) 34 WLR 210, it was held that, if the word were likely to be an incitement to an ordinary man, D was not entitled to the benefit of the steadfast loyalty of the person actually addressed.

263 (1789) 22 St Tr 300, per Eyre CB delivering the unanimous opinion of the judges.

264 (1820) 1 State Tr NS 1 at 122, 123 and 128, 139.

Earlier cases[265] supported this view but their authority was forcefully attacked by Sir James Scarlett, afterwards Lord Abinger.[266]

(iii) Sedition and freedom of speech

It is common for the judge to stress the importance of freedom of speech and of the press. In *Burns*,[267] Cave J said:

> You will recollect how valuable a blessing the liberty of the press is to all of us, and sure I am that that liberty will meet no injury – suffer no diminution at your hands

and in *Caunt*,[268] Birkett J's last words to the jury were:

> Two matters would seem to emerge over all others in this case. First of all it is in the highest degree essential that nothing should be done in this court to weaken the liberty of the press; and secondly, remember at all times that it is the duty of the prosecution to prove his case beyond all reasonable doubt.[269]

Note also the discussion of the approach to Article 10 discussed in relation to blasphemy and libel (above).

265 They are cited in argument, ibid, at 57. 266 Ibid. 267 (1886) 16 Cox CC 355 at 362.
268 (1947), reported in *An Editor on Trial* (Morecambe Press Ltd).
269 See also Coleridge J in *Aldred* (1909) 22 Cox CC 1 at 4.

27

Offences against public order

1. Offences under the Public Order Act 1986

The Public Order Act 1986 abolished the common law offences of riot, rout, unlawful assembly and affray and some statutory offences relating to public order[1] and replaced them with new offences. Three offences replace the four above-mentioned common law crimes. They are, in descending order of gravity, riot, violent disorder and affray. In addition to these more serious offences the Act created offences of inducing fear of violence, and behaviour likely to cause harassment alarm or distress. These latter offences have become some of the most commonly charged. The Act does not provide a complete code of public order offences, and some reference is made here to relevant common law offences. It should also be noted that the offences created by the 1986 Act are not all 'public' order offences: some may be committed in private. However, it is important to keep sight of the public order foundations of these offences and not treat them as merely additional offences against the person.

Though the contrary has been argued in some cases, it is clear that the general principles of secondary liability and general defences, such as private defence or the prevention of crime, are applicable to offences under the Act as they are under other statutes and at common law.

It is probable that all the offences of riot, violent disorder and affray are continuing offences. It was held that a common law affray might continue for a considerable period of time and over a wide area. An indictment was not bad for duplicity where it alleged an affray on 31 August and 1 September 'in divers streets'.[2] It appeared in evidence that the accused were milling about, armed, uttering threats and fighting, from 8.30 pm to 12.30 am, over a radius of a quarter of a mile. This was held to be a single affray. Where the ingredients of the offence ceased to exist for a time, the affray was over; and, when those ingredients came into existence again, a second affray occurred. so, where the accused travelled in a coach to a number of sites where they created terror, there was an affray at

[1] For the law before the 1986 Act, see the 5th edition of this work, ch 20; for the background to the 1986 Act, see the Home Office, *Review of the Public Order Act and Related Legislation* (1980) Cmnd 7891 and Law Commission Working Paper No 82 (1982) and Report, *Offences Relating to Public Disorder* (Law Com No 123, 1983). For detailed studies of the new law, see R. Card, *Public Order: The New Law* (1987) and A. T. H. Smith, *Offences against Public Order* (1987); For comment on the law's development since the Act see S. Bailey, D. Harris and D. Ormerod, *Civil Liberties Cases and Materials* (5th edn, 2001), ch 4; R. Card, *Public Order Law* (2000).

[2] *Woodrow* (1959) 43 Cr App R 105.

each site. During the coach journeys there was no fighting and no one was put in fear.[3] The same principles will apply to the statutory offence of affray and probably also to the offences of riot and violent disorder. Once the 12 people (in the case of riot) or the three (in violent disorder), as the case may be, have used or threatened violence, the offence is constituted and will continue so long as they remain together (in the case of riot, for a common purpose) and at least one of them is continuing to use or threaten violence. One is enough, since it is provided that the persons present need not use or threaten violence simultaneously.

(a) Riot

Riot is an indictable offence, punishable with 10 years' imprisonment, or an unlimited fine, or both. It is explained by s 1 of the Act as follows:

> (1) Where 12 or more persons who are present together use or threaten unlawful violence for a common purpose and the conduct of them (taken together) is such as would cause a person of reasonable firmness present at the scene to fear for his personal safety, each of the persons using unlawful violence for the common purpose is guilty of riot.
>
> (2) It is immaterial whether or not the 12 or more use or threaten unlawful violence simultaneously.
>
> (3) The common purpose may be inferred from conduct.
>
> (4) No person of reasonable firmness need actually be, or be likely to be, present at the scene.
>
> (5) Riot may be committed in private as well as in public places.

Riot is intended for exceptionally serious cases and no prosecution for it may be instituted except by or with the consent of the Director of Public Prosecutions. It is, nevertheless, a very widely drafted offence. In making the decision to prosecute for riot, the CPS charging standards suggest that riot might appropriately be charged where: 'the normal forces of law and order have broken down; due to the intensity of the attacks on police and other civilian authorities, normal access by emergency services is impeded by mob activity; due to the scale and ferocity of the disorder, severe disruption and fear is caused to members of the public; the violence carries with it the potential for a significant impact upon a significant number of non-participants for a significant length of time; organized or spontaneous large scale acts of violence on people and/or property'.[4]

(i) Twelve or more

The gravity of riot depends on the presence of large numbers. The number, 12, is arbitrary and it will not usually be necessary to offer evidence of a head-count, for the offence is unlikely to be used except in the case of a large crowd when well in excess of 12 are using or threatening violence.

[3] *Jones* (1974) 59 Cr App R 120.

[4] See www.cps.gov.uk/legal/section11/chapter_a.html.

(ii) Common purpose

There is no requirement that the 12 or more should have come together in pursuance of any agreement. They may have assembled by chance, one by one, and at some point when violence is used, they are present together with a common purpose and using or threatening violence. The common purpose relates to the violence not the coming together. If 12 or more people with a common purpose threaten unlawful violence but only one actually uses it, there is a riot but only one principal rioter. Since the 12 have a common purpose, the rest (the other 11 or more) may be guilty as secondary parties,[5] but this is not necessarily so. Suppose that they have all agreed – 'Threats, yes, but actual violence, no'. If D, for the common purpose, then uses violence, D commits riot but the rest are not necessarily guilty by their mere use of threats and, if D has clearly gone beyond the scope of the concerted action,[6] as by producing a knife or gun that the rest did not know he had with him, they will certainly not be guilty of riot.

The common purpose need not be an unlawful one. It might be, for example, to persuade an employer to reinstate an employee whom he has wrongfully dismissed, or to celebrate the England Test Match victory. But violence, whether used or threatened, must be unlawful. Force reasonably used or threatened by D in self-defence or for the prevention of crime cannot found a charge of riot.[7]

(iii) Violence

By s 8, in Part I of the Act 'violence' means any violent conduct, so that –

(i) it includes violent conduct towards property (except in the case of affray (below)) as well as violent conduct towards persons, and

(ii) it is not restricted to conduct causing or intended to cause injury or damage but includes any other violent conduct (for example, throwing at or towards a person a missile of a kind capable of causing injury which does not hit or falls short).

Conduct that might well have caused injury or damage will clearly be capable of amounting to violence even though it was neither intended to, nor did, cause injury or damage. 'Violent' movements of the body, where there is no possibility of any impact – as where D waves his fist at V who is across the street – is probably not 'violence' but a threat of violence.

It is immaterial whether the 12 or more use or threaten the unlawful violence simultaneously: s 1(2).

(iv) Fear for personal safety

The conduct (of the 12) must be such as would cause a person of reasonable firmness present at the scene to fear for his personal safety; no person need actually be, or even be likely to be, at the scene.[8] Where no person is present, the court or jury has to answer a

[5] The ordinary law of secondary participation applies to riot: *Jefferson* [1994] 1 All ER 270, [1993] Crim LR 880.

[6] Above, p 193.

[7] *Rothwell and Barton* [1993] Crim LR 626. This may prove especially problematical when DDs claim that they were taking pre-emptive action in self-defence.

[8] Sections 1(3) and (4), 2(3) and (4) and 3(3) and (4).

hypothetical question. It is not incumbent on the judge to direct juries on the attributes of the hypothetical reasonable person, nor to give examples of reasonable firmness.[9] The bystander who must be imagined, 'though hypothetical, is not necessarily hypothetically a white bystander'.[10]

(v) *Mens rea*

The mental element of riot includes the common purpose. A common purpose (which need not involve violence) must be proved in respect of all 12 persons, though not all of them are charged. It must be proved that a person charged with riot shared that common purpose and that he (but not necessarily the other 11 or more)[11] intended to use violence or was aware that his conduct might be violent,[12] and it is important that this is made clear to the jury.[13]

The Act wisely avoids the ambiguous word 'reckless' by its use of the word awareness. In effect this is adopting a subjective approach akin to the *Cunningham*[14] meaning of recklessness, thus keeping the law of riot, violent disorder and affray in line with offences against the person generally. There is a subtle difference since the recklessness formula requires not only that D has a subjective awareness of the risk (that his conduct may be violent) but that he has taken that risk unjustifiably. With a test of awareness alone, there is no objective assessment of the justification for his taking the risk. It is doubtful whether this has significant practical implications.

Because the meaning of violence itself is uncertain it is not entirely clear what the requirement of awareness will exclude. It is arguable that a person who was not aware that his conduct would cause any risk of injury or damage would be held to be unaware that his conduct might be violent when it did in fact cause a risk of, or actual, damage or injury.

(vi) Intoxicated rioters

Exceptionally, s 6(5) and (6) make special provision for the intoxicated defendant.

> (5) For the purposes of this section a person whose awareness is impaired by intoxication shall be taken to be aware of that of which he would be aware if not intoxicated, unless he shows either that his intoxication was not self-induced or that it was caused solely by the taking or administration of a substance in the course of medical treatment.
>
> (6) In subsection (5) 'intoxication' means any intoxication, whether caused by drink, drugs or other means, or by a combination of means.

The common law governs the position where D denies that he had the alleged 'purpose' because he was too drunk. If the indictment alleges only intent to use violence, that is presumably an allegation of a specific intent, so self-induced drunkenness would be an answer at common law; but D is still to be taken, apparently, to be aware of that of which he would be aware if not intoxicated; and, if the jury think he would have been aware that violence was a virtual certainty,[15] that is evidence on which they might find that he

9 See *Rafferty* [2004] EWCA Crim 968, 5 April, on affray.
10 *Gray v DPP* CO/5069/98, QB.
11 Section 6(7); A. T. H. Smith, above, 3–03.
12 Section 6(1).
13 *Blackwood* [2002] EWCA Crim 3102.
14 Above, p 102.
15 Above, p 94.

intended it. Thus intoxication might not be an answer even to an allegation of intentional violence.

As regard indictments alleging riot without intention – that is alleging that D was aware that his conduct may be violent, s 6 applies in full. In effect, this spells out the common law rule for offences 'of basic intent'[16] but shifts onto the defendant the onus of proving (or more probably imposes a burden on him to raise evidence) that the intoxication was involuntary.[17]

(b) Violent disorder

Violent disorder is an offence punishable on indictment with five years' imprisonment or an unlimited fine or both or, on summary conviction, with six months' imprisonment or the statutory maximum fine, or both. It is defined as follows by s 2:

> (1) Where 3 or more persons who are present together use or threaten unlawful violence and the conduct of them (taken together) is such as would cause a person of reasonable firmness present at the scene to fear for his personal safety, each of the persons using or threatening unlawful violence is guilty of violent disorder.
>
> (2) It is immaterial whether or not the 3 or more use or threaten unlawful violence simultaneously.

(i) Three or more

It is essential for the conviction of any that the jury or magistrates are sure that at least three people had been unlawfully violent during the incident.

In *Mahroof*[18] it seems to have been assumed that if three defendants are the only persons alleged to have been involved in the disorder and one of them is acquitted, the others must also be acquitted. This will usually be the case but it is submitted that it is not necessarily so. If, for example, the acquitted person was using or threatening unlawful violence but was not guilty on some other ground, there seems to be no reason why the other two accused should not be convicted. The third person may have been acquitted because he did not so intend to, and was not aware that he might, use or threaten violence (perhaps being involuntarily intoxicated) or had some other defence such as duress, insanity or that he was aged only nine. He will nevertheless have been involved in unlawful violence. Such cases are likely to be rare. In *Mechen*,[19] it was acknowledged that if the jury acquits, on the grounds of self-defence, any person potentially relied on by the prosecution to constitute one of the three persons involved, that person cannot be included to make up the necessary minimum number of people using or threatening *unlawful* violence. It is for this reason that is often important to lay alternative charges of affray.[20]

[16] Above, pp 276 and 280.

[17] See above, Ch 2, on the post-Human Rights Act 1998 approach to reverse burdens and the greater likelihood that this is merely an evidential burden.

[18] (1988) 88 Cr App R 317, [1989] Crim LR 721; cf *Fleming and Robinson* [1989] Crim LR 658; *McGuigan* [1991] Crim LR 719.

[19] [2004] EWCA Crim 388.

[20] *Hadjisavva* [2004] EWCA Crim 1316.

In *Lemon*,[21] it was emphasized that s 2 does not require that at least two others be *convicted* of the offence before any one defendant could be convicted.[22] The judge properly directed the jury that provided they found three or more used or threatened violence they could convict any one or more of the defendants even though they were unable to identify the three.

In cases of aiding and abetting violent disorder, it is crucial that the directions make clear the respective *mens rea* requirements of the principals and secondary parties.[23]

(ii) Use or threat of unlawful violence

There need be no common purpose. Each of the three or more persons may have a different purpose or no purpose. At least three must be using or threatening *unlawful* violence,[24] so if one of only three persons present is acting in self-defence or the prevention of crime, no offence is committed.[25]

It must be proved that each defendant intended to use or threaten violence or that he was aware that his conduct might be violent or threaten violence.[26] A *prima facie* case of violent disorder could be established where D was running along with a group in a populated area when D knew members of the group were armed and intent on violence.[27] There was held to be evidence of a threat of unlawful violence where three men followed another along a path for three-quarters of a mile and for three-quarters of an hour in the middle of the night, creating 'an aura of violence'.[28] Section 2 has been used diversely to deal with conduct ranging from pub brawls to violent animal rights protests.[29]

Where the evidence which led to the conviction under s 2 relates to violence to property, the court must decline to substitute verdicts under s 3 since that offence is limited to violence to people.[30] The judge must then direct the jury adequately on the relevant parts of s 4 (see below).[31]

(iii) Effect of conduct

The conduct of the three must be such as would cause a person of reasonable firmness present at the scene to fear for his personal safety, no person need actually be, or even be likely to be, at the scene.[32] Where no person is present, the court or jury has to answer a hypothetical question.

(iv) Other matters

Private defence, the prevention of crime[33] and other general defences are available to a defendant charged with this offence. The intoxicated defendant is governed by s 6(5) and (6), considered above. The offence may be committed in private as well as public.

21 [2002] EWCA Crim 1661.

22 L was one of six defendants charged under s 2. All accepted their presence at the scene, but L claimed mistaken identity, two others claimed that they had acted in self-defence and the remaining three made no comment.

23 *Blackwood* [2002] EWCA Crim 3102.

24 For the meaning of 'violence', see above, p 972.

25 *Mechen*, above p 974.

26 Section 6(2).

27 *Church* [2000] 4 Archbold News 3, CA.

28 *Brodie* [2000] Crim LR 775. See also *Casey* [2004] EWCA Crim 1853.

29 Eg *R v Oxford Crown Court, ex p Monaghan* (1998) 18 June, DC (throwing stones over the fence in an aimless manner at police and using fences as battering rams).

30 *R v McGuigan and Cameron* [1991] Crim LR 719.

31 *R v Perrins* [1995] Crim LR 432.

32 Section 2(3) and (4).

33 *Rothwell v Barton* [1993] Crim LR 626.

Violent disorder is intended to be the normal charge[34] for serious outbreaks of public disorder, riot being reserved for exceptionally serious cases, but it clearly covers many relatively minor disturbances. Consequently, it is triable either way.

(c) Affray[35]

Bingham LCJ (as he then was) described the nature of affray as follows:[36]

> It typically involves a group of people who may well be shouting, struggling, threatening, waving weapons, throwing objects, exchanging and threatening blows and so on. Again, typically, it involves a continuous course of conduct, the criminal character of which depends on the general nature and effect of the conduct as a whole and not on particular incidents and events which may take place in the course of it. Where reliance is placed on such a continuous course of conduct, it is not necessary for the Crown to identify and prove particular incidents.

Affray is punishable on indictment with three years' imprisonment or an unlimited fine or both, or, on summary conviction, with six months' imprisonment or the statutory maximum fine or both. It is defined as follows by s 3:

> (1) A person is guilty of affray if he uses or threatens unlawful violence towards another and his conduct is such as would cause a person of reasonable firmness present at the scene to fear for his personal safety.
>
> (2) Where 2 or more persons use or threaten the unlawful violence, it is the conduct of them taken together that must be considered for the purposes of subsection (1).
>
> (3) For the purposes of this section a threat cannot be made by the use of words alone.

(i) Violence

In this section, 'violence' is limited to violence towards another person and does not include violence towards property.[37] In resolving a doubt about the meaning of the section it is permissible to refer to the definition of the common law offence – but this is a practice to be approached with care.[38]

The overt act of carrying petrol bombs in the presence of those against whom the bombs are intended to be used may be a threat of violence.[39] The section makes it clear that the offence cannot be committed by the use of words alone, however aggressive and frightening the tone of voice.[40] If a mere threat to use violence were enough, affray would swallow the lesser offence under s 4(1) (considered below).[41] But the use of words to set a dog on another may amount to affray.[42] It seems that 'I am going to set the dog on you'

34 See CPS website for details of charging standards: www.cps.gov.uk/legal/section11/chapter_a.html.

35 *Smith* [1997] 1 Cr App R 14, [1996] Crim LR 893. Where an alleged affray falls into two or more sequences – eg inside, and outside, a house – the judge must give a separate direction in relation to each sequence, for the jury may be satisfied that only one is an affray.

36 *Smith* [1997] 1 Cr App R 14 at 16. Contrast the position where parties are charged with committing an offence by a specific act in the course of a joint enterprise: *Uddin* [1998] 2 All ER 744, above, p 194.

37 Section 8, above, p 972.

38 *I, M and H v DPP* [2001] Crim LR 491, HL.

39 *I, M and H v DPP*, above.

40 *Robinson* [1993] Crim LR 581.

41 It has also been noted that while affray was designed to deal with imminent violence, charges under the Offences Against the Person Act 1861 are available for threats to cause harm in the future: *Lewis* [2004] EWCA Crim 1407.

42 *Dixon* [1993] Crim LR 579, and commentary. See also *Dackers* [2000] All ER (D) 1958.

would not be the offence, but 'Seize him Fido' would – Fido being a Pitt Bull terrier whose performance would alarm a bystander.

The violence must be unlawful, so that if the jury accept that D honestly believed or may have honestly believed that it was necessary to defend himself or others there will be no unlawful violence.[43]

(ii) Participants

The offence envisages at least three persons: (i) the person using or threatening unlawful[44] violence; (ii) a person towards whom the violence or threat is directed who must be present at the scene; and (iii) a person of reasonable firmness who need not actually be, or be likely to be, present.[45] So where D swiped with a knife towards a constable, J, the question was not whether a person of reasonable firmness in J's shoes would have feared for his personal safety but whether this hypothetical third person, present in the room and seeing D's conduct towards J, would have so feared.[46] But where gang A marched to attack gang B, but dispersed on the arrival of the police before they came in sight of the Bs, there was no affray.[47] The question involves an objective assessment. As at common law, affray is a public order offence for the protection of the bystander. There are other offences for the protection of persons at whom the violence is aimed. This distinction should be observed, and charges of assault should not be elevated to affray.[48]

Subsection (2) makes it clear that, where two or more use or threaten the unlawful violence, it is the conduct of all of them which must be considered in deciding whether it would cause a person of reasonable firmness to fear for his personal safety.

(iii) *Mens rea*

The mental element is D's intention to use or threaten violence or his awareness that his conduct may be violent or threaten violence. Where reliance is placed by the prosecution on subs (2), it will probably be necessary to show that D's awareness extended to the conduct of the other persons or persons using or threatening violence.

The intoxicated defendant is governed by s 6(5) and (6), considered above.[49]

(d) Fear or provocation of violence

It is an offence under s 4, punishable on summary conviction[50] with six months' imprisonment or a fine not exceeding level 5 on the standard scale, if a person:

(i) uses towards another person threatening, abusive or insulting words or behaviour, or

43 See *Talland* [2003] EWCA Crim 2884.

44 The defences of self-defence, etc will be available – see *Rothwell* [1993] Crim LR 626; *Pulham* [1995] Crim LR 296.

45 *Thind* [1999] Crim LR 842. Hence the possibility of a conviction in a prison cell as in *Beaument and Correlli* (1999) 12 Feb, unreported, CACD.

46 *Davison* [1992] Crim LR 31, CA; *Sanchez* [1996] Crim LR 572, approving the commentary on *Davison.*

47 *I, M and H v DPP*, above.

48 *Plavecz* [2002] Crim LR 837. For details of CPS Charging standard see: www.cps.gov.uk/legal/section11/chapter_a.html.

49 P 973.

50 Note that the racially aggravated forms of the offence are triable either way.

(ii) distributes or displays to another person any writing, sign or other visible representation which is threatening, abusive or insulting

with intent to cause that person to believe that immediate unlawful violence will be used against him or another by any person, or to provoke the immediate use of unlawful violence by that person or another, or whereby that person is likely to believe that such violence will be used or it is likely that such violence will be provoked.

The section creates only one offence. It may be committed in a variety of ways. But the facts proved must correspond with the form alleged in the information. If there is a substantial discrepancy between the particulars alleged and the facts found, a conviction will be quashed.[51]

(i) Towards another

The words in s 4(1)(a), 'uses towards another person', mean 'uses in the presence of and in the direction of another person directly . . .': *Atkin v DPP*[52] where D told customs officers in his house that, if the bailiff in the car outside came in, he was 'a dead un'. The bailiff, being informed, felt threatened, but the threat was not direct. Similarly under s 4(1)(b) the distribution or display must be made directly to a person present. Writing contained in an envelope is not a 'display'.[53] For the purposes of s 4 (though not for any other offence under the Act), the words 'towards another' arguably also require that the words or behaviour be directed against that other.[54]

(ii) Threatening, abusive or insulting

This is the first of nine offences under the Act of which 'threatening, abusive or insulting' conduct is a principal constituent.[55] Whether conduct has this quality seems to be governed by an objective test. This is an element of the *actus reus*. It has been noticed above[56] that a word describing the *actus reus* element of an offence may also imply a mental element. The Act, however, assumes that conduct or material may be threatening, abusive or insulting even though there is no evidence that the actor or author intended it to have, or was aware that it might have, that quality. The effect is to create an extremely harsh offence. When proof by the prosecution of such intention or awareness is required, the Act specifically so provides;[57] and, in other cases, it puts the burden of proof (or at least an evidential one) on the defendant to show that he did not suspect or have reason to suspect that it was threatening, abusive or insulting.[58]

The words, 'threatening, abusive or insulting', which are taken from the repealed s 5 of the Public Order Act 1936, are to be given their ordinary meaning. It has been said that it is not helpful to seek to explain them by the use of synonyms or dictionary definitions because 'an ordinary sensible man knows an insult when he sees or hears it'.[59] Whether particular conduct is 'threatening', etc is a question of fact. In *Brutus v Cozens*[60] D interrupted a tennis match to protest against apartheid and thereby angered the spectators. The House of Lords, reversing the Divisional Court, held that the finding

51 *Winn v DPP* (1992) 156 JP 881.
52 (1989) 89 Cr App R 199, [1989] Crim LR 581, DC.
53 *Chappell v DPP* (1988) 89 Cr App R 82.
54 Card, above, 3.11.
55 Sections 4(1), 4A(1), 5(1), 18(1), 19(1), 20(1), 21(1), 22(1), 23(1).
56 P 152.
57 Section 6(3) and (4).
58 Sections 19, 20, 21, 22, 23.
59 *Brutus v Cozens* [1972] 2 All ER 1297 at 1300, per Lord Reid.
60 [1972] 2 All ER 1297.

of the magistrate that this was not 'insulting' behaviour could not be disturbed because it was not an unreasonable finding of fact. If the magistrates had decided that the behaviour was insulting, it may be that their decision would have been equally beyond challenge.[61]

The section is not limited to rowdy or abusive behaviour. In *Taft*,[62] the defendant was prosecuted having driven erratically alongside lone women drivers on country roads while masturbating or pretending to do so. Masturbation in the sight of a stranger while in a public lavatory is capable of being insulting behaviour because, for example, the stranger might be a heterosexual who would be insulted at being taken for a homosexual.[63] It is immaterial that the stranger is a policeman[64] who is on the look out for this sort of thing, or a man, whether homosexual or not, who is not at all insulted. Words cannot be insulting (or, presumably, threatening or abusive) unless there is 'a human target which they strike' and it seems that D must be aware of that 'human target', though he need not intend the conduct to be 'insulting': *Masterson v Holden*,[65] where intimate 'cuddling' by two homosexual men in Oxford Street at 1.55 am on a June morning, in the presence of two young men and two young women, was held capable of being insulting. It is doubtful whether this interpretation would withstand scrutiny under the Human Rights Act 1998. The gay couple could surely claim that they were being discriminated against in the exercise of their private life since it is unrealistic to assume that similar displays of heterosexual behaviour would be prosecuted. In *Vigon v DPP*,[66] surreptitious filming of people in a changing room was held to be insulting. All three decisions adopt a broad, arguably too broad, interpretation of the term insulting.

The concept of 'insulting' has also given rise to difficulty in the context of protestors. For example, in *Lewis v DPP*[67] protestors outside an abortion clinic displayed placards including one of an aborted 21-week foetus in pools of blood. The Divisional Court held that this could constitute abusive and insulting behaviour, rejecting the argument that 'the photograph on the placard was an accurate representation of the result of an abortion, and that what is truthful cannot be abusive or insulting'.[68] Again, it is doubtful whether this would withstand challenge under the ECHR. Article 10 protects the right to freedom of expression, and if the protest is peaceful and involves the depiction of factual images, it is questionable whether prosecution is a necessary and proportionate response to protect the rights of others.

The breadth of the offence and the vagueness of these elements leaves an enormous discretion to the police officer in arrest and subsequently to the magistrates and can lead to great inconsistency in the application of the law.

[61] Per Lord Kilbrandon at 1303. Lord Reid, *obiter*, agreed with the magistrates' finding; but it does not follow that he would have held a contrary finding to be unreasonable.

[62] (1997) 13 Jan, CA Cr Div, unreported.

[63] *Parkin v Norman* [1982] 2 All ER 583 at 588–589, DC.

[64] And therefore presumably one who will not be readily insulted or provoked to violence.

[65] [1986] 3 All ER 39, [1986] 1 WLR 1017.

[66] (1998) 162 JP 115.

[67] (1995) unreported, DC. Cf *DPP v Clarke* (1991) 94 Cr App R 359, DC, where acquittals were upheld following the defendants' claims that they had not intended nor were they aware that displaying abortion images to police officers on duty outside a clinic would be threatening abusive or insulting.

[68] Per Pill LJ.

(iii) *Mens rea*/effect on V

It must be proved that D:[69]

(i) intended his words or behaviour towards V to be, or was aware that they might be, threatening, abusive or insulting;[70] and

(ii) either –

(a) that he intended V to believe that immediate unlawful violence would be used against him or another; or

(b) that he intended to provoke the immediate use of unlawful violence by V or another; or

(c) that V was likely[71] to believe that such violence (that is, *immediate* unlawful violence)[72] would be used; or

(d) that it was likely that such violence would be provoked.

Although the section creates only one offence,[73] alternatives (a) and (b) require proof of intention whereas in alternatives (c) and (d) the test focuses on the effect and is objective. The belief specified must be the belief of the person threatened.[74]

Where D's awareness that his conduct might be threatening, abusive or insulting is impaired by intoxication, s 6(5) and (6)[75] apply.

(iv) Public/private

The offence may be committed in a public or private place, except where D acts inside a dwelling[76] and V is also inside that, or another, dwelling.[77] So in *Atkin v DPP*[78] the threat to the customs officers in D's house could not be the offence. Threatening gestures through the bedroom window to the neighbour in his bedroom window across the street do not amount to the offence. Where D is in a dwelling, it seems that, if the issue is raised, the prosecution must prove that D was aware that his conduct might be heard or seen by a person outside that dwelling or another dwelling.[79] The common parts, including a

[69] See *Winn* (1992) 156 JP 881.

[70] Section 6(3).

[71] In construing the word 'likely', it is the state of the mind of the victim which is crucial rather than precise probability of violence actually occurring within a short space of time: *DPP v Ramos* [2000] Crim LR 768 (D sending letter bomb). See also Auld LJ in *Chief Constable of Lancashire v Potter* [2003] EWHC 2272, para 34, considering the expression in the context of ASBOs.

[72] *Horseferry Road Metropolitan Stipendiary Magistrate, ex p Siadatan* [1991] 1 QB 260, [1990] Crim LR 598, DC (the publication of Salman Rushdie's *The Satanic Verses* was not an offence because it was not likely to provoke *immediate* violence). Immediate does not mean instantaneous, and is generously interpreted, as in *Valentine* [1991] 1 QB 260 where V had said to a neighbouring family 'next time you go [to work] we're going to burn your house. You are all going to fucking die'. The DC held that the magistrates were entitled to infer that these words gave rise to a fear of immediate violence. see also *Ramos*, above.

[73] Section 7(2).

[74] *Loade v DPP* [1990] 1 QB 1052, [1990] 1 All ER 36, DC.

[75] Above, p 973.

[76] Defined in s 8.

[77] Section 4(2). See *Barber* [2001] EWCA Crim 838. Delivery of a threatening letter to V's home is incapable of being an offence under s 4 or s 5; *Chappell v DPP* (1988) 89 Cr App R 82, cf *DPP v Ramos* [2000] Crim LR 768 where the letter went to a business address.

[78] Above, p 9.

[79] Cf s 5(3)(b), putting the onus of proof (or at least an evidential burden) on D.

landing in a block of flats, are not part of a dwelling (this emphasizes the public order nature of the offence).[80]

(e) Harassment, alarm or distress[81]

It is an offence under s 5(1), punishable on summary conviction with a fine not exceeding level 3 on the standard scale, if a person–

(i) uses threatening abusive or insulting words or behaviour, or disorderly behaviour, or

(ii) displays any writing, sign or other visible representation which is threatening, abusive or insulting, within the hearing or sight of a person likely to be caused harassment, alarm or distress thereby.

This offence is wider than that under s4 in that it includes the further alternative of 'disorderly' behaviour; and it extends beyond apprehension of violence to the causing of 'harassment, alarm or distress'. When enacted it was regarded as a controversial extension of the law.

Many of the elements are discussed above in relation to s 4. 'Disorderly' is, no doubt, another ordinary word of the English language to be given its natural meaning and it will apply to acts of hooligans likely to produce the specified effect. In *Chambers and Edwards v DPP*[82] 'disorderly' was held to be a question of fact for the trial court to determine. The CPS Charging standards suggest that the following types of conduct may at least be capable of amounting to disorderly behaviour: causing a disturbance in a residential area or common part of a block of flats; persistently shouting abuse or obscenities at passers-by; pestering people waiting to catch public transport or otherwise waiting in a queue; rowdy behaviour in a street late at night which might alarm residents or passers-by, especially those who may be vulnerable, such as the elderly or members of an ethnic minority group; causing a disturbance in a shopping precinct or other area to which the public have access or might otherwise gather; and bullying.'[83]

(i) Victim

There is no requirement that the conduct be directed 'towards another person'. The prosecution must prove that D's conduct took place within the hearing or sight of a person (who might be a policeman)[84] likely to cause harassment, alarm (for his own or a third party's[85] safety) or distress. There must be a real not merely a hypothetical victim. It has been held that the s 5 (and 4A below) offence can be committed where there is a general confrontation between the police and protesters and the fact that the victim perceives the behaviour through CCTV at the scene does not prevent a conviction.[86] It is

80 *Rukwira v DPP* [1993] Crim LR 882.

81 For research on the impact and operation of the offence, see D. Brown and T. Ellis, *Policing Low-Level Disorder: police use of s 5 of the Public Order Act 1986* (1994) HORS 135.

82 [1995] Crim LR 896 (defendants standing peacefully to block surveyor's theodolite beam convicted despite absence of threat or fear of violence).

83 See www.cps.gov.uk/legal/section11/chapter_a.html#06.

84 *DPP v Orum* [1988] 3 All ER 449, [1989] 1 WLR 88, DC.

85 *Lodge v DPP* (1988) The Times, 26 Oct. See also *Chambers v DPP* [1995] Crim LR 896.

86 *Rogers and others v DPP* (1999) 22 July, DC.

not enough for the conduct to be such that it merely might have been seen or could possibly have been seen: *Holloway v DPP*.[87]

It is for D to prove, if he can, that he had no reason to believe that there was any such person within hearing or sight, except where D acts inside a dwelling and V is also inside that, or another, dwelling.[88] The requirement of a 'true' victim operates as a significant limitation on the breadth of the offence.

The offence was intended to deal with 'minor acts of hooliganism' but it appears to have been widely interpreted in practice.[89] In *Vigon v DPP*[90] it was held that the offence was not limited to rowdy behaviour and was apt to cover the conduct of a market trader who peeped between the curtains of a changing room and watched his customers undressing. such an affront to a person's dignity or modesty was 'insulting'. The fact that D did not peep, but used a video camera, made no difference. As he attempted to conceal the camera, he cannot have intended to insult; but it would be sufficient that he knew that the camera might be seen by a customer who might be insulted thereby.[91]

(ii) *Mens rea*

It must be proved that D intended his conduct to be threatening, abusive, or insulting or disorderly or was aware that it might be so.[92] Section 6(5) and (6) apply to the intoxicated defendant.[93] The requirement at its lowest involves proof that D had an awareness of a possibility.

(iii) Defence of reasonableness

An important aspect of the crime is the defence provided in s 5(3). In addition to the opportunity to prove (a) that he had no reason to believe that there was any person within sight or hearing who was likely to be caused harassment alarm or distress or (b) that he was inside a dwelling and had no reason to believe that his conduct would be heard or seen by a person outside that or any other dwelling, it is a defence for D to prove under s 5(3)(c) that his conduct was reasonable. This test is clearly, one of an objective nature.[94]

(iv) ECHR

In a number of cases the offence has been challenged in the domestic courts as being incompatible with Article 10 of the ECHR (which guarantees the right to freedom of expression).[95] There is no doubt that the protection of freedom of expression applies

87 [2004] EWHC Admin 2621 (D videoing himself naked with group of school children on playing field in background unaware of D's presence).

88 Section 5(3)(b).

89 S. Bailey, D. Harris and D. Ormerod, *Civil Liberties, Cases and Materials* (5th edn, 2001), 490 et seq; D. Feldman, *Civil Liberties and Human Rights in England and Wales* (2nd edn, 2002), ch 18; B. Emmerson and A. Ashworth, *Criminal Justice and Human Rights* (2000), ch 8.

90 [1998] Crim LR 289.

91 For details of the CPS Charging Standard see www.cps.gov.uk/legal/section11/chapter_a.html#08.

92 Section 6(3). *Ball* (1989) 90 Cr App R 378, 381.

93 Above p 973.

94 See generally A. Geddis, 'Free Speech Martyrs or Unreasonable Threats to Social Peace? "Insulting" expression and s 5 of the Public Order Act 1986' [2004] PL 853.

95 See above, ch 2.

widely and is engaged by 'conduct' that might not normally be considered as expression. 'Expression' includes purely physical acts of protest: *Hashman and Harrup v UK*,[96] and extends to 'the irritating, the contentious, the heretical, the unwelcome and the provocative provided it does not tend to provoke violence'.[97] The domestic courts have adopted a consistently narrow application of Article 10 in this context.

In *Percy v DPP*,[98] P had desecrated the US flag as part of her protest against US defence systems in the UK. Evidence was adduced that the US military personnel witnessing P's behaviour found it distressing. The Divisional Court held that s 5 was not necessarily incompatible with Article 10 (nor could it be since the offence encompasses behaviour other than that involving freedom of expression.) The court expressly acknowledged that s 5 is drafted in such a way as to accommodate freedom of expression defences. On the facts the District Judge had attached too much weight to the fact that P could have made the protest without the flag desecration. More generally, the court suggested that Article 10 had to be narrowly construed. The court had to presume that the appellant's conduct was protected by Article 10 unless and until it was established that a restriction on her freedom of expression was strictly necessary, having regard to: P's awareness of the likely impact of her conduct, the fact that P's behaviour went beyond legitimate protest, that the behaviour had not formed part of an open expression of opinion on a matter of public interest, but had become disproportionate and unreasonable, that P knew the likely effect of her conduct upon witnesses, whom she had targeted, and the fact that she used a method of demonstration – destroying the flag – which was not necessary to convey her message or the expression of opinion.

Percy was followed in *Norwood v DPP*,[99] where N's conviction for the racially aggravated version of the offence was upheld when he displayed a British National Party poster: 'Islam out of Britain' showing an image of the terrorist attack on 11 September 2001. The Divisional Court concluded that although Article 10 was engaged, having regard to Article 10(2), the offence was a necessary and proportionate restriction on D's freedom of expression for the prevention of disorder or crime and/or for the protection of the rights of others. It was noted that where the prosecution proves that an accused's conduct was insulting and that he intended it to be, or was aware that it might be so, it would in most cases follow that his conduct was objectively unreasonable, especially where that conduct was motivated wholly or partly by hostility towards members of a religious group based on their membership of that group.

In *Hammond v DPP*[100] H, an evangelical Christian, carried a double-sided sign bearing the words 'Stop Immorality', 'Stop Homosexuality' and 'Stop Lesbianism' on each side of a pole. H's preaching with the sign on display led to a gathering of 30 to 40 people shouting and becoming angry. H refused when police requested him to remove the sign, although H admitted he was aware that his sign was insulting because he had experienced a similar reaction before. H was convicted under s 5 and the conviction was upheld by the Divisional Court who concluded that H had not established that his

96 (1999) 30 EHRR 241, para 28 (hunting sabateurs).

97 Per Sedley LJ in *DPP v Redmond-Bate* [1999] Crim LR 998, 1000; and see *Handyside v UK* (1976) 1 EHRR 737, para 49.

98 [2001] EWHC Admin 1125, [2002] Crim LR 835.

99 [2003] EWHC 1564 Admin, [2003] Crim LR 888.

100 [2004] EWHC 69, [2004] Crim LR 851.

conduct was reasonable having regard to Article 10 of the Convention and Article 9 – the right to freedom of thought, conscience and religion.

These cases demonstrate the difficulty that an accused is likely to face in pleading Article 10 as a defence. Once the elements of intentional or reckless insult have been proved, it will be an uphill struggle to demonstrate that the conduct was nonetheless reasonable. Article 10 offers little by way of a foothold for the defence unless the question of freedom of expression is also to be considered in the evaluation of whether the conduct is insulting.

It seems that to rebut the Article 10 defence, the Crown must establish that prosecuting the relevant conduct under s 5 was necessary and proportionate to pursue a legitimate aim such as the protection of the rights of others. Some of the factors to be considered when examining the prosecution's rebuttal of the Article 10 plea are ones that the prosecution will already have had to establish in proving elements of *actus reus* and *mens rea*: specifically, the intention to act, the awareness of the likely effect, that it amounted to an insult, and that people found it distressing.

(f) Intentional harassment, alarm or distress

The Criminal Justice and Public Order Act 1994 inserted a new s 4A into the 1986 Act, creating a new offence of intentional harassment, alarm or distress punishable on summary conviction with imprisonment for six months or a fine not exceeding level 5 on the standard scale, or both. It requires threatening, abusive or insulting words or behaviour, as in s 5, but it also requires an intent to cause a person harassment, alarm or distress and actual causing of harassment, alarm or distress to that or another person. As in s 5, the offence may be committed in public or in private, with the same exception relating to a dwelling. The offence, being more severely punishable than s 5, was explained in Parliamentary debates to be aimed at serious or persistent racial harassment.

The provisions relating to intoxication in s 6(5) and (6) do not apply to the offence under s 4A. The *mens rea* requires an intention, and the offence would seem therefore to be one of specific intent.

(g) Prohibited processions and assemblies

Part II of the 1986 Act makes detailed provision for the regulation of processions and assemblies. Close examination of these provisions with their significant implications for public protest and civil liberties in general lies beyond the scope of this work.[101]

(i) Advance notice requirements

Section 11 requires advance notice in writing by the organizers of a procession. A summary offence is committed if the requirements of the section are not complied with. Under s 12 'a senior police officer' may, in specified circumstances, impose conditions; and s 13 similarly empowers a chief officer of police to prohibit a procession altogether.

101 See S . Bailey, D. Harris and D. Ormerod, *Civil Liberties, Cases and Materials* (5th edn, 2001), 437 et seq; D. Feldman, *Civil Liberties and Human Rights in England and Wales* (2nd edn, 2002), ch 18; D. G. Williams, 'Processions, assemblies and the freedom of the individual' [1987] Crim LR 167.

An organizer,[102] or person taking part, who knowingly fails to comply with such a condition or to obey such a prohibition is guilty of a summary offence.[103] It is also an offence to incite a person to commit such an offence.[104]

Section 14 empowers a senior police officer to impose conditions on public assemblies. Where a Chief officer imposes conditions under s 14 he must identify on which limb of the section he is relying. Moreover, if the conditions are imposed under s 14(1)(a) the officer must identify which of the three grounds contained in that limb was being relied on.[105] There must be sufficient reasons given to enable a party to whom the decision is directed to understand it. Summary offences are provided for organizers, and those taking part who knowingly fail to comply with a condition.[106] It is also an offence to incite a person to commit such an offence. The courts have construed the powers widely. Thus, although the powers were originally triggered only by a group of 20 or more persons, it was held that the police were entitled control the movements of individuals alone.[107] The Anti Social Behaviour Act 2003, s 57[108] alters the definition of 'public assembly' to mean an assembly of two or more. This is an astonishingly wide power to control assemblies and its proportionality may well be challenged under Article 11 of the ECHR.[109]

Section 14A (inserted by the Criminal Justice and Public Order Act 1994) enables a chief officer of police in particular circumstances to apply to the council of the district for an order prohibiting trespassory assemblies in the district or part of it for a specified period. Again, a person who organizes or takes part in an assembly which he knows is prohibited commits a summary offence. The person who incites such an offence also commits an offence.[110] This applies only to *trespassory* assemblies, that is, assemblies which would be a trespass if no order had been made. So a peaceful assembly of 21 people on the verge of a highway adjacent to stonehenge did not constitute a trespassory assembly since it did not amount to an unreasonable obstruction of the highway or a public nuisance.[111]

Sections 30 to 36 of the Anti-Social Behaviour Act 2003 empower a constable, or a community support officer, to issue a direction requiring the dispersal of any group which he considers is by its presence causing members of the public to be intimidated, harassed, alarmed or distressed. There are summary offences for knowingly contravening such an order.

102 Sections 12(4), 13(7); *DPP v Baillie* [1995] Crim LR 426.
103 Sections 12(5), 13(8).
104 Sections 12(6), 13(9).
105 *R (Brehony) v CC Greater Manchester Police* [2005] EWHC 640.
106 Section 14(4), (5), (6).
107 *Broadwith v CC Thames Valley* [2000] Crim LR 924.
108 See Anti-Social Behaviour Act (Commencement No 1 and Transitional Provisions) Order 2003, SI 3300 and N. Padfield, 'The Anti-social Behaviour Act 2003: the ultimate nanny-state Act?' [2004] Crim LR 712.
109 Cf *R (Laporte) v CC Gloucestershire* [2005] 1 All ER 473, holding that conditions being limited in time rendered them compatible with Articles 10 and 11. See also *Austin v MPC* [2005] EWHC 480.
110 Section 14B(1), (2), (3).
111 *DPP v Jones* [1999] 2 All ER 257, reversing [1998] QB 563, [1997] 2 All ER 119. On which, see comments at [1999] EHRLR 223; I. Hare, 'Public Assembly: The New Highway Code' [1999] CLJ 265; H. Fenwick and G. Philipson, 'Public Protest, the Human Rights Act, and Judicial Responses to Political Expression' (2000) PL 627; G. Clayton, 'Reclaiming Public Ground: the Right to Peaceful Assembly' (2000) 63 MLR 252.

(ii) ECHR

Challenge to restrictions on public meetings and protest may include those involving freedom of religion (Article 9), freedom of expression (Article 10) and freedom of assembly (Article 11). The European Court has recognized that public authorities have a duty to protect the right to peaceful protest and assembly,[112] but has held the statutory power to restrict processions to be compatible with Article 11 in particular where there is an anticipation of violence.[113] In *Pendragon v UK*,[114] Arthur U Pendragon, a druid, challenged a banning order under s 14A relating to Stonehenge. P was arrested at a 'service' he was conducting for druids, and he claimed that his right to religion under Article 9 was infringed, along with his rights under Articles 10, 11, and 14. The European Commission found that the order under section 14A complied with a sufficiently clear procedure, was limited and could be challenged before the courts.

(h) Other public assembly related offences

Other public order offences such as those dealing with raves[115] (ss 63–66 of the Criminal Justice and Public Order Act 1994 as amended by the Anti Social Behaviour Act 2003, s 58) and aggravated trespass (ss 68 and 69 of the 1994 Act) are beyond the scope of this work. It should be noted that these are becoming increasingly important in dealing with protestors.[116]

(i) Racially aggravated public order offences[117]

The Crime and Disorder Act 1998, s 31, created new racially aggravated versions of the offences under ss 4, 4A and 5 of the 1986 Act, and the Anti-Terrorism, Crime and Security Act 2001 extended these offences to include circumstances of religious aggravation.[118] Definitions of 'racially aggravated' and 'religiously aggravated' are set out and discussed above in the chapter on offences against the person, pp 557–559.[119] Aggravated s 4 and s 4A offences are punishable on summary conviction by six months, or a fine not exceeding the statutory maximum, or both; and on indictment by two years, or a fine, or both. An aggravated s 5 offence is triable only summarily and punishable by a fine, not exceeding level 4 on the standard scale. It is CPS policy 'not to accept pleas to lesser offences, or omit or minimize admissible evidence of racial or religious aggravation for the sake of expediency'.[120]

112 *Platform Arzte fur das Leben v Austria* (1988) 13 EHRR 204.

113 See *Rai Allmond and 'Negotiate Now' v UK* (1995) 81 DR 146.

114 [1999] EHRLR 223.

115 Open air gatherings to listen to loud 'music' ('sounds wholly or predominantly characterized by the emission of a succession of repetitive beats').

116 See *DPP v Bayer* [2003] EWHC Crim 2567 (Admin); *DPP v Tilly* [2001] EWHC Admin 821; *DPP v Barnard* [2000] Crim LR 371; *Nelder v DPP* (1998) The Times, 11 June. See further, S . Bailey, D. Harris, D. Ormerod, above, ch 4; Feldman, above, ch 18.

117 See, *inter alia*, M. Malik, 'Racist Crime: Racially Aggravated Offences in the Crime and Disorder Act 1998 Part II' (1999) 62 MLR 409; F. Brennan, 'The Crime and Disorder Act 1998: (2) Racially Motivated Crime: The Response of the Criminal Justice System' [1999] Crim LR 17. Specific guidance is provided to prosecutors by the CPS on prosecuting racially or religiously motivated crime – see www.cps.gov.uk/publications/prosecution/rrpbcrpol.html.

118 See M. M. Idriss, 'Religion and the Anti-Terrorism, Crime and Security Act 2001' [2002] Crim LR 890.

119 P 557.

120 See CPS guidance on prosecuting cases of racial and religious crime: www.cps.gov.uk/publications/docs/rrpbcrpol.pd.

As noted above, it is questionable whether such aggravated offences are necessary in view of the established approach to acknowledging such matters in the sentencing process.[121] They have been described recently as having 'positive disadvanatges.'[122]

The courts have been faced with numerous issues under the new offences, particularly as to the intentions of the defendant.[123] In *CPS v Weeks*[124] a charge under s 4A failed on the facts where the defendant had said 'watch out the nights are getting dark' to his victim, and called him a 'black bastard'. Holland J noted that the question whether the use of words such as 'black bastard' indicates an *intention* to cause harassment, alarm or distress is a question of fact dependent on the context and circumstances in which they were used. In *DPP v McFarlane*,[125] Rose LJ found that once the 'basic' offence (that is, the public order element) was proved and that racist language was used that was hostile or threatening to the victim, it made no difference that the defendant may have had an additional reason for using the language, the test of racial hostility under s 28(1)(a) was satisfied.[126] In *DPP v Woods*[127] it was confirmed that the fact that the *primary* motivation for the offence was something other than a racist motivation (being refused entry by a bouncer) did not preclude conviction for the aggravated offence.[128] The point was made that ordinarily, the use of racially or religiously insulting remarks would in the normal course of events be enough to establish a demonstration of hostility.

Arguments that such offences are an illegitimate restriction on the right to freedom of expression will be most unlikely to get off the ground. The European Court has taken the view that the direct expression of racist views is not protected under Article 10.[129]

(j) Acts intended or likely to stir up racial hatred[130]

(i) Racial hatred[131]

Offences of inciting racial hatred were first introduced into the law by the Race Relations Act 1965 which required proof of an intention to stir up such hatred. Because of the difficulty of proving such intent, the law was amended by the Race Relations Act 1976

121 There is a general duty on criminal courts when sentencing an offender to treat more seriously any offence which can be shown to be aggravated by a demonstration of hostility towards a person or to be motivated by hostility based on a person's membership or presumed membership of a racial or religious group: Powers of Criminal Court (Sentencing) Act 2000, s 153.

122 See the House of Lords Select Committee on *Religious Offences in England First Report* (2004), para 124.

123 On which see E. Burney, 'Using the Law on Racially Aggravated Offences' [2003] Crim LR 28–36.

124 (2000) 14 June, DC.

125 [2002] EWHC Admin 485.

126 See also *Greene* [2004] All ER (D) 70 (May).

127 [2002] EWHC Admin 85.

128 See also *DPP v M* [2005] Crim LR 392 and commentary.

129 *X v Italy* (1976) 5 DR 83; *Jersild v Denmark* [1994] EHRR 1, on which see also J. Andrews and A. Sherlock, 'Freedom of Expression – How Far should it Go' [1995] 20(3) EL 329. See also the important limitation in Article 17 preventing any group from performing acts designed to destroy the rights and freedoms in the Convention to a greater extent than is provided for in the Convention. This has been influential in the ECtHR's reasoning. There are similar guarantees in Article 20 of the ICCPR.

130 See recently, P. S. Rumney, 'The British Experience of Racist Hate speech regulation – A lesson for First Amendment Absolutists?' [2003] Common Law World Rev 117. See also on the implications of the prevalent use of the internet to distribute racist material M. Horn, 'Racism and Cyber Law' (2003) 153 NLJ 777.

131 Related offences include making racist chants at football games: Football (Offences) Act 1991, s 3.

which replaced the requirement of intent with an objective test. It was enough that the defendant's conduct was likely to stir up racial hatred, whether he intended to do so or not. Part III of the Public Order Act 1986 replaces the old law with six new offences. These have been extended by the Anti-Terrorism, Crime and Security Act 2001.[132] They are all concerned with acts intended or likely to stir up racial hatred – the objective test is retained throughout – and, by s 17:

> In this Part, 'racial hatred' means hatred against a group of persons [. . .][133] defined by reference to colour, race, nationality (including citizenship) or ethnic or national origins.

It will be noted that the offences do not (yet) extend to stirring up hatred against religious groups as such but an attack on a particular religion, such as the Jewish religion, might be interpreted as an attack on Jews as a race.[134] Under the 1976 Act it was held that the term, 'ethnic', was to be construed relatively widely and that the Sikhs, though originally a religious community, now constituted an ethnic group because they were a separate community with a long shared history and distinctive customs.[135]

In *Mandla*, Lord Fraser of Tullybelton observed that:

> For a group to constitute an ethnic group in the sense of the Act of 1976, it must, in my opinion, regard itself, and be regarded by others, as a distinct community by virtue of certain characteristics. some of these characteristics are essential; others are not essential but one or more of them will commonly be found and will help to distinguish the group from the surrounding community. The conditions which appear to me to be essential are these: (1) a long shared history, of which the group is conscious as distinguishing it from other groups, and the memory of which it keeps alive; (2) a cultural tradition of its own, including family and social customs and manners, often but not necessarily associated with religious observance. In addition to those two essential characteristics the following characteristics are, in my opinion, relevant; (3) either a common geographical origin, or descent from a small number of common ancestors; (4) a common language, not necessarily peculiar to the group; (5) a common literature peculiar to the group; (6) a common religion different from that of neighbouring groups or from the general community surrounding it; (7) being a minority or being an oppressed or a dominant group within a larger community, for example a conquered people (say the inhabitants shortly after the Norman conquest) and their conquerors might both be ethnic groups.

It has been held in an employment context that Muslims are not a racial group under this definition.[136] In *R v DPP, ex p LBC of Merton*,[137] it was held in judicial review proceedings that a declaration that Muslims were a group covered by ss 17–19 would not be binding

132 See also the discussion in the House of Lords Select Committee on *Religious Offences in England First Report* (2004), ch 6.

133 The words 'in Great Britain', in the original formulation were repealed by the Anti-Terrorism, Crime and Security Act 2001, s 37.

134 On earlier proposals to extend the offences to include inciting religious hatred, see M. M. Idriss, 'Religion and the Anti-Terrorism, Crime and Security Act 2001' [2002] Crim LR 890. On the difficulty of definition and application of the racial hatred offences to members of home nations, see C. Munro, 'When racism is not black and white' (2001) 151 NLJ 313.

135 *Mandla v Dowell Lee* [1983] 2 AC 548, [1983] 1 All ER 1062.

136 *J. H. Walker v Hussain* [1996] IRLR 11. See for an argument that British Muslims are protected K. S. Dobe and S. S. Chokar, 'Muslims, ethnicity and the law' (2000) 4 Int J of Discrimination and Law 369. See generally Bailey, Harris and Ormerod, above, ch 11.

137 [1999] COD 358.

on the criminal courts. The law would appear to be arbitrarily discriminatory in the protection it offers to the religious groups within the jurisdiction.

Anxiety over increasingly common examples of Islamophobia, particularly since 9/11, has led to increased pressure for a new offence of *inciting religious hatred*. Defining an offence with sufficient precision, and one which will infringe to the narrowest extent possible on the right to freedom of expression is incredibly difficult and controversial.[138]

The Racial and Religious Hatred Bill 2005 is currently before Parliament. It extends the racial hatred offences in Part III of the Public Order Act 1986 to cover stirring up hatred on religious grounds.[139]

(ii) The offences

Proceedings for an offence under Part III of the 1986 Act may not be instituted except by or with the consent of the Attorney-General. Each offence is punishable on indictment with two years' imprisonment or an unlimited fine or both, or, on summary conviction with six months' imprisonment or a fine not exceeding the statutory maximum, or both.

The essence of each offence is that D does an act involving the use of threatening, abusive or insulting words, behaviour or material and either:

(i) he intends thereby to stir up racial hatred, or

(ii) having regard to all the circumstances racial hatred is likely to be stirred up thereby.[140]

The offences are:

s 18 – using threatening, abusive or insulting words or behaviour or displaying any written material which is threatening, abusive or insulting;

s 19 – publishing or distributing written material which is threatening, abusive or insulting;

s 20 – presenting or directing the public performance of a play which involves the use of threatening, abusive or insulting words or behaviour;

s 21 – distributing or showing or playing a recording of visual images or sounds which are threatening, abusive or insulting;

s 22 – providing a programme service for, or producing, or directing, a programme involving threatening, abusive or insulting visual images or sounds, or using the offending words or behaviour therein;

s 23 – possessing written material, or a recording of visual images or sounds, which is threatening, abusive or insulting, with a view to its being displayed, published, etc.

These are specific statutory offences creating inchoate liability, and as ever with inchoates,

[138] See Idriss, above, for a full discussion.

[139] P. Jepson, 'Tackling religious discrimination that stirs up racial hatred' (1999) 149 NLJ 554, considering whether English law is compatible with the ICCPR. Religious offences in England and Wales, House of Lords First Report, www.parliament.the-stationery-office.co.uk/pa/ld200203/ldselect/ldrelof/95/9501.htm and government reply www.official-documents.co.uk/document/cm60/6091/6091.pdf. Progress of Racial and Religious Hatred Bill www.commonsleader.gov.uk/output/page1228.asp.

[140] For a discussion of speech crimes as either conduct or result crimes see J. Jacconelli, 'Context Dependent Crime' [1995] Crim LR 771.

the elements of *mens rea* take on paramount importance. This part of the Act provides a variety of requirements of *mens rea* in relation to the 'threatening, abusive or insulting' quality of the material in question. We have seen that for offences under ss 4 and 5 the prosecution must prove that D intended his conduct to have, or was aware that it might have, that quality.[141] In Part III this requirement is not as simple.

Under s 18 where D is shown to have intended to stir up racial hatred the test for 'threatening, abusive or insulting' is wholly objective. Where D is not shown to have intended to stir up racial hatred the prosecution must prove that D intended his conduct to have, or was aware that it might be, 'threatening, abusive or insulting'.[142]

Under s 22, where D is shown to have an intention to stir up racial hatred the test of whether it is threatening abusive or insulting is purely objective. Where D is not shown to have intended to stir up racial hatred, the prosecution must prove that he knew or *had reason to suspect* that the material was threatening, abusive or insulting.

For offences under ss 19, 20, 21 and 23, the prosecution need prove no intention or awareness with respect to 'threatening, abusive or insulting', but it is a defence for D, who is not shown to have intended to stir up racial hatred, to prove:[143]

- for s 19, that he was not aware of the content of material and did not suspect or have reason to suspect that it was threatening, abusive or insulting;
- for s 20, that he did not know and had no reason to suspect that the offending words or behaviour were threatening, abusive or insulting;
- for s 21, that he was not aware of the content of the recording and did not suspect and had no reason to suspect that it was threatening, abusive or insulting; and
- for s 23 that he was not aware of the content of the written material or recording and did not suspect, and had no reason to suspect, that it was threatening, abusive or insulting.

Section 26 provides a defence for fair and accurate reports of proceedings in Parliament and a contemporaneous report of proceedings in open court.

(iii) ECHR

Challenges under Article 10 (freedom of expression) and Article 9 (freedom of religion) would seem inevitable, particularly since it has been held that there is no defence in English law that the words spoken or published are true.[144] As noted above, although the ECtHR has acknowledged that Article 10 protects the right to express views that offend, shock or disturb,[145] the Court has declined to extend the protection to direct expression of racist views.[146] However, in the leading case of *Jersild v Denmark*, the Court distinguished between those who had expressed racist views directly, and acts of those exposing these individuals and the beliefs they espoused (the prosecution of an undercover journalist was a disproportionate response). It is arguable that the present law under the Public Order Act fails adequately to reflect that distinction, and that a prosecution of a journalist under ss 22 or 23 would not be a proportionate response within Article 10(2).

141 Section 6(3) and (4).

142 Section 6(3) and (4).

143 Subject to the discussion in Ch 2 relating to burdens of proof resting on the accused in the light of the jurisprudence on Article 6(2) of the ECHR.

144 *Birdwood* [1995] 6 Archbold News 2.

145 *Muller v Switzerland* [1991] 13 EHRR 212.

146 See *Jersild v Denmark* [1994] EHRR 1.

2. Public nuisance[147]

Public nuisance is a misdemeanour at common law triable either way.[148] It consists in:

> . . . an act not warranted by law or an omission to discharge a legal duty, which act or omission obstructs or causes inconvenience or damage to the public in the exercise of rights common to all His Majesty's subjects.[149]

The Court of Appeal recently confirmed the continued existence of the offence in the following terms:

> A person is guilty of a public nuisance (also known as a common nuisance) who (a) does an act not warranted by law, or (b) omits to discharge a legal duty, if the effect of the act or omission is to endanger the life, health, property, morals, or comfort of the public, or to obstruct the public in the exercise or enjoyment of rights common to all Her Majesty's subjects.[150]

A person who has suffered particular damage as the result of a public nuisance can maintain an action for damages in tort, and the major importance of public nuisance today is in the civil remedy which it affords.[151]

(a) Nature of nuisance

(i) Diverse forms of offence

The most common and important instance of a public nuisance is obstruction of the highway and this is more closely considered below. But it also includes a wide variety of other interferences with the public; for example, the carrying on of an offensive trade which impregnates the air 'with noisome offensive and stinking smoke' to the common nuisance of the public passing along the highway;[152] polluting a river with gas so as to destroy the fish and render the water unfit for drinking;[153] unnecessarily, and with full knowledge of the facts, exposing in a public highway a person infected with a contagious disease;[154] taking a horse into a public place knowing that it has glanders and that that is an infectious disease;[155] sending food to market, knowing that it is to be sold for human consumption and that it is unfit for that purpose;[156] burning a dead body in such a place and such a manner as to be offensive to members of the public passing along a highway or other public place;[157] keeping a fierce and unruly bull in a field crossed by a public footpath;[158] keeping two pumas and a leopard in a garden;[159] discharging oil into the sea in such circumstances that it is likely to be carried on to English (*sic*) shores and

147 I. Brownlie, *Law of Public Order and National Security* (2nd edn, 1981), 75, 77.

148 Criminal Law Act 1977, s 16 and Sch 2.

149 Stephen, *Digest*, 184.

150 *Goldstein* [2004] 2 All ER 589, para 3. See commentary by Ashworth [2004] Crim LR 303.

151 See further on the tort W. V. H. Rogers, *Winfield and Jolowicz on Tort* (16th edn, 2003), ch 14.

152 *White and Ward* (1757) 1 Burr 333. See also *Tysoe v Davies* [1983] Crim LR 684 (QBD).

153 *Medley* (1834) 6 C & P 292.

154 *Vantandillo* (1815) 4 M & S 73.

155 *Henson* (1852) Dears CC 24.

156 *Stevenson* (1862) 3 F & F 106; otherwise if D did not intend it for human consumption: *Crawley* (1862) 3 F & F 109.

157 *Price* (1884) 12 QBD 247.

158 Archbold (2005), ss 31–53.

159 *Wheeler* (1971) The Times, 17 Dec.

beaches;[160] by causing excessive noise and dust in the course of quarrying operations;[161] by an 'acid house-party' which creates a great deal of noise so as greatly to disturb the local populace;[162] by giving false information as to the presence of explosives so as to cause actual danger or discomfort to the public;[163] by trespassing and sniffing glue in a school playground even in the absence of staff and pupils;[164] by making hundreds of obscene telephone calls to different women in a particular area;[165] making hundreds of telephone calls intended to jam the switchboards;[166] by arranging to cause the abandonment of a Premiership football match by switching off the floodlights;[167] and by sending hundreds of packages containing racially offensive material to members of the public.[168]

(ii) Certainty of offence

A great many varieties of nuisance are now the subject of special legislation and proceedings are unlikely to be brought at common law where there is a statutory remedy. But the common law may still be useful where no statute has intervened or where the penalty provided by statute is too slight.[169] It is this flexibility that renders the offence so attractive to prosecutors, and the offence has often been used as a stop-gap pending specific legislation, to prosecute activity that poses a new threat to the health and welfare of the community. Examples include prosecutions for harassing behaviour as noted above, and in some jurisdictions for such conduct as knowing HIV transmission.[170]

It is this flexibility which also renders the offence subject to cogent criticism for its potential conflict with the principle of certainty.[171] The Court of Appeal has recently confirmed in *Goldstein*,[172] that the offence is sufficiently certain to enable a person with appropriate legal advice to regulate his conduct. As such the offence was found to be sufficiently clearly prescribed to satisfy the (rather undemanding) requirements of Article 7 of the ECHR. Controversially, the court was prepared to accept that the offence would not infringe Article 7 if it was applied to novel circumstances (that is, in which conduct had not previously been criminalized as public nuisance). It is submitted that this aspect of the decision may fall for reconsideration.[173]

(iii) Isolated act or omission

A public nuisance may be committed by omission, as by permitting a house near the highway to fall into a ruinous state[174] or by allowing one's land to

160 *Southport Corpn v Esso Petroleum Co Ltd* [1954] 2 QB 182 at 197, [1954] 2 All ER 561 at 571, CA, per Denning LJ; revsd [1956] AC 218, [1955] 3 All ER 864.

161 *A-G v PYA Quarries Ltd* [1957] 2 QB 169, [1957] 1 All ER 894.

162 *Shorrock* [1994] QB 279, [1993] 3 All ER 917.

163 *Madden* [1975] 3 All ER 155, CA. The court said 'potential danger' to the public was not enough but that 'actual risk' to the comfort of the public was. This is difficult to follow. Is not 'potential' danger the same as risk? And should not risk be enough?

164 *Sykes v Holmes* [1985] Crim LR 791, DC (conduct capable of being a nuisance within s 40 of the Local Government (Miscellaneous Provisions) Act 1982).

165 *Johnson* [1996] 2 Cr App R 434, [1996] Crim LR 828.

166 *Holliday* [2004] EWCA Crim 1847.

167 *Ong* [2001] 1 Cr App R (S) 404,

168 *Goldstein*, above.

169 Cf obstruction of the highway, Highways Act 1980, s 137, Town Police Clauses Act 1847, s 28.

170 See *Kreider* (1993) 140 AR 81; *Thornton* (1991) 3 CR 4th 381.

171 See J. R. Spencer, 'Public Nuisance – a critical examination' [1989] CLJ 55.

172 [2004] 2 All ER 589, [2004] Crim LR 303.

173 See Ashworth commenting at [2004] Crim LR 303.

174 *Watts* (1703) 1 Salk 357.

accumulate filth, even though it is deposited there by others for whom D is not responsible.[175]

Whereas private nuisance always involves some degree of repetition or continuance,[176] 'an isolated act may amount to public nuisance if it is done under such circumstances that the public right to condemn it should be vindicated'.[177]

(iv) Nature of interference

The interference with the public's rights must be substantial and unreasonable. Not every obstruction of the highway is a public nuisance:

If an unreasonable time is occupied in the operation of delivering beer from a brewer's dray into the cellar of a publican, this is certainly a nuisance. A cart or wagon may be unloaded at a gateway; but this must be done with promptness. so as to the repairing of a house; – the public must submit to the inconvenience occasioned necessarily in repairing the house; but if this inconvenience is prolonged for an unreasonable time, the public have a right to complain and the party can be indicted for a nuisance.'[178]

The public right to use the highway is not limited to passing and repassing; the highway is 'a public place, on which all manner of reasonable activities may go on'. It appears to include 'such ordinary and usual activities as making a sketch, taking a photograph, handing out leaflets, collecting money for charity, singing carols, playing in a Salvation Army band, children playing a game on the pavement, having a picnic, or reading a book . . . .'[179]

The key word is 'reasonable'. Any interference with the public's rights must be caused by some unnecessary and unreasonable act or omission by D is an unlawful obstruction. In *Dwyer v Mansfield*[180] it was held that, when queues formed outside D's shop because he was selling only 1lb (454g) of potatoes per ration book in view of the wartime scarcity, he was not liable because he was carrying on his business in a normal and proper way without doing anything unreasonable or unnecessary. The nuisance, if there was one, had been created not by D's conduct, but by the short supply of potatoes.[181] The result might be different if D sold ice-cream though the window of a shop, causing a crowd to gather on the pavement, because this is not a normal and proper way of carrying on business in England.[182]

175 *A-G v Tod Heatley* [1897] 1 Ch 560. 176 Per Denning LJ [1957] 2 QB at 192.

177 Ibid. In *Mutters* (1864) Le & Ca 491, a conviction was upheld where the indictment alleged that D, on a particular day, caused an explosion which scattered pieces of rock on to neighbouring dwelling-houses and the highway; but the indictment did allege that D allowed the stones to remain on the highway for several hours.

178 *Jones* (1812) 3 Camp 230, per Lord Ellenborough. And see *Cross* (1812) 3 Camp 224: 'A stage-coach may set down or take up passengers in the street, this being necessary for the public convenience; but it must be done in a reasonable time': per Lord Ellenborough. For a similar statutory rule, see Public Service Vehicles Regulations 1936, reg 7, and *Ellis v Smith* [1962] 3 All ER 954, [1962] 1 WLR 1486.

179 *DPP v Jones* [1999] 2 All ER 257, HL, per Lord Irvine, LC.

180 [1946] KB 437, [1946] 2 All ER 247.

181 *Sed quaere.* Would it be a defence to obstructing a pavement that D's lap-dancing club was the only one in town?

182 *Fabbri v Morris* [1947] 1 All ER 315 (Highway Act 1835, s 72).

(b) The public

Blackstone says that a public nuisance must be an annoyance to all the King's subjects.[183] This is obviously too wide for, if it were so, no public nuisance could ever be established. Denning LJ declared that the test is:

> . . . that a public nuisance is a nuisance which is so widespread in its range or so indiscriminate in its effect that it would not be reasonable to expect one person to take proceedings on his own responsibility to put a stop to it, but that it should be taken on the responsibility of the community at large.[184]

Whether an annoyance or injury is sufficiently widespread to amount to a public nuisance is a question of fact. In *Lloyd*,[185] where D's carrying on his trade caused annoyance to only three houses in Clifford's Inn, Lord Ellenborough said that this, if anything,[186] was a private nuisance, not being sufficiently general to support an indictment. But in the *PYA Quarries* case the nuisance was held to be sufficiently general where the inhabitants of about 30 houses and portions of two public highways were affected by dust and vibration. In *Johnson*[187] evidence that obscene calls had been made to 13 women in the Cumbria area was enough. In *Madden* a telephone call stating that there was a bomb in a factory affected only eight security officers who could not be regarded as a class of the public.[188] If the call had stated that the bomb was in a public place, such as a highway, from which the public were consequently excluded, it would seem that there would have been a public nuisance, even if few or no members of the public were in fact affected. Probably the same result should apply if the place were one to which the public have access on payment, such as a sports ground.

(c) *Mens rea*

It was decided in *Shorrock*[189] that it is enough that D knew or *ought to have known* that a nuisance would be caused – in effect that the offence is one of negligence. The previous authorities were ambiguous and most of them were civil proceedings. D relied on *Stephens*,[190] where Mellor J said –

> in as much as the object of the indictment is not to punish the defendant, but really to prevent the nuisance from being continued, I think that the evidence which would support a civil action would be sufficient to support an indictment –

arguing that as the proceedings in *Shorrock* were indeed intended to punish, *mens rea* in the sense of actual knowledge of the nuisance was required. It was accepted, however, that whether *mens rea* was required or not could not depend on the motive of the prosecutor. In light of the recent endorsement of requirements of subjective *mens rea* for serious offences,[191] including in particular the common law offence of misconduct in public

183 *Commentaries*, iii, 216.

184 *A-G v PYA Quarries Ltd* [1957] 2 QB 169 at 191, [1957] 1 All ER 894 at 908.

185 (1802) 4 Esp 200.

186 The annoyance could be avoided by shutting the windows.

187 Above, p 992.

188 [1975] 3 All ER 155, CA. What if all the workers in the factory had been evacuated? See now, Criminal Law Act 1977, s 51(2); above, Ch 16.

189 [1994] QB 279, above, p 992.

190 (1866) LR 1 QB 702, 710.

191 See *G* [2004] 1 AC 1034, above, p 103.

offence,[192] it is arguable that the *mens rea* for the offence of public nuisance will require reconsideration by the courts.

(i) Proof

While *Shorrock* may be taken to have settled the issue of *mens rea*, it does not follow that criminal and civil proceedings for nuisance are the same in all respects. Presumably the criminal rather than the civil rules of evidence apply, particularly as to burden of proof.

Denning LJ tells us:

> In an action for a public nuisance, once the nuisance is proved, and the defendant is shown to have caused it, the legal burden is shifted to the defendant to justify or excuse himself.[193]

But in a criminal prosecution the principle of *Woolmington v DPP*[194] and the guarantees in Article 6(2) of the ECHR requires that, as a general rule, there is only an evidential burden on D who sets up justification or excuse.[195]

(d) Vicarious liability

In at least some types of public nuisance a master is liable for the acts of his servant, performed within the scope of employment, even though the mode of performance which creates the nuisance is contrary to the master's express orders. Thus in *Stephens*,[196] D was held liable for the obstruction by his servants of the navigation of a public river by depositing rubbish therein. The reason given was that the proceeding was, in substance, civil, the object being not to punish D but to prevent the continuation of the nuisance.[197] But Mellor and Shee JJ thought that there may be nuisances of such a character that this rule would not be applicable. Baty[198] criticizes the ground of this decision and pertinently asks:

> who is to decide whether [the] prosecution is 'substantially civil' or tinged with criminology [*sic*]?[199]

Certainly, prosecutions for obstructing the highway are by no means always civil in substance: frequently the object is the punishment of the offenders. In *Chisholm v Doulton*[200] Field J said that *Stephens* 'must be taken to stand upon its own facts';[201] and the court held that, on a charge under the Smoke Nuisance (Metropolis) Act 1853 D was not criminally liable for the negligence of his servant in creating a nuisance. In cases of statutory nuisance D is vicariously liable only if the words of the statute require it.[202]

192 *A-G's Reference (No 3 of 2003)* [2004] EWCA Crim 868, above.

193 *Southport Corpn v Esso Petroleum Co Ltd* [1954] 2 QB 182 at 197, [1954] 2 All ER 561 at 571.

194 [1935] AC 462; above, p 24.

195 Another obvious difference is that the civil case may be made out on a balance of probabilities, but the criminal case must be proved beyond reasonable doubt.

196 Above, n 190.

197 Does this involve an enquiry into the motives of the prosecutor? Or does it reflect the courts' own view of what is the proper remedy for the wrong in question?

198 *Vicarious Liability* (1916) 204.

199 In *Russell* (1854) 3 E & B 942, Lord Campbell thought that the obstruction of navigation by building a wall was 'a grave offence'.

200 (1889) 22 QBD 736.

201 Ibid, at 740.

202 Cf *Armitage Ltd v Nicholson* (1913) 23 Cox CC 416.

The rule imposing vicarious liability for public nuisance may thus be neither so firmly established nor so all-embracing as is sometimes supposed; but *Shorrock* suggests that the courts will not distinguish between different types of nuisance and that all will be held to impose vicarious liability.

(e) ECHR

In many instances, D's conduct will involve his expressing opinions or engaging in activity that might be regarded as an aspect of his private life. To the extent that the offence engages the rights such as the freedom of expression (Article 10) and respect for privacy (Article 8), it has been held that it is a necessary and proportionate response for the protection of the rights of others (under Articles 8(2) and 10(2)).[203]

3. The Protection from Harassment Act 1997[204]

Prior to 1997 the criminal law struggled to provide protection for those who suffered at the hands of so-called stalkers. The use of the tort to tackle behaviour which amounted to stalking was severely curtailed by the decision of the House of Lords in *Hunter v Canary Wharf*.[205] The Lords held that only those who had a right to exclusive possession of the land could sue in nuisance. Recourse was had to the criminal law and prosecutors relied on offences of public nuisance, specific offences relating to malicious communications or telecommunications where possible or public order offences and offences against the person. These efforts to combat what was perceived as a growing social menace were assisted by the courts' acceptance that psychiatric injury was a sufficient basis for a finding of actual or grievous bodily harm[206] and by the House of Lords' acceptance that assault could be committed by words alone or even by a silent telephone call.[207] These extended interpretations were not always well received[208] but led to successful convictions.

Parliament nevertheless felt that a specific offence was needed and, following consultation,[209] and an unseemly rush through Parliament the Protection of Harassment Act was enacted.[210] The draftsman faced a formidable difficulty in defining 'stalking' without overcriminalizing. The conduct complained of may include acts of apparent kindness such as repeated sending of flowers or seemingly innocuous conduct such as walking by the victim's house. As the Minister stated:

203 *Goldstein* [2003] EWCA Crim 3450, [2004] 2 All ER 589.

204 See R. Babcock in P. Infield and G. Platford, *The Law of Harassment and Stalking* (2000); N. Addison and T. Lawson-Cruttenden, *Harassment Law and Practice* (1998). See also the information collected at www.harassment-law.co.uk. The offence is further amended by the Serious Organised Crime and Police Act 2005, s 125 (not yet in force).

205 [1997] 2 All ER 426.

206 *Chan Fook* [1994] 2 All ER 552, CA; *Burstow* [1998] AC 147.

207 *Ireland* [1998] AC 147.

208 C. Wells, 'Stalking the Law's Reponse' [1997] Crim LR 1.

209 See Home Office, *Stalking the Solutions* (1996).

210 See the analysis by E. Finch, *The Criminalisation of Stalking* (2001); M. Allen, 'Look Who's Stalking' [1996] Web Jnl CLI 1. For a comparative review of stalking laws see B. Clarke and L. Meintjes-van der Valt [1998] 115 South African Law Jnl 729.

Stalkers do not stick to activities on a list. stalkers and other weirdos who pursue women, [*sic*] cause racial harassment and annoy their neighbours have a wide range of activity which it is impossible to define.'[211]

As Wells observes, the Act follows a pattern all too common in recent years of 'addressing a narrowly conceived social harm with a widely drawn provision, often supplementing and overlapping with existing offences.'[212]

(a) Course of conduct

The two offences under the Act are dependent on proof of a course of conduct, which is an element of the offence and not a crime in itself.

> 1—(1) A person must not pursue a course of conduct –
>
> (a) which amounts to harassment of another, and
>
> (b) which he knows or ought to know amounts to harassment of the other.
>
> (2) For the purposes of this section, the person whose course of conduct is in question ought to know that it amounts to harassment of another if a reasonable person in possession of the same information would think the course of conduct amounted to harassment of the other.

At the core of both crimes (and the tort of harassment) is a 'course of conduct', which is further explained in s 7(1) such that it 'must involve conduct on at least two occasions'. The provision is far from clear, with little further elaboration other than that words are sufficient (s 7(4)). One of the major problems under the Act has been in determining when two incidents are sufficiently closely associated to constitute a course of conduct. Although seeking to identify the idea of 'persistence' that lies at the heart of stalking, Parliament refrained from attempting further to define the proscribed behaviour. In debates on the Bill, Michael Howard referred to the lack of definition, but regarded harassment as a concept 'interpreted regularly by the courts since 1986'.[213] It is extremely wide in scope and applies to protest and neighborhood disputes[214] as well as what might more usually be regarded as stalking.

(i) One actor or two?

Section 7 (3A) provides:

> A person's conduct on any occasion shall be taken, if aided, abetted, counselled or procured by another –
>
> (a) to be conduct on that occasion of the other (as well as conduct of the person whose conduct it is); and
>
> (b) to be conduct in relation to which the other's knowledge and purpose, and what he ought to have known, are the same as they were in relation to what was contemplated or reasonably foreseeable at the time of the aiding, abetting, counselling or procuring.[215]

211 D. MacLean, Home Office Minister, HC, col 827 (17 Dec 1996).

212 Above, at 2.

213 HC, vol 287, col 784 (17 Dec 1996).

214 Inciting a dog to bark is sufficient to form part of a course of conduct: *Tafurelli v DPP* [2004] EWHC 25 (Nov).

215 As inserted by the Criminal Justice and Police Act 2001.

Thus where A performs an harassing act towards V aided by B, and subsequently A alone commits a further act of harassment towards V, the two may be regarded as a course of conduct. The extension of the scope of course of conduct was enacted to deal with protestors.

(ii) One act or two?

Is there a 'course of conduct' when an individual engages in one continuous activity? In *Hills*[216] it was stressed that it is not just enough to count the incidents, nor to direct the jury in such terms.[217] In *Kelly v DPP*,[218] K had had a relationship with V and 10 days after being released on licence for harassing her he made three abusive and threatening telephone calls to a mobile telephone belonging to the victim between 2.57 am and 3.02 am. The victim did not answer any of the calls at the time and they were recorded on her voice-mail facility. She listened to the messages one after the other, without pause. It was held that the shortage of time within which telephone calls were made was only *a* factor to be taken into account when determining whether there had been repetitious behaviour of the purposes of proving the commission of an offence of harassment. If calls within five minutes were held to constitute a 'course', where would the courts draw the line? D telephones V, V answers the call and immediately she identifies D she terminates the call. D calls back immediately. V sees that D's number appears on the 'caller id' facility. Is this a course of conduct? In *Hills*, Latham LJ stated that repetition was a significant factor in determining whether there is a course of conduct, but there is no requirement that acts be similar or repeated. Any combination of bouquets of flowers, menacing calls or letters, loitering outside the victim's home, etc will suffice. As was suggested in *Lau*,[219] the question should be whether there is a sufficient nexus between the two acts, taking account of all of the circumstances.

(iii) No need for temporal proximity or similarity

Is there a course of conduct where different acts are separated by a considerable period of time? For example, are two acts separated by one year, for example, two birthday cards, a 'course of conduct'? In *Lau v DPP*[220] two incidents four months apart were held to be capable of amounting to a course of conduct. The court observed that 'one can conceive of circumstances where incidents, as far apart as a year, could constitute a course of conduct.' The example given was of racial harassment outside a synagogue on the Day of Atonement. In *Baron v Crown Prosecution Service*,[221] it was accepted that less proximate in time and the more limited in number the incidents, the less likely that there was a course of conduct. In *Pratt v DPP*,[222] D first threw water over his estranged wife and three months later chased her through the matrimonial home swearing and questioning her constantly. The justices found these to be a course of conduct and the Divisional Court did not find this to be an irrational decision. However, it was noted that prosecuting authorities should be cautious in bringing charges for the offence of harassment in circumstances where only a small number of incidents had occurred. The prosecution

[216] [2001] Crim LR 318
[217] *Patel* [2005] Crim LR 649, [2004] EWCA Crim (Nov).
[218] [2003] Crim LR 43, DC.
[219] [2000] Crim LR 580 and commentary.
[220] [2000] Crim LR, [2000] 1 FLR 799.
[221] 13 June 2000, unreported.
[222] [2001] EWHC Admin 483.

should ensure not merely that two or more incidents had occurred but that such repetitious behaviour had caused harassment to the other person.

It is submitted that the events making up the 'course of conduct' under the Act require a nexus, as is implicit within the expression, which suggests a 'series' of events with some connection. The main connecting factor will be that the acts are aimed at a particular victim, but that will not of itself be sufficient, in the same way that two visits to the hospital by the same patient would not necessarily be described as a course of treatment. There must be something more connecting them – in the case of the treatment, one would expect it to be for the same ailment. The mere fact that D made two harassing calls to the same victim a year apart will not necessarily constitute a course of conduct. If the calls were made on a particular anniversary, there would be a greater nexus and the course of conduct would be more likely to be established. The question must turn on all the circumstances of the case.

(iv) Conduct towards the same victim

The course of conduct must relate to 'another'. In *DPP v Williams*[223] W had put his hand through a bathroom window startling the occupant M who was showering. She then informed H, her flatmate, who was scared by the event. Two days later he peered through the bedroom window, this time frightening H. The magistrate convicted, holding that 'another' could be read as 'others'. The Divisional Court decided the case on the basis that H had been distressed on both occasions and therefore the offence was made out. The interpretation was criticized for extending the offence considerably and for giving rise to practical problems.[224] In *Caurti v DPP*[225] it was held that in relation to the s 4 offence the course of conduct must have its impact on *one* complainant, even where it is aimed at another.

The complainant must be an individual and not a corporate body.[226]

(v) When does the course of conduct begin?

In many instances D will be involved in what might considered to be initially at least neutral conduct towards V. Does his course of conduct only begin when he is aware of the distress he is causing V, or when it causes V harassment or when the reasonable person would see it as harassing? In *King v DPP*[227] the alleged harassment was by offering the victim a plant, writing letters to her, rummaging in her rubbish and stealing her discarded underwear from those bags and filming her secretly. The Divisional Court held that 'repeated offers of unwelcome gifts or the repeated sending of letters could well amount to harassment, nevertheless, the *single* offer of a gift of modest value *and* the sending of one innocuous letter in the circumstances of this case cannot amount to harassment within the meaning of the 1997 Act. Nor could the letter and the gift be treated as the first stage or the first two stages of a course of conduct amounting to harassment . . .' The

223 *DPP v Williams* (DC, 27 July 1998, Rose LJ and Bell J).

224 A charge under the 1997 Act might be bad for duplicity where it names two complainants when they are members of a 'close knit identifiable group': *Mills v DPP* (1998) 17 Dec, DC.

225 [2002] Crim LR 131 and commentary.

226 *DPP v Dziurzynski* (2002) 166 JP 545; cf *Daiichi UK Ltd and others v Huntingdon Animal Cruelty and others; Asahi Glass UK Ltd and others v Same; Eisai Ltd and others v Same; Yamanouchi Pharma UK Ltd and others v Same; Sankyo Pharma UK Ltd and others v Same* (2003) The Times, 22 Oct, QBD.

227 20 June 2000, DC.

magistrates were wrong to treat these incidents as forming a part of a course of conduct. The decision is difficult to square with the terms of the section. There is no limitation as to the types of conduct amounting to harassment in the statute.

(vi) *Mens rea* as to the course of conduct

There is no requirement that the harasser intended or directed his conduct, it is sufficient that 'a reasonable person in possession of the same information would think the course of conduct amounted to harassment of another.'[228] The leading case is that of *Colohan*[229] where it was held that the test is entirely objective and that D's schizophrenia could not be taken into consideration in evaluating whether the reasonable person would have realized that the conduct was harassing. On the facts it was unclear whether D was denying that he knew what he was doing in writing the allegedly harassing letters, or denying that he knew that the letters constituted a course of harassing conduct, or was claiming simply that the harassment was reasonable. Given the clear policy behind the legislation it is not surprising that the court rejected the defence claims. The prosecution of mentally disordered individuals under this offence not only ensures the protection for victims of stalking, but also increases the chances of the offender receiving psychiatric assessment and treatment.

(vii) In possession of the same information

Section 1(2) is unusual in requiring that the person whose course of conduct is in question *ought to know* that it amounts to harassment of another if a reasonable person 'in possession of the same information' would do so. The section is designed to endow the reasonable person with knowledge of circumstances that would render otherwise seemingly innocuous conduct harassing (for example, when D knows that previous advances towards V have been rejected and continues to send gifts). In such cases D's inculpatory state of mind is taken into account. Should the reasonable person also be possessed with knowledge about D's exculpatory states of mind in order to assess whether the conduct is harassment? This is not the same as asking whether a reasonable person with the characteristics of the accused would regard it as harassment, particularly where the characteristic inhibits cognition of the wrongdoing. In *Colohan*, the strong policy grounds of protection on which the Act is founded justified the court's rejection of any attempt to diminish the purely objective stance.

(viii) Defences justifying the course of conduct

Section 1 provides:

> (3) Subsection (1) does not apply to a course of conduct if the person who pursued it shows –
>
> (a) that it was pursued for the purpose of preventing or detecting crime.
>
> (b) that it was pursued under any enactment or rule of law or to comply with any condition or requirement imposed by any person under any enactment, or
>
> (c) that in the particular circumstances the pursuit of the course of conduct was reasonable.

[228] Section 1(2). [229] [2001] EWCA Crim 1251, [2001] Crim LR 845.

Paragraph (a) seems clear, although debate might arise over whether it is restricted to State officials engaged in crime investigations or whether investigative journalists might also be able to rely on this defence.[230] Paragraph (b) is uncontroversial. It protects the right of free speech and expression. Picketers ought to be able to rely on the defence in (b). Indeed, one of the first cases in which the Act was considered involved anti-vivisection protesters.[231] Eady J in hearings relating to injunctive relief in that case commented that the Act was not intended to be used to stifle discussion of public interest on public demonstration.[232]

More difficult is that under para (c), particularly where D claims that his action was part of a campaign of legitimate protest. In *Baron v DPP*,[233] the court emphasized that:

> a line must be drawn between legitimate expression of disgust at the way a public agency has behaved and conduct amounting to harassment. The right to free speech requires a broad degree of tolerance in relation to communications. It is a legitimate exercise of that right to say things which are unpleasant or possibly hurtful to the recipient.

The defence under s 1(3)(c) does not involve the question whether the reasonable person regards the course of conduct as harassment, but whether it is reasonable harassment. It seems to arise only where it is accepted that the course of conduct is harassing. Furthermore, the question is whether the conduct was, as a whole 'reasonable', which suggests a purely objective assessment. In some cases involving campaigns the courts can face difficult issues of evaluating the reasonableness of a form of protest. These may involve arguments based on rights of freedom of expression under Article 10 of the ECHR.

The burden is on the defendant to prove, on the balance of probabilities,[234] that the conduct is reasonable. It has been held that pursuit of conduct in breach of an injunction will preclude a defence under s 1(3)(c).[235]

(b) The s 2 offence

> 2 (1) A person who pursues a course of conduct in breach of s 1 is guilty of an offence.
> (2) A person guilty of an offence under this section is liable on summary conviction to imprisonment for a term not exceeding six months, or a fine not exceeding level 5 on the standard scale, or both.

The offence is based on the course of conduct and it has been held that prosecutions are not therefore time barred if at least one of the incidents forming part of the course of conduct occurs within the six-month limitation period for the laying of informations in the magistrates.[236]

(i) *Actus reus*

The s 2 offence requires two or more acts by the accused constituting a course of conduct. There need be only one result from their cumulative effect – the harassment of the victim.

[230] Note also s 12 providing that the Secretary of State may issue certificates that render conduct of specified individuals conclusively reasonable (eg security service operatives).

[231] [1998] Env LR D9.

[232] *Huntingdon Life Sciences v Curtin* (1997) The Times, 11 Dec.

[233] 13 June 2000, unreported.

[234] See Ch 2 on the appropriateness of the burden under the Human Rights Act 1998 and Article 6(2).

[235] *DPP v Mosely* (1999) The Times, 23 June.

[236] *DPP v Baker* [2004] EWHC 2782 (Admin).

Section 7(2) provides that 'harassing a person' includes 'alarming the person or causing the person distress' and this has been treated as a non-exhaustive definition.[237] There is no requirement that any violence is threatened (or feared) for the offence under s 2. The section criminalizes conduct such as that in *Chambers and Edwards v DPP*[238] where protestors persistently but non-violently blocked the surveyor's theodolite beam, since the Divisional Court held that such conduct would amount to harassment for the purposes of the Public Order Act 1986. In many cases the section has been used successfully in respect of 'classic' stalking behaviour.[239]

(c) Causing a fear of violence – s 4

Section 4 provides:

(1) A person whose course of conduct causes another to fear, on at least two occasions, that violence will be used him is guilty of an offence if he knows or ought to know that his course of conduct will cause the other so to fear on each of those occasions.

(2) For the purposes of this section, the person whose course of conduct is in question ought to know that it will cause another to fear that violence will be used against him on any occasion if a reasonable person in possession of the same information would think the course of conduct would cause the other so to fear on that occasion.

(3) It is a defence for a person charged with an offence under this section to show that

(a) his course of conduct was pursued for the purpose of preventing or detecting crime,

(b) his course of conduct was pursued under any enactment or rule of law or to comply with any condition or requirement imposed by any person under any enactment, or

(c) the pursuit of his course of conduct was reasonable for the protection of himself or another or for the protection of his or another's property.

Section 4 is triable either way, carrying a maximum sentence on indictment of five years or a fine or both.

The essential differences between this offence and that in s 2 (and under tort in s 3) is that the victim must be caused to fear on at least two occasions, that violence will be used 'against him'. The other important difference is that the only defence available to this charge is that the harasser proves that his conduct was for the purpose of preventing or detecting crime, was lawfully authorized, or was reasonable for the protection of *himself or another or of property.*[240] Section 4 has been criticized as being too narrow because of this requirement.[241]

[237] *DPP v Ramsdale* (2001), *The Independent*, 19 Mar.

[238] [1995] Crim LR 896.

[239] For critical comment on the scope of the offence see E. Finch, 'Stalking the Perfect Stalking Law: An Evaluation of the Efficacy of the Protection from Harassment Act 1997' [2002] Crim LR 702. See also J. Harris Home Office Research Study No 203, *An evaluation of the use and effectiveness of the Protection from Harassment Act 1997* (2000).

[240] A failure to direct on these defences may well render a conviction unsafe – *Wilkes* [2004] EWCA Crim 3136.

[241] See Finch, 'Stalking the Perfect Stalking Law' above suggesting a new offence of intentional harassment to bridge the gap between the narrow s 4 and the wide and overused s 2.

Section 4 has no requirement of immediacy of assault. Whereas violence is defined in s 8 of the 1986 Act for the purposes of that Act, no such definition appears in the Protection from Harassment Act 1997. In *Henley*[242] H's harassment of the complainant and her family included threats to kill. He was charged under s 4. The trial judge failed properly to direct the jury wrongly suggesting that to 'seriously frighten her' would suffice and failed to clarify that the person must *himself* fear violence, not violence towards others. A direction on the *mens rea* under s 4(2) should be routinely given.

A fear of violence may be inferred from threats and behaviour other than explicit threats of violence issued to the victim in person (for example, threats to his dog) but the victim must fear that violence will be used against himself.[243]

(d) Racially and religiously aggravated harassment

The Crime and Disorder Act 1998, as amended by the Anti-Terrorism Crime and Security Act 2001, provides racially and religiously aggravated offences of harassment and putting people in fear of violence.

Section 32:

(1) A person is guilty of an offence under this section if he commits –

(a) an offence under s 2 of the Protection from Harassment Act 1997 (offence of harassment); or

(b) an offence under s 4 of that Act (putting people in fear of violence),

which is [racially or religiously aggravated] for the purposes of this section.

An aggravated offence under s 32(1)(a) is triable either way and punishable on indictment with a maximum sentence of two years' imprisonment. An offence under s 32(1)(b) is triable either way and carries a maximum seven years' imprisonment on conviction on indictment. The nature of racial and religious aggravation is discussed above in Chapter 16.

242 [2000] Crim LR 582.

243 *R v DPP* [2001] Crim LR 396; *Henley* [2000] Crim LR 582; *Caurti v DPP* [2002] Crim LR 131 and commentaries.

28

Road traffic offences[1]

The advent of the motor vehicle created problems with which the existing law was ill-equipped to deal. The threat of proceedings for manslaughter might deter the motorist from driving with wilful disregard for human life, but where some harm less than death was caused other offences against the person were hardly pertinent at all. Those offences, in the main, require that the harm should be caused intentionally or recklessly. It is rare for a motorist to intend harm to the person though perhaps not so rare for him to be reckless as to whether or not he causes such harm, particularly if recklessness does not require the driver to be aware of the obvious risk which he is taking. Though the motorist who causes harm may often be at fault, the harm he causes is ordinarily both undesired and unforeseen by him. But it must not be thought that there is little or no room for offences of intention and recklessness in road traffic. There are many offences (such as speeding, driving whilst unlicensed, driving whilst uninsured) where the offence is ordinarily committed intentionally or recklessly though it does not follow that such offences will require proof of intention or recklessness. Generally it is only in relation to the causing of harm to the person or property that the motorist is neither intentional nor reckless.

There were some provisions of statutes which applied to motorists, but only, as it were, by chance. Under the Highway Act 1835, s 72, for example, it was an offence to drive any carriage on the pavement and this could be applied to the motor carriage, and under the Town Police Clauses Act 1847, s 28, the furious driving of any horse or carriage was an offence and this was applied to motorists. And it is still an offence, triable only on indictment and punishable with two years' imprisonment, under s 35 of the Offences Against the Person Act 1861 for a person, having charge of a carriage or vehicle, to cause bodily harm by wanton or furious driving.[2] But for the main part the law barely con-

[1] A detailed review of road traffic offences lies beyond the scope of this work. Readers are referred to the leading works, in particular, K. Swift, *Wilkinson's Road Traffic Offences* (21st edn, 2003) and R. Ward (ed), *Encyclopaedia of Road Traffic Law and Practice* (2001). A major source of reference on the major offences covered in the chapter is the Department of Transport, Home Office, *Road Traffic Law Review Report*, HMSO, 1988, hereinafter referred to as the *North Report*. See further J. R. Spencer 'Road Traffic Law: A Review of the *North Report*' [1988] Crim LR 707. Details of reviews and reform proposals on the law are available at www.dft.gov.uk/stellent/groups/dft_rdsafety/documents/sectionhomepage/dft_rdsafety_page.hcsp.

[2] In *Okosi* [1996] Crim LR 666 and commentary, it was assumed, without deciding the point, that subjective, *Cunningham* recklessness must be proved. In the recent case of *Knight* [2004] All ER (D) 149 (Oct), the court held that a jury direction referring to 'driving without sufficient thought as to the possibility of risk' represented an 'unacceptable dilution' of the *mens rea* required. This endorsement of subjective *mens rea* is to be welcomed. This provision, though rarely used, is not a complete dead letter because it applies to drivers of horse-drawn vehicles and motorists or cyclists who cannot be prosecuted for dangerous driving or

cerned the motorist at all. There were no tests of driving proficiency, no registration requirements, no compulsory insurance, and virtually no driving offences. The common law could not (and rightly did not) fill gaps like these and the result is that for practical purposes the regulation of road traffic is almost entirely statutory.

The legislation is considerable, technical, and complex and it is neither possible nor appropriate in a work of this kind to deal in a comprehensive way with the plethora of offences created. Attention is accordingly concentrated on careless driving, dangerous driving and causing death by dangerous driving since a discussion of these contributes to an understanding of the general principles of the criminal law. Careless and dangerous driving are rare examples of English law providing endangerment offences.

1. Careless driving

(a) Negligence as a basis of liability

At common law, negligence is only rarely a sufficient basis for criminal liability. It is now established that manslaughter may be committed by gross negligence[3] but this is exceptional. Negligence, however gross, is not sufficient to ground liability for a non-fatal offence against the person or even of damage to property. It is, however, an offence to drive a mechanically propelled vehicle carelessly and the offence does not require (though it used to be that a prosecution was unlikely without)[4] harm to person or property. Why, if it is not an offence negligently to cause injury with 'a garden fork, hedge trimmer or even a chainsaw'[5] should it be an offence to cause harm (or even not to cause harm) by the negligent use of a motor vehicle? The *North Report* concedes that there is not a great logical difference between the careless use of a chainsaw or a vehicle but defends the offence of careless driving on the grounds that:

> . . . the careless use of chainsaws does not contribute to over 5,000 deaths every year. It is because the danger associated with the widespread use of motor vehicles is so great that society has decided to attempt to restrain the use of vehicles so as to reduce this danger. And there are parallels between road traffic law and other bodies of regulatory law covering areas of activity such as health and safety at work, and building standards. Some of these areas of law contain offences which could be the result of mere carelessness such as, for example, polluting a river or leaving a machine unguarded. The common element between such offences is the degree of danger that may be caused to innocent parties.[6]

cycling because their act was not done on a road or (in the case of drivers) a public place, or because they were not warned of intended prosecution. Cf *Cooke* [1971] Crim LR 44, QS where D could not be charged under the Road Traffic legislation because the offence was not committed on a road and *Mohan* [1976] QB 1, [1975] 2 All ER 193, CA. The *North Report* recommended the repeal of s 35 but this recommendation seems to have been rejected.

[3] *Adomako*, above, Ch 14.

[4] 'One widespread complaint was of the mechanical nature of the prosecution decision – a bad case of careless driving may not go to court because no personal injury was caused, and conversely a very trivial case of carelessness may lead to prosecution simply because injury was caused': *North Report*, 5.27.

[5] *North Report*, 5.29.

[6] *North Report*, 5.30.

Some may find this reassurance convincing, others less so. The assumption appears to be that without an offence of careless driving road deaths attributable to this source would have been significantly more than 5,000, but the assumption remains unproven.

To the suggestion that careless driving ought not to be a criminal offence because drivers are already constrained to drive as best they can by a well grounded fear for their own safety and their wish to avoid an accident and its consequences (not least the loss of a no claims bonus the cost of which may exceed any fine the court imposes) the *North Report* replied that if the offence of careless driving were to be abolished then:

> . . . at least part of it would have to be replaced or there would be some serious instances of bad driving which would go unpunished. In our view it is likely that the issues here are confused by the amount of attention which is focused on the common shorthand term for this offence – careless driving. But what is required to establish the section 3 offence is more than this. The course of driving must be found to be lacking in *due* care or *reasonable* consideration. Cases where no accident is caused, involving momentary inattention for example, by a driver with an unblemished driving career should not, in our opinion, lead to an appearance in court. But a series of bad overtaking decisions might, if such driving came to police attention, warrant prosecution, even if no accident resulted.[7]

This passage is puzzling. It suggests that the offence of careless driving should be retained because it will deal with cases of 'bad' driving which are not bad enough to qualify as 'very bad' driving within the offence of dangerous driving. It also suggests that carelessness *per se* does not suffice for the s 3 offence; the emphasis on '*due* care' and '*reasonable* consideration' suggesting that more than mere carelessness is required to constitute the offence. This is a novel suggestion and does not appear to be one articulated in the existing case law.

(b) The offence(s)

Section 3 of the Road Traffic Act 1988, as substituted by s 2 of the Road Traffic Act 1991, provides:

> If a person drives a mechanically propelled vehicle on a road or other public place without due care and attention, or without reasonable consideration for other persons using the road or place, he is guilty of an offence.

The offences are summary only and punishable by a fine at level 4.[8]

The substituted section extended the offences in two respects, first by substituting 'mechanically propelled vehicle' for 'motor vehicle', and secondly, by the addition of 'or other public place' to 'road'.[9] Otherwise the law is unchanged.

For the purposes of s 3, and no doubt for the purposes of ss 1 and 2, 'other persons using the road' includes the passengers in a vehicle driven by D.[10]

Section 3 creates two distinct offences, careless driving and inconsiderate driving. In many cases the facts would constitute either offence but they are not identical since

7 *North Report*, 5.31.

8 Disqualification is discretionary and the offence carries 3–9 penalty points.

9 The *North Report* recommended these extensions for the offence of dangerous driving (8.10, 8.12) but not for careless driving. See *May v DPP* [2005] EWHC Admin, 14 May.

10 *Pawley v Wharldall* [1966] 1 QB 373, [1965] 2 All ER 757.

the latter, unlike the former, may be committed only where other persons are using the road.

(i) Careless driving

The test of liability according to Lord Goddard CJ in *Simpson v Peat*[11] is: was D exercising that degree of care and attention that a reasonable and prudent driver would exercise in the circumstances? The relevant standard, according to Lord Hewart CJ:

is an objective standard, impersonal and universal, fixed in relation to the safety of other users of the highway. It is in no way related to the degree of proficiency or degree of experience attained by the individual driver.[12]

It is accordingly no defence that a learner driver is doing his best if the care exercised falls short of that to be expected from the reasonably competent driver;[13] nor is any special standard applicable to experienced drivers, such as police drivers who may be trained to meet exacting standards of proficiency,[14] and even though they may have to cope with emergencies which are not the lot of ordinary drivers.[15] Faced by an emergency the issue is not whether by taking some other course of action harm may have been avoided but whether D's reaction to the emergency was a reasonable one.[16] Even if D suffers an unexplained initial loss of control (for example, resulting in the vehicle skidding), it is not improper for justices to convict him of careless driving on the basis of his reaction in braking too heavily.[17]

Another view of the nature of liability for careless driving was given by Lord Diplock in *Lawrence*.[18] 'Section 3', he said:

creates an absolute offence in the sense in which that term is commonly used to denote an offence for which the only *mens rea* needed is simply that the prohibited physical act (*actus reus*) done by the accused was directed by a mind that was conscious of what his body was doing, it being unnecessary to show that his mind was also conscious of the possible consequences of his doing it. So s 3 takes care of this kind of inattention or misjudgment to which the ordinarily careful motorist is occasionally subject without its necessarily involving any moral turpitude, although it causes inconvenience and annoyance to other users of the road.

11 [1952] 2 QB 24, [1952] 1 All ER 447 at 449, DC.

12 *McCrone v Riding* [1938] 1 All ER 157 at 158, DC. The standard is the same as that applied in a civil action for negligence – 'the obligation in the criminal law on the . . . driver cannot be the subject of a more stringent test than his liability in civil law': *Scott v Warren* [1974] RTR 104, DC, per Lord Widgery CJ at 107. References in a criminal case to rules of civil law affecting the onus of proof (such as *res ipsa loquitur*) are probably best avoided though it is open to justices to infer negligence from facts affording no other reasonable explanation.

13 *McCrone v Riding* [1938] 1 All ER 157; *Preston Justices, ex p Lyons* [1982] RTR 173, [1982] Crim LR 451, DC. See M. Wasik, 'A Learner's Careless Driving' [1982] Crim LR 411. Inexperience may be relevant to sentence: *Mabley* [1965] Crim LR 377.

14 *Woods v Richards* (1977) 65 Cr App R 300, DC.

15 In coping with such emergencies the police driver owes the ordinary duty of care to other persons lawfully (*Gaynor v Allen* [1959] 2 QB 403, [1959] 2 All ER 644, DC) or unlawfully (*Marshall v Osmond* [1983] QB 1034, [1983] 2 All ER 225, DC) on the highway. The test is whether D is driving with due care *in all the circumstances*, including the emergency with which he is faced (*Woods v Richards* (1977) 65 Cr App R 300, DC) and the nature of the unlawful conduct with which he has to deal (*Marshall v Osmond*).

16 *R v Bristol Crown Court, ex p Jones* (1986) 83 Cr App R 109, DC.

17 *R (On the Application of Bingham) v Director of Public Prosecutions* (2003) 167 JP 422.

18 [1981] 1 All ER 974 at 981, HL.

This is a puzzling passage. Offences of 'absolute', perhaps more properly called 'strict', liability are ordinarily contrasted with offences requiring a fault element, including offences which require proof of negligence.[19] In the case of an absolute offence it can be no defence to show that all reasonable care was taken but where an offence, such as careless driving, requires proof of negligence the prosecution must necessarily fail unless a want of due care is established.

There is a sense in which liability for careless driving might be said to be absolute. If D's driving falls short of the standard expected from the reasonably prudent driver, not only is it no defence for D to show that he was doing his level best but also it is no defence for him to show that it was in fact impossible for him to do any better. Drivers, being human, will inevitably make some errors of judgment in their driving lives but the assumption is, and for practical reasons must be, that the reasonably prudent driver makes none. In truth, the 'reasonably prudent driver' is not the average driver but a mean standard. In this limited sense careless driving might be said to be an absolute offence but it is not clear that it is in any sense helpful to so classify it. The general basis on which persons are punished for offences of negligence is that they could have done better, whereas people may be punished for offences of absolute liability even though they have taken all reasonable care.

Lord Diplock does, however, recognize that no liability can be incurred unless what was done by D was directed by a mind conscious of what he was doing. This is merely a particular instance, of a general principle governing criminal liability. If D is unforeseeably afflicted by an epileptic seizure when driving he cannot be convicted of careless driving. D may thereby create considerable dangers for other road users, which perhaps explains why some cases seem to show a marked lack of sympathy to drivers raising automatism,[20] but without a real ability to control his actions D cannot be convicted of careless driving.[21] He may, however, find himself not guilty by reason of insanity if his disability arose from an 'internal factor' such as multiple sclerosis or epilepsy.[22]

Nor must it be thought that, as Lord Diplock's dictum might be taken to imply, the offence of careless driving requires proof of inconvenience or annoyance to other road users. Careless driving is a conduct crime and not a result crime;[23] consequently it may be committed though no one is affected by the careless driving in question.

All the circumstances (which cannot be exhaustively stated but include such factors as the state of the road, the volume of traffic, weather conditions and so on) need to be considered by the justices in determining whether D's driving falls short of the relevant standard and the question is essentially one of fact for them. Evidence of the amount of alcohol consumed by the driver is admissible. It is relevant as circumstantial evidence of

[19] Cf his Lordship's view as expressed in *Tesco Supermarkets Ltd v Nattrass* [1971] 2 All ER 127 at 155, HL: 'negligence connotes a reprehensible state of mind – a lack of care for the consequences of his physical acts on the part of the person doing them'.

[20] *Watmore v Jenkins* [1962] 2 QB 572, [1962] 2 All ER 868, DC; *Broome v Perkins* [1987] Crim LR 271, DC.

[21] But note *Moses* [2004] All ER 128 (Sept) where D was convicted of causing death by *dangerous* driving when the bus he was driving swerved onto the pavement when he was swatting a wasp that had flown into the cab.

[22] See case discussed by J. C. Smith in 'Individual incapacities and criminal liability' [1998] 6 Med L Rev 138 at 144–145.

[23] Above, Ch 4.

the manner of driving where, as in *Millington*,[24] it is in dispute; an intoxicated person is more likely to have driven in the manner alleged by the prosecution than a sober person. It may also be an element in the alleged carelessness – it might not be 'careless' for a mildly intoxicated person to drive in the particular conditions at 30 mph, nor for a sober person to drive at 45 mph, but careless for that intoxicated person to drive at 45 mph.

Only where the justices reach a decision which no reasonable bench could reach on those facts will the High Court interfere.[25] Consequently the High Court may uphold a decision to convict (or acquit) if it is one which may reasonably be reached on the facts and even though, had the decision been to acquit (or convict), that decision would equally have been upheld.[26] In criminal cases, as in civil actions for negligence, the courts resist any attempt to elevate 'to the status of propositions of law what really are particular applications to special facts of propositions of ordinary good sense'.[27]

The point may be illustrated by reference to cases involving the Highway Code.[28] While the Code contains many precepts of good driving, and while the Act itself provides[29] that a failure to observe its provisions may be relied on in both criminal and civil proceedings as tending to establish or negative liability, it does not lay down for drivers a regime of inflexible imperatives. Since each case turns on its own particular facts it does not *always* (though it may usually) follow that a driver is necessarily careless in driving at such a speed that he cannot stop in the distance he sees to be clear,[30] nor in leaving insufficient braking distance between his vehicle and another's;[31] nor in failing to look behind before reversing;[32] nor in crossing a road's dividing line[33] though these are all precepts of driving practice set out in the Code.

Nor is D's driving necessarily careless merely because it constitutes some other driving offence. While the speed at which a vehicle is driven is often a relevant factor, it does not necessarily follow that D is guilty of careless driving merely because he is exceeding a speed limit.[34] Nor does it follow that a driver who is guilty of the offence of failing to accord precedence to a pedestrian on a crossing is guilty of careless driving.[35]

Since the test is objective, and what is relevant is the driver's conduct, it cannot matter that the failure to exercise due care arose from a deliberate act of bad driving on D's part.[36] This is not to say that subjective factors must always be ruled out of account. Though no account is to be taken of such subjective factors as experience and skill,[37]

[24] [1995] Crim LR 824. [25] *Bracegirdle v Oxley* [1947] KB 349, [1947] 1 All ER 126, DC.

[26] *Jarvis v Fuller* [1974] RTR 160, DC. The same principles apply to a charge of inconsiderate driving: *Dilks v Bowman-Shaw* [1981] RTR 4.

[27] *Easson v London and North Eastern Rly Co* [1944] 2 All ER 425 at 426, CA, per du Parcq LJ.

[28] www.dft.gov.uk/stellent/groups/dft_rdsafety/documents/page/dft_rdsafety_032114.hcsp.

[29] Section 38(7). [30] *Jarvis v Fuller* [1974] RTR 160.

[31] *Scott v Warren* [1974] RTR 104, DC. Cf *Preston Justices, ex p Lyons* [1982] RTR 173, DC.

[32] *Hume v Ingleby* [1975] RTR 502, DC.

[33] *Mundi v Warwickshire Police* [2001] All ER (D) 68 (Jun), [2001] EWHC 447 (Admin).

[34] *Quinn v Scott* [1965] 2 All ER 588, [1965] 1 WLR 1004, DC.

[35] *Gibbons v Kahl* [1956] 1 QB 59, [1955] 3 All ER 345, DC.

[36] *Taylor v Rogers* (1960) 124 JP 217, [1960] Crim LR 271, DC.

[37] Presumably no account is to be taken of age although D may lawfully drive a motor car at 17 years and a motor cycle at 16. No doubt the same 'impersonal and universal' standard would be applied. But what of careless cycling under s 29 where D may be only 10 years old? In civil cases generally a child must exercise the care to be expected of a child of his age but where a child is engaged in an activity such as cycling on a road there is much to be said for holding him to the standard of the reasonably experienced cyclist.

knowledge of circumstances may be a relevant factor. It is clear, for example, that D could be convicted of careless driving where, because of his familiarity with the vehicle, he realizes that it has a tendency to pull to the right when the brakes are applied at high speed,[38] while someone who was unfamiliar with the vehicle, and who was reasonably unaware of this tendency, could not.

The CPS guidance on prosecuting careless driving emphasizes that the test is: 'what did the defendant do, or fail to do? It is not: what happened as a result of the defendant's action or inaction, even if this has serious consequences'.[39] The following are provided by the CPS as examples of driving which may amount to driving without due care and attention: overtaking on the inside; driving inappropriately close to another vehicle; driving through a red light; emerging from a side road into the path of another vehicle; conduct whilst driving, such as: using a hand held mobile telephone while the vehicle is moving; tuning a car radio; reading a newspaper/map; selecting and lighting a cigarette/cigar/pipe; talking to and looking at a passenger.

(ii) Inconsiderate driving

Whereas in cases of careless driving the prosecution need not show that any other person was inconvenienced, in cases of inconsiderate driving, there must be evidence that some other user of the road or public place was actually inconvenienced. Inconsiderate driving is the more appropriate offence where, for instance, D drives his car through a puddle which he might have avoided and drenches pedestrians. It must be the driving which is inconsiderate; other inconsiderate conduct, such as kicking a cyclist,[40] will not do.

The CPS[41] provides examples of conduct appropriate for a charge of driving without reasonable consideration: flashing of lights to *force* other drivers in front to give way; misuse of any lane to avoid queuing or gain some other advantage over other drivers; unnecessarily remaining in an overtaking lane; unnecessarily slow driving or braking without good cause; driving with un-dipped headlights which dazzle oncoming drivers; driving through a puddle causing pedestrians to be splashed; driving a bus in such a way as to scare the passengers.

2. Dangerous driving[42]

(a) Background

Until the law was amended by the Criminal Law Act 1977 it was an offence to drive a motor vehicle 'recklessly, or at a speed or in a manner dangerous to the public'. Although the offences carried the same penalty, reckless driving was considered the most serious. But it would not be unfair to say that the courts failed to find a satisfactory definition for any of the offences, nor did they articulate a clear distinction between them. Perhaps the

38 *Haynes v Swain* [1975] RTR 40, [1974] Crim LR 483, DC.

39 Available at www.cps.gov.uk/legal/section9/chapter_b.html#17.

40 *Downes v Fell* [1969] Crim LR 376, DC.

41 Available at www.cps.gov.uk/legal/section9/chapter_b.html#17.

42 See generally S. Cunningham, 'Dangerous Driving a Decade On' [2002] Crim LR 945, considering reviews of the legislation and proposed reform.

best that could be said was that dangerous driving was driving that was worse than careless driving and that reckless driving was driving that was even worse than that.

The James Committee[43] noted the confused state of the law. The Committee said:

> The most unsatisfactory motoring offence at present is dangerous driving. At one end of the scale it may verge on reckless driving, at the other it may be barely distinguishable from driving without due care and attention.

The Committee's proposed solution[44] was to have only two offences, reckless driving and 'a single composite offence covering the existing offences of dangerous driving, driving without due care and attention and driving inconsiderately'. The legislative solution adopted was simply to abolish dangerous driving.

What was still lacking was a definition of recklessness in the context of reckless driving and this was provided by the House of Lords in *Lawrence*.[45] It is no longer necessary to rehearse this decision in the context of driving offences since it is superseded by the offence of dangerous driving which, unlike its predecessor in title, is given a detailed definition. It is, however, worth noting some of the reasons[46] which led to the rejection of the *Lawrence* test because it sheds some light on the purport of the new offence of dangerous driving. Essentially the *North Report* found the *Lawrence* test to be too narrow in that it left too many cases of bad driving to be dealt with simply as careless driving.[47] The Report says:[48]

> In terms of behaviour on the road the sort of driving which we believe ought to be treated more seriously would include . . . such activities as driving in an aggressive or intimidatory fashion which might involve, for example, sudden lane changes, cutting into a line of vehicles or persistently driving much too close to a vehicle in front. The present reckless driving offence is too narrowly framed reliably to catch those guilty of this kind of bad driving, *particularly in that it requires investigation of the driver's state of mind at the relevant time, evidence of which may be hard to obtain.*

The italics have been supplied because, to some at least, it is not immediately apparent why in an offence carrying two years' imprisonment on conviction on indictment (and five years' imprisonment should death be fortuitously caused) the driver's state of mind should be irrelevant. It would surely be relevant to the sentencer who would be inclined to award a sentence towards the lower end of the scale if he concluded that the driver was merely thoughtless and towards the higher end of the scale if he concluded that the driver had deliberately put at risk the persons or properties of others. And why should it be more difficult to obtain evidence as to the driver's state of mind when he is driving a motor car than when he is wielding a garden fork, hedge-trimmer or chainsaw?

The *North Report* also criticizes the *Lawrence* test in that it exculpates the driver who gave thought to the risk but foolishly concluded there was none, the so-called lacuna or

[43] The Distribution of Criminal Business between the Crown Court and Magistrates' Courts, Cmnd 6323, paras 123, 124 and Appendix K.

[44] Appendix K, para 6.

[45] [1982] AC 510, [1981] 1 All ER 974, HL, above, Ch 5.

[46] *North Report*, 5.7–5.11.

[47] This same anxiety has led, bizzarely, to suggestions for an intermediary offence of negligent driving. For cogent criticism of these see Cunningham, above.

[48] At para 5.15.

loophole in the *Caldwell* test of recklessness.[49] This is an acceptable criticism of *Lawrence* to the extent that there is no rational ground for distinguishing between the driver who foolishly gives no thought to there being any risk and the driver who gives thought to the risk and foolishly concludes that there is none.[50]

(b) The offence

The *North Report* concluded that there should be a new 'very bad' driving offence which would be objective and would articulate the relevant standard. Section 2 of the Road Traffic Act 1988, as substituted by s 1 of the Road Traffic Act 1991, accordingly provides:

> 2A—(1) For the purposes of sections 1 and 2 above a person is to be regarded as driving dangerously if (and, subject to subsection (2) below, only if) –
>
> (a) the way he drives falls far below what would be expected of a competent and careful driver, and
>
> (b) it would be obvious to a competent and careful driver that driving in that way would be dangerous.
>
> (2) A person is also to be regarded as driving dangerously for the purposes of sections 1 and 2 above if it would be obvious to a competent and careful driver that driving the vehicle in its current state would be dangerous.
>
> (3) In subsections (1) and (2) above 'dangerous' refers to danger either of injury to any person or of serious damage to property; and in determining for the purposes of those subsections what would be expected of, or obvious to, a competent and careful driver in a particular case, regard shall be had not only to the circumstances of which he could be expected to be aware but also to any circumstances shown to have been within the knowledge of the accused.
>
> (4) In determining for the purposes of subsection (2) above the state of a vehicle, regard may be had to anything attached to or carried on or in it and to the manner in which it is attached or carried.

The CPS[51] provides the following examples of driving which may support an allegation of dangerous driving: racing or competitive driving; speed, which is highly inappropriate for the prevailing road or traffic conditions; aggressive driving, such as sudden lane changes, cutting into a line of vehicles or driving much too close to the vehicle in front; disregard of traffic lights and other road signs, which, on an objective analysis, would appear to be deliberate; or disregard of warnings from fellow passengers; overtaking which could not have been carried out safely; driving a vehicle with a load which presents a danger to other road users; where the driver is suffering from impaired ability such as having an arm or leg in plaster, or impaired eyesight; driving when too tired to stay awake; driving with actual knowledge of a dangerous defect on a vehicle; using a mobile phone whether as a phone or to compose or read text messages.[52]

49 As to which, see above, p 104.

50 Some would argue that the driver in an inadvertent state is really failing to apply latent knowledge from experiences of driving and is blameworthy in that regard. For discussion see A. Duff, *Intention, Agency and Criminal Liability* (1990) at 160.

51 www.cps.gov.uk/legal/section9/chapter_b.html#17.

52 See *Browning* (2001) EWCA Crim 1831, (2002) 1 Cr App R (S) 88.

Dangerous driving is triable either way and carries a level 5 fine and/or six months' custody on summary conviction; in the Crown Court the maximum penalty is two years' custody and/or an unlimited fine. Disqualification from driving for at least a year and an extended driving re-test are mandatory in the absence of 'special reasons'.

The offence requires a consideration of the following matters.

(i) The relevant standard for dangerous driving

In relation to the *driving* of the vehicle the relevant standard is entirely objective,[53] D doing his incompetent best might still render him liable for dangerous driving. The test is focused on the manner of driving and not on D's state of mind.[54]

It must be proved (i) that the way D drives falls 'far below' what would be expected of a competent and careful driver; *and*[55] (ii) that it would be obvious to a competent and careful driver that driving in that way would be dangerous. The requirements at (i) and (ii) are obviously intended to be additional and are not meant to be two ways of expressing the same thing. Careless driving may well create a risk of injury to the person or of serious damage to property but careless driving which does not fall 'far below' what would be expected of a competent driver does not suffice. Conversely, driving might fall far below the standard of the competent driver and yet not create a risk of injury to the person nor of serious damage to property. Moreover the danger of the relevant harm must be 'obvious' to the competent and careful driver and this requires more than that the danger would have been foreseeable to the competent and careful driver; the situation must be one where the competent and careful driver would say that the danger was plain for all to see. A single inadvertent act or omission may fall so far below the standard of driving of a competent and careful driver that it constitutes dangerous driving. It is nevertheless, intended to be a high threshold, and not one applying to every slip;[56] not every breach of the Highway Code will be sufficent to establish the offence of dangerous driving, although it will be a guide as to the standard to be expected of the careful and competent driver.[57]

Clearly the magistrates or the jury have to make a value judgement as to whether D's driving falls 'far below' the standard of the competent and careful driver. Opinions of magistrates and juries may, and no doubt will, differ on how far below is 'far below' but, as with careless driving, appellate courts are unlikely to interfere with what are said to be decisions 'of fact and degree' unless the decision is patently unreasonable. There will thus be an element of chance in whether D is convicted of dangerous or careless driving.[58] This element of the offence has been heavily criticized since members of the public do not have a 'consistent perception of what is required of a competent and careful driver'.[59]

53 *Collins* [1997] Crim LR 578.

54 But note the public attitude reported in the surveys discussed by Cunningham, above at 950. See also, B. Mitchell, 'Further Evidence of the Relationship Between Legal and Public Opinion on the Law of Homicide' [2000] Crim LR 814.

55 See *Brooks* [2001] EWCA Crim 1944.

56 *Conteh* [2004] RTR 1; *Few* [2005] EWCA Crim 728.

57 *Taylor* [2004] EWCA Crim 213.

58 It is incumbent on the trial judge to direct carefully on the difference between dangerous and careless driving, *Jeshani* [2005] EWCA Crim 146.

59 Cunningham above at 957, reviewing the findings of research surveys into the working of the 1991 Act.

Viewed as a matter of principle the driving should be considered independently of the harm in fact caused; it is the nature of the driving and its potential to cause the stated harms that is the criterion in a conduct or endangerment crime such as dangerous driving is.[60] This is supported in particular by the fact that there is a specific offence of causing death by dangerous driving.

(ii) Driving a vehicle in a dangerous state

Regardless of the manner in which a vehicle is driven, danger may be caused to the public (a) by the condition of the driver or (b) by the condition of the vehicle. Though the vehicle is presently proceeding as a well-driven vehicle should, the danger may be ever-present. Under the repealed law of reckless driving the courts held, quite inconsistently, (i) that danger arising from the driver's drunken condition could not in itself amount to the offence because the recklessness must be in the manner of the driving; but (ii) that the offence was committed merely by driving a vehicle in a dangerous condition and it was immaterial that the manner of the driving was not reckless. The *North Report* recommended that, as indeed common sense seems to require, these two cases should be treated alike and either should constitute the offence. The offence:

> should cover the fact that the vehicle is driven at all, as well as how it is driven. This is necessary so as to include within the offence those who decide to drive when either they themselves or their vehicles are wholly unfit to be on the road as well as those who, despite being fit to drive and having properly maintained vehicles, drive very badly.[61]

Section 2A(2) implemented this recommendation in respect of the state of the vehicle but not in the state of the driver. The absence of any reference to the driver's condition appears to confirm the illogical pre-Act position in this respect. It was therefore a great surprise when, in *Woodward*,[62] the court found persuasive in respect of dangerous driving the arguments which it had persistently rejected or ignored in respect of reckless driving and held that the fact that D was adversely affected by alcohol was 'a relevant circumstance' in determining whether he was driving dangerously.

> It would be strange if Parliament intended to make driving a vehicle in a dangerously defective state an offence under the section but not driving when the driver is in a dangerously defective state due to drink.[63]

[60] Cf *Krawec* (1984) 6 Cr App R (S) 367, CA, holding that in cases of careless driving leading to death, the unforeseen and unexpected consequences are not normally relevant to penalty, the primary consideration being the extent to which the driving falls below the standard of the reasonable driver. The *North Report* (para 5.22) recommended that the dangerous driving offence 'should look directly and objectively at the quality of the driving . . . – was the driving really bad? – without needing to consider how or what the driver had thought about the possible consequences . . .'.

[61] At para 5.22 (iv).

[62] [1995] 3 All ER 79, [1995] Crim LR 487. The Crim LR report wrongly treats this as a case of *reckless* driving. *Woodward* was followed in *Marison* [1997] RTR 457 (diabetic driver who was aware that there was a real risk he might have a sudden hypoglycaemic attack guilty of causing death by dangerous driving).

[63] In *Marison* [1997] RTR 457, [1996] Crim LR 909 it was held that, for the purposes of conviction of this offence there is no relevant distinction between an incapacity induced by alcohol and one which is induced by diabetes or any other cause. The question in every case is whether the incapacity is such that it would be obvious to a competent and careful driver that it would be dangerous to drive while labouring under it. The source of the disability may be relevant to sentence. See also *Constantini* [2005] EWCA Crim.

Strange, certainly, but that seems to have been Parliament's intention in rejecting half of the North Report's recommendation. It has been persuasively suggested that this is a case where the court has improved the law by misreading the statute.[64]

As regards the state of the vehicle, it has been acknowledged that latent defects in the vehicle will be insufficient to found the charge since they would not be obvious to a competent and careful driver.[65] The 'current state' of the vehicle implies a state altered from the manufactured or designed state.

In determining the state of the vehicle s 2A(4) provides that regard may be had to anything attached to or carried on or in the vehicle and to the manner in which it is attached or carried. This provision may have been unnecessary but it prevents any possible argument that the 'state' of the vehicle refers only to its mechanical state and does not extend, for example, to an improperly secured trailer or an insecure load.[66]

(iii) The relevant danger

The danger created must be of 'injury to any person or of serious damage to property'.[67] As to the latter it is odd, given that the essence of the offence is very bad driving; that the offence is committed (assuming in a particular case that no danger of personal injury is created) only where the very bad driving creates a danger of 'serious' harm to property since very bad driving remains very bad driving if it creates a danger of any damage to property. And when does damage become *serious*? £50's worth? £100's worth? £500's worth? Perhaps the courts will take refuge in the formula that 'it is all a matter of fact and degree'.

(iv) The relevance of knowledge

The test of dangerous driving is largely objective: did D's driving fall far below the standard of the competent and careful driver and would it have been obvious to a careful and competent driver that driving in that way would be dangerous? The fact that D pressed the accelerator accidentally in mistake for the brake is no defence. If no competent and careful driver would have done such a thing, the fact is evidence of dangerous driving.[68] Even in the case where the alleged offence is driving a vehicle in a dangerous state D cannot defend himself by showing that he was unaware of the defect in the vehicle, or that he thought the load was secure, if it would have been obvious to a careful and competent driver that the vehicle was defective or that the load was insecure.[69] Where D secured his bails of straw to the trailer in a manner that had been in use for over 25 years without mishap, it was not reasonably open to the jury to convict on the basis that it was an 'inherently dangerous' system under s 2.[70]

64 E. J. Griew, Archbold News [1995] Issue 2, p 4.

65 *Marchant* [2004] 1 All ER 1187, [2003] Crim LR 806.

66 Cf *Crossman* [1986] RTR 49, CA (insecure load).

67 A jury has held that a motorist driving at 145 mph, more than twice the speed limit, was not driving dangerously, apparently having regard to the high quality of the vehicle, the ability of the driver and, presumably, the prevailing road conditions: (1999) The Times, 25 Mar.

68 *A-G's Reference (No 4 of 2000)* [2001] RTR 415, [2001] Crim LR 578.

69 See *Marchant* [2004] 1 All ER 1187 on the position where the vehicle has an authorization for use on the roads from the Secretary of State.

70 *Few* [2005] EWCA Crim 728.

The danger it has been held, is 'obvious' only if it could be 'seen or realized at first glance, evident to' the competent and careful driver: *Strong*[71] where the fatal corrosion of the car, which D had bought only a few days earlier, could have been discovered only by going underneath it. The danger was not 'obvious.' The court has subsequently suggested that *Strong* was not attempting to lay down a precise formula, and that 'obvious' was an ordinary English word that did not require elaboration.[72]

If a driver is aware of facts which would not be obvious in this sense he may nevertheless be guilty since the Act provides that regard must be had to any circumstances shown to be within his knowledge. If D is reasonably unaware, for example, of the tendency of a car to swerve to the right when braked hard, D cannot be held to have driven dangerously or even carelessly, but once D becomes aware of this tendency he may properly be held to have driven dangerously if it would then be obvious to a competent and careful driver that to drive the car with this tendency would be dangerous.[73] Similarly, D's actual knowledge of an uneven road surface may count against him though other drivers would be unaware of the hazard. More may be expected of a professional driver than of the private motorist.[74] An employed driver, however, cannot generally be expected to do more than to comply with the apparently reasonable instructions of his employer.

3. Causing death by dangerous or careless driving[75]

By s 1 of the Road Traffic Act 1988, as substituted by s 1 of the Road Traffic Act 1991:

A person who causes the death of another person by driving a mechanically propelled vehicle dangerously on a road or other public place is guilty of an offence.

The offence is triable only on indictment and is punishable by imprisonment for 14 years[76] and/or a fine.

At common law a motorist who by his driving causes death may be convicted of manslaughter.[77] In practice juries have been reluctant to convict motorists of manslaughter save in the most exceptional circumstances[78] so in 1956 it was made a statutory offence to cause death by driving a motor vehicle on a road 'recklessly, or at a speed or in a manner dangerous to the public'. Following the recommendations of the James Committee this offence, like the offence of reckless and dangerous driving,[79] was truncated to causing death by reckless driving. The House of Lords at one time thought

[71] [1995] Crim LR 428. See also *Roberts and George* [1997] RTR 462, [1997] Crim LR 209.

[72] *Marsh* [2002] EWCA Crim 137.

[73] Cf *Haynes v Swain* [1975] RTR 40, DC, above, n 38.

[74] *Roberts and George* [1997] Crim LR 209.

[75] On the application of the offences see S. Cunningham, 'The Reality of Vehicular Homicides: Convictions for Murder, Manslaughter and Causing Death by Dangerous Driving' [2001] Crim LR 679.

[76] Criminal Justice Act 2003, s 285 (after 14 February 2004). Higher sentences will be imposed: *Afzal* [2005] EWCA Crim 384.

[77] *United States of America Government v Jennings* [1983] 1 AC 624, [1982] 3 All ER 104, HL.

[78] See *Seymour* [1983] 2 AC 493, [1983] 2 All ER 1058, HL. See also I. Brownlee and M. Seneveratine, 'Killing with Cars After *Adomako*: Time for Some Alternatives' [1995] Crim LR 389. On the illogicality of the offence, see B. McKenna, 'Causing Death by Reckless or Dangerous Driving' [1970] Crim LR 67.

[79] See above, p 1012.

that the offences of manslaughter and causing death by reckless driving were coextensive in law[80] but accepted that in fact juries were more likely to convict of the causing death offence. Under the law as substituted, however, causing death by reckless driving is superseded by causing death by dangerous driving, a more broadly based offence.

Clearly, following *Adomako*, a charge of manslaughter will only be appropriate where there is a risk of death from the manner of the driving; a risk of serious injury will not do. Furthermore, the CPS guidance suggests that manslaughter will very rarely be appropriate and should be reserved for 'very grave' cases. In particular, it might be appropriate where a vehicle has been used as an instrument of attack (but where D lacks the necessary intent for murder),[81] 'or to cause fright and death results'. In addition, it may be appropriate in hit and run cases where the death did not arise from the manner of the defendant's driving but the susbequent failure to comply with the duty under s 170 of the Road Traffic Act 1988 following an accident. Manslaughter should also be considered where the driving is otherwise than on a road or other public place, or when the vehicle driven was not mechanically propelled since in these cases the statutory offences do not apply.[82]

The elements of causation and what constitutes a human being have been considered above in relation to murder (see Ch 13).

The attitude of the law towards offences depending on the chance whether a particular evil consequence occurs has been considered above. This is a particularly conspicuous example of the importance attached to harm done and the *North Report*[83] canvassed the arguments for and against but concluded that the offence should be retained:

> Two main factors have influenced our thinking. To abolish the offence in the absence of compelling reasons for doing so would mean that some cases of very bad driving were not dealt with appropriate seriousness. Repeal of section 1 would be seen as a down-grading of bad driving as a criminal activity. This is not a message which we wish to convey. Secondly, though logic might pull us towards arguments in favour of abolition neither English nor Scots law in fact relies entirely on intent as the basis for offences. There seems to be a strong public acceptance that, if the consequence of a culpable act is death, then this consequence should lead to a more serious charge being brought than if death had not been the result. We concur with this view.[84]

Developments since the Report have emphasized this attitude. The penalty for causing death by dangerous driving has been increased from five to 10 years, and now to 14 years and the Road Traffic Act 1991, inserting a new s 3A into the Road Traffic Act 1988, has created new offences, triable only on indictment and punishable with 10 years' imprisonment, of causing death by careless or inconsiderate driving when under the influence of drink or drugs. The new section provides:

> If a person causes the death of another person by driving a mechanically propelled vehicle on a road or other public place without due care and attention, or without reasonable consideration for other persons using the road or place, and –
>
> (a) he is, at the time when he is driving, unfit to drive through drink or drugs, or

80 *Seymour*, supra. See above, p 482.
81 See J. Spencer, 'Motor Vehicles as Weapons of Offence' [1985] Crim LR 29.
82 www.cps.gov.uk/legal/section9/chapter_b.html#30.
83 At 6.1–6.9. 84 At 6.9.

(b) he has consumed so much alcohol that the proportion of it in his breath, blood or urine at that time exceeds the prescribed limit, or

(c) he is, within 18 hours after that time, required to provide a specimen in pursuance of section 7 of this Act, but without reasonable excuse fails to provide it,

he is guilty of an offence.

This section appears to create six offences. It is well established that simple careless and inconsiderate driving are separate offences and each is a further separate offence according to whether it is combined with (a) or (b) or (c). Where these offences are charged in the alternative to causing death by dangerous driving, the jury will need careful direction. In some instances, it will not be appropriate to leave the alternative charge of causing death by careless driving, as where the only issue is whether D was asleep.[85]

It is noteworthy that, even where the most grievous injury short of death is caused by dangerous or careless driving, the offender is punishable by only two years' imprisonment or a fine respectively.[86] Offences (a), (b) and (c), when not combined with careless or inconsiderate driving causing death, are punishable with six months, six months and a fine respectively, whatever non-fatal injuries they may have caused. Death, will have a dramatic effect on the gravity of the offence. It seems, as Lord Lowry said when explaining the court's refusal to extend the defence of duress to murder, that it is 'the stark fact of death' which weighs so heavily.

The relevant principles of causation appear to be the same as in homicide generally and these are discussed elsewhere.[87] It is however worthy of note here that, where the dangerous condition of the vehicle results in its being stationary on the road, creating an obstruction which is a contributory cause of a fatal accident, the driver who ought to have known of the vehicle's condition is guilty of causing death.[88] D may be convicted of causing death by dangerous driving even though it would not have been obvious to a careful and competent driver that there was any danger of personal injury so long as there was an obvious risk of serious damage to property; this seems a particularly unwarrantable extension of liability for an unforeseen death.[89]

4. Reform

In February 2005, the government announced proposals for reform in *Consultation Paper: Review of Road Traffic Offences Involving Bad Driving*.[90] The paper puts forward a

85 *Hart* [2003] EWCA Crim 1268.

86 There have been calls for an offence of causing serious injury by dangerous driving. See the discussion by Cunningham above. There is, it seems, nothing to prevent charges of dangerous driving and offences against the person such as grievous bodily harm being charged together: *Bain* [2005] EWCA Crim 07.

87 Above, Ch 4. In this context, however, it needs to be noted that it is not enough that D brings about a death *while* driving dangerously; the dangerous driving must be the *cause* of the death. Cf *O'Neale* [1988] Crim LR 122, CA; *Hand v DPP* [1991] Crim LR 473, DC.

88 *Skelton* [1995] Crim LR 635, rejecting an argument that, by the time of the crash, the act of dangerous driving was spent.

89 See also *Jeshani* [2005] EWCA Crim 146.

90 www.homeoffice.gov.uk/docs4/consult_roadtraffic.htm.

set of proposals including: a new offence of causing death by careless driving, with a maximum of five years' imprisonment; a new offence dealing with death resulting from illegal (disqualified and unlicensed) driving with a maximum penalty of five years; a requirement for the courts to take serious injuries into account when sentencing; to make community penalties more readily available for non-imprisonable offences; defining careless driving in statute; and allowing the courts to find defendants guilty of a statutory bad driving offence as an alternative to manslaughter so as to ensure those found not guilty of manslaughter do not escape the law altogether.

It is submitted that many of these offences are unnecessary. Sentencing powers allow for such factors to be considered.

Bibliography

Abbott, C, 'The Appropriateness of Strict Liability in Environmental Law' (2004) Environmental Law and Management 67.

Adams, JN, 'Trespass Under the Theft and Firearms Act' (1969) 119 NLJ 655.

Addison, N, and Lawson-Cruttenden, T, *Harassment Law and Practice* (1998).

Akdeniz, Y 'Section 3 of the Computer Misuse Act 1990–An Antidote for Computer Viruses' [1996] Web Jnl CLI.

Akdeniz, Y, 'Cybercrime' in *E-Commerce Law & Regulation Encyclopaedia* (2003).

Alexander, L, 'Criminal Liability for Omissions: An Inventory of Issues' in S Shute and A Simester (eds), *Criminal Law Theory: Doctrines of the General Part* (2000).

Alexander, L, and Kessler, D, '*Mens Rea* and Inchoate Crimes' (1997) 87 J Crim L and Criminology 1138.

Alldridge, P, 'Developing the Defence of Duress' [1986] Crim LR 433.

Alldridge, P, 'Incontinent Dogs and the Law' (1990) 140 NLJ 1067.

Alldridge, P, 'The Doctrine of Innocent Agency' (1990) 2 Criminal Law Forum 45.

Alldridge, P, 'Attempted Murder of the Soul: Blackmail, Privacy and Secrets' (1993) 13 OJLS 368.

Alldridge, P, 'Sex Lies and the Criminal Law' (1993) 44 NILQ 250.

Alldridge, P, 'Threat Offences the Case for Reform' [1994] Crim LR 176.

Alldridge, P, 'The Sexual Offences (Conspiracy and Incitement) Act 1996' [1997] Crim LR 30.

Alldridge, P, 'Making Criminal Law Known' in S Shute and A Simester (eds), *Criminal Law Theory* (2002)

Alldridge, P, *Money Laundering Law* (2003).

Allen, CK, 'The Nature of a Crime', Journal of Society of Comparative Legislation, February 1931, reprinted in Legal Duties, 221.

Allen, M, 'Consent and Assault' (1994) 58 J Crim Law 183.

Allen, M, 'Look Who's Stalking' [1996] Web Jnl CLI 1.

Altmann, S, 'A Patchwork Theory of Blackmail' (1993) U Pa L Rev 1639.

Amos, M, 'A Note on Contractual Restraint of Liberty' (1928) 44 LQR 464.

Andenaes, J, 'Ignorantia Juris in Scandinavian Law' in GOW Mueller *Essays in Criminal Science* (1961).

Andenaes, J, *The General Part of the Criminal Law of Norway* (1965).

Andrews, J, 'Robbery' [1966] Crim LR 524.

Andrews, JA, 'Uses and Misuses of the Jury' in P Glazebrook (ed), *Reshaping the Criminal Law: Essays in Honour of Glanville Williams* (1978).

Andrews, J, and Sherlock, A, 'Freedom of Expression–How Far Should it Go' [1995] 20(3) EL 329.

Anyangwe, C, 'Dealing with the Problem of Bad Cheques in France' [1978] Crim LR 31.

Archbold, F, *Criminal Pleading, Evidence and Practice* (2005).

Arden, M, 'Criminal Law at the Crossroads: the Impact on Human Rights from the Law Commission's Perspective and the Need for a Code' [1999] Crim LR 439.

Arlidge, A, 'The Trial of Dr David Moor' [2000] Crim LR 31.

Arlidge, A, and Parry, J, *Fraud in the Criminal Law* (2nd edn 1996).

Ashall, PA, 'Manslaughter the Impact of *Caldwell*' [1984] Crim LR 467.

Ashworth, A, 'The Doctrine of Provocation' [1976] CLJ 292.

Ashworth, A, 'Entrapment' [1978] Crim LR 137.

Ashworth, A, 'Excusable Mistake of Law' [1974] Crim LR 652.

Ashworth, A, 'Reason, Logic and Criminal Liability' (1975) 91 LQR 102.

Ashworth, A, 'Transferred Malice and Punishment for Unforeseen Consequences' in P Glazebrook (ed), *Reshaping the Criminal Law: Essays in Honour of Glanville Williams* (1978).

Ashworth, A, 'The Elasticity of Mens Rea' in C Tapper, *Crime Proof and Punishment: Essays in Memory of Sir Rupert Cross* (1981).

Ashworth, A, 'Defining Criminal Offences without Harm' in P Smith (ed), *Criminal Law: Essays in Honour of JC Smith* (1987).

Ashworth, A, 'Criminal Attempts and the Role of Resulting Harm under the Code and under the Common law' (1988) 19 Rutgers LR 725.

Ashworth, A, 'Belief Intent and Criminal Liability' in J Eekelaar and J Bell (eds) Oxford Essays in Jurisprudence (1989).

Ashworth, A, 'The Scope of Criminal Liability for Omissions' (1989) 105 LQR 424.

Ashworth, A, 'Reform of the Law of Murder' [1990] Crim LR 75.

Ashworth, A, 'Interpreting Criminal Statutes: A Crisis of Legality' (1991) 117 LQR 419.

Ashworth, A, 'Taking the Consequences' in S Shute, J Gardner, and J Horder, *Action and Value in the Criminal Law* (1993).

Ashworth, A, 'Criminal Liability in a Medical Context: the Treatment of Good Intentions' in A Simester and ATH Smith (eds), *Harm and Culpability* (1996).

Ashworth, A, and Blake, M, 'The Presumption of Innocence in English Criminal Law' [1996] Crim LR 306.

Ashworth, A, 'Is the Criminal Law a Lost Cause?' (2000) 116 LQR 225.

Ashworth A, 'HRA 1998 and Substantive Law' [2000] Crim LR 564.

Ashworth, A, 'Testing Fidelity to Legal Values: Official Involvement in Criminal Justice' (2000) 63 MLR 633.

Ashworth, A, *Sentencing and Criminal Justice* (3rd edn 2000).

Ashworth, A, 'Redrawing the Boundaries of Entrapment' [2002] Crim LR 161.

Ashworth, A, 'Testing Fidelity to Legal Values: Official Involvement and Criminal Justice' in S Shute and A Simester (eds), *Criminal Law Theory: Doctrines of the General Part* (2002).

Ashworth, A, 'Robbery Reassessed' [2002] Crim LR 851.

Ashworth, A, 'Social Control and Anti-Social Behaviour: the Subversion of Human Rights?' (2004) 120 LQR 263.

Ashworth, A, Principles of Criminal Law (4th edn 2003).

Ashworth, A, and Redmayne, M, *The Criminal Process: An Evaluative Study* (3rd edn 2005).

Ashworth, A, and Steiner, E, 'Criminal Omissions and Public Duties: The French Experience' (1990) 10 LS 153.

Atiyah, PS, *Vicarious Liability in the English Law of Torts* (1967).

Atkinson, SB, 'Life, Birth and Live Birth' (1904) 20 LQR 134.

Austin, JH, 'A Plea for Excuses' in H Morris (ed), *Freedom and Responsibility* (1961).

Babcock, R, 'The Psychology of Stalking' in P Infield and G Platford *The Law of Harassment and Stalking* (2000).

Bagshaw, R, 'Legal Proof of Knowledge' in

P Mirfield and R Smith (eds), *Essays in Honour of Colin Tapper* (2003).

Bailey, S, Ching, P, Gunn, M, and Ormerod, D, *Smith Bailey and Gunn, The Modern English Legal System* (4th edn 2001).

Bailey, S, Harris, D, and Ormerod, D, *Bailey Harris and Jones, Civil Liberties Cases and Materials* (5th edn 2001).

Bailey, V, and Blackburn, S, 'The Punishment of Incest Act 1908: A Case Study in Law Creation' [1979] Crim LR 708.

Baird, V, and Wade, C, 'The Criminal Procedure (Insanity and Unfitness to Plead) Act 1991 and the Juries Act 1974: Irreconcilable Problems' [1999] Crim LR 656.

Baker, E, 'Human Rights and McNaghten and the 1991 Act' [1994] Crim LR 84.

Baker, E, 'Taking European Criminal Law Seriously' [1998] Crim LR 361.

Baldwin, R, 'The New Punitive Regulation' (2004) 67 MLR 351.

Ball, C, 'Youth Justice: Half A Century of Responses to Youth offending' [2004] Crim LR 167.

Bamforth, N, 'Sadomasochism and Consent' [1994] Crim LR 661.

Bates, F, 'Pornography and The Expert Witness' (1978) 20 Crim LQ 250.

Baty, T, *Vicarious Liability* (1916).

Beatson, J, and Simester, A, 'Stealing One's Own Property' (1999) 115 LQR 372.

Bedford, Sybille, *The Best We Can Do* (1958).

Bell, MD, Moss E, and Murphy, PG, 'Brainstem Death Testing in the UK — Time for Reappraisal?' (2004) 92 Br J Anaesthesia 633–40.

Bennett, B, *Abortion* (2004).

Bennion, F,'The Drafting of Section 3 of the Theft Act 1978' [1980] Crim LR 670.

Bennion, F, 'Criminalising Children Under the Sexual Offences Bill' (2003) 167 JP 784.

Bentham, J, *Principles of Morals and Legislation* Harrison (ed) (1789).

Bergman, D, *The Case for Corporate Responsibility* (2000).

Beynon, H, 'Doctors as Murderers' [1982] Crim LR 17.

Beynon, H, 'Causation, Omissions and Complicity' [1987] Crim LR 539.

Bingham, T (Lord Bingham of Cornhill), 'A Criminal Code: Must We Wait For Ever?' [1998] Crim LR 694.

Binning, P, 'When Dishonesty is Not Enough' (2004) 154 NLJ 1042.

Birch, DJ, 'The Foresight Saga: The Biggest Mistake of All' [1988] Crim LR 4.

Birds, J, 'Consent of the Owner under a Motor Policy' [1998] J Bus Law 421.

Blackstone, W, *Commentaries on the Laws of England* 4 vols (17th edn 1830).

Blake, L, 'The Innocent Purchaser and Section 22 of the Theft Act' [1972] Crim LR 494.

Blake, L, 'The Erstwhile Innocent Purchaser of Stolen Goods' (1982) J Crim Law 220.

Block, W, 'The Logic of the Argument of Legalising Blackmail' [2001] Bracton LJ 61.

Block, W, and Mcgee, R, 'Blackmail as a Victimless Crime' [1999] Bracton LJ 24.

Blom-Cooper, L, 'Life Until Death' [1999] Crim LR 899.

Blom-Cooper, L, and Drewry, G, *Law and Morality* (1976).

Bogg, AL, and Stanton-Ife, J, 'Protecting the Vulnerable: Legality, Harm and Theft' (2003) 23 LS 402.

Bowers, J, *A Practical Approach to Employment Law* (7th edn 2005).

Bowland, F, 'Intoxication and Criminal Liability' (1986) J Crim Law 100.

Brabyn, M, 'A Sequel to *Seymour* Made in Hong Kong' [1987] Crim LR 84.

Brackenridge, C, and Williams, Y, 'Incest in the 'Family' of Sport' (2004) 154 NLJ 179.

Brady, J, 'Recklessness, Negligence, Indifference and Awareness' (1980) 43 MLR 381.

Brahams, D, 'Putting Arthur's Case in Perspective' [1986] Crim LR 387.

Brazier, M, 'Criminal Trustees?' (1975) 39 Conv (NS) 29.

Brennan, F, 'The Crime and Disorder Act 1998: (2) Racially Motivated Crime: The Response of the Criminal Justice System' [1999] Crim LR 17.

Brett, P, *An Inquiry into Criminal Guilt* (1963).

Brett, P, 'The Physiology of Provocation' [1970] Crim LR 634.

Brett, P, 'Strict Responsibility: Possible solutions' (1974) 37 MLR 417.

Bridge, N, 'The European Communities and the Criminal Law' [1976] Crim LR 88.

Briggs, A, 'In Defence of Manslaughter' [1983] Crim LR 764.

Briggs, H, *Euthanasia, Death with Dignity and the Law* (2002).

Bronnit, S, 'Spreading Disease and the Criminal Law' [1994] Crim LR 21.

Brown, JG, 'Blackmail as Private Justice' (1993) U Pa L Rev 1935.

Brown, D, and Ellis, T, 'Policing Low-Level Disorder: Police Use of s 5 of the Public Order Act 1986' (1994) HORS 135.

Brownlie, I, *Law of Public Order and National Security* (2nd edn 1981).

Brownlee, I, 'Superior Orders–Time for a New realism' [1989] Crim LR 396.

Brownlee, I, and Seneveratine, M, 'Killing with Cars After Adomako: Time for Some Alternatives' [1995] Crim LR 389.

Buchanan, A, and Virgo, G, 'Duress and Mental Abnormality' [1999] Crim LR 517.

Budd, M, and Lynch, A, 'Voluntariness, Causation, and Strict Liability' [1978] Crim LR 74.

Budd, T, *Burglary of Domestic Dwellings: Findings from the British Crime Survey* (1999).

Burchell, FM, Milton, JRL, and Burchell, JM, *South African Criminal Law and Procedure Vol I* (1983).

Burchell, J, 'Joint Enterprise and Common Purpose' (1997) SACJ 125.

Burnley, E, 'Using the Law on Racially Aggravated Offences' [2003] Crim LR 28–36.

Burnley, E, and Rose, G, 'Racist Offending: How Is the Law Working?' (2002) HORS 244.

Burnside, J, 'The Sexual Offences (Amendment) Act 2000: The Head of a 'Kiddy Libber' and the Torso of a 'Child-Saver'?' [2001] Crim LR 425.

Busuttill, A and McCall Smith, A, 'Fright, Stress and Homicide' (1990) 54 J Crim L 257.

Butler, Lord, *Report of the Committee on Mentally Abnormal Offenders* (1975), Cmnd 6244.

Buxton, R, 'Complicity in the Criminal Code' (1969) 85 LQR 252.

Buxton, R, 'Negligence and Constructive Crime' [1969] Crim LR 112

Buxton, R, *Annual Survey of Commonwealth Law* [1970].

Buxton, R, 'Inchoate Offences: Incitement and Attempt' [1973] Crim LR 656.

Buxton, R, 'The Working Party on Inchoate Offences: Incitement and Attempt' [1973] Crim LR 656, 662.

Buxton, R, 'The Case of Blasphemous Libel' [1978] Crim LR 673.

Buxton, R, 'The New Murder' [1980] Crim LR 521.

BUXTON, R, 'Circumstances, Consequences and Attempted Rape' [1984] Crim LR 25.

BUZZARD, J, 'Intent' [1978] Crim LR 5.

CALVERT-SMITH, D, AND O'DOHERTY, S, 'Legislative Technique and Human Rights–A Response' [2003] Crim LR 384.

CAMPBELL, A, AND KIBBLE, N, 'Dishonoured Cheques: A Comparative Analysis' [2001] JIBL 77.

CAMPBELL, C, 'Two Steps Backwards: The Criminal Justice (Terrorism and Conspiracy) Act 1998' [1999] Crim LR 941.

CAMPBELL, K, 'Offence and Defence' in I Dennis (ed) *Criminal Law and Criminal Justice* (1987).

CAMPBELL, K, 'The Test of Dishonesty in Ghosh' [1994] 43 CLJ 349, 354.

CAMPS, F, AND HARVARD, J, 'Causation in Homicide–A Medical View' [1957] Crim LR.

CARD, R, *Public Order: The New Law* (1987).

CARD, R, *Public Order Law* (2000).

CARD, R, *Sexual Offences: The New Law* (2004).

CARSON, WG, 'Some Sociological Aspects of Strict Liability and the Enforcement of Factory Legislation' (1970) 33 MLR 396.

CARTER, P, AND HARRISON, R, *Offences of Violence* (1987).

CHALMERS, J, 'Fireraising by Omission' (2004) SLT 59.

CHALMERS, J, 'Merging Provocation and Diminished Responsibility: Some Reasons for Scepticism' [2004] Crim LR 198.

CHARLESWORTH, A, 'Addiction and Hacking' (1993) 143 NLJ 540.

CHILDS, M, 'Outraging Public Decency: The Offence of Offensiveness' [1991] PL 20.

CHILDS, M, 'Medical Manslaughter and Corporate Liability' (1999) LS 316.

CHILDS, M, 'Sexual Autonomy and the Law' (2001) 64 MLR 309.

CHOO, A, *Abuse of Process and Judicial Stays of Criminal Proceedings* (1993).

CHRISTOPHER, RL, 'Unknowing Justification and the Logical Necessity of the *Dadson* Principle in Self-Defence'(1995) 15 OJLS 229.

CLARK, RS, *Essays on Criminal Law in New Zealand* (1971).

CLARKE, B, AND MEINTJES-VAN DER WALT, L. 'Stalking: Do We Need a Statute?' [1998] 115 South African Law Jnl 729.

CLARKSON, C, 'Theft and Fair Labelling' (1993) 56 MLR 554.

CLARKSON, C, 'Complicity, Powell and Manslaughter' [1998] Crim LR 556.

CLARKSON, C, 'Context and Culpability in Involuntary Manslaughter: Principle or Instinct' in A Ashworth and B Mitchell (eds) *Rethinking English Homicide Law* (2000).

CLARKSON, C, 'Necessary Action: A New Defence' [2004] Crim LR 81.

CLARKSON, C, CRETNEY, A, DAVIS, G, AND SHEPHERD, J, 'Assaults: The Relationship between Seriousness, Criminalisation and Punishment' [1994] Crim LR 4.

CLAYTON, G, 'Reclaiming Public Ground: the Right to Peaceful Assembly' (2000) 63 MLR 252.

CLAYTON, R, AND TOMLINSON, H, *Civil Actions Against the Police* (3rd edn 2003).

COHEN, I, 'Inciting the Impossible' [1979] Crim LR 239.

COHEN, MD, 'The Actus Reus and Offences of Situation' (1972) 7 Israel Law Rev 186.

COKE, SIR EDWARD, *Institutes of the Laws of England*, 4 vols (1797).

COLE-WILSON, YI, 'Old Baily Hacks: Some Reflections on R v Gold and Schifren' (1987) 137 NLJ 118.

COLEMAN, A, *Intellectual Property Law* (1994).

COOK, K, *Wildlife Law: Conservation and Biodiversity* (2004).

Cooke, Lord 'One Golden Thread' in *Turning Points in the Common Law* (The Hamlyn Lectures 1997).

Cooper, S. and Allen, M, 'Appropriation After *Gomez*' (1993) 57 J Crim Law 186.

Corbett, C, *Car Crime* (2003).

Corker, D, and Young, D, *Abuse of Process in Criminal Proceedings* (2001).

Corrado, ML (ed), *Justification and Excuse in the Criminal Law: A Collection of Essays* (1994).

Corstens, G, 'Criminal law in the first Pillar?' (2003) 11 Euro Jnl of Crime, Criminal Law and Criminal Justice 131.

Coulter, CW, 'The Unnecessary Rule of Consistency in Conspiracy Trials' (1986) 135 U Pa LR 223.

Coutts, J, 'Obstructing the Police' (1956) 19 MLR 411.

Craig, P, and De Búrca, G, *EU Law: Text, Cases and Materials* (3rd edn 2003).

Cram, I, 'Criminalising Child Pornography–A Canadian Study in Freedom of Expression and Charter-led Judicial Review of Legislative Policy Making' (2002) Journal of Criminal Law 359.

Cross, R, 'Duress and Aiding and Abetting (A Reply)' (1953) 69 LQR 354.

Cross, R, 'Specific Intent' [1961] Crim LR 510.

Cross, R, 'The Theft Bill 1: Theft and Deception' [1966] Crim LR 415.

Cross, R, 'Protecting Confidential Information under the Criminal Law of Theft and Fraud' (1991) OJLS 264.

Crystal-Kirk, D, 'Forgery Reforged' (1986) 49 MLR 608.

Cunningham, S, 'The Reality of Vehicular Homicides: Convictions for Murder, Manslaughter and Causing Death by Dangerous Driving' [2001] Crim LR 679.

Cunningham, S, 'Dangerous Driving a Decade On' [2002] Crim LR 945.

Curwood, J (ed), *A Treatise of the Pleas of the Crown* (8th edn 1795).

Cutcheon, M, 'Sports, Violence and the Criminal Law' [1994] 45 NILQ 267.

Dashwood, A, 'Logic and the Lords in Majewski' [1977] Crim LR 532 and 591.

Davies, C, 'Protection of Intellectual Property–A Myth?' [2004] J Crim Law 398.

Davies, M, 'Consent after the House of Lords: Taking and Leading Astray the House of Lords' (1993) 13 LS 308.

Davies, M, 'Filling in the Gaps' [2003] Crim LR 243.

Davies, M, 'Lawmakers, Law Lords and Legal Fault' (2004) J Crim L 130.

Davies, P, 'Computer Misuse' (1995) 145 NLJ 1776.

De Bùrca, G, and Gardner, S, 'Codification of the Criminal Law' (1990) 10 OJLS 559.

Dean, M, 'Fitness to Plead' [1960] Crim LR 79 at 82.

Dean, M, '*Hedley Byrne* and the Eager Business Man' (1968) 31 MLR 322.

Dell, S, 'Wanted; An Insanity Defence that Can be Used' [1983] Crim LR 431.

Dell, S, *Murder into Manslaughter: the Diminished Responsibility Defence in Practice* (1984).

Dennis, IH, 'The Rationale of Criminal Conspiracy' (1977) 93 LQR 39.

Dennis, IH, 'Duress Murder and Criminal Responsibility' [1980] 106 LQR 208.

Dennis, IH, 'Manslaughter by Omission' (1980) CLP 255.

Dennis, IH, 'The Criminal Attempts Act 1981' [1982] Crim LR 5.

Dennis, IH, 'The Mental Element for Accessories' in *Essays in Honour of J.C. Smith* (1987).

Dennis, IH, 'Intention and Complicity: A Reply' [1988] Crim LR 649.

DENNIS, IH, *The Law of Evidence* (2nd edn 2002).

DENNO, DW, 'How Psychological Research on Consciousness Can Enlighten the Criminal Law' [2002] Amicus Curiae 28.

Department of Health: *The Removal, Retention and Use of Human Organs and Tissue from Post-Mortem Examination* (2001).

DEVLIN, P, *Easing the Passing* (1985).

DEVLIN, P, 'Law, Democracy and Morality' (1962) 110 U Pa Law Rev 635 at 642 (reprinted in *The Enforcement of Morals* (1965)).

Devlin P Maccabaean Lecture: 'The Enforcement of Morals' (1959) 45 Proc of British Academy, 129 reprinted in *The Enforcement of Morals* (1965).

DICEY, AV, *Introduction to the Study of the Law of the Constitution* (10th edn 1959).

DICKENS, BM, *Abortion and the Law* (1966).

DINAN, D, *Ever Closer Union* (2nd edn 1999).

DINE, J, 'European Community Criminal Law' [1993] Crim LR 246.

DIXON, R, AND KHAN, K, *Archbold, International Criminal Courts. Practice, Procedure and Evidence.*

DOBBS, L, AND SUTTON, R (eds), *Fraud: Law, Practice and Procedure* (2004).

DOBE, KS, AND CHOKAR, SS, 'Muslims, ethnicity and the law' (2000) 4 Int J of Discrimination and Law 369.

DOEGAR, RC, 'Strict Liability in Criminal Law and Larsonneur Revisited' [1998] Crim LR 791.

DORAN, S, 'Alternative Defences' [1991] Crim LR 878.

DRESSLER, J, 'Provocation: Partial Justification or Partial Excuse' (1988) 51 MLR 467.

DRESSLER, J, 'Battered Women Who Kill Their Sleeping Tormentors' in S Shute and A Simester (eds), *Criminal Law Theory* (2002).

DUFF, A, 'Fitness to Plead and Fair Trials' [1994] Crim LR 419.

DUFF, RA, 'Regarding Intention: The Criminal Attempts Act 1981 s 1(3)' [1990] XII(2) Liverpool Law Review 161.

DUFF, RA, 'Can I Help You? Accessorial Liability and the Intention to Assist'(1990) LS 165.

DUFF, RA, 'The Politics of Intention: A Response to Norrie' [1990] Crim LR 637.

DUFF, RA, *Intention Agency and Criminal Liability* (1990).

DUFF, RA, 'Attempts and the Problem of the Missing Circumstance' (1991) 42 NILQR 87.

DUFF, RA, 'The Circumstances of an Attempt' (1991) 50 CLJ 100.

DUFF, RA, 'Recklessness in Attempts (Again)' (1995) 15 OJLS 309.

DUFF, RA, *Criminal Attempts* (1996).

DUFF, RA, 'Rule Violations and Wrongdoing' in S Shute and A Simester (eds), *Criminal Law Theory* (2002).

DWORKIN, R, *Life's Dominion* (1993).

EADY, D, AND SMITH, ATH, *Arlidge, Eady and Smith on Concept* (2nd edn 1999).

EAST, EH, *A Treatise of the Pleas of the Crown* 2 vols (1803).

EDWARDS, JLI, 'Another View' [1954] Crim LR 898.

EDWARDS, JLl, 'Criminal Attempts' (1952) 15 MLR 345.

EDWARDS, JLl, *Mens Rea in Statutory Offences* (1955).

EDWARDS, SM, 'A Plea for Censorship' (1991) 141 NLJ 1478.

EDWARDS, SM, 'On the Contemporary Application of the Obscene Publications Act 1959' [1998] Crim LR 843.

Edwards, SM, 'Mad Bad or Pre-Menstrual' (1988) 138 NLJ 456.

EDWARDS, SM, 'Perjury and Perverting the

Course of Justice Considered' [2003] Crim LR 525.

Edwards, SM, *Sex and Gender in the Legal Process* (1996).

Elliott, DW, 'Dishonesty Under the Theft Act' [1972] Crim LR 625.

Elliott, DW, 'Law and Fact in Theft Act Cases' [1976] Crim LR 707.

Elliott, DW, 'Theft and Related Problems–England, Australia and the USA Compared' (1977) 26 ICLQ 110.

Elliott, DW, 'Mens rea in statutory conspiracy' [1978] Crim LR 202.

Elliott, DW, 'Dialogues on the Theft Act' in P Glazebrook (ed), *Reshaping the Criminal Law: Essays in Honour of Glanville Williams* (1978).

Elliott, DW, 'Dishonesty in Theft: A Dispensable Concept' [1982] Crim LR 395 and 406.

Elliott, DW, 'Criminal Damage' [1988] Crim LR 403.

Elliott, DW, 'Necessity, Duress and Self-Defence' [1989] Crim LR 611.

Elliott, DW, ''*Brutus v Cozens*', Decline and Fall' [1989] Crim LR 323.

Elliott, DW, 'Directors' Thefts and Dishonesty' [1991] Crim LR 732.

Elliott, DW, 'Endangering Life by Destroying or Damaging Property' [1997] Crim LR 382, 393.

Elliott, ID, 'Responsibility for Involuntary Acts: *Ryan v The Queen*' (1968) 41 ALJ 497.

Emmerichs, MB, 'Trials of Women for Homicide in Nineteenth Century England' (1993) 5 Women and Criminal Justice 99.

Emmerson, B, and Ashworth, A, *Human Rights and Criminal Justice* (2001).

Emmins, C, 'Unfitness to Plead: Thoughts Prompted by Glenn Pearson's Case' [1986] Crim LR 604.

English, P, 'Provocation and Attempted Murder' [1973] Crim LR 727.

Epstein, R, 'Blackmail Inc.' (1983) 50 U Chi LR 553.

Eser, A, Fletcher, G, Cornils K, et al (eds), *Justification and Excuse: Comparative Perspectives* (1987).

Essen, R, 'Cybercrime: a Growing Problem' (2002) J Crim L 269.

Evans, C, *Freedom of Religion under the European Convention on Human Rights* (2001).

Evans, J, 'Dilemma of Proof and the Extension of Criminal Statutes' [2003] Crim LR 181.

Fairweather, F, and Levy, S, 'Assaults on the Police: A Case of Mistaken Identity' [1994] Crim LR 817.

Fearon, G, 'All Party Internet (APIG) Report on the Computer Misuse Act' (2004) 15 Comps and Law 36.

Feinberg, J, 'The Moral Limits of the Criminal Law' vol 1 in J Feinberg *Harm to Others* (1984).

Feldman, D, *Civil Liberties and Human Rights in England and Wales* (2nd edn 2002).

Fennell, P, 'The Criminal Procedure (Insanity and Unfitness to Plead) Act 1991' (1992) 55 MLR 547.

Fenwick, H, and Philipson, G, 'Public Protest, the Human Rights Act, and Judicial Responses to Political Expression' (2000) PL 627.

Ferguson, PR, 'The Limits of the Automatism Defence' (1991) 36 J Law Soc Scotland 446.

Ferguson, PR, 'Codifying Criminal Law (1): A Critique of Scots Common Law' [2004] Crim LR 49

Ferguson, PR, 'Codifying Criminal Law (2): The Scots and the English Draft Codes Compared' [2004] Crim LR 105.

Ferguson, PW, 'Intention Agreement and Statutory Conspiracy' (1986) 102 LQR 26.

Ferris, G, 'The Origins of Larceny by Trick and Constructive Possession' [1998] Crim LR 17.

Field, S, and Jorg, N, 'Corporate Liability and Manslaughter: Should We be Going Dutch?' [1991] Crim LR 156.

Field, S, and Lynn, M, 'The Capacity for Recklessness' (1992) 12 LS 74.

Field, S, and Lynn, M, 'Capacity Recklessness and the House of Lords' [1993] Crim LR 127.

Finch, E, 'Stalking the Perfect Stalking Law: An Evaluation of the Efficacy of the Protection from Harassment Act 1997' [2002] Crim LR 703, 714.

Finch, E, *The Criminalisation of Stalking* (2001).

Finch, E, and Munro, V, 'Intoxicated Consent and the Boundaries of Drug Assisted Rape' [2003] Crim LR 773.

Finch, E, and Munro, V, 'The Sexual Offences Act 2003: Intoxicated Consent and Drug Assisted Rape Revisited' [2004] Crim LR 789.

Finkelstein, C, 'Involuntary Crimes, Voluntarily Committed' in S Shute and A Simester (eds) *Criminal Law Theory* (2002).

Finnis, JM, 'The Abortion Act: What Has Changed? [1971] Crim LR 3.

Fisher, J, and Bewsey, J, 'Laundering the Proceeds of Fiscal Crime' (2000) JIBL 11.

Fisher, J, Bewsey, J, Waters, M, and Ovey, E, *The Law of Investor Protection* (2nd edn 1996).

Fitzgerald, PJ, 'A Concept of Crime' [1960] Crim LR 257.

Fitzgerald, PJ, 'The Arrest of a Motor-Car' [1965] Crim LR 23.

Fitzpatrick, B, 'Strict liability and Article 6(2) of the European Convention on Human Rights: School Non-Attendance Offence (2004) 68 J Crim Law 16–24.

Fitzpatrick, D, 'Variations on Conspiracy'(1993) 143 NLJ 1180.

Fleming, JG, *Fleming on Torts* (8th edn 1992).

Fletcher, G, 'The Nature of Justifications' in S Shute, S Gardner, and J Horder (eds), *Action and Value in Criminal Law* (1993).

Fletcher, G, 'Blackmail: The Paradigmatic Crime' (1993) U Pa L Rev 1617.

Fletcher, GP, *Rethinking Criminal Law* (1978).

Fonda, J, 'New Labour, Old Hat: Youth Justice and the Crime and Disorder Act 1998' [1999] Crim LR 36.

Fortson, R, *Misuse of Drugs and Drug Trafficking Offences* (4th edn 2002).

Foster, Sir Michael, *A Report on Crown Cases and Discourses on the Crown Law* (3rd edn 1792).

Fowles, T, and Wilson, D, 'Racist and Religious Crime Data' (2004) 43 Howard Jnl of Crim Justice 441.

Fox, D, 'Bona Fide Purchase and the Currency of Money' [1996] 55 CLJ 547.

Fox, D, 'The Transfer of Legal Title to Money' [1996] Restitution LR 60.

Freeman, M, 'Death, Dying and the Human Rights Act 1998' (1999) 52 CLP 218.

Freeman, M, 'Denying Death its Dominion' (2002) 10 Med LR 245

Fry, C, 'Forgeries and Signatures on Paintings' (1993) 143 NLJ 1233.

Funk, TM, 'Justifying Justifications' (1999) OJLS 630.

Furse M, and Nash, S, 'Partners in Crime–the General Cartel Offence in UK Law' (2004) Int. Company and Commerical Law Review 138.

Gale, M, Gale, S, and Scanlon, G, 'Fraud and the Sale of Shares' [2001] Comp Law 98.

Gallagher, B, Christmann, K, Fraser, C, and Hodgson, B, 'International and

Internet Child Sexual Abuse and Exploitation–Issues Emerging from Research' (2003) CFLQ 353.

Gandhi, S, and James, J, 'The English Law of Blasphemy and the ECHR' [1998] EHRLR 430.

Gardiner, S, 'The Law and the Sportsfield' [1994] Crim LR 513

Gardner, J, 'Rationality and the Rule of Law in Offences Against the Person' [1994] CLJ 520.

Gardner, J, 'Justifications and Reasons' in A Simester and ATH Smith (eds), *Harm and Culpability* (1996).

Gardner, J, 'The Gist of Excuses' (1998) Buffalo Crim LR 575.

Gardner, J, and Macklem, T, 'No Provocation Without Responsibility: A Reply to Mackay and Mitchell' [2004] Crim LR 213.

Gardner, S, 'Duress in Attempted Murder' (1991) 107 LQR 389.

Gardner, S, 'Necessity's Newest Invention' (1991) 11 OJLS 125.

Gardner, S, 'Reiterating the Criminal Code' (1992) MLR 839.

Gardner, S, 'Appropriation in Theft: The Last Word' (1993) 109 LQR 194.

Gardner, S, 'The Importance of Majewski' (1994) 14 OJLS 279.

Gardner, S, 'Manslaughter by Gross Negligence' (1995) 111 LQR 22.

Gardner, S, 'Appreciating Olugboja' (1996) 16 LS 275.

Gardner, S, 'Property and Theft' [1998] Crim LR 35.

Geddis, A, 'Free Speech Martyrs or Unreasonable Threats to Social Peace? 'Insulting' Expression and s 5 of the Public Order Act 1986' [2004] PL 853.

Gelsthorpe, L, 'Much Ado About Nothing' (1999) CFLQ 209.

Giles, M, 'Judicial Law-Making in the Criminal Courts: The Case of Marital Rape' [1992] Crim LR 407.

Giles, M, 'Consensual Harm and the Public Interest' (1994) 57 MLR 101.

Giles, M, and Uglow, S, 'Appropriation and Manifest Criminality in Theft' (1992) 56 J Crim L 179.

Gill, M, *Commercial Robbery* (2000).

Gillespie, A, 'Children, Chatrooms and the Law' [2001] Crim LR 435.

Gillespie, A, 'Child Protection on the Internet–Challenges for Criminal Law' (2002) CFLQ 411.

Gillespie, A, 'The Sexual Offences Act 2003: (3) Tinkering With "Child Pornography"' [2004] Crim LR 361.

Ginsburg, DH, and Shechtman, P, 'Blackmail: An Economic Analysis of the Law' (1993) U Pa L Rev 1849.

Glazebrook, P, 'Attempting to Procure' [1959] Crim LR 774.

Glazebrook, P, 'Criminal Omissions: The Duty Requirements in Offences Against the Person'(1960) 76 LQR 386.

Glazebrook, P, 'Should We Have a Law of Attempted Crime' (1969) 85 LQR 28.

Glazebrook, P, 'The Law Commission's Working Paper on Forgery: Some Further Comments' [1970] Crim LR 554.

Glazebrook, P, 'Constructive Manslaughter and The Threshold Tort' [1970] CLJ 21.

Glazebrook, P, 'The Necessity Plea in English Criminal Law' [1972] CLJ 87.

Glazebrook, P, 'Situational Liability' in *Reshaping the Criminal Law: Essays in Honour of Glanville Williams* (1978).

Glazebrook, P, 'Thief or Swindler: Who Cares?' [1991] CLJ 389.

Glazebrook, P, 'Revising the Theft Acts' [1993] CLJ 191.

Glazebrook, P, 'How Old Do *You* Think She Was?' [2001] CLJ 26, 30.

Glazebrook, P, 'A Better Way of Convicting Businesses of Avoidable Deaths and Injuries' (2002) CLJ 405.

Glazebrook, P, 'Insufficient Child Protection' [2003] Crim LR 541.

Glover, J, *Causing Death and Saving Lives* (1977).

Gobert, J, 'Corporate Criminality: four models of fault' (1994) 14 LS 393.

Gobert, J, 'Corporate Criminality: New Crimes for the Times' [1994] Crim LR 722.

Gobert, J, 'Corporate Killing at Home and Abroad: Reflections on the Government Proposals' (2002) 118 LQR 72.

Gobert, J, and Mugnai, E, 'Coping with Corporate Criminality–Some Lessons from Italy' [2002] Crim LR 617.

Gobert, J, and Punch, M, *Rethinking Corporate Crime* (2003).

Goff, R (Lord Goff), 'The Mental Element in the Crime of Murder' (1988) 104 LQR 30.

Goff, R, and Jones, G, *The Law of Restitution* (6th edn 2002).

Gold, AD, 'An Untrimmed Beard' (1976) 19 Crim LQ 34.

Goldstein, AF, *The Insanity Defence* (1967).

Goodman, RN, 'When is a Document False in the Law of Forgery' (1952) 15 MLR 11.

Gordon, GH, *Criminal Law of Scotland* (2nd edn 1978).

Goss, J, 'A Postscript to the Trial of Dr David Moor' [2000] Crim LR 568.

Gough, S, 'Intoxication and Criminal Liability' (1996) 112 LQR 335.

Gough, S, 'Taking the Heat of Provocation' (1999) 19 OJLS 481.

Gough, S, 'Surviving without Majewski' [2000] Crim LR 719.

Graham, C, 'The Enterprise Act 2002 and Competition Law' (2004) 67 MLR 273.

Grantham, R, 'Corporate Knowledge: Identification or Attribution?' (1996) 59 MLR 732.

Gray, K, and Gray, S, 'Civil Rights, Civil Wrongs and Quasi-Public Space' [1999] 1 EHRLR 46.

Greaves, CS, *The Criminal Law Consolidation and Amendment Acts* (2nd edn 1862).

Greenfield, S, and Osborn, G (eds), *Law and Sport in Contemporary Society* (2000).

Gregory, J, and Lees, S, *Policing Sexual Assault* (1999).

Griew, E, 'It Must Have Been One of Them' [1989] Crim LR 129.

Griew, EJ, 'The Law Commission's Working Paper on Forgery: A General Comment' [1970] Crim LR 548.

Griew, EJ, 'Annotations on the Act', in *Current Law Statutes* (1978).

Griew, EJ, 'Consistency, Communication and Codification–Reflections on Two *Mens Rea* Words' in P Glazebrook (ed), *Reshaping the Criminal Law: Essays in Honour of Glanville Williams* (1978).

Griew, EJ, 'Reckless Damage and Reckless Driving–Living with Caldwell and Lawrence' [1981] Crim LR 743

Griew, EJ, 'Dishonesty–the Objections to Feely and Ghosh' [1985] Crim LR 341.

Griew, EJ, 'Stealing and Obtaining Bank Credits' [1986] Crim LR 356.

Griew, EJ, 'Unauthorised Overdrawing by Use of Cheque Card Abroad' [1987] 2 JIBL 116.

Griew, EJ, 'The Future of Diminished Responsibility' [1988] Crim LR 75.

Griew, EJ, *The Theft Acts* (7th edn 1995).

Griffiths, J, 'Assisted Suicide in the Netherlands' (1995) 58 MLR 232.

Griffiths, M, 'Internet Corporate Blackmail: a Growing Problem' (2004) 168 JP 632.

Gross, H, *A Theory of Criminal Justice* (1979).

GRUBB, A, 'The New Law on Abortion: Clarification or Ambiguity' [1991] Crim LR 659.

GRUBIN, D, 'What Constitutes Unfitness to Plead' [1993] Crim LR 748.

GUNN, M, AND ORMEROD, D, 'The Legality of Boxing' (1995) 15 LS 181.

GUNN M, AND SMITH, JC, 'Arthur's Case and the Right to Life of a Down's Syndrome Child' [1985] Crim LR 705.

HADDEN, T, 'Conspiracy to Defraud' [1996] CLJ 248.

HALE, LADY, 'A Pretty Pass–When Is There a Rights to Die?' [2003] 32 Common Law World Review 1.

HALE, M, *The History of the Pleas of the Crown* (1736).

HALL, J, 'Negligent Behaviour Should be Excluded from Criminal Liability' (1963) 63 Col LR 632.

HALL, J, *General Principles of Criminal Law* (2nd edn 1960).

HALL, J, *Theft Law and Society* (1952).

HALPIN, A, 'The Appropriate Appropriation' [1991] Crim LR 426.

HALPIN, A, 'The Test for Dishonesty' [1996] Crim LR 283, 294, and 289.

HALPIN, A, *Definitions in the Criminal Law* (2004).

HALSBURY, EARL OF, *The Laws of England* (4th edn: Lord Hailsham 1990 reissue).

HAMILTON, A, 'Live Streamed Sex Videos' (2003) 14(2) Computers and the Law 29.

HAMMOND, R, 'Theft of Information' (1984) 100 LQR 252.

HARDING C, AND JOSHUA, J, 'Breaking up the Hand Core: the Prospects for the Proposed Cartel Offence [2002] Crim LR 933.

HARE, I, 'A Compelling Case for the Code' (1993) 56 MLR 74.

HARE, I, 'Public Assembly: The New Highway Code' [1999] CLJ 265.

HARRIS, J, *An Evaluation of the Use and effectiveness of the Protection from Harassment Act 1997* Home Office Research Study 203 (2000).

HARRIS, J, AND GRACE, S, 'A Question of Evidence? Investigating and Prosecuting Rapes in the 1990s' (1999) HORS No 196.

HARRISON, R, 'Handling Stolen Goods for the Benefit of Another' (2000) 64 J Crim L 156.

HART, HLA, 'Law, Liberty and Morality; Hughes, "Morals and the Criminal Law"' (1962) 71 YLJ 662.

HART, HLA, 'Negligence, Mens Rea, and Criminal Responsibility' in *Punishment and Responsibility* (1968).

HART, HLA, *Punishment and Responsibility* (1968).

HART, HLA, 'Abortion Law Reform: The English Experience' (1972) 8 MULR 389.

HART, HLA, 'The House of Lords on Attempting the Impossible' in C Tapper (ed) *Crime Proof and Punishment: Essays in Honour of Sir Rupert Cross* (1981).

HART, HLA, AND HONORÉ, A, *Causation in the Law* (2nd edn 1985).

HART, HLA, *Jubilee Lectures* (1960).

HART, HLA, *The Morality of the Criminal Law* (1965).

HART, HM, 'The Aims of the Criminal Law' (1958) 23 Law and Contemporary Problems, 401 and 404.

HARTLEY, TC 'The Impact of European Community Law on the Criminal Process' [1981] Crim LR 75.

HARTLEY, TC, *The Foundations of European Community Law* (5th edn 2003).

HAWKINS, W, *A Treatise of the Pleas of the Crown* 2 vols (2nd edn 1960).

HAVARD, J, 'Therapeutic Abortion' [1958] Crim LR 600.

HEATON, R, 'Deceiving without Thieving' [2001] Crim LR 712.

HEATON, R, 'Dealing in Death' [2003] Crim LR 497.

HEPWORTH, M, 'The British Conception of Blackmail' (1975) Int Jnl of Criminology and Penology 1.

HEPWORTH, M, *Blackmail, Publicity and Secrecy in Everyday Life* (1975).

HEYDON, J, 'The Problems of Entrapment' [1973] CLJ 268.

HICKS, M, AND BRANSTON, G, 'Transexual Rape-A Loophole Closed?' [1997] Crim LR 526.

HIRSCH, A VON, AND JAREBORG, N, 'Gauging Criminal Harm: A Living Standard Analysis' (1991) 11 OJLS 1.

HIRST, M, 'Murder in England or Murder in Scotland' [1995] CLJ 488.

HIRST, M, 'Preventing the Lawful Burial of a Body' [1996] Crim LR 96.

HIRST, M, 'Assault, Battery and Indirect Violence' [1999] Crim LR 577.

HIRST, M, 'Guilty but of what' (2000) 4 E&P 31.

HIRST, M, *Jurisdiction and the Ambit of the Criminal Law* (2003).

HMSO: *Valuing People: A New Strategy for the 21st Century* (Cm 5086.2001).

HMSO: Report No 186 *Computer Misuse* (1989) Cmnd 819.

HOBHOUSE OF WOODBOROUGH, LORD, 'AGENCY AND THE CRIMINAL LAW' IN *Lex Mercatoria* (*Essays in Honour of Francis Reynolds*) (2000).

HOGAN, B, 'Victims as Parties to Crime' [1962] Crim LR 683.

HOGAN, B, 'Blackmail' [1966] Crim LR 474.

HOGAN, B, *Criminal Liability without Fault* (1969).

HOGAN, B, 'A Note on Death' [1972] Crim LR 80.

HOGAN, B, 'On Modernising the Law of Sexual Offences' in P Glazebrook (ed) *Reshaping the Criminal Law: Essays in Honour of Glanville Williams* (1978).

HOGAN, B, 'The Criminal Attempts Act and Attempting the Impossible' [1984] Crim LR 584.

HOGAN, B, 'The Principle of Legality' (1986) NLJ 267.

HOGAN, B, 'Omissions and the Duty Myth' in P Smith (ed), *Criminal Law: Essays in Honour of JC Smith* (1987).

HOGAN, B, 'The Dadson Principle' [1989] Crim LR 679

HOGGETT, J, 'The Abortion Act 1967' [1968] Crim LR 247.

HOLDER, C, 'Staying One Step Ahead of the Criminals' (2002) 10(3) IT Law 17.

HOLDSWORTH, Sir William, *A History of English Law* 14 vols (1923–64).

HOLROYD, J, 'The Reform of Jurisdiction over International Conspiracy' (2000) 64 J Crim L 323.

HOLROYD, J, 'Incitement, A Tale of Three Agents' (2001) J Crim Law 515.

Home Office: *Fraud Law Reform Consultation Paper on Proposals for Legislation* (2004).

Home Office: *New Measures to Control Prostitutes' Cards in Phone Boxes* (1999).

Home Office: *Entitlement Card and Identity Fraud* (2002).

Home Office: *Legislation on Identity Cards* (2004).

Home Office: *Violence: Reforming the Law of Offences against the Person* (1998).

HORDER, J, 'The Problem of Provocative Children' [1987] Crim LR 655.

HORDER, J, 'Cognition, Emotion and Criminal Culpability' (1990) 106 LQR 469.

HORDER, J, *Provocation and Responsibility* (1992).

HORDER, J, 'Pleading Involuntary Lack of Capacity' (1993) 52 CLJ 298.

HORDER, J, 'Occupying the Moral High Ground' [1994] Crim LR 334.

HORDER, J, 'Varieties of Intention, Criminal Attempts and Endangerment' (1994) 14 LS 335.

Horder, J, 'A Critique of the Correspondence Principle in Criminal Law' [1995] Crim LR 759.

Horder, J, 'Sobering Up' (1995) 58 MLR 534.

Horder, J, 'Intention in the Criminal Law: A Rejoinder' [1995] MLR 678 and 688.

Horder, J, 'Crimes of Ulterior Intent' in A Simester and ATH Smith, *Harm and Culpability* (1996).

Horder, J, 'Two Histories and Four Hidden Principles of Mens Rea' (1997) 113 LQR 95.

Horder, J, 'Reconsidering Psychic Assault' [1998] Crim LR 392.

Horder, J, 'Questioning the Correspondence Principle: A Reply' [1999] Crim LR 206.

Horder, J, 'On the Irrelevance of Motive in Criminal Law' in J Horder (ed), *Oxford Essays in Jurisprudence* (2000).

Horder, J, 'How Culpability Can and Can't be Denied in Under Age Sex Crimes' [2001] Crim LR 15.

Horder, J, 'Killing the Passive Abuser: A Theoretical Defence' in S Shute and A Sinister (eds) *Criminal Law Theory* (2002).

Horder, J, 'Strict Liability, Statutory Construction and the Spirit of Liberty' (2002) 118 LQR 458.

Horder, J, *Excusing Crime* (2003).

Horder, J, 'Reshaping the Subjective Element in the Provocation Defence' (2005) OJLS 123.

Horder, J, and Shute, S, 'The Wrongness of Rape' in J Horder (ed), *Oxford Essays in Jurisprudence* (2000).

Horn, M, 'Racism and Cyber law' (2003) 153 NLJ 777.

Hornby, J, 'On What's Intentionally Done' in S Shute, J Gardner, and J Horder *Action and Value in Criminal Law* (1993) 60.

House of Lords Select Committee: *Religious Offences in England: First Report* (2004).

Howard, C, *Australian Criminal Law* (2nd edn 1970).

Howard, C, 'The Reasonableness of Mistake in the Criminal Law' (1961), 4 Univ QLJ 45.

Howard, C, *Strict Liability* (1963).

Howard, C, 'Escaping the Fool' [1967] Crim LR 406.

Hughes, G, 'Criminal Omissions' (1958) 67 Yale LJ 590.

Hughes, G, 'The Concept of Crime: An American View' [1959] Crim LR 239 and 331.

Hull, J, 'Stealing Secrets: A Review of the Law Commission's Consultation Paper on the Misuse of Trade Secrets' [1998] Crim LR 246.

Hurd, H, 'The Moral Magic of Consent' (1996) 2 Legal Theory 168.

Huxley, R, 'Proposals and Counter-Proposals on the Defence of Necessity' [1978] Crim LR 141.

Idriss, M, 'Religion and the Anti-Terrorism Crime and Security Act 2001' [2002] Crim LR 890.

Irish Law Reform Commission: LRC CP 27, *Consultation Paper on Homicide: The Plea of Provocation* (2003).

Isenbergh, J, 'Blackmail from A to C' (1993) U Pa L Rev 1905.

Jackson, BS, 'Storkwein: A Case Study in Strict Liability and Self Regulation' [1991] Crim LR 892.

Jackson, M, 'Infanticide: Historical Perspectives' (1996) 146 NLJ 416.

Jaconelli, J, 'Context-Dependent Crime' [1995] Crim LR 771.

Jefferson, M, 'Corporate Criminal Liability: The Problems of Sanctions' (2001) 65 J Crim Law 235.

Jepson, P, 'Tackling Religious Discrimination that Stirs Up Racial Hatred' (1999) 149 NLJ, 554.

Jeremy, AW, 'Religious Offences' [2003] Ecc LJ 127.

Johnson, PE, 'The Unnecessary Crime of Conspiracy' (1973) Calif LR 1137.

Jones, T, 'Insanity, Automatism and the Burden of Proof on the Accused' 1995 111 LQR 475.

Jung, H, 'Criminal Justice–a European Perspective' [1993] Crim LR 237.

Kadish, SH, *Essays* (1987).

Katkin, DM, and Ogle, R, 'A Rationale for Infanticide Laws' [1993] Crim LR 903.

Katz, L, 'Blackmail and Other Forms of Arm-Twisting' (1993) U Pa L Rev 1567.

Katz, L, *Ill-Gotten Gains: Evasion, Blackmail, Fraud, and Kindred Puzzles of the Law* (1996).

Kaveny, MC, 'Inferring Intention from Foresight' (2004) 120 LQR 81.

Kaye, JM, 'Early History of Murder and Manslaughter' (1967) 83 LQR 365.

Kaye, M, 'Excessive Force in Self Defence After Clegg' (1996) J Crim L 448.

Kearns, P, 'Obscene and Blasphemous Libel: Misunderstanding Art' [2000] Crim LR 652.

Kearns, P, 'The Uncultured God: Blasphemy Law's Reprieve and the Art Matrix' [2000] EHRLR 512.

Kearns, P, 'Religion and the Human Rights Act 1998' (2001) 151 NLJ 498.

Keating, H, 'The Restoration of a Serious Crime' [1996] Crim LR 535

Keating, H, 'The Law Commission Report on Involuntary Manslaughter: (1) The Restoration of a Serious Crime' [1998] Crim LR 535.

Keedy, E, 'Ignorance and Mistake in the Criminal Law' (1908) 22 Harv LR 75.

Keith, Lord, 'Some Observations on Diminished Responsibility' [1959] Jur Rev 109.

Kell, D, 'Social Disutility and Consent' (1994) OJLS 121.

Kennedy, IM, 'Alive or Dead?' (1969) 22 CLP 102.

Kennedy IM, 'Switching Off Life Support Machines: The Legal Implications' [1977] Crim LR 443.

Kennedy, IM, *Treat Me Right* (1991).

Kennedy, IM, and Grubb, A, *Medical Law: Text and Materials* (3rd edn 2000).

Kenny, CS, 'The Evolution of the Law of Blasphemy' [1922] 1 CLJ 127.

Kenny, CS, *Outlines of Criminal Law* (19th edn 1965).

Keown, J, 'The Scope of the Offence of Child Destruction' [1988] 104 LQR 120.

Keown, J, 'Restoring Moral and Intellectual Shape to the Law After Bland' (1997) 113 LQR 481.

Keown, J, 'Beyond Bland: A Critique of the BMA Guidance on Withholding and Withdrawing Medical Treatment' (2000) 20 LS 66.

Kiernan, P, and Scanlon, G, 'Fraud and the Law Commission: The Future of Dishonesty' (2003) 24 Comp Law 4.

Klang, M, 'A Critical Look at the Regulation of Computer Viruses' (2003) Int J of Law and IT 162.

Klockars, CB, *The Professional Fence* (1975).

Koffman, L, 'The Nature of Appropriation' [1982] Crim LR 331.

Kugler, I, 'Conditional Oblique Intention' [2004] Crim LR 284.

Kuhl, L, 'The Criminal Law Protection of the Communities' Financial Interests against Fraud' [1998] Crim LR 259 and 323.

Lacey, N, 'A Clear Concept of Intention' (1993) 56 MLR 621.

Lacey, N, 'In(de)terminable Intentions' (1995) 58 MLR 692.

Lacey, N, *Unspeakable Subjects* (1998).

Lacey, N, *State Punishment* (1988).

Lacey, N, 'Partial Defences to Homicide' in A Ashworth and B Mitchell (eds), *Rethinking English Homicide Law* (2000).

LACEY, N, 'Beset by Boundaries' [2001] Crim LR 3.

LACEY, N, WELLS, C, AND QUICK, O, *Reconstructing Criminal Law* (3rd edn 2003).

LAMOND, G, 'Coercion, Threats and the Puzzle of Blackmail' in A Simester and ATH Smith (eds), *Harm and Culpability* (1996).

LANHAM, D, 'Arrest, Detention and Compulsion' [1974] Crim LR 288.

LANHAM, D, 'Delegated Legislation and Publication' (1974) 37 MLR 510.

LANHAM, D, 'Larsonneur Revisited' [1976] Crim LR 276.

LANHAM, D, 'Accomplices and Transferred Malice' (1980) 96 LQR 110.

LANHAM, D, 'Complicity, Concert and Conspiracy' [1980] 4 Crim LJ 276.

LANHAM, D, 'Accomplices and Withdrawal' (1981) 97 LQR 575.

LANHAM, D, 'Drivers Control and Accomplices' [1982] Crim LR 419.

LANHAM, D, 'Danger Down Under' [1999] Crim LR 960.

LANHAM, D, 'Primary and Derivative Criminal Liability: An Australian Perspective' [2000] Crim LR 707.

LANHAM, D, 'Offensive Weapons and Self Defence' [2005] Crim LR 85.

Law Commission: Consultation Paper, No 136, *The Year and a Day Rule in Homicide* (1994).

Law Commission: Consultation Paper, No 150, *Legislating the Criminal Code: Misuse of Trade Secrets* (1997).

Law Commission: Consultation Paper , No 155, *Legislating the Criminal Code: Fraud and Deception* (1999).

Law Commission: Report, No 26, *Forgery* (1970).

Law Commission: Report, No 29, *Offences of Damage to Property* (1970).

Law Commission: Report, No 79, *Offences Against Religion and Public Worship* (1981).

Law Commission: Report, No 83, *Report on Defences of General Applications* (1977).

Law Commission: Report, No 123, *Offences Relating to Public Disorder* (1983).

Law Commission: Report, No 145, *Offences Against Religion and Public Worship* (1985).

Law Commission: Report, No 218, *Legislating the Criminal Code Offences Against the Person and General Principles* (1992).

Law Commission: Report, No 243, *Offences of Dishonesty: Money Transfers* (1996).

Law Commission: Report, No 276, *Fraud* (2002).

Law Commission: Report, No 282, *Children: Their Non-Accidental Death or Serious Injury (Criminal Trials)* (2003).

Law Commission: Report, No 290, *Partial Defences to Murder* (2004).

Law Commission: Working Paper, No 23, *Malicious Damage* (1969).

Law Commission: Working Paper, No 79, *Offences against Religion and Public Worship* (1981).

Law Commission: Working Paper, No 110, *Computer Misuse* (1988).

Law Commission: Working Paper, No 145 *Offences against Religion and Public Worship* (1985).

LEAVENS, A, 'A Causation Approach to Criminal Omissions' (1988) 76 Cal LR 547.

LEIGH, LH, 'Sado-Masochism, Consent and the Reform of the Criminal Law' (1976) 39 MLR 130.

LEIGH, LH, 'Some Remarks on Appropriation in the Law of Theft after Morris' (1985) 48 MLR 167.

LEIGH, LH, 'Necessity and the Case of Dr Morgentaler' [1978] Crim LR 151.

LEIGH, LH, *Strict and Vicarious Liability* (1982).

LEIGH, LH, 'Recklessness after Reid' (1993) 56 MLR 208.

LEIGH, LH, 'Liability for Inadvertence a Lordly Legacy' (1995) 58 MLR 457, 459.

LEIGH, LH, *Strict and Vicarious Liability* (1982).

LENG, R, 'Incitement–An Objective Approach to the Definition of Crime' (1978) 41 MLR 725.

LENG, R, 'Falsity in Forgery' [1989] Crim LR 687.

LESTER, A, AND PANNICK, D, *Human Rights Law and Practice* (2004).

LEVERICK, F, 'The Use of Force in Public or Private Defence and Article 2: a Reply to Professor Sir John Smith' [2002] Crim LR 963.

LEVI, M, 'The Costs of Transnational and Other Financial Crime: Making Sense of the Worldwide Data' (2001) 1 Int Jnl of Comp. Criminology 8.

LEVI, M, AND SMITH, A, *Comparative Analysis of Organised Crime Conspiracy Legislation and Practice and their Relevance to England and Wales* (2002) HO Research Study 17/02, 16.

LIDSTONE, K, 'A Maze in Law!' [1978] Crim LR 332.

LINDGREN, J, 'Unravelling the Paradox of Blackmail' (1984) 84 Col L Rev 670.

LINDGREN, J, 'The Theory, History, and Practice of the Bribery-Extortion Distinction' (1993) 141(5) U Pa L Rev 1695.

LIPTON, J, 'A Revised Property Concept for the New Millennium' (1999) Int Jnl of Law and IT 171.

LLOYD, I, *Information Technology Law* (4th edn 2004).

LLOYD-BOSTOCK, S, 'The Effects on Juries of Hearing about the Defendant's Previous Criminal Record: A Simulation Study' [2000] Crim LR 734.

LOVELAND, I, 'Back to the Future' (2000) 150 NLJ 1220.

LOVELL, E, *Children and Young People who Display Sexually Harmful Behaviour* (NSPCC 2002).

LOWE, WING-COMMANDER 'The Fraudulent Intent in Larceny' [1956] Crim LR 78.

LYNCH, ACE, 'The Mental Element in the Actus Reus' (1982) 98 LQR 109.

LYNCH, ACE, 'The Scope of Intoxication' [1982] Crim LR 139.

MACCORMACK, G, 'Mistaken Payments and Proprietary Claims' [1996] Conv 86.

MACDONALD K, AND THOMPSON, R, 'Dishonest Agreements' (2003) Competition Law Journal 94.

MACDOUGALL, I, 'Automatism–Negation of *Mens Rea*' (1992) 37 J Law Soc Scotland 57.

MACKAY, IRENE, 'The Sleepwalker Is Not Insane' (1992) 55 MLR 714.

MACKAY, RD, 'Non-Organic Automatism' [1980] Crim LR 350.

MACKAY, RD, 'Fact and Fiction About the Insanity Defence' [1990] Crim LR 247.

MACKAY, RD, 'The Consequences of Killing Very Young Children' [1993] Crim LR 21.

MACKAY, RD, *Mental Condition Defences in Criminal Law* (1996).

MACKAY, RD, 'The Abnormality of Mind Factor in Diminished Responsibility' [1999] Crim LR 117.

MACKAY, RD, 'Diminished Responsibility and Mentally Disordered Killers' in A Ashworth and B Mitchell (eds), *Rethinking English Homicide Law* (2000).

MACKAY, RD, 'On Being Insane in Jersey Part Two' [2002] Crim LR 728.

MACKAY, RD, 'On Being Insane in Jersey Part Three–the Case of the Attorney General v O'Driscoll' [2004] Crim LR 219.

MACKAY, RD, AND KEARNS, G, 'The Continued Underuse of Unfitness to Plead and the Insanity Defence' [1994] Crim LR 546.

MACKAY, RD, AND KEARNS, G, 'The Trial of the Facts and Unfitness to Plead' [1997] Crim LR 644.

MACKAY, RD, AND KEARNS, G, 'More Fact(s) About the Insanity Defence' [1999] Crim LR 714.

MACKAY, RD, AND KEARNS, G, 'An Upturn in Unfitness to Plead?' [2000] Crim LR 532.

MACKAY, RD, AND MITCHELL, B, 'Provoking Diminished Responsibility: Two Pleas Merging into One?' [2003] Crim LR 745.

MACKAY, RD, AND MITCHELL, B, 'Replacing Provocation: More on A Combined Plea' [2004] Crim LR 219.

MACKAY, RD, AND MITCHELL, B, 'But is this Provocation? Some Thoughts on Law Commission Report No 290' [2005] Crim LR 44.

MACKAY, S, 'Entrapment, Competing Views on the Effect of the HRA on the English Criminal Law' [2002] EHRLR 764.

MACKENNA, B, 'Blackmail' [1966] Crim LR 467.

MACKENNA, B, 'Causing Death by Reckless or Dangerous Driving' [1970] Crim LR 67.

MACKLEM, T, AND GARDNER, J, 'Provocation and Pluralism' (2001) 64 MLR 815.

MACKLEM, T, AND GARDNER, J, 'Compassion without Respect: Nine Fallacies in R v Smith' [2001] Crim LR 623

MACLEAN, A, 'Resurrection of the Body Snatchers' (2000) 150 NLJ 174.

MAEIR-KATKIN, D, AND OGLE, R, 'A Rationale for Infanticide Laws' [1993] Crim LR 903.

MAHONEY, P, 'Universality and Subsidiarity in the Strasbourg caselaw on Free Speech: Explaining Some Recent Judgments' [1997] EHRLR 364.

MALIK, M, 'Racist Crime: Racially Aggravated Offences in the Crime and Disorder Act 1998' (1999) 62 MLR 409.

MANCHESTER, C, 'A History of the Crime of Obscene Libel' [1991] Lournal of Legal History 31.

MARSTON, G, 'Contemporaneity of Act and Intention' (1970) 86 LQR 208.

MARSTON, J, AND ROSS, L, 'Treasure and Portable Antiquities in the 1990s Still Chained to the Ghosts of the Past: The Treasure Act 1996' [1997] Conv 273.

MATTHEWS, M, 'Ignorance of the Law is no Excuse' (1983) 3 LS 174.

MCAULEY, F, 'Anticipating the Past: The Defences of Provocation in Irish Law' (1987) 50 MLR 133.

MCCALL SMITH, A, 'The Duty to Rescue and the Common law' in M Menlove and A McCall Smith (eds), *The Duty to Rescue: The Jurisprudence of Aid* (1993).

MCCLEAN, JD, 'Informers and Agents Provocateurs' [1969] Crim LR 527.

MCCOLGAN, A, 'In Defence of Battered Women Who Kill' (1993) J Law and Soc 508.

MCCOLGAN, A, 'Heralding Corporate Liability' [1994] Crim LR 547.

MCCUTCHEON, JP, AND QUINN, K, 'Codifying Criminal Law in Ireland' (1998) Statute Law Review 131.

MCEWAN, J, 'Murder by Design: The Feel-Good Factor and the Criminal Law' [2001] Med LR 246.

MCEWAN, J, AND ROBILLIARD, J, 'Recklessness: the House of Lords and the Criminal Law' (1981) LS 267.

MCGOLDRICK, D, 'The Permanent ICC–An End to the Culture of Impunity' [1999] Crim LR 627.

MCGREGOR, J, 'Why When She Says No She Doesn't Mean Maybe and Doesn't Mean Yes' (1996) 2 Legal Theory 175.

MCSHERRY, B, 'Voluntariness, Intention and the Defence of Mental Disorder: Towards a Rational Approach' (2003) 21(5) Behavioural Sciences and the Law 581.

MEAD, G, 'Contracting into Crime: A Theory of Criminal Omissions' (1991) OJLS 147.

MEHIGAN, S, PHILLIPS, J, AND SAUNDERS, J (eds), *The Licensing Act 2003* (2004).

MEHIGAN, S, PHILLIPS, J, AND SAUNDERS, J (eds), *Paterson's Licensing Acts 2005* (113th edn 2005).

MENLOVE, M, 'The Philosophical Foundations of a Duty to Rescue' in M Menlove and A McCall Smith (eds) *The Duty to Rescue: The Jurisprudence of Aid* (1993).

MILGATE, H, 'Duress and the Criminal Law; Another About Turn by the House of Lords' [1988] CLJ 61.

MILMO, P, AND ROGERS, WVH (eds), *Gatley on Libel and Slander* (10th edn 2004).

MITCHELL, A, TAYLOR, S, AND TALBOT, K, *On Confiscation and the Proceeds of Crime* (2002).

MITCHELL, B, *Murder and Penal Policy* (1990).

MITCHELL, B, 'Thinking About Murder' (1992) J Crim L 78.

MITCHELL, B, 'Culpably Indifferent Murder' (1996) 25 Anglo Am LR 64.

MITCHELL, B, 'Public Perceptions of Homicide and Criminal Justice' (1998) 38 Cr J Crim, 453.

MITCHELL, B, 'In Defence of a Principle of Correspondence' [1999] Crim LR 195.

MITCHELL, B, 'Further Evidence of the Relationship Between Legal and Public Opinion on the Law of Homicide' [2000] Crim LR 814.

MITCHELL, B, 'Multiple Wrongdoing and Offence Structure' (2001) 64 MLR 393.

MONTROSE, J, 'The M'Naghten Rules' (1954) 17 MLR 383.

MOORE, MS, *Act and Crime: The Philosophy of Action and its Implications for Criminal Law* (1993).

MORAN, L, 'Learning the Limits of Privacy' (1998) 61 MLR 77.

MORRIS, N, '"Wrong" in the M'Naghten Rules' (1953) 16 MLR 435.

MORSE, SJ, 'Diminished Capacity' in S Shute, S Gardner, and J Horder (eds), *Action and Value in Criminal Law* (1993).

MUNDAY, R, 'Handling the Evidential Exception' [1988] Crim LR 345.

MUNRO, C, 'When Racism Is Not Black and White' (2001) 151 NLJ 313.

MURPHY, J (ed), *Street on Torts* (11th edn 2003).

MURPHY, P et al (eds), *Blackstone's Criminal Practice* (2005).

MYHILL, A, AND ALLEN, J, 'Rape and Sexual Assault on Women: The Extent and Nature of the Problem–findings from the British Crime Survey' (2002) HORS No 237.

NAPIER, D, 'Detention Offences at Common Law' in P Glazebrook (ed), *Reshaping the Criminal Law: Essays in Honour of Glanville Williams* (1978).

New South Wales Law Reform Commission: Report No 83, *Partial Defences to Murder: Provocation and Infanticide* (1997).

NICHOLS, DB, 'Untying the Soldier by Refurbishing the Common Law' [1976] Crim LR 181.

NICHOLSON, D, 'The Citizen's Legal Duty to Assist the Police' [1992] Crim LR 611.

NICHOLSON, D, AND SANGHVI, R, 'Battered Women and Provocation: The Implications of R v Ahluwalia' [1993] Crim LR 728.

NICOL, A, 'Child Offenders: UK and International Practice' (1995) Howard League for Penal Reform.

NOKES, GD, *History of the Crime of Blasphemy* (1928).

NORRIE, AW, 'Subjectivism, Objectivism and the Limits of Criminal Recklessness' (1992) 12 OJLS 45.

NORRIE, AW, *Crime, Reason and History* (2nd edn 2000).

NORRIE, AW, 'From Criminal law to Legal Theory: The Mysterious Case of the Reasonable Glue Sniffer' (2002) 65 MLR 538, 547.

NORRIE, AW, 'Oblique Intention and Legal Politics' [1989] Crim LR 793.

NORRIE, AW, 'Intention–More Loose Talk' [1990] Crim LR 642.

NORRIE, AW, 'After *Woollin*' [1999] Crim LR 532.

NOWLIN, C, 'Expert Evidence in English Obscenity Law: Implications of the Human Rights Act 1998' (2001) Common Law World Review 94.

O'DONNELL, I, AND MORRISON, S, 'Armed and Dangerous: the Use of Firearms in Robbery' (1997) 36(3) Howard Jnl 305.

O'DONOVAN, K, 'The Medicalisation of Infanaticide' [1984] Crim LR 259.

O'DONOVAN, K, 'Defences for Battered Women Who Kill?' (1991) 18 J Law and Soc 219.

O'REGAN, RS, 'Indirect Provocation and Misdirected Retaliation' [1968] Crim LR 319.

OLIVER, S, 'Provocation and Non-Violent Homosexual Advances' (1999) J Crim L 586.

ORCHARD, G, 'Drunkenness, Drugs and Manslaughter' [1970] Crim LR 132.

ORCHARD, G, 'Agreement in Criminal Conspiracy' [1974] Crim LR 297 at 335.

ORCHARD, G, 'The Defence of Absence of Fault in Australia and Canada' in P Smith (ed), *Essays in Honour of JC Smith* (1987).

ORCHARD, G, 'Surviving without Majewski' [1993] Crim LR 426.

ORMEROD, D, 'A Victim's Mistaken Consent in Rape' (1992) J Crim L 407.

ORMEROD, D, 'Consent and Offences Against the Person: LCCP No 134' (1994) 57 MLR 928.

ORMEROD, D, 'Cheating the Public Revenue' [1998] Crim LR 627.

ORMEROD, D, 'A Bit of a Con–The Law Commission's Proposals on Fraud' [1999] Crim LR 789.

ORMEROD, D, 'Criminalising HIV Transmission–Still No Effective Solutions' [2001] Common Law World Review 135–68.

ORMEROD, D, 'Summary Evasion of Income Tax' [2002] Crim LR 3.

ORMEROD, D, 'A Presumption of Intercourse' (2003) Archbold News, 2.

ORMEROD, D, AND GUNN, M, 'Consent–A Second Bash' [1996] Crim LR 694.

ORMEROD, D, AND GUNN, M, 'Criminal Liability for the Transmission of HIV' [1996] 1 Web Jnl Current Legal Issues.

ORMEROD, D, AND GUNN, M, 'In Defence of Ireland' [1996] 3 Web Jnl CLI.

ORMEROD, D, AND ROBERTS, A, 'The Trouble with *Teixera*: Developing a Principled Approach to Entrapment' [2002] Int Jnl E&P 38.

ORMEROD, D, AND ROBERTS, A, 'The Police Reform Act 2002–Increasing Centralisation, Maintaining Confidence and Contracting Out Crime Control' [2003] Crim LR 141.

PACE, PJ, 'Demanding with Menaces' (1971) 121 NLJ 242.

PACE, PJ, '"Impeding Arrest". A Wife's Right as a Spouse?' [1978] Crim LR 82.

PACE, PJ, 'Delegation–A Doctrine in Search of a Definition' [1982] Crim LR 627.

PACE, PJ, 'Burglarious Trespass' [1985] Crim LR 716.

PACKER, H, *The Limits of the Criminal Sanction* (1969).

PADFIELD, N, 'Clean Water and Muddy Causation' [1995] Crim LR 683.

PADFIELD, N, 'Tariffs in Murder' [2002] Crim LR 192.

PADFIELD, N, 'The Anti-Social Behaviour Act 2003: the Ultimate Nanny-State Act?' [2004] Crim LR 712.

PALFREY, T, 'Is Fraud Dishonest?' (2000) J Crim L 518.

PALLIS, C, AND HARLEY, D, *ABC of Brain Stem Death* (2nd edn 1996).

PALMER, H, 'Dr Adams Trial for Murder' [1957] Crim LR 365.

PALMER, P, 'Attempt by Act or Omission: Causation and the Problem of the Hypothetical Nurse' (1999) J Crim L 158.

PALMER, T, *The Trials of OZ* (1971).

PANNICK, D, 'Religious Freedom and the European Court' [1995] PL 7.

PARRY, DL, 'Judicial Approaches to Due Diligence' [1995] Crim LR 695.

PATON, E, 'Reformulating the Intoxication Rule' [1995] Crim LR 382.

PAWLOWSKI, M, 'Dead Bodies as Property' (1996) 146 NLJ 1828.

PEDAIN, A, 'Intention and the Terrorist Example' [2003] Crim LR

PEERS, S, *EU Justice and Home Affairs Law* (2000).

PENNINGTON, R, *Company Law* (8th edn 2001).

PERKINS, RM, 'A Rationale of Mens Rea' (1939) 52 Harv L Rev 905, 924.

PERKINS, RM, *Criminal Law* (2nd edn 1969).

PERKINS, RM, AND BOYCE, RN, *Criminal Law* (3rd edn 1982).

PHILLIPS, A, 'Criminal and Civil Aspects of Wheel Clamping on Private Property' (1993) 38 Jnl of the Law Soc of Scotland 187.

PHILLIPS, B, 'The Case for Corporal Punishment in the UK–Beaten into Submission in Europe' (1994) 43 ICLQ 153.

PICKARD, T, 'Culpable Mistakes' (1980) 30 U Toronto J 75.

POLLARD, RSW, *Abolish the Blasphemy Laws* (1957).

POLLOCK, SIR FREDERICK, AND MAITLAND, FW, *The History of English Law before the Time of Edward I*, 2 vols (1895).

POOLE, AR, 'Standing Mute and Fitness to Plead' [1966] Crim LR 6.

POOLE, D, 'Arthur's Case: A Comment' [1986] Crim LR 383.

POSNER, R, 'Blackmail, Privacy and Freedom of Contract' (1993) U Pa L Rev 1817.

POULTER, SM, 'Foreign Customs and the English Criminal Law' (1975) 24 ICLQ 136.

POULTER, SM, 'Towards Legislative Reform of the Blasphemy and Racial Hatred Laws' [1991] PL 371.

POWER, H, 'Towards a Redefinition of the Mens Rea of Rape'(2003) 23 OJLS 379.

PREVEZER, S, 'Criminal Homicides Other Than Murder' [1980] Crim LR 530.

PRICE, D, 'How Viable Is the Present Scope of the Offence of Child Destruction' (1987) 16 Anglo Am LR 220.

PRICE, D, 'Fairly Bland: An Alternative View of a Supposed New 'Death Ethic' and the BMA Guidelines' (2001) 21 LS 618.

RADZINOWICZ, L, AND TURNER, JWC (eds), *The Modern Approach to Criminal Law* (1948).

REED, A, 'Analysis of Fraud Vitiating Consent in Rape Cases' (1995) 59 J Crim LR 310.

REED, A, 'The Need for a New Anglo American Approach to Duress' [1996] J Crim L 209.

REES, E, AND HALL, A, *The Blackstone's Guide to the Proceeds of Crime Act 2002* (2003).

REID, K, AND MACLEOD, J, 'Ticket Touts or Theft of Tickets and Related Offences' (1999) 63(6) J Crim Law 593.

REVILLE, NJ, 'Mischief of Aggravated Burglary' (1989) 139 NLJ 835.

RICHARDSON, G, 'Effective Means of Regulating Industry Strict Liability for

Regulating Crime: the Empirical Evidence' [1987] Crim LR 295.

Richardson, T, 'Crimes without Frontiers? The War Crimes Act 1991' in I Loveland (ed), *Frontiers of Criminality* (1995).

Roberts, A, 'Law Reform Defences to Murder' [2005] Crim LR 256.

Roberts, P, 'The Philosophical Foundations of Consent in the Criminal Law' (1997) 17 OJLS 389.

Roberts, P, 'The Presumption of Innocence Brought Home? Kebilene Deconstructed' (2002) LQR 41.

Robertson, G, 'Blasphemy: The Law Commission Working Paper' [1981] PL 295.

Robertson, G, *Freedom, the Individual and the Law* (7th edn 1993).

Robilliard, AStJ, 'Offences Against Religion and Public Worship' (1981) 44 MLR 556.

Robinson, P, 'Criminal Law Defences: A Systematic Analysis' (1982) 82 Col LR 199.

Robinson, PH, 'Causing the Condition of Ones Own Defense: A Study in the Limits of the Criminal Law Doctrine' (1985) 71 Virg LR.

Robinson, PH, 'Should the Criminal Law Abandon the Actus Reus—Mens Rea Distinction?' in S Shute, J Gardner, and J Horder (eds), *Action and Value in Criminal Law* (1993).

Robinson, PH, 'Competing Theories of Justification' in A Simester and ATH Smith (eds), *Harm and Culpability* (1996).

Robinson, PH, *Structure and Function of Criminal Law* (1998).

Robinson, PH, 'The Modern General Part: Three Illusions' in S Shute and A Simester, *Criminal Law Theory: Doctrines of the General Part* (2002).

Rodwell QC, HHD 'Problems with the Sexual Offences Act 2003' [2005] Crim LR 290.

Rogers, AP, *Law on the Battlefield* (1996).

Rogers, J, 'A Criminal Lawyer's Response to Chastisement in European Court' [2002] Crim LR 98.

Rogers, WVH, *Winfield and Jolowicz on Tort* (16th edn 2004).

Rolph, CH, *The Trial of Lady Chatterley; Robertson, Freedom, the Individual and the Law* (7th edn 1993).

Rook, P, and Ward, R, *Sexual Offences: Law and Practice* (2004).

Room, S, 'Criminalising Cybercrime' (2004) 154 NLJ 950.

Ross, U, 'Two Cases on Obstructing a Constable' [1977] Crim LR 187.

Rostow, EV, 'The Enforcement of Morals' [1960] CLJ 174 at 189.

Rowe, P, 'Murder and the Law of War' (1991) NILQ 216.

Rowlands, P, 'Minors: Can They Make Off Without Payment' (1981) JP 410.

Rubin, GR, 'New Light on Steane's Case' (2003) Legal History 143.

Rumney, P, 'The Review of Sex Offences and Rape Law Reform: Another False Dawn' (2001) 64 MLR.

Rumney, P, 'Progress at a Price: The Construction of Non-Stranger Rape in the Millbery Sentencing Guidelines' (2003) 66 MLR 870.

Rumney, P, 'The British Experience of Racist Hate Speech regulation–A Lesson for First Amendment Absolutists?' [2003] Common Law World Rev 117.

Rumney, P, and Morgan-Taylor, M, 'Recognising the Male Victim: Gender Neutrality and the Law of Rape'(1997) 26 Anglo American Law Review 198.

Russell, Sir WO, *Crime*, 2 vols (12th edn 1964: JWC Turner).

Salmond, J, *Salmond on Jurisprudence* (11th edn 1957).

Salmond, J, *Salmond on Torts* (21st edn 1996).

Samuels, A, 'Can the Prosecution Allege that the Accused Is Insane?' [1960] Crim LR 453, [1961] Crim LR 308.

Saunders, K, 'Voluntary Acts and the Criminal Law: Justifying Culpability Based on the Existence of Volition' (1988) 49 U Pitt LR 443.

Sayre, F, 'Public Welfare Offences' (1933) 33 Col LR 55.

Sayre, FB, 'Criminal Responsibility for the Acts of Another' (1930) 43 Harv LR 689.

Scarman, Lord, *Codification and Judge-Made Law* (1966).

Schopp, R, *Automatism, Insanity and the Psychology of Criminal Responsibility: A Philosophical Inquiry* (1991).

Schopp, R, *Justification Defences and Just Convictions* (1988).

Schulhofer, S, *Unwanted Sex: The Culture of Intimidation and the Failure of Law* (1998).

Scottish Law Commission: Report No 195, *Insanity and Diminished Responsibility* (2004).

Seaborne Davies, D, *Annual Survey of English Law* (1932).

Seaborne Davies, D, 'Child-Killing in English Law' (1937) 1 MLR 203.

Sheldon, S, *Beyond Control* (1977).

Shields, R, *Offensive Weapons* (2nd edn 1996).

Shute, S, 'Something Old, Something New, Something Borrowed–Three Aspects of the Consent Project' [1996] Crim LR 684.

Shute, S, 'Appropriation and the Law of Theft' [2002] Crim LR 445 and 455.

Shute, S, 'Knowledge and Belief in the Criminal Law' in S Shute and A Simester (eds) *Criminal Law Theory: Doctrines of the General Part* (2002).

Shute, S, 'New Civil Preventative Orders: Sexual Offences Prevention orders; Foreign Travel Orders; Risk of Sexual Harm Orders' [2004] Crim LR 417.

Shute, S, 'Punishing Murderers: Release Procedures and the 'Tarriff'' [2004] Crim LR 873.

Shute, S, and Horder, J, 'Thieving and Deceiving: What is the Difference' (1993) 56 MLR 548.

Silber, S, 'The Law Commission, Conspiracy to Defraud and the Dishonesty Project' [1995] Crim LR 461.

Simester, A, and Sullivan, GR, *Criminal Law Theory and Doctrine* (2nd edn 2003).

Simms, M, 'Abortion Law Reform: Has the Controversy Changed' [1970] Crim LR 567, 573

Simms, M, 'The Abortion Act: A Reply' [1971] Crim LR 86.

Simpson, WB, *Cannibalism and the Common Law* (1984).

Skegg, P, 'Irreversibly Comatose Individuals: Alive or Dead?' [1964] CLJ 130.

Skegg, P, 'Medical Procedures and the Crime of Battery' [1974] Crim LR 693 and (1973) 36 MLR 370.

Skegg, P, 'Criminal Liability for the Unauthorised Use of Corpses for Medical Education and Research' (1992) 32 Med Sci Law 51.

Skinner, S, 'Citizens in Uniform: Public Defence, Reasonableness and Human Rights' [2000] PL 266.

Smart, A, 'Criminal Responsibility for failing to do the Impossible' (1987) 103 LQR 532.

Smith, ATH, 'Stealing the Body and its Parts' [1976] Crim LR 622.

Smith, ATH, 'Theft and/or Handling' [1977] Crim LR 517.

Smith, ATH, 'Reforming Section 16 of the Theft Act' [1977] Crim LR 259.

Smith, ATH, 'The Idea of Criminal Deception' [1982] Crim LR 721.

Smith, ATH, 'On Actus Reus and Mens Rea' in P Glazebrook (ed), *Reshaping the Criminal Law: Essays in Honour of Glanville Williams* (1978).

Smith, ATH, 'Shoplifting and the Theft Acts' [1981] Crim LR 586.

SMITH, ATH, *Offences against Public Order* (1987).

SMITH, ATH, 'Conspiracy to Defraud [1988] Crim LR 508.

SMITH, ATH, 'Legislating the Criminal Code' [1992] Crim LR 396.

SMITH, ATH, *Property Offences* (1994).

SMITH, ATH, 'The Human Rights Act and the Criminal Lawyer, the Constitutional Context' [1999] CLR 251.

SMITH, ATH, 'Theft or Sharp Practice: Who Cares Now' [2001] CLJ 21.

SMITH, J, *The Nature of Personal Robbery* (2003).

SMITH, JC, 'The Fraudulent Intent to Larceny: Another View' [1956] Crim LR 238.

SMITH, JC, 'Embezzlement and the Disobedient Servant' (1956) 19 MLR 39.

SMITH JC, 'Two Problems in Criminal Attempts' (1957) 70 Harv LR 422.

SMITH, JC, 'The Guilty Mind in the Criminal Law' (1960) 76 LQR 78.

SMITH, JC, 'Two Problems in Criminal Attempts Re-examined' [1962] Crim LR 135.

SMITH, JC, 'Burglary under the Theft Bill' [1968] Crim LR 367.

SMITH, JC, 'Assault: *Donnelly v Jackson*' [1970] Crim LR 219 at 220.

SMITH, JC, 'Civil Law Concepts in the Criminal Law' [1972] CLJ 197.

SMITH, JC, 'Intention in Criminal Law' (1974) 27 CLP 93.

SMITH, JC, 'Conspiracy under the Criminal Law Act 1977' [1977] Crim LR 598 and 638.

SMITH, JC, 'A Reply' [1978] Crim LR 14.

SMITH, JC, 'Theft, Conspiracy and Jurisdiction: Tarling's Case' [1979] Crim LR 220.

SMITH, JC, 'Secondary Participation and Inchoate Offences' in *Crime, Proof and Punishment: Essays in Memory of Sir Rupert Cross* (1981).

SMITH, JC, 'Liability for Omissions in Criminal Law' (1984) 4 LS 88.

SMITH, JC, 'Responsibility in Criminal Law', in Barbara Wootton, *Essays in Her Honour* (1986).

SMITH, JC, 'Satisfying the Jury' [1988] Crim LR 335.

SMITH, JC, *Justifications and Excuses in Criminal Law* (1989).

SMITH, JC, 'A Note on Intention' [1990] Crim LR 85.

SMITH, JC, 'Secondary Participation in Crime–Can we do without it?' (1994) 144 NLJ 679.

SMITH, JC, 'The Right to Life and the Right to Kill in Law Enforcement' (1994) 144 NLJ 354.

SMITH, JC, 'Conspiracy to Defraud: Some Comments on the Law Commission's Report' [1995] Crim LR 209–10.

SMITH, JC, 'Fraud and the Criminal Law' in P Birks (ed), *Pressing Problems in the Law* vol 1 (1995)

SMITH, JC, 'Proving Conspiracy' [1996] Crim LR 386.

SMITH, JC, 'Criminal Liability of Accessories: Law and Law Reform' (1997) 113 LQR 453

SMITH, JC, 'More on Proving Conspiracy' [1997] Crim LR 333.

SMITH, JC, 'Obtaining Cheques by Deception or Theft' [1997] Crim LR 396.

SMITH, JC, *The Law of Theft* (8th edn 1997).

SMITH JC, 'Stealing Tickets' [1998] Crim LR 723.

SMITH, JC, 'Offences Against the Person: The Home Office Consultation Paper' [1998] Crim LR 317.

SMITH, JC, 'Home Office Consultation Paper of February 1998' [1998] Crim LR 317.

SMITH, JC, 'Individual Incapacities and Criminal Liability' [1999] Med L Rev 138.

Smith, JC 'The Sad Fate of the Theft Act 1968 in W Swadling and G Jones, *The Search for Principle, Essays in Honour of Lord Goff of Chieveley* (1999).

Smith, JC, 'A Comment on Dr Moor's Case' [2000] Crim LR 41.

Smith, JC, 'The Triumph of Inexorable Logic' in Eoin O'Dell (ed), *Leading Cases of the Twentieth Century* (2000).

Smith, JC, 'The Use of Force in Public or Private Defence and Article 2' [2002] Crim LR 958.

Smith, KJM, 'Assisting Suicide–The Attorney-General and the Voluntary Euthanasia Society' [1983] Crim LR 579.

Smith, KJM, 'Liability for Endangerment: English Ad Hoc Pragmatism and American Innovation' [1983] Crim LR 127.

Smith, KJM, 'Complicity and Causation' [1986] Crim LR 663.

Smith, KJM, *A Modern Treatise on the Law of Complicity* (1991).

Smith, KJM, 'Proximity in Attempt: Lord Lane's Midway Course' [1991] Crim LR 576.

Smith, KJM, 'Duress and Steadfastness: In Pursuit of the Unintelligible' [1999] Crim LR 363.

Smith, KJM, 'Withdrawal in Complicity: A Restatement of Principles' [2001] Crim LR 769.

Smith, KJM, and Wilson, W, 'Impaired Voluntariness and Criminal Responsibility' (1993) 13 OJLS 69.

Smith, PF, 'Excessive Defence–A Rejection of Australian Initiative' [1972] Crim LR 524.

Smith, M, and Perason, A, 'The Value of Strict Liability' [1969] Crim LR 5.

Smith, R, and Clements, L, 'Involuntary Intoxication, The Threshold of Inhibition and the Instigation of Crime' (1995) 46 NILQ 210.

Smith, TB, 'Diminished Responsibility' [1957] Crim LR 354.

Sparks, R, 'The Elusive Element of Unlawfulness' (1965) 28 MLR 601.

Sparks, TB, 'Diminished Responsibility in Theory and Practice' (1964) 27 MLR 9.

Spencer, JN, 'The Aggravated Vehicle Taking Act 1992' [1992] Crim LR 69.

Spencer, JR, 'The Metamorphosis of Section 6 of the Theft Act' [1977] Crim LR 653.

Spencer, JR, 'Criminal Libel: A Skeleton in the Cupboard' [1977] Crim LR 383 and 465.

Spencer, JR, 'The Theft Act 1978' [1979] Crim LR 24.

Spencer, JR, 'The Press and the Reform of Criminal Libel' in P Glazebrook (ed), *Reshaping the Criminal Law: Essays in Honour of Glanville Williams* (1978).

Spencer, JR, 'Blasphemy: The Law Commission Working Paper' [1981] Crim LR 810.

Spencer, JR, 'The Mishandling of Handling' [1981] Crim LR 682.

Spencer, JR, 'Handling and Taking Risks: A Reply to Professor Williams' [1985] Crim LR 440.

Spencer, JR, 'Handling, Theft and the Mala Fide Purchaser' [1985] Crim LR 92.

Spencer, JR, 'Motor Vehicles as Weapons of Offence' [1985] Crim LR 29.

Spencer, JR, 'Road Traffic Law: A Review of the North Report' [1988] Crim LR 707.

Spencer, JR, 'Public Nuisance–a Critical Examination' [1989] CLJ 55.

Spencer, JR, 'Child and Family Offences' [2004] Crim LR 34.

Spencer, JR, 'Liability for Reckless Infection' (2004) 154 NLJ 384–5 (part 1) and 448–71 (part 2).

Spencer, JR, 'Retrial for Reckless Infection' (2004) NLJ 762.

SPENCER, S, 'Assault with Intent to Rape–Dead or Alive' [1986] Crim LR 110.

ST JOHN STEVAS, N, 'Obscenity and the Law' [1954] Crim LR 817.

ST JOHN STEVAS, N, *Life, Death and the Law* (1961).

ST JOHN, V, 'Premenstrual Syndrome in the Criminal Law' [1997] Auckland Uni LR 331.

STALLWORTHY, M, 'Can Death by Shock be Manslaughter' (1986) 136 NLJ 51.

STALLWORTHY, M, 'Damage to Crops' (2000) 150 NLJ 728, 801.

STANNARD, J, 'Making up for the Missing Element: A Sideways Look at Attempts' (1987) 7 LS 194.

STANNARD, J, 'From Andrews to Seymour and Back Again' [1996] 47 NILQ 1.

STANNARD, J, 'Towards a Normative Defence of Provocation in England and Ireland' (2002) J Crim L 528.

STEPHEN, SIR JF, *A History of the Criminal Law of England* 3 vols (1883).

STEPHEN, SIR JF, *A Digest of the Criminal Law* (9th edn 1950).

STEVENSON, K, DAVIES, A, AND GUNN, M, *Blackstone's Guide to the Sexual Offences Act 2003* (2004).

STEWART, N, 'The New ICC' (2001) 151 NLJ 1381.

STOKES, S, 'Blasphemy and Freedom of Expression Under the ECHR: Two Recent Cases' (1996) 7 Ent LR.

STONE, RTH, 'Obscene Publications: The Problems Persist' [1986] Crim LR 139.

STREET, H, *Freedom, the Individual and the Law* (5th edn 1984).

STUART, D, 'Reform of the Law of Theft' (1967) 30 MLR 609.

STUART, D, 'Mens Rea, Negligence and Attempts' [1968] Crim LR 647.

STUART, D, 'The Actus Reus in Attempts' [1970] Crim LR 505, 519–28.

SULLIVAN, GR, 'Fraud and Efficacy in the Criminal Law: A Proposal for a Wide Residual Offence' [1985] Crim LR 616.

SULLIVAN, GR, 'Intent, Purpose and Complicity' [1988] Crim LR 641.

SULLIVAN, GR, 'The Need for A Crime of Sexual Assault' [1989] Crim LR 331.

SULLIVAN, GR, 'Intent, Subjective Recklessness and Culpability' (1992) 12 OJLS 381, 385.

SULLIVAN, GR, 'Intoxicants and Diminished Responsibility' [1994] Crim LR 156.

SULLIVAN, GR, 'Involuntary Intoxication and Beyond' [1994] Crim LR 272.

SULLIVAN, GR, 'Expressing Corporate Guilt (1995) 15 OJLS 281.

SULLIVAN, GR, 'Making Excuses', in S Shute and A Simester (eds), *Harm and Culpability* (1996).

SULLIVAN, GR, 'The Attribution of Culpability to a Limited Company' [1996] CLJ 515.

SULLIVAN, GR, 'Corporate Killing–Some Government Proposals' [2001] Crim LR 31.

SULLIVAN, GR, 'Knowledge, Belief and Culpability' Law' in S Shute and A Simester (eds), *Criminal Law Theory: Doctrines of the General Part* (2002).

SULLIVAN, GR, 'Fraud the Latest Law Commission Proposals' (2003) 67 J Crim L 139.

SULLIVAN, GR, AND WARBRICK, C, 'Territoriality, Theft and Atakpu' [1994] Crim LR 650 and 659

SUTHERLAND, P, AND GEARTY, C, 'Insanity and the ECHR' [1992] Crim LR 418.

SUTTON, M, 'Supply by Theft: Does the Market for Second-Hand Goods Play a Role in Keeping Crime Figures High? (1995) 35 Brit Jnl Criminology 400.

SUTTON, M, JOHNSTON, K, AND LOCKWOOD, H, *Handling Stolen Goods and Theft: A Market Reduction Approach* (1998).

SUTTON, R, AND DOBBS, L, *Fraud Law, Practice and Procedure* (2004).

SWIFT, K, *Wilkinson's Road Traffic Offences* (21st edn 2003).

SYROTA, G, *Current Law Statutes* (1978).

SYROTA, G, 'Are Cheque Frauds Covered by Section 3 of the Theft Act 1978' [1980] Crim LR 413.

SYROTA, G, 'A Radical Change in the Law of Recklessness' [1982] Crim LR 97.

SYROTA, G, 'Mens Rea in Gross Negligence Manslaughter' [1983] Crim LR 776.

TADROS, V, 'The Characters of Excuses' (2001) 21 OJLS 495.

TADROS, V, 'Recklessness and the Duty to Take Care' in S Shute and A Simester (eds), *Criminal Law Theory* (2002).

TAN, KF, 'A Misconceived Issue in the Tort of False Imprisonment' (1981) 44 MLR 166.

TAO, LS, 'Legal Problems of Alcoholism' (1969) 37(3) Fordham LR 405.

TAPPER, C, 'Computer Crime: Scotch Mist?' [1987] Crim LR 4.

TAPPER, C, *Cross and Tapper on Evidence* (10th edn 2004).

TAYLOR, PR, 'Provocation and Mercy Killing' 1991] Crim LR 111.

TAYLOR, R, 'Complicity and Excuses' [1983] Crim LR 656.

TELLING, D, 'Arrest and Detention–The Conceptual Maze' [1978] Crim LR 320.

TEMKIN, J, 'Impossible Attempts: Another View' (1976) 39 MLR 55.

TEMKIN, J, 'Towards a Modern Law of Rape' (1982) MLR 399.

TEMKIN, J, 'Pre-natal Injury, Homicide and the Draft Criminal Code' [1986] CLJ 414.

TEMKIN, J, 'Do We Need a Crime of Incest?' (1988) CLP 185.

TEMKIN, J, *Rape and the Legal Process* (2nd edn 2002).

TEMKIN, J, AND ASHWORTH, A, 'Rape, Sexual Assaults and the Problems of Consent' [2004] Crim LR 328.

TENNANT, E, *The Future of the Diminished Responsibility defence to Murder* (2001)

THOMAS, D, AND LOADER, BD, *Cybercrime* (2000).

THOMAS, DA , 'Form and Function in Criminal Law' in P Glazebrook (ed), *Reshaping the Criminal Law: Essays in Honour of Glanville Williams* (1978).

THOMAS, DA, *Principles of Sentencing* (2nd edn 1979).

THOMAS, DA, 'Sentencing: The Basic Principles' [1967] Crim LR.

THOMAS, DA, *Sentencing Referencer 2005/2006* (2005).

THOMPSON, M, 'Criminal Law and Property Law: an Unhappy Combination' (2002) 66 Conv 387.

THORNTON, GC, *Legislative Drafting* (1987).

THORNTON, R, 'Dishonest Assistance: Guilty Conduct or a Guilty Mind' (2002) 61 CLJ 524.

TICEHURST R, 'Jurisdiction in Sex Tourism Cases' (1996) 146 NLJ 1826.

TOCZEK, L, 'Never Plead Guilty!' (2002) 146 SJ 455.

TOLMIE, J, 'Alcoholism and Criminal Liability' (2001) 64 MLR 688.

TOMKINS, A, 'Legislating Against Terror: The Anti-terrorism Crime and Security Act 2001' [2002] PL 205.

TREGILAS-DAVEY M, 'An Opportunity Missed' (1991) 54 MLR 294.

TREITEL, GH, 'Contract and Crime' in C Tapper (ed), *Crime, Proof and Punishment: Essays in Memory of Sir Rupert Cross* (1981)

TREVALYEN, HM (LADY MACCAULEY) (ed), *The Works of Lord MacCauley: Volume 7* (1866).

TRIDIMAS, T, *The General Principles of EC Law* (1999).

TUR, R, 'Dishonesty and the Jury Question' in A Phillips Griffiths (ed) *Philosophy and Practice* (1985).

TUR, R, 'Subjectivism and Objectivism : Towards Synthesis' in S Shute, J Gardner, and J Horder (eds), *Action and Value in Criminal Law* (1993) 213.

TUR, R, 'Legislative Techniques and Human Rights–The Sad Case of Assisted Suicide' [2003] Crim LR 3.

TURNER, JWG, 'The Mental Element in Crimes at Common Law', MACL 195.

UNSWORTH, C, 'Blasphemy, Cultural Divergence and Legal Relativism' (1995) 58 MLR 658.

VICKERS, L, 'Circumcision–The Unkindest Cut of All?' (2000) 150 NLJ 1694.

VIRGO, G, 'Reconciling Principle and Policy' [1993] Crim LR 415.

VIRGO, G, 'Offences Against the Person–Do-It-Yourself Law Reform' [1997] CLJ 251.

WALKER, C, *The Prevention of Terrorism in British Law* (2nd edn 1992).

WALKER, C, *The Anti-Terrorism Legislation* (2002).

WALKER, L, *Battered Women Syndrome* (1st edn 1984; 2nd edn 2000).

WALKER, N, *The Aims of a Penal System* (1966).

WALKER, N, *Crime and Insanity in England* (1968).

WALKER, N, *Punishment, Danger and Stigma* (1980).

WALKER, N, 'The End of an Old Song' (1999) 149 NLJ 64.

WALKER, N, AND MARSH, C, 'Do Sentences Affect Public Disapproval?' (1984) British Journal of Criminology 27.

WALL, DS (ed), Criminal Law Review [1998] (special edition).

WALTER, N, *Blasphemy Ancient and Modern* (1990).

WALTERS, L, 'Murder under Duress and Judicial Decision Making in the House of Lords' (1988) 18 LS 61.

WARD, A, 'Making Some Sense of Self Induced Intoxication' [1986] CLJ 247.

WARD, R (ed), *Encyclopaedia of Road Traffic Law and Practice* (2001).

WARD, O, *Information Technology Watch Out, There's a Hacker About* (2000).

WASIK, M, 'Duress and Criminal Responsibility' [1977] Crim LR 453.

WASIK, M 'Abandoning Criminal Intent' [1980] Crim LR 785.

WASIK, M, 'A Learner's Careless Driving' [1982] Crim LR 411.

WASIK, M, 'Cumulative Provocation and Domestic Killing' [1982] Crim LR 29.

WASIK, M, 'Definitions of Crimes in Insurance Contracts' [1986] J Bus Law 45.

WASIK, M, 'Law Reform Proposals on Computer Misuse' [1989] Crim LR 257.

WASIK, M, 'The Computer Misuse Act 1990' [1990] Crim LR 767.

WASIK, M, *Crime and the Computer* (1991).

WASIK, M, 'Form and Function in the Law of Involuntary Manslaughter' [1994] Crim LR 883.

WASIK, M, 'Sentencing in Homicide' in A Ashworth and B Mitchell (eds), *Rethinking English Homicide Law* (2000).

WASIK, M, *Emmins on Sentencing* (4th edn 2001).

WATSON, M, 'Cannabis and the Defence of Necessity' (1998) 148 NLJ 1260.

WATSON, M, 'Graffiti–Popular Art, Anti Social Behaviour or Criminal Damage' (2004) 168 JP 668.

WEAIT, M, 'Dica: Knowledge, consent and the transmission of HIV' (2004) NLJ 826.

WEAIT, M, 'Criminal Law and the Transmission of HIV: *R v Dica*' (2005) MLR 121.

WEATHERILL, S, AND BEAUMONT, P, *EU Law* (3rd edn 1999).

WEBSTER, R, *A Brief History of Blasphemy* (1990).

WECHSLER, H, 'The Model Penal Code', in JLI Edwards, *Modern Advances in Criminology* (1965).

WEINREIB, L, 'Information and Property' (1988) 38 UTLJ 117.

WELLER, M, AND SOMERS, W, 'Differences in the Medical and Legal Viewpoint Illustrated by *Hardie*' [1991] 31 Med Sci Law 152.

WELLS, C, 'The Death Penalty for Provocation' [1978] Crim LR 662.

WELLS, C, 'Culture, Risk and Criminal Liability' [1993] Crim LR 551, 563.

WELLS, C, 'Battered Women's Syndrome, and Defences to Homicide: Where Now?' (1994) LS 266.

WELLS, C, 'A Quiet Revolution in Corporate Liability for Crime' (1995) 145 NLJ 1326.

WELLS, C, 'The Corporate Manslaughter Proposals: Pragmatism, Paradox and Peninsularity' [1996] Crim LR 545.

WELLS, C, 'Stalking: the Criminal Law's Response' [1997] Crim LR 463.

WELLS, C, 'Swatting the Subjectivist Bug' [1982] Crim LR 209.

WELLS, C, 'Provocation the Case for Abolition' in A Ashworth and B Mitchell (eds) *Rethinking English Homicide Law* (2000).

WELLS, C, *Corporations and Criminal Responsibility* (2nd edn 2001).

WELSH, R, 'The Criminal Liability of Corporations (1946) 62 LQR 345.

WELSTEAD, M, 'Seasons of Mists and Mellow Fruitfulness' (1995) 145 NLJ 1499.

WHEAT, K, 'The Law's Treatment of the Suicidal' [2000] Med LR 182.

WHITE, AR, *Misleading Cases* (1991).

WHITE, AR, 'The Identity and Time of the *Actus Reus*' [1977] Crim LR 148.

WHITE, D, 'Attempts: Initiatives in the Common Law Caribbean' [1980] Crim LR 780.

WHITE, S, 'A Note on Provocation' [1970] Crim LR 446.

WHITE, S, 'Continuing Representations in the Criminal Law' (1986) 37 NILQ 255.

WHITE, S, 'Lurkers, Draggers and Kidnappers' (1986) 150 JP 37, 56.

WHITE, S 'Taking the Joy Out of Joy-Riding' [1980] Crim LR 609.

WHITE, S, 'Three Points on Pigg' [1989] Crim LR 539 and 541.

WHITE, S, 'The Criminal Procedure (Insanity and Unfitness to Plead) Act 1991' [1992] Crim LR 4.

WILCZYNSKI, A, AND MORRIS, A, 'Parents Who Kill Their Children' [1993] Crim LR 31.

Wilkinson's Road Traffic Encyclopaedia (21st edn 2003).

WILLIAMS, CR, 'Demanding with Menaces: A Survey of the Australian Law of Blackmail' (1975) 10 Melb LR 118.

WILLIAMS, DG, 'The Control of Obscenity' [1965] Crim LR 471, 522.

WILLIAMS, DG, 'Processions, Assemblies and the Freedom of the Individual' [1987] Crim LR 167.

WILLIAMS, G, 'Homicide and the Supernatural' (1949) 65 LQR 491.

WILLIAMS, G, 'Blackmail' [1954] Crim LR 7.

WILLIAMS, G, 'Provocation and the Reasonable Man' [1954] Crim LR 740.

WILLIAMS, G, 'The Criminal Responsibility of Children' [1954] Crim LR 493.

WILLIAMS, G, 'The Definition of Crime' (1955) 8 CLP 107.

WILLIAMS, G, 'Mens Rea and Vicarious Responsibility' (1956) 9 CLP 57.

WILLIAMS, G, 'Causation in Homicide' [1957] Crim LR 429, 431, and 510.

WILLIAMS, G, *The Sanctity of Life and the Criminal Law* (1957).

WILLIAMS, G, 'Diminished Responsibility' (1960–1) 1 Med Sci & L 41.

Williams, G, *Criminal Law: The General Part* (2nd edn 1961).

Williams, G, 'Consent and Public Policy' [1962] Crim LR 74, 75, and 154.

Williams, G, 'Victims as Parties to Crimes–A Further Comment' [1964] Crim LR 686.

Williams, G, 'The Legalization of Medical Abortion' (1964) The Eugenics Review.

Williams, G, 'Criminal Law–The Duty Not To Obstruct Your Own Conviction' [1972] CLJ 193.

Williams, G, 'Evading Justice' [1975] Crim LR 430 and 609.

Williams, G, 'Intoxication of Specific Intent' (1976) 126ii NLJ 658

Williams, G, 'Law and Fact' [1976] Crim LR 472.

Williams, G, 'The New Statutory Offence of Conspiracy' (1977) 127 NLJ 1164 and 1188.

Williams, G, 'Theft, Consent and Illegality' [1977] Crim LR 127 and 205.

Williams, G, 'The Evidential Burden' (1977) 127 NLJ 156.

Williams, G, 'Appropriation: A Single or Continuous Act' [1978] Crim LR 69.

Williams, G, 'Necessity' [1978] Crim LR 128

Williams, G, 'The Three Rogues Charter' [1980] Crim LR 263.

Williams, G, 'Recklessness Redefined' [1981] CLJ 252.

Williams, G, 'Theft and Voidable Title' [1981] Crim LR 666.

Williams, G, 'Temporary Appropriation Should Be Theft' [1981] Crim LR 129.

Williams, G, 'Offences and Defences' (1982) 2 LS 233.

Williams, G, 'The Theory of Excuses' [1982] Crim LR 722 and 732.

Williams, G, *Textbook of Criminal Law* (2nd edn 1983).

Williams, G, 'Convictions and Fair Labelling' [1983] CLJ 85.

Williams, G, 'Innocuously Dipping into trust funds' (1983) LS 183.

Williams, G, 'The Problem of Reckless Attempts' [1983] Crim LR 365.

Williams, G, 'Alternative Elements and Included Offences' [1984] CLJ 290 and commentary at [1984] Crim LR 37.

Williams G, 'Handling, Theft and the Purchaser who Takes a Chance' [1985] Crim LR 432.

Williams, G, 'Attempting the Impossible–the Last Round?' (1985) 135 NLJ 337.

Williams, G, 'Oblique Intention' [1987] CLJ 417.

Williams, G, 'What Should the Code Do About Omissions?' (1987) 7 LS 92.

Williams, G, 'The Unresolved Problem of Recklessness' (1988) 8 LS 74.

Williams, G, 'Can Babies be Kidnapped?' [1989] Crim LR 473.

Williams, G, '*Finis for Novus Actus*' (1989) 48 CLJ 391.

Williams, G, 'The Draft Code and Relevance of Official Statements' (1989) 9 LS 177.

Williams, G, 'The Mens Rea for Murder: Leave it Alone' (1989) 105 LQR 387.

Williams, G, 'Which of You Did It?'(1989) 52 MLR 179.

Williams, G, 'The Meaning of Indecency' (1990) LS 20.

Williams, G, 'Complicity, Purpose and the Draft Code–1' [1990] Crim LR 4, 12.

Williams, G, 'Obedience to Law as a Crime' (1990) 53 MLR 445.

Williams, G, 'Two Nocturnal Blunders' (1990) 140 NLJ 1564.

Williams, G, 'Victims and Other Exempt Parties in Crime' (1990) 10 LS 245.

Williams, G, 'Intents in the Alternative' [1991] 50 CLJ 120.

WILLIAMS, G, 'Criminal Complicity' [1991] Crim LR 930.

WILLIAMS, G, 'Wrong Turnings on the Law of Attempt' [1991] Crim LR 416.

WILLIAMS, G, 'Criminal Omissions–the Conventional View' (1991) 107 LQR 86.

WILLIAMS, G, 'Misadventures of Manslaughter' [1993] 153 NLJ 1413.

WILLIAMS, G, *The Proof of Guilt* (3rd edn 1963).

WILLIAMS, M, AND WEINBERG, C, *The Australian Law of Theft* (3rd edn 1986).

WILSON, W, 'Murder and the Structure of Homicide' in A Ashworth and B Mitchell (eds), *Rethinking English Homicide Law* (2000).

WILSON, W, *Central Issues in Criminal Theory* (2002).

WILSON, W, *Criminal Law Doctrine* (2003).

WILSON, W, 'The Structure of Defences' [2005] Crim LR 108.

WINDER, W, 'The Development of Blackmail' (1941) 5 MLR 21.

WOLFRAM, S, 'Eugenics and the Punishment of Incest Act 1908' [1983] Crim LR 308.

WOOTTON, B, 'Diminished Responsibility–A Layman's View' (1960) 76 LQR 224.

WRIGHT, G, 'Capable of Being Born Alive?' (1981) 131 NLJ 188.

WRIGHT, G, 'The Legality of Abortion by Prostaglandin' [1984] Crim LR 347.

YALE, D, 'A Year and A Day in Homicide' [1989] CLJ 202.

YEO, S, *Compulsion in the Criminal Law* (1990).

YEO, S, *Fault in Homicide* (1997)

YEO, S, *Unrestrained Killings and the Law: Provocation and Excessive Self Defence in India, England and Australia* (1998).

YEO, S, 'Killing in Defence of Property' (2000) 150 NLJ 730.

ZELLICK, G, 'The Forcible Feeding of Prisoners: An Examination of the Legality of England Therapy' [1976] PL 153.

SYMPOSIUM

'Blackmail—A Symposium' (1993) 141(5) V Pa L Rev.

Index